**PROPERTY OF
BARNEY WELLS**

THE

ANTE-NICENE FATHERS

TRANSLATIONS OF

The Writings of the Fathers down to A.D. 325

THE REV. ALEXANDER ROBERTS, D.D.,

AND

JAMES DONALDSON, LL.D.,

EDITORS

AMERICAN REPRINT OF THE EDINBURGH EDITION

REVISED AND CHRONOLOGICALLY ARRANGED, WITH BRIEF PREFACES AND
OCCASIONAL NOTES,

BY

A. CLEVELAND COXE, D.D.

VOLUME II

FATHERS OF THE SECOND CENTURY:

HERMAS, TATIAN, ATHENAGORAS, THEOPHILUS, AND CLEMENT OF
ALEXANDRIA (ENTIRE).

WM. B. EERDMANS PUBLISHING COMPANY
GRAND RAPIDS   MICHIGAN

Reprinted, February 1975

ISBN 0-8028-8088-6

FATHERS OF THE SECOND CENTURY:

HERMAS, TATIAN, ATHENAGORAS, THEOPHILUS, AND CLEMENT OF ALEXANDRIA (ENTIRE).

AMERICAN EDITION

CHRONOLOGICALLY ARRANGED, WITH NOTES, PREFACES, AND ELUCIDATIONS,

BY

A. CLEVELAND COXE, D.D.

Τὰ ἀρχαῖα ἔθη κρατείτω.
THE NICENE COUNCIL.

CONTENTS OF VOLUME II

THE PASTOR OF HERMAS

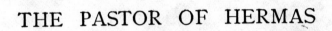

INTRODUCTORY NOTE

TO

THE PASTOR OF HERMAS

[TRANSLATED BY THE REV. F. CROMBIE, M.A.]

[A.D. 160.] THE fragment known as the "Muratorian Canon" is the historic ground for the date I give to this author.[1] I desired to prefix *The Shepherd* to the writings of Irenæus, but the limits of the volume would not permit. *The Shepherd* attracted my attention, even in early youth, as a specimen of primitive romance; but of course it disappointed me, and excited repugnance. As to its form, it is even now distasteful. But more and more, as I have studied it, and cleared up the difficulties which surround it, and the questions it has started, it has become to me a most interesting and suggestive relic of the primitive age. Dr. Bunsen[2] calls it "a good but dull novel," and reminds us of a saying of Niebuhr (Bunsen's master), that "he pitied the Athenian[3] Christians for being obliged to hear it read in their assemblies." A very natural, but a truly superficial, thought, as I trust I shall be able to show.

At first sight, Hermas might seem to have little in common with Irenæus; and, on many accounts, it would be preferable to pair him with Barnabas. But I feel sure that chronology forbids, and that the age of Irenæus, and of the martyrs of Lyons and Vienne, is the period which called for this work, and which accounts for its popularity and its diffusion among the churches. Its pacific spirit in dealing with a rising heresy, which at first was a puzzle to the Latins,[4] which Pius was disposed to meet by this gentle antidote, with which Eleutherus, in the spirit of a pacificator, tampered to his own hurt, and by which Victor was temporarily compromised, met precisely what the case seemed to demand in the judgment of Western Christians. They could not foresee the results of Montanism: it was not yet a defined heresy. And even the wise prudence of Irenæus shows anxiety not too hastily to denounce it; "seeing," as Eusebius affirms, "there were many other wonderful powers of divine grace yet exhibited, *even at that time*, in different churches."

Bunsen pronounces magisterially on the Muratorian fragment as an ill-translated excerpt from Hegesippus, written about A.D. 165. This date may be inaccurate, but the evidence is that of a contemporary on which we may rely. "Very recently," he says, "*in our own times*, in the city of Rome, Hermas compiled *The Shepherd;* his brother, Bishop Pius,[5] then sitting in the *cathedra*

---

[1] To be found, with copious annotations, in Routh's *Reliquiæ*, vol. i. pp. 389–434, Oxford, 1846. See also Westcott, *On the Canon of the New Testament*, Cambridge, 1855.

[2] *Hippolytus and His Age*, vol. i. p. 315.

[3] Why "Athenian"? It was read everywhere. But possibly this is a specification based on Acts xvii. 21. They may have welcomed it as *a novel* and a novelty.

[4] More of this in Athenagoras; but see Kaye's *Justin Martyr*, p. 179, note 3, ed. 1853.

[5] Roman fabulists know all about Pius, of course, and give us this history: "He was a native of Aquileia, and was elected bishop on the 15th of January, A.D. 158. . . . He governed the Church nine years, five months, and twenty-seven days." So affirms that favourite of Popes, Artaud de Montor (*Histoire de Pie VIII.*, p. xi. Paris, 1830).

of the Roman Church." With the period thus assigned, the internal evidence agrees. It accounts for the anti-Montanism of the whole allegory, and not less for the choice of this non-controversial form of antidote. Montanism is not named ; but it is opposed by a reminder of better "prophesyings," and by setting the pure spirit of the apostolic age over against the fren-zied and pharisaical pretensions of the fanatics. The pacific policy at first adopted by the Roman bishops, dictated, no doubt, this effort of Hermas to produce such a refutation as his brother [1] might commend to the churches.

Let me present, in outline, the views which seem to me necessary to a good understanding of the work ; and as I am so unfortunate as to differ with the Edinburgh editors, who are entitled, *primâ facie*, to be supposed correct, I shall venture to apologize for my own conceptions, by a few notes and elucidations.[2]

As Eusebius informs us, the *charismata* were not extinct in the churches when the Phrygian imitations began to puzzle the faithful. Bunsen considers its first propagators specimens of the *clairvoyant* art, and pointedly cites the manipulations they were said to practise (like persons playing on the harp), in proof of this. We must place ourselves in those times to comprehend the difficulties of early Christians in dealing with the counterfeit. "Try the spirits," said St. John ; and St. Paul had said more expressly, "Quench not the Spirit ; *despise not* prophesyings ; *prove* all things," etc. This very expression suggests that there might often be something *despicable* in the form and manner of uttering what was excellent. To borrow a phrase of our days, "the human element" was painfully predominant at times, even among those who spoke by the Spirit. The smoke of personal infirmity discoloured genuine scintillations from hearts in which still smoul-dered the fire of Pentecostal gifts. The reticence of Irenæus is therefore not to be marvelled at. He cautioned Eleutherus no doubt, but probably felt, with him, that the rumours from Phrygia needed further examination. The prophetic gifts were said to be lodged in men and women austere as John the Baptist, and professing a mission to rebuke the carnal and self-indulgent degeneracy of a generation that knew not the apostles.

It would not be a very bold conjecture, that Hermas and his brother were elderly grand-children of the original Hermas, the friend of St. Paul. *The Shepherd*, then, might be based upon personal recollections, and upon the traditions of a family which the spirit of prophecy had reproved, and who were monuments of its power. The book supplies us with evidences of the awakened conscience with which Hermas strove to "bless his household." But, be this as it may, this second Hermas, with his brother's approbation, undertakes to revive the memory of those primal days portrayed in the Epistle to Diognetus, when Christians, though *sorrowful*, were "always rejoicing." He compiles accordingly a non-metrical idyl ; reproducing, no doubt, tradi-tional specimens of those "prophesyings," on which St. Paul remarks. Hence we infer, that such outpourings as became the subject of apostolic censure, when they confused the order of the Corinthian Church,[3] were, in their nobler examples, such "visions," "mandates" and "simili-tudes" as these ; more or less human as to form, but, in their moral teachings, an impressive testimony against heathen oracles, and their obscene or blasphemous suggestions.

The permissive wisdom of the Spirit granting, while restraining, such manifestations, is seen in thus counterbalancing Sibylline and other ethnic utterances. (Acts xvi. 16–19.) With this in view, Hermas makes his compilation. He casts it into an innocent fiction, as Cowper wrote in the name of Alexander Selkirk, and introduces Hermas and Clement to identify the times which are idealized in his allegory. Very gently, but forcibly, therefore, he brings back the original

---

[1] The latest learned authority among Roman Catholics, a Benedictine, gives us the dates A.D. 142-156, respectively, as those of his election and decease. See *Series Episcoporum*, etc. P. B. Gams, Ratisbonæ, 1873.

[2] Relying upon the invaluable aid of Dr. Routh, I had not thought of looking into Westcott, till I had worked out my own conclusions. I am greatly strengthened by his elaborate and very able argument. See his work on the *Canon*, pp. 213-235.

[3] 1 Cor. xiv. The value of Hermas in helping us to comprehend this mysterious chapter appears to me very great. Celsus reproached Christians as *Sibyllists*. See Origen, *Against Celsus*, book v. cap. lxi.

Christians as antagonists of the Montanistic opinions ; and so exclusively does this idea predominate in the whole work, as Tertullian's scornful comment implies, that one wonders to find Wake, with other very learned men, conceding that the Pauline Hermas was its actual author. Were it so, he must have been a prophet indeed. No doubt those of the ancients who knew nothing of the origin of the work, and accepted it as the production of the first Hermas, were greatly influenced by this idea. It seemed to them a true oracle from God, like those of the Apocalypse, though sadly inferior ; preparing the Church for one of its great trials and perils, and fulfilling, as did the Revelation of St. John, that emphatic promise concerning the Spirit, " He shall show you things to come."

This view of the subject, moreover, explains historical facts which have been so unaccountable to many critics ; such as the general credit it obtained, and that its influence was greater in the East than among Latins. But once commended to the Asiatic churches by Pius, as a useful instruction for the people, and a safeguard against the Phrygian excesses, it would easily become current wherever the Greek language prevailed. Very soon it would be popularly regarded as the work of the Pauline Hermas, and as embodying genuine *prophesyings* of the apostolic age. A qualified inspiration would thus be attributed to them, precisely such as the guarded language of Origen [1] suggested afterwards : hence the deutero-canonical repute of the book, read, like the Apocrypha, for instruction and edification, but not cited to establish any doctrine as of the faith.[2] It must be remembered, that, although the Roman Church was at first a Grecian colony, and largely composed of those Hellenistic Jews to whom St. Paul's arguments in his Epistle to the Romans were personally appropriate, yet in the West, generally, it was not so : hence the greater diffusion of *The Shepherd* written in Greek, through the Greek churches. There, too, the Montanists were a raging pestilence long before the West really felt the contagion through the influence of the brilliant Tertullian. These facts account for the history of the book, its early currency and credit in the Church. Nor must we fail to observe, that the tedious allegorizing of Hermas, though not acceptable to us, was by no means displeasing to Orientals. To this day, the common people, even with us, seem to be greatly taken with story-telling and " similitudes," especially when there is an interpreter to give them point and application.

After reading Irenæus *Against Heresies*, then, we may not inappropriately turn to this mild protest against the most desolating and lasting delusion of primitive times. Most bitterly this will be felt when we reach the great founder of " Latin Christianity," whose very ashes breathed contagion into the life of such as handled his relics with affection, save only those, who, like Cyprian, were gifted with a character as strong as his own. The genius of Tertullian inspired his very insanity with power, and, to the discipline of the Latin churches, he communicated something of the rigour of Montanism, with the natural re-actionary relaxation of morals in actual life. Of this, we shall learn enough when we come to read the fascinating pages of that splendid but infatuated author. Montanism itself, and the Encratite heresy which we are soon to consider in the melancholy case of Tatian, were re-actions from those abominations of the heathen with which Christians were daily forced to be conversant. These Fathers erred through a temptation in which Satan was " transformed as an angel of light." Let us the more admire the penetrating foresight, and the holy moderation, of Hermas. To our scornful age, indeed, glutted with reading of every sort, and alike over-cultivated and superficial, taking little time for thought, and almost as little for study, *The Shepherd* can furnish nothing attractive. He who brings nothing to it, gets nothing from it. But let the fastidious who desire at the same time to be competent judges, put themselves into the times of the Antonines, and make themselves, for the moment, Christians of that period, and they will awaken to a new world of thought. Let such go into the assemblies of the primitive faithful, in which it was evident that " not many wise men after the flesh, not many mighty, not many noble, were called." There they were, " as sheep appointed to be slain,"

---

[1] Westcott, p. 219.   Ed. 1855, London.   [2] Hieron., tom. i. p. 988, Benedictine ed.

"dying daily," and, like their blessed Master, "the scorn of men, and outcast of the people," as they gathered on the day of the Lord to "eat of that bread, and drink of that cup." After the manner of the synagogue, there came a moment when the "president" said, "Brethren, if ye have any word of exhortation for the people, say on." But the tongues were ceasing, as the apostle foretold; and they who professed to speak by the Spirit were beginning to be doubted. "Your fathers, where are they? and the prophets, do they live forever?" It was gratifying to the older men, and excited the curiosity of the young, when the reader stood up, and said, "Hear, then, the words of Hermas." Blessed were the simple folk, those "lambs among wolves," who hungered and thirsted after righteousness, and who eagerly drank in the pure and searching Scriptural morality of *The Shepherd,* and then went forth to "shine as lights in the world," in holy contrast with the gross darkness that surrounded them.

It has been objected, indeed, that the morals of Hermas have a legalizing tone. The same is said of St. James, and the Sermon on the Mount. Most unjustly and cruelly is this objection made to *The Shepherd.* Granted its language is not formulated after Augustine, as it could not be: its text is St. James, but, like St. James, harmonized always with St. Paul.[1] Faith is always honoured in its primary place; and penitence, in its every evangelical aspect, is thoroughly defined. He exposes the emptiness of formal works, such as mere physical fastings, and the carnal observance of set times and days. That in one instance he favours "works of supererogation" is an entire mistake, made by reading into the words of Hermas a heresy of which he never dreamed. His whole teaching conflicts with such a thought. His orthodoxy in other respects, is sustained by such masters as Pearson and Bull.[2] And then, the positive side of his teaching is a precious testimony to the godly living exacted of believers in the second century. How suitable to all times are the maxims he extracts from the New Law. How searching his exposure of the perils of lax family discipline, and of wealth unsanctified. What heavenly precepts of life he lays down for all estates of men. To the clergy, what rules he prescribes against ambition and detraction and worldly-mindedness. Surely such reproofs glorify the epoch, when they who had cast off, so recently, the lusts and passions of heathenism, were, as the general acceptance of this book must lead us to suppose, eager to be fed with "truth, severe in *rugged* fiction drest."

But the reader will now be eager to examine the following INTRODUCTORY NOTICE of the translator: —

THE Pastor of Hermas was one of the most popular books, if not the most popular book, in the Christian Church during the second, third, and fourth centuries. It occupied a position analogous in some respects to that of Bunyan's *Pilgrim's Progress* in modern times; and critics have frequently compared the two works.

In ancient times two opinions prevailed in regard to the authorship. The most widely spread was, that the Pastor of Hermas was the production of the Hermas mentioned in the Epistle to the Romans. Origen[3] states this opinion distinctly, and it is repeated by Eusebius[4] and Jerome.[5]

Those who believed the apostolic Hermas to be the author, necessarily esteemed the book very highly; and there was much discussion as to whether it was inspired or not. The early writers are of opinion that it was really inspired. Irenæus quotes it as Scripture;[6] Clemens Alexandrinus speaks of it as making its statements "divinely;"[7] and Origen, though a few of his expressions are regarded by some as implying doubt, unquestionably gives it as his opinion that it is "divinely inspired."[8] Eusebius mentions that difference of opinion prevailed in his day as to the inspiration of the book, some opposing its claims, and others maintaining its divine origin, especially

[1] Bull (and Grabe), *Harmonia Apostolica;* Works, vol. iii.
[2] Pearson, *Vindiciæ Ignat.,* i. cap. 4. Bull, *Defens. Fid. Nicæn.,* i. cap. 2. sec. 3; Works, vol. v. part i. p. 15.
[3] Comment. in Rom. xvi. 14, lib. x. 31. [But see Westcott's fuller account of all this, pp. 219, 220.]
[4] *Hist. Eccl.* iii. 3.   [5] *De Viris Illustribus,* c. x.   [6] *Contra Hæres.,* iv. 20, 2.
[7] *Strom.,* i. xxi. p. 426.   [8] *Ut supra.*

because it formed an admirable introduction to the Christian faith. For this latter reason it was read publicly, he tells us, in the churches.

The only voice of antiquity decidedly opposed to the claim is that of Tertullian. He designates it apocryphal,[1] and rejects it with scorn, as favouring anti-Montanistic opinions. Even *his* words, however, show that it was regarded in many churches as Scripture.

The second opinion as to the authorship is found in no writer of any name. It occurs only in two places : a poem falsely ascribed to Tertullian, and a fragment published by Muratori, on the Canon, the authorship of which is unknown, and the original language of which is still a matter of dispute.[2] The fragment says, " The Pastor was written very lately in our times, in the city of Rome, by Hermas, while Bishop Pius, his brother, sat in the chair of the Church of the city of Rome."

A third opinion has had advocates in modern times. The Pastor of Hermas is regarded as a fiction, and the person Hermas, who is the principal character, is, according to this opinion, merely the invention of the fiction-writer.

Whatever opinion critics may have in regard to the authorship, there can be but one opinion as to the date. The Pastor of Hermas must have been written at an early period. The fact that it was recognised by Irenæus as Scripture shows that it must have been in circulation long before his time. The most probable date assigned to its composition is the reign of Hadrian, or of Antoninus Pius.

The work is very important in many respects ; but especially as reflecting the tone and style of books which interested and instructed the Christians of the second and third centuries.

The Pastor of Hermas was written in Greek. It was well known in the Eastern Churches : it seems to have been but little read in the Western. Yet the work bears traces of having been written in Italy.

For a long time the Pastor of Hermas was known to scholars only in a Latin version, occurring in several MSS. with but slight variations. But within recent times the difficulty of settling the text has been increased by the discovery of various MSS. A Latin translation has been edited, widely differing from the common version. Then a Greek MS. was said to have been found in Mount Athos, of which Simonides affirmed that he brought away a portion of the original and a copy of the rest. Then a MS. of the Pastor of Hermas was found at the end of the Sinaitic Codex of Tischendorf. And in addition to all these, there is an Æthiopic translation. The discussion of the value of these discoveries is one of the most difficult that can fall to the lot of critics ; for it involves not merely an examination of peculiar forms of words and similar criteria, but an investigation into statements made by Simonides and Tischendorf respecting events in their own lives. But whatever may be the conclusions at which the critic arrives, the general reader does not gain or lose much. In all the Greek and Latin forms the Pastor of Hermas is substantially the same. There are many minute differences ; but there are scarcely any of importance, — perhaps we should say none.

In this translation the text of Hilgenfeld, which is based on the Sinaitic Codex, has been followed.

The letters *Vat.* mean the *Vatican* manuscript, the one from which the common or vulgate version was usually printed.

The letters *Pal.* mean the *Palatine* manuscript edited by Dressel, which contains the Latin version, differing considerably from the common version.

The letters *Lips.* refer to the *Leipzig* manuscript, partly original and partly copied, furnished by Simonides from Athos. The text of Anger and Dindorf (Lips., 1856) has been used, though reference has also been made to the text of Tischendorf in Dressel.

---

[1] *De Pudicitia*, c. xx., also c. x.; *De Oratione*, c. xvi.
[2] [This statement should be compared with Westcott's temperate and very full account of the Muratorian Fragment, pp. 235-245.]

The letters *Sin.* refer to the *Sinaitic* Codex, as given in Dressel and in Hilgenfeld's notes.

The letters *Æth.* refer to the *Æthiopic* version, edited, with a Latin translation, by Antonius D'Abbadie. Leipzig, 1860.

No attempt has been made to give even a tithe of the various readings. Only the most important have been noted.

[It is but just to direct the reader's attention to an elaborate article of Dr. Donaldson, in the (London) *Theological Review*, vol. xiv. p. 564; in which he very ingeniously supports his opinions with regard to Hermas, and also touching the Muratorian Canon. In one important particular he favours my own impression; viz., that *The Shepherd* is a compilation, traditional, or reproduced from memory. He supposes its sentiments "must have been expressed in innumerable oral communications delivered in the churches throughout the world."]

THE PASTOR

BOOK FIRST.—VISIONS

VISION FIRST.

AGAINST FILTHY AND PROUD THOUGHTS, AND THE CARELESSNESS OF HERMAS IN CHASTISING HIS SONS.

CHAP. I.

HE who had brought me up, sold me to one Rhode in Rome.[1] Many years after this I recognised her, and I began to love her as a sister. Some time after, I saw her bathe in the river Tiber; and I gave her my hand, and drew her out of the river. The sight of her beauty made me think with myself, "I should be a happy man if I could but get a wife as handsome and good as she is." This was the only thought that passed through me: this and nothing more. A short time after this, as I was walking on my road to the villages,[2] and magnifying the creatures of God, and thinking how magnificent, and beautiful, and powerful they are,[3] I fell asleep. And the Spirit carried me away, and took me through a pathless place,[4] through which a man could not travel, for it was situated in the midst of rocks; it was rugged and impassible on account of water. Having passed over this river, I came to a plain. I then bent down on my knees, and began to pray to the Lord,[5] and to confess my sins. And as I prayed, the heavens were opened, and I see the woman whom I had desired saluting me from the sky, and saying, "Hail, Hermas!" And looking up to her, I said, "Lady, what doest thou here?" And she answered me, "I have been taken up here to accuse you of your sins before the Lord." "Lady," said I, "are you to be the subject of my accusation?"[6] "No," said she; "but hear the words which I am going to speak to you. God, who dwells in the heavens, and made out of nothing the things that exist, and multiplied and increased them on account of His holy Church,[7] is angry with you for having sinned against me." I answered her, "Lady, have I sinned against you? How?[8] or when spoke I an unseemly word to you? Did I not always think of you as a lady? Did I not always respect you as a sister? Why do you falsely accuse me of this wickedness and impurity?" With a smile she replied to me, "The desire of wickedness[9] arose within your heart. Is it not your opinion that a righteous man commits sin when an evil desire arises in his heart? There is sin in such a case, and the sin is great," said she; "for the thoughts of a righteous man should be righteous. For by thinking righteously his character is established in the heavens,[10] and he has the Lord merciful to him in every business. But such as entertain wicked thoughts in their minds are bringing upon themselves death and captivity; and especially is this the case with those who set their affections on this world,[11] and glory in their riches, and look not forward to the blessings of the life to come. For many will their regrets be; for they have no hope, but have despaired of themselves and their life.[12] But do thou pray to God, and He will

---

[1] The commencement varies. In the Vatican: "He who had brought me up, sold a certain young woman at Rome. Many years after this I saw her and recognised her." So Lips.; Pal. has the name of the woman, Rada. The name Rhode occurs in Acts xii. 13.

[2] "On my road to the villages." This seems to mean: as I was taking a walk into the country, or spending my time in travelling amid rural scenes. So the Æthiopic version. "Proceeding with these thoughts in my mind."—*Vat.* After I had come to the city of Ostia."—*Pal.* "Proceeding to some village."—*Lips.* [The Christian religion begetting this enthusiasm for nature, and love for nature's God, is to be noted. Where in all heathendom do we find spirit or expression like this?]

[3] *Creatures.* Creature or creation.—*Lips., Vat., Æth.*

[4] *Pathless place.* Place on the right hand.—*Vat.* [Rev. xvii. 3, xxi. 10. Dante, *Inferno*, i. 1–5.]

[5] *Lord.* God.—*Sin.* alone.

[6] *Are you to be the subject of my accusation?* Are you to accuse me?—*Vat., Lips., Æth.*

[7] [Eph. iii. 9, 10.]

[8] *How?* In what place?—*Vat., Sin.*

[9] *Wickedness.* The desire of fornication.—*Lips.* [Prov. xxi. 10, xxiv. 9; Matt. v. 28.]

[10] Literally, his glory is made straight in the heavens. As long as his thoughts are righteous and his way of life correct, he will have the Lord in heaven merciful to him.—*Vat.* When he thinks righteously, he corrects himself, and his grace will be in heaven, and he will have the Lord merciful in every business.—*Pal.* His dignity will be straight in the skies.—*Æth.* [Prov. x. 24, xi. 23.]

[11] [Col. iii. 2; Ps. xlix. 6.]

[12] *For many . . . life.* For the minds of such become empty. Now this is what the doubters do who have no hope in the Lord, and despise and neglect their life.—*Vat.* Their souls not having the hope of life, do not resist these luxuries: for they despair of themselves and their life.—*Pal.* [Eph. ii. 12.]

9

heal thy sins, and the sins of thy whole house, and of all the saints." [1]

CHAP. II.

After she had spoken these words, the heavens were shut. I was overwhelmed with sorrow and fear, and said to myself, " If this sin is assigned to me, how can I be saved, or how shall I propitiate God in regard to my sins,[2] which are of the grossest character ? With what words shall I ask the Lord to be merciful to me? While I was thinking over these things, and discussing them in my mind, I saw opposite to me a chair, white, made of white wool,[3] of great size. And there came up an old woman, arrayed in a splendid robe, and with a book in her hand ; and she sat down alone, and saluted me, " Hail, Hermas ! " And in sadness and tears [4] I said to her, " Lady, hail ! " And she said to me, " Why are you downcast, Hermas? for you were wont to be patient and temperate, and always smiling. Why are you so gloomy, and not cheerful? " I answered her and said, " O Lady, I have been reproached by a very good woman, who says that I sinned against her." And she said, " Far be such a deed from a servant of God. But perhaps a desire after her has arisen within your heart. Such a wish, in the case of the servants of God, produces sin. For it is a wicked and horrible wish in an all-chaste and already well-tried spirit [5] to desire an evil deed ; and especially for Hermas so to do, who keeps himself from all wicked desire, and is full of all simplicity, and of great guilelessness.

CHAP. III.

" But God is not angry with you on account of this, but that you may convert your house,[6] which have committed iniquity against the Lord, and against you, their parents. And although you love your sons, yet did you not warn your house, but permitted them to be terribly corrupted.[7] On this account is the Lord angry with you, but He will heal all the evils which have been done in your house. For, on account of their sins and iniquities, you have been destroyed by the affairs of this world. But now the mercy

of the Lord [8] has taken pity on you and your house, and will strengthen you, and establish you in his glory.[9] Only be not easy-minded,[10] but be of good courage and comfort your house. For as a smith hammers out his work, and accomplishes whatever he wishes,[11] so shall righteous daily speech overcome all iniquity.[12] Cease not therefore to admonish your sons ; for I know that, if they will repent with all their heart, they will be enrolled in the Books of Life with the saints." [13] Having ended these words, she said to me, " Do you wish to hear me read ? " I say to her, " Lady, I do." " Listen then, and give ear to the glories of God." [14] And then I heard from her, magnificently and admirably, things which my memory could not retain. For all the words were terrible, such as man could not endure.[15] The last words, however, I did remember ; for they were useful to us, and gentle.[16] " Lo, the God of powers, who by His invisible strong power and great wisdom has created the world, and by His glorious counsel has surrounded His creation with beauty, and by His strong word has fixed the heavens and laid the foundations of the earth upon the waters, and by His own wisdom and providence [17] has created His holy [18] Church, which He has blessed, lo ! He removes [19] the heavens and the mountains,[20] the hills and the seas, and all things become plain to His elect, that He may bestow on them the blessing which He has promised them,[21] with much glory and joy, if only they shall keep the commandments of God which they have received in great faith."

CHAP. IV.

When she had ended her reading, she rose from the chair, and four young men came and carried off the chair and went away to the east. And she called me to herself and touched my breast, and said to me, " Have you been pleased with my reading ? " And I say to her, " Lady,

---

[1] [Job xlii. 8.]

[2] Literally, perfect. *How . . . sins.* How shall I entreat the Lord in regard to my very numerous sins ? — *Vat.* How can I propitiate the Lord God in these my sins ? — *Pal.* How then shall I be saved, and beg pardon of the Lord for these my many sins ? — *Æth.* [Mic. vi. 6, 7, 8.]

[3] A chair made of white wool, like snow. — *Vat.* A chair for reclining, and on it a covering of wool, white as hail. — *Æth.*

[4] *And . . . sorrow.* I leaping in spirit with joy at her salutation. — *Lips.* [The Montanist austerity glanced at.]

[5] *For . . . spirit.* For this hateful thought ought not to be in a servant of God, nor ought a well-tried spirit to desire an evil deed. — *Vat.* [The praise here bestowed on Hermas favours the idea that a second Hermas was the author.]

[6] *But that.* But God is not angry with you on your own account, but on account of your house, which has. — *Vat.*

[7] *Corrupted.* To live riotously. — *Vat.* [1 Sam. iii. 11, 14. Traditions of the Pauline Hermas may be here preserved.]

[8] *Lord.* God. — *Vat.* [The Montanist dogma representing God as the reverse of (Neh. ix. 17) " gentle and easy to be entreated " is rebuked.]

[9] *Will strengthen.* Has preserved you in glory. — *Vat.* Strengthened and established. — *Lips.* Has saved your house. — *Pal.*

[10] *Easy-minded.* Only wander not, but be calm. — *Vat.* Omitted in Pal.

[11] *Accomplishes . . . wishes.* And exhibits it to any one to whom he wishes. — *Vat.*

[12] So shall you also, teaching the truth daily, cut off great sin. — *Vat.*

[13] *I know . . . saints.* For the Lord knows that they will repent with all their heart, and He will write you in the Book of Life. — *Vat.* See Phil. iv. 3 ; Rev. xx. 15. [He contrasts the mild spirit of the Gospel with the severity of the Law in the case of Eli.]

[14] *And give ear to the glories of God,* omitted in Vat.

[15] *And then . . . her.* And unfolding a book, she read gloriously, magnificently, and admirably. — *Vat.* [Dan. x. 9.]

[16] *Gentle.* For they were few and useful to us. — *Vat.*

[17] *By His own wisdom and providence.* By His mighty power. — *Vat., Pal.* [Scripture is here distilled like the dew. Prov. iii. 19. Ps. xxiv. 2, and marginal references.]

[18] *Holy* omitted by Lips.

[19] *Removes.* He will remove. — *Vat.*

[20] See 2 Pet. iii. 5.

[21] [Isa. lxv. 22. See Faber's *Historical Inquiry,* as to the primitive idea of the elect, book ii. 2. New York, 1840.]

the last words please me, but the first are cruel and harsh." Then she said to me, "The last are for the righteous : the first are for heathens and apostates." And while she spoke to me, two men appeared and raised her on their shoulders, and they went to where the chair was in the east. With joyful countenance did she depart ; and as she went, she said to me, " Behave like a man,[1] Hermas."

VISION SECOND.

AGAIN, OF HIS NEGLECT IN CHASTISING HIS TALKATIVE WIFE AND HIS LUSTFUL SONS, AND OF HIS CHARACTER.

CHAP. I.

As I was going to the country[2] about the same time as on the previous year, in my walk I recalled to memory the vision of that year. And again the Spirit carried me away, and took me to the same place where I had been the year before.[3] On coming to that place, I bowed my knees and began to pray to the Lord, and to glorify His name, because He had deemed me worthy, and had made known to me my former sins. On rising from prayer, I see opposite me that old woman, whom I had seen the year before, walking and reading some book. And she says to me, " Can you carry a report of these things to the elect of God ? " I say to her, " Lady, so much I cannot retain in my memory, but give me the book and I shall transcribe it." " Take it," says she, " and you will give it back to me." Thereupon I took it, and going away into a certain part of the country, I transcribed the whole of it letter by letter ;[4] but the syllables of it I did not catch. No sooner, however, had I finished the writing of the book, than all of a sudden it was snatched from my hands ; but who the person was that snatched it, I saw not.

CHAP. II.

Fifteen days after, when I had fasted and prayed much to the Lord, the knowledge of the writing was revealed to me. Now the writing was to this effect : " Your seed, O Hermas, has sinned against God, and they have blasphemed against[5] the Lord, and in their great wickedness they have betrayed their parents. And they passed as traitors of their parents, and by their treachery did they not[6] reap profit. And even now they have added to their sins lusts and iniquitous pollutions, and thus their iniquities have

been filled up. But make known[7] these words to all your children, and to your wife, who is to be your sister. For she does not[8] restrain her tongue, with which she commits iniquity ; but, on hearing these words, she will control herself, and will obtain mercy. For after you have made known to them these words which my Lord has commanded me to reveal to you,[9] then shall they be forgiven all the sins which in former times they committed, and forgiveness will be granted to all the saints who have sinned even to the present day, if they repent with all their heart, and drive all doubts from their minds.[10] For the Lord has sworn by His glory, in regard to His elect, that if any one of them sin after a certain day which has been fixed, he shall not be saved. For the repentance of the righteous has limits.[11] Filled up are the days of repentance to all the saints ; but to the heathen, repentance will be possible even to the last day. You will tell, therefore, those who preside over the Church, to direct their ways in righteousness, that they may receive in full the promises with great glory. Stand stedfast, therefore, ye who work righteousness, and doubt not,[12] that your passage[13] may be with the holy angels. Happy ye who endure the great tribulation that is coming on, and happy they who shall not deny their own life.[14] For the Lord hath sworn by His Son, that those who denied their Lord have abandoned their life in despair, for even now these are to deny Him in the days that are coming.[15] To those who denied in earlier times, God became[16] gracious, on account of His exceeding tender mercy.

CHAP. III.

" But as for you, Hermas, remember not the wrongs done to you by your children, nor neglect your sister, that they may be cleansed from their former sins. For they will be instructed with righteous instruction, if you remember not the wrongs they have done you. For the re-

---

[7] *Make known.* Rebuke with these words. — *Vat.* [Your sister in Christ, i.e., when converted.]
[8] Let her restrain her tongue. — *Vat.* [Jas. iii. 5-10.]
[9] *For . . . you.* For she will be instructed, after you have rebuked her with those words which the Lord has commanded to be revealed to you. — *Vat.*
[10] [Against Montanism. Matt. xii. 31, xviii. 22.]
[11] [To show that the Catholic doctrine does not make Christ the minister of sin. Gal. ii. 17.]
[12] *Doubt not.* [Jas. i. 5.] And so act. — *Vat.*
[13] *Passage.* [Luke xvi. 22.] Your journey. — *Pal.*
[14] And whosoever shall not deny his own life. — *Vat.* [Seeking one's life was losing it : hating one's own life was finding it (Matt. x. 39 ; Luke xiv. 26.) The great tribulation here referred to, is probably that mystery of St. Paul (2 Thess. ii. 3), which they supposed nigh at hand. Our author probably saw signs of it in Montanus and his followers.]
[15] *Those . . . coming.* The meaning of this sentence is obscure. The Vat. is evidently corrupt, but seems to mean : "The Lord has sworn by His Son, that whoever will deny Him and His Son, promising themselves life thereby, they [God and His Son] will deny them in the days that are to come." The days that are to come would mean the day of judgment and the future state. See Matt. x. 33. [This they supposed would soon follow the great apostasy and tribulation. The words " earlier times " are against the Pauline date.]
[16] *Became gracious.* Will be gracious. — *Pal.*

---

[1] Be strong, or be made strong. — *Vat.* [1 Cor. xvi. 13.]
[2] *Country;* lit. *to the villages.* From Cumæ. — *Vat.* While I was journeying in the district of the Cumans. — *Pal.*
[3] [Ezek. i. 1, iii. 23.]
[4] *Going . . . letter.* [Ezek. ii. 9 ; Rev. x. 4.] Now taking the book, I sat down in one place and wrote the whole of it in order. — *Pal.* In the ancient MSS. there was nothing to mark out where one word ended and another commenced.
[5] *God . . . against,* omitted in Vat.
[6] *Not,* omitted in Vat.

membrance of wrongs worketh death.[1] And you, Hermas, have endured great personal[2] tribulations on account of the transgressions of your house, because you did not attend to them, but were careless,[3] and engaged in your wicked transactions. But[4] you are saved, because you did not depart from the living God, and on account of your simplicity and great self-control. These have saved you, if you remain stedfast. And they will save all who act in the same manner, and walk in guilelessness and simplicity. Those who possess such virtues will wax strong against every form of wickedness, and will abide unto eternal life. Blessed are all they who practise righteousness, for they shall never be destroyed. Now you will tell Maximus: Lo![5] tribulation cometh on. If it seemeth good to thee, deny again. The Lord is near to them who return unto Him, as it is written in Eldad and Modat,[6] who prophesied to the people in the wilderness."

CHAP. IV.

Now a revelation was given to me, my brethren, while I slept, by a young man of comely appearance, who said to me, "Who do you think that old woman is from whom you received the book?" And I said, "The Sibyl." "You are in a mistake," says he; "it is not the Sibyl." "Who is it then?" say I. And he said, "It is the Church."[7] And I said to him, "Why then is she an old woman?" "Because," said he, "she was created first of all. On this account is she old. And for her sake was the world made." After that I saw a vision in my house, and that old woman came and asked me, if I had yet given the book to the presbyters. And I said that I had not. And then she said, "You have done well, for I have some words to add. But when I finish all the words, all the elect will then become acquainted with them through you. You will write therefore two books, and you will send the one to Clemens and the other to Grapte.[8] And Clemens will send his to foreign countries,

for permission has been granted to him to do so.[9] And Grapte will admonish the widows and the orphans. But you will read the words in this city, along with the presbyters who preside over the Church.

VISION THIRD.

CONCERNING THE BUILDING OF THE TRIUMPHANT CHURCH, AND THE VARIOUS CLASSES OF REPROBATE MEN.

CHAP. I.

The vision which I saw, my brethren, was of the following nature. Having fasted frequently, and having prayed to the Lord that He would show me the revelation which He promised to show me through that old woman, the same night that old woman appeared to me, and said to me, "Since you are so anxious and eager to know all things, go into the part of the country where you tarry; and about the fifth[10] hour I shall appear unto you, and show you all that you ought to see." I asked her, saying "Lady, into what part of the country am I to go?" And she said, "Into any part you wish." Then I chose a spot which was suitable, and retired. Before, however, I began to speak and to mention the place, she said to me, "I will come where you wish." Accordingly, I went to the country, and counted the hours, and reached the place where I had promised to meet her. And I see an ivory seat ready placed, and on it a linen cushion, and above the linen cushion was spread a covering of fine linen.[11] Seeing these laid out, and yet no one in the place, I began to feel awe, and as it were a trembling seized hold of me, and my hair stood on end, and as it were a horror came upon me when I saw that I was all alone. But on coming back to myself and calling to mind the glory of God, I took courage, bent my knees, and again confessed my sins to God as I had done before.[12] Whereupon the old woman approached, accompanied by six young men whom I had also seen before; and she stood behind me, and listened to me, as I prayed and confessed my sins to the Lord. And touching me she said, "Hermas, cease praying continually for your sins; pray for righteousness,[13] that you may

---

[1] The Vat. adds: but forgetfulness of them, eternal life. [Lev. xix. 18. See Jeremy Taylor, *Of Forgiveness*, Discourse xi. vol. i. p. 217. London, Bohn, 1844.]

[2] *Personal.* Worldly.— *Vat.*

[3] *You . . . careless.* You neglected them as if they did not belong to you.— *Vat.* [See cap. iii. *supra*, "easy-minded."]

[4] But you will be saved for not having departed from the living God. And your simplicity and singular self-control will save you, if you remain stedfast.— *Vat.*

[5] Now you will say: Lo! great tribulation cometh on.— *Vat.* Lo! exceedingly great tribulation cometh on.— *Lips.* [Maximus seems to have been a lapser, thus warned in a spirit of orthodoxy in contrast with Montanism, but with irony.]

[6] [The sense is: This is the temptation of those who pervert the promises made to the penitent. They may say, "we are threatened with terrible persecution; let us save our lives by momentarily denying Christ: we can *turn again*, and the Lord is nigh to all who thus turn, as Eldad and Medad told the Israelites."] Eldad (or Eldat or Heldat or Heldam) and Modat (Mudat or Modal) are mentioned in Num. xi. 26, 27. The apocryphal book inscribed with their name is now lost. Cotelerius compares, for the passage, Ps. xxxiv. 9.

[7] *The Church.* The Church of God.— *Vat.* [See Grabe's note, Bull's *Defens. Fid. Nicæn.*, i. cap. 2. sec. 6; Works, vol. v. part i. p. 67.]

[8] Grapte is supposed to have been a deaconess.

[9] [Here, as in places that follow, is to be noted a development of canon law, that could hardly have existed in the days of the Pauline Hermas. He is supposed to be a lector, who might read for the edification of the elect, if permitted by the presbyters. Grapte, the deaconess, is supposed to have charge of widows and orphans; while Clement, only, has canonical right to authenticate books to foreign churches, as the Eastern bishops were accustomed to authenticate canonical Scriptures to him and others. The second Hermas falls into such anachronisms innocently, but they betray the fiction of his work. Compare the *Apost. Constitutions* with (apocryphal) authentications by Clement.]

[10] *Fifth.* Sixth.— *Vat.* [Here is a probable reference to canonical hours, borrowed from apostolic usage (Acts iii. 1), but not reflected in written constitutions in Clement's day.]

[11] [Compare *Cyprian's Life and Martyrdom*, by Pontius the deacon (sec. 16). This is doubtless a picture of the bishop's *cathedra* in the days of Pius, but, for the times of the Pauline Hermas, a probable anachronism.]

[12] [Ezek. i. 28.]

[13] [For justification and sanctification.]

have a portion of it immediately in your house."
On this, she took me up by the hand, and brought
me to the seat, and said to the young men, "Go
and build." When the young men had gone and
we were alone, she said to me, "Sit here." I
say to her, "Lady, permit my elders ¹ to be seated
first." "Do what I bid you," said she; "sit
down." When I would have sat down on her
right, she did not permit me, but with her hand
beckoned to me to sit down on the left. While
I was thinking about this, and feeling vexed that
she did not let me sit on the right, she said,
"Are you vexed, Hermas? The place to the
right is for others who have already pleased God,
and have suffered for His name's sake; and you
have yet much to accomplish before you can sit
with them. But abide as you now do in your
simplicity, and you will sit with them, and with
all who do their deeds and bear what they have
borne."

CHAP. II.

"What have they borne?" said I. "Listen,"
said she: "scourges, prisons, great tribulations,
crosses, wild beasts,² for God's name's sake. On
this account is assigned to them the division of
santification on the right hand, and to every one
who shall suffer for God's name: to the rest is
assigned the division on the left. But both for
those who sit on the right, and those who sit on
the left, there are the same gifts and promises;
only those sit on the right, and have some glory.
You then are eager to sit on the right with them,
but your shortcomings are many. But you will
be cleansed from your shortcomings; and all
who are not given to doubts shall be cleansed
from all their iniquities up till this day." Saying
this, she wished to go away. But falling down at
her feet, I begged her by the Lord that she would
show me the vision which she had promised to
show me. And then she again took hold of me
by the hand, and raised me, and made me sit
on the seat to the left; and lifting up a splendid
rod,³ she said to me, "Do you see something
great?" And I say, "Lady, I see nothing."
She said to me, "Lo! do you not see opposite
to you a great tower, built upon the waters, of
splendid square stones?" For the tower was
built square ⁴ by those six young men who had
come with her. But myriads of men were carrying stones to it, some dragging them from the
depths, others removing them from the land, and
they handed them to these six young men.
They were taking them and building; and those
of the stones that were dragged out of the
depths, they placed in the building just as they

were: for they were polished and fitted exactly
into the other stones, and became so united one
with another that the lines of juncture could not
be perceived.⁵ And in this way the building of
the tower looked as if it were made out of one
stone. Those stones, however, which were taken
from the earth suffered a different fate; for the
young men rejected some of them, some they
fitted into the building, and some they cut down,
and cast far away from the tower. Many other
stones, however, lay around the tower, and the
young men did not use them in building; for
some of them were rough, others had cracks
in them, others had been made too short,⁶ and
others were white and round, but did not fit into
the building of the tower. Moreover, I saw
other stones thrown far away from the tower, and
falling into the public road; yet they did not remain on the road, but were rolled into a pathless
place. And I saw others falling close to the water,
and burning, others falling close to the water, and
yet not capable of being rolled into the water,
though they wished to be rolled down, and to
enter the water.

CHAP. III.

On showing me these visions, she wished to
retire. I said to her, "What is the use of my
having seen all this, while I do not know what it
means?" She said to me, "You are a cunning
fellow, wishing to know everything that relates
to the tower." "Even so, O Lady," said I,
"that I may tell it to my brethren, that, hearing
this, they may know the Lord in much glory." ⁷
And she said, "Many indeed shall hear, and
hearing, some shall be glad, and some shall weep.
But even these, if they hear and repent, shall
also rejoice. Hear, then, the parables of the
tower; for I will reveal all to you, and give me
no more trouble in regard to revelation: for
these revelations have an end, for they have been
completed. But you will not cease praying for
revelations, for you are shameless.⁸ The tower
which you see building is myself, the Church,
who have appeared to you now and on the former occasion. Ask, then, whatever you like in
regard to the tower, and I will reveal it to you,
that you may rejoice with the saints." I said
unto her, "Lady, since you have vouchsafed
to reveal all to me this once, reveal it." She
said to me, "Whatsoever ought to be revealed,
will be revealed; only let your heart be with
God,⁹ and doubt not whatsoever you shall see."

---

¹ *My elders.* Perhaps the translation should be: the presbyters.
[No doubt; for here also is a reference to canon law. See *Apost.
Constitutions* (so called), book ii. sec. vii. 57.]
² [Heb. xi. 36, 37.]
³ [Rev. xi. 1.]
⁴ [Rev. xxi. 16.]

⁵ [1 Kings vi. 7; 1 Pet. ii. 4–8. The apostle interprets his own
name,—shows Christ to be the Rock, himself a *stone* laid upon the
foundation, by which also all believers are made lively *stones*, like the
original *Cephas.*]
⁶ *Others had been made too short*, not in Vat.
⁷ *That . . . glory.* And that they may be made more joyful,
and, hearing this, may greatly glorify the Lord. — *Vat.*
⁸ [2 Cor. xii. 1–11. The apostle is *ashamed* to glory in revelations, and this seems to be the reference.]
⁹ *God.* Lord. — *Vat.*

I asked her, "Why was the tower built upon the waters, O Lady?" She answered, "I told you before,[1] and you still inquire carefully : therefore inquiring you shall find the truth. Hear then why the tower is built upon the waters. It is because your life has been, and will be, saved through water. For the tower was founded on the word of the almighty and glorious Name, and it is kept together by the invisible power of the Lord."[2]

CHAP. IV.

In reply I said to her, "This is magnificent and marvellous. But who are the six young men who are engaged in building?" And she said, "These are the holy angels of God, who were first created, and to whom the Lord handed over His whole creation, that they might increase and build up and rule over the whole creation. By these will the building of the tower be finished." "But who are the other persons who are engaged in carrying the stones?" "These also are holy angels of the Lord, but the former six are more excellent than these. The building of the tower will be finished,[3] and all will rejoice together around the tower, and they will glorify God, because the tower is finished." I asked her, saying, "Lady, I should like to know what became of the stones, and what was meant by the various kinds of stones?" In reply she said to me, "Not because you are[4] more deserving than all others that this revelation should be made to you — for there are others before you, and better than you, to whom these visions should have been revealed — but that the name of God may be glorified, has the revelation been made to you, and it will be made on account of the doubtful who ponder in their hearts whether these things will be or not. Tell them that all these things are true, and that none of them is beyond the truth. All of them are firm and sure, and established on a strong foundation.

CHAP. V.

"Hear now with regard to the stones which are in the building. Those square white stones which fitted exactly into each other, are apostles, bishops, teachers, and deacons, who have lived in godly purity, and have acted as bishops and teachers and deacons chastely and reverently to the elect of God. Some of them have fallen asleep, and some still remain alive.[5] And they have always agreed with each other, and

been at peace among themselves,[6] and listened to each other. On account of this, they join exactly into the building of the tower." "But who are the stones that were dragged from the depths, and which were laid into the building and fitted in with the rest of the stones previously placed in the tower?" "They are those[7] who suffered for the Lord's sake." "But I wish to know, O Lady, who are the other stones which were carried from the land." "Those," she said, "which go into the building without being polished, are those whom God has approved of, for they walked in the straight ways of the Lord and practised His commandments." "But who are those who are in the act of being brought and placed in the building?" "They are those who are young in faith and are faithful. But they are admonished by the angels to do good, for no iniquity has been found in them." "Who then are those whom they rejected and cast away?"[8] "These are they who have sinned, and wish to repent. On this account they have not been thrown far from the tower, because they will yet be useful in the building, if they repent. Those then who are to repent, if they do repent, will be strong in faith, if they now repent while the tower is building. For if the building be finished, there will not be more room for any one, but he will be rejected.[9] This privilege, however, will belong only to him who has now been placed near the tower.

CHAP. VI.

"As to those who were cut down and thrown far away from the tower, do you wish to know who they are? They are the sons of iniquity, and they believed in hypocrisy, and wickedness did not depart from them. For this reason they are not saved, since they cannot be used in the building on account of their iniquities. Wherefore they have been cut off and cast far away on account of the anger of the Lord, for they have roused Him to anger. But I shall explain to you the other stones which you saw lying in great numbers, and not going into the building. Those which are rough are those who have known the truth and not remained in it, nor have they been joined to the saints.[10] On this account are they unfit for use." "Who are those that have rents?" "These are they who are at discord in their hearts one with another, and are not at peace amongst themselves : they indeed keep peace before each other, but when they separate one from the other, their wicked thoughts remain in

---

[1] I said to you before, that you were cunning, diligently inquiring in regard to the Scriptures. — *Vat.* You are cunning in regard to the Scriptures. — *Lips* In some of the mss. of the common Latin version, "structures" is read instead of "Scriptures."

[2] *The Lord.* God. — *Vat.* [1 Pet. iii. 20; Eph. v. 26. Both these texts seem in the author's mind, but perhaps, also, Num. xxiv. 6, 7.]

[3] *The building.* When therefore the building of the tower is finished, all. — *Vat.*

[4] *Not because you are better.* Are you better? — *Vat.* [See note 8, preceding chapter.]

[5] [1 Cor. xv. 6, 18.]

[6] [Phil. ii. 2, iii. 16; 1 Thess. v. 13.]

[7] *Are those.* They are those who have already fallen asleep, and who suffered. — *Vat.*

[8] *Cast away.* Placed near the tower. — *Vat.*

[9] [Heb. vi. 6-8; xii. 17.]

[10] [Heb. x. 25. Barnabas (cap. iv.) reproves the same fault, almost as if directing his words against anchorites, vol. i. p. 139, this series.]

their hearts. These, then, are the rents which are in the stones. But those which are shortened are those who have indeed believed, and have the larger share of righteousness; yet they have also a considerable share of iniquity, and therefore they are shortened and not whole." "But who are these, Lady, that are white and round, and yet do not fit into the building of the tower?" She answered and said, "How long will you be foolish and stupid, and continue to put every kind of question and understand nothing? These are those who have faith indeed, but they have also the riches of this world. When, therefore, tribulation comes, on account of their riches and business they deny the Lord."[1] I answered and said to her, "When, then, will they be useful for the building, Lady?" "When the riches that now seduce them have been circumscribed, then will they be of use to God.[2] For as a round stone cannot become square unless portions be cut off and cast away, so also those who are rich in this world cannot be useful to the Lord unless their riches be cut down. Learn this first from your own case. When you were rich, you were useless; but now you are useful and fit for life. Be ye useful to God; for you also will be used as one of these stones.[3]

CHAP. VII.

"Now the other stones which you saw cast far away from the tower, and falling upon the public road and rolling from it into pathless places, are those who have indeed believed, but through doubt have abandoned the true road. Thinking, then, that they could find a better, they wander and become wretched, and enter upon pathless places. But those which fell into the fire and were burned,[4] are those who have departed for ever from the living God; nor does the thought of repentance ever come into their hearts, on account of their devotion to their lusts and to the crimes which they committed. Do you wish to know who are the others which fell near the waters, but could not be rolled into them? These are they who have heard the word, and wish to be baptized in the name of the Lord; but when the chastity demanded by the truth comes into their recollection, they draw back,[5] and again walk after their own wicked desires." She finished her exposition of the tower. But I, shameless as I yet was, asked her, "Is repent-

ance possible for all those stones which have been cast away and did not fit into the building of the tower, and will they yet have a place in this tower?" "Repentance," said she, "is yet possible, but in this tower they cannot find a suitable place. But in another[6] and much inferior place they will be laid, and that, too, only when they have been tortured and completed the days of their sins. And on this account will they be transferred, because they have partaken of the righteous Word.[7] And then only will they be removed from their punishments when the thought of repenting of the evil deeds which they have done has come into their hearts. But if it does not come into their hearts, they will not be saved, on account of the hardness of their heart."

CHAP. VIII.

When then I ceased asking in regard to all these matters, she said to me, "Do you wish to see anything else?" And as I was extremely eager to see something more, my countenance beamed with joy. She looked towards me with a smile, and said, "Do you see seven women around the tower?" "I do, Lady," said I. "This tower," said she, "is supported by them according to the precept of the Lord. Listen now to their functions. The first of them, who is clasping her hands, is called Faith. Through her the elect of God are saved.[8] Another, who has her garments tucked up[9] and acts with vigour, is called Self-restraint. She is the daughter of Faith. Whoever then follows her will become happy in his life, because he will restrain himself from all evil works, believing that, if he restrain himself from all evil desire, he will inherit eternal life." "But the others," said I, "O Lady, who are they?" And she said to me, "They are daughters of each other. One of them is called Simplicity, another Guilelessness, another Chastity, another Intelligence, another Love. When then you do all the works of their mother,[10] you will be able to live." "I should like to know," said I, "O Lady, what power each one of them possesses." "Hear," she said, "what power they have. Their powers are regulated[11] by each other, and follow each other in the

---

[1] [Matt. xiii. 21.]

[2] *Use . . . God.* Then will they be of use for the building of the Lord.—*Vat.* [1 Cor. iii. 9-15. But, instead of *circumscribed,* let us read *circumcised* (with the Latin); with reference to the circumcision of wealth (*of trees* under the law, Lev. xix. 23), Luke xi. 41. The Greek of Hermas is ὅταν περικοπῇ αὐτῶν ὁ πλοῦτος.]

[3] *For . . . stones.* For you yourself were also one of these stones.—*Vat.*

[4] [Heb. iii. 12, vi. 8.]

[5] The words " draw back" are represented in Greek by the word elsewhere translated " repent ; " μετανοεῖν is thus used for a change of mind, either from evil to good, or good to evil.

[6] [Perhaps the earliest reference to the penitential discipline which was developed after the Nicene Council, and to the separation of the *Flentes* and others from the faithful, in public worship. But compare Irenæus (vol. i. p. 335, this series), who refers to this discipline; also *Apost. Constitutions,* book ii. cap. 39. I prefer in this chapter Wake's rendering; and see Bingham, book xviii. cap. 1.]

[7] [Greek, ῥῆμα not λόγος. To translate this as if it referred to the Word (St. John i. 1) is a great mistake (Heb. xi. 3). Compare Wake's rendering. It seems a reference to the *audientes,* separated from the *faithful,* but admitted to hear the Word. See Bingham, and *Apost. Constit.,* as above.]

[8] [Salvation is ascribed to faith; and works of faith follow after, being faith in action.]

[9] [*Girded* rather, the loins compressed.]

[10] [Their mother is Faith (*ut supra*), and works of faith are here represented as deriving their value from faith only.]

[11] *Regulated.* They have equal powers, but their powers are connected with each other.—*Vat.*

order of their birth. For from Faith arises Self-restraint; from Self-restraint, Simplicity; from Simplicity, Guilelessness; from Guilelessness, Chastity; from Chastity, Intelligence; and from Intelligence, Love. The deeds, then, of these are pure, and chaste, and divine. Whoever devotes himself to these, and is able to hold fast by their works, shall have his dwelling in the tower with the saints of God." Then I asked her in regard to the ages, if now there is the conclusion. She cried out with a loud voice, "Foolish man! do you not see the tower yet building? When the tower is finished and built, then comes the end; and I assure you it will be soon finished. Ask me no more questions. Let you and all the saints be content with what I have called to your remembrance, and with my renewal of your spirits. But observe that it is not for your own sake only that these revelations have been made to you, but they have been given you that you may show them to all. For[1] after three days — this you will take care to remember — I command you to speak all the words which I am to say to you into the ears of the saints, that hearing them and doing them, they may be cleansed from their iniquities, and you along with them."

CHAP. IX.

Give ear unto me, O Sons: I have brought you up in much simplicity, and guilelessness, and chastity, on account of the mercy of the Lord,[2] who has dropped His righteousness down upon you, that ye may be made righteous and holy[3] from all your iniquity and depravity; but you do not wish to rest from your iniquity. Now, therefore, listen to me, and be at peace one with another, and visit each other, and bear each other's burdens, and do not partake of God's creatures alone,[4] but give abundantly of them to the needy. For some through the abundance of their food produce weakness in their flesh, and thus corrupt their flesh; while the flesh of others who have no food is corrupted, because they have not sufficient nourishment. And on this account their bodies waste away. This intemperance in eating is thus injurious to you who have abundance and do not distribute among those who are needy. Give heed to the judgment that is to come. Ye, therefore, who are high in position, seek out the hungry as long as the tower is not yet finished; for after the tower is finished, you will wish to do good, but will find no opportunity. Give heed, therefore,

ye who glory in your wealth, lest those who are needy should groan, and their groans should ascend to the Lord,[5] and ye be shut out with all your goods beyond the gate of the tower. Wherefore I now say to you who preside over the Church and love the first seats,[6] "Be not like to drug-mixers. For the drug-mixers carry their drugs in boxes, but ye carry your drug and poison in your heart. Ye are hardened, and do not wish to cleanse your hearts, and to add unity of aim to purity of heart, that you may have mercy from the great King. Take heed, therefore, children, that these dissensions of yours do not deprive you of your life. How will you instruct the elect of the Lord, if you yourselves have not instruction? Instruct each other therefore, and be at peace among yourselves, that[7] I also, standing joyful before your Father, may give an account of you all to your Lord."[8]

CHAP. X.

On her ceasing to speak to me, those six young men who were engaged in building came and conveyed her to the tower, and other four lifted up the seat and carried it also to the tower. The faces of these last I did not see, for they were turned away from me. And as she was going, I asked her to reveal to me the meaning of the three forms in which she appeared to me. In reply she said to me: "With regard to them, you must ask another to reveal their meaning to you." For she had appeared to me, brethren, in the first vision the previous year under the form of an exceedingly old woman, sitting in a chair. In the second vision her face was youthful, but her skin and hair betokened age, and she stood while she spoke to me. She was also more joyful than on the first occasion. But in the third vision she was entirely youthful and exquisitely beautiful, except only that she had the hair of an old woman; but her face beamed with joy, and she sat on a seat. Now I was exceeding sad in regard to these appearances, for I longed much to know what the visions meant. Then I see the old woman in a vision of the night saying unto me: "Every prayer should be accompanied with humility: fast,[9] therefore, and you will obtain from the Lord what you beg." I fasted therefore for one day.

That very night there appeared to me a young man, who said, "Why do you frequently ask revelations in prayer? Take heed lest by asking many things you injure your flesh: be content

---

[1] [Apparently for fasting, and to wait for the appearance of the interpreter, in cap. x.]
[2] *The Lord.* God. — *Vat.* [See Hos. x. 12.]
[3] Or, that ye may be justified and sanctified.
[4] I have translated the Vat. reading here. The Greek seems to mean, "Do not partake of God's creatures alone by way of mere relish." The Pal. has, "Do not partake of God's creatures alone joylessly, in a way calculated to defeat enjoyment of them."

[5] [Jas. v. 1–4.]
[6] *Those that love the first seats*, omitted in Æth. [Greek, τοῖς προηγουμένοις τῆς ἐκκλησίας καὶ τοῖς πρωτοκαθεδρίταις. Hermas seems, purposely, colourless as to technical distinctions in the clergy; giving a more primitive cast to his fiction, by this feature. Matt. xxiii. 6; Mark xii. 39; Luke xi. 43, xx. 46.]
[7] [Rom. ii. 21; 1 Thess. v. 13.]
[8] [Heb. xiii. 17.]
[9] *Fast.* Believe. — *Pal.*

with these revelations. Will you be able to see greater[1] revelations than those which you have seen?" I answered and said to him, "Sir, one thing only I ask, that in regard to these three forms the revelation may be rendered complete." He answered me, "How long are ye senseless?[2] But your doubts make you senseless, because you have not your hearts turned towards the Lord." But I answered and said to him, "From you, sir, we shall learn these things more accurately."

CHAP. XI.

"Hear then," said he, "with regard to the three forms, concerning which you are inquiring. Why in the first vision did she appear to you as an old woman seated on a chair? Because your spirit is now old and withered up, and has lost its power in consequence of your infirmities and doubts. For, like elderly men who have no hope of renewing their strength, and expect nothing but their last sleep, so you, weakened by worldly occupations, have given yourselves up to sloth, and have not cast your cares upon the Lord.[3] Your spirit therefore is broken, and you have grown old in your sorrows." "I should like then to know, sir, why she sat on a chair?" He answered, "Because every weak person sits on a chair on account of his weakness, that his weakness may be sustained. Lo! you have the form of the first vision.

CHAP. XII.

"Now in the second vision you saw her standing with a youthful countenance, and more joyful than before; still she had the skin and hair of an aged woman. Hear," said he, "this parable also. When one becomes somewhat old, he despairs of himself on account of his weakness and poverty, and looks forward to nothing but the last day of his life. Then suddenly an inheritance is left him: and hearing of this, he rises up, and becoming exceeding joyful, he puts on strength. And now he no longer reclines, but stands up; and his spirit, already destroyed by his previous actions, is renewed,[4] and he no longer sits, but acts with vigour. So happened it with you on hearing the revelation which God gave you. For the Lord had compassion on you, and renewed your spirit, and ye laid aside your infirmities. Vigour arose within you, and ye grew strong in faith; and the Lord,[5] seeing your strength, rejoiced. On this account He showed you the building of the tower; and He will show you other things, if you continue at peace with each other with all your heart.

CHAP. XIII.

"Now, in the third vision, you saw her still younger, and she was noble and joyful, and her shape was beautiful.[6] For, just as when some good news comes suddenly to one who is sad, immediately he forgets his former sorrows, and looks for nothing else than the good news which he has heard, and for the future is made strong for good, and his spirit is renewed on account of the joy which he has received; so ye also have received the renewal of your spirits by seeing these good things. As to your seeing her sitting on a seat, that means that her position is one of strength, for a seat has four feet and stands firmly. For the world also is kept together by means of four elements. Those, therefore, who repent completely and with the whole heart, will become young and firmly established. You now have the revelation completely given you.[7] Make no further demands for revelations. If anything ought to be revealed, it will be revealed to you."

VISION FOURTH.

CONCERNING THE TRIAL AND TRIBULATION THAT ARE TO COME UPON MEN.

CHAP. I.

Twenty days after the former vision I saw another vision, brethren[8] — a representation of the tribulation[9] that is to come. I was going to a country house along the Campanian road. Now the house lay about ten furlongs from the public road. The district is one rarely[10] traversed. And as I walked alone, I prayed the Lord to complete the revelations which He had made to me through His holy Church, that He might strengthen me,[11] and give repentance to all His servants who were going astray, that His great and glorious name might be glorified because He vouchsafed to show me His marvels.[12] And while I was glorifying Him and giving Him thanks, a voice, as it were, answered me, "Doubt not, Hermas;" and I began to think with myself, and to say, "What reason have I to doubt — I who have been established by the Lord, and who have seen such glorious sights?" I advanced a little, brethren, and, lo! I see dust rising even to the heavens. I began to say to myself, "Are cattle approaching and raising the dust?" It was about a furlong's distance from me. And,

1 Literally, "stronger," and therefore more injurious to the body.
2 *How long.* Ye are not senseless. — *Vat.* [Matt. xvii. 17; Luke xxiv. 25.]
3 [1 Pet. v. 7.]
4 *His spirit . . . renewed.* He is freed from his former sorrows. — *Vat.*
5 *The Lord.* God. — *Vat.*

6 *Shape . . . beautiful.* Her countenance was serene. — *Vat.*
7 [As Dupin suggests of *The Shepherd*, generally, one may feel that these "revelations" would be better without the symbolical part.]
8 [This address to "brethren" sustains the form of the primitive *prophesyings*, in the congregation.]
9 [One of the tribulations spoken of in the Apocalypse is probably intended. This Vision is full of the imagery of the Book of Revelation.]
10 *Rarely.* Easily. — *Lips., Sin.*
11 *He might strengthen me*, omitted in Vat.
12 *For . . . marvels.* This clause is connected with the subsequent sentence in Vat.

lo ! I see the dust rising more and more, so that I imagined that it was something sent from God. But the sun now shone out a little, and, lo ! I see a mighty beast like a whale, and out of its mouth fiery locusts[1] proceeded. But the size of that beast was about a hundred feet, and it had a head like an urn.[2] I began to weep, and to call on the Lord to rescue me from it. Then I remembered the word which I had heard, "Doubt not, O Hermas." Clothed, therefore, my brethren, with faith in the Lord,[3] and remembering the great things which He had taught me, I boldly faced the beast. Now that beast came on with such noise and force, that it could itself have destroyed a city.[4] I came near it, and the monstrous beast stretched itself out on the ground, and showed nothing but its tongue, and did not stir at all until I had passed by it. Now the beast had four colours on its head — black, then fiery and bloody, then golden, and lastly white.

CHAP. II.

Now after I had passed by the wild beast, and had moved forward about thirty feet, lo ! a virgin meets me, adorned as if she were proceeding from the bridal chamber, clothed entirely in white, and with white sandals, and veiled up to her forehead, and her head was covered by a hood.[5] And she had white hair. I knew from my former visions that this was the Church, and I became more joyful. She saluted me, and said, "Hail, O man !" And I returned her salutation, and said, "Lady, hail !" And she answered. and said to me, "Has nothing crossed your path?" I say, "I was met by a beast of such a size that it could destroy peoples, but through the power of the Lord[6] and His great mercy I escaped from it." "Well did you escape from it," says she, "because you cast your care[7] on God,[8] and opened your heart to the Lord, believing that you can be saved by no other than by His great and glorious name.[9] On this account the Lord has sent His angel, who has rule over the beasts, and whose name is Thegri,[10] and has shut up its mouth, so that it cannot tear you. You have escaped from great tribulation on account of your faith, and because you did not doubt in the presence of such a beast. Go, therefore, and tell the elect of the Lord[11] His mighty deeds, and say to them that this beast is a type of the great tribulation that is coming. If then ye prepare yourselves, and repent with all your heart, and turn to the Lord, it will be possible for you to escape it, if your heart be pure and spotless, and ye spend the rest of the days of your life in serving the Lord blamelessly. Cast your cares upon the Lord, and He will direct them. Trust the Lord, ye who doubt, for He is all-powerful, and can turn His anger away from you, and send scourges[12] on the doubters. Woe to those who hear these words, and despise them : [13] better were it for them not to have been born." [14]

CHAP. III.

I asked her about the four colours which the beast had on his head. And she answered, and said to me, "Again you are inquisitive in regard to such matters." "Yea, Lady," said I, "make known to me what they are." "Listen," said she : "the black is the world in which we dwell : but the fiery and bloody points out that the world must perish through blood and fire : but the golden part are you who have escaped from this world. For as gold is tested by fire, and thus becomes useful, so are you tested who dwell in it. Those, therefore, who continue stedfast, and are put through the fire, will be purified by means of it. For as gold casts away its dross, so also will ye cast away all sadness and straitness, and will be made pure so as to fit into the building of the tower. But the white part is the age that is to come, in which the elect of God will dwell, since those elected by God to eternal life will be spotless and pure. Wherefore cease not speaking these things into the ears of the saints. This then is the type of the great tribulation that is to come. If ye wish it, it will be nothing. Remember those things which were written down before." And saying this, she departed. But I saw not into what place she retired. There was a noise, however, and I turned round in alarm, thinking that that beast was coming.[15]

VISION FIFTH.

CONCERNING THE COMMANDMENTS.[16]

After I had been praying at home, and had sat down on my couch, there entered a man of

---

[1] [Rev. ix. 3.]
[2] Comp. Rev. xi. 7, xii. 3, 4, xiii. 1, xvii. 8, xxii. 2. [The beast was "like a whale" in size and proportion. It was not a sea-monster. This whole passage is *Dantesque*. See *Inferno*, canto xxxi., and, for the colours, canto xvii. 15.]
[3] God. — *Lips.*, *Vat.*
[4] The Vat. adds: with a stroke.
[5] [Those who remember the Vatican collection and other *antiques*, will recall the exquisite figure and veiling of the *Pudicitia*.]
[6] *The Lord.* God. — *Vat.*
[7] *Care.* Loneliness and anxiety. — *Vat.*
[8] *God.* The Lord. — *Vat.*
[9] [Acts iv. 12.]
[10] *Thegri.* [Perhaps compounded from θήρ and ἀγρεύω.] The name of this angel is variously written, Hegrin [*Query. Quasi* ἐγρηγορεῖν, or corrupted from (*Sept.*) εἰρ καὶ ἅγιος; *Hir* in Daniel's Chaldee], Tegri. Some have supposed the word to be for ἄγριον, *the wild;* some have taken it to mean "the watchful," as in Dan. iv. 10, 23: and some take it to be the name of a fabulous lion. [See, also, Dan. vi. 22.]

[11] *The Lord.* God. — *Vat.*
[12] *Send scourges.* Send you help. But woe to the doubters who. — *Vat.*
[13] [1 Thess. v. 20.]
[14] Matt. xxvi. 24.
[15] [Very much resembling Dante, again, in many passages. *Inferno*, xxi. "Allor mi volsi," etc.]
[16] [This vision naturally belongs to book ii., to which it is a preface.]

glorious aspect, dressed like a shepherd, with a white goat's skin, a wallet on his shoulders, and a rod in his hand, and saluted me. I returned his salutation. And straightway he sat down beside me, and said to me, "I have been sent by a most venerable angel to dwell with you the remaining days of your life." And I thought that he had come to tempt me, and I said to him, "Who are you? For I know him to whom I have been entrusted." He said to me, "Do you not know me?" "No," said I. "I," said he, "am that shepherd to whom you have been entrusted." And while he yet spake, his figure was changed; and then I knew that it was he to whom I had been entrusted. And straightway I became confused, and fear took hold of me, and I was overpowered with deep sorrow that I had answered him so wickedly and foolishly. But he answered, and said to me, "Do not be confounded, but receive strength from the commandments which I am going to give you. For I have been sent," said he, "to show you again all the things which you saw before, especially those of them which are useful to you. First of all, then, write down my commandments and similitudes, and you will write the other things as I shall show you. For this purpose," said he, "I command you to write down the commandments and similitudes first, that you may read them easily, and be able to keep them."[1] Accordingly I wrote down the commandments and similitudes, exactly as he had ordered me. If then, when you have heard these, ye keep them and walk in them, and practise them with pure minds, you will receive from the Lord all that He has promised to you. But if, after you have heard them, ye do not repent, but continue to add to your sins, then shall ye receive from the Lord the opposite things. All these words did the shepherd, even the angel of repentance, command me to write.[2]

---

[1] *Keep them.* That you may be able to keep them more easily by reading them from time to time. — *Vat.*

[2] ["The Shepherd," then, is the "angel of repentance," here represented as a guardian angel. This gives the work its character, as enforcing primarily the anti-Montanist principle of the value of true repentance in the sight of God.]

THE PASTOR

BOOK SECOND. — COMMANDMENTS

COMMANDMENT FIRST.

ON FAITH IN GOD.

First of all, believe [1] that there is one God who created and finished all things, and made all things out of nothing. He alone is able to contain the whole, but Himself cannot be contained.[2] Have faith therefore in Him, and fear Him; and fearing Him, exercise self-control. Keep these commands, and you will cast away from you all wickedness, and put on the strength of righteousness, and live to God, if you keep this commandment.

COMMANDMENT SECOND.

ON AVOIDING EVIL-SPEAKING, AND ON GIVING ALMS IN SIMPLICITY.

He said to me, "Be simple and guileless, and you will be as the children who know not the wickedness that ruins the life of men. First, then, speak evil of no one, nor listen with pleasure to any one who speaks evil of another. But if you listen, you will partake of the sin of him who speaks evil, if you believe the slander which you hear;[3] for believing it, you will also have something to say against your brother. Thus, then, will you be guilty of the sin of him who slanders. For slander is evil[4] and an unsteady demon. It never abides in peace, but always remains in discord. Keep yourself from it, and you will always be at peace with all. Put on a holiness in which there is no wicked cause of offence, but all deeds that are equable and joyful. Practise goodness; and from the rewards of your labours, which God gives you, give to all the needy in simplicity, not hesitating as to whom you are to give or not to give. Give to all, for God wishes His gifts to be shared amongst all. They who receive, will render an account to God why and for what they have received. For the afflicted who receive will not be condemned,[5] but they who receive on false pretences will suffer punishment. He, then, who gives is guiltless. For as he received from the Lord, so has he accomplished his service in simplicity, not hesitating as to whom he should give and to whom he should not give. This service, then, if accomplished in simplicity, is glorious with God. He, therefore, who thus ministers in simplicity, will live to God.[6] Keep therefore these commandments, as I have given them to you, that your repentance and the repentance of your house may be found in simplicity, and your heart [7] may be pure and stainless."

---

[1] [These first words are quoted by Irenæus, vol. i. p. 488, this series. Note that this book begins with the fundamental principle of faith, which is everywhere identified by Hermas (as in Vision ii. cap. 2) with faith in the Son of God. The Holy Spirit is also everywhere exhibited in this work. But the careful student will discover a very deep plan in the treatment of this subject. Repentance and faith are the great themes, and the long-suffering of God, against the Montanists. But he begins by indicating the divine character and the law of God. He treats of sin in its relations to the law and the gospel: little by little, opening the way, he reaches a point, in the Eighth Similitude, where he introduces the New Law, identifying it, indeed, with the old, but magnifying the gospel of the Son of God. Hermas takes for granted the "Son of man;" but everywhere he avoids the names of His humanity, and brings out "the Son of God" with emphasis, in the spirit of St. John's Gospel (cap. i.) and of the Epistle to the Hebrews (cap. i.), as if he feared the familiarities even of believers in speaking of Jesus or of Christ, without recognising His eternal power and Godhead.]

[2] *Contained.* — Vat. and Pal. add: and who cannot be defined in words, nor conceived by the mind. [Here we have the "Incomprehensible," so familiar in the liturgic formula improperly called the *Athanasian Creed.* In the Latin *immensus*, in the Greek ἄπειρος; i. e., "non mensurabilis, quiâ *inlocalis*, incircumscriptus, ubique totus, ubique prœsens, ubique potens." *Not intelligible* is too frequently supposed to be the sense, but this is feeble and ambiguous. See Waterland, Works, iv. p. 320. London, 1823.]

[3] *If . . . brother.* [Jas. iv. 11.] And if you believe the slanderer, you will also be guilty of sin, in that you have believed one who speaks evil of your brother. — *Vat.* For if you give your assent to the detractor, and believe what is said of one in his absence, you also will be like to him, and acting ruinously towards your brother, and you are guilty of the same sin as the person who slanders. — *Pal.*

[4] For slander is ruihous. — *Vat.* For it is wicked to slander any one. — *Pal.*

[5] *For . . . condemned,* omitted in Vat.

[6] *This service . . . God.* And he has accomplished this service to God simply and gloriously. — *Vat.* [Rom. xii. 8.]

[7] The Vat. adds: and a blessing may fall on your house.

COMMANDMENT THIRD.

ON AVOIDING FALSEHOOD, AND ON THE REPENTANCE OF HERMAS FOR HIS DISSIMULATION.

Again he said to me, "Love the truth, and let nothing but truth proceed from your mouth,[1] that the spirit which God has placed in your flesh may be found truthful before all men; and the Lord, who dwelleth in you,[2] will be glorified, because the Lord is truthful in every word, and in Him is no falsehood. They therefore who lie deny the Lord, and rob Him, not giving back to Him the deposit which they have received. For they received from Him a spirit free from falsehood.[3] If they give him back this spirit untruthful, they pollute the commandment of the Lord, and become robbers." On hearing these words, I wept most violently. When he saw me weeping, he said to me, "Why do you weep?" And I said, "Because, sir, I know not if I can be saved." "Why?" said he. And I said, "Because, sir, I never spake a true word in my life, but have ever spoken cunningly to all,[4] and have affirmed a lie for the truth to all; and no one ever contradicted me, but credit was given to my word. How then can I live, since I have acted thus?" And he said to me, "Your feelings are indeed right and sound, for you ought as a servant of God to have walked in truth, and not to have joined an evil conscience with the spirit of truth, nor to have caused sadness to the holy and true Spirit."[5] And I said to him, "Never, sir, did I listen to these words with so much attention." And he said to me, "Now you hear them, and keep them, that even the falsehoods which you formerly told in your transactions may come to be believed through the truthfulness of your present statements. For even they can become worthy of credit. If you keep these precepts, and from this time forward you speak nothing but the truth,[6] it will be possible for you to obtain life. And whosoever shall hear this commandment, and depart from that great wickedness falsehood, shall live to God."

COMMANDMENT FOURTH.

ON PUTTING ONE'S WIFE AWAY FOR ADULTERY.

CHAP. I.

"I charge you," said he, "to guard your chastity, and let no thought enter your heart of another man's wife, or of fornication, or of similar iniquities; for by doing this you commit a great sin. But if you always remember your own wife, you will never sin. For if this thought[7] enter your heart, then you will sin; and if, in like manner, you think other wicked thoughts, you commit sin. For this thought is great sin in a servant of God. But if any one commit this wicked deed, he works death for himself. Attend, therefore, and refrain from this thought; for where purity dwells, there iniquity ought not to enter the heart of a righteous man." I said to him, "Sir, permit me to ask you a few questions."[8] "Say on," said he. And I said to him, "Sir, if any one has a wife who trusts in the Lord, and if he detect her in adultery, does the man sin if he continue to live with her?" And he said to me, "As long as he remains ignorant of her sin, the husband commits no transgression in living with her. But if the husband know that his wife has gone astray, and if the woman does not repent, but persists in her fornication, and yet the husband continues to live with her, he also is guilty of her crime, and a sharer in her adultery." And I said to him, "What then, sir, is the husband to do, if his wife continue in her vicious practices?" And he said, "The husband should put her away, and remain by himself. But if he put his wife away and marry another, he also commits adultery."[9] And I said to him, "What if the woman put away should repent, and wish to return to her husband: shall she not be taken back by her husband?" And he said to me, "Assuredly. If the husband do not take her back, he sins, and brings a great sin upon himself; for he ought to take back the sinner who has repented. But not frequently.[10] For there is but one repentance to the servants of God. In case, therefore, that the divorced wife may repent, the husband ought not to marry another, when his wife has been put away. In this matter man and woman are to be treated exactly in the same way. Moreover, adultery is committed not only by those who pollute their flesh, but by those who imitate the heathen in their actions.[11] Wherefore if any one[12]

---

1 [Eph. iv. 25, 29.]
2 *Dwelleth in you.* Who put the spirit within you. — *Vat.*
3 [The seven gifts of the Spirit are here referred to, especially the gift of "true godliness," with a reference to the parable of the talents (Matt. xxv. 15), and also to 1 John ii. 20–27.]
4 *Cunningly to all.* Have ever lived in dissimulation. — *Vat.* Lived cunningly with all. — *Pal.* [Custom-house oaths and business lies among moderns.]
5 The Vat. adds: of God. [1 John iii. 19–21, iv. 6, and Eph. iv. 30.]
6 *For . . . truth.* For even they can become worthy of credit, if you will speak the truth in future; and if you keep the truth. — *Vat.* [See, under the Tenth Mandate, p. 26, in this book.]

7 *This thought.* [Matt. v. 28. See, further, Simil. ix. cap. 11.] The thought of another man's wife or of fornication.
8 *Questions.* "I charge you," said he, "to guard your chastity, and let no thought enter your heart of another man's marriage (i.e., wife), or of fornication, for this produces a great transgression. But be always mindful of the Lord at all hours, and you will never sin. For if this very wicked thought enter your heart, you commit a great sin, and they who practise such deeds follow the way of death. Take heed, therefore, and refrain from this thought. For where chastity remains in the heart of a righteous man, never ought there to arise any evil thought." I said to him, "Sir, permit me to say a few words to you." "Say on," said he. — *Vat.*
9 Matt. v. 32, xix. 9.
10 [*Not frequently . . . one repentance.* True penitence is a habit of life. An apparent safe-guard against the reproaches of Montanism, and a caution not to turn forgiveness into a momentary sponge without avoiding renewed transgression.]
11 *Who . . . actions.* But he who makes an image also commits adultery. — *Vat.*
12 *Any one.* She. — *Vat.* [2 Thess. iii. 14; 2 John 11.]

persists in such deeds, and repents not, withdraw from him, and cease to live with him, otherwise you are a sharer in his sin. Therefore has the injunction been laid on you, that you should remain by yourselves, both man and woman, for in such persons repentance can take place. But I do not," said he, "give opportunity for the doing of these deeds, but that he who has sinned may sin no more. But with regard to his previous transgressions, there is One who is able to provide a cure;[1] for it is He, indeed, who has power over all."

CHAP. II.

I asked him again, and said, "Since the Lord has vouchsafed to dwell always with me, bear with me while I utter a few words;[2] for I understand nothing, and my heart has been hardened by my previous mode of life. Give me understanding, for I am exceedingly dull, and I understand absolutely nothing." And he answered and said unto me, "I am set over repentance, and I give understanding to all who repent. Do you not think," he said, "that it is great wisdom to repent? for repentance is great wisdom.[3] For he who has sinned understands that he acted wickedly in the sight of the Lord, and remembers the actions he has done, and he repents, and no longer acts wickedly, but does good munificently, and humbles and torments his soul because he has sinned. You see, therefore, that repentance is great wisdom." And I said to him, "It is for this reason, sir, that I inquire carefully into all things, especially because I am a sinner; that I may know what works I should do, that I may live: for my sins are many and various." And he said to me, "You shall live if you keep my commandments,[4] and walk in them; and whosoever shall hear and keep these commandments, shall live to God."

CHAP. III.

And I said to him, "I should like to continue my questions." "Speak on," said he. And I said, "I heard, sir, some teachers maintain that there is no other repentance than that which takes place, when we descended into the water[5] and received remission of our former sins." He said to me, "That was sound doctrine which you heard; for that is really the case. For he who has received remission of his sins ought not to sin any more, but to live in purity. Since,

however, you inquire diligently into all things, I will point this also out to you, not as giving occasion for error to those who are to believe, or have lately believed, in the Lord. For those who have now believed, and those who are to believe, have not repentance for their sins; but they have remission of their previous sins. For to those who have been called before these days, the Lord has set repentance. For the Lord, knowing the heart, and foreknowing all things, knew the weakness of men and the manifold wiles of the devil, that he would inflict some evil on the servants of God, and would act wickedly towards them.[6] The Lord, therefore, being merciful, has had mercy on the work of His hand, and has set repentance for them; and He has entrusted to me power over this repentance. And therefore I say to you, that if any one is tempted by the devil, and sins after that great and holy calling in which the Lord has called His people to everlasting life,[7] he has opportunity to repent but once. But if he should sin frequently after this, and then repent, to such a man his repentance will be of no avail; for with difficulty will he live."[8] And I said, "Sir, I feel that life has come back to me in listening attentively to these commandments; for I know that I shall be saved, if in future I sin no more." And he said, "You will be saved, you and all who keep these commandments."

CHAP. IV.

And again I asked him, saying, "Sir, since you have been so patient in listening to me, will you show me this also?" "Speak," said he. And I said, "If a wife or husband die, and the widower or widow marry, does he or she commit sin?" "There is no sin in marrying again," said he; "but if they remain unmarried, they gain greater honour and glory with the Lord; but if they marry, they do not sin.[9] Guard, therefore, your chastity and purity, and you will live to God. What commandments I now give you, and what I am to give, keep from henceforth, yea, from the very day when you were entrusted to me, and I will dwell in your house. And your former sins will be forgiven, if you keep my commandments. And all shall be forgiven who keep these my commandments, and walk in this chastity."

---

1 *There . . . cure.* God, who has power to heal, will provide a remedy. — *Vat.* [This whole passage seems to refer to the separation of penitents under canonical discipline. Tertullian, *Pudicit.*, capp. 5, 13, and *De Penitent.*, cap. 9. 2 Thess. iii. 14.]
2 *Bear . . . words.* Give me a few words of explanation. — *Vat.*
3 *Repentance . . . wisdom.* For he who repents obtains great intelligence. For he feels that he has sinned and acted wickedly. — *Vat.* ["Wisdom and understanding;" spiritual gifts here instanced as requisite to true penitence and spiritual life.]
4 [Matt. xix. 17. Saint-Pierre, *Harm. de la Nature*, iii. p. 150.]
5 [Immersion continues to be the usage, then, even in the West, at this epoch.]

6 *For . . . them.* Since God knows the thoughts of all hearts, and the weakness of men, and the manifold wickedness of the devil which he practises in plotting against the servants of God, and in malignant designs against them. — *Vat.*
7 *In . . . life.* These words occur only in Pal. [Can the following words be genuine? They reflect the very Montanism here so strictly opposed. Wake has followed a very different text. The Scriptures, it is true, use very awful language of the same kind: Heb. x. 26, 27, xii. 16, 17; 1 John iii. 9.]
8 *With . . . live.* With difficulty will he live to God. — *Vat.* and *Pal.*
9 [1 Cor. vii. 39; Rom. vii. 3. See my note on Simil. ix. cap. 28. Here are touching illustrations of the new spirit as to the sanctity of marriage, to which the Gospel was awakening the heathen mind.]

COMMANDMENT FIFTH.

OF SADNESS OF HEART, AND OF PATIENCE.

CHAP. I.

"Be patient," said he, "and of good understanding, and you will rule over every wicked work, and you will work all righteousness. For if you be patient, the Holy Spirit that dwells in you will be pure. He will not be darkened by any evil spirit, but, dwelling in a broad region,[1] he will rejoice and be glad ; and with the vessel in which he dwells he will serve God in gladness, having great peace within himself.[2] But if any outburst of anger take place, forthwith the Holy Spirit, who is tender, is straitened, not having a pure place, and He seeks to depart. For he is choked by the vile spirit, and cannot attend on the Lord as he wishes, for anger pollutes him. For the Lord dwells in long-suffering, but the devil in anger.[3] The two spirits, then, when dwelling in the same habitation, are at discord with each other, and are troublesome to that man in whom they dwell.[4] For if an exceedingly small piece of wormwood be taken and put into a jar of honey, is not the honey entirely destroyed, and does not the exceedingly small piece of wormwood entirely take away the sweetness of the honey, so that it no longer affords any gratification to its owner, but has become bitter, and lost its use? But if the wormwood be not put into the honey, then the honey remains sweet, and is of use to its owner. You see, then, that patience is sweeter than honey, and useful to God, and the Lord dwells in it. But anger is bitter and useless. Now, if anger be mingled with patience, the patience is polluted,[5] and its prayer is not then useful to God."
"I should like, sir," said I, "to know the power of anger, that I may guard myself against it." And he said, "If you do not guard yourself against it, you and your house lose all hope of salvation. Guard yourself, therefore, against it. For I am with you, and all will depart from it who repent with their whole heart.[6] For I will be with them, and I will save them all. For all are justified by the most holy angel.[7]

CHAP. II.

"Hear now," said he, "how wicked is the action of anger, and in what way it overthrows the servants of God by its action, and turns them from righteousness. But it does not turn away those who are full of faith, nor does it act on them, for the power of the Lord is with them. It is the thoughtless and doubting that it turns away.[8] For as soon as it sees such men standing stedfast, it throws itself into their hearts, and for nothing at all the man or woman becomes embittered on account of occurrences in their daily life, as for instance on account of their food, or some superfluous word that has been uttered, or on account of some friend, or some gift or debt, or some such senseless affair. For all these things are foolish and empty and unprofitable to the servants of God. But patience is great, and mighty, and strong, and calm in the midst of great enlargement, joyful, rejoicing, free from care, glorifying God at all times, having no bitterness in her, and abiding continually meek and quiet. Now this patience dwells with those who have complete faith. But anger is foolish, and fickle, and senseless. Now, of folly is begotten bitterness, and of bitterness anger, and of anger frenzy. This frenzy, the product of so many evils, ends in great and incurable sin. For when all these spirits dwell in one vessel in which the Holy Spirit also dwells, the vessel cannot contain them, but overflows. The tender Spirit, then, not being accustomed to dwell with the wicked spirit, nor with hardness, withdraws from such a man, and seeks to dwell with meekness and peacefulness. Then, when he withdraws from the man in whom he dwelt, the man is emptied of the righteous Spirit ; and being henceforward filled with evil spirits,[9] he is in a state of anarchy in every action, being dragged hither and thither by the evil spirits, and there is a complete darkness in his mind as to everything good. This, then, is what happens to all the angry. Wherefore do you depart from that most wicked spirit anger, and put on patience, and resist anger and bitterness, and you will be found in company with the purity which is loved by the Lord.[10] Take care, then, that you neglect not by any chance this commandment: for if you obey this commandment, you will be able to keep all the other commandments which I am to give you. Be strong, then, in these commandments, and put on power, and

---

[1] It will be noticed that space is attributed to the heart or soul, and that joy and goodness expand the heart, and produce width, while sadness and wickedness contract and straiten.

[2] *But . . . himself.* But rejoicing he will be expanded, and he will feast in the vessel in which he dwells, and he will serve the Lord joyfully in the midst of great peace. — *Vat.* He will serve the Lord in great gladness, having abundance of all things within himself. — *Pal.*

[3] *For . . . anger,* omitted in Vat.; fuller in Pal.: For the Lord dwells in calmness and greatness of mind, but anger is the devil's house of entertainment. [Eph. iv. 26, 27.]

[4] [Jas. iii. 11.]

[5] *Patience is polluted.* The mind is distressed. — *Vat.* ; omitted in Pal.

[6] *I . . . heart.* I, the angel [or messenger] of righteousness, am with you, and all who depart from anger, and repent with their whole heart, will live to God. — *Vat.*

[7] *Are justified.* Are received into the number of the just by the most holy angel (or messenger). — *Pal.* [i.e., As the *instrument* of justification ; but the superlative here used seems to identify this angel with that of the covenant (Mal. iii. 1); i.e., the meritorious cause, "the Lord."]

[8] *Hear . . . away.* "Hear now," said he, "how great is the wickedness of anger, and how injurious, and in what way it overthrows the servants of God. For they who are full of faith receive no harm from it, for the power of God is with them; for it is the doubters and those destitute [of faith] that it overturns." — *Vat.* [The philosophic difference between anger and indignation is here in view.]

[9] [Matt. xii. 45; Luke xi. 26.]

[10] *You . . . Lord.* You will be found by God in the company of purity and chastity. — *Vat.*

let all put on power, as many as wish to walk in them." [1]

COMMANDMENT SIXTH.

HOW TO RECOGNISE THE TWO SPIRITS ATTENDANT ON EACH MAN, AND HOW TO DISTINGUISH THE SUGGESTIONS OF THE ONE FROM THOSE OF THE OTHER.

CHAP. I.

"I gave you," he said, "directions in the first commandment to attend to faith, and fear, and self-restraint." "Even so, sir," said I. And he said, "Now I wish to show you the powers of these, that you may know what power each possesses. For their powers are double, and have relation alike to the righteous and the unrighteous. Trust you, therefore, the righteous, but put no trust in the unrighteous. For the path of righteousness is straight, but that of unrighteousness is crooked. But walk in the straight and even way, and mind not the crooked. For the crooked path has no roads, but has many pathless places and stumbling-blocks in it, and it is rough and thorny. It is injurious to those who walk therein. But they who walk in the straight road walk evenly without stumbling, because it is neither rough nor thorny. You see, then, that it is better to walk in this road." "I wish to go by this road," said I. "You will go by it," said he; "and whoever turns to the Lord with all his heart will walk in it."

CHAP. II.

"Hear now," said he, "in regard to faith. There are two angels [2] with a man — one of righteousness, and the other of iniquity." And I said to him, "How, sir, am I to know the powers of these, for both angels dwell with me?" "Hear," said he, and "understand them. The angel of righteousness is gentle and modest, meek and peaceful. When, therefore, he ascends into your heart, forthwith [3] he talks to you of righteousness, purity, chastity, contentment, and of every righteous deed and glorious virtue. When all these ascend into your heart, know that the angel of righteousness is with you. These are the deeds of the angel of righteousness. Trust him, then, and his works. Look now at the works of the angel of iniquity. First, he is wrathful, and bitter, and foolish, and his works are evil, and ruin the servants of God. When, then, he ascends into your heart, know him by his works."

And I said to him, "How, sir, I shall perceive him, I do not know." "Hear and understand," said he. "When anger comes upon you, or harshness, know that he is in you; and you will know this to be the case also, when you are attacked by a longing after many transactions,[4] and the richest delicacies, and drunken revels, and divers luxuries, and things improper, and by a hankering after women, and by overreaching, and pride, and blustering, and by whatever is like to these. When these ascend into your heart, know that the angel of iniquity is in you. Now that you know his works, depart from him, and in no respect trust him, because his deeds are evil, and unprofitable to the servants of God. These, then, are the actions of both angels. Understand them, and trust the angel of righteousness; but depart from the angel of iniquity, because his instruction is bad in every deed.[5] For though a man be most faithful,[6] and the thought of this angel ascend into his heart, that man or woman must sin. On the other hand, be a man or woman ever so bad, yet, if the works of the angel of righteousness ascend into his or her heart, he or she must do something good. You see, therefore, that it is good to follow the angel of righteousness, but to bid farewell [7] to the angel of iniquity.

"This commandment exhibits the deeds of faith, that you may trust the works of the angel of righteousness, and doing them you may live to God. But believe the works of the angel of iniquity are hard. If you refuse to do them, you will live to God."

COMMANDMENT SEVENTH.

ON FEARING GOD, AND NOT FEARING THE DEVIL.

"Fear," said he, "the Lord, and keep His commandments.[8] For if you keep the commandments of God, you will be powerful in every action, and every one of your actions will be incomparable. For, fearing the Lord, you will do all things well. This is the fear which you ought to have, that you may be saved. But fear not the devil; for, fearing the Lord, you will have dominion over the devil, for there is no power in him. But he in whom there is no power ought on no account to be an object of fear; but He in whom there is glorious power is truly to be feared. For every one that has power ought to be feared; but he who has not

---

[1] *And put . . . them.* That you may live to God, and they who keep these commandments will live to God. — *Vat.* [The beauty of this chapter must be felt by all, especially in the eulogy on *patience.* A pious and learned critic remarks on the emphasis and frequent recurrence of scriptural exhortations to *patience*, which he thinks have been too little enlarged upon in Christian literature.]

[2] [See Tob. iii. 8, 17. The impure spirit, and the healing angel. This apocryphal book greatly influenced the Church's ideas of angels, and may have suggested this early reference to one's good and evil angel. The mediæval ideas on this subject are powerfully illustrated in the German legends preserved by Sir W. Scott in *The Wild Huntsman* and *The Fire-King.*]

[3] *Forthwith . . . heart,* omitted in Lips.

[4] *Transactions.* I think the writer means, when a longing is felt to engage with too great devotedness to business and the pursuit of wealth. [" That ye may attend upon the Lord without distraction." 1 Cor. vii. 35.]

[5] *Trust . . . deed.* Trust the angel of righteousness, because his instruction is good. — *Vat.*

[6] *Faithful.* Most happy. — *Vat.*

[7] *But to bid farewell.* The Vat. ends quite differently from this point: If, then, you follow him, and trust to his works, you will live to God; and they who trust to his works will live to God. — *Vat.*

[8] Eccles. xii. 13.

power is despised by all. Fear, therefore, the deeds of the devil, since they are wicked. For, fearing the Lord, you will not do these deeds, but will refrain from them. For fears are of two kinds: [1] for if you do not wish to do that which is evil, fear the Lord, and you will not do it; but, again, if you wish to do that which is good, fear the Lord, and you will do it. Wherefore the fear of the Lord is strong, and great, and glorious. Fear, then, the Lord, and you will live to Him, and as many as fear Him and keep His commandments will live to God." "Why," [2] said I, "sir, did you say in regard to those that keep His commandments, that they will live to God?" "Because," says he, "all creation fears the Lord, but all creation does not keep His commandments. They only who fear the Lord and keep His commandments have life with God; [3] but as to those who keep not His commandments, there is no life in them."

COMMANDMENT EIGHTH.

WE OUGHT TO SHUN THAT WHICH IS EVIL, AND DO THAT WHICH IS GOOD.

"I told you," said he, "that the creatures of God are double,[4] for restraint also is double; for in some cases restraint has to be exercised, in others there is no need of restraint." "Make known to me, sir," say I, "in what cases restraint has to be exercised, and in what cases it has not." "Restrain yourself in regard to evil, and do it not; but exercise no restraint in regard to good, but do it. For if you exercise restraint in the doing of good, you will commit a great sin; [5] but if you exercise restraint, so as not to do that which is evil, you are practising great righteousness. Restrain yourself, therefore, from all iniquity, and do that which is good." "What, sir," say I, "are the evil deeds from which we must restrain ourselves?" "Hear," says he: "from adultery and fornication, from unlawful revelling,[6] from wicked luxury, from indulgence in many kinds of food and the extravagance of riches, and from boastfulness, and haughtiness, and insolence, and lies, and backbiting, and hypocrisy, from the remembrance of wrong, and from all slander. These are the deeds that are most wicked in the life of men. From all these deeds, therefore, the servant of God must restrain himself. For he who does not restrain himself from these, cannot live to God. Listen, then, to the deeds that accompany these." "Are there, sir," said I, "any other evil deeds?" "There

are," says he; "and many of them, too, from which the servant of God must restrain himself — theft, lying, robbery, false witness, overreaching, wicked lust, deceit, vainglory, boastfulness, and all other vices like to these." "Do you not think that these are really wicked?" "Exceedingly wicked in the servants of God. From all of these the servant of God must restrain himself. Restrain yourself, then, from all these, that you may live to God, and you will be enrolled amongst those who restrain themselves in regard to these matters. These, then, are the things from which you must restrain yourself.

"But listen," says he, "to the things in regard to which you have not to exercise self-restraint, but which you ought to do. Restrain not yourself in regard to that which is good, but do it." "And tell me, sir," say I, "the nature of the good deeds, that I may walk in them and wait on them, so that doing them I can be saved." "Listen," says he, "to the good deeds which you ought to do, and in regard to which there is no self-restraint requisite. First of all [7] there is faith, then fear of the Lord, love, concord, words of righteousness, truth, patience. Than these, nothing is better in the life of men. If any one attend to these, and restrain himself not from them, blessed is he in his life. Then there are the following attendant on these: helping widows, looking after orphans and the needy, rescuing the servants of God from necessities, the being hospitable — for in hospitality good-doing finds a field — never opposing any one, the being quiet, having fewer needs than all men, reverencing the aged, practising righteousness, watching the brotherhood, bearing insolence, being long-suffering, encouraging those who are sick in soul, not casting those who have fallen into sin from the faith, but turning them back and restoring them to peace of mind, admonishing sinners, not oppressing debtors and the needy, and if there are any other actions like these.[8] Do these seem to you good?" says he. "For what, sir," say I, "is better than these?" "Walk then in them," says he, "and restrain not yourself from them, and you will live to God.[9] Keep, therefore, this commandment. If you do good, and restrain not yourself from it, you will live to God. All who act thus will live to God. And, again, if you refuse to do evil, and restrain yourself from it, you will live to God. And all will live to God who keep these commandments, and walk in them."

---

[1] [Prov. xxviii. 14; 1 John iv. 18. This chapter seems based on Jas. iv. 7.]

[2] Why . . . they only who fear the Lord, omitted in Vat.

[3] God. Lord.— Vat.

[4] [Command. vi. cap. 1. p. 24, supra. The idea taken from Ecclus. xxxiii. 15, and Eccles. vii. 14.]

[5] For . . . sin, omitted in Lips.

[6] [Gal. v. 19, 21; 1 Pet. iv. 3.]

[7] [First of all, faith, holy fear, love, etc. Then, works of mercy. Could evangelical morality be more beautifully illustrated?]

[8] [1 Pet. iv. 9. Who does not feel humbled and instructed by these rules of holy living. No wonder Athanasius, while rejecting it from the canon (Contra hæresim Arian., p. 380) calls this a "most useful book." De Incarnatione, p. 38. Paris, 1573.]

[9] From them . . . all who act thus will live to God, omitted in Vat., which ends thus: If you keep all these commandments, you will live to God, and all who keep these commandments will live to God.

COMMANDMENT NINTH.

PRAYER MUST BE MADE TO GOD WITHOUT CEASING, AND WITH UNWAVERING CONFIDENCE.

He says to me, " Put away doubting from you, and do not hesitate to ask of the Lord, saying to yourself, ' How can I ask of the Lord and receive from Him, seeing I have sinned so much against Him?' Do not thus reason with yourself, but with all your heart turn to the Lord, and ask of Him without doubting, and you will know the multitude of His tender mercies; that He will never leave you, but fulfil the request of your soul. For He is not like men, who remember evils done against them; but He Himself remembers not evils, and has compassion on His own creature. Cleanse, therefore, your heart from all the vanities of this world, and from the words already mentioned, and ask of the Lord and you will receive all, and in none of your requests will you be denied which you make to the Lord without doubting. But if you doubt in your heart, you will receive none of your requests. For those who doubt regarding God are double-souled, and obtain not one of their requests.[1] But those who are perfect in faith ask everything, trusting in the Lord; and they obtain, because they ask nothing doubting, and not being double-souled. For every double-souled man, even if he repent, will with difficulty be saved.[2] Cleanse your heart, therefore, from all doubt, and put on faith, because it is strong, and trust God that you will obtain from Him all that you ask. And if at any time, after you have asked of the Lord, you are slower in obtaining your request [than you expected], do not doubt because you have not soon obtained the request of your soul; for invariably it is on account of some temptation or some sin of which you are ignorant that you are slower in obtaining your request. Wherefore do not cease to make the request of your soul, and you will obtain it. But if you grow weary and waver in your request, blame yourself, and not Him who does not give to you. Consider this doubting state of mind, for it is wicked and senseless, and turns many away entirely from the faith, even though they be very strong. For this doubting is the daughter of the devil, and acts exceedingly wickedly to the servants of God. Despise, then, doubting, and gain the mastery over it in everything; clothing yourself with faith, which is strong and powerful. For faith promises all things, perfects all things; but doubt having no thorough faith in itself, fails in every work which it undertakes. You see, then," says he, " that faith is from above — from the Lord [3] — and has

great power; but doubt is an earthly spirit, coming from the devil, and has no power. Serve, then, that which has power, namely faith, and keep away from doubt, which has no power, and you will live to God. And all will live to God whose minds have been set on these things."

COMMANDMENT TENTH.

OF GRIEF, AND NOT GRIEVING THE SPIRIT OF GOD WHICH IS IN US.

CHAP. I.

" Remove from you," says he, " grief; for she is the sister of doubt and anger." " How, sir," say I, " is she the sister of these? for anger, doubt, and grief seem to be quite different from each other." " You are senseless, O man. Do you not perceive that grief is more wicked than all the spirits, and most terrible to the servants of God, and more than all other spirits destroys man and crushes out the Holy Spirit, and yet, on the other hand, she saves him?" " I am senseless, sir," say I, " and do not understand these parables. For how she can crush out, and on the other hand save, I do not perceive." " Listen," says he. " Those who have never searched for the truth, nor investigated the nature of the Divinity, but have simply believed, when they devote themselves to and become mixed up with business, and wealth, and heathen friendships, and many other actions of this world,[4] do not perceive the parables of Divinity; for their minds are darkened by these actions, and they are corrupted and become dried up. Even as beautiful vines, when they are neglected, are withered up by thorns and divers plants, so men who have believed, and have afterwards fallen away into many of those actions above mentioned, go astray in their minds, and lose all understanding in regard to righteousness; for if they hear of righteousness, their minds are occupied with their business,[5] and they give no heed at all. Those, on the other hand, who have the fear of God, and search after Godhead and truth, and have their hearts turned to the Lord, quickly perceive and understand what is said to them, because they have the fear of the Lord in them. For where the Lord dwells, there is much understanding. Cleave, then, to the Lord, and you will understand and perceive all things.

CHAP. II.

" Hear, then," says he, " foolish man, how grief crushes out the Holy Spirit, and on the

---

[1] [Jas. i. 6–8 is here the text of the Shepherd's comment.]
[2] *With difficulty be saved.* Will with difficulty live to God. — Vat.
[3] *Lord.* God. — Vat.

[4] The Vat. has here a considerable number of sentences, found in the Greek, the Palatine, and the Æthiopic, in Commandment Eleventh. In consequence of this transference, the Eleventh Commandment in the Vatican differs considerably from the others in the position of the sentences, but otherwise it is substantially the same.
[5] *And . . . business.* This part is omitted in the Leipzig Codex, and is supplied from the Latin and Æthiopic translations. [Luke viii. 14.]

other hand saves. When the doubting man attempts any deed, and fails in it on account of his doubt, this grief enters into the man, and grieves the Holy Spirit, and crushes him out. Then, on the other hand, when anger attaches itself to a man in regard to any matter, and he is embittered, then grief enters into the heart of the man who was irritated, and he is grieved at the deed which he did, and repents that he has wrought a wicked deed. This grief, then, appears to be accompanied by salvation, because the man, after having done a wicked deed, repented.[1] Both actions grieve the Spirit : doubt, because it did not accomplish its object ; and anger grieves the Spirit, because it did what was wicked. Both these are grievous to the Holy Spirit — doubt and anger. Wherefore remove grief from you, and crush not the Holy Spirit which dwells in you, lest he entreat God[2] against you, and he withdraw from you. For the Spirit of God which has been granted to us to dwell in this body does not endure grief nor straitness. Wherefore put on cheerfulness, which always is agreeable and acceptable to God,[3] and rejoice in it. For every cheerful man does what is good, and minds what is good, and despises grief ;[4] but the sorrowful man always acts wickedly. First, he acts wickedly because he grieves the Holy Spirit, which was given to man a cheerful Spirit. Secondly, Grieving the Holy Spirit,[5] he works iniquity, neither entreating the Lord nor confessing[6] to Him. For the entreaty of the sorrowful man has no power to ascend to the altar of God." "Why," say I, "does not the entreaty of the grieved man ascend to the altar?" "Because," says he, "grief sits in his heart. Grief, then, mingled with his entreaty, does not permit the entreaty to ascend pure to the altar of God. For as vinegar and wine, when mixed in the same vessel, do not give the same pleasure [as wine alone gives], so grief mixed with the Holy Spirit does not produce the same entreaty [as would be produced by the Holy Spirit alone]. Cleanse yourself from this wicked grief, and you will live to God ; and all will live to God who drive away grief from them, and put on all cheerfulness."[7]

COMMANDMENT ELEVENTH.

THE SPIRIT AND PROPHETS TO BE TRIED BY THEIR WORKS; ALSO OF THE TWO KINDS OF SPIRIT.

He pointed out to me some men sitting on a seat, and one man sitting on a chair. And he says to me, "Do you see the persons sitting on the seat?" "I do, sir," said I. "These," says he, "are the faithful, and he who sits on the chair is a false prophet, ruining the minds of the servants of God.[8] It is the doubters, not the faithful, that he ruins. These doubters then go to him as to a soothsayer, and inquire of him what will happen to them ; and he, the false prophet, not having the power of a Divine Spirit in him, answers them according to their inquiries, and according to their wicked desires, and fills their souls with expectations, according to their own wishes. For being himself empty, he gives empty answers to empty inquirers ; for every answer is made to the emptiness of man. Some true words he does occasionally utter ; for the devil fills him with his own spirit, in the hope that he may be able to overcome some of the righteous. As many, then, as are strong in the faith of the Lord, and are clothed with truth, have no connection with such spirits, but keep away from them ; but as many as are of doubtful minds and frequently repent, betake themselves to soothsaying, even as the heathen, and bring greater sin upon themselves by their idolatry. For he who inquires of a false prophet in regard to any action is an idolater, and devoid of the truth, and foolish. For no spirit given by God requires to be asked ; but such a spirit having the power of Divinity speaks all things of itself, for it proceeds from above from the power of the Divine Spirit. But the spirit which is asked and speaks according to the desires of men is earthly,[9] light, and powerless, and it is altogether silent if it is not questioned." "How then, sir," say I, "will a man know which of them is the prophet, and which the false prophet?" "I will tell you," says he, "about both the prophets, and then you can try the true and the false prophet according to my directions. Try the man who has the Divine Spirit by his life. First, he who has the Divine Spirit proceeding from above is meek, and peaceable, and humble, and refrains from all iniquity and the vain desire of this world, and contents himself with fewer wants than those of other men, and when asked he makes no reply ; nor does he speak privately, nor when man wishes the spirit to speak does the Holy Spirit speak, but it speaks only when God wishes it to speak. When, then, a man having the Divine Spirit comes into an assembly of righteous men who

---

[1] *This . . . repented,* omitted in Vat. [2 Cor. vii. 10. Compare this Commandment in Wake's translation and notes.]
[2] *God.* The Lord. — *Vat., Æth.*
[3] *God.* The Lord. — *Vat.*
[4] *Grief.* Injustice. — *Vat.*
[5] [Eph. iv. 30.]
[6] ἐξομολογούμενος one would expect here to mean "giving thanks," a meaning which it has in the New Testament; but as ἐξομολογοῦμαι means to "confess" throughout the *Pastor of Hermas,* it is likely that it means "confessing" here also.
[7] [Matt. vi. 16, 17: Is. lviii. 5; 2 Cor. vi. 10; John xvi. 33; Rom. xii. 8.]

[8] *Is . . . God.* He who sits in the chair is a terrestrial spirit. — *Vat.* And then follows the dislocation of sentences noticed above.
[9] *The spirit of all men is earthly,* etc. This passage, down to "it is not possible that the prophet of God should do this," is found in the Vat. and other MSS. of the common translation, with the exception of the Lambeth, in Commandment Twelfth. [Consult Wake upon omissions and transpositions in this and the former Commandment. And note, especially, his valuable caution against confounding what is here said, so confusedly, of the Spirit in man, and of the Spirit of God in his essence (1 Cor. ii. 11, 12).]

have faith in the Divine Spirit, and this assembly of men offers up prayer to God, then the angel of the prophetic Spirit,[1] who is destined for him, fills the man ; and the man being filled with the Holy Spirit, speaks to the multitude as the Lord wishes. Thus, then, will the Spirit of Divinity become manifest. Whatever power therefore comes from the Spirit of Divinity belongs to the Lord. Hear, then," says he, "in regard to the spirit which is earthly, and empty, and power-less, and foolish. First, the man[2] who seems to have the Spirit exalts himself, and wishes to have the first seat, and is bold, and impudent, and talkative, and lives in the midst of many luxuries and many other delusions, and takes rewards for his prophecy; and if he does not receive rewards, he does not prophesy. Can, then, the Divine Spirit take rewards and prophesy? It is not possible that the prophet of God should do this, but prophets of this character are possessed by an earthly spirit. Then it never approaches an assembly of righteous men, but shuns them. And it associates with doubters and the vain, and prophesies to them in a corner, and deceives them, speaking to them, according to their desires, mere empty words : for they are empty to whom it gives its answers. For the empty vessel, when placed along with the empty, is not crushed, but they correspond to each other. When, therefore, it comes into an assembly of righteous men who have a Spirit of Divinity, and they offer up prayer, that man is made empty, and the earthly spirit flees from him through fear, and that man is made dumb, and is entirely crushed, being unable to speak. For if you pack closely a storehouse with wine or oil, and put an empty jar in the midst of the vessels of wine or oil, you will find that jar empty as when you placed it, if you should wish to clear the storehouse. So also the empty prophets, when they come to the spirits of the righteous, are found [on leaving] to be such as they were when they came. This, then, is the mode of life of both prophets. Try by his deeds and his life the man who says that he is inspired. But as for you, trust the Spirit which comes from God, and has power; but the spirit which is earthly and empty trust not at all, for there is no power in it : it comes from the devil. Hear, then, the parable which I am to tell you. Take a stone, and throw it to the sky, and see if you can touch it. Or again, take a squirt of water and squirt into the sky, and see if you can penetrate the sky." "How, sir," say I, "can these things take place? for both of them are impossible." "As these things," says he, "are impossible, so also are the earthly spirits powerless

and pithless. But look, on the other hand, at the power which comes from above. Hail is of the size of a very small grain, yet when it falls on a man's head how much annoyance it gives him ! Or, again, take the drop which falls from a pitcher to the ground, and yet it hollows a stone.[3] You see, then, that the smallest things coming from above have great power when they fall upon the earth.[4] Thus also is the Divine Spirit, which comes from above, powerful. Trust, then, that Spirit, but have nothing to do with the other."

COMMANDMENT TWELFTH.

ON THE TWOFOLD DESIRE. THE COMMANDMENTS OF GOD CAN BE KEPT, AND BELIEVERS OUGHT NOT TO FEAR THE DEVIL.

CHAP. I.

He says to me, "Put away from you all wicked desire, and clothe yourself with good and chaste desire ; for clothed with this desire you will hate wicked desire,[5] and will rein your-self in even as you wish. For wicked desire is wild, and is with difficulty tamed. For it is ter-rible, and consumes men exceedingly by its wild-ness. Especially is the servant of God terribly consumed by it, if he falls into it and is devoid of understanding. Moreover, it consumes all such as have not on them the garment of good desire, but are entangled and mixed up with this world. These it delivers up to death." "What then, sir," say I, "are the deeds of wicked desire which deliver men over to death? Make them known to me, and I will refrain from them." "Listen, then, to the works in which evil desire slays the servants of God."[6]

CHAP. II.

" Foremost of all is the desire after another's wife or husband, and after extravagance, and many useless dainties and drinks, and many other foolish luxuries ; for all luxury is foolish and empty in the servants of God. These, then, are the evil desires which slay the servants of God. For this evil desire is the daughter of the devil. You must refrain from evil desires, that by refraining ye may live to God.[7] But as many as are mastered by them, and do not resist them, will perish at last, for these desires are fatal. Put you on, then, the desire of righteousness ; and arming yourself with the fear of the Lord,

---

[1] *Angel of the prophetic Spirit.* The holy messenger (angel) of Divinity. — *Vat.* [1 Cor. xiv. *passim*.]
[2] [Here is a caution against divers Phrygian *prophesyings*.]

[3] [This proverb is found in many languages. Hermas may have been familiar with Ovid, or with the Greek of the poetaster Chœrilus, from whom Ovid, with other Latin poets, condescended to borrow it.]
[4] *Earth.* After this the Vatican reads: Join yourself, therefore, to that which has power, and withdraw from that one which is empty. [Hermas seems to apply to the Spirit, in carrying out his figure, those words of the Psalmist, lxxii. 6.]
[5] [Concupiscence is here shown to have the nature of sin.]
[6] [See the Greek of Athanasius, and Grabe's transposition, in Wake's version of the Eleventh and Twelfth Commandments.]
[7] *For . . . God.* This desire, therefore, is wicked and destruc-tive, bringing death on the servants of God. Whoever, therefore, shall abstain from evil desire, shall live to God. — *Vat.*

resist them. For the fear of the Lord dwells in good desire. But if evil desire see you armed with the fear of God,[1] and resisting it, it will flee far from you, and it will no longer appear to you, for it fears your armour. Go, then, garlanded with the crown which you have gained for victory over it, to the desire of righteousness, and, delivering up to it the prize which you have received, serve it even as it wishes.[2] If you serve good desire, and be subject to it, you will gain the mastery over evil desire, and make it subject to you even as you wish." [3]

CHAP. III.

" I should like to know," say I, " in what way I ought to serve good desire." " Hear," says he : " You will practise righteousness and virtue, truth and the fear of the Lord, faith and meekness, and whatsoever excellences are like to these. Practising these, you will be a well-pleasing servant of God,[1] and you will live to Him ; and every one who shall serve good desire, shall live to God."

He concluded the twelve commandments, and said to me, " You have now these commandments. Walk in them, and exhort your hearers that their repentance may be pure during the remainder of their life. Fulfil carefully this ministry which I now entrust to you, and you will accomplish much.[4] For you will find favour among those who are to repent, and they will give heed to your words ; for I will be with you, and will compel them to obey you." I say to him, " Sir, these commandments are great, and good, and glorious, and fitted to gladden the heart of the man who can perform them. But I do not know if these commandments can be kept by man, because they are exceeding hard." He answered and said to me, " If you lay it down as certain that they can be kept,[5] then you will easily keep them, and they will not be hard. But if you come to imagine that they cannot be kept by man, then you will not keep them. Now I say to you, If you do not keep them, but neglect them, you will not be saved, nor your children, nor your house, since you have already determined for yourself that these commandments cannot be kept by man."

CHAP. IV.

These things he said to me in tones of the deepest anger, so that I was confounded and exceedingly afraid of him, for his figure was altered so that a man could not endure his anger. But seeing me altogether agitated and confused, he began to speak to me in more gentle tones ; and he said : " O fool,. senseless and doubting, do you not perceive how great is the glory of God, and how strong and marvellous, in that He created the world for the sake of man,[6] and subjected all creation to him, and gave him power to rule over everything under heaven? If, then, man is lord of the creatures of God, and rules over all, is he not able to be lord also of these commandments? For," says he, " the man who has the Lord in his heart can also be lord of all, and of every one of these commandments. But to those who have the Lord only on their lips,[7] but their hearts hardened,[8] and who are far from the Lord, the commandments are hard and difficult. Put, therefore, ye who are empty and fickle in your faith, the Lord in your heart, and ye will know that there is nothing easier or sweeter, or more manageable, than these commandments. Return, ye who walk in the commandments of the devil, in hard, and bitter, and wild licentiousness, and fear not the devil ; for there is no power in him against you, for I will be with you, the angel of repentance, who am lord over him. The devil has fear only, but his fear has no strength.[9] Fear him not, then, and he will flee from you."

CHAP. V.

I say to him, " Sir, listen to me for a moment." " Say what you wish," says he. " Man, sir," say I, " is eager to keep the commandments of God, and there is no one who does not ask of the Lord that strength may be given him for these commandments, and that he may be subject to them ; but the devil is hard, and holds sway over them." " He cannot," says he, " hold sway over the servants of God, who with all their heart place their hopes in Him. The devil can wrestle against these, overthrow them he cannot. If, then, ye resist him, he will be conquered, and flee in disgrace from you. As many, therefore," says he, " as are empty, fear the devil, as possessing power. When a man has filled very suitable jars with good wine, and a few among those jars are left empty,[10] then he comes to the jars, and does not look at the full jars, for he knows that they are full ; but he looks at the empty, being afraid lest they have become sour. For empty jars quickly become sour, and the goodness of the wine is gone. So also the devil goes to all

---

[1] *God.* The Lord.— *Vat.*
[2] *Go . . . wishes.* And you will obtain the victory, and will be crowned on account of it, and you will arrive at good desire, and you will deliver up the victory which you have obtained to God, and you will serve Him by acting even as you yourself wish to act. — *Vat.*
[3] Chapters third, fourth, and a part of fifth, are omitted in the Palatine. [This chapter seems based on Heb. v. 14.]
[4] [Here is the commission to be a prophet, and to speak *prophesyings* in the congregation. If the Montanists resisted these teachings, they were self-condemned. Such is the idea here conveyed 1 Cor. xiv. 32, 37.]
[5] *If . . . kept,* omitted in Vat.

[6] [Boyle beautifully reconciles " those two current assertions, that (1) God made all things for His own glory, and that (2) He made all things for man." See *Usefulness of Nat. Philos.*, part i., essay 3, or Leighton's Works, vol. iii. p. 235, London, 1870.]
[7] Isa. xxix. 13; Matt. xv. 8.
[8] John xii. 40; 2 Cor. iii. 14.
[9] [Jas. ii. 19, iv. 6, 7.]
[10] *Empty.* Half full. — *Vat.*

the servants of God to try them. As many, then, as are full in the faith, resist him strongly, and he withdraws from them, having no way by which he might enter them. He goes, then, to the empty, and finding a way of entrance, into them, he produces in them whatever he wishes, and they become his servants.[1]

CHAP. VI.

"But I, the angel of repentance, say to you Fear not the devil; for I was sent," says he, "to be with you who repent with all your heart, and to make you strong in faith. Trust God,[2] then, ye who on account of your sins have despaired of life, and who add to your sins and weigh down your life; for if ye return to the Lord with all your heart, and practise righteousness the rest of your days,[3] and serve Him according to His will, He will heal your former sins, and you will have power to hold sway over the works of the devil. But as to the threats of the devil, fear them not at all, for he is powerless as the sinews of a dead man. Give ear to me, then, and fear Him who has all power, both to save and destroy,[4] and keep His commandments, and ye will live to God." I say to him, "Sir, I am now made strong in all the ordinances of the Lord, because you are with me; and I know that you will crush all the power of the devil, and we shall have rule over him, and shall prevail against all his works. And I hope, sir, to be able to keep all these commandments[5] which you have enjoined upon me, the Lord strengthening me." "You will keep them," says he, "if your heart be pure towards the Lord; and all will keep them who cleanse their hearts from the vain desires of this world, and they will live to God."

---

[1] [Eph. iv. 27.]
[2] *Trust God.* Believe ye, then, who on account of your sins have forgotten God. — *Vat.*
[3] *Practise . . . days*, omitted in Vat.

[4] Matt. x. 28 ; Luke xii. 5.
[5] *Rule over . . . commandments.* But we shall conquer him completely, if we can keep these commandments. — *Vat.*

THE PASTOR.

BOOK THIRD. — SIMILITUDES.

SIMILITUDE FIRST.[1]

AS IN THIS WORLD WE HAVE NO ABIDING CITY, WE
OUGHT TO SEEK ONE TO COME.

HE says to me, " You know that you who are
the servants of God dwell in a strange land ; for
your city is far away from this one.[2] If, then,"
he continues, " you know your city in which you
are to dwell, why do ye here provide lands, and
make expensive preparations, and accumulate
dwellings and useless buildings ? He who makes
such preparations for this city cannot return
again to his own. Oh foolish, and unstable, and
miserable man ! Dost thou not understand that
all these things belong to another, and are under
the power of another ? for the lord of this city
will say, ' I do not wish thee to dwell in my city ;
but depart from this city, because thou obeyest
not my laws.' Thou, therefore, although having
fields and houses, and many other things, when
cast out by him, what wilt thou do with thy land,
and house, and other possessions which thou
hast gathered to thyself ? For the lord of this
country justly says to thee, ' Either obey my laws
or depart from my dominion.' What, then, dost
thou intend to do, having a law in thine own city,
on account of thy lands, and the rest of thy possessions ?[3] Thou shalt altogether deny thy law,
and walk according to the law of this city. See
lest it be to thy hurt to deny thy law ;[4] for if
thou shalt desire to return to thy city, thou wilt
not be received, because thou hast denied the
law of thy city, but wilt be excluded from it.
Have a care, therefore : as one living in a foreign land, make no further preparations for thyself than such merely as may be sufficient ; and
be ready, when the master of this city shall come
to cast thee out for disobeying his law, to leave
his city, and to depart to thine own, and to obey
thine own law without being exposed to annoyance, but in great joy. Have a care, then, ye
who serve the Lord, and have Him in your
heart, that ye work the works of God, remembering His commandments and promises which
He promised, and believe that He will bring
them to pass if His commandments be observed.
Instead of lands, therefore, buy afflicted souls,
according as each one is able, and visit[5] widows
and orphans, and do not overlook them ; and
spend your wealth and all your preparations,
which ye received from the Lord, upon such
lands and houses. For to this end did the
Master make you rich, that you might perform
these services unto Him ; and it is much better
to purchase such lands, and possessions, and
houses, as you will find in your own city, when
you come to reside in it. This is a noble and
sacred expenditure, attended neither with sorrow
nor fear, but with joy. Do not practise the ex-

---

[1] [We have seen in Justin and Irenæus what seem to us an overstrained allegorizing, and more will be encountered in Origen. On
this whole subject, however, as it struck the Oriental and primitive
instincts, take the following very illustrative remarks, attributed to
Hartley of Winwick: —
"Nature, in its proper order, is the book of God, and exhibits
spiritual things in material forms. The knowledge of *correspondences* being so little understood, is one main cause of the obscurity
of the Scriptures of the Old Testament, *which were chiefly written
by the rules of this science :* and not Scripture alone, but man, also,
as an image of the spiritual and natural worlds, contains in himself the
correspondences of both : of the former, in his interior, and of the latter in his exterior or bodily, part, and so is called the *microcosm,* or
little world."
Such texts as Heb. ix. 24, 1 Cor. ii. 13, 14, go far to explain to
us the childlike faith of the Fathers. See note on *Leighton's St.
Peter,* p. 238, vol. iii. Ed. of William West, B.A. 1870.]
[2] [Heb. xiii. 14 is the text of this very beautiful chapter. But the
original Greek of Phil. iii. 20 seems, also, to be in the author's mind.
St. Paul addressed it to the church of a Roman "colony," whose
citizenship was not Macedonian but Roman : hence its beautiful
propriety.]

[3] This sentence may be also rendered thus, giving ἕνεκεν the
meaning of " as regards," " respecting "—a usual enough signification : " What then do you intend to do, as you have a law in your
own city regarding your lands and the rest of your possessions ?"
The Vatican punctuates the passage so that it runs as follows :
" What then will you do, who have a law in your own city ? Will
you, on account of your land, or any other of your preparations, be
able to deny your law ?" The Vatican also omits several clauses that
are in the Greek, down to " for if thou shalt deny, and shalt desire to
return," etc.
[4] *See . . . law,* omitted in Lips. [The θρησκεία of Jas., i. 27.]
[5] The Vatican has : " Acquit widows, and do justice to orphans."

31

penditure of the heathen,[1] for it is injurious to you who are the servants of God ; but practise an expenditure of your own, in which ye can rejoice ; and do not corrupt[2] nor touch what is another's nor covet it, for it is an evil thing to covet the goods of other men ; but work thine own work, and thou wilt be saved."

SIMILITUDE SECOND.

AS THE VINE IS SUPPORTED BY THE ELM, SO IS THE RICH MAN HELPED BY THE PRAYER OF THE POOR.

As I was walking in the field, and observing an elm and vine, and determining in my own mind respecting them and their fruits, the Shepherd appears to me, and says, "What is it that you are thinking about the elm and vine ? " " I am considering," I reply, " that they become each other exceedingly well." " These two trees," he continues, " are intended as an example for the servants of God." " I would like to know," said I, " the example which these trees, you say, are intended to teach." " Do you see," he says, " the elm and the vine ? " " I see them, sir," I replied. " This vine," he continued, " produces fruit, and the elm is an unfruitful tree ; but unless the vine be trained upon the elm, it cannot bear much fruit when extended at length upon the ground ;[3] and the fruit which it does bear is rotten, because the plant is not suspended upon the elm. When, therefore, the vine is cast upon the elm, it yields fruit both from itself and from the elm. You see, moreover, that the elm also produces much fruit, not less than the vine, but even more ; because,"[4] he continued, " the vine, when suspended upon the elm, yields much fruit, and good ; but when thrown upon the ground, what it produces is small and rotten. This similitude,[5] therefore, is for the servants of God — for the poor man and for the rich." " How so, sir ? " said I ; " explain the matter to me." " Listen," he said : " The rich man has much wealth, but is poor in matters relating to the Lord, because he is distracted about his riches ; and he offers very few confessions and intercessions to the Lord, and those which he does offer are small and weak, and have no power above. But when the rich man refreshes[6] the poor, and assists him in his necessities, believing that what he does to the poor man will be able to find its reward with God — because the poor man is rich in intercession and confession, and his intercession has great power with God — then the rich man helps the poor in all things without hesitation ; and the poor man, being helped by the rich, intercedes for him, giving thanks to God for him who bestows gifts upon him. And he still continues to interest himself zealously for the poor man, that his wants may be constantly supplied. For he knows that the intercession of the poor man is acceptable and influential[7] with God. Both, accordingly, accomplish their work. The poor man makes intercession ; a work in which he is rich, which he received from the Lord, and with which he recompenses the master who helps him. And the rich man, in like manner, unhesitatingly bestows upon the poor man the riches which he received from the Lord. And this is a great work, and acceptable before God, because he understands the object of his wealth, and has given to the poor of the gifts of the Lord, and rightly discharged his service to Him.[8] Among men, however, the elm appears not to produce fruit, and they do not know nor understand that if a drought come, the elm, which contains water, nourishes the vine ; and the vine, having an unfailing supply of water, yields double fruit both for itself and for the elm. So also poor men interceding with the Lord on behalf of the rich, increase their riches ; and the rich, again, aiding the poor in their necessities, satisfy their souls. Both, therefore, are partners in the righteous work. He who does these things shall not be deserted by God, but shall be enrolled in the books of the living. Blessed are they who have riches, and who understand that they are from the Lord. [For they who are of that mind will be able to do some good.[9]]"

SIMILITUDE THIRD.

AS IN WINTER GREEN TREES CANNOT BE DISTINGUISHED FROM WITHERED, SO IN THIS WORLD NEITHER CAN THE JUST FROM THE UNJUST.

He showed me many trees having no leaves,

---

[1] The Vatican renders, " Do not covet, therefore, the riches of the heathen." [Here follows, in the Lambeth MS., an allusion to Luke xix. 15, which Wake renders : " Trade with your own riches." See, also, Luke xii. 33.]

[2] The Vatican, rendering παραχαράσσετε, *adulterare*, proceeds as if the reference were to adultery. " Neither touch another man's wife, nor lust after her, but desire your own work, and you will be saved."

[3] The Vatican reads : " Unless this vine be attached to the elm, and rest upon it, it cannot bear much fruit. For, lying upon the ground, it produces bad fruit, because it is not suspended upon the elm."

[4] The Vatican here makes Hermas interrupt the Shepherd, and ask, " How greater than the vine ? "

[5] [Based on Jas. i. 9-11, 27, and ii. 1-9 ; introducing the heathen world to just ideas of human brotherhood, and the mutual relations of the poor and the rich]

[6] The translation of the text is based on the Palatine. Lips. reads : " When the rich man fills out upon the poor." Hilgenfeld amends this : " When the rich man recovers breath upon the poor." Neither gives sense. The Æthiopic has : " But if the rich man lean on the poor ; " and the Greek of Hilgenfeld might mean : " When the rich man recovers his breath by leaning on the poor." The Vatican is quite different : " When, therefore, the rich man helps the poor in those things which he needs, the poor man prays to the Lord for the rich man, and God bestows all blessings upon the rich man, because the poor man is rich in prayer, and his prayer has great merit with God. Then the rich man accordingly assists the poor man's things, because he feels that he is fully heard (*exaudiri*) by the Lord ; and the more willingly and unhesitatingly does he give him every help, and takes care that he wants for nothing. The poor man gives thanks to God for the rich man, because they do their duty in respect to the Lord (*a Domino*)."

[7] [I note this use of the word " influential," because it was formerly denounced as an Americanism.]

[8] [Luke xii. 42.]

[9] The sentence in brackets is not in Lips. It is taken from Pal.

but withered, as it seemed to me; for all were alike. And he said to me, "Do you see those trees?" "I see, sir," I replied, "that all are alike, and withered." He answered me, and said, "These trees which you see are those who dwell in this world." "Why, then, sir," I said, "are they withered, as it were, and alike?"[1] "Because," he said, "neither are the righteous manifest in this life, nor sinners, but they are alike; for this life is a winter to the righteous, and they do not manifest themselves, because they dwell with sinners: for as in winter trees that have cast their leaves are alike, and it is not seen which are dead and which are living, so in this world neither do the righteous show themselves, nor sinners, but all are alike one to another."[2]

SIMILITUDE FOURTH.

AS IN SUMMER LIVING TREES ARE DISTINGUISHED
FROM WITHERED BY FRUIT AND LIVING LEAVES,
SO IN THE WORLD TO COME THE JUST DIFFER
FROM THE UNJUST IN HAPPINESS.

He showed me again many trees, some budding, and others withered. And he said to me, "Do you see these trees?" "I see, sir," I replied, "some putting forth buds, and others withered." "Those," he said, "which are budding are the righteous who are to live in the world to come; for the coming world is the summer[3] of the righteous, but the winter of sinners. When, therefore, the mercy of the Lord shines forth, then shall they be made manifest who are the servants of God, and all men shall be made manifest. For as in summer the fruits of each individual tree appear, and it is ascertained of what sort they are, so also the fruits of the righteous shall be manifest, and all who have been fruitful in that world shall be made known.[4] But the heathen and sinners, like the withered trees which you saw, will be found to be those who have been withered and unfruitful in that world, and shall be burnt as wood, and [so] made manifest, because their actions were evil during their lives. For the sinners shall be consumed because they sinned and did not repent, and the heathen shall be burned because they knew not Him who created them. Do you therefore bear fruit, that in that summer your fruit may be known. And refrain from much business, and you will never sin: for they who are occupied with much business commit also many sins, being distracted about their affairs, and not at all serving their Lord.[5] How, then," he continued, "can such

a one ask and obtain anything from the Lord, if he serve Him not? They who serve Him shall obtain their requests, but they who serve Him not shall receive nothing. And in the performance even of a single action a man can serve the Lord; for his mind will not be perverted from the Lord, but he will serve Him, having a pure mind. If, therefore, you do these things, you shall be able to bear fruit for the life to come. And every one who will do these things shall bear fruit."

SIMILITUDE FIFTH.
OF TRUE FASTING AND ITS REWARD: ALSO OF
PURITY OF BODY.

CHAP. I.

While fasting and sitting on a certain mountain, and giving thanks to the Lord for all His dealings with me, I see the Shepherd sitting down beside me, and saying, "Why have you come hither [so] early in the morning?" "Because, sir," I answered, "I have a station."[6] "What is a station?" he asked. "I am fasting, sir," I replied. "What is this fasting," he continued, "which you are observing?" "As I have been accustomed, sir," I reply, "so I fast." "You do not know," he says, "how to fast unto the Lord: this useless fasting which you observe to Him is of no value." "Why, sir," I answered, "do you say this?" "I say to you," he continued, "that the fasting which you think you observe is not a fasting. But I will teach you what is a full and acceptable fasting to the Lord. Listen," he continued: "God does not desire such an empty fasting.[7] For fasting to God in this way you will do nothing for a righteous life; but offer to God a fasting of the following kind: Do no evil in your life, and serve the Lord with a pure heart: keep His commandments, walking in His precepts, and let no evil desire arise in your heart; and believe in God. If you do these things, and fear Him, and abstain from every evil thing, you will live unto God; and if you do these things, you will keep a great fast, and one acceptable before God.

CHAP. II.

"Hear the similitude which I am about to narrate to you relative to fasting. A certain man had a field and many slaves, and he planted a certain part of the field with a vineyard,[8] and selecting a faithful and beloved and much valued slave, he called him to him, and said, 'Take

---

[1] The Vatican renders this thus: "Why do they resemble those that are, as it were, withered?"
[2] [Matt. xiii. 29.]
[3] *Summer.* Throne. — *Lips.* [Rom. viii. 22-24.]
[4] The Vatican has, "And all the merry and joyful shall be restored in that age."
[5] [1 Cor. vii. 30-35; Rom. xii. 11.]

[6] [This anachronism betrays the later origin of "The Pastor." The Pauline Hermas would not have used this technical term. These fasts were very early fixed by canon for Wednesdays and Fridays. See Canon lxix. of canons called "Apostolical;" also Bingham, book xiii. cap. 9, and this volume, p. 34, note 4.]
[7] [See cap. iii. of this similitude.]
[8] The Vatican adds, "for his successors."

this vineyard which I have planted, and stake [1] it until I come, and do nothing else to the vineyard; and attend to this order of mine, and you shall receive your freedom from me.' And the master of the slave departed to a foreign country. And when he was gone, the slave took and staked the vineyard; and when he had finished the staking of the vines, he saw that the vineyard was full of weeds. He then reflected, saying, 'I have kept this order of my master: I will dig up the rest of this vineyard, and it will be more beautiful when dug up; and being free of weeds, it will yield more fruit, not being choked by them.' He took, therefore, and dug up the vineyard, and rooted out all the weeds that were in it. And that vineyard became very beautiful and fruitful, having no weeds to choke it. And after a certain time the master of the slave and of the field returned, and entered into the vineyard. And seeing that the vines were suitably supported on stakes, and the ground, moreover, dug up, and all the weeds rooted out, and the vines fruitful, he was greatly pleased with the work of his slave. And calling his beloved son who was his heir, and his friends who were his councillors, he told them what orders he had given his slave, and what he had found performed. And they rejoiced along with the slave at the testimony which his master bore to him. And he said to them, 'I promised this slave freedom if he obeyed the command which I gave him; and he has kept my command, and done besides a good work to the vineyard, and has pleased me exceedingly. In return, therefore, for the work which he has done, I wish to make him co-heir with my son, because, having good thoughts, he did not neglect them, but carried them out.' With this resolution of the master his son and friends were well pleased, viz., that the slave should be co-heir with the son. After a few days the master made a feast, [2] and sent to his slave many dishes from his table. And the slave receiving the dishes that were sent him from his master, took of them what was sufficient for himself, and distributed the rest among his fellow-slaves. And his fellow-slaves rejoiced to receive the dishes, and began to pray for him, that he might find still greater favour with his master for having so treated them. His master heard all these things that were done, and was again greatly pleased with his conduct. And the master again calling together his friends and his son, reported to them the slave's proceeding with regard to the dishes which he had sent him. And they were

still more satisfied that the slave should become co-heir with his son."

CHAP. III.

I said to him, "Sir, I do not see the meaning of these similitudes, nor am I able to comprehend them, unless you explain them to me." "I will explain them all to you," he said, "and whatever I shall mention in the course of our conversations I will show you. [Keep the commandments of the Lord, and you will be approved, and inscribed amongst the number of those who observe His commands.] And if you do any good beyond what is commanded by God,[3] you will gain for yourself more abundant glory, and will be more honoured by God than you would otherwise be. If, therefore, in keeping the commandments of God, you do, in addition, these services, you will have joy if you observe them according to my command." I said to him, "Sir, whatsoever you enjoin upon me I will observe, for I know that you are with me." "I will be with you," he replied, "because you have such a desire for doing good; and I will be with all those," he added, "who have such a desire. This fasting," he continued, "is very good, provided the commandments of the Lord be observed. Thus, then, shall you observe the fasting which you intend to keep.[4] First of all,[5] be on your guard against every evil word, and every evil desire, and purify your heart from all the vanities of this world. If you guard against these things, your fasting will be perfect. And you will do also as follows.[6] Having fulfilled what is written, in the day on which you fast you will taste nothing but bread and water; and having reckoned up the price of the dishes of that day which you intended to have eaten, you will give it to a widow, or an orphan, or to some person in want, and thus you will exhibit humility of mind, so that he who has received benefit from your humility may fill his own soul, and pray for you to the Lord. If you observe fasting, as I have commanded you, your sacrifice

---

[1] i.e., attach the vines to stakes.

[2] The Vatican adds, " Having called together his friends." [The gospel parables of the vineyard, and of the sower, and of the man travelling into a far country, are here reflected *passim*. I cannot but refer to a parable which greatly resembles this, and is yet more beautiful, occurring in Mrs. Sherwood's *Stories on the Catechism* (*Fijou*), a book for children. It is not unworthy of Bunyan.]

[3] [To read into this passage the idea of " supererogatory merit " is an unpardonable anachronism. (Compare Command. iv. 4.) The writer everywhere denies human merit, extols mercy, and imputes good works to grace. He has in view St. Paul's advice (1 Cor. vii. 25-28), or our blessed Lord's saying (Matt. xix. 12). The *abuse* of such Scriptures propped up a false system (2 Pet. iii. 16) after it had been invented by Pelagians and monastic enthusiasts. But it has no place in the mind of Hermas, nor in the mind of Christ.]

[4] [Thus he does not object to the "station," if kept with evangelical acts of devotion and penitence. Isa. lviii. 5-8.]

[5] Pseudo-Athanasius gives this paragraph as follows: " First of all be on your guard to fast from every evil word and evil report, and purify your heart from every defilement and revenge, and base covetousness. And on the day on which you fast, be content with bread, and herbs, and water, giving thanks to God. And having calculated the amount of the cost of the meal which you intended to have eaten on that day, give it to a widow, or an orphan, or to some one in want, so that, having clearly filled his own soul, he shall pray to the Lord on your behalf. If you therefore perform your fasting as I enjoined you, your sacrifice will be acceptable before the Lord, and inscribed in the heavens in the day of the requital of the good things that have been prepared for the righteous."

[6] [Note this detailed account of primitive fasting (2 Cor. vi. 5, ix. 27, xi. 27). Amid all the apostle's sufferings and dying daily, he adds *fastings* to involuntary hunger and thirst.]

will be acceptable to God, and this fasting will be written down; and the service thus performed is noble, and sacred, and acceptable to the Lord. These things, therefore, shall you thus observe with your children, and all your house, and in observing them you will be blessed; and as many as hear these words and observe them shall be blessed; and whatsoever they ask of the Lord they shall receive."

CHAP. IV.

I prayed him much that he would explain to me the similitude of the field, and of the master of the vineyard, and of the slave who staked the vineyard, and of the stakes, and of the weeds that were plucked out of the vineyard, and of the son, and of the friends who were fellow-councillors, for I knew that all these things were a kind of parable. And he answered me, and said, "You are exceedingly persistent[1] with your questions. You ought not," he continued, "to ask any questions at all; for if it is needful to explain anything, it will be made known to you." I said to him, "Sir, whatsoever you show me, and do not explain, I shall have seen to no purpose, not understanding its meaning. In like manner, also, if you speak parables to me, and do not unfold them, I shall have heard your words in vain." And he answered me again, saying, "Every one who is the servant of God, and has his Lord in his heart, asks of Him understanding, and receives it, and opens up every parable; and the words of the Lord become known to him which are spoken in parables.[2] But those who are weak and slothful in prayer, hesitate to ask anything from the Lord; but the Lord is full of compassion, and gives without fail to all who ask Him. But you, having been strengthened by the holy Angel,[3] and having obtained from Him such intercession, and not being slothful, why do not you ask of the Lord understanding, and receive it from Him?" I said to him, "Sir, having you with me, I am necessitated to ask questions of you, for you show me all things, and converse with me; but if I were to see or hear these things without you, I would then ask the Lord to explain them."

CHAP. V.

"I said to you a little ago," he answered, "that you were cunning and obstinate in asking explanations of the parables; but since you are so persistent, I shall unfold to you the meaning of the similitudes of the field, and of all the others that follow, that you may make them known to every one.[4] Hear now," he said, "and

understand them. The field is this world; and the Lord of the field is He who created, and perfected, and strengthened all things; [and the son is the Holy Spirit;[5]] and the slave is the Son of God; and the vines are this people, whom He Himself planted; and the stakes are the holy angels of the Lord, who keep His people together; and the weeds that were plucked out of the vineyard are the iniquities of God's servants; and the dishes which He sent Him from His table are the commandments which He gave His people through His Son; and the friends and fellow-councillors are the holy angels who were first created; and the Master's absence from home is the time that remains until His appearing." I said to him, "Sir, all these are great, and marvellous, and glorious things. Could I, therefore," I continued, "understand them? No, nor could any other man, even if exceedingly wise. Moreover," I added, "explain to me what I am about to ask you." "Say what you wish," he replied. "Why, sir," I asked, "is the Son of God in the parable in the form of a slave?"

CHAP. VI.

"Hear," he answered: "the Son of God is not in the form[6] of a slave, but in great power and might." "How so, sir?" I said; "I do not understand." "Because," he answered, "God planted the vineyard, that is to say, He created the people, and gave them to His Son; and the Son appointed His angels over them to keep them; and He Himself purged away their sins, having suffered many trials and undergone many labours, for no one is able to dig without labour and toil. He Himself, then, having purged away the sins of the people, showed them the paths of life[7] by giving them the law which He received from His Father. [You see," he said, "that He is the Lord of the people, having received all authority from His Father.[8]] And why the Lord took His Son as councillor, and the glorious angels, regarding the heirship of the slave, listen. The holy, pre-existent Spirit, that created every creature, God made to dwell in flesh, which He chose.[9] This flesh, accordingly, in which the Holy Spirit dwelt, was nobly subject to that Spirit, walking reli-

---

[1] Literally, "self-willed" (αὐθάδης).
[2] [Matt. xiii. 11; Jas. i. 5.]
[3] [Luke xxii. 43.]
[4] [Part of the commission again.]

[5] This clause occurs only in the Vatican. It does not occur in Lips., Pal., or in the Æth.
[6] [Phil. ii. 7. But no longer is He such.]
[7] [Heb. i. 3; Ps. xvi. 11.]
[8] The sentence in brackets is omitted in Lips. and Æth., occurs in Vat. and Pal.
[9] This passage varies in each of the forms in which it has come down, and is corrupt in most, if not in all. The Vatican (Lat.) has, "Because the messenger hears the Holy Spirit, which was the first of all that was poured (*infusus*) into a body in which God might dwell. For understanding (*intellectus*) placed it in a body as seemed proper to Him." The Pal. reads: "For that Holy Spirit which was created pure [first] of all in a body in which it might dwell, God made and appointed a chosen body which pleased Him." The Æth. reads: "The Holy Spirit, who created all things, dwelt in a body in which He wished to dwell." [See Grabe's collation and emendation here, in Wake's translation.]

giously and chastely, in no respect defiling the Spirit; and accordingly, after living [1] excellently and purely, and after labouring and co-operating with the Spirit, and having in everything acted vigorously and courageously along with the Holy Spirit, He assumed it as a partner with it. For this conduct [2] of the flesh pleased Him, because it was not defiled on the earth while having the Holy Spirit. He took, therefore, as fellow-councillors His Son and the glorious angels, in order that this flesh, which had been subject to the body without a fault, might have some place of tabernacle, and that it might not appear that the reward [of its servitude had been lost [3]], for the flesh that has been found without spot or defilement, in which the Holy Spirit dwelt, [will receive a reward [3]]. You have now the explanation [4] of this parable also."

CHAP. VII.

"I rejoice, sir," I said, "to hear this explanation." "Hear," again he replied: "Keep this flesh pure and stainless, that the Spirit which inhabits it may bear witness to it, and your flesh may be justified. See that the thought never arise in your mind that this flesh of yours is corruptible, and you misuse it by any act of defilement. If you defile your flesh, you will also defile the Holy Spirit; and if you defile your flesh [and spirit], you will not live." [5] "And if any one, sir," I said, "has been hitherto ignorant, before he heard these words, how can such a man be saved who has defiled his flesh?" "Respecting former sins [6] of ignorance," he said, "God alone is able to heal them, for to Him belongs all power. [But be on your guard now, and the all-powerful and compassionate God will heal former transgressions [7]], if for the time to come you defile not your body nor your spirit; for both are common, and cannot be defiled, the one without the other: keep both therefore pure, and you will live unto God."

SIMILITUDE SIXTH.

OF THE TWO CLASSES OF VOLUPTUOUS MEN, AND OF THEIR DEATH, FALLING AWAY, AND THE DURATION OF THEIR PUNISHMENT.

CHAP. I.

Sitting in my house, and glorifying the Lord for all that I had seen, and reflecting on the commandments, that they are excellent, and powerful, and glorious, and able to save a man's soul, I said within myself, "I shall be blessed if I walk in these commandments, and every one who walks in them will be blessed." While I was saying these words to myself, I suddenly see him sitting beside me, and hear him thus speak: "Why are you in doubt about the commandments which I gave you? They are excellent: have no doubt about them at all, but put on faith in the Lord, and you will walk in them, for I will strengthen you in them. These commandments are beneficial to those who intend to repent: for if they do not walk in them, their repentance is in vain. You, therefore, who repent cast away the wickedness of this world which wears you out; and by putting on all the virtues of a holy life, you will be able to keep these commandments, and will no longer add to the number of your sins. Walk,[8] therefore, in these commandments of mine, and you will live unto God. All these things have been spoken to you by me." And after he had uttered these words, he said to me, "Let us go into the fields, and I will show you the shepherds of the flocks." "Let us go, sir," I replied. And we came to a certain plain, and he showed me a young man, a shepherd, clothed in a suit of garments of a yellow colour: and he was herding very many sheep, and these sheep were feeding luxuriously, as it were, and riotously, and merrily skipping hither and thither. The shepherd himself was merry, because of his flock; and the appearance of the shepherd was joyous, and he was running about amongst his flock. [And other sheep I saw rioting and luxuriating in one place, but not, however, leaping about.[9]]

CHAP. II.

And he said to me, "Do you see this shepherd?" "I see him, sir," I said. "This," he answered, "is the angel [10] of luxury and deceit:

---

[1] The Vatican renders this sentence: "This body, therefore, into which the Holy Spirit was led, was subject to that Spirit, walking rightly, modestly, and chastely, and did not at all defile that Spirit. Since, then, that body had always obeyed the Holy Spirit, and had laboured rightly and chastely with it, and had not at any time given way, that wearied body passed its time as a slave; but having strongly approved itself along with the Holy Spirit, it was received unto God." The Palatine is similar. The Æth. reads: "That body served well in righteousness and purity, nor did it ever defile that Spirit, and it became His partner, since that body pleased God."

[2] πορεία. Vatican, potens cursus.

[3] The passages within brackets are omitted by Lips. and Æth.

[4] [If the reader feels that the explanation itself needs to be explained, let him attribute it to the confused and inaccurate state of the text. Grabe says emphatically, that "the created Spirit of Christ as a man and not the Holy Ghost, the third person of the Trinity," is spoken of in this chapter chiefly. The apparent confusion of words and phrases must be the result of ignorant copying. It is a sufficient answer to certain German critics to cite the providential approval of Athanasius, a fact of the utmost moment. Nobody doubts that Athanasius was sensitive to any discoloration of the Nicene Faith. In the text of Hermas, therefore, as it was in his copy, there could have been nothing heretical, or favouring heresy. That Hermas was an artist, and purposely gave his fiction a very primitive air, is evident. He fears to name the Scriptures he quoted, lest any one should doubt their use, in the days of Clement, in the Western churches.]

[5] [1 Cor. iii. 16, 17. Owen, On the Spirit, passim. Ambiguities, cap. ii.]

[6] [Acts xvii. 30.]

[7] Omitted in Lips. Æth. has simply, "But be on your guard now."

[8] The Vatican has a sentence before this: "For if you sin not afterwards, you will greatly fall away from your former [transgressions]."

[9] Found only in Pseudo-Athanasius. It occurs in none of the translations.

[10] [The use of the word "angel," here, may possibly coincide with that in the Apocalypse, rebuking an unfaithful and luxurious pastor, like the angel of Sardis (Rev. iii. 1-5). The "yellow" raiment may be introduced as a contrast to the words, "thou hast a few names even in Sardis which have not defiled their garments, and they shall walk with me in white."]

he wears out the souls of the servants of God, and perverts them from the truth, deceiving them with wicked desires, through which they will perish; for they forget the commandments of the living God, and walk in deceits and empty luxuries; and they are ruined by the angel, some being brought to death, others to corruption." [1] I said to him, "Sir, I do not know the meaning of these words, 'to death, and to corruption.'" "Listen," he said. "The sheep which you saw merry and leaping about, are those which have torn themselves away from God for ever, and have delivered themselves over to luxuries and deceits [2] [of this world. Among them there is no return to life through repentance, because they have added to their other sins, and blasphemed the name of the Lord. Such men, therefore, are appointed unto death.[3] And the sheep which you saw not leaping, but feeding in one place, are they who have delivered themselves over to luxury and deceit], but have committed no blasphemy against the Lord. These have been perverted from the truth: among them there is the hope of repentance, by which it is possible to live. Corruption, then, has a hope of a kind of renewal,[4] but death has everlasting ruin." Again I went forward a little way, and he showed me a tall shepherd, somewhat savage in his appearance, clothed in a white goatskin, and having a wallet on his shoulders, and a very hard staff with branches, and a large whip. And he had a very sour look, so that I was afraid of him, so forbidding was his aspect. This shepherd, accordingly, was receiving the sheep from the young shepherd, those, viz., that were rioting and luxuriating, but not leaping; and he cast them into a precipitous place, full of thistles and thorns, so that it was impossible to extricate the sheep from the thorns and thistles; but they were completely entangled amongst them. These, accordingly, thus entangled, pastured amongst the thorns and thistles, and were exceedingly miserable, being beaten by him; and he drove them hither and thither, and gave them no rest; and, altogether, these sheep were in a wretched plight.

CHAP. III.

Seeing them, therefore, so beaten and so badly used, I was grieved for them, because they were so tormented, and had no rest at all. And I said to the Shepherd who talked with me, "Sir, who is this shepherd, who is so pitiless and severe,

and so completely devoid of compassion for these sheep?" "This," he replied, "is the angel of punishment; [5] and he belongs to the just angels, and is appointed to punish. He accordingly takes those who wander away from God, and who have walked in the desires and deceits of this world, and chastises them as they deserve with terrible and diverse punishments." "I would know, sir," I said, "Of what nature are these diverse tortures and punishments?" "Hear," he said, "the various tortures and punishments. The tortures are such as occur during life.[6] For some are punished with losses, others with want, others with sicknesses of various kinds, and others with all kinds of disorder and confusion; others are insulted by unworthy persons, and exposed to suffering in many other ways: for many, becoming unstable in their plans, try many things, and none of them at all succeed, and they say they are not prosperous in their undertakings; and it does not occur to their minds that they have done evil deeds, but they blame the Lord.[7] When, therefore, they have been afflicted with all kinds of affliction, then are they delivered unto me for good training, and they are made strong in the faith of the Lord; and [8] for the rest of the days of their life they are subject to the Lord with pure hearts, and are successful in all their undertakings, obtaining from the Lord everything they ask; and then they glorify the Lord, that they were delivered to me, and no longer suffer any evil."

CHAP. IV.

I said to him, "Sir, explain this also to me." "What is it you ask?" he said. "Whether, sir," I continued, "they who indulge in luxury, and who are deceived, are tortured for the same period of time that they have indulged in luxury and deceit?" He said to me, "They are tortured in the same manner." [9] ["They are tor-

---

[1] καταφθοράν, translated in Pal. and Vat. by *defectio*, apostasy, as departure from goodness and truth. The Æthiopic has "ruin."

[2] *Of . . . deceit*, omitted in Lips. Our translation is made from the Vat.

[3] Pseudo-Athanasius has, "of such men the life is death."

[4] Pseudo-Athanasius has, "Corruption, therefore, has a hope of resurrection up to a certain point." [Death here must mean final apostasy (Heb. vi. 4-6, x. 26-31, xii. 15-17). But a certain death-in-life, which is not final, is instanced in Rev. iii. 1; note also 1 John iii. 14, 15, v. 16, 17.]

[5] [The idea is, the *minister of discipline*, as St. Ambrose is represented with a scourge in his hand. The Greek (ἐκ τῶν ἀγγέλων τῶν δικαίων) favours the idea that faithful pastors are here symbolized, — just stewards and righteous men.]

[6] βιωτικαί. The Vatican and Pal. render this, "the various punishments and tortures which men suffer daily in their lives." Pseudo-Athanasius has: "For when they revolt from God, thinking to be in rest and in wealth, then they are punished, some meeting with losses," etc. [1 Tim. i. 20. Remedial discipline is thus spoken of, 1 Cor. v. 5.]

[7] Pseudo-Athanasius has: "And they cannot bear for the rest of their days to turn and serve the Lord with a pure heart. But if they repent and become sober again, then they understand that they were not prosperous on account of their evil deeds; and so they glorify the Lord, because He is a just Judge, and because they suffered justly, and were punished (ἐπαιδεύθησαν) according to their deeds."

[8] The Vatican inserts the following sentence before this: "And when they begin to repent of their sins, then the works in which they have wickedly exercised themselves arise in their hearts; and then they give honour to God, saying that He is a just Judge, and that they have deservedly suffered everything according to their deeds." So does Pal. The Æthiopic becomes very condensed in this portion. [Note this class of offenders, having suffered remedial chastisement, are not delivered over to Satan finally, but "delivered unto me (the angel of repentance) for good training."]

[9] τρόπον. The Vat. and Pal. have, "for the same time" (*per idem tempus*).

mented much less, sir," I replied ; ¹] " for those who are so luxurious and who forget God ought to be tortured seven-fold." He said to me, " You are foolish, and do not understand the power of torment." " Why, sir," I said, " if I had understood it, I would not have asked you to show me." " Hear," he said, " the power of both. The time of luxury and deceit is one hour ; but the hour of torment is equivalent to thirty days. If, accordingly, a man indulge in luxury for one day, and be deceived and be tortured for one day, the day of his torture is equivalent to a whole year. For all the days of luxury, therefore, there are as many years of torture to be undergone. You see, then," he continued, " that the time of luxury and deceit is very short,² but that of punishment and torture long."

CHAP. V.

" Still," I said, " I do not quite understand about the time of deceit, and luxury, and torture ; explain it to me more clearly." He answered, and said to me, " Your folly is persistent ; and you do not wish to purify your heart, and serve God. Have a care," he added, " lest the time be fulfilled, and you be found foolish. Hear now," he added, " as you desire, that you may understand these things. He who indulges in luxury, and is deceived for one day, and who does what he wishes, is clothed with much foolishness, and does not understand the act which he does until the morrow ; for he forgets what he did the day before. For luxury and deceit have no memories, on account of the folly with which they are clothed ; but when punishment and torture cleave to a man for one day, he is punished and tortured for a year ; for punishment and torture have powerful memories. While tortured and punished, therefore, for a whole year, he remembers at last ³ his luxury and deceit, and knows that on their account he suffers evil. Every man, therefore, who is luxurious and deceived is thus tormented, because, although having life, they have given themselves over to death." " What kinds of luxury, sir," I asked, " are hurtful?" " Every act of a man which he performs with pleasure," he replied, " is an act of luxury ; for the sharp-tempered man, when gratifying his tendency, indulges in luxury ; and the adulterer, and the drunkard, and the backbiter, and the liar, and the covetous man, and the thief, and he who does things like these, gratifies his peculiar propensity, and in so doing indulges in luxury. All these acts of luxury are hurtful to the servants of God. On account of

these deceits, therefore, do they suffer, who are punished and tortured. And there are also acts of luxury which save men ; for many who do good indulge in luxury, being carried away by their own pleasure : ⁴ this luxury, however, is beneficial to the servants of God, and gains life for such a man ; but the injurious acts of luxury before enumerated bring tortures and punishment upon them ; and if they continue in them and do not repent, they bring death upon themselves."

SIMILITUDE SEVENTH.

THEY WHO REPENT MUST BRING FORTH FRUITS WORTHY OF REPENTANCE.

After a few days I saw him in the same plain where I had also seen the shepherds ; and he said to me, " What do you wish with me ? " I said to him, " Sir, that you would order the shepherd who punishes to depart out of my house, because he afflicts me exceedingly." " It is necessary," he replied, " that you be afflicted ; for thus," he continued, " did the glorious angel command concerning you, as he wishes you to be tried." " What have I done which is so bad, sir," I replied, " that I should be delivered over to this angel ? " " Listen," he said : " Your sins are many, but not so great as to require that *you* be delivered over to this angel ; but your household has committed great iniquities and sins, and the glorious angel has been incensed at them on account of their deeds ; and for this reason he commanded you to be afflicted for a certain time, that they also might repent, and purify themselves from every desire of this world. When, therefore, they repent and are purified, then the angel of punishment will depart." I said to him, " Sir, if they have done such things as to incense the glorious angel against them, yet what have I done ? " He replied, " They cannot be afflicted at all, unless you, the head of the house, be afflicted : for when you are afflicted, of necessity they also suffer affliction ; but if you are in comfort, they can feel no affliction." " Well, sir," I said, " they have repented with their whole heart." " I know, too," he answered, " that they have repented with their whole heart : do you think, however, that the sins of those who repent are remitted ? ⁵ Not altogether, but he who repents must torture his own soul, and be exceedingly humble in all his conduct, and be afflicted with many kinds of affliction ; and if he endure the afflictions that come upon him, He who created all things, and endued them with power, will assuredly have compassion, and will heal him ; and this will He do when He sees the heart

---

¹ Omitted in Lips.
² Pseudo-Athanasius has " nothing " (οὐδέν) instead of ἐλάχιστος.
³ ποτέ. [The pleasures of sin are " for a season " (Heb. xi. 25), at most : impenitence is the " treasuring up of wrath against the day of wrath " (Rom. ii. 5).]

⁴ [Ps. iv. 6, 7, cxix. 14, lxxxiv. 10. Dr. Doddridge's epigram on *Dum Vivimus Vivamus* will be brought to mind.]
⁵ The Vat. and Pal. have *protinus*, " immediately." [Wake adopts this reading, which appears to be required by the context.]

of every penitent pure from every evil thing : [1] and it is profitable for you and for your house to suffer affliction now. But why should I say much to you? You must be afflicted, as that angel of the Lord commanded who delivered you to me. And for this give thanks to the Lord, because He has deemed you worthy of showing you beforehand this affliction, that, knowing it before it comes, you may be able to bear it with courage." [2] I said to him, "Sir, be thou with me, and I will be able to bear all affliction." "I will be with you," he said, "and I will ask the angel of punishment to afflict you more lightly; nevertheless, you will be afflicted for a little time, and again you will be re-established in your house. Only continue humble, and serve the Lord in all purity of heart, you and your children, and your house, and walk in my commands which I enjoin upon you, and your repentance will be deep and pure ; and if you observe these things with your household, every affliction will depart from you.[3] And affliction," he added, "will depart from all who walk in these my commandments."

SIMILITUDE EIGHTH.

THE SINS OF THE ELECT AND OF THE PENITENT ARE OF MANY KINDS, BUT ALL WILL BE REWARDED ACCORDING TO THE MEASURE OF THEIR REPENTANCE AND GOOD WORKS.

CHAP. I.

He showed me a large willow tree overshadowing plains and mountains, and under the shade of this willow had assembled all those who were called by the name of the Lord. And a glorious angel of the Lord, who was very tall, was standing beside the willow, having a large pruning-knife, and he was cutting little twigs from the willow and distributing them among the people that were overshadowed by the willow ; and the twigs which he gave them were small, about a cubit, as it were, in length. And after they had all received the twigs, the angel laid down the pruning-knife, and that tree was sound, as I had seen it at first. And I marvelled within myself, saying, "How is the tree sound, after so many branches have been cut off?" And the Shepherd said to me, "Do not be surprised if the tree remains sound after so many branches were lopped off ; [but wait,[4]] and when you shall have seen everything, then it will be explained to you what it means." The angel

who had distributed the branches among the people again asked them from them, and in the order in which they had received them were they summoned to him, and each one of them returned his branch. And the angel of the Lord took and looked at them. From some he received the branches withered and moth-eaten ; those who returned branches in that state the angel of the Lord ordered to stand apart. Others, again, returned them withered, but not moth-eaten ; and these he ordered to stand apart. And others returned them half-withered, and these stood apart ; and others returned their branches half-withered and having cracks in them, and these stood apart. [And others returned their branches green and having cracks in them ; and these stood apart.[5]] And others returned their branches, one-half withered and the other green ; and these stood apart. And others brought their branches two-thirds green and the remaining third withered ; and these stood apart. And others returned them two-thirds withered and one-third green ; and these stood apart. And others returned their branches nearly all green, the smallest part only, the top, being withered, but they had cracks in them ; and these stood apart. And of others very little was green, but the remaining parts withered ; and these stood apart. And others came bringing their branches green, as they had received them from the angel. And the majority of the crowd returned branches of that kind, and with these the angel was exceedingly pleased ; and these stood apart. [And others returned their branches green and having offshoots ; and these stood apart, and with these the angel was exceedingly delighted.[6]] And others returned their branches green and with offshoots, and the offshoots had some fruit, as it were ; [7] and those men whose branches were found to be of that kind were exceedingly joyful. And the angel was exultant because of them ; and the Shepherd also rejoiced greatly because of them.

CHAP. II.

And the angel of the Lord ordered crowns to be brought ; [8] and there were brought crowns, formed, as it were, of palms ; and he crowned the men who had returned the branches which had offshoots and some fruit, and sent them away into the tower. And the others also he sent into the tower, those, namely, who had returned branches that were green and had offshoots but no fruit, having given them seals.[9] And all who went into the tower had the same

---

[1] The Lips. has lost here a few words, which are supplied from the Latin translations. [Mal. iii. 3; Isa. i. 22; Ps. xxvi. 2, cxxxix. 23, 24. Is there not much teaching here for our easy living, and light ideas of the sinfulness of sin?]
[2] The Vatican has: "But rather give thanks to the Lord, that He, knowing what is to come to pass, has deemed you worthy to tell you beforehand that affliction is coming upon those who are able to bear it." [1 Cor. x. 13. But the whole argument turns on Jas. i. 2, as Hermas delights in this practical apostle.]
[3] [Sam. iii. 31, 32, 33.]
[4] Omitted by Lips.

[5] Omitted in Lips. and Vat.
[6] Omitted in Lips.
[7] Num. xvii. 8. [Willows are chosen, perhaps, with reference to Isa. xliv. 4; but Ezekiel's willow supplies the thought here (Ezek. xvii. 5, 6).]
[8] 2 Esdras ii. 43.
[9] [Eph. i. 13, iv. 30.]

clothing — white as snow.[1] And those who returned their branches green, as they had received them, he set free, giving them clothing and seals. Now after the angel had finished these things, he said to the Shepherd, "I am going away, and you will send these away within the walls, according as each one is worthy to have his dwelling. And examine their branches carefully, and so dismiss them; but examine them with *care*. See that no one escape you," he added; "and if any escape you, I will try them at the altar."[2] Having said these words to the Shepherd, he departed. And after the angel had departed, the Shepherd said to me, "Let us take the branches of all these and plant them, and see if any of them will live." I said to him, "Sir, how can these withered branches live?" He answered, and said, "This tree is a willow, and of a kind that is very tenacious of life. If, therefore, the branches be planted, and receive a little moisture, many of them will live. And now let us try, and pour water[3] upon them; and if any of them live I shall rejoice with them, and if they do not I at least will not be found neglectful." And the Shepherd bade me call them as each one was placed. And they came, rank by rank, and gave their branches to the Shepherd. And the Shepherd received the branches, and planted them in rows; and after he had planted them he poured much water upon them, so that the branches could not be seen for the water; and after the branches had drunk it in, he said to me, "Let us go, and return after a few days, and inspect all the branches; for He who created this tree wishes all those to live who received branches[4] from it. And I also hope that the greater part of these branches which received moisture and drank of the water will live."

CHAP. III.

I said to him, "Sir, explain to me what this tree means, for I am perplexed about it, because, after so many branches have been cut off, it continues sound, and nothing appears to have been cut away from it. By this, now, I am perplexed." "Listen," he said: "This great tree[5] that casts its shadow over plains, and mountains, and all the earth, is the law of God that was given to the whole world; and this law is the Son of God,[6] proclaimed to the ends of the earth; and the people who are under its shadow are they who have heard the proclamation, and have believed upon Him. And the great and glorious angel Michael is he who has authority over this people, and governs them;[7] for this is he who gave them the law[8] into the hearts of believers: he accordingly superintends them to whom he gave it, to see if they have kept the same. And you see the branches of each one, for the branches are the law You see, accordingly, many branches that have been rendered useless, and you will know them all — those who have not kept the law; and you will see the dwelling of each one." I said to him, "Sir, why did he dismiss some into the tower, and leave others to you?" "All," he answered, "who transgressed the law which they received from him, he left under my power for repentance; but all who have satisfied the law, and kept it, he retains under his own authority." "Who, then," I continued, "are they who were crowned, and who go to the tower?" "These are they who have suffered on account of the law; but the others, and they who returned their branches green, and with offshoots, but without fruit, are they who have been afflicted on account of the law, but who have not suffered nor denied[9] their law; and they who returned their branches green as they had received them, are the venerable, and the just, and they who have walked carefully in a pure heart, and have kept the commandments of the Lord. And the rest you will know when I have examined those branches which have been planted and watered."

CHAP. IV.

And after a few days we came to the place, and the Shepherd sat down in the angel's place, and I stood beside him. And he said to me, "Gird yourself with pure, undressed linen made of sackcloth;" and seeing me girded, and ready to minister to him, "Summon," he said, "the men to whom belong the branches that were planted, according to the order in which each one gave them in." So I went away to the plain, and summoned them all, and they all stood in their ranks. He said to them, "Let each one pull out his own branch, and bring it to me." The first to give in were those who had them withered and cut; and[10] because they were found to be thus withered and cut, he commanded them to stand apart. And next they gave them in who had them withered, but not cut. And some of them gave in their branches green, and some withered and eaten as by a moth. Those that gave them in green, accordingly, he ordered to stand apart; and those who gave them in dry and cut, he ordered to stand along with the first. Next they gave them

---

1 [Rev. xix. 8.]
2 [Rev. viii. 3; Num. xvii. 7.]
3 [Ezek. xxxix. 29.]
4 [Rom. xi. 16.]
5 [Matt. xiii. 32.]
6 " And by this law the Son of God was preached to all the ends of the earth." — *Vat.* [Hermas again introduces here the name which he made his base in Vision ii. 2.]

7 [Dan. x. 21, xii 1; Rev. xii. 7. It is not necessary to accept this statement as doctrine, but the idea may be traced to these texts.]
8 [That is, the New Law, the gospel of the Son of God.]
9 [Vision ii. 2. Denying the Son.]
10 *And . cut*, omitted in Pal.

in who had them half-withered and cracked;[1] and many of them gave them in green and without cracks; and some green and with offshoots, and fruits upon the offshoots, such as they had who went, after being crowned, into the tower. And some handed them in withered and eaten, and some withered and uneaten; and some as they were, half-withered and cracked. And he commanded them each one to stand apart, some towards their own rows, and others apart from them.

CHAP. V.

Then they gave in their branches who had them green, but cracked: all these gave them in green, and stood in their own row. And the Shepherd was pleased with these, because they were all changed, and had lost their cracks.[2] And they also gave them in who had them half-green and half-withered: of some, accordingly, the branches were found completely green; of others, half-withered; of others, withered and eaten; of others, green, and having offshoots. All these were sent away, each to his own row. [Next they gave in who had them two parts green and one-third withered. Many of them gave them half-withered; and others withered and rotten; and others half-withered and cracked, and a few green. These all stood in their own row.[3]] And they gave them in who had them green, but to a very slight extent withered and cracked.[4] Of these, some gave them in green, and others green and with offshoots. And these also went away to their own row. Next they gave them who had a very small part green and the other parts withered. Of these the branches were found for the most part green and having offshoots, and fruit upon the offshoots, and others altogether green. With these branches the Shepherd was exceedingly pleased, because they were found in this state. And these went away, each to his own row.

CHAP. VI.

After the Shepherd had examined the branches of them all, he said to me, "I told you that this tree was tenacious of life. You see," he continued, "how many repented and were saved." "I see, sir," I replied. "That you may behold," he added, "the great mercy of the Lord, that it is great and glorious, and that He has given His Spirit to those who are worthy of repentance." "Why then, sir," I said, "did not all these repent?" He answered, "To them whose heart He saw would become pure, and obedient to Him, He gave power to repent with the whole heart. But to them whose deceit and wickedness He perceived, and saw that they intended to repent hypocritically, He did not grant repentance,[5] lest they should again profane His name." I said to him, "Sir, show me now, with respect to those who gave in the branches, of what sort they are, and their abode, in order that they hearing it who believed, and received the seal, and broke it, and did not keep it whole, may, on coming to a knowledge of their deeds, repent, and receive from you a seal, and may glorify the Lord because He had compassion upon them, and sent you to renew their spirits." "Listen," he said: "they whose branches were found withered and moth-eaten are the apostates and traitors of the Church, who have blasphemed the Lord in their sins, and have, moreover, been ashamed of the name of the Lord by which they were called.[6] These, therefore, at the end were lost unto God. And you see that not a single one of them repented, although they heard the words which I spake to them, which I enjoined upon you. From such life departed.[7] And they who gave them in withered and undecayed, these also were near to them; for they were hypocrites, and introducers of strange doctrines, and subverters of the servants of God, especially of those who had sinned, not allowing them to repent, but persuading them by foolish doctrines.[8] These, accordingly, have a hope of repentance. And you see that many of them also have repented since I spake to them, and they will still repent. But all who will not repent have lost their lives; and as many of them as repented became good, and their dwelling was appointed within the first walls; and some of them ascended even into the tower. You see, then," he said, "that repentance involves life to sinners, but non-repentance death."

CHAP. VII.

"And as many as gave in the branches half-withered and cracked, hear also about them. They whose branches were half-withered to the same extent are the wavering; for they neither live, nor are they dead. And they who have them half-withered and cracked are both waverers and slanderers, [railing against the absent,] and never at peace with one another, but always at variance. And yet to these also," he continued, "repentance is possible. You see," he said, "that some of them have repented, and there is still remaining in them," he continued, "a hope of repentance. And as many of them," he added, "as have repented, shall have their

---

1 [Wake reads "cleft."]
2 [Clefts.]
3 Omitted in Lips. Translation is made from Vat.
4 The versions vary in some of the minute particulars.

5 [The by-gone quarrels about foreknowledge and predestination are innocently enough anticipated here.]
6 [Jas. ii. 7.]
7 [Heb. x. 39.]
8 [Here is a note of Hermas' time. Not only does it imply the history of heresies as of some progress, but it marks the Montanist refusal to receive penitent lapsers.]

dwelling in the tower. And those of them who have been slower in repenting shall dwell within the walls. And as many as do not repent at all, but abide in their deeds, shall utterly perish. And they who gave in their branches green and cracked were always faithful and good, though emulous of each other about the foremost places, and about fame : [1] now all these are foolish, in indulging in such a rivalry. Yet they also, being naturally good,[2] on hearing my commandments, purified themselves, and soon repented. Their dwelling, accordingly, was in the tower. But if any one relapse into strife, he will be cast out of the tower, and will lose his life.[3] Life is the possession of all who keep the commandments of the Lord ; but in the commandments there is no rivalry in regard to the first places, or glory of any kind, but in regard to patience and personal humility. Among such persons, then, is the life of the Lord, but amongst the quarrelsome and transgressors, death.

CHAP. VIII.

" And they who gave in their branches half-green and half-withered, are those who are immersed in business, and do not cleave to the saints. For this reason, the one half of them is living, and the other half dead.[4] Many, accordingly, who heard my commands repented, and those at least who repented had their dwelling in the tower. But some of them at last fell away : these, accordingly, have not repentance, for on account of their business they blasphemed the Lord, and denied Him. They therefore lost their lives through the wickedness which they committed. And many of them doubted. These still have repentance in their power, if they repent speedily ; and their abode will be in the tower. But if they are slower in repenting, they will dwell in the walls ; and if they do not repent, they too have lost their lives. And they who gave in their branches two-thirds withered and one-third green, are those who have denied [the Lord] in various ways. Many, however, repented, but some of them hesitated and were in doubt. These, then, have repentance within their reach, if they repent quickly, and do not remain in their pleasures ;[5] but if they abide in their deeds, these, too, work to themselves death.

CHAP. IX.

" And they who returned their branches two-thirds withered and one-third green, are those that were faithful indeed ; but after acquiring

wealth, and becoming distinguished amongst the heathen, they clothed themselves with great pride, and became lofty-minded, and deserted the truth, and did not cleave to the righteous, but lived with the heathen, and this way of life became more agreeable to them.[6] They did not, however, depart from God, but remained in the faith, although not working the works of faith. Many of them accordingly repented, and their dwelling was in the tower. And others continuing to live until the end with the heathen, and being corrupted by their vain glories, [departed from God, serving the works and deeds of the heathen.[7]] These were reckoned with the heathen. But others of them hesitated, not hoping to be saved on account of the deeds which they had done ; while others were in doubt, and caused divisions among themselves. To those, therefore, who were in doubt on account of their deeds, repentance is still open ; but their repentance ought to be speedy, that their dwelling may be in the tower. And to those who do not repent, but abide in their pleasures, death is near.

CHAP. X.

" And they who give in their branches green, but having the tips withered and cracked, these were always good, and faithful, and distinguished before God ; but they sinned a very little through indulging small desires, and finding little faults with one another. But on hearing my words the greater part of them quickly repented, and their dwelling was upon the tower. Yet some of them were in doubt ; and certain of them who were in doubt wrought greater dissension. Among these, therefore, is hope of repentance, because they were always good ; and with difficulty will any one of them perish. And they who gave up their branches withered,[8] but having a very small part green, are those who believed only, yet continue working the works of iniquity. They never, however, departed from God, but gladly bore His name, and joyfully received His servants into their houses.[9] Having accordingly heard of this repentance, they unhesitatingly repented, and practise all virtue and righteousness ; and some of them even [suffered, being willingly put to death[10]], knowing their deeds which they had done. Of all these, therefore, the dwelling shall be in the tower."

CHAP. XI.

And after he had finished the explanations of

---

[1] [He has in view the passages Matt. xx. 23, Luke xxii. 24, and hence is lenient in judgment.]
[2] [Why "naturally" ? Latin, " de ipsis tamen qui boni fuerunt." Greek, ἀγαθοὶ ὄντες. Gebhardt and Harnack, Lips. 1877.]
[3] [Jas. iii. 16.]
[4] [Jas. ii. 26.]
[5] [1 Tim. v. 6.]

[6] [A note of the time of composing *The Shepherd*. This chapter speaks of experiences of life among heathen and of worldly Christians, inconsistent with the times of Clement.]
[7] Omitted in Lips.; supplied from Vat.
[8] " Withered, all but their tops, which alone were green." — *Vat.* and *Pal.*
[9] [Matt. x. 40-42 influences this judgment of Hermas.]
[10] Omitted in Lips., which has, instead, " are afraid."

all the branches, he said to me, " Go and tell them to every one, that they may repent, and they shall live unto God.¹ Because the Lord, having had compassion on all men, has sent me to give repentance, although some are not worthy of it on account of their works ; but the Lord, being long-suffering, desires those who were called by His Son to be saved." ²   I said to him, " Sir, I hope that all who have heard them will repent ; for I am persuaded that each one, on coming to a knowledge of his own works, and fearing the Lord, will repent."   He answered me, and said, " All who with their whole heart shall purify themselves from their wickedness before enumerated, and shall add no more to their sins, will receive healing from the Lord for their former transgressions, if they do not hesitate at these commandments ; and they will live unto God.   But do you walk in my commandments, and live."   Having shown me these things, and spoken all these words, he said to me, " And the rest I will show you after a few days."

SIMILITUDE NINTH.

THE GREAT MYSTERIES IN THE BUILDING OF THE MILITANT AND TRIUMPHANT CHURCH.

CHAP. I.

After I had written down the commandments and similitudes of the Shepherd, the angel of repentance, he came to me and said, " I wish to explain to you what the Holy Spirit ³ that spake with you in the form of the Church showed you, for that Spirit is the Son of God.   For, as you were somewhat weak in the flesh, it was not explained to you by the angel.   When, however, you were strengthened by the Spirit, and your strength was increased, so that you were able to see the angel also, then accordingly was the building of the tower shown you by the Church. In a noble and solemn manner did you see everything as if shown you by a virgin ; but now you see [them] through the same Spirit as if shown by an angel.   You must, however, learn everything from me with greater accuracy.   For I was sent for this purpose by the glorious angel to dwell in your house, that you might see all things with power, entertaining no fear, even as it was before."   And he led me away into Arcadia, to a round hill ; ⁴ and he placed me on

the top of the hill, and showed me a large plain, and round about the plain twelve mountains, all having different forms.   The first was black as soot ; and the second bare, without grass ; and the third full of thorns and thistles ; and the fourth with grass half-withered, the upper parts of the plants green, and the parts about the roots withered ; and some of the grasses, when the sun scorched them, became withered.   And the fifth mountain had green grass, and was rugged.   And the sixth mountain was quite full of clefts, some small and others large ; and the clefts were grassy, but the plants were not very vigorous, but rather, as it were, decayed.   The seventh mountain, again, had cheerful pastures, and the whole mountain was blooming, and every kind of cattle and birds were feeding upon that mountain ; and the more the cattle and the birds ate, the more the grass of that mountain flourished.   And the eighth mountain was full of fountains, and every kind of the Lord's creatures drank of the fountains of that mountain.   But the ninth mountain [had no water at all, and was wholly a desert, and had within it deadly serpents, which destroy men.   And the tenth mountain ⁵] had very large trees, and was completely shaded, and under the shadow of the trees sheep lay resting and ruminating.   And the eleventh mountain was very thickly wooded, and those trees were productive, being adorned with various sorts of fruits, so that any one seeing them would desire to eat of their fruits.   The twelfth mountain, again, was wholly white, and its aspect was cheerful, and the mountain in itself was very beautiful.

CHAP. II.

And in the middle of the plain he showed me a large white rock that had arisen out of the plain.   And the rock was more lofty than the mountains, rectangular in shape, so as to be capable of containing the whole world : and that rock was old, having a gate cut out of it ; and the cutting out of the gate seemed to me as if recently done.   And the gate glittered to such a degree under the sunbeams, that I marvelled at the splendour of the gate ; ⁶ and round about the gate were standing twelve virgins.   The four who stood at the corners seemed to me more distinguished than the others — they were all, however, distinguished — and they were standing at the four parts of the gate ; two virgins between each part.   And they were clothed with linen tunics, and gracefully girded, having their right shoulders exposed, as if about to bear some burden.   Thus they stood ready ; for they were exceedingly cheerful and eager.   After I had seen these things, I marvelled in myself,

---

¹ [A cheering conclusion of his severe judgments, and aimed at the despair created by Montanist prophesyings.]
² Literally, " the calling that was made by His Son to be saved." The Vatican renders this, " He wishes to preserve the invitation made by His Son."   The Pal. has, " wishes to save His Church, which belongs to His Son."   In the text, κλῆσις is taken as = κλητοί.
³ The Spirit. — Vat.   [He is called " the Spirit of Christ " by St. Peter (i. 11) ; and perhaps this is a key to the non-dogmatic language of Hermas, if indeed he is here speaking of the Holy Spirit personally, and not of the Son exclusively.   See Simil. v. 6.   Isa. v. i.]
⁴ To a fruitful hill. — Pal.   Omitted in Vat.   [Hermas delights in the picturesque, and introduces Arcadia in harmony with his pastoral fiction.]

⁵ Omitted in Lips.
⁶ [As of Eden.   Gen. iii. 24 ; Rev. xxi. 11.   The Tsohar.]

because I was beholding great and glorious sights. And again I was perplexed about the virgins, because, although so delicate, they were standing courageously, as if about to carry the whole heavens. And the Shepherd said to me, "Why are you reasoning in yourself, and perplexing your mind, and distressing yourself? for the things which you cannot understand, do not attempt to comprehend, as if you were wise; but ask the Lord, that you may receive understanding and know them. You cannot see what is behind you, but you see what is before. Whatever, then, you cannot see, let alone, and do not torment yourself about it: but what you see, make yourself master of it, and do not waste your labour about other things; and I will explain to you everything that I show you. Look, therefore, on the things that remain."

CHAP. III.

I saw six men come, tall, and distinguished, and similar in appearance, and they summoned a multitude of men. And they who came were also tall men, and handsome, and powerful; and the six men commanded them to build a tower[1] above the rock. And great was the noise of those men who came to build the tower, as they ran hither and thither around the gate. And the virgins who stood around the gate told the men to hasten to build the tower. Now the virgins had spread out their hands, as if about to receive something from the men. And the six men commanded stones to ascend out of a certain pit, and to go to the building of the tower. And there went up ten shining rectangular stones, not hewn in a quarry. And the six men called the virgins, and bade them carry all the stones that were intended for the building, and to pass through the gate, and give them to the men who were about to build the tower. And the virgins put upon one another the ten first stones which had ascended from the pit, and carried them together, each stone by itself.

CHAP. IV.

And as they stood together around the gate, those who seemed to be strong carried them, and they stooped down under the corners of the stone; and the others stooped down under the sides of the stones. And in this way they carried all the stones.[2] And they carried them through the gate as they were commanded, and gave them to the men for the tower; and they took the stones and proceeded with the building. Now the tower was built upon the great rock, and above the gate. Those ten stones were prepared as the foundation for the building of the tower. And the rock and gate were the support of the whole of the tower. And after the ten stones other twenty [five] came up out of the pit, and these were fitted into the building of the tower, being carried by the virgins as before. And after these ascended thirty-five. And these in like manner were fitted into the tower. And after these other forty stones came up; and all these were cast into the building of the tower, [and there were four rows in the foundation of the tower,[3]] and they ceased ascending from the pit. And the builders also ceased for a little. And again the six men commanded the multitude of the crowd to bear stones from the mountains for the building of the tower. They were accordingly brought from all the mountains of various colours, and being hewn by the men were given to the virgins; and the virgins carried them through the gate, and gave them for the building of the tower. And when the stones of various colours were placed in the building, they all became white alike, and lost their different colours. And certain stones were given by the men for the building, and these did not become shining; but as they were placed, such also were they found to remain: for they were not given by the virgins, nor carried through the gate. These stones, therefore, were not in keeping with the others in the building of the tower. And the six men, seeing these unsuitable stones in the building, commanded them to be taken away, and to be carried away down to their own place whence they had been taken; [and being removed one by one, they were laid aside; and] they say to the men who brought the stones, "Do not ye bring any stones at all for the building, but lay them down beside the tower, that the virgins may carry them through the gate, and may give them for the building. For unless," they said, "they be carried through the gate by the hands of the virgins, they cannot change their colours: do not toil, therefore," they said, "to no purpose."

CHAP. V.

And on that day the building was finished, but the tower was not completed; for additional building was again about to be added, and there was a cessation in the building. And the six men commanded the builders all to withdraw a little distance, and to rest, but enjoined the virgins not to withdraw from the tower; and it seemed to me that the virgins had been left to guard the tower. Now after all had withdrawn, and were resting themselves, I said to the Shepherd, "What is the reason that the building of the tower was not finished?" "The tower," he answered, "cannot be finished just yet, until the Lord of it come and examine the building, in

---

[1] [Vision iii. 1, 2.]
[2] All carried the gate. — Pal.

[3] Omitted in Lips.

order that, if any of the stones be found to be decayed, he may change them : for the tower is built according to his pleasure." " I would like to know, sir," I said, " what is the meaning of the building of this tower, and what the rock and gate, and the mountains, and the virgins mean, and the stones that ascended from the pit, and were not hewn, but came as they were to the building. Why, in the first place, were ten stones placed in the foundation, then twenty-five, then thirty-five, then forty? and I wish also to know about the stones that went to the building, and were again taken out and returned to their own place? On all these points put my mind at rest, sir, and explain them to me." " If you are not found to be curious about trifles," he replied, " you shall know everything. For after a few days [we shall come hither, and you will see the other things that happen to this tower, and will know accurately all the similitudes." After a few days [1]] we came to the place where we sat down. And he said to me, " Let us go to the tower; for the master of the tower is coming to examine it." And we came to the tower, and there was no one at all near it, save the virgins only. And the Shepherd asked the virgins if perchance the master of the tower had come ; and they replied that he was about to come [2] to examine the building.

CHAP. VI.

And, behold, after a little I see an array of many men coming, and in the midst of them one man [3] of so remarkable a size as to overtop the tower. And the six men who had worked upon the building were with him, and many other honourable men were around him. And the virgins who kept the tower ran forward and kissed him, and began to walk near him around the tower. And that man examined the building carefully, feeling every stone separately ; and holding a rod in his hand, he struck every stone in the building three times. And when he struck them, some of them became black as soot, and some appeared as if covered with scabs, and some cracked, and some mutilated, and some neither white nor black, and some rough and not in keeping with the other stones, and some having [very many] stains : such were the varieties of decayed stones that were found in the building. He ordered all these to be taken out of the tower, and to be laid down beside it, and other stones to be brought and put in their stead. [And the builders asked him from what mountain he wished them to be brought and put in their place.[4]] And he did

not command them to be brought from the mountains, [but he bade them be brought from a certain plain which was near at hand.[5]] And the plain was·dug up, and shining rectangular stones were found, and some also of a round shape ; and all the stones which were in that plain were brought, and carried through the gate by the virgins. And the rectangular stones were hewn, and put in place of those that were taken away ; but the rounded stones were not put into the building, because they were hard to hew, and appeared to yield slowly to the chisel ; they were deposited, however, beside the tower, as if intended to be hewn and used in the building, for they were exceedingly brilliant.

CHAP. VII.

The glorious man, the lord of the whole tower, having accordingly finished these alterations, called to him the Shepherd, and delivered to him all the stones that were lying beside the tower, that had been rejected from the building, and said to him, " Carefully clean all these stones, and put aside such for the building of the tower as may harmonize with the others; and those that do not, throw far away from the tower." [Having given these orders to the Shepherd, he departed from the tower[6]], with all those with whom he had come. · Now the virgins were standing around the tower, keeping it. I said again to the Shepherd, " Can these stones return to the building of the tower, after being rejected?" He answered me, and said, " Do you see these stones?" " I see them, sir," I replied. " The greater part of these stones," he said, " I will hew, and put into the building, and they will harmonize with the others." " How, sir," I said, " can they, after being cut all round about, fill up the same space?" He answered, " Those that shall be found small will be thrown into the middle of the building, and those that are larger will be placed on the outside, and they will hold them together." Having spoken these words, he said to me, " Let us go, and after two days let us come and clean these stones, and cast them into the building; for all things around the tower must be cleaned, lest the Master come suddenly,[7] and find the places about the tower dirty, and be displeased, and these stones be not returned for the building of the tower, and I also shall seem to be neglectful towards the Master." And after two days we came to the tower, and he said to me, " Let us examine all the stones, and ascertain those which may return to the building." I said to him, " Sir, let us examine them ! "

---

1 Omitted in Lips.
2 And they replied that he would forthwith come. — *Vat.*
3 2 Esdras ii. 43.
4 Omitted in Lips. The text is from Vat.; slight variations in Pal. and Æth.

5 Also omitted from Lips. The text is in all the translations.
6 Omitted in Lips. The text in all the translations.
7 [Mark xiii. 36; Matt. xxiv. 46-51.]

CHAP. VIII.

And beginning, we first examined the black stones. And such as they had been taken out of the building, were they found to remain; and the Shepherd ordered them to be removed out of the tower, and to be placed apart. Next he examined those that had scabs; and he took and hewed many of these, and commanded the virgins to take them up and cast them into the building. And the virgins lifted them up, and put them in the middle of the building of the tower. And the rest he ordered to be laid down beside the black ones; for these, too, were found to be black. He next examined those that had cracks; and he hewed many of these, and commanded them to be carried by the virgins to the building: and they were placed on the outside, because they were found to be sounder than the others; but the rest, on account of the multitude of the cracks, could not be hewn, and for this reason, therefore, they were rejected from the building of the tower. He next examined the chipped stones, and many amongst these were found to be black, and some to have great cracks. And these also he commanded to be laid down along with those which had been rejected. But the remainder, after being cleaned and hewn, he commanded to be placed in the building. And the virgins took them up, and fitted them into the middle of the building of the tower, for they were somewhat weak. He next examined those that were half white and half black, and many of them were found to be black. And he commanded these also to be taken away along with those which had been rejected. And the rest were all taken away by the virgins; for, being white, they were fitted by the virgins themselves into the building. And they were placed upon the outside, because they were found to be sound, so as to be able to support those which were placed in the middle, for no part of them at all was chipped. He next examined those that were rough and hard; and a few of them were rejected because they could not be hewn, as they were found exceedingly hard. But the rest of them were hewn, and carried by the virgins, and fitted into the middle of the building of the tower; for they were somewhat weak. He next examined those that had stains; and of these a very few were black, and were thrown aside with the others; but the greater part were found to be bright, and these were fitted by the virgins into the building, but on account of their strength were placed on the outside.

CHAP. IX.

He next came to examine the white and rounded stones, and said to me, "What are we to do with these stones?" "How do I know, sir?" I replied. "Have you no intentions regarding them?" "Sir," I answered, "I am not acquainted with this art, neither am I a stone-cutter, nor can I tell." "Do you not see," he said, "that they are exceedingly round? and if I wish to make them rectangular, a large portion of them must be cut away; for some of them must of necessity be put into the building." "If therefore," I said, "they must, why do you torment yourself, and not at once choose for the building those which you prefer, and fit them into it?" He selected the larger ones among them, and the shining ones, and hewed them; and the virgins carried and fitted them into the outside parts of the building. And the rest which remained over were carried away, and laid down on the plain from which they were brought. They were not, however, rejected, "because," he said, "there remains yet a little addition to be built to the tower. And the lord of this tower wishes all the stones to be fitted into the building, because they are exceedingly bright." And twelve women were called, very beautiful in form, clothed in black, and with dishevelled hair. And these women seemed to me to be fierce. But the Shepherd commanded them to lift the stones that were rejected from the building, and to carry them away to the mountains from which they had been brought. And they were merry, and carried away all the stones, and put them in the place whence they had been taken. Now after all the stones were removed, and there was no longer a single one lying around the tower, he said, "Let us go round the tower and see, lest there be any defect in it." So I went round the tower along with him. And the Shepherd, seeing that the tower was beautifully built, rejoiced exceedingly; for the tower was built in such a way, that, on seeing it, I coveted the building of it, for it was constructed as if built of one stone, without a single joining. And the stone seemed as if hewn out of the rock; having to me the appearance of a monolith.

CHAP. X.

And as I walked along with him, I was full of joy, beholding so many excellent things. And the Shepherd said to me, "Go and bring unslacked lime and fine-baked clay, that I may fill up the forms of the stones that were taken and thrown into the building; for everything about the tower must be smooth." And I did as he commanded me, and brought it to him. "Assist me," he said, "and the work will soon be finished." He accordingly filled up the forms of the stones that were returned to the building, and commanded the places around the tower to be swept and to be cleaned; and the virgins took brooms and swept the place, and carried all the dirt out of the tower, and brought water, and the ground around the tower became cheerful and very beautiful. Says the Shepherd to me, " Everything has been cleared away ; if the lord of the tower come to inspect it, he can have no fault to find with us." Having spoken these words, he wished to depart ; but I laid hold of him by the wallet, and began to adjure him by the Lord that he would explain what he had showed me. He said to me, " I must rest a little, and then I shall explain to you everything ; wait for me here until I return." I said to him, " Sir, what can I do here alone ? " " You are not alone," he said, " for these virgins are with you." " Give me in charge to them, then," I replied. The Shepherd called them to him, and said to them, " I entrust him to you until I come," and went away. And I was alone with the virgins ; and they were rather merry, but were friendly to me, especially the four more distinguished of them.

CHAP. XI.

The virgins said to me, " The Shepherd does not come here to-day." " What, then," said I, " am I to do ? " They replied, " Wait for him until he comes ; and if he comes he will converse with you, and if he does not come you will remain here with us until he does come." I said to them, " I will wait for him until it is late ; and if he does not arrive, I will go away into the house, and come back early in the morning." And they answered and said to me, " You were entrusted to us ; you cannot go away from us." " Where, then," I said, " am I to remain ? " " You will sleep with us," they replied, " as a brother, and not as a husband : for you are our brother, and for the time to come we intend to abide with you, for we love you exceedingly ! " But I was ashamed to remain with them. And she who seemed to be the first among them began to kiss me. [And the others seeing her kissing me, began also to kiss me], and to lead me round the tower, and to play with me.[1] And I, too, became like a young man, and began to play with them : for some of them formed a chorus, and others danced, and others

sang ; and I, keeping silence, walked with them around the tower, and was merry with them. And when it grew late I wished to go into the house ; and they would not let me, but detained me. So I remained with them during the night, and slept beside the tower. Now the virgins spread their linen tunics on the ground, and made me lie down in the midst of them ; and they did nothing at all but pray ; and I without ceasing prayed with them, and not less than they. And the virgins rejoiced because I thus prayed. And I remained there with the virgins until the next day at the second hour. Then the Shepherd returned, and said to the virgins, " Did you offer him any insult ? " " Ask him," they said. I said to him, " Sir, I was delighted that I remained with them." " On what," he asked, " did you sup ? " " I supped, sir," I replied, " on the words of the Lord the whole night." " Did they receive you well ? " he inquired. " Yes, sir," I answered. " Now," he said, " what do you wish to hear first ? " " I wish to hear in the order," I said, " in which you showed me from the beginning. I beg of you, sir, that as I shall ask you, so also you will give me the explanation." " As you wish," he replied, " so also will I explain to you, and will conceal nothing at all from you."

CHAP. XII.

" First of all, sir," I said, " explain this to me : What is the meaning of the rock and the gate ? " " This rock," he answered, " and this gate are the Son of God." " How, sir ? " I said ; " the rock is old, and the gate is new." " Listen," he said, " and understand, O ignorant man. The Son of God is older than all His creatures, so that He was a fellow-councillor with the Father in His work of creation :[2] for this reason is He old." " And why is the gate new, sir ? " I said. " Because," he answered, " He became manifest[3] in the last days of the dispensation : for this reason the gate was made new, that they who are to be saved by it might enter into the kingdom of God. You saw," he said, " that those stones which came in through the gate were used for the building of the tower, and that those which did not come, were again thrown back to their own place ? " " I saw, sir," I replied. " In like manner," he continued, " no one shall enter into the kingdom of God unless he receive His holy name. For if you desire to enter into a city, and that city is surrounded by a wall, and has but one gate, can you enter into that city save through the gate which it has ? " " Why, how can it be otherwise, sir ? " I said. " If, then, you cannot enter

---

[1] [This curious chapter, be it remembered, is but a dream and a similitude. In the pure homes of Christians, it is almost unintelligible. Amid the abominations of heathenism, it taught a lesson which afterwards required enforcement by the canons and stern discipline of the whole Church. The lesson is, that what " begins in the spirit " may " end in the flesh." Those who shunning the horrible impurities of the pagans abused spiritual relationships as " brothers and sisters," were on the verge of a precipice. ' To the pure, all things are pure;" but they who presume on this great truth to indulge in kissings and like familiarities are tempting a dangerous downfall. In this vision, Hermas resorted to " watching and praying;" and the virgins rejoiced because he thus saved himself. The behaviour of the maidens was what heathen women constantly practised, and what Christian women, bred in such habits of life, did, perhaps, without evil thought, relying on their " sun-clad power of chastity." Nothing in this picture is the product of Christianity, except the *self-mastery* inculcated as the only safeguard even amongst good women. But see " Elucidation," at end of this book.]

[2] [Hermas confirms the doctrine of St. John (i. 3); also Col. i, 15, 16. Of this Athanasius would approve.]
[3] [1 Pet. i. 20.]

into the city except through its gate, so, in like manner, a man cannot otherwise enter into the kingdom of God than by the name of His beloved Son. You saw," he added, "the multitude who were building the tower?" "I saw them, sir," I said. "Those," he said, "are all glorious angels, and by them accordingly is the Lord surrounded. And the gate is the Son of God. This is the one entrance to the Lord. In no other way, then, shall any one enter in to Him except through His Son. You saw," he continued, "the six men, and the tall and glorious man in the midst of them, who walked round the tower, and rejected the stones from the building?" "I saw him, sir," I answered. "The glorious man," he said, "is the Son of God, and those six glorious angels are those who support Him on the right hand and on the left. None of these glorious angels," he continued, "will enter in unto God apart from Him. Whosoever does not receive His [1] name, shall not enter into the kingdom of God."

CHAP. XIII.

"And the tower," I asked, "what does it mean?" "This tower," he replied, "is the Church." "And these virgins, who are they?" "They are holy spirits, and men cannot otherwise be found in the kingdom of God unless these have put their clothing upon them : for if you receive the name only, and do not receive from them the clothing, they are of no advantage to you. For these virgins are the powers of the Son of God. If you bear His name but possess not His power, it will be in vain that you bear His name. Those stones," he continued, "which you saw rejected bore His name, but did not put on the clothing of the virgins." "Of what nature is their clothing, sir?" I asked. "Their very names," he said, "are their clothing. Every one who bears the name of the Son of God, ought to bear the names also of these ; for the Son Himself bears the names [2] of these virgins. As many stones," he continued, "as you saw [come into the building of the tower through the hands [3]] of these virgins, and remaining, have been clothed with their strength. For this reason you see that the tower became of one stone with the rock. So also they who have believed on the Lord [4] through His Son, and are clothed with these spirits, shall become one spirit, one body, and the colour of their garments shall be one. And the dwelling of such as bear the names of the virgins is in the tower." "Those stones, sir, that were rejected," I inquired, "on what account were they re-

jected? for they passed through the gate, and were placed by the hands of the virgins in the building of the tower." "Since you take an interest in everything," he replied, "and examine minutely, hear about the stones that were rejected. These all," he said, "received the name of God, and they received also the strength of these virgins. Having received, then, these spirits, they were made strong, and were with the servants of God ; and theirs was one spirit, and one body, and one clothing. For they were of the same mind, and wrought righteousness. After a certain time, however, they were persuaded by the women whom you saw clothed in black, and having their shoulders exposed and their hair dishevelled, and beautiful in appearance. Having seen these women, they desired to have them, and clothed themselves with their strength, and put off the strength of the virgins. These, accordingly, were rejected from the house of God, and were given over to these women. But they who were not deceived by the beauty of these women remained in the house of God. You have," he said, "the explanation of those who were rejected."

CHAP. XIV.

"What, then, sir," I said, "if these men, being such as they are, repent and put away their desires after these women, and return again to the virgins, and walk in their strength and in their works, shall they not enter into the house of God?" "They shall enter in," he said, "if they put away the works of these women, and put on again the strength of the virgins, and walk in their works. For on this account was there a cessation in the building, in order that, if these repent, they may depart into the building of the tower. But if they do not repent, then others will come in their place, and these at the end will be cast out. For all these things I gave thanks to the Lord, because He had pity on all that call upon His name ; and sent the angel of repentance to us who sinned against Him, and renewed our spirit ; and when we were already destroyed, and had no hope of life, He restored us to newness of life." "Now, sir," I continued, "show me why the tower was not built upon the ground, but upon the rock and upon the gate." "Are you still," he said, "without sense and understanding?" "I must, sir," I said, "ask you of all things, because I am wholly unable to understand them ; for all these things are great and glorious, and difficult for man to understand." "Listen," he said : "the name of the Son of God is great, and cannot be contained, and supports the whole world.[5] If, then, the whole creation is supported by the

---

[1] *His.* God's. — *Lips.*
[2] [Ex. xxviii. 12, 29.]
[3] Omitted in Lips. The text in Vat. and Pal. The Æth. different in form, but in meaning the same.
[4] *Lord.* God. — *Vat.*

[5] [Heb. i. 3. Hermas drips with Scripture like a honeycomb.]

Son of God, what think ye of those who are called by Him, and bear the name of the Son of God, and walk in His commandments? do you see what kind of persons He supports? Those who bear His name with their whole heart. He Himself, accordingly, became a foundation[1] to them, and supports them with joy, because they are not ashamed to bear His name."

CHAP. XV.[2]

"Explain to me, sir," I said, "the names of these virgins, and of those women who were clothed in black raiment." "Hear," he said, "the names of the stronger virgins who stood at the corners. The first is Faith,[3] the second Continence, the third Power, the fourth Patience. And the others standing in the midst of these have the following names: Simplicity, Innocence, Purity, Cheerfulness, Truth, Understanding, Harmony, Love. He who bears these names and that of the Son of God will be able to enter into the kingdom of God. Hear, also," he continued, "the names of the women who had the black garments; and of these four are stronger than the rest. The first is Unbelief, the second Incontinence, the third Disobedience, the fourth Deceit. And their followers are called Sorrow, Wickedness, Wantonness, Anger, Falsehood, Folly, Backbiting, Hatred. The servant of God who bears these names shall see, indeed, the kingdom of God, but shall not enter into it." "And the stones, sir," I said, "which were taken out of the pit and fitted into the building: what are they?" "The first," he said, "the ten, viz., that were placed as a foundation, are the first generation, and the twenty-five the second generation, of righteous men; and the thirty-five are the prophets of God and His ministers; and the forty are the apostles and teachers of the preaching of the Son of God."[4] "Why, then, sir," I asked, "did the virgins carry these stones also through the gate, and give them for the building of the tower?" "Because," he answered, "these were the first who bore these spirits, and they never departed from each other, neither the spirits from the men nor the men from the spirits, but the spirits remained with them until their falling asleep. And unless they had had these spirits with them, they would not have been of use for the building of this tower."

CHAP. XVI.

"Explain to me a little further, sir," I said.

"What is it that you desire?" he asked. "Why, sir," I said, "did these stones ascend out of the pit, and be applied to the building of the tower, after having borne these spirits?" "They were obliged," he answered, "to ascend through water in order that they might be made alive; for, unless they laid aside the deadness of their life, they could not in any other way enter into the kingdom of God. Accordingly, those also who fell asleep received the seal of the Son of God. For," he continued, "before a man bears the name of the Son of God[5] he is dead; but when he receives the seal he lays aside his deadness, and obtains life. The seal, then, is the water: they descend into the water dead, and they arise alive. And to them, accordingly, was this seal preached, and they made use of it that they might enter into the kingdom of God." "Why, sir," I asked, "did the forty stones also ascend with them out of the pit, having already received the seal?" "Because," he said, "these apostles and teachers who preached the name of the Son of God, after falling asleep in the power and faith of the Son of God, preached it not only to those who were asleep, but themselves also gave them the seal of the preaching. Accordingly they descended with them into the water, and again ascended. [But these descended alive and rose up again alive; whereas they who had previously fallen asleep descended dead, but rose up again alive.[6]] By these, then, were they quickened and made to know the name of the Son of God. For this reason also did they ascend with them, and were fitted along with them into the building of the tower, and, untouched by the chisel, were built in along with them. For they slept in righteousness and in great purity, but only they had not this seal. You have accordingly the explanation of these also."

CHAP. XVII.

"I understand, sir," I replied. "Now, sir," I continued, "explain to me, with respect to the mountains, why their forms are various and diverse." "Listen," he said: "these mountains are the twelve tribes, which inhabit the whole world.[7] The Son of God, accordingly, was preached unto them by the apostles." "But why are the mountains of various kinds, some having one form, and others another? Explain that to me, sir." "Listen," he answered: "these twelve tribes that inhabit the whole world are twelve nations. And they vary in prudence and understanding. As numerous, then, as are the varieties of the mountains which you saw,

---

1 [Isa. xxviii. 16; 1 Cor. iii. 11.]
2 This portion of the Leipzig Codex is much eaten away, and therefore the text is derived to a considerable extent from the translations.
3 [The tenacity with which Hermas everywhere exalts the primary importance of Faith, makes it inexcusable that he should be charged with mere legalizing morality.]
4 [Eph. ii. 20; Rev. xxi. 14.]

5 *The name of the Son of God.* The name of God.—*Lips.* [1 John v. 11, 12.]
6 All the translations and Clemens Alexandrinus (*Strom.*, vi. 6, 46) have this passage. It is omitted in Lips.
7 [Rev. vii. 4.]

are also the diversities of mind and understanding among these nations. And I will explain to you the actions of each one." "First, sir," I said, "explain this: why, when the mountains are so diverse, their stones, when placed in the building, became one colour, shining like those also that had ascended out of the pit." "Because," he said, "all the nations that dwell under heaven were called by hearing and believing upon the name of the Son of God.[1] Having, therefore, received the seal, they had one understanding and one mind; and their faith became one, and their love one, and with the name they bore also the spirits of the virgins.[2] On this account the building of the tower became of one colour, bright as the sun. But after they had entered into the same place, and became one body, certain of these defiled themselves, and were expelled from the race of the righteous, and became again what they were before, or rather worse."

CHAP. XVIII.

"How, sir," I said, "did they become worse, after having known God?"[3] "He that does not know God," he answered, "and practises evil, receives a certain chastisement for his wickedness; but he that has known God, ought not any longer to do evil, but to do good. If, accordingly, when he ought to do good, he do evil, does not he appear to do greater evil than he who does not know God? For this reason, they who have not known God and do evil are condemned to death; but they who have known God, and have seen His mighty works, and still continue in evil, shall be chastised doubly, and shall die for ever.[4] In this way, then, will the Church of God be purified. For as you saw the stones rejected from the tower, and delivered to the evil spirits, and cast out thence, so [they also shall be cast out, and[5]] there shall be one body of the purified, as the tower also became, as it were, of one stone after its purification. In like manner also shall it be with the Church of God, after it has been purified, and has rejected the wicked, and the hypocrites, and the blasphemers, and the waverers, and those who commit wickedness of different kinds. After these have been cast away, the Church of God shall be one body, of one mind, of one understanding, of one faith, of one love. And then the Son of God will be exceeding glad, and shall rejoice over them, because He has received His people pure."[6] "All these things, sir," I said, "are great and glorious.

"Moreover, sir," I said, "explain to me the power and the actions of each one of the mountains, that every soul, trusting in the Lord, and hearing it, may glorify His great, and marvellous, and glorious name." "Hear," he said, "the diversity of the mountains and of the twelve nations.

CHAP. XIX.

"From the first mountain, which was black, they that believed are the following: apostates and blasphemers against the Lord, and betrayers of the servants of God. To these repentance is not open; but death lies before them, and on this account also are they black, for their race is a lawless one. And from the second mountain, which was bare, they who believed are the following: hypocrites, and teachers of wickedness. And these, accordingly, are like the former, not having any fruits of righteousness; for as their mountain was destitute of fruit, so also such men have a name indeed, but are empty of faith, and there is no fruit of truth in them. They indeed have repentance in their power, if they repent quickly; but if they are slow in so doing, they shall die along with the former." "Why, sir," I said, "have these repentance, but the former not? for their actions are nearly the same." "On this account," he said, "have these repentance, because they did not blaspheme their Lord, nor become betrayers of the servants of God; but on account of their desire of possessions they became hypocritical, and each one taught according to the desires of men that were sinners. But they will suffer a certain punishment; and repentance is before them, because they were not blasphemers or traitors.

CHAP. XX.

"And from the third mountain, which had thorns and thistles, they who believed are the following. There are some of them rich, and others immersed in much business. The thistles are the rich, and the thorns are they who are immersed in much business. Those, [accordingly, who are entangled in many various kinds of business, do not[7]] cleave to the servants of God, but wander away, being choked by their business transactions; and the rich cleave with difficulty to the servants of God, fearing lest these should ask something of them. Such persons, accordingly, shall have difficulty in entering the kingdom of God. For as it is disagreeable to walk among thistles with naked feet, so also it is hard for such to enter the kingdom of God.[8] But to all these repentance, and that speedy, is open, in order that what they did not do in former

---

[1] *Name of the Son of God.* Name of God.—*Lips.* [Rom. x. 17.]
[2] [Rev. xiv. 4.]
[3] *God* in Pal.; *Lord* in Vat. and Æth.; *Christ* in Lips.
[4] [Luke xii. 47, 48.]
[5] Omitted in Vat., Æth., Lips.
[6] [Eph. v. 27.]

[7] Omitted in Lips. The text from Vat. Substantially the same in the other two. [Matt. xiii. 5.]
[8] Matt. xix. 23, 24. [Mark x. 23.]

times they may make up for in these days, and do some good, and they shall live unto God. But if they abide in their deeds, they shall be delivered to those women, who will put them to death.

CHAP. XXI.

"And from the fourth mountain, which had much grass, the upper parts of the plants green, and the parts about the roots withered, and some also scorched by the sun, they who believed are the following: the doubtful, and they who have the Lord upon their lips, but have Him not in their heart. On this account their foundations are withered, and have no strength; and their words alone live, while their works are dead. Such persons are [neither alive nor [1]] dead. They resemble, therefore, the waverers: for the wavering are neither withered nor green, being neither living nor dead. For as their blades, on seeing the sun, were withered, so also the wavering, when they hear of affliction, on account of their fear, worship idols, and are ashamed of the name of their Lord.[2] Such, then, are neither alive nor dead. But these also may yet live, if they repent quickly; and if they do not repent, they are already delivered to the women, who take away their life.

CHAP. XXII.

"And from the fifth mountain, which had green grass, and was rugged, they who believed are the following: believers, indeed, but slow to learn, and obstinate, and pleasing themselves, wishing to know everything, and knowing nothing at all. On account of this obstinacy of theirs, understanding departed from them, and foolish senselessness entered into them. And they praise themselves as having wisdom, and desire to become teachers, although destitute of sense. On account, therefore, of this loftiness of mind, many became vain, exalting themselves: for self-will and empty confidence is a great demon. Of these, accordingly, many were rejected, but some repented and believed, and subjected themselves to those that had understanding, knowing their own foolishness. And to the rest of this class repentance is open; for they were not wicked, but rather foolish, and without understanding. If these therefore repent, they will live unto God; but if they do not repent, they shall have their dwelling with the women who wrought wickedness among them.

CHAP. XXIII.

"And those from the sixth mountain, which had clefts large and small, and decayed grass in the clefts, who believed, were the following:

they who occupy the small clefts are those who bring charges against one another, and by reason of their slanders have decayed in the faith. Many of them, however, repented; and the rest also will repent when they hear my commandments, for their slanders are small, and they will quickly repent. But they who occupy the large clefts are persistent in their slanders, and vindictive in their anger against each other. These, therefore, were thrown away from the tower, and rejected from having a part in its building. Such persons, accordingly, shall have difficulty in living. If our God and Lord, who rules over all things, and has power over all His creation, does not remember evil against those who confess their sins, but is merciful, does man, who is corruptible and full of sins, remember evil against a fellow-man, as if he were able to destroy or to save him?[3] I, the angel of repentance, say unto you, As many of you as are of this way of thinking, lay it aside, and repent, and the Lord will heal your former sins, if you purify yourselves from this demon; but if not, you will be delivered over to him for death.

CHAP. XXIV.

"And those who believed from the seventh mountain, on which the grass was green and flourishing, and the whole of the mountain fertile, and every kind of cattle and the fowls of heaven were feeding on the grass on this mountain, and the grass on which they pastured became more abundant, were the following: they were always simple, and harmless, and blessed, bringing no charges against one another, but always rejoicing greatly because of the servants of God, and being clothed with the holy spirit of these virgins, and always having pity on every man, and giving aid from their own labour to every man, without reproach and without hesitation.[4] The Lord, therefore, seeing their simplicity and all their meekness, multiplied them amid the labours of their hands, and gave them grace in all their doings. And I, the angel of repentance, say to you who are such, Continue to be such as these, and your seed will never be blotted out; for the Lord has made trial of you, and inscribed you in the number of us, and the whole of your seed will dwell with the Son of God; for ye have received of His Spirit.

CHAP. XXV.

"And they who believed from the eighth mountain, where were the many fountains, and where all the creatures of God drank of the fountains, were the following: apostles, and teachers, who preached to the whole world, and who taught solemnly and purely the word of the Lord, and

---

[1] Omitted in Lips.
[2] [The imagery of our Lord's parables everywhere apparent. Also, the words of Scripture recur constantly.]

[3] Jas. iv. 12. [Matt. xviii. 33.]
[4] Ecclus. xx. 15, xli. 22; Jas. i. 5.

did not at all fall into evil desires, but walked always in righteousness and truth, according as they had received the Holy Spirit. Such persons, therefore, shall enter in with the angels.[1]

CHAP. XXVI.

" And they who believed from the ninth mountain, which was deserted, and had in it creeping things and wild beasts which destroy men, were the following : they who had the stains as servants,[2] who discharged their duty ill, and who plundered widows and orphans of their livelihood, and gained possessions for themselves from the ministry, which they had received.[3] If, therefore, they remain under the dominion of the same desire, they are dead, and there is no hope of life for them; but if they repent, and finish their ministry in a holy manner, they shall be able to live. And they who were covered with scabs are those who have denied their Lord, and have not returned to Him again; but becoming withered and desert-like, and not cleaving to the servants of God, but living in solitude, they destroy their own souls. For as a vine, when left within an enclosure, and meeting with neglect, is destroyed, and is made desolate by the weeds, and in time grows wild, and is no longer of any use to its master, so also are such men as have given themselves up, and become useless to their Lord, from having contracted savage habits. These men, therefore, have repentance in their power, unless they are found to have denied from the heart; but if any one is found to have denied from the heart, I do not know if he may live. And I say this not for these present days, in order that any one who has denied may obtain repentance, for it is impossible for him to be saved who now intends to deny his Lord; but to those who denied Him long ago, repentance seems to be possible. If, therefore, any one intends to repent, let him do so quickly, before the tower is completed; for if not, he will be utterly destroyed by the women. And the chipped stones are the deceitful and the slanderers; and the wild beasts, which you saw on the ninth mountain, are the same. For as wild beasts destroy and kill a man by their poison, so also do the words of such men destroy and ruin a man. These, accordingly, are mutilated in their faith, on account of the deeds which they have done in themselves; yet some repented, and were saved. And the rest, who are of such a character, can be saved if they repent; but if they do not repent, they will perish with those women, whose strength they have assumed.

CHAP. XXVII.

" And from the tenth mountain, where were trees which overshadowed certain sheep, they who believed were the following: bishops[4] given to hospitality, who always gladly received into their houses the servants of God, without dissimulation. And the bishops never failed to protect, by their service, the widows, and those who were in want, and always maintained a holy conversation. All these, accordingly, shall be protected by the Lord for ever. They who do these things are honourable before God, and their place is already with the angels, if they remain to the end serving God.

CHAP. XXVIII.

" And from the eleventh mountain, where were trees full of fruits, adorned with fruits of various kinds, they who believed were the following: they who suffered for the name of the Son of God, and who also suffered cheerfully with their whole heart, and laid down their lives." " Why, then, sir," I said, " do all these trees bear fruit, and some of them fairer than the rest?" " Listen," he said: " all who once suffered for the name of the Lord are honourable before God; and of all these the sins were remitted, because they suffered for the name of the Son of God.[5] And why their fruits are of various kinds, and some of them superior, listen. All," he continued, " who were brought before the authorities and were examined, and did not deny, but suffered cheerfully—these are held in greater honour with God, and of these the fruit is superior; but all who were cowards, and in doubt, and who reasoned in their hearts whether they would deny or confess, and yet suffered, of these the fruit is less, because that suggestion came into their hearts; for that suggestion—that a servant should deny his Lord—is evil. Have a care, therefore, ye who are planning such things, lest that suggestion remain in your hearts, and

---

[1] *Cf.* Donaldson's *Hist. of Christ. Lit.*, vol i. p. 291. [This beautiful chapter, and its parable of the fountains of living water, may well be read with that passage of Leighton which delighted Coleridge: Com. on 1 Pet. i. 10-12.]

[2] διάκονοι. [*Deacons*, evidently, or *stewards*. Acts vi. 1.]

[3] [Ezek. xxxiv. 3.]

[4] *Bishops.* Bishops, that is, presidents of the churches.—*Vat.* [This textual peculiarity must have originated at the period when the Ignatian use of *episcopus* was becoming naturalized in Rome. It was originally common to all *pastors*, local or regionary.]

[5] [This passage (with Vision iii. 2, and especially Similitude v. 3) has been pressed into the service of those who seek to find " supererogatory merit " in the Fathers. See 1 Cor. vii. 38. But why not begin with the Scriptures which Hermas doubtless has in mind, such as Rev. iii. 4, 5, " They are worthy " ? Does this ascribe to them any merit apart from (" worthy is the Lamb ") the only meritorious cause of salvation? So also Rev. vii. 14, xiv. 4, 5. The primitive Fathers accepted such truths like innocent children, and loved them. They believed St. Paul as to degrees of glory (1 Cor. xv. 41), and our Lord Himself as to the awards (Matt. xx. 21-23) of mercy to fruits of grace ; ' and they are no more responsible for forced constructions that have been put upon them by afterthought and subsequent heresy, than our blessed Lord can be charged with all that has overloaded His precious sayings (Matt. xix. 12 or xvi. 18). The principle of deficient works of faith, which is the corresponding idea on the negative side, appears in St. Paul (1 Cor. iii. 13-15), and has been abused to sustain the whole system of creature merit, and the monstrous afterthought of purgatory. Those, therefore, who read such ideas into " The Ante-Nicene Fathers," to diminish their credit, often, unintentionally, (1) help the perverters of truth to claim the Fathers, and (2) give them the like aid in claiming the Scriptures. See p. 34, *supra*, note 3.]

ye perish unto God. And ye who suffer for His name ought to glorify God, because He deemed you worthy to bear His name, that all your sins might be healed. [Therefore, rather deem yourselves happy], and think that ye have done a great thing, if any of you suffer on account of God. The Lord bestows upon you life, and ye do not understand, for your sins were heavy; but if you had not suffered for the name of the Lord, ye would have died to God on account of your sins. These things I say to you who are hesitating about denying or confessing: acknowledge that ye have the Lord, lest, denying Him, ye be delivered up to prison. If the heathen chastise their slaves, when one of them denies his master, what, think ye, will your Lord do, who has authority over all men? Put away these counsels out of your hearts, that you may live continually unto God.

CHAP. XXIX.

"And they who believed from the twelfth mountain, which was white, are the following: they are as infant children, in whose hearts no evil originates; nor did they know what wickedness is, but always remained as children. Such accordingly, without doubt, dwell in the kingdom of God, because they defiled in nothing the commandments of God; but they remained like children all the days of their life in the same mind. All of you, then, who shall remain stedfast, and be as children,[1] without doing evil, will be more honoured than all who have been previously mentioned; for all infants are honourable before God, and are the first persons with Him.[2] Blessed, then, are ye who put away wickedness from yourselves, and put on innocence. As the first of all will you live unto God."

After he had finished the similitudes of the mountains, I said to him, "Sir, explain to me now about the stones that were taken out of the plain, and put into the building instead of the stones that were taken out of the tower; and about the round stones that were put into the building; and those that still remain round."

CHAP. XXX.

"Hear," he answered, "about all these also. The stones taken out of the plain and put into the building of the tower instead of those that were rejected, are the roots of this white mountain. When, therefore, they who believed from the white mountain were all found guileless, the Lord of the tower commanded those from the roots of this mountain to be cast into the building of the tower; for he knew that if these stones were to go to the building of the tower, they would remain bright, and not one of them

become black.[3] But if he had so resolved with respect to the other mountains, it would have been necessary for him to visit that tower again, and to cleanse it. Now all these persons were found white who believed, and who will yet believe, for they are of the same race. This is a happy race, because it is innocent. Hear now, further, about these round and shining stones. All these also are from the white mountain. Hear, moreover, why they were found round: because their riches had obscured and darkened them a little from the truth, although they never departed from God; nor did any evil word proceed out of their mouth, but all justice, virtue, and truth. When the Lord, therefore, saw the mind of these persons, that they were born good,[4] and could be good, He ordered their riches to be cut down, not to be taken[5] away for ever, that they might be able to do some good with what was left them; and they will live unto God, because they are of a good race. Therefore were they rounded a little by the chisel, and put in the building of the tower.

CHAP. XXXI.

"But the other round stones, which had not yet been adapted to the building of the tower, and had not yet received the seal, were for this reason put back into their place, because they are exceedingly round. Now this age must be cut down in these things, and in the vanities of their riches, and then they will meet in the kingdom of God; for they must of necessity enter into the kingdom of God, because the Lord has blessed this innocent race. Of this race, therefore, no one will perish; for although any of them be tempted by the most wicked devil, and commit sin, he will quickly return to his Lord. I deem you happy, I, who am the messenger of repentance, whoever of you are innocent as children,[6] because your part is good, and honourable before God. Moreover, I say to you all, who have received the seal of the Son of God, be clothed with simplicity, and be not mindful of offences, nor remain in wickedness. Lay aside, therefore, the recollection of your offences and bitternesses, and you will be formed in one spirit. And heal and take away from you those wicked schisms, that if the Lord of the flocks come, He may rejoice concerning you. And He will rejoice, if He find all things sound, and none of you shall perish. But if He find any one of these sheep strayed, woe to the shepherds! And if the shepherds themselves have

---

[1] Matt. xviii. 3.
[2] [Mark. ix. 36.]

[3] Here ends Codex Lipsiensis. The rest of the text is from the common translation corrected by the Palatine and Æthiopic.
[4] [Born good. Not in the text of Gebhardt and Harnack (the Greek is wanting); nor do they note any such text, though the Æthiopic favours it. See p. 42, supra, note 2.]
[5] [Here again the Latin has the reading before noted, on the circumcision of wealth, p. 15, note 2, supra.]
[6] Matt. xviii. 3, xix. 14.

strayed, what answer will they give Him for their flocks?[1] Will they perchance say that they were harassed by their flocks? They will not be believed, for the thing is incredible that a shepherd could suffer from his flock; rather will he be punished on account of his falsehood. And I myself am a shepherd, and I am under a most stringent necessity of rendering an account of you.

CHAP. XXXII.

"Heal yourselves, therefore, while the tower is still building. The Lord dwells in men that love peace, because He loved peace; but from the contentious and the utterly wicked He is far distant. Restore to Him, therefore, a spirit sound as ye received it. For when you have given to a fuller a new garment, and desire to receive it back entire at the end, if, then, the fuller return you a torn garment, will you take it from him, and not rather be angry, and abuse him, saying, 'I gave you a garment that was entire: why have you rent it, and made it useless, so that it can be of no use on account of the rent which you have made in it?' Would you not say all this to the fuller about the rent which you found in your garment? If, therefore, you grieve about your garment, and complain because you have not received it entire, what do you think the Lord will do to you, who gave you a sound spirit, which you have rendered altogether useless, so that it can be of no service to its possessor? for its use began to be unprofitable, seeing it was corrupted by you. Will not the Lord, therefore, because of this conduct of yours regarding His Spirit, act in the same way, and deliver you over to death? Assuredly, I say, he will do the same to all those whom He shall find retaining a recollection of offences.[2] Do not trample His mercy under foot, He says, but rather honour Him, because He is so patient with your sins, and is not as ye are. Repent, for it is useful to you.

CHAP. XXXIII.

"All these things which are written above, I, the Shepherd, the messenger of repentance, have showed and spoken to the servants of God.[3] If therefore ye believe, and listen to my words, and walk in them, and amend your ways, you shall have it in your power to live: but if you remain in wickedness, and in the recollection of offences, no sinner of that class will live unto God. All these words which I had to say have been spoken unto you."

The Shepherd said to me, "Have you asked me everything?" And I replied, "Yes, sir." "Why did you not ask me about the shape of

the stones that were put into the building, that I might explain to you why we filled up the shapes?" And I said, "I forgot, sir." "Hear now, then," he said, "about this also. These are they who have now heard my commandments, and repented with their whole hearts. And when the Lord saw that their repentance was good and pure, and that they were able to remain in it, He ordered their former sins to be blotted out.[4] For these shapes were their sins, and they were levelled down, that they might not appear."

SIMILITUDE TENTH.

CONCERNING REPENTANCE AND ALMS-GIVING.

CHAP. I.

After I had fully written down this book, that messenger who had delivered me to the Shepherd came into the house in which I was, and sat down upon a couch, and the Shepherd stood on his right hand. He then called me, and spoke to me as follows: "I have delivered you and your house to the Shepherd, that you may be protected by him." "Yes, sir," I said. "If you wish, therefore, to be protected," he said, "from all annoyance, and from all harsh treatment, and to have success in every good work and word, and to possess all the virtues of righteousness, walk in these commandments which he has given you, and you will be able to subdue all wickedness. For if you keep those commandments, every desire and pleasure of the world will be subject to you, and success will attend you in every good work. Take unto yourself his experience and moderation, and say to all that he is in great honour and dignity with God, and that he is a president with great power, and mighty in his office. To him alone throughout the whole world is the power of repentance assigned. Does he seem to you to be powerful? But you despise his experience, and the moderation which he exercises towards you."

CHAP. II.

I said to him, "Ask himself, sir, whether from the time that he has entered my house I have done anything improper, or have offended him in any respect." He answered, "I also know that you neither have done nor will do anything improper, and therefore I speak these words to you, that you may persevere. For he had a good report of you to me, and you will say these words to others, that they also who have either repented or will still repent may entertain the same feelings with you, and he may report well of these to me, and I to the Lord." And I

[1] [Jer. xiii. 20; Zech. xi. 15-17.]
[2] [Jas. v. 9. Who can fail to feel the searching spirit of the gospel here? Matt. v. 23, 24, vi. 14.]
[3] *Servants of God.* Servant of the Lord. — *Æth.*

[4] [Heb. viii 12, x. 17.]

said, "Sir, I make known to every man the great works of God: and I hope that all those who love them, and have sinned before, on hearing these words, may repent, and receive life again." "Continue, therefore, in this ministry, and finish it. And all who follow out his commands shall have life, and great honour with the Lord.[1] But those who do not keep his commandments, flee from his life, and despise him. But he has his own honour with the Lord. All, therefore, who shall despise him,[2] and not follow his commands, deliver themselves to death, and every one of them will be guilty of his own blood. But I enjoin you, that you obey his commands, and you will have a cure for your former sins.

CHAP. III.

"Moreover, I sent you these virgins, that they may dwell with you.[3] For I saw that they were courteous to you. You will therefore have them as assistants, that you may be the better able to keep his commands: for it is impossible that these commandments can be observed without these virgins. I see, moreover, that they abide with you willingly; but I will also instruct them not to depart at all from your house: do you only keep your house pure, as they will delight to dwell in a pure abode. For they are pure, and chaste, and industrious, and have all influence with the Lord. Therefore, if they find your house to be pure, they will remain with you; but if any defilement, even a little, befall it, they will immediately withdraw from your house. For these virgins do not at all like any defilement." I said to him, "I hope, sir, that I will please them, so that they may always be willing to inhabit my house. And as he to whom you entrusted me has no complaint against me, so neither will they have." He said to the Shepherd, "I see that the servant of God wishes to live, and to keep these commandments, and will place these virgins in a pure habitation."[4] When he had spoken these words he again delivered me to the Shepherd, and called those virgins, and said to them, "Since I see that you are willing to dwell in his house, I commend him and his house to you, asking that you withdraw

not at all from it." And the virgins heard these words with pleasure.

CHAP. IV.

The angel[5] then said to me, "Conduct yourself manfully in this service, and make known to every one the great things of God,[6] and you will have favour in this ministry. Whoever, therefore, shall walk in these commandments, shall have life, and will be happy in his life; but whosoever shall neglect them shall not have life, and will be unhappy in this life. Enjoin all, who are able to act rightly, not to cease well-doing; for, to practise good works, is useful to them.[7] And I say that every man ought to be saved from inconveniences. For both he who is in want, and he who suffers inconveniences in his daily life, is in great torture and necessity. Whoever, therefore, rescues a soul of this kind from necessity, will gain for himself great joy. For he who is harassed by inconveniences of this kind, suffers equal torture with him who is in chains. Moreover many, on account of calamities of this sort, when they could not endure them, hasten their own deaths. Whoever, then, knows a calamity of this kind afflicting a man, and does not save him, commits a great sin, and becomes guilty of his blood.[8] Do good works, therefore, ye who have received good from the Lord; lest, while ye delay to do them, the building of the tower be finished, and you be rejected from the edifice: there is now no other tower a-building. For on your account was the work of building suspended. Unless, then, you make haste to do rightly, the tower will be completed, and you will be excluded."

After he had spoken with me he rose up from the couch, and taking the Shepherd and the virgins, he departed. But he said to me that he would send back the Shepherd and the virgins to my dwelling. Amen.[9]

---

1 *Lord.* God. — *Pal.*
2 *But he has his own honour . . . despise him,* omitted in Vat.
3 [Cap. xiii. p. 48, *supra.*]
4 [1 Pet. i. 22.]

5 Angel, *Æth.;* Pastor, *Pal.;* omitted in Vat.
6 *God,* common version; Lord, *Æth., Ral.;* Lord God, *Vat.*
7 [Here might follow that beautiful fragment of Irenæus, on God's goodness accepting the feeblest efforts of the soul in drawing near to Him. Vol. i. Frag. lv. p. 577, this series.]
8 [Jas. v. 19, 20. As St. James concludes with this principle, so also Hermas, who evidently delights in this apostle's teaching and has thrown it into this allegorical metaphrase.]
9 The Vatican has: "Here ends the Book of the Shepherd, the disciple of the blessed apostle Paul. Thanks be to God." The Æthiopic has: "May the name of him who wrote this book be written on a pillar of gold. With thanksgiving to Father, Son, and Holy Spirit, this book of the prophet Hermas has been finished. Amen. Finished are the visions, and commandments, and similitudes of the prophet Hermas, who is Paul, in the year 191 of mercy, 23d night and 22d day of the month," etc. The writer goes on [fruitlessly] to show that Hermas is Paul, appealing to Acts xiv. 12.

ELUCIDATIONS.

I.

THE reader has now had an opportunity of judging for himself whether the internal evidence favours any other view of the authorship of *The Shepherd*, than that which I have adopted. Its apparent design is to meet the rising pestilence of Montanism, and the perils of a secondary stage of Christianity. This it attempts to do by an imaginary voice from the first period. Avoiding controversy, Hermas presents, in the name of his earlier synonyme, a portraiture of the morals and practical godliness which were recognised as "the way of holiness" in the apostolic days. In so doing, he falls into anachronisms, of course, as poets and romancers must. These are sufficiently numerous to reveal the nature of his production, and to prove that the author was not the Hermas of the story.

The authorship was a puzzle and a problem during the earlier discussions of the learned. An anonymous poem (falsely ascribed to Tertullian, but very ancient) did, indeed, give a clue to the solution : —

> "—— deinde Pius, Hermas cui germine frater,
> Angelicus Pastor, quia tradita verba locutus."

To say that there was no evidence to sustain this, is to grant that it doubles the evidence when sufficient support for it is discovered. This was supplied by the fragment found in Milan, by the erudite and indefatigable Muratori, about a hundred and fifty years ago. Its history, with very valuable notes on the fragment itself, which is given entire, may be found in Routh's *Reliquiæ*.[1] Or the English reader may consult Westcott's very luminous statement of the case.[2] I am sorry that Dr. Donaldson doubts and objects; but he would not deny that experts, at least his equals,[3] accept the Muratorian Canon, which carries with it the historic testimony needed in the case of Hermas. All difficulties disappear in the light of this evidence. Hermas was brother of Pius, ninth Bishop of Rome (after Hyginus, *circ.* A.D. 157), and wrote his prose idyl under the fiction of his *Pauline* predecessor's name and age. This accounts (1) for the existence of the work, (2) for its form of allegory and prophesying, (3) for its anachronisms, (4) for its great currency, and (5) for its circulation among the Easterns, which was greater than it enjoyed in the West; and also (6) for their innocent mistake in ascribing it to the elder Hermas.

1. The Phrygian enthusiasm, like the convulsionism of Paris[4] in the last century, was a phenomenon not to be trifled with; especially when it began to threaten the West. This work was produced to meet so great an emergency.

2. "Fire fights fire," and prophesyings are best met by prophesyings. These were rare among the Orthodox, but Hermas undertook to restore those of the apostolic age; and I think this is what is meant by the *tradita verba* of the old poem, i.e., words "transmitted or bequeathed traditionally" from the times of Clement. Irenæus, the contemporary of this Hermas, had received the traditions of the same age from Polycarp: hence the greater probability of my conjecture that the brother of Pius compiled many traditional prophesyings of the first age.

3. Supposing the work to be in fact what it is represented to be in fiction, we have seen that it abounds with anachronisms. As now explained, we can account for them: the second Hermas forgets himself, like other poets, and mixes up his own period with that which he endeavours to portray.

---

[1] Tom. i. pp. 393-434.   [2] *On the Canon*, p. 235. Ed. 1855.   [3] Such as Lightfoot, Westcott, Canon Cook, and others.
[4] Candidly treated by Guettée, *L'Église de France*, vol. xii. p. 15. See also Parton's *Voltaire*, vol. i. pp. 260-270.

4 and 5. Written in Greek, its circulation in the West was necessarily limited; but, as the plague of Montanism was raging in the East, its Greek was a godsend, and enabled the Easterns to introduce it everywhere as a *useful* book. Origen values it as such; and, taking it without thought to be the work of the Pauline Hermas, attributes to it, as a fancy of his own,[1] that kind of inspiration which pertained to early "prophesyings." This conjecture once started, "it satisfied curiosity," says Westcott, "and supplied the place of more certain information; but, though it found acceptance, it acquired no new strength."[2]

6. Eusebius and Jerome[3] merely repeat the report as an *on dit*, and on this slender authority it travelled down. The Pauline Hermas was credited with it; and the critics, in their researches, find multiplied traces of the one mistake, as did the traveller whose circuits became a beaten road under the hoofs of his own horse.

If the reader will now turn back to the Introductory Note of the Edinburgh editors, he will find that the three views of which they take any serious notice are harmonized by that we have reached. (1) The work is unquestionably, on its face, the work of the Pauline Hermas. (2) But this is attributable to the fact that it is a fiction, or prose poem. (3) And hence it must be credited to the later Hermas, whose name and authorship are alone supported by external testimony, as well as internal evidence.

II.

(Similitude Ninth, cap. xi. p. 47, note 1.)

Westcott is undoubtedly correct in connecting this strange passage with one of the least defensible experiments of early Christian living. Gibbon finds in this experiment nothing but an opportunity for his scurrility.[4] A true philosopher will regard it very differently; and here, once and for all, we may speak of it somewhat at length. The young believer, a member, perhaps, of a heathen family, daily mixed up with abominable manners, forced to meet everywhere, by day, the lascivious *hetæræ* of the Greeks or those who are painted by Martial among the Latins, had no refuge but in flying to the desert, or practising the most heroic self-restraint if he remained with the relations and companions of his youth. If he went to the bath, it was to see naked women wallowing with vile men: if he slept upon the housetop, it was to throw down his mat or rug in a promiscuous stye of men and women.[5] This alike with rich and poor; but the latter were those among whom the Gospel found its more numerous recruits, and it was just these who were least able to protect themselves from pollutions. Their only resource was in that self-mastery, out of which sprung the Encraty of Tatian and the Montanism of Tertullian. Angelic purity was supposed to be attainable in this life; and the experiment was doubtless attended with some success, among the more resolute in fastings and prayer. Inevitably, however, what was "begun in the spirit," ended "in the flesh," in many instances. To live as brothers and sisters in the family of Christ, was a daring experiment; especially in such a social atmosphere, and amid the domestic habits of the heathen. Scandals ensued. Canonical censures were made stringent by

---

[1] Comment., book x. sec. 31, as quoted in Westcott, p. 219.

[2] I subjoin Westcott's references: Clem. Alex., *Stromata*, i. 17, sec. 85; *Ibid.*, i. 29, sec. 29; *Ibid.*, ii. 1, sec. 3. Also *Ibid.*, ii. 12, sec. 55; iv. 9, sec 76; vi. 6, sec. 46. Also Tertull., *Pudicitia*, capp. 10 and 20. These I have verified in *Ed.* Oehler, pp. 468, 488. I add *De Oratione*, capp. xvi. p. 311. Let me also add Athanasius, *De Incarnatione*, p. 38; *Contra Hæresim Arian.*, p. 369; *Ibid.*, 380. To the testimony of this great Father and defender of the faith I attach the greatest importance; because his approval shows that there was nothing in the book, as he had it in its pure text, to justify the attempts of moderns to disprove its orthodoxy. Athanasius calls it "a most useful book," and quotes it again ("although that book is not in the Canon") with great respect. *Ed.* Paris, 1572.

Modern theories of inspiration appear to me untenable, with reference to canonical Scripture; but they precisely illustrate the sort of inspiration with which these *prophesyings* were probably first credited. The human element is largely intermixed with divine suggestions; or you may state the proposition conversely.

[3] Eusebius, iii. 3, and Hieronym., catal. x. See Westcott, p. 220.

[4] Milman's *Gibbon*, vol. i. p. 550. The editor's notes are not over severe, and might be greatly strengthened as refutations.

[5] Van Lennep, *Bible-lands*, p. 440.

the Church ; and, while the vices of men and the peril of persecution multiplied the anchorites of the desert, this mischief was crushed out, and made impossible for Christians. " The sun-clad power of chastity," which Hermas means to depict, was no doubt gloriously exemplified among holy men and women, in those heroic ages. The power of the Holy Ghost demonstrated, in many instances, how true it is, that, " to the pure, all things are pure." But the Gospel proscribes everything like presumption and " leading into temptation." The Church, in dealing with social evils, often encouraged a recourse to monasticism, in its pure form ; but this also tended to corruption. To charge Christianity, however, with rash experiments of living which it never tolerated, is neither just nor philosophical. We have in it an example of the struggles of individuals out of heathenism, — by no means an institution of Christianity itself. It was a struggle, which, in its spirit, demands sympathy and respect. The Gospel has taught us to nauseate what even a regenerated heathen conceived to be praiseworthy, until the Christian family had become a developed product of the Church.[1]

The Gospel arms its enemies against itself, by elevating them infinitely above what they would have been without its influences. Refined by its social atmosphere, but refusing its sanctifying power, they gloat over the failures and falls of those with whom their own emancipation was begun. Let us rather admire those whom she lifted out of an abyss of moral degradation, but whose struggles to reach the high levels of her precepts were not always successful. Yet these very struggles were heroic ; for all their original habits, and all their surroundings, were of the sort " which hardens all within, and petrifies the feeling."

The American editor has devoted more than his usual amount of annotation to Hermas, and he affectionately asks the student not to overlook the notes, in which he has condensed rather than amplified exposition. It has been a labour of love to contribute something to a just conception of *The Shepherd*, because the Primitive Age has often been reproached with its good repute in the early churches. So little does one generation comprehend another ! When Christians conscientiously rejected the books of the heathen, and had as yet none of their own, save the Sacred Scriptures, or such scanty portions of the New Testament as were the treasures of the churches, is it wonderful that the first effort at Christian allegory was welcomed, especially in a time of need and perilous temptation?

---

[1] See Vision iii. cap. 8, for the relation of *encraty* to faith, in the view of Hermas; also (cap. 7 and *passim*) note his uncompromising reproofs of lust, and his beautiful delineations of chastity. The third canon of the Nicene Synod proscribed the *syneisactæ*, and also the nineteenth of Ancyra, adopted at Chalcedon into the Catholic discipline.

TATIAN'S ADDRESS TO THE GREEKS.

[TRANSLATED BY J. E. RYLAND.]

INTRODUCTORY NOTE

TO

TATIAN THE ASSYRIAN.

[TRANSLATED BY J. E. RYLAND.]

[A.D. 110–172.] It was my first intention to make this author a mere appendix to his master, Justin Martyr; for he stands in an equivocal position, as half Father and half heretic. His good seems to have been largely due to Justin's teaching and influence. One may trust that his falling away, in the decline of life, is attributable to infirmity of mind and body; his severe asceticism countenancing this charitable thought. Many instances of human frailty, which the experience of ages has taught Christians to view with compassion rather than censure, are doubtless to be ascribed to mental aberration and decay. Early Christians had not yet been taught this lesson; for, socially, neither Judaism nor Paganism had wholly surrendered their unloving influences upon their minds. Moreover, their high valuation of discipline, as an essential condition of self-preservation amid the fires of surrounding scorn and hatred, led them to practise, perhaps too sternly, upon offenders, what they often heroically performed upon themselves, — the amputation of the scandalous hand, or the plucking out of the evil eye.

In Tatian, another Assyrian follows the Star of Bethlehem, from Euphrates and the Tigris. The scanty facts of his personal history are sufficiently detailed by the translator, in his Introductory Note. We owe to himself the pleasing story of his conversion from heathenism. But I think it important to qualify the impressions the translation may otherwise leave upon the student's mind, by a little more sympathy with the better side of his character, and a more just statement of his great services to the infant Church.

His works, which were very numerous, have perished, in consequence of his lapse from orthodoxy. Give him due credit for his *Diatessaron*, of which the very name is a valuable testimony to the Four Gospels as recognised by the primitive churches. It is lost, with the "infinite number" of other books which St. Jerome attributes to him. All honour to this earliest harmonist for such a work; and let us believe, with Mill and other learned authorities, that, if Eusebius had seen the work he censures, he might have expressed himself more charitably concerning it.

We know something of Tatian, already, from the melancholy pages of Irenæus. Theodoret finds no other fault with his *Diatessaron* than its omission of the genealogies, which he, probably, could not harmonize on any theory of his own. The errors into which he fell in his old age [1] were so absurd, and so contrary to the Church's doctrine and discipline, that he could not be tolerated as one of the faithful, without giving to the heathen new grounds for the malignant slanders with which they were ever assailing the Christians. At the same time, let us reflect,

---

[1] "Paul the aged" was only *sixty* when he gives himself this title (Philem. 9). See the additional note, *Speaker's Commentary*, vol. iii. 843.

that his fall is to be attributed to extravagant ideas of that encraty which is a precept of the Gospel, and which a pure abhorrence of pagan abominations led many of the orthodox to practise with extreme rigidity. And this is the place to say, once for all, that the figures of Elijah upon Mt. Carmel and of John Baptist in the wilderness, approved by our Lord's teachings, but moderated, as a lesson to others, by his own holy but less austere example, justify the early Church in making room for the two classes of Christians which must always be found in earnest religion, and which seem to have their warrant in the fundamental constitution of human nature. There must be men like St. Paul, living in the world, though not of it; and there must be men like the Baptist, of whom the world will say, " he hath a devil." Marvellously the early Catholics were piloted between the rocks and the whirlpools, in the narrow drift of the Gospel; and always the Holy Spirit of counsel and might was their guardian, amid their terrible trials and temptations. This must suggest, to every reflecting mind, a gratitude the most profound. To preserve evangelical encraty, and to restrain fanatical asceticism, was the spirit of early Christianity, as one sees in the ethics of Hermas. But the awful malaria of Montanism was even now rising like a fog of the marshes, and was destined to leave its lasting impress upon Western Christianity; " forbidding to marry, and commanding to abstain from meats." Our author, alas, laid the egg which Tertullian hatched, and invented terms which that great author raised to their highest power; for he was rather the disciple of Tatian than of the Phrygians, though they kindled his strange fire. After Tertullian, the whole subject of marriage became entangled with sophistries, which have ever since adhered to the Latin churches, and introduced the most corrosive results into the vitals of individuals and of nations. Southey suggests, that, in the Roman Communion, John Wesley would have been accommodated with full scope for his genius, and canonized as a saint, while his Anglican mother had no place for him.[1] But, on the other hand, let us reflect that while Rome had no place for Wiclif and Hus, or Jerome of Prague, she has used and glorified and canonized many fanatics whose errors were far more disgraceful than those of Tatian and Tertullian. In fact, she would have utilized and beatified these very enthusiasts, had they risen in the Middle Ages, to combine their follies with equal extravagance in persecuting the Albigenses, while aggrandizing the papal ascendency.

I have enlarged upon the equivocal character of Tatian with melancholy interest, because I shall make sparing use of notes, in editing his sole surviving work, pronounced by Eusebius his masterpiece. I read it with sympathy, admiration, and instruction. I enjoy his biting satire of heathenism, his Pauline contempt for all philosophy save that of the Gospel, his touching reference to his own experiences, and his brilliant delineation of Christian innocence and of his own emancipation from the seductions of a deceitful and transient world. In short, I feel that Tatian deserves critical editing, in the original, at the hand and heart of some expert who can thoroughly appreciate his merits, and his relations to primitive Christianity.

The following is the original INTRODUCTORY NOTICE : —

WE learn from several sources that Tatian was an Assyrian, but know nothing very definite either as to the time or place of his birth. Epiphanius (*Hær.*, xlvi.) declares that he was a native of Mesopotamia; and we infer from other ascertained facts regarding him, that he flourished about the middle of the second century. He was at first an eager student of heathen literature, and seems to have been especially devoted to researches in philosophy. But he found no satisfaction in the bewildering mazes of Greek speculation, while he became utterly disgusted with what heathenism presented to him under the name of religion. In these circumstances, he happily met with the sacred books of the Christians, and was powerfully attracted by the purity of morals which these inculcated, and by the means of deliverance from the bondage of sin which

---

[1] See (vol. ii. p. 331.) Southey's *Life of Wesley;* an invaluable work, and one which presents this eminent saint in a most interesting light, even to worldly men. Ed. New York, Harpers, 1853.

they revealed.   He seems to have embraced Christianity at Rome, where he became acquainted with Justin Martyr, and enjoyed the instructions of that eminent teacher of the Gospel.   After the death of Justin, Tatian unfortunately fell under the influence of the Gnostic heresy, and founded an ascetic sect, which, from the rigid principles it professed, was called that of the Encratites, that is, " *The self-controlled*," or, " *The masters of themselves*."   Tatian latterly established himself at Antioch, and acquired a considerable number of disciples, who continued after his death to be distinguished by the practice of those austerities which he had enjoined.   The sect of the Encratites is supposed to have been established about A.D. 166, and Tatian appears to have died some few years afterwards.

The only extant work of Tatian is his " Address to the Greeks."   It is a most unsparing and direct exposure of the enormities of heathenism.   Several other works are said to have been composed by Tatian ; and of these, a *Diatessaron*, or *Harmony of the Four Gospels*, is specially mentioned.   His Gnostic views led him to exclude from the continuous narrative of our Lord's life, given in this work, all those passages which bear upon the incarnation and true humanity of Christ.   Not withstanding this defect, we cannot but regret the loss of this earliest Gospel harmony ; but the very title it bore is important, as showing that the Four Gospels, and these only, were deemed authoritative about the middle of the second century.

ADDRESS OF TATIAN TO THE GREEKS.

CHAP. I. — THE GREEKS CLAIM, WITHOUT REASON, THE INVENTION OF THE ARTS.

BE not, O Greeks, so very hostilely disposed towards the Barbarians, nor look with ill will on their opinions. For which of your institutions has not been derived from the Barbarians? The most eminent of the Telmessians invented the art of divining by dreams; the Carians, that of prognosticating by the stars; the Phrygians and the most ancient Isaurians, augury by the flight of birds; the Cyprians, the art of inspecting victims. To the Babylonians you owe astronomy; to the Persians, magic; to the Egyptians, geometry; to the Phœnicians, instruction by alphabetic writing. Cease, then, to miscall these imitations inventions of your own. Orpheus, again, taught you poetry and song; from him, too, you learned the mysteries. The Tuscans taught you the plastic art; from the annals of the Egyptians you learned to write history; you acquired the art of playing the flute from Marsyas and Olympus, — these two rustic Phrygians constructed the harmony of the shepherd's pipe. The Tyrrhenians invented the trumpet; the Cyclopes, the smith's art; and a woman who was formerly a queen of the Persians, as Hellanicus tells us, the method of joining together epistolary tablets:[1] her name was Atossa. Wherefore lay aside this conceit, and be not ever boasting of your elegance of diction; for, while you applaud yourselves, your own people will of course side with you. But it becomes a man of sense to wait for the testimony of others, and it becomes men to be of one accord also in the pronunciation of their language. But, as matters stand, to you alone it has happened not to speak alike even in common intercourse; for the way of speaking among the Dorians is not the same as that of the inhabitants of Attica, nor do the Æolians speak like the Ionians. And, since such a discrepancy exists where it ought not to be, I am at a loss whom to call a Greek. And, what is strangest of all, you hold in honour expressions not of native growth, and by the intermixture of barbaric words have made your language a medley. On this account we have renounced your wisdom, though I was once a great proficient in it; for, as the comic poet[2] says, —

> These are gleaners' grapes and small talk, —
> Twittering places of swallows, corrupters of art.

Yet those who eagerly pursue it shout lustily, and croak like so many ravens. You have, too, contrived the art of rhetoric to serve injustice and slander, selling the free power of your speech for hire, and often representing the same thing at one time as right, at another time as not good. The poetic art, again, you employ to describe battles, and the amours of the gods, and the corruption of the soul.

CHAP. II. — THE VICES AND ERRORS OF THE PHILOSOPHERS.

What noble thing have you produced by your pursuit of philosophy? Who of your most eminent men has been free from vain boasting? Diogenes, who made such a parade of his independence with his tub, was seized with a bowel complaint through eating a raw polypus, and so lost his life by gluttony. Aristippus, walking about in a purple robe, led a profligate life, in accordance with his professed opinions. Plato, a philosopher, was sold by Dionysius for his gormandizing propensities. And Aristotle, who absurdly placed a limit to Providence and made happiness to consist in the things which give pleasure, quite contrary to his duty as a preceptor flattered Alexander, forgetful that he was but a youth; and he, showing how well he had learned the lessons of his master, because his friend would not worship him shut him up and and carried him about like a bear or a leopard. He in fact obeyed strictly the precepts of his

---

[1] ἐπιστολὰς συντάττειν, i.e., for transmission by letter-carriers. — OTTO.

[2] Aristoph., Ranæ, 92, 93.

teacher in displaying manliness and courage by feasting, and transfixing with his spear his intimate and most beloved friend, and then, under a semblance of grief, weeping and starving himself, that he might not incur the hatred of his friends. I could laugh at those also who in the present day adhere to his tenets, — people who say that sublunary things are not under the care of Providence ; and so, being nearer the earth than the moon, and below its orbit, they themselves look after what is thus left uncared for ; and as for those who have neither beauty, nor wealth, nor bodily strength, nor high birth, they have no happiness, according to Aristotle. Let such men philosophize, for me !

CHAP. III. — RIDICULE OF THE PHILOSOPHERS.

I cannot approve of Heraclitus, who, being self-taught and arrogant, said, " I have explored myself." Nor can I praise him for hiding his poem[1] in the temple of Artemis, in order that it might be published afterwards as a mystery ; and those who take an interest in such things say that Euripides the tragic poet came there and read it, and, gradually learning it by heart, carefully handed down to posterity this darkness[2] of Heraclitus. Death, however, demonstrated the stupidity of this man ; for, being attacked by dropsy, as he had studied the art of medicine as well as philosophy, he plastered himself with cow-dung, which, as it hardened, contracted the flesh of his whole body, so that he was pulled in pieces, and thus died. Then, one cannot listen to Zeno, who declares that at the conflagration the same man will rise again to perform the same actions as before ; for instance, Anytus and Miletus to accuse, Busiris to murder his guests, and Hercules to repeat his labours ; and in this doctrine of the conflagration he introduces more wicked than just persons — one Socrates and a Hercules, and a few more of the same class, but not many, for the bad will be found far more numerous than the good. And according to him the Deity will manifestly be the author of evil, dwelling in sewers and worms, and in the perpetrators of impiety. The eruptions of fire in Sicily, moreover, confute the empty boasting of Empedocles, in that, though he was no god, he falsely almost gave himself out for one. I laugh, too, at the old wife's talk of Pherecydes, and the doctrine inherited from him by Pythagoras, and that of Plato, an imitation of his, though some think otherwise. And who would give his approval to the cynogamy of Crates, and not rather, repudiating the wild and tumid speech of those who resemble him, turn to the investigation of what truly deserves attention? Wherefore be

not led away by the solemn assemblies of philosophers who are no philosophers, who dogmatize one against the other, though each one vents but the crude fancies of the moment. They have, moreover, many collisions among themselves ; each one hates the other ; they indulge in conflicting opinions, and their arrogance makes them eager for the highest places. It would better become them, moreover, not to pay court to kings unbidden, nor to flatter men at the head of affairs, but to wait till the great ones come to them.

CHAP. IV. — THE CHRISTIANS WORSHIP GOD ALONE.

For what reason, men of Greece, do you wish to bring the civil powers, as in a pugilistic encounter, into collision with us? And, if I am not disposed to comply with the usages of some of them, why am I to be abhorred as a vile miscreant?[3] Does the sovereign order the payment of tribute, I am ready to render it. Does my master command me to act as a bondsman and to serve, I acknowledge the serfdom. Man is to be honoured as a fellow-man ;[4] God alone is to be feared, — He who is not visible to human eyes, nor comes within the compass of human art. Only when I am commanded to deny Him, will I not obey, but will rather die than show myself false and ungrateful. Our God did not begin to be in time :[5] He alone is without beginning, and He Himself is the beginning of all things. God is a Spirit,[6] not pervading matter, but the Maker of material spirits,[7] and of the forms that are in matter ; He is invisible, impalpable, being Himself the Father of both sensible and invisible things. Him we know from His creation, and apprehend His invisible power by His works.[8] I refuse to adore that workmanship which He has made for our sakes. The sun and moon were made for us : how, then, can I adore my own servants? How can I speak of stocks and stones as gods? For the Spirit that pervades matter[7] is inferior to the more divine spirit ; and this, even when assimilated to the soul, is not to be honoured equally with the perfect God. Nor even ought the ineffable God to be presented with gifts ; for He who is in want of nothing is not to be misrepresented by us as though He were indigent. But I will set forth our views more distinctly.

---

3 [Dear Christians of those times; so Justin and all the rest appeal against this odium. Their name an offence, " cast out as evil," but fragrant with unrequited love. Matt. x. 22–39.]

4 [1 Pet. ii. 17. This claim for man *as man* is the inspiration of Christianity. Terence breathes it from his wounded soul in slavery; and his immortal line, " Homo sum: humani nihil a me alienum puto " (*Heauntontimor.*, act i. sc. 1, verse 25), looks as if it had been written in the second century of illumination.]

5 [Kaye's *Justin*, pp. 56, 158.]

6 John iv. 24.

7 [Over again Tatian asserts spirits to be *material*, though not *fleshly ;* and I think with reference to 1 Cor. xv. 44.]

8 Rom. i. 20.

---

1 περὶ φύσεως.

2 He was called ὁ σκοτεινός for his obscurity.

CHAP. V. — THE DOCTRINE OF THE CHRISTIANS AS TO THE CREATION OF THE WORLD.

God was in the beginning; but the beginning, we have been taught, is the power of the Logos. For the Lord of the universe, who is Himself the necessary ground (ὑπόστασις) of all being, inasmuch as no creature was yet in existence, was alone; but inasmuch as He was all power, Himself the necessary ground of things visible and invisible, with Him were all things; with Him, by Logos-power (διὰ λογικῆς δυνάμεως), the Logos Himself also, who was in Him, subsists.[1] And by His simple will the Logos springs forth; and the Logos, not coming forth in vain, becomes the first-begotten work of the Father. Him (the Logos) we know to be the beginning of the world. But He came into being by participation,[2] not by abscission; for what is cut off is separated from the original substance, but that which comes by participation, making its choice of function,[3] does not render him deficient from whom it is taken. For just as from one torch many fires are lighted, but the light of the first torch is not lessened by the kindling of many torches, so the Logos, coming forth from the Logos-power of the Father, has not divested of the Logos-power Him who begat Him. I myself, for instance, talk, and you hear; yet, certainly, I who converse do not become destitute of speech (λόγος) by the transmission of speech, but by the utterance of my voice I endeavour to reduce to order the unarranged matter in your minds. And as the Logos,[4] begotten in the beginning, begat in turn our world, having first created for Himself the necessary matter, so also I, in imitation of the Logos, being begotten again,[5] and having become possessed of the truth, am trying to reduce to order the confused matter which is kindred with myself. For matter is not, like God, without beginning, nor, as having no beginning, is of equal power with God; it is begotten, and not produced by any other being, but brought into existence by the Framer of all things alone.

CHAP. VI. — CHRISTIANS' BELIEF IN THE RESURRECTION.

And on this account we believe that there will be a resurrection of bodies after the consumma-

tion of all things; not, as the Stoics affirm, according to the return of certain cycles, the same things being produced and destroyed for no useful purpose, but a resurrection once for all,[6] when our periods of existence are completed, and in consequence solely of the constitution of things under which men alone live, for the purpose of passing judgment upon them. Nor is sentence upon us passed by Minos or Rhadamanthus, before whose decease not a single soul, according to the mythic tales, was judged; but the Creator, God Himself, becomes the arbiter. And, although you regard us as mere triflers and babblers, it troubles us not, since we have faith in this doctrine. For just as, not existing before I was born, I knew not who I was, and only existed in the potentiality (ὑπόστασις) of fleshly matter, but being born, after a former state of nothingness, I have obtained through my birth a certainty of my existence; in the same way, having been born, and through death existing no longer, and seen no longer, I shall exist again, just as before I was not, but was afterwards born. Even though fire destroy all traces of my flesh, the world receives the vaporized matter;[7] and though dispersed through rivers and seas, or torn in pieces by wild beasts, I am laid up in the storehouses of a wealthy Lord. And, although the poor and the godless know not what is stored up, yet God the Sovereign, when He pleases, will restore the substance that is visible to Him alone to its pristine condition.

CHAP. VII. — CONCERNING THE FALL OF MAN.

For the heavenly Logos, a spirit emanating from the Father and a Logos from the Logos-power, in imitation of the Father who begat Him made man an image of immortality, so that, as incorruption is with God, in like manner, man, sharing in a part of God, might have the immortal principle also. The Logos,[8] too, before the creation of men, was the Framer of angels. And each of these two orders of creatures was made free to act as it pleased, not having the nature of good, which again is with God alone, but is brought to perfection in men through their freedom of choice, in order that the bad man may be justly punished, having become depraved through his own fault, but the just man be deservedly praised for his virtuous deeds, since in the exercise of his free choice he refrained from transgressing the will of God. Such is the constitution of things in reference to angels and men. And the power of the Logos, having in itself a faculty to foresee future events, not as

---

[1] [See Kaye's *Justin Martyr*, p. 161, note; and observe his stricture on Bull and Waterland.]
[2] κατὰ μερισμόν. Some translate, "by division," but the above is preferable. The sense, according to Otto, is that the Logos, having received a peculiar nature, shares in the *rational power* of the Father as a lighted torch partakes of the light of the torch from which it is kindled Comp. Just. Mar., *Dial. c. T.*, chap. lxi.
[3] οἰκονομίας τὴν αἵρεσιν προσλαβόν. The above seems the simplest rendering of this difficult passage, but several others have been proposed. [See note 4, cap. ix., *infra*, p. 69.]
[4] [Matter not eternal. He seems to have understood Gen. i. 1, of the creation of matter; and verse 2, as beginning the history of our planet and the visible universe.]
[5] [Supposed to be a personal reference to his conversion and baptism. As to "*confused*" matter," it should be *kindred* matter, and must be set over "*kindred spirit.*" See p. 71, cap. xiii., *infra*]

[6] [Comp. cap. xvii., *infra*, note 5, p. 72. ἐν ἡμέρᾳ συντελείας.]
[7] [A supposed discovery of modern science. See *Religion and Chemistry*, by Professor Cook of Harvard, pp. 79, 101. *Revised Edition*, Scribners, 1880.]
[8] [Kaye's rendering of this passage should be compared. See his *Justin*, p. 182.]

fated, but as taking place by the choice of free agents, foretold from time to time the issues of things to come ; it also became a forbidder of wickedness by means of prohibitions, and the encomiast of those who remained good. And, when men attached themselves to one who was more subtle than the rest, having regard to his being the first-born,[1] and declared him to be God, though he was resisting the law of God, then the power of the Logos excluded the beginner of the folly and his adherents from all fellowship with Himself. And so he who was made in the likeness of God, since the more powerful spirit is separated from him, becomes mortal ; but that first-begotten one through his transgression and ignorance becomes a demon ; and they who imitated him, that is his illusions, are become a host of demons, and through their freedom of choice have been given up to their own infatuation.

CHAP. VIII. — THE DEMONS SIN AMONG MANKIND.

But men form the material (ὑπόθεσις) of their apostasy. For, having shown them a plan of the position of the stars, like dice-players, they introduced Fate, a flagrant injustice. For the judge and the judged are made so by Fate ; the murderers and the murdered, the wealthy and the needy, are the offspring of the same Fate ; and every nativity is regarded as a theatrical entertainment by those beings of whom Homer says, —

> "Among the gods
> Rose laughter irrepressible."[2]

But must not those who are spectators of single combats and are partisans on one side or the other, and he who marries and is a pæderast and an adulterer, who laughs and is angry, who flees and is wounded, be regarded as mortals? For, by whatever actions they manifest to men their characters, by these they prompt their hearers to copy their example. And are not the demons themselves, with Zeus at their head, subjected to Fate, being overpowered by the same passions as men? And, besides, how are those beings to be worshipped among whom there exists such a great contrariety of opinions? For Rhea, whom the inhabitants of the Phrygian mountains call Cybele, enacted emasculation on account of Attis, of whom she was enamoured ; but Aphrodite is delighted with conjugal embraces. Artemis is a poisoner ; Apollo heals diseases. And after the decapitation of the Gorgon, the beloved of Poseidon, whence sprang the horse Pegasus and Chrysaor, Athené and Asclepios divided between them the drops of blood ; and, while he saved men's lives by means of them, she, by the same blood, became a homicide and the instigator of wars. From regard to her reputation, as it appears to me, the Athenians attributed to the earth the son born of her connection with Hephæstos, that Athene might not be thought to be deprived of her virility by Hephæstos, as Atalanta by Meleager. This limping manufacturer of buckles and earrings, as is likely, deceived the motherless child and orphan with these girlish ornaments. Poseidon frequents the seas ; Ares delights in wars ; Apollo is a player on the cithara ; Dionysus is absolute sovereign of the Thebans ; Kronos is a tyrannicide ; Zeus has intercourse with his own daughter, who becomes pregant by him. I may instance, too, Eleusis, and the mystic Dragon, and Orpheus, who says, —

> "Close the gates against the profane !"

Aïdoneus carries off Koré, and his deeds have been made into mysteries ; Demeter bewails her daughter, and some persons are deceived by the Athenians. In the precincts of the temple of the son of Leto is a spot called Omphalos ; but Omphalos is the burial-place of Dionysus. You now I laud, O Daphne ! — by conquering the incontinence of Apollo, you disproved his power of vaticination ; for, not foreseeing what would occur to you,[3] he derived no advantage from his art. Let the far-shooting god tell me how Zephyrus slew Hyacinthus. Zephyrus conquered him ; and in accordance with the saying of the tragic poet, —

> "A breeze is the most honourable chariot of the
> gods,"[4] —

conquered by a slight breeze, Apollo lost his beloved.

CHAP. IX. — THEY GIVE RISE TO SUPERSTITIONS.

Such are the demons ; these are they who laid down the doctrine of Fate. Their fundamental principle was the placing of animals in the heavens. For the creeping things on the earth, and those that swim in the waters, and the quadrupeds on the mountains, with which they lived when expelled from heaven, — these they dignified with celestial honour, in order that they might themselves be thought to remain in heaven, and, by placing the constellations there, might make to appear rational the irrational course of life on earth.[5] Thus the high-spirited and he who is crushed with toil, the temperate and the intemperate, the indigent and the wealthy, are what they are simply from the controllers of their nativity. For the delineation of the zodiacal circle is the work of gods. And, when the light of one of them predominates, as they express it, it deprives all the rest

---

[1] Gen. iii. 1. [*First-born.* ἄγγελος πρωτόγονος.]
[2] *Il.,* i. 599; *Od.,* viii. 326.

[3] On fleeing from Apollo, she became a bay-tree.
[4] It is uncertain from whom this line is quoted.
[5] Comp. ch. viii. init.

of their honour; and he who now is conquered, at another time gains the predominance. And the seven planets are well pleased with them,[1] as if they were amusing themselves with dice. But we are superior to Fate, and instead of wandering ($\pi\lambda\alpha\nu\eta\tau\hat{\omega}\nu$) demons, we have learned to know one Lord who wanders not; and, as we do not follow the guidance of Fate, we reject its lawgivers. Tell me, I adjure you,[2] did Triptolemus sow wheat and prove a benefactor to the Athenians after their sorrow? And why was not Demeter, before she lost her daughter, a benefactress to men? The Dog of Erigone is shown in the heavens, and the Scorpion the helper of Artemis, and Chiron the Centaur, and the divided Argo, and the Bear of Callisto. Yet how, before these performed the aforesaid deeds, were the heavens unadorned? And to whom will it not appear ridiculous that the Deltotum[3] should be placed among the stars, according to some, on account of Sicily, or, as others say, on account of the first letter in the name of Zeus ($\Delta\iota\acute{o}\varsigma$)? For why are not Sardinia and Cyprus honoured in heaven? And why have not the letters of the names of the brothers of Zeus, who shared the kingdom with him, been fixed there too? And how is it that Kronos, who was put in chains and ejected from his kingdom, is constituted a manager[4] of Fate? How, too, can he give kingdoms who no longer reigns himself? Reject, then, these absurdities, and do not become transgressors by hating us unjustly.

CHAP. X. — RIDICULE OF THE HEATHEN DIVINITIES.

There are legends of the metamorphosis of men: with you the gods also are metamorphosed. Rhea becomes a tree; Zeus a dragon, on account of Persephone; the sisters of Phaëthon are changed into poplars, and Leto into a bird of little value, on whose account what is now Delos was called Ortygia. A god, forsooth, becomes a swan, or takes the form of an eagle, and, making Ganymede his cupbearer, glories in a vile affection. How can I reverence gods who are eager for presents, and angry if they do not receive them? Let them have their Fate! I am not willing to adore wandering stars. What is that hair of Berenicé? Where were her stars before her death? And how was the dead Antinoüs fixed as a beautiful youth in the moon? Who carried him thither: unless perchance, as men, perjuring themselves for hire, are credited when they say in ridicule of the gods that kings have ascended into heaven, so some one, in like manner, has put this man also among the gods,[5] and been recompensed with honour and reward? Why have you robbed God? Why do you dishonour His workmanship? You sacrifice a sheep, and you adore the same animal. The Bull is in the heavens, and you slaughter its image. The Kneeler[6] crushes a noxious animal; and the eagle that devours the man-maker Prometheus is honoured. The swan is noble, forsooth, because it was an adulterer; and the Dioscuri, living on alternate days, the ravishers of the daughters of Leucippus, are also noble! Better still is Helen, who forsook the flaxen-haired Menelaus, and followed the turbaned and gold-adorned Paris. A just man also is Sophron,[7] who transported this adulteress to the Elysian fields! But even the daughter of Tyndarus is not gifted with immortality, and Euripides has wisely represented this woman as put to death by Orestes.

CHAP. XI. — THE SIN OF MEN DUE NOT TO FATE, BUT TO FREE-WILL.

How, then, shall I admit this nativity according to Fate, when I see such managers of Fate? I do not wish to be a king; I am not anxious to be rich; I decline military command; I detest fornication; I am not impelled by an insatiable love of gain to go to sea; I do not contend for chaplets; I am free from a mad thirst for fame; I despise death; I am superior to every kind of disease; grief does not consume my soul. Am I a slave, I endure servitude. Am I free, I do not make a vaunt of my good birth. I see that the same sun is for all, and one death for all, whether they live in pleasure or destitution. The rich man sows, and the poor man partakes of the same sowing. The wealthiest die, and beggars have the same limits to their life. The rich lack many things, and are glorious only through the estimation they are held in;[8] but the poor man and he who has very moderate desires, seeking as he does only the things suited to his lot, more easily obtains his purpose. How is it that you are fated to be sleepless through avarice? Why are you fated to grasp at things often, and often to die? Die to the world, repudiating the madness that is in it. Live to God, and by apprehending Him lay aside your old nature.[9] We were not created to die, but we die by our own

---

[1] The signs of the Zodiac (Gesner).
[2] Literally, "Tell me by God," or, "in the name of God."
[3] The Deltotum was a star of the shape of a triangle. — OTTO.
[4] [οἰκόνομος. So cap. xii., *infra*: "the constitution of the body is under one *management*," μιᾶς ἐστὶν οἰκονομίας. Also cap. xxi., p. 74, *infra*, note 5.]

[5] [He uses the verb θεολογεῖν as = θεοποιεῖν; but Kaye directs attention to Justin's use of the same as = *to discourse on divine things*, and again in *calling* Christ God.]
[6] Hercules — a sign in the sky. Leaning on his right knee, he tries to crush with his left foot the right side of the dragon's head.
[7] A writer of mimes.
[8] Or, reading with Maranus, κἂν . . . γεν., "even though," etc.
[9] [Think of a Chaldean heathen, by the power of grace, thus transformed. *Sapiens solus liber*, but the Christian alone is *wise*. This chapter compares favourably with the eloquence of Chrysostom in his letter to Cyriac, which, if spurious, is made up of passages to be found elsewhere in his works. Tom. iii. p. 683. *Ed.* Migne, Paris, 1859.]

fault.[1] Our free-will has destroyed us ; we who were free have become slaves ; we have been sold through sin. Nothing evil has been created by God ; we ourselves have manifested wickedness ; but we, who have manifested it, are able again to reject it.

CHAP. XII. — THE TWO KINDS OF SPIRITS.

We recognise two varieties of spirit, one of which is called the soul[2] ($\psi\upsilon\chi\acute{\eta}$), but the other is greater than the soul, an image and likeness of God : both existed in the first men, that in one sense they might be material ($\upsilon\lambda\iota\kappa o\acute{\iota}$), and in another superior to matter. The case stands thus : we can see that the whole structure of the world, and the whole creation, has been produced from matter, and the matter itself brought into existence[3] by God ; so that on the one hand it may be regarded as rude and unformed before it was separated into parts, and on the other as arranged in beauty and order after the separation was made. Therefore in that separation the heavens were made of matter, and the stars that are in them ; and the earth and all that is upon it has a similar constitution : so that there is a common origin of all things. But, while such is the case, there yet are certain differences in the things made of matter, so that one is more beautiful, and another is beautiful but surpassed by something better. For as the constitution of the body is under one management, and is engaged in doing that which is the cause of its having been made,[4] yet though this is the case, there are certain differences of dignity in it, and the eye is one thing, and another the ear, and another the arrangement of the hair and the distribution of the intestines, and the compacting together of the marrow and the bones and the tendons ; and though one part differs from another, there is yet all the harmony of a concert of music in their arrangement ; — in like manner the world, according to the power of its Maker containing some things of superior splendour, but some unlike these, received by the will of the Creator a material spirit. And these things severally it is possible for him to perceive who does not conceitedly reject those most divine explanations which in the course of time have been consigned to writing, and make those who study them great lovers of God. Therefore the demons,[5] as you call them, hav-

ing received their structure from matter and obtained the spirit which inheres in it, became intemperate and greedy ; some few, indeed, turning to what was purer, but others choosing what was inferior in matter, and conforming their manner of life to it. These beings, produced from matter, but very remote from right conduct, you, O Greeks, worship. For, being turned by their own folly to vaingloriousness, and shaking off the reins [of authority], they have been forward to become robbers of Deity ; and the Lord of all has suffered them to besport themselves, till the world, coming to an end, be dissolved, and the Judge appear, and all those men who, while assailed by the demons, strive after the knowledge of the perfect God obtain as the result of their conflicts a more perfect testimony in the day of judgment. There is, then, a spirit in the stars, a spirit in angels, a spirit in plants and the waters, a spirit in men, a spirit in animals ; but, though one and the same, it has differences in itself.[6] And while we say these things not from mere hearsay, nor from probable conjectures and sophistical reasoning, but using words of a certain diviner speech, do you who are willing hasten to learn. And you who do not reject with contempt the Scythian Anacharsis, do not disdain to be taught by those who follow a barbaric code of laws. Give at least as favourable a reception to our tenets as you would to the prognostications of the Babylonians. Hearken to us when we speak, if only as you would to an oracular oak. And yet the things just referred to are the trickeries of frenzied demons, while the doctrines we inculcate are far beyond the apprehension of the world.

CHAP. XIII. — THEORY OF THE SOUL'S IMMORTALITY.

The soul is not in itself immortal, O Greeks, but mortal.[7] Yet it is possible for it not to die. If, indeed, it knows not the truth, it dies, and is dissolved with the body, but rises again at last at the end of the world with the body, receiving death by punishment in immortality. But, again, if it acquires the knowledge of God, it dies not, although for a time it be dissolved. In itself it is darkness, and there is nothing luminous in it. And this is the meaning of the saying, "The darkness comprehendeth not the light."[8] For the soul does not preserve the spirit, but is preserved by it, and the light comprehends the darkness. The Logos, in truth, is the light of God, but the ignorant soul is darkness. On this account, if it continues solitary, it tends downward towards matter, and dies with the flesh ; but, if it enters into union with the Divine Spirit,

---

1 [Comp. cap. xv., *infra*, and the note 6, p. 71.]
2 [See cap. xv., *infra*.]
3 Literally, "brought forth" or "forward." The word does not imply that matter was created by God.
4 Tatian's words are somewhat obscure. We have given substantially the opinion of Worth, as expressed in his translation. The sense is: The body is evidently a unity in its organization and its activity, and the ultimate end which it serves in creation is that with which it is occupied, yet there are differences in respect of the parts. Otto renders: "For as the constitution of the body is of one plan, and in reference to the body the cause of its origin is occupied."
5 [*Demons.* The Paris editors have a note here, bidding us to read with caution; as our author seems rashly to imagine the demons to be material creatures. P. 151, ed. 1615.]

6 ["Which, though one and the same, is thus variously modified." Kaye's rendering in his *Justin*, p. 184.]
7 [Here Bishop Kaye has a very full note, quoting a beautiful passage textually from Beausobre, with whom, however, he does not entirely coincide. *Justin*, p. 184.]
8 John i. 5.

it is no longer helpless, but ascends to the regions whither the Spirit guides it: for the dwelling-place of the spirit is above, but the origin of the soul is from beneath. Now, in the beginning the spirit was a constant companion of the soul, but the spirit forsook it because it was not willing to follow. Yet, retaining as it were a spark of its power, though unable by reason of the separation to discern the perfect, while seeking for God it fashioned to itself in its wandering many gods, following the sophistries of the demons. But the Spirit of God is not with all, but, taking up its abode with those who live justly, and intimately combining with the soul, by prophecies it announced hidden things to other souls. And the souls that are obedient to wisdom have attracted to themselves the cognate spirit;[1] but the disobedient, rejecting the minister of the suffering God,[2] have shown themselves to be fighters against God, rather than His worshippers.

CHAP. XIV. — THE DEMONS SHALL BE PUNISHED MORE SEVERELY THAN MEN.

And such are you also, O Greeks, — profuse in words, but with minds strangely warped; and you acknowledge the dominion of many rather than the rule of one, accustoming yourselves to follow demons as if they were mighty. For, as the inhuman robber is wont to overpower those like himself by daring; so the demons, going to great lengths in wickedness, have utterly deceived the souls among you which are left to themselves by ignorance and false appearances. These beings do not indeed die easily, for they do not partake of flesh; but while living they practise the ways of death, and die themselves as often as they teach their followers to sin. Therefore, what is now their chief distinction, that they do not die like men, they will retain when about to suffer punishment: they will not partake of everlasting life, so as to receive this instead of death in a blessed immortality. And as we, to whom it now easily happens to die, afterwards receive the immortal with enjoyment, or the painful with immortality, so the demons, who abuse the present life to purposes of wrong-doing, dying continually even while they live, will have hereafter the same immortality, like that which they had during the time they lived, but in its nature like that of men, who voluntarily performed what the demons prescribed to them during their lifetime. And do not fewer kinds of sin break out among men owing to the brevity of their lives,[3] while on the part of these demons transgression is more abundant owing to their boundless existence?

CHAP. XV. — NECESSITY OF A UNION WITH THE HOLY SPIRIT.

But further, it becomes us now to seek for what we once had, but have lost, to unite the soul with the Holy Spirit, and to strive after union with God. The human soul consists of many parts, and is not simple; it is composite, so as to manifest itself through the body; for neither could it ever appear by itself without the body, nor does the flesh rise again without the soul. Man is not, as the croaking philosophers say, merely a rational animal, capable of understanding and knowledge; for, according to them, even irrational creatures appear possessed of understanding and knowledge. But man alone is the image and likeness of God; and I mean by man, not one who performs actions similar to those of animals, but one who has advanced far beyond mere humanity — to God Himself. This question we have discussed more minutely in the treatise concerning animals. But the principal point to be spoken of now is, what is intended by the image and likeness of God. That which cannot be compared is no other than abstract being; but that which is compared is no other than that which is like. The perfect God is without flesh; but man is flesh. The bond of the flesh is the soul;[4] that which encloses the soul is the flesh. Such is the nature of man's constitution; and, if it be like a temple, God is pleased to dwell in it by the spirit, His representative; but, if it be not such a habitation, man excels the wild beasts in articulate language only, — in other respects his manner of life is like theirs, as one who is not a likeness of God. But none of the demons possess flesh; their structure is spiritual, like that of fire or air. And only by those whom the Spirit of God dwells in and fortifies are the bodies of the demons easily seen, not at all by others, — I mean those who possess only soul;[5] for the inferior has not the ability to apprehend the superior. On this account the nature of the demons has no place for repentance; for they are the reflection of matter and of wickedness. But matter desired to exercise lordship over the soul; and according to their free-will these gave laws of death to men; but men, after the loss of immortality, have conquered death by submitting to death in faith;[6] and by repentance a call has been given to them, according to the word which says, "Since they were made a little lower than the angels."[7] And,

---

[1] [See cap. v., note, *supra*, p. 67.]
[2] [τοῦ πεπονθότος Θεοῦ. A very noteworthy testimony to the mystery of the Cross, and an early specimen of the *Communicatio idiomatum*: the ἀντίδοσις or ἀντιμετάστασις of the Greek theologians. Pearson, *On the Creed*, p. 314. London, 1824.]
[3] [The shortening of human life is a gracious limitation of transgression and of the peril of probation. "Let not our years be multiplied to increase our guilt."]

[4] [δεσμὸς δὲ τοῦ σαρκὸς ψυχή.]
[5] Comp. 1 Cor. ii. 14, 15. [The ψυχικοί, of whom we are to hear so much in Tertullian. Comp. cap. xii., *supra*, p. 70.]
[6] [But Kaye would translate, "by dying *to the world* through faith."]
[7] Ps. viii. 5

for every one who has been conquered, it is possible again to conquer, if he rejects the condition which brings death. And what that is, may be easily seen by men who long for immortality.

CHAP. XVI. — VAIN DISPLAY OF POWER BY THE DEMONS.

But the demons[1] who rule over men are not the souls of men ; for how should these be capable of action after death? unless man, who while living was void of understanding and power, should be believed when dead to be endowed with more of active power. But neither could this be the case, as we have shown elsewhere.[2] And it is difficult to conceive that the immortal soul, which is impeded by the members of the body, should become more intelligent when it has migrated from it. For the demons, inspired with frenzy against men by reason of their own wickedness, pervert their minds, which already incline downwards, by various deceptive scenic representations, that they may be disabled from rising to the path that leads to heaven. But from us the things which are in the world are not hidden, and the divine is easily apprehended by us if the power that makes souls immortal visits us. The demons are seen also by the men possessed of soul, when, as sometimes, they exhibit themselves to men, either that they may be thought to be something, or as evil-disposed friends may do harm to them as to enemies, or afford occasions of doing them honour to those who resemble them. For, if it were possible, they would without doubt pull down heaven itself with the rest of creation. But now this they can by no means effect, for they have not the power ; but they make war by means of the lower matter against the matter that is like themselves. Should any one wish to conquer them, let him repudiate matter. Being armed with the breastplate[3] of the celestial Spirit, he will be able to preserve all that is encompassed by it. There are, indeed, diseases and disturbances of the matter that is in us ; but, when such things happen, the demons ascribe the causes of them to themselves, and approach a man whenever disease lays hold of him. Sometimes they themselves disturb the habit of the body by a tempest of folly ; but, being smitten by the word of God, they depart in terror, and the sick man is healed.

CHAP. XVII. — THEY FALSELY PROMISE HEALTH TO THEIR VOTARIES.

Concerning the sympathies and antipathies of Democritus what can we say but this, that, according to the common saying, the man of

Abdera is Abderiloquent? But, as he who gave the name to the city, a friend of Hercules as it is said, was devoured by the horses of Diomedes, so he who boasted of the Magian Ostanes[4] will be delivered up in the day of consummation[5] as fuel for the eternal fire. And you, if you do not cease from your laughter, will gain the same punishment as the jugglers. Wherefore, O Greeks, hearken to me, addressing you as from an eminence, nor in mockery transfer your own want of reason to the herald of the truth. A diseased affection ($\pi\acute{a}\theta$os) is not destroyed by a counter-affection ($\dot{a}\nu\tau\iota\pi\acute{a}\theta\epsilon\iota a$), nor is a maniac cured by hanging little amulets of leather upon him. There are visitations of demons ; and he who is sick, and he who says he is in love, and he who hates, and he who wishes to be revenged, accept them as helpers. And this is the method of their operation : just as the forms of alphabetic letters and the lines composed of them cannot of themselves indicate what is meant, but men have invented for themselves signs of their thoughts, knowing by their peculiar combination what the order of the letters was intended to express ; so, in like manner, the various kinds of roots and the mutual relation of the sinews and bones can effect nothing of themselves, but are the elemental matter with which the depravity of the demons works, who have determined for what purpose each of them is available. And, when they see that men consent to be served by means of such things, they take them and make them their slaves. But how can it be honourable to minister to adulteries? How can it be noble to stimulate men in hating one another? Or how is it becoming to ascribe to matter the relief of the insane, and not to God? For by their art they turn men aside from the pious acknowledgment of God, leading them to place confidence in herbs and roots.[6] But God, if He had prepared these things to effect just what men wish, would be a Producer of evil things ; whereas He Himself produced everything which has good qualities, but the profligacy of the demons has made use of the productions of nature for evil purposes, and the appearance of evil which these wear is from them, and not from the perfect God. For how comes it to pass that when alive I was in no wise evil, but that now I am dead and can do nothing, my remains, which are incapable of motion or even sense, should effect something cognizable by the senses? And how shall he who has died by the most miserable death be able to assist in avenging any one? If this were possible, much more might he defend

---

1 [For a learned and valuable comparison of early patristic *Demonologies*, see Kaye's *Justin Martyr*, pp. 201-210.]
2 Perhaps in his treatise " On Animals."
3 Comp. Eph. vi. 13, 14, 17.

4 Democritus. [The Paris editors add, *vide Laertium*. As to *Ostanes*, see that invaluable thesaurus, *Hofmann's Lex. Universale*, vol. ii. p. 6. Leyden, 1698.]
5 [Comp. cap. vi., note 6, *supra*, p. 67.]
6 [*Naviget Anticyras*. On hellebore, see otherwise useless learning but illustrative of this place, in Burton, *Anat. Melanchol.*, p. 400. *Ed.* New York, 1847.]

himself from his own enemy; being able to assist others, much more might he constitute himself his own avenger.

CHAP. XVIII. — THEY DECEIVE, INSTEAD OF HEALING.

But medicine and everything included in it is an invention of the same kind. If any one is healed by matter, through trusting to it, much more will he be healed by having recourse to the power of God. As noxious preparations are material compounds, so are curatives of the same nature. If, however, we reject the baser matter, some persons often endeavour to heal by a union of one of these bad things with some other, and will make use of the bad to attain the good. But, just as he who dines with a robber, though he may not be a robber himself, partakes of the punishment on account of his intimacy with him, so he who is not bad but associates with the bad, having dealings with them for some supposed good, will be punished by God the Judge for partnership in the same object. Why is he who trusts in the system of matter [1] not willing to trust in God? For what reason do you not approach the more powerful Lord, but rather seek to cure yourself, like the dog with grass, or the stag with a viper, or the hog with river-crabs, or the lion with apes? Why do you deify the objects of nature? And why, when you cure your neighbour, are you called a benefactor? Yield to the power of the Logos! The demons don ot cure, but by their art make men their captives. And the most admirable Justin [2] has rightly denounced them as robbers. For, as it is the practice of some to capture persons and then to restore them to their friends for a ransom, so those who are esteemed gods, invading the bodies of certain persons, and producing a sense of their presence by dreams, command them to come forth into public, and in the sight of all, when they have taken their fill of the things of this world, fly away from the sick, and, destroying the disease which they had produced, restore men to their former state

CHAP. XIX. — DEPRAVITY LIES AT THE BOTTOM OF DEMON-WORSHIP.

But do you, who have not the perception of these things, be instructed by us who know them: though you do profess to despise death, and to be sufficient of yourselves for everything. But this is a discipline in which your philosophers are so greatly deficient, that some of them receive from the king of the Romans 600 aurei yearly, for no useful service they perform, but that they may not even wear a long beard without being paid for it! Crescens, who made his nest in the great city, surpassed all men in unnatural love (παιδεραστία), and was strongly addicted to the love of money. Yet this man, who professed to despise death, was so afraid of death, that he endeavoured to inflict on Justin, and indeed on me, the punishment of death, as being an evil, because by proclaiming the truth he convicted the philosophers of being gluttons and cheats. But whom of the philosophers, save you only, was he accustomed to inveigh against? If you say, in agreement with our tenets, that death is not to be dreaded, do not court death from an insane love of fame among men, like Anaxagoras, but become despisers of death by reason of the knowledge of God. The construction of the world is excellent, but the life men live in it is bad; and we may see those greeted with applause as in a solemn assembly who know not God. For what is divination? and why are ye deceived by it? It is a minister to thee of worldly lusts. You wish to make war, and you take Apollo as a counsellor of slaughter. You want to carry off a maiden by force, and you select a divinity to be your accomplice. You are ill by your own fault; and, as Agamemnon [3] wished for ten councillors, so you wish to have gods with you. Some woman by drinking water gets into a frenzy, and loses her senses by the fumes of frankincense, and you say that she has the gift of prophecy. Apollo was a prognosticator and a teacher of soothsayers: in the matter of Daphne he deceived himself. An oak, forsooth, is oracular, and birds utter presages! And so you are inferior to animals and plants! It would surely be a fine thing for you to become a divining rod, or to assume the wings of a bird! He who makes you fond of money also foretells your getting rich; he who excites to seditions and wars also predicts victory in war. If you are superior to the passions, you will despise all worldly things. Do not abhor us who have made this attainment, but, repudiating the demons,[4] follow the one God. "All things [5] were made by Him, and without Him not one thing was made." If there is poison in natural productions, this has supervened through our sinfulness. I am able to show the perfect truth of these things; only do you hearken, and he who believes will understand.

CHAP. XX. — THANKS ARE EVER DUE TO GOD.

Even if you be healed by drugs (I grant you that point by courtesy), yet it behoves you to give testimony of the cure to God. For the world still draws us down, and through weakness I incline towards matter. For the wings of the

---

[1] [ὑλης οἰκονομία. Comp. cap. ix., supra, note 4, p. 69]
[2] [The language of an affectionate pupil: ὁ θαυμασιώτατος Ἰουστῖνος.]
[3] Comp. Hom., Il., ii. 372.
[4] [The baptismal renunciation.]
[5] John i. 3.

soul were the perfect spirit, but, having cast this off through sin, it flutters like a nestling and falls to the ground. Having left the heavenly companionship, it hankers after communion with inferior things. The demons were driven forth to another abode; the first created human beings were expelled from their place: the one, indeed, were cast down from heaven; but the other were driven from earth, yet not out of this earth, but from a more excellent order of things than exists here now. And now it behoves us, yearning after that pristine state, to put aside everything that proves a hindrance. The heavens are not infinite, O man, but finite and bounded; and beyond them are the superior worlds which have not a change of seasons, by which various diseases are produced, but, partaking of every happy temperature, have perpetual day, and light unapproachable by men below.[1] Those who have composed elaborate descriptions of the earth have given an account of its various regions so far as this was possible to man; but, being unable to speak of that which is beyond, because of the impossibility of personal observation, they have assigned as the cause the existence of tides; and that one sea is filled with weed, and another with mud; and that some localities are burnt up with heat, and others cold and frozen. We, however, have learned things which were unknown to us, through the teaching of the prophets, who, being fully persuaded that the heavenly spirit[2] along with the soul will acquire a clothing of mortality, foretold things which other minds were unacquainted with. But it is possible for every one who is naked to obtain this apparel, and to return to its ancient kindred.

CHAP. XXI. — DOCTRINES OF THE CHRISTIANS AND GREEKS RESPECTING GOD COMPARED.

We do not act as fools, O Greeks, nor utter idle tales, when we announce that God was born in the form of a man. I call on you who reproach us to compare your mythical accounts with our narrations. Athené, as they say, took the form of Deïphobus for the sake of Hector,[3] and the unshorn Phœbus for the sake of Admetus fed the trailing-footed oxen, and the spouse of Zeus came as an old woman to Semele. But, while you treat seriously such things, how can you deride us? Your Asclepios died, and he who ravished fifty virgins in one night at Thespiæ lost his life by delivering himself to the devouring flame. Prometheus, fastened to Caucasus, suffered punishment for his good deeds to men. According to you, Zeus is envious, and hides the dream[4] from men, wishing their destruction. Wherefore, looking at your own memorials, vouchsafe us your approval, though it were only as dealing in legends similar to your own. We, however, do not deal in folly, but your legends are only idle tales. If you speak of the origin of the gods, you also declare them to be mortal. For what reason is Hera now never pregnant? Has she grown old? or is there no one to give you information? Believe me now, O Greeks, and do not resolve your myths and gods into allegory. If you attempt to do this, the divine nature as held by you is overthrown by your own selves; for, if the demons with you are such as they are said to be, they are worthless as to character; or, if regarded as symbols of the powers of nature, they are not what they are called. But I cannot be persuaded to pay religious homage to the natural elements, nor can I undertake to persuade my neighbour. And Metrodorus of Lampsacus, in his treatise concerning Homer, has argued very foolishly, turning everything into allegory. For he says that neither Hera, nor Athené, nor Zeus are what those persons suppose who consecrate to them sacred enclosures and groves, but parts of nature and certain arrangements of the elements. Hector also, and Achilles, and Agamemnon, and all the Greeks in general, and the Barbarians with Helen and Paris, being of the same nature, you will of course say are introduced merely for the sake of the machinery[5] of the poem, not one of these personages having really existed. But these things we have put forth only for argument's sake; for it is not allowable even to compare our notion of God with those who are wallowing in matter and mud.

CHAP. XXII. — RIDICULE OF THE SOLEMNITIES OF THE GREEKS.

And of what sort are your teachings? Who must not treat with contempt your solemn festivals, which, being held in honour of wicked demons, cover men with infamy? I have often

---

[1] [The flavour of this passage comes out with more sweetness in Kaye's note (p. 198, *Justin M.*), thus: "Above the visible heavens exist the better ages, αἰῶνες οἱ κρείττονες, having no change of seasons from which various diseases take their origin; but, blest with a uniform goodness of temperature, they enjoy perpetual day, and light inaccessible to men who dwell here below."
Here Tatian seems to me to have had in mind a noble passage from Pindar, one of the most exquisite specimens of Greek poetry, which he baptizes and sanctifies.

Ἴσον δὲ νύκτεσσιν αἰεὶ
Ἴσα δ᾽ ἐν ἁμέραις ἅλι-
ον ἔχοντες, ἀπονέστερον
Ἐσθλοὶ νέμονται βίο-
τον, οὐ χθόνα ταράσσον-
τες ἀλκᾷ χερῶν,
Οὐδὲ πόντιον ὕδωρ,
Κεινὰν παρὰ δίαιταν· κ.τ.λ.   *Olymp.* ii.

Truly the Gentiles reflect some light from the window in the ark of their father Noah. How sweet what follows: ἀδακρυν νέμονται αἰῶνα. Comp. Rev. vii. 7, xxi. 4, xxii.]

[2] [Kaye thus renders this passage: "the spirit together with the soul will receive immortality, the heavenly covering of mortality." *Justin*, p. 288.]

[3] *Il.*, xxii. 227.

[4] *Il.*, ii. init.

[5] [Χάριν οἰκουμίας. Compare divers uses of this word in Kaye's *Justin*, p. 174.]

seen a man [1] — and have been amazed to see, and the amazement has ended in contempt, to think how he is one thing internally, but outwardly counterfeits what he is not — giving himself excessive airs of daintiness and indulging in all sorts of effeminacy; sometimes darting his eyes about; sometimes throwing his hands hither and thither, and raving with his face smeared with mud; sometimes personating Aphrodité, sometimes Apollo; a solitary accuser of all the gods, an epitome of superstition, a vituperator of heroic deeds, an actor of murders, a chronicler of adultery, a storehouse of madness, a teacher of cynædi, an instigator of capital sentences; — and yet such a man is praised by all. But I have rejected all his falsehoods, his impiety, his practices, — in short, the man altogether. But you are led captive by such men, while you revile those who do not take a part in your pursuits. I have no mind to stand agape at a number of singers, nor do I desire to be affected in sympathy with a man when he is winking and gesticulating in an unnatural manner. What wonderful or extraordinary thing is performed among you? They utter ribaldry in affected tones, and go through indecent movements; your daughters and your sons behold them giving lessons in adultery on the stage. Admirable places, forsooth, are your lecture-rooms, where every base action perpetrated by night is proclaimed aloud, and the hearers are regaled with the utterance of infamous discourses! Admirable, too, are your mendacious poets, who by their fictions beguile their hearers from the truth!

CHAP. XXIII. — OF THE PUGILISTS AND GLADIATORS.

I have seen men weighed down by bodily exercise, and carrying about the burden of their flesh, before whom rewards and chaplets are set, while the adjudicators cheer them on, not to deeds of virtue, but to rivalry in violence and discord; and he who excels in giving blows is crowned. These are the lesser evils; as for the greater, who would not shrink from telling them? Some, giving themselves up to idleness for the sake of profligacy, sell themselves to be killed; and the indigent barters himself away, while the rich man buys others to kill him. And for these the witnesses take their seats, and the boxers meet in single combat, for no reason whatever, nor does any one come down into the arena to succour. Do such exhibitions as these redound to your credit? He who is chief among you collects a legion of blood-stained murderers, engaging to maintain them; and these ruffians are sent forth by him, and you assemble at the

spectacle to be judges, partly of the wickedness of the adjudicator, and partly of that of the men who engage in the combat. And he who misses the murderous exhibition is grieved, because he was not doomed to be a spectator of wicked and impious and abominable deeds. You slaughter animals for the purpose of eating their flesh, and you purchase men to supply a cannibal banquet for the soul, nourishing it by the most impious bloodshedding. The robber commits murder for the sake of plunder, but the rich man purchases gladiators for the sake of their being killed.[2]

CHAP. XXIV. — OF THE OTHER PUBLIC AMUSEMENTS.

What advantage should I gain from him who is brought on the stage by Euripides raving mad, and acting the matricide of Alcmæon; who does not even retain his natural behaviour, but with his mouth wide open goes about sword in hand, and, screaming aloud, is burned to death, habited in a robe unfit for man? Away, too, with the mythical tales of Acusilaus, and Menander, a versifier of the same class! And why should I admire the mythic piper? Why should I busy myself about the Theban Antigenides,[3] like Aristoxenus? We leave you to these worthless things; and do you either believe our doctrines, or, like us, give up yours.

CHAP. XXV. — BOASTINGS AND QUARRELS OF THE PHILOSOPHERS.

What great and wonderful things have your philosophers effected? They leave uncovered one of their shoulders; they let their hair grow long; they cultivate their beards; their nails are like the claws of wild beasts. Though they say that they want nothing, yet, like Proteus,[4] they need a currier for their wallet, and a weaver for their mantle, and a wood-cutter for their staff, and the rich,[5] and a cook also for their gluttony. O man competing with the dog,[6] you know not God, and so have turned to the imitation of an irrational animal. You cry out in public with an assumption of authority, and take upon you to avenge your own self; and if you receive nothing, you indulge in abuse, and philosophy is with you the art of getting money. You follow the doctrines of Plato, and a disciple of Epicurus lifts up his voice to oppose you. Again, you wish to be a disciple of Aristotle, and a follower of Democritus rails at you. Pythagoras says that he was Euphorbus, and he is the heir of the

---

[1] Tatian here describes an actor. [And in America heathenism has returned upon us in most of the indecencies here exposed. Are we Christians?]

[2] [Here Christianity began to avenge itself on the brutal spectacles of the Coliseum, which stands a gigantic monument of the religious system of which they were a part. See Athenagoras, *Embassy*, cap. xxxv.]
[3] Antigenides was a flute-player, and Aristoxenus a writer on music and musical instruments.
[4] The Cynic Peregrinus is meant.
[5] They need the rich to invite them to banquets.
[6] The Cynic.

doctrine of Pherecydes; but Aristotle impugns the immortality of the soul. You who receive from your predecessors doctrines which clash with one another, you the inharmonious, are fighting against the harmonious. One of you asserts that God is body, but I assert that He is without body; that the world is indestructible, but I say that it is to be destroyed; that a conflagration will take place at various times, but I say that it will come to pass once for all; that Minos and Rhadamanthus are judges, but I say that God Himself is Judge; that the soul alone is endowed with immortality, but I say that the flesh also is endowed with it.[1] What injury do we inflict upon you, O Greeks? Why do you hate those who follow the word of God, as if they were the vilest of mankind? It is not we who eat human flesh[2]—they among you who assert such a thing have been suborned as false witnesses; it is among you that Pelops is made a supper for the gods, although beloved by Poseidon, and Kronos devours his children, and Zeus swallows Metis.

CHAP. XXVI. — RIDICULE OF THE STUDIES OF THE GREEKS.

Cease to make a parade of sayings which you have derived from others, and to deck yourselves like the daw in borrowed plumes. If each state were to take away its contribution to your speech, your fallacies would lose their power. While inquiring what God is, you are ignorant of what is in yourselves; and, while staring all agape at the sky, you stumble into pitfalls. The reading of your books is like walking through a labyrinth, and their readers resemble the cask of the Danaïds. Why do you divide time, saying that one part is past, and another present, and another future? For how can the future be passing when the present exists? As those who are sailing imagine in their ignorance, as the ship is borne along, that the hills are in motion, so you do not know that it is you who are passing along, but that time (ὁ αἰών) remains present as long as the Creator wills it to exist. Why am I called to account for uttering my opinions, and why are you in such haste to put them all down? Were not you born in the same manner as ourselves, and placed under the same government of the world? Why say that wisdom is with you alone, who have not another sun, nor other risings of the stars, nor a more distinguished origin, nor a death preferable to that of other men? The grammarians have been the beginning of this idle talk; and you who parcel out wisdom are

cut off from the wisdom that is according to truth, and assign the names of the several parts to particular men; and you know not God, but in your fierce contentions destroy one another. And on this account you are all nothing worth. While you arrogate to yourselves the sole right of discussion, you discourse like the blind with the deaf. Why do you handle the builder's tools without knowing how to build? Why do you busy yourselves with words, while you keep aloof from deeds, puffed up with praise, but cast down by misfortunes? Your modes of acting are contrary to reason, for you make a pompous appearance in public, but hide your teaching in corners. Finding you to be such men as these, we have abandoned you, and no longer concern ourselves with your tenets, but follow the word of God. Why, O man, do you set the letters of the alphabet at war with one another? Why do you, as in a boxing match, make their sounds clash together with your mincing Attic way of speaking, whereas you ought to speak more according to nature? For if you adopt the Attic dialect though not an Athenian, pray why do you not speak like the Dorians? How is it that one appears to you more rugged, the other more pleasant for intercourse?

CHAP. XXVII. — THE CHRISTIANS ARE HATED UNJUSTLY.

And if you adhere to *their* teaching, why do you fight against me for choosing such views of doctrine as I approve? Is it not unreasonable that, while the robber is not to be punished for the name he bears,[3] but only when the truth about him has been clearly ascertained, yet we are to be assailed with abuse on a judgment formed without examination? Diagoras was an Athenian, but you punished him for divulging the Athenian mysteries; yet you who read his Phrygian discourses hate us. You possess the commentaries of Leo, and are displeased with our refutations of them; and having in your hands the opinions of Apion concerning the Egyptian gods, you denounce us as most impious. The tomb of Olympian Zeus is shown among you,[4] though some one says that the Cretans are liars.[5] Your assembly of many gods is nothing. Though their despiser Epicurus acts as a torch-bearer,[6] I do not any the more conceal from the rulers that view of God which I hold in relation to His government of the universe. Why do you advise me to be false to my principles? Why do you who say that you despise death exhort us to use art in order to escape it? I have not the heart of a deer; but your zeal

---

[1] [The vigor of this passage, and the impact of its truths upon heathen idols, are noble specimens of our author's power.]
[2] [They ate and drank bread and wine hallowed to be the κοινωνία of the flesh and blood of Christ (1 Cor. x. 16); but they knew nothing of the modern doctrine of the Latin churches, which is precisely what Tatian denies.]

[3] [Athenagoras, *Embassy*, cap. ii., *infra*.]
[4] In Crete.
[5] Comp. Tit. i. 12. Callimachus is probably the author referred to, though others express the same opinion respecting the Cretans.
[6] Accommodating himself to the popular opinions, through fear.

for dialectics resembles the loquacity of Thersites. How can I believe one who tells me that the sun is a red-hot mass and the moon an earth? Such assertions are mere logomachies, and not a sober exposition of truth. How can it be otherwise than foolish to credit the books of Herodotus relating to the history of Hercules, which tell of an upper earth from which the lion came down that was killed by Hercules? And what avails the Attic style, the sorites of philosophers, the plausibilities of syllogisms, the measurements of the earth, the positions of the stars, and the course of the sun? To be occupied in such inquiries is the work of one who imposes opinions on himself as if they were laws.

CHAP. XXVIII. — CONDEMNATION OF THE GREEK LEGISLATION.

On this account I reject your legislation also ; for there ought to be one common polity for all ; but now there are as many different codes as there are states, so that things held disgraceful in some are honourable in others. The Greeks consider intercourse with a mother as unlawful, but this practice is esteemed most becoming by the Persian Magi ; pæderasty is condemned by the Barbarians, but by the Romans, who endeavour to collect herds of boys like grazing horses, it is honoured with certain privileges.

CHAP. XXIX. — ACCOUNT OF TATIAN'S CONVERSION.

Wherefore, having seen these things, and moreover also having been admitted to the mysteries, and having everywhere examined the religious rites performed by the effeminate and the pathic, and having found among the Romans their Latiarian Jupiter delighting in human gore and the blood of slaughtered men, and Artemis not far from the great city [1] sanctioning acts of the same kind, and one demon here and another there instigating to the perpetration of evil, — retiring by myself, I sought how I might be able to discover the truth. And, while I was giving my most earnest attention to the matter, I happened to meet with certain barbaric writings, too old to be compared with the opinions of the Greeks, and too divine to be compared with their errors ; and I was led to put faith in these by the unpretending cast of the language, the inartificial character of the writers, the foreknowledge displayed of future events, the excellent quality of the precepts, and the declaration of the government of the universe as centred in one Being.[2] And, my soul being taught of God, I discern that the former class of writings lead to condemnation, but that these put an end to the slavery that is in the world, and rescue us from a multiplicity of rulers and ten thousand tyrants, while they give us, not indeed what we had not before received, but what we had received but were prevented by error from retaining.

CHAP. XXX. — HOW HE RESOLVED TO RESIST THE DEVIL.

Therefore, being initiated and instructed in these things, I wish to put away my former errors as the follies of childhood. For we know that the nature of wickedness is like that of the smallest seeds ; since it has waxed strong from a small beginning, but will again be destroyed if we obey the words of God and do not scatter ourselves. For He has become master of all we have by means of a certain "hidden treasure,"[3] which while we are digging for we are indeed covered with dust, but we secure it as our fixed possession. He who receives the whole of this treasure has obtained command of the most precious wealth. Let these things, then, be said to our friends. But to you Greeks what can I say, except to request you not to rail at those who are better than yourselves, nor if they are called Barbarians to make that an occasion of banter? For, if you are willing, you will be able to find out the cause of men's not being able to understand one another's language ; for to those who wish to examine our principles I will give a simple and copious account of them.

CHAP. XXXI. — THE PHILOSOPHY OF THE CHRISTIANS MORE ANCIENT THAN THAT OF THE GREEKS.

But now it seems proper for me to demonstrate that our philosophy is older than the systems of the Greeks. Moses and Homer shall be our limits, each of them being of great antiquity ; the one being the oldest of poets and historians, and the other the founder of all barbarian wisdom. Let us, then, institute a comparison between them ; and we shall find that our doctrines are older, not only than those of the Greeks, but than the invention of letters.[3] And I will not bring forward witnesses from among ourselves, but rather have recourse to Greeks. To do the former would be foolish, because it would not be allowed by you ; but the other will surprise you, when, by contending against you with your own weapons, I adduce arguments of which you had no suspicion. Now the poetry of Homer, his parentage, and the time in which he flourished have been investigated by the most ancient writers, — by Theagenes of Rhegium, who lived in the time of Cambyses, Stesimbrotus

---

[1] At Aricia, near Rome.
[2] [A memorable tribute to the light-giving power of the Holy Scriptures. "Barbarian books" (*barbaric* means something else) they were ; but well says Dr. Watts in a paraphrase of Ps. cxix. 96 (and comp. capp. xl , xli., *infra*), —

"Let all the heathen writers join to form one perfect book,
Great God if once compared with thine, how mean their writings look !"

See his *Hymns*, p. 238. *Ed.* Worcester, 1836.]

[3] Comp. Matt. xiii. 44. [Cogent reasoning with Greeks.]

of Thasos and Antimachus of Colophon, Herodotus of Halicarnassus, and Dionysius the Olynthian; after them, by Ephorus of Cumæ, and Philochorus the Athenian, Megaclides and Chamæleon the Peripatetics; afterwards by the grammarians, Zenodotus, Aristophancs, Callimachus, Crates, Eratosthenes, Aristarchus, and Apollodorus. Of these, Crates says that he flourished before the return of the Heraclidæ, and within 80 years after the Trojan war; Eratosthenes says that it was after the 100th year from the taking of Ilium; Aristarchus, that it was about the time of the Ionian migration, which was 140 years after that event; but, according to Philochorus, after the Ionian migration, in the archonship of Archippus at Athens, 180 years after the Trojan war; Apollodorus says it was 100 years after the Ionian migration, which would be 240 years after the Trojan war. Some say that he lived 90 years before the Olympiads, which would be 317 years after the taking of Troy. Others carry it down to a later date, and say that Homer was a contemporary of Archilochus; but Archilochus flourished about the 23d Olympiad, in the time of Gyges the Lydian, 500 years after Troy. Thus, concerning the age of the aforesaid poet, I mean Homer, and the discrepancies of those who have spoken of him, we have said enough in a summary manner for those who are able to investigate with accuracy. For it is possible to show that the opinions held about the facts themselves also are false. For, where the assigned dates do not agree together, it is impossible that the history should be true. For what is the cause of error in writing, but the narrating of things that are not true?

CHAP. XXXII.—THE DOCTRINE OF THE CHRISTIANS, IS OPPOSED TO DISSENSIONS, AND FITTED FOR ALL.

But with us there is no desire of vainglory, nor do we indulge in a variety of opinions. For having renounced the popular and earthly, and obeying the commands of God, and following the law of the Father of immortality, we reject everything which rests upon human opinion. Not only do the rich among us pursue our philosophy, but the poor enjoy instruction gratuitously; [1] for the things which come from God surpass the requital of worldly gifts. Thus we admit all who desire to hear, even old women and striplings; and, in short, persons of every age are treated by us with respect, but every kind of licentiousness is kept at a distance. And in speaking we do not utter falsehood. It would be an excellent thing if your continuance in unbelief should receive a check; but, however that

may be, let our cause remain confirmed by the judgment pronounced by God. Laugh, if you please; but you will have to weep hereafter. Is it not absurd that Nestor,[2] who was slow at cutting his horses' reins owing to his weak and sluggish old age, is, according to you, to be admired for attempting to rival the young men in fighting, while you deride those among us who struggle against old age and occupy themselves with the things pertaining to God? Who would not laugh when you tell us that the Amazons, and Semiramis, and certain other warlike women existed, while you cast reproaches on our maidens? Achilles was a youth, yet is believed to have been very magnanimous; and Neoptolemus was younger, but strong; Philoctetes was weak, but the divinity had need of him against Troy. What sort of man was Thersites? yet he held a command in the army, and, if he had not through doltishness had such an unbridled tongue, he would not have been reproached for being peak-headed and bald. As for those who wish to learn our philosophy, we do not test them by their looks, nor do we judge of those who come to us by their outward appearance; for we argue that there may be strength of mind in all, though they may be weak in body. But your proceedings are full of envy and abundant stupidity.

CHAP. XXXIII. — VINDICATION OF CHRISTIAN WOMEN.

Therefore I have been desirous to prove from the things which are esteemed honourable among you, that our institutions are marked by sobermindedness, but that yours are in close affinity with madness.[3] You who say that we talk nonsense among women and boys, among maidens and old women, and scoff at us for not being with you, hear what silliness prevails among the Greeks. For their works of art are devoted to worthless objects, while they are held in higher estimation by you than even your gods; and you behave yourselves unbecomingly in what relates to woman. For Lysippus cast a statue of Praxilla, whose poems contain nothing useful, and Menestratus one of Learchis, and Selanion one of Sappho the courtezan, and Naucydes one of Erinna the Lesbian, and Boiscus one of Myrtis, and Cephisodotus one of Myro of Byzantium, and Gomphus one of Praxigoris, and Amphistratus one of Clito. And what shall I say about Anyta, Telesilla, and Mystis? Of the first Euthycrates and Cephisodotus made a statue, and of the second Niceratus, and of the third Aristodotus; Euthycrates made one of Mnesiarchis the Ephesian, Selanion one of Corinna, and Euthycrates one of Thalarchis the Argive. My object in referring to these women is, that you may not regard as something strange what

_____
[1] [Compare cap. xi. p. 69. And note, thus early, the Christian free-schools, such as Julian closed and then imitated, confessing their power.]

[2] Il., ix.
[3] [See note 2, next page.]

you find among us, and that, comparing the statues which are before your eyes, you may not treat the women with scorn who among us pursue philosophy. This Sappho is a lewd, love-sick female, and sings her own wantonness;[1] but all our women are chaste, and the maidens at their distaffs sing of divine things[2] more nobly than that damsel of yours. Wherefore be ashamed, you who are professed disciples of women yet scoff at those of the sex who hold our doctrine, as well as at the solemn assemblies they frequent.[2] What a noble infant did Glaucippé present to you, who brought forth a prodigy, as is shown by her statue cast by Niceratus, the son of Euctemon the Athenian! But, if Glaucippé brought forth an elephant, was that a reason why she should enjoy public honours? Praxiteles and Herodotus made for you Phryné the courtezan, and Euthycrates cast a brazen statue of Panteuchis, who was pregnant by a whoremonger; and Dinomenes, because Besantis queen of the Pæonians gave birth to a black infant, took pains to preserve her memory by his art. I condemn Pythagoras too, who made a figure of Europa on the bull; and you also, who honour the accuser of Zeus on account of his artistic skill. And I ridicule the skill of Myron, who made a heifer and upon it a Victory because by carrying off the daughter of Agenor it had borne away the prize for adultery and lewdness. The Olynthian Herodotus made statues of Glycera the courtezan and Argeia the harper. Bryaxis made a statue of Pasiphaë; and, by having a memorial of her lewdness, it seems to have been almost your desire that the women of the present time should be like her.[3] A certain Melanippë was a wise woman, and for that reason Lysistratus made her statue. But, forsooth, you will not believe that among us there are wise women!

CHAP. XXXIV. — RIDICULE OF THE STATUES ERECTED BY THE GREEKS.

Worthy of very great honour, certainly, was the tyrant Bhalaris, who devoured sucklings, and accordingly is exhibited by the workmanship of Polystratus the Ambraciot, even to this day, as a very wonderful man! The Agrigentines dreaded to look on that countenance of his, because of his cannibalism; but people of culture now make it their boast that they behold him in his statue! Is it not shameful that fratricide is honoured by you who look on the statues of Polynices and Eteocles, and that you have not rather buried them with their maker Pythagoras? Destroy these memorials of iniquity! Why should I contemplate with admiration the figure of the woman who bore thirty children, merely for the sake of the artist Periclymenus? One ought to turn away with disgust from one who bore off the fruits of great incontinence, and whom the Romans compared to a sow, which also on a like account, they say, was deemed worthy of a mystic worship. Ares committed adultery with Aphrodité, and Andron made an image of their offspring Harmonia. Sophron, who committed to writing trifles and absurdities, was more celebrated for his skill in casting metals, of which specimens exist even now. And not only have his tales kept the fabulist Æsop in everlasting remembrance, but also the plastic art of Aristodemus has increased his celebrity. How is it then that you, who have so many poetesses whose productions are mere trash, and innumerable courtezans, and worthless men, are not ashamed to slander the reputation of our women? What care I to know that Euanthé gave birth to an infant in the Peripatus, or to gape with wonder at the art of Callistratus, or to fix my gaze on the Neæra of Calliades? For she was a courtezan. Laïs was a prostitute, and Turnus made her a monument of prostitution. Why are you not ashamed of the fornication of Hephæstion, even though Philo has represented him very artistically? And for what reason do you honour the hermaphrodite Ganymede by Leochares, as if you possessed something admirable? Praxiteles even made a statue of a woman with the stain of impurity upon it. It behoved you, repudiating everything of this kind, to seek what is truly worthy of attention, and not to turn with disgust from our mode of life while receiving with approval the shameful productions of Philænis and Elephantis.

CHAP. XXXV. — TATIAN SPEAKS AS AN EYE-WITNESS.

The things which I have thus set before you I have not learned at second hand. I have visited many lands; I have followed rhetoric, like yourselves; I have fallen in with many arts and inventions; and finally, when sojourning in the city of the Romans, I inspected the multiplicity of statues brought thither by you: for I do not attempt, as is the custom with many, to strengthen

---

1 [St. Chrysostom speaks of the heathen as ὁι ταῖς σατανικαῖς ᾠδαῖς κατασηπόμενοι. In Psalmum, cxvii. tom. v. p. 533. Ed. Migne.]

2 [Such as the Magnificat of the Virgin, the Twenty-third Psalm, or the Christian Hymn for Eventide, which they learned in the Christian schools (cap. xxxii. p. 78). Cold is the heart of any mother's son that does not warm over such a chapter as this on the enfranchisement of womanhood by Christ. Observe our author's scorn for the heathen "affinity with unreason" (this chapter, supra), and then enjoy this glimpse of the contrast afforded by the Gospel in its influence upon women. Intensely should we delight in the pictures of early Christian society, of which the Fathers give us these suggestive outlines. Rejecting the profane and wanton songs they heard around them, — "satanic minstrelsies," as St. Chrysostom names them, — they beguiled their toils and soothed their sorrows with "Psalms and hymns and spiritual songs." As St. Jerome relates, "You could not go into the field, but you might hear the ploughman's hallelujahs, the mower's hymns, and the vine-dresser's chant of the Psalms of David." See Cave's Primitive Christianity, p. 132.]

3 [St. Paul's spirit was stirred within him, beholding the abominable idolatries of the Athenians; and who can wonder at the loathing of Christians, whose wives and children could not escape from these shameful spectacles. The growing asceticism and fanatical views of sexual relations, which were now rising in the Church, were a morbid but virtuous revolt of faith against these impurities.]

my own views by the opinions of others, but I wish to give you a distinct account of what I myself have seen and felt. So, bidding farewell to the arrogance of Romans and the idle talk of Athenians, and all their ill-connected opinions, I embraced our barbaric philosophy. I began to show how this was more ancient than your institutions,[1] but left my task unfinished, in order to discuss a matter which demanded more immediate attention; but now it is time I should attempt to speak concerning its doctrines. Be not offended with our teaching, nor undertake an elaborate reply filled with trifling and ribaldry, saying, "Tatian, aspiring to be above the Greeks, above the infinite number of philosophic inquirers, has struck out a new path, and embraced the doctrines of Barbarians." For what grievance is it, that men manifestly ignorant should be reasoned with by a man of like nature with themselves? Or how can it be irrational, according to your own sophist,[2] to grow old always learning something?

CHAP. XXXVI. — TESTIMONY OF THE CHALDEANS TO THE ANTIQUITY OF MOSES.

But let Homer be not later than the Trojan war; let it be granted that he was contemporary with it, or even that he was in the army of Agamemnon, and, if any so please, that he lived before the invention of letters. The Moses before mentioned will be shown to have been many years older than the taking of Troy, and far more ancient than the building of Troy, or than Tros and Dardanus. To demonstrate this I will call in as witnesses the Chaldeans, the Phœnicians, and the Egyptians. And what more need I say? For it behoves one who professes to persuade his hearers to make his narrative of events very concise. Berosus, a Babylonian, a priest of their god Belus, born in the time of Alexander, composed for Antiochus, the third after him, the history of the Chaldeans in three books; and, narrating the acts of the kings, he mentions one of them, Nabuchodonosor by name, who made war against the Phœnicians and the Jews, — events which we know were announced by our prophets, and which happened much later than the age of Moses, seventy years before the Persian empire. But Berosus is a very trustworthy man, and of this Juba is a witness, who, writing concerning the Assyrians, says that he learned the history from Berosus : there are two books of his concerning the Assyrians.

CHAP. XXXVII. — TESTIMONY OF THE PHŒNICIANS.

After the Chaldeans, the testimony of the

Phœnicians is as follows. There were among them three men, Theodotus, Hypsicrates, and Mochus; Chaitus translated their books into Greek, and also composed with exactness the lives of the philosophers. Now, in the histories of the aforesaid writers it is shown that the abduction of Europa happened under one of the kings, and an account is given of the coming of Menelaus into Phœnicia, and of the matters relating to Chiramus,[3] who gave his daughter in marriage to Solomon the king of the Jews, and supplied wood of all kind of trees for the building of the temple. Menander of Pergamus composed a history concerning the same things. But the age of Chiramus is somewhere about the Trojan war; but Solomon, the contemporary of Chiramus, lived much later than the age of Moses.

CHAP. XXXVIII. — THE EGYPTIANS PLACE MOSES IN THE REIGN OF INACHUS.

Of the Egyptians also there are accurate chronicles. Ptolemy, not the king, but a priest of Mendes, is the interpreter of their affairs. This writer, narrating the acts of the kings, says that the departure of the Jews from Egypt to the places whither they went occurred in the time of king Amosis, under the leadership of Moses. He thus speaks : "Amosis lived in the time of king Inachus." After him, Apion the grammarian, a man most highly esteemed, in the fourth book of his Ægyptiaca (there are five books of his), besides many other things, says that Amosis destroyed Avaris in the time of the Argive Inachus, as the Mendesian Ptolemy wrote in his annals. But the time from Inachus to the taking of Troy occupies twenty generations. The steps of the demonstration are the following : —

CHAP. XXXIX. — CATALOGUE OF THE ARGIVE KINGS.

The kings of the Argives were these : Inachus, Phoroneus, Apis, Criasis, Triopas, Argeius, Phorbas, Crotopas, Sthenelaus, Danaus, Lynceus, Prœtus, Abas, Acrisius, Perseus, Sthenelaus, Eurystheus, Atreus, Thyestes, and Agamemnon, in the eighteenth year of whose reign Troy was taken. And every intelligent person will most carefully observe that, according to the tradition of the Greeks, they possessed no historical composition; for Cadmus, who taught them letters, came into Bœotia many generations later. But after Inachus, under Phoroneus, a check was with difficulty given to their savage and nomadic life, and they entered upon a new order of things. Wherefore, if Moses is shown to be contemporary with Inachus, he is four hundred years older than the Trojan war. But this is demonstrated from the succession of the Attic, [and of the

---

[1] Chap. xxxi. [With what calm superiority he professes himself a *barbarian!* I honour the eye-witness who tells not only what he had seen, but what he *felt* amid such evidences of man's degradation and impiety.]
[2] Solon. Bergh., *Poetæ Græc. Lyr*, fr. 18. [The interest and biographical importance of this chapter must be apparent.]

[3] Called Hiram in our authorized translation.

Macedonian, the Ptolemaic, and the Antiochian]¹ kings. Hence, if the most illustrious deeds among the Greeks were recorded and made known after Inachus, it is manifest that this must have been after Moses. In the time of Phoroneus, who was after Inachus, Ogygus is mentioned among the Athenians, in whose time was the first deluge; and in the time of Phorbas was Actæus, from whom Attica was called Actæa; and in the time of Triopas were Prometheus, and Epimetheus, and Atlas, and Cecrops of double nature, and Io; in the time of Crotopas was the burning of Phaëthon and the flood of Deucalion; in the time of Sthenelus was the reign of Amphictyon and the coming of Danaus into Peloponnesus, and the founding of Dardania by Dardanus, and the return of Europa from Phœnicia to Crete; in the time of Lynceus was the abduction of Koré, and the founding of the temple in Eleusis, and the husbandry of Triptolemus, and the coming of Cadmus to Thebes, and the reign of Minos; in the time of Prœtus was the war of Eumolpus against the Athenians; in the time of Acrisius was the coming over of Pelops from Phrygia, and the coming of Ion to Athens, and the second Cecrops, and the deeds of Perseus and Dionysus, and Musæus, the disciple of Orpheus; and in the reign of Agamemnon Troy was taken.

CHAP. XL. — MOSES MORE ANCIENT AND CREDIBLE THAN THE HEATHEN HEROES.

Therefore, from what has been said it is evident that Moses was older than the ancient heroes, wars, and demons. And we ought rather to believe him, who stands before them in point of age, than the Greeks, who, without being aware of it,² drew his doctrines [as] from a fountain. For many of the sophists among them, stimulated by curiosity, endeavoured to adulterate whatever they learned from Moses,³ and from those who have philosophized like him, first that they might be considered as having something of their own, and secondly, that covering up by a certain rhetorical artifice whatever things they did not understand, they might misrepresent the truth as if it were a fable. But what the learned among the Greeks have said concerning our polity and the history of our laws, and how many and what kind of men have written of these things, will be shown in the treatise against those who have discoursed of divine things.⁴

¹ The words within brackets, though they occur in the MSS. and in Eusebius, are supposed by some scholars to be a very old interpolation.
² This expression admits of several meanings: "Without properly understanding them,"—WORTH; "not with a proper sense of gratitude."—MARANUS.
³ [There is increasing evidence of the obligations of the Greek sages to that "light shining in a dark place," i.e., amid an idolatrous world.]
⁴ [Let it be noted as the moral of our author's review, that there is no self-degradation of which man is not capable when he rejects the true God. Rom. i. 28.]

CHAP. XLI.

But the matter of principal importance is to endeavour with all accuracy to make it clear that Moses is not only older than Homer, but than all the writers that were before him — older than Linus, Philammon, Thamyris, Amphion, Musæus, Orpheus, Demodocus, Phemius, Sibylla, Epimenides of Crete, who came to Sparta, Aristæus of Proconnesus, who wrote the Arimaspia, Asbolus the Centaur, Isatis, Drymon, Euclus the Cyprian, Horus the Samian, and Pronapis the Athenian. Now, Linus was the teacher of Hercules, but Hercules preceded the Trojan war by one generation; and this is manifest from his son Tlepolemus, who served in the army against Troy. And Orpheus lived at the same time as Hercules; moreover, it is said that all the works attributed to him were composed by Onomacritus the Athenian, who lived during the reign of the Pisistratids, about the fiftieth Olympiad. Musæus was a disciple of Orpheus. Amphion, since he preceded the siege of Troy by two generations, forbids our collecting further particulars about him for those who are desirous of information. Demodocus and Phemius lived at the very time of the Trojan war; for the one resided with the suitors, and the other with the Phæacians. Thamyris and Philammon were not much earlier than these. Thus, concerning their several performances in each kind, and their times and the record of them, we have written very fully, and, as I think, with all exactness. But, that we may complete what is still wanting, I will give my explanation respecting the men who are esteemed wise. Minos, who has been thought to excel in every kind of wisdom, and mental acuteness, and legislative capacity, lived in the time of Lynceus, who reigned after Danaus in the eleventh generation after Inachus. Lycurgus, who was born long after the taking of Troy, gave laws to the Lacedemonians. Draco is found to have lived about the thirty-ninth Olympiad, Solon about the forty-sixth, and Pythagoras about the sixty-second. We have shown that the Olympiads commenced 407 years after the taking of Troy. These facts being demonstrated, we shall briefly remark concerning the age of the seven wise men. The oldest of these, Thales, lived about the fiftieth Olympiad; and I have already spoken briefly of those who came after him.

CHAP. XLII. — CONCLUDING STATEMENT AS TO THE AUTHOR.

These things, O Greeks, I Tatian, a disciple of the barbarian philosophy,⁵ have composed for you. I was born in the land of the Assyrians, having been first instructed in your doctrines,

⁵ [Comp. cap. xxix. p. 77, supra.]

and afterwards in those which I now undertake to proclaim. Henceforward, knowing who God is and what is His work, I present myself to you prepared for an examination [1] concerning my doctrines, while I adhere immoveably to that mode of life which is according to God.[2]

FRAGMENTS.[3]

I.

In his treatise, *Concerning Perfection according to the Saviour,* he writes, "Consent indeed fits for prayer, but fellowship in corruption weakens supplication. At any rate, by the permission he certainly, though delicately, forbids; for while he permits them to return to the same on account of Satan and incontinence, he exhibits a man who will attempt to serve two masters — God by the 'consent' (1 Cor. vii. 5), but by want of consent, incontinence, fornication, and the devil." — Clem. Alex. : *Strom.,* iii. c. 12.

II.

A certain person inveighs against generation, calling it corruptible and destructive; and some one does violence [to Scripture], applying to pro-creation the Saviour's words, "Lay not up treasure on earth, where moth and rust corrupt;" and he is not ashamed to add to these the words of the prophet: "You all shall grow old as a garment, and the moth shall devour you."

And, in like manner, they adduce the saying concerning the resurrection of the dead, "The sons of that world neither marry nor are given in marriage." — Clem. Alex. : iii. c. 12, § 86.

III.

Tatian, who maintaining the imaginary flesh of Christ, pronounces all sexual connection impure, who was also the very violent heresiarch of the Encratites, employs an argument of this sort: "If any one sows to the flesh, of the flesh he shall reap corruption;" but he sows to the flesh who is joined to a woman; therefore he who takes a wife and sows in the flesh, of the flesh he shall reap corruption.— Hieron. : *Com. in Ep. ad Gal.*

IV.

Seceding from the Church, and being elated and puffed up by a conceit of his teacher,[4] as if he were superior to the rest, he formed his own peculiar type of doctrine. Imagining certain invisible Æons like those of Valentinus, and denouncing marriage as defilement and fornication in the same way as Marcion and Saturninus, and denying the salvation of Adam as an opinion of his own. — Irenæus : *Adv. Hær.,* i. 28.

V.

Tatian attempting from time to time to make use of Paul's language, that in Adam all die, but ignoring that "where sin abounded, grace has much more abounded." — Irenæus : *Adv. Heres.,* iii. 37.

VI.

Against Tatian, who says that the words, "Let there be light," are to be taken as a prayer. If He who uttered it knew a superior God, how is it that He says, "I am God, and there is none beside me"?

He said that there are punishments for blasphemies, foolish talking, and licentious words, which are punished and chastised by the Logos. And he said that women were punished on account of their hair and ornaments by a power placed over those things, which also gave strength to Samson by his hair, and punishes those who by the ornament of their hair are urged on to fornication. — Clem. Alex. : *Frag.*

VII.

But Tatian, not understanding that the expression "Let there be" is not always precative but sometimes imperative, most impiously imagined concerning God, who said "Let there be light," that He prayed rather than commanded light to be, as if, as he impiously thought, God was in darkness. — Origen : *De Orat.*

VIII.

Tatian separates the old man and the new, but not, as we say, understanding the old man to be the law, and the new man to be the Gospel. We agree with him in saying the same thing, but not in the sense he wishes, abrogating the law as if it belonged to another God. — Clem. Alex. : *Strom.,* iii. 12.

IX.

Tatian condemns and rejects not only marriage, but also meats which God has created for use. — Hieron. : *Adv. Jovin.,* i. 3.

X.

"But ye gave the Nazarites wine to drink, and commanded the prophets, saying, Prophesy not." On this, perhaps, Tatian the chief of the Encratites endeavours to build his heresy, asserting that wine is not to be drunk, since it was

---

[1] [Compare the boastful Rousseau: "Que la trompette du jugement sonne quand elle voudra, je viendrai *ce livre à la main,* me presenter devant le souverain Juge." *Confessions,* livre i. p. 2.]

[2] ["Adhere *immoveably."* Alas! "let him that thinketh he standeth", etc. But I cannot part with Tatian nor think of Tertullian without recalling David's threnode: "There the shield of the mighty is vilely cast away. . . . I am distressed for thee, my brother: . . . very pleasant hast thou been unto me. . . . How are the mighty fallen, and the weapons of war perished!" Our own sad times have taught us similar lamentations for some who seemed for a time to be "burning and shining lights." God be merciful to poor frail men.]

[3] From the lost works of Tatian. Ed. *Otto.*

[4] i.e., Justin Martyr.

commanded in the law that the Nazarites were not to drink wine, and now those who give the Nazarites wine are accused by the prophet. — HIERON.: *Com. in Amos.*

XI.

Tatian, the patriarch of the Encratites, who himself rejected some of Paul's Epistles, believed this especially, that is [addressed] to Titus, ought to be declared to be the apostle's, thinking little of the assertion of Marcion and others, who agree with him on this point. — HIERON.: *Præf. in Com. ad Tit.*

XII.

[Archelaus (A.D. 280), Bishop of Carrha in Mesopotamia, classes his countryman Tatian with "Marcion, Sabellius, and others who have made up for themselves a peculiar science," i.e., a theology of their own. — ROUTH: *Reliquiæ*, tom. v. p. 137. But see Edinburgh Series of this work, vol. xx. p. 267.]

THEOPHILUS OF ANTIOCH

INTRODUCTORY NOTE

TO

THEOPHILUS OF ANTIOCH.

[TRANSLATED BY THE REV. MARCUS DODS, A.M.]

[A.D. 115–168–181.] Eusebius praises the pastoral fidelity of the primitive pastors, in their unwearied labours to protect their flocks from the heresies with which Satan contrived to endanger the souls of believers. By exhortations and admonitions, and then again by *oral discussions* and refutations, contending with the heretics themselves, they were prompt to ward off the devouring beasts from the fold of Christ. Such is the praise due to Theophilus, in his opinion; and he cites especially his lost work against Marcion as "of no mean character."[1] He was one of the earliest commentators upon the Gospels, if not the first; and he seems to have been the earliest Christian historian of the Church of the Old Testament. His only remaining work, here presented, seems to have originated in an "oral discussion," such as Eusebius instances. But nobody seems to accord him due praise as the founder of the science of *Biblical Chronology* among Christians, save that his great successor in modern times, Abp. Usher, has not forgotten to pay him this tribute in the *Prolegomena* of his Annals. (*Ed.* Paris, 1673.)

Theophilus occupies an interesting position, after Ignatius, in the succession of faithful men who represented Barnabas and other prophets and teachers of Antioch,[2] in that ancient seat, from which comes our name as Christians. I cannot forbear another reference to those recent authors who have so brilliantly illustrated and depicted the Antioch of the early Christians;[3] because, if we wish to understand Autolycus, we must *feel* the state of society which at once fascinated him, and disgusted Theophilus. The Fathers are dry to those only who lack imagination to reproduce their age, or who fail to study them geographically and chronologically. Besides this, one should bring to the study of their works, that sympathy springing from a burning love to Christ, which borrows its motto, in slightly altered words, from the noble saying of the African poet: "I am a *Christian*, and nothing which concerns *Christianity* do I consider foreign to myself."

Theophilus comes down to us only as an apologist intimately allied in spirit to Justin and Irenæus; and he should have been placed with Tatian between these two, in our series, had not the inexorable laws of our compilation brought them into this volume. I need add no more to what follows from the translator, save only the expression of a hope that others will enjoy this author as I do, rating him very highly, even at the side of Athenagoras. He is severe, yet gentle too, in dealing with his antagonist; and he cannot be charged with a more sublime contempt for heathenism than St. Paul betrays in all his writings, abjuring even Plato and Socrates, and accen-

---

[1] Book iv. cap. 24. Thus he with others met the "grievous wolves" foretold by St. Paul "night and day with tears," three years continually (Acts xx. 29–31).

[2] Acts xiii. 1.   [3] Renan, *St Paul*, cap. i., Ferrar, *Life of St. Paul*, cap. xvi.

87

tuating his maxim, "The world by wisdom knew not God." For him it was *Christ* to live; and I love Theophilus for this very fault, if it be such. He was of Antioch; and was content to be, simply and altogether, nothing but a Christian.

The following is the original INTRODUCTORY NOTICE:—

LITTLE is known of the personal history of Theophilus of Antioch. We gather from the following treatise that he was born a pagan (i. 14), and owed his conversion to Christianity to the careful study of the Holy Scriptures. Eusebius (*Hist. Eccl.*, iv. 20) declares that he was the sixth bishop of Antioch in Syria from the apostles, the names of his supposed predecessors being Eros, Cornelius, Hero, Ignatius, and Euodius. We also learn from the same writer, that Theophilus succeeded to the bishopric of Antioch in the eighth year of the reign of Marcus Aurelius, that is, in A.D. 168. He is related to have died either in A.D. 181, or in A.D. 188; some assigning him an episcopate of thirteen, and others of twenty-one, years.

Theophilus is said by Eusebius, Jerome, and others, to have written several works against the heresies which prevailed in his day. He himself refers in the following treatise (ii. 30) to another of his compositions. Commentaries on the Gospels, arranged in the form of a harmony, and on the Book of Proverbs, are also ascribed to him by Jerome; but the sole remaining specimen of his writings consists of the three books that follow, addressed to his friend Autolycus. The occasion which called these forth is somewhat doubtful. It has been thought that they were written in refutation of a work which Autolycus had published against Christianity; but the more probable opinion is, that they were drawn forth by disparaging remarks made in conversation. The language of the writer (ii. 1) leads to this conclusion.

In handling his subject, Theophilus goes over much the same ground as Justin Martyr and the rest of the early apologists. He is somewhat fond of fanciful interpretations of Scripture; but he evidently had a profound acquaintance with the inspired writings, and he powerfully exhibits their immense superiority in every respect over the heathen poetry and philosophy. The whole treatise was well fitted to lead on an intelligent pagan to the cordial acceptance of Christianity.

[I venture to assign to Theophilus a conjectural date of birth, *circiter* A. D. 115.[1]]

---

[1] [Our chronological arrangement must yield in minute accuracy to other considerations; and we may borrow an excuse from our author, who notes the difficulty of microscopic ἀκριβεία in his own chronological labours (book iii. cap 29). It was impossible to crowd Tatian and Theophilus into vol. i. of this series, without dividing Irenæus, and putting part of his works in vol. ii. But, in the case of contemporaries, this dislocation is trifling, and creates no confusion.]

THEOPHILUS TO AUTOLYCUS.

BOOK I.

CHAP. I. — AUTOLYCUS AN IDOLATER AND SCORNER OF CHRISTIANS.

A FLUENT tongue and an elegant style afford pleasure and such praise as vainglory delights in, to wretched men who have been corrupted in mind; the lover of truth does not give heed to ornamented speeches, but examines the real matter of the speech, what it is, and what kind it is. Since, then, my friend, you have assailed me with empty words, boasting of your gods of wood and stone, hammered and cast, carved and graven, which neither see nor hear, for they are idols, and the works of men's hands; and since, besides, you call me a Christian, as if this were a damning name to bear, I, for my part, avow that I am a Christian,[1] and bear this name beloved of God, hoping to be serviceable[2] to God. For it is not the case, as you suppose, that the name of God is hard to bear; but possibly you entertain this opinion of God, because you are yourself yet unserviceable to Him.

CHAP. II. — THAT THE EYES OF THE SOUL MUST BE PURGED ERE GOD CAN BE SEEN.

But if you say, "Show me thy God," I would reply, "Show me yourself,[3] and I will show you my God." Show, then, that the eyes of your soul are capable of seeing, and the ears of your heart able to hear; for as those who look with the eyes of the body perceive earthly objects and what concerns this life, and discriminate at the same time between things that differ, whether light or darkness, white or black, deformed or beautiful, well-proportioned and symmetrical or disproportioned and awkward, or monstrous or mutilated; and as in like manner also, by the sense of hearing, we discriminate either sharp, or deep, or sweet sounds; so the same holds good regarding the eyes of the soul and the ears of the heart, that it is by them we are able to behold God. For God is seen by those who are enabled to see Him when they have the eyes of their soul opened: for all have eyes; but in some they are overspread,[4] and do not see the light of the sun. Yet it does not follow, because the blind do not see, that the light of the sun does not shine; but let the blind blame themselves and their own eyes. So also thou, O man, hast the eyes of thy soul overspread by thy sins and evil deeds. As a burnished mirror, so ought man to have his soul pure. When there is rust on the mirror, it is not possible that a man's face be seen in the mirror; so also when there is sin in a man, such a man cannot behold God. Do you, therefore, show me yourself, whether you are not an adulterer, or a fornicator, or a thief, or a robber, or a purloiner; whether you do not corrupt boys; whether you are not insolent, or a slanderer, or passionate, or envious, or proud, or supercilious; whether you are not a brawler, or covetous, or disobedient to parents; and whether you do not sell your children; for to those who do these things God is not manifest, unless they have first cleansed themselves from all impurity. All these things, then, involve you in darkness, as when a filmy defluxion on the eyes prevents one from beholding the light of the sun: thus also do iniquities, O man, involve you in darkness, so that you cannot see God.

CHAP. III. — NATURE OF GOD.

You will say, then, to me, "Do you, who see God, explain to me the appearance of God." Hear, O man. The appearance of God is ineffable and indescribable, and cannot be seen by eyes of flesh. For in glory He is incomprehensible, in greatness unfathomable, in height inconceivable, in power incomparable, in wisdom

---

[1] [Acts xi 26 Note this as from *an Antiochian*, glorying in the name of Christian]

[2] Εὐχρηστος, punning on the name *Christian*. [Comp cap xii., *infra*. So Justin, p. 164, vol. i., this series. But he also puns on his own name, "beloved of God," in the text φορῶ τὸ Θεοφιλὲς ὄνομα τοῦτο, κ.τ.λ.]

[3] Literally, "your man:" the invisible soul, as the noblest part of man, being probably intended.

[4] The technical word for a disease of the eye, like cataract.

unrivalled, in goodness inimitable, in kindness unutterable. For if I say He is Light, I name but His own work; if I call Him Word, I name but His sovereignty; if I call Him Mind, I speak but of His wisdom; if I say He is Spirit, I speak of His breath; if I call Him Wisdom, I speak of His offspring; if I call Him Strength, I speak of His sway; if I call Him Power, I am mentioning His activity; if Providence, I but mention His goodness; if I call Him Kingdom, I but mention His glory; if I call Him Lord, I mention His being judge; if I call Him Judge, I speak of Him as being just; if I call Him Father, I speak of all things as being from Him;[1] if I call Him Fire, I but mention His anger. You will say, then, to me, "Is God angry?" Yes; He is angry with those who act wickedly, but He is good, and kind, and merciful, to those who love and fear Him; for He is a chastener[1] of the godly, and father of the righteous; but he is a judge and punisher of the impious.

CHAP. IV. — ATTRIBUTES OF GOD.

And He is without beginning, because He is unbegotten; and He is unchangeable, because He is immortal. And he is called God [Θεός] on account of His having placed [τεθεικέναι] all things on security afforded by Himself; and on account of [θέειν], for θέειν means running, and moving, and being active, and nourishing, and foreseeing, and governing, and making all things alive. But he is Lord, because He rules over the universe; Father, because he is before all things; Fashioner and Maker, because He is creator and maker of the universe; the Highest, because of His being above all; and Almighty, because He Himself rules and embraces all. For the heights of heaven, and the depths of the abysses, and the ends of the earth, are in His hand, and there is no place of His rest. For the heavens are His work, the earth is His creation, the sea is His handiwork; man is His formation and His image; sun, moon, and stars are His elements, made for signs, and seasons, and days, and years, that they may serve and be slaves to man; and all things God has made out of things that were not[3] into things that are, in order that through His works His greatness may be known and understood.

CHAP. V. — THE INVISIBLE GOD PERCEIVED THROUGH HIS WORKS.

For as the soul in man is not seen, being invisible to men, but is perceived through the motion of the body, so God cannot indeed be seen by human eyes, but is beheld and perceived through His providence and works. For, in like manner, as any person, when he sees a ship on the sea rigged and in sail, and making for the harbour, will no doubt infer that there is a pilot in her who is steering her; so we must perceive that God is the governor [pilot] of the whole universe, though He be not visible to the eyes of the flesh, since He is incomprehensible. For if a man cannot look upon the sun, though it be a very small heavenly body, on account of its exceeding heat and power, how shall not a mortal man be much more unable to face the glory of God, which is unutterable? For as the pomegranate, with the rind containing it, has within it many cells and compartments which are separated by tissues, and has also many seeds dwelling in it, so the whole creation is contained by the spirit[4] of God, and the containing spirit is along with the creation contained by the hand of God. As, therefore, the seed of the pomegranate, dwelling inside, cannot see what is outside the rind, itself being within; so neither can man, who along with the whole creation is enclosed by the hand of God, behold God. Then again, an earthly king is believed to exist, even though he be not seen by all, for he is recognised by his laws and ordinances, and authorities, and forces, and statues; and are you unwilling that God should be recognised by His works and mighty deeds?

CHAP. VI.— GOD IS KNOWN BY HIS WORKS.

Consider, O man, His works, — the timely rotation of the seasons, and the changes of temperature; the regular march of the stars; the well-ordered course of days and nights, and months, and years; the various beauty of seeds, and plants, and fruits; and the divers species[5] of quadrupeds, and birds, and reptiles, and fishes, both of the rivers and of the sea; or consider the instinct implanted in these animals to beget and rear offspring, not for their own profit, but for the use of man; and the providence with which God provides nourishment for all flesh, or the subjection in which He has ordained that all things subserve mankind. Consider, too, the flowing of sweet fountains and never-failing rivers, and the seasonable supply of dews, and showers, and rains; the manifold movement of the heavenly bodies, the morning star rising and heralding the approach of the perfect luminary; and the constellation of Pleiades, and Orion, and Arcturus, and the orbit of the other stars that circle through the heavens, all of which the manifold wisdom of

---

[1] The translation here follows the Hamburg editor, others read, "If Father, I say everything"
[2] Maranus observes that Theophilus means to indicate the difference between God's chastisement of the righteous and His punishment of the wicked.
[3] [Kaye's *Justin*, p. 173.]

[4] The reference here is not to the Holy Spirit, but to that vital power which is supposed to be diffused throughout the universe. Comp. book ii. 4.
[5] Literally, "propagation."

God has called by names of their own. He is God alone who made light out of darkness, and brought forth light from His treasures, and formed the chambers of the south wind,[1] and the treasure-houses of the deep, and the bounds of the seas, and the treasuries of snows and hail-storms, collecting the waters in the store-houses of the deep, and the darkness in His treasures, and bringing forth the sweet, and desirable, and pleasant light out of His treas-ures; "who causeth the vapours to ascend from the ends of the earth: He maketh lightnings for the rain;"[2] who sends forth His thunder to terrify, and foretells by the lightning the peal of the thunder, that no soul may faint with the sudden shock; and who so moderates the vio-lence of the lightning as it flashes out of heaven, that it does not consume the earth; for, if the lightning were allowed all its power, it would burn up the earth; and were the thunder allowed all its power, it would overthrow all the works that are therein.

CHAP. VII. — WE SHALL SEE GOD WHEN WE PUT ON IMMORTALITY.

This is my God, the Lord of all, who alone stretched out the heaven, and established the breadth of the earth under it; who stirs the deep recesses of the sea, and makes its waves roar; who rules its power, and stills the tumult of its waves; who founded the earth upon the waters, and gave a spirit to nourish it; whose breath giveth light to the whole, who, if He with-draw His breath, the whole will utterly fail. By Him you speak, O man; His breath you breathe, yet Him you know not. And this is your condi-tion, because of the blindness of your soul, and the hardness of your heart. But, if you will, you may be healed. Entrust yourself to the Physician, and He will couch the eyes of your soul and of your heart. Who is the Physician? God, who heals and makes alive through His word and wisdom. God by His own word and wisdom made all things; for "by His word were the heavens made, and all the host of them by the breath of His mouth."[3] Most excellent is His wisdom. By His wisdom God founded the earth; and by knowledge He prepared the heavens; and by understanding were the foun-tains of the great deep broken up, and the clouds poured out their dews. If thou perceivest these things, O man, living chastely, and holily, and righteously, thou canst see God. But before all let faith and the fear of God have rule in thy heart, and then shalt thou understand these things. When thou shalt have put off the mor-tal, and put on incorruption, then shalt thou see

God worthily. For God will raise thy flesh immortal with thy soul; and then, having be-come immortal, thou shalt see the Immortal, if now you believe on Him; and then you shall know that you have spoken unjustly against Him.

CHAP. VIII. — FAITH REQUIRED IN ALL MATTERS.

But you do not believe that the dead are raised. When the resurrection shall take place, then you will believe, whether you will or no; and your faith shall be reckoned for unbelief, unless you believe now. And why do you not believe? Do you not know that faith is the leading principle in all matters? For what hus-bandman can reap, unless he first trust his seed to the earth? Or who can cross the sea, unless he first entrust himself to the boat and the pilot? And what sick person can be healed, unless first he trust himself to the care of the physician? And what art or knowledge can any one learn, unless he first apply and entrust himself to the teacher? If, then, the husbandman trusts the earth, and the sailor the boat, and the sick the physician, will you not place confidence in God, even when you hold so many pledges at His hand? For first He created you out of nothing, and brought you into existence (for if your father was not, nor your mother, much more were you yourself at one time not in being), and formed you out of a small and moist substance, even out of the least drop, which at one time had itself no being; and God introduced you into this life. Moreover, you believe that the images made by men are gods, and do great things; and can you not believe that the God who made you is able also to make you after-wards?[4]

CHAP. IX. — IMMORALITIES OF THE GODS.

And, indeed, the names of those whom you say you worship, are the names of dead men. And these, too, who and what kind of men were they? Is not Saturn found to be a cannibal, destroying and devouring his own children? And if you name his son Jupiter, hear also his deeds and conduct — first, how he was suckled by a goat on Mount Ida, and having slain it, accord-ing to the myths, and flayed it, he made him-self a coat of the hide. And his other deeds, — his incest, and adultery, and lust, — will be bet-ter recounted by Homer and the rest of the poets. Why should I further speak of his sons? How Hercules burnt himself; and about the drunk and raging Bacchus; and of Apollo fear-ing and fleeing from Achilles, and falling in love with Daphne, and being unaware of the fate of Hyacinthus; and of Venus wounded, and of

---

[1] Job ix 9
[2] Ps. cxxxv. 7.
[3] Ps xxxiii. 6.

[4] i.e , in the resurrection.

Mars, the pest of mortals; and of the ichor flowing from the so-called gods. And these, indeed, are the milder kinds of legends; since the god who is called Osiris is found to have been torn limb from limb, whose mysteries are celebrated annually, as if he had perished, and were being found, and sought for limb by limb. For neither is it known whether he perished, nor is it shown whether he is found. And why should I speak of Atys mutilated, or of Adonis wandering in the wood, and wounded by a boar while hunting; or of Æsculapius struck by a thunderbolt; or of the fugitive Serapis chased from Sinope to Alexandria; or of the Scythian Diana, herself, too, a fugitive, and a homicide, and a huntress, and a passionate lover of Endymion? Now, it is not we who publish these things, but your own writers and poets.

CHAP. X. — ABSURDITIES OF IDOLATRY.

Why should I further recount the multitude of animals worshipped by the Egyptians, both reptiles, and cattle, and wild beasts, and birds, and river-fishes; and even wash-pots [1] and disgraceful noises? [2] But if you cite the Greeks and the other nations, they worship stones and wood, and other kinds of material substances, — the images, as we have just been saying, of dead men. For Phidias is found in Pisa making for the Eleians the Olympian Jupiter, and at Athens the Minerva of the Acropolis. And I will inquire of you, my friend, how many Jupiters exist. For there is, firstly, Jupiter surnamed Olympian, then Jupiter Latiaris, and Jupiter Cassius, and Jupiter Tonans, and Jupiter Propator, and Jupiter Pannychius, and Jupiter Poliuchus, and Jupiter Capitolinus; and that Jupiter, the son of Saturn, who is king of the Cretans, has a tomb in Crete, but the rest, possibly, were not thought worthy of tombs. And if you speak of the mother of those who are called gods, far be it from me to utter with my lips her deeds, or the deeds of those by whom she is worshipped (for it is unlawful for us so much as to name such things), and what vast taxes and revenues she and her sons furnish to the king. For these are not gods, but idols, as we have already said, the works of men's hands and unclean demons. And such may all those become who make them and put their trust in them!

CHAP. XI. — THE KING TO BE HONOURED, GOD TO BE WORSHIPPED.

Wherefore I will rather honour the king [than your gods], not, indeed, worshipping him, but praying for him. But God, the living and true God, I worship, knowing that the king is made by Him. You will say, then, to me, "Why do you not worship the king?" Because he is not made to be worshipped, but to be reverenced with lawful honour, for he is not a god, but a man appointed by God, not to be worshipped, but to judge justly. For in a kind of way his government is committed to him by God: as He will not have those called kings whom He has appointed under Himself; for "king" is his title, and it is not lawful for another to use it; so neither is it lawful for any to be worshipped but God only. Wherefore, O man, you are wholly in error. Accordingly, honour the king, be subject to him, and pray for him with loyal mind; for if you do this, you do the will of God. For the law that is of God, says, "My son, fear thou the Lord and the king, and be not disobedient to them; for suddenly they shall take vengeance on their enemies." [3]

CHAP. XII. — MEANING OF THE NAME CHRISTIAN.

And about your laughing at me and calling me "Christian," you know not what you are saying. First, because that which is anointed [4] is sweet and serviceable, and far from contemptible. For what ship can be serviceable and seaworthy, unless it be first caulked [anointed]? Or what castle or house is beautiful and serviceable when it has not been anointed? And what man, when he enters into this life or into the gymnasium, is not anointed with oil? And what work has either ornament or beauty unless it be anointed and burnished? Then the air and all that is under heaven is in a certain sort anointed by light and spirit; and are you unwilling to be anointed with the oil of God? Wherefore we are called Christians on this account, because we are anointed with the oil of God. [5]

CHAP. XIII. — THE RESURRECTION PROVED BY EXAMPLES.

Then, as to your denying that the dead are raised — for you say, [6] "Show me even one who has been raised from the dead, that seeing I may believe," — first, what great thing is it if you believe when you have seen the thing done? Then, again, you believe that Hercules, who burned himself, lives; and that Æsculapius, who

---

[1] [Foot-baths. A reference to Amasis, and his story in Herodotus, ii. 172. See *Rawlinson's Version and Notes*, vol. ii. p. 221, *ed.* Appletons, 1859. See also Athenagoras, *infra*, *Embassy*, cap. xxvi.]

[2] [The fable of Echo and her shameful gossip may serve for an example.]

[3] Prov. xxiv. 21, 22. The Greek of Theophilus has "honour" instead of "fear."

[4] "The argumentation of this chapter depends on the literal meaning which Theophilus attaches to *Christos*, the Anointed One; and he plays on this meaning, and also on the similarity of pronunciation between χρηστός, 'useful,' and χριστός, 'anointed.'" — DONALDSON.

[5] [Not material oil probably, for it is not mentioned in such Scriptures as Acts viii. 17, xix 6, Heb. vi. 2; but the anointing (1 John ii. 20) of the Holy Ghost. As a symbol, oil was used at an early period, however; and the Latins are not slow to press this in favour of material oil in the *chrism*, or confirmation.]

[6] [This is the famous challenge which affords Gibbon (cap. xv.) a most pleasing opportunity for his cavils. But our author was not asserting that the dead was raised in his day, but only that they should be at the last day.]

was struck with lightning, was raised; and do you disbelieve the things that are told you by God? But, suppose I should show you a dead man raised and alive, even this you would disbelieve. God indeed exhibits to you many proofs that you may believe Him. For consider, if you please, the dying of seasons, and days, and nights, how these also die and rise again. And what? Is there not a resurrection going on of seeds and fruits, and this, too, for the use of men? A seed of wheat, for example, or of the other grains, when it is cast into the earth, first dies and rots away, then is raised, and becomes a stalk of corn. And the nature of trees and fruit-trees, — is it not that according to the appointment of God they produce their fruits in their seasons out of what has been unseen and invisible? Moreover, sometimes also a sparrow or some of the other birds, when in drinking it has swallowed a seed of apple or fig, or something else, has come to some rocky hillock or tomb, and has left the seed in its droppings, and the seed, which was once swallowed, and has passed though so great a heat, now striking root, a tree has grown up. And all these things does the wisdom of God effect, in order to manifest even by these things, that God is able to effect the general resurrection of all men. And if you would witness a more wonderful sight, which may prove a resurrection not only of earthly but of heavenly bodies, consider the resurrection of the moon, which occurs monthly; how it wanes, dies, and rises again. Hear further, O man, of the work of resurrection going on in yourself, even though you are unaware of it. For perhaps you have sometimes fallen sick, and lost flesh, and strength, and beauty; but when you received again from God mercy and healing, you picked up again in flesh and appearance, and recovered also your strength. And as you do not know where your flesh went away and disappeared to, so neither do you know whence it grew, or whence it came again. But you will say, "From meats and drinks changed into blood." Quite so; but this, too, is the work of God, who thus operates, and not of any other.

CHAP. XIV. — THEOPHILUS AN EXAMPLE OF CONVERSION.

Therefore, do not be sceptical, but believe; for I myself also used to disbelieve that this would take place, but now, having taken these things into consideration, I believe. At the same time, I met with the sacred Scriptures [1] of the holy prophets, who also by the Spirit of God foretold the things that have already happened, just as they came to pass, and the things now occurring as they are now happening, and things future in the order in which they shall be accomplished. Admitting, therefore, the proof which events happening as predicted afford, I do not disbelieve, but I believe, obedient to God, whom, if you please, do you also submit to, believing Him, lest if now you continue unbelieving, you be convinced hereafter, when you are tormented with eternal punishments; which punishments, when they had been foretold by the prophets, the later-born poets and philosophers stole from the holy Scriptures, to make their doctrines worthy of credit. Yet these also have spoken beforehand of the punishments that are to light upon the profane and unbelieving, in order that none be left without a witness, or be able to say, "We have not heard, neither have we known." But do you also, if you please, give reverential attention to the prophetic Scriptures, [2] and they will make your way plainer for escaping the eternal punishments, and obtaining the eternal prizes of God. For He who gave the mouth for speech, and formed the ear to hear, and made the eye to see, will examine all things, and will judge righteous judgment, rendering merited awards to each. To those who by patient continuance in well-doing [3] seek immortality, He will give life everlasting, joy, peace, rest, and abundance of good things, which neither hath eye seen, nor ear heard, nor hath it entered into the heart of man to conceive. [4] But to the unbelieving and despisers, who obey not the truth, but are obedient to unrighteousness, when they shall have been filled with adulteries and fornications, and filthiness, and covetousness, and unlawful idolatries, there shall be anger and wrath, tribulation and anguish, [5] and at the last everlasting fire shall possess such men. Since you said, "Show me thy God," this is my God, and I counsel you to fear Him and to trust Him.

---

[1] [Ps. cxix. 130. Note this tribute to the inspired Scriptures and their converting power; I might almost say their sacramental energy, referring to John vi. 63.]

[2] [Rev. xix. 10. I cannot reconcile what Scripture says of itself with the modern *refinements* as to the human and divine element, while fully admitting that there are such elements, intermixed and interpenetrated mutually, beyond all power of dissection by us. I prefer the childlike docility of the Fathers.]

[3] Rom. ii. 7.

[4] 1 Cor. ii. 9.

[5] Rom. ii. 8, 9.

THEOPHILUS TO AUTOLYCUS

BOOK II

CHAP. I. — OCCASION OF WRITING THIS BOOK.

WHEN we had formerly some conversation, my very good friend Autolycus, and when you inquired who was my God, and for a little paid attention to my discourse, I made some explanations to you concerning my religion; and then having bid one another adieu, we went with much mutual friendliness each to his own house, although at first you had borne somewhat hard upon me. For you know and remember that you supposed our doctrine was foolishness. As you then afterwards urged me to do, I am desirous, though not educated to the art of speaking, of more accurately demonstrating, by means of this tractate, the vain labour and empty worship in which you are held; and I wish also, from a few of your own histories which you read, and perhaps do not yet quite understand, to make the truth plain to you.

CHAP. II. — THE GODS ARE DESPISED WHEN THEY ARE MADE; BUT BECOME VALUABLE WHEN BOUGHT.

And in truth it does seem to me absurd that statuaries and carvers, or painters, or moulders, should both design and paint, and carve, and mould, and prepare gods, who, when they are produced by the artificers, are reckoned of no value; but as soon as they are purchased[1] by some and placed in some so-called temple, or in some house, not only do those who bought them sacrifice to them, but also those who made and sold them come with much devotion, and apparatus of sacrifice, and libations, to worship them; and they reckon them gods, not seeing that they are just such as when they were made by themselves, whether stone, or brass, or wood, or colour, or some other material. And this is your case, too, when you read the histories and genealogies of the so-called gods. For when you read of their births, you think of them as men, but afterwards you call them gods, and worship them, not reflecting nor understanding that, when born, they are exactly such beings as ye read of before.

CHAP. III. — WHAT HAS BECOME OF THE GODS?

And of the gods of former times, if indeed they were begotten, the generation was sufficiently prolific. But now, where is their generation exhibited? For if of old they begot and were begotten, it is plain that even to the present time there should be gods begotten and born; or at least if it be not so, such a race will be reckoned impotent. For either they have waxed old, and on that account no longer beget, or they have died out and no longer exist. For if the gods were begotten, they ought to be born even until now, as men, too, are born; yea, much more numerous should the gods be than men, as the Sibyl says: —

"For if the gods beget, and each remains
    Immortal, then the race of gods must be
    More numerous than mortals, and the throng
    So great that mortals find no room to stand."

For if the children begotten of men who are mortal and short-lived make an appearance even until now, and men have not ceased to be born, so that cities and villages are full, and even the country places also are inhabited, how ought not the gods, who, according to your poets, do not die, much rather to beget and be begotten, since you say that the gods were produced by generation? And why was the mount which is called Olympus formerly inhabited by the gods, but now lies deserted? Or why did Jupiter, in days of yore, dwell on Ida, and was known to dwell there, according to Homer and other poets, but now is beyond ken? And why was he found only in one part of the earth, and not everywhere? For either he neglected the other parts, or was not able to be present everywhere and provide for all. For if he were, e.g., in an eastern place, he was not in the western; and if, on the other hand, he were present in the western

---

[1] The words "by some and placed in" are omitted in some editions, but occur in the best MSS.

parts, he was not in the eastern. But this is the attribute of God, the Highest and Almighty, and the living God, not only to be everywhere present, but also to see all things and to hear all, and by no means to be confined in a place; for if He were, then the place containing Him would be greater than He; for that which contains is greater than that which is contained. For God is not contained, but is Himself the place of all. But why has Jupiter left Ida? Was it because he died, or did that mountain no longer please him? And where has he gone? To heaven? No. But you will perhaps say, To Crete? Yes, for there, too, his tomb is shown to this day. Again, you will say, To Pisa, where he reflects glory on the hands of Phidias to this day. Let us, then, proceed to the writings of the philosophers and poets.

CHAP. IV. — ABSURD OPINIONS OF THE PHILOSOPHERS CONCERNING GOD.

Some of the philosophers of the Porch say that there is no God at all; or, if there is, they say that He cares for none but Himself; and these views the folly of Epicurus and Chrysippus has set forth at large. And others say that all things are produced without external agency, and that the world is uncreated, and that nature is eternal;[1] and have dared to give out that there is no providence of God at all, but maintain that God is only each man's conscience. And others again maintain that the spirit which pervades all things is God. But Plato and those of his school acknowledge indeed that God is uncreated, and the Father and Maker of all things; but then they maintain that matter as well as God is uncreated, and aver that it is coeval with God. But if God is uncreated and matter uncreated, God is no longer, according to the Platonists, the Creator of all things, nor, so far as their opinions hold, is the monarchy[2] of God established. And further, as God, because He is uncreated, is also unalterable; so if matter, too, were uncreated, it also would be unalterable, and equal to God; for that which is created is mutable and alterable, but that which is uncreated is immutable and unalterable. And what great thing is it if God made the world out of existent materials?[3] For even a human artist, when he gets material from some one, makes of it what he pleases. But the power of God is manifested in this, that out of things that are not He makes whatever He pleases; just as the bestowal of life and motion is the prerogative of no other than God alone. For even man makes indeed an image, but reason and breath, or feeling, he cannot give to what he

has made. But God has this property in excess of what man can do, in that He makes a work, endowed with reason, life, sensation. As, therefore, in all these respects God is more powerful than man, so also in this; that out of things that are not He creates and has created things that are, and whatever He pleases, as He pleases.

CHAP. V. — OPINIONS OF HOMER AND HESIOD CONCERNING THE GODS.

So that the opinion of your philosophers and authors is discordant; for while the former have propounded the foregoing opinions, the poet Homer is found explaining the origin not only of the world, but also of the gods, on quite another hypothesis. For he says somewhere:[4]—

"Father of Gods, Oceanus, and she
　Who bare the gods, their mother Tethys, too,
　From whom all rivers spring, and every sea."

In saying which, however, he does not present God to us. For who does not know that the ocean is water? But if water, then not God. God indeed, if He is the creator of all things, as He certainly is, is the creator both of the water and of the seas. And Hesiod himself also declared the origin, not only of the gods, but also of the world itself. And though he said that the world was created, he showed no inclination to tell us by whom it was created. Besides, he said that Saturn, and his sons Jupiter, Neptune, and Pluto, were gods, though we find that they are later born than the world. And he also relates how Saturn was assailed in war by his own son Jupiter; for he says:[5]—

"His father Saturn he by might o'ercame,
　And 'mong th' immortals ruled with justice wise,
　And honours fit distributed to each.

Then he introduces in his poem the daughters of Jupiter, whom he names Muses, and as whose suppliant he appears, desiring to ascertain from them how all things were made; for he says:[6]—

"Daughters of Jove, all hail! Grant me your aid
　That I in numbers sweet and well-arrayed,
　Of the immortal gods may sing the birth;
　Who of the starry heav'ns were born, and earth;
　Who, springing from the murky night at first,
　Were by the briny ocean reared and nursed.
　Tell, too, who form unto the earth first gave,
　And rivers, and the boundless sea whose wave
　Unwearied sinks, then rears its crest on high;
　And how was spread yon glittering canopy
　Of glistening stars that stud the wide-spread heaven.
　Whence sprang the gods by whom all good is given?
　Tell from their hands what varied gifts there came,
　Riches to some, to others wealth, or fame;
　How they have dwelt from the remotest time
　In many-nooked Olympus' sunny clime.
　These things, ye Muses, say, who ever dwell
　Among Olympian shades — since ye can tell:
　From the beginning there thy feet have strayed;
　Then tell us which of all things first was made.

---

[1] This is according to the Benedictine reading: the reading of Wolf, "nature is left to itself," is also worthy of consideration.
[2] That is, the existence of God as sole first principle.
[3] Literally, "subject-matter."

[4] *Il.*, xiv. 201.
[5] Hesiod, *Theog.*, 74.
[6] *Theog.*, 104.

But how could the Muses, who are younger than the world, know these things? Or how could they relate to Hesiod [what was happening], when their father was not yet born?

CHAP. VI. — HESIOD ON THE ORIGIN OF THE WORLD.

And in a certain way he indeed admits matter [as self-existent] and the creation of the world [without a creator], saying : [1] —

" First of all things was chaos made, and next
Broad-bosom'd earth's foundations firm were fixed,
Where safely the immortals dwell for aye,
Who in the snowy-peak'd Olympus stay.
Afterwards gloomy Tartarus had birth
In the recesses of broad-pathwayed earth,
And Love, ev'n among gods most beauteous still,
Who comes all-conquering, bending mind and will,
Delivering from care, and giving then
Wise counsel in the breasts of gods and men.
From chaos Erebus and night were born,
From night and Erebus sprung air and morn.
Earth in her likeness made the starry heaven,
That unto all things shelter might be given,
And that the blessed gods might there repose.
The lofty mountains by her power arose,
For the wood-nymphs she made the pleasant caves,
Begot the sterile sea with all his waves,
Loveless; but when by heaven her love was sought,
Then the deep-eddying ocean forth she brought."

And saying this, he has not yet explained by whom all this was made. For if chaos existed in the beginning, and matter of some sort, being uncreated, was previously existing, who was it that effected the change on its condition, and gave it a different order and shape? Did matter itself alter its own form and arrange itself into a world (for Jupiter was born, not only long after matter, but long after the world and many men ; and so, too, was his father Saturn), or was there some ruling power which made it ; I mean, of course, God, who also fashioned it into a world? Besides, he is found in every way to talk nonsense, and to contradict himself. For when he mentions earth, and sky, and sea, he gives us to understand that from these the gods were produced ; and from these again [the gods] he declares that certain very dreadful men were sprung, — the race of the Titans and the Cyclopes, and a crowd of giants, and of the Egyptian gods, — or, rather, vain men, as Apollonides, surnamed Horapius, mentions in the book entitled *Semenouthi*, and in his other histories concerning the worship of the Egyptians and their kings, and the vain labours in which they engaged.[2]

CHAP. VII. — FABULOUS HEATHEN GENEALOGIES.

Why need I recount the Greek fables, — of Pluto, king of darkness, of Neptune descending beneath the sea, and embracing Melanippe and begetting a cannibal son, — or the many tales your writers have woven into their tragedies concerning the sons of Jupiter, and whose pedigree they register because they were born men, and not gods? And the comic poet Aristophanes, in the play called " The Birds," having taken upon him to handle the subject of the Creation, said that in the beginning the world was produced from an egg, saying : [3] —

" A windy egg was laid by black-winged night
At first."

But Satyrus, also giving a history of the Alexandrine families, beginning from Philopator, who was also named Ptolemy, gives out that Bacchus was his progenitor ; wherefore also Ptolemy was the founder of this [4] family. Satyrus then speaks thus : That Dejanira was born of Bacchus and Althea, the daughter of Thestius ; and from her and Hercules the son of Jupiter there sprang, as I suppose, Hyllus ; and from him Cleodemus, and from him Aristomachus, and from him Temenus, and from him Ceisus, and from him Maron, and from him Thestrus, and from him Acous, and from him Aristomidas, and from him Caranus, and from him Cœnus, and from him Tyrimmas, and from him Perdiccas, and from him Philip, and from him Æropus, and from him Alcetas, and from him Amyntas, and from him Bocrus, and from him Meleager, and from him Arsinoë, and from her and Lagus Ptolemy Soter, and from him and Arsinoe Ptolemy Euergetes, and from him and Berenice, daughter of Maga, king of Cyrene, Ptolemy Philopator. Thus, then, stands the relationship of the Alexandrine kings to Bacchus. And therefore in the Dionysian tribe there are distinct families : the Althean from Althea, who was the wife of Dionysus and daughter of Thestius ; the family of Dejanira also, from her who was the daughter of Dionysus and Althea, and wife of Hercules ; — whence, too, the families have their names : the family of Ariadne, from Ariadne, daughter of Minos and wife of Dionysus, a dutiful daughter, who had intercourse with Dionysus in another form ; the Thestian, from Thestius, the father of Althea ; the Thoantian, from Thoas, son of Dionysus ; the Staphylian, from Staphylus, son of Dionysus ; the Euænian, from Eunous, son of Dionysus ; the Maronian, from Maron, son of Ariadne and Dionysus ; — for all these are sons of Dionysus. And, indeed, many other names were thus originated, and exist to this day ; as the Heraclidæ from Hercules, and the Apollonidæ from Apollo, and the Poseidonii from Poseidon, and from Zeus the Dii and Diogenæ.

---

[1] [*Theog.*, 116-133. S.]
[2] The Benedictine editor proposes to read these words after the first clause of c. 7. We follow the reading of Wolf and Fell, who understand the pyramids to be referred to.

[3] Aristoph., *Av.*, 694. A wind-egg being one produced without impregnation, and coming to nothing.
[4] The Dionysian family taking its name from Dionysus or Bacchus.

CHAP. VIII. — OPINIONS CONCERNING PROVIDENCE.

And why should I recount further the vast array of such names and genealogies? So that all the authors and poets, and those called philosophers, are wholly deceived; and so, too, are they who give heed to them. For they plentifully composed fables and foolish stories about their gods, and did not exhibit them as gods, but as men, and men, too, of whom some were drunken, and others fornicators and murderers. But also concerning the origin of the world, they uttered contradictory and absurd opinions. First, some of them, as we before explained, maintained that the world is uncreated. And those that said it was uncreated and self-producing contradicted those who propounded that it was created. For by conjecture and human conception they spoke, and not knowing the truth. And others, again, said that there was a providence, and destroyed the positions of the former writers. Aratus, indeed, says:[1] —

"From Jove begin my song; nor ever be
The name unuttered: all are full of thee;
The ways and haunts of men; the heavens and sea:
On thee our being hangs; in thee we move;
All are thy offspring and the seed of Jove.
Benevolent, he warns mankind to good,
Urges to toil and prompts the hope of food.
He tells where cattle best may graze, and where
The soil, deep-furrowed, yellow grain will bear.
What time the husbandman should plant or sow,
'Tis his to tell, 'tis his alone to know."

Who, then, shall we believe: Aratus as here quoted, or Sophocles, when he says:[2] —

"And foresight of the future there is none;
'Tis best to live at random, as one can"?

And Homer, again, does not agree with this, for he says[3] that virtue

"Waxes or wanes in men as Jove decrees."

And Simonides says: —

"No man nor state has virtue save from God;
Counsel resides in God; and wretched man
Has in himself nought but his wretchedness."

So, too, Euripides: —

"Apart from God, there's nothing owned by men."

And Menander: —

"Save God alone, there's none for us provides."

And Euripides again: —

"For when God wills to save, all things He'll bend
To serve as instruments to work His end."

And Thestius: —

"If God design to save you, safe you are,
Though sailing in mid-ocean on a mat."[4]

And saying numberless things of a like kind, they contradicted themselves. At least Sophocles, who in another place denied Providence, says: —

"No mortal can evade the stroke of God."

Besides, they both introduced a multitude of gods, and yet spoke of a Unity; and against those who affirmed a Providence they maintained in opposition that there was no Providence. Wherefore Euripides says: —

"We labour much and spend our strength in vain,
For empty hope, not foresight, is our guide."

And without meaning to do so, they acknowledge that they know not the truth; but being inspired by demons and puffed up by them, they spoke at their instance whatever they said. For indeed the poets, — Homer, to wit, and Hesiod, being, as they say, inspired by the Muses, — spoke from a deceptive fancy,[5] and not with a pure but an erring spirit. And this, indeed, clearly appears from the fact, that even to this day the possessed are sometimes exorcised in the name of the living and true God; and these spirits of error themselves confess that they are demons who also formerly inspired these writers. But sometimes some of them wakened up in soul, and, that they might be for a witness both to themselves and to all men, spoke things in harmony with the prophets regarding the monarchy of God, and the judgment and such like.

CHAP. IX. — THE PROPHETS INSPIRED BY THE HOLY GHOST.

But men of God carrying in them a holy spirit[6] and becoming prophets, being inspired and made wise by God, became God-taught, and holy, and righteous. Wherefore they were also deemed worthy of receiving this reward, that they should become instruments of God, and contain the wisdom that is from Him, through which wisdom they uttered both what regarded the creation of the world and all other things. For they predicted also pestilences, and famines, and wars. And there was not one or two, but many, at various times and seasons among the Hebrews; and also among the Greeks there was the Sibyl; and they all have spoken things consistent and harmonious with each other, both what happened before them and what happened in their own time, and what things are now being fulfilled in our own day: wherefore we are persuaded also concerning the future things that they will fall out, as also the first have been accomplished.

CHAP. X. — THE WORLD CREATED BY GOD THROUGH THE WORD.

And first, they taught us with one consent that

---

[1] The following lines are partly from the translation of Hughes.
[2] Œdipus Rex, line 978.
[3] Il., xx. 242.
[4] This verse is by Plutarch hesitatingly attributed to Pindar. The expression, "Though you swim in a wicker basket," was proverbial.

[5] Literally, "in fancy and error."
[6] Wolf prefers πνευματόφοροι, carried or borne along by the Spirit. [Kaye's Justin M., p. 180, comparing this view of the inspiration of prophets, with those of Justin and Athenagoras.]

God made all things out of nothing; for nothing was coeval with God: but He being His own place, and wanting nothing, and existing before the ages, willed to make man by whom He might be known; for him, therefore, He prepared the world. For he that is created is also needy; but he that is uncreated stands in need of nothing. God, then, having His own Word internal[1] within His own bowels, begat Him, emitting[2] Him along with His own wisdom before all things. He had this Word as a helper in the things that were created by Him, and by Him He made all things. He is called "governing principle" [ἀρχή], because He rules, and is Lord of all things fashioned by Him. He, then, being Spirit of God, and governing principle, and wisdom, and power of the highest, came down upon the prophets, and through them spake of the creation of the world and of all other things. For the prophets were not when the world came into existence, but the wisdom of God which was in Him, and His holy Word which was always present with Him. Wherefore He speaks thus by the prophet Solomon: "When He prepared the heavens I was there, and when He appointed the foundations of the earth I was by Him as one brought up with Him."[3] And Moses, who lived many years before Solomon, or, rather, the Word of God by him as by an instrument, says, "In the beginning God created the heavens and the earth." First he named the "beginning,"[4] and "creation,"[5] then he thus introduced God; for not lightly and on slight occasion is it right to name God. For the divine wisdom foreknew that some would trifle and name a multitude of gods that do not exist. In order, therefore, that the living God might be known by His works, and that [it might be known that] by His Word God created the heavens and the earth, and all that is therein, he said, "In the beginning God created the heavens and the earth." Then having spoken of their creation, he explains to us: "And the earth was without form, and void, and darkness was upon the face of the deep; and the Spirit of God moved upon the water." This, sacred Scripture teaches at the outset, to show that matter, from which God made and fashioned the world, was in some manner created, being produced by God.[6]

CHAP. XI. — THE SIX DAYS' WORK DESCRIBED.

Now, the beginning of the creation is light; since light manifests the things that are created. Wherefore it is said: "And God said, Let light be,[7] and light was; and God saw the light, that it was good," manifestly made good for man. "And God divided the light from the darkness; and God called the light Day, and the darkness He called Night. And the evening and the morning were the first day. And God said, Let there be a firmament in the midst of the waters, and let it divide the waters from the waters: and it was so. And God made the firmament, and divided the waters which were under the firmament from the waters which were above the firmament. And God called the firmament Heaven: and God saw that it was good. And the evening and the morning were the second day. And God said, Let the water under the heaven be gathered into one place, and let the dry land appear: and it was so. And the waters were gathered together into their places, and the dry land appeared. And God called the dry land Earth, and the gathering together of the waters He called Seas: and God saw that it was good. And God said, Let the earth bring forth grass, the herb yielding seed after his kind and in his likeness, and the fruit-tree yielding fruit after his kind, whose seed is in itself, in his likeness: and it was so. And the earth brought forth grass, the herb yielding seed after his kind, and the fruit-tree yielding fruit, whose seed was in itself, after his kind, on the earth: and God saw that it was good. And the evening and the morning were the third day. And God said, Let there be lights in the firmament of the heaven, to give light on earth, to divide the day from the night; and let them be for signs, and for seasons, and for days, and for years; and let them be for lights in the firmament of the heaven, to give light upon the earth: and it was so. And God made two great lights; the greater light to rule the day, and the lesser light to rule the night: He made the stars also. And God set them in the firmament of the heaven to give light upon the earth, and to rule over the day and over the night, and to divide the light from the darkness: and God saw that it was good. And the evening and the morning were the fourth day. And God said, Let the waters bring forth the creeping things that have life, and fowl flying over the earth in the firmament of

---

[1] ἐνδιάθετον. [Here the Logos is spoken of in the entire spirit of the Nicene Council. Ps. xlv. i is a favourite text against Arius; and (*Advs. Judæos.* b. ii. 3) Cyprian presses it against the Jews, which shows that they accepted the *Hebrew* and the *LXX.* in a mystical sense.]

[2] Literally, belching or vomiting. [The reference is to Ps. xlv. where the LXX. read ἐξηρεύξατο ἡ καρδία μου λόγον ἀγαθόν, and the Latin *eructavit cor meum bonum Verbum*; i.e., "My heart hath breathed forth a glorious Word." The well-chosen language of the translator (emitted) is degraded by his note.]

[3] Prov. viii. 27. Theophilus reads with the Septuagint, "I was with Him, putting things into order," instead of "I was by Him as one brought up with Him." [Here the Logos is the σοφία as with the Fathers generally; e.g., Cyprian, *Advs. Judæos*, book ii. 2. But see cap. xv. p. 101, *infra*.]

[4] That is, the first principle, whom he has just shown to be the Word.

[5] In the Greek version of Gen. i. 1, the word "created" stands before "God."

[6] Theophilus, therefore, understands that when in the first verse it is said that God created the earth, it is meant that He created the matter of which the earth is formed.

[7] The words, "and light was; and God saw the light, that it was good," are omitted in the two best MSS. and in some editions; but they seem to be necessary, and to have fallen out by the mistake of transcribers.

heaven: and it was so. And God created great whales, and every living creature that creepeth, which the waters brought forth after their kind, and every winged fowl after his kind: and God saw that it was good. And God blessed them, saying, Increase and multiply, and fill the waters of the sea, and let fowl multiply in the earth. And the evening and the morning were the fifth day. And God said, Let the earth bring forth the living creature after his kind, cattle, and creeping thing, and beast of the earth after his kind: and it was so. And God made the beasts of the earth after their kind, and the cattle after their kind, and all the creeping things of the earth. And God said, Let us make man in our image, after our likeness; and let them have dominion over the fish of the sea, and over the fowl of the heaven, and over the cattle, and over all the earth, and over every creeping thing that creepeth upon the earth. And God created man: in the image of God created He him; male and female created He them. And God blessed them, saying, Be fruitful, and multiply, and replenish the earth, and subdue it, and have dominion over the fish of the sea, and over the fowl of the heaven, and over all cattle, and over all the earth, and over all the creeping things that creep upon the earth. And God said, Behold I have given you every herb bearing seed, which is upon the face of all the earth, and every tree in the which is the fruit of a tree yielding seed; to you it shall be for meat, and to all the beasts of the earth, and to all the fowls of heaven, and to every creeping thing that creepeth upon the earth, which has in it the breath of life; every green herb for meat: and it was so. And God saw everything that He had made, and, behold, it was very good. And the evening and the morning were the sixth day. And the heaven and the earth were finished, and all the host of them. And on the sixth day God finished His works which He made, and rested on the seventh day from all His works which He made. And God blessed the seventh day, and sanctified it; because in it He rested from all His works which God began to create."

CHAP. XII. — THE GLORY OF THE SIX DAYS' WORK.

Of this six days' work no man can give a worthy explanation and description of all its parts, not though he had ten thousand tongues and ten thousand mouths; nay, though he were to live ten thousand years, sojourning in this life, not even so could he utter anything worthy of these things, on account of the exceeding greatness and riches of the wisdom of God which there is in the six days' work above narrated. Many writers indeed have imitated [the narration], and essayed to give an explanation of these things; yet, though they thence derived

some suggestions, both concerning the creation of the world and the nature of man, they have emitted no slightest spark of truth. And the utterances of the philosophers, and writers, and poets have an appearance of trustworthiness, on account of the beauty of their diction; but their discourse is proved to be foolish and idle, because the multitude of their nonsensical frivolities is very great; and not a stray morsel of truth is found in them. For even if any truth seems to have been uttered by them, it has a mixture of error. And as a deleterious drug, when mixed with honey or wine, or some other thing, makes the whole [mixture] hurtful and profitless; so also eloquence is in their case found to be labour in vain; yea, rather an injurious thing to those who credit it. Moreover, [they spoke] concerning the seventh day, which all men acknowledge; but the most know not that what among the Hebrews is called the "Sabbath," is translated into Greek the "Seventh" (ἑβδομάς), a name which is adopted by every nation, although they know not the reason of the appellation. And as for what the poet Hesiod says of Erebus being produced from chaos, as well as the earth and love which lords it over his [Hesiod's] gods and men, his dictum is shown to be idle and frigid, and quite foreign to the truth. For it is not meet that God be conquered by pleasure; since even men of temperance abstain from all base pleasure and wicked lust.

CHAP. XIII. — REMARKS ON THE CREATION OF THE WORLD.

Moreover, his [Hesiod's] human, and mean, and very weak conception, so far as regards God, is discovered in his beginning to relate the creation of all things from the earthly things here below. For man, being below, begins to build from the earth, and cannot in order make the roof, unless he has first laid the foundation. But the power of God is shown in this, that, first of all, He creates out of nothing, according to His will, the things that are made. "For the things which are impossible with men are possible with God."[1] Wherefore, also, the prophet mentioned that the creation of the heavens first of all took place, as a kind of roof, saying: "At the first God created the heavens"—that is, that by means of the "first" principle the heavens were made, as we have already shown. And by "earth" he means the ground and foundation, as by "the deep" he means the multitude of waters; and "darkness" he speaks of, on account of the heaven which God made covering the waters and the earth like a lid. And by the Spirit which is borne above the waters,

---

[1] Luke xviii. 27.

he means that which God gave for animating the creation, as he gave life to man,[1] mixing what is fine with what is fine. For the Spirit is fine, and the water is fine, that the Spirit may nourish the water, and the water penetrating everywhere along with the Spirit, may nourish creation. For the Spirit being one, and holding the place of light,[2] was between the water and the heaven, in order that the darkness might not in any way communicate with the heaven, which was nearer God, before God said, "Let there be light." The heaven, therefore, being like a dome-shaped covering, comprehended matter which was like a clod. And so another prophet, Isaiah by name, spoke in these words : "It is God who made the heavens as a vault, and stretched them as a tent to dwell in."[3] The command, then, of God, that is, His Word, shining as a lamp in an enclosed chamber, lit up all that was under heaven, when He had made light apart from the world.[4] And the light God called Day, and the darkness Night. Since man would not have been able to call the light Day, or the darkness Night, nor, indeed, to have given names to the other things, had not he received the nomenclature from God, who made the things themselves. In the very beginning, therefore, of the history and genesis of the world, the holy Scripture spoke not concerning this firmament [which we see], but concerning another heaven, which is to us invisible, after which this heaven which we see has been called "firmament," and to which half the water was taken up that it might serve for rains, and showers, and dews to mankind. And half the water was left on earth for rivers, and fountains, and seas. The water, then, covering all the earth, and specially its hollow places, God, through His Word, next caused the waters to be collected into one collection, and the dry land to become visible, which formerly had been invisible. The earth thus becoming visible, was yet without form. God therefore formed and adorned it[5] with all kinds of herbs, and seeds and plants.

CHAP. XIV.—THE WORLD COMPARED TO THE SEA.

Consider, further, their variety, and diverse beauty, and multitude, and how through them resurrection is exhibited, for a pattern of the resurrection of all men which is to be. For who that considers it will not marvel that a fig-tree is produced from a fig-seed, or that very huge trees grow from the other very little seeds? And we say that the world resembles the sea. For as the

sea, if it had not had the influx and supply of the rivers and fountains to nourish it, would long since have been parched by reason of its saltness ; so also the world, if it had not had the law of God and the prophets flowing and welling up sweetness, and compassion, and righteousness, and the doctrine of the holy commandments of God, would long ere now have come to ruin, by reason of the wickedness and sin which abound in it. And as in the sea there are islands, some of them habitable, and well-watered, and fruitful, with havens and harbours in which the storm-tossed may find refuge,—so God has given to the world which is driven and tempest-tossed by sins, assemblies[6]—we mean holy churches[7]—in which survive the doctrines of the truth, as in the island-harbours of good anchorage ; and into these run those who desire to be saved, being lovers of the truth, and wishing to escape the wrath and judgment of God. And as, again, there are other islands, rocky and without water, and barren, and infested by wild beasts, and uninhabitable, and serving only to injure navigators and the storm-tossed, on which ships are wrecked, and those driven among them perish,—so there are doctrines of error—I mean heresies[7]—which destroy those who approach them. For they are not guided by the word of truth ; but as pirates, when they have filled their vessels,[8] drive them on the fore-mentioned places, that they may spoil them : so also it happens in the case of those who err from the truth, that they are all totally ruined by their error.

CHAP. XV.—OF THE FOURTH DAY.

On the fourth day the luminaries were made ; because God, who possesses foreknowledge, knew the follies of the vain philosophers, that they were going to say, that the things which grow on the earth are produced from the heavenly bodies, so as to exclude God. In order, therefore, that the truth might be obvious, the plants and seeds were produced prior to the heavenly bodies, for what is posterior cannot produce that which is prior. And these contain the pattern and type of a great mystery. For the sun is a type of God, and the moon of man. And as the sun far surpasses the moon in power and glory, so far does God surpass man. And as the sun remains ever full, never becoming less, so does God always abide perfect, being full of all power, and understanding, and wisdom, and immortality, and all good. But the moon wanes monthly, and in a manner dies, being a type of man ; then it is born again, and is crescent, for a pattern of the future resurrection. In like manner also the

---

[1] [See book i. cap. v., *supra*, note 2; also, the important remark of Kaye, *Justin Martyr*, p. 179.]
[2] This follows the Benedictine reading. Other editors, as Humphrey, read [φωτὸς] τὼπον, " resembling light."
[3] Isa. xl. 22.
[4] Following Wolf's rendering.
[5] Or, suitably arranged and appointed it.

[6] Literally, synagogues.
[7] [The ports and happy havens beautifully contrasted with rocks and shoals and barren or inhospitable isles.]
[8] That is, as the Benedictine edition suggests, when they have filled them with unsuspecting passengers.

three days which were before the luminaries,[1] are types of the Trinity,[2] of God, and His Word, and His wisdom.[3] And the fourth is the type of man, who needs light, that so there may be God, the Word, wisdom, man. Wherefore also on the fourth day the lights were made. The disposition of the stars, too, contains a type of the arrangement and order of the righteous and pious, and of those who keep the law and commandments of God. For the brilliant and bright stars are an imitation of the prophets, and therefore they remain fixed, not declining, nor passing from place to place. And those which hold the second place in brightness, are types of the people of the righteous. And those, again, which change their position, and flee from place to place, which also are called planets,[4] they too are a type of the men who have wandered from God, abandoning His law and commandments.

CHAP. XVI. — OF THE FIFTH DAY.

On the fifth day the living creatures which proceed from the waters were produced, through which also is revealed the manifold wisdom of God in these things ; for who could count their multitude and very various kinds? Moreover, the things proceeding from the waters were blessed by God, that this also might be a sign of men's being destined to receive repentance and remission of sins, through the water and laver of regeneration, — as many as come to the truth, and are born again, and receive blessing from God. But the monsters of the deep and the birds of prey are a similitude of covetous men and transgressors. For as the fish and the fowls are of one nature, — some indeed abide in their natural state, and do no harm to those weaker than themselves, but keep the law of God, and eat of the seeds of the earth ; others of them, again, transgress the law of God, and eat flesh, and injure those weaker than themselves : thus, too, the righteous, keeping the law of God, bite and injure none, but live holily and righteously. But robbers, and murderers, and godless persons are like monsters of the deep, and wild beasts, and birds of prey ; for they virtually devour those weaker than themselves. The race, then, of fishes and of creeping things, though partaking of God's blessing, received no very distinguishing property.

CHAP. XVII. — OF THE SIXTH DAY.

And on the sixth day, God having made the quadrupeds, and wild beasts, and the land reptiles, pronounced no blessing upon them, reserving His blessing for man, whom He was about to create on the sixth day. The quadrupeds, too, and wild beasts, were made for a type of some men, who neither know nor worship God, but mind earthly things, and repent not. For those who turn from their iniquities and live righteously, in spirit fly upwards like birds, and mind the things that are above, and are well-pleasing to the will of God. But those who do not know nor worship God, are like birds which have wings, but cannot fly nor soar to the high things of God. Thus, too, though such persons are called men, yet being pressed down with sins, they mind grovelling and earthly things. And the animals are named wild beasts [θηρία], from their being hunted [θηρεύεσθαι], not as if they had been made evil or venomous from the first — for nothing was made evil by God,[5] but all things good, yea, very good, — but the sin in which man was concerned brought evil upon them. For when man transgressed, they also transgressed with him. For as, if the master of the house himself acts rightly, the domestics also of necessity conduct themselves well ; but if the master sins, the servants also sin with him ; so in like manner it came to pass, that in the case of man's sin, he being master, all that was subject to him sinned with him. When, therefore, man again shall have made his way back to his natural condition, and no longer does evil, those also shall be restored to their original gentleness.

CHAP. XVIII. — THE CREATION OF MAN.

But as to what relates to the creation of man, his own creation cannot be explained by man, though it is a succinct account of it which holy Scripture gives. For when God said, "Let Us make man in Our image, after Our likeness," He first intimates the dignity of man. For God having made all things by His Word, and having reckoned them all mere bye-works, reckons the creation of man to be the only work worthy of His own hands. Moreover, God is found, as if needing help, to say, "Let Us make man in Our image, after Our likeness." But to no one else than to His own Word and wisdom did He say, "Let Us make." And when He had made and blessed him, that he might increase and replenish the earth, He put all things under his dominion, and at his service ; and He appointed from the first that he should find nutriment from the fruits of the earth, and from seeds, and herbs, and acorns, having at the same time appointed that

---

[1] Following Wolf's reading.

[2] Τριάδος. [The earliest use of this word "Trinity." It seems to have been used by this writer in his lost works, also; and, as a learned friend suggests, the use he makes of it is familiar. He does not lug it in as something novel : "types of the Trinity," he says, illustrating an accepted word, not introducing a new one.]

[3] [An eminent authority says, "It is certain, that, according to the notions of Theophilus, God, His Word, and His wisdom constitute a Trinity; and it should seem a Trinity of persons." He notes that the title σοφία, is here assigned to the Holy Spirit, although he himself elsewhere gives this title to the Son (book ii. cap. x., *supra*), as is more usual with the Fathers." Consult Kaye's *Justin Martyr*, p. 157. Ed. 1853.]

[4] i.e., wandering stars.

[5] [Note the solid truth that God is not the author of evil, and the probable suggestion that all nature sympathized with man's transgression. Rom. viii. 22.]

the animals be of habits similar tom an's, that they also might eat of all the seeds of the earth.

CHAP. XIX. — MAN IS PLACED IN PARADISE.

God having thus completed the heavens, and the earth, and the sea, and all that are in them, on the sixth day, rested on the seventh day from all His works which He made. Then holy Scripture gives a summary in these words: "This is the book of the generation of the heavens and the earth, when they were created, in the day that the LORD made the heavens and the earth, and every green thing of the field, before it was made, and every herb of the field before it grew. For God had not caused it to rain upon the earth, and there was not a man to till the ground."[1] By this He signifies to us, that the whole earth was at that time watered by a divine fountain, and had no need that man should till it; but the earth produced all things spontaneously by the command of God, that man might not be wearied by tilling it. But that the creation of man might be made plain, so that there should not seem to be an insoluble problem existing among men, since God had said, "Let Us make man;" and since His creation was not yet plainly related, Scripture teaches us, saying: "And a fountain went up out of the earth, and watered the face of the whole earth; and God made man of the dust of the earth, and breathed into his face the breath of life, and man became a living soul."[2] Whence also by most persons the soul is called immortal.[3] And after the formation of man, God chose out for him a region among the places of the East, excellent for light, brilliant with a very bright atmosphere, [abundant] in the finest plants; and in this He placed man.

CHAP. XX. — THE SCRIPTURAL ACCOUNT OF PARADISE.

Scripture thus relates the words of the sacred history: "And God planted Paradise, eastward, in Eden; and there He put the man whom He had formed. And out of the ground made God to grow every tree that is pleasant to the sight, and good for food; the tree of life also in the midst of Paradise, and the tree of the knowledge of good and evil. And a river flows out of Eden, to water the garden; thence it is parted into four heads. The name of the first is Pison:

that is it which compasseth the whole land of Havilah, where there is gold; and the gold of that land is good, and there is bdellium and the onyx stone. And the name of the second river is Gihon: the same is it that compasseth the whole land of Ethiopia. And the third river is Tigris: this is it which goeth toward Syria. And the fourth river is Euphrates. And the LORD God took the man whom He had made, and put him in the garden, to till and to keep it. And God commanded Adam, saying, Of every tree that is in the garden thou mayest freely eat; but of the tree of the knowledge of good and evil, ye shall not eat of it; for in the day ye eat of it ye shall surely die. And the LORD God said, It is not good that the man should be alone; let Us make him an helpmeet for him. And out of the ground God formed all the beasts of the field, and all the fowls of heaven, and brought them to Adam. And whatsoever Adam called every living creature, that was the name thereof. And Adam gave names to all cattle, and to the fowls of the air, and to all the beasts of the field. But for Adam there was not found an helpmeet for him. And God caused an ecstasy to fall upon Adam, and he slept; and He took one of his ribs, and closed up the flesh instead thereof. And the rib, which the LORD God had taken from man, made He a woman, and brought her unto Adam. And Adam said, This is now bone of my bones, and flesh of my flesh; she shall be called Woman, because she was taken out of man. Therefore shall a man leave his father and his mother, and shall cleave unto his wife, and they two shall be one flesh. And they were both naked, Adam and his wife, and were not ashamed.

CHAP. XXI. — OF THE FALL OF MAN.

"Now the serpent was more subtle than any beast of the field which the LORD God had made. And the serpent said to the woman, Why hath God said, Ye shall not eat of every tree of the garden? And the woman said unto the serpent, We eat of every tree of the garden, but of the fruit of the tree which is in the midst of the garden God hath said, Ye shall not eat of it, neither shall ye touch it, lest ye die. And the serpent said unto the woman, Ye shall not surely die. For God doth know that in the day ye eat thereof, then your eyes shall be opened, and ye shall be as gods, knowing good and evil. And the woman saw that the tree was good for food, and that it was pleasant to the eyes, and a tree to be desired to make one wise; and having taken of the fruit thereof, she did eat, and gave also unto her husband with her: and they did eat. And the eyes of them both were opened, and they knew that they were naked; and they sewed fig leaves together, and made themselves aprons. And they heard the voice of the LORD God walk-

---

[1] Gen. ii. 4, 5.
[2] Gen. ii. 7. [The Hebrew must not be overlooked: "the breath of *lives*," *spiraculum vitarum*; on which see Bartholinus, in Delitzsch, *System of Bib. Psychol.*, p. 27. Also, Luther's *Trichotomy*, *ibid.*, p. 460. With another work of similar character I am only slightly acquainted, but, recall with great satisfaction a partial examination of it when it first appeared. I refer to *The Tripartite Nature of Man*, by the Rev. J. B. Heard, M.A. 3d ed. Edinburgh, 1871, T. & T. Clark.]
[3] [But compare Tatian (cap. xiii. p. 70), and the note of the Parisian editors in margin (p. 152), where they begin by *distinctions* to make him orthodox, but at last accuse him of downright heresy. *Ed.* Paris, 1615.]

ing in the garden in the cool of the day, and Adam and his wife hid themselves from the presence of the LORD God amongst the trees of the garden. And the LORD God called unto Adam, and said unto him, Where art thou? And he said unto Him, I heard Thy voice in the garden, and I was afraid, because I was naked, and I hid myself. And He said unto him, Who told thee that thou wast naked, unless thou hast eaten of the tree whereof I commanded thee that thou shouldest not eat? And Adam said, The woman whom Thou gavest to be with me, she gave me of the tree, and I did eat. And God said to the woman, What is this that thou hast done? And the woman said, The serpent beguiled me, and I did eat. And the LORD God said unto the serpent, Because thou hast done this, thou art accursed above all the beasts of the earth; on thy breast and belly shalt thou go, and dust shalt thou eat all the days of thy life: and I will put enmity between thee and the woman, and between thy seed and her seed; it shall bruise thy head, and thou shalt bruise his heel.[1] And to the woman He said, I will greatly multiply thy sorrow and thy travail: in sorrow shalt thou bring forth children; and thy desire shall be to thy husband, and he shall rule over thee. And unto Adam He said, Because thou hast hearkened unto the voice of thy wife, and hast eaten of the tree of which I commanded thee, saying, Thou shalt not eat of it; cursed is the ground in[2] thy works: in sorrow shalt thou eat of it all the days of thy life; thorns and thistles shall it bring forth to thee; and thou shalt eat the herb of the field. In the sweat of thy face shalt thou eat thy bread, till thou return unto the earth; for out of it wast thou taken: for dust thou art, and unto dust shalt thou return."[3] Such is the account given by holy Scripture of the history of man and of Paradise.

CHAP. XXII. — WHY GOD IS SAID TO HAVE WALKED.

You will say, then, to me: "You said that God ought not to be contained in a place, and how do you now say that He walked in Paradise?" Hear what I say. The God and Father, indeed, of all cannot be contained, and is not found in a place, for there is no place of His rest; but His Word, through whom He made all things, being His power and His wisdom, assuming the person[4] of the Father and Lord of all, went to the garden in the person of God, and conversed with Adam. For the divine writing

itself teaches us that Adam said that he had heard the voice. But what else is this voice but the Word of God, who is also His Son? Not as the poets and writers of myths talk of the sons of gods begotten from intercourse [with women], but as truth expounds, the Word, that always exists, residing within the heart of God. For before anything came into being He had Him as a counsellor, being His own mind and thought. But when God wished to make all that He determined on, He begot this Word, uttered,[5] the first-born of all creation, not Himself being emptied of the Word[Reason], but having begotten Reason, and always conversing with His Reason. And hence the holy writings teach us, and all the spirit-bearing [inspired] men, one of whom, John, says, "In the beginning was the Word, and the Word was with God,"[6] showing that at first God was alone, and the Word in Him. Then he says, "The Word was God; all things came into existence through Him; and apart from Him not one thing came into existence." The Word, then, being God, and being naturally[7] produced from God, whenever the Father of the universe wills, He sends Him to any place; and He, coming, is both heard and seen, being sent by Him, and is found in a place.

CHAP. XXIII. — THE TRUTH OF THE ACCOUNT IN GENESIS.

Man, therefore, God made on the sixth day, and made known this creation after the seventh day, when also He made Paradise, that he might be in a better and distinctly superior place. And that this is true, the fact itself proves. For how can one miss seeing that the pains which women suffer in childbed, and the oblivion of their labours which they afterwards enjoy, are sent in order that the word of God may be fulfilled, and that the race of men may increase and multiply?[8] And do we not see also the judgment of the serpent, — how hatefully he crawls on his belly and eats the dust, — that we may have this, too, for a proof of the things which were said aforetime?

CHAP. XXIV. — THE BEAUTY OF PARADISE.

God, then, caused to spring out of the earth every tree that is beautiful in appearance, or good for food. For at first there were only those things which were produced on the third day, — plants, and seeds, and herbs; but the things which were in Paradise were made of a

---

[1] Theophilus reads, "It shall watch thy head, and thou shalt watch his heel."

[2] Or, "by thy works."

[3] Gen. ii 8–iii. 19. [See Justin M., *Dial.*, cap. lvi. p. 223, vol. i. this series.]

[4] The annotators here warn us against supposing that "person" is used as it was afterwards employed in discussing the doctrine of the Trinity, and show that the word is used in its original meaning, and with reference to an actor taking up a mask and personating a character.

[5] Προφορικός, the term used of the Logos as manifested; the Word as uttered by the Father, in distinction from the Word immanent in Him. [Theophilus is the first author who distinguishes between the *Logos ἐνδιάθετος* (cap. x., *supra*) and the *Logos προφορικός*; the Word *internal*, and the Word emitted. Kaye's *Justin*, p. 171.]

[6] John i. 1.

[7] That is, being produced by generation, not by creation.

[8] The Benedictine editor remarks: "Women bring forth with labour and pain as the punishment awarded to sin: they forget the pain, that the propagation of the race may not be hindered."

superior loveliness and beauty, since in it the plants were said to have been planted by God. As to the rest of the plants, indeed, the world contained plants like them ; but the two trees,— the tree of life and the tree of knowledge,— the rest of the earth possessed not, but only Paradise. And that Paradise is earth, and is planted on the earth, the Scripture states, saying : [1] "And the LORD God planted Paradise in Eden eastwards, and placed man there ; and out of the ground made the LORD God to grow every tree that is pleasant to the sight and good for food." By the 'expressions, therefore, "out of the ground," and "eastwards," the holy writing clearly teaches us that Paradise is under this heaven, under which the east and the earth are. And the Hebrew word Eden signifies " delight." And it was signified that a river flowed out of Eden to water Paradise, and after that divides into four heads ; of which the two called Pison and Gihon water the eastern parts, especially Gihon, which encompasses the whole land of Ethiopia, and which, they say, reappears in Egypt under the name of Nile. And the other two rivers are manifestly recognisable by us — those called Tigris and Euphrates — for these border on our own regions. And God having placed man in Paradise, as has been said, to till and keep it, commanded him to eat of all the trees, — manifestly of the tree of life also ; but only of the tree of knowledge He commanded him not to taste. And God transferred him from the earth, out of which he had been produced, into Paradise, giving him means of advancement, in order that, maturing and becoming perfect, and being even declared a god, he might thus ascend into heaven in possession of immortality. For man had been made a middle nature, neither wholly mortal, nor altogether immortal, but capable of either ; so also the place, Paradise, was made in respect of beauty intermediate between earth and heaven. And by the expression, " till it," [2] no other kind of labour is implied than the observance of God's command, lest, disobeying, he should destroy himself, as indeed he did destroy himself, by sin.

CHAP. XXV. — GOD WAS JUSTIFIED IN FORBIDDING MAN TO EAT OF THE TREE OF KNOWLEDGE.

The tree of knowledge itself was good, and its fruit was good. For it was not the tree, as some think, but the disobedience, which had death in it. For there was nothing else in the fruit than only knowledge ; but knowledge is good when one uses it discreetly.[3] But Adam,

being yet an infant in age, was on this account as yet unable to receive knowledge worthily. For now, also, when a child is born it is not at once able to eat bread, but is nourished first with milk, and then, with the increment of years, it advances to solid food. Thus, too, would it have been with Adam ; for not as one who grudged him, as some suppose, did God command him not to eat of knowledge. But He wished also to make proof of him, whether he was submissive to His commandment. And at the same time He wished man, infant as he was,[4] to remain for some time longer simple and sincere. For this is holy, not only with God, but also with men, that in simplicity and guilelessness subjection be yielded to parents. But if it is right that children be subject to parents, how much more to the God and Father of all things ? Besides, it is unseemly that children in infancy be wise beyond their years ; for as in stature one increases in an orderly progress, so also in wisdom. But as when a law has commanded abstinence from anything, and some one has not obeyed, it is obviously not the law which causes punishment, but the disobedience and transgression ; — for a father sometimes enjoins on his own child abstinence from certain things, and when he does not obey the paternal order, he is flogged and punished on account of the disobedience ; and in this case the actions themselves are not the [cause of] stripes, but the disobedience procures punishment for him who disobeys ; — so also for the first man, disobedience procured his expulsion from Paradise. Not, therefore, as if there were any evil in the tree of knowledge ; but from his disobedience did man draw, as from a fountain, labour, pain, grief, and at last fall a prey to death.

CHAP. XXVI. — GOD'S GOODNESS IN EXPELLING MAN FROM PARADISE.

And God showed great kindness to man in this, that He did not suffer him to remain in sin for ever ; but, as it were, by a kind of banishment, cast him out of Paradise, in order that, having by punishment expiated, within an appointed time, the sin, and having been disciplined, he should afterwards be restored. Wherefore also, when man had been formed in this world, it is mystically written in Genesis, as if he had been twice placed in Paradise ; so that the one was fulfilled when he was placed there, and the second will be fulfilled after the resurrection and judgment. For just as a vessel, when on being fashioned it has some flaw, is remoulded or remade, that it may become new and entire ; so also it happens to man by death. For somehow

---

[1] Gen. ii. 8.
[2] In the Greek the word is, "work" or "labour," as we also speak of working land.
[3] ["Pulchra, si quis ea recte utatur," is the rendering of the Paris translators. A noble motto for a college.]

[4] [No need of a long argument here, to show, as some editors have done, that our author calls Adam an *infant*, only with reference to time, not physical development. He was but a few days old.]

or other he is broken up, that he may rise in the resurrection whole ; I mean spotless, and righteous, and immortal. And as to God's calling, and saying, Where art thou, Adam? God did this, not as if ignorant of this ; but, being long-suffering, He gave him an opportunity of repentance and confession.

CHAP. XXVII. — THE NATURE OF MAN.

But some one will say to us, Was man made by nature mortal? Certainly not. Was he, then, immortal? Neither do we affirm this. But one will say, Was he, then, nothing? Not even this hits the mark. He was by nature neither mortal nor immortal. For if He had made him immortal from the beginning, He would have made him God. Again, if He had made him mortal, God would seem to be the cause of his death. Neither, then, immortal nor yet mortal did He make him, but, as we have said above, capable of both ; so that if he should incline to the things of immortality, keeping the commandment of God, he should receive as reward from Him immortality, and should become God ; but if, on the other hand, he should turn to the things of death, disobeying God, he should himself be the cause of death to himself. For God made man free, and with power over himself.[1] That, then, which man brought upon himself through carelessness and disobedience, this God now vouchsafes to him as a gift through His own philanthropy and pity, when men obey Him.[2] For as man, disobeying, drew death upon himself ; so, obeying the will of God, he who desires is able to procure for himself life everlasting. For God has given us a law and holy commandments ; and every one who keeps these can be saved, and, obtaining the resurrection, can inherit incorruption.

CHAP. XXVIII. — WHY EVE WAS FORMED OF ADAM'S RIB.

And Adam having been cast out of Paradise, in this condition knew Eve his wife, whom God had formed into a wife for him out of his rib. And this He did, not as if He were unable to make his wife separately, but God foreknew that man would call upon a number of gods. And having this prescience, and knowing that through the serpent error would introduce a number of gods which had no existence, — for there being but one God, even then error was striving to disseminate a multitude of gods, saying, " Ye shall be as gods ; " — lest, then, it should be supposed that one God made the man and another the woman, therefore He made them both ; and God made the woman together with the man,

not only that thus the mystery of God's sole government might be exhibited, but also that their mutual affection might be greater. Therefore said Adam to Eve, " This is now bone of my bones, and flesh of my flesh." And besides, he prophesied, saying, " For this cause shall a man leave his father and his mother, and shall cleave unto his wife ; and they two shall be one flesh ; "[3] which also itself has its fulfilment in ourselves. For who that marries lawfully does not despise mother and father, and his whole family connection, and all his household, cleaving to and becoming one with his own wife, fondly preferring her? So that often, for the sake of their wives, some submit even to death. This Eve, on account of her having been in the beginning deceived by the serpent, and become the author of sin, the wicked demon, who also is called Satan, who then spoke to her through the serpent, and who works even to this day in those men that are possessed by him, invokes as Eve.[4] And he is called " demon " and " dragon," on account of his [ἀποδεδρακέναι] revolting from God. For at first he was an angel. And concerning his history there is a great deal to be said ; wherefore I at present omit the relation of it, for I have also given an account of him in another place.

CHAP. XXIX. — CAIN'S CRIME.

When, then, Adam knew Eve his wife, she conceived and bare a son, whose name was Cain ; and she said, " I have gotten a man from God." And yet again she bare a second son, whose name was Abel, " who began to be a keeper of sheep, but Cain tilled the ground."[5] Their history receives a very full narration, yea, even a detailed explanation :[6] wherefore the book itself, which is entitled " The Genesis of the World," can more accurately inform those who are anxious to learn their story. When, then, Satan saw Adam and his wife not only still living, but also begetting children — being carried away with spite because he had not succeeded in putting them to death, — when he saw that Abel was well-pleasing to God, he wrought upon the heart of his brother called Cain, and caused him to kill his brother Abel. And thus did death get a beginning in this world, to find its way into every race of man, even to this day. But God, being pitiful, and wishing to afford to Cain, as to Adam, an opportunity of repentance and confession, said, " Where is Abel thy brother?" But Cain answered God contuma-

---

[1] [A noble sentence: ἐλεύθερον γὰρ καὶ αὐτεξούσιον ἐποίησεν ὁ Θεὸς τὸν ἄνθρωπον.]

[2] Apparently meaning, that God turns death, which man brought on himself by disobedience, into a blessing.

[3] Gen. ii 24. [Kaye justly praises our author's high estimate of Christian marriage. See his *Justin M.*, p. 128.]

[4] Referring to the bacchanalian orgies in which " Eva " was shouted, and which the Fathers professed to believe was an unintentional invocation of Eve, the authoress of all sin.

[5] Gen. iv. 1, 2.

[6] [He speaks of the *œconomy* of the narrative; τὴν οἰκονομίαν τῆς ἐξηγήσεως. Kaye's *Justin*, p. 175.]

ciously, saying, "I know not; am I my brother's keeper?" God, being thus made angry with him, said, "What hast thou done? The voice of thy brother's blood crieth to me from the earth, which opened her mouth to receive thy brother's blood from thy hand. Groaning and trembling shalt thou be on the earth." From that time the earth, through fear, no longer receives human blood,[1] no, nor the blood of any animal; by which it appears that it is not the cause [of death], but man, who transgressed.

CHAP. XXX. — CAIN'S FAMILY AND THEIR INVENTIONS.

Cain also himself had a son, whose name was Enoch; and he built a city, which he called by the name of his son, Enoch. From that time was there made a beginning of the building of cities, and this before the flood; not as Homer falsely says:[2] —

> "Not yet had men a city built."

And to Enoch was born a son, by name Gaidad; who begat a son called Meel; and Meel begat Mathusala; and Mathusala, Lamech. And Lamech took unto him two wives, whose names were Adah and Zillah. At that time there was made a beginning of polygamy, and also of music. For Lamech had three sons: Jabal, Jubal, Tubal. And Jabal became a keeper of cattle, and dwelt in tents; but Jubal is he who made known the psaltery and the harp; and Tubal became a smith, a forger in brass and iron. So far the seed of Cain is registered; and for the rest, the seed of his line has sunk into oblivion, on account of his fratricide of his brother. And, in place of Abel, God granted to Eve to conceive and bear a son, who was called Seth; from whom the remainder of the human race proceeds until now. And to those who desire to be informed regarding all generations, it is easy to give explanations by means of the holy Scriptures. For, as we have already mentioned, this subject, the order of the genealogy of man, has been partly handled by us in another discourse, in the first book of *The History*.[3] And all these things the Holy Spirit teaches us, who speaks through Moses and the rest of the prophets, so that the writings which belong to us godly people are more ancient, yea, and are shown to be more truthful, than all writers and poets. But also, concerning music, some have fabled that Apollo was the inventor, and others say that Orpheus discovered the art of music from the sweet voices of the birds. Their story is shown to

be empty and vain, for these inventors lived many years after the flood. And what relates to Noah, who is called by some Deucalion, has been explained by us in the book before mentioned, and which, if you wish it, you are at liberty to read.

CHAP. XXXI. — THE HISTORY AFTER THE FLOOD.

After the flood was there again a beginning of cities and kings, in the following manner: — The first city was Babylon, and Erech, and Accad, and Calneh, in the land of Shinar. And their king was called Nebroth [Nimrod]. From these came Asshur, from whom also the Assyrians receive their name. And Nimrod built the cities Nineveh and Rehoboth, and Calah, and Resen, between Nineveh and Calah; and Nineveh became a very great city. And another son of Shem, the son of Noah, by name Mizraim, begat Ludim, and those called Anamim, and Lehabim, and Naphtuhim, and Pathrusim, and Casluhim, out of whom came Philistin. Of the three sons of Noah, however, and of their death and genealogy, we have given a compendious register in the above-mentioned book. But now we will mention the remaining facts both concerning cities and kings, and the things that happened when there was one speech and one language. Before the dividing of the languages these fore-mentioned cities existed. But when men were about to be dispersed, they took counsel of their own judgment, and not at the instigation of God, to build a city, a tower whose top might reach into heaven, that they might make a glorious name to themselves. Since, therefore, they had dared, contrary to the will of God, to attempt a grand work, God destroyed their city, and overthrew their tower. From that time He confounded the languages of men, giving to each a different dialect. And similarly did the Sibyl speak, when she declared that wrath would come on the world. She says: —

> "When are fulfilled the threats of the great God,
> With which He threatened men, when formerly
> In the Assyrian land they built a tower,
> And all were of one speech, and wished to rise
> Even till they climbed unto the starry heaven,
> Then the Immortal raised a mighty wind
> And laid upon them strong necessity;
> For when the wind threw down the mighty tower,
> Then rose among mankind fierce strife and hate.
> One speech was changed to many dialects,
> And earth was filled with divers tribes and kings."

And so on. These things, then, happened in the land of the Chaldæans. And in the land of Canaan there was a city, by name Haran. And in these days, Pharaoh, who by the Egyptians was also called Nechaoth, was first king of Egypt, and thus the kings followed in succession.[4] And in the land of Shinar, among those called Chal-

---

1 Fell remarks, " Blood shed at once coagulates, and does not easily enter the earth." [On the field of Antietam, after the battle, I observed the blood *flaked* upon the soil, not absorbed by it.]
2 *Il.*, xx. 216. But Homer refers only to Troy.
3 [Of the founder of Christian chronology this must be noted.]

4 But the Benedictine editor understands the words to mean, that the succeeding kings were in like manner called Pharaoh.

dæans, the first king was Arioch, and next after him Ellasar, and after him Chedorlaomer, king of Elam, and after him Tidal, king of the nations called Assyrians. And there were five other cities in the territory of Ham, the son of Noah; the first called Sodom, then Gomorrah, Admah, Zeboiim, and Balah, which was also called Zoar. And the names of their kings are these: Bera, king of Sodom; Birsha, king of Gomorrah; Shinab, king of Admah; Shemeber, king of Zeboiim; Bela, king of Zoar, which is also called Kephalac.[1] These served Chedorlaomer, the king of the Assyrians, for twelve years, and in the thirteenth year they revolted from Chedorlaomer; and thus it came to pass at that time that the four Assyrian kings waged war upon the five kings. This was the first commencement of making war on the earth; and they destroyed the giants Karnaim, and the strong nations that were with them in their city, and the Horites of the mountains called Seir, as far as the plain of Paran, which is by the wilderness. And at that time there was a righteous king called Melchisedek, in the city of Salem, which now is Jerusalem. This was the first priest of all priests[2] of the Most High God; and from him the above-named city Hierosolyma was called Jerusalem.[3] And from his time priests were found in all the earth. And after him reigned Abimelech in Gerar; and after him another Abimelech. Then reigned Ephron, surnamed the Hittite. Such are the names of the kings that were in former times. And the rest of the kings of the Assyrians, during an interval of many years, have been passed over in silence unrecorded, all writers narrating the events of our recent days. There were these kings of Assyria: Tiglath-Pileser, and after him Shalmaneser, then Sennacherib; and Adrammelech the Ethiopian, who also reigned over Egypt, was his triarch; — though these things, in comparison with our books, are quite recent.

CHAP. XXXII. — HOW THE HUMAN RACE WAS DISPERSED.

Hence, therefore, may the lovers of learning and of antiquity understand the history, and see that those things are recent which are told by us apart from the holy prophets.[4] For though at first there were few men in the land of Arabia and Chaldæa, yet, after their languages were divided, they gradually began to multiply and spread over all the earth; and some of them tended towards the east to dwell there, and others to the parts of the great continent, and others northwards, so as to extend as far as Britain, in the Arctic regions. And others went to the land of Canaan, which is called Judæa, and Phœnicia, and the region of Ethiopia, and Egypt, and Libya, and the country called torrid, and the parts stretching towards the west; and the rest went to places by the sea, and Pamphylia, and Asia, and Greece, and Macedonia, and, besides, to Italy, and the whole country called Gaul, and Spain, and Germany; so that now the whole world is thus filled with inhabitants. Since then the occupation of the world by men was at first in three divisions, — in the east, and south, and west: afterwards, the remaining parts of the earth were inhabited, when men became very numerous. And the writers, not knowing these things, are forward to maintain that the world is shaped like a sphere, and to compare it to a cube. But how can they say what is true regarding these things, when they do not know about the creation of the world and its population? Men gradually increasing in number and multiplying on the earth, as we have already said, the islands also of the sea and the rest of the countries were inhabited.

CHAP. XXXIII. — PROFANE HISTORY GIVES NO ACCOUNT OF THESE MATTERS.

Who, then, of those called sages, and poets, and historians, could tell us truly of these things, themselves being much later born, and introducing a multitude of gods, who were born so many years after the cities, and are more modern than kings, and nations, and wars? For they should have made mention of all events, even those which happened before the flood; both of the creation of the world and the formation of man, and the whole succession of events. The Egyptian or Chaldæan prophets, and the other writers, should have been able accurately to tell, if at least they spoke by a divine and pure spirit, and spoke truth in all that was uttered by them; and they should have announced not only things past or present, but also those that were to come upon the world. And therefore it is proved that all others have been in error; and that we Christians alone have possessed the truth, inasmuch as we are taught by the Holy Spirit, who spoke in the holy prophets, and foretold all things.

CHAP. XXXIV. — THE PROPHETS ENJOINED HOLINESS OF LIFE.

And, for the rest, would that in a kindly spirit

---

[1] Theophilus spells some of the names differently from what they are given in our text. For Tidal he has Thargal; for Bera, Ballas; for Birsha, Barsas; for Shinab, Senaar; for Shemeber, Hymoor. Kephalac is taken to be a corruption for Balak, which in the previous sentence is inserted by many editors, though it is not in the best MSS.

[2] [St. Paul seems to teach that the whole story of Melchisedek is a "similitude," and that the one Great High Priest of our profession appeared to Abraham in that character, as to Joshua in another, the "Captain of our salvation" (Heb. vii. 1-3; Josh. v. 13-15). We need a carefully digested work on the apparitions of the Word before His incarnation, or the theophanies of the *Old Testament*.]

[3] [Certainly a striking etymon, "Salem of the priest." But we can only accept it as a beautiful play upon words.]

[4] Proving the antiquity of Scripture, by showing that no recent occurrences are mentioned in it. Wolf, however, gives another reading, which would be rendered, "understand whether those things are recent which we utter on the authority of the holy prophets."

you would investigate divine things [1] — I mean the things that are spoken by the prophets — in order that, by comparing what is said by us with the utterances of the others, you may be able to discover the truth. We [2] have shown from their own histories, which they have compiled, that the names of those who are called gods, are found to be the names of men who lived among them, as we have shown above. And to this day their images are daily fashioned, idols, "the works of men's hands." And these the mass of foolish men serve, whilst they reject the maker and fashioner of all things and the nourisher of all breath of life, giving credit to vain doctrines through the deceitfulness of the senseless tradition received from their fathers. But God at least, the Father and Creator of the universe, did not abandon mankind, but gave a law, and sent holy prophets to declare and teach the race of men, that each one of us might awake and understand that there is one God. And they also taught us to refrain from unlawful idolatry, and adultery, and murder, fornication, theft, avarice, false swearing, wrath, and every incontinence and uncleanness; and that whatever a man would not wish to be done to himself, he should not do to another; and thus he who acts righteously shall escape the eternal punishments, and be thought worthy of the eternal life from God.

CHAP. XXXV. — PRECEPTS FROM THE PROPHETIC BOOKS.

The divine law, then, not only forbids the worshipping of idols, but also of the heavenly bodies, the sun, the moon, or the other stars; yea, not heaven, nor earth, nor the sea, nor fountains, nor rivers, must be worshipped, but we must serve in holiness of heart and sincerity of purpose only the living and true God, who also is Maker of the universe. Wherefore saith the holy law: "Thou shalt not commit adultery; thou shalt not steal; thou shalt not bear false witness; thou shalt not desire thy neighbour's wife." So also the prophets. Solomon indeed teaches us that we must not sin with so much as a turn of the eye,[3] saying, "Let thine eyes look right on, and let thy eyelids look straight before thee." [4] And Moses, who himself also was a prophet, says, concerning the sole government of God: "Your God is He who establishes the heaven, and forms the earth, whose hands have brought forth all the host of heaven; and He has not set these things before you that you should go after them." [5] And Isaiah himself also says: "Thus saith the LORD God who es-

tablished the heavens, and founded the earth and all that is therein, and giveth breath unto the people upon it, and spirit to them that walk therein. This is the LORD your God." [6] And again, through him He says: "I have made the earth, and man upon it. I by my hand have established the heavens." [7] And in another chapter, "This is your God, who created the ends of the earth; He hungereth not, neither is weary, and there is no searching of His understanding." [8] So, too, Jeremiah says: "Who hath made the earth by His power, and established the world by His wisdom, and by His discretion hath stretched out the heavens, and a mass of water in the heavens, and He caused the clouds to ascend from the ends of the earth; He made lightnings with rain, and brought forth winds out of His treasures." [9] One can see how consistently and harmoniously all the prophets spoke, having given utterance through one and the same spirit concerning the unity of God, and the creation of the world, and the formation of man. Moreover, they were in sore travail, bewailing the godless race of men, and they reproached those, who seemed to be wise, for their error and hardness of heart. Jeremiah, indeed, said: "Every man is brutishly gone astray from the knowledge of Him; every founder is confounded by his graven images; in vain the silversmith makes his molten images; there is no breath in them: in the day of their visitation they shall perish." [10] The same, too, says David: "They are corrupt, they have done abominable works; there is none that doeth good, no, not one; they have all gone aside, they have together become profitless." [11] So also Habakkuk: "What profiteth the graven image that he has graven it a lying image? Woe to him that saith to the stone, Awake; and to the wood, Arise." [12] Likewise spoke the other prophets of the truth. And why should I recount the multitude of prophets, who are numerous, and said ten thousand things consistently and harmoniously? For those who desire it, can, by reading what they uttered, accurately understand the truth, and no longer be carried away by opinion and profitless labour. These, then, whom we have already mentioned, were prophets among the Hebrews, — illiterate, and shepherds, and uneducated.

CHAP. XXXVI. — PROPHECIES OF THE SIBYL.

And the Sibyl, who was a prophetess among the Greeks and the other nations, in the beginning of her prophecy, reproaches the race of men, saying: —

---

1 [Comp. book i. cap. xiv., *supra*, p. 93.]
2 Benedictine editor proposes "they."
3 Literally, "a nod."
4 Prov. iv. 25.
5 Cf. Deut. iv. 19.

6 Isa. xlii. 5.
7 Isa. xlv. 12.
8 Isa. xl. 28.
9 Jer. x. 12, 13.
10 Jer. li. 17, 18.
11 Ps. xiv. 1, 3.
12 Hab. ii. 18.

" How are ye still so quickly lifted up,
And how so thoughtless of the end of life,
Ye mortal men of flesh, who are but nought?
Do ye not tremble, nor fear God most high?
Your Overseer, the Knower, Seer of all,
Who ever keeps those whom His hand first made,
Puts His sweet Spirit into all His works,
And gives Him for a guide to mortal men.
There is one only uncreated God,
Who reigns alone, all-powerful, very great,
From whom is nothing hid.   He sees all things,
Himself unseen by any mortal eye.
Can mortal man see the immortal God,
Or fleshly eyes, which shun the noontide beams,
Look upon Him who dwells beyond the heavens?
Worship Him, then, the self-existent God,
The unbegotten Ruler of the world,
Who only was from everlasting time,
And shall to everlasting still abide.
Of evil counsels ye shall reap the fruit,
Because ye have not honoured the true God,
Nor offered to Him sacred hecatombs.
To those who dwell in Hades ye make gifts,
And unto demons offer sacrifice.
In madness and in pride ye have your walk;
And leaving the right way, ye wander wide,
And lose yourselves in pitfalls and in thorns.
Why do ye wander thus, O foolish men?
Cease your vain wanderings in the black, dark night;
Why follow darkness and perpetual gloom
When, see, there shines for you the blessed light?
Lo, He is clear — in Him there is no spot.
Turn, then, from darkness, and behold the day;
Be wise, and treasure wisdom in your breasts.
There is one God who sends the winds and rains,
The earthquakes, and the lightnings, and the plagues,
The famines, and the snow-storms, and the ice,
And all the woes that visit our sad race.
Nor these alone, but all things else He gives,
Ruling omnipotent in heaven and earth,
And self-existent from eternity."

And regarding those [gods] that are said to have been born, she said : —

" If all things that are born must also die,
God cannot be produced by mortal man.
But there is only One, the All-Supreme,
Who made the heavens, with all their starry host,
The sun and moon; likewise the fruitful earth,
With all the waves of ocean, and the hills,
The fountains, and the ever flowing streams;
He also made the countless multitude
Of ocean creatures, and He keeps alive
All creeping things, both of the earth and sea;
And all the tuneful choir of birds He made,
Which cleave the air with wings, and with shrill pipe
Trill forth at morn their tender, clear-voiced song.
Within the deep glades of the hills He placed
A savage race of beasts; and unto men
He made all cattle subject, making man
The God-formed image, ruler over all,
And putting in subjection to his sway
Things many and incomprehensible.
For who of mortals can know all these things?
He only knows who made them at the first,
He the Creator, incorruptible,
Who dwells in upper air eternally;
Who proffers to the good most rich rewards,
And against evil and unrighteous men
Rouses revenge, and wrath, and bloody wars,
And pestilence, and many a tearful grief.
O man exalted vainly — say why thus
Hast thou so utterly destroyed thyself?
Have ye no shame worshipping beasts for gods?
And to believe the gods should steal your beasts,

Or that they need your vessels — is it not
Frenzy's most profitless and foolish thought?
Instead of dwelling in the golden heavens,
Ye see your gods become the prey of worms,
And hosts of creatures noisome and unclean.
O, fools! ye worship serpents, dogs, and cats,
Birds, and the creeping things of earth and sea,
Images made with hands, statues of stone,
And heaps of rubbish by the wayside placed.
All these, and many more vain things, ye serve,
Worshipping things disgraceful even to name:
These are the gods who lead vain men astray,
From whose mouth streams of deadly poison flow.
But unto Him in whom alone is life,
Life, and undying, everlasting light;
Who pours into man's cup of life a joy
Sweeter than sweetest honey to his taste, —
Unto Him bow the head, to Him alone,
And walk in ways of everlasting peace.
Forsaking Him, ye all have turned aside,
And, in your raving folly, drained the cup
Of justice quite unmixed, pure, mastering, strong;
And ye will not again be sober men,
Ye will not come unto a sober mind,
And know your God and King, who looks on all:
Therefore, upon you burning fire shall come,
And ever ye shall daily burn in flames,
Ashamed for ever of your useless gods.
But those who worship the eternal God,
They shall inherit everlasting life,
Inhabiting the blooming realms of bliss,
And feasting on sweet food from starry heaven."

That these things are true, and useful, and just, and profitable to all men, is obvious. Even the poets have spoken of the punishments of the wicked.

CHAP. XXXVII. — THE TESTIMONIES OF THE POETS.

And that evil-doers must necessarily be punished in proportion to their deeds, has already been, as it were, oracularly uttered by some of the poets, as a witness both against themselves and against the wicked, declaring that they shall be punished. Æschylus said : —

" He who has done must also suffer."

And Pindar himself said : —

" It is fit that suffering follow doing."

So, too, Euripides : —

" The deed rejoiced you — suffering endure;
The taken enemy must needs be pain'd."

And again : —

" The foe's pain is the hero's meed."

And, similarly, Archilochus : —

" One thing I know, I hold it ever true,
The evil-doer evil shall endure."

And that God sees all, and that nothing escapes His notice, but that, being long-suffering, He refrains until the time when He is to judge — concerning this, too, Dionysius said : —

" The eye of Justice seeing all,
Yet seemeth not to see."

And that God's judgment is to be, and that evils will suddenly overtake the wicked, — this, too, Æschylus declared, saying : —

" Swift-footed is the approach of fate,
    And none can justice violate,
    But feels its stern hand soon or late.

" 'Tis with you, though unheard, unseen ;
    You draw night's curtain in between,
    But even sleep affords no screen.

" 'Tis with you if you sleep or wake ;
    And if abroad your way you take,
    Its still, stern watch you cannot break.

" 'Twill follow you, or cross your path ;
    And even night no virtue hath
    To hide you from th' Avenger's wrath.

" To show the ill the darkness flees ;
    Then, if sin offers joy or ease,
    Oh stop, and think that some one sees ! "

And may we not cite Simonides also ? —

" To men no evil comes unheralded ;
    But God with sudden hand transforms all things."

Euripides again : —

" The wicked and proud man's prosperity
    Is based on sand : his race abideth not ;
    And time proclaims the wickedness of men."

Once more Euripides : —

" Not without judgment is the Deity,
    But sees when oaths are struck unrighteously,
    And when from men unwilling they are wrung."

And Sophocles : —

" If ills you do, ills also you must bear."

That God will make inquiry both concerning false swearing and concerning every other wickedness, they themselves have well-nigh predicted. And concerning the conflagration of the world, they have, willingly or unwillingly, spoken in conformity with the prophets, though they were much more recent, and stole these things from the law and the prophets. The poets corroborate the testimony of the prophets.

CHAP. XXXVIII. — THE TEACHINGS OF THE GREEK POETS AND PHILOSOPHERS CONFIRMATORY OF THOSE OF THE HEBREW PROPHETS.

But what matters it whether they were before or after them ? Certainly they did at all events utter things confirmatory of the prophets. Concerning the burning up of the world, Malachi the prophet foretold : " The day of the Lord cometh as a burning oven, and shall consume all the wicked." [1] And Isaiah : " For the wrath of God is as a violent hail-storm, and as a rushing mountain torrent." [2] The Sibyl, then, and the other prophets, yea, and the poets and philoso-phers, have clearly taught both concerning right-eousness, and judgment, and punishment ; and also concerning providence, that God cares for us, not only for the living among us, but also for those that are dead : though, indeed, they said this unwillingly, for they were convinced by the truth. And among the prophets indeed, Solo-mon said of the dead, " There shall be healing to thy flesh, and care taken of thy bones." [3] And the same says David, " The bones which Thou hast broken shall rejoice." [4] And in agreement with these sayings was that of Timocles : —

" The dead are pitied by the loving God."

And the writers who spoke of a multiplicity of gods came at length to the doctrine of the unity of God, and those who asserted chance spoke also of providence ; and the advocates of im-punity confessed there would be a judgment, and those who denied that there is a sensation after death acknowledged that there is. Homer, ac-cordingly, though he had said, —

" Like fleeting vision passed the soul away," [5]

says in another place : —

" To Hades went the disembodied soul ; " [6]

And again : —

" That I may quickly pass through Hades' gates,
    Me bury." [7]

And as regards the others whom you have read, I think you know with sufficient accuracy how they have expressed themselves. But all these things will every one understand who seeks the wisdom of God, and is well pleasing to Him through faith and righteousness and the doing of good works. For one of the prophets whom we already mentioned, Hosea by name, said, " Who is wise, and he shall understand these things ? prudent, and he shall know them ? for the ways of the Lord are right, and the just shall walk in them : but the transgressors shall fall therein." [8] He, then, who is desirous of learn-ing, should learn much.[9] Endeavour therefore to meet [with me] more frequently, that, by hearing the living voice, you may accurately ascertain the truth.

---

1 Mal. iv. 1.
2 Isa. xxx. 30.

3 Prov. iii. 8.
4 Ps. li. 8.
5 *Od.*, xi. 222.
6 *Il.*, xvi. 856.
7 xxiii. 71.
8 Hos. xiv. 9.
9 We have adopted the reading of Wolf in the text. The read-ing of the MSS. is, " He who desires to learn should desire to learn." Perhaps the most satisfactory emendation is that of Heumann, who reads φιλομυθεῖν instead of φιλομαθεῖν : " He who desires to learn should also desire to discuss subjects, and hold conversations on them." In this case, Theophilus most probably borrows his remark from Aristotle, *Metaphysic.* i. c. 2.

THEOPHILUS TO AUTOLYCUS.

BOOK III.

CHAP. I. — AUTOLYCUS NOT YET CONVINCED.

THEOPHILUS to Autolycus, greeting: Seeing that writers are fond of composing a multitude of books for vainglory, — some concerning gods, and wars, and chronology, and some, too, concerning useless legends, and other such labour in vain, in which you also have been used to employ yourself until now, and do not grudge to endure that toil; but though you conversed with me, are still of opinion that the word of truth is an idle tale, and suppose that our writings are recent and modern; — on this account I also will not grudge the labour of compendiously setting forth to you, God helping me, the antiquity of our books, reminding you of it in few words, that you may not grudge the labour of reading it, but may recognise the folly of the other authors.

CHAP. II. — PROFANE AUTHORS HAD NO MEANS OF KNOWING THE TRUTH.

For it was fit that they who wrote should themselves have been eye-witnesses of those things concerning which they made assertions, or should accurately have ascertained them from those who had seen them; for they who write of things unascertained beat the air. For what did it profit Homer to have composed the Trojan war, and to have deceived many; or Hesiod, the register of the theogony of those whom he calls gods; or Orpheus, the three hundred and sixty-five gods, whom in the end of his life he rejects, maintaining in his precepts that there is one God? What profit did the sphærography of the world's circle confer on Aratus, or those who held the same doctrine as he, except glory among men? And not even that did they reap as they deserved. And what truth did they utter? Or what good did their tragedies do to Euripides and Sophocles, or the other tragedians? Or their comedies to Menander and Aristophanes, and the other comedians? Or their histories to Herodotus and Thucydides?

Or the shrines[1] and the pillars of Hercules to Pythagoras, or the Cynic philosophy to Diogenes? What good did it do Epicurus to maintain that there is no providence; or Empedocles to teach atheism; or Socrates to swear by the dog, and the goose, and the plane-tree, and Æsculapius struck by lightning, and the demons whom he invoked? And why did he willingly die? What reward, or of what kind, did he expect to receive after death? What did Plato's system of culture profit him? Or what benefit did the *rest* of the philosophers derive from their doctrines, not to enumerate the whole of them, since they are numerous? But these things we say, for the purpose of exhibiting their useless and godless opinions.

CHAP. III. — THEIR CONTRADICTIONS.

For all these, having fallen in love with vain and empty reputation, neither themselves knew the truth, nor guided others to the truth: for the things which they said themselves convict them of speaking inconsistently; and most of them demolished their own doctrines. For not only did they refute one another, but some, too, even stultified their own teachings; so that their reputation has issued in shame and folly, for they are condemned by men of understanding. For either they made assertions concerning the gods, and afterwards taught that there was no god; or if they spoke even of the creation of the world, they finally said that all things were produced spontaneously. Yea, and even speaking of providence, they taught again that the world was not ruled by providence. But what? Did they not, when they essayed to write even of honourable conduct, teach the perpetration of lasciviousness, and fornication, and adultery; and did they not introduce hateful and unutterable wickedness? And they proclaim that their gods took the lead in committing unutterable acts of

---

[1] While in Egypt, Pythagoras was admitted to the penetralia of the temples and the arcana of religion.

adultery, and in monstrous banquets. For who does not sing Saturn devouring his own children, and Jove his son gulping down Metis, and preparing for the gods a horrible feast, at which also they say that Vulcan, a lame blacksmith, did the waiting; and how Jove not only married Juno, his own sister, but also with foul mouth did abominable wickedness? And the rest of his deeds, as many as the poets sing, it is likely you are acquainted with. Why need I further recount the deeds of Neptune and Apollo, or Bacchus and Hercules, of the bosom-loving Minerva, and the shameless Venus, since in another place[1] we have given a more accurate account of these?

CHAP. IV. — HOW AUTOLYCUS HAD BEEN MISLED BY FALSE ACCUSATIONS AGAINST THE CHRISTIANS.

Nor indeed was there any necessity for my refuting these, except that I see you still in dubiety about the word of the truth. For though yourself prudent, you endure fools gladly. Otherwise you would not have been moved by senseless men to yield yourself to empty words, and to give credit to the prevalent rumor wherewith godless lips falsely accuse us, who are worshippers of God, and are called Christians, alleging that the wives of us all are held in common and made promiscuous use of; and that we even commit incest with our own sisters, and, what is most impious and barbarous of all, that we eat human flesh.[2] But further, they say that our doctrine has but recently come to light, and that we have nothing to allege in proof of what we receive as truth, nor of our teaching, but that our doctrine is foolishness. I wonder, then, chiefly that you, who in other matters are studious, and a scrutinizer of all things, give but a careless hearing to us. For, if it were possible for you, you would not grudge to spend the night in the libraries

CHAP. V. — PHILOSOPHERS INCULCATE CANNIBALISM.

Since, then, you have read much, what is your opinion of the precepts of Zeno, and Diogenes, and Cleanthes, which their books contain, inculcating the eating of human flesh: that fathers be cooked and eaten by their own children; and that if any one refuse or reject a part of this infamous food, he himself be devoured who will not eat? An utterance even more godless than these is found,— that, namely, of Diogenes, who teaches children to bring their own parents in sacrifice, and devour them. And does not

the historian Herodotus narrate that Cambyses,[3] when he had slaughtered the children of Harpagus, cooked them also, and set them as a meal before their father? And, still further, he narrates that among the Indians the parents are eaten by their own children. Oh! the godless teaching of those who recorded, yea, rather, inculcated such things! Oh! their wickedness and godlessness! Oh! the conception of those who thus accurately philosophized, and profess philosophy! For they who taught these doctrines have filled the world with iniquity.

CHAP. VI. — OTHER OPINIONS OF THE PHILOSOPHERS.

And regarding lawless conduct, those who have blindly wandered into the choir of philosophy have, almost to a man, spoken with one voice. Certainly Plato, to mention him first who seems to have been the most respectable philosopher among them, expressly, as it were, legislates in his first book,[4] entitled *The Republic*, that the wives of all be common, using the precedent of the son[5] of Jupiter and the lawgiver of the Cretans, in order that under this pretext there might be an abundant offspring from the best persons, and that those who were worn with toil might be comforted by such intercourse.[6] And Epicurus himself, too, as well as teaching atheism, teaches along with it incest with mothers and sisters, and this in transgression of the laws which forbid it; for Solon distinctly legislated regarding this, in order that from a married parent children might lawfully spring, that they might not be born of adultery, so that no one should honour as his father him who was not his father, or dishonour him who was really his father, through ignorance that he was so. And these things the other laws of the Romans and Greeks also prohibit. Why, then, do Epicurus and the Stoics teach incest and sodomy, with which doctrines they have filled libraries, so that from boyhood[7] this lawless intercourse is learned? And why should I further spend time on them, since even of those they call gods they relate similar things?

CHAP. VII. — VARYING DOCTRINE CONCERNING THE GODS.

For after they had said that these are gods, they again made them of no account. For

---

[1] Viz., in the first book to Autolycus.

[2] [The body of Christ is human flesh. If, then, it had been the primitive doctrine, that the bread and wine cease to exist in the Eucharist, and are changed into natural flesh and blood, our author could not have resented this charge as "most barbarous and impious."]

[3] It was not Cambyses, but Astyages, who did this; see Herod. i. 119.

[4] Not in the first, but the fifth book of the *Republic*, p. 460.

[5] Minos.

[6] As this sentence cannot be intelligibly rendered without its original in Plato, we subjoin the latter: "As for those youths who excel either in war or other pursuits, they ought both to have other rewards and prizes given them; and specially this, of being allowed the freest intercourse with women, that, at the same time, under this pretext the greatest number of children may spring from such parents."

[7] [This statement reflects light upon some passages of Hermas, and shows with what delicacy he has reproved the gross vices with which Christians could not escape familiarity.]

some said that they were composed of atoms; and others, again, that they eventuate in atoms; and they say that the gods have no more power than men. Plato, too, though he says these are gods, would have them composed of matter. And Pythagoras, after he had made such a toil and moil about the gods, and travelled up and down [for information], at last determines that all things are produced naturally and spontaneously, and that the gods care nothing for men. And how many atheistic opinions Clitomachus the academician introduced, [I need not recount.] And did not Critias and Protagoras of Abdera say, "For whether the gods exist, I am not able to affirm concerning them, nor to explain of what nature they are; for there are many things would prevent me"? And to speak of the opinions of the most atheistical, Euhemerus, is superfluous. For having made many daring assertions concerning the gods, he at last would absolutely deny their existence, and have all things to be governed by self-regulated action.[1] And Plato, who spoke so much of the unity of God and of the soul of man, asserting that the soul is immortal, is not he himself afterwards found, inconsistently with himself, to maintain that some souls pass into other men, and that others take their departure into irrational animals? How can his doctrine fail to seem dreadful and monstrous — to those at least who have any judgment — that he who was once a man shall afterwards be a wolf, or a dog, or an ass, or some other irrational brute? Pythagoras, too, is found venting similar nonsense, besides his demolishing providence. Which of them, then, shall we believe? Philemon, the comic poet, who says, —

"Good hope have they who praise and serve the gods;"

or those whom we have mentioned — Euhemerus, and Epicurus, and Pythagoras, and the others who deny that the gods are to be worshipped, and who abolish providence? Concerning God and providence, Ariston said: —

"Be of good courage: God will still preserve
And greatly help all those who so deserve.
If no promotion waits on faithful men,
Say what advantage goodness offers then.
'Tis granted — yet I often see the just
Faring but ill, from ev'ry honour thrust;
While they whose own advancement is their aim,
Oft in this present life have all they claim.
But we must look beyond, and wait the end,
That consummation to which all things tend.
'Tis not, as vain and wicked men have said,
By an unbridled destiny we're led:
It is not blinded chance that rules the world,
Nor uncontrolled are all things onward hurled.
The wicked blinds himself with this belief;
But be ye sure, of all rewards, the chief
Is still reserved for those who holy live;
And Providence to wicked men will give

Only the just reward which is their meed,
And fitting punishment for each bad deed."

And one can see how inconsistent with each other are the things which others, and indeed almost the majority, have said about God and providence. For some have absolutely cancelled God and providence; and others, again, have affirmed God, and have avowed that all things are governed by providence. The intelligent hearer and reader must therefore give minute attention to their expressions; as also Simylus said: "It is the custom of the poets to name by a common designation the surpassingly wicked and the excellent; we therefore must discriminate." As also Philemon says: "A senseless man who sits and merely hears is a troublesome feature; for he does not blame himself, so foolish is he." We must then give attention, and consider what is said, critically inquiring into what has been uttered by the philosophers and the poets.

CHAP. VIII. — WICKEDNESS ATTRIBUTED TO THE GODS BY HEATHEN WRITERS.

For, denying that there are gods, they again acknowledge their existence, and they said they committed grossly wicked deeds. And, first, of Jove the poets euphoniously sing the wicked actions. And Chrysippus, who talked a deal of nonsense, is he not found publishing that Juno had the foulest intercourse with Jupiter? For why should I recount the impurities of the so-called mother of the gods, or of Jupiter Latiaris thirsting for human blood, or the castrated Attis; or of Jupiter, surnamed Tragedian, and how he defiled himself, as they say, and now is worshipped among the Romans as a god? I am silent about the temples of Antinous, and of the others whom you call gods. For when related to sensible persons, they excite laughter. They who elaborated such a philosophy regarding either the non-existence of God, or promiscuous intercourse and beastly concubinage, are themselves condemned by their own teachings. Moreover, we find from the writings they composed that the eating of human flesh was received among them; and they record that those whom they honour as gods were the first to do these things.

CHAP. IX. — CHRISTIAN DOCTRINE OF GOD AND HIS LAW.

Now we also confess that God exists, but that He is one, the creator, and maker, and fashioner of this universe; and we know that all things are arranged by His providence, but by Him alone. And we have learned a holy law; but we have as lawgiver Him who is really God, who teaches us to act righteously, and to be pious, and to do good. And concerning piety [1] He says, "Thou shalt have no other gods before me. Thou shalt not make unto thee any graven image, or any likeness of anything that is in heaven above, or that is in the earth beneath, or that is in the water under the earth : thou shalt not bow down thyself to them, nor serve them : for I am the LORD thy God." [2] And of doing good He said : "Honour thy father and thy mother ; that it may be well with thee, and that thy days may be long in the land which I the LORD God give thee." Again, concerning righteousness : "Thou shalt not commit adultery. Thou shalt not kill. Thou shalt not steal. Thou shalt not bear false witness against thy neighbour. Thou shalt not covet thy neighbour's wife, thou shalt not covet thy neighbour's house, nor his land, nor his man-servant, nor his maid-servant, nor his ox, nor his beast of burden, nor any of his cattle, nor any-thing that is thy neighbour's. Thou shalt not wrest the judgment of the poor in his cause.[3] From every unjust matter keep thee far. The innocent and righteous thou shalt not slay ; thou shalt not justify the wicked ; and thou shalt not take a gift, for gifts blind the eyes of them that see and pervert righteous words." Of this divine law, then, Moses, who also was God's servant, was made the minister both to all the world, and chiefly to the Hebrews, who were also called Jews, whom an Egyptian king had in ancient days enslaved, and who were the righteous seed of godly and holy men — Abraham, and Isaac, and Jacob. God, being mindful of them, and doing marvellous and strange miracles by the hand of Moses, delivered them, and led them out of Egypt, leading them through what is called the desert ; whom He also settled again in the land of Canaan, which afterwards was called Judæa, and gave them a law, and taught them these things. Of this great and wonderful law, which tends to all righteousness, the ten heads are such as we have already rehearsed.

CHAP. X. — OF HUMANITY TO STRANGERS.

Since therefore they were strangers in the land of Egypt, being by birth Hebrews from the land of Chaldæa, — for at that time, there being a famine, they were obliged to migrate to Egypt for the sake of buying food there, where also for a time they sojourned ; and these things befell them in accordance with a predic-tion of God, — having sojourned, then, in Egypt for 430 years, when Moses was about to lead them out into the desert, God taught them by the law, saying, " Ye shall not afflict a stranger ; for ye know the heart of a stranger : for your-selves were strangers in the land of Egypt." [4]

CHAP. XI. — OF REPENTANCE.

And when the people transgressed the law which had been given to them by God, God being good and pitiful, unwilling to destroy them, in addition to His giving them the law, afterwards sent forth also prophets to them from among their brethren, to teach and remind them of the contents of the law, and to turn them to repentance, that they might sin no more. But if they persisted in their wicked deeds, He fore-warned them that they should be delivered into subjection to all the kingdoms of the earth ; and that this has already happened them is manifest. Concerning repentance, then, Isaiah the prophet, generally indeed to all, but expressly to the peo-ple, says : " Seek ye the LORD while He may be found, call ye upon Him while He is near : let the wicked forsake his ways, and the unright-eous man his thoughts : and let him return unto the LORD his God, and he will find mercy, for He will abundantly pardon." [5] And another prophet, Ezekiel, says : " If the wicked will turn from all his sins that he hath committed, and keep all My statutes, and do that which is right in My sight, he shall surely live, he shall not die. All his transgressions that he hath committed, they shall not be mentioned unto him ; but in his righteousness that he hath done he shall live : for I desire not the death of the sinner, saith the Lord, but that he turn from his wicked way, and live." [6] Again Isaiah : " Ye who take deep and wicked counsel, turn ye, that ye may be saved." [7] And another prophet, Jeremiah : " Turn to the LORD your God, as a grape-gath-erer to his basket, and ye shall find mercy." [8] Many therefore, yea rather, countless are the sayings in the Holy Scriptures regarding repent-ance, God being always desirous that the race of men turn from all their sins.

CHAP. XII. — OF RIGHTEOUSNESS.

Moreover, concerning the righteousness which the law enjoined, confirmatory utterances are found both with the prophets and in the Gospels, because they all spoke inspired by one Spirit of God. Isaiah accordingly spoke thus : " Put away the evil of your doings from your souls ; learn to do well, seek judgment, relieve the oppressed, judge the fatherless, plead for the widow." [9] And again the same prophet said : " Loose every band of wickedness, dissolve every oppressive contract, let the oppressed go free, and tear up every un-righteous bond. Deal out thy bread to the hungry, and bring the houseless poor to thy home. When thou seest the naked, cover him, and hide not thyself from thine own flesh. Then shall thy light

---

[1] Or, right worship.
[2] Ex. xx. 3.
[3] Ex. xxiii. 6.
[4] Ex. xxii. 21.

[5] Isa. lv. 6.
[6] Ezek. xviii. 21.
[7] Isa. xxxi. 6.
[8] Jer. vi. 9.
[9] Isa. i. 16, 17.

break forth as the morning, and thine health shall spring forth speedily, and thy righteousness shall go before thee." [1]   In like manner also Jeremiah says : " Stand in the ways, and see, and ask which is the good way of the LORD your God, and walk in it and ye shall find rest for your souls. Judge just judgment, for in this is the will of the LORD your God." [2]   So also says Hosea : " Keep judgment, and draw near to your God, who established the heavens and created the earth." [3]   And another, Joel, spoke in agreement with these : " Gather the people, sanctify the congregation, assemble the elders, gather the children that are in arms ; let the bridegroom go forth of his chamber, and the bride out of her closet, and pray to the LORD thy God urgently that he may have mercy upon you, and blot out your sins." [4] In like manner also another, Zachariah : " Thus saith the LORD Almighty, Execute true judgment, and show mercy and compassion every man to his brother ; and oppress not the widow, nor the fatherless, nor the stranger ; and let none of you imagine evil against his brother in your heart, saith the LORD Almighty." [5]

CHAP. XIII. — OF CHASTITY.

And concerning chastity, the holy word teaches us not only not to sin in act, but not even in thought, not even in the heart to think of any evil, nor look on another man's wife with our eyes to lust after her. Solomon, accordingly, who was a king and a prophet, said : " Let thine eyes look right on, and let thine eyelids look straight before thee : make straight paths for your feet." [6] And the voice of the Gospel teaches still more urgently concerning chastity, saying : " Whosoever looketh on a woman who is not his own wife, to lust after her, hath committed adultery with her already in his heart." [7]   " And he that marrieth," says [the Gospel], " her that is divorced from her husband, committeth adultery ; and whosoever putteth away his wife, saving for the cause of fornication, causeth her to commit adultery." [8] Because Solomon says : " Can a man take fire in his bosom, and his clothes not be burned? Or can one walk upon hot coals, and his feet not be burned? So he that goeth in to a married woman shall not be innocent." [9]

CHAP. XIV. — OF LOVING OUR ENEMIES.

And that we should be kindly disposed, not only towards those of our own stock, as some suppose, Isaiah the prophet said : " Say to those that hate you, and that cast you out, Ye are our brethren, that the name of the LORD may be glorified, and be apparent in their joy." [10]   And the Gospel says : " Love your enemies, and pray for them that despitefully use you. For if ye love them who love you, what reward have ye? This do also the robbers and the publicans." [11]   And those that do good it teaches not to boast, lest they become men-pleasers. For it says : " Let not your left hand know what your right hand doeth." [12]   Moreover, concerning subjection to authorities and powers, and prayer for them, the divine word gives us instructions, in order that " we may lead a quiet and peaceable life." [13]   And it teaches us to render all things to all, [14] " honour to whom honour, fear to whom fear, tribute to whom tribute ; to owe no man anything, but to love all."

CHAP. XV. — THE INNOCENCE OF THE CHRISTIANS DEFENDED.

Consider, therefore, whether those who teach such things can possibly live indifferently, and be commingled in unlawful intercourse, or, most impious of all, eat human flesh, especially when we are forbidden so much as to witness shows of gladiators, lest we become partakers and abettors of murders. But neither may we see the other spectacles, [15] lest our eyes and ears be defiled, participating in the utterances there sung. For if one should speak of cannibalism, in these spectacles the children of Thyestes and Tereus are eaten ; and as for adultery, both in the case of men and of gods, whom they celebrate in elegant language for honours and prizes, this is made the subject of their dramas. But far be it from Christians to conceive any such deeds ; for with them temperance dwells, self-restraint is practised, monogamy is observed, chastity is guarded, iniquity exterminated, sin extirpated, righteousness exercised, law administered, worship performed, God acknowledged : truth governs, grace guards, peace screens them ; the holy word guides, wisdom teaches, life directs, God reigns. Therefore, though we have much to say regarding our manner of life, and the ordinances of God, the maker of all creation, we yet consider that we have for the present reminded you of enough to induce you to study these things, especially since you can now read [our writings] for yourself, that as you have been fond of acquiring information, you may still be studious in this direction also.

---

[1] Isa. lviii. 6.
[2] Jer. vi. 16.
[3] Hos. xii. 6.
[4] Joel ii. 16.
[5] Zech. vii. 9, 10.
[6] Prov. iv. 25.
[7] Matt. v. 28.
[8] Matt. v. 32.
[9] Prov. vi. 27-29.

[10] Isa. lxvi. 5.
[11] Matt. v. 44, 46.
[12] Matt. vi. 3.
[13] 1 Tim. ii. 2.
[14] Rom. xiii. 7, 8.
[15] At the theatres. [N.B. — Let the easy Christians of our age be reminded of this warning; frequenting, as they do, plays and operas equally defiling, impure in purport often, even when not gross in language.]

CHAP. XVI. — UNCERTAIN CONJECTURES OF THE
PHILOSOPHERS.

But I wish now to give you a more accurate demonstration, God helping me, of the historical periods, that you may see that our doctrine is not modern nor fabulous, but more ancient and true than all poets and authors who have written in uncertainty. For some, maintaining that the world was uncreated, went into infinity;[1] and others, asserting that it was created, said that already 153, 075 years had passed. This is stated by Apollonius the Egyptian. And Plato, who is esteemed to have been the wisest of the Greeks, into what nonsense did he run? For in his book entitled *The Republic*,[2] we find him expressly saying: "For if things had in all time remained in their present arrangement, when ever could any new thing be discovered? For ten thousand times ten thousand years elapsed without record, and one thousand or twice as many years have gone by since some things were discovered by Dædalus, and some by Orpheus, and some by Palamedes." And when he says that these things happened, he implies that ten thousand times ten thousand years elapsed from the flood to Dædalus. And after he has said a great deal about the cities of the world, and the settlements, and the nations, that he has said these things conjecturally. For he says, "If then, my friend, some god should promise us, that if we attempted to make a survey of legislation, the things now said,"[3] etc., which shows that he was speaking by guess; and if by guess, then what he says is not true.

CHAP. XVII. — ACCURATE INFORMATION OF THE
CHRISTIANS.

It behoved, therefore, that he should the rather become a scholar of God in this matter of legislation, as he himself confessed that in no other way could he gain accurate information than by God's teaching him through the law. And did not the poets Homer and Hesiod and Orpheus profess that they themselves had been instructed by Divine Providence? Moreover, it is said that among your writers there were prophets and prognosticators, and that those wrote accurately who were informed by them. How much more, then, shall *we* know the truth who are instructed by the holy prophets, who were possessed by[4] the Holy Spirit of God! On this account all the prophets spoke harmoniously and in agreement with one another, and foretold the things that would come to pass in all the world. For

the very accomplishment of predicted and already consummated events should demonstrate to those who are fond of information, yea rather, who are lovers of truth, that those things are really true which they declared concerning the epochs and eras before the deluge:[5] to wit, how the years have run on since the world was created until now, so as to manifest the ridiculous mendacity of your authors, and show that their statements are not true.

CHAP. XVIII. — ERRORS OF THE GREEKS ABOUT
THE DELUGE.

For Plato, as we said above, when he had demonstrated that a deluge had happened, said that it extended not over the whole earth, but only over the plains, and that those who fled to the highest hills saved themselves. But others say that there existed Deucalion and Pyrrha, and that they were preserved in a chest; and that Deucalion, after he came out of the chest, flung stones behind him, and that men were produced from the stones; from which circumstance they say that men in the mass are named "people."[6] Others, again, say that Clymenus existed in a second flood. From what has already been said, it is evident that they who wrote such things and philosophized to so little purpose are miserable, and very profane and senseless persons. But Moses, our prophet and the servant of God, in giving an account of the genesis of the world, related in what manner the flood came upon the earth, telling us, besides, how the details of the flood came about, and relating no fable of Pyrrha nor of Deucalion or Clymenus; nor, forsooth, that only the plains were submerged, and that those only who escaped to the mountains were saved.

CHAP. XIX. — ACCURATE ACCOUNT OF THE DELUGE.

And neither does he make out that there was a second flood: on the contrary, he said that never again would there be a flood of water on the world; as neither indeed has there been, nor ever shall be. And he says that eight human beings were preserved in the ark, in that which had been prepared by God's direction, not by Deucalion, but by Noah; which Hebrew word means in English[7] "rest," as we have elsewhere shown that Noah, when he announced to the men then alive that there was a flood coming, prophesied to them, saying, Come thither, God calls you to repentance. On this account he was fitly called Deucalion.[8] And this Noah had three sons (as we mentioned in the second book), whose names

---

[1] i.e., tracing back its history through an infinite duration.
[2] The following quotation is not from the *Republic*, but from the third book of the *Laws*, p. 676.
[3] Plato goes on to say, that if he had this pledge of divine assistance, he would go further in his speculation; and therefore Theophilus argues that what he said without this assistance he felt to be unsafe.
[4] Literally, "contained."

[5] [See *supra*, book i. cap. 14, p. 93, the author's account of his own conversion.]
[6] λαός, from λᾶας, stone.
[7] Literally, in Greek, ἀνάπαυσις.
[8] Deucalion, from Δεῦτε, come, and καλέω, I call.

were Shem, and Ham, and Japhet; and these had three wives, one wife each; each man and his wife. This man some have surnamed Eunuchus. All the eight persons, therefore, who were found in the ark were preserved. And Moses showed that the flood lasted forty days and forty nights, torrents pouring from heaven, and from the fountains of the deep breaking up, so that the water overtopped every high hill 15 cubits. And thus the race of all the men that then were was destroyed, and those only who were protected in the ark were saved; and these, we have already said, were eight. And of the ark, the remains are to this day to be seen in the Arabian mountains. This, then, is in sum the history of the deluge.

CHAP. XX. — ANTIQUITY OF MOSES.

And Moses, becoming the leader of the Jews, as we have already stated, was expelled from the land of Egypt by the king, Pharaoh, whose name was Amasis, and who, they say, reigned after the expulsion of the people 25 years and 4 months, as Manetho assumes. And after him [reigned] Chebron, 13 years. And after him Amenophis, 20 years 7 months. And after him his sister Amessa, 21 years 1 month. And after her Mephres, 12 years 9 months. And after him Methramuthosis, 20 years and 10 months. And after him Tythmoses, 9 years 8 months. And after him Damphenophis, 30 years 10 months. And after him Orus, 35 years 5 months. And after him his daughter, 10 years 3 months. After her Mercheres, 12 years 3 months. And after him his son Armais, 30 years 1 month. After him Messes, son of Miammus, 6 years 2 months. After him Rameses, 1 year 4 months. After him Amenophis, 19 years 6 months. After him his sons Thoessus and Rameses, 10 years, who, it is said, had a large cavalry force and naval equipment. The Hebrews, indeed, after their own separate history, having at that time migrated into the land of Egypt, and been enslaved by the king Tethmosis, as already said, built for him strong cities, Peitho, and Rameses, and On, which is Heliopolis; so that the Hebrews, who also are our ancestors, and from whom we have those sacred books which are older than all authors, as already said, are proved to be more ancient than the cities which were at that time renowned among the Egyptians. And the country was called Egypt from the king Sethos. For the word Sethos, they say, is pronounced "Egypt."[1] And Sethos had a brother, by name Armais. He is called Danaus, the same who passed from Egypt to Argos, whom the other authors mention as being of very ancient date.

CHAP. XXI. — OF MANETHO'S INACCURACY.

And Manetho, who among the Egyptians gave out a great deal of nonsense, and even impiously charged Moses and the Hebrews who accompanied him with being banished from Egypt on account of leprosy, could give no accurate chronological statement. For when he said they were shepherds, and enemies of the Egyptians, he uttered truth indeed, because he was forced to do so. For our forefathers who sojourned in Egypt were truly shepherds, but not lepers. For when they came into the land called Jerusalem, where also they afterwards abode, it is well known how their priests, in pursuance of the appointment of God, continued in the temple, and there healed every disease, so that they cured lepers and every unsoundness. The temple was built by Solomon the king of Judæa. And from Manetho's own statement his chronological error is manifest. (As it is also in respect of the king who expelled them, Pharaoh by name. For he no longer ruled them. For having pursued the Hebrews, he and his army were engulphed in the Red Sea. And he is in error still further, in saying that the shepherds made war against the Egyptians.) For they went out of Egypt, and thenceforth dwelt in the country now called Judæa, 313[2] years before Danaus came to Argos. And that most people consider him older than any other of the Greeks is manifest. So that Manetho has unwillingly declared to us, by his own writings, two particulars of the truth: first, avowing that they were shepherds; secondly, saying that they went out of the land of Egypt. So that even from these writings Moses and his followers are proved to be 900 or even 1000 years prior to the Trojan war.[3]

CHAP. XXII. — ANTIQUITY OF THE TEMPLE.

Then concerning the building of the temple in Judæa, which Solomon the king built 566 years after the exodus of the Jews from Egypt, there is among the Tyrians a record how the temple was built; and in their archives writings have been preserved, in which the temple is proved to have existed 143[4] years 8 months before the Tyrians founded Carthage (and this record was made by Hiram[5] (that is the name of the king of the Tyrians), the son of Abimalus, on account of the hereditary friendship which existed between Hiram and Solomon, and at the same time on account of the surpassing wisdom possessed by Solomon. For they continually engaged with each other in discussing difficult problems. And proof of this exists in their correspondence, which to this day is preserved

---

[1] Or, reading ὁ γὰρ Σέθως, "Sethos is also called Egyptus."

[2] The Benedictine editor shows that this should be 393 years.
[3] The correct date would be about 400 years.
[4] Others read 134 years.
[5] Literally, Hieromus.

among the Tyrians, and the writings that passed between them) ; as Menander the Ephesian, while narrating the history of the Tyrian kingdom, records, speaking thus : " For when Abimalus the king of the Tyrians died, his son Hiram succeeded to the kingdom. He lived 53 years. And Bazorus succeeded him, who lived 43, and reigned 17 years. And after him followed Methuastartus, who lived 54 years, and reigned 12. And after him succeeded his brother Atharymus, who lived 58 years, and reigned 9. He was slain by his brother of the name of Helles, who lived 50 years, and reigned 8 months. He was killed by Juthobalus, priest of Astarte, who lived 40 years, and reigned 12. He was succeeded by his son Bazorus, who lived 45 years, and reigned 7. And to him his son Metten succeeded, who lived 32 years, and reigned 29. Pygmalion, son of Pygmalius succeeded him, who lived 56 years, and reigned 7.[1] And in the 7th year of his reign, his sister, fleeing to Libya, built the city which to this day is called Carthage." The whole period, therefore, from the reign of Hiram to the founding of Carthage, amounts to 155 years and 8 months. And in the 12th year of the reign of Hiram the temple in Jerusalem was built. So that the entire time from the building of the temple to the founding of Carthage was 143 years and 8 months.

CHAP. XXIII. — PROPHETS MORE ANCIENT THAN GREEK WRITERS.

So then let what has been said suffice for the testimony of the Phœnicians and Egyptians, and for the account of our chronology given by the writers Manetho the Egyptian, and Menander the Ephesian, and also Josephus, who wrote the Jewish war, which they waged with the Romans. For from these very old records it is proved that the writings of the rest are more recent than the writings given to us through Moses, yes, and than the subsequent prophets. For the last of the prophets, who was called Zechariah, was contemporary with the reign of Darius. But even the lawgivers themselves are all found to have legislated subsequently to that period. For if one were to mention Solon the Athenian, he lived in the days of the kings Cyrus and Darius, in the time of the prophet Zechariah first mentioned, who was by many years the last of the prophets.[2] Or if you mention the lawgivers Lycurgus, or Draco, or Minos, Josephus tells us in his writings that the sacred books take precedence of them in antiquity, since even before the reign of Jupiter over the Cretans, and before the Trojan war, the writings of the divine law which has been given to us through Moses were in existence. And

that we may give a more accurate exhibition of eras and dates, we will, God helping us, now give an account not only of the dates after the deluge, but also of those before it, so as to reckon the whole number of all the years, as far as possible ; tracing up to the very beginning of the creation of the world, which Moses the servant of God recorded through the Holy Spirit. For having first spoken of what concerned the creation and genesis of the world, and of the first man, and all that happened after in the order of events, he signified also the years that elapsed before the deluge. And I pray for favour from the only God, that I may accurately speak the whole truth according to His will, that you and every one who reads this work may be guided by His truth and favour. I will then begin first with the recorded genealogies, and I begin my narration with the first man.[3]

CHAP. XXIV. — CHRONOLOGY FROM ADAM.

Adam lived till he begat a son,[4] 230 years. And his son Seth, 205. And his son Enos, 190. And his son Cainan, 170. And his son Mahaleel, 165. And his son Jared, 162. And his son Enoch, 165. And his son Methuselah, 167. And his son Lamech, 188. And Lamech's son was Noah, of whom we have spoken above, who begat Shem when 500 years old. During Noah's life, in his 600th year, the flood came. The total number of years, therefore, till the flood, was 2242. And immediately after the flood, Shem, who was 100 years old, begat Arphaxad. And Arphaxad, when 135 years old, begat Salah. And Salah begat a son when 130. And his son Eber, when 134. And from him the Hebrews name their race. And his son Phaleg begat a son when 130. And his son Reu, when 132. And his son Serug, when 130. And his son Nahor, when 75. And his son Terah, when 70. And his son Abraham, our patriarch, begat Isaac when he was 100 years old. Until Abraham, therefore, there are 3278 years. The fore-mentioned Isaac lived until he begat a son, 60 years, and begat Jacob. Jacob, till the migration into Egypt, of which we have spoken above, lived 130 years. And the sojourning of the Hebrews in Egypt lasted 430 years ; and after their departure from the land of Egypt they spent 40 years in the wilderness, as it is called. All these years, therefore, amount to 3,938. And at that time, Moses having died, Jesus the sun of Nun succeeded to his rule, and governed them 27 years. And after Jesus, when the people had transgressed the commandments of God, they served the king of Mesopotamia, by name Chusarathon, 8 years. Then, on the

---

[1] In this register it seems that the number of years during which each person lived does not include the years of his reign.
[2] But the meaning here is obscure in the original. Malachi was much later than Zechariah.

[3] [Usher, in his *Annals*, honours our author as the father of Christian chronology, p. 3. Paris, 1673.]
[4] i.e., till he begat Seth. [A fragment of the *Chronicon* of Julius Africanus, A.D. 232, is given in Routh's *Reliquiæ*, tom. ii. p. 238, with very rich annotations. pp. 357–509.]

repentance of the people, they had judges: Gothonoel, 40 years; Eglon, 18 years; Aoth, 8 years. Then having sinned, they were subdued by strangers for 20 years. Then Deborah judged them 40 years. Then they served the Midianites 7 years. Then Gideon judged them 40 years; Abimelech, 3 years; Thola, 22 years; Jair, 22 years. Then the Philistines and Ammonites ruled them 18 years. After that Jephthah judged them 6 years; Esbon, 7 years; Ailon, 10 years; Abdon, 8 years. Then strangers ruled them 40 years. Then Samson judged them 20 years. Then there was peace among them for 40 years. Then Samera judged them one year; Eli, 20 years; Samuel, 12 years.

CHAP. XXV. — FROM SAUL TO THE CAPTIVITY.

And after the judges they had kings, the first named Saul, who reigned 20 years; then David, our forefather, who reigned 40 years. Accordingly, there are to the reign of David [from Isaac] 496 years. And after these kings Solomon reigned, who also, by the will of God, was the first to build the temple in Jerusalem; he reigned 40 years. And after him Rehoboam, 17 years; and after him Abias, 7 years; and after him Asa, 41 years; and after him Jehoshaphat, 25 years; and after him Joram, 8 years; and after him Ahaziah, 1 year; and after him Athaliah, 6 years; and after her Josiah, 40 years; and after him Amaziah, 39 years; and after him Uzziah, 52 years; and after him Jotham, 16 years; and after him Ahaz, 17 years; and after him Hezekiah, 29 years; and after him Manasseh, 55 years; and after him Amon, 2 years; and after him Josiah, 31 years; and after him Jehoahaz, 3 months; and after him Jehoiakim, 11 years. Then another Jehoiakim, 3 months 10 days; and after him Zedekiah, 11 years. And after these kings, the people, continuing in their sins, and not repenting, the king of Babylon, named Nebuchadnezzar, came up into Judæa, according to the prophecy of Jeremiah. He transferred the people of the Jews to Babylon, and destroyed the temple which Solomon had built. And in the Babylonian banishment the people passed 70 years. Until the sojourning in the land of Babylon, there are therefore, in all, 4954 years 6 months and 10 days. And according as God had, by the prophet Jeremiah, foretold that the people should be led captive to Babylon, in like manner He signified beforehand that they should also return into their own land after 70 years. These 70 years then being accomplished, Cyrus becomes king of the Persians, who, according to the prophecy of Jeremiah, issued a decree in the second year of his reign, enjoining by his edict that all Jews who were in his kingdom should return to their own country, and rebuild their temple to God, which the fore-

mentioned king of Babylon had demolished. Moreover, Cyrus, in compliance with the instructions of God, gave orders to his own body-guards, Sabessar and Mithridates, that the vessels which had been taken out of the temple of Judæa by Nebuchadnezzar should be restored, and placed again in the temple. In the second year, therefore, of Darius are fulfilled the 70 years which were foretold by Jeremiah.

CHAP. XXVI. — CONTRAST BETWEEN HEBREW AND GREEK WRITINGS.

Hence one can see how our sacred writings are shown to be more ancient and true than those of the Greeks and Egyptians, or any other historians. For Herodotus and Thucydides, as also Xenophon, and most other historians, began their relations from about the reign of Cyrus and Darius, not being able to speak with accuracy of prior and ancient times. For what great matters did they disclose if they spoke of Darius and Cyrus, barbarian kings, or of the Greeks Zopyrus and Hippias, or of the wars of the Athenians and Lacedæmonians, or the deeds of Xerxes or of Pausanias, who ran the risk of starving to death in the temple of Minerva, or the history of Themistocles and the Peloponnesian war, or of Alcibiades and Thrasybulus? For my purpose is not to furnish mere matter of much talk, but to throw light upon the number of years from the foundation of the world, and to condemn the empty labour and trifling of these authors, because there have neither been twenty thousand times ten thousand years from the flood to the present time, as Plato said, affirming that there had been so many years; nor yet 15 times 10,375 years, as we have already mentioned Apollonius the Egyptian gave out; nor is the world uncreated, nor is there a spontaneous production of all things, as Pythagoras and the rest dreamed; but, being indeed created, it is also governed by the providence of God, who made all things; and the whole course of time and the years are made plain to those who wish to obey the truth.[1] Lest, then, I seem to have made things plain up to the time of Cyrus, and to neglect the subsequent periods, as if through inability to exhibit them, I will endeavour, by God's help, to give an account, according to my ability, of the course of the subsequent times.

CHAP. XXVII. — ROMAN CHRONOLOGY TO THE DEATH OF M. AURELIUS.

When Cyrus, then, had reigned twenty-nine years, and had been slain by Tomyris in the country of the Massagetæ, this being in the 62d Olympiad, then the Romans began to increase

---

[1] [Usher notes this as affirmed in general terms only, and qualified afterwards, in cap. xxix , *infra*, note 1, p. 121.]

in power, God strengthening them, Rome having been founded by Romulus, the reputed child of Mars and Ilia, in the 7th Olympiad, on the 21st day of April, the year being then reckoned as consisting of ten months. Cyrus, then, having died, as we have already said, in the 62d Olympiad, this date falls 220 A.U.C., in which year also Tarquinius, surnamed Superbus, reigned over the Romans, who was the first who banished Romans and corrupted the youth, and made eunuchs of the citizens, and, moreover, first defiled virgins, and then gave them in marriage. On this account he was fitly called Superbus in the Roman language, and that is translated "the Proud." For he first decreed that those who saluted him should have their salute acknowledged by some one else. He reigned twenty-five years. After him yearly consuls were introduced, tribunes also and ediles for 453 years, whose names we consider it long and superfluous to recount. For if any one is anxious to learn them, he will ascertain them from the tables which Chryserus the nomenclator compiled: he was a freedman of Aurelius Verus, who composed a very lucid record of all things, both names and dates, from the founding of Rome to the death of his own patron, the Emperor Verus. The annual magistrates ruled the Romans, as we say, for 453 years. Afterwards those who are called emperors began in this order: first, Caius Julius, who reigned 3 years 4 months 6 days; then Augustus, 56 years 4 months 1 day; Tiberius, 22 years; then another Caius, 3 years 8 months 7 days; Claudius, 23 years 8 months 24 days; Nero, 13 years 6 months 28 days; Galba, 2 years 7 months 6 days; Otho, 3 months 5 days; Vitellius, 6 months 22 days; Vespasian, 9 years 11 months 22 days; Titus, 2 years 22 days; Domitian, 15 years 5 months 6 days; Nerva, 1 year 4 months 10 days; Trajan, 19 years 6 months 16 days; Adrian, 20 years 10 months 28 days; Antoninus, 22 years 7 months 6 days; Verus, 19 years 10 days. The time therefore of the Cæsars to the death of the Emperor Verus is 237 years 5 days. From the death of Cyrus, therefore, and the reign of Tarquinius Superbus, to the death of the Emperor Verus, the whole time amounts to 744 years.

CHAP. XXVIII. — LEADING CHRONOLOGICAL EPOCHS.

And from the foundation of the world the whole time is thus traced, so far as its main epochs are concerned. From the creation of the world to the deluge were 2242 years. And from the deluge to the time when Abraham our forefather begat a son, 1036 years. And from Isaac, Abraham's son, to the time when the people dwelt with Moses in the desert, 660 years. And from the death of Moses and the rule of Joshua the son of Nun, to the death of the patriarch David, 498 years. And from the death of David and the reign of Solomon to the sojourning of the people in the land of Babylon, 518 years 6 months 10 days. And from the government of Cyrus to the death of the Emperor Aurelius Verus, 744 years. All the years from the creation of the world amount to a total of 5698 years, and the odd months and days.[1]

CHAP. XXIX. — ANTIQUITY OF CHRISTIANITY.

These periods, then, and all the above-mentioned facts, being viewed collectively, one can see the antiquity of the prophetical writings and the divinity of our doctrine, that the doctrine is not recent, nor our tenets mythical and false, as some think, but very ancient and true. For Thallus mentioned Belus, king of the Assyrians, and Saturn, son of Titan, alleging that Belus with the Titans made war against Jupiter and the so-called gods in his alliance; and on this occasion he says that Gyges, being defeated, fled to Tartessus. At that time Gyges ruled over that country, which then was called Acte, but now is named Attica. And whence the other countries and ·cities derived their names, we think it unnecessary to recount, especially to you who are acquainted with history. That Moses, and not he only, but also most of the prophets who followed him, is proved to be older than all writers, and than Saturn and Belus and the Trojan war, is manifest. For according to the history of Thallus, Belus is found to be 322 years prior to the Trojan war. But we have shown above that Moses lived somewhere about 900 or 1000 years before the sack of Troy. And as Saturn and Belus flourished at the same time, most people do not know which is Saturn and which is Belus. Some worship Saturn, and call him Bel or Bal, especially the inhabitants of the eastern countries, for they do not know who either Saturn or Belus is. And among the Romans he is called Saturn, for neither do they know which of the two is more ancient — Saturn or Bel. So far as regards the commencement of the Olympiads, they say that the observance dates from Iphitus, but according to others from Linus, who is also called Ilius. The order which the whole number of years and Olympiads holds, we have shown above. I think I have now, according to my ability, accurately discoursed both of the godlessness of your practices,[2] and of the whole number of the epochs of history. For if even a chronological error has been committed by us, of, e.g., 50 or 100, or even 200 years, yet

---

[1] [As Verus died A.D. 169, the computation of our author makes the creation, B.C. 5529. Hales, who says B.C. 5411, inspires us with great respect for Theophilus, by the degree of accuracy he attained, using (the LXX.) the same authority as his base. Slight variations in the copies used in his day might have led, one would think, to greater discrepancies.]

[2] Another reading gives, "both of the antiquity of our religion."

not of thousands and tens of thousands, as Plato and Apollonius and other mendacious authors have hitherto written. And perhaps our knowledge of the whole number of the years is not quite accurate, because the odd months and days are not set down in the sacred books.[1] But so far as regards the periods we speak of, we are corroborated by Berosus,[2] the Chaldæan philosopher, who made the Greeks acquainted with the Chaldæan literature, and uttered some things concerning the deluge, and many other points of history, in agreement with Moses; and with the prophets Jeremiah and Daniel also, he spoke in a measure of agreement. For he mentioned what happened to the Jews under the king of the Babylonians, whom he calls Abobassor, and who is called by the Hebrews Nebuchadnezzar. And he also spoke of the temple of Jerusalem, how it was desolated by the king of the Chaldæans, and that the foundations of the temple having been laid the second year of the reign of Cyrus, the temple was completed in the second year of the reign of Darius.

CHAP. XXX. — WHY THE GREEKS DID NOT MEN-
TION OUR HISTORIES.

But the Greeks make no mention of the histories which give the truth: first, because they themselves only recently became partakers of the knowledge of letters; and they themselves own it, alleging that letters were invented, some say among the Chaldæans, and others with the Egyptians, and others again say that they are derived from the Phœnicians. And secondly, because they sinned, and still sin, in not making mention of God, but of vain and useless matters. For thus they most heartily celebrate Homer and Hesiod, and the rest of the poets, but the glory of the incorruptible and only God they not only omit to mention, but blaspheme; yes, and they persecuted, and do daily persecute, those who worship Him. And not only so, but they even bestow prizes and honours on those who in harmonious language insult God; but of those who are zealous in the pursuit of virtue and practise a holy life, some they stoned, some they put to death, and up to the present time they subject them to savage tortures. Wherefore such men have necessarily lost the wisdom of God, and have not found the truth.

If you please, then, study these things carefully, that you may have a compendium[3] and pledge of the truth.

---

[1] [Usher quotes this concession as to the ἀκριβεία or minute delicacy he could not attain. *Ut supra*, p. 119, note 1.]
[2] Berosus flourished in the reign of Alexander the Great.

[3] Otto prefers σύμβουλον instead of σύμβολον, on the authority of one MS. The sense then is, "that you may have a counsellor and pledge of the truth," — the counsellor and pledge of the truth being the book written by Theophilus for Autolycus. [This has been supposed to mean, "that you may have a token and pledge (or earnest) of the truth," i.e., in Christian baptism. Our author uses St. Paul's word (ἀῤῥαβὼν), "the earnest of the spirit," as in 2 Cor. i. 22, and Eph. i. 14.]

WRITINGS OF ATHENAGORAS

INTRODUCTORY NOTE

TO THE

WRITINGS OF ATHENAGORAS

[TRANSLATED BY THE REV. B. P. PRATTEN.]

[A.D. 177.] In placing Athenagoras here, somewhat out of the order usually accepted, I commit no appreciable violence against chronology, and I gain a great advantage for the reader. To some extent we must recognise, in collocation, the principles of affinity and historic growth. Closing up the bright succession of the earlier Apologists, this favourite author affords also a fitting introduction to the great founder of the Alexandrian School, who comes next into view. His work opens the way for Clement's elaboration of Justin's claim, that the whole of philosophy is embraced in Christianity. It is charming to find the primal fountains of Christian thought uniting here, to flow on for ever in the widening and deepening channel of Catholic orthodoxy, as it gathers into itself all human culture, and enriches the world with products of regenerated mind, harvested from its overflow into the fields of philosophy and poetry and art and science. More of this when we come to Clement, that man of genius who introduced Christianity to itself, as reflected in the burnished mirror of his intellect. Shackles are falling from the persecuted and imprisoned faculties of the faithful, and soon the Faith is to speak out, no more in tones of apology, but as mistress of the human mind, and its pilot to new worlds of discovery and broad domains of conquest. All hail the freedom with which, henceforth, Christians are to assume the overthrow of heathenism as a foregone conclusion. The distasteful exposure of heresies was the inevitable task after the first victory. It was the chase and following-up of the adversary in his limping and cowardly retreat, "the scattering of the rear of darkness." With Athenagoras, we touch upon tokens of things to come ; we see philosophy yoked to the chariot of Messiah ; we begin to realize that sibylline surrender of outworn Paganism, and its forecast of an era of light : —

> " Magnus ab integro sæclorum nascitur ordo,
> . . . . quo ferrea primum
> Desinet, ac toto surget gens aurea mundo."

In Athenagoras, whose very name is a retrospect, we discover a remote result of St. Paul's speech on Mars Hill. The apostle had cast his bread upon the waters of Ilissus and Cephisus to find it after many days. "When they heard of the resurrection of the dead, some mocked ; " but here comes a philosopher, from the Athenian *agora*, a convert to St. Paul's argument in his Epistle to the Corinthians, confessing " the unknown God," demolishing the marble mob of deities that so " stirred the apostle's spirit within him," and teaching alike the Platonist and the Stoic to sit at the feet of Jesus. " Dionysius the Areopagite, and the woman named Damaris," are no longer to be despised as the scanty first-fruits of Attica. They too have found a voice in this splendid trophy of the Gospel ; and, " being dead, they yet speak " through him.

To the meagre facts of his biography, which appear below, there is nothing to be added; [1] and I shall restrain my disposition to be a commentator, within the limits of scanty annotations. In the notes to Tatian and Theophilus, I have made the student acquainted with that useful addition to his treatise on *Justin Martyr*, in which the able and judicious Bishop Kaye harmonizes those authors with Justin. The same harmony enfolds the works of Athenagoras,[2] and thus affords a synopsis of Christian teaching under the Antonines; in which precision of theological language is yet unattained, but identity of faith is clearly exhibited. While the Germans are furnishing the scholar with critical editions of the ancients, invaluable for their patient accumulations of fact and illustration, they are so daring in theory and conjecture when they come to exposition, that one enjoys the earnest and wholesome tone of sober comment that distinguishes the English theologian. It has the great merit of being inspired by profound sympathy with primitive writers, and unadulterated faith in the Scriptures. Too often a German critic treats one of these venerable witnesses, who yet live and yet speak, as if they were dead subjects on the dissecting-table. They cut and and carve with anatomical display, and use the microscope with scientific skill; but, oh! how frequently they surrender the saints of God as mere corpses, into the hands of those who count them victims of a blind faith in a dead Christ.

It will not be necessary, after my quotations from Kaye in the foregoing sheets, to do more than indicate similar illustrations of Athenagoras to be found in his pages. The dry version often requires lubrications of devoutly fragrant exegesis; and providentially they are at hand in that elaborate but modest work, of which even this generation should not be allowed to lose sight.

The annotations of Conrad Gesner and Henry Stephans would have greatly enriched this edition, had I been permitted to enlarge the work by adding a version of them. They are often curious, and are supplemented by the interesting letter of Stephans to Peter Nannius, "the eminent pillar of Louvain," on the earliest copies of Athenagoras, from which modern editions have proceeded. The Paris edition of Justin Martyr (1615) contains these notes, as well as the Greek of Tatian, Theophilus, and Athenagoras, with a Latin rendering. As Bishop Kaye constantly refers to this edition, I have considered myself fortunate in possessing it; using it largely in comparing his learned comments with the Edinburgh Version.

A few words as to the noble treatise of our author, on the Resurrection. As a firm and loving voice to this keynote of Christian faith, it rings like an anthem through all the variations of his thought and argument. Comparing his own blessed hope with the delusions of a world lying in wickedness, and looking stedfastly to the life of the world to come, what a sublime contrast we find in this figure of Christ's witness to the sensual life of the heathen, and even to the groping wisdom of the Attic sages. I think this treatise a sort of growth from the mind of one who had studied in the Academe, pitying yet loving poor Socrates and his disciples. Yet more, it is the outcome of meditation on that sad history in the Acts, which expounds St. Paul's bitter reminiscences, when he says that his gospel was, "to the Greeks, foolishness." They never "heard him again on this matter." He left them under the confused impressions they had expressed in the *agora*, when they said, "he seemeth to be a setter-forth of new gods." St. Luke allows himself a smile only half suppressed when he adds, "because he preached unto them *Jesus and Anastasis*," which in their ears was only a barbarian echo to their own *Phœbus and Artemis;* and what did Athenians want of any more wares of that sort, especially under the introduction of a poor Jew from parts unknown? Did the apostle's prophetic soul foresee Athenagoras, as he "departed from among them"? However that may be, his blessed Master "knew what he would do." He could let none of Paul's words fall to the ground, without taking care that some seeds should bring forth fruit a thousand-fold. Here come the sheaves at last. Athenagoras proves, also, what our Saviour meant, when he said to the Galileans, "Ye are the light of the world."

---

[1] But Lardner tells the whole story much better. *Credibility*, vol. ii. p. 193.

[2] The dogmatic value of a patristic quotation depends on the support it finds in other Fathers, under the supremacy of Scripture: hence the utility of Kaye's collocations.

The following is the original INTRODUCTORY NOTICE : —

IT is one of the most singular facts in early ecclesiastical history, that the name of Athenagoras is scarcely ever mentioned. Only two references to him and his writings have been discovered. One of these occurs in the work of Methodius, *On the Resurrection of the Body,* as preserved by Epiphanius (*Hær.,* lxiv.) and Photius (*Biblioth.,* ccxxxiv.). The other notice of him is found in the writings [1] of Philip of Side, in Pamphylia, who flourished in the early part of the fifth century. It is very remarkable that Eusebius should have been altogether silent regarding him ; and that writings, so elegant and powerful as are those which still exist under his name, should have been allowed in early times to sink into almost entire oblivion.

We know with certainty regarding Athenagoras, that he was an Athenian philosopher who had embraced Christianity, and that his *Apology,* or, as he styles it, "Embassy" ($\pi\rho\epsilon\sigma\beta\epsilon\iota a$), was presented to the Emperors Aurelius and Commodus about A.D. 177. He is supposed to have written a considerable number of works, but the only other production of his extant is his treatise on the Resurrection. It is probable that this work was composed somewhat later than the *Apology* (see chap. xxxvi.), though its exact date cannot be determined. Philip of Side also states that he preceded Pantænus as head of the catechetical school at Alexandria ; but this is probably incorrect, and is contradicted by Eusebius. A more interesting and perhaps well-founded statement is made by the same writer respecting Athenagoras, to the effect that he was won over to Christianity while reading the Scriptures in order to controvert them.[2] Both his *Apology* and his treatise on the Resurrection display a practised pen and a richly cultured mind. He is by far the most elegant, and certainly at the same time one of the ablest, of the early Christian Apologists.

---

[1] The fragment in which the notice occurs was extracted from the works of Philip by some unknown writer. It is published as an appendix to Dodwell's *Dissertationes in Irenæum.*

[2] [Here a picture suggests itself. We go back to the times of Hadrian. A persecution is raging against the "Nazarenes." A boyish, but well-cultured Athenian saunters into the market-place to hear some new thing. They are talking of those enemies of the human race, the Christians. Curiosity leads him to their assemblies. He finds them keeping the feast of the resurrection. Quadratus is preaching. He mocks, but is persuaded to open one of St. Paul's Epistles. "What will this babbler say ?" He reads the fifteenth chapter of First Corinthians, and resents it with all the objections still preserved in his pages. One can see him inquiring more about this Paul, and reading the seventeenth chapter of the Acts. What an animated description of his own Athens, and in what a new light it reflects the familiar scenes! He must refute this Paul. But, when he undertakes it, he falls in love with the intrepid assailant of the gods of Greece. Scales fall from his own eyes. How he sees it all at last, we find in the two works here presented, corresponding as they do, first and last, with the two parts of the apostle's speech to the men of Athens.]

A PLEA[1] FOR THE CHRISTIANS

BY ATHENAGORAS THE ATHENIAN: PHILOSOPHER AND CHRISTIAN

To the Emperors Marcus Aurelius Anoninus and Lucius Aurelius Commodus, conquerors of Armenia and Sarmatia, and more than all, philosophers.

CHAP. I. — INJUSTICE SHOWN TOWARDS THE CHRISTIANS.

In your empire, greatest of sovereigns, different nations have different customs and laws ; and no one is hindered by law or fear of punishment from following his ancestral usages, however ridiculous these may be. A citizen of Ilium calls Hector a god, and pays divine honours to Helen, taking her for Adrasteia. The Lacedæmonian venerates Agamemnon as Zeus, and Phylonoë the daughter of Tyndarus; and the man of Tenedos worships Tennes.[2] The Athenian sacrifices to Erechtheus as Poseidon. The Athenians also perform religious rites and celebrate mysteries in honour of Agraulus and Pandrosus, women who were deemed guilty of impiety for opening the box. In short, among every nation and people, men offer whatever sacrifices and celebrate whatever mysteries they please. The Egyptians reckon among their gods even cats, and crocodiles, and serpents, and asps, and dogs. And to all these both you and the laws give permission so to act, deeming, on the one hand, that to believe in no god at all is impious and wicked, and on the other, that it is necessary for each man to worship the gods he prefers, in order that, through fear of the deity, men may be kept from wrong-doing. But why — for do not, like the multitude, be led astray by hearsay — why is a mere name odious to you?[3] Names are not deserving of hatred : it is the unjust act that calls for penalty and punishment. And accordingly, with admiration of your mildness and gentleness, and your peaceful and benevolent disposition towards every man, individuals live in the possession of equal rights ; and the cities, according to their rank, share in equal honour ; and the whole empire, under your intelligent sway, enjoys profound peace. But for us who are called Christians[4] you have not in like manner cared ; but although we commit no wrong—nay, as will appear in the sequel of this discourse, are of all men most piously and righteously disposed towards the Deity and towards your government— you allow us to be harassed, plundered, and persecuted, the multitude making war upon us for our name alone. We venture, therefore, to lay a statement of our case before you—and you will learn from this discourse that we suffer unjustly, and contrary to all law and reason—and we beseech you to bestow some consideration upon us also, that we may cease at length to be slaughtered at the instigation of false accusers. For the fine imposed by our persecutors does not aim merely at our property, nor their insults at our reputation, nor the damage they do us at any other of our greater interests. These we hold in contempt, though to the generality they appear matters of great importance ; for we have learned, not only not to return blow for blow, nor to go to law with those who plunder and rob us, but to those who smite us on one side of the face to offer the other side also, and to those who take away our coat to give likewise our cloak. But, when we have surrendered our property, they plot against our very bodies and souls,[5] pouring

---

[1] Literally, " embassy." [By this name best known to scholars.]
[2] There are here many varieties of reading: we have followed the text suggested by Gesner.
[3] We here follow the text of Otto: others read ἡμῖν.

[4] [Kaye, 153.]
[5] [For three centuries the faithful were made witnesses for Jesus and the resurrection, even unto death; with " spoiling of their goods," not only, but dying daily, and " counted as sheep for the slaughter." What can refute such testimony? They conquered through suffering.

The reader will be pleased with this citation from an author, the neglect of whose heavenly writings is a sad token of spiritual decline in the spirit of our religion: —

" The Lord is sure of His designed advantages out of the sufferings of His Church and of His saints for His name. He loses nothing, and they lose nothing; but their enemies, when they rage most and prevail most, are ever the greatest losers. His own glory grows, the graces of His people grow; *yea, their very number grows*, and that, sometimes, most by their greatest sufferings. This was evident in the first ages of the Christian Church. Where were *the glory of so much invincible love and patience*, if they had not been so put to it ? " Leighton, *Comm. on St. Peter*, Works, vol. iv. p. 478. West's admirable edition, London, Longmans, 1870.]

upon us wholesale charges of crimes of which we are guiltless even in thought, but which belong to these idle praters themselves, and to the whole tribe of those who are like them.

CHAP. II. — CLAIM TO BE TREATED AS OTHERS ARE WHEN ACCUSED.

If, indeed, any one can convict us of a crime, be it small or great, we do not ask to be excused from punishment, but are prepared to undergo the sharpest and most merciless inflictions. But if the accusation relates merely to our name — and it is undeniable, that up to the present time the stories told about us rest on nothing better than the common undiscriminating popular talk, nor has any Christian [1] been convicted of crime — it will devolve on you, illustrious and benevolent and most learned sovereigns, to remove by law this despiteful treatment, so that, as throughout the world both individuals and cities partake of your beneficence, we also may feel grateful to you, exulting that we are no longer the victims of false accusation. For it does not comport with your justice, that others when charged with crimes should not be punished till they are convicted, but that in our case the name we bear should have more force than the evidence adduced on the trial, when the judges, instead of inquiring whether the person arraigned have committed any crime, vent their insults on the name, as if that were itself a crime.[2] But no name in and by itself is reckoned either good or bad; names appear bad or good according as the actions underlying them are bad or good. You, however, have yourselves a clear knowledge of this, since you are well instructed in philosophy and all learning. For this reason, too, those who are brought before you for trial, though they may be arraigned on the gravest charges, have no fear, because they know that you will inquire respecting their previous life, and not be influenced by names if they mean nothing, nor by the charges contained in the indictments if they should be false: they accept with equal satisfaction, as regards its fairness, the sentence whether of condemnation or acquittal. What, therefore, is conceded as the common right of all, we claim for ourselves, that we shall not be hated and punished because we are called Christians (for what has the name [2] to do with our being bad men?), but be tried on any charges which may be brought against us, and either be released on our disproving them, or punished if convicted of crime — not for the name (for no Christian is a bad man unless he falsely profess our doctrines), but for the wrong which has been done. It is thus that we see the philosophers judged. None of them

before trial is deemed by the judge either good or bad on account of his science or art, but if found guilty of wickedness he is punished, without thereby affixing any stigma on philosophy (for he is a bad man for not cultivating philosophy in a lawful manner, but science is blameless), while if he refutes the false charges he is acquitted. Let this equal justice, then, be done to us. Let the life of the accused persons be investigated, but let the name stand free from all imputation. I must at the outset of my defence entreat you, illustrious emperors, to listen to me impartially: not to be carried away by the common irrational talk and prejudge the case, but to apply your desire of knowledge and love of truth to the examination of our doctrine also. Thus, while you on your part will not err through ignorance, we also, by disproving the charges arising out of the undiscerning rumour of the multitude, shall cease to be assailed.

CHAP. III. — CHARGES BROUGHT AGAINST THE CHRISTIANS.

Three things are alleged against us: atheism, Thyestean feasts,[3] Œdipodean intercourse. But if these charges are true, spare no class: proceed at once against our crimes; destroy us root and branch, with our wives and children, if any Christian [4] is found to live like the brutes. And yet even the brutes do not touch the flesh of their own kind; and they pair by a law of nature, and only at the regular season, not from simple wantonness; they also recognise those from whom they receive benefits. If any one, therefore, is more savage than the brutes, what punishment that he can endure shall be deemed adequate to such offences? But, if these things are only idle tales and empty slanders, originating in the fact that virtue is opposed by its very nature to vice, and that contraries war against one another by a divine law (and you are yourselves witnesses that no such iniquities are committed by us, for you forbid informations to be laid against us), it remains for you to make inquiry concerning our life, our opinions, our loyalty and obedience to you and your house and government, and thus at length to grant to us the same rights (we ask nothing more) as to those who persecute us. For we shall then conquer them, unhesitatingly surrendering, as we now do, our very lives for the truth's sake.

CHAP. IV. — THE CHRISTIANS ARE NOT ATHEISTS, BUT ACKNOWLEDGE ONE ONLY GOD.

As regards, first of all, the allegation that we are atheists — for I will meet the charges one

---

[1] [Kaye, 154.]
[2] [Tatian, cap. xxvii., *supra*, p. 76.]

[3] [See cap. xxxi. Our Lord was "perfect man," yet our author resents the idea of eating the flesh of one's own kind as worse than brutal. As to the Eucharist the inference is plain.]
[4] Thus Otto: others read, "if any one of men."

by one, that we may not be ridiculed for having no answer to give to those who make them — with reason did the Athenians adjudge Diagoras guilty of atheism, in that he not only divulged the Orphic doctrine, and published the mysteries of Eleusis and of the Cabiri, and chopped up the wooden statue of Hercules to boil his turnips, but openly declared that there was no God at all. But to us, who distinguish God from matter,[1] and teach that matter is one thing and God another, and that they are separated by a wide interval (for that the Deity is uncreated and eternal, to be beheld by the understanding and reason alone, while matter is created and perishable), is it not absurd to apply the name of atheism? If our sentiments were like those of Diagoras, while we have such incentives to piety — in the established order, the universal harmony, the magnitude, the colour, the form, the arrangement of the world — with reason might our reputation for impiety, as well as the cause of our being thus harassed, be charged on ourselves. But, since our doctrine acknowledges one God, the Maker of this universe, who is Himself uncreated (for that which is does not come to be, but that which is not) but has made all things by the Logos which is from Him, we are treated unreasonably in both respects, in that we are both defamed and persecuted.

CHAP. V. — TESTIMONY OF THE POETS TO THE UNITY OF GOD.[2]

Poets and philosophers have not been voted atheists for inquiring concerning God. Euripides, speaking of those who, according to popular preconception, are ignorantly called gods, says doubtingly : —

"If Zeus indeed does reign in heaven above,
He ought not on the righteous ills to send."[3]

But speaking of Him who is apprehended by the understanding as matter of certain knowledge, he gives his opinion decidedly, and with intelligence, thus : —

"Seest thou on high him who, with humid arms,
Clasps both the boundless ether and the earth?
Him reckon Zeus, and him regard as God."[4]

For, as to these so-called gods, he neither saw any real existences, to which a name is usually assigned, underlying them ("Zeus," for instance : "who Zeus is I know not, but by report"), nor that any names were given to realities which actually do exist (for of what use are names to those who have no real existences underlying them?) ; but Him he did see by means of His works, considering with an eye to things unseen the things which are manifest in air, in ether, on earth. Him therefore, from whom proceed all created things, and by whose Spirit they are governed, he concluded to be God ; and Sophocles agrees with him, when he says : —

"There is one God, in truth there is but one,
Who made the heavens, and the broad earth beneath."[5]

[Euripides is speaking] of the nature of God, which fills His works with beauty, and teaching both where God must be, and that He must be One.

CHAP. VI. — OPINIONS OF THE PHILOSOPHERS AS TO THE ONE GOD.

Philolaus, too, when he says that all things are included in God as in a stronghold, teaches that He is one, and that He is superior to matter. Lysis and Opsimus[6] thus define God : the one says that He is an ineffable number, the other that He is the excess of the greatest number beyond that which comes nearest to it. So that since ten is the greatest number according to the Pythagoreans, being the Tetractys,[7] and containing all the arithmetic and harmonic principles, and the Nine stands next to it, God is a unit — that is, one. For the greatest number exceeds the next least by one. Then there are Plato and Aristotle — not that I am about to go through all that the philosophers have said about God, as if I wished to exhibit a complete summary of their opinions ; for I know that, as you excel all men in intelligence and in the power of your rule, in the same proportion do you surpass them all in an accurate acquaintance with all learning, cultivating as you do each several branch with more success than even those who have devoted themselves exclusively to any one. But, inasmuch as it is impossible to demonstrate without the citation of names that we are not alone in confining the notion of God to unity, I have ventured on an enumeration of opinions. Plato, then, says, "To find out the Maker and Father of this universe is difficult ; and, when found, it is impossible to declare Him to all,"[8] conceiving of one uncreated and

---

[1] [Kaye, p. 7.]
[2] [De Maistre, who talks nothing but sophistry when he rides his hobby, and who shocked the pope himself by his fanatical effort to demonstrate the papal system, is, nevertheless, very suggestive and interesting when he condescends to talk simply as a Christian. See his citations showing the heathen consciousness of one Supreme Being. *Soirées de St. Pétersbourg*, vol. i. pp. 225, 280; vol. ii. pp. 379, 380.]
[3] From an unknown play.
[4] From an unknown play; the original is ambiguous; comp. Cic., *De Nat Deorum*, ii. c. 25, where the words are translated — "Seest thou this boundless ether on high which embraces the earth in its moist arms? Reckon this Zeus." Athenagoras cannot so have understood Euripides.

[5] Not found in his extant works.
[6] Common text has ὄψει: we follow the text of Otto. [Gesner notes this corruption, and conjectures that it should be the name of some philosopher.]
[7] One, two, three, and four together forming *ten*.
[8] *Timæus*, p. 28, C.

eternal God. And if he recognises others as well, such as the sun, moon, and stars, yet he recognises them as created: "gods, offspring of gods, of whom I am the Maker, and the Father of works which are indissoluble apart from my will; but whatever is compounded can be dissolved." [1] If, therefore, Plato is not an atheist for conceiving of one uncreated God, the Framer of the universe, neither are we atheists who acknowledge and firmly hold that He is God who has framed all things by the Logos, and holds them in being by His Spirit. Aristotle, again, and his followers, recognising the existence of one whom they regard as a sort of compound living creature ($\zeta\hat{\omega}o\nu$), speak of God as consisting of soul and body, thinking His body to be the etherial space and the planetary stars and the sphere of the fixed stars, moving in circles; but His soul, the reason which presides over the motion of the body, itself not subject to motion, but becoming the cause of motion to the other. The Stoics also, although by the appellations they employ to suit the changes of matter, which they say is permeated by the Spirit of God, they multiply the Deity in name, yet in reality they consider God to be one.[2] For, if God is an artistic fire advancing methodically to the production of the several things in the world, embracing in Himself all the seminal principles by which each thing is produced in accordance with fate, and if His Spirit pervades the whole world, then God is one according to them, being named Zeus in respect of the fervid part ($\tau\grave{o}\ \zeta\acute{e}o\nu$) of matter, and Hera in respect of the air ($\acute{o}\ \grave{a}\acute{\eta}\rho$), and called by other names in respect of that particular part of matter which He pervades.

CHAP. VII.—SUPERIORITY OF THE CHRISTIAN DOCTRINE RESPECTING GOD.

Since, therefore, the unity of the Deity is confessed by almost all, even against their will, when they come to treat of the first principles of the universe, and we in our turn likewise assert that He who arranged this universe is God, — why is it that they can say and write with impunity what they please concerning the Deity, but that against us a law lies in force, though we are able to demonstrate what we apprehend and justly believe, namely that there is one God, with proofs and reason accordant with truth? For poets and philosophers, as to other subjects so also to this, have applied themselves in the way of conjecture, moved, by reason of their affinity with the afflatus

from God,[3] each one by his own soul, to try whether he could find out and apprehend the truth; but they have not been found competent fully to apprehend it, because they thought fit to learn, not from God concerning God, but each one from himself; hence they came each to his own conclusion respecting God, and matter, and forms, and the world. But we have for witnesses of the things we apprehend and believe, prophets, men who have pronounced concerning God and the things of God, guided by the Spirit of God. And you too will admit, excelling all others as you do in intelligence and in piety towards the true God ($\tau\grave{o}\ \check{o}\nu\tau\omega\varsigma\ \theta\epsilon\hat{\iota}o\nu$), that it would be irrational for us to cease to believe in the Spirit from God, who moved the mouths of the prophets like musical instruments, and to give heed to mere human opinions.

CHAP. VIII.—ABSURDITIES OF POLYTHEISM.

As regards, then, the doctrine that there was from the beginning one God, the Maker of this universe, consider it in this wise, that you may be acquainted with the argumentative grounds also of our faith. If there were from the beginning two or more gods, they were either in one and the same place, or each of them separately in his own. In one and the same place they could not be. For, if they are gods, they are not alike; but because they are uncreated they are unlike: for created things are like their patterns; but the uncreated are unlike, being neither produced from any one, nor formed after the pattern of any one. Hand and eye and foot are parts of one body, making up together one man: is God in this sense one?[4] And indeed Socrates was compounded and divided into parts, just because he was created and perishable; but God is uncreated, and, impassible, and indivisible—does not, therefore, consist of parts. But if, on the contrary, each of them exists separately, since He that made the world is above the things created, and about the things He has made and set in order, where can the other or the rest be? For if the world, being made spherical, is confined within the circles of heaven, and the Creator of the world is above the things created, managing that[5] by His providential care of these, what place is there for the second god, or for the other gods? For he is not in the world, because it belongs to the other; nor about the world, for God the Maker of the world is above it. But if he is neither in the world nor about the world (for

[1] *Timæus*, p. 41, A.
[2] [We must not wonder at the scanty praise accorded by the Apologists to the truths embedded everywhere in Plato and other heathen writers. They felt intensely, that "the world, by wisdom, knew not God; and that it was their own mission to lead men to the only source of true philosophy.]

[3] [See cap. xxx., *infra*. Important, as showing the degree of value attributed by the Fathers to the Sibylline and Orphic sayings. Comp. Kaye, p. 177.]
[4] i. e., Do several gods make up one God? — OTTO. Others read affirmatively, "God is one."
[5] i.e., the world.

all that surrounds it is occupied by this one [1]), where is he? Is he above the world and [the first] God? In another world, or about another? But if he is in another or about another, then he is not about us, for he does not govern the world; nor is his power great, for he exists in a circumscribed space. But if he is neither in another world (for all things are filled by the other), nor about another (for all things are occupied by the other), he clearly does not exist at all, for there is no place in which he can be. Or what does he do, seeing there is another to whom the world belongs, and he is above the Maker of the world, and yet is neither in the world nor about the world? Is there, then, some other place where he can stand? But God, and what belongs to God, are above him. And what, too, shall be the place, seeing that the other fills the regions which are above the world? Perhaps he exerts a providential care? [By no means.] And yet, unless he does so, he has done nothing. If, then, he neither does anything nor exercises providential care, and if there is not another place in which he is, then this Being of whom we speak is the one God from the beginning, and the sole Maker of the world.

CHAP. IX. — THE TESTIMONIES OF THE PROPHETS.

If we satisfied ourselves with advancing such considerations as these, our doctrines might by some be looked upon as human. But, since the voices of the prophets confirm our arguments — for I think that you also, with your great zeal for knowledge, and your great attainments in learning, cannot be ignorant of the writings either of Moses or of Isaiah and Jeremiah, and the other prophets, who, lifted in ecstasy above the natural operations of their minds by the impulses of the Divine Spirit, uttered the things with which they were inspired, the Spirit making use of them as a flute-player [2] breathes into a flute; — what, then, do these men say? "The LORD is our God; no other can be compared with Him." [3] And again: "I am God, the first and the last, and besides Me there is no God." [4] In like manner: "Before Me there was no other God, and after Me there shall be none; I am God, and there is none besides Me." [5] And as to His greatness: "Heaven is My throne, and the earth is the footstool of My feet: what house will ye build for Me, or what is the place of My rest?" [6] But I leave it to you, when you meet with the books themselves, to examine carefully the prophecies contained in them, that you may

on fitting grounds defend us from the abuse cast upon us.

CHAP. X. — THE CHRISTIANS WORSHIP THE FATHER, SON, AND HOLY GHOST.

That we are not atheists, therefore, seeing that we acknowledge one God, uncreated, eternal, invisible, impassible, incomprehensible, illimitable, who is apprehended by the understanding only and the reason, who is encompassed by light, and beauty, and spirit, and power ineffable, by whom the universe has been created through His Logos, and set in order, and is kept in being — I have sufficiently demonstrated. [I say "His Logos"], for we acknowledge also a Son of God. Nor let any one think it ridiculous that God should have a Son. For though the poets, in their fictions, represent the gods as no better than men, our mode of thinking is not the same as theirs, concerning either God the Father or the Son. But the Son of God is the Logos of the Father, in idea and in operation; for after the pattern of Him and by Him [7] were all things made, the Father and the Son being one. And, the Son being in the Father and the Father in the Son, in oneness and power of spirit, the understanding and reason (νοῦς καὶ λόγος) of the Father is the Son of God. But if, in your surpassing intelligence, [8] it occurs to you to inquire what is meant by the Son, I will state briefly that He is the first product of the Father, not as having been brought into existence (for from the beginning, God, who is the eternal mind [νοῦς], had the Logos in Himself, being from eternity instinct with Logos [λογικός]); but inasmuch as He came forth to be the idea and energizing power of all material things, which lay like a nature without attributes, and an inactive earth, the grosser particles being mixed up with the lighter. The prophetic Spirit also agrees with our statements. "The Lord," it says, "made me, the beginning of His ways to His works." [9] The Holy Spirit Himself also, which operates in the prophets, we assert to be an effluence of God, flowing from Him, and returning back again like a beam of the sun. Who, then, would not be astonished to hear men who speak of God the Father, and of God the Son, and of the Holy Spirit, [10] and who declare both their power in union and their distinction in order, called atheists? Nor is our teaching in what relates to the divine nature confined to these points; but we recognise also a multitude of angels and ministers, [11] whom God the Maker and Framer of the world distributed and ap-

---

[1] i. e., the Creator, or first God.
[2] [Kaye, 179. An important comment; comp. cap. vii., *supra*.]
[3] Isa. xli. 4; Ex. xx. 2, 3 (as to sense).
[4] Isa. xliv. 6.
[5] Isa. xliii. 10, 11.
[6] Isa. lxvi. 1.

[7] "Or, by Him and through Him." [Kaye, pp. 155, 175.]
[8] [Kaye, p. 166.]
[9] Prov. viii. 22.
[10] [Compare Theophilus, *supra*, p. 101, and Kaye's note, p. 156.]
[11] [Heb. i. 14, the express doctrine of St. Paul. They are *ministers* to men, not objects of any sort of worship. "Let no man beguile you," etc. Col. ii. 4, 18.]

pointed to their several posts by His Logos, to occupy themselves about the elements, and the heavens, and the world, and the things in it, and the goodly ordering of them all.

CHAP. XI. — THE MORAL TEACHING OF THE CHRISTIANS REPELS THE CHARGE BROUGHT AGAINST THEM.

If I go minutely into the particulars of our doctrine, let it not surprise you. It is that you may not be carried away by the popular and irrational opinion, but may have the truth clearly before you. For presenting the opinions themselves to which we adhere, as being not human, but uttered and taught by God, we shall be able to persuade you not to think of us as atheists. What, then, are those teachings in which we are brought up? "I say unto you, Love your enemies; bless them that curse you; pray for them that persecute you; that ye may be the sons of your Father who is in heaven, who causes His sun to rise on the evil and the good, and sends rain on the just and the unjust." [1] Allow me here to lift up my voice boldly in loud and audible outcry, pleading as I do before philosophic princes. For who of those that reduce syllogisms, and clear up ambiguities, and explain etymologies,[2] or of those who teach homonyms and synonyms, and predicaments and axioms, and what is the subject and what the predicate, and who promise their disciples by these and such like instructions to make them happy: who of them have so purged their souls as, instead of hating their enemies, to love them; and, instead of speaking ill of those who have reviled them (to abstain from which is of itself an evidence of no mean forbearance), to bless them; and to pray for those who plot against their lives? On the contrary, they never cease with evil intent to search out skilfully the secrets of their art,[3] and are ever bent on working some ill, making the art of words and not the exhibition of deeds their business and profession. But among us you will find uneducated persons, and artisans, and old women, who, if they are unable in words to prove the benefit of our doctrine, yet by their deeds exhibit the benefit arising from their persuasion of its truth: they do not rehearse speeches, but exhibit good works; when struck, they do not strike again; when robbed, they do not go to law; they give to those that ask of them, and love their neighbours as themselves.

CHAP. XII. — CONSEQUENT ABSURDITY OF THE CHARGE OF ATHEISM.

Should we, then, unless we believed that a God presides over the human race, thus purge ourselves from evil? Most certainly not. But because we are persuaded that we shall give an account of everything in the present life to God who made us and the world, we adopt a temperate and benovolent and generally despised method of life, believing that we shall suffer no such great evil here, even should our lives be taken from us, compared with what we shall there receive for our meek and benevolent and moderate life from the great Judge. Plato indeed has said that Minos and Rhadamanthus will judge and punish the wicked; but we say that, even if a man be Minos or Rhadamanthus himself, or their father, even he will not escape the judgment of God. Are, then, those who consider life to be comprised in this, "Let us eat and drink, for to-morrow we die," and who regard death as a deep sleep and forgetfulness ("sleep and death, twin-brothers"[4]), to be accounted pious; while men who reckon the present life of very small worth indeed, and who are conducted to the future life by this one thing alone, that they know God and His Logos, what is the oneness of the Son with the Father, what the communion of the Father with the Son, what is the Spirit, what is the unity of these three, the Spirit, the Son, the Father, and their distinction in unity; and who know that the life for which we look is far better than can be described in words, provided we arrive at it pure from all wrong-doing; who, moreover, carry our benevolence to such an extent, that we not only love our friends ("for if ye love them," He says, "that love you, and lend to them that lend to you, what reward will ye have?"[5]), — shall we, I say, when such is our character, and when we live such a life as this, that we may escape condemnation at last, not be accounted pious? These, however, are only small matters taken from great, and a few things from many, that we may not further trespass on your patience; for those who test honey and whey, judge by a small quantity whether the whole is good.

CHAP. XIII. — WHY THE CHRISTIANS DO NOT OFFER SACRIFICES.

But, as most of those who charge us with atheism, and that because they have not even the dreamiest conception of what God is, and are doltish and utterly unacquainted with natural and divine things, and such as measure piety by the rule of sacrifices, charges us with not acknowledging the same gods as the cities, be pleased to attend to the following considerations, O emperors, on both points. And first, as to our not sacrificing: the Framer and Father of

---

[1] Luke vi. 27, 28; Matt. v. 44, 45.
[2] [Kaye, pp. 212–217.]
[3] The meaning is here doubtful; but the probable reference is to the practices of the Sophists.

[4] Hom., *Il.*, xvi. 672.
[5] Luke vi. 32, 34; Matt. v. 46.

this universe does not need blood, nor the odour of burnt-offerings, nor the fragrance of flowers and incense,[1] forasmuch as He is Himself perfect fragrance, needing nothing either within or without; but the noblest sacrifice [2] to Him is for us to know who stretched out and vaulted the heavens, and fixed the earth in its place like a centre, who gathered the water into seas and divided the light from the darkness, who adorned the sky with stars and made the earth to bring forth seed of every kind, who made animals and fashioned man. When, holding God to be this Framer of all things, who preserves them in being and superintends them all by knowledge and administrative skill, we "lift up holy hands" to Him, what need has He further of a hecatomb?

> "For they, when mortals have transgress'd or fail'd
> To do aright, by sacrifice and pray'r,
> Libations and burnt-offerings, may be soothed."[3]

And what have I to do with holocausts, which God does not stand in need of?— though indeed it does behove us to offer a bloodless sacrifice and "the service of our reason." [4]

CHAP. XIV. — INCONSISTENCY OF THOSE WHO ACCUSE THE CHRISTIANS.

Then, as to the other complaint, that we do not pray to and believe in the same gods as the cities, it is an exceedingly silly one. Why, the very men who charge us with atheism for not admitting the same gods as they acknowledge, are not agreed among themselves concerning the gods. The Athenians have set up as gods Celeus and Metanira: the Lacedæmonians Menelaus; and they offer sacrifices and hold festivals to him, while the men of Ilium cannot endure the very sound of his name, and pay their adoration to Hector. The Ceans worship Aristæus, considering him to be the same as Zeus and Apollo; the Thasians Theagenes, a man who committed murder at the Olympic games; the Samians Lysander, notwithstanding all the slaughters and all the crimes perpetrated by him; Alcman and Hesiod Medea, and the Cilicians Niobe; the Sicilians Philip the son of Butacides; the Amathusians Onesilus; the Carthaginians Hamilcar. Time would fail me to enumerate the whole. When, therefore, they differ among themselves concerning their gods, why do they bring the charge against us of not agreeing with them? Then look at the practices prevailing among the Egyptians: are they not perfectly ridiculous? For in the temples at their solemn festivals they beat their breasts as for the dead, and sacrifice to the same beings as gods; and no wonder, when they look upon the brutes as gods, and shave themselves when they die, and bury them in temples, and make public lamentation. If, then, we are guilty of impiety because we do not practise a piety corresponding with theirs, then all cities and all nations are guilty of impiety, for they do not all acknowledge the same gods.

CHAP. XV. — THE CHRISTIANS DISTINGUISH GOD FROM MATTER.

But grant that they acknowledge the same. What then? Because the multitude, who cannot distinguish between matter and God, or see how great is the interval which lies between them, pray to idols made of matter, are we therefore, who do distinguish and separate the uncreated and the created, that which is and that which is not, that which is apprehended by the understanding and that which is perceived by the senses, and who give the fitting name to each of them,— are we to come and worship images? If, indeed, matter and God are the same, two names for one thing, then certainly, in not regarding stocks and stones, gold and silver, as gods, we are guilty of impiety. But if they are at the greatest possible remove from one another — as far asunder as the artist and the materials of his art — why are we called to account? For as is the potter and the clay (matter being the clay, and the artist the potter), so is God, the Framer of the world, and matter, which is subservient to Him for the purposes of His art.[5] But as the clay cannot become vessels of itself without art, so neither did matter, which is capable of taking all forms, receive, apart from God the Framer, distinction and shape and order. And as we do not hold the pottery of more worth than him who made it, nor the vessels of glass and gold than him who wrought them; but if there is anything about them elegant in art we praise the artificer, and it is he who reaps the glory of the vessels: even so with matter and God — the glory and honour of the orderly arrangement of the world belongs of right not to matter, but to God, the Framer of matter. So that, if we were to regard the various forms of matter as gods, we should seem to be without any sense of the true God, because we should be putting the things which are dissoluble and perishable on a level with that which is eternal.

---

[1] [Harmless as flowers and incense may be, the Fathers disown them in this way continually.]
[2] [This brilliant condensation of the *Benedicite* (*Song of the Three Children*) affords Kaye occasion to observe that our author is silent as to the sacraments. p. 195.]
[3] Hom., *Il.*, ix. 499 sq., Lord Derby's translation, which version the translator has for the most part used.
[4] Comp. Rom. xii. 1. [Mal. i. 11. "A pure *Mincha*" (Lev. ii. 1) was the unbloody sacrifice of the Jews. This was to be the Christian oblation: hence the offering of Christ's natural blood, as the Latins now teach, was unknown to Theophilus.]

[5] [Kaye, p. 172.]

CHAP. XVI. — THE CHRISTIANS DO NOT WORSHIP
THE UNIVERSE.

Beautiful without doubt is the world, excelling,[1] as well in its magnitude as in the arrangement of its parts, both those in the oblique circle and those about the north, and also in its spherical form.[2] Yet it is not this, but its Artificer, that we must worship. For when any of your subjects come to you, they do not neglect to pay their homage to you, their rulers and lords, from whom they will obtain whatever they need, and address themselves to the magnificence of your palace ; but, if they chance to come upon the royal residence, they bestow a passing glance of admiration on its beautiful structure : but it is to you yourselves that they show honour, as being " all in all." You sovereigns, indeed, rear and adorn your palaces for yourselves ; but the world was not created because God needed it ; for God is Himself everything to Himself, — light unapproachable, a perfect world, spirit, power, reason. If, therefore, the world is an instrument in tune, and moving in well-measured time, I adore the Being who gave its harmony, and strikes its notes, and sings the accordant strain, and not the instrument. For at the musical contests the adjudicators do not pass by the lute-players and crown the lutes. Whether, then, as Plato says, the world be a product of divine art, I admire its beauty, and adore the Artificer ; or whether it be His essence and body, as the Peripatetics affirm, we do not neglect to adore God, who is the cause of the motion of the body, and descend " to the poor and weak elements," adoring in the impassible [3] air (as they term it), passible matter ; or, if any one apprehends the several parts of the world to be powers of God, we do not approach and do homage to the powers, but their Maker and Lord. I do not ask of matter what it has not to give, nor passing God by do I pay homage to the elements, which can do nothing more than what they were bidden ; for, although they are beautiful to look upon, by reason of the art of their Framer, yet they still have the nature of matter. And to this view Plato also bears testimony ; " for," says he, " that which is called heaven and earth has received many blessings from the Father, but yet partakes of body ; hence it cannot possibly be free from change."[4] If, therefore, while I admire the heavens and the elements in respect of their art, I do not worship them as gods, knowing that the law of dissolution is upon them, how can I call those objects gods of which I know the makers to be men? Attend, I beg, to a few words on this subject.

CHAP. XVII. — THE NAMES OF THE GODS AND
THEIR IMAGES ARE BUT OF RECENT DATE.

An apologist must adduce more precise arguments than I have yet given, both concering the names of the gods, to show that they are of recent origin, and concerning their images, to show that they are, so to say, but of yesterday. You yourselves, however, are thoroughly acquainted with these matters, since you are versed in all departments of knowledge, and are beyond all other men familiar with the ancients. I assert, then, that it was Orpheus, and Homer, and Hesiod who [5] gave both genealogies and names to those whom they call gods. Such, too, is the testimony of Herodotus.[6] " My opinion," he says, " is that Hesiod and Homer preceded me by four hundred years, and no more ; and it was they who framed a theogony for the Greeks, and gave the gods their names, and assigned them their several honours and functions, and described their forms." Representations of the gods, again, were not in use at all, so long as statuary, and painting, and sculpture were unknown ; nor did they become common until Saurias the Samian, and Crato the Sicyonian, and Cleanthes the Corinthian, and the Corinthian damsel [7] appeared, when drawing in outline was invented by Saurias, who sketched a horse in the sun, and painting by Crato, who painted in oil on a whitened tablet the outlines of a man and woman ; and the art of making figures in relief (κοροπλαθική) was invented by the damsel,[7] who, being in love with a person, traced his shadow on a wall as he lay asleep, and her father, being delighted with the exactness of the resemblance (he was a potter), carved out the sketch and filled it up with clay : this figure is still preserved at Corinth. After these, Dædalus and Theodorus the Milesian further invented sculpture and statuary. You perceive, then, that the time since representations of form and the making of images began is so short, that we can name the artist of each particular god. The image of Artemis at Ephesus, for example, and that of Athenâ (or rather of Athelâ, for so is she named by those who speak more in the style of the mysteries ; for thus was the ancient image made of the olive-tree called), and the sitting figure of the same goddess, were made by Endœus, a pupil of Dædalus ; the Pythian god was the work of Theodorus and Telecles ; and the Delian

---

[1] Thus Otto; others render " comprising."
[2] [The Ptolemaic universe is conceived of as a sort of hollow ball, or bubble, within which are the spheres moving about the earth. Milton adopts from Homer the idea of such a globe, or bubble, hanging by a chain from heaven (*Paradise Lost*, ii. 10, 51). The oblique circle is the zodiac. The *Septentriones* are referred to also. See *Paradise Lost*, viii. 65-168.]
[3] Some refer this to the human spirit.
[4] *Polit.*, p. 269, D.

[5] We here follow the text of Otto; others place the clause in the following sentence.
[6] ii. 53.
[7] Or, Koré. It is doubtful whether or not this should be regarded as a proper name.

god and Artemis are due to the art of Tectæus and Angelio ; Hera in Samos and in Argos came from the hands of Smilis, and the other statues [1] were by Phidias ; Aphrodité the courtezan in Cnidus is the production of Praxiteles ; Asclepius in Epidaurus is the work of Phidias. In a word, of not one of these statues can it be said that it was not made by man. If, then, these are gods, why did they not exist from the beginning? Why, in sooth, are they younger than those who made them? Why, in sooth, in order to their coming into existence, did they need the aid of men and art? They are nothing but earth, and stones, and matter, and curious art.[2]

CHAP. XVIII. — THE GODS THEMSELVES HAVE BEEN CREATED, AS THE POETS CONFESS.

But, since it is affirmed by some that, although these are only images, yet there exist gods in honour of whom they are made ; and that the supplications and sacrifices presented to the images are to be referred to the gods, and are in fact made to the gods ;[3] and that there is not any other way of coming to them, for

> " 'Tis hard for man
> To meet in presence visible a God ; "[4]

and whereas, in proof that such is the fact, they adduce the eneregies possessed by certain images, let us examine into the power attached to their names. And I would beseech you, greatest of emperors, before I enter on this discussion, to be indulgent to me while I bring forward true considerations ; for it is not my design to show the fallacy of idols, but, by disproving the calumnies vented against us, to offer a reason for the course of life we follow. May you, by considering yourselves, be able to discover the heavenly kingdom also ! For as all things are subservient to you, father and son,[5] who have received the kingdom from above (for " the king's soul is in the hand of God,"[6] saith the prophetic Spirit), so to the one God and the Logos proceeding from Him, the Son, apprehended by us as inseparable from Him, all things are in like manner subjected. This then especially I beg you carefully to consider. The gods, as they affirm, were not from the beginning, but every one of them has come into existence just like ourselves. And in this opinion they all agree. Homer speaks of

> " Old Oceanus,
> The sire of gods, and Tethys ; "[7]

and Orpheus (who, moreover, was the first to invent their names, and recounted their births, and narrated the exploits of each, and is believed by them to treat with greater truth than others of divine things, whom Homer himself follows in most matters, especially in reference to the gods) — he, too, has fixed their first origin to be from water : —

> " Oceanus, the origin of all."

For, according to him, water was the beginning of all things, and from water mud was formed, and from both was produced an animal, a dragon with the head of a lion growing to it, and between the two heads there was the face of a god, named Heracles and Kronos. This Heracles generated an egg of enormous size, which, on becoming full, was, by the powerful friction of its generator, burst into two, the part at the top receiving the form of heaven ($o\mathring{v}\rho a\nu \acute{o}s$), and the lower part that of earth ($\gamma \tilde{\eta}$). The goddess Gê, moreover, came forth with a body ; and Ouranos, by his union with Gê, begat females, Clotho, Lachesis, and Atropos ; and males, the hundred-handed Cottys, Gyges, Briareus, and the Cyclopes Brontes, and Steropes, and Argos, whom also he bound and hurled down to Tartarus, having learnt that he was to be ejected from his government by his children ; whereupon Gê, being enraged, brought forth the Titans.[8]

> " The godlike Gaia bore to Ouranos
> Sons who are by the name of Titans known,
> Because they vengeance [9] took on Ouranos,
> Majestic, glitt'ring with his starry crown." [10]

CHAP. XIX. — THE PHILOSOPHERS AGREE WITH THE POETS RESPECTING THE GODS.

Such was the beginning of the existence both of their gods and of the universe. Now what are we to make of this? For each of those things to which divinity is ascribed is conceived of as having existed from the first. For, if they have come into being, having previously had no existence, as those say who treat of the gods, they do not exist. For, a thing is either uncreated and eternal, or created and perishable. Nor do I think one thing and the philosophers another. " What is that which always is, and has no origin ; or what is that which has been originated, yet never is ? " [11] Discoursing of the intelligible and the sensible, Plato teaches that

---

[1] The reading is here doubtful.
[2] [There were no images or pictures, therefore, in the earliest Christian places of prayer.]
[3] [This was a heathen justification of image-worship, and entirely foreign to the Christian mind. Leighton, *Works*, vol. v. p. 323.]
[4] Hom., *Il.*, xx. 131.
[5] [See Kaye's very important note, refuting Gibbon's cavil, and illustrating the purpose of Bishop Bull, in his quotation. On the περιχώρησις, see Bull, *Fid. Nicænæ*, iv. cap. 4.]
[6] Prov. xxi. 1.

[7] Hom., *Il.*, xiv. 201, 302.
[8] Hom., *Il.*, xiv. 246.
[9] τισάσθην.
[10] Orpheus, *Fragments*.
[11] Plat., *Tim.*, p. 27, D.

that which always is, the intelligible, is unoriginated, but that that which is not, the sensible, is originated, beginning to be and ceasing to exist. In like manner, the Stoics also say that all things will be burnt up and will again exist, the world receiving another beginning. But if, although there is, according to them, a twofold cause, one active and governing, namely providence, the other passive and changeable, namely matter, it is nevertheless impossible for the world, even though under the care of Providence, to remain in the same state, because it is created — how can the constitution of these gods remain, who are not self-existent,[1] but have been originated? And in what are the gods superior to matter, since they derive their constitution from water? But not even water, according to them, is the beginning of all things. From simple and homogeneous elements what could be constituted? Moreover, matter requires an artificer, and the artificer requires matter. For how could figures be made without matter or an artificer? Neither, again, is it reasonable that matter should be older than God; for the efficient cause must of necessity exist before the things that are made.

CHAP. XX. — ABSURD REPRESENTATIONS OF THE GODS.

If the absurdity of their theology were confined to saying that the gods were created, and owed their constitution to water, since I have demonstrated that nothing is made which is not also liable to dissolution, I might proceed to the remaining charges. But, on the one hand, they have described their bodily forms: speaking of Hercules, for instance, as a god in the shape of a dragon coiled up; of others as hundred-handed; of the daughter of Zeus, whom he begat of his mother Rhea; or of Demeter, as having two eyes in the natural order, and two in her forehead, and the face of an animal on the back part of her neck, and as having also horns, so that Rhea, frightened at her monster of a child, fled from her, and did not give her the breast (θηλή), whence mystically she is called Athêlâ, but commonly Phersephoné and Koré, though she is not the same as Athênâ,[2] who is called Koré from the pupil of the eye; — and, on the other hand, they have described their admirable[3] achievements, as they deem them: how Kronos, for instance, mutilated his father, and hurled him down from his chariot, and how he murdered his children, and swallowed the males of them; and how Zeus bound his father, and cast him down to Tartarus, as did Ouranos

also to his sons, and fought with the Titans for the government; and how he persecuted his mother Rhea when she refused to wed him, and, she becoming a she-dragon, and he himself being changed into a dragon, bound her with what is called the Herculean knot, and accomplished his purpose, of which fact the rod of Hermes is a symbol; and again, how he violated his daughter Phersephoné, in this case also assuming the form of a dragon, and became the father of Dionysus. In face of narrations like these, I must say at least this much, What that is becoming or useful is there in such a history, that we must believe Kronos, Zeus, Koré, and the rest, to be gods? Is it the descriptions of their bodies? Why, what man of judgment and reflection will believe that a viper was begotten by a god (thus Orpheus: —

"But from the sacred womb Phanes begat
Another offspring, horrible and fierce,
In sight a frightful viper, on whose head
Were hairs: its face was comely; but the rest,
From the neck downwards, bore the aspect dire
Of a dread dragon"[4]);

or who will admit that Phanes himself, being a first-born god (for he it was that was produced from the egg), has the body or shape of a dragon, or was swallowed by Zeus, that Zeus might be too large to be contained? For if they differ in no respect from the lowest brutes (since it is evident that the Deity must differ from the things of earth and those that are derived from matter), they are not gods. How, then, I ask, can we approach them as suppliants, when their origin resembles that of cattle, and they themselves have the form of brutes, and are ugly to behold?

CHAP. XXI. — IMPURE LOVES ASCRIBED TO THE GODS.

But should it be said that they only had fleshly forms, and possess blood and seed, and the affections of anger and sexual desire, even then we must regard such assertions as nonsensical and ridiculous; for there is neither anger, nor desire and appetite, nor procreative seed, in gods. Let them, then, have fleshly forms, but let them be superior to wrath and anger, that Athênâ may not be seen

"Burning with rage and inly wroth with Jove;"[5]

nor Hera appear thus: —

"Juno's breast
Could not contain her rage."[6]

And let them be superior to grief: —

---

[1] Literally, "by nature."
[2] i.e., Minerva.
[3] Or, "have accurately described."

[4] *Fragments.*
[5] Hom., *Il.,* iv. 23.
[6] *Ibid.,* iv. 24.

"A woful sight mine eyes behold: a man
   I love in flight around the walls! My heart
   For Hector grieves."[1]

For I call even men rude and stupid who give way to anger and grief. But when the "father of men and gods" mourns for his son, —

"Woe, woe! that fate decrees my best belov'd
   Sarpedon, by Patroclus' hand to fall;"[2]

and is not able while he mourns to rescue him from his peril : —

"The son of Jove, yet Jove preserv'd him not;"[3]

who would not blame the folly of those who, with tales like these, are lovers of the gods, or rather, live without any god? Let them have fleshly forms, but let not Aphrodité be wounded by Diomedes in her body : —

"The haughty son of Tydeus, Diomed,
   Hath wounded me;"[4]

or by Arês in her soul : —

"Me, awkward me, she scorns; and yields her charms
   To that fair lecher, the strong god of arms."[5]

"The weapon pierced the flesh."[6]

He who was terrible in battle, the ally of Zeus against the Titans, is shown to be weaker than Diomedes : —

"He raged, as Mars, when brandishing his spear."[7]

Hush! Homer, a god never rages. But you describe the god to me as blood-stained, and the bane of mortals : —

"Mars, Mars, the bane of mortals, stained with blood;"[8]

and you tell of his adultery and his bonds : —

"Then, nothing loth, th' enamour'd fair he led,
   And sunk transported on the conscious bed.
   Down rushed the toils."[9]

Do they not pour forth impious stuff of this sort in abundance concerning the gods? Ouranos is mutilated ; Kronos is bound, and thrust down to Tartarus ; the Titans revolt ; Styx dies in battle : yea, they even represent them as mortal ; they are in love with one another ; they are in love with human beings : —

"Æneas, amid Ida's jutting peaks,
   Immortal Venus to Anchises bore."[10]

Are they not in love? Do they not suffer? Nay, verily, they are gods, and desire cannot touch them! Even though a god assume flesh in pur-

suance of a divine purpose,[11] he is therefore the slave of desire.

"For never yet did such a flood of love,
   For goddess or for mortal, fill my soul;
   Not for Ixion's beauteous wife, who bore
   Pirithöus, sage in council as the gods ;
   Nor the neat-footed maiden Danäe,
   Acrisius' daughter, her who Perséus bore,
   Th' observ'd of all ; nor noble Phœnix' child ;
   . . . . . . nor for Semele ;
   Nor for Alcmena fair ; . . .
   No, nor for Ceres, golden-tressèd queen ;
   Nor for Latona bright ; nor for thyself."[12]

He is created, he is perishable, with no trace of a god in him. Nay, they are even the hired servants of men : —

"Admetus' halls, in which I have endured
   To praise the menial table, though a god."[13]

And they tend cattle : —

"And coming to this land, I cattle fed,
   For him that was my host, and kept this house."[14]

Admetus, therefore, was superior to the god. O prophet and wise one, and who canst foresee for others the things that shall be, thou didst not divine the slaughter of thy beloved, but didst even kill him with thine own hand, dear as he was : —

"And I believed Apollo's mouth divine
   Was full of truth, as well as prophet's art.

(Æschylus is reproaching Apollo for being a false prophet :) —

"The very one who sings while at the feast,
   The one who said these things, alas! is he
   Who slew my son."[15]

CHAP. XXII. — PRETENDED SYMBOLICAL EXPLANATIONS.

But perhaps these things are poetic vagary, and there is some natural explanation of them, such as this by Empedocles : —

"Let Jove be fire, and Juno source of life,
   With Pluto and Nêstis, who bathes with tears
   The human founts."

If, then, Zeus is fire, and Hera the earth, and Aïdoneus the air, and Nêstis water, and these are elements — fire, water, air — none of them is a god, neither Zeus, nor Hera, nor Aïdoneus ; for from matter separated into parts by God is their constitution and origin : —

"Fire, water, earth, and the air's gentle height,
   And harmony with these."

Here are things which without harmony cannot abide ; which would be brought to ruin by strife : how then can any one say that they are

---

1 Ibid., xxii. 168 sq.
2 Ibid., xvi. 433 sq.
3 Ibid., xvi. 522.
4 Ibid., v. 376.
5 Hom., Od., viii. 308 sq., Pope's transl.
6 Hom., Il., v. 858.
7 Hom., Il., xv. 605.
8 Hom., Il., v. 31, 455.
9 Hom., Od., viii. 296-298, Pope's transl.
10 Hom., Il., ii. 820.

11 [οἰκονομίαν. Kaye, p. 174. And see Paris ed., 1615.]
12 Hom., Il., xiv. 315 sqq.
13 Eurip., Alcest., 1 sq.
14 Ibid., 8 sq.
15 From an unknown play of Æschylus.

gods? Friendship, according to Empedocles, has an aptitude to govern, things that are compounded are governed, and that which is apt to govern has the dominion; so that if we make the power of the governed and the governing one and the same, we shall be, unawares to ourselves, putting perishable and fluctuating and changeable matter on an equality with the uncreated, and eternal, and ever self-accordant God. Zeus is, according to the Stoics, the fervid part of nature; Hera is the air (ἀήρ) — the very name, if it be joined to itself, signifying this;[1] Poseidon is what is drunk (water, πόσις). But these things are by different persons explained of natural objects in different ways. Some call Zeus twofold masculine-feminine air; others the season which brings about mild weather, on which account it was that he alone escaped from Kronos. But to the Stoics it may be said, If you acknowledge one God, the supreme and uncreated and eternal One, and as many compound bodies as there are changes of matter, and say that the Spirit of God, which pervades matter, obtains according to its variations a diversity of names, the forms of matter will become the body of God; but when the elements are destroyed in the conflagration, the names will necessarily perish along with the forms, the Spirit of God alone remaining. Who, then, can believe that those bodies, of which the variation according to matter is allied to corruption, are gods? But to those who say that Kronos is time, and Rhea the earth, and that she becomes pregnant by Kronos, and brings forth, whence she is regarded as the mother of all; and that he begets and devours his offspring; and that the mutilation is the intercourse of the male with the female, which cuts off the seed and casts it into the womb, and generates a human being, who has in himself the sexual desire, which is Aphrodité; and that the madness of Kronos is the turn of season, which destroys animate and inanimate things; and that the bonds and Tartarus are time, which is changed by seasons and disappears;—to such persons we say, If Kronos is time, he changes; if a season, he turns about; if darkness, or frost, or the moist part of nature, none of these is abiding; but the Deity is immortal, and immoveable, and unalterable: so that neither is Kronos nor his image God. As regards Zeus again: If he is air, born of Kronos, of which the male part is called Zeus and the female Hera (whence both sister and wife), he is subject to change; if a season, he turns about: but the Deity neither changes nor shifts about. But why should I trespass on your patience by saying more, when you know so well what has been said by each of those who have resolved these things into nature, or what

various writers have thought concerning nature, or what they say concerning Athênâ, whom they affirm to be the wisdom (φρόνησις) pervading all things; and concerning Isis, whom they call the birth of all time (φύσις αἰῶνος), from whom all have sprung, and by whom all exist; or concerning Osiris, on whose murder by Typhon his brother Isis with her son Orus sought after his limbs, and finding them honoured them with a sepulchre, which sepulchre is to this day called the tomb of Osiris? For whilst they wander up and down about the forms of matter, they miss to find the God who can only be beheld by the reason, while they deify the elements and their several parts, applying different names to them at different times: calling the sowing of the corn, for instance, Osiris (hence they say, that in the mysteries, on the finding of the members of his body, or the fruits, Isis is thus addressed: We have found, we wish thee joy), the fruit of the vine Dionysus, the vine itself Semelé, the heat of the sun the thunderbolt. And yet, in fact, they who refer the fables to actual gods, do anything rather than add to their divine character; for they do not perceive, that by the very defence they make for the gods, they confirm the things which are alleged concerning them. What have Europa, and the bull, and the swan, and Leda, to do with the earth and air, that the abominable intercourse of Zeus with them should be taken for the intercourse of the earth and air? But missing to discover the greatness of God, and not being able to rise on high with their reason (for they have no affinity for the heavenly place), they pine away among the forms of matter, and rooted to the earth, deify the changes of the elements: just as if any one should put the ship he sailed in in the place of the steersman. But as the ship, although equipped with everything, is of no use if it have not a steersman, so neither are the elements, though arranged in perfect order, of any service apart from the providence of God. For the ship will not sail of itself; and the elements without their Framer will not move.

CHAP. XXIII. — OPINIONS OF THALES AND PLATO.

You may say, however, since you excel all men in understanding, How comes it to pass, then, that some of the idols manifest power, if those to whom we erect the statues are not gods? For it is not likely that images destitute of life and motion can of themselves do anything without a mover. That in various places, cities, and nations, certain effects are brought about in the name of idols, we are far from denying. None the more, however, if some have received benefit, and others, on the contrary, suffered harm, shall we deem those to be gods who have produced the effects in either

---

[1] Perhaps ἤρ (αηρ) α.

case. But I have made careful inquiry, both why it is that you think the idols to have this power, and who they are that, usurping their names, produce the effects. It is necessary for me, however, in attempting to show who they are that produce the effects ascribed to the idols, and that they are not gods, to have recourse to some witnesses from among the philosophers. First Thales, as those who have accurately examined his opinions report, divides [superior beings] into God, demons, and heroes. God he recognises as the Intelligence (νοῦς) of the world; by demons he understands beings possessed of soul (ψυχικαί); and by heroes the separated souls of men, the good being the good souls, and the bad the worthless. Plato again, while withholding his assent on other points, also divides [superior beings] into the uncreated God and those produced by the uncreated One for the adornment of heaven, the planets, and the fixed stars, and into demons; concerning which demons, while he does not think fit to speak himself, he thinks that those ought to be listened to who have spoken about them. "To speak concerning the other demons, and to know their origin, is beyond our powers; but we ought to believe those who have before spoken, the descendants of gods, as they say — and surely they must be well acquainted with their own ancestors: it is impossible, therefore, to disbelieve the sons of gods, even though they speak without probable or convincing proofs; but as they profess to tell of their own family affairs, we are bound, in pursuance of custom, to believe them. In this way, then, let us hold and speak as they do concerning the origin of the gods themselves. Of Gê and Ouranos were born Oceanus and Tethys; and of these Phorcus, Kronos, and Rhea, and the rest; and of Kronos and Rhea, Zeus, Hera, and all the others, who, we know, are all called their brothers; besides other descendants again of these." [1] Did, then, he who had contemplated the eternal Intelligence and God who is apprehended by reason, and declared His attributes — His real existence, the simplicity of His nature, the good that flows forth from Him that is truth, and discoursed of primal power, and how "all things are about the King of all, and all things exist for His sake, and He is the cause of all;" and about two and three, that He is "the second moving about the seconds, and the third about the thirds;" [2] — did this man think, that to learn the truth concerning those who are said to have been produced from sensible things, namely earth and heaven, was a task transcending his powers? It is not to be believed for a moment. But because he thought

it impossible to believe that gods beget and are brought forth, since everything that begins to be is followed by an end, and (for this is much more difficult) to change the views of the multitude, who receive the fables without examination, on this account it was that he declared it to be beyond his powers to know and to speak concerning the origin of the other demons, since he was unable either to admit or teach that gods were begotten. And as regards that saying of his, "The great sovereign in heaven, Zeus, driving a winged car, advances first, ordering and managing all things, and there follow him a host of gods and demons," [3] this does not refer to the Zeus who is said to have sprung from Kronos; for here the name is given to the Maker of the universe. This is shown by Plato himself: not being able to designate Him by another title that should be suitable, he availed himself of the popular name; not as peculiar to God, but for distinctness, because it is not possible to discourse of God to all men as fully as one might; and he adds at the same time the epithet "Great," so as to distinguish the heavenly from the earthly, the uncreated from the created, who is younger than heaven and earth, and younger than the Cretans, who stole him away, that he might not be killed by his father.

CHAP. XXIV. — CONCERNING THE ANGELS AND GIANTS.

What need is there, in speaking to you who have searched into every department of knowledge, to mention the poets, or to examine opinions of another kind? Let it suffice to say thus much. If the poets and philosophers did not acknowledge that there is one God, and concerning these gods were not of opinion, some that they are demons, others that they are matter, and others that they once were men, — there might be some show of reason for our being harassed as we are, since we employ language which makes a distinction between God and matter, and the natures of the two. For, as we acknowledge a God, and a Son his Logos, and a Holy Spirit, united in essence, — the Father, the Son, the Spirit, because the Son is the Intelligence, Reason, Wisdom of the Father, and the Spirit an effluence, as light from fire; so also do we apprehend the existence of other powers, which exercise dominion about matter, and by means of it, and one in particular, which is hostile to God: not that anything is really opposed to God, like strife to friendship, according to Empedocles, and night to day, according to the appearing and disappearing of the stars (for even if anything had placed itself in opposition to God, it would have ceased to

---

[1] *Tim.*, p. 40, D. E.
[2] Pseudo-Plat., *Epist.*, ii. p. 312, D. E. The meaning is very obscure.

[3] Plat., *Phædr.*, p. 246, E.

exist, its structure being destroyed by the power and might of God), but that to the good that is in God, which belongs of necessity to Him, and co-exists with Him, as colour with body, without which it has no existence (not as being part of it, but as an attendant property co-existing with it, united and blended, just as it is natural for fire to be yellow and the ether dark blue),— to the good that is in God, I say, the spirit which is about matter,[1] who was created by God, just as the other angels were created by Him, and entrusted with the control of matter and the forms of matter, is opposed. For this is the office of the angels,— to exercise providence for God over the things created and ordered by Him; so that God may have the universal and general providence of the whole, while the particular parts are provided for by the angels appointed over them.[2] Just as with men, who have freedom of choice as to both virtue and vice (for you would not either honour the good or punish the bad, unless vice and virtue were in their own power; and some are diligent in the matters entrusted to them by you, and others faithless), so is it among the angels. Some, free agents, you will observe, such as they were created by God, continued in those things for which God had made and over which He had ordained them; but some outraged both the constitution of their nature and the government entrusted to them: namely, this ruler of matter and its various forms, and others of those who were placed about this first firmament (you know that we say nothing without witnesses, but state the things which have been declared by the prophets); these fell into impure love of virgins, and were subjugated by the flesh, and he became negligent and wicked in the management of the things entrusted to him. Of these lovers of virgins, therefore, were begotten those who are called giants.[3] And if something has been said by the poets, too, about the giants, be not surprised at this: worldly wisdom and divine differ as much from each other as truth and plausibility: the one is of heaven and the other of earth; and indeed, according to the prince of matter,—

" We know we oft speak lies that look like truths."[4]

CHAP. XXV. — THE POETS AND PHILOSOPHERS HAVE DENIED A DIVINE PROVIDENCE.

These angels, then, who have fallen from heaven, and haunt the air and the earth, and are no longer able to rise to heavenly things, and the souls of the giants, which are the demons who wander about the world, perform actions similar, the one (that is, the demons) to the natures they have received, the other (that is, the angels) to the appetites they have indulged. But the prince of matter, as may be seen merely from what transpires, exercises a control and management contrary to the good that is in God : —

" Ofttimes this anxious thought has crossed my mind,
    Whether 'tis chance or deity that rules
    The small affairs of men; and, spite of hope
    As well as justice, drives to exile some
    Stripped of all means of life, while others still
    Continue to enjoy prosperity."[5]

Prosperity and adversity, contrary to hope and justice, made it impossible for Euripides to say to whom belongs the administration of earthly affairs, which is of such a kind that one might say of it :—

" How then, while seeing these things, can we say
    There is a race of gods, or yield to laws ? "[6]

The same thing led Aristotle to say that the things below the heaven are not under the care of Providence, although the eternal providence of God concerns itself equally with us below, —

" The earth, let willingness move her or not,
    Must herbs produce, and thus sustain my flocks,"[7]—

and addresses itself to the deserving individually, according to truth and not according to opinion ; and all other things, according to the general constitution of nature, are provided for by the law of reason. But because the demoniac movements and operations proceeding from the adverse spirit produce these disorderly sallies, and moreover move men, some in one way and some in another, as individuals and as nations, separately and in common, in accordance with the tendency of matter on the one hand, and of the affinity for divine things on the other, from within and from without,— some who are of no mean reputation have therefore thought that this universe is constituted without any definite order, and is driven hither and thither by an irrational chance. But they do not understand, that of those things which belong to the constitution of the whole world there is nothing out of order or neglected, but that each one of them has been produced by reason, and that, therefore, they do not transgress the order prescribed to them ; and that man himself, too, so far as He that made him is concerned, is well ordered, both by his original nature, which has one common character for all, and by the constitution of his body, which does not transgress the law imposed upon

---

[1] [Comp. cap. xxvii., *infra.*]
[2] [Kaye, 192. And see cap. x., *supra*, p. 133. Divine Providence does not exclude the ministry of angels by divine appointment. *Resurrection,* cap. xviii., *infra.*]
[3] [The Paris editors caution us against yielding to this interpretation of Gen. vi. 1-4. It was the Rabbinical interpretation. See Josephus, book i. cap. 3.]
[4] Hesiod, *Theog.,* 27. [Traces of the *Nephilim* are found in all mythologies.]

[5] Eurip.: from an unknown play.
[6] *Ibid.*
[7] Eurip., *Cycl.,* 332 sq.

it, and by the termination of his life, which remains equal and common to all alike ; [1] but that, according to the character peculiar to himself and the operation of the ruling prince and of the demons his followers, he is impelled and moved in this direction or in that, notwithstanding that all possess in common the same original constitution of mind.[2]

CHAP. XXVI. — THE DEMONS ALLURE MEN TO THE WORSHIP OF IMAGES.

They who draw men to idols, then, are the aforesaid demons, who are eager for the blood of the sacrifices, and lick them ; but the gods that please the multitude, and whose names are given to the images, were men, as may be learned from their history. And that it is the demons who act under their names, is proved by the nature of their operations. For some castrate, as Rhea ; others wound and slaughter, as Artemis ; the Tauric goddess puts all strangers to death. I pass over those who lacerate with knives and scourges of bones, and shall not attempt to describe all the kinds of demons ; for it is not the part of a god to incite to things against nature.

"But when the demon plots against a man,
He first inflicts some hurt upon his mind."[3]

But God, being perfectly good, is eternally doing good. That, moreover, those who exert the power are not the same as those to whom the statues are erected, very strong evidence is afforded by Troas and Parium. The one has statues of Neryllinus, a man of our own times ; and Parium of Alexander and Proteus : both the sepulchre and the statue of Alexander are still in the forum. The other statues of Neryllinus, then, are a public ornament, if indeed a city can be adorned by such objects as these ; but one of them is supposed to utter oracles and to heal the sick, and on this account the people of the Troad offer sacrifices to this statue, and overlay it with gold, and hang chaplets upon it. But of the statues of Alexander and Proteus (the latter, you are aware, threw himself into the fire near Olympia), that of Proteus is likewise said to utter oracles ; and to that of Alexander —

"Wretched Paris, though in form so fair,
Thou slave of woman"[4] —

sacrifices are offered and festivals are held at the public cost, as to a god who can hear. Is it, then, Neryllinus, and Proteus, and Alexander who exert these energies in connection with the statues, or is it the nature of the matter itself? But

the matter is brass. And what can brass do of itself, which may be made again into a different form, as Amasis treated the footpan,[5] as told by Herodotus? And Neryllinus, and Proteus, and Alexander, what good are they to the sick? For what the image is said now to effect, it effected when Neryllinus was alive and sick.

CHAP. XXVII. — ARTIFICES OF THE DEMONS.

What then? In the first place, the irrational and fantastic movements of the soul about opinions produce a diversity of images (εἴδωλα) from time to time : some they derive from matter, and some they fashion and bring forth for themselves ; and this happens to a soul especially when it partakes of the material spirit[6] and becomes mingled with it, looking not at heavenly things and their Maker, but downwards to earthly things, wholly at the earth, as being now mere flesh and blood, and no longer pure spirit.[7] These irrational and fantastic movements of the soul, then, give birth to empty visions in the mind, by which it becomes madly set on idols. When, too, a tender and susceptible soul, which has no knowledge or experience of sounder doctrines, and is unaccustomed to contemplate truth, and to consider thoughtfully the Father and Maker of all things, gets impressed with false opinions respecting itself, then the demons who hover about matter, greedy of sacrificial odours and the blood of victims, and ever ready to lead men into error, avail themselves of these delusive movements of the souls of the multitude ; and, taking possession of their thoughts, cause to flow into the mind empty visions as if coming from the idols and the statues ; and when, too, a soul of itself, as being immortal,[8] moves comformably to reason, either predicting the future or healing the present, the demons claim the glory for themselves.

CHAP. XXVIII. — THE HEATHEN GODS WERE SIMPLY MEN.

But it is perhaps necessary, in accordance with what has already been adduced, to say a little about their names. Herodotus, then, and Alexander the son of Philip, in his letter to his mother (and each of them is said to have conversed with the priests at Heliopolis, and Memphis, and Thebes), affirm that they learnt from them that the gods had been men. Herodotus speaks thus : "Of such a nature were, they said, the beings represented by these images, they were very far indeed from being gods. However, in the times anterior to them it was otherwise ; then

---

1 [Kaye, p. 190.]
2 Or, "powers of reasoning" (λογισμός).
3 From an unknown tragedian. [A passage which I cannot but apply to the lapse of Tatian.]
4 Hom., *Il.*, iii. 39.

5 [See note to Theophilus, cap. x., *supra*, p. 92.]
6 [Kaye, p. 191; and comp. cap. xxiv., *supra*, p. 142.]
7 [Comp. *On the Resurrection*, cap. xiii., *infra*, p. 439 of *ed.* Edinburgh. Also Kaye, p. 199.]
8 [Kaye, p. 190.]

Egypt had gods for its rulers, who dwelt upon the earth with men, one being always supreme above the rest. The last of these was Horus the son of Osiris, called by the Greeks Apollo. He deposed Typhon, and ruled over Egypt as its last god-king. Osiris is named Dionysus (Bacchus) by the Greeks."[1] "Almost all the names of the gods came into Greece from Egypt."[2] Apollo was the son of Dionysus and Isis, as He rodotus likewise affirms: "According to the Egyptians, Apollo and Diana are the children of Bacchus and Isis; while Latona is their nurse and their preserver."[3] These beings of heavenly origin they had for their first kings: partly from ignorance of the true worship of the Deity, partly from gratitude for their government, they esteemed them as gods together with their wives. "The male kine, if clean, and the male calves, are used for sacrifice by the Egyptians universally; but the females, they are not allowed to sacrifice, since they are sacred to Isis. The statue of this goddess has the form of a woman, but with horns like a cow, resembling those of the Greek representations of Io."[4] And who can be more deserving of credit in making these statements, than those who in family succession, son from father, received not only the priesthood, but also the history? For it is not likely that the priests, who make it their business to commend the idols to men's reverence, would assert falsely that they were men. If Herodotus alone had said that the Egyptians spoke in their histories of the gods as of men, when he says, "What they told me concerning their religion it is not my intention to repeat, except only the names of their deities, things of very trifling importance,"[5] it would behove us not to credit even Herodotus as being a fabulist. But as Alexander and Hermes surnamed Trismegistus, who shares with them in the attribute of eternity, and innumerable others, not to name them individually, [declare the same], no room is left even for doubt that they, being kings, were esteemed gods. That they were men, the most learned of the Egyptians also testify, who, while saying that ether, earth, sun, moon, are gods, regard the rest as mortal men, and the temples as their sepulchres. Apollodorus, too, asserts the same thing in his treatise concerning the gods. But Herodotus calls even their sufferings mysteries. "The ceremonies at the feast of Isis in the city of Busiris have been already spoken of. It is there that the whole multitude, both of men and women, many thousands in number, beat themselves at the close of the sacrifice in honour of a god whose name a religious scruple forbids me to mention."[6] If they are gods, they are also immortal; but if people are beaten for them, and their sufferings are mysteries, they are men, as Herodotus himself says: "Here, too, in this same precinct of Minerva at Saïs, is the burial-place of one whom I think it not right to mention in such a connection. It stands behind the temple against the back wall, which it entirely covers. There are also some large stone obelisks in the enclosure, and there is a lake near them, adorned with an edging of stone. In form it is circular, and in size, as it seemed to me, about equal to the lake at Delos called the Hoop. On this lake it is that the Egyptians represent by night his sufferings whose name I refrain from mentioning, and this representation they call their mysteries."[7] And not only is the sepulchre of Osiris shown, but also his embalming: "When a body is brought to them, they show the bearer various models of corpses made in wood, and painted so as to resemble nature. The most perfect is said to be after the manner of him whom I do not think it religious to name in connection with such a matter."[8]

CHAP. XXIX. — PROOF OF THE SAME FROM THE POETS.

But among the Greeks, also, those who are eminent in poetry and history say the same thing. Thus of Heracles: —

" That lawless wretch, that man of brutal strength,
    Deaf to Heaven's voice, the social rite transgressed."[9]

Such being his nature, deservedly did he go mad, and deservedly did he light the funeral pile and burn himself to death. Of Asklepius, Hesiod says: —

" The mighty father both of gods and men
    Was filled with wrath, and from Olympus' top
    With flaming thunderbolt cast down and slew
    Latona's well-lov'd son — such was his ire."[10]

And Pindar: —

" But even wisdom is ensnared by gain.
    The brilliant bribe of gold seen in the hand
    Ev'n him [11] perverted: therefore Kronos' son
    With both hands quickly stopp'd his vital breath.
    And by a bolt of fire ensured his doom."[12]

Either, therefore, they were gods and did not hanker after gold —

" O gold, the fairest prize to mortal men,
    Which neither mother equals in delight,
    Nor children dear " [13] —

---

[1] ii. 144. Mr. Rawlinson's translation is used in the extracts from Herodotus.
[2] ii. 50.
[3] ii. 156.
[4] ii. 41.
[5] ii. 3. The text is here uncertain, and differs from that of Herodotus. [Herodotus, initiated in Egyptian mysteries, was doubtless sworn to maintain certain secrets of the priests of Osiris.]

[6] ii. 61. [The name of Osiris.]
[7] ii. 170.
[8] ii. 86.
[9] Hom., Od., xxi. 28 sq.
[10] Hesiod, Frag.
[11] i.e., Æsculapius.
[12] Pyth., iii. 96 sq.
[13] Ascribed by Seneca to the Bellerophon of Eurip.

for the Deity is in want of nought, and is superior to carnal desire, nor did they die; or, having been born men, they were wicked by reason of ignorance, and overcome by love of money. What more need I say, or refer to Castor, or Pollux, or Amphiaraus, who, having been born, so to speak, only the other day, men of men, are looked upon as gods, when they imagine even Ino after her madness and its consequent sufferings to have become a goddess?

"Sea-rovers will her name Leucothea." [1]

And her son : —

"August Palæmon, sailors will invoke."

CHAP. XXX. — REASONS WHY DIVINITY HAS BEEN ASCRIBED TO MEN.

For if detestable and god-hated men had the reputation of being gods, and the daughter of Derceto, Semiramis, a lascivious and blood-stained woman, was esteemed a Syrian goddess; and if, on account of Derceto, the Syrians worship doves and Semiramis (for, a thing impossible, a woman was changed into a dove : the story is in Ctesias), what wonder if some should be called gods by their people on the ground of their rule and sovereignty (the Sibyl, of whom Plato also makes mention, says : —

"It was the generation then the tenth,
  Of men endow'd with speech, since forth the flood
Had burst upon the men of former times,
  And Kronos, Japetus, and Titan reigned,
Whom men, of Ouranos and Gaïa
Proclaimed the noblest sons, and named them so,[2]
Because of men endowed with gift of speech
They were the first ") ; [3]

and others for their strength, as Heracles and Perseus ; and others for their art, as Asclepius? Those, therefore, to whom either the subjects gave honour or the rulers themselves [assumed it], obtained the name, some from fear, others from revenge. Thus Antinous, through the benevolence of your ancestors towards their subjects, came to be regarded as a god. But those who came after adopted the worship without examination.

"The Cretans always lie; for they, O king,
  Have built a tomb to thee who art not dead." [4]

Though you believe, O Callimachus, in the nativity of Zeus, you do not believe in his sepulchre ; and whilst you think to obscure the truth, you in fact proclaim him dead, even to those who are ignorant ; and if you see the cave, you call to mind the childbirth of Rhea ; but when you see the coffin, you throw a shadow over his death, not considering that the unbegotten God alone is eternal. For either the tales told by the multitude and the poets about the gods are unworthy of credit, and the reverence shown them is superfluous (for those do not exist, the tales concerning whom are untrue) ; or if the births, the amours, the murders, the thefts, the castrations, the thunderbolts, are true, they no longer exist, having ceased to be since they were born, having previously had no being. And on what principle must we believe some things and disbelieve others, when the poets have written their stories in order to gain greater veneration for them? For surely those through whom they have got to be considered gods, and who have striven to represent their deeds as worthy of reverence, cannot have invented their sufferings. That, therefore, we are not atheists, acknowledging as we do God the Maker of this universe and His Logos, has been proved according to my ability, if not according to the importance of the subject.

CHAP. XXXI. — CONFUTATION OF THE OTHER CHARGES BROUGHT AGAINST THE CHRISTIANS.

But they have further also made up stories against us of impious feasts [5] and forbidden intercourse between the sexes, both that they may appear to themselves to have rational grounds of hatred, and because they think either by fear to lead us away from our way of life, or to render the rulers harsh and inexorable by the magnitude of the charges they bring. But they lose their labour with those who know that from of old it has been the custom, and not in our time only, for vice to make war on virtue. Thus Pythagoras, with three hundred others, was burnt to death ; Heraclitus and Democritus were banished, the one from the city of the Ephesians, the other from Abdera, because he was charged with being mad ; and the Athenians condemned Socrates to death. But as they were none the worse in respect of virtue because of the opinion of the multitude, so neither does the undiscriminating calumny of some persons cast any shade upon us as regards rectitude of life, for with God we stand in good repute. Nevertheless, I will meet these charges also, although I am well assured that by what has been already said I have cleared myself to you. For as you excel all men in intelligence, you know that those whose life is directed towards God as its rule, so that each one among

---

1 From the *Ino*, a lost play of Eurip.
2 i.e., after Gaïa and Ouranos, *Earth* and *Heaven*.
3 Oracc., *Sibyll.*, iii. 108-113. [Kaye, p. 220, and compare cap. vii., *supra*. The inspiration of Balaam, and likewise that of the ass, must, in my opinion, illustrate that of the Sibyls.]
4 Callim., *Hym. Jov.*, 8 sq. [Tit. i. 12. But St. Paul's quotation is from Epimenides.]

5 [Thyestian feasts" (p. 130, *supra*); a charge which the Christian Fathers perpetually repel. Of course the sacrament of the Lord's Supper lent colour to this charge; but it could not have been repelled, had they believed the material body and blood of the "man Christ Jesus," present in this sacrament. See cap. iii., note.]

us may be blameless and irreproachable before Him, will not entertain even the thought of the slightest sin.   For if we believed that we should live only the present life, then we might be suspected of sinning, through being enslaved to flesh and blood, or overmastered by gain or carnal desire ; but since we know that God is witness to what we think and what we say both by night and by day, and that He, being Himself light, sees all things in our heart, we are persuaded that when we are removed from the present life we shall live another life, better than the present one, and heavenly, not earthly (since we shall abide near God, and with God, free from all change or suffering in the soul, not as flesh, even though we shall have flesh,[1] but as heavenly spirit), or, falling with the rest, a worse one and in fire ; for God has not made us as sheep or beasts of burden, a mere by-work, and that we should perish and be annihilated.   On these grounds it is not likely that we should wish to do evil, or deliver ourselves over to the great Judge to be punished.

CHAP. XXXII. — ELEVATED MORALITY OF THE CHRISTIANS.

It is, however, nothing wonderful that they should get up tales about us such as they tell of their own gods, of the incidents of whose lives they make mysteries.   But it behoved them, if they meant to condemn shameless and promiscuous intercourse, to hate either Zeus, who begat children of his mother Rhea and his daughter Koré, and took his own sister to wife, or Orpheus, the inventor of these tales, which made Zeus more unholy and detestable than Thyestes himself; for the latter defiled his daughter in pursuance of an oracle, and when he wanted to obtain the kingdom and avenge himself.   But we are so far from practising promiscuous intercourse, that it is not lawful among us to indulge even a lustful look.   " For," saith He, " he that looketh on a woman to lust after her, hath committed adultery already in his heart."[2]   Those, then, who are forbidden to look at anything more than that for which God formed the eyes, which were intended to be a light to us, and to whom a wanton look is adultery, the eyes being made for other purposes, and who are to be called to account for their very thoughts, how can any one doubt that such persons practise self-control?   For our account lies not with human laws, which a bad man can evade (at the outset I proved to you, sovereign lords, that our doctrine is from the teaching of God), but we have a law which makes the measure of rectitude to consist in dealing with our neighbour as our-

selves.[3]   On this account, too, according to age, we recognise some as sons and daughters, others we regard as brothers and sisters,[4] and to the more advanced in life we give the honour due to fathers and mothers.   On behalf of those, then, to whom we apply the names of brothers and sisters, and other designations of relationship, we exercise the greatest care that their bodies should remain undefiled and uncorrupted ; for the Logos[5] again says to us, " If any one kiss a second time because it has given him pleasure, [he sins] ; " adding, "Therefore the kiss, or rather the salutation, should be given with the greatest care, since, if there be mixed with it the least defilement of thought, it excludes us from eternal life."[6]

CHAP. XXXIII. — CHASTITY OF THE CHRISTIANS WITH RESPECT TO MARRIAGE.

Therefore, having the hope of eternal life, we despise the things of this life, even to the pleasures of the soul, each of us reckoning her his wife whom he has married according to the laws laid down by us, and that only for the purpose of having children.   For as the husbandman throwing the seed into the ground awaits the harvest, not sowing more upon it, so to us the procreation of children is the measure of our indulgence in appetite.   Nay, you would find many among us, both men and women, growing old unmarried, in hope of living in closer communion with God.[7]   But if the remaining in virginity and in the state of an eunuch brings nearer to God, while the indulgence of carnal thought and desire leads away from Him, in those cases in which we shun the thoughts, much more do we reject the deeds.   For we bestow our attention, not on the study of words, but on the exhibition and teaching of actions, — that a person should either remain as he was born, or be content with one marriage ; for a second marriage is only a specious adultery.[8]   " For whosoever puts away his wife," says He, " and

---

[1] [1 Cor. xv. 44.   A very clear representation of the apostle's doctrine.   See Kaye, 199; and compare *On the Resurrection*, cap. xiii.]
[2] Matt. v. 28.

[3] Otto translates: " which has made us and our neighbours attain the highest degree of rectitude."   The text is obscure, but the above seems the probable meaning: comp. Matt. xxii. 39, etc.
[4] [Hermas, p. 47, note, and p. 57, this volume; Elucidation, ii.]
[5] [The Logos never said, " it excludes *us* from eternal life: " that is sure: and the passage, though ambiguous, is not so interpreted in the Latin of Gesner.   Jones remarks that Athenagoras never introduces a saying of our Lord in this way.   Compare Clem. Alexandrin. (*Pædagogue*, b. iii. cap. v. p. 297, Edinburgh Series), where he quotes Matt. v. 28, with variation.   Lardner (cap. xviii. sec. 20) gives a probable explanation.   Jones on *The Canon* (vol. i. p. 436) is noteworthy.   Kaye (p. 221) does not solve the puzzle.]
[6] Probably from some apocryphal writing.   [Come from what source it may, it suggests a caution of the utmost importance to Americans.   In the newer parts of the country, the practice, here corrected, has cropped out among " brothers and sisters " of divers religious names, and consequent scandals have arisen.   To all Christians comes the apostolic appeal, " Let it not be once named among you."]
[7] [This our Lord commends (Matt. xix. 12) as a voluntary act of private self-devotion.]
[8] [There is perhaps a touch of the rising Phrygian influence in this passage; yet the language of St. Paul (1 Tim. v. 9) favoured this view, no doubt, in primitive opinion.   See *Speaker's Comm.* on 1 Tim. iii. 2.   *Ed.* Scribners, New York.]

marries another, commits adultery;"[1] not permitting a man to send her away whose virginity he has brought to an end, nor to marry again. For he who deprives himself of his first wife, even though she be dead, is a cloaked adulterer,[2] resisting the hand of God, because in the beginning God made one man and one woman, and dissolving the strictest union of flesh with flesh, formed for the intercourse of the race.

CHAP. XXXIV. — THE VAST DIFFERENCE IN MORALS BETWEEN THE CHRISTIANS AND THEIR ACCUSERS.

But though such is our character (Oh! why should I speak of things unfit to be uttered?), the things said of us are an example of the proverb, "The harlot reproves the chaste." For those who have set up a market for fornication, and established infamous resorts for the young for every kind of vile pleasure, — who do not abstain even from males, males with males committing shocking abominations, outraging all the noblest and comeliest bodies in all sorts of ways, so dishonouring the fair workmanship of God (for beauty on earth is not self-made, but sent hither by the hand and will of God), — these men, I say, revile us for the very things which they are conscious of themselves, and ascribe to their own gods, boasting of them as noble deeds, and worthy of the gods. These adulterers and pæderasts defame the eunuchs and the once-married (while they themselves live like fishes;[3] for these gulp down whatever falls in their way, and the stronger chases the weaker: and, in fact, this is to feed upon human flesh, to do violence in contravention of the very laws which you and your ancestors, with due care for all that is fair and right, have enacted), so that not even the governors of the provinces sent by you suffice for the hearing of the complaints against those, to whom it even is not lawful, when they are struck, not to offer themselves for more blows, nor when defamed not to bless: for it is not enough to be just (and justice is to return like for like), but it is incumbent on us to be good and patient of evil.

CHAP. XXXV. — THE CHRISTIANS CONDEMN AND DETEST ALL CRUELTY.

What man of sound mind, therefore, will affirm, while such is our character, that we are murderers? For we cannot eat human flesh till we have killed some one. The former charge, therefore, being false, if any one should ask them in regard to the second, whether they have seen what they assert, not one of them would be so barefaced

as to say that he had. And yet we have slaves, some more and some fewer, by whom we could not help being seen; but even of these, not one has been found to invent even such things against us. For when they know that we cannot endure even to see a man put to death, though justly, who of them can accuse us of murder or cannibalism? Who does not reckon among the things of greatest interest the contests of gladiators and wild beasts, especially those which are given by you? But we, deeming that to see a man put to death is much the same as killing him, have abjured such spectacles.[4] How, then, when we do not even look on, lest we should contract guilt and pollution, can we put people to death? And when we say that those women who use drugs to bring on abortion commit murder, and will have to give an account to God[5] for the abortion, on what principle should we commit murder? For it does not belong to the same person to regard the very fœtus in the womb as a created being, and therefore an object of God's care, and when it has passed into life, to kill it; and not to expose an infant, because those who expose them are chargeable with child-murder, and on the other hand, when it has been reared to destroy it. But we are in all things always alike and the same, submitting ourselves to reason, and not ruling over it.

CHAP. XXXVI. — BEARING OF THE DOCTRINE OF THE RESURRECTION ON THE PRACTICES OF THE CHRISTIANS.

Who, then, that believes in a resurrection, would make himself into a tomb for bodies that will rise again? For it is not the part of the same persons to believe that our bodies will rise again, and to eat them as if they would not; and to think that the earth will give back the bodies held by it, but that those which a man has entombed in himself will not be demanded back. On the contrary, it is reasonable to suppose, that those who think they shall have no account to give of the present life, ill or well spent, and that

---

[1] Matt. xix. 9.
[2] [But Callistus, heretical Bishop of Rome (A.D. 218.), authorized even third marriages in the clergy. Hippolytus, vol. vi. p. 343, *Ante-Nicene Fathers*, Edinburgh Series.]
[3] [An allusion to the fable of the *Sargus;* and see Burton's *Anat. Mel.*, p. 445.]

[4] [See Tatian, cap xxiii., *supra*, p. 75. But here the language of Gibbon is worthy to be quoted; though the icy-hearted infidel failed to understand that just such philosophers as he enjoyed these spectacles, till Christianity taught even such to profess a refined abhorrence of what the Gospel abolished, with no help from them. He says, "the first Christian emperor may claim the honour of the first edict which condemned the art and *amusement* of shedding human blood; but this benevolent law expressed the wishes of the prince, without reforming an inveterate abuse which degraded a civilized(?) nation *below the condition of savage cannibals.* Several hundred, *perhaps several thousand,* victims were annually slaughtered in the great cities of the empire." He tells the story of the heroic Telemachus, without eulogy; how his death, while struggling to separate the combatants abolished for ever the inhuman sports and sacrifices of the amphitheatre. This happened under Honorius. Milman's *Gibbon,* iii. 210.]
[5] [Let Americans read this, and ask whether a relapse into heathenism is not threatening our civilization, in this respect. May I venture to refer to *Moral Reforms* (ed. 1869, Lippincotts, Philadelphia), a little book of my own, rebuking this iniquity, and tracing the earliest violation of this law of Christian morals, and of nature itself, to an unhappy Bishop of Rome, rebuked by Hippolytus. See vol. vi. p. 345, Edinburgh Series of *Ante-Nicene Fathers.*]

there is no resurrection, but calculate on the soul perishing with the body, and being as it were quenched in it, will refrain from no deed of daring; but as for those who are persuaded that nothing will escape the scrutiny of God, but that even the body which has ministered to the irrational impulses of the soul, and to its desires, will be punished along with it, it is not likely that they will commit even the smallest sin. But if to any one it appears sheer nonsense that the body which has mouldered away, and been dissolved, and reduced to nothing, should be reconstructed, we certainly cannot with any reason be accused of wickedness with reference to those that believe not, but only of folly; for with the opinions by which we deceive ourselves we injure no one else. But that it is not our belief alone that bodies will rise again, but that many philosophers also hold the same view, it is out of place to show just now, lest we should be thought to introduce topics irrelevant to the matter in hand, either by speaking of the intelligible and the sensible, and the nature of these respectively, or by contending that the incorporeal is older than the corporeal, and that the intelligible precedes the sensible, although we become acquainted with the latter earliest, since the corporeal is formed from the incorporeal, by the combination with it of the intelligible, and that the sensible is formed from the intelligible; for nothing hinders, according to Pythagoras and Plato, that when the dissolution of bodies takes place, they should, from the very same elements of which they were constructed at first, be constructed again.[1] But let us defer the discourse concerning the resurrection.[2]

CHAP. XXXII. — ENTREATY TO BE FAIRLY JUDGED.

And now do you, who are entirely in everything, by nature and by education, upright, and moderate, and benevolent, and worthy of your rule, now that I have disposed of the several accusations, and proved that we are pious, and gentle, and temperate in spirit, bend your royal head in approval. For who are more deserving to obtain the things they ask, than those who, like us, pray for your government, that you may, as is most equitable, receive the kingdom, son from father, and that your empire may receive increase and addition, all men becoming subject to your sway? And this is also for our advantage, that we may lead a peaceable and quiet life, and may ourselves readily perform all that is commanded us.[3]

---

[1] [Comp. cap. xxxi., *supra*, p. 146. The science of their times lent itself to the notions of the Fathers necessarily; but neither Holy Scripture nor theology binds us to any theory of the *how*, in this great mystery: hence Plato and Pythagoras are only useful, as showing that even they saw nothing impossible in the resurrection of the dead. As to "the same elements," identity does not consist in the same particles of material, but in the continuity of material, by which every seed reproduces "its own body." 1 Cor. xv. 38.]
[2] [It is a fair inference that *The Discourse* was written after the *Embassy* "In it," says Kaye, "may be found nearly all the arguments which human reason has been able to advance in support of the resurrection." p. 200.]
[3] [1 Tim. ii. 1, 2. Kaye, p. 154. They refused worship, however, to imperial images; and for this they suffered. "Bend your royal head" is an amusing reference to the *nod* of the Thunderer.]

THE TREATISE OF ATHENAGORAS

THE ATHENIAN, PHILOSOPHER AND CHRISTIAN, ON THE RESURRECTION OF THE DEAD.

CHAP. I. — DEFENCE OF THE TRUTH SHOULD PRE-CEDE DISCUSSIONS REGARDING IT.[1]

By the side of every opinion and doctrine which agrees with the truth of things, there springs up some falsehood; and it does so, not because it takes its rise naturally from some fundamental principle, or from some cause peculiar to the matter in hand, but because it is invented on purpose by men who set a value on the spurious seed, for its tendency to corrupt the truth. This is apparent, in the first place, from those who in former times addicted themselves to such inquiries, and their want of agreement with their predecessors and contemporaries, and then, not least, from the very confusion which marks the discussions that are now going on. For such men have left no truth free from their calumnious attacks — not the being of God, not His knowledge, not His operations, not those books which follow by a regular and strict sequence from these, and delineate for us the doctrines of piety. On the contrary, some of them utterly, and once for all, give up in despair the truth concerning these things, and some distort it to suit their own views, and some of set purpose doubt even of things which are palpably evident. Hence I think that those who bestow attention on such subjects should adopt two lines of argument, one in defence of the truth, another concerning the truth: that in defence of the truth, for disbelievers and doubters; that concerning the truth, for such as are candid and receive the truth with readiness. Accordingly it behoves those who wish to investigate these matters, to keep in view that which the necessity of the case in each instance requires, and to regulate their discussion by this; to accommodate the order of their treatment of these subjects to what is suitable to the occasion, and not for the sake of appearing always to preserve the same method, to disregard fitness and the place which properly belongs to each topic. For, so far as proof and the natural order are concerned, dissertations concerning the truth always take precedence of those in defence of it; but, for the purpose of greater utility, the order must be reversed, and arguments in defence of it precede those concerning it. For the farmer could not properly cast the seed into the ground, unless he first extirpated the wild wood, and whatever would be hurtful to the good seed; nor the physician introduce any wholesome medicines into the body that needed his care, if he did not previously remove the disease within, or stay that which was approaching. Neither surely can he who wishes to teach the truth persuade any one by speaking about it, so long as there is a false opinion lurking in the mind of his hearers, and barring the entrance of his arguments. And, therefore, from regard to greater utility, I myself sometimes place arguments in defence of the truth before those concerning the truth; and on the present occasion it appears to me, looking at the requirements of the case, not without advantage to follow the same method in treating of the resurrection. For in regard to this subject also we find some utterly disbelieving, and some others doubting, and even among those who have accepted the first principles some who are as much at a loss what to believe as those who doubt; the most unaccountable thing of all being, that they are in this state of mind without having any ground whatsoever in the matters themselves for their disbelief, or finding it possible to assign any

---

[1] [This argument was adapted to the times, and to those to whom it was addressed, with great rhetorical art and concealment of art. Its faults arise from the defective science of the age, and from the habits of thought and of public instruction then in fashion. He does not address himself to believers, but to sceptics, and meets them on their highest levels of speech and of reason.]

reasonable cause why they disbelieve or experience any perplexity.

CHAP. II. — A RESURRECTION IS NOT IMPOSSIBLE.

Let us, then, consider the subject in the way I have indicated. If all disbelief does not arise from levity and inconsideration, but if it springs up in some minds on strong grounds and accompanied by the certainty which belongs to truth, [well and good] ; for it then maintains the appearance of being just, when the thing itself to which their disbelief relates appears to them unworthy of belief ; but to disbelieve things which are not deserving of disbelief, is the act of men who do not employ a sound judgment about the truth. It behoves, therefore, those who disbelieve or doubt concerning the resurrection, to form their opinion on the subject, not from any view they have hastily adopted, and from what is acceptable to profligate men, but either to assign the origin of men to no cause (a notion which is very easily refuted), or, ascribing the cause of all things to God, to keep steadily in view the principle involved in this article of belief, and from this to demonstrate that the resurrection is utterly unworthy of credit. This they will succeed in, if they are able to show that it is either impossible for God, or contrary to His will, to unite and gather together again bodies that are dead, or even entirely dissolved into their elements, so as to constitute the same persons. If they cannot do this, let them cease from this godless disbelief, and from this blasphemy against sacred things : for, that they do not speak the truth when they say that it is impossible, or not in accordance with the divine will, will clearly appear from what I am about to say. A thing is in strictness of language considered impossible to a person, when it is of such a kind that he either does not know what is to be done, or has not sufficient power for the proper doing of the thing known. For he who is ignorant of anything that requires to be done, is utterly unable either to attempt or to do what he is ignorant of ; and he, too, who knows ever so well what has to be done, and by what means, and how, but either has no power at all to do the thing known, or not power sufficient, will not even make the attempt, if he be wise and consider his powers ; and if he did attempt it without due consideration, he would not accomplish his purpose. But it is not possible for God to be ignorant, either of the nature of the bodies that are to be raised, as regards both the members entire and the particles of which they consist, or whither each of the dissolved particles passes, and what part of the elements has received that which is dissolved and has passed into that with which it has affinity, although to men it may appear quite impossible that what has again combined according to its nature with the universe should be separable from it again. For He from whom, antecedently to the peculiar formation of each, was not concealed either the nature of the elements of which the bodies of men were to consist, or the parts of these from which He was about to take what seemed to Him suitable for the formation of the human body, will manifestly, after the dissolution of the whole, not be ignorant whither each of the particles has passed which He took for the construction of each. For, viewed relatively to the order of things now obtaining among us, and the judgment we form concerning other matters, it is a greater thing to know beforehand that which has not yet come to pass ; but, viewed relatively to the majesty and wisdom of God, both are according to nature, and it is equally easy to know beforehand things that have not yet come into existence, and to know things which have been dissolved.

CHAP. III. — HE WHO COULD CREATE, CAN ALSO RAISE UP THE DEAD.

Moreover also, that His power is sufficient for the raising of dead bodies, is shown by the creation of these same bodies. For if, when they did not exist, He made at their first formation the bodies of men, and their original elements, He will, when they are dissolved, in whatever manner that may take place, raise them again with equal ease : for this, too, is equally possible to Him. And it is no damage to the argument, if some suppose the first beginnings to be from matter, or the bodies of men at least to be derived from the elements as the first materials, or from seed. For that power which could give shape to what is regarded by them as shapeless matter, and adorn it, when destitute of form and order, with many and diverse forms, and gather into one the several portions of the elements, and divide the seed which was one and simple into many, and organize that which was unorganized, and give life to that which had no life, — that same power can reunite what is dissolved, and raise up what is prostrate, and restore the dead to life again, and put the corruptible into a state of incorruption. And to the same Being it will belong, and to the same power and skill, to separate that which has been broken up and distributed among a multitude of animals of all kinds which are wont to have recourse to such bodies, and glut their appetite upon them, — to separate this, I say, and unite it again with the proper members and parts of members, whether it has passed into some one of those animals, or into many, or thence into others, or, after being dissolved along with these, has been carried back again to the original elements, resolved into these according to a natural law — a matter this which seems to have exceedingly confounded some, even of those admired for wisdom, who, I cannot tell why, think those doubts worthy of serious attention which are brought forward by the many.

CHAP. IV. — OBJECTION FROM THE FACT THAT SOME HUMAN BODIES HAVE BECOME PART OF OTHERS.

These persons, to wit, say that many bodies of those who have come to an unhappy death in shipwrecks and rivers have become food for fishes, and many of those who perish in war, or who from some other sad cause or state of things are deprived of burial, lie exposed to become the food of any animals which may chance to light upon them. Since, then, bodies are thus consumed, and the members and parts composing them are broken up and distributed among a great multitude of animals, and by means of nutrition become incorporated with the bodies of those that are nourished by them, — in the first place, they say, their separation from these is impossible ; and besides this, in the second place, they adduce another circumstance more difficult still. When animals of the kind suitable for human food, which have fed on the bodies of men, pass through their stomach, and become incorporated with the bodies of those who have partaken of them, it is an absolute necessity, they say, that the parts of the bodies of men which have served as nourishment to the animals which have partaken of them should pass into other bodies of men, since the animals which meanwhile have been nourished by them convey the nutriment derived from those by whom they were nourished into those men of whom they become the nutriment. Then to this they tragically add the devouring of offspring perpetrated by people in famine and madness, and the children eaten by their own parents through the contrivance of enemies, and the celebrated Median feast, and the tragic banquet of Thyestes ; and they add, moreover, other such like unheard-of occurrences which have taken place among Greeks and barbarians : and from these things they establish, as they suppose, the impossibility of the resurrection, on the ground that the same parts cannot rise again with one set of bodies, and with another as well ; for that either the bodies of the former possessors cannot be reconstituted, the parts which composed them having passed into others, or that, these having been restored to the former, the bodies of the last possessors will come short.

CHAP. V. — REFERENCE TO THE PROCESSES OF DIGESTION AND NUTRITION.

But it appears to me that such persons, in the first place, are ignorant of the power and skill of Him that fashioned and regulates this universe, who has adapted to the nature and kind of each animal the nourishment suitable and correspondent to it, and has neither ordained that everything in nature shall enter into union and combination with every kind of body, nor is at any loss to separate what has been so united, but grants to the nature of each several created being or thing to do or to suffer what is naturally suited to it, and sometimes also hinders and allows or forbids whatever He wishes, and for the purpose He wishes ; and, moreover, that they have not considered the power and nature of each of the creatures that nourish or are nourished. Otherwise they would have known that not everything which is taken for food under the pressure of outward necessity turns out to be suitable nourishment for the animal, but that some things no sooner come into contact with the plicatures of the stomach than they are wont to be corrupted, and are vomited or voided, or disposed of in some other way, so that not even for a little time do they undergo the first and natural digestion, much less become incorporated with that which is to be nourished ; as also, that not even everything which has been digested in the stomach and received the first change actually arrives at the parts to be nourished, since some of it loses its nutritive power even in the stomach, and some during the second change, and the digestion that takes place in the liver is separated and passes into something else which is destitute of the power to nourish ; nay, that the change which takes place in the liver does not all issue in nourishment to men, but the matter changed is separated as refuse according to its natural purpose ; and that the nourishment which is left in the members and parts themselves that have to be nourished sometimes changes to something else, according as that predominates which is present in greater or less [1] abundance, and is apt to corrupt or to turn into itself that which comes near it.

CHAP. VI. — EVERYTHING THAT IS USELESS OR HURTFUL IS REJECTED.

Since, therefore, great difference of nature obtains in all animals, and the very nourishment which is accordant with nature is varied to suit each kind of animal, and the body which is nourished ; and as in the nourishment of every animal there is a threefold cleansing and separation, it follows that whatever is alien from the nourishment of the animal must be wholly destroyed and carried off to its natural place, or change into something else, since it cannot coalesce with it ; that the power of the nourishing body must be suitable to the nature of the animal to be nourished, and accordant with its powers ; and that this, when it has passed

---

[1] The common reading is " excessive."

through the strainers appointed for the purpose, and been thoroughly purified by the natural means of purification, must become a most genuine addition to the substance, — the only thing, in fact, which any one calling things by their right names would call nourishment at all; because it rejects everything that is foreign and hurtful to the constitution of the animal nourished, and that mass of superfluous food introduced merely for filling the stomach and gratifying the appetite. This nourishment, no one can doubt, becomes incorporated with the body that is nourished, interwoven and blended with all the members and parts of members; but that which is different and contrary to nature is speedily corrupted if brought into contact with a stronger power, but easily destroys that which is overcome by it, and is converted into hurtful humours and poisonous qualities, because producing nothing akin or friendly to the body which is to be nourished. And it is a very clear proof of this, that in many of the animals nourished, pain, or disease, or death follows from these things, if, owing to a too keen appetite, they take in mingled with their food something poisonous and contrary to nature; which, of course, would tend to the utter destruction of the body to be nourished, since that which is nourished is nourished by substances akin to it and which accord with its nature, but is destroyed by those of a contrary kind. If, therefore, according to the different nature of animals, different kinds of food have been provided suitable to their nature, and none of that which the animal may have taken, not even an accidental part of it, admits of being blended with the body which is nourished, but only that part which has been purified by an entire digestion, and undergone a complete change for union with a particular body, and adapted to the parts which are to receive nourishment, — it is very plain that none of the things contrary to nature can be united with those bodies for which it is not a suitable and correspondent nourishment, but either passes off by the bowels before it produces some other humour, crude and corrupted; or, if it continue for a longer time, produces suffering or disease hard to cure, destroying at the same time the natural nourishment, or even the flesh itself which needs nourishment. But even though it be expelled at length, overcome by certain medicines, or by better food, or by the natural forces, it is not got rid of without doing much harm, since it bears no peaceful aspect towards what is natural, because it cannot coalesce with nature.

CHAP. VII. — THE RESURRECTION-BODY DIFFERENT FROM THE PRESENT.

Nay, suppose we were to grant that the nour-ishment coming from these things (let it be so called, as more accordant with the common way of speaking), although against nature, is yet separated and changed into some one of the moist or dry, or warm or cold, matters which the body contains, our opponents would gain nothing by the concession: for the bodies that rise again are reconstituted from the parts which properly belong to them, whereas no one of the things mentioned is such a part, nor has it the form or place of a part; nay, it does not remain always with the parts of the body which are nourished, or rise again with the parts that rise, since no longer does blood, or phlegm, or bile, or breath, contribute anything to the life. Neither, again, will the bodies nourished then require the things they once required, seeing that, along with the want and corruption of the bodies nourished, the need also of those things by which they were nourished is taken away. To this must be added, that if we were to suppose the change arising from such nourishment to reach as far as flesh, in that case too there would be no necessity that the flesh recently changed by food of that kind, if it became united to the body of some other man, should again as a part contribute to the formation of that body, since neither the flesh which takes it up always retains what it takes, nor does the flesh so incorporated abide and remain with that to which it was added, but is subject to a great variety of changes, — at one time being dispersed by toil or care, at another time being wasted by grief or trouble or disease, and by the distempers arising from being heated or chilled, the humours which are changed with the flesh and fat not receiving the nourishment so as to remain what they are. But while such are the changes to which the flesh is subject, we should find that flesh, nourished by food unsuited to it, suffers them in a much greater degree; now swelling out and growing fat by what it has received, and then again rejecting it in some way or other, and decreasing in bulk, from one or more of the causes already mentioned; and that that alone remains in the parts which is adapted to bind together, or cover, or warm the flesh that has been chosen by nature, and adheres to those parts by which it sustains the life which is according to nature, and fulfils the labours of that life. So that whether the investigation in which we have just been engaged be fairly judged of, or the objections urged against our position be conceded, in neither case can it be shown that what is said by our opponents is true, nor can the bodies of men ever combine with those of the same nature, whether at any time, through ignorance and being cheated of their perception by some one else, men have partaken of such a body, or of their own accord, impelled by want or madness, they have defiled themselves with the body of one of like form; for we are very well aware that some brutes have human forms, or have a nature compounded of men and brutes, such as the more daring of the poets are accustomed to represent.

CHAP. VIII. — HUMAN FLESH NOT THE PROPER OR NATURAL FOOD OF MEN.

But what need is there to speak of bodies not allotted to be the food of any animal, and destined only for a burial in the earth in honour of nature, since the Maker of the world has not alloted any animal whatsoever as food to those of the same kind, although some others of a different kind serve for food according to nature? If, indeed, they are able to show that the flesh of men was alloted to men for food, there will be nothing to hinder its being according to nature that they should eat one another, just like anything else that is allowed by nature, and nothing to prohibit those who dare to say such things from regaling themselves with the bodies of their dearest friends as delicacies, as being espcially suited to them, and to entertain their living friends with the same fare. But if it be unlawful even to speak of this, and if for men to partake of the flesh of men is a thing most hateful and abominable, and more detestable than any other unlawful and unnatural food or act; and if what is against nature can never pass into nourishment for the limbs and parts requiring it, and what does not pass into nourishment can never become united with that which it is not adapted to nourish, — then can the bodies of men never combine with bodies like themselves, to which this nourishment would be against nature, even though it were to pass many times through their stomach, owing to some most bitter mischance; but, removed from the influence of the nourishing power, and scattered to those parts of the universe again from which they obtained their first origin, they are united with these for as long a period of time as may be the lot of each; and, separated thence again by the skill and power of Him who has fixed the nature of every animal, and furnished it with its peculiar powers, they are united suitably, each to each, whether they have been burnt up by fire, or rotted by water, or consumed by wild beasts, or by any other animals, or separated from the entire body and dissolved before the other parts; and, being again united with one another, they occupy the same place for the exact construction and formation of the same body, and for the resurrection and life of that which was dead, or even entirely dissolved. To expatiate further, however, on these topics, is not suitable; for all men are agreed in their decision respecting them, — those at least who are not half brutes.

CHAP. IX. — ABSURDITY OF ARGUING FROM MAN'S IMPOTENCY.

As there are many things of more importance to the inquiry before us, I beg to be excused from replying for the present to those who take refuge in the works of men, and even the constructors of them, who are unable to make anew such of their works as are broken in pieces, or worn out by time, or otherwise destroyed, and then from the analogy of potters and carpenters attempt to show that God neither can will, nor if He willed would be able, to raise again a body that is dead, or has been dissolved, — not considering that by such reasoning they offer the grossest insult to God, putting, as they do, on the same level the capabilities of things which are altogether different, or rather the natures of those who use them, and comparing the works of art with those of nature. To bestow any serious attention on such arguments would be not undeserving of censure, for it is really foolish to reply to superficial and trifling objections. It is surely far more probable, yea, most absolutely true, to say that what is impossible with men is possible with God. And if by this statement of itself as probable, and by the whole investigation in which we have just been engaged reason shows it to be possible, it is quite clear that it is not impossible. No, nor is it such a thing as God could not will.

CHAP. X. — IT CANNOT BE SHOWN THAT GOD DOES NOT WILL A RESURRECTION.

For that which is not accordant with His will is so either as being unjust or as unworthy of Him. And again, the injustice regards either him who is to rise again, or some other than he. But it is evident that no one of the beings exterior to him, and that are reckoned among the things that have existence, is injured. Spiritual natures (νοηταὶ φύσεις) cannot be injured by the resurrection of men, for the resurrection of men is no hindrance to their existing, nor is any loss or violence inflicted on them by it; nor, again, would the nature of irrational or inanimate beings sustain wrong, for they will have no existence after the resurrection, and no wrong can be done to that which is not. But even if any one should suppose them to exist for ever, they would not suffer wrong by the renewal of human bodies: for if now, in being subservient to the nature of men and their necessities while they require them, and subjected to the yoke and every kind of drudgery, they suffer no wrong, much more, when men have become immortal and free from want, and no longer need their service, and when they are themselves liberated from bondage, will they suffer no wrong. For if they had the gift of speech, they would not bring against the Creator the charge of making them, contrary to justice, inferior to men because they did not share in the same resurrection. For to creatures whose nature is not alike the Just Being does not assign a like end. And, besides, with creatures that have no notion of justice there can be no complaint of injustice. Nor can it be said either that there is any injustice done as regards the man to be raised, for he consists of soul and body, and he suffers no wrong as to either soul or body. No person in his senses will affirm that his soul suffers wrong, because, in speaking so, he would at the same time be unawares reflecting on the present life also; for if now, while dwelling in a body subject to corruption and suffering, it has had no wrong done to it, much less will it suffer wrong when living in conjunction with a body which is free from corruption and suffering. The body, again, suffers no wrong; for if no wrong is done to it now while united a corruptible thing with an incorruptible, manifestly will it not be wronged when united an incorruptible with an incorruptible. No; nor can any one say that it is a work unworthy of God to raise up and bring together again a body which has been dissolved: for if the worse was not unworthy of Him, namely, to make the body which is subject to corruption and suffering, much more is the better not unworthy, to make one not liable to corruption or suffering.

CHAP. XI. — RECAPITULATION.

If, then, by means of that which is by nature first and that which follows from it, each of the points investigated has been proved, it is very evident that the resurrection of dissolved bodies is a work which the Creator can perform, and can will, and such as is worthy of Him: for by these considerations the falsehood of the contrary opinion has been shown, and the absurdity of the position taken by disbelievers. For why should I speak of their correspondence each with each, and of their connection with one another? If indeed we ought to use the word connection, as though they were separated by some difference of nature; and not rather say, that what God can do He can also will, and that what God can will it is perfectly possible for Him to do, and that it is accordant with the dignity of Him who wills it. That to discourse concerning the truth is one thing, and to discourse in defence of it is another, has been sufficiently explained in the remarks already made, as also in what respects they differ from each other, and when and in dealing with whom they are severally useful; but perhaps there is no reason why, with a view to the general certainty, and because of the connection of what has been said with what remains, we should not make a fresh beginning from these same points

and those which are allied to them. To the one kind of argument it naturally pertains to hold the foremost place, to the other to attend upon the first, and clear the way, and to remove whatever is obstructive or hostile. The discourse concerning the truth, as being necessary to all men for certainty and safety, holds the first place, whether in nature, or order, or usefulness: in nature, as furnishing the knowledge of the subject; in order, as being in those things and along with those things which it informs us of; in usefulness, as being a guarantee of certainty and safety to those who become acquainted with it. The discourse in defence of the truth is inferior in nature and force, for the refutation of falsehood is less important than the establishment of truth; and second in order, for it employs its strength against those who hold false opinions, and false opinions are an aftergrowth from another sowing and from degeneration. But, notwithstanding all this, it is often placed first, and sometimes is found more useful, because it removes and clears away beforehand the disbelief which disquiets some minds, and the doubt or false opinion of such as have but recently come over. And yet each of them is referrible to the same end, for the refutation of falsehood and the establishment of truth both have piety for their object: not, indeed, that they are absolutely one and the same, but the one is necessary, as I have said, to all who believe, and to those who are concerned about the truth and their own salvation; but the other proves to be more useful on some occasions, and to some persons, and in dealing with some. Thus much by way of recapitulation, to recall what has been already said. We must now pass on to what we proposed, and show the truth of the doctrine concerning the resurrection, both from the cause itself, according to which, and on account of which, the first man and his posterity were created, although they were not brought into existence in the same manner, and from the common nature of all men as men; and further, from the judgment of their Maker upon them according to the time each has lived, and according to the rules by which each has regulated his behaviour, — a judgment which no one can doubt will be just.

CHAP. XII. — ARGUMENT FOR THE RESURRECTION FROM THE PURPOSE CONTEMPLATED IN MAN'S CREATION.

The argument from the cause will appear, if we consider whether man was made at random and in vain, or for some purpose; and if for some purpose, whether simply that he might live and continue in the natural condition in which he was created, or for the use of another; and if with a view to use, whether for that of the

Creator Himself, or of some one of the beings who belong to Him, and are by Him deemed worthy of greater care. Now, if we consider this in the most general way, we find that a person of sound mind, and who is moved by a rational judgment to do anything, does nothing in vain which he does intentionally, but either for his own use, or for the use of some other person for whom he cares, or for the sake of the work itself, being moved by some natural inclination and affection towards its production. For instance (to make use of an illustration, that our meaning may be clear), a man makes a house for his own use, but for cattle and camels and other animals of which he has need he makes the shelter suitable for each of them; not for his own use, if we regard the appearance only, though for that, if we look at the end he has in view, but as regards the immediate object, from concern for those for whom he cares. He has children, too, not for his own use, nor for the sake of anything else belonging to him, but that those who spring from him may exist and continue as long as possible, thus by the succession of children and grandchildren comforting himself respecting the close of his own life, and hoping in this way to immortalize the mortal. Such is the procedure of men. But God can neither have made man in vain, for He is wise, and no work of wisdom is in vain; nor for His own use, for He is in want of nothing. But to a Being absolutely in need of nothing, no one of His works can contribute anything to His own use. Neither, again, did He make man for the sake of any of the other works which He has made. For nothing that is endowed with reason and judgment has been created, or is created, for the use of another, whether greater or less than itself, but for the sake of the life and continuance of the being itself so created. For reason cannot discover any use which might be deemed a cause for the creation of men, since immortals are free from want, and in need of no help from men in order to their existence; and irrational beings are by nature in a state of subjection, and perform those services for men for which each of them was intended, but are not intended in their turn to make use of men: for it neither was nor is right to lower that which rules and takes the lead to the use of the inferior, or to subject the rational to the irrational, which is not suited to rule. Therefore, if man has been created neither without cause and in vain (for none of God's works is in vain, so far at least as the purpose of their Maker is concerned), nor for the use of the Maker Himself, or of any of the works which have proceeded from Him, it is quite clear that although, according to the first and more general view of the subject, God made man for Himself, and in

pursuance of the goodness and wisdom which are conspicuous throughout the creation, yet, according to the view which more nearly touches the beings created, He made him for the sake of the life of those created, which is not kindled for a little while and then extinguished. For to creeping things, I suppose, and birds, and fishes, or, to speak more generally, all irrational creatures, God has assigned such a life as that; but to those who bear upon them the image of the Creator Himself, and are endowed with understanding, and blessed with a rational judgment, the Creator has assigned perpetual duration, in order that, recognising their own Maker, and His power and skill, and obeying law and justice, they may pass their whole existence free from suffering, in the possession of those qualities with which they have bravely borne their preceding life, although they lived in corruptible and earthly bodies. For whatever has been created for the sake of something else, when that has ceased to be for the sake of which it was created, will itself also fitly cease to be, and will not continue to exist in vain, since, among the works of God, that which is useless can have no place; but that which was created for the very purpose of existing and living a life naturally suited to it, since the cause itself is bound up with its nature, and is recognised only in connection with existence itself, can never admit of any cause which shall utterly annihilate its existence. But since this cause is seen to lie in perpetual existence, the being so created must be preserved for ever, doing and experiencing what is suitable to its nature, each of the two parts of which it consists contributing what belongs to it, so that the soul may exist and remain without change in the nature in which it was made, and discharge its appropriate functions (such as presiding over the impulses of the body, and judging and measuring that which occurs from time to time by the proper standards and measures), and the body be moved according to its nature towards its appropriate objects, and undergo the changes allotted to it, and, among the rest (relating to age, or appearance, or size), the resurrection. For the resurrection is a species of change, and the last of all, and a change for the better of what still remains in existence at that time.

CHAP. XIII. — CONTINUATION OF THE ARGUMENT.

[1] Confident of these things, no less than of those which have already come to pass, and reflecting on our own nature, we are content with a life associated with neediness and corruption, as suited to our present state of existence, and

---

[1] [The calm sublimity of this paragraph excels all that ever came from an Athenian before. In the Phœdon we have conjectures: here is certain hope and patient submission as our reasonable service.]

we stedfastly hope for a continuance of being in immortality ; and this we do not take without foundation from the inventions of men, feeding ourselves on false hopes, but our belief rests on a most infallible guarantee — the purpose of Him who fashioned us, according to which He made man of an immortal soul[1] and a body, and furnished him with understanding and an innate law for the preservation and safeguard of the things given by Him as suitable to an intelligent existence and a rational life : for we know well that He would not have fashioned such a being, and furnished him with everything belonging to perpetuity, had He not intended that what was so created should continue in perpetuity. If, therefore, the Maker of this universe made man with a view to his partaking of an intelligent life, and that, having become a spectator of His grandeur, and of the wisdom which is manifest in all things, he might continue always in the contemplation of these ; then, according to the purpose of his Author, and the nature which he has received, the cause of his creation is a pledge of his continuance for ever, and this continuance is a pledge of the resurrection, without which man could not continue. So that, from what has been said, it is quite clear that the resurrection is plainly proved by the cause of man's creation, and the purpose of Him who made him. Such being the nature of the cause for which man has been brought into this world, the next thing will be to consider that which immediately follows, naturally or in the order proposed ; and in our investigation the cause of their creation is followed by the nature of the men so created, and the nature of those created by the just judgment of their Maker upon them, and all these by the end of their existence. Having investigated therefore the point placed first in order, we must now go on to consider the nature of men.

CHAP. XIV. — THE RESURRECTION DOES NOT REST SOLELY ON THE FACT OF A FUTURE JUDGMENT.

The proof[2] of the several doctrines of which the truth consists, or of any matters whatsoever proposed for examination, if it is to produce an unwavering confidence in what is said, must begin, not from anything without, nor from what certain persons think or have thought,[3] but from the common and natural notion[4] of the matter, or from the connection of secondary truths with primary ones. For the question relates either to primary beliefs, and then all that is necessary is

reminiscence, so as to stir up the natural notion ; or to things which naturally follow from the first and to their natural sequence. And in these things we must observe order, showing what strictly follows from the first truths, or from those which are placed first, so as neither to be unmindful of the truth, or of our certainty respecting it, nor to confound the things arranged by nature and distinguished from each other, or break up the natural order. Hence I think it behoves those who desire to handle the subject with fairness, and who wish to form an intelligent judgment whether there is a resurrection or not, first to consider attentively the force of the arguments contributing to the proof of this, and what place each of them holds — which is first, which second, which third, and which last. And in the arrangement of these they should place first the cause of the creation of men, — namely, the purpose of the Creator in making man ; and then connect with this, as is suitable, the nature of the men so created ; not as being second in order, but because we are unable to pass our judgment on both at the same time, although they have the closest natural connection with each other, and are of equal force in reference to the subject before us. But while from these proofs as the primary ones, and as being derived from the work of creation, the resurrection is clearly demonstrated, none the less can we gain conviction respecting it from the arguments taken from providence, — I mean from the reward or punishment due to each man in accordance with just judgment, and from the end of human existence. For many, in discussing the subject of the resurrection, have rested the whole cause on the third argument alone, deeming that the cause of the resurrection is the judgment. But the fallacy of this is very clearly shown, from the fact that, although all human beings who die rise again, yet not all who rise again are to be judged : for if only a just judgment were the cause of the resurrection, it would of course follow that those who had done neither evil nor good — namely, very young children[5] — would not rise again ; but seeing that all are to rise again, those who have died in infancy as well as others, they too justify our conclusion that the resurrection takes place not for the sake of the judgment as the primary reason, but in consequence of the purpose of God in forming men, and the nature of the beings so formed.

CHAP. XV. — ARGUMENT FOR THE RESURRECTION FROM THE NATURE OF MAN.

But while the cause discoverable in the creation of men is of itself sufficient to prove that the resurrection follows by natural sequence on

---

[1] [Kaye, p. 199. Compare *Embassy*, cap. xxvii., *supra*, p. 143.]
[2] [This chapter of itself establishes the fact that Christians have a right to demand the evidence for what they are required to believe. It refutes the idea that what any single bishop or saint has said or thought is doctrine, for that reason only ; but it leaves the fact that concurrent testimony is evidence, on certain conditions, in all its force.]
[3] [Not strong enough for the force of the original: οὐδ' ἐκ τῶν τισι δοκούντων ἢ δεδογμένων.]
[4] [From the natural common sense of the thing.]

[5] [A beautiful and cogent argument for his proposition, and a precious testimony to the innocence of babes falling asleep in Christ. See Kaye, 190.]

the dissolution of bodies, yet it is perhaps right not to shrink from adducing either of the proposed arguments, but, agreeably to what has been said, to point out to those who are not able of themselves to discern them, the arguments from each of the truths evolved from the primary; and first and foremost, the nature of the men created, which conducts us to the same notion, and has the same force as evidence of the resurrection. For if the whole nature of men in general is composed of an immortal soul and a body which was fitted to it in the creation, and if neither to the nature of the soul by itself, nor to the nature of the body separately, has God assigned such a creation or such a life and entire course of existence as this, but to men compounded of the two, in order that they may, when they have passed through their present existence, arrive at one common end, with the same elements of which they are composed at their birth and during life, it unavoidably follows, since one living-being is formed from the two, experiencing whatever the soul experiences and whatever the body experiences, doing and performing whatever requires the judgment of the senses or of the reason, that the whole series of these things must be referred to some one end, in order that they all, and by means of all, — namely, man's creation, man's nature, man's life, man's doings and sufferings, his course of existence, and the end suitable to his nature, — may concur in one harmony and the same common experience. But if there is some one harmony and community of experience belonging to the whole being, whether of the things which spring from the soul or of those which are accomplished by means of the body, the end for all these must also be one. And the end will be in strictness one, if the being whose end that end is remains the same in its constitution; and the being will be exactly the same, if all those things of which the being consists as parts are the same. And they will be the same in respect of their peculiar union, if the parts dissolved are again united for the constitution of the being. And the constitution of the same men of necessity proves that a resurrection will follow of the dead and dissolved bodies; for without this, neither could the same parts be united according to nature with one another, nor could the nature of the same men be reconstituted. And if both understanding and reason have been given to men for the discernment of things which are perceived by the understanding, and not of existences only, but also of the goodness and wisdom and rectitude of their Giver, it necessarily follows that, since those things continue for the sake of which the rational judgment is given, the judgment given for these things should also continue. But it is impossible for this to continue, unless the nature which has received it, and in which it adheres, continues. But that which has received both understanding and reason is man, not the soul by itself. Man, therefore, who consists of the two parts, must continue for ever. But it is impossible for him to continue unless he rise again. For if no resurrection were to take place, the nature of men as men would not continue. And if the nature of men does not continue, in vain has the soul been fitted to the need of the body and to its experiences; in vain has the body been fettered so that it cannot obtain what it longs for, obedient to the reins of the soul, and guided by it as with a bridle; in vain is the understanding, in vain is wisdom, and the observance of rectitude, or even the practice of every virtue, and the enactment and enforcement of laws, — to say all in a word, whatever is noble in men or for men's sake, or rather the very creation and nature of men. But if vanity is utterly excluded from all the works of God, and from all the gifts bestowed by Him, the conclusion is unavoidable, that, along with the interminable duration of the soul, there will be a perpetual continuance of the body according to its proper nature.

CHAP. XVI. — ANALOGY OF DEATH AND SLEEP, AND CONSEQUENT ARGUMENT FOR THE RESURRECTION.

And let no one think it strange that we call by the name of life a continuance of being which is interrupted by death and corruption; but let him consider rather that this word has not one meaning only, nor is there only one measure of continuance, because the nature also of the things that continue is not one. For if each of the things that continue has its continuance according to its peculiar nature, neither in the case of those who are wholly incorruptible and immortal shall we find the continuance like ours, because the natures of superior beings do not take the level of such as are inferior; nor in men is it proper to look for a continuance invariable and unchangeable; inasmuch as the former are from the first created immortal, and continue to exist without end by the simple will of their Maker, and men, in respect of the soul, have from their first origin an unchangeable continuance, but in respect of the body obtain immortality by means of change. This is what is meant by the doctrine of the resurrection; and, looking to this, we both await the dissolution of the body, as the sequel to a life of want and corruption, and after this we hope for a continuance with immortality, [1]not putting either our death

---

[1] [Job xix. 25. On which see St. Jerome, *Ad Paulinum*, cap. 10, tom. iv. 569, ed. Bened. And, on the text itself, see Pusey on *Daniel*, p. 504, London, 1864. A fine passage in Calvin, *ad locum:* "En igitur qualis debate esse nostra Fides," etc. *Opp.*, tom. ii. p. 260, ed. Amsterdam, 1676.]

on a level with the death of the irrational animals, or the continuance of man with the continuance of immortals, lest we should unawares in this way put human nature and life on a level with things with which it is not proper to compare them. It ought not, therefore, to excite dissatisfaction, if some inequality appears to exist in regard to the duration of men; nor, because the separation of the soul from the members of the body and the dissolution of its parts interrupts the continuity of life, must we therefore despair of the resurrection. For although the relaxation of the senses and of the physical powers, which naturally takes place in sleep, seems to interrupt the sensational life when men sleep at equal intervals of time, and, as it were, come back to life again, yet we do not refuse to call it life; and for this reason, I suppose, some call sleep the brother of death,[1] not as deriving their origin from the same ancestors and fathers, but because those who are dead and those who sleep are subject to similar states, as regards at least the stillness and the absence of all sense of the present or the past, or rather of existence itself and their own life. If, therefore, we do not refuse to call by the name of life the life of men full of such inequality from birth to dissolution, and interrupted by all those things which we have before mentioned, neither ought we to despair of the life succeeding to dissolution, such as involves the resurrection, although for a time it is interrupted by the separation of the soul from the body.

CHAP. XVII. — THE SERIES OF CHANGES WE CAN NOW TRACE IN MAN RENDERS A RESURRECTION PROBABLE.

For this nature of men, which has inequality allotted to it from the first, and according to the purpose of its Maker, has an unequal life and continuance, interrupted sometimes by sleep, at another time by death, and by the changes incident to each period of life, whilst those which follow the first are not clearly seen beforehand. Would any one have believed, unless taught by experience, that in the soft seed alike in all its parts there was deposited such a variety and number of great powers, or of masses, which in this way arise and become consolidated — I mean of bones, and nerves, and cartilages, of muscles too, and flesh, and intestines, and the other parts of the body? For neither in the yet moist seed is anything of this kind to be seen, nor even in infants do any of those things make their appearance which pertain to adults, or in the adult period what belongs to those who are past their prime, or in these what belongs to such as have grown old. But although some of the things I have said exhibit not at all, and

others but faintly, the natural sequence and the changes that come upon the nature of men, yet all who are not blinded in their judgment of these matters by vice or sloth, know that there must be first the depositing of the seed, and that when this is completely organized in respect of every member and part and the progeny comes forth to the light, there comes the growth belonging to the first period of life, and the maturity which attends growth, and after the maturity the slackening of the physical powers till old age, and then, when the body is worn out, its dissolution. As, therefore, in this matter, though neither the seed has inscribed upon it the life or form of men, nor the life the dissolution into the primary elements, the succession of natural occurrences makes things credible which have no credibility from the phenomena themselves, much more does reason, tracing out the truth from the natural sequence, afford ground for believing in the resurrection, since it is safer and stronger than experience for establishing the truth.

CHAP. XVIII. — JUDGMENT MUST HAVE REFERENCE BOTH TO SOUL AND BODY : THERE WILL THEREFORE BE A RESURRECTION.

The arguments I just now proposed for examination, as establishing the truth of the resurrection, are all of the same kind, since they all start from the same point; for their starting-point is the origin of the first men by creation. But while some of them derive their strength from the starting-point itself from which they take their rise, others, consequent upon the nature and the life of men, acquire their credibility from the superintendence of God over us; for the cause according to which, and on account of which, men have come into being, being closely connected with the nature of men, derives its force from creation; but the argument from rectitude, which represents God as judging men according as they have lived well or ill, derives its force from the end of their existence : they come into being on the former ground, but their state depends more on God's superintendence. And now that the matters which come first have been demonstrated by me to the best of my ability, it will be well to prove our proposition by those also which come after — I mean by the reward or punishment due to each man in accordance with righteous judgment, and by the final cause of human existence ; and of these I put foremost that which takes the lead by nature, and inquire first into the argument relating to the judgment : premising only one thing, from concern for the principle which appertains to the matters before us, and for order — namely, that it is incumbent on those who admit God to be the Maker of this universe,

---

[1] [Homer, *Iliad*, b. xiv. 231, and Virgil, *Æn.*, vi. 278.]

to ascribe to His wisdom and rectitude the preservation and care of all that has been created, if they wish to keep to their own principles; and with such views to hold that nothing either in earth or in heaven is without guardianship or providence, but that, on the contrary, to everything, invisible and visible alike, small and great, the attention of the Creator reaches; for all created things require the attention of the Creator,[1] and each one in particular, according to its nature and the end for which it was made: though I think it would be a useless expenditure of trouble to go through the list now, or distinguish between the several cases, or mention in detail what is suitable to each nature. Man, at all events, of whom it is now our business to speak, as being in want, requires food; as being mortal, posterity; as being rational, a process of judgment. But if each of these things belongs to man by nature, and he requires food for his life, and requires posterity for the continuance of the race, and requires a judgment in order that food and posterity may be according to law, it of course follows, since food and posterity refer to both together, that the judgment must be referred to them too (by both together I mean man, consisting of soul and body), and that such man becomes accountable for all his actions, and receives for them either reward or punishment. Now, if the righteous judgment awards to both together its retribution for the deeds wrought; and if it is not proper that either the soul alone should receive the wages of the deeds wrought in union with the body (for this of itself has no inclination to the faults which are committed in connection with the pleasure or food and culture of the body), or that the body alone should (for this of itself is incapable of distinguishing law and justice), but man, composed of these, is subjected to trial for each of the deeds wrought by him; and if reason does not find this happening either in this life (for the award according to merit finds no place in the present existence, since many atheists and persons who practise every iniquity and wickedness live on to the last, unvisited by calamity, whilst, on the contrary, those who have manifestly lived an exemplary life in respect of every virtue, live in pain, in insult, in calumny and outrage, and suffering of all kinds) or after death (for both together no longer exist, the soul being separated from the body, and the body itself being resolved again into the materials out of which it was composed, and no longer retaining anything of its former structure or form, much less the remembrance of its actions): the result of all this is very plain

to every one, — namely, that, in the language of the apostle, "this corruptible (and dissoluble) must put on incorruption,"[2] in order that those who were dead, having been made alive by the resurrection, and the parts that were separated and entirely dissolved having been again united, each one may, in accordance with justice, receive what he has done by the body, whether it be good or bad.

CHAP. XIX. — MAN WOULD BE MORE UNFAVOURABLY SITUATED THAN THE BEASTS IF THERE WERE NO RESURRECTION.

In replying, then, to those who acknowledge a divine superintendence, and admit the same principles as we do, yet somehow depart from their own admissions, one may use such arguments as those which have been adduced, and many more than these, should he be disposed to amplify what has been said only concisely and in a cursory manner. But in dealing with those who differ from us concerning primary truths, it will perhaps be well to lay down another principle antecedent to these, joining with them in doubting of the things to which their opinions relate, and examining the matter along with them in this manner — whether the life of men, and their entire course of existence, is overlooked, and a sort of dense darkness is poured down upon the earth, hiding in ignorance and silence both the men themselves and their actions; or whether it is much safer to be of opinion that the Maker presides over the things which He Himself has made, inspecting all things whatsoever which exist, or come into existence, Judge of both deeds and purposes. For if no judgment whatever were to be passed on the actions of men, men would have no advantage over the irrational creatures, but rather would fare worse than these do, inasmuch as they keep in subjection their passions, and concern themselves about piety, and righteousness, and the other virtues; and a life after the manner of brutes would be the best, virtue would be absurd, the threat of judgment a matter for broad laughter, indulgence in every kind of pleasure the highest good, and the common resolve of all these and their one law would be that maxim, so dear to the intemperate and lewd, "Let us eat and drink, for to-morrow we die." For the termination of such a life is not even pleasure, as some suppose, but utter insensibility. But if the Maker of men takes any concern about His own works, and the distinction is anywhere to be found between those who have lived well and ill, it must be either in the present life, while men are still living who have conducted themselves virtuously or vicious-

---

[1] [Noble testimony to a minute and particular Providence. Kaye, p 191.]

[2] 1 Cor. xv. 54.

ly, or after death, when men are in a state of separation and dissolution. But according to neither of these suppositions can we find a just judgment taking place ; for neither do the good in the present life obtain the rewards of virtue, nor yet do the bad receive the wages of vice. I pass over the fact, that so long as the nature we at present possess is preserved, the moral nature is not able to bear a punishment commensurate with the more numerous or more serious faults. For the robber, or ruler, or tyrant, who has unjustly put to death myriads on myriads, could not by one death make restitution for these deeds ; and the man who holds no true opinion concerning God, but lives in all outrage and blasphemy, despises divine things, breaks the laws, commits outrage against boys and women alike, razes cities unjustly, burns houses with their inhabitants, and devastates a country, and at the same time destroys inhabitants of cities and peoples, and even an entire nation — how in a mortal body could he endure a penalty adequate to these crimes, since death prevents the deserved punishment, and the mortal nature does not suffice for any single one of his deeds? It is proved, therefore, that neither in the present life is there a judgment according to men's deserts, nor after death.

CHAP. XX. — MAN MUST BE POSSESSED BOTH OF A BODY AND SOUL HEREAFTER, THAT THE JUDGMENT PASSED UPON HIM MAY BE JUST.

For either death is the entire extinction of life, the soul being dissolved and corrupted along with the body, or the soul remains by itself, incapable of dissolution, of dispersion, of corruption, whilst the body is corrupted and dissolved, retaining no longer any remembrance of past actions, nor sense of what it experienced in connection with the soul. If the life of men is to be utterly extinguished, it is manifest there will be no care for men who are not living, no judgment respecting those who have lived in virtue or in vice ; but there will rush in again upon us whatever belongs to a lawless life, and the swarm of absurdities which follow from it, and that which is the summit of this lawlessness — atheism. But if the body were to be corrupted, and each of the dissolved particles to pass to its kindred element, yet the soul to remain by itself as immortal, neither on this supposition would any judgment on the soul take place, since there would be an absence of equity : for it is unlawful to suspect that any judgment can proceed out of God and from God which is wanting in equity. Yet equity *is* wanting to the judgment, if the being is not preserved in existence who practised righteousness or lawlessness : for that which practised each of the things in life on which the judgment is passed was man, not soul by itself. To sum up all in a word, this view will in no case consist with equity.

CHAP. XXI. — CONTINUATION OF THE ARGUMENT.

For if good deeds are rewarded, the body will clearly be wronged, inasmuch as it has shared with the soul in the toils connected with well-doing, but does not share in the reward of the good deeds, and because, though the soul is often excused for certain faults on the ground of the body's neediness and want, the body itself is deprived of all share in the good deeds done, the toils on behalf of which it helped to bear during life. Nor, again, if faults are judged, is the soul dealt fairly with, supposing it alone to pay the penalty for the faults it committed through being solicited by the body and drawn away by it to its own appetites and motions, at one time being seized upon and carried off, at another attracted in some very violent manner, and sometimes concurring with it by way of kindness and attention to its preservation. How can it possibly be other than unjust for the soul to be judged by itself in respect of things towards which in its own nature it feels no appetite, no motion, no impulse, such as licentiousness, violence, covetousness, injustice, and the unjust acts arising out of these? For if the majority of such evils come from men's not having the mastery of the passions which solicit them, and they are solicited by the neediness and want of the body, and the care and attention required by it (for these are the motives for every acquisition of property, and especially for the using of it, and moreover for marriage and all the actions of life, in which things, and in connection with which, is seen what is faulty and what is not so), how can it be just for the soul alone to be judged in respect of those things which the body is the first to be sensible of, and in which it draws the soul away to sympathy and participation in actions with a view to things which it wants ; and that the appetites and pleasures, and moreover the fears and sorrows, in which whatever exceeds the proper bounds is amenable to judgment, should be set in motion by the body, and yet that the sins arising from these, and the punishments for the sins committed, should fall upon the soul alone, which neither needs anything of this sort, nor desires nor fears or suffers of itself any such thing as man is wont to suffer? But even if we hold that these affections do not pertain to the body alone, but to man, in saying which we should speak correctly, because the life of man is one, though composed of the two, yet surely we shall not assert that these things belong to the soul, if we only look simply at its peculiar nature. For if it is absolutely without need of food, it can never desire those things which it does not in the least require for its subsistence ; nor can it feel any impulse towards any of those things which it is not at all fitted to use ; nor, again, can it be grieved at the want of money or other property, since these are not suited to it. And if, too, it is superior to corruption, it fears nothing whatever as destructive of itself : it has no dread of famine, or disease, or mutilation, or blemish, or fire, or sword, since it cannot suffer from any of these any hurt or pain, because neither bodies nor bodily powers touch it at all. But if it is absurd to attach the passions to the soul as belonging specially to it, it is in the highest degree unjust and unworthy of the judgment of God to lay upon the soul alone the sins which spring from them, and the consequent punishments.

CHAP. XXII. — CONTINUATION OF THE ARGUMENT.

In addition to what has been said, is it not absurd that, while we cannot even have the notion of virtue and vice as existing separately in the soul (for we recognise the virtues as man's virtues, even as in like manner vice, their opposite, as not belonging to the soul in separation from the body, and existing by itself), yet that the reward or punishment for these should be assigned to the soul alone? How can any one have even the notion of courage or fortitude as existing in the soul alone, when it has no fear of death, or wounds, or maiming, or loss, or maltreatment, or of the pain connected with these, or the suffering resulting from them? And what shall we say of self-control and temperance, when there is no desire drawing it to food or sexual intercourse, or other pleasures and enjoyments, nor any other thing soliciting it from within or exciting it from without? And what of practical wisdom, when things are not proposed to it which may or may not be done, nor things to be chosen or avoided, or rather when there is in it no motion at all or natural impulse towards the doing of anything? And how in any sense can equity be an attribute of souls, either in reference to one another or to anything else, whether of the same or of a different kind, when they are not able from any source, or by any means, or in any way, to bestow that which is equal according to merit or according to analogy, with the exception of the honour rendered to God, and, moreover, have no impulse or motion towards the use of their own things, or abstinence from those of others, since the use of those things which are according to nature, or the abstinence from them, is considered in reference to those who are so constituted as to use them, whereas the soul neither wants anything, nor is so constituted as to use any things or any single thing, and therefore what is called the independent action of the parts cannot be found in the soul so constituted?

CHAP. XXIII. — CONTINUATION OF THE ARGUMENT.

But the most irrational thing of all is this : to impose properly sanctioned laws on men, and then to assign to their souls alone the recompense of their lawful or unlawful deeds. For if he who receives the laws would also justly receive the recompense of the transgression of the laws, and if it was man that received the laws, and not the soul by itself, man must also bear the recompense for the sins committed, and not the soul by itself, since God has not enjoined on souls to abstain from things which have no relation to them, such as adultery, murder, theft, rapine, dishonour to parents, and every desire in general that tends to the injury and loss of our neighbours. For neither the command, " Honour thy father and thy mother," is adapted to souls alone, since such names are not applicable to them, for souls do not produce souls, so as to appropriate the appellation of father or mother, but men produce men ; nor could the command, " Thou shalt not commit adultery," ever be properly addressed to souls, or even thought of in such a connection, since the difference of male and female does not exist in them, nor any aptitude for sexual intercourse, nor appetite for it ; and where there is no appetite, there can be no intercourse ; and where there is no intercourse at all, there can be no legitimate intercourse, namely marriage ; and where there is no lawful intercourse, neither can there be unlawful desire of, or intercourse with, another man's wife, namely adultery. Nor, again, is the prohibition of theft, or of the desire of having more, applicable to souls, for they do not need those things, through the need of which, by reason of natural indigence or want, men are accustomed to steal or to rob, such as gold, or silver, or an animal, or something else adapted for food, or shelter, or use ; for to an immortal nature everything which is desired by the needy as useful is useless. But let the fuller discussion of these matters be left to those who wish to investigate each point more exactly, or to contend more earnestly with opponents. But, since what has just been said, and that which concurs with this to guarantee the resurrection, suffices for us, it would not be seasonable to dwell any longer upon them ; for we have not made it our aim to omit nothing that might be said, but to point out in a summary manner to those who have assembled what ought to be thought concerning the resurrection, and to adapt to the capacity of those present the arguments bearing on this question.

CHAP. XXIV. — ARGUMENT FOR THE RESURRECTION FROM THE CHIEF END OF MAN.

The points proposed for consideration having been to some extent investigated, it remains to examine the argument from the end or final cause, which indeed has already emerged in what has been said, and only requires just so much attention and further discussion as may enable us to avoid the appearance of leaving unmentioned any of the matters briefly referred to by us, and thus indirectly damaging the subject or the division of topics made at the outset. For the sake of those present, therefore, and of others who may pay attention to this subject, it may be well just to signify that each of those things which are constituted by nature, and of those which are made by art, must have an end peculiar to itself, as indeed is taught us by the common sense of all men, and testified by the things that pass before our eyes. For do we not see that husbandmen have one end, and physicians another; and again, the things which spring out of the earth another, and the animals nourished upon it, and produced according to a certain natural series, another? If this is evident, and natural and artificial powers, and the actions arising from these, must by all means be accompanied by an end in accordance with nature, it is absolutely necessary that the end of men, since it is that of a peculiar nature, should be separated from community with the rest; for it is not lawful to suppose the same end for beings destitute of rational judgment, and of those whose actions are regulated by the innate law and reason, and who live an intelligent life and observe justice. Freedom from pain, therefore, cannot be the proper end for the latter, for this they would have in common with beings utterly devoid of sensibility: nor can it consist in the enjoyment of things which nourish or delight the body, or in an abundance of pleasures; else a life like that of the brutes must hold the first place, while that regulated by virtue is without a final cause. For such an end as this, I suppose, belongs to beasts and cattle, not to men possessed of an immortal soul and rational judgment.

CHAP. XXV. — ARGUMENT CONTINUED AND CONCLUDED.

Nor again is it the happiness of soul separated from body: for we are not inquiring about the life or final cause of either of the parts of which man consists, but of the being who is composed of both; for such is every man who has a share in this present existence, and there must be some appropriate end proposed for this life. But if it is the end of both parts together, and this can be discovered neither while they are still living in the present state of existence through the numerous causes already mentioned, nor yet when the soul is in a state of separation, because the man cannot be said to exist when the body is dissolved, and indeed entirely scattered abroad, even though the soul continue by itself — it is absolutely necessary that the end of a man's being should appear in some reconstitution of the two together, and of the same living being. And as this follows of necessity, there must by all means be a resurrection of the bodies which are dead, or even entirely dissolved, and the same men must be formed anew, since the law of nature ordains the end not absolutely, nor as the end of any men whatsoever, but of the same men who passed through the previous life; but it is impossible for the same men to be reconstituted unless the same bodies are restored to the same souls. But that the same soul should obtain the same body is impossible in any other way, and possible only by the resurrection; for if this takes place, an end befitting the nature of men follows also. And we shall make no mistake in saying, that the final cause of an intelligent life and rational judgment, is to be occupied uninterruptedly with those objects to which the natural reason is chiefly and primarily adapted, and to delight unceasingly in the contemplation of *Him who is*, and of His decrees, notwithstanding that the majority of men, because they are affected too passionately and too violently by things below, pass through life without attaining this object. For the large number of those who fail of the end that belongs to them does not make void the common lot, since the examination relates to individuals, and the reward or punishment of lives ill or well spent is proportioned to the merit of each.

[This concluding chapter is of itself a masterpiece, and comforts my own soul unspeakably, as proving that this life is very precious, if only directed to the end for which we are created. Blest be Athenagoras for completing what St. Paul began on the Areopagus, and for giving us "beauty for ashes" out of the gardens of Plato. Now we find what power there was in the apostle's word, when he preached to the Athenians, "Jesus and the resurrection."]

CLEMENT OF ALEXANDRIA.

INTRODUCTORY NOTE

TO

CLEMENT OF ALEXANDRIA

[A.D. 153–193–217.] The second century of illumination is drawing to a close, as the great name of this Father comes into view, and introduces us to a new stage of the Church's progress. From Britain to the Ganges it had already made its mark. In all its Oriental identity, we have found it vigorous in Gaul and penetrating to other regions of the West. From its primitive base on the Orontes, it has extended itself to the deltas of the Nile; and the Alexandria of Apollos and of St. Mark has become the earliest seat of Christian learning. There, already, have the catechetical schools gathered the finest intellectual trophies of the Cross; and under the aliment of its library springs up something like a Christian university. Pantænus, "the Sicilian bee" from the flowery fields of Enna, comes to frame it by his industry, and store it with the sweets of his eloquence and wisdom. Clement, who had followed Tatian to the East, tracks Pantænus to Egypt, and comes with his Attic scholarship to be his pupil in the school of Christ. After Justin and Irenæus, he is to be reckoned the founder of Christian literature; and it is noteworthy how sublimely he begins to treat Paganism as a creed outworn, to be dismissed with contempt, rather than seriously wrestled with any longer.

His merciless exposure of the entire system of "lords many and gods many," seems to us, indeed, unnecessarily offensive. Why not spare us such details? But let us reflect, that, if such are our Christian instincts of delicacy, we owe it to this great reformer in no small proportion. For not content to show the Pagans that the very atmosphere was polluted by their mythologies, so that Christians, turn which way they would, must encounter pestilence, he becomes the ethical philosopher of Christians; and while he proceeds to dictate, even in minute details, the transformations to which the faithful must subject themselves in order "to escape the pollutions of the world," he sketches in outline the reformations which the Gospel imposes on society, and which nothing but the Gospel has ever enabled mankind to realize. "For with a celerity unsurpassable, and a benevolence to which we have ready access," says Clement, "the Divine Power hath filled the universe with the seed of salvation." Socrates and Plato had talked sublimely four hundred years before; but Lust and Murder were yet the gods of Greece, and men and women were like what they worshipped. Clement had been their disciple; but now, as the disciple of Christ, he was to exert a power over men and manners, of which they never dreamed.

Alexandria becomes the brain of Christendom: its heart was yet beating at Antioch, but the West was still receptive only, its hands and arms stretched forth towards the sunrise for further enlightenment. From the East it had obtained the Scriptures and their authentication, and from the same source was deriving the canons, the liturgies, and the creed of Christendom. The universal language of Christians is Greek. To a pagan emperor who had outgrown the ideas of

Nero's time, it was no longer Judaism ; but it was not less an Oriental superstition, essentially Greek in its features and its dress. "All the churches of the West," [1] says the historian of Latin Christianity, "were Greek religious colonies. Their language was Greek, their organization Greek, their writers Greek, their Scriptures and their ritual were Greek. Through Greek, the communications of the churches of the West were constantly kept up with the East. . . . Thus the Church at Rome was but one of a confederation of Greek religious republics founded by Christianity." Now this confederation was the Holy Catholic Church.

Every Christian must recognise the career of Alexander, and the history of his empire, as an immediate precursor of the Gospel. The patronage of letters by the Ptolemies at Alexandria, the translation of the Hebrew Scriptures into the dialect of the Hellenes, the creation of a new terminology in the language of the Greeks, by which ideas of faith and of truth might find access to the mind of a heathen world, — these were preliminaries to the preaching of the Gospel to mankind, and to the composition of the New Testament of our Lord and Saviour. He Himself had prophetically visited Egypt, and the idols were now to be removed before his presence. There a powerful Christian school was to make itself felt for ever in the definitions of orthodoxy ; and in a new sense was that prophecy to be understood, "Out of Egypt have I called my Son."

The genius of Apollos was revived in his native city. A succession of doctors was there to arise, like him, "eloquent men, and mighty in the Scriptures." Clement tells us of his masters in Christ, and how, coming to Pantænus, his soul was filled with a deathless element of divine knowledge.[2] He speaks of the apostolic tradition as received through his teachers hardly at second-hand. He met in that school, no doubt, some, at least, who recalled Ignatius and Polycarp ; some, perhaps, who as children had heard St. John when he could only exhort his congregations to "love one another." He could afterwards speak of himself as in the next succession after the apostles.

He became the successor of Pantænus in the catechetical school, and had Origen for his pupil, with other eminent men. He was also ordained a presbyter. He seems to have compiled his *Stromata* in the reigns of Commodus and Severus. If, at this time, he was about forty years of age, as seems likely, we must conceive of his birth at Athens, while Antoninus Pius was emperor, while Polycarp was yet living, and while Justin and Irenæus were in their prime.

Alexander, bishop of Jerusalem, speaks of Clement, in turn, as his master : "for we acknowledge as fathers those blessed saints who are gone before us, and *to whom we shall go after a little time ;* the truly blest Pantænus, I mean, and the holy Clemens, my teacher, who was to me so greatly useful and helpful." St. Cyril of Alexandria calls him "a man admirably learned and skilful, and one that searched to the depths all the learning of the Greeks, with an exactness rarely attained before." So Theodoret says, "He surpassed all others, and *was a holy man.*" St. Jerome pronounces him the most learned of all the ancients ; while Eusebius testifies to his theological attainments, and applauds him as an "incomparable master of Christian philosophy." But the rest shall be narrated by our translator, Mr. Wilson.

The following is the original INTRODUCTORY NOTICE : —

TITUS FLAVIUS CLEMENS, the illustrious head of the Catechetical School at Alexandria at the close of the second century, was originally a pagan philosopher. The date of his birth is unknown. It is also uncertain whether Alexandria or Athens was his birthplace.[3]

On embracing Christianity, he eagerly sought the instructions of its most eminent teachers ; for this purpose travelling extensively over Greece, Italy, Egypt, Palestine, and other regions of the East.

Only one of these teachers (who, from a reference in the *Stromata,* all appear to have been

---

[1] Milman, vol. i. pp. 28, 29, condensed. He fails, however, to observe the immense importance of the facts he chronicles.
[2] I have felt that Pantænus and his school require a few words in my elucidations.
[3] Epiph., *Hær.,* xxxii. 6.

alive when he wrote [1]) can be with certainty identified, viz., Pantænus, of whom he speaks in terms of profound reverence, and whom he describes as the greatest of them all. Returning to Alexandria, he succeeded his master Pantænus in the catechetical school, probably on the latter departing on his missionary tour to the East, somewhere about A.D. 189.[2] He was also made a presbyter of the Church, either then or somewhat later.[3] He continued to teach with great distinction till A.D. 202, when the persecution under Severus compelled him to retire from Alexandria. In the beginning of the reign of Caracalla we find him at Jerusalem, even then a great resort of Christian, and especially clerical, pilgrims. We also hear of him travelling to Antioch, furnished with a letter of recommendation by Alexander, bishop of Jerusalem.[4] The close of his career is covered with obscurity. He is supposed to have died about A.D. 220.

Among his pupils were his distinguished successor in the Alexandrian school, Origen, Alexander bishop of Jerusalem, and, according to Baronius, Combefisius, and Bull, also Hippolytus.

The above is positively the sum of what we know of Clement's history.

His three great works, *The Exhortation to the Heathen* (λόγος ὁ προτρεπτικὸς πρὸς Ἕλληνας), *The Instructor*, or *Pædagogus* (παιδαγωγός), *The Miscellanies*, or *Stromata* (Στρωματεῖς), are among the most valuable remains of Christian antiquity, and the largest that belong to that early period.

The Exhortation, the object of which is to win pagans to the Christian faith, contains a complete and withering exposure of the abominable licentiousness, the gross imposture and sordidness of paganism. With clearness and cogency of argument, great earnestness and eloquence, Clement sets forth in contrast the truth as taught in the inspired Scriptures, the true God, and especially the personal Christ, the living Word of God, the Saviour of men. It is an elaborate and masterly work, rich in felicitous classical allusion and quotation, breathing throughout the spirit of philosophy and of the Gospel, and abounding in passages of power and beauty.

The *Pædagogus*, or *Instructor*, is addressed to those who have been rescued from the darkness and pollutions of heathenism, and is an exhibition of Christian morals and manners, — a guide for the formation and development of Christian character, and for living a Christian life. It consists of three books. It is the grand aim of the whole work to set before the converts Christ as the only Instructor, and to expound and enforce His precepts. In the first book Clement exhibits the person, the function, the means, methods, and ends of the Instructor, who is the Word and Son of God ; and lovingly dwells on His benignity and philanthropy, His wisdom, faithfulness, and righteousness.

The second and third books lay down rules for the regulation of the Christian, in all the relations, circumstances, and actions of life, entering most minutely into the details of dress, eating, drinking, bathing, sleeping, etc. The delineation of a life in all respects agreeable to the Word, a truly Christian life, attempted here, may, now that the Gospel has transformed social and private life to the extent it has, appear unnecessary, or a proof of the influence of ascetic tendencies. But a code of Christian morals and manners (a sort of " whole duty of man " and manual of good breeding combined) was eminently needed by those whose habits and characters had been moulded under the debasing and polluting influences of heathenism ; and who were bound, and were aiming, to shape their lives according to the principles of the Gospel, in the midst of the all but incredible licentiousness and luxury by which society around was incurably tainted. The disclosures which Clement, with solemn sternness, and often with caustic wit, makes of the

---

[1] *Strom.*, lib. i. c. v.

[2] Eusebius, *Hist. Eccl.*, vi. 6.

[3] Hieron., *Lib. de Viris Illustribus*, c. 38; Ph., *Bibl.*, 111.

[4] [The reader is already acquainted (Hermas, p. 12, note 9) with permissive canons, by which bishops might commend to their brethren, books fit to be read, which they sent, authenticated, not only by hand and seal, but by a clerical messenger whose duty it was (in the language of Bingham) " to go on the bishop's embassies, with his letters or messages to foreign churches; for in those days, by reason of the persecutions, a bishop did not so much as send a letter to a foreign church, but by the hands of one of his clergy. Whence Cyprian calls them *literæ clericæ.*" *Antiquties*, book iii. cap. ii. 3.]

prevalent voluptuousness and vice, form a very valuable contribution to our knowledge of that period.

The full title of the *Stromata*, according to Eusebius and Photius, was Τίτου Φλαυίου Κλήμεντος τῶν κατὰ τὴν ἀληθῆ φιλοσοφίαν γνωστικῶν ὑπομνημάτων στρωματεῖς [1] — "Titus Flavius Clement's miscellaneous collections of speculative (gnostic) notes bearing upon the true philosophy." The aim of the work, in accordance with this title, is, in opposition to Gnosticism, to furnish the materials for the construction of a true gnosis, a Christian philosophy, on the basis of faith, and to lead on to this higher knowledge those who, by the discipline of the Pædagogus, had been trained for it. The work consisted originally of eight books. The eighth book is lost; that which appears under this name has plainly no connection with the rest of the *Stromata*. Various accounts have been given of the meaning of the distinctive word in the title (Στρωματεύς); but all agree in regarding it as indicating the miscellaneous character of its contents. And they are very miscellaneous. They consist of the speculations of Greek philosophers, of heretics, and of those who cultivated the true Christian gnosis, and of quotations from sacred Scripture. The latter he affirms to be the source from which the higher Christian knowledge is to be drawn; as it was that from which the germs of truth in Plato and the Hellenic philosophy were derived. He describes philosophy as a divinely ordered preparation of the Greeks for faith in Christ, as the law was for the Hebrews; and shows the necessity and value of literature and philosophic culture for the attainment of true Christian knowledge, in opposition to the numerous body among Christians who regarded learning as useless and dangerous. He proclaims himself an eclectic, believing in the existence of fragments of truth in all systems, which may be separated from error; but declaring that the truth can be found in unity and completeness only in Christ, as it was from Him that all its scattered germs originally proceeded. The *Stromata* are written carelessly, and even confusedly; but the work is one of prodigious learning, and supplies materials of the greatest value for understanding the various conflicting systems which Christianity had to combat.

It was regarded so much as the author's great work, that, on the testimony of Theodoret, Cassiodorus, and others, we learn that Clement received the appellation of Στρωματεύς (the Stromatist). In all probability, the first part of it was given to the world about A.D. 194. The latest date to which he brings down his chronology in the first book is the death of Commodus, which happened in A.D. 192; from which Eusebius [2] concludes that he wrote this work during the reign of Severus, who ascended the imperial throne in A.D. 193, and reigned till A.D. 211. It is likely that the whole was composed ere Clement quitted Alexandria in A.D. 202. The publication of the *Pædagogus* preceded by a short time that of the *Stromata*; and the *Cohortatio* was written a short time before the *Pædagogus*, as is clear from statements made by Clement himself.

So multifarious is the erudition, so multitudinous are the quotations and the references to authors in all departments, and of all countries, the most of whose works have perished, that the works in question could only have been composed near an extensive library — hardly anywhere but in the vicinity of the famous library of Alexandria. They are a storehouse of curious ancient lore, — a museum of the fossil remains of the beauties and monstrosities of the world of pagan antiquity, during all the epochs and phases of its history. The three compositions are really parts of one whole. The central connecting idea is that of the Logos — the Word — the Son of God; whom in the first work he exhibits drawing men from the superstitions and corruptions of heathenism to faith; in the second, as training them by precepts and discipline; and in the last, as conducting them to that higher knowledge of the things of God, to which those only who devote themselves assiduously to spiritual, moral, and intellectual culture can attain. Ever before his eye is the grand form of the living personal Christ, — the Word, who "was with God, and who was God, but who became man, and dwelt among us."

---

[1] Eusebius, *Hist. Eccl.*, vi. 13; Phot. *Bibl.*, 111.
[2] *Hist. Eccl.*, vi. 6.

Of course there is throughout plenty of false science, and frivolous and fanciful speculation.

Who is the rich man that shall be saved? (τίς ὁ σωζόμενος πλούσιος ;) is the title of a practical treatise, in which Clement shows, in opposition to those who interpreted our Lord's words to the young ruler as requiring the renunciation of worldly goods, that the disposition of the soul is the great essential. Of other numerous works of Clement, of which only a few stray fragments have been preserved, the chief are the eight books of *The Hypotyposes*, which consisted of expositions of all the books of Scripture. Of these we have a few undoubted fragments. *The Adumbrations*, or *Commentaries on some of the Catholic Epistles*, and *The Selections from the Prophetic Scriptures*, are compositions of the same character, as far as we can judge, as *The Hypotyposes*, and are supposed by some to have formed part of that work.

Other lost works of Clement are : —

The Treatise of Clement, the Stromatist, on the Prophet Amos.

On Providence.

Treatise on Easter.

On Evil-speaking.

Discussion on Fasting.

Exhortation to Patience ; or, To the newly baptized.

Ecclesiastical Canon ; or, Against the Judaizers.

Different Terms.

The following are the names of treatises which Clement refers to as written or about to be written by him, but of which otherwise we have no trace or mention : — *On First Principles ; On Prophecy ; On the Allegorical Interpretation of Members and Affections when ascribed to God ; On Angels ; On the Devil ; On the Origin of the Universe ; On the Unity and Excellence of the Church ; On the Offices of Bishops, Presbyters, Deacons, and Widows ; On the Soul ; On the Resurrection ; On Marriage ; On Continence ; Against Heresies.*

Preserved among Clement's works is a fragment called *Epitomes of the Writings of Theodotus, and of the Eastern Doctrine*, most likely abridged extracts made by Clement for his own use, and giving considerable insight into Gnosticism.

Clement's quotations from Scripture are made from the Septuagint version, often inaccurately from memory, sometimes from a different text from what we possess, often with verbal adaptations ; and not rarely different texts are blended together.[1]

The works of Clement present considerable difficulties to the translator ; and one of the chief is the state of the text, which greatly needs to be expurgated and amended. For this there are abundant materials, in the copious annotations and disquisitions, by various hands, collected together in Migne's edition ; where, however, corruptions the most obvious have been allowed to remain in the text.

The publishers are indebted to Dr. W. L. ALEXANDER for the poetical translations of the Hymns of Clement.

---

[1] [I am glad that our learned translator makes nothing of the statement of Photius, that one of the works of Clement (now lost) contained many things unworthy of his orthodoxy and piety; but it may be well to say here, that Photius himself suggests that heretics had corrupted some of his writings, and that his genuine works testify against these very corruptions. Dupin thinks that if Clement ever wrote such things they must have crept into his works from fragments of his earlier writings, while he was a mere Platonist, at most an inquirer into Christianity. But his great repute in the Catholic Church after his decease, is sufficient to place his character far above all suspicions of his having ever swerved from the " faith of the Church."]

EXHORTATION TO THE HEATHEN

CHAP. I. — EXHORTATION TO ABANDON THE IMPIOUS MYSTERIES OF IDOLATRY FOR THE ADORATION OF THE DIVINE WORD AND GOD THE FATHER.

AMPHION of Thebes and Arion of Methymna were both minstrels, and both were renowned in story. They are celebrated in song to this day in the chorus of the Greeks; the one for having allured the fishes, and the other for having surrounded Thebes with walls by the power of music. Another, a Thracian, a cunning master of his art (he also is the subject of a Hellenic legend), tamed the wild beasts by the mere might of song; and transplanted trees — oaks — by music. I might tell you also the story of another, a brother to these — the subject of a myth, and a minstrel — Eunomos the Locrian and the Pythic grasshopper. A solemn Hellenic assembly had met at Pytho, to celebrate the death of the Pythic serpent, when Eunomos sang the reptile's epitaph. Whether his ode was a hymn in praise of the serpent, or a dirge, I am not able to say. But there was a contest, and Eunomos was playing the lyre in the summer time: it was when the grasshoppers, warmed by the sun, were chirping beneath the leaves along the hills; but they were singing not to that dead dragon, but to God All-wise, — a lay unfettered by rule, better than the numbers of Eunomos. The Locrian breaks a string. The grasshopper sprang on the neck of the instrument, and sang on it as on a branch; and the minstrel, adapting his strain to the grasshopper's song, made up for the want of the missing string. The grasshopper then was attracted by the song of Eunomos, as the fable represents, according to which also a brazen statue of Eunomos with his lyre, and the Locrian's ally in the contest, was erected at Pytho. But of its own accord it flew to the lyre, and of its own accord sang, and was regarded by the Greeks as a musical performer.

How, let me ask, have you believed vain fables, and supposed animals to be charmed by music; while Truth's shining face alone, as would seem, appears to you disguised, and is looked on with incredulous eyes? And so Cithæron, and Helicon, and the mountains of the Odrysi, and the initiatory rites of the Thracians, mysteries of deceit, are hallowed and celebrated in hymns. For me, I am pained at such calamities as form the subjects of tragedy, though but myths; but by you the records of miseries are turned into dramatic compositions.

But the dramas and the raving poets, now quite intoxicated, let us crown with ivy; and distracted outright as they are, in Bacchic fashion, with the satyrs, and the frenzied rabble, and the rest of the demon crew, let us confine to Cithæron and Helicon, now antiquated.

But let us bring from above out of heaven, Truth, with Wisdom in all its brightness, and the sacred prophetic choir, down to the holy mount of God; and let Truth, darting her light to the most distant points, cast her rays all around on those that are involved in darkness, and deliver men from delusion, stretching out her very strong [1] right hand, which is wisdom, for their salvation. And raising their eyes, and looking above, let them abandon Helicon and Cithæron, and take up their abode in Sion. "For out of Sion shall go forth the law, and the word of the LORD from Jerusalem," [2] — the celestial Word, the true athlete crowned in the theatre of the whole universe. What my Eunomos sings is not the measure of Terpander, nor that of Capito, nor the Phrygian, nor Lydian, nor Dorian, but the immortal measure of the new harmony which bears God's name — the new, the Levitical song. [3]

"Soother of pain, calmer of wrath, producing forgetfulness of all ills." [4]

Sweet and true is the charm of persuasion which blends with this strain.

To me, therefore, that Thracian Orpheus, that Theban, and that Methymnæan, — men,

---

[1] The Greek is ὑπερτάτην, lit. highest. Potter appeals to the use of ὑπέρτερος in Sophocles, *Electr.* 455, in the sense of *stronger*, as giving a clue to the meaning here. The scholiast in Klotz takes the words to mean that the hand is held over them.
[2] Isa. ii. 3.
[3] Ps. xcvi. 1, xcviii. 1.
[4] *Odyssey*, iv. 220.

and yet unworthy of the name, — seem to have been deceivers, who, under the pretence of poetry corrupting human life, possessed by a spirit of artful sorcery for purposes of destruction, celebrating crimes in their orgies, and making human woes the materials of religious worship, were the first to entice men to idols; nay, to build up the stupidity of the nations with blocks of wood and stone, — that is, statues and images, — subjecting to the yoke of extremest bondage the truly noble freedom of those who lived as free citizens under heaven, by their songs and incantations. But not such is my song, which has come to loose, and that speedily, the bitter bondage of tyrannizing demons; and leading us back to the mild and loving yoke of piety, recalls to heaven those that had been cast prostrate to the earth. It alone has tamed men, the most intractable of animals; the frivolous among them answering to the fowls of the air, deceivers to reptiles, the irascible to lions, the voluptuous to swine, the rapacious to wolves. The silly are stocks and stones, and still more senseless than stones is a man who is steeped in ignorance. As our witness, let us adduce the voice of prophecy accordant with truth, and bewailing those who are crushed in ignorance and folly: "For God is able of these stones to raise up children to Abraham;"[1] and He, commiserating their great ignorance and hardness of heart who are petrified against the truth, has raised up a seed of piety, sensitive to virtue, of those stones — of the nations, that is, who trusted in stones. Again, therefore, some venomous and false hypocrites, who plotted against righteousness, He once called "a brood of vipers."[2] But if one of those serpents even is willing to repent, and follows the Word, he becomes a man of God.

Others he figuratively calls wolves, clothed in sheep-skins, meaning thereby monsters of rapacity in human form. And so all such most savage beasts, and all such blocks of stone, the celestial song has transformed into tractable men. "For even we ourselves were sometime foolish, disobedient, deceived, serving divers lusts and pleasures, living in malice and envy, hateful, hating one another." Thus speaks the apostolic Scripture: "But after that the kindness and love of God our Saviour to man appeared, not by works of righteousness which we have done, but according to His mercy, He saved us."[3] Behold the might of the new song! It has made men out of stones, men out of beasts. Those, moreover, that were as dead, not being partakers of the true life, have come to life again, simply by becoming listeners to this song. It also composed the universe into melodious order, and tuned the discord of the elements to harmonious arrangement, so that the whole world might become harmony. It let loose the fluid ocean, and yet has prevented it from encroaching on the land. The earth, again, which had been in a state of commotion, it has established, and fixed the sea as its boundary. The violence of fire it has softened by the atmosphere, as the Dorian is blended with the Lydian strain; and the harsh cold of the air it has moderated by the embrace of fire, harmoniously arranging these the extreme tones of the universe. And this deathless strain, — the support of the whole and the harmony of all, — reaching from the centre to the circumference, and from the extremities to the central part, has harmonized this universal frame of things, not according to the Thracian music, which is like that invented by Jubal, but according to the paternal counsel of God, which fired the zeal of David. And He who is of David, and yet before him, the Word of God, despising the lyre and harp, which are but lifeless instruments, and having tuned by the Holy Spirit the universe, and especially man, — who, composed of body and soul, is a universe in miniature, — makes melody to God on this instrument of many tones; and to this intrument — I mean man — he sings accordant: "For thou art my harp, and pipe, and temple."[4] — a harp for harmony — a pipe by reason of the Spirit — a temple by reason of the word; so that the first may sound, the second breathe, the third contain the Lord. And David the king, the harper whom we mentioned a little above, who exhorted to the truth and dissuaded from idols, was so far from celebrating demons in song, that in reality they were driven away by his music. Thus, when Saul was plagued with a demon, he cured him by merely playing. A beautiful breathing instrument of music the Lord made man, after His own image. And He Himself also, surely, who is the supramundane Wisdom, the celestial Word, is the all-harmonious, melodious, holy instrument of God. What, then, does this instrument — the Word of God, the Lord, the New Song — desire? To open the eyes of the blind, and unstop the ears of the deaf, and to lead the lame or the erring to righteousness, to exhibit God to the foolish, to put a stop to corruption, to conquer death, to reconcile disobedient children to their father. The instrument of God loves mankind. The Lord pities, instructs, exhorts, admonishes, saves, shields, and of His bounty promises us the kingdom of heaven as a reward for learning; and the only advantage He reaps is, that we are

---

[1] Matt. iii. 9; Luke iii. 8.
[2] Matt. iii. 7; Luke iii. 7.
[3] Tit. iii. 3-5.

[4] Probably a quotation from a hymn.

aved. For wickedness feeds on men's destruc-ion; but truth, like the bee, harming nothing, lelights only in the salvation of men.

You have, then, God's promise; you have His ove: become partaker of His grace. And do not suppose the song of salvation to be new, as . vessel or a house is new. For "before the norning star it was;"[1] and "in the beginning vas the Word, and the Word was with God, and he Word was God."[2]   Error seems old, but ruth seems a new thing.

Whether, then, the Phrygians are shown to)e the most ancient people by the goats of the able; or, on the other hand, the Arcadians by he poets, who describe them as older than the noon; or, finally, the Egyptians by those who lream that this land first gave birth to gods and nen: yet none of these at least existed before :he world. But before the foundation of the vorld were we, who, because destined to be in Him, pre-existed in the eye of God before, — we :he rational creatures of the Word of God, on whose account we date from the beginning; for " in the beginning was the Word." Well, inas-much as the Word was from the first, He was and is the divine source of all things; but inas-much as He has now assumed the name Christ, consecrated of old, and worthy of power, he has been called by me the New Song. This Word, then, the Christ, the cause of both our being at first (for He was in God) and of our well-being, this very Word has now appeared as man, He alone being both, both God and man — the Au-thor of all blessings to us; by whom we, being taught to live well, are sent on our way to life eternal. For, according to that inspired apostle of the Lord, " the grace of God which bringeth salvation hath appeared to all men, teaching us, that, denying ungodliness and worldly lusts, we should live soberly, righteously, and godly, in this present world; looking for the blessed hope, and appearing of the glory of the great God and our Saviour Jesus Christ."[3]

This is the New Song,[4] the manifestation of the Word that was in the beginning, and before the beginning. The Saviour, who existed before, has in recent days appeared. He, who is in Him that truly is, has appeared; for the Word, who " was with God," and by whom all things were created, has appeared as our Teacher. The Word, who in the beginning bestowed on us life as Creator when He formed us, taught us to live well when He appeared as our Teacher; that as God He might afterwards conduct us to the life which never ends. He did not now for the first

time pity us for our error; but He pitied us from the first, from the beginning. But now, at His appearance, lost as we already were, He accom-plished our salvation. For that wicked reptile monster, by his enchantments, enslaves and plagues men even till now; inflicting, as seems to me, such barbarous vengeance on them as those who are said to bind the captives to corpses till they rot together. This wicked tyrant and serpent, accordingly, binding fast with the mis-erable chain of superstition whomsoever he can draw to his side from their birth, to stones, and stocks, and images, and such like idols, may with truth be said to have taken and buried living men with those dead idols, till both suffer cor-ruption together.

Therefore (for the seducer is one and the same) he that at the beginning brought Eve down to death, now brings thither the rest of mankind. Our ally and helper, too, is one and the same — the Lord, who from the beginning gave revelations by prophecy, but now plainly calls to salvation. In obedience to the apostolic injunction, therefore, let us flee from " the prince of the power of the air, the spirit that now work-eth in the children of disobedience,"[5] and let us run to the Lord the Saviour, who now exhorts to salvation, as He has ever done, as He did by signs and wonders in Egypt and the desert, both by the bush and the cloud, which, through the favour of divine love, attended the Hebrews like a handmaid. By the fear which these inspired He addressed the hard-hearted; while by Moses, learned in all wisdom, and Isaiah, lover of truth, and the whole prophetic choir, in a way appealing more to reason, He turns to the Word those who have ears to hear. Sometimes He upbraids, and sometimes He threatens. Some men He mourns over, others He addresses with the voice of song, just as a good physician treats some of his patients with cataplasms, some with rubbing, some with fomentations; in one case cuts open with the lancet, in another cauterizes, in another amputates, in order if possible to cure the patient's diseased part or member. The Saviour has many tones of voice, and many methods for the salvation of men; by threaten-ing He admonishes, by upbraiding He converts, by bewailing He pities, by the voice of song He cheers. He spake by the burning bush, for the men of that day needed signs and wonders.

He awed men by the fire when He made flame to burst from the pillar of cloud — a token at once of grace and fear: if you obey, there is the light; if you disobey, there is the fire; but, since humanity is nobler than the pillar or the bush, after them the prophets uttered their voice, — the Lord Himself speaking in Isaiah,

---

[1] Ps. cx. 3.   Septuagint has, " before the morning star."
[2] John i. 1.
[3] Tit. ii. 11–13.
[4] [Isa. xlii 10. Note that in all the Psalms where this expres-sion is used, there is a foretaste of the New Covenant and of the mani-festation of the Word.]

[5] Eph. ii. 2.

in Elias, — speaking Himself by the mouth of the prophets. But if thou dost not believe the prophets, but supposest both the men and the fire a myth, the Lord Himself shall speak to thee, " who, being in the form of God, thought it not robbery to be equal with God, but humbled Himself," [1] — He, the merciful God, exerting Himself to save man. And now the Word Himself clearly speaks to thee, shaming thy unbelief; yea, I say, the Word of God became man, that thou mayest learn from man how man may become God. Is it not then monstrous, my friends, that while God is ceaselessly exhorting us to virtue, we should spurn His kindness and reject salvation?

Does not John also invite to salvation, and is he not entirely a voice of exhortation? Let us then ask him, " Who of men art thou, and whence?" He will not say Elias. He will deny that he is Christ, but will profess himself to be " a voice crying in the wilderness." Who, then, is John? [2] In a word, we may say, " The beseeching voice of the Word crying in the wilderness." What criest thou, O voice? Tell us also. " Make straight the paths of the LORD." [3] John is the forerunner, and that voice the precursor of the Word; an inviting voice, preparing for salvation, — a voice urging men on to the inheritance of the heavens, and through which the barren and the desolate is childless no more. This fecundity the angel's voice foretold; and this voice was also the precursor of the Lord preaching glad tidings to the barren woman, as John did to the wilderness. By reason of this voice of the Word, therefore, the barren woman bears children, and the desert becomes fruitful. The two voices which heralded the Lord's — that of the angel and that of John — intimate, as I think, the salvation in store for us to be, that on the appearance of this Word we should reap, as the fruit of this productiveness, eternal life. The Scripture makes this all clear, by referring both the voices to the same thing : " Let her hear who has not brought forth, and let her who has not had the pangs of childbirth utter her voice : for more are the children of the desolate, than of her who hath an husband." [4]

The angel announced to us the glad tidings of a husband. John entreated us to recognise the husbandman, to seek the husband. For this husband of the barren woman, and this husbandman of the desert — who filled with divine power the barren woman and the desert — is one and the same. For because many were the children of the mother of noble race, yet the Hebrew woman, once blessed with many children, was made childless because of unbelief: the barren woman receives the husband, and the desert the husbandman ; then both become mothers through the word, the one of fruits, the other of believers. But to the unbelieving the barren and the desert are still reserved. For this reason John, the herald of the Word, besought men to make themselves ready against the coming of the Christ of God.[5] And it was this which was signified by the dumbness of Zacharias, which waited for fruit in the person of the harbinger of Christ, that the Word, the light of truth, by becoming the Gospel, might break the mystic silence of the prophetic enigmas. But if thou desirest truly to see God, take to thyself means of purification worthy of Him, not leaves of laurel fillets interwoven with wool and purple ; but wreathing thy brows with righteousness, and encircling them with the leaves of temperance, set thyself earnestly to find Christ. " For I am," He says, " the door," [6] which we who desire to understand God must discover, that He may throw heaven's gates wide open to us. For the gates of the Word being intellectual, are opened by the key of faith. No one knows God but the Son, and he to whom the Son shall reveal Him.[7] And I know well that He who has opened the door hitherto shut, will afterwards reveal what is within ; and will show what we could not have known before, had we not entered in by Christ, through whom alone God is beheld.

CHAP. II. — THE ABSURDITY AND IMPIETY OF THE HEATHEN MYSTERIES AND FABLES ABOUT THE BIRTH AND DEATH OF THEIR GODS.

Explore not then too curiously the shrines of impiety, or the mouths of caverns full of monstrosity, or the Thesprotian caldron, or the Cirrhæan tripod, or the Dodonian copper. The Gerandryon,[8] once regarded sacred in the midst of desert sands, and the oracle there gone to decay with the oak itself, consigned to the region of antiquated fables. The fountain of Castalia is silent, and the other fountain of Colophon ; and, in like manner, all the rest of the springs of divination are dead, and stripped of their vainglory, although at a late date, are shown with their fabulous legends to have run dry. Recount to us also the useless [9] oracles of that other kind of divination, or rather madness, the Clarian, the Pythian, the Didymæan, that of Amphiaraus, of Apollo, of Amphilochus ; and if you will, couple [10]

---

[1] Phil. ii. 6, 7.
[2] John i. 23.
[3] Isa. xl. 3.
[4] Isa. liv. 1.

[5] This may be translated, " of God the Christ."
[6] John x. 9.
[7] Matt. xi. 27.
[8] What this is, is not known; but it is likely that the word is a corruption of ἱερὰν δρῦν, the sacred oak.
[9] ἀχρηστα χρηστήρια.
[10] The text has ἀνίερου, the imperative of ἀνιερόω, which in classical Greek means " to hallow; " but the verb here must be derived from the adjective ἀνίερος, and be taken in the sense " deprive of their holiness," " no longer count holy." Eusebius reads ἀνιέρους; " unholy interpreters."

with them the expounders of prodigies, the augurs, and the interpreters of dreams. And bring and place beside the Pythian those that divine by flour, and those that divine by barley, and the ventriloquists still held in honour by many. Let the secret shrines of the Egyptians and the necromancies of the Etruscans be consigned to darkness. Insane devices truly are they all of unbelieving men. Goats, too, have been confederates in this art of soothsaying, trained to divination; and crows taught by men to give oracular responses to men.

And what if I go over the mysteries? I will not divulge them in mockery, as they say Alcibiades did, but I will expose right well by the word of truth the sorcery hidden in them; and those so-called gods of yours, whose are the mystic rites, I shall display, as it were, on the stage of life, to the spectators of truth. The bacchanals hold their orgies in honour of the frenzied Dionysus, celebrating their sacred frenzy by the eating of raw flesh, and go through the distribution of the parts of butchered victims, crowned with snakes, shrieking out the name of that Eva by whom error came into the world. The symbol of the Bacchic orgies is a consecrated serpent. Moreover, according to the strict interpretation of the Hebrew term, the name Hevia, aspirated, signifies a female serpent.

Demeter and Proserpine have become the heroines of a mystic drama; and their wanderings, and seizure, and grief, Eleusis celebrates by torchlight processions. I think that the derivation of orgies and mysteries ought to be traced, the former to the wrath (ὀργή) of Demeter against Zeus, the latter to the nefarious wickedness (μύσος) relating to Dionysus; but if from Myus of Attica, who Pollodorus says was killed in hunting — no matter, I don't grudge your mysteries the glory of funeral honours. You may understand mysteria in another way, as mytheria (hunting fables), the letters of the two words being interchanged; for certainly fables of this sort hunt after the most barbarous of the Thracians, the most senseless of the Phrygians, and the superstitious among the Greeks.

Perish, then, the man who was the author of this imposture among men, be he Dardanus, who taught the mysteries of the mother of the gods, or Eetion, who instituted the orgies and mysteries of the Samothracians, or that Phrygian Midas who, having learned the cunning imposture from Odrysus, communicated it to his subjects. For I will never be persuaded by that Cyprian Islander Cinyras, who dared to bring forth from night to the light of day the lewd orgies of Aphrodite in his eagerness to deify a strumpet of his own country. Others say that Melampus the son of Amythaon imported the festivals of Ceres from Egypt into Greece, celebrating her grief in song.

These I would instance as the prime authors of evil, the parents of impious fables and of deadly superstition, who sowed in human life that seed of evil and ruin — the mysteries.

And now, for it is time, I will prove their orgies to be full of imposture and quackery. And if you have been initiated, you will laugh all the more at these fables of yours which have been held in honour. I publish without reserve what has been involved in secrecy, not ashamed to tell what you are not ashamed to worship.

There is then the foam-born and Cyprus-born, the darling of Cinyras, — I mean Aphrodite, lover of the virilia, because sprung from them, even from those of Uranus, that were cut off, — those lustful members, that, after being cut off, offered violence to the waves. Of members so lewd a worthy fruit — Aphrodite — is born. In the rites which celebrate this enjoyment of the sea, as a symbol of her birth a lump of salt and the phallus are handed to those who are initiated into the art of uncleanness. And those initiated bring a piece of money to her, as a courtesan's paramours do to her.

Then there are the mysteries of Demeter, and Zeus's wanton embraces of his mother, and the wrath of Demeter; I know not what for the future I shall call her, mother or wife, on which account it is that she is called Brimo, as is said; also the entreaties of Zeus, and the drink of gall, the plucking out of the hearts of sacrifices, and deeds that we dare not name. Such rites the Phrygians perform in honour of Attis and Cybele and the Corybantes. And the story goes, that Zeus, having torn away the orchites of a ram, brought them out and cast them at the breasts of Demeter, paying thus a fraudulent penalty for his violent embrace, pretending to have cut out his own. The symbols of initiation into these rites, when set before you in a vacant hour, I know will excite your laughter, although on account of the exposure by no means inclined to laugh. "I have eaten out of the drum, I have drunk out of the cymbal, I have carried the Cernos,[1] I have slipped into the bedroom." Are not these tokens a disgrace? Are not the mysteries absurdity?

What if I add the rest? Demeter becomes a mother, Core[2] is reared up to womanhood. And, in course of time, he who begot her, — this same Zeus has intercourse with his own daughter Pherephatta, — after Ceres, the mother, — forgetting his former abominable wickedness. Zeus is both the father and the seducer of Core,

---

[1] The cernos some take to be a vessel containing poppy, etc., carried in sacrificial processions. The scholiast says that it is a fan. [I have marked this as a quotation. See below: Eleusinian rites.]
[2] Proserpine or Pherephatta.

and shamefully courts her in the shape of a dragon; his identity, however, was discovered. The token of the Sabazian mysteries to the initiated is " the deity gliding over the breast,"— the deity being this serpent crawling over the breasts of the initiated. Proof surely this of the unbridled lust of Zeus. Pherephatta has a child, though, to be sure, in the form of a bull, as an idolatrous poet says, —

> " The bull
> The dragon's father, and the father of the bull the dragon,
> On a hill the herdsman's hidden ox-goad," —

alluding, as I believe, under the name of the herdsman's ox-goad, to the reed wielded by bacchanals. Do you wish me to go into the story of Persephatta's gathering of flowers, her basket, and her seizure by Pluto (Aidoneus), and the rent in the earth, and the swine of Eubouleus that were swallowed up with the two goddesses; for which reason, in the Thesmophoria, speaking the Megaric tongue, they thrust out swine? This mythological story the women celebrate variously in different cities in the festivals called Thesmophoria and Scirophoria; dramatizing in many forms the rape of Pherephatta or Persephatta (Proserpine).

The mysteries of Dionysus are wholly inhuman; for while still a child, and the Curetes danced around [his cradle] clashing their weapons, and the Titans having come upon them by stealth, and having beguiled him with childish toys, these very Titans tore him limb from limb when but a child, as the bard of this mystery, the Thracian Orpheus, says : —

> " Cone, and spinning-top, and limb-moving rattles,
> And fair golden apples from the clear-toned Hesperides."

And the useless symbols of this mystic rite it will not be useless to exhibit for condemnation. These are dice, ball, hoop, apples, top,[1] looking-glass, tuft of wool.

Athene (Minerva), to resume our account, having abstracted the heart of Dionysus, was called Pallas, from the vibrating of the heart; and the Titans who had torn him limb from limb, setting a caldron on a tripod, and throwing into it the members of Dionysus, first boiled them down, and then fixing them on spits, " held them over the fire." But Zeus having appeared, since he was a god, having speedily perceived the savour of the pieces of flesh that were being cooked, — that savour which your gods agree to have assigned to them as their perquisite, — assails the Titans with his thunderbolt, and consigns the members of Dionysus to his son Apollo to be interred. And he — for he did not disobey

Zeus — bore the dismembered corpse to Parnassus, and there deposited it.

If you wish to inspect the orgies of the Corybantes, then know that, having killed their third brother, they covered the head of the dead body with a purple cloth, crowned it, and carrying it on the point of a spear, buried it under the roots of Olympus. These mysteries are, in short, murders and funerals. And the priests of these rites, who are called kings of the sacred rites by those whose business it is to name them, give additional strangeness to the tragic occurrence, by forbidding parsley with the roots from being placed on the table, for they think that parsley grew from the Corybantic blood that flowed forth; just as the women, in celebrating the Thesmophoria, abstain from eating the seeds of the pomegranate which have fallen on the ground, from the idea that pomegranates sprang from the drops of the blood of Dionysus. Those Corybantes also they call Cabiric; and the ceremony itself they announce as the Cabiric mystery.

For those two identical fratricides, having abstracted the box in which the phallus of Bacchus was deposited, took it to Etruria — dealers in honourable wares truly. They lived there as exiles, employing themselves in communicating the precious teaching of their superstition, and presenting phallic symbols and the box for the Tyrrhenians to worship. And some will have it, not improbably, that for this reason Dionysus was called Attis, because he was mutilated. And what is surprising at the Tyrrhenians, who were barbarians, being thus initiated into these foul indignities, when among the Athenians, and in the whole of Greece — I blush to say it — the shameful legend about Demeter holds its ground? For Demeter, wandering in quest of her daughter Core, broke down with fatigue near Eleusis, a place in Attica, and sat down on a well overwhelmed with grief. This is even now prohibited to those who are initiated, lest they should appear to mimic the weeping goddess. The indigenous inhabitants then occupied Eleusis : their names were Baubo, and Dusaules, and Triptolemus; and besides, Eumolpus and Eubouleus. Triptolemus was a herdsman, Eumolpus a shepherd, and Eubouleus a swineherd; from whom came the race of the Eumolpidæ and that of the Heralds — a race of Hierophants — who flourished at Athens.

Well, then (for I shall not refrain from the recital), Baubo having received Demeter hospitably, reaches to her a refreshing draught; and on her refusing it, not having any inclination to drink (for she was very sad), and Baubo having become annoyed, thinking herself slighted, uncovered her shame, and exhibited her nudity to the goddess. Demeter is delighted at the sight, and takes, though with difficulty, the draught —

---

[1] The scholiast takes the ῥίμβος to mean a piece of wood attached to a cord, and swung round so as to cause a whistling noise.

pleased, I repeat, at the spectacle. These are the secret mysteries of the Athenians; these Orpheus records. I shall produce the very words of Orpheus, that you may have the great authority on the mysteries himself, as evidence for this piece of turpitude : —

" Having thus spoken, she drew aside her garments,
    And showed all that shape of the body which it is
      improper to name,
And with her own hand Baubo stripped herself under
      the breasts.
Blandly then the goddess laughed and laughed in her
      mind,
And received the glancing cup in which was the
      draught."

And the following is the token of the Eleusinian mysteries : *I have fasted, I have drunk the cup; I have received from the box; having done, I put it into the basket, and out of the basket into the chest.*[1] Fine sights truly, and becoming a goddess ; mysteries worthy of the night, and flame, and the magnanimous or rather silly people of the Erechthidæ, and the other Greeks besides, " whom a fate they hope not for awaits after death." And in truth against these Heraclitus the Ephesian prophesies, as " the night-walkers, the magi, the bacchanals, the Lenæan revellers, the initiated." These he threatens with what will follow death, and predicts for them fire. For what are regarded among men as mysteries, they celebrate sacrilegiously. Law, then, and opinion, are nugatory. And the mysteries of the dragon are an imposture, which celebrates religiously mysteries that are no mysteries at all, and observes with a spurious piety profane rites. What are these mystic chests ?— for I must expose their sacred things, and divulge things not fit for speech. Are they not sesame cakes, and pyramidal cakes, and globular and flat cakes, embossed all over, and lumps of salt, and a serpent the symbol of Dionysus Bassareus ? And besides these, are they not pomegranates, and branches, and rods, and ivy leaves ? and besides, round cakes and poppy seeds ? And further, there are the unmentionable symbols of Themis, marjoram, a lamp, a sword, a woman's comb, which is a euphemism and mystic expression for the *muliebria*.

O unblushing shamelessness ! Once on a time night was silent, a veil for the pleasure of temperate men ; but now for the initiated, the holy night is the tell-tale of the rites of licentiousness ; and the glare of torches reveals vicious indulgences. Quench the flame, O Hierophant ; reverence, O Torch-bearer, the torches. That light exposes Iacchus ; let thy mysteries be honoured, and command the orgies to be hidden in night and darkness.[2]

The fire dissembles not ; it exposes and punishes what it is bidden.

Such are the mysteries of the Atheists.[3] And with reason I call those Atheists who know not the true God, and pay shameless worship to a boy torn in pieces by the Titans, and a woman in distress, and to parts of the body that in truth cannot be mentioned for shame, held fast as they are in the double impiety, first in that they know not God, not acknowledging as God Him who truly is ; the other and second is the error of regarding those who exist not, as existing and calling those gods that have no real existence, or rather no existence at all, who have nothing but a name. Wherefore the apostle reproves us, saying, " And ye were strangers to the covenants of promise, having no hope, and without God in the world." [4]

All honour to that king of the Scythians, whoever Anacharsis was, who shot with an arrow one of his subjects who imitated among the Scythians the mystery of the Mother of the gods, as practised by the inhabitants of Cyzicus, beating a drum and sounding a cymbal strung from his neck like a priest of Cybele, condemning him as having become effeminate among the Greeks, and a teacher of the disease of effeminacy to the rest of the Cythians.

Wherefore (for I must by no means conceal it) I cannot help wondering how Euhemerus of Agrigentum, and Nicanor of Cyprus, and Diagoras, and Hippo of Melos, and besides these, that Cyrenian of the name of Theodorus, and numbers of others, who lived a sober life, and had a clearer insight than the rest of the world into the prevailing error respecting those gods, were called Atheists ; for if they did not arrive at the knowledge of the truth, they certainly suspected the error of the common opinion ; which suspicion is no insignificant seed, and becomes the germ of true wisdom. One of these charges the Egyptians thus : " If you believe them to be gods, do not mourn or bewail them ; and if you mourn and bewail them, do not any more regard them as gods." And another, taking an image of Hercules made of wood (for he happened most likely to be cooking something at home), said, " Come now, Hercules ; now is the time to undergo for us the thirteenth labour, as you did the twelve for Eurystheus, and make this ready for Diagoras," and so cast it into the fire as a log of wood. For the extremes of ignorance are atheism and superstition, from which we must endeavour to keep. And do you not see Moses, the hierophant of the truth, enjoining that no eunuch, or emasculated man, or son of a harlot, should enter the congregation ? By the two first

---

[1] [See *supra*, p 175, where I have affixed quotation-marks, and adopted the word " tokens" (instead of " signs ") to harmonize these two places]

[2] This sentence is read variously in various editions.

[3] [A scathing retort upon those who called Christians *atheists*, and accused them of shameful rites.]

[4] Eph. ii. 12.

he alludes to the impious custom by which men were deprived both of divine energy and of their virility; and by the third, to him who, in place of the only real God, assumes many gods falsely so called, — as the son of a harlot, in ignorance of his true father, may claim many putative fathers.

There was an innate original communion between men and heaven, obscured through ignorance, but which now at length has leapt forth instantaneously from the darkness, and shines resplendent; as has been expressed by one[1] in the following lines : —

"See'st thou this lofty, this boundless ether,
Holding the earth in the embrace of its humid arms."

And in these : —

"O Thou, who makest the earth Thy chariot, and in the earth hast Thy seat,
Whoever Thou be, baffling our efforts to behold Thee."

And whatever else the sons of the poets sing.

But sentiments erroneous, and deviating from what is right, and certainly pernicious, have turned man, a creature of heavenly origin, away from the heavenly life, and stretched him on the earth, by inducing him to cleave to earthly objects. For some, beguiled by the contemplation of the heavens, and trusting to their sight alone, while they looked on the motions of the stars, straightway were seized with admiration, and deified them, calling the stars gods from their motion ($\theta\epsilon\acute{o}\varsigma$ from $\theta\epsilon\hat{\iota}\nu$); and worshipped the sun, — as, for example, the Indians; and the moon, as the Phrygians. Others, plucking the benignant fruits of earth-born plants, called grain Demeter, as the Athenians, and the vine Dionysus, as the Thebans. Others, considering the penalties of wickedness, deified them, worshipping various forms of retribution and calamity. Hence the Erinnyes, and the Eumenides, and the piacular deities, and the judges and avengers of crime, are the creations of the tragic poets.

And some even of the philosophers, after the poets, make idols of forms of the affections in your breasts, — such as fear, and love, and joy, and hope; as, to be sure, Epimenides of old, who raised at Athens the altars of Insult and Impudence. Other objects deified by men take their rise from events, and are fashioned in bodily shape, such as a Dike, a Clotho, and Lachesis, and Atropos, and Heimarmene, and Auxo, and Thallo, which are Attic goddesses. There is a sixth mode of introducing error and of manufacturing gods, according to which they number the twelve gods, whose birth is the theme of which Hesiod sings in his Theogony, and of whom Homer speaks in all that he says of the gods. The last mode remains (for there are seven in all) — that which takes its rise from the divine beneficence towards men. For, not understanding that it is God that does us good, they have invented saviours in the persons of the Dioscuri and Hercules the averter of evil, and Asclepius the healer. These are the slippery and hurtful deviations from the truth which draw man down from heaven, and cast him into the abyss.

wish to show thoroughly what like these gods of yours are, that now at length you may abandon your delusion, and speed your flight back to heaven. "For we also were once children of wrath even as others; but God, being rich in mercy for the great love wherewith He loved us, when we were now dead in trespasses, quickened us together with Christ."[2] For the Word is living and having been buried with Christ, is exalted with God. But those who are still unbelieving are called children of wrath, reared for wrath. We who have been rescued from error, and restored to the truth, are no longer the nurslings of wrath. Thus, therefore, we who were once the children of lawlessness, have through the philanthropy of the Word now become the sons of God.

But to you a poet of your own, Empedocles of Agrigentum, comes and says : —

"Wherefore, distracted with grievous evils,
You will never ease your soul of its miserable woes."

The most of what is told of your gods is fabled and invented; and those things which are supposed to have taken place, are recorded of vile men who lived licentious lives : —

"You walk in pride and madness,
And leaving the right and straight path, you have gone away
Through thorns and briars. Why do ye wander?
Cease, foolish men, from mortals;
Leave the darkness of night, and lay hold on the light."

These counsels the Sibyl, who is at once prophetic and poetic, enjoins on us; and truth enjoins them on us too, stripping the crowd of deities of those terrifying and threatening masks of theirs, disproving the rash opinions formed of them by showing the similarity of names. For there are those who reckon three Jupiters : him of Æther in Arcadia, and the other two sons of Kronos; and of these, one in Crete, and the others again in Arcadia. And there are those that reckon five Athenes : the Athenian, the daughter of Hephæstus; the second, the Egyptian, the daughter of Nilus; the third the inventor of war, the daughter of Kronos; the fourth, the daughter of Zeus, whom the Messenians have named Coryphasia, from her mother; above all, the daughter of Pallas and Titanis, the daughter of Oceanus, who, having wickedly killed her father, adorned

---

[1] Euripides.

[2] Eph. ii. 3-5.

erself with her father's skin, as if it had been the fleece of a sheep. Further, Aristotle calls the first Apollo, the son of Hephæstus and Athene (consequently Athene is no more a virgin) ; the second, that in Crete, the son of Corybas ; the third, the son Zeus ; the fourth, the Arcadian, the son of Silenus (this one is called by the Arcadians Nomius) ; and in addition to these, he specifies the Libyan Apollo, the son of Ammon ; and to these Didymus the grammarian adds a sixth, the son of Magnes. And now how many Apollos are there ? They are numberless, mortal men, all helpers of their fellow-men, who similarly with those already mentioned have been so called. And what were I to mention the many Asclepiuses, or all the Mercuries that are reckoned up, or the Vulcans of fable ? Shall I not appear extravagant, deluging your ears with these numerous names ?

At any rate, the native countries of your gods, and their arts and lives, and besides especially their sepulchres, demonstrate them to have been men. Mars, accordingly, who by the poets is held in the highest possible honour : —

Mars, Mars, bane of men, blood-stained stormer of walls," [1] —

His deity, always changing sides, and implacable, as Epicharmus says, was a Spartan ; Sophocles knew him for a Thracian ; others say he was an Arcadian. This god, Homer says, was bound thirteen months : —

> " Mars had his suffering ; by Alöeus' sons,
> Otus and Ephialtes, strongly bound,
> He thirteen months in brazen fetters lay." [2]

Good luck attend the Carians, who sacrifice dogs to him ! And may the Scythians never leave off sacrificing asses, as Apollodorus and Callimachus relate : —

> " Phœbus rises propitious to the Hyperboreans,
> Then they offer sacrifices of asses to him."

And the same in another place : —

> " Fat sacrifices of asses' flesh delight Phœbus."

Hephæstus, whom Jupiter cast from Olympus, from its divine threshold, having fallen on Lemnos, practised the art of working in brass, maimed in his feet : —

His tottering knees were bowed beneath his weight." [3]

You have also a doctor, and not only a brass-worker among the gods. And the doctor was greedy of gold ; Asclepius was his name. I shall produce as a witness your own poet, the Bœotian Pindar : —

> Him even the gold glittering in his hands,
> Amounting to a splendid fee, persuaded
> To rescue a man, already death's capture, from his
>   grasp ;

But Saturnian Jove, having shot his bolt through both,
Quickly took the breath from their breasts,
And his flaming thunderbolt sealed their doom."

And Euripides : —

" For Zeus was guilty of the murder of my son
Asclepius, by casting the lightning flame at his breast."

He therefore lies struck with lightning in the regions of Cynosuris. Philochorus also says, that Poseidon was worshipped as a physician in Tenos ; and that Kronos settled in Sicily, and there was buried. Patroclus the Thurian, and Sophocles the younger, in three tragedies, have told the story of the Dioscuri ; and these Dioscuri were only two mortals, if Homer is worthy of of credit : —

> " . . . . . . but they beneath the teeming earth,
> In Lacedæmon lay, their native land." [4]

And, in addition, he who wrote the Cyprian poems says Castor was mortal, and death was decreed to him by fate ; but Pollux was immortal, being the progeny of Mars. This he has poetically fabled. But Homer is more worthy of credit, who spoke as above of both the Dioscuri ; and, besides, proved Herucles to be a mere phantom : —

> " The man Hercules, expert in mighty deeds."

Hercules, therefore, was known by Homer himself as only a mortal man. And Hieronymus the philosopher describes the make of his body, as tall,[5] bristling-haired, robust ; and Dicæarchus says that he was square-built, muscular, dark, hook-nosed, with greyish eyes and long hair. This Hercules, accordingly, after living fifty-two years, came to his end, and was burned in a funeral pyre in Œta.

As for the Muses, whom Alcander calls the daughters of Zeus and Mnemosyne, and the rest of the poets and authors deify and worship,— those Muses, in honour of whom whole states have already erected museums, being handmaids, were hired by Megaclo, the daughter of Macar. This Macar reigned over the Lesbians, and was always quarrelling with his wife ; and Megaclo was vexed for her mother's sake. What would she not do on her account ? Accordingly she hires those handmaids, being so many in number, and calls them Mysæ, according to the dialect of the Æolians. These she taught to sing deeds of the olden time, and play melodiously on the lyre. And they, by assiduously playing the lyre, and singing sweetly to it, soothed Macar, and put a stop to his ill-temper. Wherefore Megaclo, as a token of gratitude to them, on her mother's account erected brazen pillars, and ordered them to be held in honour in all the temples. Such, then, are the Muses. This account is in Myrsilus of Lesbos.

---

[1] *Iliad*, v. 31.
[2] *Iliad*, v. 385.
[3] *Iliad*, xviii. 411.

[4] *Iliad*, iii. 243. Lord Derby's translation is used in extracts from the *Iliad*.
[5] The MSS. read " *small*," but the true reading is doubtless " *tall*."

And now, then, hear the loves of your gods, and the incredible tales of their licentiousness, and their wounds, and their bonds, and their laughings, and their fights, their servitudes too, and their banquets ; and furthermore, their embraces, and tears, and sufferings, and lewd delights. Call me Poseidon, and the troop of damsels deflowered by him, Amphitrite Amymone, Alope, Melanippe, Alcyone, Hippothoe, Chione, and myriads of others ; with whom, though so many, the passions of your Poseidon were not satiated.

Call me Apollo ; this is Phœbus, both a holy prophet and a good adviser. But Sterope will not say that, nor Æthousa, nor Arsinoe, nor Zeuxippe, nor Prothoe, nor Marpissa, nor Hypsipyle. For Daphne alone escaped the prophet and seduction.

And, above all, let the father of gods and men, according to you, himself come, who was so given to sexual pleasure, as to lust after all, and indulge his lust on all, like the goats of the Thmuitæ. And thy poems, O Homer, fill me with admiration !

" He said, and nodded with his shadowy brows ;
  Waved on the immortal head the ambrosial locks,
  And all Olympus trembled at his nod." [1]

Thou makest Zeus venerable, O Homer ; and the nod which thou dost ascribe to him is most reverend. But show him only a woman's girdle, and Zeus is exposed, and his locks are dishonoured. To what a pitch of licentiousness did that Zeus of yours proceed, who spent so many nights in voluptuousness with Alcmene? For not even these nine nights were long to this insatiable monster. But, on the contrary, a whole lifetime were short enough for his lust ; that he might beget for us the evil-averting god.

Hercules, the son of Zeus — a true son of Zeus — was the offspring of that long night, who with hard toil accomplished the twelve labours in a long time, but in one night deflowered the fifty daughters of Thestius, and thus was at once the debaucher and the bridegroom of so many virgins. It is not, then, without reason that the poets call him a cruel wretch and a nefarious scoundrel. It were tedious to recount his adulteries of all sorts, and debauching of boys. For your gods did not even abstain from boys, one having loved Hylas, another Hyacinthus, another Pelops, another Chrysippus, and another Ganymede. Let such gods as these be worshipped by your wives, and let them pray that their husbands be such as these — so temperate ; that, emulating them in the same practices, they may be like the gods. Such gods let your boys be trained to worship, that they may grow up to be men with the accursed likeness of fornication on them received from the gods.

But it is only the male deities, perhaps, that are impetuous in sexual indulgence.

"The female deities stayed each in the house for shame," [2] says Homer ; the goddesses blushing, for modesty's sake, to look on Aphrodite when she had been guilty of adultery. But these are more passionately licentious, bound in the chains of adultery ; Eos having disgraced herself with Tithonus, Selene with Endymion, Nereis with Æacus, Thetis with Peleus, Demeter with Jason, Persephatta with Adonis. And Aphrodite having disgraced herself with Ares, crossed over to Cinyra and married Anchises, and laid snare for Phaëthon, and loved Adonis. She contended with the ox-eyed Juno ; and the goddesses un robed for the sake of the apple, and presented themselves naked before the shepherd, that he might decide which was the fairest.

But come, let us briefly go the round of the games, and do away with those solemn assemblages at tombs, the Isthmian, Nemean, and Pythian, and finally the Olympian. At Pytho the Pythian dragon is worshipped, and the festival-assemblage of the serpent is called by the name Pythia. At the Isthmus the sea spit out a piece of miserable refuse ; and the Isthmian games bewail Melicerta.

At Nemea another — a little boy, Archemorus — was buried ; and the funeral games of the child are called Nemea. Pisa is the grave of the Phrygian charioteer, O Hellenes of all tribes ; and the Olympian games, which are nothing else than the funeral sacrifices of Pelops, the Zeus of Phidias claims for himself. The mysteries were then, as is probable, games held in honour of the dead ; so also were the oracles, and both became public. But the mysteries at Sagra [3] and in Alimus of Attica were confined to Athens. But those contests and *phalloi* consecrated to Dionysus were a world's shame, pervading life with their deadly influence. For Dionysus eagerly desiring to descend to Hades, did not know the way ; a man, by name Prosymnus, offers to tell him, not without reward. The reward was a disgraceful one, though not so in the opinion of Dionysus : it was an Aphrodisian favour that was asked of Dionysus as a reward. The god was not reluctant to grant the request made to him, and promises to fulfil it should he return, and confirms his promise with an oath. Having learned the way, he departed and again returned : he did not find Prosymnus, for he had died. In order to acquit himself of his promise to his lover, he rushes to his tomb, and burns with unnatural lust. Cutting a fig-branch that came to his hand, he shaped the phallus, and so performed his promise to the dead man. As a mystic memorial of this incident, *phalloi* are

---

[1] *Iliad*, i. 528.

[2] *Odyss.*, viii. 324.
[3] Meursius proposed to read, " at Agra."

raised aloft in honour of Dionysus through the various cities. "For did they not make a procession in honour of Dionysus, and sing most shameless songs in honour of the pudenda, all would go wrong," says Heraclitus. This is that Pluto and Dionysus in whose honour they give themselves up to frenzy, and play the bacchanal, — not so much, in my opinion, for the sake of intoxication, as for the sake of the shameless ceremonial practised. With reason, therefore, such as have become slaves of their passions are your gods !

Furthermore, like the Helots among the Lacedemonians, Apollo came under the yoke of slavery to Admetus in Pheræ, Hercules to Omphale in Sardis. Poseidon was a drudge to Laomedon ; and so was Apollo, who, like a good-for-nothing servant, was unable to obtain his freedom from his former master ; and at that time the walls of Troy were built by them for the Phrygian. And Homer is not ashamed to speak of Athene as appearing to Ulysses with a golden lamp in her hand. And we read of Aphrodite, like a wanton serving-wench, taking and setting a seat for Helen opposite the adulterer, in order to entice him.

Panyasis, too, tells us of gods in plenty besides those who acted as servants, writing thus : —

" Demeter underwent servitude, and so did the famous lame god;
Poseidon underwent it, and Apollo too, of the silver bow,
With a mortal man for a year. And fierce Mars
Underwent it at the compulsion of his father."

And so on.

Agreeably to this, it remains for me to bring before you those amatory and sensuous deities of yours, as in every respect having human feelings.

" For theirs was a mortal body."

This Homer most distinctly shows, by introducing Aphrodite uttering loud and shrill cries on account of her wound ; and describing the most warlike Ares himself as wounded in the stomach by Diomede. Polemo, too, says that Athene was wounded by Ornytus ; nay, Homer says that Pluto even was struck with an arrow by Hercules ; and Panyasis relates that the beams of Sol were struck by the arrows of Hercules ; [1] and the same Panyasis relates, that by the same Hercules Hera the goddess of marriage was wounded in sandy Pylos. Sosibius, too, relates that Hercules was wounded in the hand by the sons of Hippocoon. And if there are wounds, there is blood. For the *ichor* of the poets is more repulsive than blood ; for the putrefaction of blood is called *ichor*. Wherefore cures and means of sustenance of which they stand in need

must be furnished. Accordingly mention is made of tables, and potations, and laughter, and intercourse ; for men would not devote themselves to love, or beget children, or sleep, if they were immortal, and had no wants, and never grew old. Jupiter himself, when the guest of Lycaon the Arcadian, partook of a human table among the Ethiopians — a table rather inhuman and forbidden. For he satiated himself with human flesh unwittingly ; for the god did not know that Lycaon the Arcadian, his entertainer, had slain his son (his name was Nyctimus), and served him up cooked before Zeus.

This is Jupiter the good, the prophetic, the patron of hospitality, the protector of suppliants, the benign, the author of omens, the avenger of wrongs ; rather the unjust, the violater of right and of law, the impious, the inhuman, the violent, the seducer, the adulterer, the amatory. But perhaps when he was such he was a man ; but now these fables seem to have grown old on our hands. Zeus is no longer a serpent, a swan, nor an eagle, nor a licentious man ; the god no longer flies, nor loves boys, nor kisses, nor offers violence, although there are still many beautiful women, more comely than Leda, more blooming than Semele, and boys of better looks and manners than the Phrygian herdsman. Where is now that eagle? where now that swan? where now is Zeus himself? He has grown old with his feathers ; for as yet he does not repent of his amatory exploits, nor is he taught continence. The fable is exposed before you : Leda is dead, the swan is dead. Seek your Jupiter. Ransack not heaven, but earth. The Cretan, in whose country he was buried, will show him to you, — I mean Callimachus, in his hymns : —

" For thy tomb, O king,
The Cretans fashioned ! "

For Zeus is dead, be not distressed, as Leda is dead, and the swan, and the eagle, and the libertine, and the serpent. And now even the superstitious seem, although reluctantly, yet truly, to have come to understand their error respecting the Gods.

" For not from an ancient oak, nor from a rock,
But from men, is thy descent." [2]

But shortly after this, they will be found to be but oaks and stones. One Agamemnon is said by Staphylus to be worshipped as a Jupiter in Sparta ; and Phanocles, in his book of the *Brave and Fair*, relates that Agamemnon king of the Hellenes erected the temple of Argennian Aphrodite, in honour of Argennus his friend. An Artemis, named the Strangled, is worshipped by the Arcadians, as Callimachus says in his *Book of Causes ;* and at Methymna another Artemis had divine honours paid her, viz., Artemis Con-

---

[1] *The beams of Sol or the Sun* is an emendation of Potter's. The MSS. read "*the Elean Augeas.*"

[2] *Odyss.,* xix. 163.

dylitis. There is also the temple of another Artemis — Artemis Podagra (or, the gout) — in Laconica, as Sosibius says. Polemo tells of an image of a yawning Apollo ; and again of another image, reverenced in Elis, of the guzzling Apollo. Then the Eleans sacrifice to Zeus, the averter of flies ; and the Romans sacrifice to Hercules, the averter of flies ; and to Fever, and to Terror, whom also they reckon among the attendants of Hercules. (I pass over the Argives, who worshipped Aphrodite, opener of graves.) The Argives and Spartans reverence Artemis Chelytis, or the cougher, from χελύττειν, which in their speech signifies to cough.

Do you imagine from what source these details have been quoted? Only such as are furnished by yourselves are here adduced ; and you do not seem to recognise your own writers, whom I call as witnesses against your unbelief. Poor wretches that ye are, who have filled with unholy jesting the whole compass of your life — a life in reality devoid of life !

Is not Zeus the Baldhead worshipped in Argos ; and another Zeus, the avenger, in Cyprus? Do not the Argives sacrifice to Aphrodite Peribaso (the protectress),[1] and the Athenians to Aphrodite Hetæra (the courtesan), and the Syracusans to Aphrodite Kallipygos, whom Nicander has somewhere called Kalliglutos (with beautiful rump). I pass over in silence just now Dionysus Choiropsales.[2] The Sicyonians reverence this deity, whom they have constituted the god of the muliebria — the patron of filthiness — and religiously honour as the author of licentiousness. Such, then, are their gods ; such are they also who make mockery of the gods, or rather mock and insult themselves. How much better are the Egyptians, who in their towns and villages pay divine honours to the irrational creatures, than the Greeks, who worship such gods as these?

For if they are beasts, they are not adulterous or libidinous, and seek pleasure in nothing that is contrary to nature. And of what sort these deities are, what need is there further to say, as they have been already sufficiently exposed? Furthermore, the Egyptians whom I have now mentioned are divided in their objects of worship. The Syenites worship the braize-fish ; and the maiotes — this is another fish — is worshipped by those who inhabit Elephantine : the Oxyrinchites likewise worship a fish which takes its name from their country. Again, the Heraclitopolites worship the ichneumon, the inhabitants of Sais and of Thebes a sheep, the Leucopolites a wolf, the Cynopolites a dog, the

Memphites Apis, the Mendesians a goat. And you, who are altogether better than the Egyptians (I shrink from saying worse), who never cease laughing every day of your lives at the Egyptians, what are some of you, too, with regard to brute beasts? For of your number the Thessalians pay divine homage to storks, in accordance with ancient custom ; and the Thebans to weasels, for their assistance at the birth of Hercules. And again, are not the Thessalians reported to worship ants, since they have learned that Zeus in the likeness of an ant had intercourse with Eurymedusa, the daughter of Cletor, and begot Myrmidon? Polemo, too, relates that the people who inhabit the Troad worship the mice of the country, which they call Sminthoi, because they gnawed the strings of their enemies' bows ; and from those mice Apollo has received his epithet of Sminthian. Heraclides, in his work, *Regarding the Building of Temples in Acarnania*, says that, at the place where the promontory of Actium is, and the temple of Apollo of Actium, they offer to the flies the sacrifice of an ox.

Nor shall I forget the Samians : the Samians, as Euphorion says, reverence the sheep. Nor shall I forget the Syrians, who inhabit Phœnicia, of whom some revere doves, and others fishes, with as excessive veneration as the Eleans do Zeus. Well, then, since those you worship are not gods, it seems to me requisite to ascertain if those are really demons who are ranked, as you say, in this second order [next the gods]. For if the lickerish and impure are demons, indigenous demons who have obtained sacred honours may be discovered in crowds throughout your cities : Menedemus among the Cythnians ; among the Tenians, Callistagoras ; among the Delians, Anius ; among the Laconians, Astrabacus ; at Phalerus, a hero affixed to the prow of ships is worshipped ; and the Pythian priestess enjoined the Platæans to sacrifice to Androcrates and Democrates, and Cyclæus and Leuco while the Median war was at its height. Other demons in plenty may be brought to light by any one who can look about him a little.

" For thrice ten thousand are there in the all-nourishing earth
  Of demons immortal, the guardians of articulate-speaking men." [3]

Who these guardians are, do not grudge, O Bœotian, to tell. Is it not clear that they are those we have mentioned, and those of more renown, the great demons, Apollo, Artemis, Leto, Demeter, Core, Pluto, Hercules, and Zeus himself?

But it is from running away that they guard us, O Ascræan, or perhaps it is from sinning, as forsooth they have never tried their hand at sin

---

[1] So Liddell and Scott. Commentators are generally agreed that the epithet is an obscene one, though what its precise meaning is they can only conjecture.
[2] An obscene epithet, derived from χοῖρος, a sow, and θλίβω, to press.

[3] Hesiod, *Works and Days*, I. i. 250.

emselves! In that case verily the proverb ay fitly be uttered:—

The father who took no admonition admonishes his son."

If these are our guardians, it is not because ey have any ardour of kindly feeling towards s, but intent on your ruin, after the manner of atterers, they prey on your substance, enticed y the smoke. These demons themselves indeed onfess their own gluttony, saying:—

"For with drink-offerings due, and fat of lambs,
My altar still hath at their hands been fed;
Such honour hath to us been ever paid."[1]

What other speech would they utter, if indeed e gods of the Egyptians, such as cats and easels, should receive the faculty of speech, an that Homeric and poetic one which proaims their liking for savoury odours and cookry? Such are your demons and gods, and emigods, if there are any so called, as there re demi-asses (mules); for you have no want f terms to make up compound names of imiety.

HAP. III. — THE CRUELTY OF THE SACRIFICES TO
THE GODS.

Well, now, let us say in addition, what inhuan demons, and hostile to the human race, our gods were, not only delighting in the inanity of men, but gloating over human slaugher, — now in the armed contests for superiority n the stadia, and now in the numberless conests for renown in the wars providing for themelves the means of pleasure, that they might e able abundantly to satiate themselves with he murder of human beings.

And now, like plagues invading cities and ations, they demanded cruel oblations. Thus, ristomenes the Messenian slew three hundred uman beings in honour of Ithometan Zeus, hinking that hecatombs of such a number and uality would give good omens; among whom as Theopompos, king of the Lacedemonians, noble victim.

The Taurians, the people who inhabit the auric Chersonese, sacrifice to the Tauric Arteis forthwith whatever strangers they lay hands n on their coasts who have been cast adrift on he sea. These sacrifices Euripides represents n tragedies on the stage. Monimus relates, in is treatise on marvels, that at Pella, in Thessaly, man of Achaia was slain in sacrifice to Peleus nd Chiron. That the Lyctii, who are a Cretan ace, slew men in sacrifice to Zeus, Anticlides hows in his *Homeward Journeys;* and that the esbians offered the like sacrifice to Dionysus, s said by Dosidas. The Phocæans also (for will not pass over such as they are), Pytho-

cles informs us in his third book, *On Concord,* offer a man as a burnt-sacrifice to the Taurian Artemis.

Erechtheus of Attica and Marius the Roman[2] sacrificed their daughters, — the former to Pherephatta, as Demaratus mentions in his first book on *Tragic Subjects;* the latter to the evil-averting deities, as Dorotheus relates in his first book of *Italian Affairs.* Philanthropic, assuredly, the demons appear, from these examples; and how shall those who revere the demons not be correspondingly pious? The former are called by the fair name of saviours; and the latter ask for safety from those who plot against their safety, imagining that they sacrifice with good omens to them, and forget that they themselves are slaying men. For a murder does not become a sacrifice by being committed in a particular spot. You are not to call it a sacred sacrifice, if one slays a man either at the altar or on the highway to Artemis or Zeus, any more than if he slew him for anger or covetousness, — other demons very like the former; but a sacrifice of this kind is murder and human butchery. Then why is it, O men, wisest of all creatures, that you avoid wild beasts, and get out of the way of the savage animals, if you fall in with a bear or lion?

"..... As when some traveller spies,
Coiled in his path upon the mountain side,
A deadly snake, back he recoils in haste,—
His limbs all trembling, and his cheek all pale."[3]

But though you perceive and understand demons to be deadly and wicked, plotters, haters of the human race, and destroyers, why do you not turn out of their way, or turn them out of yours? What truth can the wicked tell, or what good can they do any one?

I can then readily demonstrate that man is better than these gods of yours, who are but demons; and can show, for instance, that Cyrus and Solon were superior to oracular Apollo. Your Phœbus was a lover of gifts, but not a lover of men. He betrayed his friend Crœsus, and forgetting the reward he had got (so careful was he of his fame), led him across the Halys to the stake. The demons love men in such a way as to bring them to the fire [unquenchable].

But O man, who lovest the human race better, and art truer than Apollo, pity him that is bound on the pyre. Do thou, O Solon, declare truth; and thou, O Cyrus, command the fire to be extinguished. Be wise, then, at last, O Crœsus, taught by suffering. He whom you worship is an ingrate; he accepts your reward, and after taking the gold plays false. "Look again to the end," O Solon. It is not the demon, but the man that tells you this. It is not ambiguous

---

[1] *Iliad,* iv. 48.

[2] Plutarch, xx.
[3] *Iliad,* iii. 33.

oracles that Solon utters. You shall easily take him up. Nothing but true, O Barbarian, shall you find by proof this oracle to be, when you are placed on the pyre. Whence I cannot help wondering, by what plausible reasons those who first went astray were impelled to preach superstition to men, when they exhorted them to worship wicked demons, whether it was Phoroneus or Merops, or whoever else that raised temples and altars to them; and besides, as is fabled, were the first to offer sacrifices to them. But, unquestionably, in succeeding ages men invented for themselves gods to worship. It is beyond doubt that this Eros, who is said to be among the oldest of the gods, was worshipped by no one till Charmus took a little boy and raised an altar to him in Academia, — a thing more seemly [1] than the lust he had gratified; and the lewdness of vice men called by the name of Eros, deifying thus unbridled lust. The Athenians, again, knew not who Pan was till Philippides told them.

Superstition, then, as was to be expected, having taken its rise thus, became the fountain of insensate wickedness; and not being subsequently checked, but having gone on augmenting and rushing along in full flood, it became the originator of many demons, and was displayed in sacrificing hecatombs, appointing solemn assemblies, setting up images, and building temples, which were in reality tombs: for I will not pass these over in silence, but make a thorough exposure of them, though called by the august name of temples; that is, the tombs which got the name of temples. But do ye now at length quite give up your superstition, feeling ashamed to regard sepulchres with religious veneration. In the temple of Athene in Larissa, on the Acropolis, is the grave of Acrisius; and at Athens, on the Acropolis, is that of Cecrops, as Antiochus says in the ninth book of his *Histories*. What of Erichthonius? was he not buried in the temple of Polias? And Immarus, the son of Eumolpus and Daira, were they not buried in the precincts of the Elusinium, which is under the Acropolis; and the daughters of Celeus, were they not interred in Eleusis? Why should I enumerate to you the wives of the Hyperboreans? They were called Hyperoche and Laodice; they were buried in the Artemisium in Delos, which is in the temple of the Delian Apollo. Leandrius says that Clearchus was buried in Miletus, in the Didymæum. Following the Myndian Zeno, it were unsuitable in this connection to pass over the sepulchre of Leucophryne, who was buried in the temple of Artemis in Magnesia; or the altar of Apollo in Telmessus, which is reported to be the tomb of Telmisseus the seer. Further Ptolemy the son of Agesarchus, in his first book about Philopator, says that Cinyras and the descendants of Cinyras were interred in the temple of Aphrodite in Paphos. But all time would not be sufficient for me, were I to go over the tombs which are held sacred by you. And if no shame for these audacious impieties steals over you, it comes to this, that you are completely dead, putting, as really you do, your trust in the dead.

"Poor wretches, what misery is this you suffer?
Your heads are enveloped in the darkness of night." [2]

CHAP. IV. — THE ABSURDITY AND SHAMEFULNESS OF THE IMAGES BY WHICH THE GODS ARE WORSHIPPED.

If, in addition, I take and set before you for inspection these very images, you will, as you go over them, find how truly silly is the custom in which you have been reared, of worshipping the senseless works of men's hands.

Anciently, then, the Scythians worshipped their sabres, the Arabs stones, the Persians rivers. And some, belonging to other races still more ancient, set up blocks of wood in conspicuous situations, and erected pillars of stone, which were called Xoana, from the carving of the material of which they were made. The image of Artemis in Icarus was doubtless unwrought wood, and that of the Cithæronian Here was a felled tree-trunk; and that of the Samian Here, as Aethlius says, was at first a plank, and was afterwards during the government of Proclus carved into human shape. And when the Xoana began to be made in the likeness of men, they got the name of Brete, — a term derived from Brotos (man). In Rome, the historian Varro says that in ancient times the Xoaron of Mars — the idol by which he was worshipped — was a spear, artists not having yet applied themselves to this specious pernicious art; but when art flourished, error increased. That of stones and stocks — and, to speak briefly, of dead matter — you have made images of human form, by which you have produced a counterfeit of piety, and slandered the truth, is now as clear as can be; but such proof as the point may demand must not be declined.

That the statue of Zeus at Olympia, and that of Polias at Athens, were executed of gold and ivory by Phidias, is known by everybody; and that the image of Here in Samos was formed by the chisel of Euclides, Olympichus relates in his *Samiaca*. Do not, then, entertain any doubt, that of the gods called at Athens venerable, Scopas made two of the stone called Lychnis, and Calos the one which they are reported to have had placed between them, as Polemon shows in the fourth of his books addressed to

---

[1] If we read χαριέστερον, this is the only sense that can be put on the words. But if we read χαριστήριον, we may translate "a memorial of gratified lust."

[2] *Odyss.*, xx. 351.

Timæus. Nor need you doubt respecting the images of Zeus and Apollo at Patara, in Lycia, which Phidias executed, as well as the lions that recline with them ; and if, as some say, they were the work of Bryxis, I do not dispute, — you have in him another maker of images. Whichever of these you like, write down. Furthermore, the statues nine cubits in height of Poseidon and Amphitrite, worshipped in Tenos, are the work of Telesius the Athenian, as we are told by Philochorus. Demetrius, in the second book of his *Argolics*, writes of the image of Here in Tiryns, both that the material was pear-tree and the artist was Argus.

Many, perhaps, may be surprised to learn that the Palladium which is called the Diopetes — that is, fallen from heaven — which Diomede and Ulysses are related to have carried off from Troy and deposited at Demophoon, was made of the bones of Pelops, as the Olympian Jove of other bones — those of the Indian wild beast. I adduce as my authority Dionysius, who relates this in the fifth part of his *Cycle*. And Apellas, in the *Delphics*, says that there were two Palladia, and that both were fashioned by men. But that no one may suppose that I have passed over them through ignorance, I shall add that the image of Dionysus Morychus at Athens was made of the stones called Phellata, and was the work of Simon the son of Eupalamus, as Polemo says in a letter. There were also two other sculptors of Crete, as I think : they were called Scyles and Dipoenus ; and these executed the statues of the Dioscuri in Argos, and the image of Hercules in Tiryns, and the effigy of the Munychian Artemis in Sicyon. Why should I linger over these, when I can point out to you the great deity himself, and show you who he was, — whom indeed, conspicuously above all, we hear to have been considered worthy of veneration? Him they have dared to speak of as made without hands — I mean the Egyptian Serapis. For some relate that he was sent as a present by the people of Sinope to Ptolemy Philadelphus, king of the Egyptians, who won their favour by sending them corn from Egypt when they were perishing with famine ; and that this idol was an image of Pluto ; and Ptolemy, having received the statue, placed it on the promontory which is now called Racotis ; where the temple of Serapis was held in honour, and the sacred enclosure borders on the spot ; and that Blistichis the courtesan having died in Canopus, Ptolemy had her conveyed there, and buried beneath the fore-mentioned shrine.

Others say that the Serapis was a Pontic idol, and was transported with solemn pomp to Alexandria. Isidore alone says that it was brought from the Seleucians, near Antioch, who also had been visited with a dearth of corn, and had been fed by Ptolemy. But Athenodorus the son of Sandon, while wishing to make out the Serapis to be ancient, has somehow slipped into the mistake of proving it to be an image fashioned by human hands. He says that Sesostris the Egyptian king, having subjugated the most of the Hellenic races, on his return to Egypt brought a number of craftsmen with him. Accordingly he ordered a statue of Osiris, his ancestor, to be executed in sumptuous style ; and the work was done by the artist Bryaxis, not the Athenian, but another of the same name, who employed in its execution a mixture of various materials. For he had filings of gold, and silver, and lead, and in addition, tin ; and of Egyptian stones not one was wanting, and there were fragments of sapphire, and hematite, and emerald, and topaz. Having ground down and mixed together all these ingredients, he gave to the composition a blue colour, whence the darkish hue of the image ; and having mixed the whole with the colouring matter that was left over from the funeral of Osiris and Apis, moulded the Serapis, the name of which points to its connection with sepulture and its construction from funeral materials, compounded as it is of Osiris and Apis, which together make Osirapis.

Another new deity was added to the number with great religious pomp in Egypt, and was near being so in Greece by the king of the Romans, who deified Antinous, whom he loved as Zeus loved Ganymede, and whose beauty was of a very rare order : for lust is not easily restrained, destitute as it is of fear ; and men now observe the sacred nights of Antinous, the shameful character of which the lover who spent them with him knew well. Why reckon him among the gods, who is honoured on account of uncleanness? And why do you command him to be lamented as a son? And why should you enlarge on his beauty? Beauty blighted by vice is loathsome. Do not play the tyrant, O man, over beauty, nor offer foul insult to youth in its bloom. Keep beauty pure, that it may be truly fair. Be king over beauty, not its tyrant. Remain free, and then I shall acknowledge thy beauty, because thou hast kept its image pure : then will I worship that true beauty which is the archetype of all who are beautiful. Now the grave of the debauched boy is the temple and town of Antinous. For just as temples are held in reverence, so also are sepulchres, and pyramids, and mausoleums, and labyrinths, which are temples of the dead, as the others are sepulchres of the gods. As teacher on this point, I shall produce to you the Sibyl prophetess : —

" Not the oracular lie of Phœbus,
  Whom silly men called God, and falsely termed
    Prophet ;
But the oracles of the great God, who was not made
    by men's hands,
Like dumb idols of sculptured stone." [1]

---

[1] Vulg., *Sibyllini*, p. 253.

She also predicts the ruin of the temple, fore-telling that that of the Ephesian Artemis would be engulphed by earthquakes and rents in the ground, as follows : —

"Prostrate on the ground Ephesus shall wail, weeping
    by the shore,
And seeking a temple that has no longer an inhabit-
    ant."

She says also that the temple of Isis and Serapis would be demolished and burned : —

"Isis, thrice-wretched goddess, thou shalt linger by the
  · streams of the Nile ;
Solitary, frenzied, silent, on the sands of Acheron."

Then she proceeds : —

"And thou, Serapis, covered with a heap of white
    stones,
Shalt lie a huge ruin in thrice-wretched Egypt."

But if you attend not to the prophetess, hear at least your own philosopher, the Ephesian Hera-clitus, upbraiding images with their senselessness : "And to these images they pray, with the same result as if one were to talk to the walls of his house." For are they not to be wondered at who worship stones, and place them before the doors, as if capable of activity? They worship Hermes as a god, and place Aguieus as a door-keeper. For if people upbraid them with being devoid of sensation, why worship them as gods? And if they are thought to be endowed with sensation, why place them before the door? The Romans, who ascribed their greatest successes to Fortune, and regarded her as a very great deity, took her statue to the privy, and erected it there, assigning to the goddess as a fitting temple — the necessary. But senseless wood and stone, and rich gold, care not a whit for either savoury odour, or blood, or smoke, by which, being at once honoured and fumigated, they are blackened ; no more do they for honour or insult. And these images are more worthless than any animal. I am at a loss to conceive how objects devoid of sense were deified, and feel compelled to pity as miserable wretches those that wander in the mazes of this folly : for if some living creatures have not all the senses, as worms and caterpillars, and such as even from the first appear imperfect, as moles and the shrew-mouse, which Nicander says is blind and uncouth ; yet are they superior to those utterly senseless idols and images. For they have some one sense, — say, for example, hearing, or touch-ing, or something analogous to smell or taste ; while images do not possess even one sense. There are many creatures that have neither sight, nor hearing, nor speech, such as the genus of oysters, which yet live and grow, and are affected by the changes of the moon. But images, being motionless, inert, and senseless, are bound, nailed, glued, — are melted, filed, sawed, polished, carved. The senseless earth is dishonoured by

the makers of images, who change it by their art from its proper nature, and induce men to worship it ; and the makers of gods worship not gods and demons, but in my view earth and art, which go to make up images. For, in sooth, the image is only dead matter shaped by the craftsman's hand. But *we* have no sensible image of sensible matter, but an image that is perceived by the mind alone, — God, who alone is truly God.[1]

And again, when involved in calamities, the superstitious worshippers of stones, though they have learned by the event that senseless matter is not to be worshipped, yet, yielding to the pressure of misfortune, become the victims of their superstition ; and though despising the images, yet not wishing to appear wholly to neglect them, are found fault with by those gods by whose names the images are called.

For Dionysius the tyrant, the younger, having stripped off the golden mantle from the statue of Jupiter in Sicily, ordered him to be clothed in a woollen one, remarking facetiously that the latter was better than the golden one, being lighter in summer and warmer in winter. And Antiochus of Cyzicus, being in difficulties for money, ordered the golden statue of Zeus, fifteen cubits in height, to be melted ; and one like it, of less valuable material, plated with gold, to be erected in place of it. And the swallows and most birds fly to these statues, and void their excrement on them, paying no respect either to Olympian Zeus, or Epidaurian Asclepius, or even to Athene Polias, or the Egyptian Serapis ; but not even from them have you learned the sense-lessness of images.[1] But it has happened that miscreants or enemies have assailed and set fire to temples, and plundered them of their votive gifts, and melted even the images themselves, from base greed of gain. And if a Cambyses or a Darius, or any other madman, has made such attempts, and if one has killed the Egyp-tian Apis, I laugh at him killing their god, while pained at the outrage being perpetrated for the sake of gain. I will therefore willingly forget such villany, looking on acts like these more as deeds of covetousness, than as a proof of the impotence of idols. But fire and earthquakes are shrewd enough not to feel shy or frightened at either demons or idols, any more than at peb-bles heaped by the waves on the shore.

I know fire to be capable of exposing and curing superstition. If thou art willing to aban-don this folly, the element of fire shall light thy way. This same fire burned the temple in Argos, with Chrysis the priestess ; and that of Artemis in Ephesus the second time after the Amazons.

---

[1] [The Trent Creed makes the saints and *their images* objects of worship. It is evident that Clement never imagined the existence of an image among Christians. See p. 188, *infra*.]

And the Capitol in Rome was often wrapped in flames; nor did the fire spare the temple of Serapis, in the city of the Alexandrians. At Athens it demolished the temple of the Eleutherian Dionysus; and as to the temple of Apollo at Delphi, first a storm assailed it, and then the discerning fire utterly destroyed it. This is told as the preface of what the fire promises. And the makers of images, do they not shame those of you who are wise into despising matter? The Athenian Phidias inscribed on the finger of the Olympian Jove, Pantarkes [1] is beautiful. It was not Zeus that was beautiful in his eyes, but the man he loved. And Praxiteles, as Posidippus relates in his book about Cnidus, when he fashioned the statue of Aphrodite of Cnidus, made it like the form of Cratine, of whom he was enamoured, that the miserable people might have the paramour of Praxiteles to worship. And when Phryne the courtesan, the Thespian, was, in her bloom, all the painters made their pictures of Aphrodite copies of the beauty of Phryne; as, again, the sculptors at Athens made their Mercuries like Alcibiades. It remains for you to judge whether you ought to worship courtesans. Moved, as I believe, by such facts, and despising such fables, the ancient kings unblushingly proclaimed themselves gods, as this involved no danger from men, and thus taught that on account of their glory they were made immortal. Ceux, the son of Éolus, was styled Zeus by his wife Alcyone; Alcyone, again, being by her husband styled Hera. Ptolemy the Fourth was called Dionysus; and Mithridates of Pontus was also called Dionysus; and Alexander wished to be considered the son of Ammon, and to have his statue made horned by the sculptors — eager to disgrace the beauty of the human form by the addition of a horn. And not kings only, but private persons dignified themselves with the names of deities, as Menecrates the physician, who took the name of Zeus. What need is there for me to instance Alexarchus? He, having been by profession a grammarian, assumed the character of the sun-god, as Aristus of Salamis relates. And why mention Nicagorus? He was a native of Zela [in Pontus], and lived in the days of Alexander. Nicagorus was styled Hermes, and used the dress of Hermes, as he himself testifies. And whilst whole nations, and cities with all their inhabitants, sinking into self-flattery, treat the myths about the gods with contempt, at the same time men themselves, assuming the air of equality with the gods, and being puffed up with vainglory, vote themselves extravagant honours. There is the case of the Macedonian Philip of Pella, the son of Amyntor,

to whom they decreed divine worship in Cynosargus, although his collar-bone was broken, and he had a lame leg, and had one of his eyes knocked out. And again that of Demetrius, who was raised to the rank of the gods; and where he alighted from his horse on his entrance into Athens is the temple of Demetrius the Alighter; and altars were raised to him everywhere, and nuptials with Athene assigned to him by the Athenians. But he disdained the goddess, as he could not marry the statue; and taking the courtesan Lamia, he ascended the Acropolis, and lay with her on the couch of Athene, showing to the old virgin the postures of the young courtesan.

There is no cause for indignation, then, at Hippo, who immortalized his own death. For this Hippo ordered the following elegy to be inscribed on his tomb :—

"This is the sepulchre of Hippo, whom Destiny
    Made, through death, equal to the immortal gods."

Well done, Hippo! thou showest to us the delusion of men. If they did not believe thee speaking, now that thou art dead, let them become thy disciples. This is the oracle of Hippo; let us consider it. The objects of your worship were once men, and in process of time died; and fable and time have raised them to honour. For somehow, what is present is wont to be despised through familiarity; but what is past, being separated through the obscurity of time from the temporary censure that attached to it, is invested with honour by fiction, so that the present is viewed with distrust, the past with admiration. Exactly in this way is it, then, that the dead men of antiquity, being reverenced through the long prevalence of delusion respecting them, are regarded as gods by posterity. As grounds of your belief in these, there are your mysteries, your solemn assemblies, bonds and wounds, and weeping deities.

"Woe, woe! that fate decrees my best-belov'd,
    Sarpedon, by Patroclus' hand to fall." [2]

The will of Zeus was overruled; and Zeus being worsted, laments for Sarpedon. With reason, therefore, have you yourselves called them shades and demons, since Homer, paying Athene and the other divinities sinister honour, has styled them demons : —

"She her heavenward course pursued
To join the immortals in the abode of Jove." [3]

How, then, can shades and demons be still reckoned gods, being in reality unclean and impure spirits, acknowledged by all to be of an earthly and watery nature, sinking downwards by their own weight, and flitting about graves and tombs, about which they appear dimly, being but

---

[1] Pantarkes is said to have been the name of a boy loved by Phidias; but as the word signifies " all-assisting," " all-powerful," it might also be made to apply to Zeus.

[2] Iliad, xvi. 433.
[3] Iliad, i. 221; μετὰ δαίμονας ἄλλους.

shadowy phantasms? Such things are your gods—shades and shadows; and to these add those maimed, wrinkled, squinting divinities the Litæ, daughters of Thersites rather than of Zeus. So that Bion—wittily, as I think—says, How in reason could men pray Zeus for a beautiful progeny,—a thing he could not obtain for himself?

The incorruptible being, as far as in you lies, you sink in the earth; and that pure and holy essence you have buried in the grave, robbing the divine of its true nature.

Why, I pray you, have you assigned the prerogatives of God to what are no gods? Why, let me ask, have you forsaken heaven to pay divine honour to earth? What else is gold, or silver, or steel, or iron, or brass, or ivory, or precious stones? Are they not earth, and of the earth?

Are not all these things which you look on the progeny of one mother—the earth?

Why, then, foolish and silly men (for I will repeat it), have you, defaming the super-celestial region, dragged religion to the ground, by fashioning to yourselves gods of earth, and by going after those created objects, instead of the uncreated Deity, have sunk into deepest darkness?

The Parian stone is beautiful, but it is not yet Poseidon. The ivory is beautiful, but it is not yet the Olympian Zeus. Matter always needs art to fashion it, but the deity needs nothing. Art has come forward to do its work, and the matter is clothed with its shape; and while the preciousness of the material makes it capable of being turned to profitable account, it is only on account of its form that it comes to be deemed worthy of veneration. Thy image, if considered as to its origin, is gold, it is wood, it is stone, it is earth, which has received shape from the artist's hand. But I have been in the habit of walking on the earth, not of worshipping it. For I hold it wrong to entrust my spirit's hopes to things destitute of the breath of life. We must therefore approach as close as possible to the images. How peculiarly inherent deceit is in them, is manifest from their very look. For the forms of the images are plainly stamped with the characteristic nature of demons. If one go round and inspect the pictures and images, he will at a glance recognise your gods from their shameful forms: Dionysus from his robe; Hephæstus from his art; Demeter from her calamity; Ino from her head-dress; Poseidon from his trident; Zeus from the swan; the pyre indicates Heracles; and if one sees a statue of a naked woman without an inscription, he understands it to be the golden Aphrodite. Thus that Cyprian Pygmalion became enamoured of an image of ivory: the image was Aphrodite, and it was nude. The Cyprian is made a conquest of by the mere shape, and embraces the image.

This is related by Philostephanus. A different Aphrodite in Cnidus was of stone, and beautiful. Another person became enamoured of it, and shamefully embraced the stone. Posidippus relates this. The former of these authors, in his book on Cyprus, and the latter in his book on Cnidus. So powerful is art to delude, by seducing amorous men into the pit. Art is powerful, but it cannot deceive reason, nor those who live agreeably to reason. The doves on the picture were represented so to the life by the painter's art, that the pigeons flew to them; and horses have neighed to well-executed pictures of mares. They say that a girl became enamoured of an image, and a comely youth of the statue at Cnidus. But it was the eyes of the spectators that were deceived by art; for no one in his senses ever would have embraced a goddess, or entombed himself with a lifeless paramour, or become enamoured of a demon and a stone. But it is with a different kind of spell that art deludes you, if it leads you not to the indulgence of amorous affections: it leads you to pay religious honour and worship to images and pictures.

The picture is like. Well and good! Let art receive its meed of praise, but let it not deceive man by passing itself off for truth. The horse stands quiet; the dove flutters not, its wing is motionless. But the cow of Dædalus, made of wood, allured the savage bull; and art having deceived him, compelled him to meet a woman full of licentious passion. Such frenzy have mischief-working arts created in the minds of the insensate. On the other hand, apes are admired by those who feed and care for them, because nothing in the shape of images and girls' ornaments of wax or clay deceives them. You then will show yourselves inferior to apes by cleaving to stone, and wood, and gold, and ivory images, and to pictures. Your makers of such mischievous toys—the sculptors and makers of images, the painters and workers in metal, and the poets—have introduced a motley crowd of divinities: in the fields, Satyrs and Pans; in the woods, Nymphs, and Oreads, and Hamadryads; and besides, in the waters, the rivers, and fountains, the Naiads; and in the sea the Nereids. And now the Magi boast that the demons are the ministers of their impiety, reckoning them among the number of their domestics, and by their charms compelling them to be their slaves. Besides, the nuptials of the deities, their begetting and bringing forth of children that are recounted, their adulteries celebrated in song, their carousals represented in comedy, and bursts of laughter over their cups, which your authors introduce, urge me to cry out, though I would fain be silent. Oh the godlessness! You have turned heaven into a stage;

the Divine has become a drama; and what is sacred you have acted in comedies under the masks of demons, travestying true religion by your demon-worship [superstition].

"But he, striking the lyre, began to sing beautifully." [1]

Sing to us, Homer, that beautiful song

"About the amours of Ares and Venus with the beautiful crown:
   How first they slept together in the palace of Hephæstus
   Secretly; and he gave many gifts, and dishonoured the bed and chamber of king Hephæstus."

Stop, O Homer, the song! It is not beautiful; it teaches adultery, and we are prohibited from polluting our ears with hearing about adultery: for we are they who bear about with us, in this living and moving image of our human nature, the likeness of God, — a likeness which dwells with us, takes counsel with us, associates with us, is a guest with us, feels with us, feels for us. We have become a consecrated offering to God for Christ's sake: we are the chosen generation, the royal priesthood, the holy nation, the peculiar people, who once were not a people, but are now the people of God; who, according to John, are not of those who are beneath, but have learned all from Him who came from above; who have come to understand the dispensation of God; who have learned to walk in newness of life. But these are not the sentiments of the many; but, casting off shame and fear, they depict in their houses the unnatural passions of the demons. Accordingly, wedded to impurity, they adorn their bed-chambers with painted tablets [2] hung up in them, regarding licentiousness as religion; and lying in bed, in the midst of their embraces, they look on that Aphrodite locked in the embrace of her paramour. And in the hoops of their rings they cut a representation of the amorous bird that fluttered round Leda, — having a strong predilection for representations of effeminacy, — and use a seal stamped with an impression of the licentiousness of Zeus. Such are examples of your voluptuousness, such are the theologies of vice, such are the instructions of your gods, who commit fornication along with you; for what one wishes, that he thinks, according to the Athenian orator. And of what kind, on the other hand, are your other images? Diminutive Pans, and naked girls, and drunken Satyrs, and phallic tokens, painted naked in pictures disgraceful for filthiness. And more than this: you are not ashamed in the eyes of all to look at representations of all forms of licentiousness which are portrayed in public places, but set them up and guard them with scrupulous care, consecrating these pillars of shamelessness

at home, as if, forsooth, they were the images of your gods, depicting on them equally the postures of Philænis and the labours of Heracles. Not only the use of these, but the sight of them, and the very hearing of them, we denounce as deserving the doom of oblivion. Your ears are debauched, your eyes commit fornication, your looks commit adultery before you embrace. O ye that have done violence to man, and have devoted to shame what is divine in this handiwork of God, you disbelieve everything that you may indulge your passions, and that ye may believe in idols, because you have a craving after their licentiousness, but disbelieve God, because you cannot bear a life of self-restraint. You have hated what was better, and valued what was worse, having been spectators indeed of virtue, but actors of vice. Happy, therefore, so to say, alone are all those with one accord, —

"Who shall refuse to look on any temples
   And altars, worthless seats of dumb stones,
   And idols of stone, and images made by hands,
   Stained with the life's-blood, and with sacrifices
   Of quadrupeds, and bipeds, and fowls, and butcheries of wild beasts." [3]

For we are expressly prohibited from exercising a deceptive art: "For thou shalt not make," says the prophet, "the likeness of anything which is in heaven above or in the earth beneath." [4]

For can we possibly any longer suppose the Demeter, and the Core, and the mystic Iacchus of Praxiteles, to be gods, and not rather regard the art of Leucippus, or the hands of Apelles, which clothed the material with the form of the divine glory, as having a better title to the honour? But while you bestow the greatest pains that the image may be fashioned with the most exquisite beauty possible, you exercise no care to guard against your becoming like images for stupidity. Accordingly, with the utmost clearness and brevity, the prophetic word condemns this practice: "For all the gods of the nations are the images of demons; but God made the heavens, and what is in heaven." [5] Some, however, who have fallen into error, I know not how, worship God's work instead of God Himself, — the sun and the moon, and the rest of the starry choir, — absurdly imagining these, which are but instruments for measuring time, to be gods; "for by His word they were established, and all their host by the breath of His mouth." [6]

Human art, moreover, produces houses, and ships, and cities, and pictures. But how shall I tell what God makes? Behold the whole universe; it is His work: and the heaven, and

---

[1] Odyss., viii. 266.
[2] [Is not this a rebuke to many of the figures and pictures which vulgarize abodes of wealth in America?]

[3] Sibyl. Justin Martyr, Cohort. ad Græcos, p. 81. See p. 280, vol. i of this series.
[4] Ex. xx. 4. [Clement even regards the art of painters and sculptors as unlawful for Christians.]
[5] Ps. xcvi. 5.
[6] Ps. xxxiii. 6.

the sun, and angels, and men, are the works of His fingers.¹ How great is the power of God! His bare volition was the creation of the universe. For God alone made it, because He alone is truly God. By the bare exercise of volition He creates; His mere willing was followed by the springing into being of what He willed. Consequently the choir of philosophers are in error, who indeed most nobly confess that man was made for the contemplation of the heavens, but who worship the objects that appear in the heavens and are apprehended by sight. For if the heavenly bodies are not the works of men, they were certainly created for man. Let none of you worship the sun, but set his desires on the Maker of the sun; nor deify the universe, but seek after the Creator of the universe. The only refuge, then, which remains for him who would reach the portals of salvation is divine wisdom. From this, as from a sacred asylum, the man who presses after salvation, can be dragged by no demon.

CHAP. V. — THE OPINIONS OF THE PHILOSOPHERS RESPECTING GOD.

Let us then run over, if you choose, the opinions of the philosophers, to which they give boastful utterance, respecting the gods; that we may discover philosophy itself, through its conceit making an idol of matter; although we are able to show, as we proceed, that even while deifying certain demons, it has a dream of the truth. The elements were designated as the first principles of all things by some of them: by Thales of Miletus, who celebrated water, and Anaximenes, also of Miletus, who celebrated air as the first principle of all things, and was followed afterwards by Diogenes of Apollonia. Parmenides of Elia introduced fire and earth as gods; one of which, namely fire, Hippasus of Metapontum and Heraclitus of Ephesus supposed a divinity. Empedocles of Agrigentum fell in with a multitude, and, in addition to those four elements, enumerates disagreement and agreement. Atheists surely these are to be reckoned, who through an unwise wisdom worshipped matter, who did not indeed pay religious honour to stocks and stones, but deified earth, the mother of these, — who did not make an image of Poseidon, but revered water itself. For what else, according to the original signification, is Poseidon, but a moist substance? the name being derived from *posis* (drink); as, beyond doubt, the warlike Ares is so called, from *arsis* (rising up) and *anæresis* (destroying). For this reason mainly, I think, many fix a sword into the ground, and sacrifice to it as to Ares. The Scythians have a practice of this

nature, as Eudoxus tells us in the second book of his *Travels*. The Sauromatæ, too, a tribe of the Scythians, worship a sabre, as Ikesius says in his work on *Mysteries*.

This was also the case with Heraclitus and his followers, who worshipped fire as the first cause; for this fire others named Hephæstus. The Persian Magi, too, and many of the inhabitants of Asia, worshipped fire; and besides them, the Macedonians, as Diogenes relates in the first book of his *Persica*. Why specify the Sauromatæ, who are said by Nymphodorus, in his *Barbaric Customs*, to pay sacred honours to fire? or the Persians, or the Medes, or the Magi? These, Dino tells us, sacrifice beneath the open sky, regarding fire and water as the only images of the gods.

Nor have I failed to reveal their ignorance; for, however much they think to keep clear of error in one form, they slide into it in another.

They have not supposed stocks and stones to be images of the gods, like the Greeks; nor ibises and ichneumons, like the Egyptians; but fire and water, as philosophers. Berosus, in the third book of his *Chaldaics*, shows that it was after many successive periods of years that men worshipped images of human shape, this practice being introduced by Artaxerxes, the son of Darius, and father of Ochus, who first set up the image of Aphrodite Anaitis at Babylon and Susa; and Ecbatana set the example of worshipping it to the Persians; the Bactrians, to Damascus and Sardis.

Let the philosophers, then, own as their teachers the Persians, or the Sauromatæ, or the Magi, from whom they have learned the impious doctrine of regarding as divine certain first principles, being ignorant of the great First Cause, the Maker of all things, and Creator of those very first principles, the unbeginning God, but reverencing "these weak and beggarly elements,"² as the apostle says, which were made for the service of man. And of the rest of the philosophers who, passing over the elements, have eagerly sought after something higher and nobler, some have discanted on the Infinite, of whom were Anaximander of Miletus, Anaxagoras of Clazomenæ, and the Athenian Archelaus, both of whom set Mind ($\nu o \hat{\upsilon} \varsigma$) above Infinity; while the Milesian Leucippus and the Chian Metrodorus apparently inculcated two first principles — fulness and vacuity. Democritus of Abdera, while accepting these two, added to them images ($\epsilon \check{\iota} \delta \omega \lambda a$); while Alcmæon of Crotona supposed the stars to be gods, and endowed with life (I will not keep silence as to their effrontery). Xenocrates of Chalcedon indicates that the planets are seven gods, and that the universe, composed of all these, is an eighth. Nor will I pass over those of the Porch, who say that the Divinity pervades all matter, even the vilest, and thus clumsily disgrace philosophy. Nor do I think will it be taken ill, having reached this point, to advert to the Peripatetics. The father of this sect, not knowing the Father of all things, thinks that He who is called the Highest is the soul of the universe ; that is, he supposes the soul of the world to be God, and so is pierced by his own sword. For by first limiting the sphere of Providence to the orbit of the moon, and then by supposing the universe to be God, he confutes himself, inasmuch as he teaches that that which is without God is God. And that Eresian Theophrastus, the pupil of Aristotle, conjectures at one time heaven, and at another spirit, to be God. Epicurus alone I shall gladly forget, who carries impiety to its full length, and thinks that God takes no charge of the world. What, moreover, of Heraclides of Pontus ? He is dragged everywhere to the images — the εἴδωλα — of Democritus.

CHAP. VI. — BY DIVINE INSPIRATION PHILOSOPHERS SOMETIMES HIT ON THE TRUTH.

A great crowd of this description rushes on my mind, introducing, as it were, a terrifying apparition of strange demons, speaking of fabulous and monstrous shapes, in old wives' talk. Far from enjoining men to listen to such tales are we, who avoid the practice of soothing our crying children, as the saying is, by telling them fabulous stories, being afraid of fostering in their minds the impiety professed by those who, though wise in their own conceit, have no more knowledge of the truth than infants. For why (in the name of truth !) do you make those who believe you subject to ruin and corruption, dire and irretrievable ? Why, I beseech you, fill up life with idolatrous images, by feigning the winds, or the air, or fire, or earth, or stones, or stocks, or steel, or this universe, to be gods ; and, prating loftily of the heavenly bodies in this much vaunted science of astrology, not astronomy, to those men who have truly wandered, talk of the wandering stars as gods ? It is the Lord of the spirits, the Lord of the fire, the Maker of the universe, Him who lighted up the sun, that I long for. I seek after God, not the works of God. Whom shall I take as a helper in my inquiry ? We do not, if you have no objection, wholly disown Plato. How, then, is God to be searched out, O Plato ? "For both to find the Father and Maker of this universe is a work of difficulty ; and having found Him, to declare Him fully, is impossible." [1]

Why so? by Himself, I beseech you ! For He can by no means be expressed. Well done, Plato ! Thou hast touched on the truth. But do not flag. Undertake with me the inquiry respecting the Good. For into all men whatever, especially those who are occupied with intellectual pursuits, a certain divine effluence has been instilled ; wherefore, though reluctantly, they confess that God is one, indestructible, unbegotten, and that somewhere above in the tracts of heaven, in His own peculiar appropriate eminence, whence He surveys all things, He has an existence true and eternal.

"Tell me what I am to conceive God to be,
    Who sees all things, and is Himself unseen,"

Euripides says. Accordingly, Menander seems to me to have fallen into error when he said : —

"O sun ! for thou, first of gods, ought to be worshipped,
    By whom it is that we are able to see the other gods."

For the sun never could show me the true God ; but that healthful Word, that is the Sun of the soul, by whom alone, when He arises in the depths of the soul, the eye of the soul itself is irradiated. Whence accordingly, Democritus, not without reason, says, "that a few of the men of intellect, raising their hands upwards to what we Greeks now call the air (ἀήρ), called the whole expanse Zeus, or God : He, too, knows all things, gives and takes away, and He is King of all."

Of the same sentiments is Plato, who somewhere alludes to God thus : "Around the King of all are all things, and He is the cause of all good things." Who, then, is the King of all ? God, who is the measure of the truth of all existence. As, then, the things that are to be measured are contained in the measure, so also the knowledge of God measures and comprehends truth. And the truly holy Moses says : "There shall not be in thy bag a balance and a balance, great or small, but a true and just balance shall be to thee," [2] deeming the balance and measure and number of the whole to be God. For the unjust and unrighteous idols are hid at home in the bag, and, so to speak, in the polluted soul. But the only just measure is the only true God, always just, continuing the selfsame ; who measures all things, and weighs them by righteousness as in a balance, grasping and sustaining universal nature in equilibrium. "God, therefore, as the old saying has it, occupying the beginning, the middle, and the end of all that is in being, keeps the straight course, while He makes the circuit of nature ; and justice always follows Him, avenging those who violate the divine law."

Whence, O Plato, is that hint of the truth which thou givest ? Whence this rich copious-

---

[1] Timæus.

[2] Deut. xxv. 13, 15.

ness of diction, which proclaims piety with oracular utterance? The tribes of the barbarians, he says, are wiser than these; I know thy teachers, even if thou wouldst conceal them. You have learned geometry from the Egyptians, astronomy from the Babylonians; the charms of healing you have got from the Thracians; the Assyrians also have taught you many things; but for the laws that are consistent with truth, and your sentiments respecting God, you are indebted to the Hebrews,[1]

" Who do not worship through vain deceits
The works of men, of gold, and brass, and silver, and ivory,
And images of dead men, of wood and stone,
Which other men, led by their foolish inclinations, worship;
But raise to heaven pure arms:
When they rise from bed, purifying themselves with water,
And worship alone the Eternal, who reigns for ever more."

And let it not be this one man alone — Plato; but, O philosophy, hasten to produce many others also, who declare the only true God to be God, through His inspiration, if in any measure they have grasped the truth. For Antisthenes did not think out this doctrine of the Cynics; but it is in virtue of his being a disciple of Socrates that he says, "that God is not like to any; wherefore no one can know Him from an image." And Xenophon the Athenian would have in his own person committed freely to writing somewhat of the truth, and given the same testimony as Socrates, had he not been afraid of the cup of poison, which Socrates had to drink. But he hints nothing less; he says: "How great and powerful He is who moves all things, and is Himself at rest, is manifest; but what He is in form is not revealed. The sun himself, intended to be the source of light to all around, does not deem it fitting to allow himself to be looked at; but if any one audaciously gazes on him, he is deprived of sight." Whence, then, does the son of Gryllus learn his wisdom? Is it not manifestly from the prophetess of the Hebrews,[2] who prophesies in the following style? —

" What flesh can see with the eye the celestial,
The true, the immortal God, who inhabits the vault of heaven?
Nay, men born mortal cannot even stand
Before the rays of the sun."

Cleanthes Pisadeus,[3] the Stoic philosopher, who exhibits not a poetic theogony, but a true theology, has not concealed what sentiments he entertained respecting God: —

" If you ask me what is the nature of the good, listen:
That which is regular, just, holy, pious.

Self-governing, useful, fair, fitting,
Grave, independent, always beneficial;
That feels no fear or grief; profitable, painless,
Helpful, pleasant, safe, friendly;
Held in esteem, agreeing with itself, honourable;
Humble, careful, meek, zealous,
Perennial, blameless, ever-during:
Mean is every one who looks to opinion
With the view of obtaining some advantage from it."

Here, as I think, he clearly teaches of what nature God is; and that the common opinion and religious customs enslave those that follow them, but seek not after God.

We must not either keep the Pythagoreans in the back-ground, who say: "God is one; and He is not, as some suppose, outside of this frame of things, but within it; but, in all the entireness of His being, is in the whole circle of existence, surveying all nature, and blending in harmonious union the whole, — the author of all His own forces and works, the giver of light in heaven, and Father of all, — the mind and vital power of the whole world, — the mover of all things." For the knowledge of God, these utterances, written by those we have mentioned through the inspiration of God, and selected by us, may suffice even for the man that has but small power to examine into truth.

CHAP. VII. — THE POETS ALSO BEAR TESTIMONY TO THE TRUTH.

Let poetry also approach to us (for philosophy alone will not suffice): poetry which is wholly occupied with falsehood — which scarcely will make confession of the truth, but will rather own to God its deviations into fable. Let whoever of those poets chooses advance first. Aratus considers that the power of God pervades all things: —

" That all may be secure,
Him ever they propitiate first and last,
Hail, Father! great marvel, great gain to man."

Thus also the Ascræan Hesiod dimly speaks of God: —

" For He is the King of all, and monarch
Of the immortals; and there is none that may vie with Him in power."

Also on the stage they reveal the truth: —

" Look on the ether and heaven, and regard that as God,"

says Euripides. And Sophocles, the son of Sophilus, says: —

" One, in truth, one is God,
Who made both heaven and the far-stretching earth,
And ocean's blue wave, and the mighty winds;
But many of us mortals, deceived in heart,
Have set up for ourselves, as a consolation in our afflictions,
Images of the gods of stone, or wood, or brass,
Or gold, or ivory;
And, appointing to those sacrifices and vain festal assemblages,
Are accustomed thus to practise religion."

---

[1] [This great truth comes forcibly from an Attic scholar. Let me refer to a very fine passage in another Christian scholar, William Cowper (Task, book ii.): "All truth is from the sempiternal source," etc.]

[2] The Sibyl.

[3] Or Asseus, native of Asso.

In this venturous manner has he on the stage brought truth before the spectators. But the Thracian Orpheus, the son of Œagrus, hierophant and poet at once, after his exposition of the orgies, and his theology of idols, introduces a palinode of truth with true solemnity, though tardily singing the strain : —

> "I shall utter to whom it is lawful ; but let the doors
>   be closed,
> Nevertheless, against all the profane. But do thou
>   hear,
> O Musæus, offspring of the light-bringing moon,
> For I will declare what is true. And let not these
>   things
> Which once appeared in your breast rob you of dear
>   life ;
> But looking to the divine word, apply yourself to it,
> Keeping right *the seat of intellect and feeling ;* and
>   walk well
> In the straight path, and to the immortal King of the
>   universe alone
> Direct your gaze."

Then proceeding, he clearly adds : —

> "He is one, self-proceeding ; and from Him alone all
>   things proceed,
> And in them He Himself exerts his activity : no mor-
>   tal
> Beholds Him, but He beholds all."

Thus far Orpheus at last understood that he had been in error : —

> "But linger no longer, O man, endued with varied wis-
>   dom ;
> But turn and retrace your steps, and propitiate God."

For if, at the most, the Greeks, having received certain scintillations of the divine word, have given forth some utterances of truth, they bear indeed witness that the force of truth is not hidden, and at the same time expose their own weakness in not having arrived at the end. For I think it has now become evident to all, that those who do or speak aught without the word of truth are like people compelled to walk without feet. Let the strictures on your gods, which the poets, impelled by the force of truth, introduce in their comedies, shame you into salvation. Menander, for instance, the comic poet, in his drama of the *Charioteer*, says : —

> "No God pleases me that goes about
>   With an old woman, and enters houses
>   Carrying a trencher."

For such are the begging priests of Cybele. Hence Antisthenes replies appropriately to their request for alms : —

> "I do not maintain the mother of the gods,
>   For the gods maintain her."

Again, the same writer of comedy, expressing his dissatisfaction with the common usages, tries to expose the impious arrogance of the prevailing error in the drama of the *Priestess*, sagely declaring : —

> "If a man drags the Deity
> Whither he will by the sound of cymbals,
> He that does this is greater than the Deity ;
> But these are the instruments of audacity and means
>   of living
> Invented by men."

And not only Menander, but Homer also, and Euripides, and other poets in great numbers, expose your gods, and are wont to rate them, and that soundly too. For instance, they call Aphrodite dog-fly, and Hephæstus a cripple. Helen says to Aphrodite : —

> "Thy godship abdicate !
>   Renounce Olympus ! " [1]

And of Dionysus, Homer writes without reserve : —

> "He, mid their frantic orgies, in the groves
>   Of lovely Nyssa, put to shameful rout
>   The youthful Bacchus' nurses ; they in fear,
>   Dropped each her thyrsus, scattered by the hand
>   Of fierce Lycurgus, with an ox-goad armed." [2]

Worthy truly of the Socratic school is Euripides, who fixes his eye on truth, and despises the spectators of his plays. On one occasion, Apollo,

> "Who inhabits the sanctuary that is in the middle of
>   the earth,
> Dispensing most certain oracles to mortals, "

is thus exposed : —

> "It was in obedience to him that I killed her who
>   brought me forth ;
> Him do you regard as stained with guilt — put him
>   to death ;
> It was he that sinned, not I, uninstructed as I was
> In right and justice." [3]

He introduces Heracles, at one time mad, at another drunk and gluttonous. How should he not so represent the god who, when entertained as a guest, ate green figs to flesh, uttering discordant howls, that even his barbarian host remarked it? In his drama of *Ion*, too, he barefacedly brings the gods on the stage : —

> "How, then, is it right for you, who have given laws
>   to mortals,
> To be yourselves guilty of wrong?
> And if — what will never take place, yet I will state
>   the supposition —
> You will give satisfaction to men for your adulteries,
> You, Poseidon, and you, Zeus, the ruler of heaven,—
> You will, in order to make recompense for your mis-
>   deeds,
> Have to empty your temples." [4]

CHAP. VIII. — THE TRUE DOCTRINE IS TO BE
SOUGHT IN THE PROPHETS.

It is now time, as we have despatched in order the other points, to go to the prophetic Scriptures ; for the oracles present us with the appliances necessary for the attainment of piety,

[1] *Il.*, iii. 406.
[2] *Il.*, vi 132.
[3] *Orestes*, 590.
[4] *Ion*, 442.

and so establish the truth. The divine Scriptures and institutions of wisdom form the short road to salvation. Devoid of embellishment, of outward beauty of diction, of wordiness and seductiveness, they raise up humanity strangled by wickedness, teaching men to despise the casualties of life; and with one and the same voice remedying many evils, they at once dissuade us from pernicious deceit, and clearly exhort us to the attainment of the salvation set before us. Let the Sibyl [1] prophetess, then, be the first to sing to us the song of salvation: —

"So He is all sure and unerring:
Come, follow no longer darkness and gloom;
See, the sun's sweet-glancing light shines gloriously.
Know, and lay up wisdom in your hearts:
There is one God, who sends rains, and winds, and
      earthquakes,
Thunderbolts, famines, plagues, and dismal sorrows,
And snows and ice. But why detail particulars?
He reigns over heaven, He rules earth,
      He truly is;" —

where, in remarkable accordance with inspiration [2] she compares delusion to darkness, and the knowledge of God to the sun and light, and subjecting both to comparison, shows the choice we ought to make. For falsehood is not dissipated by the bare presentation of the truth, but by the practical improvement of the truth it is ejected and put to flight.

Jeremiah the prophet, gifted with consummate wisdom, [3] or rather the Holy Spirit in Jeremiah, exhibits God. "Am I a God at hand," he says, " and not a God afar off? Shall a man do ought in secret, and I not see him? Do I not fill heaven and earth? Saith the LORD. " [4]

And again by Isaiah, "Who shall measure heaven with a span, and the whole earth with his hand? " [5] Behold God's greatness, and be filled with amazement. Let us worship Him of whom the prophet says, " Before Thy face the hills shall melt, as wax melteth before the fire ! " [6] This, says he, is the God "whose throne is heaven, and His footstool the earth ; and if He open heaven, quaking will seize thee." [7] Will you hear, too, what this prophet says of idols? "And they shall be made a spectacle of in the face of the sun, and their carcases shall be meat for the fowls of heaven and the wild beasts of the earth ; and they shall putrefy before the sun and

the moon, which they have loved and served ; and their city shall be burned down." [8] He says, too, that the elements and the world shall be destroyed. "The earth," he says, " shall grow old, and the heaven shall pass away ; but the word of the Lord endureth for ever." What, then, when again God wishes to show Himself by Moses : " Behold ye, behold ye, that I AM, and there is no other God beside Me. I will kill, and I will make to live ; I will strike, and I will heal ; and there is none who shall deliver out of My hands." [9] But do you wish to hear another seer? You have the whole prophetic choir, the associates of Moses. What the Holy Spirit says by Hosea, I will not shrink from quoting : " Lo, I am He that appointeth the thunder, and createth spirit ; and His hands have established the host of heaven." [10] And once more by Isaiah. And this utterance I will repeat : " I am," he says, " I am the LORD ; I who speak righteousness, announce truth. Gather yourselves together, and come. Take counsel together, ye that are saved from the nations. They have not known, they who set up the block of wood, their carved work, and pray to gods who will not save them." [11] Then proceeding : " I am God, and there is not beside Me a just God, and a Saviour : there is none except Me. Turn to Me, and ye will be saved, ye that are from the end of the earth. I am God, and there is no other ; by Myself I swear." [12] But against the worshippers of idols he is exasperated, saying, " To whom will ye liken the LORD, or to what likeness will ye compare Him? Has not the artificer made the image, or the goldsmith melted the gold and plated it with gold ? " [13] — and so on. Be not therefore idolaters, but even now beware of the threatenings ; " for the graven images and the works of men's hands shall wail, or rather they that trust in them," [14] for matter is devoid of sensation. Once more he says, " The LORD will shake the cities that are inhabited, and grasp the world in His hand like a nest." [15] Why repeat to you the mysteries of wisdom, and sayings from the writings of the son of the Hebrews, the master of wisdom? " The LORD created me the beginning of His ways, in order to His works." [16] And, " The LORD giveth wisdom, and from His face proceed knowledge and understanding." [17] " How long wilt thou lie in bed, O sluggard ; and when wilt thou be aroused from sleep ? " [18] " but if thou show thyself no

---

[1] [Note her remarkable *accord* with inspiration, clearly distinguishing between such and the oracles of God. But see, *supra*, p. 132 and p. 145.]
[2] [Having shown what truth there is to be found in heathen poets, he ascends to the Sibyl, and thus comes to the prophets; showing them how to climb upward in this way, and cleverly inducing them to make the best use of their own prophets and poets, by following them to the sources of their noblest ideas.]
[3] [How sublimely he now introduces the oracles of truth.]
[4] Jer. xxiii. 23.
[5] Isa. xl. 12.
[6] Isa. lxiv. 1, 2.
[7] Isa. lxvi. 1.

[8] Jer. viii. 2, xxx. 20, iv. 6.
[9] Deut. xxxii. 39.
[10] Amos iv. 13.
[11] Isa. xlv. 19, 20.
[12] Isa. xlv. 21-23.
[13] Isa. xl. 18, 19.
[14] Isa. x. 10, 11.
[15] Isa. x. 14.
[16] Prov. viii. 22.
[17] Prov. ii. 6.
[18] Prov. vi. 9.

sluggard, as a fountain thy harvest shall come," [1] the "Word of the Father, the benign light, the Lord that bringeth light, faith to all, and salvation." [2] For " the LORD who created the earth by His power," as Jeremiah says, " has raised up the world by His wisdom ; " [3] for wisdom, which is His word, raises us up to the truth, who have fallen prostrate before idols, and is itself the first resurrection from our fall. Whence Moses, the man of God, dissuading from all idolatry, beautifully exclaims, " Hear, O Israel, the LORD thy God is one LORD ; and thou shalt worship the LORD thy God, and Him only shalt thou serve." [4] " Now therefore be wise, O men," according to that blessed psalmist David ; " lay hold on instruction, lest the Lord be angry, and ye perish from the way of righteousness, when His wrath has quickly kindled. Blessed are all they who put their trust in Him." [5] But already the Lord, in His surpassing pity, has inspired the song of salvation, sounding like a battle march, " Sons of men, how long will ye be slow of heart? Why do you love vanity, and seek after a lie ? " [6] What, then, is the vanity, and what the lie? The holy apostle of the Lord, reprehending the Greeks, will show thee : " Because that, when they knew God, they glorified Him not as God, neither were thankful ; but became vain in their imaginations, and changed the glory of God into the likeness of corruptible man, and worshipped and served the creature more than the Creator." [7] And verily this is the God who " in the beginning made the heaven and the earth." [8] But you do not know God, and worship the heaven, and how shall you escape the guilt of impiety? Hear again the prophet speaking : " The sun shall suffer eclipse, and the heaven be darkened ; but the Almighty shall shine for ever : while the powers of the heavens shall be shaken, and the heavens stretched out and drawn together shall be rolled as a parchment-skin (for these are the prophetic expressions), and the earth shall flee away from before the face of the Lord." [9]

CHAP. IX. — " THAT THOSE GRIEVOUSLY SIN WHO DESPISE OR NEGLECT GOD'S GRACIOUS CALLING."

I could adduce ten thousand Scriptures of which not " one tittle shall pass away " [10] without being fulfilled ; for the mouth of the Lord the Holy Spirit hath spoken these things. " Do not any longer," he says, " my son, despise the chastening of the LORD, nor faint when thou art rebuked of Him." [11] O surpassing love for man ! Not as a teacher speaking to his pupils, not as a master to his domestics, nor as God to men, but as a father, does the Lord gently admonish his children. Thus Moses confesses that " he was filled with quaking and terror " [12] while he listened to God speaking concerning the Word. And art not thou afraid as thou hearest the voice of the Divine Word? Art not thou distressed? Do you not fear, and hasten to learn of Him, — that is, to salvation, — dreading wrath, loving grace, eagerly striving after the hope set before us, that you may shun the judgment threatened? Come, come, O my young people ! For if you become not again as little children, and be born again, as saith the Scripture, you shall not receive the truly existent Father, nor shall you ever enter into the kingdom of heaven. For in what way is a stranger permitted to enter? Well, as I take it, then, when he is enrolled and made a citizen, and receives one to stand to him in the relation of father, then will he be occupied with the Father's concerns, then shall he be deemed worthy to be made His heir, then will he share the kingdom of the Father with His own dear Son. For this is the first-born Church, composed of many good children ; these are " the first-born enrolled in heaven, who hold high festival with so many myriads of angels." We, too, are first-born sons, who are reared by God, who are the genuine friends of the First-born, who first of all other men attained to the knowledge of God, who first were wrenched away from our sins, first severed from the devil. And now the more benevolent God is, the more impious men are ; for He desires us from slaves to become sons, while they scorn to become sons. O the prodigious folly of being ashamed of the Lord ! He offers freedom, you flee into bondage ; He bestows salvation, you sink down into destruction ; He confers everlasting life, you wait for punishment, and prefer the fire which the Lord " has prepared for the devil and his angels." [13] Wherefore the blessed apostle says : " I testify in the Lord, that ye walk no longer as the Gentiles walk, in the vanity of their mind ; having their understanding darkened, being alienated from the life of God through the ignorance that is in them, because of the hardness of their heart : who, being past feeling, have given themselves over to lasciviousness, to work all uncleanness and concupiscence." [14] After the accusation of such a witness, and his invocation of God, what else remains for the unbelieving than judgment and condemnation? And the Lord, with ceaseless assiduity, exhorts, terrifies, urges, rouses,

---

[1] Prov. vi. 11.
[2] Prov. vi. 23.
[3] Jer. x. 12.
[4] Deut. vi. 4, 13, x. 20.
[5] Ps. ii. 10, 12.
[6] Ps. iv. 2.
[7] Rom. i. 21, 23, 25.
[8] Gen. i. 1.
[9] This is made up of several passages, as Isa. xiii. 10, Ezek. xxxii. 7, Joel ii. 10, 31, iii. 15.
[10] Matt. v. 18.

[11] Prov. iii. 11.
[12] Heb. xii. 21.
[13] Matt. xxv. 41, 46.
[14] Eph. iv. 17-19.

admonishes; He awakes from the sleep of darkness, and raises up those who have wandered in error. "Awake," He says, "thou that sleepest, and arise from the dead, and Christ shall give thee light," [1] — Christ, the Sun of the Resurrection, He "who was born before the morning star," [2] and with His beams bestows life. Let no one then despise the Word, lest he unwittingly despise himself. For the Scripture somewhere says, "To-day, if ye will hear His voice, harden not your hearts, as in the provocation, in the day of temptation in the wilderness, when your fathers proved Me by trial." [3] And what was the trial? If you wish to learn, the Holy Spirit will show you: "And saw my works," He says, "forty years. Wherefore I was grieved with that generation, and said, They do always err in heart, and have not known My ways. So I sware in my wrath, they shall not enter into My rest." [4] Look to the threatening! Look to the exhortation! Look to the punishment! Why, then, should we any longer change grace into wrath, and not receive the word with open ears, and entertain God as a guest in pure spirits? For great is the grace of His promise, "if to-day we hear His voice." [5] And that to-day is lengthened out day by day, while it is called to-day. And to the end the to-day and the instruction continue; and then the true to-day, the never-ending day of God, extends over eternity. Let us then ever obey the voice of the divine word. For the to-day signifies eternity. And day is the symbol of light; and the light of men is the Word, by whom we behold God. Rightly, then, to those that have believed and obey, grace will superabound; while with those that have been unbelieving, and err in heart, and have not known the Lord's ways, which John commanded to make straight and to prepare, God is incensed, and those He threatens.

And, indeed, the old Hebrew wanderers in the desert received typically the end of the threatening; for they are said not to have entered into the rest, because of unbelief, till, having followed the successor of Moses, they learned by experience, though late, that they could not be saved otherwise than by believing on Jesus. But the Lord, in His love to man, invites all men to the knowledge of the truth, and for this end sends the Paraclete. What, then, is this knowledge? Godliness; and "godliness," according to Paul, "is profitable for all things, having the promise of the life that now is, and of that which is to come." [6] If eternal salvation were to be sold, for how much, O men, would you propose to purchase it? Were one to estimate the value of the whole of Pactolus, the fabulous river of gold, he would not have reckoned up a price equivalent to salvation.

Do not, however, faint. You may, if you choose, purchase salvation, though of inestimable value, with your own resources, love and living faith, which will be reckoned a suitable price. This recompense God cheerfully accepts; "for we trust in the living God, who is the Saviour of all men, especially of those who believe." [7]

But the rest, round whom the world's growths have fastened, as the rocks on the sea-shore are covered over with sea-weed, make light of immortality, like the old man of Ithaca, eagerly longing to see, not the truth, not the fatherland in heaven, not the true light, but smoke. But godliness, that makes man as far as can be like God, designates God as our suitable teacher, who alone can worthily assimilate man to God. This teaching the apostle knows as truly divine. "Thou, O Timothy," he says, "from a child hast known the holy letters, which are able to make thee wise unto salvation, through faith that is in Christ Jesus." [8] For truly holy are those letters that sanctify and deify; and the writings or volumes that consist of those holy letters and syllables, the same apostle consequently calls "inspired of God, being profitable for doctrine, for reproof, for correction, for instruction in righteousness, that the man of God may be perfect, thoroughly furnished to every good work." [9] No one will be so impressed by the exhortations of any of the saints, as he is by the words of the Lord Himself, the lover of man. For this, and nothing but this, is His only work — the salvation of man. Therefore He Himself, urging them on to salvation, cries, "The kingdom of heaven is at hand." [10] Those men that draw near through fear, He converts. Thus also the apostle of the Lord, beseeching the Macedonians, becomes the interpreter of the divine voice, when he says, "The Lord is at hand; take care that ye be not apprehended empty." [11] But are ye so devoid of fear, or rather of faith, as not to believe the Lord Himself, or Paul, who in Christ's stead thus entreats: "Taste and see that Christ is God?" [12] Faith will lead you in; experience will teach you; Scripture will train you, for it says, "Come hither, O children; listen to me, and I will teach you the fear of the LORD." Then, as to those who already believe, it briefly adds, "What man is he that desireth life, that loveth to see good days?" [13] It is we, we shall

---

[1] Eph. v. 14.
[2] Ps. cx. 3.
[3] Ps. xcv. 8, 9.
[4] Ps. xcv. 9-11.
[5] Ps. xcv. 7.
[6] 1 Tim. iv. 8.

[7] 1 Tim. iv. 10.
[8] 2 Tim. iii. 15.
[9] 2 Tim. iii. 16, 17.   [Here note the testimony of Clement to the universal diffusion and study of the Scriptures.]
[10] Matt. iv. 17.
[11] Phil. iv. 5.
[12] Ps. xxxiv. 8, where Clem. has read Χριστός for χρηστός.
[13] Ps. xxxiv. 11.

say — we who are the devotees of good, we who eagerly desire good things. Hear, then, ye who are far off, hear ye who are near : the word has not been hidden from any ; light is common, it shines " on all men." No one is a Cimmerian in respect to the word. Let us haste to salvation, to regeneration ; let us who are many haste that we may be brought together into one love, according to the union of the essential unity ; and let us, by being made good, conformably follow after union, seeking after the good Monad.

The union of many in one, issuing in the production of divine harmony out of a medley of sounds and division, becomes one symphony following one choir-leader and teacher,[1] the Word, reaching and resting in the same truth, and crying Abba, Father. This, the true utterance of His children, God accepts with gracious welcome — the first-fruits He receives from them.

CHAP. X. — ANSWER TO THE OBJECTION OF THE HEATHEN, THAT IT WAS NOT RIGHT TO ABANDON THE CUSTOMS OF THEIR FATHERS.

But you say it is not creditable to subvert the customs handed down to us from our fathers. And why, then, do we not still use our first nourishment, milk, to which our nurses accustomed us from the time of our birth? Why do we increase or diminish our patrimony, and not keep it exactly the same as we got it? Why do we not still vomit on our parents' breasts, or still do the things for which, when infants, and nursed by our mothers, we were laughed at, but have corrected ourselves, even if we did not fall in with good instructors? Then, if excesses in the indulgence of the passions, though pernicious and dangerous, yet are accompanied with pleasure, why do we not in the conduct of life abandon that usage which is evil, and provocative of passion, and godless, even should our fathers feel hurt, and betake ourselves to the truth, and seek Him who is truly our Father, rejecting custom as a deleterious drug? For of all that I have undertaken to do, the task I now attempt is the noblest, viz., to demonstrate to you how inimical this insane and most wretched custom is to godliness. For a boon so great, the greatest ever given by God to the human race, would never have been hated and rejected, had not you been carried away by custom, and then shut your ears against us ; and just as unmanageable horses throw off the reins, and take the bit between their teeth, you rush away from the arguments addressed to you, in your eager desire to shake yourselves clear of us, who seek to guide

the chariot of your life, and, impelled by your folly, dash towards the precipices of destruction, and regard the holy word of God as an accursed thing. The reward of your choice, therefore, as described by Sophocles, follows : —

" The mind a blank, useless ears, vain thoughts."

And you know not that, of all truths, this is the truest, that the good and godly shall obtain the good reward, inasmuch as they held goodness in high esteem ; while, on the other hand, the wicked shall receive meet punishment. For the author of evil, torment has been prepared ; and so the prophet Zecharias threatens him : " He that hath chosen Jerusalem rebuke thee ; lo, is not this a brand plucked from the fire ?"[2] What an infatuated desire, then, for voluntary death is this, rooted in men's minds ! Why do they flee to this fatal brand, with which they shall be burned, when it is within their power to live nobly according to God, and not according to custom? For God bestows life freely ; but evil custom, after our departure from this world, brings on the sinner unavailing remorse with punishment. *By sad experience, even a child knows* how superstition destroys and piety saves. Let any of you look at those who minister before the idols, their hair matted, their persons disgraced with filthy and tattered clothes ; who never come near a bath, and let their nails grow to an extraordinary length, like wild beasts ; many of them castrated, who show the idol's temples to be in reality graves or prisons. These appear to me to bewail the gods, not to worship them, and their sufferings to be worthy of pity rather than piety. And seeing these things, do you still continue blind, and will you not look up to the Ruler of all, the Lord of the universe ? And will you not escape from those dungeons, and flee to the mercy that comes down from heaven ? For God, of His great love to man, comes to the help of man, as the mother-bird flies to one of her young that has fallen out of the nest ; and if a serpent open its mouth to swallow the little bird, " the mother flutters round, uttering cries of grief over her dear progeny ; "[3] and God the Father seeks His creature, and heals his transgression, and pursues the serpent, and recovers the young one, and incites it to fly up to the nest.

Thus dogs that have strayed, track out their master by the scent ; and horses that have thrown their riders, come to their master's call if he but whistle. " The ox," it is said, " knoweth his owner, and the ass his master's crib ; but Israel hath not known Me."[4] What, then, of the Lord? He remembers not our ill desert ; He still pities, He still urges us to repentance.

<hr>

[1] [Here seems to be a running allusion to the privileges of the Christian Church in its unity, and to the " Psalms and hymns and spiritual songs," which were so charming a feature of Christian worship. Bunsen, *Hippolytus*, etc., vol. ii. p. 157.]

[2] Zech. iii. 2.
[3] *Iliad*, ii. 315.
[4] Isa. i. 3.

And I would ask you, if it does not appear to you monstrous, that you men who are God's handiwork, who have received your souls from Him, and belong wholly to God, should be subject to another master, and, what is more, serve the tyrant instead of the rightful King — the evil one instead of the good? For, in the name of truth, what man in his senses turns his back on good, and attaches himself to evil? What, then, is he who flees from God to consort with demons? Who, that may become a son of God, prefers to be in bondage? Or who is he that pursues his way to Erebus, when it is in his power to be a citizen of heaven, and to cultivate Paradise, and walk about in heaven and partake of the tree of life and immortality, and, cleaving his way through the sky in the track of the luminous cloud, behold, like Elias, the rain of salvation? Some there are, who, like worms wallowing in marshes and mud in the streams of pleasure, feed on foolish and useless delights — swinish men. For swine, it is said, like mud better than pure water; and, according to Democritus, "doat upon dirt."

Let us not then be enslaved or become swinish; but, as true children of the light, let us raise our eyes and look on the light, lest the Lord discover us to be spurious, as the sun does the eagles. Let us therefore repent, and pass from ignorance to knowledge, from foolishness to wisdom, from licentiousness to self-restraint, from unrighteousness to righteousness, from godlessness to God. It is an enterprise of noble daring to take our way to God; and the enjoyment of many other good things is within the reach of the lovers of righteousness, who pursue eternal life, specially those things to which God Himself alludes, speaking by Isaiah: "There is an inheritance for those who serve the LORD." [1] Noble and desirable is this inheritance: not gold, not silver, not raiment, which the moth assails, and things of earth which are assailed by the robber, whose eye is dazzled by worldly wealth; but it is that treasure of salvation to which we must hasten, by becoming lovers of the Word. Thence praise-worthy works descend to us, and fly with us on the wing of truth. This is the inheritance with which the eternal covenant of God invests us, conveying the everlasting gift of grace; and thus our loving Father — the true Father — ceases not to exhort, admonish, train, love us. For He ceases not to save, and advises the best course: "Become righteous," says the Lord.[2] Ye that thirst, come to the water; and ye that have no money, come, and buy and drink without money.[3] He invites to the laver, to salvation, to illumination, all but crying out and saying,

The land I give thee, and the sea, my child, and heaven too; and all the living creatures in them I freely bestow upon thee. Only, O child, thirst for thy Father; God shall be revealed to thee without price; the truth is not made merchandise of. He gives thee all creatures that fly and swim, and those on the land. These the Father has created for thy thankful enjoyment. What the bastard, who is a son of perdition, foredoomed to be the slave of mammon, has to buy for money, He assigns to thee as thine own, even to His own son who loves the Father; for whose sake He still works, and to whom alone He promises, saying, "The land shall not be sold in perpetuity," for it is not destined to corruption. "For the whole land is mine;" and it is thine too, if thou receive God. Wherefore the Scripture, as might have been expected, proclaims good news to those who have believed. "The saints of the Lord shall inherit the glory of God and His power." What glory, tell me, O blessed One, which "eye hath not seen, nor ear heard, nor hath it entered into the heart of man;"[4] and "they shall be glad in the kingdom of their Lord for ever and ever! Amen." You have, O men, the divine promise of grace; you have heard, on the other hand, the threatening of punishment: by these the Lord saves, teaching men by fear and grace. Why do we delay? Why do we not shun the punishment? Why do we not receive the free gift? Why, in fine, do we not choose the better part, God instead of the evil one, and prefer wisdom to idolatry, and take life in exchange for death? "Behold," He says, "I have set before your face death and life."[5] The Lord tries you, that "you may choose life." He counsels you as a father to obey God. "For if ye hear Me," He says, "and be willing, ye shall eat the good things of the land:"[6] this is the grace attached to obedience. "But if ye obey Me not, and are unwilling, the sword and fire shall devour you:"[7] this is the penalty of disobedience. For the mouth of the Lord — the law of truth, the word of the Lord — hath spoken these things. Are you willing that I should be your good counsellor? Well, do you hear. I, if possible, will explain. You ought, O men, when reflecting on the Good, to have brought forward a witness inborn and competent, viz., faith, which of itself, and from its own resources, chooses at once what is best, instead of occupying yourselves in painfully inquiring whether what is best ought to be followed. For, allow me to tell you, you ought to doubt whether you should get drunk, but you get drunk before reflecting on the matter; and whether

---

[1] Isa. liv. 17.
[2] Isa. liv. 17, where Sept. reads, "ye shall be righteous."
[3] Isa. lv. 1.

[4] 1 Cor. ii. 9.
[5] Deut. xxx. 15.
[6] Isa. i. 19.
[7] Isa. i. 20, xxxiii. 11.

you ought to do an injury, but you do injury with the utmost readiness. The only thing you make the subject of question is, whether God should be worshipped, and whether this wise God and Christ should be followed : and this you think requires deliberation and doubt, and know not what is worthy of God. Have faith in us, as you have in drunkenness, that you may be wise ; have faith in us, as you have in injury, that you may live. But if, acknowledging the conspicuous trustworthiness of the virtues, you wish to trust them, come and I will set before you in abundance, materials of persuasion respecting the Word. But do you — for your ancestral customs, by which your minds are preoccupied, divert you from the truth, — do you now hear what is the real state of the case as follows.

And let not any shame of this name preoccupy you, which does great harm to men, and seduces them from salvation. Let us then openly strip for the contest, and nobly strive in the arena of truth, the holy Word being the judge, and the Lord of the universe prescribing the contest. For 'tis no insignificant prize, the guerdon of immortality which is set before us. Pay no more regard, then, if you are rated by some of the low rabble who lead the dance of impiety, and are driven on to the same pit by their folly and insanity, makers of idols and worshippers of stones. For these have dared to deify men, — Alexander of Macedon, for example, whom they canonized as the thirteenth god, whose pretensions Babylon confuted, which showed him dead. I admire, therefore, the divine sophist. Theocritus was his name. After Alexander's death, Theocritus, holding up the vain opinions entertained by men respecting the gods, to ridicule before his fellow-citizens, said : "Men, keep up your hearts as long as you see the gods dying sooner than men." And, truly, he who worships gods that are visible, and the promiscuous rabble of creatures begotten and born, and attaches himself to them, is a far more wretched object than the very demons. For God is by no manner of means unrighteous, as the demons are, but in the very highest degree righteous ; and nothing more resembles God than one of us when he becomes righteous in the highest possible degree : —

"Go into the way, the whole tribe of you handicrafts-men,
Who worship Jove's fierce-eyed daughter,[1] the working goddess,
With fans duly placed, fools that ye are "—

fashioners of stones, and worshippers of them. Let your Phidias, and Polycletus, and your Praxiteles and Apelles too, come, and all that are engaged in mechanical arts, who, being themselves of the earth, are workers of the earth. "For then," says a certain prophecy, "the affairs here turn out unfortunately, when men put their trust in images." Let the meaner artists, too — for I will not stop calling — come. None of these ever made a breathing image, or out of earth moulded soft flesh. Who liquefied the marrow? or who solidified the bones? Who stretched the nerves? who distended the veins? Who poured the blood into them? Or who spread the skin? Who ever could have made eyes capable of seeing? Who breathed spirit into the lifeless form? Who bestowed righteousness? Who promised immortality? The Maker of the universe alone ; the Great Artist and Father has formed us, such a living image as man is. But your Olympian Jove, the image of an image, greatly out of harmony with truth, is the senseless work of Attic hands. For the image of God is His Word, the genuine Son of Mind, the Divine Word, the archetypal light of light ; and the image of the Word is the true man, the mind which is in man, who is therefore said to have been made "in the image and likeness of God,"[2] assimilated to the Divine Word in the affections of the soul, and therefore rational ; but effigies sculptured in human form, the earthly image of that part of man which is visible and earth-born, are but a perishable impress of humanity, manifestly wide of the truth. That life, then, which is occupied with so much earnestness about matter, seems to me to be nothing else than full of insanity. And custom, which has made you taste bondage and unreasonable care, is fostered by vain opinion ; and ignorance, which has proved to the human race the cause of unlawful rites and delusive shows, and also of deadly plagues and hateful images, has, by devising many shapes of demons, stamped on all that follow it the mark of long-continued death. Receive, then, the water of the word ; wash, ye polluted ones ; purify yourselves from custom, by sprinkling yourselves with the drops of truth.[3] The pure must ascend to heaven. Thou art a man, if we look to that which is most common to thee and others — seek Him who created thee ; thou art a son, if we look to that which is thy peculiar prerogative — acknowledge thy Father. But do you still continue in your sins, engrossed with pleasures? To whom shall the Lord say, "Yours is the kingdom of heaven?" Yours, whose choice is set on God, if you will ; yours, if you will only believe, and comply with the brief terms of the announcement ; which the Ninevites having obeyed, instead of the destruction they looked for, obtained a signal deliverance. How, then,

---

[1] Minerva.

[2] Gen. i. 26.

[3] [Immersion was surely the form of primitive baptism, but these words, if not a reference to that sacrament, must recall Isa. lii. 15.]

may I ascend to heaven, is it said? The Lord is the way; a strait way, but leading from heaven, strait in truth, but leading back to heaven, strait, despised on earth; broad, adored in heaven.

Then, he that is uninstructed in the word, has ignorance as the excuse of his error; but as for him into whose ears instruction has been poured, and who deliberately maintains his incredulity in his soul, the wiser he appears to be, the more harm will his understanding do him; for he has his own sense as his accuser for not having chosen the best part. For man has been otherwise constituted by nature, so as to have fellowship with God. As, then, we do not compel the horse to plough, or the bull to hunt, but set each animal to that for which it is by nature fitted; so, placing our finger on what is man's peculiar and distinguishing characteristic above other creatures, we invite him — born, as he is, for the contemplation of heaven, and being, as he is, a truly heavenly plant — to the knowledge of God, counselling him to furnish himself with what is his sufficient provision for eternity, namely piety. Practise husbandry, we say, if you are a husbandman; but while you till your fields, know God. Sail the sea, you who are devoted to navigation, yet call the whilst on the heavenly Pilot.[1] Has knowledge taken hold of you while engaged in military service? Listen to the commander, who orders what is right. As those, then, who have been overpowered with sleep and drunkenness, do ye awake; and using your eyes a little, consider what mean those stones which you worship, and the expenditure you frivolously lavish on matter. Your means and substance you squander on ignorance, even as you throw away your lives to death, having found no other end of your vain hope than this. Not only unable to pity yourselves, you are incapable even of yielding to the persuasions of those who commiserate you; enslaved as you are to evil custom, and, clinging to it voluntarily till your last breath, you are hurried to destruction: "because light is come into the world, and men have loved the darkness rather than the light,"[2] while they could sweep away those hindrances to salvation, pride, and wealth, and fear, repeating this poetic utterance: —

"Whither do I bear these abundant riches? and whither
Do I myself wander?"[3]

If you wish, then, to cast aside these vain phantasies, and bid adieu to evil custom, say to vain opinion: —

"Lying dreams, farewell; you were then nothing."

For what, think you, O men, is the Hermes of Typho, and that of Andocides, and that of Amye-

tus? Is it not evident to all that they are stones, as is the veritable Hermes himself? As the Halo is not a god, and as the Iris is not a god, but are states of the atmosphere and of the clouds; and as, likewise, a day is not a god, nor a year, nor time, which is made up of these, so neither is sun nor moon, by which each of those mentioned above is determined. Who, then, in his right senses, can imagine Correction, and Punishment, and Justice, and Retribution to be gods? For neither the Furies, nor the Fates, nor Destiny are gods, since neither Government, nor Glory, nor Wealth are gods, which last [as Plutus] painters represent as blind. But if you deify Modesty, and Love, and Venus, let these be followed by Infamy, and Passion, and Beauty, and Intercourse. Therefore Sleep and Death cannot reasonably any more be regarded as twin deities, being merely changes which take place naturally in living creatures; no more will you with propriety call Fortune, or Destiny, or the Fates goddesses. And if Strife and Battle be not gods, no more are Ares and Enyo. Still further, if the lightnings, and thunderbolts, and rains are not gods, how can fire and water be gods? how can shooting stars and comets, which are produced by atmospheric changes? He who calls Fortune a god, let him also so call Action. If, then, none of these, nor of the images formed by human hands, and destitute of feeling, is held to be a God, while a providence exercised about us is evidently the result of a divine power,[4] it remains only to acknowledge this, that He alone who is truly God, only truly is and subsists. But those who are insensible to this are like men who have drunk mandrake or some other drug. May God grant that you may at length awake from this slumber, and know God; and that neither Gold, nor Stone, nor Tree, nor Action, nor Suffering, nor Disease, nor Fear, may appear in your eyes as a god. For there are, in sooth, "on the fruitful earth thrice ten thousand" demons, not immortal, nor indeed mortal; for they are not endowed with sensation, so as to render them capable of death, but only things of wood and stone, that hold despotic sway over men insulting and violating life through the force of custom. "The earth is the LORD'S," it is said, "and the fulness thereof."[5] Then why darest thou, while luxuriating in the bounties of the Lord, to ignore the Sovereign Ruler? "Leave my earth," the Lord will say to thee. "Touch not the water which I bestow. Partake not of the fruits of the earth produced by my hus-

---

[1] [This fine passage will be recalled by what Clement afterward, in the *Stromata*, says of prayer. Book vii. vol. ii. p. 432. *Edin.*]
[2] John iii. 19.
[3] *Odyss.*, xiii. 203.

[4] A translation in accordance with the Latin version would run thus: "While a certain previous conception of divine power is nevertheless discovered within us." But adopting that in the text the argument is: there is unquestionably a providence implying the exertion of divine power. That power is not exercised by idols or heathen gods. The only other alternative is, that it is exercised by the one self-existent God.
[5] Ps. xxiv. 1; 1 Cor. x. 26, 28.

bandry." Give to God recompense for your sustenance; acknowledge thy Master. Thou art God's creature. What belongs to Him, how can it with justice be alienated? For that which is alienated, being deprived of the properties that belonged to it, is also deprived of truth. For, after the fashion of Niobe, or, to express myself more mystically, like the Hebrew woman called by the ancients Lot's wife, are ye not turned into a state of insensibility? This woman, we have heard, was turned into stone for her love of Sodom. And those who are godless, addicted to impiety, hard-hearted and foolish, are Sodomites. Believe that these utterances are addressed to you from God. For think not that stones, and stocks, and birds, and serpents are sacred things, and men are not; but, on the contrary, regard men as truly sacred,[1] and take beasts and stones for what they are. For there are miserable wretches of human kind, who consider that God utters His voice by the raven and the jackdaw, but says nothing by man; and honour the raven as a messenger of God. But the man of God, who croaks not, nor chatters, but speaks rationally and instructs lovingly, alas, they persecute; and while he is inviting them to cultivate righteousness, they try inhumanly to slay him, neither welcoming the grace which comes from above, nor fearing the penalty. For they believe not God, nor understand His power, whose love to man is ineffable; and His hatred of evil is inconceivable. His anger augments punishment against sin; His love bestows blessings on repentance. It is the height of wretchedness to be deprived of the help which comes from God. Hence this blindness of eyes and dulness of hearing are more grievous than other inflictions of the evil one; for the one deprives them of heavenly vision, the other robs them of divine instruction. But ye, thus maimed as respects the truth, blind in mind, deaf in understanding, are not grieved, are not pained, have had no desire to see heaven and the Maker of heaven, nor, by fixing your choice on salvation, have sought to hear the Creator of the universe, and to learn of Him; for no hindrance stands in the way of him who is bent on the knowledge of God. Neither childlessness, nor poverty, nor obscurity, nor want, can hinder him who eagerly strives after the knowledge of God; nor does any one who has conquered[2] by brass or iron the true wisdom for himself choose to exchange it, for it is vastly preferred to everything else. Christ is able to save in every place. For he that is fired with ardour and admiration for righteousness, being the lover of One who needs

nothing, needs himself but little, having treasured up his bliss in nothing but himself and God, where is neither moth,[3] robber, nor pirate, but the eternal Giver of good. With justice, then, have you been compared to those serpents who shut their ears against the charmers. For "their mind," says the Scripture, "is like the serpent, like the deaf adder, which stoppeth her ear, and will not hear the voice of the charmers."[4] But allow yourselves to feel the influence of the charming strains of sanctity, and receive that mild word of ours, and reject the deadly poison, that it may be granted to you to divest yourselves as much as possible of destruction, as they[5] have been divested of old age. Hear me, and do not stop your ears; do not block up the avenues of hearing, but lay to heart what is said. Excellent is the medicine of immortality! Stop at length your grovelling reptile motions.[4] "For the enemies of the Lord," says Scripture, "shall lick the dust."[6] Raise your eyes from earth to the skies, look up to heaven, admire the sight, cease watching with outstretched head the heel of the righteous, and hindering the way of truth. Be wise and harmless. Perchance the Lord will endow you with the wing of simplicity (for He has resolved to give wings to those that are earth-born), that you may leave your holes and dwell in heaven. Only let us with our whole heart repent, that we may be able with our whole heart to contain God. "Trust in Him, all ye assembled people; pour out all your hearts before Him."[7] He says to those that have newly abandoned wickedness, "He pities them, and fills them with righteousness." Believe Him who is man and God; believe, O man. Believe, O man, the living God, who suffered and is adored. Believe, ye slaves,[8] Him who died; believe, all ye of human kind, Him who alone is God of all men. Believe, and receive salvation as your reward. Seek God, and your soul shall live. He who seeks God is busying himself about his own salvation. Hast thou found God?—then thou hast life. Let us then seek, in order that we may live. The reward of seeking is life with God. "Let all who seek Thee be glad and rejoice in Thee; and let them say continually, God be magnified."[9] A noble hymn of God is an immortal man, established in righteousness, in whom the oracles of truth are engraved. For where but in a soul that is wise can you write truth? where love? where reverence? where meekness? Those who have had these divine

---

[1] [1 Pet. ii. 17. This appeal in behalf of the sanctity of man as man, shows the workings of the apostolic precept.]

[2] The expression "conquered by brass or iron" is borrowed from Homer (*Il.*, viii. 534). Brass, or copper, and iron were the metals of which arms were made.

[3] Matt. vi. 20, 21.

[4] Ps. lviii. 4, 5. [It was supposed that adders deafened themselves by laying one ear on the earth, and closing the other with the tail.]

[5] "They" seems to refer to sanctity and the word.

[6] Ps. lxxii. 9.

[7] Ps. lxii. 8.

[8] [The impact of the Gospel on the slavery and *helotism* of the Pagans.]

[9] Ps. lxx. 4.

characters impressed on them, ought, I think, to regard wisdom as a fair port whence to embark, to whatever lot in life they turn; and likewise to deem it the calm haven of salvation: wisdom, by which those who have betaken themselves to the Father, have proved good fathers to their children; and good parents to their sons, those who have known the Son; and good husbands to their wives, those who remember the Bridegroom; and good masters to their servants,[1] those who have been redeemed from utter slavery. Oh, happier far the beasts than men involved in error! who live in ignorance as you, but do not counterfeit the truth. There are no tribes of flatterers among them. Fishes have no superstition: the birds worship not a single image; only they look with admiration on heaven, since, deprived as they are of reason, they are unable to know God. So are you not ashamed for living through so many periods of life in impiety, making yourselves more irrational than irrational creatures? You were boys, then striplings, then youths, then men, but never as yet were you good. If you have respect for old age, be wise, now that you have reached life's sunset; and albeit at the close of life, acquire the knowledge of God, that the end of life may to you prove the beginning of salvation. You have become old in superstition; as young, enter on the practice of piety. God regards you as innocent children. Let, then, the Athenian follow the laws of Solon, and the Argive those of Phoroneus, and the Spartan those of Lycurgus: but if thou enrol thyself as one of God's people, heaven is thy country, God thy lawgiver. And what are the laws? "Thou shalt not kill; thou shalt not commit adultery; thou shalt not seduce boys; thou shalt not steal; thou shalt not bear false witness; thou shalt love the Lord thy God."[2] And the complements of these are those laws of reason and words of sanctity which are inscribed on men's hearts: "Thou shalt love thy neighbour as thyself; to him who strikes thee on the cheek, present also the other;"[3] "thou shalt not lust, for by lust alone thou hast committed adultery."[4] How much better, therefore, is it for men from the beginning not to wish to desire things forbidden, than to obtain their desires! But ye are not able to endure the austerity of salvation; but as we delight in sweet things, and prize them higher for the agreeableness of the pleasure they yield, while, on the other hand, those bitter things which are distasteful to the palate are curative and healing, and the harshness of medicines strengthens people of weak stomach, thus custom pleases and

tickles; but custom pushes into the abyss, while truth conducts to heaven. Harsh it is at first, but a good nurse of youth; and it is at once the decorous place where the household maids and matrons dwell together, and the sage councilchamber. Nor is it difficult to approach, or impossible to attain, but is very near us in our very homes; as Moses, endowed with all wisdom, says, while referring to it, it has its abode in three departments of our constitution — in the hands, the mouth, and the heart: a meet emblem this of truth, which is embraced by these three things in all — will, action, speech. And be not afraid lest the multitude of pleasing objects which rise before you withdraw you from wisdom. You yourself will spontaneously surmount the frivolousness of custom, as boys when they have become men throw aside their toys. For with a celerity unsurpassable, and a benevolence to which we have ready access, the divine power, casting its radiance on the earth, hath filled the universe with the seed of salvation. For it was not without divine care that so great a work was accomplished in so brief a space by the Lord, who, though despised as to appearance, was in reality adored, the expiator of sin, the Saviour, the clement, the Divine Word, He that is truly most manifest Deity, He that is made equal to the Lord of the universe; because He was His Son, and the Word was in God, not disbelieved in by all when He was first preached, nor altogether unknown when, assuming the character of man, and fashioning Himself in flesh, He enacted the drama of human salvation: for He was a true champion and a fellow-champion with the creature. And being communicated most speedily to men, having dawned from His Father's counsel quicker than the sun, with the most perfect ease He made God shine on us. Whence He was and what He was, He showed by what He taught and exhibited, manifesting Himself as the Herald of the Covenant, the Reconciler, our Saviour, the Word, the Fount of life, the Giver of peace, diffused over the whole face of the earth; by whom, so to speak, the universe has already become an ocean of blessings.[5]

CHAP. XI. — HOW GREAT ARE THE BENEFITS CONFERRED ON MAN THROUGH THE ADVENT OF CHRIST.

Contemplate a little, if agreeable to you, the divine beneficence. The first man, when in Paradise, sported free, because he was the child of God; but when he succumbed to pleasure (for the serpent allegorically signifies pleasure crawling on its belly, earthly wickedness nour-

---

[1] [See above, p. 201, and below, the command " thou shalt love thy neighbour."]
[2] Ex. xx. 13-16; Deut. vi. 5.
[3] Luke vi. 29.
[4] Matt. v. 28.

[5] [*Good will to men* made emphatic. Slavery already modified, free-schools established, and homes created. As soon as persecution ceased, we find the Christian hospital. Forster ascribes the first foundation of this kind to Ephraim Syrus. A friend refers me to his *Mohammedanism Unveiled*, vol. i. p. 283.]

ished for fuel to the flames), was as a child seduced by lusts, and grew old in disobedience; and by disobeying his Father, dishonoured God. Such was the influence of pleasure. Man, that had been free by reason of simplicity, was found fettered to sins. The Lord then wished to release him from his bonds, and clothing Himself with flesh — O divine mystery! — vanquished the serpent, and enslaved the tyrant death; and, most marvellous of all, man that had been deceived by pleasure, and bound fast by corruption, had his hands unloosed, and was set free. O mystic wonder! The Lord was laid low, and man rose up; and he that fell from Paradise receives as the reward of obedience something greater [than Paradise] — namely, heaven itself. Wherefore, since the Word Himself has come to us from heaven, we need not, I reckon, go any more in search of human learning to Athens and the rest of Greece, and to Ionia. For if we have as our teacher Him that filled the universe with His holy energies in creation, salvation, beneficence, legislation, prophecy, teaching, we have the Teacher from whom all instruction comes; and the whole world, with Athens and Greece, has already become the domain of the Word.[1] For you, who believed the poetical fable which designated Minos the Cretan as the bosom friend of Zeus, will not refuse to believe that we who have become the disciples of God have received the only true wisdom; and that which the chiefs of philosophy only guessed at, the disciples of Christ have both apprehended and proclaimed. And the one whole Christ is not divided: "There is neither barbarian, nor Jew, nor Greek, neither male nor female, but a new man,"[2] transformed by God's Holy Spirit. Further, the other counsels and precepts are unimportant, and respect particular things, — as, for example, if one may marry, take part in public affairs, beget children; but the only command that is universal, and over the whole course of existence, at all times and in all circumstances, tends to the highest end, viz., life, is piety,[3] — all that is necessary, in order that we may live for ever, being that we live in accordance with it. Philosophy, however, as the ancients say, is "a long-lived exhortation, wooing the eternal love of wisdom;" while the commandment of the Lord is far-shining, "enlightening the eyes." Receive Christ, receive sight, receive thy light,

"In order that you may know well both God and man."[4]

"Sweet is the Word that gives us light, precious above gold and gems; it is to be desired above honey and the honey-comb."[5]

For how can it be other than desirable, since it has filled with light the mind which had been buried in darkness, and given keenness to the "light-bringing eyes" of the soul? For just as, had the sun not been in existence, night would have brooded over the universe notwithstanding the other luminaries of heaven; so, had we not known the Word, and been illuminated by Him, we should have been nowise different from fowls that are being fed, fattened in darkness, and nourished for death. Let us then admit the light, that we may admit God; let us admit the light, and become disciples to the Lord. This, too, He has been promised to the Father: "I will declare Thy name to my brethren; in the midst of the Church will I praise Thee."[6] Praise and declare to me Thy Father God; Thy utterances save; Thy hymn teaches[7] that hitherto I have wandered in error, seeking God. But since Thou leadest me to the light, O Lord, and I find God through Thee, and receive the Father from Thee, I become "Thy fellow-heir,"[8] since Thou "wert not ashamed of me as Thy brother."[9] Let us put away, then, let us put away oblivion of the truth, viz., ignorance; and removing the darkness which obstructs, as dimness of sight, let us contemplate the only true God, first raising our voice in this hymn of praise:[10] Hail, O light! For in us, buried in darkness, shut up in the shadow of death, light has shone forth from heaven, purer than the sun, sweeter than life here below. That light is eternal life; and whatever partakes of it lives. But night fears the light, and hiding itself in terror, gives place to the day of the Lord. Sleepless light is now over all, and the west has given credence to the east. For this was the end of the new creation. For "the Sun of Righteousness," who drives His chariot over all, pervades equally all humanity, like "His Father, who makes His sun to rise on all men," and distils on them the dew of the truth. He hath changed sunset into sunrise, and through the cross brought death to life; and having wrenched man from destruction, He hath raised him to the skies, transplanting mortality into immortality, and translating earth to heaven — He, the husbandman of God,

"Pointing out the favourable signs and rousing the nations
To good works, putting them in mind of the true sustenance;"[11]

having bestowed on us the truly great, divine, and inalienable inheritance of the Father, deifying man by heavenly teaching, putting His laws

---

[1] [The Catholic instinct is here; and an all-embracing benevolence is its characteristic, not worldly empire.]
[2] Gal. iii. 28, vi. 15.
[3] [He seems to be thinking of 1 Tim. vi. 6, and 1 Tim. iv. 8.]
[4] *Iliad*, v. 128.
[5] Ps. xix. 10.

[6] Ps. xxii. 22.
[7] [Eph. v. 14, is probably from a hymn of the Church, which is here referred to as His, as it is adopted into Scripture.]
[8] Rom. viii. 17.
[9] Heb. ii. 11.
[10] [A quotation from another hymn, in all probability.]
[11] Aratus.

into our minds, and writing them on our hearts. What laws does He inscribe? "That all shall know God, from small to great;" and, "I will be merciful to them," says God, "and will not remember their sins."[1] Let us receive the laws of life, let us comply with God's expostulations; let us become acquainted with Him, that He may be gracious. And though God needs nothing let us render to Him the grateful recompense of a thankful heart and of piety, as a kind of house-rent for our dwelling here below.

> "Gold for brass,
> A hundred oxen's worth for that of nine;"[2]

that is, for your little faith He gives you the earth of so great extent to till, water to drink and also to sail on, air to breathe, fire to do your work, a world to dwell in; and He has permitted you to conduct a colony from here to heaven: with these important works of His hand, and benefits in such numbers, He has rewarded your little faith. Then, those who have put faith in necromancers, receive from them amulets and charms, to ward off evil forsooth; and will you not allow the heavenly Word, the Saviour, to be bound on to you as an amulet, and, by trusting in God's own charm, be delivered from passions which are the diseases of the mind, and rescued from sin? —for sin is eternal death. Surely utterly dull and blind, and, like moles, doing nothing but eat, you spend your lives in darkness, surrounded with corruption. But it is truth which cries, "The light shall shine forth from the darkness." Let the light then shine in the hidden part of man, that is, the heart; and let the beams of knowledge arise to reveal and irradiate the hidden inner man, the disciple of the Light, the familiar friend and fellow-heir of Christ; especially now that we have come to know the most precious and venerable name of the good Father, who to a pious and good child gives gentle counsels, and commands what is salutary for His child. He who obeys Him has the advantage in all things, follows God, obeys the Father, knows Him through wandering, loves God, loves his neighbour, fulfils the commandment, seeks the prize, claims the promise. But it has been God's fixed and constant purpose to save the flock of men: for this end the good God sent the good Shepherd. And the Word, having unfolded the truth, showed to men the height of salvation, that either repenting they might be saved, or refusing to obey, they might be judged. This is the proclamation of righteousness: to those that obey, glad tidings; to those that disobey, judgment. The loud trumpet, when sounded, collects the soldiers, and proclaims war. And

shall not Christ, breathing a strain of peace to the ends of the earth, gather together His own soldiers, the soldiers of peace? Well, by His blood, and by the word, He has gathered the bloodless host of peace, and assigned to them the kingdom of heaven. The trumpet of Christ is His Gospel. He hath blown it, and we have heard. "Let us array ourselves in the armour of peace, putting on the breastplate of righteousness, and taking the shield of faith, and binding our brows with the helmet of salvation; and the sword of the Spirit, which is the word of God,"[3] let us sharpen. So the apostle in the spirit of peace commands. These are our invulnerable weapons: armed with these, let us face the evil one; "the fiery darts of the evil one" let us quench with the sword-points dipped in water, that have been baptized by the Word, returning grateful thanks for the benefits we have received, and honouring God through the Divine Word. "For while thou art yet speaking," it is said, "He will say, Behold, I am beside thee."[4] O this holy and blessed power, by which God has fellowship with men! Better far, then, is it to become at once the imitator and the servant of the best of all beings; for only by holy service will any one be able to imitate God, and to serve and worship Him only by imitating Him. The heavenly and truly divine love comes to men thus, when in the soul itself the spark of true goodness, kindled in the soul by the Divine Word, is able to burst forth into flame; and, what is of the highest importance, salvation runs parallel with sincere willingness—choice and life being, so to speak, yoked together. Wherefore this exhortation of the truth alone, like the most faithful of our friends, abides with us till our last breath, and is to the whole and perfect spirit of the soul the kind attendant on our ascent to heaven. What, then, is the exhortation I give you? I urge you to be saved. This Christ desires. In one word, He freely bestows life on you. And who is He? Briefly learn. The Word of truth, the Word of incorruption, that regenerates man by bringing him back to the truth—the goad that urges to salvation—He who expels destruction and pursues death—He who builds up the temple of God in men, that He may cause God to take up His abode in men. Cleanse the temple; and pleasures and amusements abandon to the winds and the fire, as a fading flower; but wisely cultivate the fruits of self-command, and present thyself to God as an offering of first-fruits, that there may be not the work alone, but also the grace of God; and both are requisite, that the friend of Christ may be rendered worthy of the kingdom, and be counted worthy of the kingdom.

---

[1] Heb. viii. 10–12; Jer. xxxi. 33, 34.
[2] Il., vi. 236. [The exchange of Glaucus.]
[3] Eph. vi. 14–17.
[4] Isa. lviii. 9.

CHAP. XII. — EXHORTATION TO ABANDON THEIR OLD ERRORS AND LISTEN TO THE INSTRUCTIONS OF CHRIST.

Let us then avoid custom as we would a dangerous headland, or the threatening Charybdis, or the mythic sirens. It chokes man, turns him away from truth, leads him away from life : custom is a snare, a gulf, a pit, a mischievous winnowing fan.

"Urge the ship beyond that smoke and billow." [1]

Let us shun, fellow-mariners, let us shun this billow ; it vomits forth fire : it is a wicked island, heaped with bones and corpses, and in it sings a fair courtesan, Pleasure, delighting with music for the common ear.

"Hie thee hither, far-famed Ulysses, great glory of the Achæans ;
Moor the ship, that thou mayest hear a diviner voice." [2]

She praises thee, O mariner, and calls the eillustrious ; and the courtesan tries to win to herself the glory of the Greeks. Leave her to prey on the dead ; a heavenly spirit comes to thy help : pass by Pleasure, she beguiles.

"Let not a woman with flowing train cheat you of your senses,
With her flattering prattle seeking your hurt."

Sail past the song ; it works death. Exert your will only, and you have overcome ruin ; bound to the wood of the cross, thou shalt be freed from destruction : the word of God will be thy pilot, and the Holy Spirit will bring thee to anchor in the haven of heaven. Then shalt thou see my God, and be initiated into the sacred mysteries, and come to the fruition of those things which are laid up in heaven reserved for me, which "ear hath not heard, nor have they entered into the heart of any." [3]

"And in sooth methinks I see two suns,
And a double Thebes," [4]

said one frenzy-stricken in the worship of idols, intoxicated with mere ignorance. I would pity him in his frantic intoxication, and thus frantic I would invite him to the sobriety of salvation ; for the Lord welcomes a sinner's repentance, and not his death.

Come, O madman, not leaning on the thyrsus, not crowned with ivy ; throw away the mitre, throw away the fawn-skin ; come to thy senses. I will show thee the Word, and the mysteries of the Word, expounding them after thine own fashion. This is the mountain beloved of God, not the subject of tragedies like Cithæron, but consecrated to dramas of the truth, — a mount of sobriety, shaded with forests of purity ; and there revel on it not the Mænades, the sisters

of Semele, who was struck by the thunderbolt, practising in their initiatory rites unholy division of flesh, but the daughters of God, the fair lambs, who celebrate the holy rites of the Word, raising a sober choral dance. The righteous are the chorus ; the music is a hymn of the King of the universe. The maidens strike the lyre, the angels praise, the prophets speak ; the sound of music issues forth, they run and pursue the jubilant band ; those that are called make haste, eagerly desiring to receive the Father.

Come thou also, O aged man, leaving Thebes, and casting away from thee both divination and Bacchic frenzy, allow thyself to be led to the truth. I give thee the staff [of the cross] on which to lean. Haste, Tiresias ; believe, and thou wilt see. Christ, by whom the eyes of the blind recover sight, will shed on thee a light brighter than the sun ; night will flee from thee, fire will fear, death will be gone ; thou, old man, who saw not Thebes, shalt see the heavens. O truly sacred mysteries ! O stainless light ! My way is lighted with torches, and I survey the heavens and God ; I become holy whilst I am initiated. The Lord is the hierophant, and seals while illuminating him who is initiated, and presents to the Father him who believes, to be kept safe for ever. Such are the reveries of my mysteries. If it is thy wish, be thou also initiated ; and thou shalt join the choir along with angels around the unbegotten and indestructible and the only true God, the Word of God, raising the hymn with us. [5] This Jesus, who is eternal, the one great High Priest of the one God and of His Father, prays for and exhorts men.

"Hear, ye myriad tribes, rather whoever among men are endowed with reason, both barbarians and Greeks. I call on the whole race of men, whose Creator I am, by the will of the Father. Come to Me, that you may be put in your due rank under the one God and the one Word of God ; and do not only have the advantage of the irrational creatures in the possession of reason ; for to you of all mortals I grant the enjoyment of immortality. For I want, I want to impart to you this grace, bestowing on you the perfect boon of immortality ; and I confer on you both the Word and the knowledge of God, My complete self. This am I, this God wills, this is symphony, this the harmony of the Father, this is the Son, this is Christ, this the Word of God, the arm of the Lord, the power of the universe, the will of the Father ; of which things there were images of old, but not all adequate. I desire to restore you according to the original model, that ye may become also like Me. I anoint you with the ungent of faith, by which you throw off corrup-

---

[1] *Odyss.*, xii. 219.
[2] *Odyss.*, xii. 184.
[3] 1 Cor. ii. 9.
[4] Eurip., *Bacch.*, 918.

[5] [Here are references to baptism and the Eucharist, and to the *Trisagion*, "Therefore with angels and archangels," which was universally diffused in the Christian Church. Bunsen, *Hippol.*, iii. 63.]

tion, and show you the naked form of righteousness by which you ascend to God. Come to Me, all ye that labour and are heavy laden, and I will give you rest. Take My yoke upon you, and learn of Me ; for I am meek and lowly in heart : and ye shall find rest to your souls. For My yoke is easy, and My burden light." [1]

Let us haste, let us run, my fellow-men — us, who are God-loving and God-like images of the Word. Let us haste, let us run, let us take His yoke, let us receive, to conduct us to immortality, the good charioteer of men. Let us love Christ. He led the colt with its parent ; and having yoked the team of humanity to God, directs His chariot to immortality, hastening clearly to fulfil, by driving now into heaven, what He shadowed forth before by riding into Jerusalem. A spectacle most beautiful to the Father is the eternal Son crowned with victory.[2] Let us aspire, then, after what is good ; let us become God-loving men, and obtain the greatest of all things which are incapable of being harmed — God and life. Our helper is the Word ; let us put confidence in Him ; and never let us be visited with such a craving for silver and gold, and glory, as for the Word of truth Himself. For it will not, it will not be pleasing to God Himself if we value least those things which are worth most, and hold in the highest estimation the manifest enormities and the utter impiety of folly, and ignorance, and thoughtlessness, and idolatry. For not improperly the sons of the philosophers consider that the foolish are guilty of profanity and impiety in whatever they do ; and describing ignorance itself as a species of madness, allege that the multitude are nothing but madmen. There is therefore no room to doubt, the Word will say, whether it is better to be sane or insane ; but holding on to truth with our teeth, we must with all our might follow God, and in the exercise of wisdom regard all things to be, as they are, His ; and besides, having learned that we are the most excellent of His possessions, let us commit ourselves to God, loving the Lord God, and regarding this as our business all our life long. And if what belongs to friends be reckoned common property, and man be the friend of God — for through the mediation of the Word has he been made the friend of God — then accordingly all things become man's, because all things are God's, and the common property of both the friends, God and man.

It is time, then, for us to say that the pious Christian alone is rich and wise, and of noble birth, and thus call and believe him to be God's image, and also His likeness,[3] having become righteous and holy and wise by Jesus Christ, and so far already like God. Accordingly this grace is indicated by the prophet, when he says, " I said that ye are gods, and all sons of the Highest." [4] For us, yea us, He has adopted, and wishes to be called the Father of us alone, not of the unbelieving. Such is then our position who are the attendants of Christ.

> " As are men's wishes, so are their words ;
> As are their words, so are their deeds ;
> And as their works, such is their life."

Good is the whole life of those who have known Christ.

Enough, methinks, of words, though, impelled by love to man, I might have gone on to pour out what I had from God, that I might exhort to what is the greatest of blessings — salvation.[5] For discourses concerning the life which has no end, are not readily brought to the end of their disclosures. To you still remains this conclusion, to choose which will profit you most — judgment or grace. For I do not think there is even room for doubt which of these is the better ; nor is it allowable to compare life with destruction.

---

[1] Matt. xi. 28, 29, 30.
[2] [" Who is this that cometh from Edom," seems to be in mind. Isa. lxiii. 1.]

[3] Clement here draws a distinction, frequently made by early Christian writers, between the image and likeness of God. Man never loses the image of God; but as the likeness consists in moral resemblance, he may lose it, and he recovers it only when he becomes righteous, holy, and wise.
[4] Ps. lxxxii. 6.
[5] [Let me quote from an excellent author: " We ought to give the Fathers credit for knowing what arguments were best calculated to affect the minds of those whom they were addressing. It was unnecessary for them to establish, by a long train of reasoning, the *probability* that a revelation may be made from heaven to man, or to prove the credibility of miracles. . . . The majority, both of the learned and unlearned, were fixed in the belief that the Deity exercised an immediate control over the human race, and consequently felt no predisposition to reject that which purported to be a communication of His will. . . . Accustomed as they were, however, to regard the various systems proposed by philosophers as matters of curious speculation, designed to exercise the understanding, *not to influence* the conduct, the chief difficulty of the advocate of Christianity was to prevent them from treating it *with the same levity*, and to induce them to view it in its true light as a revelation declaring truths of the highest practical importance."
This remark of Bishop Kaye is a hint of vast importance in our study of the early Apologists. It is taken from that author's *Account of the Writings of Clement of Alexandria* (London, 1835), to which I would refer the student, as the best introduction to these works that I know of. It is full of valuable comment and exposition I make only sparing reference to it, however, in these pages, as otherwise I should hardly know what to omit, or to include.]

THE INSTRUCTOR.

[PÆDAGOGUS.]

THE INSTRUCTOR

BOOK I

CHAP. I. THE OFFICE OF THE INSTRUCTOR.

As there are these three things in the case of man, habits, actions, and passions; habits are the department appropriated by *hortatory* discourse the guide to piety, which, like the ship's keel, is laid beneath for the building up of faith; in which, rejoicing exceedingly, and abjuring our old opinions, through salvation we renew our youth, singing with the hymning prophecy, "How good is God to Israel, to such as are upright in heart!"[1] All actions, again, are the province of *preceptive* discourse; while *persuasive* discourse applies itself to heal the passions. It is, however, one and the self-same word which rescues man from the custom of this world in which he has been reared, and trains him up in the one salvation of faith in God.

When, then, the heavenly guide, the Word, was inviting[2] men to salvation, the appellation of *hortatory* was properly applied to Him: his same word was called rousing (the whole from a part). For the whole of piety is hortatory, engendering in the kindred faculty of reason a yearning after true life now and to come. But now, being at once curative and preceptive, following in His own steps, He makes what had been prescribed the subject of persuasion, promising the cure of the passions within us. Let us then designate this Word appropriately by the one name *Tutor* (or *Pædagogue*, or *Instructor*).

The Instructor being practical, not theoretical, His aim is thus to improve the soul, not to teach, and to train it up to a virtuous, not to an intellectual life. Although this same word is didactic, but not in the present instance. For the word which, in matters of doctrine, explains and reveals, is that whose province it is to teach. But our Educator[3] being practical, first exhorts to the attainment of right dispositions and character, and then persuades us to the energetic practice of our duties, enjoining on us pure commandments, and exhibiting to such as come after representations of those who formerly wandered in error. Both are of the highest utility, — that which assumes the form of counselling to obedience, and that which is presented in the form of example; which latter is of two kinds, corresponding to the former duality, — the one having for its purpose that we should choose and imitate the good, and the other that we should reject and turn away from the opposite.

Hence accordingly ensues the healing of our passions, in consequence of the assuagements of those examples; the Pædagogue strengthening our souls, and by His benign commands, as by gentle medicines, guiding the sick to the perfect knowledge of the truth.

There is a wide difference between health and knowledge; for the latter is produced by learning, the former by healing. One, who is ill, will not therefore learn any branch of instruction till he is quite well. For neither to learners nor to the sick is each injunction invariably expressed similarly; but to the former in such a way as to lead to knowledge, and to the latter to health. As, then, for those of us who are diseased in body a physician is required, so also those who are diseased in soul require a pædagogue to cure our maladies; and then a teacher, to train and guide the soul to all requisite knowledge when it is made able to admit the revelation of the Word. Eagerly desiring, then, to perfect us by a gradation conducive to salvation, suited for efficacious discipline, a beautiful arrangement is observed by the all-benignant Word, who first exhorts, then trains, and finally teaches.

CHAP. II. — OUR INSTRUCTOR'S TREATMENT OF OUR SINS.

Now, O you, my children, our Instructor is like His Father God, whose son He is, sinless,

---

[1] Ps. lxxiii. 1.
[2] [See *Exhortation to the Heathen*, cap. xi. p. 203, *supra*.]
[3] The pædagogus. [This word seems to be used by Clement, with frequent allusion, at least, to its original idea, of one who leads the child to his instructor; which is the true idea, I suppose, in Gal. iii. 24.]

blameless, and with a soul devoid of passion; God in the form of man, stainless, the minister of His Father's will, the Word who is God, who is in the Father, who is at the Father's right hand, and with the form of God is God. He is to us a spotless image; to Him we are to try with all our might to assimilate our souls. He is wholly free from human passions; wherefore also He alone is judge, because He alone is sinless. As far, however, as we can, let us try to sin as little as possible. For nothing is so urgent in the first place as deliverance from passions and disorders, and then the checking of our liability to fall into sins that have become habitual. It is best, therefore, not to sin at all in any way, which we assert to be the prerogative of God alone; next to keep clear of voluntary transgressions, which is characteristic of the wise man; thirdly, not to fall into many involuntary offences, which is peculiar to those who have been excellently trained. Not to continue long in sins, let that be ranked last. But this also is salutary to those who are called back to repentance, to renew the contest.

And the Instructor, as I think, very beautifully says, through Moses: "If any one die suddenly by him, straightway the head of his consecration shall be polluted, and shall be shaved,"[1] designating involuntary sin as sudden death. And He says that it pollutes the soul by defiling it: wherefore He prescribes the cure with all speed, advising the head to be instantly shaven; that is, counselling the locks of ignorance which shade the reason to be shorn clean off, that reason (whose seat is in the brain), being left bare of the dense stuff of vice, may speed its way to repentance. Then after a few remarks He adds, "The days before are not reckoned irrational,"[2] by which manifestly sins are meant which are contrary to reason. The involuntary act He calls "*sudden*," the sin He calls "irrational." Wherefore the Word, the Instructor, has taken the charge of us, in order to the prevention of sin, which is contrary to reason.

Hence consider the expression of Scripture, "Therefore these things saith the Lord;" the sin that had been committed before is held up to reprobation by the succeeding expression "therefore," according to which the righteous judgment follows. This is shown conspicuously by the prophets, when they said, "Hadst thou not sinned, He would not have uttered these threatenings." "Therefore thus saith the Lord;" "Because thou hast not heard these words, therefore these things the Lord;" and, "Therefore, behold, the Lord saith." For prophecy is given by reason both of obedience and disobedience: for obedience, that we may

be saved; for disobedience, that we may b corrected.

Our Instructor, the Word, therefore cures th unnatural passions of the soul by means of ex hortations. For with the highest propriety th help of bodily diseases is called the healing a — an art acquired by human skill. But th paternal Word is the only Pæonian physician o human infirmities, and the holy charmer of th sick soul. "Save," it is said, "Thy servant, (my God, who trusteth in Thee. Pity me, (Lord; for I will cry to Thee all the day." For a while the "physician's art," according t Democritus, "heals the diseases of the body wisdom frees the soul from passion." But th good Instructor, the Wisdom, the Word of th Father, who made man, cares for the whol nature of His creature; the all-sufficient Physi cian of humanity, the Saviour, heals both bod and soul. "Rise up," He said to the paralytic "take the bed on which thou liest, and go awa home;"[4] and straightway the infirm man re ceived strength. And to the dead He said "Lazarus, go forth;"[5] and the dead man is sued from his coffin such as he was ere he died having undergone resurrection. Further, He heals the soul itself by precepts and gifts — b precepts indeed, in course of time, but being liberal in His gifts, He says to us sinners, "Thy sins be forgiven thee."[6]

We, however, as soon as He conceived the thought, became His children, having had as signed us the best and most secure rank by His orderly arrangement, which first circles about the world, the heavens, and the sun's circuits, and occupies itself with the motions of the rest of the stars for man's behoof, and then busies itself with man himself, on whom all its care is concentrated; and regarding him as its greatest work, regulated his soul by wisdom and temperance, and tempered the body with beauty and proportion. And whatever in human actions is right and regular, is the result of the inspiration of its rectitude and order.

CHAP. III. — THE PHILANTHROPY OF THE INSTRUCTOR.

The Lord ministers all good and all help, both as man and as God: as God, forgiving our sins; and as man, training us not to sin. Man is therefore justly dear to God, since he is His workmanship. The other works of creation He made by the word of command alone, but man He framed by Himself, by His own hand, and breathed into him what was peculiar to Himself. What, then, was fashioned by Him, and after He likeness, either was created by God Himself as

---

[1] Num. vi. 9.
[2] Num. vi. 12.

[3] Ps. lxxxvi. 2, 3.
[4] Mark ii. 11.
[5] John xi. 43.
[6] Matt. ix. 2.

being desirable on its own account, or was formed as being desirable on account of something else. If, then, man is an object desirable for itself, then He who is good loved what is good, and the love-charm is within even in man, and is that very thing which is called the inspiration [or breath] of God; but if man was a desirable object on account of something else, God had no other reason for creating him, than that unless he came into being, it was not possible for God to be a good Creator, or for man to arrive at the knowledge of God. For God would not have accomplished that on account of which man was created otherwise than by the creation of man; and what hidden power in willing God possessed, He carried fully out by the forth-putting of His might externally in the act of creating, receiving from man what He made man;[1] and whom He had He saw, and what He wished that came to pass; and there is nothing which God cannot do. Man, then, whom God made, is desirable for himself, and that which is desirable on his account is allied to him to whom it is desirable on his account; and this, too, is acceptable and liked.

But what is loveable, and is not also loved by Him? And man has been proved to be loveable; consequently man is loved by God. For how shall he not be loved for whose sake the only-begotten Son is sent from the Father's bosom, the Word of faith, the faith which is superabundant; the Lord Himself distinctly confessing and saying, "For the Father Himself loveth you, because ye have loved Me;"[2] and again, "And hast loved them as Thou hast loved Me?"[3] What, then, the Master desires and declares, and how He is disposed in deed and word, how He commands what is to be done, and forbids the opposite, has already been shown.

Plainly, then, the other kind of discourse, the didactic, is powerful and spiritual, observing precision, occupied in the contemplation of mysteries. But let it stand over for the present. Now, it is incumbent on us to return His love, who lovingly guides us to that life which is best; and to live in accordance with the injunctions of His will, not only fulfilling what is commanded, or guarding against what is forbidden, but turning away from some examples, and imitating others as much as we can, and thus to perform the works of the Master according to His similitude, and so fulfil what Scripture says as to our being made in His image and likeness. For, wandering in life as in deep darkness, we need a guide that cannot stumble or stray; and our guide is the best, not blind, as the Scripture says, "leading the blind into pits."[4] But the Word is keen-sighted, and scans the recesses of the heart. As, then, that is not light which enlightens not, nor motion that moves not, nor loving which loves not, so neither is that good which profits not, nor guides to salvation. Let us then aim at the fulfilment of the commandments by the works of the Lord; for the Word Himself also, having openly become flesh,[5] exhibited the same virtue, both practical and contemplative. Wherefore let us regard the Word as law, and His commands and counsels as the short and straight paths to immortality; for His precepts are full of persuasion, not of fear.

CHAP. IV.— MEN AND WOMEN ALIKE UNDER THE INSTRUCTOR'S CHARGE.

Let us, then, embracing more and more this good obedience, give ourselves to the Lord, clinging to what is surest, the cable of faith in Him, and understanding that the virtue of man and woman is the same. For if the God of both is one, the master of both is also one; one church, one temperance, one modesty; their food is common, marriage an equal yoke; respiration, sight, hearing, knowledge, hope, obedience, love all alike. And those whose life is common, have common graces and a common salvation; common to them are love and training. "For in this world," he says, "they marry, and are given in marriage,"[6] in which alone the female is distinguished from the male; "but in that world it is so no more." There the rewards of this social and holy life, which is based on conjugal union, are laid up, not for male and female, but for man, the sexual desire which divides humanity being removed. Common therefore, too, to men and women, is the name of man. For this reason I think the Attics called, not boys only, but girls, παιδάριον, using it as a word of common gender; if Menander the comic poet, in *Rhapizomena*, appears to any one a sufficient authority, who thus speaks: —

> "My little daughter; for by nature
> The child (παιδάριον) is most loving."

Ἄρνες, too, the word for lambs, is a common name of simplicity for the male and female animal.

Now the Lord Himself will feed us as His flock forever. Amen. But without a sheperd, neither

---

1 Bishop Kaye (*Some Account of the Writings and Opinions of Clement of Alexandria*, p. 48) translates, "receiving from man that which made man (that on account of which man was made)." But it seems more likely that Clement refers to the ideal man in the divine mind, whom he identifies elsewhere with the Logos, the ἄνθρωπος παθής, of whom man was the image. The reader will notice that Clement speaks of man as existing in the divine mind before his creation, and creation is represented by God's *seeing* what He had previously within Him merely as a hidden power.

2 John xvi. 27.
3 John xvii. 23.
4 Matt. xv. 14.
5 John i. 14.
6 Luke xx. 34.

can sheep nor any other animal live, nor children without a tutor, nor domestics without a master.

CHAP. V. — ALL WHO WALK ACCORDING TO TRUTH ARE CHILDREN OF GOD.

That, then, Pædagogy is the training of children (παίδων ἀγωγή), is clear from the word itself. It remains for us to consider the children whom Scripture points to ; then to give the pædagogue charge of them. We are the children. In many ways Scripture celebrates us, and describes us in manifold figures of speech, giving variety to the simplicity of the faith by diverse names. Accordingly, in the Gospel, " the Lord, standing on the shore, says to the disciples " — they happened to be fishing — " and called aloud, Children, have ye any meat ? " [1] — addressing those that were already in the position of disciples as children. " And they brought to Him," it is said, " children, that He might put His hands on them and bless them ; and when His disciples hindered them, Jesus said, Suffer the children, and forbid them not to come to Me, for of such is the kingdom of heaven." [2] What the expression means, the Lord Himself shall declare, saying, " Except ye be converted, and become as little children, ye shall not enter into the kingdom of heaven ; " [3] not in that place speaking figuratively of regeneration, but setting before us, for our imitation, the simplicity that is in children.[4]

The prophetic spirit also distinguishes us as children. " Plucking," it is said, " branches of olives or palms, the children went forth to meet the Lord, and cried, saying, Hosanna to the Son of David ! Blessed is He that cometh in the name of the Lord ; " [5] light, and glory, and praise, with supplication to the Lord : for this is the meaning of the expression Hosanna when rendered in Greek. And the Scripture appears to me, in allusion to the prophecy just mentioned, reproachfully to upbraid the thoughtless : " Have ye never read, Out of the mouths of babes and sucklings Thou hast perfected praise ? " [6] In this way the Lord in the Gospels spurs on His disciples, urging them to attend to Him, hastening as He was to the Father ; rendering His hearers more eager by the intimation that after a little He was to depart, and showing them that it was requisite that they should take more unsparing advantage of the truth than ever before, as the Word was to ascend to heaven. Again, therefore, He calls them children ; for He says, "Children, a little while I am with you." [7] And, again, He likens the kingdom

of heaven to children sitting in the market-place and saying, " We have piped unto you, and ye have not danced ; we have mourned, and ye have not lamented ; " [8] and whatever else He added agreeably thereto. And it is not alone the Gospel that holds these sentiments. Prophecy also agrees with it. David accordingly says, "Praise, O children, the LORD ; praise the name of the LORD." [9] It says also by Esaias, " Here am I and the children that God hath given me." [10] Are you amazed, then, to hear that men who belong to the nations are sons in the Lord's sight ? You do not in that case appear to give ear to the Attic dialect, from which you may learn that beautiful, comely, and freeborn young maidens are still called παιδίσκαι, and servant-girls παιδισκάρια; and that those last also are, on account of the bloom of youth, called by the flattering name of young maidens.

And when He says, " Let my lambs stand on my right," [11] He alludes to the simple children, as if they were sheep and lambs in nature, not men ; and the lambs He counts worthy of preference, from the superior regard He has to that tenderness and simplicity of disposition in men which constitutes innocence. Again, when He says, " as suckling calves," He again alludes figuratively to us ; and " as an innocent and gentle dove," [12] the reference is again to us. Again by Moses, He commands " two young pigeons or a pair of turtles to be offered for sin ; " [13] thus saying, that the harmlessness and innocence and placable nature of these tender young birds are acceptable to God, and explaining that like is an expiation for like. Further, the timorousness of the turtle-doves typifies fear in reference to sin.

And that He calls us chickens the Scripture testifies : " As a hen gathereth her chickens under her wings." [14] Thus are we the Lord's chickens ; the Word thus marvellously and mystically describing the simplicity of childhood. For sometimes He calls us children, sometimes chickens, sometimes infants, and at other times sons, and " a new people," and " a recent people." " And my servants shall be called by a new name " [15] (a new name, He says, fresh and eternal, pure and simple, and childlike and true) which shall be blessed on the earth. And again He figuratively calls us colts unyoked to vice, not broken in by wickedness ; but simple, and bounding joyously to the Father alone ; not such horses " as neigh after their neighbours' wives,

---

[1] John xxi. 4, 5.
[2] Matt. xix. 14.
[3] Matt. xviii. 3.
[4] [The dignity ascribed to Christian childhood in this chapter is something noteworthy. The Gospel glorifying children, sanctifies marriage, and creates the home.]
[5] Matt. xxi. 9.
[6] Matt. xxi. 16; Ps. viii. 2.
[7] John xiii. 33.

[8] Matt. xi. 16, 17. [In the Peshito-Syriac version, where are probably found the very words our Saviour thus quotes from children in Nazareth, this saying is seen to be metrical and alliterative.]
[9] Ps. cxiii. 1.
[10] Isa. viii. 18.
[11] Matt. xxv. 33.
[12] Matt. x. 16.
[13] Lev. xv. 29, xii. 8; Luke ii. 24.
[14] Matt. xxiii. 37.
[15] Isa. lxv. 15, 16.

that are under the yoke, and are female-mad;"[1] but free and new-born, jubilant by means of faith, ready to run to the truth, swift to speed to salvation, that tread and stamp under foot the things of the world.

"Rejoice greatly, O daughter of Sion; tell aloud, O daughter of Jerusalem: behold, thy King cometh, just, meek, and bringing salvation; meek truly is He, and riding on a beast of burden, and a young colt."[2] It was not enough to have said colt alone, but He added to it also *young*, to show the youth of humanity in Christ, and the eternity of simplicity, which shall know no old age. And we who are little ones being such colts, are reared up by our divine colt-tamer. But if the new man in Scripture is represented by the ass, this ass is also a colt. "And he bound," it is said, "the colt to the vine," having bound this simple and childlike people to the word, whom He figuratively represents as a vine. For the vine produces wine, as the Word produces blood, and both drink for health to men — wine for the body, blood for the spirit.

And that He also calls us lambs, the Spirit by the mouth of Isaiah is an unimpeachable witness: "He will feed His flock like a shepherd, He will gather the lambs with His arm,"[3] — using the figurative appellation of lambs, which are still more tender than sheep, to express simplicity. And we also in truth, honouring the fairest and most perfect objects in life with an appellation derived from the word child, have named training παιδεία, and discipline παιδαγωγία. Discipline (παιδαγωγία) we declare to be right guiding from childhood to virtue. Accordingly, our Lord revealed more distinctly to us what is signified by the appellation of children. On the question arising among the apostles, "which of them should be the greater," Jesus placed a little child in the midst, saying, "Whosoever shall humble himself as this little child, the same shall be the greater in the kingdom of heaven."[4] He does not then use the appellation of children on account of their very limited amount of understanding from their age, as some have thought. Nor, if He says, "Except ye become as these children, ye shall not enter into the kingdom of God," are His words to be understood as meaning "without learning." We, then, who are infants, no longer roll on the ground, nor creep on the earth like serpents as before, crawling with the whole body about senseless lusts; but, stretching upwards in soul, loosed from the world and our sins, touching the earth on tiptoe so as to appear to be in the world, we pursue holy wisdom, although this seems folly to those whose wits are whetted for wickedness. Rightly, then, are those called children who know Him who is God alone as their Father, who are simple, and infants, and guileless, who are lovers of the horns of the unicorns.[5]

To those, therefore, that have made progress in the word, He has proclaimed this utterance, bidding them dismiss anxious care of the things of this world, and exhorting them to adhere to the Father alone, in imitation of children. Wherefore also in what follows He says: "Take no anxious thought for the morrow; sufficient unto the day is the evil thereof."[6] Thus He enjoins them to lay aside the cares of this life, and depend on the Father alone. And he who fulfils this commandment is in reality a child and a son to God and to the world, — to the one as deceived, to the other as beloved. And if we have one Master in heaven, as the Scripture says, then by common consent those on the earth will be rightly called disciples. For so is the truth, that perfection is with the Lord, who is always teaching, and infancy and childishness with us, who are always learning. Thus prophecy hath honoured *perfection*, by applying to it the appellation *man*. For instance, by David, He says of the devil: "The LORD abhors the man of blood;"[7] he calls him man, as perfect in wickedness. And the Lord is called man, because He is perfect in righteousness. Directly in point is the instance of the apostle, who says, writing the Corinthians: "For I have espoused you to one man, that I may present you as a chaste virgin to Christ,"[8] whether as children or saints, but to the Lord alone. And writing to the Ephesians, he has unfolded in the clearest manner the point in question, speaking to the following effect: "Till we all attain to the unity of the faith, and of the knowledge of God, to a perfect man, to the measure of the stature of the fulness of Christ: that we be no longer children, tossed to and fro by every wind of doctrine, by the craft of men, by their cunning in stratagems of deceit; but, speaking the truth in love, may grow up to Him in all things,"[9] — saying these things in order to the edification of the body of Christ, who is the head and man, the only one perfect in righteousness; and we who are children guarding against the blasts of heresies, which blow to our inflation; and not putting our trust in fathers who teach us otherwise, are then made perfect when we are the church, having received Christ the head. Then it is right to notice, with respect to the appellation of infant (νήπιος), that

---

[5] Theodoret explains this to mean that, as the animal referred to has only one horn, so those brought up in the practice of piety worship only one God. [It might mean lovers of those promises which are introduced by these words in the marvellous twenty-second Psalm.]
[6] Matt. vi. 34.
[7] Ps. v. 6.
[8] 2 Cor. xi. 2.
[9] Eph. iv. 13-15.

[1] Jer. v. 8.
[2] Zech. ix. 9; Gen. xlix. 11.
[3] Isa. xl. 11.
[4] Matt. xviii. 4.

τὸ νήπιον is not predicated of the silly : for the silly man is called νηπύτιος : and νήπιος is νεήπιος (since he that is tender-hearted is called ἤπιος), as being one that has newly become gentle and meek in conduct. This the blessed Paul most clearly pointed out when he said, "When we might have been burdensome as the apostles of Christ, we were gentle (ἤπιοι) among you, as a nurse cherisheth her children."[1] The child (νήπιος) is therefore gentle (ἤπιος), and therefore more tender, delicate, and simple, guileless, and destitute of hypocrisy, straightforward and upright in mind, which is the basis of simplicity and truth. For He says, "Upon whom shall I look, but upon him who is gentle and quiet?"[2] For such is the virgin speech, tender, and free of fraud ; whence also a virgin is wont to be called "a tender bride," and a child "tender-hearted." And we are tender who are pliant to the power of persuasion, and are easily drawn to goodness, and are mild, and free of the stain of malice and perverseness, for the ancient race was perverse and hard-hearted ; but the band of infants, the new people which we are, is delicate as a child. On account of the hearts of the innocent, the apostle, in the Epistle to the Romans, owns that he rejoices, and furnishes a kind of definition of children, so to speak, when he says, "I would have you wise toward good, but simple towards evil."[3] For the name of child, νήπιος, is not understood by us privatively, though the sons of the grammarians make the νη a privative particle. For if they call us who follow after childhood foolish, see how they utter blasphemy against the Lord, in regarding those as foolish who have betaken themselves to God. But if, which is rather the true sense, they themselves understand the designation children of simple ones, we glory in the name. For the new minds, which have newly become wise, which have sprung into being according to the new covenant, are infantile in the old folly. Of late, then, God was known by the coming of Christ : "For no man knoweth God but the Son, and he to whom the Son shall reveal Him."[4]

In contradistinction, therefore, to the older people, the new people are called young, having learned the new blessings ; and we have the exuberance of life's morning prime in this youth which knows no old age, in which we are always growing to maturity in intelligence, are always young, always mild, always new : for those must necessarily be new, who have become partakers of the new Word. And that which participates in eternity is wont to be assimilated to the incorruptible : so that to us appertains the designation of the age of childhood, a lifelong spring-time, because the truth that is in us, and our habits saturated with the truth, cannot be touched by old age ; but Wisdom is ever blooming, ever remains consistent and the same, and never changes. "Their children," it is said, "shall be borne upon their shoulders, and fondled on their knees ; as one whom his mother comforteth, so also shall I comfort you."[5] The mother draws the children to herself ; and we seek our mother the Church. Whatever is feeble and tender, as needing help on account of its feebleness, is kindly looked on, and is sweet and pleasant, anger changing into help in the case of such : for thus horses' colts, and the little calves of cows, and the lion's whelp, and the stag's fawn, and the child of man, are looked upon with pleasure by their fathers and mothers. Thus also the Father of the universe cherishes affection towards those who have fled to Him ; and having begotten them again by His Spirit to the adoption of children, knows them as gentle, and loves those alone, and aids and fights for them ; and therefore He bestows on them the name of child. The word Isaac I also connect with child. Isaac means laughter. He was seen sporting with his wife and helpmeet Rebecca by the prying king.[6] The king, whose name was Abimelech, appears to me to represent a supramundane wisdom contemplating the mystery of sport. They interpret Rebecca to mean endurance. O wise sport, laughter also assisted by endurance, and the king as spectator ! The spirit of those that are children in Christ, whose lives are ordered in endurance, rejoice. And this is the divine sport. "Such a sport, of his own, Jove sports," says Heraclitus. For what other employment is seemly for a wise and perfect man, than to sport and be glad in the endurance of what is good — and, in the administration of what is good, holding festival with God? That which is signified by the prophet may be interpreted differently, — namely, of our rejoicing for salvation, as Isaac. He also, delivered from death, laughed, sporting and rejoicing with his spouse, who was the type of the Helper of our salvation, the Church, to whom the stable name of endurance is given ; for this cause surely, because she alone remains to all generations, rejoicing ever, subsisting as she does by the endurance of us believers, who are the members of Christ. And the witness of those that have endured to the end, and the rejoicing on their account, is the mystic sport, and the salvation accompanied with decorous solace which brings us aid.

---

[1] 1 Thess. ii. 6, 7.
[2] Isa. lxvi. 2.
[3] Rom. xvi. 19.
[4] Matt. xi. 27: Luke x. 22.

[5] Isa. lxvi. 12, 13.
[6] Gen. xxvi. 8.

The King, then, who is Christ, beholds from above our laughter, and looking through the window, as the Scripture says, views the thanksgiving, and the blessing, and the rejoicing, and the gladness, and furthermore the endurance which works together with them and their embrace : views His Church, showing only His face, which was wanting to the Church, which is made perfect by her royal Head. And where, then, was the door by which the Lord showed Himself? The flesh by which He was manifested. He is Isaac (for the narrative may be interpreted otherwise), who is a type of the Lord, a child as a son ; for he was the son of Abraham, as Christ the Son of God, and a sacrifice as the Lord, but he was not immolated as the Lord. Isaac only bore the wood of the sacrifice, as the Lord the wood of the cross. And he laughed mystically, prophesying that the Lord should fill us with joy, who have been redeemed from corruption by the blood of the Lord. Isaac did everything but suffer, as was right, yielding the precedence in suffering to the Word. Furthermore, there is an intimation of the divinity of the Lord in His not being slain. For Jesus rose again after His burial, having suffered no harm, like Isaac released from sacrifice. And in defence of the point to be established, I shall adduce another consideration of the greatest ·weight. The Spirit calls the Lord Himself a child, thus prophesying by Esaias : " Lo, to us a child has been born, to us a son has been given, on whose own shoulder the government shall be ; and His name has been called the Angel of great Counsel." Who, then, is this infant child? He according to whose image we are made little children. By the same prophet is declared His greatness : "Wonderful, Counsellor, Mighty God, Everlasting Father, Prince of Peace ; that He might fulfil His discipline : and of His peace there shall be no end." [1]　O the great God ! O the perfect child ! The Son in the Father, and the Father in the Son. And how shall not the discipline of this child be perfect, which extends to all, leading as a schoolmaster us as children, who are His little ones? He has stretched forth to us those hands of His that are conspicuously worthy of trust. To this child additional testimony is borne by John, " the greatest prophet among those born of women : " [2]　" Behold the Lamb of God ! " [3]　For since Scripture calls the infant children lambs, it has also called Him — God the Word — who became man for our sakes, and who wished in all points to be made like to us — " the Lamb of God " — Him, namely, that is the Son of God, the child of the Father.

CHAP. VI. — THE NAME CHILDREN DOES NOT IMPLY INSTRUCTION IN ELEMENTARY PRINCIPLES.

We have ample means of encountering those who are given to carping. For we are not termed children and infants with reference to the childish and contemptible character of our education, as those who are inflated on account of knowledge have calumniously alleged. Straightway, on our regeneration, we attained that perfection after which we aspired. For we were illuminated, which is to know God. He is not then imperfect who knows what is perfect. And do not reprehend me when I profess to know God ; for so it was deemed right to speak to the Word, and He is free.[4] For at the moment of the Lord's baptism there sounded a voice from heaven, as a testimony to the Beloved, " Thou art My beloved Son, to-day have I begotten Thee." Let us then ask the wise, Is Christ, begotten to-day, already perfect, or — what were most monstrous — imperfect? If the latter, there is some addition He requires yet to make. But for Him to make any addition to His knowledge is absurd, since He is God. For none can be superior to the Word, or the teacher of the only Teacher. Will they not then own, though reluctant, that the perfect Word born of the perfect Father was begotten in perfection, according to œconomic fore-ordination? And if He was perfect, why was He, the perfect one, baptized? It was necessary, they say, to fulfil the profession that pertained to humanity. Most excellent. Well, I assert, simultaneously with His baptism by John, He becomes perfect? Manifestly. He did not then learn anything more from him? Certainly not. But He is perfected by the washing — of baptism — alone, and is sanctified by the descent of the Spirit? Such is the case. The same also takes place in our case, whose exemplar Christ became. Being baptized, we are illuminated ; illuminated, we become sons ; being made sons, we are made perfect ; being made perfect, we are made immortal. " I," says He, " have said that ye are gods, and all sons of the Highest." [5]　This work is variously called grace,[6] and illumination, and perfection, and washing : washing, by which we cleanse away our sins ; grace, by which the penalties accruing to transgressions are remitted ; and illumination, by which that holy light of salvation is beheld, that is, by which we see God clearly. Now we call that perfect which wants nothing. For what is yet wanting to him who knows God? For it were truly monstrous that that which is not complete should be called a gift (or act) of God's grace. Being perfect, He consequently bestows perfect gifts. As at

---

[1] Isa. ix. 6.
[2] Luke vii. 28.
[3] John i. 29, 36.

[4] In allusion apparently to John viii. 35, 36.
[5] Ps. lxxxii. 6.
[6] χάρισμα.

His command all things were made, so on His bare wishing to bestow grace, ensues the perfecting of His grace. For the future of time is anticipated by the power of His volition.

Further release from evils is the beginning of salvation. We then alone, who first have touched the confines of life, are already perfect; and we already live who are separated from death. Salvation, accordingly, is the following of Christ: "For that which is in Him is life." [1] "Verily, verily, I say unto you, He that heareth My words, and believeth on Him that sent Me, hath eternal life, and cometh not into condemnation, but hath passed from death to life." [2] Thus believing alone, and regeneration, is perfection in life; for God is never weak. For as His will is work, and this [3] is named the world; so also His counsel is the salvation of men, and this has been called the church. He knows, therefore, whom He has called, and whom He has saved; and at one and the same time He called and saved them. "For ye are," says the apostle, "taught of God." [4] It is not then allowable to think of what is taught by Him as imperfect; and what is learned from Him is the eternal salvation of the eternal Saviour, to whom be thanks for ever and ever. Amen. And he who is only regenerated — as the name necessarily indicates — and is enlightened, is delivered forthwith from darkness, and on the instant receives the light.

As, then, those who have shaken off sleep forthwith become all awake within; or rather, as those who try to remove a film that is over the eyes, do not supply to them from without the light which they do not possess, but removing the obstacle from the eyes, leave the pupil free; thus also we who are baptized, having wiped off the sins which obscure the light of the Divine Spirit, have the eye of the spirit free, unimpeded, and full of light, by which alone we contemplate the Divine, the Holy Spirit flowing down to us from above. This is the eternal adjustment of the vision, which is able to see the eternal light, since like loves like; and that which is holy, loves that from which holiness proceeds, which has appropriately been termed light. "Once ye were darkness, now are ye light in the Lord." [5] Hence I am of opinion man was called by the ancients φώς.[6] But he has not yet received, say they, the perfect gift. I also assent to this; but he is in the light, and the darkness comprehendeth him not. There is nothing intermediate between light and darkness. But the end is reserved till the resurrection of those who believe; and it is not the reception of some other thing, but the obtaining of the promise previously made. For we do not say that both take place together at the same time — both the arrival at the end, and the anticipation of that arrival. For eternity and time are not the same, neither is the attempt and the final result; but both have reference to the same thing, and one and the same person is concerned in both. Faith, so to speak, is the attempt generated in time; the final result is the attainment of the promise, secured for eternity. Now the Lord Himself has most clearly revealed the equality of salvation, when He said: "For this is the will of my Father, that every one that seeth the Son, and believeth on Him, should have everlasting life; and I will raise him up in the last day." [7] As far as possible in this world, which is what he means by the last day, and which is preserved till the time that it shall end, we believe that we are made perfect. Wherefore He says, "He that believeth on the Son hath everlasting life." [8] If, then, those who have believed have life, what remains beyond the possession of eternal life? Nothing is wanting to faith, as it is perfect and complete in itself. If aught is wanting to it, it is not wholly perfect. But faith is not lame in any respect; nor after our departure from this world does it make us who have believed, and received without distinction the earnest of future good, wait; but having in anticipation grasped by faith that which is future, after the resurrection we receive it as present, in order that that may be fulfilled which was spoken, "Be it according to thy faith." [9] And where faith is, there is the promise; and the consummation of the promise is rest. So that in illumination what we receive is knowledge, and the end of knowledge is rest — the last thing conceived as the object of aspiration. As, then, inexperience comes to an end by experience, and perplexity by finding a clear outlet, so by illumination must darkness disappear. The darkness is ignorance, through which we fall into sins, purblind as to the truth. Knowledge, then, is the illumination we receive, which makes ignorance disappear, and endows us with clear vision. Further, the abandonment of what is bad is the adopting [10] of what is better. For what ignorance has bound ill, is by knowledge loosed well; those bonds are with all speed slackened by human faith and divine grace, our transgressions being taken away by one Pœonian [11] medicine, the baptism of the Word. We are washed from all our sins, and are no longer entangled in evil. This is the one grace of illu-

---

[1] John i. 4.
[2] John v. 24.
[3] viz., the result of His will.
[4] 1 Thess. iv. 9.
[5] Eph. v. 8.
[6] φώς, light; φώς, a man.

[7] John vi. 40.
[8] John iii. 36.
[9] Matt. ix. 29.
[10] Migne's text has ἀποκάλυψις. The emendation ἀπόληψις is preferable.
[11] [*Iliad*, v. 401.]

nination, that our characters are not the same as before our washing. And since knowledge springs up with illumination, shedding its beams around the mind, the moment we hear, we who were untaught become disciples. Does this, I ask, take place on the advent of this instruction? You cannot tell the time. For instruction leads to faith, and faith with baptism is trained by the Holy Spirit. For that faith is the one universal salvation of humanity, and that there is the same equality before the righteous and loving God, and the same fellowship between Him and all, the apostle most clearly showed, speaking to the following effect: "Before faith came, we were kept under the law, shut up unto the faith which should afterwards be revealed, so that the law became our schoolmaster to bring us to Christ, that we might be justified by faith; but after that faith is come, we are no longer under a schoolmaster." [1] Do you not hear that we are no longer under that law which was accompanied with fear, but under the Word, the master of free choice? Then he subjoined the utterance, clear of all partiality: "For ye are all the children of God through faith in Christ Jesus. For as many as were baptized into Christ have put on Christ. There is neither Jew nor Greek, there is neither bond nor free, there is neither male nor female: for ye are all one in Christ Jesus." [2] There are not, then, in the same Word some "illuminated (gnostics); and some animal (or natural) men;" but all who have abandoned the desires of the flesh are equal and spiritual before the Lord. And again he writes in another place: "For by one spirit are we all baptized into one body, whether Jews or Greeks, whether bond or free, and we have all drunk of one cup." [3] Nor were it absurd to employ the expressions of those who call the reminiscence of better things the filtration of the spirit, understanding by filtration the separation of what is baser, that results from the reminiscence of what is better. There follows of necessity, in him who has come to the recollection of what is better, repentance for what is worse. Accordingly, they confess that the spirit in repentance retraces its steps. In the same way, therefore, we also, repenting of our sins, renouncing our iniquities, purified by baptism, speed back to the eternal light, children to the Father. Jesus therefore, rejoicing in the spirit, said: "I thank Thee, O Father, God of heaven and earth, that Thou hast hid these things from the wise and prudent, and hast revealed them to babes;" [4] the Master and Teacher applying the name babes to us, who are readier to embrace salvation than the wise in the world, who, thinking themselves wise, are inflated with pride. And He exclaims in exultation and exceeding joy, as if lisping with the children, "Even so, Father; for so it seemed good in Thy sight." [5] Wherefore those things which have been concealed from the wise and prudent of this present world have been revealed to babes. Truly, then, are we the children of God, who have put aside the old man, and stripped off the garment of wickedness, and put on the immortality of Christ; that we may become a new, holy people by regeneration, and may keep the man undefiled. And a babe, as God's little one, [6] is cleansed from fornication and wickedness. With the greatest clearness the blessed Paul has solved for us this question in his First Epistle to the Corinthians, writing thus: "Brethren, be not children in understanding; howbeit in malice be children, but in understanding be men." [7] And the expression, "When I was a child, I thought as a child, I spake as a child," [8] points out his mode of life according to the law, according to which, thinking childish things, he persecuted, and speaking childish things he blasphemed the Word, not as having yet attained to the simplicity of childhood, but as being in its folly; for the word νήπιον has two meanings. [9] "When I became a man," again Paul says, "I put away childish things." [10] It is not incomplete size of stature, nor a definite measure of time, nor additional secret teachings in things that are manly and more perfect, that the apostle, who himself professes to be a preacher of childishness, alludes to when he sends it, as it were, into banishment; but he applies the name "children" to those who are under the law, who are terrified by fear as children are by bugbears; and "men" to us who are obedient to the Word and masters of ourselves, who have believed, and are saved by voluntary choice, and are rationally, not irrationally, frightened by terror. Of this the apostle himself shall testify, calling as he does the Jews heirs according to the first covenant, and us heirs according to promise: "*Now I say, as long as the heir is a child, he differeth nothing from a servant, though he be lord of all; but is under tutors and governors, till the time appointed by the father. So also we, when we were children, were in bondage under the rudiments of the world: but when the fulness of the time was come, God sent forth His Son, made of a woman, made under the law, to*

---

[1] Gal. iii. 23-25. [Here the *schoolmaster* should be the *child-guide*; for the law leads us to the Master, says Clement, and we are no longer under the disciplinary guide, but " under the Word, the master of our free choice." The schoolmaster then is the Word, and the law merely led us to his school.]

[2] Gal. iii. 26-28.

[3] 1 Cor. xii. 13.

[4] Luke x. 21.

[5] Luke x. 21.

[6] [Clement here considers all believers as babes, in the sense he explains; but the tenderness towards children of the allusions running through this chapter are not the less striking.]

[7] 1 Cor. xiv. 20.

[8] 1 Cor. xiii. 11. [A text much misused by the heretical gnostics whom Clement confutes.]

[9] viz., simple or innocent as a child, and *foolish* as a child.

[10] 1 Cor. xiii. 11.

redeem them that were under the law, that we might receive the adoption of sons"[1] by Him. See how He has admitted those to be children who are under fear and sins; but has conferred manhood on those who are under faith, by calling them sons, in contradistinction from the children that are under the law: "For thou art no more a servant," he says, "but a son; and if a son, then an heir through God."[2] What, then, is lacking to the son after inheritance? Wherefore the expression, "When I was a child," may be elegantly expounded thus: that is, when I was a Jew (for he was a Hebrew by extraction) I thought as a child, when I followed the law; but after becoming a man, I no longer entertain the sentiments of a child, that is, of the law, but of a man, that is, of Christ, whom alone the Scripture calls man, as we have said before. "I put away childish things." But the childhood which is in Christ is maturity, as compared with the law. Having reached this point, we must defend our childhood. And we have still to explain what is said by the apostle: "I have fed you with milk (as children in Christ), not with meat; for ye were not able, neither yet are ye now able."[3] For it does not appear to me that the expression is to be taken in a Jewish sense; for I shall oppose to it also that Scripture, "I will bring you into that good land which flows with milk and honey."[4] A very great difficulty arises in reference to the comparison of these Scriptures, when we consider. For if the infancy which is characterized by the milk is the beginning of faith in Christ, then it is disparaged as childish and imperfect. How is the rest that comes after the meat, the rest of the man who is perfect and endowed with knowledge, again distinguished by infant milk? Does not this, as explaining a parable, mean something like this, and is not the expression to be read somewhat to the following effect: "*I have fed you with milk in Christ;*" and after a slight stop, let us add, "as children," that by separating the words in reading we may make out some such sense as this: I have instructed you in Christ with simple, true, and natural nourishment, — namely, that which is spiritual: for such is the nourishing substance of milk swelling out from breasts of love. So that the whole matter may be conceived thus: As nurses nourish new-born children on milk, so do I also by the Word, the milk of Christ, instilling into you spiritual nutriment.

Thus, then, the milk which is perfect is perfect nourishment, and brings to that consummation which cannot cease. Wherefore also the same milk and honey were promised in the rest.

Rightly, therefore, the Lord again promises milk to the righteous, that the Word may be clearly shown to be both, "the Alpha and Omega, beginning and end;"[5] the Word being figuratively represented as milk. Something like this Homer oracularly declares against his will, when he calls righteous men milk-fed ($\gamma\alpha\lambda\alpha\kappa\tauο\phi\acute{\alpha}\gammaο\iota$).[6] So also may we take the Scripture: "And I, brethren, could not speak unto you as unto spiritual, but as unto carnal, even as unto babes in Christ;"[7] so that the carnal may be understood as those recently instructed, and still babes in Christ. For he called those who had already believed on the Holy Spirit spiritual, and those newly instructed and not yet purified carnal; whom with justice he calls still carnal, as minding equally with the heathen the things of the flesh: "For whereas there is among you envy and strife, are ye not carnal, and walk as men?"[8] "Wherefore also I have given you milk to drink," he says; meaning, I have instilled into you the knowledge which, from instruction, nourishes up to life eternal. But the expression, "I have given you to drink" ($\grave{ε}\pi\acute{ο}\tau\iota\sigma\alpha$), is the symbol of perfect appropriation. For those who are full-grown are said to drink, babes to suck. "For my blood," says the Lord, "is true drink."[9] In saying, therefore, "I have given you milk to drink," has he not indicated the knowledge of the truth, the perfect gladness in the Word, who is the milk? And what follows next, "not meat, for ye were not able," may indicate the clear revelation in the future world, like food, face to face. "For now we see as through a glass," the same apostle says, "but then face to face."[10] Wherefore also he has added, "neither yet are ye now able, for ye are still carnal," minding the things of the flesh, — desiring, loving, feeling jealousy, wrath, envy. "For we are no more in the flesh,"[11] as some suppose. For with it [they say], having the face which is like an angel's, we shall see the promise face to face. How then, if that is truly the promise after our departure hence, say they that they know "what eye hath not known, nor hath entered into the mind of man," who have not perceived by the Spirit, but received from instruction "what ear hath not heard,"[12] or that ear alone which "was rapt up into the third heaven?"[13] But it even then was commanded to preserve it unspoken.

But if human wisdom, as it remains to understand, is the glorying in knowledge, hear the law

---

[1] Gal. iv. 1–5.
[2] Gal. iv. 7.
[3] 1 Cor. iii. 2.
[4] Ex. iii. 8.

[5] Rev. i. 8.
[6] [*Iliad,* xiii. 6. S.]
[7] 1 Cor. iii. 1.
[8] 1 Cor. iii. 3.
[9] John vi. 55.
[10] 1 Cor. xiii. 12.
[11] Rom. viii. 9.
[12] Cor. ii. 9.
[13] Cor. xii. 2–4.

of Scripture : " Let not the wise man glory in his wisdom, and let not the mighty man glory in his might ; but let him that glorieth glory in the Lord." [1] But we are God-taught, and glory in the name of Christ. How then are we not to regard the apostle as attaching this sense to the milk of the babes? And if we who preside over the Churches are shepherds after the image of the good Shepherd, and you the sheep, are we not to regard the Lord as preserving consistency in the use of figurative speech, when He speaks also of the milk of the flock? And to this meaning we may secondly accommodate the expression, " I have given you milk to drink, and not given you food, for ye are not yet able," regarding the meat not as something different from the milk, but the same in substance. For the very same Word is fluid and mild as milk, or solid and compact as meat. And entertaining this view, we may regard the proclamation of the Gospel, which is universally diffused, as milk ; and as meat, faith, which from instruction is compacted into a foundation, which, being more substantial than hearing, is likened to meat, and assimilates to the soul itself nourishment of this kind. Elsewhere the Lord, in the Gospel according to John, brought this out by symbols, when He said : " Eat ye my flesh, and drink my blood ; " [2] describing distinctly by metaphor the drinkable properties of faith and the promise, by means of which the Church, like a human being consisting of many members, is refreshed and grows, is welded together and compacted of both, — of faith, which is the body, and of hope, which is the soul ; as also the Lord of flesh and blood. For in reality the blood of faith is hope, in which faith is held as by a vital principle. And when hope expires, it is as if blood flowed forth ; and the vitality of faith is destroyed. If, then, some would oppose, saying that by milk is meant the first lessons — as it were, the first food — and that by meat is meant those spiritual cognitions to which they attain by raising themselves to knowledge, let them understand that, in saying that meat is solid food, and the flesh and blood of Jesus, they are brought by their own vainglorious wisdom to the true simplicity. For the blood is found to be an original product in man, and some have consequently ventured to call it the substance of the soul. And this blood, transmuted by a natural process of assimilation in the pregnancy of the mother, through the sympathy of parental affection, effloresces and grows old, in order that there may be no fear for the child. Blood, too, is the moister part of flesh, being a kind of liquid flesh ; and milk is the sweeter and finer part of blood. For whether it be the blood supplied to the fœtus,

and sent through the navel of the mother, or whether it be the menses themselves shut out from their proper passage, and by a natural diffusion, bidden by the all-nourishing and creating God, proceed to the already swelling breasts, and by the heat of the spirits transmuted, [whether it be the one or the other] that is formed into food desirable for the babe, that which is changed is the blood. For of all the members, the breasts have the most sympathy with the womb. When there is parturition, the vessel by which blood was conveyed to the fœtus is cut off : there is an obstruction of the flow, and the blood receives an impulse towards the breasts ; and on a considerable rush taking place, they are distended, and change the blood to milk in a manner analogous to the change of blood into pus in ulceration. Or if, on the other hand, the blood from the veins in the vicinity of the breasts, which have been opened in pregnancy, is poured into the natural hollows of the breasts ; and the spirit discharged from the neighbouring arteries being mixed with it, the substance of the blood, still remaining pure, it becomes white by being agitated like a wave ; and by an interruption such as this is changed by frothing it, like what takes place with the sea, which at the assaults of the winds, the poets say, " spits forth briny foam." Yet still the essence is supplied by the blood.

In this way also the rivers, borne on with rushing motion, and fretted by contact with the surrounding air, murmur forth foam. The moisture in our mouth, too, is whitened by the breath. What an absurdity [3] is it, then, not to acknowledge that the blood is converted into that very bright and white substance by the breath ! The change it suffers is in quality, not in essence. You will certainly find nothing else more nourishing, or sweeter, or whiter than milk. In every respect, accordingly, it is like spiritual nourishment, which is sweet through grace, nourishing as life, bright as the day of Christ.

The blood of the Word has been also exhibited as milk. Milk being thus provided in parturition, is supplied to the infant ; and the breasts, which till then looked straight towards the husband, now bend down towards the child, being taught to furnish the substance elaborated by nature in a way easily received for salutary nourishment. For the breasts are not like fountains full of milk, flowing in ready prepared ; but, by effecting a change in the nutriment, form the milk in themselves, and discharge it. And the nutriment suitable and wholesome for the new-formed and new-born babe is elaborated by God, the nourisher and the Father of all that are generated and regenerated, — as manna, the celestial food of

---

[1] Jer. ix. 23; 1 Cor. i. 31; 2 Cor. x. 17.
[2] John vi. 34.

[3] The emendation ἀπολήρησις is adopted instead of the reading in the text.

angels, flowed down from heaven on the ancient Hebrews. Even now, in fact, nurses call the first-poured drink of milk by the same name as that food — manna. Further, pregnant women, on becoming mothers, discharge milk. But the Lord Christ, the fruit of the Virgin, did not pronounce the breasts of women blessed, nor selected them to give nourishment; but when the kind and loving Father had rained down the Word, Himself became spiritual nourishment to the good. O mystic marvel! The universal Father is one, and one the universal Word; and the Holy Spirit is one and the same everywhere, and one is the only virgin mother. I love to call her the Church. This mother, when alone, had not milk, because alone she was not a woman. But she is once virgin and mother — pure as a virgin, loving as a mother. And calling her children to her, she nurses them with holy milk, viz., with the Word for childhood. Therefore she had not milk; for the milk was this child fair and comely, the body of Christ, which nourishes by the Word the young brood, which the Lord Himself brought forth in throes of the flesh, which the Lord Himself swathed in His precious blood. O amazing birth! O holy swaddling bands! The Word is all to the child, both father and mother, and tutor and nurse. "Eat ye my flesh," He says, "and drink my blood." [1] Such is the suitable food which the Lord ministers, and He offers His flesh and pours forth His blood, and nothing is wanting for the children's growth. O amazing mystery! We are enjoined to cast off the old and carnal corruption, as also the old nutriment, receiving in exchange another new regimen, that of Christ, receiving Him if we can, to hide Him within; and that, enshrining the Saviour in our souls, we may correct the affections of our flesh.

But you are not inclined to understand it thus, but perchance more generally. Hear it also in the following way. The flesh figuratively represents to us the Holy Spirit; for the flesh was created by Him. The blood points out to us the Word, for as rich blood the Word has been infused into life; and the union of both is the Lord, the food of the babes — the Lord who is Spirit and Word. The food — that is, the Lord Jesus — that is, the Word of God, the Spirit made flesh, the heavenly flesh sanctified. The nutriment is the milk of the Father, by which alone we infants are nourished. The Word Himself, then, the beloved One, and our nourisher, hath shed His own blood for us, to save humanity; and by Him, we, believing on God, flee to the Word, "the care-soothing breast" of the Father. And He alone, as is befitting, supplies us children with the milk of love, and those only

are truly blessed who suck this breast. Wherefore also Peter says: "Laying therefore aside all malice, and all guile, and hypocrisy, and envy, and evil speaking, as new-born babes, desire the milk of the word, that ye may grow by it to salvation; if ye have tasted that the Lord is Christ." [2] And were one to concede to them that the meat was something different from the milk, then how shall they avoid being transfixed on their own spit, through want of consideration of nature? [3] For in winter, when the air is condensed, and prevents the escape of the heat enclosed within, the food, transmuted and digested and changed into blood, passes into the veins, and these, in the absence of exhalation, are greatly distended, and exhibit strong pulsations; consequently also nurses are then fullest of milk. And we have shown a little above, that on pregnancy blood passes into milk by a change which does not affect its substance, just as in old people yellow hair changes to grey. But again in summer, the body, having its pores more open, affords greater facility for diaphoretic action in the case of the food, and the milk is least abundant, since neither is the blood full, nor is the whole nutriment retained. If, then, the digestion of the food results in the production of blood, and the blood becomes milk, then blood is a preparation for milk, as blood is for a human being, and the grape for the vine. With milk, then, the Lord's nutriment, we are nursed directly we are born; and as soon as we are regenerated, we are honoured by receiving the good news of the hope of rest, even the Jerusalem above, in which it is written that milk and honey fall in showers, receiving through what is material the pledge of the sacred food. "For meats are done away with," [4] as the apostle himself says; but this nourishment on milk leads to the heavens, rearing up citizens of heaven, and members of the angelic choirs. And since the Word is the gushing fountain of life, and has been called a river of olive oil, Paul, using appropriate figurative language, and calling Him milk, adds: "I have given you to drink;" [5] for we drink in the word, the nutriment of the truth. In truth, also liquid food is called drink; and the same thing may somehow be both meat and drink, according to the different aspects in which it is considered, just as cheese is the solidification of milk or milk solidified; for I am not concerned here to make a nice selection of an expression, only to say that one substance supplies both articles of food. Besides, for children at the breast, milk alone suffices; it serves both for meat and drink. "I,"

---

[1] John vi. 53, 54.

[2] 1 Pet. ii. 1-3. Clement here reads Χριστός, *Christ*, for χρηστός, *gracious*, in Text. Rec.
[3] [Clement here argues from what was scientific in his day, introducing a curious, but to us not very pertinent, episode.]
[4] 1 Cor. vi. 13.
[5] 1 Cor. iii. 2.

says the Lord, "have meat to eat that ye know not of. My meat is to do the will of Him that sent Me." [1] You see another kind of food which, similarly with milk, represents figuratively the will of God. Besides, also, the completion of His own passion He called catachrestically " a cup," [2] when He alone had to drink and drain it. Thus to Christ the fulfilling of His Father's will was food ; and to us infants, who drink the milk of the word of the heavens, Christ Himself is food. Hence seeking is called sucking ; for to those babes that seek the Word, the Father's breasts of love supply milk.

Further, the Word declares Himself to be the bread of heaven. " For Moses," He says, " gave you not that bread from heaven, but My Father giveth you the true bread from heaven. For the bread of God is He that cometh down from heaven, and giveth life to the world. And the bread which I will give is My flesh, which I will give for the life of the world." [3] Here is to be noted the mystery of the bread, inasmuch as He speaks of it as flesh, and as flesh, consequently, that has risen through fire, as the wheat springs up from decay and germination ; and, in truth, it has risen through fire for the joy of the Church, as bread baked. But this will be shown by and by more clearly in the chapter on the resurrection. But since He said, " And the bread which I will give is My flesh," and since flesh is moistened with blood, and blood is figuratively termed wine, we are bidden to know that, as bread, crumbled into a mixture of wine and water, seizes on the wine and leaves the watery portion, so also the flesh of Christ, the bread of heaven, absorbs the blood ; that is, those among men who are heavenly, nourishing them up to immortality, and leaving only to destruction the lusts of the flesh.

Thus in many ways the Word is figuratively described, as meat, and flesh, and food, and bread, and blood, and milk. The Lord is all these, to give enjoyment to us who have believed on Him. Let no one then think it strange, when we say that the Lord's blood is figuratively represented as milk. For is it not figuratively represented as wine ? " Who washes," it is said, " His garment in wine, His robe in the blood of the grape." [4] In His own Spirit He says He will deck the body of the Word ; as certainly by His own Spirit He will nourish those who hunger for the Word.

And that the blood is the Word, is testified by the blood of Abel,[5] the righteous interceding with God. For the blood would never have uttered a voice, had it not been regarded as the

Word : for the righteous man of old is the type of the new righteous one ; and the blood of old that interceded, intercedes in the place of the new blood. And the blood that is the Word cries to God, since it intimated that the Word was to suffer.

Further, this flesh, and the blood in it, are by a mutual sympathy moistened and increased by the milk. And the process of formation of the seed in conception ensues when it has mingled with the pure residue of the menses, which remains. For the force that is in the seed coagulating the substances of the blood, as the rennet curdles milk, effects the essential part of the formative process. For a suitable blending conduces to fruitfulness ; but extremes are adverse, and tend to sterility. For when the earth itself is flooded by excessive rain, the seed is swept away, while in consequence of scarcity it is dried up ; but when the sap is viscous, it retains the seed, and makes it germinate. Some also hold the hypothesis, that the seed of an animal is in substance the foam of the blood, which being by the natural heat of the male agitated and shaken out is turned into foam, and deposited in the seminal veins. For Diogenes Apollionates will have it, that hence is derived the word *aphrodisia*.[6]

From all this it is therefore evident, that the essential principle of the human body is blood. The contents of the stomach, too, at first are milky, a coagulation of fluid ; then the same coagulated substance is changed into blood ; but when it is formed into a compact consistency in the womb, by the natural and warm spirit by which the embryo is fashioned, it becomes a living creature. Further also, the child after birth is nourished by the same blood. For the flow of milk is the product of the blood ; and the source of nourishment is the milk ; by which a woman is shown to have brought forth a child, and to be truly a mother, by which also she receives a potent charm of affection. Wherefore the Holy Spirit in the apostle, using the voice of the Lord, says mystically, " I have given you milk to drink." [7] For if we have been regenerated unto Christ, He who has regenerated us nourishes us with His own milk, the Word ; for it is proper that what has procreated should forthwith supply nourishment to that which has been procreated. And as the regeneration was conformably spiritual, so also was the nutriment of man spiritual. In all respects, therefore, and in all things, we are brought into union with Christ, into relationship through His blood, by which we are redeemed ; and into sympathy, in consequence of the nourishment which flows from

---

[1] John iv. 32–34.
[2] Matt. xx. 22, etc.
[3] John vi. 32, 33, 51.
[4] Gen. xlix. 11.
[5] [Matt. xxiii. 35. S.]

[6] [i.e., Not from the ἀφρὸς, of the sea, but of the blood.]
[7] 1 Cor. iii. 2.

the Word ; and into immortality, through His guidance : —

" Among men the bringing up of children
    Often produces stronger impulses to love than the
    procreating of them."

The same blood and milk of the Lord is therefore the symbol of the Lord's passion and teaching. Wherefore each of us babes is permitted to make our boast in the Lord, while we proclaim : —

" Yet of a noble sire and noble blood I boast me
    sprung." [1]

And that milk is produced from blood by a change, is already clear ; yet we may learn it from the flocks and herds. For these animals, in the time of the year which we call spring, when the air has more humidity, and the grass and meadows are juicy and moist, are first filled with blood, as is shown by the distension of the veins of the swollen vessels ; and from the blood the milk flows more copiously. But in summer, again, the blood being burnt and dried up by the heat, prevents the change, and so they have less milk.

Further, milk has a most natural affinity for water, as assuredly the spiritual washing has for the spiritual nutriment. Those, therefore, that swallow a little cold water, in addition to the above-mentioned milk, straightway feel benefit ; for the milk is prevented from souring by its combination with water, not in consequence of any antipathy between them, but in consequence of the water taking kindly to the milk while it is undergoing digestion.

And such as is the union of the Word with baptism, is the agreement of milk with water ; for it receives it alone of all liquids, and admits of mixture with water, for the purpose of cleansing, as baptism for the remission of sins. And it is mixed naturally with honey also, and this for cleansing along with sweet nutriment. For the Word blended with love at once cures our passions and cleanses our sins ; and the saying,

" Sweeter than honey flowed the stream of speech," [2]

seems to me to have been spoken of the Word, who is honey. And prophecy oft extols Him " above honey and the honeycomb." [3]

Furthermore, milk is mixed with sweet wine ; and the mixture is beneficial, as when suffering is mixed in the cup in order to immortality. For the milk is curdled by the wine, and separated, and whatever adulteration is in it is drained off. And in the same way, the spiritual communion of faith with suffering man, drawing off

as serous matter the lusts of the flesh, commits man to eternity, along with those who are divine, immortalizing him.

Further, many also use the fat of milk, called butter, for the lamp, plainly indicating by this enigma the abundant unction of the Word, since He alone it is who nourishes the infants, makes them grow, and enlightens them. Wherefore also the Scripture says respecting the Lord, " He fed them with the produce of the fields ; they sucked honey from the rock, and oil from the solid rock, butter of kine, and milk of sheep, with fat of lambs ; " [4] and what follows He gave them. But he that prophesies the birth of the child says : " Butter and honey shall He eat." [5] And it occurs to me to wonder how some dare call themselves perfect and gnostics, with ideas of themselves above the apostle, inflated and boastful, when Paul even owned respecting himself, " Not that I have already attained, or am already perfect ; but I follow after, if that I may apprehend that for which I am apprehended of Christ. Brethren, I count not myself to have apprehended : but this one thing I do, forgetting the things which are behind, and stretching forth to those that are before, I press toward the mark, for the prize of the high calling in Christ Jesus." [6] And yet he reckons himself perfect, because he has been emancipated from his former life, and strives after the better life, not as perfect in knowledge, but as aspiring after perfection. Wherefore also he adds, " As many of us as are perfect, are thus minded," [7] manifestly describing perfection as the renunciation of sin, and regeneration into the faith of the only perfect One, and forgetting our former sins.

CHAP. VII. — WHO THE INSTRUCTOR IS, AND RESPECTING HIS INSTRUCTION.

Since, then, we have shown that all of us are by Scripture called children ; and not only so, but that we who have followed Christ are figuratively called babes ; and that the Father of all alone is perfect, for the Son is in Him, and the Father is in the Son ; it is time for us in due course to say who our Instructor is.

He is called Jesus. Sometimes He calls Himself a shepherd, and says, " I am the good Shepherd." [8] According to a metaphor drawn from shepherds, who lead the sheep, is hereby understood the Instructor, who leads the children — the Shepherd who tends the babes. For the babes are simple, being figuratively described as sheep. " And they shall all," it is said, " be one flock, and one shepherd." [9] The Word, then,

---

[1] *Il.*, xiv. 113.
[2] *Il.*, i. 248.
[3] Ps. xix. 10.

[4] Deut. xxxii. 13, 14.
[5] Isa. vii. 15.
[6] Phil. iii. 12-14.
[7] Phil. iii. 15.
[8] John x. 11.
[9] John x. 16.

who leads the children to salvation, is appropriately called *the Instructor*[1] (Pædagogue).

With the greatest clearness, accordingly, the Word has spoken respecting Himself by Hosea: " I am your Instructor."[2] Now piety is instruction, being the learning of the service of God, and training in the knowledge of the truth, and right guidance which leads to heaven. And the word " instruction "[3] is employed variously. For there is the instruction of him who is led and learns, and that of him who leads and teaches ; and there is, thirdly, the guidance itself; and fourthly, what is taught, as the commandments enjoined.

Now the instruction which is of God is the right direction of truth to the contemplation of God, and the exhibition of holy deeds in everlasting perseverance.

As therefore the general directs the phalanx, consulting the safety of his soldiers, and the pilot steers the vessel, desiring to save the passengers ; so also the Instructor guides the children to a saving course of conduct, through solicitude for us ; and, in general, whatever we ask in accordance with reason from God to be done for us, will happen to those who believe in the Instructor. And just as the helmsman does not always yield to the winds, but sometimes, turning the prow towards them, opposes the whole force of the hurricanes ; so the Instructor never yields to the blasts that blow in this world, nor commits the child to them like a vessel to make shipwreck on a wild and licentious course of life ; but, wafted on by the favouring breeze of the Spirit of truth, stoutly holds on to the child's helm, — his ears, I mean, — until He bring him safe to anchor in the haven of heaven.

What is called by men an ancestral custom passes away in a moment, but the divine guidance is a possession which abides for ever.

They say that Phœnix was the instructor of Achilles, and Adrastus of the children of Crœsus ; and Leonides of Alexander, and Nausithous of Philip. But Phœnix was women-mad, Adrastus was a fugitive. Leonides did not curtail the pride of Alexander, nor Nausithous reform the drunken Pellæan. No more was the Thracian Zopyrus able to check the fornication of Alcibiades ; but Zopyrus was a bought slave, and Sicinnus, the tutor of the children of Themistocles, was a lazy domestic. They say also that he invented the Sicinnian dance. Those have not escaped our attention who are called royal instructors among the Persians ; whom, in number four, the kings of the Persians select with the greatest care from all the Persians, and set over their sons. But the children only

learn the use\ of the bow, and on reaching maturity have sexual intercourse with sisters, and mothers, and women, wives and courtesans innumerable, practised in intercourse like the wild boars.

But our Instructor is the holy God Jesus, the Word, who is the guide of all humanity. The loving God Himself is our Instructor. Somewhere in song the Holy Spirit says with regard to Him, " He provided sufficiently for the people in the wilderness. He led him about in the thirst of summer heat in a dry land, and instructed him, and kept him as the apple of His eye, as an eagle protects her nest, and shows her fond solicitude for her young, spreads abroad her wings, takes them, and bears them on her back. The Lord alone led them, and there was no strange god with them."[4] Clearly, I trow, has the Scripture exhibited the Instructor in the account it gives of His guidance.

Again, when He speaks in His own person, He confesses Himself to be the Instructor : " I am the Lord thy God, who brought thee out of the land of Egypt."[5] Who, then, has the power of leading in and out? Is it not the Instructor? This was He who appeared to Abraham, and said to him, " I am thy God, be accepted before Me ; "[6] and in a way most befitting an instructor, forms him into a faithful child, saying, " And be blameless ; and I will make My covenant between Me and thee, and thy seed." There is the communication of the Instructor's friendship. And He most manifestly appears as Jacob's instructor. He says accordingly to him, " Lo, I am with thee, to keep thee in all the way in which thou shalt go ; and I will bring thee back into this land : for I will not leave thee till I do what I have told thee."[7] He is said, too, to have wrestled with Him. " And Jacob was left alone, and there wrestled with him a man (the Instructor) till the morning."[8] This was the man who led, and brought, and wrestled with, and anointed the athlete Jacob against evil.[9] Now that the Word was at once Jacob's trainer and the Instructor of humanity [appears from this] — " He asked," it is said, " His name, and said to him, Tell me what is Thy name." And he said, " Why is it that thou askest My name ? " For He reserved the new name for the new people — the babe ; and was as yet unnamed, the Lord God not having yet become man. Yet Jacob called the name of the place, " Face of God." " For I have seen," he says, " God face to face ; and my life is preserved."[10] The face of God is the Word by whom God is manifested

---

1 παιδαγωγός.
2 παιδευτής; Hos. v. 2.
3 παιδαγωγία.

4 Deut. xxxii. 10-12.
5 Ex. xx. 2.
6 Gen. xvii. 1, 2.
7 Gen. xxviii. 15.
8 Gen. xxxii. 24.
9 Or, " against the evil one."
10 Gen. xxxii. 30.

and made known. Then also was he named Israel, because he saw God the Lord. It was God, the Word, the Instructor, who said to him again afterwards, "Fear not to go down into Egypt."[1] See how the Instructor follows the righteous man, and how He anoints the athlete, teaching him to trip up his antagonist.

It is He also who teaches Moses to act as instructor. For the Lord says, "If any one sin before Me, him will I blot out of My book; but now, go and lead this people into the place which I told thee."[2] Here He is the teacher of the art of instruction. For it was really the Lord that was the instructor of the ancient people by Moses; but He is the instructor of the new people by Himself, face to face. "For behold," He says to Moses, "My angel shall go before thee," representing the evangelical and commanding power of the Word, but guarding the Lord's prerogative. "In the day on which I will visit them,"[3] He says, "I will bring their sins on them; that is, on the day on which I will sit as judge I will render the recompense of their sins." For the same who is Instructor is judge, and judges those who disobey Him; and the loving Word will not pass over their transgression in silence. He reproves, that they may repent. For "the Lord willeth the repentance of the sinner rather than his death."[4] And let us as babes, hearing of the sins of others, keep from similar transgressions, through dread of the threatening, that we may not have to undergo like sufferings. What, then, was the sin which they committed? "For in their wrath they slew men, and in their impetuosity they hamstrung bulls. Cursed be their anger."[5] Who, then, would train us more lovingly than He? Formerly the older people had an old covenant, and the law disciplined the people with fear, and the Word was an angel; but to the fresh and new people has also been given a new covenant, and the Word has appeared, and fear is turned to love, and that mystic angel is born — Jesus. For this same Instructor said then, "Thou shalt fear the Lord God;"[6] but to us He has addressed the exhortation, "Thou shalt love the Lord thy God."[7] Wherefore also this is enjoined on us: "Cease from your own works, from your old sins;" "Learn to do well;" "Depart from evil, and do good;" "Thou hast loved righteousness, and hated iniquity." This is my new covenant written in the old letter. The newness of the word must not, then, be made ground of reproach. But the Lord hath also said in Jeremiah: "Say not that I am a youth: before I formed thee in the belly I knew thee, and before I brought thee out of the womb I sanctified thee."[8] Such allusions prophecy can make to us, destined in the eye of God to faith before the foundation of the world; but now babes, through the recent fulfilment of the will of God, according to which we are born now to calling and salvation. Wherefore also He adds, "I have set thee for a prophet to the nations,"[9] saying that he must prophesy, so that the appellation of "youth" should not become a reproach to those who are called babes.

Now the law is ancient grace given through Moses by the Word. Wherefore also the Scripture says, "The law was given through Moses,"[10] not by Moses, but by the Word, and through Moses His servant. Wherefore it was only temporary; but eternal grace and truth were by Jesus Christ. Mark the expressions of Scripture: of the law only is it said "was given;" but truth being the grace of the Father, is the eternal work of the Word; and it is not said to *be given*, but *to be* by Jesus, *without whom nothing was*.[11] Presently, therefore, Moses prophetically, giving place to the perfect Instructor the Word, predicts both the name and the office of Instructor, and committing to the people the commands of obedience, sets before them the Instructor. "A prophet," says he, "like Me shall God raise up to you of your brethren," pointing out Jesus the Son of God, by an allusion to Jesus the son of Nun; for the name of Jesus predicted in the law was a shadow of Christ. He adds, therefore, consulting the advantage of the people, "Him shall ye hear;"[12] and, "The man who will not hear that Prophet,"[13] him He threatens. Such a name, then, he predicts as that of the Instructor, who is the author of salvation. Wherefore prophecy invests Him with a rod, a rod of discipline, of rule, of authority; that those whom the persuasive word heals not, the threatening may heal; and whom the threatening heals not, the rod may heal; and whom the rod heals not, the fire may devour. "There shall come forth," it is said, "a rod out of the root of Jesse."[14]

See the care, and wisdom, and power of the Instructor: "He shall not judge according to opinion, nor according to report; but He shall dispense judgment to the humble, and reprove the sinners of the earth." And by David: "The Lord instructing, hath instructed me, and not given me over to death."[15] For to be chastised of the Lord, and instructed, is deliverance from death. And by the same prophet He says:

---

1 Gen. xlvi. 3.
2 Ex. xxxii. 33, 34.
3 Ex. xxxii. 33, 34.
4 Ezek. xviii. 23, 32.
5 Gen. xlix. 6.
6 Deut. vi. 2.
7 Matt. xxii. 37.

8 Jer. i. 7.
9 Jer. i. 5.
10 John i. 17.
11 John i. 3.
12 Deut. xviii. 15.
13 Deut. xviii. 19.
14 Isa. xi. 1, 3, 4.
15 Ps. cxviii. 18.

"Thou shalt rule them with a rod of iron." [1] Thus also the apostle, in the Epistle to the Corinthians, being moved, says, "What will ye? Shall I come unto you with a rod, or in love, in the spirit of meekness?" [2] Also, "The Lord shall send the rod of strength out of Sion," [3] He says by another prophet. And this same rod of instruction, "Thy rod and staff have comforted me," [4] said some one else. Such is the power of the Instructor — sacred, soothing, saving.

CHAP. VIII. — AGAINST THOSE WHO THINK THAT WHAT IS JUST IS NOT GOOD.

At this stage some rise up, saying that the Lord, by reason of the rod, and threatening, and fear, is not good; misapprehending, as appears, the Scripture which says, "And he that feareth the Lord will turn to his heart;" [5] and most of all, oblivious of His love, in that for us He became man. For more suitably to Him, the prophet prays in these words: "Remember us, for we are dust;" [6] that is, Sympathize with us; for Thou knowest from personal experience of suffering the weakness of the flesh. In this respect, therefore, the Lord the Instructor is most good and unimpeachable, sympathizing as He does from the exceeding greatness of His love with the nature of each man. "For there is nothing which the Lord hates." [7] For assuredly He does not hate anything, and yet wish that which He hates to exist. Nor does He wish anything not to exist, and yet become the cause of existence to that which He wishes not to exist. Nor does He wish anything not to exist which yet exists. If, then, the Word hates anything, He does not wish it to exist. But nothing exists, the cause of whose existence is not supplied by God. Nothing, then, is hated by God, nor yet by the Word. For both are one — that is, God. For He has said, "In the beginning the Word was in God, and the Word was God." [8] If then He hates none of the things which He has made, it follows that He loves them. Much more than the rest, and with reason, will He love man, the noblest of all objects created by Him, and a God-loving being. Therefore God is loving; consequently the Word is loving.

But he who loves anything wishes to do it good. And that which does good must be every way better than that which does not good. But nothing is better than the Good. The Good, then, does good. And God is admitted to be good. God therefore does good. And the Good, in virtue of its being good, does nothing else than do good. Consequently God does all good. And He does no good to man without caring for him, and He does not care for him without taking care of him. For that which does good purposely, is better than what does not good purposely. But nothing is better than God. And to do good purposely, is nothing else than to take care of man. God therefore cares for man, and takes care of him. And He shows this practically, in instructing him by the Word, who is the true coadjutor of God's love to man. But the good is not said to be good, on account of its being possessed of virtue; as also righteousness is not said to be good on account of its possessing virtue — for it is itself virtue — but on account of its being in itself and by itself good.

In another way the useful is called good, not on account of its pleasing, but of its doing good. All which, therefore, is righteousness, being a good thing, both as virtue and as desirable for its own sake, and not as giving pleasure; for it does not judge in order to win favour, but dispenses to each according to his merits. And the beneficial follows the useful. Righteousness, therefore, has characteristics corresponding to all the aspects in which goodness is examined, both possessing equal properties equally. And things which are characterized by equal properties are equal and similar to each other. Righteousness is therefore a good thing.

"How then," say they, "if the Lord loves man, and is good, is He angry and punishes?" We must therefore treat of this point with all possible brevity; for this mode of treatment is advantageous to the right training of the children, occupying the place of a necessary help. For many of the passions are cured by punishment, and by the inculcation of the sterner precepts, as also by instruction in certain principles. For reproof is, as it were, the surgery of the passions of the soul; and the passions are, as it were, an abscess of the truth, [9] which must be cut open by an incision of the lancet of reproof.

Reproach is like the application of medicines, dissolving the callosities of the passions, and purging the impurities of the lewdness of the life; and in addition, reducing the excrescences of pride, restoring the patient to the healthy and true state of humanity.

Admonition is, as it were, the regimen of the diseased soul, prescribing what it must take, and forbidding what it must not. And all these tend to salvation and eternal health.

Furthermore, the general of an army, by inflicting fines and corporeal punishments with chains and the extremest disgrace on offenders,

---

[1] Ps. ii. 9.
[2] 1 Cor. iv. 21.
[3] Ps. cx. 2.
[4] Ps. xxiii. 4.
[5] Ecclus. xxi. 6.
[6] Ps. ciii. 14.
[7] Wisd. xi. 24.
[8] John i. 1.

[9] For ἀληθείας, there are the readings ἀπαθείας and ἀτιμίας.

and sometimes even by punishing individuals with death, aims at good, doing so for the admonition of the officers under him.

Thus also He who is our great General, the Word, the Commander-in-chief of the universe, by admonishing those who throw off the restraints of His law, that He may effect their release from the slavery, error, and captivity of the adversary, brings them peacefully to the sacred concord of citizenship.

As, therefore in addition to persuasive discourse, there is the hortatory and the consolatory form; so also, in addition to the laudatory, there is the inculpatory and reproachful. And this latter constitutes the art of censure. Now censure is a mark of good-will, not of ill-will. For both he who is a friend and he who is not, reproach; but the enemy does so in scorn, the friend in kindness. It is not, then, from hatred that the Lord chides men; for He Himself suffered for us, whom He might have destroyed for our faults. For the Instructor also, in virtue of His being good, with consummate art glides into censure by rebuke; rousing the sluggishness of the mind by His sharp words as by a scourge. Again in turn He endeavours to exhort the same persons. For those who are not induced by praise are spurred on by censure; and those whom censure calls not forth to salvation, being as dead, are by denunciation roused to the truth. "For the stripes and correction of wisdom are in all time." "For teaching a fool is gluing a potsherd; and sharpening to sense a hopeless blockhead is bringing earth to sensation." [1] Wherefore He adds plainly, "rousing the sleeper from deep sleep," which of all things else is likest death.

Further, the Lord shows very clearly of Himself, when, describing figuratively His manifold and in many ways serviceable culture, — He says, " I am the true vine, and my Father is the husbandman." Then He adds, " Every branch in me that beareth not fruit He taketh away; and every branch that beareth fruit He pruneth, that it may bring forth more fruit." [2] For the vine that is not pruned grows to wood. So also man. The Word — the knife — clears away the wanton shoots; compelling the impulses of the soul to fructify, not to indulge in lust. Now, reproof addressed to sinners has their salvation for its aim, the word being harmoniously adjusted to each one's conduct; now with tightened, now with relaxed cords. Accordingly it was very plainly said by Moses, " Be of good courage: God has drawn near to try you, that His fear may be among you, that ye sin not." [3] And Plato, who had learned from this source, says

beautifully : " For all who suffer punishment are in reality treated well, for they are benefited; since the spirit of those who are justly punished is improved." And if those who are corrected receive good at the hands of justice, and, according to Plato, what is just is acknowledged to be good, fear itself does good, and has been found to be for men's good. " For the soul that feareth the Lord shall live, for their hope is in Him who saveth them." [4] And this same Word who inflicts punishment is judge; regarding whom Esaias also says, " The Lord has assigned Him to our sins," [5] plainly as a corrector and reformer of sins. Wherefore He alone is able to forgive our iniquities, who has been appointed by the Father, Instructor of us all; He alone it is who is able to distinguish between disobedience and obedience. And while He threatens, He manifestly is unwilling to inflict evil to execute His threatenings; but by inspiring men with fear, He cuts off the approach to sin, and shows His love to man, still delaying, and declaring what they shall suffer if they continue sinners, and is not as a serpent, which the moment it fastens on its prey devours it.

God, then, is good. And the Lord speaks many a time and oft before He proceeds to act. " For my arrows," He says, " will make an end of them; they shall be consumed with hunger, and be eaten by birds; and there shall be incurable tetanic incurvature. I will send the teeth of wild beasts upon them, with the rage of serpents creeping on the earth. Without, the sword shall make them childless; and out of their chambers shall be fear." [6] For the Divine Being is not angry in the way that some think; but often restrains, and always exhorts humanity, and shows what ought to be done. And this is a good device, to terrify lest we sin. " For the fear of the Lord drives away sins, and he that is without fear cannot be justified," [7] says the Scripture. And God does not inflict punishment from wrath, but for the ends of justice; since it is not expedient that justice should be neglected on our account. Each one of us, who sins, with his own free-will chooses punishment, and the blame lies with him who chooses. [8] God is without blame. " But if our unrighteousness commend the righteousness of God, what shall we say? Is God unrighteous, who taketh vengeance? God forbid." [9] He says, therefore, threatening, " I will sharpen my sword, and my hand shall lay hold on judgment; and I will render justice to mine enemies, and requite those who hate me. I will make mine arrows drunk with blood, and my sword shall devour

---

[1] Ecclus. xxii. 6–8.
[2] John xv. 1, 2.
[3] Ex. xx. 20.

[4] Ecclus. xxxiv. 14, 15.
[5] Isa. liii. 6.
[6] Deut. xxxii. 23–25.
[7] Ecclus. i. 21, 22.
[8] Plato, *Rep.*, x. 617 E.
[9] Rom. iii. 5, 6.

flesh from the blood of the wounded." [1]   It is clear, then, that those who are not at enmity with the truth, and do not hate the Word, will not hate their own salvation, but will escape the punishment of enmity.   "The crown of wisdom," then, as the book of Wisdom says, "is the fear of the Lord." [2]   Very clearly, therefore, by the prophet Amos has the Lord unfolded His method of dealing, saying, "I have overthrown you, as God overthrew Sodom and Gomorrah ; and ye shall be as a brand plucked from the fire : and yet ye have not returned unto me, saith the LORD." [3]

See how God, through His love of goodness, seeks repentance ; and by means of the plan He pursues of threatening silently, shows His own love for man.   "I will avert," He says, "My face from them, and show what shall happen to them." [4]   For where the face of the Lord looks, there is peace and rejoicing ; but where it is averted, there is the introduction of evil.   The Lord, accordingly, does not wish to look on evil things ; for He is good.   But on His looking away, evil arises spontaneously through human unbelief.   "Behold, therefore," says Paul, "the goodness and severity of God : on them that fell, severity ; but upon thee, goodness, if thou continue in His goodness," [5] that is, in faith in Christ.

Now hatred of evil attends the good man, in virtue of His being in nature good.   Wherefore I will grant that He punishes the disobedient (for punishment is for the good and advantage of him who is punished, for it is the correction of a refractory subject) ; but I will not grant that He wishes to take vengeance.   Revenge is retribution for evil, imposed for the advantage of him who takes the revenge.   He will not desire us to take revenge, who teaches us "to pray for those that despitefully use us." [6]   But that God is good, all willingly admit ; and that the same God is just, I require not many more words to prove, after adducing the evangelical utterance of the Lord ; He speaks of Him as one, "That they all may be one ; as Thou, Father, art in Me, and I in Thee, that they also may be one in Us : that the world also may believe that Thou hast sent Me.   And the glory which Thou hast given Me I have given them ; that they may be one, as We are one : I in them, and Thou in Me, that they may be made perfect in one." [7]   God is one, and beyond the one and above the Monad itself.   Wherefore also the particle "Thou," having a demonstrative emphasis, points out God, who alone truly is, "who was, and is, and is to come," in which three divisions of time the one name (ὁ ὤν), "who is," [8]

has its place.   And that He who alone is God is also alone and truly righteous, our Lord in the Gospel itself shall testify, saying "Father, I will that they also whom Thou hast given Me be with Me where I am ; that they may behold My glory, which Thou hast given Me : For Thou lovedst Me before the foundation of the world.   O righteous Father, the world hath not known Thee : but I have known Thee, and these have known that Thou hast sent Me.   And I have declared to them Thy name, and will declare it." [9]   This is He "that visits the iniquities of the fathers upon the children, to them that hate Him, and shows mercy to those that love Him." [10]   For He who placed some "on the right hand, and others on the left," [11] conceived as Father, being good, is called that which alone He is — "good ; " [12] but as He is the Son in the Father, being his Word, from their mutual relation, the name of power being measured by equality of love, He is called righteous.   "He will judge," He says, "a man according to his works," [13] — a good balance, even God having made known to us the face of righteousness in the person of·Jesus, by whom also, as by even scales, we know God.   Of this also the book of Wisdom plainly says,. "For mercy and wrath are with Him, for He alone is Lord of both," Lord of propitiations, and pouring forth wrath according to the abundance of His mercy.   "So also is His reproof." [14]   For the aim of mercy and of reproof is the salvation of those who are reproved.

Now, that the God and Father of our Lord Jesus is good, the Word Himself will again avouch : "For He is kind to the unthankful and the evil ; " and further, when He says, "Be merciful, as your Father is merciful." [15]   Still further also He plainly says, "None is good, but My Father, who is in heaven." [16]   In addition to these, again He says, "My Father makes His sun to shine on all." [17]   Here it is to be noted that He proclaims His Father to be good, and to be the Creator.   And that the Creator is just, is not disputed.   And again he says, "My Father sends rain on the just, and on the unjust."   In respect of His sending rain, He is the Creator of the waters, and of the clouds.   And in respect of His doing so on all, He holds an even balance justly and rightly.   And as being good, He does so on just and unjust alike.

Very clearly, then, we conclude Him to be one and the same God, thus.   For the Holy Spirit has sung, "I will look to the heavens, the works

---

1   Deut. xxxii. 41, 42.
2   Ecclus. i. 18.
3   Amos iv. 11.
4   Deut. xxxii. 20.
5   Rom. xi. 22.
6   Matt. v. 44.
7   John xvii. 21–23
8   Ex. iii. 14.

9   John xvii. 24–26.
10   Ex. xx. 5, 6.
11   Matt. xx. 21, xxv. 33.
12   Matt. xix. 17.
13   Ecclus. xvi. 12.
14   Ecclus. xvi. 12.
15   Luke vi. 35, 36.
16   Matt. xix. 17.
17   Matt. v. 45.

of Thy hands;"[1] and, "He who created the heavens dwells in the heavens;" and, "Heaven is Thy throne."[2] And the Lord says in His prayer, "Our Father, who art in heaven."[3] And the heavens belong to Him, who created the world. It is indisputable, then, that the Lord is the Son of the Creator. And if the Creator above all is confessed to be just, and the Lord to be the Son of the Creator; then the Lord is the Son of Him who is just. Wherefore also Paul says, "But now the righteousness of God without the law is manifested;"[4] and again, that you may better conceive of God, "even the righteousness of God by the faith of Jesus Christ upon all that believe; for there is no difference."[5] And, witnessing further to the truth, he adds after a little, "through the forbearance of God, in order to show that He is just, and that Jesus is the justifier of him who is of faith." And that he knows that what is just is good, appears by his saying, "So that the law is holy, and the commandment holy, and just, and good,"[6] using both names to denote the same power. But "no one is good," except His Father. It is this same Father of His, then, who being one is manifested by many powers. And this was the import of the utterance, "No man knew the Father,"[7] who was Himself everything before the coming of the Son. So that it is veritably clear that the God of all is only one good, just Creator, and the Son in the Father, to whom be glory for ever and ever, Amen. But it is not inconsistent with the saving Word, to administer rebuke dictated by solicitude; for this is the medicine of the divine love to man, by which the blush of modesty breaks forth, and shame at sin supervenes. For if one must censure, it is necessary also to rebuke; when it is the time to wound the apathetic soul not mortally, but salutarily, securing exemption from everlasting death by a little pain.

Great is the wisdom displayed in His instruction, and manifold the modes of His dealing in order to salvation. For the Instructor testifies to the good, and summons forth to better things those that are called; dissuades those that are hastening to do wrong from the attempt, and exhorts them to turn to a better life. For the one is not without testimony, when the other has been testified to; and the grace which proceeds from the testimony is very great. Besides, the feeling of anger (if it is proper to call His admonition anger) is full of love to man, God condescending to emotion on man's account; for whose sake also the Word of God became man.

CHAP. IX. — THAT IT IS THE PREROGATIVE OF THE SAME POWER TO BE BENEFICENT AND TO PUNISH JUSTLY. ALSO THE MANNER OF THE INSTRUCTION OF THE LOGOS.

With all His power, therefore, the Instructor of humanity, the Divine Word, using all the resources of wisdom, devotes Himself to the saving of the children, admonishing, upbraiding, blaming, chiding, reproving, threatening, healing, promising, favouring; and as it were, by many reins, curbing the irrational impulses of humanity. To speak briefly, therefore, the Lord acts towards us as we do towards our children. "Hast thou children? correct them," is the exhortation of the book of Wisdom, "and bend them from their youth. Hast thou daughters? attend to their body, and let not thy face brighten towards them,"[8]—although we love our children exceedingly, both sons and daughters, above aught else whatever. For those who speak with a man merely to please him, have little love for him, seeing they do not pain him; while those that speak for his good, though they inflict pain for the time, do him good for ever after. It is not immediate pleasure, but future enjoyment, that the Lord has in view.

Let us now proceed to consider the mode of His loving discipline, with the aid of the prophetic testimony.

Admonition, then, is the censure of loving care, and produces understanding. Such is the Instructor in His admonitions, as when He says in the Gospel, "How often would I have gathered thy children, as a bird gathers her young ones under her wings, and ye would not!"[9] And again, the Scripture admonishes, saying, "And they committed adultery with stock and stone, and burnt incense to Baal."[10] For it is a very great proof of His love, that, though knowing well the shamelessness of the people that had kicked and bounded away, He notwithstanding exhorts them to repentance, and says by Ezekiel, "Son of man, thou dwellest in the midst of scorpions; nevertheless, speak to them, if peradventure they will hear."[11] Further, to Moses He says, "Go and tell Pharaoh to send My people forth; but I know that he will not send them forth."[12] For He shows both things: both His divinity in His foreknowledge of what would take place, and His love in affording an opportunity for repentance to the self-determination of the soul. He admonishes also by Esaias, in His care for the people, when He says, "This people honour Me with their lips, but their heart is far from Me." What follows is reproving censure: "In vain do they worship

---

[1] Ps. viii. 4.
[2] Ps. ii. 4, xi. 5, ciii. 19.
[3] Matt. vi. 9
[4] Rom. iii. 21, 22.
[5] Rom. iii. 26.
[6] Rom. vii. 12.
[7] Luke x. 22; John xvii. 25.

[8] Ecclus. vii. 23, 24.
[9] Matt. xxiii. 37.
[10] Jer. iii. 9, vii. 9, xi. 13, xxxii. 29.
[11] Ezek. ii. 6, 7.
[12] Ex. iii. 18, 19.

Me, teaching for doctrines the commandments of men." [1] Here His loving care, having shown their sin, shows salvation side by side.

Upbraiding is censure on account of what is base, conciliating to what is noble. This is shown by Jeremiah: "They were female-mad horses; each one neighed after his neighbour's wife. Shall I not visit for these things? saith the LORD: shall not my soul be avenged on such a nation as this?" [2] He everywhere interweaves fear, because "the fear of the LORD is the beginning of sense." [3] And again, by Hosea, He says, "Shall I not visit them? for they themselves were mingled with harlots, and sacrificed with the initiated; and the people that understood embraced a harlot." [4] He shows their offence to be clearer, by declaring that they understood, and thus sinned wilfully. Understanding is the eye of the soul; wherefore also Israel means, "he that sees God"—that is, he that understands God.

Complaint is censure of those who are regarded as despising or neglecting. He employs this form when He says by Esaias: "Hear, O heaven; and give ear, O earth: for the LORD hath spoken, I have begotten and brought up children, but they have disregarded Me. The ox knoweth his owner, and the ass his master's crib: but Israel hath not known Me." [5] For how shall we not regard it fearful, if he that knows God, shall not recognise the Lord; but while the ox and the ass, stupid and foolish animals, will know him who feeds them, Israel is found to be more irrational than these? And having, by Jeremiah, complained against the people on many grounds, He adds: "And they have forsaken Me, saith the LORD." [6]

Invective [7] is a reproachful upbraiding, or chiding censure. This mode of treatment the Instructor employs in Isaiah, when He says, "Woe to you, children revolters. Thus saith the LORD, Ye have taken counsel, but not by Me; and made compacts, but not by My Spirit." [8] He uses the very bitter mordant of fear in each case repressing [9] the people, and at the same time turning them to salvation; as also wool that is undergoing the process of dyeing is wont to be previously treated with mordants, in order to prepare it for taking on a fast colour.

Reproof is the bringing forward of sin, laying it before one. This form of instruction He employs as in the highest degree necessary, by reason of the feebleness of the faith of many.

For He says by Esaias, "Ye have forsaken the LORD, and have provoked the Holy One of Israel to anger." [10] And He says also by Jeremiah: "Heaven was astonished at this, and the earth shuddered exceedingly. For My people have committed two evils; they have forsaken Me, the fountain of living waters, and have hewn out to themselves broken cisterns, which will not be able to hold water." [11] And again, by the same: "Jerusalem hath sinned a sin; therefore it became commotion. All that glorified her dishonoured her, when they saw her baseness." [12] And He uses the bitter and biting [13] language of reproof in His consolations by Solomon, tacitly alluding to the love for children that characterizes His instruction: "My son, despise not thou the chastening of the LORD; nor faint when thou art rebuked of Him: for whom the LORD loveth He chasteneth, and scourgeth every son whom He receiveth;" [14] "For a man who is a sinner escapes reproof." [15] Consequently, therefore, the Scripture says, "Let the righteous reprove and correct me; but let not the oil of the sinner anoint my head." [16]

Bringing one to his senses (φρένωσις) is censure, which makes a man think. Neither from this form of instruction does he abstain, but says by Jeremiah, "How long shall I cry, and you not hear? So your ears are uncircumcised." [17] O blessed forbearance! And again, by the same: "All the heathen are uncircumcised, but this people is uncircumcised in heart:" [18] "for the people are disobedient; children," says He, "in whom is not faith." [19]

Visitation is severe rebuke. He uses this species in the Gospel: "O Jerusalem, Jerusalem, that killest the prophets, and stonest them that are sent unto thee!" The reduplication of the name gives strength to the rebuke. For he that knows God, how does he persecute God's servants? Wherefore He says, "Your house is left desolate; for I say unto you, Henceforth ye shall not see Me, till ye shall say, Blessed is He that cometh in the name of the Lord." [20] For if you do not receive His love, ye shall know His power.

Denunciation is vehement speech. And He employs denunciation as medicine, by Isaiah, saying, "Ah, sinful nation, lawless sons, people full of sins, wicked seed!" [21] And in the Gospel by John He says, "Serpents, brood of vipers." [22]

---

[1] Isa. xxix. 13.
[2] Jer. v. 8, 9.
[3] Prov. i. 7.
[4] Hos. iv. 14: "understood not" in the A.V.
[5] Isa. i. 2, 3.
[6] Jer i. 16, ii. 13, 29.
[7] Or, rebuke.
[8] Isa. xxx. 1.
[9] Lowth conjectures ἐπιστομῶν or ἐπιστομίζων, instead of ἀναστομῶν.
[10] Isa. i. 4.
[11] Jer. ii. 12, 13.
[12] Lam. i. 8.
[13] H. reads δηκτικόν, for which the text has ἐπιδεικτικόν.
[14] Prov. iii. 11, 12
[15] Ecclus. xxxii. 21.
[16] Ps. cxli. 5.
[17] Jer. vi. 10.
[18] Jer. ix. 26.
[19] Isa. xxx. 9.
[20] Matt. xxiii. 37-39.
[21] Isa. i. 4.
[22] Nothing similar to this is found in the fourth Gospel; the reference may be to the words of the Baptist, Matt. iii. 7, Luke iii. 7.

Accusation is censure of wrong-doers. This mode of instruction He employs by David, when He says : ." The people whom I knew not served me, and at the hearing of the ear obeyed me. Sons of strangers lied to me, and halted from their ways." [1] And by Jeremiah : "And I gave her a writing of divorcement, and covenant-breaking Judah feared not." [2] And again : "And the house of Israel disregarded Me ; and the house of Judah lied to the LORD." [3]

Bewailing one's fate is latent censure, and by artful aid ministers salvation as under a veil. He made use of this by Jeremiah : "How did the city sit solitary that was full of people ! She that ruled over territories became as a widow ; she came under tribute ; weeping, she wept in the night." [4]

Objurgation is objurgatory censure. Of this help the Divine Instructor made use by Jeremiah, saying, "Thou hadst a whore's forehead ; thou wast shameless towards all ; and didst not call me to the house, who am thy father, and lord of thy virginity." [5] "And a fair and graceful harlot skilled in enchanted potions." [6] With consummate art, after applying to the virgin the opprobrious name of whoredom, He thereupon calls her back to an honourable life by filling her with shame.

Indignation is a rightful upbraiding ; or upbraiding on account of ways exalted above what is right. In this way He instructed by Moses, when He said, "Faulty children, a generation crooked and perverse, do ye thus requite the LORD? This people is foolish, and not wise. Is not this thy father who acquired thee?" [7] He says also by Isaiah, "Thy princes are disobedient, companions of thieves, loving gifts, following after rewards, not judging the orphans." [8]

In fine, the system He pursues to inspire fear is the source of salvation. And it is the prerogative of goodness to save : "The mercy of the Lord is on all flesh, while He reproves, corrects, and teaches as a shepherd His flock. He pities those who receive His instruction, and those who eagerly seek union with Him." [9] And with such guidance He guarded the six hundred thousand footmen that were brought together in the hardness of heart in which they were found ; scourging, pitying, striking, healing, in compassion and discipline : "For according to the greatness of His mercy, so is His rebuke." [10] For it is indeed noble not to sin ; but it is good also for the sinner to repent ; just as it is best to be always in good health, but well to recover from disease. So He commands by Solomon : "Strike thou thy. son with the rod, that thou mayest deliver his soul from death." [11] And again : "Abstain not from chastising thy son, but correct him with the rod ; for he will not die." [12]

For reproof and rebuke, as also the original term implies, are the stripes of the soul, chastizing sins, preventing death, and leading to self-control those carried away to licentiousness. Thus also Plato, knowing reproof to be the greatest power for reformation, and the most sovereign purification, in accordance with what has been said, observes, "that he who is in the highest degree impure is uninstructed and base, by reason of his being unreproved in those respects in which he who is destined to be truly happy ought to be the purest and best."

For if rulers are not a terror to a good work, how shall God, who is by nature good, be a terror to him who sins not? "If thou doest evil, be afraid," [13] says the apostle. Wherefore the apostle himself also in every case uses stringent language to the Churches, after the Lord's example ; and conscious of his own boldness, and of the weakness of his hearers, he says to the Galatians : "Am I your enemy, because I tell you the truth?" [14] Thus also people in health do not require a physician, do not require him as long as they are strong ; but those who are ill need his skill. Thus also we who in our lives are ill of shameful lusts and reprehensible excesses, and other inflammatory effects of the passions, need the Saviour. And He administers not only mild, but also stringent medicines. The bitter roots of fear then arrest the eating sores of our sins. Wherefore also fear is salutary, if bitter. Sick, we truly stand in need of the Saviour ; having wandered, of one to guide us ; blind, of one to lead us to the light ; thirsty, "of the fountain of life, of which whosoever partakes, shall no longer thirst ;" [15] dead, we need life ; sheep, we need a shepherd ; we who are children need a tutor, while universal humanity stands in need of Jesus ; so that we may not continue intractable and sinners to the end, and thus fall into condemnation, but may be separated from the chaff, and stored up in the paternal garner. "For the fan is in the Lord's hand, by which the chaff due to the fire is separated from the wheat." [16] You may learn, if you will, the crowning wisdom of the all-holy Shepherd and Instructor, of the omnipotent and paternal Word, when He figuratively represents Himself as the Shepherd of the sheep. And He is the Tutor of the

---

[1] Ps. xviii. 43-45.
[2] Jer. iii. 8.
[3] Jer. v. 11, 12.
[4] Lam. i. 1, 2.
[5] Jer. iii. 3, 4.
[6] Nahum iii. 4.
[7] Deut. xxxii. 5, 6.
[8] Isa. i. 23.
[9] Ecclus. xviii. 13, 14.
[10] Ecclus. xvi. 12.

[11] Prov. xxiii. 14.
[12] Prov. xxiii. 13.
[13] Rom. xiii. 3, 4.
[14] Gal. iv. 16.
[15] John iv. 13, 14.
[16] Matt. iii. 12; Luke iii. 17.

children. He says therefore by Ezekiel, directing His discourse to the elders, and setting before them a salutary description of His wise solicitude : " And that which is lame I will bind up, and that which is sick I will heal, and that which has wandered I will turn back ; and I will feed them on my holy mountain." [1] Such are the promises of the good Shepherd.

Feed us, the children, as sheep. Yea, Master, fill us with righteousness, Thine own pasture ; yea, O Instructor, feed us on Thy holy mountain the Church, which towers aloft, which is above the clouds, which touches heaven. " And I will be," He says, " their Shepherd," [2] and will be near them, as the garment to their skin. He wishes to save my flesh by enveloping it in the robe of immortality, and He hath anointed my body. " They shall call Me," He says, " and I will say, Here am I." [3] Thou didst hear sooner than I expected, Master. " And if they pass over, they shall not slip," [4] saith the Lord. For we who are passing over to immortality shall not fall into corruption, for He shall sustain us. For so He has said, and so He has willed. Such is our Instructor, righteously good. " I came not," He says, " to be ministered unto, but to minister." [5] Wherefore He is introduced in the Gospel " wearied," [6] because toiling for us, and promising " to give His life a ransom for many." [7] For him alone who does so He owns to be the good shepherd. Generous, therefore, is He who gives for us the greatest of all gifts, His own life ; and beneficent exceedingly, and loving to men, in that, when He might have been Lord, He wished to be a brother man ; and so good was He that He died for us.

Further, His righteousness cried, " If ye come straight to me, I also will come straight to you ; but if ye walk crooked, I also will walk crooked, saith the Lord of hosts ; " [8] meaning by the crooked ways the chastisements of sinners. For the straight and natural way which is indicated by the *Iota* of the name of Jesus is His goodness, which is firm and sure towards those who have believed at hearing : " When I called, ye obeyed not, saith the Lord ; but set at nought my counsels, and heeded not my reproofs." [9] Thus the Lord's reproof is most beneficial. David also says of them, " A perverse and provoking race ; a race which set not their heart aright, and whose spirit was not faithful with God : they kept not the covenant of God, and would not walk in His law." [10]

Such are the causes of provocation for which the Judge comes to inflict punishment on those that would not choose a life of goodness. Wherefore also afterwards He assailed them more roughly ; in order, if possible, to drag them back from their impetuous rush towards death. He therefore tells by David the most manifest cause of the threatening : " They believed not in His wonderful works. When He slew them, they sought after Him, and turned and inquired early after God ; and remembered that God was their Helper, and God the Most High their Redeemer." [11] Thus He knew that they turned for fear, while they despised His love : for, for the most part, that goodness which is always mild is despised ; but He who admonishes by the loving fear of righteousness is reverenced.

There is a twofold species of fear, the one of which is accompanied with reverence, such as citizens show towards good rulers, and we towards God, as also right-minded children towards their fathers. " For an unbroken horse turns out unmanageable, and a son who is let take his own way turns out reckless." [12] The other species of fear is accompanied with hatred, which slaves feel towards hard masters, and the Hebrews felt, who made God a master, not a father. And as far as piety is concerned, that which is voluntary and spontaneous differs much, nay entirely, from what is forced. " For He," it is said, " is merciful ; He will heal their sins, and not destroy them, and fully turn away His anger, and not kindle all His wrath." [13] See how the justice of the Instructor, which deals in rebukes, is shown ; and the goodness of God, which deals in compassions. Wherefore David — that is, the Spirit by him — embracing them both, sings of God Himself, " Justice and judgment are the preparation of His throne : mercy and truth shall go before Thy face." [14] He declares that it belongs to the same power both to judge and to do good. For there is power over both together, and judgment separates that which is just from its opposite. And He who is truly God is just and good ; who is Himself all, and all is He ; for He is God, the only God.

For as the mirror is not evil to an ugly man because it shows him what like he is ; and as the physician is not evil to the sick man because he tells him of his fever, — for the physician is not the cause of the fever, but only points out the fever ; — so neither is He, that reproves, ill-disposed towards him who is diseased in soul. For He does not put the transgressions on him, but only shows the sins which are there ; in order to turn him away from similar practices. So

---

[1] Ezek. xxxiv. 14, 15, 16.
[2] Ezek. xxxiv. 14–16.
[3] Isa. lviii. 9.
[4] Isa. xliii. 2.
[5] Matt. xx. 28; Mark x. 45.
[6] John iv. 6.
[7] Matt. xx. 28.
[8] Here Clement gives the sense of various passages, e.g., Jer. vi., Lev. xxvi.
[9] Prov. i. 24, 25.
[10] Ps. lxxviii. 8, 10.

[11] Ps. lxxviii. 32–35.
[12] Ecclus. xxx. 8.
[13] Ps. lxxviii. 38.
[14] Ps. lxxxix. 14.

God is good on His own account, and just also on ours, and He is just because He is good. And His justice is shown to us by His own Word from there from above, whence the Father was. For before He became Creator He was God; He was good. And therefore He wished to be Creator and Father. And the nature of all that love was the source of righteousness — the cause, too, of His lighting up His sun, and sending down His own Son. And He first announced the good righteousness that is from heaven, when He said, "No man knoweth the Son, but the Father; nor the Father, but the Son."[1] This mutual and reciprocal knowledge is the symbol of primeval justice. Then justice came down to men both in the letter and in the body, in the Word and in the law, constraining humanity to saving repentance; for it was good. But do you not obey God? Then blame yourself, who drag to yourself the judge.

CHAP. X. — THAT THE SAME GOD, BY THE SAME WORD, RESTRAINS FROM SIN BY THREATENING, AND SAVES HUMANITY BY EXHORTING.

If, then, we have shown that the plan of dealing stringently with humanity is good and salutary, and necessarily adopted by the Word, and conducive to repentance and the prevention of sins; we shall have now to look in order at the mildness of the Word. For He has been demonstrated to be just. He sets before us His own inclinations which invite to salvation; by which, in accordance with the Father's will, He wishes to make known to us the good and the useful. Consider these. The good ($\tau\grave{o}$ $\kappa\alpha\lambda\acute{o}\nu$) belongs to the panegyrical form of speech, the useful to the persuasive. For the hortatory and the dehortatory are a form of the persuasive, and the laudatory and inculpatory of the panegyrical.

For the persuasive style of sentence in one form becomes hortatory, and in another dehortatory. So also the panegyrical in one form becomes inculpatory, and in another laudatory. And in these exercises the Instructor, the Just One, who has proposed our advantage as His aim, is chiefly occupied. But the inculpatory and dehortatory forms of speech have been already shown us; and we must now handle the persuasive and the laudatory, and, as on a beam, balance the equal scales of justice. The exhortation to what is useful, the Instructor employs by Solomon, to the following effect: " I exhort you, O men; and I utter my voice to the sons of men. Hear me; for I will speak of excellent things;"[2] and so on. And He counsels what is salutary: for counsel has for its end, choosing or refusing a certain course; as He does by David, when He says, "Blessed is the man who

walketh not in the counsels of the ungodly, and standeth not in the way of sinners, and sitteth not in the chair of pestilences; but his will is in the law of the LORD."[3] And there are three departments of counsel: That which takes examples from past times; as what the Hebrews suffered when they worshipped the golden calf, and what they suffered when they committed fornication, and the like. The second, whose meaning is understood from the present times, as being apprehended by perception; as it was said to those who asked the Lord, "If He was the Christ, or shall we wait for another? Go and tell John, the blind receive their sight, the deaf hear, the lepers are cleansed, the dead are raised up; and blessed is he who shall not be offended in Me."[4] Such was that which David said when he prophesied, "As we have heard, so have we seen."[5] And the third department of counsel consists of what is future, by which we are bidden guard against what is to happen; as also that was said, "They that fall into sins shall be cast into outer darkness, where there shall be wailing and gnashing of teeth,"[6] and the like. So that from these things it is clear that the Lord, going the round of all the methods of curative treatment, calls humanity to salvation.

By encouragement He assuages sins, reducing lust, and at the same time inspiring hope for salvation. For He says by Ezekiel, "If ye return with your whole heart, and say, Father, I will hear you, as a holy people."[7] And again He says, "Come all to Me, who labour, and are heavy laden, and I will give you rest;"[8] and that which is added the Lord speaks in His own person. And very clearly He calls to goodness by Solomon, when He says, "Blessed is the man who hath found wisdom, and the mortal who hath found understanding."[9] "For the good is found by him who seeks it, and is wont to be seen by him who has found it."[10] By Jeremiah, too, He sets forth prudence, when he says, "Blessed are we, Israel; for what is pleasing to God is known by us;"[11] — and it is known by the Word, by whom we are blessed and wise. For wisdom and knowledge are mentioned by the same prophet, when he says, "Hear, O Israel, the commandments of life, and give ear to know understanding."[12] By Moses, too, by reason of the love He has to man, He promises a gift to those who hasten to salvation. For He says, "And I will bring you into the good land,

---

[1] Luke x. 22.
[2] Prov. viii. 4, 6.

[3] Ps. i. 1, 2.
[4] Matt. xi. 3-6; Luke vii. 19, 22, 23.
[5] Ps. xlviii. 8.
[6] Matt. xxii. 13, xxv. 30.
[7] Ezek. xviii., xxxiii.
[8] Matt. xi. 28.
[9] Prov. iii. 13.
[10] In Prov. ii. 4, 5, iii. 15, Jer. ii. 24, we have the sense of these verses.
[11] Baruch iv. 4.
[12] Baruch iii. 9.

which the Lord sware to your fathers."[1] And further, "And I will bring you into the holy mountain, and make you glad,"[2] He says by Isaiah. And still another form of instruction is benediction. "And blessed is he," He saith by David, "who has not sinned; and he shall be as the tree planted near the channels of the waters, which will yield its fruit in its season, and his leaf shall not wither"[3] (by this He made an allusion to the resurrection); "and whatsoever he shall do shall prosper with him." Such He wishes us to be, that we may be blessed. Again, showing the opposite scale of the balance of justice, He says, "But not so the ungodly — not so; but as the dust which the wind sweeps away from the face of the earth."[4] By showing the punishment of sinners, and their easy dispersion, and carrying off by the wind, the Instructor dissuades from crime by means of punishment; and by holding up the merited penalty, shows the benignity of His beneficence in the most skilful way, in order that we may possess and enjoy its blessings. He invites us to knowledge also, when He says by Jeremiah, "Hadst thou walked in the way of God, thou wouldst have dwelt for ever in peace;"[5] for, exhibiting there the reward of knowledge, He calls the wise to the love of it. And, granting pardon to him who has erred, He says, "Turn, turn, as a grape-gatherer to his basket."[6] Do you see the goodness of justice, in that it counsels to repentance? And still further, by Jeremiah, He enlightens in the truth those who have erred. "Thus saith the LORD, Stand in the ways, and look, and ask for the eternal paths of the Lord, what is the good path, and walk in it, and ye shall find purification for your souls."[7] And in order to promote our salvation, He leads us to repentance. Wherefore He says, "If thou repent, the LORD will purify thy heart, and the heart of thy seed."[8] We might have adduced, as supporters on this question, the philosophers who say that only the perfect man is worthy of praise, and the bad man of blame. But since some slander beatitude, as neither itself taking any trouble, nor giving any to any one else, thus not understanding its love to man; on their account, and on account of those who do not associate justice with goodness, the following remarks are added. For it were a legitimate inference to say, that rebuke and censure are suitable to men, since they say that all men are bad; but God alone is wise, from whom cometh wisdom, and alone perfect, and therefore alone

worthy of praise. But I do not employ such language. I say, then, that praise or blame, or whatever resembles praise or blame, are medicines most essential of all to men. Some are ill to cure, and, like iron, are wrought into shape with fire, and hammer, and anvil, that is, with threatening, and reproof, and chastisement; while others, cleaving to faith itself, as self-taught, and as acting of their own free-will, grow by praise: —

> "For virtue that is praised
> Grows like a tree."

And comprehending this, as it seems to me, the Samian Pythagoras gives the injunction: —

> "When you have done base things, rebuke *yourself*;
> But when you have done good things, be glad."

Chiding is also called admonishing; and the etymology of admonishing ($\nu o \upsilon \theta \acute{\epsilon} \tau \eta \sigma \iota \varsigma$) is ($\nu o \hat{\upsilon}$ $\acute{\epsilon} \nu \theta \epsilon \mu \alpha \tau \iota \sigma \mu \acute{o} \varsigma$) putting of understanding into one; so that rebuking is bringing one to one's senses.

But there are myriads of injunctions to be found, whose aim is the attainment of what is good, and the avoidance of what is evil. "For there is no peace to the wicked, saith the LORD."[9] Wherefore by Solomon He commands the children to beware: "My son, let not sinners deceive thee, and go not after their ways; and go not, if they entice thee, saying, Come with us, share with us in innocent blood, and let us hide unjustly the righteous man in the earth; let us put him out of sight, all alive as he is into Hades."[10] This is accordingly likewise a prediction concerning the Lord's passion. And by Ezekiel, the life supplies commandments: "The soul that sinneth shall die; but he that doeth righteousness shall be righteous. He eateth not upon the mountains, and hath not set his eyes on the devices of the house of Israel, and will not defile his neighbour's wife, and will not approach to a woman in her separation, and will not oppress a man, and will restore the debtor's pledge, and will not take plunder: he will give his bread to the hungry, and clothe the naked. His money he will not give on usury, and will not take interest; and he will turn away his hand from wrong, and will execute righteous judgment between a man and his neighbour. He has walked in my statutes, and kept my judgments to do them. This is a righteous man. He shall surely live, saith the Lord."[11] These words contain a description of the conduct of Christians, a notable exhortation to the blessed life, which is the reward of a life of goodness — everlasting life.

---

[1] Deut. xxxi. 20.
[2] Isa. lvi. 7.
[3] Ps. i. 1-3.
[4] Ps. i. 4.
[5] Baruch iii. 13.
[6] Jer. vi. 9.
[7] Jer. vi. 16.
[8] Deut. xxx. 6.

[9] Isa. lvii. 21, xlviii. 22.
[10] Prov. i. 10-12.
[11] Ezek. xviii. 4-9.

CHAP. XI. — THAT THE WORD INSTRUCTED BY THE LAW AND THE PROPHETS.

The mode of His love and His instruction we have shown as we could. Wherefore He Himself, declaring Himself very beautifully, likened Himself to a grain of mustard-seed;[1] and pointed out the spirituality of the word that is sown, and the productiveness of its nature, and the magnificence and conspicuousness of the power of the word; and besides, intimated that the pungency and the purifying virtue of punishment are profitable on account of its sharpness. By the little grain, as it is figuratively called, He bestows salvation on all humanity abundantly. Honey, being very sweet, generates bile, as goodness begets contempt, which is the cause of sinning. But mustard lessens bile, that is, anger, and stops inflammation, that is, pride. From which Word springs the true health of the soul, and its eternal happy temperament (εὐκρασία).

Accordingly, of old He instructed by Moses, and then by the prophets. Moses, too, was a prophet. For the law is the training of refractory children. "Having feasted to the full," accordingly, it is said, "they rose up to play;"[2] senseless repletion with victuals being called χόρτασμα (fodder), not βρῶμα (food). And when, having senselessly filled themselves, they senselessly played; on that account the law was given them, and terror ensued for the prevention of transgressions and for the promotion of right actions, securing attention, and so winning to obedience to the true Instructor, being one and the same Word, and reducing to conformity with the urgent demands of the law. For Paul says that it was given to be a "schoolmaster to bring us to Christ."[3] So that from this it is clear, that one alone, true, good, just, in the image and likeness of the Father, His Son Jesus, the Word of God, is our Instructor; to whom God hath entrusted us, as an affectionate father commits his children to a worthy tutor, expressly charging us, "This is my beloved Son: hear Him."[4] The divine Instructor is trustworthy, adorned as He is with three of the fairest ornaments — knowledge, benevolence, and authority of utterance; — with knowledge, for He is the paternal wisdom: "All Wisdom is from the Lord, and with Him for evermore;" — with authority of utterance, for He is God and Creator: "For all things were made by Him, and without Him was not anything made;"[5] — and with benevolence, for He alone gave Himself a sacrifice for us: "For the good Shepherd giveth His life for the sheep;"[6] and He has so given it. Now, benevolence is nothing but wishing to do good to one's neighbour for his sake.

CHAP. XII. — THE INSTRUCTOR CHARACTERIZED BY THE SEVERITY AND BENIGNITY OF PATERNAL AFFECTION.

Having now accomplished those things, it were a fitting sequel that our instructor Jesus should draw for us the model of the true life, and train humanity in Christ.

Nor is the cast and character of the life He enjoins very formidable; nor is it made altogether easy by reason of His benignity. He enjoins His commands, and at the same time gives them such a character that they may be accomplished.

The view I take is, that He Himself formed man of the dust, and regenerated him by water; and made him grow by his Spirit; and trained him by His word to adoption and salvation, directing him by sacred precepts; in order that, transforming earth-born man into a holy and heavenly being by His advent, He might fulfil to the utmost that divine utterance, "Let Us make man in Our own image and likeness."[7] And, in truth, Christ became the perfect realization of what God spake; and the rest of humanity is conceived as being created merely in His image.

But let us, O children of the good Father — nurslings of the good Instructor — fulfil the Father's will, listen to the Word, and take on the impress of the truly saving life of our Saviour; and meditating on the heavenly mode of life according to which we have been deified, let us anoint ourselves with the perennial immortal bloom of gladness — that ointment of sweet fragrance — having a clear example of immortality in the walk and conversation of the Lord; and following the footsteps of God, to whom alone it belongs to consider, and whose care it is to see to, the way and manner in which the life of men may be made more healthy. Besides, He makes preparation for a self-sufficing mode of life, for simplicity, and for girding up our loins, and for free and unimpeded readiness of our journey; in order to the attainment of an eternity of beatitude, teaching each one of us to be his own storehouse. For He says, "Take no anxious thought for to-morrow,"[8] meaning that the man who has devoted himself to Christ ought to be sufficient to himself, and servant to himself, and moreover lead a life which provides for each day by itself. For it is not in war, but in peace, that

---

[1] Matt. xiii. 31; Luke xiii. 19.
[2] Ex. xxxii. 6; 1 Cor. x. 7.
[3] Gal. iii 24.
[4] Matt. xvii. 5.
[5] John i. 3.

[6] John x. 11.
[7] Gen. i. 26.
[8] Matt. vi. 34.

we are trained. War needs great preparation, and luxury craves profusion; but peace and love, simple and quiet sisters, require no arms nor excessive preparation. The Word is their sustenance.

Our superintendence in instruction and discipline is the office of the Word, from whom we learn frugality and humility, and all that pertains to love of truth, love of man, and love of excellence. And so, in a word, being assimilated to God by a participation in moral excellence, we must not retrograde into carelessness and sloth. But labour, and faint not. Thou shalt be what thou dost not hope, and canst not conjecture. And as there is one mode of training for philosophers, another for orators, and another for athletes; so is there a generous disposition, suitable to the choice that is set upon moral loveliness, resulting from the training of Christ. And in the case of those who have been trained according to this influence, their gait in walking, their sitting at table, their food, their sleep, their going to bed, their regimen, and the rest of their mode of life, acquire a superior dignity.[1] For such a training as is pursued by the Word is not overstrained, but is of the right tension. Thus, therefore, the Word has been called also the Saviour, seeing He has found out for men those rational medicines which produce vigour of the senses and salvation; and devotes Himself to watching for the favourable moment, reproving evil, exposing the causes of evil affections, and striking at the roots of irrational lusts, pointing out what we ought to abstain from, and supplying all the antidotes of salvation to those who are diseased. For the greatest and most regal work of God is the salvation of humanity. The sick are vexed at a physician, who gives no advice bearing on their restoration to health. But how shall we not acknowledge the highest gratitude to the divine Instructor, who is not silent, who omits not those threatenings that point towards destruction, but discloses them, and cuts off the impulses that tend to them; and who indoctrinates in those counsels which result in the true way of living? We must confess, therefore, the deepest obligations to Him. For what else do we say is incumbent on the rational creature — I mean man — than the contemplation of the Divine? I say, too, that it is requisite to contemplate human nature, and to live as the truth directs, and to admire the Instructor and His injunctions, as suitable and harmonious to each other. According to which image also we ought, conforming ourselves to the Instructor, and making the word and our deeds agree, to live a real life.

CHAP. XIII. — VIRTUE RATIONAL, SIN IRRATIONAL.

Everything that is contrary to right reason is sin. Accordingly, therefore, the philosophers think fit to define the most generic passions thus: lust, as desire disobedient to reason; fear, as weakness disobedient to reason; pleasure, as an elation of the spirit disobedient to reason. If, then, disobedience in reference to reason is the generating cause of sin, how shall we escape the conclusion, that obedience to reason — the Word — which we call faith, will of necessity be the efficacious cause of duty? For virtue itself is a state of the soul rendered harmonious by reason in respect to the whole life. Nay, to crown all, philosophy itself is pronounced to be the cultivation of right reason; so that, necessarily, whatever is done through error of reason is transgression, and is rightly called. (ἁμάρτημα) sin. Since, then, the first man sinned and disobeyed God, it is said, "And man became like to the beasts:"[2] being rightly regarded as irrational, he is likened to the beasts. Whence Wisdom says: "The horse for covering; the libidinous and the adulterer is become like to an irrational beast."[3] Wherefore also it is added: "He neighs, whoever may be sitting on him." The man, it is meant, no longer speaks; for he who transgresses against reason is no longer rational, but an irrational animal, given up to lusts by which he is ridden (as a horse by his rider).

But that which is done right, in obedience to reason, the followers of the Stoics call προσῆκον and καθῆκον, that is, incumbent and fitting. What is fitting is incumbent. And obedience is founded on commands. And these being, as they are, the same as counsels — having truth for their aim, train up to the ultimate goal of aspiration, which is conceived of as the end (τέλος). And the end of piety is eternal rest in God. And the beginning of eternity is our end. The right operation of piety perfects duty by works; whence, according to just reasoning, duties consist in actions, not in sayings. And Christian conduct is the operation of the rational soul in accordance with a correct judgment and aspiration after the truth, which attains its destined end through the body, the soul's consort and ally.[4] Virtue is a will in conformity to God and Christ in life, rightly adjusted to life everlasting. For the life of Christians, in which we are now trained, is a system of reasonable actions — that is, of those things taught by the Word — an unfailing energy which we have called faith. The system is the commandments of the Lord, which, being divine statues and spiritual counsels, have been written for ourselves, being adapted for ourselves and our neighbours. Moreover, they

---

[1] [The secondary, civilizing, and socializing power of the Gospel, must have already produced all this change from heathen manners, under Clement's own observation.]

[2] Ps. xlix. 12, 20.
[3] Ecclus. xxxiii. 6.
[4] [Note this definition in Christian ethics.]

turn back on us, as the ball rebounds on him that throws it by the repercussion. Whence also duties are essential for divine discipline, as being enjoined by God, and furnished for our salvation. And since, of those things which are necessary, some relate only to life here, and others, which relate to the blessed life yonder, wing us for flight hence; so, in an analogous manner, of duties, some are ordained with reference to life, others for the blessed life. The commandments issued with respect to natural life are published to the multitude; but those that are suited for living well, and from which eternal life springs, we have to consider, as in a sketch, as we read them out of the Scriptures.

THE INSTRUCTOR

BOOK II.

CHAP. I. — ON EATING.

KEEPING, then, to our aim, and selecting the Scriptures which bear on the usefulness of training for life, we must now compendiously describe what the man who is called a Christian ought to be during the whole of his life. We must accordingly begin with ourselves, and how we ought to regulate ourselves. We have therefore, preserving a due regard to the symmetry of this work, to say how each of us ought to conduct himself in respect to his body, or rather how to regulate the body itself. For whenever any one, who has been brought away by the Word from external things, and from attention to the body itself to the mind, acquires a clear view of what happens according to nature in man, he will know that he is not to be earnestly occupied about external things, but about what is proper and peculiar to man — to purge the eye of the soul, and to sanctify also his flesh. For he that is clean rid of those things which constitute him still dust, what else has he more serviceable than himself for walking in the way which leads to the comprehension of God.

Some men, in truth, live that they may eat, as the irrational creatures, "whose life is their belly, and nothing else." But the Instructor enjoins us to eat that we may live. For neither is food our business, nor is pleasure our aim ; but both are on account of our life here, which the Word is training up to immortality. Wherefore also there is discrimination to be employed in reference to food. And it is to be simple, truly plain, suiting precisely simple and artless children — as ministering to life, not to luxury. And the life to which it conduces consists of two things — health and strength ; to which plainness of fare is most suitable, being conducive both to digestion and lightness of body, from which come growth, and health, and right strength, not strength that is wrong or dangerous and wretched, as is that of athletes produced by compulsory feeding.

We must therefore reject different varieties, which engender various mischiefs, such as a depraved habit of body and disorders of the stomach, the taste being vitiated by an unhappy art — that of cookery, and the useless art of making pastry. For people dare to call by the name of food their dabbling in luxuries, which glides into mischievous pleasures. Antiphanes, the Delian physician, said that this variety of viands was the one cause of disease ; there being people who dislike the truth, and through various absurd notions abjure moderation of diet, and put themselves to a world of trouble to procure dainties from beyond seas.

For my part, I am sorry for this disease, while they are not ashamed to sing the praises of their delicacies, giving themselves great trouble to get lampreys in the Straits of Sicily, the eels of the Mæander, and the kids found in Melos, and the mullets in Sciathus, and the mussels of Pelorus, the oysters of Abydos, not omitting the sprats found in Lipara, and the Mantinican turnip ; and furthermore, the beetroot that grows among the Ascræans : they seek out the cockles of Methymna, the turbots of Attica, and the thrushes of Daphnis, and the reddish-brown dried figs, on account of which the ill-starred Persian marched into Greece with five hundred thousand men. Besides these, they purchase birds from Phasis, the Egyptian snipes, and the Median peafowl. Altering these by means of condiments, the gluttons gape for the sauces. "Whatever earth and the depths of the sea, and the unmeasured space of the air produce," they cater for their gluttony. In their greed and solicitude, the gluttons seem absolutely to sweep the world with a drag-net to gratify their luxurious tastes. These gluttons, surrounded with the sound of hissing frying-pans, and wearing their whole life away at the pestle and mortar, cling to matter like fire. More than that, they emasculate plain food, namely bread, by straining off the nourishing part of the grain, so that

237

the necessary part of food becomes matter of reproach to luxury. There is no limit to epicurism among men. For it has driven them to sweetmeats, and honey-cakes, and sugar-plums; inventing a multitude of desserts, hunting after all manner of dishes. A man like this seems to me to be all jaw, and nothing else. "Desire not," says the Scripture, "rich men's dainties;"[1] for they belong to a false and base life. They partake of luxurious dishes, which a little after go to the dunghill. But we who seek the heavenly bread must rule the belly, which is beneath heaven, and much more the things which are agreeable to it, which "God shall destroy,"[2] says the apostle, justly execrating gluttonous desires. For "meats are for the belly,"[3] for on them depends this truly carnal and destructive life; whence[4] some, speaking with unbridled tongue, dare to apply the name agape,[5] to pitiful suppers, redolent of savour and sauces. Dishonouring the good and saving work of the Word, the consecrated agape, with pots and pouring of sauce; and by drink and delicacies and smoke desecrating that name, they are deceived in their idea, having expected that the promise of God might be bought with suppers. Gatherings for the sake of mirth, and such entertainments as are called by ourselves, we name rightly suppers, dinners, and banquets, after the example of the Lord. But such entertainments the Lord has not called agapæ. He says accordingly somewhere, "When thou art called to a wedding, recline not on the highest couch; but when thou art called, fall into the lowest place;"[6] and elsewhere, "When thou makest a dinner or a supper;" and again, "But when thou makest an entertainment, call the poor,"[7] for whose sake chiefly a supper ought to be made. And further, "A certain man made a great supper, and called many."[8] But I perceive whence the specious appellation of suppers flowed: "from the gullets and furious love for suppers"— according to the comic poet. For, in truth, "to many, many things are on account of the supper." For they have not yet learned that God has provided for His creature (man I mean) food and drink, for sustenance, not for pleasure; since the body derives no advantage from extravagance in viands. For, quite the contrary, those who use the most frugal fare are the strongest and the healthiest, and the noblest; as domestics are healthier and stronger than their masters, and husbandmen than the proprietors;

and not only more robust, but wiser, as philosophers are wiser than rich men. For they have not buried the mind beneath food, nor deceived it with pleasures. But love (agape) is in truth celestial food, the banquet of reason. "It beareth all things, endureth all things, hopeth all things. Love never faileth."[9] "Blessed is he who shall eat bread in the kingdom of God."[10] But the hardest of all cases is for charity, which faileth not, to be cast from heaven above to the ground into the midst of sauces. And do you imagine that I am thinking of a supper that is to be done away with? "For if," it is said, "I bestow all my goods, and have not love, I am nothing."[11] On this love alone depend the law and the Word; and if "thou shalt love the Lord thy God and thy neighbour," this is the celestial festival in the heavens. But the earthly is called a supper, as has been shown from Scripture. For the supper is made for love, but the supper is not love (agape); only a proof of mutual and reciprocal kindly feeling. "Let not, then, your good be evil spoken of; for the kingdom of God is not meat and drink," says the apostle, in order that the meal spoken of may not be conceived as ephemeral, "but righteousness, and peace, and joy in the Holy Ghost."[12] He who eats of this meal, the best of all, shall possess the kingdom of God, fixing his regards here on the holy assembly of love, the heavenly Church. Love, then, is something pure and worthy of God, and its work is communication. "And the care of discipline is love," as Wisdom says; "and love is the keeping of the law."[13] And these joys have an inspiration of love from the public nutriment, which accustoms to everlasting dainties. Love (agape), then, is not a supper. But let the entertainment depend on love. For it is said, "Let the children whom Thou hast loved, O Lord, learn that it is not the products of fruits that nourish man; but it is Thy word which preserves those who believe on Thee."[14] "For the righteous shall not live by bread."[15] But let our diet be light and digestible, and suitable for keeping awake, unmixed with diverse varieties. Nor is this a point which is beyond the sphere of discipline. For love is a good nurse for communication; having as its rich provision sufficiency, which, presiding over diet measured in due quantity, and treating the body in a healthful way, distributes something from its resources to those near us. But the diet which exceeds sufficiency injures a man, deteriorates his spirit, and renders his body prone to disease. Besides, those dainty tastes,

---

1 Prov. xxiii. 3.
2 1 Cor. vi. 13.
3 1 Cor. vi. 13.
4 ὅθεν, an emendation for ὅν.
5 Love, or love-feast, a name applied by the ancients to public entertainments. [But surely he is here rebuking, with St. Jude (v. 12), abuses of the Christian agapæ by heretics and others.]
6 Luke xiv. 8, 10.
7 Luke xiv. 12, 13.
8 Luke xiv. 16.

9 1 Cor. xiii. 7, 8.
10 Luke xiv. 15.
11 1 Cor. xiii. 3.
12 Rom. xiv. 16, 17.
13 Wisd. vi. 17, 18.
14 Wisd. xvi. 26.
15 Deut. viii. 3; Matt. iv. 4.

which trouble themselves about rich dishes, drive to practices of ill-repute, daintiness, gluttony, greed, voracity, insatiability. Appropriate designations of such people as so indulge are flies, weasels, flatterers, gladiators, and the monstrous tribes of parasites — the one class surrendering reason, the other friendship, and the other life, for the gratification of the belly ; crawling on their bellies, beasts in human shape after the image of their father, the voracious beast. People first called the abandoned ἀσώτους, and so appear to me to indicate their end, understanding them as those who are (ἀσώστους) unsaved, excluding the σ. For those that are absorbed in pots, and exquisitely prepared niceties of condiments, are they not plainly abject, earth-born, leading an ephemeral kind of life, as if they were not to live [hereafter] ? Those the Holy Spirit, by Isaiah, denounces as wretched, depriving them tacitly of the name of love (*agape*), since their feasting was not in accordance with the word. " But they made mirth, killing calves, and sacrificing sheep, saying, Let us eat and drink, for to-morrow we die." And that He reckons such luxury to be sin, is shown by what He adds, " And your sin shall not be forgiven you till you die," [1] — not conveying the idea that death, which deprives of sensation, is the forgiveness of sin, but meaning that death of salvation which is the recompense of sin. " Take no pleasure in abominable delicacies," says Wisdom.[2] At this point, too, we have to advert to what are called things sacrificed to idols, in order to show how we are enjoined to abstain from them. Polluted and abominable those things seem to me, to the blood of which, fly

" Souls from Erebus of inanimate corpses." [3]

" For I would not that ye should have fellowship with demons," [4] says the apostle ; since the food of those who are saved and those who perish is separate. We must therefore abstain from these viands not for fear (because there is no power in them) ; but on account of our conscience, which is holy, and out of detestation of the demons to which they are dedicated, are we to loathe them ; and further, on account of the instability of those who regard many things in a way that makes them prone to fall, " whose conscience, being weak, is defiled : for meat commendeth us not to God." [5] " For it is not that which entereth in that defileth a man, but that which goeth out of his mouth." [6] The natural use of food is then indifferent. " For neither if we eat are we the better," it is said, " nor if we

eat not are we the worse." [7] But it is inconsistent with reason, for those that have been made worthy to share divine and spiritual food, to partake of the tables of demons. " Have we not power to eat and to drink," says the apostle, " and to lead about wives " ? But by keeping pleasures under command we prevent lusts. See, then, that this power of yours never " become a stumbling-block to the weak."

For it were not seemly that we, after the fashion of the rich man's son in the Gospel,[8] should, as prodigals, abuse the Father's gifts ; but we should use them, without undue attachment to them, as having command over ourselves. For we are enjoined to reign and rule over meats, not to be slaves to them. It is an admirable thing, therefore, to raise our eyes aloft to what is true, to depend on that divine food above, and to satiate ourselves with the exhaustless contemplation of that which truly exists, and so taste of the only sure and pure delight. For such is the *agape*, which, the food that comes from Christ shows that we ought to partake of. But totally irrational, futile, and not human is it for those that are of the earth, fattening themselves like cattle, to feed themselves up for death ; looking downwards on the earth, and bending ever over tables ; leading a life of gluttony ; burying all the good of existence here in a life that by and by will end ; courting voracity alone, in respect to which cooks are held in higher esteem than husbandmen. For we do not abolish social intercourse, but look with suspicion on the snares of custom, and regard them as a calamity. Wherefore daintiness is to be shunned, and we are to partake of few and necessary things. " And if one of the unbelievers call us to a feast, and we determine to go " (for it is a good thing not to mix with the dissolute), the apostle bids us " eat what is set before us, asking no questions for conscience sake." [9] Similarly he has enjoined to purchase " what is sold in the shambles," without curious questioning.[10]

We are not, then, to abstain wholly from various kinds of food, but only are not to be taken up about them. We are to partake of what is set before us, as becomes a Christian, out of respect to him who has invited us, by a harmless and moderate participation in the social meeting ; regarding the sumptuousness of what is put on the table as a matter of indifference, despising the dainties, as after a little destined to perish. " Let him who eateth, not despise him who eateth not ; and let him who eateth not, not judge him who eateth." [11] And a little way on he explains the reason of the command, when

---

[1] Isa. xxii. 13, 14.
[2] Ecclus xviii. 32.
[3] *Odyss.*, xi. 37.
[4] 1 Cor. x. 20.
[5] 1 Cor. viii. 7, 8.
[6] Matt. xv. 11.

[7] 1 Cor. viii. 8.
[8] Luke xv. 11.
[9] 1 Cor. x. 27.
[10] 1 Cor. x. 25.
[11] Rom. xiv. 3.

he says, " He that eateth, eateth to the Lord, and giveth God thanks; and he that eateth not, to the Lord he eateth not, and giveth God thanks." [1] So that the right food is thanksgiving. And he who gives thanks does not occupy his time in pleasures. And if we would persuade any of our fellow-guests to virtue, we are all the more on this account to abstain from those dainty dishes; and so exhibit ourselves as a bright pattern of virtue, such as we ourselves have in Christ. " For if any of such meats make a brother to stumble, I shall not eat it as long as the world lasts," says he, " that I may not make my brother stumble." [2] I gain the man by a little self-restraint. " Have we not power to eat and to drink?" [3] And "we know "—he says the truth—" that an idol is nothing in the world; but we have only one true God, of whom are all things, and one Lord Jesus. But," he says, " through thy knowledge thy weak brother perishes, for whom Christ died; and they that wound the conscience of the weak brethren sin against Christ." [4] Thus the apostle, in his solicitude for us, discriminates in the case of entertainments, saying, that " if any one called a brother be found a fornicator, or an adulterer, or an idolater, with such an one not to eat; " [5] neither in discourse or food are we to join, looking with suspicion on the pollution thence proceeding, as on the tables of the demons. " It is good, then, neither to eat flesh nor to drink wine," [6] as both he and the Pythagoreans acknowledge. For this is rather characteristic of a beast; and the fumes arising from them being dense, darken the soul. If one partakes of them, he does not sin. Only let him partake temperately, not dependent on them, nor gaping after fine fare. For a voice will whisper to him, saying, " Destroy not the work of God for the sake of food." [7] For it is the mark of a silly mind to be amazed and stupified at what is presented at vulgar banquets, after the rich fare which is in the Word; and much sillier to make one's eyes the slaves of the delicacies, so that one's greed is, so to speak, carried round by the servants. And how foolish for people to raise themselves on the couches, all but pitching their faces into the dishes, stretching out from the couch as from a nest, according to the common saying, " that they may catch the wandering steam by breathing it in!" And how senseless, to besmear their hands with the condiments, and to be constantly reaching to the sauce, cramming themselves immoderately and shamelessly, not like people tasting, but ravenously seizing! For you may see such

people, liker swine or dogs for gluttony than men, in such a hurry to feed themselves full, that both jaws are stuffed out at once, the veins about the face raised, and besides, the perspiration running all over, as they are tightened with their insatiable greed, and panting with their excess; the food pushed with unsocial eagerness into their stomach, as if they were stowing away their victuals for provision for a journey, not for digestion. Excess, which in all things is an evil, is very highly reprehensible in the matter of food. Gluttony, called ὀψοφαγία, is nothing but excess in the use of relishes (ὄψον); and λαιμαργία is insanity with respect to the gullet; and γαστριμαργία is excess with respect to food — insanity in reference to the belly, as the name implies; for μάργος is a madman. The apostle, checking those that transgress in their conduct at entertainments, [8] says: " For every one taketh beforehand in eating his own supper; and one is hungry, and another drunken. Have ye not houses to eat and to drink in? Or despise ye the church of God, and shame those who have not?" [9] And among those who have, they, who eat shamelessly and are insatiable, shame themselves. And both act badly; the one by paining those who have not, the other by exposing their own greed in the presence of those who have. Necessarily, therefore, against those who have cast off shame and unsparingly abuse meals, the insatiable to whom nothing is sufficient, the apostle, in continuation, again breaks forth in a voice of displeasure: "So that, my brethren, when ye come together to eat, wait for one another. And if any one is hungry, let him eat at home, that ye come not together to condemnation." [10]

From all slavish habits [11] and excess we must abstain, and touch what is set before us in a decorous way; keeping the hand and couch and chin free of stains; preserving the grace of the countenance undisturbed, and committing no indecorum in the act of swallowing; but stretching out the hand at intervals in an orderly manner. We must guard against speaking anything while eating: for the voice becomes disagreeable and inarticulate when it is confined by full jaws; and the tongue, pressed by the food and impeded in its natural energy, gives forth a compressed utterance. Nor is it suitable to eat and to drink simultaneously. For it is the very extreme of intemperance to confound the times whose uses are discordant. And "whether ye eat or drink, do all to the glory of God," [12] aiming after true frugality, which the Lord also seems to me to have hinted at when He blessed

---

1 Rom. xiv. 6.
2 1 Cor. viii. 13.
3 1 Cor. ix. 14.
4 1 Cor. viii. 6, 11, 12.
5 1 Cor. v 11.
6 Rom. xiv. 21.
7 Rom. xiv. 20.

8 [Clement seems to think this abuse was connected with the agapæ, not — one might trust — with the Lord's supper.]
9 1 Cor. xi. 21, 22.
10 1 Cor. xi. 33, 34.
11 Literally, " slave-manners," the conduct to be expected from slaves.
12 1 Cor. x. 31.

the loaves and the cooked fishes with which He feasted the disciples, introducing a beautiful example of simple food. That fish then which, at the command of the Lord, Peter caught, points to digestible and God-given and moderate food. And by those who rise from the water to the bait of righteousness, He admonishes us to take away luxury and avarice, as the coin from the fish ; in order that He might displace vainglory ; and by giving the stater to the tax-gatherers, and "rendering to Cæsar the things which are Cæsar's," might preserve "to God the things which are God's." [1] The stater is capable of other explanations not unknown to us, but the present is not a suitable occasion for their treatment. Let the mention we make for our present purpose suffice, as it is not unsuitable to the flowers of the Word ; and we have often done this, drawing to the urgent point of the question the most beneficial fountain, in order to water those who have been planted by the Word. "For if it is lawful for me to partake of all things, yet all things are not expedient." [2] For those that do all that is lawful, quickly fall into doing what is unlawful. And just as righteousness is not attained by avarice, nor temperance by excess ; so neither is the regimen of a Christian formed by indulgence ; for the table of truth is far from lascivious dainties. For though it was chiefly for men's sake that all things were made, yet it is not good to use all things, nor at all times. For the occasion, and the time, and the mode, and the intention, materially turn the balance with reference to what is useful, in the view of one who is rightly instructed ; and this is suitable, and has influence in putting a stop to a life of gluttony, which wealth is prone to choose, not that wealth which sees clearly, but that abundance which makes a man blind with reference to gluttony. No one is poor as regards necessaries, and a man is never overlooked. For there is one God who feeds the fowls and the fishes, and, in a word, the irrational creatures ; and not one thing whatever is wanting to them, though "they take no thought for their food." [3] And we are better than they, being their lords, and more closely allied to God, as being wiser ; and we were made, not that we might eat and drink, but that we might devote ourselves to the knowledge of God. "For the just man who eats is satisfied in his soul, but the belly of the wicked shall want," [4] filled with the appetites of insatiable gluttony. Now lavish expense is adapted not for enjoyment alone, but also for social communication. Wherefore we must guard against those articles of food which

persuade us to eat when we are not hungry, bewitching the appetite. For is there not within a temperate simplicity a wholesome variety of eatables ? Bulbs, [5] olives, certain herbs, milk, cheese, fruits, all kinds of cooked food without sauces ; and if flesh is wanted, let roast rather than boiled be set down. Have you anything to eat here ? said the Lord [6] to the disciples after the resurrection ; and they, as taught by Him to practise frugality, "gave Him a piece of broiled fish ; " and having eaten before them, says Luke, He spoke to them what He spoke. And in addition to these, it is not to be overlooked that those who feed according to the Word are not debarred from dainties in the shape of honey-combs. For of articles of food, those are the most suitable which are fit for immediate use without fire, since they are readiest ; and second to these are those which are simplest, as we said before. But those who bend around inflammatory tables, nourishing their own diseases, are ruled by a most lickerish demon, whom I shall not blush to call the Belly-demon, and the worst and most abandoned of demons. He is therefore exactly like the one who is called the Ventriloquist-demon. It is far better to be happy [7] than to have a demon dwelling with us. And happiness is found in the practice of virtue. Accordingly, the apostle Matthew partook of seeds, and nuts, [8] and vegetables, without flesh. And John, who carried temperance to the extreme, "ate locusts and wild honey." Peter abstained from swine ; "but a trance fell on him," as is written in the Acts of the Apostles, "and he saw heaven opened, and a vessel let down on the earth by the four corners, and all the four-footed beasts and creeping things of the earth and the fowls of heaven in it ; and there came a voice to him, Rise, and slay, and eat. And Peter said, Not so, Lord, for I have never eaten what is common or unclean. And the voice came again to him the second time, What God hath cleansed, call not thou common." [9] The use of them is accordingly indifferent to us. "For not what entereth into the mouth defileth the man," [10] but the vain opinion respecting uncleanness. For God, when He created man, said, "All things shall be to you for meat." [11] "And herbs, with love, are better than a calf with fraud." [12] This well reminds us of what was said above, that herbs are not love, but that our meals are to be taken with love ; [13] and in these the medium state is

---

[1] Matt. xxii. 21.
[2] 1 Cor. x. 23.
[3] Matt. vi. 25, etc.
[4] Prov. xiii. 5.

[5] A bulbous root, much prized in Greece, which grew wild.
[6] Luke xxiv. 41-44.
[7] A play here on the words εὐδαίμων and δαίμων.
[8] ἀκρόδρυα, hard-shelled fruits.
[9] Acts x. 10-15.
[10] Matt. xv. 11.
[11] Gen. ix. 2, 3.
[12] Prov. xv. 17.
[13] In allusion to the agapæ, or love-feasts.

good. In all things, indeed, this is the case, and not least in the preparation made for feasting, since the extremes are dangerous, and middle courses good. And to be in no want of necessaries is the medium. For the desires which are in accordance with nature are bounded by sufficiency. The Jews had frugality enjoined on them by the law in the most systematic manner. For the Instructor, by Moses, deprived them of the use of innumerable things, adding reasons — the spiritual ones hidden ; the carnal ones apparent, to which indeed they have trusted ; in the case of some animals, because they did not part the hoof, and others because they did not ruminate their food, and others because alone of aquatic animals they were devoid of scales ; so that altogether but a few were left appropriate for their food. And of those that he permitted them to touch, he prohibited such as had died, or were offered to idols, or had been strangled ; for to touch these was unlawful. For since it is impossible for those who use dainties to abstain from partaking of them, he appointed the opposite mode of life, till he should break down the propensity to indulgence arising from habit. Pleasure has often produced in men harm and pain ; and full feeding begets in the soul uneasiness, and forgetfulness, and foolishness. And they say that the bodies of children, when shooting up to their height, are made to grow right by deficiency in nourishment. For then the spirit, which pervades the body in order to its growth, is not checked by abundance of food obstructing the freedom of its course. Whence that truth-seeking philosopher Plato, fanning the spark of the Hebrew philosophy when condemning a life of luxury, says : "On my coming hither, the life which is here called happy, full of Italian and Syracusan tables, pleased me not by any means, [consisting as it did] in being filled twice a day, and never sleeping by night alone, and whatever other accessories attend the mode of life. For not one man under heaven, if brought up from his youth in such practices, will ever turn out a wise man, with however admirable a natural genius he may be endowed." For Plato was not unacquainted with David, who " placed the sacred ark in his city in the midst of the tabernacle ; " and bidding all his subjects rejoice " before the Lord, divided to the whole host of Israel, man and woman, to each a loaf of bread, and baked bread, and a cake from the frying-pan." [1]

This was the sufficient sustenance of the Israelites. But that of the Gentiles was overabundant. No one who uses it will ever study to become temperate, burying as he does his mind in his belly, very like the fish called ass,[2] which, Aristotle says, alone of all creatures has its heart in its stomach. This fish Epicharmus the comic poet calls " monster-paunch."

Such are the men who believe in their belly, " whose God is their belly, whose glory is in their shame, who mind earthly things." To them the apostle predicted no good when he said, " whose end is destruction." [3]

CHAP. II. — ON DRINKING.

" Use a little wine," says the apostle to Timothy, who drank water, " for thy stomach's sake ; " [4] most properly applying its aid as a strengthening tonic suitable to a sickly body enfeebled with watery humours ; and specifying " a little," lest the remedy should, on account of its quantity, unobserved, create the necessity of other treatment.

The natural, temperate, and necessary beverage, therefore, for the thirsty is water.[5] This was the simple drink of sobriety, which, flowing from the smitten rock, was supplied by the Lord to the ancient Hebrews.[6] It was most requisite that in their wanderings they should be temperate.[7]

Afterwards the sacred vine produced the prophetic cluster. This was a sign to them, when trained from wandering to their rest ; representing the great cluster the Word, bruised for us. For the blood of the grape — that is, the Word — desired to be mixed with water, as His blood is mingled with salvation.

And the blood of the Lord is twofold. For there is the blood of His flesh, by which we are redeemed from corruption ; and the spiritual, that by which we are anointed. And to drink the blood of Jesus, is to become partaker of the Lord's immortality ; the Spirit being the energetic principle of the Word, as blood is of flesh.[8]

Accordingly, as wine is blended with water,[9] so is the Spirit with man. And the one, the mixture of wine and water, nourishes to faith ; while the other, the Spirit, conducts to immortality.

And the mixture of both — of the water and of the Word — is called *Eucharist*, renowned and glorious grace ; and they who by faith partake of it are sanctified both in body and soul. For the divine mixture, man, the Father's will

---

[1] 2 Kings vi. 17-19, Septuagint: 2 Sam. vi. 17-19. A. V.

[2] ὄνος, perhaps the hake or cod.
[3] Phil. iii. 19.
[4] 1 Tim. v. 23.
[5] [This remarkable chapter seems to begin with the author's recollections of Pindar (ἄριστον μὲν ὕδωρ), but to lay down very justly the Scriptural ideas of temperance and abstinence.]
[6] Ex. xvii.; Num. xx.
[7] [Clement reckons only two classes as living faithfully with respect to drink, the *abstinent* and the *totally abstinent*.]
[8] [This seems Clement's exposition of St. John (vi. 63), and a clear statement as to the Eucharist, which he pronounces spiritual food.]
[9] [A plain reference to the use of the mixed cup in the Lord's supper.]

as mystically compounded by the Spirit and the Word. For, in truth, the spirit is joined to the soul, which is inspired by it ; and the flesh, by reason of which the Word became flesh, to the Word.

I therefore admire those who have adopted an austere life, and who are fond of water, the medicine of temperance, and flee as far as possible from wine, shunning it as they would the danger of fire.[1] It is proper, therefore, that boys and girls should keep as much as possible away from this medicine. For it is not right to pour into the burning season of life the hottest of all liquids — wine — adding, as it were, fire to fire.[2] For hence wild impulses and burning lusts and fiery habits are kindled ; and young men inflamed from within become prone to the indulgence of vicious propensities ; so that signs of injury appear in their body, the members of lust coming to maturity sooner than they ought. The breasts and organs of generation, inflamed with wine, expand and swell in a shameful way, already exhibiting beforehand the image of fornication ; and the body compels the wound of the soul to inflame, and shameless pulsations follow abundance, inciting the man of correct behaviour to transgression ; and hence the voluptuousness of youth overpasses the bounds of modesty. And we must, as far as possible, try to quench the impulses of youth by removing the Bacchic fuel of the threatened danger ; and by pouring the antidote to the inflammation, so keep down the burning soul, and keep in the swelling members, and allay the agitation of lust when it is already in commotion. And in the case of grown-up people, let those with whom it agrees sometimes partake of dinner, tasting bread only, and let them abstain wholly from drink ; in order that their superfluous moisture may be absorbed and drunk up by the eating of dry food. For constant spitting and wiping off perspiration, and hastening to evacuations, is the sign of excess, from the immoderate use of liquids supplied in excessive quantity to the body. And if thirst come on, let the appetite be satisfied with a little water. For it is not proper that water should be supplied in too great profusion ; in order that the food may not be drowned, but ground down in order to digestion ; and this takes place when the victuals are collected into a mass, and only a small portion is evacuated.

And, besides, it suits divine studies not to be heavy with wine. " For unmixed wine is far from compelling a man to be wise, much less temperate," according to the comic poet. But towards evening, about supper-time, wine may be used, when we are no longer engaged in more serious readings. Then also the air becomes colder than it is during the day ; so that the failing natural warmth requires to be nourished by the introduction of heat. But even then it must only be a little wine that is to be used ; for we must not go on to intemperate potations. Those who are already advanced in life may partake more cheerfully of the draught, to warm by the harmless medicine of the vine the chill of age, which the decay of time has produced. For old men's passions are not, for the most part, stirred to such agitation as to drive them to the shipwreck of drunkenness. For being moored by reason and time, as by anchors, they stand with greater ease the storm of passions which rushes down from intemperance. They also may be permitted to indulge in pleasantry at feasts. But to them also let the limit of their potations be the point up to which they keep their reason unwavering, their memory active, and their body unmoved and unshaken by wine. People in such a state are called by those who are skilful in these matters, *acrothorakes*.[3] It is well, therefore, to leave off betimes, for fear of tripping.

One Artorius, in his book *On Long Life* (for so I remember), thinks that drink should be taken only till the food be moistened, that we may attain to a longer life. It is fitting, then, that some apply wine by way of physic, for the sake of health alone, and others for purposes of relaxation and enjoyment. For first wine makes the man who has drunk it more benignant than before, more agreeable to his boon companions, kinder to his domestics, and more pleasant to his friends. But when intoxicated, he becomes violent instead. For wine being warm, and having sweet juices when duly mixed, dissolves the foul excrementitious matters by its warmth, and mixes the acrid and base humours with the agreeable scents.

It has therefore been well said, " A joy of the soul and heart was wine created from the beginning, when drunk in moderate sufficiency."[4] And it is best to mix the wine with as much water as possible, and not to have recourse to it as to water, and so get enervated to drunkenness, and not pour it in as water from love of wine. For both are works of God ; and so the mixture of both, of water and of wine, conduces together to health, because life consists of what is necessary and of what is useful. With water, then, which is the necessary of life, and to be used in abundance, there is also to be mixed the useful.

By an immoderate quantity of wine the tongue

[1] [If the *temperate* do well, he thinks, the *abstinent* do better ; but nobody is temperate who does not often and habitually abstain.]

[2] [A very important principle ; for, if wine be " the milk of age," the use of it in youth deprives age of any benefit from its sober use].

[3] The exact derivation of *acrothorakes* is matter of doubt. But we have the authority of Aristotle and Erotian for believing that it was applied to those who were slightly drunk. Some regard the clause here as an interpolation.

[4] Ecclus. xxxi. 27.

is impeded ; the lips are relaxed ; the eyes roll wildly, the sight, as it were, swimming through the quantity of moisture ; and compelled to deceive, they think that everything is revolving round them, and cannot count distant objects as single. "And, in truth, methinks I see two suns,"[1] said the Theban old man in his cups. For the sight, being disturbed by the heat of the wine, frequently fancies the substance of one object to be manifold. And there is no difference between moving the eye or the object seen. For both have the same effect on the sight, which, on account of the fluctuation, cannot accurately obtain a perception of the object. And the feet are carried from beneath the man as by a flood, and hiccuping and vomiting and maudlin nonsense follow ; "for every intoxicated man," according to the tragedy,[2] —

> "Is conquered by anger, and empty of sense,
> And likes to pour forth much silly speech ;
> And is wont to hear unwillingly,
> What evil words he with his will hath said."

And before tragedy, Wisdom cried, "Much wine drunk abounds in irritation and all manner of mistakes."[3] Wherefore most people say that you ought to relax over your cups, and postpone serious business till morning. I however think that then especially ought reason to be introduced to mix in the feast, to act the part of director (pædagogue) to wine-drinking, lest conviviality imperceptibly degenerate to drunkenness. For as no sensible man ever thinks it requisite to shut his eyes before going to sleep, so neither can any one rightly wish reason to be absent from the festive board, or can well study to lull it asleep till business is begun. But the Word can never quit those who belong to Him, not even if we are asleep ; for He ought to be invited even to our sleep.[4] For perfect wisdom, which is knowledge of things divine and human, which comprehends all that relates to the oversight of the flock of men, becomes, in reference to life, art ; and so, while we live, is constantly with us, always accomplishing its own proper work, the product of which is a good life.

But the miserable wretches who expel temperance from conviviality, think excess in drinking to be the happiest life ; and their life is nothing but revel, debauchery, baths, excess, urinals, idleness, drink. You may see some of them, half-drunk, staggering, with crowns round their necks like wine jars, vomiting drink on one another in the name of good fellowship ; and others, full of the effects of their debauch, dirty, pale in the face, livid, and still above yesterday's bout pouring another bout to last till next morning. It is

well, my friends, it is well to make our acquaintance with this picture at the greatest possible distance from it, and to frame ourselves to what is better, dreading lest we also become a like spectacle and laughing-stock to others.

It has been appropriately said, "As the furnace proveth the steel blade in the process of dipping, so wine proveth the heart of the haughty."[5] A debauch is the immoderate use of wine, intoxication the disorder that results from such use ; crapulousness (κραιπάλη) is the discomfort and nausea that follow a debauch, so called from the head shaking (κάρα πάλλειν).

Such a life as this (if life it must be called, which is spent in idleness, in agitation about voluptuous indulgences, and in the hallucinations of debauchery) the divine Wisdom looks on with contempt, and commands her children, "Be not a wine-bibber, nor spend your money in the purchase of flesh ; for every drunkard and fornicator shall come to beggary, and every sluggard shall be clothed in tatters and rags."[6] For every one that is not awake to wisdom, but is steeped in wine, is a sluggard. "And the drunkard," he says, "shall be clothed in rags, and be ashamed of his drunkenness in the presence of onlookers."[7] For the wounds of the sinner are the rents of the garment of the flesh, the holes made by lusts, through which the shame of the soul within is seen — namely sin, by reason of which it will not be easy to save the garment, that has been torn away all round, that has rotted away in many lusts, and has been rent asunder from salvation.

So he adds these most monitory words. "Who has woes, who has clamour, who has contentions, who has disgusting babblings, who has unavailing remorse?"[8] You see, in all his raggedness, the lover of wine, who despises the Word Himself, and has abandoned and given himself to drunkenness. You see what threatening Scripture has pronounced against him. And to its threatening it adds again : "Whose are red eyes? Those, is it not, who tarry long at their wine, and hunt out the places where drinking goes on?" Here he shows the lover of drink to be already dead to the Word, by the mention of the blood-shot eyes, — a mark which appears on corpses, announcing to him death in the Lord. For forgetfulness of the things which tend to true life turns the scale towards destruction. With reason therefore, the Instructor, in His solicitude for our salvation, forbids us, "Drink not wine to drunkenness." Wherefore? you will ask. Because, says He, "thy mouth will then speak perverse things, and thou liest down as in the heart of the

---

1 Pentheus in Euripides, *Bacch.*, 918.
2 Attributed to Sophocles.
3 Ecclus. xxxi. 29.
4 [A beautiful maxim, and proving the habit of early Christians to use completory prayers. This the drunkard is in no state to do.]

5 Ecclus. xxxi. 26.
6 Prov. xxiii. 20.
7 Prov. xxiii. 21.
8 Prov. xxiii. 29, 30.

,ea, and as the steersman of a ship in the midst of huge billows." Hence, too, poetry comes to our help, and says : —

" Let wine which has strength equal to fire come to men.
Then will it agitate them, as the north or south wind
    agitates the Libyan waves."

And further : —

" Wine wandering in speech shows all secrets.
Soul-deceiving wine is the ruin of those who drink it."

And so on.

You see the danger of shipwreck. The heart is drowned in much drink. The excess of drunkenness is compared to the danger of the sea, in which when the body has once been sunken like a ship, it descends to the depths of turpitude, overwhelmed in the mighty billows of wine ; and the helmsman, the human mind, is tossed about on the surge of drunkenness, which swells aloft ; and buried in the trough of the sea, is blinded by the darkness of the tempest, having drifted away from the haven of truth, till, dashing on the rocks beneath the sea, it perishes, driven by itself into voluptuous indulgences.

With reason, therefore, the apostle enjoins, " Be not drunk with wine, in which there is much excess ; " by the term excess (ἀσωτία) intimating the inconsistence of drunkenness with salvation (τὸ ἄσωστον). For if He made water wine at the marriage, He did not give permission to get drunk. He gave life to the watery element of the meaning of the law, filling with His blood the doer of it who is of Adam, that is, the whole world ; supplying piety with drink from the vine of truth, the mixture of the old law and of the new word, in order to the fulfilment of the pre-destined time. The Scripture, accordingly, has named wine the symbol of the sacred blood ; [1] but reproving the base tippling with the dregs of wine, it says : " Intemperate is wine, and insolent is drunkenness." [2] It is agreeable, therefore, to right reason, to drink on account of the cold of winter, till the numbness is dispelled from those who are subject to feel it ; and on other occasions as a medicine for the intestines. For, as we are to use food to satisfy hunger, so also are we to use drink to satisfy thirst, taking the most careful precautions against a slip : " for the introduction of wine is perilous." And thus shall our soul be pure, and dry, and luminous ; and the soul itself is wisest and best when dry. And thus, too, is it fit for contemplation, and is not humid with the exhalations, that rise from wine, forming a mass like a cloud. We must not therefore trouble ourselves to procure Chian wine if it is absent, or Ariousian when it is not at hand. For thirst is a sensation of want, and craves means suitable for supplying the want, and not

sumptuous liquor. Importations of wines from beyond seas are for an appetite enfeebled by excess, where the soul even before drunkenness is insane in its desires. For there are the fragrant Thasian wine, and the pleasant-breathing Lesbian, and a sweet Cretan wine, and sweet Syracusan wine, and Mendusian, an Egyptian wine, and the insular Naxian, the " highly per-fumed and flavoured," [3] another wine of the land of Italy. These are many names. For the temperate drinker, one wine suffices, the product of the cultivation of the one God. For why should not the wine of their own country satisfy men's desires, unless they were to import water also, like the foolish Persian kings? The Choaspes, a river of India so called, was that from which the best water for drinking — the Choaspian — was got. As wine, when taken, makes people lovers of it, so does water too. The Holy Spirit, uttering His voice by Amos, pronounces the rich to be wretched on account of their luxury : [4] " Those that drink strained wine, and recline on an ivory couch," he says ; and what else similar he adds by way of reproach.

Especial regard is to be paid to decency [5] (as the myth represents Athene, whoever she was, out of regard to it, giving up the pleasure of the flute because of the unseemliness of the sight) : so that we are to drink without contortions of the face, not greedily grasping the cup, nor before drinking making the eyes roll with unseemly motion ; nor from intemperance are we to drain the cup at a draught ; nor besprinkle the chin, nor splash the garments while gulping down all the liquor at once, — our face all but filling the bowl, and drowned in it. For the gurgling occasioned by the drink rushing with violence, and by its being drawn in with a great deal of breath, as if it were being poured into an earthenware vessel, while the throat makes a noise through the rapidity of ingurgitation, is a shameful and unseemly spectacle of intemperance. In addition to this, eagerness in drinking is a practice injurious to the the partaker. Do not haste to mischief, my friend. Your drink is not being taken from you. It is given you, and waits you. Be not eager to burst, by draining it down with gaping throat. Your thirst is satiated, even if you drink slower, observing decorum, by taking the beverage in small portions, in an orderly way. For that which intemperance greedily seizes, is not taken away by taking time.

" Be not mighty," he says, " at wine ; for wine has overcome many." [6] The Scythians, the Celts, the Iberians, and the Thracians, all of them war-

---

[3] ἀνθοσμίας. Some suppose the word to be derived from the name of a town: " The Anthosmian."
[4] Amos vi. 4, 6.
[5] [Here Clement satirizes heathen manners, and quotes *Athene*, to shame Christians who imitate them.]
[6] Ecclus. xxxi. 25.

[1] [A passage not to be overlooked. *Greek*, μυστικὸν σύμβολον.]
[2] Prov. xx. 1.

like races, are greatly addicted to intoxication, and think that it is an honourable, happy pursuit to engage in. But we, the people of peace, feasting for lawful enjoyment, not to wantonness, drink sober cups of friendship, that our friendships may be shown in a way truly appropriate to the name.

In what manner do you think the Lord drank when He became man for our sakes? As shamelessly as we? Was it not with decorum and propriety? Was it not deliberately? For rest assured, He Himself also partook of wine; for He, too, was man. And He blessed the wine, saying, "Take, drink: this is my blood"—the blood of the vine.[1] He figuratively calls the Word "shed for many, for the remission of sins"—the holy stream of gladness. And that he who drinks ought to observe moderation, He clearly showed by what He taught at feasts. For He did not teach affected by wine. And that it was wine which was the thing blessed, He showed again, when He said to His disciples, "I will not drink of the fruit of this vine, till I drink it with you in the kingdom of my Father."[2] But that it was wine which was drunk by the Lord, He tells us again, when He spake concerning Himself, reproaching the Jews for their hardness of heart: "For the Son of man," He says, "came, and they say, Behold a glutton and a wine-bibber, a friend of publicans."[3] Let this be held fast by us against those that are called Encratites.

But women, making a profession, forsooth, of aiming at the graceful, that their lips may not be rent apart by stretching them on broad drinking cups, and so widening the mouth, drinking in an unseemly way out of alabastra quite too narrow in the mouth, throw back their heads and bare their necks indecently, as I think; and distending the throat in swallowing, gulp down the liquor as if to make bare all they can to their boon companions; and drawing hiccups like men, or rather like slaves, revel in luxurious riot. For nothing disgraceful is proper for man, who is endowed with reason; much less for woman, to whom it brings modesty even to reflect of what nature she is.

"An intoxicated woman is great wrath," it is said, as if a drunken woman were the wrath of God. Why? "Because she will not conceal her shame."[4] For a woman is quickly drawn down to licentiousness, if she only set her choice on pleasures. And we have not prohibited drinking from alabastra; but we forbid studying to drink from them alone, as arrogant; counselling women to use with indifference what comes

in the way, and cutting up by the roots the dangerous appetites that are in them. Let the rush of air, then, which regurgitates so as to produce hiccup, be emitted silently.

But by no manner of means are women to be allowed to uncover and exhibit any part of their person, lest both fall,—the men by being excited to look, they by drawing on themselves the eyes of the men.

But always must we conduct ourselves as in the Lord's presence, lest He say to us, as the apostle in indignation said to the Corinthians, "When ye come together, this is not to eat the Lord's supper."[5]

To me, the star called by the mathematicians Acephalus (headless), which is numbered before the wandering star, his head resting on his breast, seems to be a type of the gluttonous, the voluptuous, and those that are prone to drunkenness. For in such[6] the faculty of reasoning is not situated in the head, but among the intestinal appetites, enslaved to lust and anger. For just as Elpenor broke his neck through intoxication,[7] so the brain, dizzied by drunkenness, falls down from above, with a great fall to the liver and the heart, that is, to voluptuousness and anger: as the sons of the poets say Hephæstus was hurled by Zeus from heaven to earth.[8] "The trouble of sleeplessness, and bile, and cholic, are with an insatiable man," it is said.[9]

Wherefore also Noah's intoxication was recorded in writing, that, with the clear and written description of his transgression before us, we might guard with all our might against drunkenness. For which cause they who covered the shame[10] of his drunkenness are blessed by the Lord. The Scripture accordingly, giving a most comprehensive compend, has expressed all in one word: "To an instructed man sufficiency is wine, and he will rest in his bed."[11]

CHAP. III.—ON COSTLY VESSELS.

And so the use of cups made of silver and gold, and of others inlaid with precious stones, is out of place, being only a deception of the vision. For if you pour any warm liquid into them, the vessels becoming hot, to touch them is painful. On the other hand, if you pour in what is cold, the material changes its quality, injuring the mixture, and the rich potion is hurtful. Away, then, with Thericleian cups and

---

[1] [The blood of the vine is Christ's blood. According to Clement, then, it remains in the Eucharist unchanged.]
[2] Mark xvi. 25; Matt. xxvi. 29. [This also is a noteworthy use of the text.]
[3] Matt. xi. 19.
[4] Ecclus. xxvi. 8.

[5] 1 Cor. xi. 20. [Clement has already hinted his opinion, that this referred to a shameful custom of the Corinthians to let an *agape* precede the Eucharist; an abuse growing out of our Lord's eating of the Passover before he instituted the Eucharist.]
[6] τούτοις, an emendation for τούτῳ.
[7] *Odyss.*, xi. 65.
[8] *Iliad*, i. 591.
[9] Ecclus. xxxi. 20.
[10] Shem and Japheth.
[11] See Ecclus. xxxi. 19, where, however, we have a different reading.

ntigonides, and Canthari, and goblets, and Le-astæ,[1] and the endless shapes of drinking ves-els, and wine-coolers, and wine-pourers also. or, on the whole, gold and silver, both publicly nd privately, are an invidious possession when iey exceed what is necessary, seldom to be ac-uired, difficult to keep, and not adapted for se. The elaborate vanity, too, of vessels in lass chased, more apt to break on account of ie art, teaching us to fear while we drink, is to e banished from our well-ordered constitution. nd silver couches, and pans and vinegar-saucers, nd trenchers and bowls; and besides these, essels of silver and gold, some for serving food, nd others for other uses which I am ashamed o name, of easily cleft cedar and thyine wood, nd ebony, and tripods fashioned of ivory, and ouches with silver feet and inlaid with ivory, nd folding-doors of beds studded with gold and ariegated with tortoise-shell, and bed-clothes of urple and other colours difficult to produce, roofs of tasteless luxury, cunning devices of nvy and effeminacy, — are all to be relinquished, s having nothing whatever worth our pains. " For the time is short," as says the apostle. This then remains that we do not make a ridicu-ous figure, as some are seen in the public spec-acles outwardly anointed strikingly for imposing ffect, but wretched within. Explaining this nore clearly, he adds, " It remains that they that ave wives be as though they had none, and they hat buy as though they possessed not."[2] And f he speaks thus of marriage, in reference to vhich God says, " Multiply," how do you not hink that senseless display is by the Lord's uthority to be banished? Wherefore also the Lord says, " Sell what thou hast, and give to he poor; and come, follow me."[3]

Follow God, stripped of arrogance, stripped of fading display, possessed of that which is thine, which is good, what alone cannot be taken away — faith towards god, confession towards Him who suffered, beneficence towards men, which is he most precious of possessions. For my part, I approve of Plato, who plainly lays it down as a aw, that a man is not to labour for wealth of gold or silver, nor to possess a useless vessel which is not for some necessary purpose, and moderate; so that the same thing may serve for many purposes, and the possession of a variety of things may be done away with. Excellently, therefore, the Divine Scripture, addressing boast-ers and lovers of their own selves, says, " Where are the rulers of the nations, and the lords of the wild beasts of the earth, who sport among the birds of heaven, who treasured up silver and gold, in whom men trusted, and there was no end of their substance, who fashioned silver and gold, and were full of care? There is no finding of their works. They have vanished, and gone down to Hades."[4] Such is the reward of dis-play. For though such of us as cultivate the soil need a mattock and plough, none of us will make a pickaxe of silver or a sickle of gold, but we employ the material which is serviceable for agriculture, not what is costly. What prevents those who are capable of considering what is sim-ilar from entertaining the same sentiments with respect to household utensils, of which let use, not expense, be the measure? For tell me, does the table-knife not cut unless it be studded with silver, and have its handle made of ivory? Or must we forge Indian steel in order to divide meat, as when we call for a weapon for the fight? What if the basin be earthenware? will it not receive the dirt of the hands? or the footpan the dirt of the foot? Will the table that is fashioned with ivory feet be indignant at bearing a three-halfpenny loaf? Will the lamp not dispense light because it is the work of the potter, not of the goldsmith? I affirm that truckle-beds afford no worse repose than the ivory couch; and the goatskin coverlet being amply sufficient to spread on the bed, there is no need of purple or scarlet coverings. Yet to condemn, notwithstanding, frugality, through the stupidity of luxury, the author of mischief, what a prodigious error, what senseless conceit! See. The Lord ate from a common bowl, and made the disciples recline on the grass on the ground, and washed their feet, girded with a linen towel — He, the lowly-minded God, and Lord of the universe. He did not bring down a silver foot-bath from heaven. He asked to drink of the Samaritan woman, who drew the water from the well in an earthenware vessel, not seeking regal gold, but teaching us how to quench thirst easily. For He made use, not extravagance His aim. And He ate and drank at feasts, not digging metals from the earth, nor using vessels of gold and silver, that is, ves-sels exhaling the odour of rust — such fumes as the rust of smoking[5] metal gives off.

For in fine, in food, and clothes, and vessels, and everything else belonging to the house, I say comprehensively, that one must follow the institutions of the Christian[6] man, as is service-able and suitable to one's person, age, pursuits, time of life. For it becomes those that are servants of one God, that their possessions and furniture should exhibit the tokens of one beau-tiful[7] life; and that each individually should be seen in faith, which shows no difference, practis-ing all other things which are conformable to

---

1 Limpet-shaped cups. [On this chapter consult Kaye, p. 74.]
2 1 Cor. vii. 29, 30.
3 Matt. xix. 21.

4 Baruch iii. 16–19.
5 Or, proud.
6 [See Elucidation I. ἐνστάσεσιν τοῦ Χριστιανοῦ.]
7 καλοῦ.

this uniform mode of life, and harmonious with this one scheme.

What we acquire without difficulty, and use with ease, we praise, keep easily, and communicate freely. The things which are useful are preferable, and consequently cheap things are better than dear. In fine, wealth, when not properly governed, is a stronghold of evil, about which many casting their eyes, they will never reach the kingdom of heaven, sick for the things of the world, and living proudly through luxury. But those who are in earnest about salvation must settle this beforehand in their mind, "that all that we possess is given to us for use, and use for sufficiency, which one may attain to by a few things." For silly are they who, from greed, take delight in what they have hoarded up. "He that gathereth wages," it is said, "gathereth into a bag with holes." [1] Such is he who gathers corn and shuts it up; and he who giveth to no one, becomes poorer.

It is a farce, and a thing to make one laugh outright, for men to bring in silver urinals and crystal *vases de nuit*, as they usher in their counsellors, and for silly rich women to get gold receptacles for excrements made; so that being rich, they cannot even ease themselves except in superb way. I would that in their whole life they deemed gold fit for dung.

But now love of money is found to be the stronghold of evil, which the apostle says "is the root of all evils, which, while some coveted, they have erred from the faith, and pierced themselves through with many sorrows." [2]

But the best riches is poverty of desires; and the true magnanimity is not to be proud of wealth, but to despise it. Boasting about one's plate is utterly base. For it is plainly wrong to care much about what any one who likes may buy from the market. But wisdom is not bought with coin of earth, nor is it sold in the market-place, but in heaven. And it is sold for true coin, the immortal Word, the regal gold.

CHAP. IV. — HOW TO CONDUCT OURSELVES AT FEASTS.

Let revelry keep away from our rational entertainments, and foolish vigils, too, that revel in intemperance. For revelry is an inebriating pipe, the chain [3] of an amatory bridge, that is, of sorrow. And let love, and intoxication, and senseless passions, be removed from our choir. Burlesque singing is the boon companion of drunkenness. A night spent over drink invites drunkenness, rouses lust, and is audacious in deeds of shame. For if people occupy their time with pipes, and psalteries, and choirs, and dances, and Egyptian clapping of hands, and such disorderly frivolities, they become quite immodest and intractable, beat on cymbals and drums, and make a noise on instruments of delusion; for plainly such a banquet, as seems to me, is a theatre of drunkenness. For the apostle decrees that, "putting off the works of darkness, we should put on the armour of light, walking honestly as in the day, not spending our time in rioting and drunkenness, in chambering and wantonness." [4] Let the pipe be resigned to the shepherds, and the flute to the superstitious who are engrossed in idolatry. For, in truth, such instruments are to be banished from the temperate banquet, being more suitable to beasts than men, and the more irrational portion of mankind. For we have heard of stags being charmed by the pipe, and seduced by music into the toils, when hunted by the huntsmen. And when mares are being covered, a tune is played on the flute — a nuptial song, as it were. And every improper sight and sound, to speak in a word, and every shameful sensation of licentiousness — which, in truth, is privation of sensation — must by all means be excluded; and we must be on our guard against whatever pleasure titillates eye and ear, and effeminates. For the various spells of the broken strains and plaintive numbers of the Carian muse corrupt men's morals, drawing to perturbation of mind, by the licentious and mischievous art of music. [5]

The Spirit, distinguishing from such revelry the divine service, sings, "Praise Him with the sound of trumpet;" for with sound of trumpet He shall raise the dead. "Praise Him on the psaltery;" for the tongue is the psaltery of the Lord. "And praise Him on the lyre." [6] By the lyre is meant the mouth struck by the Spirit, as it were by a plectrum. "Praise with the timbrel and the dance," refers to the Church meditating on the resurrection of the dead in the resounding skin. "Praise Him on the chords and organ." Our body He calls an organ, and its nerves are the strings, by which it has received harmonious tension, and when struck by the Spirit, it gives forth human voices. "Praise Him on the clashing cymbals." He calls the tongue the cymbal of the mouth, which resounds with the pulsation of the lips. Therefore He cried to humanity, "Let every breath praise the LORD," because He cares for every breathing thing which He hath made. For man is truly a pacific instrument; while other instruments, if you investigate, you will find to be warlike, inflaming to lusts, or kindling up amours, or rousing wrath.

In their wars, therefore, the Etruscans use the trumpet, the Arcadians the pipe, the Sicilians the

---

[1] Hag. i. 6.
[2] 1 Tim. vi. 10.
[3] The reading ἅλυσις is here adopted. The passage is obscure.

[4] Rom. iiix. 12, 13.
[5] [He distinguishes between the lewd music of *Satanic odes* (Tatian, cap. xxxiii. p. 79, *supra*), and another art of music of which he will soon speak.]
[6] Ps. cl. 3, 5.

ectides, the Cretans the lyre, the Lacedæmo-ians the flute, the Thracians the horn, the Egyp-ans the drum, and the Arabians the cymbal. he one instrument of peace, the Word alone by hich we honour God, is what we employ. We o longer employ the ancient psaltery, and trum-et, and timbrel, and flute, which those expert in ar and contemners of the fear of God were vont to make use of also in the choruses at their estive assemblies; that by such strains they might aise their dejected minds. But let our genial eeling in drinking be twofold, in accordance with he law. For "if thou shalt love the Lord thy God," and then "thy neighbour," let its first manifestation be towards God in thanksgiving and psalmody, and the second toward our neigh-our in decorous fellowship. For says the apos-le, "Let the Word of the Lord dwell in you ichly."[1] And this Word suits and conforms Himself to seasons, to persons, to places.

In the present instance He is a guest with us. For the apostle adds again, "Teaching and ad-monishing one another in all wisdom, in psalms, and hymns, and spiritual songs, singing with grace in your heart to God." And again, "What-oever ye do in word or deed, do all in the name of the Lord Jesus, giving thanks to God and His Father." This is our thankful revelry. And even if you wish to sing and play to the harp or lyre, there is no blame.[2] Thou shalt imitate the righteous Hebrew king in his thanksgiving to God. "Rejoice in the Lord, ye righteous; praise is comely to the upright,"[3] says the prophecy. "Confess to the Lord on the harp; play to Him on the psaltery of ten strings. Sing to Him a new song." And does not the ten-stringed psal-tery indicate the Word Jesus, who is manifested by the element of the decad? And as it is be-fitting, before partaking of food, that we should bless the Creator of all; so also in drinking it is suitable to praise Him on partaking of His crea-tures.[4] For the psalm is a melodious and sober blessing. The apostle calls the psalm "a spirit-ual song."[5]

Finally, before partaking of sleep, it is a sacred duty to give thanks to God, having enjoyed His grace and love, and so go straight to sleep.[6] "And confess to Him in songs of the lips," he says, "because in His command all His good pleasure is done, and there is no deficiency in His salvation."[7]

Further, among the ancient Greeks, in their banquets over the brimming cups, a song was sung called a skolion, after the manner of the Hebrew psalms, all together raising the pæan with the voice, and sometimes also taking turns in the song while they drank healths round; while those that were more musical than the rest sang to the lyre. But let amatory songs be banished far away, and let our songs be hymns to God. "Let them praise," it is said, "His name in the dance, and let them play to Him on the timbrel and psaltery."[8] And what is the choir which plays? The Spirit will show thee: "Let His praise be in the congregation (church) of the saints; let them be joyful in their King."[9] And again he adds, "The LORD will take pleasure in His people."[10] For temperate harmonies[11] are to be admitted; but we are to banish as far as possi-ble from our robust mind those liquid harmonies, which, through pernicious arts in the modulations of tones, train to effeminacy and scurrility. But grave and modest strains say farewell to the tur-bulence of drunkenness.[12] Chromatic harmonies are therefore to be abandoned to immodest rev-els, and to florid and meretricious music.

CHAP. V. — ON LAUGHTER.

People who are imitators of ludicrous sensa-tions, or rather of such as deserve derision, are to be driven from our polity.[13]

For since all forms of speech flow from mind and manners, ludicrous expressions could not be uttered, did they not proceed from ludicrous practices. For the saying, "It is not a good tree which produces corrupt fruit, nor a corrupt tree which produces good fruit,"[14] is to be ap-plied in this case. For speech is the fruit of the mind. If, then, wags are to be ejected from our society, we ourselves must by no manner of means be allowed to stir up laughter. For it were absurd to be found imitators of things of which we are prohibited to be listeners; and still more absurd for a man to set about making himself a laughing-stock, that is, the but of insult and derision. For if we could not endure to make a ridiculous figure, such as we see some do in processions, how could we with any propriety bear to have the inner man made a ridiculous figure of, and that to one's face? Wherefore we ought never of our own accord to assume a ludicrous character. And how, then, can we devote ourselves to being and appearing ridicu-

---

[1] Col. iii. 16.
[2] [Here instrumental music is allowed, though he turns everything into a type.]
[3] Ps. xxxiii. 1-3.
[4] [Even the heathen had such forms. The Christian grace before and after meat is here recognised as a matter of course. 1 Tim. iv. 3, 4.]
[5] Eph. v. 19; Col. iii. 16.
[6] [Besides the hymn on *lighting the lamps*, he notes *completory* prayer at bedtime.]
[7] Wisd. Sirach (Ecclus.) xxxix. 15, 16.

[8] Ps. cxlix. 3.
[9] Ps. cxlix. 1, 2.
[10] Ps. clxix. 4.
[11] [Observe the contrast between the modest harmonies he praises, and the *operatic* strains he censures. Yet modern Christians delight in these florid and meretricious compositions, and they have intruded into the solemnities of worship. In Europe, dramatic composers of a sensual school have taken possession of the Latin ceremonial.]
[12] [On gluttony and drinking, our author borrows much from Plato. Kaye, p. 74.]
[13] Or, society.
[14] Matt. vii. 18; Luke vi. 43.

lous in our conversation, thereby travestying speech, which is the most precious of all human endowments? It is therefore disgraceful to set one's self to do this; since the conversation of wags of this description is not fit for our ears, inasmuch as by the very expressions used it familiarizes us with shameful actions.[1]

Pleasantry is allowable, not waggery. Besides, even laughter must be kept in check; for when given vent to in the right manner it indicates orderliness, but when it issues differently it shows a want of restraint.

For, in a word, whatever things are natural to men we must not eradicate from them, but rather impose on them limits and suitable times. For man is not to laugh on all occasions because he is a laughing animal, any more than the horse neighs on all occasions because he is a neighing animal. But as rational beings, we are to regulate ourselves suitably, harmoniously relaxing the austerity and over-tension of our serious pursuits, not inharmoniously breaking them up altogether.

For the seemly relaxation of the countenance in a harmonious manner — as of a musical instrument — is called a smile. So also is laughter on the face of well-regulated men termed. But the discordant relaxation of countenance in the case of women is called a giggle, and is meretricious laughter; in the case of men, a guffaw, and is savage and insulting laughter. "A fool raises his voice in laughter,"[2] says the Scripture; but a clever man smiles almost imperceptibly. The clever man in this case he calls wise, inasmuch as he is differently affected from the fool. But, on the other hand, one needs not be gloomy, only grave. For I certainly prefer a man to smile who has a stern countenance than the reverse; for so his laughter will be less apt to become the object of ridicule.

Smiling even requires to be made the subject of discipline. If it is at what is disgraceful, we ought to blush rather than smile, lest we seem to take pleasure in it by sympathy; if at what is painful, it is fitting to look sad rather than to seem pleased. For to do the former is a sign of rational human thought; the other infers suspicion of cruelty.

We are not to laugh perpetually, for that is going beyond bounds; nor in the presence of elderly persons, or others worthy of respect, unless they indulge in pleasantry for our amusement. Nor are we to laugh before all and sundry, nor in every place, nor to every one, nor about everything. For to children and women especially laughter is the cause of slipping into scandal. And even to appear stern serves to keep those about us at their distance. For gravity can ward off the approaches of licentiousness by a mere look. All senseless people, to speak in a word, wine

"Commands both to laugh luxuriously and to dance," changing effeminate manners to softness. We must consider, too, how consequently freedom of speech leads impropriety on to filthy speaking.

"And he uttered a word which had been better unsaid."[3]

Especially, therefore, in liquor crafty men's characters are wont to be seen through, stripped as they are of their mask through the caitiff licence of intoxication, through which reason, weighed down in the soul itself by drunkenness, is lulled to sleep, and unruly passions are roused, which overmaster the feebleness of the mind.

CHAP. VI. — ON FILTHY SPEAKING.

From filthy speaking we ourselves must entirely abstain, and stop the mouths of those who practise it by stern looks and averting the face, and by what we call making a mock of one: often also by a harsher mode of speech. "For what proceedeth out of the mouth," He says, "defileth a man,"[4] — shows him to be unclean, and heathenish, and untrained, and licentious, and not select, and proper, and honourable, and temperate.[5]

And as a similar rule holds with regard to hearing and seeing in the case of what is obscene, the divine Instructor, following the same course with both, arrays those children who are engaged in the struggle in words of modesty, as ear-guards, so that the pulsation of fornication may not penetrate to the bruising of the soul; and He directs the eyes to the sight of what is honourable, saying that it is better to make a slip with the feet than with the eyes. This filthy speaking the apostle beats off, saying, "Let no corrupt communication proceed out of your mouth, but what is good."[6] And again, "As becometh saints, let not filthiness be named among you, nor foolish talking, nor jesting, which things are not seemly, but rather giving of thanks."[7] And if "he that calls his brother a fool be in danger of the judgment," what shall we pronounce regarding him who speaks what is foolish? Is it not written respecting such: "Whosoever shall speak an idle word, shall give an account to the Lord in the day of judgment?"[8] And again, "By thy speech thou

---

[1] [Our author is a terrible satirist; but it is instructive to see Christianity thus prescribing the minor morals, and banishing pagan brutality with holy scorn.]
[2] Ecclus. xxi. 20.
[3] *Odyss.*, xiv 463-466.
[4] Matt. xv. 18.
[5] [May the young Christian who reads this passage learn to abhor all freedom of speech of this kind. This is a very precious chapter.]
[6] Eph. iv. 29.
[7] Eph. v. 3, 4.
[8] Matt. v. 22, xii. 36

shalt be justified," He says, "and by thy speech thou shalt be condemned."[1] What, then, are the salutary ear-guards, and what the regulations for slippery eyes? Conversations with the righteous, preoccupying and forearming the ears against those that would lead away from the truth.

"Evil communications corrupt good manners," says Poetry. More nobly the apostle says, "Be haters of the evil; cleave to the good."[2] For he who associates with the saints shall be sanctified. From shameful things addressed to the ears, and words and sights, we must entirely abstain.[3] And much more must we keep pure from shameful deeds : on the one hand, from exhibiting and exposing parts of the body which we ought not ; and on the other, from beholding what is forbidden. For the modest son could not bear to look on the shameful exposure of the righteous man ; and modesty covered what intoxication exposed — the spectacle of the transgression of ignorance.[4] No less ought we to keep pure from calumnious reports, to which the ears of those who have believed in Christ ought to be inaccessible.

It is on this account, as appears to me, that the Instructor does not permit us to give utterance to aught unseemly, fortifying us at an early stage against licentiousness. For He is admirable always at cutting out the roots of sins, such as, "Thou shalt not commit adultery," by "Thou shalt not lust."[5] For adultery is the fruit of lust, which is the evil root. And so likewise also in this instance the Instructor censures licence in names, and thus cuts off the licentious intercourse of excess. For licence in names produces the desire of being indecorous in conduct ; and the observance of modesty in names is a training in resistance to lasciviousness. We have shown in a more exhaustive treatise, that neither in the names nor in the members to which appellations not in common use are applied, is there the designation of what is really obscene.

For neither are knee and leg, and such other members, nor are the names applied to them, and the activity put forth by them, obscene. And even the *pudenda* are to be regarded as objects suggestive of modesty, not shame. It is their unlawful activity that is shameful, and deserving ignominy, and reproach, and punishment. For the only thing that is in reality shameful is wickedness, and what is done through it. In accordance with these remarks, conversation about deeds of wickedness is appropriately termed filthy [shameful] speaking, as talk about adultery and pæderasty and the like. Frivolous prating, too, is to be put to silence.[6] "For," it is said, " in much speaking thou shalt not escape sin."[7] "Sins of the tongue, therefore, shall be punished." "There is he who is silent, and is found wise ; and there is that is hated for much speech."[8] But still more, the prater makes himself the object of disgust. "For he that multiplieth speech abominates his own soul."[9]

CHAP. VII. — DIRECTIONS FOR THOSE WHO LIVE TOGETHER.

Let us keep away from us jibing, the originator of insult, from which strifes and contentions and enmities burst forth. Insult, we have said, is the servant of drunkenness. A man is judged, not from his deeds alone, but from his words. "In a banquet," it is said, "reprove not thy neighbour, nor say to him a word of reproach."[10] For if we are enjoined especially to associate with saints, it is a sin to jibe at a saint : "For from the mouth of the foolish," says the Scripture, "is a staff of insult,"[11] — meaning by staff the prop of insult, on which insult leans and rests. Whence I admire the apostle, who, in reference to this, exhorts us not to utter " scurrilous nor unsuitable words."[12] For if the assemblies at festivals take place on account of affection, and the end of a banquet is friendliness towards those who meet, and meat and drink accompany affection, how should not conversation be conducted in a rational manner, and puzzling people with questions be avoided from affection? For if we meet together for the purpose of increasing our good-will to each other, why should we stir up enmity by jibing? It is better to be silent than to contradict, and thereby add sin to ignorance. "Blessed," in truth, " is the man who has not made a slip with his mouth, and has not been pierced by the pain of sin ; "[13] or has repented of what he has said amiss, or has spoken so as to wound no one. On the whole, let young men and young women altogether keep away from such festivals, that they may not make a slip in respect to what is unsuitable. For things to which their ears are unaccustomed, and unseemly sights, inflame the mind, while faith within them is still wavering ; and the instability of their age conspires to make them easily carried away by lust. Sometimes also they are the cause of others stumbling, by

---

[1] Matt. xii. 37.
[2] Rom. xii. 9.
[3] [How then can Christians frequent theatrical shows, and listen to lewd and profane plays?]
[4] Gen. ix. 23.
[5] Ex. xx. 14, 17.

[6] [An example may not be out of place, as teaching how we may put such things to silence. " Since the ladies have withdrawn," said one, " I will tell a little anecdote." " But," interposed a dignified person, " let me ask you to count me as representing the ladies; for I am the husband of one of them, and should be sorry to hear what would degrade me in her estimation."]
[7] Prov. x. 19.
[8] Ecclus. xx. 5.
[9] Ecclus. xx. 8.
[10] Ecclus. xxxi 31.
[11] Prov. xiv. 3.
[12] Eph. v. 4.
[13] Ecclus. xiv. 1.

displaying the dangerous charms of their time of life. For Wisdom appears to enjoin well : " Sit not at all with a married woman, and recline not on the elbow with her ; " [1] that is, do not sup nor eat with her frequently. Wherefore he adds, " And do not join company with her in wine, lest thy heart incline to her, and by thy blood slide to ruin." [2] For the licence of intoxication is dangerous, and prone to deflower. And he names " a married woman," because the danger is greater to him who attempts to break the connubial bond.

But if any necessity arises, commanding the presence of married women, let them be well clothed — without by raiment, within by modesty. But as for such as are unmarried, it is the extremest scandal for them to be present at a banquet of men, especially men under the influence of wine. And let the men, fixing their eyes on the couch, and leaning without moving on their elbows, be present with their ears alone ; and if they sit, let them not have their feet crossed, nor place one thigh on another, nor apply the hand to the chin. For it is vulgar not to bear one's self without support, and consequently a fault in a young man. And perpetually moving and changing one's position is a sign of frivolousness. It is the part of a temperate man also, in eating and drinking, to take a small portion, and deliberately, not eagerly, both at the beginning and during the courses, and to leave off betimes, and so show his indifference. " Eat," it is said, " like a man what is set before you. Be the first to stop for the sake of regimen ; and, if seated in the midst of several people, do not stretch out your hand before them." [3] You must never rush forward under the influence of gluttony ; nor must you, though desirous, reach out your hand till some time, inasmuch as by greed one shows an uncontrolled appetite. Nor are you, in the midst of the repast, to exhibit yourselves hugging your food like wild beasts ; nor helping yourselves to too much sauce, for man is not by nature a sauce-consumer, but a bread-eater. A temperate man, too, must rise before the general company, and retire quietly from the banquet. " For at the time for rising," it is said, " be not the last ; haste home." [4] The twelve, having called together the multitude of the disciples, said, " It is not meet for us to leave the word of God and serve tables." [5] If they avoided this, much more did they shun gluttony. And the apostles themselves, writing to the brethren at Antioch, and in Syria and Cilicia, said : " It seemed good to the Holy Ghost, and to us, to lay upon you no other burden than these necessary things, to abstain from things offered to idols, and from blood, and from things strangled, and from fornication, from which, if you keep yourselves, ye shall do well." [6] But we must guard against drunkenness as against hemlock ; for both drag down to death. We must also check excessive laughter and immoderate tears. For often people under the influence of wine, after laughing immoderately, then are, I know not how, by some impulse of intoxication moved to tears ; for both effeminacy and violence are discordant with the word. And elderly people, looking on the young as children, may, though but very rarely, be playful with them, joking with them to train them in good behaviour. For example, before a bashful and silent youth, one might by way of pleasantry speak thus : " This son of mine (I mean one who is silent) is perpetually talking." For a joke such as this enhances the youth's modesty, by showing the good qualities that belong to him playfully, by censure of the bad quatities, which do not. For this device is instructive, confirming as it does what is present by what is not present. Such, certainly, is the intention of him who says that a water-drinker and a sober man gets intoxicated and drunk. But if there are those who like to jest at people, we must be silent, and dispense with superfluous words like full cups. For such sport is dangerous. " The mouth of the impetuous approaches to contrition." [7] " Thou shalt not receive a foolish report, nor shalt thou agree with an unjust person to be an unjust witness," [8] neither in calumnies nor in injurious speeches, much less evil practices. I also should think it right to impose a limit on the speech of rightly regulated persons, who are impelled to speak to one who maintains a conversation with them. " For silence is the excellence of women, and the safe prize of the young ; but good speech is characteristic of experienced, mature age. Speak, old man, at a banquet, for it is becoming to you. But speak without embarrassment, and with accuracy of knowledge. Youth, Wisdom also commands thee. Speak, if you must, with hesitation, on being twice asked ; sum up your discourse in a few words." [9] But let both speakers regulate their discourse according to just proportion. For loudness of utterance is most insane ; while an inaudible utterance is characteristic of a senseless man, for people will not hear : the one is the mark of pusillanimity, the other of arrogance. Let contentiousness in words, for the sake of a useless triumph, be banished ; for our aim is to be free from pertur-

---

[1] Ecclus. ix. 9. [i.e., reclining at the table.]
[2] Ecclus. ix. 9.
[3] Ecclus. xxxi. 16–18.
[4] Ecclus. xxxii. 11.
[5] Acts vi. 2.

[6] Acts xv. 23, 28, 29.
[7] Prov. x. 14.
[8] Prov. xxiv. 28; Ex. xxiii. 1.
[9] Ecclus. xxxii. 3, 4, 8.

bation. Such is the meaning of the phrase,[1] "Peace to thee." Answer not a word before you hear. An enervated voice is the sign of effeminacy. But modulation in the voice is characteristic of a wise man, who keeps his utterance from loudness, from drawling, from rapidity, from prolixity. For we ought not to speak long or much, nor ought we to speak frivolously. Nor must we converse rapidly and rashly. For the voice itself, so to speak, ought to receive its just dues; and those who are vociferous and clamorous ought to be silenced. For this reason, the wise Ulysses chastised Thersites with stripes:—

> "Only Thersites, with unmeasured words,
> Of which he had good store, to rate the chiefs,
> Not over-seemly, but wherewith he thought
> To move the crowd to laughter, brawled aloud." [2]

"For dreadful in his destruction is a loquacious man." [3] And it is with triflers as with old shoes: all the rest is worn away by evil; the tongue only is left for destruction. Wherefore Wisdom gives these most useful exhortations: "Do not talk trifles in the multitude of the elders." Further, eradicating frivolousness, beginning with God, it lays down the law for our regulation somewhat thus: "Do not repeat your words in your prayer." [4] Chirruping and whistling, and sounds made through the fingers, by which domestics are called, being irrational signs, are to be given up by rational men. Frequent spitting, too, and violent clearing of the throat, and wiping one's nose at an entertainment, are to be shunned. For respect is assuredly to be had to the guests, lest they turn in disgust from such filthiness, which argues want of restraint. For we are not to copy oxen and asses, whose manger and dunghill are together. For many wipe their noses and spit even whilst supping.

If any one is attacked with sneezing, just as in the case of hiccup, he must not startle those near him with the explosion, and so give proof of his bad breeding; but the hiccup is to be quietly transmitted with the expiration of the breath, the mouth being composed becomingly, and not gaping and yawning like the tragic masks. So the disturbance of hiccup may be avoided by making the respirations gently; for thus the threatening symptoms of the ball of wind will be dissipated in the most seemly way, by managing its egress so as also to conceal anything which the air forcibly expelled may bring up with it. To wish to add to the noises, instead of diminishing them, is the sign of arrogance and disorderliness. Those, too, who scrape their teeth, bleeding the wounds, are disagreeable to themselves and detestable to their neighbours. Scratching the ears and the irritation of sneezing are swinish itchings, and attend unbridled fornication. Both shameful sights and shameful conversation about them are to be shunned. Let the look be steady, and the turning and movement of the neck, and the motions of the hands in conversation, be decorous. In a word, the Christian is characterized by composure, tranquillity, calmness, and peace.[5]

CHAP. VIII.—ON THE USE OF OINTMENTS AND CROWNS.

The use of crowns and ointments is not necessary for us; for it impels to pleasures and indulgences, especially on the approach of night. I know that the woman brought to the sacred supper "an alabaster box of ointment," [6] and anointed the feet of the Lord, and refreshed Him; and I know that the ancient kings of the Hebrews were crowned with gold and precious stones. But the woman not having yet received the Word (for she was still a sinner), honoured the Lord with what she thought the most precious thing in her possession—the ointment; and with the ornament of her person, with her hair, she wiped off the superfluous ointment, while she expended on the Lord tears of repentance: "wherefore her sins are forgiven." [7]

This may be a symbol of the Lord's teaching, and of His suffering. For the feet anointed with fragrant ointment mean divine instruction travelling with renown to the ends of the earth. "For their sound hath gone forth to the ends of the earth." [8] And if I seem not to insist too much, the feet of the Lord which were anointed are the apostles, having, according to prophecy, received the fragrant unction of the Holy Ghost. Those, therefore, who travelled over the world and preached the Gospel, are figuratively called the feet of the Lord, of whom also the Holy Spirit foretells in the psalm, "Let us adore at the place where His feet stood," [9] that is, where the apostles, His feet, arrived; since, preached by them, He came to the ends of the earth. And tears are repentance; and the loosened hair proclaimed deliverance from the love of finery, and the affliction in patience which, on account of the Lord, attends preaching, the old vainglory being done away with by reason of the new faith.[10]

Besides, it shows the Lord's passion, if you understand it mystically thus: the oil (ἔλαιον) is the Lord Himself, from whom comes the mercy (ἔλεος) which reaches us. But the ointment,

---

[1] [A primitive form of Christian salutation, borrowed from the great Example. John xx. 19.]
[2] *Iliad*, ii. 213.
[3] Ecclus. ix. 18.
[4] Ecclus. ix. 15.

[5] ["Against such there is no law." *Emollit mores*, etc.]
[6] Matt. xxvi. 7, etc.
[7] Luke vii. 47.
[8] Ps. xix. 4; Rom. x. 18.
[9] Ps. cxxxii.
[10] [We need not refuse this efflorescence as poetry, nor accept it as exposition.]

which is adulterated oil, is the traitor Judas, by whom the Lord was anointed on the feet, being released from His sojourn in the world. For the dead are anointed. And the tears are we repentant sinners, who have believed in Him, and to whom He has forgiven our sins. And the dishevelled hair is mourning Jerusalem, the deserted, for whom the prophetic lamentations were uttered. The Lord Himself shall teach us that Judas the deceitful is meant : " He that dippeth with Me in the dish, the same shall betray Me." [1] You see the treacherous guest, and this same Judas betrayed the Master with a kiss. For he was a hypocrite, giving a treacherous kiss, in imitation of another hypocrite of old. And He reproves that people respecting whom it was said, " This people honour Me with their lips ; but their heart is far from Me." [2] It is not improbable, therefore, that by the oil He means that disciple to whom was shown mercy, and by the tainted and poisoned oil the traitor.

This was, then, what the anointed feet prophesied — the treason of Judas, when the Lord went to His passion. And the Saviour Himself washing the feet of the disciples,[3] and despatching them to do good deeds, pointed out their pilgrimage for the benefit of the nations, making them beforehand fair and pure by His power. Then the ointment breathed on them its fragrance, and the work of sweet savour reaching to all was proclaimed ; for the passion of the Lord has filled us with sweet fragrance, and the Hebrews with guilt. This the apostle most clearly showed, when he said, " thanks be to God, who always makes us to triumph in Christ, and maketh manifest the savour of His knowledge by us in every place. For we are to God a sweet savour of the Lord, in them that are saved, and them that are lost ; to one a savour of death unto death, to the other a savour of life unto life." [4] And the kings of the Jews using gold and precious stones and a variegated crown, the anointed ones wearing Christ symbolically on the head, were unconsciously adorned with the head of the Lord. The precious stone, or pearl, or emerald, points out the Word Himself. The gold, again, is the incorruptible Word, who admits not the poison of corruption. The Magi, accordingly, brought to Him on His birth, gold, the symbol of royalty. And this crown, after the image of the Lord, fades not as a flower.

I know, too, the words of Aristippus the Cyrenian. Aristippus was a luxurious man. He asked an answer to a sophistical proposition in the following terms : " A horse anointed with ointment is not injured in his excellence as a horse, nor is a dog which has been anointed, in his excellence as a dog ; no more is a man," he added, and so finished. But the dog and horse take no account of the ointment, whilst in the case of those whose perceptions are more rational, applying girlish scents to their persons, its use is more censurable. Of these ointments there are endless varieties, such as the Brenthian, the Metallian, and the royal ; the Plangonian and the Psagdian of Egypt. Simonides is not ashamed in Iambic lines to say, —

" I was anointed with ointments and perfumes,
And with nard."

For a merchant was present. They use, too, the unguent made from lilies, and that from the cypress. Nard is in high estimation with them, and the ointment prepared from roses and the others which women use besides, both moist and dry, scents for rubbing and for fumigating ; for day by day their thoughts are directed to the gratification of insatiable desire, to the exhaustless variety of fragrance. Wherefore also they are redolent of an excessive luxuriousness. And they fumigate and sprinkle their clothes, their bed-clothes, and their houses. Luxury all but compels vessels for the meanest uses to smell of perfume.

There are some who, annoyed at the attention bestowed on this, appear to me to be rightly so averse to perfumes on account of their rendering manhood effeminate, as to banish their compounders and vendors from well-regulated states, and banish, too, the dyers of flower-coloured wools. For it is not right that ensnaring garments and unguents should be admitted into the city of truth ; but it is highly requisite for the men who belong to us to give forth the odour not of ointments, but of nobleness and goodness. And let woman breathe the odour of the true royal ointment, that of Christ, not of unguents and scented powders ; and let her always be anointed with the ambrosial chrism of modesty, and find delight in the holy unguent, the Spirit. This ointment of pleasant fragrance Christ prepares for His disciples, compounding the ointment of celestial aromatic ingredients.

Wherefore also the Lord Himself is anointed with an ointment, as is mentioned by David : " Wherefore God, thy God, hath anointed thee with the oil of gladness above thy fellows ; myrrh, and stacte, and cassia from thy garments." [5] But let us not unconsciously abominate unguents, like vultures or like beetles (for these, they say, when smeared with ointment, die) ; and let a few unguents be selected by women, such as will not be overpowering to a husband. For excessive anointings with unguents savour of a funeral

---

[1] Matt. xxvi. 23.
[2] Isa. xxix. 13.
[3] John xiii. 5.
[4] 2 Cor. ii. 14-16.

[5] Ps. xlv. 7, 8.

and not of connubial life. Yet oil itself is inimical to bees and insects; and some men it benefits, and some it summons to the fight; and those who were formerly friends, when anointed with it, it turns out to deadly combat.

Ointment being smooth oil, do you not think that it is calculated to render noble manners effeminate? Certainly. And as we have abandoned luxury in taste, so certainly do we renounce voluptuousness in sights and odours; lest through the senses, as through unwatched doors, we unconsciously give access into the soul to that excess which we have driven away. If, then, we say that the Lord the great High Priest offers to God the incense of sweet fragrance, let us not imagine that this is a sacrifice and sweet fragrance of incense; [1] but let us understand it to mean, that the Lord lays the acceptable offering of love, the spiritual fragrance, on the altar.

To resume: oil itself suffices to lubricate the skin, and relax the nerves, and remove any heavy smell from the body, if we require oil for this purpose. But attention to sweet scents is a bait which draws us in to sensual lust. For the licentious man is led on every hand, both by his food, his bed, his conversation, by his eyes, his ears, his jaws, and by his nostrils too. As oxen are pulled by rings and ropes, so is the voluptuary by fumigations and unguents, and the sweet scents of crowns. But since we assign no place to pleasure which is linked to no use serviceable to life, come let us also distinguish here too, selecting what is useful. For there are sweet scents which neither make the head heavy nor provoke love, and are not redolent of embraces and licentious companionship, but, along with moderation, are salutary, nourishing the brain when labouring under indisposition, and strengthening the stomach. One must not therefore refrigerate himself with flowers when he wishes to supple his nerves. For their use is not wholly to be laid aside, but ointment is to be employed as a medicine and help in order to bring up the strength when enfeebled, and against catarrhs, and colds, and ennui, as the comic poet says:—

> " The nostrils are anointed; it being
> A most essential thing for health to fill the brain with
> good odours."

The rubbing of the feet also with the fatness of warming or cooling unguents is practised on account of its beneficial effects; so consequently, in the case of those who are thus saturated, an attraction and flow take place from the head to the inferior members. But pleasure to which no utility attaches, induces the suspicion of meretricious habits, and is a drug provocative of the passions. Rubbing one's self with ointment is entirely different from anointing one's self with ointment. The former is effeminate, while anointing with ointment is in some cases beneficial. Aristippus the philosopher, accordingly, when anointed with ointment, said " that the wretched Cinœdi deserved to perish miserably for bringing the utility of ointment into bad repute." " Honour the physician for his usefulness," says the Scripture, " for the Most High made him; and the art of healing is of the Lord." Then he adds, " And the compounder of unguents will make the mixture," [2] since unguents have been given manifestly for use, not for voluptuousness. For we are by no means to care for the exciting properties of unguents, but to choose what is useful in them, since God hath permitted the production of oil for the mitigation of men's pains.

And silly women, who dye their grey hair and anoint their locks, grow speedily greyer by the perfumes they use, which are of a drying nature. Wherefore also those that anoint themselves become drier, and the dryness makes them greyer. For if greyness is an exsiccation of the hair, or defect of heat, the dryness drinking up the moisture which is the natural nutriment of the hair, and making it grey, how can we any longer retain a liking for unguents, through which ladies, in trying to escape grey hair, become grey? And as dogs with fine sense of smell track the wild beasts by the scent, so also the temperate scent the licentious by the superfluous perfume of unguents.

Such a use of crowns, also, has degenerated to scenes of revelry and intoxication. Do not encircle my head with a crown, for in the springtime it is delightful to while away the time on the dewy meads, while soft and many-coloured flowers are in bloom, and, like the bees, enjoy a natural and pure fragrance.[3] But to adorn one's self with " a crown woven from the fresh mead," and wear it at home, were unfit for a man of temperance. For it is not suitable to fill the wanton hair with rose-leaves, or violets, or lilies, or other such flowers, stripping the sward of its flowers. For a crown encircling the head cools the hair, both on account of its moisture and its coolness. Accordingly, physicians, determining by physiology that the brain is cold, approve of anointing the breast and the points of the nostrils, so that the warm exhalation passing gently through, may salutarily warm the chill. A man ought not therefore to cool himself with flowers. Besides, those who crown themselves destroy the pleasure there is in flowers: for they enjoy neither the sight of them, since they wear the crown

---

[1] [Considering the use of incense in Hebrew worship, and the imagery of the Apocalypse, the emphasis with which the Fathers reject material incense, is to be noted.]

[2] Ecclus. xxxviii. 1, 2, 8.
[3] [An idyllic passage illustrative of our author's delight in rural scenes and pleasures.]

above their eyes; nor their fragrance, since they put the flowers away above the organs of respiration. For the fragrance ascending and exhaling naturally, the organ of respiration is left destitute of enjoyment, the fragrance being carried away. As beauty, so also the flower delights when looked at; and it is meet to glorify the Creator by the enjoyment of the sight of beautiful objects.[1] The use of them is injurious, and passes swiftly away, avenged by remorse. Very soon their evanescence is proved; for both fade, both the flower and beauty. Further, whoever touches them is cooled by the former, inflamed by the latter. In one word, the enjoyment of them except by sight is a crime, and not luxury. It becomes us who truly follow the Scripture to enjoy ourselves temperately, as in Paradise. We must regard the woman's crown to be her husband, and the husband's crown to be marriage; and the flowers of marriage the children of both, which the divine husbandman plucks from meadows of flesh. "Children's children are the crown of old men."[2] And the glory of children is their fathers, it is said; and our glory is the Father of all; and the crown of the whole church is Christ. As roots and plants, so also have flowers their individual properties, some beneficial, some injurious, some also dangerous. The ivy is cooling; nux emits a stupefying effluvium, as the etymology shows. The narcissus is a flower with a heavy odour; the name evinces this, and it induces a torpor (νάρκην) in the nerves. And the effluvia of roses and violets being mildly cool, relieve and prevent headaches. But we who are not only not permitted to drink with others to intoxication, but not even to indulge in much wine,[3] do not need the crocus or the flower of the cypress to lead us to an easy sleep. Many of them also, by their odours, warm the brain, which is naturally cold, volatilizing the effusions of the head. The rose is hence said to have received its name (ῥόδον) because it emits a copious stream (ῥεῦμα) of odour (ὀδωδή). Wherefore also it quickly fades.

But the use of crowns did not exist at all among the ancient Greeks; for neither the suitors nor the luxurious Phæacians used them. But at the games there was at first the gift to the athletes; second, the rising up to applaud; third, the strewing with leaves; lastly, the crown, Greece after the Median war having given herself up to luxury.

Those, then, who are trained by the Word are restrained from the use of crowns; and do not think that this Word, which has its seat in the brain, ought to be bound about, not because the crown is the symbol of the recklessness of revelry, but because it has been dedicated to idols. Sophocles accordingly called the narcissus "the ancient coronet of the great gods," speaking of the earth-born divinities; and Sappho crowns the Muses with the rose:—

"For thou dost not share in roses from Pieria."

They say, too, that Here delights in the lily, and Artemis in the myrtle. For if the flowers were made especially for man, and senseless people have taken them not for their own proper and grateful use, but have abused them to the thankless service of demons, we must keep from them for conscience sake. The crown is the symbol of untroubled tranquillity. For this reason they crown the dead, and idols, too, on the same account, by this fact giving testimony to their being dead. For revellers do not without crowns celebrate their orgies; and when once they are encircled with flowers, at last they are inflamed excessively. We must have no communion with demons. Nor must we crown the living image of God after the manner of dead idols. For the fair crown of amaranth is laid up for those who have lived well. This flower the earth is not able to bear; heaven alone is competent to produce it.[4] Further, it were irrational in us, who have heard that the Lord was crowned with thorns,[5] to crown ourselves with flowers, insulting thus the sacred passion of the Lord. For the Lord's crown prophetically pointed to us, who once were barren, but are placed around Him through the Church of which He is the Head. But it is also a type of faith, of life in respect of the substance of the wood, of joy in respect of the appellation of crown, of danger in respect of the thorn, for there is no approaching to the Word without blood. But this platted crown fades, and the plait of perversity is untied, and the flower withers. For the glory of those who have not believed on the Lord fades. And they crowned Jesus raised aloft, testifying to their own ignorance. For being hard of heart, they understood not that this very thing, which they called the disgrace of the Lord, was a prophecy wisely uttered: "The Lord was not known by the people"[6] which erred, which was not circumcised in understanding, whose darkness was not enlightened, which knew not God, denied the Lord, forfeited the place of the true Israel, persecuted God, hoped to reduce the Word to disgrace; and Him whom they crucified as a malefactor they crowned as a king. Wherefore the Man on whom they believed not, they shall

---

[1] [Christianity delights in natural beauty, and always associates its enjoyment with praise to its Author. Ecclus. xliii. 11.]

[2] Prov. xvii. 6.

[3] [This was a marked characteristic of Christian manners at war with heathenism.]

[4] [" Immortal amaranth, a flower which once
　In Paradise fast by the tree of life
　Began to bloom."
　　　　　　　　　　　　Paradise Lost, iii. 352.]

[5] Matt. xxvii. 29.

[6] Isa. i. 3.

know to be the loving God the Lord, the Just. Whom they provoked to show Himself to be the Lord, to Him when lifted up they bore witness, by encircling Him, who is exalted above every name, with the diadem of righteousness by the ever-blooming thorn. This diadem, being hostile to those who plot against Him, coerces them; and friendly to those who form the Church, defends them. This crown is the flower of those who have believed on the glorified One, but covers with blood and chastises those who have not believed. It is a symbol, too, of the Lord's successful work, He having borne on His head, the princely part of His body, all our iniquities by which we were pierced. For He by His own passion rescued us from offences, and sins, and such like thorns; and having destroyed the devil, deservedly said in triumph, "O Death, where is thy sting?" [1] And we eat grapes from thorns, and figs from thistles; while those to whom He stretched forth His hands — the disobedient and unfruitful people — He lacerates into wounds. I can also show you another mystic meaning in it.[2] For when the Almighty Lord of the universe began to legislate by the Word, and wished His power to be manifested to Moses, a godlike vision of light that had assumed a shape was shown him in the burning bush (the bush is a thorny plant); but when the Word ended the giving of the law and His stay with men, the Lord was again mystically crowned with thorn. On His departure from this world to the place whence He came, He repeated the beginning of His old descent, in order that the Word beheld at first in the bush, and afterwards taken up crowned by the thorn, might show the whole to be the work of one power, He Himself being one, the Son of the Father, who is truly one, the beginning and the end of time.

But I have made a digression from the pædagogic style of speech, and introduced the didactic.[3] I return accordingly to my subject.

To resume, then: we have showed that in the department of medicine, for healing, and sometimes also for moderate recreation, the delight derived from flowers, and the benefit derived from unguents and perfumes, are not to be overlooked. And if some say, What pleasure, then, is there in flowers to those that do not use them? let them know, then, that unguents are prepared from them, and are most useful. The Susinian ointment is made from various kinds of lilies; and it is warming, aperient, drawing, moistening, abstergent, subtle, antibilious, emollient. The Narcissinian is made from the narcissus, and is equally beneficial with the Susinian. The Myrsinian, made of myrtle and myrtle berries, is a styptic, stopping effusions from the body; and that from roses is refrigerating. For, in a word, these also were created for our use. "Hear me," it is said, "and grow as a rose planted by the streams of waters, and give forth a sweet fragrance like frankincense, and bless the Lord for His works." [4] We should have much to say respecting them, were we to speak of flowers and odours as made for necessary purposes, and not for the excesses of luxury. And if a concession must be made, it is enough for people to enjoy the fragrance of flowers; but let them not crown themselves with them. For the Father takes great care of man, and gives to him alone His own art. The Scripture therefore says, "Water, and fire, and iron, and milk, and fine flour of wheat, and honey, the blood of the grape, and oil, and clothing, — all these things are for the good of the godly." [5]

CHAP. IX. — ON SLEEP.

How, in due course, we are to go to sleep, in remembrance of the precepts of temperance, we must now say. For after the repast, having given thanks to God for our participation in our enjoyments, and for the [happy] passing of the day,[6] our talk must be turned to sleep. Magnificence of bed-clothes, gold-embroidered carpets, and smooth carpets worked with gold, and long fine robes of purple, and costly fleecy cloaks, and manufactured rugs of purple, and mantles of thick pile, and couches softer than sleep, are to be banished.

For, besides the reproach of voluptuousness, sleeping on downy feathers is injurious, when our bodies fall down as into a yawning hollow, on account of the softness of the bedding. For they are not convenient for sleepers turning in them, on account of the bed rising into a hill on either side of the body. Nor are they suitable for the digestion of the food, but rather for burning it up, and so destroying the nutriment. But stretching one's self on even couches, affording a kind of natural gymnasium for sleep, contributes to the digestion of the food. And those that can roll on other beds, having this, as it were, for a natural gymnasium for sleep, digest food more easily, and render themselves fitter for emergencies. Moreover, silver-footed couches argue great ostentation; and the ivory on beds, the body having left the soul,[7] is not permissible for holy men, being a lazy contrivance for rest.

---

[1] 1 Cor. xv. 55.
[2] [See note 10, p. 253. The beauty of this mysticism need not be pointed out, but it need not be pressed as exposition.]
[3] [This illustrates, in part, the difference between the *esoteric*, or mystic, and the more popular teaching of our author.]

[4] Ecclus. xxxix. 13, 14.
[5] Ecclus. xxxix. 26, 27.
[6] [Family prayers, apparently.]
[7] [See p. 258, *infra*. Sleep, he supposes, frees the soul as really, not so absolutely, as death:—

"Th' immortal mind that hath forsook
Her mansion in this fleshly nook."

Penseroso, line 91.]

We must not occupy our thoughts about these things, for the use of them is not forbidden to those who possess them ; but solicitude about them is prohibited, for happiness is not to be found in them. On the other hand, it savours of cynic vanity for a man to act as Diomede, —

" And he stretched himself under a wild bull's hide," [1] —

unless circumstances compel.

Ulysses rectified the unevenness of the nuptial couch with a stone. Such frugality and self-help was practised not by private individuals alone, but by the chiefs of the ancient Greeks. But why speak of these ? Jacob slept on the ground, and a stone served him for a pillow ; and then was he counted worthy to behold the vision — that was above man. And in conformity with reason, the bed which we use must be simple and frugal, and so constructed that, by avoiding the extremes [of too much indulgence and too much endurance], it may be comfortable : if it is warm, to protect us ; if cold, to warm us. But let not the couch be elaborate, and let it have smooth feet ; for elaborate turnings form occasionally paths for creeping things which twine themselves about the incisions of the work, and do not slip off.

Especially is a moderate softness in the bed suitable for manhood ; for sleep ought not to be for the total enervation of the body, but for its relaxation. Wherefore I say that it ought not to be allowed to come on us for the sake of indulgence, but in order to rest from action. We must therefore sleep so as to be easily awaked. For it is said, " Let your loins be girt about, and your lamps burning ; and ye yourselves like to men that watch for their lord, that when he returns from the marriage, and comes and knocks, they may straightway open to him. Blessed are those servants whom the Lord, when He cometh, shall find watching." [2] For there is no use of a sleeping man, as there is not of a dead man. Wherefore we ought often to rise by night and bless God.[3] For blessed are they who watch for Him, and so make themselves like the angels, whom we call " watchers." But a man asleep is worth nothing, any more than if he were not alive.

But he who has the light watches, " and darkness seizes not on him," [4] nor sleep, since darkness does not. He that is illuminated is therefore awake towards God ; and such an one lives. " For what was made in Him was life." [5] " Blessed is the man," says Wisdom, " who shall

hear me, and the man who shall keep my ways, watching at my doors, daily observing the posts of my entrances." [6] " Let us not then sleep, as do others, but let us watch," says the Scripture, " and be sober. For they that sleep, sleep in the night ; and they that be drunken, are drunken in the night," that is, in the darkness of ignorance. " But let us who are of the day be sober. For ye are all children of the light, and children of the day ; we are not of the night, nor of the darkness." [7] But whoever of us is most solicitous for living the true life, and for entertaining noble sentiments, will keep awake for as long time as possible, reserving to himself only what in this respect is conducive to his own health ; and that is not very usual.

But devotion to activity begets an everlasting vigil after toils. Let not food weigh us down, but lighten us ; that we may be injured as little as possible by sleep, as those that swim with weights hanging to them are weighed down. But, on the other hand, let temperance raise us as from the abyss beneath to the enterprises of wakefulness. For the oppression of sleep is like death, which forces us into insensibility, cutting off the light by the closing of the eyelids. Let not us, then, who are sons of the true light, close the door against this light ; but turning in on ourselves, illumining the eyes of the hidden man, and gazing on the truth itself, and receiving its streams, let us clearly and intelligibly reveal such dreams as are true.

But the hiccuping of those who are loaded with wine, and the snortings of those who are stuffed with food, and the snoring rolled in the bed-clothes, and the rumblings of pained stomachs, cover over the clear-seeing eye of the soul, by filling the mind with ten thousand phantasies. And the cause is too much food, which drags the rational part of man down to a condition of stupidity. For much sleep brings advantage neither to our bodies nor our souls ; nor is it suitable at all to those processes which have truth for their object, although agreeable to nature.

Now, just Lot (for I pass over at present the account of the economy of regeneration [8]) would not have been drawn into that unhallowed intercourse, had he not been intoxicated by his daughters, and overpowered by sleep. If, therefore, we cut off the causes of great tendency to sleep, we shall sleep the more soberly. For those who have the sleepless Word dwelling in

---

[1] *Iliad*, x. 155. [Note the Scriptural moderation with which he censures, recognising what is allowable, and rejecting the " pride that apes humility."]
[2] Luke xii. 35-37. [Concerning " sleep," see p. 259, *infra*.]
[3] [Holy men, on waking in the night, have always used ejaculations, even when unable to rise. Ps. cxix. 62; Acts xvi. 25.]
[4] John i. 5
[5] John i. 3, 4.

[6] Prov. viii. 34.
[7] I Thess. v. 5-8.
[8] [Does our author here use the term " regeneration " with reference to the restitution of all things ? (Matt. xix. 20; Acts iii. 21.) He touched upon the subject above, speaking of one that is *illuminated:* then he begins upon the true life, and to this he may refer. But it strikes me, that naming Lot, his place in the dispensations of grace strikes him as needing some comment, and so he apologizes for passing on.]

them, ought not to sleep the livelong night ; but they ought to rise by night, especially when the days are coming to an end, and one devote himself to literature, another begin his art, the women handle the distaff, and all of us should, so to speak, fight against sleep, accustoming ourselves to this gently and gradually, so that through wakefulness we may partake of life for a longer period.

We, then, who assign the best part of the night to wakefulness, must by no manner of means sleep by day ; and fits of uselessness, and napping and stretching one's self, and yawning, are manifestations of frivolous uneasiness of soul. And in addition to all, we must know this, that the need of sleep is not in the soul. For it is ceaselessly active. But the body is relieved by being resigned to rest, the soul whilst not acting through the body, but exercising intelligence within itself.[1] Thus also, such dreams as are true, in the view of him who reflects rightly, are the thoughts of a sober soul, undistracted for the time by the affections of the body, and counselling with itself in the best manner. For the soul to cease from activity within itself, were destruction to it. Wherefore always contemplating God, and by perpetual converse with Him inoculating the body with wakefulness, it raises man to equality with angelic grace, and from the practice of wakefulness it grasps the eternity of life.[2]

CHAP. X.[3] — QUÆNAM DE PROCREATIONE LIBERORUM TRACTANDA SINT.[4]

Tempus autem opportunum conjunctionis solis iis relinquitur considerandum, qui juncti sunt matrimonio ; qui autem matrimonio juncti sunt, iis scopus est et institutum, liberorum susceptio : finis autem, ut boni sint liberi : quemadmodum agricolæ seminis quidem dejectionis causa est, quod nutrimenti habendi curam gerat ; agriculturæ autem finis est, fructuum perceptio. Multo autem melior est agricola, qui terram colit animatam : ille enim ed tempus alimentum expetens, hic vero ut universum permaneat, curam gerens, agricolæ officio fungitur : et ille quidem propter se, hic vero propter Deum plantat ac seminat. Dixit enim : " Multiplicemini ; "[5] ubi hoc subaudiendum est : " Et ea ratione fit homo Dei imago, quatenus homo co-operatur ad generationem hominis." Non est quælibet terra apta ad suscipienda semina : quod si etiam sit

quælibet, non tamen eidem agricolæ. Neque vero seminandum est supra petram, neque semen est contumlia afficiendum, quod quidem dux est et princeps generationis, estque substantia, quæ simul habet insitas naturæ rationes. Quæ sunt autem secundum naturam rationes, absque ratione præternaturalibus mandando meatibus, ignominia afficere, valde est impium. Videte itaque quomodo sapientissimus Moyses infrugiferam aliquando sationem symbolice repulerit : "Non comedes, inquiens, leporem, nec hyænam."[6] Non vult homines esse qualitatis eorum participes, neque eis æqualem gustare libidinem : hæc enim animalia ad explendum coitum venereum feruntur insano quodam furore. Ac leporem quidem dicunt quotannis multiplicare anum, pro numero annorum, quos vixit, habentem foramina : et ea ratione dum leporis esum prohibet, significat se dehortari puerorum amorem. Hyænam autem vicissim singulis annis masculinum sexum mutare in femininum : significare autem non esse illi ad adulteria prorumpendum, qui ab hyæna abstinet.[7]

Well, I also agree that the consummately wise Moses confessedly indicates by the prohibition before us, that we must not resemble these animals ; but I do not assent to the explanation of what has been symbolically spoken. For nature never can be forced to change. What once has been impressed on it, may not be transformed into the opposite by passion. For passion is not nature, and passion is wont to deface the form, not to cast it into a new shape. Though many birds are said to change with the seasons, both in colour and voice, as the blackbird (κόσσυφος), which becomes yellow from black, and a chatterer from a singing-bird. Similarly also the nightingale changes by turns both its colour and note. But they do not alter their nature itself, so as in the transformation to become female from male. But the new crop of feathers, like new clothes, produces a kind of colouring of the feathers, and a little after it evaporates in the rigour of winter, as a flower when its colour fades. And in like manner the voice itself, injured by the cold, is enfeebled. For, in consequence of the outer skin being thickened by the surrounding air, the arteries about the neck being compressed and filled, press hard on the breath ; which being very much confined, emits a stifled sound. When, again, the breath is assimilated to the surrounding air and relaxed in spring, it is freed from its confined condition, and is carried through the dilated, though till then obstructed arteries, it warbles no longer a dying melody, but now gives forth a shrill note ; and the voice

---

[1] [See note, 7 *supra*, p. 257. Here the immaterial soul is recognised as wholly independent of bodily organs, and sleep is expounded as the image of death freeing the mind.]

[2] [The psychology of Clement is noteworthy, but his ethical reflections are pure gold.]

[3] For obvious reasons, we have given the greater part of this chapter in the Latin version. [Much of this chapter requires this sacrifice to a proper *verecundia;* but the learned translators have possibly been too cautious, erring, however, on the right side of the question.]

[4] [For the substance of this chapter, see Kaye, p. 84.]

[5] Gen. i. 27, 28.

[6] Deut. xiv. 7.

[7] [He lays down the law, that marriage was instituted for the one result of replenishing the earth; and he thinks certain unclean animals of the Mosaic system to be types of the sensuality which is not less forbidden to the married than to others.]

flows wide, and spring now becomes the song of the voice of birds.

Nequaquam ergo credendum est, hyænam unquam mutare naturam : idem enim animal non habet simul ambo pudenda maris et feminæ, sicut nonnulli existimarunt, qui prodigiose hermaphroditos finxerunt, et inter marem et feminam, hanc masculo-feminam naturam innovarunt. Valde autem falluntur, ut qui non animadverterint, quam sit filiorum amans omnium mater et genetrix Natura : quoniam enim hoc animal, hyæna inquam, est salacissimum, sub cauda ante excrementi meatum, adnatum est ei quoddam carneum tuberculum, feminino pudendo figura persimile. Nullum autem meatum habet hæc figura carnis, qui in utilem aliquam desinat partem, vel in matricem inquam, vel in rectum intestinum : tantum habet magnam concavitatem, quæ inanem excipiat libidinem, quando aversi fuerint meatus, qui in concipiendo fetu occupati sunt. Hoc ipsum autem et masculo et feminæ hyænæ adnatum est, quod sit insigniter pathica : masculus enim vicissim et agit, et patitur : unde etiam rarissime inveniri potest hyæna femina : non enim frequenter concipit hoc animal, cum in eis largiter redundet ea, quæ præter naturam est, satio. Hac etiam ratione mihi videtur Plato in *Phædro*, amorem puerorum repellens, eum appellare bestiam, quod frenum mordentes, qui se voluptatibus dedunt, libidinosi, quadrupedum coeunt more, et filios seminare conantur. Impios "autem tradidit Deus," ut ait Apostolus,[1] "in perturbationes ignominiæ : nam et feminæ eorum mutaverunt naturalem usum in eum, qui est præter naturam : similiter autem et masculi eorum, relicto usu naturali, exarserunt in desiderio sui inter se invicem, masculi in masculos turpitudinem operantes, et mercedem, quam oportuit, erroris sui in se recipientes." At vero ne libidinosissimis quidem animantibus concessit natura in excrementi meatum semen immittere : urina enim in vesicam excernitur, humefactum alimentum in ventrum, lacryma vero in oculum, sanguis in venas, sordes in aures, mucus in nares defertur : fini autem recti intestini, sedes cohæret, per quam excrementa exponuntur. Sola ergo varia in hyænis natura, superfluo coitui superfluam hanc partem excogitavit, et ideo est etiam aliquantisper concavum, ut prurientibus partibus inserviat, exinde autem excæcatur concavitas : non fuit enim res fabricata ad generationem. Hinc nobis manifestum atque adeo in confesso est, vitandos esse cum masculis concubitus, et infrugiferas sationes, et Venerem præposteram, et quæ natura coalescere non possunt, androgynorum conjunctiones, ipsam naturam sequentibus, quæ id per partium prohibet constitutionem, ut quæ masculum non ad semen suscipiendum, sed ad id

effundendum fecerit. Jeremias autem, hoc est, per ipsum loquens Spiritus, quando dicit : " Spelunca hyænæ facta est domus mea,"[2] id quod ex mortuis constabat corporibus detestans alimentum, sapienti allegoria reprehendit cultum simulacrorum : vere enim oportet ab idolis esse puram domum Dei viventis. Rursus Moyses lepore quoque vesci prohibet. Omni enim tempore coit lepus, et salit, assidente femina, a tergo aggrediens : est enim ex iis, quæ retro insiliunt. Concipit autem singulis mensibus, et superfetat ; init autem, et parit ; postquam autem peperit, statim a quovis initur lepore (neque enim uno contenta est matrimonio) et rursus concipit, adhuc lactans : habet enim matricem, cui sunt duo sinus, et non unus solus matricis vacuus sinus, est ei sufficiens sedes ad receptaculum coitus (quidquid enim est vacuum, desiderat repleri) ; verum accidit, ut cum uterum gerunt, altera pars matricis desiderio teneatur et libidine furiat ; quocirca fiunt eis superfetationes. A vehementibus ergo appetitionibus, mutuisque congressionibus, et cum prægnantibus feminis conjunctionibus, alternisque initibus, puerorumque stupris, adulteriis et libidine abstinere, hujus nos ænigmatis adhortata est prohibitio. Idcirco aperte, et non per ænigmata Moyses prohibuit, " Non fornicaberis ; non mœchaberis ; pueris stuprum non inferes,"[3] inquiens. Logi itaque præscriptum totis viribus observandum, neque quidquam contra leges ullo modo faciendum est, neque mandata sunt infirmanda. Malæ enim cupiditati nomen est ὕβρις, "petulantia ;" et equum cupiditatis, "petulantem" vocavit Plato, cum legissit, "Facti estis mihi equi furentes in feminas."[4] Libidines autem supplicium notum nobis facient illi, qui Sodomam accesserunt, angeli. Li eos, qui probro illos afficere voluerunt, una cum ipsa civitate combusserunt, evidenti hoc indicio ignem, qui est fructus libidinis, describentes. Quæ enim veteribus acciderunt, sicut ante diximus, ad nos admonendos scripta sunt, ne eisdem teneamur vitiis, et caveamus, ne in pœnas similes incidamus. Oportet autem filios existimare, pueros ; uxores autem alienas intueri tanquam proprias filias : voluptates quippe continere, ventrique et iis quæ sunt infra ventrem, dominari, est maximi imperii. Si enim ne digitum quidem temere movere permittit sapienti ratio, ut confitentur Stoici, quomodo non multo magis iis, qui sapientiam persequuntur, in eam, qua coitur, particulam dominatus est obtinendus ? Atque hac quidem de causa videtur esse nominatum pudendum, quod hac corporis parte magis, quam qualibet alia, cum pudore utendum sit ; natura enim sicut alimentis, ita etiam legitimis

---

[1] Rom. i. 26, 27.

[2] Jer. xii. 9. [The empirical science of the day is here enlarged upon, by Clement, for he cannot forbear to make lust detestable by a natural parable of the foul hyæna.]

[3] Ex. xx. 14.

[4] Jer. v. 8.

nuptiis, quantum convenit, utile est, et decet, nobis uti permisit: permisit autem appetere liberorum procreationem. Quicumque autem, quod modum excedit, persequuntur, labuntur in eo quod est secundum naturam, per congressus, qui sunt præter leges, seipsos lædentes. Ante omnia enim recte habet, ut nunquam cum adolescentibus perinde ac cum feminis, Veneris utamur consuetudine. Et ideo "non esse in petris et lapidibus seminandum" dicit, qui a Moyse factus est philosophus, "quoniam nunquam actis radicibus genitalem sit semen naturam suscept15rum." Logos itaque per Moysen appertissime præcepit: "Et cum masculo non dormies feminino concubitu: est enim abominatio."[1] Accedit his, quod "ab omni quoque arvo feminino esse abstinendum" præterquam a proprio, ex divinis Scripturis colligens præclarus Plato consuluit lege illinc accepta: "Et uxori proximi tui non dabis concubitum seminis, ut polluaris apud ipsam.[2] Irrita autem sunt et adulterina concubinarum semina. Ne semina, ubi non vis tibi nasci quod seminatum est. Neque ullam omnino tange mulierem, præterquam tuam ipsius uxorem," ex qua sola tibi licet carnis voluptates percipere ad suscipiendam legitimam successionem. Hæc enim Logo sola sunt legitima. Eis quidem certe, qui divini muneris in producendo opificio sunt participes, semen non est abjiciendum, neque injuria afficiendum, neque tanquam si cornibus semen mandes seminandum est. Hic ipse ergo Moyses cum ipsis quoque prohibet uxoribus congredi, si forte eas detineant purgationes menstruæ. Non enim purgamento corporis genitale semen, et quod mox homo futurum est, polluere est æquum, nec sordido materiæ profluvio, et, quæ expurgantur, inquinamentis inundare ac obruere; semen autem generationis degenerat, ineptumque redditur, si matricis sulcis privetur. Neque vero ullum unquam induxit veterum Hebræorum coeuntem cum sua uxore prægnante. Sola enim voluptas, si quis ea etiam utatur in conjugio, est præter leges, et injusta, et a ratione aliena. Rursus autem Moyses abducit viros a prægnantibus, quousque pepererint. Revera enim matrix sub vesica quidem collocata, super intestinum autem, quod rectum appellatur, posita, extendit collum inter humeros in vesica; et os colli, in quod venit semen, impletum occluditur, illa autem rursus inanis redditur, cum partu purgata fuerit: fructu autem deposito, deinde semen suscipit. Neque vero nobis turpe est ad auditorum utilitatem nominare partes, in quibus fit fetus conceptio, quæ quidem Deum fabricari non puduit. Matrix itaque sitiens filiorum procreationem, semen suscipit, probrosumque et vituperandum negat coitum, post sationem ore clauso omnino jam libidinem excludens. Ejus autem appetitiones, quæ prius in amicis versabantur complexibus, intro conversæ, in procreatione sobolis occupatæ, operantur una cum Opifice. Nefas est ergo operantem jam naturam adhuc molestia afficere, superflue ad petulantem prorumpendo libidinem. Petulantia autem, quæ multa quidem habet nomina, et multas species, cum ad hanc veneream intemperantiam deflexerit, λαγνεία, id est "lascivia," dicitur; quo nomine significatur libidinosa, publica, et incesta in coitum propensio: quæ cum aucta fuerit, magna simul morborum convenit multitudo, obsoniorum desiderium, vinolentia et amor in mulieres; luxus quoque, et simul universarum voluptatum studium; in quæ omnia tyrannidem obtinet cupiditas. His autem cognatæ innumerabiles augentur affectiones, ex quibus mores intemperantes ad summum provehuntur. Dicit autem Scriptura: "Parantur intemperantibus flagella, et supplicia humeris insipientium:"[3] vires intemperantiæ, ejusque constantem tolerantiam, vocans "humeros insipientium." Quocirca, "Amove a servis tuis spes inanes, et indecoras," inquit, "cupiditates averte a me. Ventris appetitio et coitus ne me apprehendant."[4] Longe ergo sunt arcenda multifaria insidiatorum maleficia; non ad solam enim Cratetis Peram, sed etiam ad nostram civitatem non navigat stultus parasitus, nec scortator libidinosus, qui posteriori delectatur parte: non dolosa meretrix, nec ulla ejusmodi alia voluptatis bellua. Multa ergo nobis per totam vitam seminetur, quæ bona sit et honesta, occupatio. In summa ergo, vel jungi matrimonio, vel omnino a matrimonio purum esse oportet; in quæstione enim id versatur, et hoc a nobis declaratum est in libro *De continentia*. Quod si hoc ipsum, an ducenda sit uxor. veniat in considerationem: quomodo libere permittetur, quemadmodum nutrimento, ita etiam coitu semper uti, tanquam re necessaria? Ex eo ergo videri possunt nervi tanquam stamina distrahi, et in vehementi congressus intensione disrumpi. Jam vero offundit etiam caliginem sensibus, et vires enervat. Patet hoc et in animantibus rationis expertibus, et in iis, quæ in exercitatione versantur, corporibus; quorum hi quidem, qui abstinent, in certaminibus superant adversarios; illa vero a coitu abducta circumaguntur, et tantum non trahuntur, omnibus viribus et omni impetu tandem quasi enervata. "Parvam epilepsiam" dicebat "coitum" sophista Abderites morbum immedicabilem existimans. Annon enim consequuntur resolutiones, quæ exinanitionis ejusque, quod abscedit, magnitudini ascribuntur? "homo enim ex homine nascitur et evellitur." Vide damni magnitudinem: totus homo per exinanitionem coitus abstrahitur. Dicit enim: "Hoc nunc os ex ossibus meis, et caro ex carne mea."[1]   Homo ergo tantum exinanitur semine, quantus videtur corpore; est enim generationis initium id, quod recedit: quin etiam conturbat ebullitio materiæ et compagem corporis labefactat et commovet. Lepide ergo ille, qui interroganti, "Quomodo adhuc se haberet ad res venereas," respondit: "Bona verba, quæso: ego vero lubentissime isthinc, tanquam ab agresti et insano domino, profugi." Verum concedatur quidem et admittatur matrimonium: vult enim Dominus humanum genus repleri; sed non dicit, Estote libidinosi: nec vos, tanquam ad coitum natos, voluit esse deditos voluptati. Pudore autem nos afficiat Pædagogus, clamans per Ezechielem: "Circumcidamini fornicationem vestram." Aliquod tempus ad seminandum opportunum habent quoque rationis expertia animantia. Aliter autem coire, quam ad liberorum procreationem, est facere injuriam naturæ;[2] qua quidem oportet magistra, quas prudenter introducit temporis commoditates, diligenter observare, senectutem, inquam, et puerilem ætatem. His enim nondum concessit, illos autem non vult amplius uxores ducere. Sed non vult homines semper dare operam matrimonio. Matrimonium autem est filiorum procreationis appetitio, non inordinata seminis excretio, quæ est et præter leges et a ratione aliena. Secundum naturam autem nobis vita universa processerit,[3] si et ab initio cupiditates contineamus, et hominum genus, quod ex divina providentia nascitur, improbis et malitiosis non tollamus artibus: eæ enim, ut fornicationem celent, exitialia medicamenta adhibentes, quæ prorsus in perniciem ducunt, simul cum fetu omnem humanitatem perdunt. Cæterum, quibus uxores ducere concessum est, iis Pædagogo opus fuerit, ut non interdiu mystica naturæ celebrentur orgia, nec ut aliquis ex ecclesia, verbi gratia, aut ex foro mane rediens, galli more coeat, quando orationis, et lectionis, et eorum quæ interdiu facere convenit, operum tempus est. Vespere autem oportet post convivium quiescere, et post gratiarum actionem, quæ fit Deo pro bonis quæ percepimus. Non semper autem concedit tempus natura, ut peragatur congressus matrimonii; est enim eo desiderabilior conjunctio, quo diuturnior. Neque vero noctu, tanquam in tenebris, immodeste sese ac imtemperanter gerere oportet, sed verecundia, ut quæ sit lux rationis, in animo est includenda. Nihil enim a Penelope telam texente differemus, si interdiu quidem texamus dogmata temperantiæ; noctu autem ea resolvamus, cum in cubile venerimus. Si enim honestatem exercere oportet,

multo magis tuæ uxori honestas est ostendenda, inhonestas vitando conjunctiones: et quod caste cum proximis verseris, fide dignum e domo adsit testimonium. Non enim potest aliquid honestum ab ea existimari, apud quam honestas in acribus illis non probatur certo quasi testimonio voluptatibus. Benevolentia autem quæ præceps fertur ad congressionem, exiguo tempore floret, et cum corpore consenescit; nonnunquam autem etiam præsenescit, flaccescente jam libidine, quando matrimonialem temperantiam meretriciæ vitiaverint libidines. Amantium enim corda sunt volucria, amorisque irritamenta exstinguuntur sæpe pœnitentia; amorque sæpe vertitur in odium, quando reprehensionem senserit satietas. Impudicorum vero verborum, et turpium figurarum, meretriciorumque osculorum, et hujusmodi lasciviarum nomina ne sunt quidem memoranda, beatum sequentibus Apostolum, qui aperte dicit: "Fornicatio autem et omnis immunditia, vel plura habendi cupiditas, ne nominetur quidem in vobis, sicut decet sanctos."[4]   Recte ergo videtur dixisse quispiam: "Nulli quidem profuit coitus, recte autem cum eo agitur, quem non læserit." Nam et qui legitimus, est periculosus, nisi quatenus in liberorum procreatione versatur. De eo autem, qui est præter leges, dicit Scriptura: "Mulier meretrix apro similis reputabitur. Quæ autem viro subjecta est, turris est mortis iis, qui ea utuntur." Capro, vel apro, meretricis comparavit affectionem. "Mortem" autem dixit "quæsitam," adulterium, quod committitur in meretrice, quæ custoditur. "Domum" autem, et "urbem," in qua suam exercent intemperantiam. Quin etiam quæ est apud vos poetica, quodammodo ea exprobrans, scribit:—

Tecum et adulterium est, tecum coitusque nefandus,
Fœdus, femineusque, urbs pessima, plane impura.

Econtra autem pudicos admiratur:—

Quos desiderium tenuit nec turpe cubilis
Alterius, nec tetra invisaque stupra tulerunt
Ulla unquam maribus.

[5] For many think such things to be pleasures only which are against nature, such as these sins of theirs. And those who are better than they, know them to be sins, but are overcome by pleasures, and darkness is the veil of their vicious practices. For he violates his marriage adulterously who uses it in a meretricious way, and hears not the voice of the Instructor, crying, "The man who ascends his bed, who says in his soul, Who seeth me? darkness is around me, and the walls are my covering, and no one sees my sins. Why do I fear lest the Highest will remember?"[6]   Most wretched is such a

---

[1] Gen. ii. 23.
[2] [Tamen possunt senes et steriles matrimonium sanctum contrahere, et de re conjugali aliter docet Lactantius de naturâ singulari mulierum argute disserens: q. v. in libro ejus *de vero cultu*, vi. cap. 23, p. 280, ed. Basiliæ, 1521.]
[3] [Naturâ duce, sub lege Logi, omnia fidelibus licent non omnia tamen expediunt. Conf Paulum, I., *Ad Corinth*, vi 12.]

[4] Eph. v. 3.
[5] [He has argued powerfully on the delicacy and refinement which should be observed in Christian marriage, to which Lactantius in the next age will be found attributing the *glory of chastity*, as really as to a pure celibacy. He now continues the argument in a form which our translators do not scruple to English.]
[6] Ecclus. xxiii. 18, 19.

man, dreading men's eyes alone, and thinking that he will escape the observation of God. "For he knoweth not," says the Scripture, "that brighter ten thousand times than the sun are the eyes of the Most High, which look on all the ways of men, and cast their glance into hidden parts." Thus again the Instructor threatens them, speaking by Isaiah: "Woe be to those who take counsel in secret, and say, Who seeth us?"[1] For one may escape the light of sense, but that of the mind it is impossible to escape. For how, says Heraclitus, can one escape the notice of that which never sets? Let us by no means, then, veil our selves with the darkness; for the light dwells in us. "For the darkness," it is said, "comprehendeth it not."[2] And the very night itself is illuminated by temperate reason. The thoughts of good men Scripture has named "sleepless lamps;"[3] although for one to attempt even to practise concealment, with reference to what he does, is confessedly to sin. And every one who sins, directly wrongs not so much his neighbour if he commits adultery, as himself, because he has committed adultery, besides making himself worse and less thought of. For he who sins, in the degree in which he sins, becomes worse and is of less estimation than before; and he who has been overcome by base pleasures, has now licentiousness wholly attached to him. Wherefore he who commits fornication is wholly dead to God, and is abandoned by the Word as a dead body by the spirit. For what is holy, as is right, abhors to be polluted. But it is always lawful for the pure to touch the pure. Do not, I pray, put off modesty at the same time that you put off your clothes; because it is never right for the just man to divest himself of continence. For, lo, this mortal shall put on immortality; when the insatiableness of desire, which rushes into licentiousness, being trained to self-restraint, and made free from the love of corruption, shall consign the man to everlasting chastity. "For in this world they marry and and are given in marriage."[4] But having done with the works of the flesh, and having been clothed with immortality, the flesh itself being pure, we pursue after that which is according to the measure of the angels.

Thus in the *Philebus*, Plato, who had been the disciple of the barbarian[5] philosophy, mystically called those Atheists who destroy and pollute, as far as in them lies, the Deity dwelling in them — that is, the Logos — by association with their vices. Those, therefore, who are consecrated to God must never live mortally (θνητῶς). "Nor," as Paul says, "is it meet to make the members of Christ the members of an harlot; nor must the temple of God be made the temple of base affections."[6] Remember the four and twenty thousand that were rejected for fornication.[7] But the experiences of those who have committed fornication, as I have already said, are types which correct our lusts. Moreover, the Pædagogue warns us most distinctly: "Go not after thy lusts, and abstain from thine appetites;[8] for wine and women will remove the wise; and he that cleaves to harlots will become more daring. Corruption and the worm shall inherit him, and he shall be held up as public example to greater shame."[9] And again — for he wearies not of doing good — "He who averts his eyes from pleasure crowns his life."

Non est ergo justum vinci a rebus venereis, nec libidinibus stolide inhiare, nec a ratione alienis appetitionibus moveri, nec desiderare pollui. Ei autem soli, qui uxorem duxit, ut qui tunc sit agricola, serere permissum est; quando tempus sementem admittit. Adversus aliam autem intemperantiam, optimum quidem est medicamentum, ratio.[10] Fert etiam auxilium penuria satietatis, per quam accensæ libidines prosiliunt ad voluptates.

CHAP. XI.[11] — ON CLOTHES.

Wherefore neither are we to provide for ourselves costly clothing any more than variety of food. The Lord Himself, therefore, dividing His precepts into what relates to the body, the soul, and thirdly, external things, counsels us to provide external things on account of the body; and manages the body by the soul (ψυχή), and disciplines the soul, saying, "Take no thought for your life (ψυχῇ), what ye shall eat; nor yet for your body, what ye shall put on; for the life is more than meat, and the body more than raiment."[12] And He adds a plain example of instruction: "Consider the ravens: for they neither sow nor reap, which have neither storehouse nor barn; and God feedeth them."[13] "Are ye not better than the fowls?"[14] Thus far as to food. Similarly He enjoins with respect to clothing, which belongs to the third division, that of things external, saying, "Consider the lilies, how they spin not, nor weave. But I say unto you, that

---

[1] Isa. xxix. 15.
[2] John i. 5.
[3] Wisd. vii. 10 is probably referred to.
[4] Matt xxii. 30.
[5] That is, the Jewish.

[6] 1 Cor. vi. 15.
[7] [1 Cor. x. 8; Num. xxv. 1-9. Clement says twenty-four thousand, with the Old Testament, but St. Paul says twenty-three thousand; on which, *ad locum*, see *Speaker's Commentary*.]
[8] Ecclus. xviii. 30.
[9] Ecclus. xix. 2, 3, 5.
[10] [Right reason is the best remedy against all excesses, argues our author, but always subject to the express law of the Gospel.]
[11] Chap. xi. is not a separate chapter in the Greek, but appears as part of chap. x.
[12] Luke xii. 22, 23.
[13] Luke xii. 24.
[14] Luke xii. 24.

not even Solomon was arrayed as one of these." [1] And Solomon the king plumed himself exceedingly on his riches.

What, I ask, more graceful, more gay-coloured, than flowers? What, I say, more delightful than lilies or roses? "And if God so clothe the grass, which is to-day in the field, and to morrow is cast into the oven, how much more will He clothe you, O ye of little faith!" [2] Here the particle *what* (τί) banishes variety in food. For this is shown from the Scripture, "Take no thought what things ye shall eat, or what things ye shall drink." For to take thought of these things argues greed and luxury. Now eating, considered merely by itself, is the sign of necessity; repletion, as we have said, of want. Whatever is beyond that, is the sign of superfluity. And what is superfluous, Scripture declares to be of the devil. The subjoined expression makes the meaning plain. For having said, "Seek not what ye shall eat, or what ye shall drink," He added, "Neither be ye of doubtful (or lofty) [3] mind." Now pride and luxury make men waverers (or raise them aloft) from the truth; and the voluptuousness, which indulges in superfluities, leads away from the truth. Wherefore He says very beautifully, "And all these things do the nations of the world seek after." [4] The nations are the dissolute and the foolish. And what are these things which He specifies? Luxury, voluptuousness, rich cooking, dainty feeding, gluttony. These are the "What?" And of bare sustenance, dry and moist, as being necessaries, He says, "Your Father knoweth that ye need these." And if, in a word, we are naturally given to seeking, let us not destroy the faculty of seeking by directing it to luxury, but let us excite it to the discovery of truth. For He says, "Seek ye the kingdom of God, and the materials of sustenance shall be added to you."

If, then, He takes away anxious care for clothes and food, and superfluities in general, as unnecessary; what are we to imagine ought to be said of love of ornament, and dyeing of wool, and variety of colours, and fastidiousness about gems, and exquisite working of gold, and still more, of artificial hair and wreathed curls; and furthermore, of staining the eyes, and plucking out hairs, and painting with rouge and white lead, and dyeing of the hair, and the wicked arts that are employed in such deceptions? May we not very well suspect, that what was quoted a little above respecting the grass, has been said of those unornamental lovers of ornaments? For the field is the world, and we who are bedewed by the grace of God are the grass; and though cut down,

we spring up again, as will be shown at greater length in the book *On the Resurrection*. But hay figuratively designates the vulgar rabble, attached to ephemeral pleasure, flourishing for a little, loving ornament, loving praise, and being everything but truth-loving, good for nothing but to be burned with fire. "There was a certain man," said the Lord, narrating, "very rich, who was clothed in purple and scarlet, enjoying himself splendidly every day." This was the hay. "And a certain poor man named Lazarus was laid at the rich man's gate, full of sores, desiring to be filled with the crumbs which fell from the rich man's table." This is the grass. Well, the rich man was punished in Hades, being made partaker of the fire; while the other flourished again in the Father's bosom. I admire that ancient city of the Lacedæmonians which permitted harlots alone to wear flowered clothes, and ornaments of gold, interdicting respectable women from love of ornament, and allowing courtesans alone to deck themselves. On the other hand, the archons of the Athenians, who affected a polished mode of life, forgetting their manhood, wore tunics reaching to the feet, and had on the crobulus — a kind of knot of the hair — adorned with a fastening of gold grasshoppers, to show their origin from the soil, forsooth, in the ostentation of licentiousness. Now rivalry of these archons extended also to the other Ionians, whom Homer, to show their effeminancy, calls "Long-robed." Those, therefore, who are devoted to the image of the beautiful, that is, love of finery, not the beautiful itself, and who under a fair name again practise idolatry, are to be banished far from the truth, as those who by opinion, [5] not knowledge, dream of the nature of the beautiful; and so life here is to them only a deep sleep of ignorance; from which it becomes us to rouse ourselves and haste to that which is truly beautiful and comely, and desire to grasp this alone, leaving the ornaments of earth to the world, and bidding them farewell before we fall quite asleep. I say, then, that man requires clothes for nothing else than the covering of the body, for defence against excess of cold and intensity of heat, lest the inclemency of the air injure us. And if this is the object of clothing, see that one kind be not assigned to men and another to women. For it is common to both to be covered, as it is to eat and drink. The necessity, then, being common, we judge that the provision ought to be similar. For as it is common to both to require things to cover them, so also their coverings ought to be similar; although such a covering ought to be assumed

---

[1] Luke xii. 27.
[2] Luke xii. 28.
[3] μετέωρος.
[4] Matt. vi. 32.

[5] Clement uses here Platonic language, δόξα meaning opinion established on no scientific basis, which may be true or may be false, and ἐπιστήμη knowledge sure and certain, because based on the reasons of things.

as is requisite for covering the eyes of women. For if the female sex, on account of their weakness, desire more, we ought to blame · the habit of that evil training, by which often men reared up in bad habits become more effeminate than women. But this must not be yielded to. And if some accommodation is to be made, they may be permitted to use softer clothes, provided they put out of the way fabrics foolishly thin, and of curious texture in weaving ; bidding farewell to embroidery of gold and Indian silks and elaborate Bombyces (silks), which is at first a worm, then from it is produced a hairy caterpillar ; after which the creature suffers' a new transformation into a third form which they call lava, from which a long filament is produced, as the spider's thread from the spider. For these superfluous and diaphanous materials are the proof of a weak mind, covering as they do the shame of the body with a slender veil. For luxurious clothing, which cannot conceal the shape of the body, is no more a covering. For such clothing, falling close to the body, takes its form more easily, and adhering as it were to the flesh, receives its shape, and marks out the woman's figure, so that the whole make of the body is visible to spectators, though not seeing the body itself.[1]

Dyeing of clothes is also to be rejected. For it is remote both from necessity and truth, in addition to the fact that reproach in manners spring from it.[2] For the use of colours is not beneficial, for they are of no service against cold ; nor has it anything for covering more than other clothing, except the opprobrium alone. And the agreeableness of the colour afflicts greedy eyes, inflaming them to senseless blindness. But for those who are white and unstained within, it is most suitable to use white and simple garments. Clearly and plainly, therefore, Daniel the prophet says, "Thrones were set, and upon them sat one like the Ancient of days, and His vesture was white as snow."[3] The Apocalypse says also that the Lord Himself appeared wearing such a robe. It says also, "I saw the souls of those that had witnessed, beneath the altar, and there was given to each a white robe."[4] And if it were necessary to seek for any other colour, the natural colour of truth should suffice.[5] But garments which are like flowers are to be abandoned to Bacchic fooleries, and to those of the rites of initiation, along with purple and silver plate, as the comic poet says : —

"Useful for tragedians, not for life."

And our life ought to be anything rather than a pageant. Therefore the dye of Sardis, and another of olive, and another green, a rose-coloured, and scarlet, and ten thousand other dyes, have been invented with much trouble for mischievous voluptuousness. Such clothing is for looking at, not for covering. Garments, too, variegated with gold, and those that are purple, and that piece of luxury which has its name from beasts (figured on it), and that saffron-coloured ointment-dipped robe, and those costly and many-coloured garments of flaring membranes, we are to bid farewell to, with the art itself. "For what prudent thing can these women have done," says the comedy, "who sit covered with flowers, wearing a saffron-coloured dress,[6] painted ?"

The Instructor expressly admonishes, "Boast not of the clothing of your garment, and be not elated on account of any glory, as it is unlawful."[7]

Accordingly, deriding those who are clothed in luxurious garments, He says in the Gospel : "Lo, they who live in gorgeous apparel and luxury are in earthly palaces."[8] He says in perishable palaces, where are love of display, love of popularity, and flattery and deceit. But those that wait at the court of heaven around the King of all, are sanctified in the immortal vesture of the Spirit, that is, the flesh, and so put on incorruptibility.

As therefore she who is unmarried devotes herself to God alone, and her care is not divided, but the chaste married woman divides her life between God and her husband, while she who is otherwise disposed is devoted entirely to marriage, that is, to passion : in the same way I think the chaste wife, when she devotes herself to her husband, sincerely serves God ; but when she becomes fond of finery, she falls away from God and from chaste wedlock, exchanging her husband for the world, after the fashion of that Argive courtesan, I mean Eriphyle, —

"Who received gold prized above her dear husband."

Wherefore I admire the Ceian sophist,[9] who delineated like and suitable images of Virtue and Vice, representing the former of these, viz., Virtue, standing simply, white-robed and pure, adorned with modesty alone (for such ought to be the true wife, dowered with modesty). But the other, viz., Vice, on the contrary, he introduces dressed in superfluous attire, brightened up with colour not her own ; and her gait and mien are depicted as studiously framed to give pleasure, forming a sketch of wanton women. But he who follows the Word will not addict

---

1 [Martial, *Epigrams, passim.*]
2 [The reproach and opprobrium of foppery.]
3 Dan. vii. 9.
4 Rev. vi. 9, 11.
5 [This refers to the natural tint of unbleached linen, or to wool not whitened by the art of the fuller. Hermas speaks of "*pure* undressed linen." Book iii. 4, p. 40, *supra*.]

6 [The colour (probably, for MSS. differ) reprehended as the dress of the false shepherd in Hermas. See note 10, book iii. Simil. 6. cap. 1. p. 30, this volume.]
7 Ecclus. xi. 4.
8 Luke vii. 25.
9 Prodicus, of the island of Ceus.

himself to any base pleasure ; wherefore also what is useful in the article of dress is to be preferred. And if the Word, speaking of the Lord by David, sings, " The daughters of kings made Thee glad by honour ; the queen stood at Thy right hand, clad in cloth of gold, girt with golden fringes," it is not luxurious raiment that he indicates ; but he shows the immortal adornment, woven of faith, of those that have found mercy, that is, the Church ; in which the guileless Jesus shines conspicuous as gold, and the elect are the golden tassels. And if such must be woven[1] for the women, let us weave apparel pleasant and soft to the touch, not flowered, like pictures, to delight the eye. For the picture fades in course of time, and the washing and steeping in the medicated juices of the dye wear away the wool, and render the fabrics of the garments weak ; and this is not favourable to economy. It is the height of foolish ostentation to be in a flutter about peploi, and xystides, and ephaptides,[2] and " cloaks," and tunics, and " what covers shame," says Homer. For, in truth, I am ashamed when I see so much wealth lavished on the covering of the nakedness. For primeval man in Paradise provided a covering for his shame of branches and leaves ; and now, since sheep have been created for us, let us not be as silly as sheep, but trained by the Word, let us condemn sumptuousness of clothing, saying, " Ye are sheep's wool." Though Miletus boast, and Italy be praised, and the wool, about which many rave, be protected beneath skins,[3] yet are we not to set our hearts on it.

The blessed John, despising the locks of sheep as savouring of luxury, chose " camel's hair," and was clad in it, making himself an example of frugality and simplicity of life. For he also " ate locusts and wild honey,"[4] sweet and spiritual fare ; preparing, as he was, the lowly and chaste ways of the Lord. For how possibly could he have worn a purple robe, who turned away from the pomp of cities, and retired to the solitude of the desert, to live in calmness with God, far from all frivolous pursuits — from all false show of good — from all meanness ? Elias used a sheepskin mantle, and fastened the sheepskin with a girdle made of hair.[5] And Esaias, another prophet, was naked and barefooted,[6] and often was clad in sackcloth, the garb of humility. And if you call Jeremiah, he had only " a linen girdle."[7]

For as well-nurtured bodies, when stripped, show their vigour more manifestly, so also beauty of character shows its magnanimity, when not involved in ostentatious fooleries. But to drag one's clothes, letting them down to the soles of his feet, is a piece of consummate foppery, impeding activity in walking, the garment sweeping the surface dirt of the ground like a broom ; since even those emasculated creatures the dancers, who transfer their dumb shameless profligacy to the stage, do not despise the dress which flows away to such indignity ; whose curious vestments, and appendages of fringes, and elaborate motions of figures, show the trailing of sordid effeminacy.[8]

If one should adduce the garment of the Lord reaching down to the foot, that many-flowered coat[9] shows the flowers of wisdom, the varied and unfading Scriptures, the oracles of the Lord, resplendent with the rays of truth. In such another robe the Spirit arrayed the Lord through David, when he sang thus : " Thou wert clothed with confession and comeliness, putting on light as a garment."[10]

As, then, in the fashioning of our clothes, we must keep clear of all strangeness, so in the use of them we must beware of extravagance. For neither is it seemly for the clothes to be above the knee, as they say was the case with the Lacedæmonian virgins ;[11] nor is it becoming for any part of a woman to be exposed. Though you may with great propriety use the language addressed to him who said, " Your arm is beautiful ; yes, but it is not for the public gaze. Your thighs are beautiful ; but, was the reply, for my husband alone. And your face is comely. Yes ; but only for him who has married me." But I do not wish chaste women to afford cause for such praises to those who, by praises, hunt after grounds of censure ; and not only because it is prohibited to expose the ankle, but because it has also been enjoined that the head should be veiled and the face covered ; for it is a wicked thing for beauty to be a snare to men. Nor is it seemly for a woman to wish to make herself conspicuous, by using a purple veil. Would it were possible to abolish purple in dress, so as not to turn the eyes of spectators on the face of those that wear it ! But the women, in the manufacture of all the rest of their dress, have made everything of purple, thus inflaming the lusts. And, in truth, those women who are crazy

---

[1] Or by a conjectural emendation of the text, " If in this we must relax somewhat in the case of women."

[2] Various kinds of robes. [The *peplus*, or shawl of fine wool, seems to be specified in condemning the boast below, which asserts real wool and no imitation.]

[3] Alluding to the practice of covering the fleeces of sheep with skins, when the wool was very fine, to prevent it being soiled by exposure.

[4] Mark i. 6.

[5] 2 Kings i. 8.

[6] Isa. xx. 2.

[7] Jer. xiii. 1.

[8] [The bearing of this chapter on ecclesiastical vestments must be evident. It is wholly inconsistent with aught but very simple attire in public worship ; and rebukes even the fashionable costumes of women and much of our mediæval æstheticism, with primitive severity. On the whole subject, see the *Vestiarium Christianum* of the Rev. Wharton B. Marriott. London, *Rivingtons*, 1868.]

[9] [Based upon the idea that Joseph's coat of many colours, which was afterwards dipped in blood, was a symbol of our Lord's raiment, on which lots were cast.]

[10] Ps. civ. 2.

[11] [Women's tunics tucked up to give freedom to the knee, are familiar objects in ancient art.]

about these stupid and luxurious purples, "purple (dark) death has seized,"[1] according to the poetic saying. On account of this purple, then, Tyre and Sidon, and the vicinity of the Lacedæmonian Sea, are very much desired; and their dyers and purple-fishers, and the purple fishes themselves, because their blood produces purple, are held in high esteem. But crafty women and effeminate men, who blend these deceptive dyes with dainty fabrics, carry their insane desires beyond all bounds, and export their fine linens no longer from Egypt, but some other kinds from the land of the Hebrews and the Cilicians. I say nothing of the linens made of Amorgos[2] and Byssus. Luxury has outstripped nomenclature.

The covering ought, in my judgment, to show that which is covered to be better than itself, as the image is superior to the temple, the soul to the body, and the body to the clothes.[3] But now, quite the contrary, the body of these ladies, if sold, would never fetch a thousand Attic drachms. Buying, as they do, a single dress at the price of ten thousand talents, they prove themselves to be of less use and less value than cloth. Why in the world do you seek after what is rare and costly, in preference to what is at hand and cheap? It is because you know not what is really beautiful, what is really good, and seek with eagerness shows instead of realities, from fools who, like people out of their wits, imagine black to be white.

CHAP. XII. — ON SHOES.

Women fond of display act in the same manner with regard to shoes, showing also in this matter great luxuriousness. Base, in truth, are those sandals on which golden ornaments are fastened; but they are thought worth having nails driven into the soles in winding rows. Many, too, carve on them[4] amorous embraces, as if they would by their walk communicate to the earth harmonious movement, and impress on it the wantonness of their spirit. Farewell, therefore, must be bidden to gold-plated and jewelled mischievous devices of sandals, and Attic and Sicyonian half-boots, and Persian and Tyrrhenian buskins; and setting before us the right aim, as is the habit with our truth, we are bound to select what is in accordance with nature.

For the use of shoes is partly for covering, partly for defence in case of stumbling against objects, and for saving the sole of the foot from the roughness of hilly paths.

Women are to be allowed a white shoe, except

when on a journey, and then a greased shoe must be used. When on a journey, they require nailed shoes. Further, they ought for the most part to wear shoes; for it is not suitable for the foot to be shown naked: besides, woman is a tender thing, easily hurt. But for a man bare feet are quite in keeping, except when he is on military service. "For being shod is near neighbour to being bound."[5]

To go with bare feet is most suitable for exercise, and best adapted for health and ease, unless where necessity prevents. But if we are not on a journey, and cannot endure bare feet, we may use slippers or white shoes; dusty-foots[6] the Attics called them, on account of their bringing the feet near the dust, as I think. As a witness for simplicity in shoes let John suffice, who avowed that "he was not worthy to unloose the latchet of the Lord's shoes."[7] For he who exhibited to the Hebrews the type of the true philosophy wore no elaborate shoes. What else this may imply, will be shown elsewhere.

CHAP. XIII. — AGAINST EXCESSIVE FONDNESS FOR JEWELS AND GOLD ORNAMENTS.

It is childish to admire excessively dark or green stones, and things cast out by the sea on foreign shores, particles of the earth.[8] For to rush after stones that are pellucid and of peculiar colours, and stained glass, is only characteristic of silly people, who are attracted by things that have a striking show. Thus children, on seeing the fire, rush to it, attracted by its brightness; not understanding through senselessness the danger of touching it. Such is the case with the stones which silly women wear fastened to chains and set in necklaces, amethysts, ceraunites, jaspers, topaz, and the Milesian

"Emerald, most precious ware."

And the highly prized pearl has invaded the woman's apartments to an extravagant extent. This is produced in a kind of oyster like mussels, and is about the bigness of a fish's eye of large size. And the wretched creatures are not ashamed at having bestowed the greatest pains about this little oyster, when they might adorn themselves with the sacred jewel, the Word of God, whom the Scripture has somewhere called a pearl, the pure and pellucid Jesus, the eye that watches in the flesh, — the transparent Word, by whom the flesh, regenerated by water, becomes precious. For that oyster that is in

---

[1] *Iliad*, v. 83.
[2] Flax grown in the island of Amorgos.
[3] [Matt. vi. 25.]
[4] [It was such designs which early Christian art endeavoured to supplant, by the devices on lamps, ΧΡ. ΑΩ., etc.]

[5] ὑποδεδέσθαι τῷ δεδέσθαι. "Wearing boots is near neighbour to wearing bonds."
[6] κονιποδες.
[7] Mark i. 7: Luke iii. 16. [It was reserved for Chrysostom to give a more terrible counterblast against costly *chaussure*, in commenting upon Matt. xvi. 13, *et seq. Opera*, tom. vii. p. 502, ed. Migne.]
[8] [Amber is referred to, and the extravagant values attributed to it. The mysterious enclosure of bees and other insects in amber, gave it superstitious importance. Clement may have fancied these to be remnants of a pre-adamite earth.]

the water covers the flesh all round, and out of it is produced the pearl.

We have heard, too, that the Jerusalem above is walled with sacred stones; and we allow that the twelve gates of the celestial city, by being made like precious stones, indicate the transcendent grace of the apostolic voice. For the colours are laid on in precious stones, and these colours are precious; while the other parts remain of earthy material. With these symbolically, as is meet, the city of the saints, which is spiritually built, is walled. By that brilliancy of stones, therefore, is meant the inimitable brilliancy of the spirit, the immortality and sanctity of being. But these women, who comprehend not the symbolism of Scripture, gape all they can for jewels, adducing the astounding apology, "Why may I not use what God hath exhibited?" and, "I have it by me, why may I not enjoy it?" and, "For whom were these things made, then, if not for us?" Such are the utterances of those who are totally ignorant of the will of God. For first necessaries, such as water and air, He supplies free to all; and what is not necessary He has hid in the earth and water. Wherefore ants dig, and griffins guard gold, and the sea hides the pearl-stone. But ye busy yourselves about what you need not. Behold, the whole heaven is lighted up, and ye seek not God; but gold which is hidden, and jewels, are dug up by those among us who are condemned to death.

But you also oppose Scripture, seeing it expressly cries, "Seek first the kingdom of heaven, and all these things shall be added unto you."[1] But if all things have been conferred on you, and all things allowed you, and "if all things are lawful, yet all things are not expedient,"[2] says the apostle. God brought our race into communion by first imparting what was His own, when He gave His own Word, common to all, and made all things for all. All things therefore are common, and not for the rich to appropriate an undue share. That expression, therefore, " I possess, and possess in abundance: why then should I not enjoy?" is suitable neither to the man, nor to society. But more worthy of love is that: "I have: why should I not give to those who need?" For such an one — one who fulfils the command, "Thou shalt love thy neighbour as thyself" — is perfect. For this is the true luxury — the treasured wealth. But that which is squandered on foolish lusts is to be reckoned waste, not expenditure. For God has given to us, I know well, the liberty of use, but only so far as necessary; and He has determined that the use should be common. And it is monstrous for one to live in luxury, while many are in want. How much more glorious is it to do good to

many, than to live sumptuously! How much wiser to spend money on human beings,[3] than on jewels and gold! How much more useful to acquire decorous friends, than lifeless ornaments! Whom have lands ever benefited so much as conferring favours has? It remains for us, therefore, to do away with this allegation: Who, then, will have the more sumptuous things, if all select the simpler? Men, I would say, if they make use of them impartially and indifferently. But if it be impossible for all to exercise self-restraint, yet, with a view to the use of what is necessary, we must seek after what can be most readily procured, bidding a long farewell to these superfluities.

In fine, they must accordingly utterly cast off ornaments as girls' gewgaws, rejecting adornment itself entirely. For they ought to be adorned within, and show the inner woman beautiful. For in the soul alone are beauty and deformity shown. Wherefore also only the virtuous man is really beautiful and good. And it is laid down as a dogma, that only the beautiful is good. And excellence alone appears through the beautiful body, and blossoms out in the flesh, exhibiting the amiable comeliness of self-control, whenever the character like a beam of light gleams in the form. For the beauty of each plant and animal consists in its individual excellence. And the excellence of man is righteousness, and temperance, and manliness, and godliness. The beautiful man is, then, he who is just, temperate, and in a word, good, not he who is rich. But now even the soldiers wish to be decked with gold, not having read that poetical saying: —

"With childish folly to the war he came,
    Laden with store of gold."[4]

But the love of ornament, which is far from caring for virtue, but claims the body for itself, when the love of the beautiful has changed to empty show, is to be utterly expelled. For applying things unsuitable to the body, as if they were suitable, begets a practice of lying and a habit of falsehood; and shows not what is decorous, simple, and truly childlike, but what is pompous, luxurious, and effeminate. But these women obscure true beauty, shading it with gold. And they know not how great is their transgression, in fastening around themselves ten thousand rich chains; as they say that among the barbarians malefactors are bound with gold. The women seem to me to emulate these rich prisoners. For is not the golden necklace a collar, and do not the necklets which they call catheters[5] occupy the place of chains? and in-

---

[1] Matt. vi. 33.
[2] 1 Cor. x. 23.

[3] [Chrysostom enlarges on this Christian thought most eloquently, in several of his homilies; e.g., on the First Epistle to the Corinthians. Hom. xxi. tom. x. p. 178. *Opp.*, ed. Migne.]
[4] *Iliad*, ii. 872.
[5] [The necklace called κάθεμα or κάθημα seems to be referred to. Ezek. xvi. 11, and Isa. iii. 19, *Sept.*]

deed among the Attics they are called by this very name. The ungraceful things round the feet of women, Philemon in the *Synephebus* called ankle-fetters : —

"Conspicuous garments, and a kind of a golden fetter."

What else, then, is this coveted adorning of yourselves, O ladies, but the exhibiting of yourselves fettered? For if the material does away with the reproach, the endurance [of your fetters] is a thing indifferent. To me, then, those who voluntarily put themselves into bonds seem to glory in rich calamities.

Perchance also it is such chains that the poetic fable says were thrown around Aphrodite when committing adultery, referring to ornaments as nothing but the badge of adultery. For Homer called those, too, golden chains. But now women are not ashamed to wear the most manifest badges of the evil one. For as the serpent deceived Eve, so also has ornament of gold maddened other women to vicious practices, using as a bait the form of the serpent, and by fashioning lampreys and serpents for decoration. Accordingly the comic poet Nicostratus says, "Chains, collars, rings, bracelets, serpents, anklets, earrings." [1]

In terms of strongest censure, therefore, Aristophanes in the *Thesmophoriazousæ* exhibits the whole array of female ornament in a catalogue : —

> "Snoods, fillets, natron, and steel;
> Pumice-stone, band, back-band,
> Back-veil, paint, necklaces,
> Paints for the eyes, soft garment, hair-net,
> Girdle, shawl, fine purple border,
> Long robe, tunic, Barathrum, round tunic."

But I have not yet mentioned the principal of them. Then what?

> "Ear-pendants, jewelry, ear-rings;
> Mallow-coloured cluster-shaped anklets;
> Buckles, clasps, necklets,
> Fetters, seals, chains, rings, powders,
> Bosses, bands, olisbi, Sardian stones,
> Fans, helicters."

I am weary and vexed at enumerating the multitude of ornaments; [2] and I am compelled to wonder how those who bear such a burden are not worried to death. O foolish trouble! O silly craze for display! They squander meretriciously wealth on what is disgraceful; and in their love for ostentation disfigure God's gifts, emulating the art of the evil one. The rich man hoarding up in his barns, and saying to himself, "Thou hast much goods laid up for many years; eat, drink, be merry," the Lord in the Gospel plainly called "fool." "For this night they shall take of thee thy soul; whose then shall those things which thou hast prepared be?" [3]

Apelles, the painter, seeing one of his pupils painting a figure loaded with gold colour to represent Helen, said to him, "Boy, being incapable of painting her beautiful, you have made her rich."

Such Helens are the ladies of the present day, not truly beautiful, but richly got up. To these the Spirit prophesies by Zephaniah: "And their silver and their gold shall not be able to deliver them in the day of the LORD's anger." [4]

But for those women who have been trained under Christ, it is suitable to adorn themselves not with gold, but with the Word, through whom alone the gold comes to light. [5]

Happy, then, would have been the ancient Hebrews, had they cast away their women's ornaments, or only melted them; but having cast their gold into the form of an ox, and paid it idolatrous worship, they consequently reap no advantage either from their art or their attempt. But they taught our women most expressively to keep clear of ornaments. The lust which commits fornication with gold becomes an idol, and is tested by fire; for which alone luxury is reserved, as being an idol, not a reality. [6] Hence the Word, upbraiding the Hebrews by the prophet, says, "They made to Baal things of silver and gold," that is, ornaments. And most distinctly threatening, He says, "I will punish her for the days of Baalim, in which they offered sacrifice for her, and she put on her ear-rings and her necklaces." [7] And He subjoined the cause of the adornment, when He said, "And she went after her lovers, but forgot Me, saith the LORD. [8]

Resigning, therefore, these baubles to the wicked master of cunning himself, let us not take part in this meretricious adornment, nor commit idolatry through a specious pretext. Most admirably, therefore, the blessed Peter [9] says, "In like manner also, that women adorn themselves not with braids, or gold, or costly array, but (which becometh women professing godliness) with good works." For it is with reason that he bids decking of themselves to be kept far from them. For, granting that they are beautiful, nature suffices. Let not art contend against nature; that is, let not falsehood strive with truth. And if they are by nature ugly, they are convicted, by the things they apply to themselves, of what they do not possess [i.e., of the want of beauty]. It is

---

[1] Ἐλλόβιον by conjecture, as more suitable to the connection than Ἑλλέβορον or Ἑλεβορον, Hellebore of the MS., though Hellebore may be intended as a comic ending.
[2] [The Greek satirist seems to have borrowed Isaiah's catalogue. cap. iii. 18–23.]
[3] Luke xii. 19, 20.
[4] Zeph. i. 18.
[5] Logos is identified with reason; and it is by reason, or the ingenuity of man, that gold is discovered and brought to light. [But here he seems to have in view the comparisons between gold and wisdom, in Job xxviii.]
[6] εἴδωλον, an appearance, an image.
[7] Hos. ii. 8.
[8] Hos. ii. 13.
[9] By mistake for Paul. Clement quotes here, as often, from memory (1 Tim. ii. 9, 10).

suitable, therefore, for women who serve Christ to adopt simplicity. For in reality simplicity provides for sanctity, by reducing redundancies to equality, and by furnishing from whatever is at hand the enjoyment sought from superfluities. For simplicity, as the name shows, is not conspicuous, is not inflated or puffed up in aught, but is altogether even, and gentle, and equal, and free of excess, and so is sufficient. And sufficiency is a condition which reaches its proper end without excess or defect. The mother of these is Justice, and their nurse "Independence;" and this is a condition which is satisfied with what is necessary, and by itself furnishes what contributes to the blessed life.

Let there, then, be in the fruits of thy hands, sacred order, liberal communication, and acts of economy. "For he that giveth to the poor, lendeth to God." [1] "And the hands of the manly shall be enriched." [2] Manly He calls those who despise wealth, and are free in bestowing it. And on your feet [3] let active readiness to well-doing appear, and a journeying to righteousness. Modesty and chastity are collars and necklaces; such are the chains which God forges. "Happy is the man who hath found wisdom, and the mortal who knows understanding," says the Spirit by Solomon: "for it is better to buy her than treasures of gold and silver; and she is more valuable than precious stones." [4] For she is the true decoration.

And let not their ears be pierced, contrary to nature, in order to attach to them ear-rings and ear-drops. For it is not right to force nature against her wishes. Nor could there be any better ornament for the ears than true instruction, which finds its way naturally into the passages of hearing. And eyes anointed by the Word, and ears pierced for perception, make a man a hearer and contemplator of divine and sacred things, the Word truly exhibiting the true beauty "which eye hath not seen nor ear heard before." [5]

[1] Prov. xix. 17.
[2] Prov. x. 4.
[3] [Eph. vi. 15.]
[4] Prov. iii. 13-15.
[5] 1 Cor. ii. 9.

THE INSTRUCTOR.

BOOK III.

CHAP. I. — ON THE TRUE BEAUTY.

It is then, as appears, the greatest of all lessons to know one's self. For if one knows himself, he will know God; and knowing God, he will be made like God, not by wearing gold or long robes, but by well-doing, and by requiring as few things as possible.[1]

Now, God alone is in need of nothing, and rejoices most when He sees us bright with the ornament of intelligence; and then, too, rejoices in him who is arrayed in chastity, the sacred stole of the body. Since then the soul consists of three divisions;[2] the intellect, which is called the reasoning faculty, is the inner man, which is the ruler of this man that is seen. And that one, in another respect, God guides. But the irascible part, being brutal, dwells near to insanity. And appetite, which is the third department, is many-shaped above Proteus, the varying sea-god, who changed himself now into one shape, now into another; and it allures to adulteries, to licentiousness, to seductions.

"At first he was a lion with ample beard."[3]

While he yet retained the ornament, the hair of the chin showed him to be a man.

"But after that a serpent, a pard, or a big sow."

Love of ornament has degenerated to wantonness. A man no longer appears like a strong wild beast,

"But he became moist water, and a tree of lofty branches."

Passions break out, pleasures overflow; beauty fades, and falls quicker than the leaf on the ground, when the amorous storms of lust blow on it before the coming of autumn, and is withered by destruction. For lust becomes and fabricates all things, and wishes to cheat, so as to conceal the man. But that man with whom the Word dwells does not alter himself, does not get himself up: he has the form which is of the Word; he is made like to God; he is beautiful; he does not ornament himself: his is beauty, the true beauty, for it is God; and that man becomes God, since God so wills. Heraclitus, then, rightly said, "Men are gods, and gods are men." For the Word Himself is the manifest mystery: God in man, and man God. And the Mediator executes the Father's will; for the Mediator is the Word, who is common to both — the Son of God, the Saviour of men; His Servant, our Teacher. And the flesh being a slave, as Paul testifies, how can one with any reason adorn the handmaid like a pimp? For that which is of flesh has the form of a servant. Paul says, speaking of the Lord, "Because He emptied Himself, taking the form of a servant,"[4] calling the outward man servant, previous to the Lord becoming a servant and wearing flesh. But the compassionate God Himself set the flesh free, and releasing it from destruction, and from bitter and deadly bondage, endowed it with incorruptibility, arraying the flesh in this, the holy embellishment of eternity — immortality.

There is, too, another beauty of men — love. "And love," according to the apostle, "suffers long, and is kind; envieth not; vaunteth not itself, is not puffed up."[5] For the decking of one's self out — carrying, as it does, the look of superfluity and uselessness — is vaunting one's self. Wherefore he adds, "doth not behave itself unseemly:" for a figure which is not one's own, and is against nature, is unseemly; but what is artificial is not one's own, as is clearly explained: "seeketh not," it is said, "what is not her own." For truth calls that its own which belongs to it; but the love of finery seeks what is not its own, being apart from God, and the Word, from love.

---

[1] [On this book, Kaye's comments extend from p. 91 to p. 111 of his analysis.]
[2] [Note this psychological dissection. Compare Aristotle, *Nicomachean Ethics*, book vi. cap. 2, αἰσθησις, νοῦς, ὄρεξις, sense, intellect, appetition. Also, book i. cap. 11, or 13 in some editions.]
[3] *Odyss.*, iv. 456–458.
[4] Phil. ii. 7.
[5] 1 Cor. xiii. 4.

And that the Lord Himself was uncomely in aspect, the Spirit testifies by Esaias : "And we saw Him, and He had no form nor comeliness ; but His form was mean, inferior to men."[1] Yet who was more admirable than the Lord? But it was not the beauty of the flesh visible to the eye, but the true beauty of both soul and body, which He exhibited, which in the former is beneficence ; in the latter — that is, the flesh — immortality.

CHAP. II. — AGAINST EMBELLISHING THE BODY.

It is not, then, the aspect of the outward man, but the soul that is to be decorated with the ornament of goodness ; we may say also the flesh with the adornment of temperance. But those women who beautify the outside, are unawares all waste in the inner depths, as is the case with the ornaments of the Egyptians ; among whom temples with their porticos and vestibules are carefully constructed, and groves and sacred fields adjoining ; the halls are surrounded with many pillars ; and the walls gleam with foreign stones, and there is no want of artistic painting ; and the temples gleam with gold, and silver, and amber, and glitter with parti-coloured gems from India and Ethiopia ; and the shrines are veiled with gold-embroidered hangings.

But if you enter the penetralia of the enclosure, and, in haste to behold something better, seek the image that is the inhabitant of the temple, and if any priest of those that offer sacrifice there, looking grave, and singing a pæan in the Egyptian tongue, remove a little of the veil to show the god, he will give you a hearty laugh at the object of worship. For the deity that is sought, to whom you have rushed, will not be found within, but a cat, or a crocodile, or a serpent of the country, or some such beast unworthy of the temple, but quite worthy of a den, a hole, or the dirt. The god of the Egyptians appears a beast rolling on a purple couch.

So those women who wear gold, occupying themselves in curling at their locks, and engaged in anointing their cheeks, painting their eyes, and dyeing their hair, and practising the other pernicious arts of luxury, decking the covering of flesh, — in truth, imitate the Egyptians, in order to attract their infatuated lovers.

But if one withdraw the veil of the temple, — I mean the head-dress, the dye, the clothes, the gold, the paint, the cosmetics, — that is, the web

consisting of them, the veil, with the view of finding within the true beauty, he will be disgusted, I know well. For he will not find the image of God dwelling within, as is meet ; but instead of it a fornicator and adulteress has occupied the shrine of the soul. And the true beast will thus be detected — an ape smeared with white paint. And that deceitful serpent, devouring the understanding part of man through vanity, has the soul as its hole, filling all with deadly poisons ; and injecting his own venom of deception, this pander of a dragon has changed women into harlots. For love of display is not for a lady, but a courtesan. Such women care little for keeping at home with their husbands ; but loosing their husbands' purse-strings, they spend its supplies on their lusts, that they may have many witnesses of their seemingly fair appearance ; and, devoting the whole day to their toilet, they spend their time with their bought slaves. Accordingly they season the flesh like a pernicious sauce ; and the day they bestow on the toilet shut up in their rooms, so as not to be caught decking themselves. But in the evening this spurious beauty creeps out to candle-light as out of a hole ; for drunkenness and the dimness of the light aid what they have put on. The woman who dyes her hair yellow, Menander the comic poet expels from the house : —

"Now get out of this house, for no chaste
Woman ought to make her hair yellow,"

nor, I would add, stain her cheeks, nor paint her eyes. Unawares the poor wretches destroy their own beauty, by the introduction of what is spurious. At the dawn of day, mangling, racking, and plastering themselves over with certain compositions, they chill the skin, furrow the flesh with poisons, and with curiously prepared washes, thus blighting their own beauty. Wherefore they are seen to be yellow from the use of cosmetics, and susceptible to disease, their flesh, which has been shaded with poisons, being now in a melting state. So they dishonour the Creator of men, as if the beauty given by Him were nothing worth. As you might expect, they become lazy in housekeeping, sitting like painted things to be looked at, not as if made for domestic economy. Wherefore in the comic poet the sensible woman says, "What can we women do wise or brilliant, who sit with hair dyed yellow, outraging the character of gentlewomen ; causing the overthrow of houses, the ruin of nuptials, and accusations on the part of children?"[2] In the same way, Antiphanes the comic poet, in *Malthaca*, ridicules the meretriciousness of women in words that apply to them all, and are framed against the rubbing of themselves with cosmetics, saying : —

---

[1] Isa. liii. 2, 3. [But see also Ps. xlv. 2, which was often cited by the ancients to prove the reverse. Both may be reconciled: he was a fair and comely child like his father David; but, as "the man of sorrows," he became old in looks, and his countenance was marred. For David's beauty, see 1 Sam. xvi. 12. For our Lord's at twelve years of age, when the virgin was seeking her child, Canticles, v. 7–16. For his appearance at three and thirty, when the Jews only ventured to credit him with less than fifty years, John viii. 57. See also Irenæus, *Against Heresies*, cap. xxii. note 12, p. 391, this series.]

[2] Aristophanes, *Lysistrata*.

'She comes,
She goes back, she approaches, she goes back.
She has come, she is here, she washes herself, she advances,
She is soaped, she is combed, she goes out, is rubbed,
She washes herself, looks in the glass, robes herself,
Anoints herself, decks herself, besmears herself;
And if aught is wrong, chokes [with vexation]."

Thrice, I say, not once, do they deserve to perish, who use crocodiles' excrement, and anoint themselves with the froth of putrid humours, and stain their eyebrows with soot, and rub their cheeks with white lead.

These, then, who are disgusting even to the heathen poets for their fashions, how shall they not be rejected by the truth?[1] Accordingly another comic poet, Alexis, reproves them. For I shall adduce his words, which with extravagance of statement shame the obstinacy of their impudence. For he was not very far beyond the mark. And I cannot for shame come to the assistance of women held up to such ridicule in comedy.

Then she ruins her husband.

" For first, in comparison with gain and the spoiling of
        neighbours,
All else is in their eyes superfluous."

" Is one of them little? She stitches cork into her shoe-
        sole.
Is one tall? She wears a thin sole,
And goes out keeping her head down on her shoulder:
This takes away from her height. Has one no flanks?
She has something sewed on to her, so that the
        spectators
May exclaim on her fine shape behind. Has she a
        prominent stomach?
By making additions, to render it straight, such as the
        nurses we see in the comic poets,
She draws back, as it were, by these poles, the protu-
        berance of the stomach in front.
Has one yellow eyebrows? She stains them with
        soot.
Do they happen to be black? She smears them with
        ceruse.
Is one very white-skinned? She rouges.
Has one any part of the body beautiful? She shows
        it bare.
Has she beautiful teeth? She must needs laugh,
That those present may see what a pretty mouth she
        has;
But if not in the humour for laughing, she passes the
        day within,
With a slender sprig of myrtle between her lips,
Like what cooks have always at hand when they have
        goats' heads to sell,
So that she must keep them apart the whilst, whether
        she will or not."

I set these quotations from the comic poets[2] before you, since the Word most strenuously wishes to save us. And by and by I will fortify them with the divine Scriptures. For he who does not escape notice is wont to abstain from sins, on account of the shame of reproof. Just as the plastered hand and the anointed eye exhibit from their very look the suspicion of a person in illness, so also cosmetics and dyes indicate that the soul is deeply diseased.

The divine Instructor enjoins us not to approach to another's river, meaning by the figurative expression "another's river," "another's wife;" the wanton that flows to all, and out of licentiousness gives herself up to meretricious enjoyment with all. "Abstain from water that is another's," He says, "and drink not of another's well," admonishing us to shun the stream of "voluptuousness," that we may live long, and that years of life may be added to us;[3] both by not hunting after pleasure that belongs to another, and by diverting our inclinations.

Love of dainties and love of wine, though great vices, are not of such magnitude as fondness for finery.[4] "A full table and repeated cups " are enough to satisfy greed. But to those who are fond of gold, and purple, and jewels, neither the gold that is above the earth and below it is sufficient, nor the Tyrian Sea, nor the freight that comes from India and Ethiopia, nor yet Pactolus flowing with gold; not even were a man to become a Midas would he be satisfied, but would be still poor, craving other wealth. Such people are ready to die with their gold.

And if Plutus[5] is blind, are not those women that are crazy about him, and have a fellow-feeling with him, blind too? Having, then, no limit to their lust, they push on to shamelessness. For the theatre, and pageants, and many spectators, and strolling in the temples, and loitering in the streets, that they may be seen conspicuously by all, are necessary to them. For those that glory in their looks, not in heart,[6] dress to please others. For as the brand shows the slave, so do gaudy colours the adulteress. " For though thou clothe thyself in scarlet, and deck thyself with ornaments of gold, and anoint thine eyes with stibium, in vain is thy beauty,"[7] says the Word by Jeremiah. Is it not monstrous, that while horses, birds, and the rest of the animals, spring and bound from the grass and meadows, rejoicing in ornament that is their own, in mane, and natural colour, and varied plumage; woman, as if inferior to the brute creation, should think herself so unlovely as to need foreign, and bought, and painted beauty?

Head-dresses and varieties of head-dresses, and elaborate braidings, and infinite modes of dressing the hair, and costly specimens of mir-

---

[1] [John xvii. 17. " Thy word is truth," is here in mind; and, soon after, he speaks of the Scriptures and the Word (*Logos*) in the same way.]
[2] [He rebukes heathen women out of their own poets; while he warns Christian women also to resist the contagion of their example, fortified by the Scriptures.]
[3] Prov. ix. 11.
[4] [This is worth noting. Worse than love of wine, because he regards a love for finery as tending to loss of chastity.]
[5] Wealth.
[6] 1 Thess. ii. 17.
[7] Jer. iv. 30.

rors, in which they arrange their costume, — hunting after those that, like silly children, are crazy about their figures, — are characteristic of women who have lost all sense of shame. If any one were to call these courtesans, he would make no mistake, for they turn their faces into masks. But us the Word enjoins " to look not on the things that are seen, but the things that are not seen ; for the things that are seen are temporal, but the things that are not seen are eternal." [1]

But what passes beyond the bounds of absurdity, is that they have invented mirrors for this artificial shape of theirs, as if it were some excellent work or masterpiece. The deception rather requires a veil thrown over it. For as the Greek fable has it, it was not a fortunate thing for the beautiful Narcissus to have been the beholder of his own image. And if Moses commanded men to make not an image to represent God by art, how can these women be right, who by their own reflection produce an imitation of their own likeness, in order to the falsifying of their faces? Likewise also, when Samuel the prophet was sent to anoint one of the sons of Jesse for king, and on seeing the eldest of his sons to be fair and tall, produced the anointing oil, being delighted with him, the Lord said to him, " Look not to his appearance, nor the height of his stature : for I have rejected him. For man looketh on the eyes, but the LORD into the heart." [2]

And he anointed not him that was comely in person, but him that was comely in soul. If, then, the Lord counts the natural beauty of the body inferior to that of the soul, what thinks He of spurious beauty, rejecting utterly as He does all falsehood? " For we walk by faith, not by sight." [3] Very clearly the Lord accordingly teaches by Abraham, that he who follows God must despise country, and relations, and possessions, and all wealth, by making him a stranger. And therefore also He called him His friend, who had despised the substance which he had possessed at home. For he was of good parentage, and very opulent ; and so with three hundred and eighteen servants of his own he subdued the four kings who had taken Lot captive.

Esther alone we find justly adorned. The spouse adorned herself mystically for her royal husband ; but her beauty turns out the redemption price of a people that were about to be massacred. And that decoration makes women courtesans, and men effeminate and adulterers, the tragic poet is a witness ; thus discoursing : —

" He that judged the goddesses,
  As the myth of the Argives has it, having come from Phrygia
  To Lacedæmon, arrayed in flowery vestments,
  Glittering with gold and barbaric luxury,
  Loving, departed, carrying away her he loved,
  Helen, to the folds of Ida, having found that
  Menelaus was away from home." [4]

O adulterous beauty ! Barbarian finery and effeminate luxury overthrew Greece ; Lacedæmonian chastity was corrupted by clothes, and luxury, and graceful beauty ; barbaric display proved Jove's daughter a courtesan.

They had no instructor [5] to restrain their lusts, nor one to say, " Do not commit adultery ; " nor, " Lust not ; " or, " Travel not by lust into adultery ; " or further, " Influence not thy passions by desire of adornment."

What an end was it that ensued to them, and what woes they endured, who would not restrain their self-will ! Two continents were convulsed by unrestrained pleasures, and all was thrown into confusion by a barbarian boy. The whole of Hellas puts to sea ; the ocean is burdened with the weight of continents ; a protracted war breaks out, and fierce battles are waged, and the plains are crowded with dead : the barbarian assails the fleet with outrage ; wickedness prevails, and the eye of that poetic Jove looks on the Thracians : —

" The barbarian plains drink noble blood,
  And the streams of the rivers are choked with dead bodies."

Breasts are beaten in lamentations, and grief desolates the land ; and all the feet, and the summits of many-fountained Ida, and the cities of the Trojans, and the ships of the Achæans shake.

Where, O Homer, shall we flee and stand? Show us a spot of ground that is not shaken ! —

" Touch not the reins, inexperienced boy,
  Nor mount the seat, not having learned to drive." [6]

Heaven delights in two charioteers, by whom alone the chariot of fire is guided. For the mind is carried away by pleasure ; and the unsullied principle of reason, when not instructed by the Word, slides down into licentiousness, and gets a fall as the due reward of its transgression. An example of this are the angels who renounced the beauty of God for a beauty which fades, and so fell from heaven to earth. [7]

The Shechemites, too, were punished by an overthrow for dishonouring the holy virgin. The grave was their punishment, and the monument of their ignominy leads to salvation.

---

[1] 2 Cor. iv. 18.
[2] 1 Sam. xvi. 7.
[3] 2 Cor. v. 7.

[4] *Iphigenia in Aulis*, 71–77.
[5] [The law was the pædagogue of the Jews (Gal. iii. 24) ; and therefore, as to Gentiles, they were a law unto themselves (Rom. ii. 14, 15), with some truth in their philosophy to guide them.]
[6] *Phaethon* of Euripides.
[7] Gen. vi. 1, 2. [It is surprising with what tenacity this interpretation clings to the ancient mind of the Church. The *Nephilim* and *Gibborim* need a special investigation. The Oriental tales of the genii are probably connected with their fabulous history.]

CHAP. III. — AGAINST MEN WHO EMBELLISH
THEMSELVES.

To such an extent, then, has luxury advanced,
hat not only are the female sex deranged about
his frivolous pursuit, but men also are infected
vith the disease.[1] For not being free of the
ove of finery, they are not in health; but in-
lining to voluptuousness, they become effem-
nate, cutting their hair in an ungentlemanlike
nd meretricious way, clothed in fine and trans-
arent garments, chewing mastich,[2] smelling of
erfume.[3] What can one say on seeing them?
.ike one who judges people by their foreheads,
ve will divine them to be adulterers and effem-
nate, addicted to both kinds of venery, haters
f hair, destitute of hair, detesting the bloom
f manliness, and adorning their locks like
vomen. "Living for unholy acts of audacity,
hese fickle wretches do reckless and nefarious
leeds," says the Sibyl. For their service the
owns are full of those who take out hair by
itch-plasters, shave, and pluck out hairs from
hese womanish creatures. And shops are erect-
d and opened everywhere; and adepts at this
neretricious fornication make a deal of money
openly by those who plaster themselves, and
give their hair to be pulled out in all ways by
hose who make it their trade, feeling no shame
before the onlookers or those who approach, nor
before themselves, being men. Such are those
addicted to base passions, whose whole body is
made smooth by the violent tuggings of pitch-
plasters. It is utterly impossible to get beyond
such effrontery. If nothing is left undone by
them, neither shall anything be left unspoken by
me. Diogenes, when he was being sold, chiding
like a teacher one of these degenerate creatures,
said very manfully, "Come, youngster, buy for
yourself a man," chastising his meretriciousness by an ambiguous speech. But for those
who are men to shave and smooth themselves,
how ignoble! As for dyeing of hair, and
anointing of grey locks, and dyeing them yellow,
these are practices of abandoned effeminates;
and their feminine combing of themselves is a
thing to be let alone. For they think, that like
serpents they divest themselves of the old age
of their head by painting and renovating themselves. But though they do doctor the hair
cleverly, they will not escape wrinkles, nor will
they elude death by tricking time. For it is not
dreadful, it is not dreadful to appear old, when
you are not able to shut your eyes to the fact
that you are so.

The more, then, a man hastes to the end, the
more truly venerable is he, having God alone
as his senior, since He is the eternal aged One,
He who is older than all things. Prophecy
has called him the "Ancient of days; and the
hair of His head was as pure wool," says the
prophet.[4] "And none other," says the Lord,
"can make the hair white or black."[5] How,
then, do these godless ones work in rivalry with
God, or rather violently oppose Him, when they
transmute the hair made white by Him? "The
crown of old men is great experience,"[6] says
Scripture; and the hoary hair of their countenance is the blossom of large experience.
But these dishonour the reverence of age, the
head covered with grey hairs. It is not, it is not
possible for him to show the head true who has
a fraudulent head. "But ye have not so learned
Christ; if so be that ye have heard Him, and
have been taught by Him, as the truth is in
Jesus: that ye put off, concerning the former
conversation, the old man (not the hoary man,
but him that is) corrupt according to deceitful
lusts; and be renewed (not by dyeings and
ornaments), but in the spirit of your mind;
and put on the new man, which after God is
created in righteousness and true holiness."[7]

But for one who is a man to comb himself and
shave himself with a razor, for the sake of fine
effect, to arrange his hair at the looking-glass, to
shave his cheeks, pluck hairs out of them, and
smooth them, how womanly! And, in truth,
unless you saw them naked, you would suppose
them to be women. For although not allowed
to wear gold, yet out of effeminate desire they
enwreath their latches and fringes with leaves
of gold; or, getting certain spherical figures of
the same metal made, they fasten them to their
ankles, and hang them from their necks. This
is a device of enervated men, who are dragged
to the women's apartments, amphibious and
lecherous beasts. For this is a meretricious
and impious form of snare. For God wished
women to be smooth, and rejoice in their locks
alone growing spontaneously, as a horse in his
mane; but has adorned man, like the lions, with
a beard, and endowed him, as an attribute of
manhood, with shaggy breasts, — a sign this
of strength and rule. So also cocks, which
fight in defence of the hens, he has decked with
combs, as it were helmets; and so high a value
does God set on these locks, that He orders
them to make their appearance on men simultaneously with discretion, and delighted with a
venerable look, has honoured gravity of countenance with grey hairs. But wisdom, and
discriminating judgments that are hoary with

---

[1] [Heathen manners are here depicted as a warning to Christians.
We cannot suppose Christians, as yet, to any extent, corrupted in
their manners by fashion and frivolity; for to be a Christian excluded
one from temptations of this kind.]
[2] [Query, de re Nicotiana?]
[3] [Smelling of Nicotine?]

[4] Dan. vii. 9. [A truly eloquent passage.]
[5] Matt. v. 36.
[6] Ecclus. xxv. 6.
[7] Eph. iv. 20-24.

wisdom, attain maturity with time, and by the vigour of long experience give strength to old age, producing grey hairs, the admirable flower of venerable wisdom, conciliating confidence. This, then, the mark of the man, the beard, by which he is seen to be a man, is older than Eve, and is the token of the superior nature. In this God deemed it right that he should excel, and dispersed hair over man's whole body. Whatever smoothness and softness was in him He abstracted from his side when He formed the woman Eve, physically receptive, his partner in parentage, his help in household management, while he (for he had parted with all smoothness) remained a man, and shows himself man. And to him has been assigned action, as to her suffering; for what is shaggy is drier and warmer than what is smooth. Wherefore males have both more hair and more heat than females, animals that are entire than the emasculated, perfect than imperfect. It is therefore impious to desecrate the symbol of manhood, hairiness.[1] But the embellishment of smoothing (for I am warned by the Word), if it is to attract men, is the act of an effeminate person, — if to attract women, is the act of an adulterer; and both must be driven as far as possible from our society. "But the very hairs of your head are all numbered," says the Lord;[2] those on the chin, too, are numbered, and those on the whole body. There must be therefore no plucking out, contrary to God's appointment, which has counted[3] them in according to His will. "Know ye not yourselves," says the apostle, "that Christ Jesus is in you?"[4] Whom, had we known as dwelling in us, I know not how we could have dared to dishonour. But the using of pitch to pluck out hair (I shrink from even mentioning the shamelessness connected with this process), and in the act of bending back and bending down, the violence done to nature's modesty by stepping out and bending backwards in shameful postures, yet the doers not ashamed of themselves, but conducting themselves without shame in the midst of the youth, and in the gymnasium, where the prowess of man is tried; the following of this unnatural practice, is it not the extreme of licentiousness? For those who engage in such practices in public will scarcely behave with modesty to any at home. Their want of shame in public attests their unbridled licentiousness in private.[5]

For he who in the light of day denies his manhood, will prove himself manifestly a woman by night. "There shall not be," said the Word by Moses, "a harlot of the daughters of Israel; there shall not be a fornicator of the sons of Israel."[6]

But the pitch does good, it is said. Nay, it defames, say I. No one who entertains right sentiments would wish to appear a fornicator, were he not the victim of that vice, and study to defame the beauty of his form. No one would, I say, voluntarily choose to do this. "For if God foreknew those who are called, according to His purpose, to be conformed to the image of His Son," for whose sake, according to the blessed apostle, He has appointed "Him to be the first-born among many brethren,"[7] are they not godless who treat with indignity the body which is of like form with the Lord?

The man, who would be beautiful, must adorn that which is the most beautiful thing in man, his mind, which every day he ought to exhibit in greater comeliness; and should pluck out not hairs, but lusts. I pity the boys possessed by the slave-dealers, that are decked for dishonour. But they are not treated with ignominy by themselves, but by command the wretches are adorned for base gain. But how disgusting are those who willingly practise the things to which, if compelled, they would, if they were men, die rather than do?

But life has reached this pitch of licentiousness through the wantonness of wickedness, and lasciviousness is diffused over the cities, having become law. Beside them women stand in the stews, offering their own flesh for hire for lewd pleasure, and boys, taught to deny their sex, act the part of women.

Luxury has deranged all things; it has disgraced man. A luxurious niceness seeks everything, attempts everything, forces everything, coerces nature. Men play the part of women, and women that of men, contrary to nature; women are at once wives and husbands: no passage is closed against libidinousness; and their promiscuous lechery is a public institution, and luxury is domesticated. O miserable spectacle! horrible conduct! Such are the trophies of your social licentiousness which are exhibited: the evidence of these deeds are the prostitutes. Alas for such wickedness! Besides, the wretches know not how many tragedies the uncertainty of intercourse produces. For fathers, unmindful of children of theirs that have been exposed, often without their knowledge, have intercourse with a son that has debauched himself, and daughters that are prostitutes; and licence in lust shows them to be the men that have begotten them.

---

1 [On the other hand, this was Esau's symbol; and the sensual "satyrs" (Isa. xiii. 2) are "hairy goats," in the original. So also the originals of "devils" in Lev. xvii. 7, and 2 Chron. xi. 15. See the learned note of Mr. West, in his edition of Leighton, vol. v. p. 161.]

2 Matt. x. 30.

3 ἐγκαταριθμημένην seems to be here used in a middle, not a passive sense, as καταριθμημένος is sometimes.

4 2 Cor. xiii. 5.

5 [Such were the manners with which the Gospel was forced everywhere to contend. That they were against nature is sufficiently clear from the remains of decency in some heathen. Herodotus (book i. cap. 8) tells us that the Lydians counted it disgraceful even for a man to be seen naked.]

6 Deut. xxiii. 17.

7 Rom. viii. 28, 29.

These things your wise laws allow : people may sin legally ; and the execrable indulgence in pleasure they call a thing indifferent. They who commit adultery against nature think themselves free from adultery. Avenging justice follows their audacious deeds, and, dragging on themselves inevitable calamity, they purchase death for a small sum of money. The miserable dealers in these wares sail, bringing a cargo of fornication, like wine or oil ; and others, far more wretched, traffic in pleasures as they do in bread and sauce, not heeding the words of Moses, " Do not prostitute thy daughter, to cause her to be a whore, lest the land fall to whoredom, and the land become full of wickedness." [1]

Such was predicted of old, and the result is notorious : the whole earth has now become full of fornication and wickedness. I admire the ancient legislators of the Romans : these detested effeminacy of conduct ; and the giving of the body to feminine purposes, contrary to the law of nature, they judged worthy of the extremest penalty, according to the righteousness of the law.

For it is not lawful to pluck out the beard,[2] man's natural and noble ornament.

" A youth with his first beard : for with this, youth is most graceful."

By and by he is anointed, delighting in the beard " on which descended " the prophetic " ointment " [3] with which Aaron was honoured.

And it becomes him who is rightly trained, on whom peace has pitched its tent, to preserve peace also with his hair.

What, then, will not women with strong propensities to lust practise, when they look on men perpetrating such enormities ? Rather we ought not to call such as these men, but lewd wretches (βατάλοι), and effeminate (γύνιδες), whose voices are feeble, and whose clothes are womanish both in feel and dye. And such creatures are manifestly shown to be what they are from their external appearance, their clothes, shoes, form, walk, cut of their hair, look. " For from his look shall a man be known," says the Scripture, " and from meeting a man the man is known : the dress of a man, the step of his foot, the laugh of his teeth, tell tales of him." [4]

For these, for the most part, plucking out the rest of their hair, only dress that on the head, all but binding their locks with fillets like women. Lions glory in their shaggy hair, but are armed by their hair in the fight ; and boars even are made imposing by their mane ; the hunters are afraid of them when they see them bristling their hair.

" The fleecy sheep are loaded with their wool." [5]

And their wool the loving Father has made abundant for thy use, O man, having taught thee to sheer their fleeces. Of the nations, the Celts and Scythians wear their hair long, but do not deck themselves. The bushy hair of the barbarian has something fearful in it ; and its auburn (ξανθόν) colour threatens war, the hue being somewhat akin to blood. Both these barbarian races hate luxury. As clear witnesses will be produced by the German, the Rhine ; [6] and by the Scythian, the waggon. Sometimes the Scythian despises even the waggon : its size seems sumptuousness to the barbarian ; and leaving its luxurious ease, the Scythian man leads a frugal life. For a house sufficient, and less encumbered than the waggon, he takes his horse, and mounting it, is borne where he wishes. And when faint with hunger, he asks his horse for sustenance ; and he offers his veins, and supplies his master with all he possesses — his blood. To the nomad the horse is at once conveyance and sustenance ; and the warlike youth of the Arabians (these are other nomads) are mounted on camels. They sit on breeding camels ; and these feed and run at the same time, carrying their masters the whilst, and bear the house with them. And if drink fail the barbarians, they milk them ; and after that their food is spent, they do not spare even their blood, as is reported of furious wolves. And these, gentler than the barbarians, when injured, bear no remembrance of the wrong, but sweep bravely over the desert, carrying and nourishing their masters at the same time.

Perish, then, the savage beasts whose food is blood ! For it is unlawful for men, whose body is nothing but flesh elaborated of blood, to touch blood. For human blood has become a partaker of the Word : [7] it is a participant of grace by the Spirit ; and if any one injure him, he will not escape unnoticed. Man may, though naked in body, address the Lord. But I approve the simplicity of the barbarians : loving an unencumbered life, the barbarians have abandoned luxury. Such the Lord calls us to be — naked of finery, naked of vanity, wrenched from our sins, bearing only the wood of life, aiming only at salvation.

CHAP. IV. — WITH WHOM WE ARE TO ASSOCIATE.

But really I have unwittingly deviated in spirit from the order, to which I must now revert, and must find fault with having large numbers of domestics. For, avoiding working with their own

---

[1] Lev. xix. 29.
[2] [When the loss of the beard was a token of foppery and often of something worse, shaving would be frivolity ; but here he treats of extirpation.]
[3] Ps. cxxxiii. 2.
[4] Ecclus. xix. 29, 30.

[5] Hesiod, *Works and Days*, i. 232.
[6] Of which they drink.
[7] [He took upon him our nature, flesh and blood. Heb. ii. 14-16.]

hands and serving themselves, men have recourse to servants, purchasing a great crowd of fine cooks, and of people to lay out the table, and of others to divide the meat skilfully into pieces. And the staff of servants is separated into many divisions; some labour for their gluttony, carvers and seasoners, and the compounders and makers of sweetmeats, and honey-cakes, and custards; others are occupied with their too numerous clothes; others guard the gold, like griffins; others keep the silver, and wipe the cups, and make ready what is needed to furnish the festive table; others rub down the horses; and a crowd of cup-bearers exert themselves in their service, and herds of beautiful boys, like cattle, from whom they milk away their beauty. And male and female assistants at the toilet are employed about the ladies — some for the mirrors, some for the head-dresses, others for the combs. Many are eunuchs; and these panders serve without suspicion those that wish to be free to enjoy their pleasures, because of the belief that they are unable to indulge in lust. But a true eunuch is not one who is unable, but one who is unwilling, to indulge in pleasure. The Word, testifying by the prophet Samuel to the Jews, who had transgressed when the people asked for a king, promised not a loving lord, but threatened to give them a self-willed and voluptuous tyrant, "who shall," He says, "take your daughters to be perfumers, and cooks, and bakers,"[1] ruling by the law of war, not desiring a peaceful administration. And there are many Celts, who bear aloft on their shoulders women's litters. But workers in wool, and spinners, and weavers, and female work and housekeeping, are nowhere.

But those who impose on the women, spend the day with them, telling them silly amatory stories, and wearing out body and soul with their false acts and words. "Thou shalt not be with many," it is said, "for evil, nor give thyself to a multitude;"[2] for wisdom shows itself among few, but disorder in a multitude. But it is not for grounds of propriety, on account of not wishing to be seen, that they purchase bearers, for it were commendable if out of such feelings they put themselves under a covering; but it is out of luxuriousness that they are carried on their domestics' shoulders, and desire to make a show.

So, opening the curtain, and looking keenly round on all that direct their eyes towards them, they show their manners; and often bending forth from within, disgrace this superficial propriety by their dangerous restlessness. "Look not round," it is said, "in the streets of the city, and wander not in its lonely places."[3] For that is, in truth, a lonely place, though there be a crowd of the licentious in it, where no wise man is present.

And these women are carried about over the temples, sacrificing and practising divination day by day, spending their time with fortune-tellers, and begging priests, and disreputable old women; and they keep up old wives' whisperings over their cups, learning charms and incantations from soothsayers, to the ruin of the nuptial bonds. And some men they keep; by others they are kept; and others are promised them by the diviners. They know not that they are cheating themselves, and giving up themselves as a vessel of pleasure to those that wish to indulge in wantonness; and exchanging their purity for the foulest outrage, they think what is the most shameful ruin a great stroke of business. And there are many ministers to this meretricious licentiousness, insinuating themselves, one from one quarter, another from another. For the licentious rush readily into uncleanness, like swine rushing to that part of the hold of the ship which is depressed. Whence the Scripture most strenuously exhorts, "Introduce not every one into thy house, for the snares of the crafty are many."[4] And in another place, "Let just men be thy guests, and in the fear of the Lord let thy boast remain."[5] Away with fornication. "For know this well," says the apostle, "that no fornicator, or unclean person, or covetous man, who is an idolater, hath any inheritance in the kingdom of Christ and of God."[6]

But these women delight in intercourse with the effeminate. And crowds of abominable creatures (κιναίδες) flow in, of unbridled tongue, filthy in body, filthy in language; men enough for lewd offices, ministers of adultery, giggling and whispering, and shamelessly making through their noses sounds of lewdness and fornication to provoke lust, endeavouring to please by lewd words and attitudes, inciting to laughter, the precursor of fornication. And sometimes, when inflamed by any provocation, either these fornicators, or those that follow the rabble of abominable creatures to destruction, make a sound in their nose like a frog, as if they had got anger dwelling in their nostrils. But those who are more refined than these keep Indian birds and Median pea-fowls, and recline with peak-headed[7] creatures; playing with satyrs, delighting in monsters. They laugh when they hear Thersites; and these women, purchasing Thersiteses highly valued, pride themselves not in their husbands, but in those wretches which are a burden on the earth, and overlook the chaste widow, who is of far higher value than a Melitæan pup, and look

---

[1] 1 Sam. viii. 13.
[2] Ex. xxiii. 2.
[3] Ecclus. ix. 7.
[4] Ecclus. xi. 29.
[5] Ecclus. ix. 16.
[6] Eph. v. 5.
[7] φοξός, in allusion to Thersites, to which Homer applies this epithet.

askance at a just old man, who is lovelier in my estimation than a monster purchased for money. And though maintaining parrots and curlews, they do not receive the orphan child;[1] but they expose children that are born at home, and take up the young of birds, and prefer irrational to rational creatures; although they ought to undertake the maintenance of old people with a character for sobriety, who are fairer in my mind than apes, and capable of uttering something better than nightingales; and to set before them that saying, "He that pitieth the poor lendeth to the LORD;"[2] and this, "Inasmuch as ye have done it unto the least of these My brethren, ye have done it to Me."[3] But these, on the other hand, prefer ignorance to wisdom, turning their wealth into stone, that is, into pearls and Indian emeralds. And they squander and throw away their wealth on fading dyes, and bought slaves; like crammed fowls scraping the dung of life. "Poverty," it is said, "humbles a man."[4] By poverty is meant that niggardliness by which the rich are poor, having nothing to give away.

CHAP. V. — BEHAVIOUR IN THE BATHS.

And of what sort are their baths? Houses skilfully constructed, compact, portable, transparent, covered with fine linen. And gold-plated chairs, and silver ones, too, and ten thousand vessels of gold and silver, some for drinking, some for eating, some for bathing, are carried about with them. Besides these, there are even braziers of coals; for they have arrived at such a pitch of self-indulgence, that they sup and get drunk while bathing. And articles of silver with which they make a show, they ostentatiously set out in the baths, and thus display perchance their wealth out of excessive pride, but chiefly the capricious ignorance, through which they brand effeminate men, who have been vanquished by women; proving at least that they themselves cannot meet and cannot sweat without a multitude of vessels, although poor women who have no display equally enjoy their baths. The dirt of wealth, then, has an abundant covering of censure. With this, as with a bait, they hook the miserable creatures that gape at the glitter of gold. For dazzling thus those fond of display, they artfully try to win the admiration of their lovers, who after a little insult them naked. They will scarce strip before their own husbands, affecting a plausible pretence of modesty; but any others who wish, may see them at home shut up naked in their baths. For there they are not ashamed to strip before spectators, as if exposing their persons for sale. But Hesiod advises

"Not to wash the skin in the women's bath."[5]

The baths are opened promiscuously to men and women; and there they strip for licentious indulgence (for from looking, men get to loving), as if their modesty had been washed away in the bath.[6] Those who have not become utterly destitute of modesty shut out strangers; but bathe with their own servants, and strip naked before their slaves, and are rubbed by them; giving to the crouching menial liberty to lust, by permitting fearless handling. For those who are introduced before their naked mistresses while in the bath, study to strip themselves in order to audacity in lust, casting off fear in consequence of the wicked custom. The ancient athletes,[7] ashamed to exhibit a man naked, preserved their modesty by going through the contest in drawers; but these women, divesting themselves of their modesty along with their tunic, wish to appear beautiful, but contrary to their wish are simply proved to be wicked.[8] For through the body itself the wantonness of lust shines clearly; as in the case of dropsical people, the water covered by the skin. Disease in both is known from the look. Men, therefore, affording to women a noble example of truth, ought to be ashamed at their stripping before them, and guard against these dangerous sights; "for he who has looked curiously," it is said, "hath sinned already."[9] At home, therefore, they ought to regard with modesty parents and domestics; in the ways, those they meet; in the baths, women; in solitude, themselves; and everywhere the Word, who is everywhere, "and without Him was not anything."[10] For so only shall one remain without falling, if he regard God as ever present with him.

CHAP. VI. — THE CHRISTIAN ALONE RICH.

Riches are then to be partaken of rationally, bestowed lovingly, not sordidly, or pompously; nor is the love of the beautiful to be turned into self-love and ostentation; lest perchance some one say to us, "His horse, or land, or domestic, or gold, is worth fifteen talents; but the man himself is dear at three coppers."

[1] [The wasting on pet dogs, pups, and other animals, expense and pains which might help an orphan child, is a sin not yet uprooted. Here Clement's plea for widows, orphans, and aged men, prepares the way for Christian institutions in behalf of these classes. The same arguments should prevail with Christians in America.]
[2] Prov. xix. 17.
[3] Matt. xxv. 40.
[4] Prov. x. 4.
[5] Hesiod, *Works and days*, ii. 371.
[6] [Such were women before the Gospel came. See note to Hermas, cap. xi. note 1, p. 47, this volume, and Elucidation (p. 57) of the same.]
[7] [The barbarians were more decent than the Greeks, being nearer to the state of nature, which is a better guide than pagan civilization. But see the interesting note of Rawlinson (*Herod.*, vol. i. p. 125, ed. New York), who quotes Thucydides (i. 6) to prove the recent invasion of immodest exposure even among athletes. Our author has this same quotation in mind, for he almost translates it here.]
[8] [Attic girls raced in the games quite naked. Spartan girls wore only the linen *chiton*, even in the company of men; and this was esteemed *nudity*, not unjustly. David's "uncovering himself" (2 Sam. vi. 20) was *nudity* of the same sort. Married women assumed the *peplus*.]
[9] Matt. v. 28.
[10] John i. 3.

Take away, then, directly the ornaments from women, and domestics from masters, and you will find masters in no respect different from bought slaves in step, or look, or voice, so like are they to their slaves. But they differ in that they are feebler than their slaves, and have a more sickly upbringing.

This best of maxims, then, ought to be perpetually repeated, "That the good man, being temperate and just," treasures up his wealth in heaven. He who has sold his worldly goods, and given them to the poor, finds the imperishable treasure, "where is neither moth nor robber." Blessed truly is he, "though he be insignificant, and feeble, and obscure;" and he is truly rich with the greatest of all riches. "Though a man, then, be richer than Cinyras and Midas, and is wicked," and haughty as he who was luxuriously clothed in purple and fine linen, and despised Lazarus, "he is miserable, and lives in trouble," and shall not live. Wealth seems to me to be like a serpent, which will twist round the hand and bite; unless one knows how to lay hold of it without danger by the point of the tail. And riches, wriggling either in an experienced or inexperienced grasp, are dexterous at adhering and biting; unless one, despising them, use them skilfully, so as to crush the creature by the charm of the Word, and himself escape unscathed.

But, as is reasonable, he alone, who possesses what is worth most, turns out truly rich, though not recognised as such. And it is not jewels, or gold, or clothing, or beauty of person, that are of high value, but virtue; which is the Word given by the Instructor to be put in practice. This is the Word, who abjures luxury, but calls self-help as a servant, and praises frugality, the progeny of temperance. "Receive," he says, "instruction, and not silver, and knowledge rather than tested gold; for Wisdom is better than precious stones, nor is anything that is valuable equal in worth to her."[1] And again: "Acquire me rather than gold, and precious stones, and silver; for my produce is better than choice silver."[2]

But if we must distinguish, let it be granted that he is rich who has many possessions, loaded with gold like a dirty purse; but the righteous alone is graceful, because grace is order, observing a due and decorous measure in managing and distributing. "For there are those who sow and reap more,"[3] of whom it is written, "He hath dispersed, he hath given to the poor; his righteousness endureth for ever."[4] So that it is not he who has and keeps, but he who gives away, that is rich; and it is giving away, not possession, which renders a man happy and the fruit of the Spirit is generosity. I is in the soul, then, that riches are. Let it then, be granted that good things are the property only of good men; and Christians are good. Now, a fool or a libertine can neither have any perception of what is good, nor obtain possession of it. Accordingly, good things are possessed by Christians alone. And nothing is richer than these good things; therefore these alone are rich. For righteousness is true riches; and the Word is more valuable than all treasure, not accruing from cattle and fields, but given by God — riches which cannot be taken away. The soul alone is its treasure. It is the best possession to its possessor, rendering man truly blessed. For he whose it is to desire nothing that is not in our power, and to obtain by asking from God what he piously desires, does he not possess much, nay all, having God as his everlasting treasure? "To him that asks," it is said, "shall be given, and to him that knocketh it shall be opened."[5] If God denies nothing, all things belong to the godly.

CHAP. VII. — FRUGALITY A GOOD PROVISION FOR THE CHRISTIAN.

Delicacies spent on pleasures become a dangerous shipwreck to men; for this voluptuous and ignoble life of the many is alien to true love for the beautiful and to refined pleasures. For man is by nature an erect and majestic being, aspiring after the good as becomes the creature of the One. But the life which crawls on its belly is destitute of dignity, is scandalous, hateful, ridiculous. And to the divine nature voluptuousness is a thing most alien; for this is for a man to be like sparrows in feeding, and swine and goats in lechery. For to regard pleasure as a good thing, is the sign of utter ignorance of what is excellent. Love of wealth displaces a man from the right mode of life, and induces him to cease from feeling shame at what is shameful; if only, like a beast, he has power to eat all sorts of things, and to drink in like manner, and to satiate in every way his lewd desires. And so very rarely does he inherit the kingdom of God. For what end, then, are such dainty dishes prepared, but to fill one belly? The filthiness of gluttony is proved by the sewers into which our bellies discharge the refuse of our food. For what end do they collect so many cupbearers, when they might satisfy themselves with one cup? For what the chests of clothes? and the gold ornaments for what? Those things are prepared for clothes-stealers, and scoundrels, and for greedy eyes. "But let alms and faith not fail thee,"[6] says the Scripture.

---

[1] Prov. viii. 10, 11.
[2] Prov. viii. 19.
[3] Prov. xi. 24.
[4] Ps. cxii. 9.

[5] Matt. vii. 7, 8.
[6] Prov. iii. 5.

Look, for instance, to Elias the Thesbite, in whom we have a beautiful example of frugality, when he sat down beneath the thorn, and the angel brought him food. "It was a cake of barley and a jar of water."[1] Such the Lord sent as best for him. We, then, on our journey to the truth, must be unencumbered. "Carry not," said the Lord, "purse, nor scrip, nor shoes;"[2] that is, possess not wealth, which is only treasured up in a purse; fill not your own stores, as if laying up produce in a bag, but communicate to those who have need. Do not trouble yourselves about horses and servants, who, as bearing burdens when the rich are travelling, are allegorically called shoes.

We must, then, cast away the multitude of vessels, silver and gold drinking cups, and the crowd of domestics, receiving as we have done from the Instructor the fair and grave attendants, Self-help and Simplicity. And we must walk suitably to the Word; and if there be a wife and children, the house is not a burden, having learned to change its place along with the sound-minded traveller. The wife who loves her husband must be furnished for travel similarly to her husband. A fair provision for the journey to heaven is theirs who bear frugality with chaste gravity. And as the foot is the measure of the shoe, so also is the body of what each individual possesses. But that which is superfluous, what they call ornaments and the furniture of the rich, is a burden, not an ornament to the body. He who climbs to the heavens by force, must carry with him the fair staff of beneficence, and attain to the true rest by communicating to those who are in distress. For the Scripture avouches, "that the true riches of the soul are a man's ransom,"[3] that is, if he is rich, he will be saved by distributing it. For as gushing wells, when pumped out, rise again to their former measure,[4] so giving away, being the benignant spring of love, by communicating of its drink to the thirsty, again increases and is replenished, just as the milk is wont to flow into the breasts that are sucked or milked. For he who has the almighty God, the Word, is in want of nothing, and never is in straits for what he needs. For the Word is a possession that wants nothing, and is the cause of all abundance. If one say that he has often seen the righteous man in need of food, this is rare, and happens only where there is not another righteous man.[5] Notwithstanding let him read what follows: "For the righteous man shall not live by bread alone, but by the word of the Lord,"[6] who is the true bread, the bread of

the heavens. The good man, then, can never be in difficulties so long as he keeps intact his confession towards God. For it appertains to him to ask and to receive whatever he requires from the Father of all; and to enjoy what is his own, if he keep the Son. And this also appertains to him, to feel no want.

This Word, who trains us, confers on us the true riches. Nor is the growing rich an object of envy to those who possess through Him the privilege of wanting nothing. He that has this wealth shall inherit the kingdom of God.

CHAP. VIII. — SIMILITUDES AND EXAMPLES A MOST IMPORTANT PART OF RIGHT INSTRUCTION.

And if any one of you shall entirely avoid luxury, he will, by a frugal upbringing, train himself to the endurance of involuntary labours, by employing constantly voluntary afflictions as training exercises for persecutions; so that when he comes to compulsory labours, and fears, and griefs, he will not be unpractised in endurance.

Wherefore we have no country on earth, that we may despise earthly possessions. And frugality[7] is in the highest degree rich, being equal to unfailing expenditure, bestowed on what is requisite, and to the degree requisite. For τέλη has the meaning of expenses.

How a husband is to live with his wife, and respecting self-help, and housekeeping, and the employment of domestics; and further, with respect to the time of marriage, and what is suitable for wives, we have treated in the discourse concerning marriage. What pertains to discipline alone is reserved now for description, as we delineate the life of Christians. The most indeed has been already said, and laid down in the form of disciplinary rules. What still remains we shall subjoin; for examples are of no small moment in determining to salvation.[8]

See, says the tragedy,

"The consort of Ulysses was not killed
By Telemachus; for she did not take a husband in addition to a husband,
But in the house the marriage-bed remains unpolluted."[9]

Reproaching foul adultery, he showed the fair image of chastity in affection to her husband.

The Lacedæmonians compelling the Helots, their servants (Helots is the name of their servants), to get drunk, exhibited their drunken pranks before themselves, who were temperate, for cure and correction.

Observing, accordingly, their unseemly behaviour, in order that they themselves might not fall into like censurable conduct, they trained them-

---

[1] 1 Kings xix. 4, 6.
[2] Luke x. 4.
[3] Prov. xiii. 8.
[4] [Kaye, p. 97.]
[5] [A beautiful apophthegm, and admirably interpretative of Ps. xxxvii. 25.]
[6] Deut. viii. 3; Matt. iv. 4.

[7] The word used by Clement here for frugality is εὐτέλεια, and he supposes the word to mean originally "spending well." A proper way of spending money is as good as unfailing riches, since it always has enough for all that is necessary.
[8] [This plea for *similitudes* illustrates the principle of Hermas, and the ground of the currency of his *Pastor*.]
[9] Euripides, *Orestes*, 588–590.

selves, turning the reproach of the drunkards to the advantage of keeping themselves free from fault.

For some men being instructed are saved; and others, self-taught, either aspire after or seek virtue.

"He truly is the best of all who himself perceives all things." [1]

Such is Abraham, who sought God.

"And good, again, is he who obeys him who advises well." [2]

Such are those disciples who obeyed the Word. Wherefore the former was called "friend," the latter "apostles;" the one diligently seeking, and the other preaching one and the same God. And both are peoples, and both these have hearers, the one who is profited through seeking, the other who is saved through finding.

"But whoever neither himself perceives, nor, hearing another,
Lays to heart — he is a worthless man." [3]

The other people is the Gentile — useless; this is the people that followeth not Christ. Nevertheless the Instructor, lover of man, helping in many ways, partly exhorts, partly upbraids. Others having sinned, He shows us their baseness, and exhibits the punishment consequent upon it, alluring while admonishing, planning to dissuade us in love from evil, by the exhibition of those who have suffered from it before. By which examples He very manifestly checked those who had been evil-disposed, and hindered those who were daring like deeds; and others He brought to a foundation of patience; others He stopped from wickedness; and others He cured by the contemplation of what is like, bringing them over to what is better.

For who, when following one in the way, and then on the former falling into a pit, would not guard against incurring equal danger, by taking care not to follow him in his slip? What athlete, again, who has learned the way to glory, and has seen the combatant who had preceded him receiving the prize, does not exert himself for the crown, imitating the elder one?

Such images of divine wisdom are many; but I shall mention one instance, and expound it in a few words. The fate of the Sodomites was judgment to those who had done wrong, instruction to those who hear. The Sodomites having, through much luxury, fallen into uncleanness, practising adultery shamelessly, and burning with insane love for boys; the All-seeing Word, whose notice those who commit impieties cannot escape, cast His eye on them. Nor did the sleepless guard of humanity observe their licen-

tiousness in silence; but dissuading us from the imitation of them, and training us up to His own temperance, and falling on some sinners, lest lust being unavenged, should break loose from all the restraints of fear, ordered Sodom to be burned, pouring forth a little of the sagacious fire on licentiousness; lest lust, through want of punishment, should throw wide the gates to those that were rushing into voluptuousness. Accordingly, the just punishment of the Sodomites became to men an image of the salvation which is well calculated for men. For those who have not committed like sins with those who are punished, will never receive a like punishment. By guarding against sinning, we guard, against suffering. "For I would have you know," says Jude, "that God, having once saved His people from the land of Egypt, afterwards destroyed them that believed not; and the angels which kept not their first estate, but left their own habitation, He hath reserved to the judgment of the great day, in everlasting chains under darkness of the savage angels." [4] And a little after he sets forth, in a most instructive manner, representations of those that are judged: "Woe unto them, for they have gone in the way of Cain, and run greedily after the error of Balaam, and perished in the gainsaying of Core." For those, who cannot attain the privilege of adoption, fear keeps from growing insolent. For punishments and threats are for this end, that fearing the penalty we may abstain from sinning. I might relate to you punishments for ostentation, and punishments for vainglory, not only for licentiousness; and adduce the censures pronounced on those whose hearts are bad through wealth, [5] in which censures the Word through fear restrains from evil acts. But sparing prolixity in my treatise, I shall bring forward the following precepts of the Instructor, that you may guard against His threatenings.

CHAP. IX. — WHY WE ARE TO USE THE BATH.

There are, then, four reasons for the bath (for from that point I digressed in my oration), for which we frequent it: for cleanliness, or heat, or health, or lastly, for pleasure. Bathing for pleasure is to be omitted. For unblushing pleasure must be cut out by the roots; and the bath is to be taken by women for cleanliness and health, by men for health alone. [6] To bathe for the sake of heat is a superfluity, since one may restore what is frozen by the cold in other ways. Constant use of the bath, too, impairs strength and relaxes the physical energies, and often induces debility and fainting. For in a

---

[1] Hesiod, *Works and Days*, i. 291.
[2] *Ibid.*
[3] *Ibid.*

[4] Jude 5, 6.
[5] Following Lowth's conjecture of κακοφρόνων instead of that of the text, κακόφρονας.
[6] [The morals of Clement as to decency in bathing need to be enforced among modern Christians, at seaside places of resort.]

way the body drinks, like trees, not only by the mouth, but also over the whole body in bathing, by what they call the pores. In proof of this, often people, when thirsty, by going afterwards into the water, have assuaged their thirst. Unless, then, the bath is for some use, we ought not to indulge in it. The ancients called them places for fulling [1] men, since they wrinkle men's bodies sooner than they ought, and by cooking them, as it were, compel them to become prematurely old. The flesh, like iron, being softened by the heat, hence we require cold, as it were, to temper and give an edge. Nor must we bathe always; but if one is a little exhausted, or, on the other hand, filled to repletion, the bath is to be forbidden, regard being had to the age of the body and the season of the year. For the bath is not beneficial to all, or always, as those who are skilled in these things own. But due proportion, which on all occasions we call as our helper in life, suffices for us. For we must not so use the bath as to require an assistant, nor are we to bathe constantly and often in the day as we frequent the market-place. But to have the water poured over us by several people is an outrage on our neighbours, through fondness for luxuriousness, and is done by those who will not understand that the bath is common to all the bathers equally.

But most of all is it necessary to wash the soul in the cleansing Word (sometimes the body too, on account of the dirt which gathers and grows to it, sometimes also to relieve fatigue). "Woe unto you, scribes and Pharisees, hypocrites!" saith the Lord, "for ye are like to whited sepulchres. Without, the sepulchre appears beautiful, but within it is full of dead men's bones and all uncleanness." [2] And again He says to the same people, "Woe unto you! for ye cleanse the outside of the cup and platter, but within are full of uncleanness. Cleanse first the inside of the cup, that the outside may be clean also." [3] The best bath, then, is what rubs off the pollution of the soul, and is spiritual. Of which prophecy speaks expressly: "The Lord will wash away the filth of the sons and daughters of Israel, and will purge the blood from the midst of them" [4] — the blood of crime and the murders of the prophets. And the mode of cleansing, the Word subjoined, saying, "by the spirit of judgment and the spirit of burning." The bathing which is carnal, that is to say, of the body, is accomplished by water alone, as often in the country where there is not a bath. [5]

CHAP. X. — THE EXERCISES SUITED TO A GOOD LIFE.

The gymnasium is sufficient for boys, even if a bath is within reach. And even for men to prefer gymnastic exercises by far to the baths, is perchance not bad, since they are in some respects conducive to the health of young men, and produce exertion — emulation at not only a healthy habit of body, but courageousness of soul. When this is done without dragging a man away from better employments, it is pleasant, and not unprofitable. Nor are women to be deprived of bodily exercise. But they are not to be encouraged to engage in wrestling or running, but are to exercise themselves in spinning, and weaving, and superintending the cooking if necessary. And they are, with their own hand, to fetch from the store what we require. And it is no disgrace for them to apply themselves to the mill. Nor is it a reproach to a wife — housekeeper and helpmeet — to occupy herself in cooking, so that it may be palatable to her husband. And if she shake up the couch, reach drink to her husband when thirsty, set food on the table as neatly as possible, and so give herself exercise tending to sound health, the Instructor will approve of a woman like this, who "stretches forth her arms to useful tasks, rests her hands on the distaff, opens her hand to the poor, and extends her wrist to the beggar." [6]

She who emulates Sarah is not ashamed of that highest of ministries, helping wayfarers. For Abraham said to her, "Haste, and knead three measures of meal, and make cakes." [7] "And Rachel, the daughter of Laban, came," it is said, "with her father's sheep." [8] Nor was this enough; but to teach humility it is added, "for she fed her father's sheep." [9] And innumerable such examples of frugality and self-help, and also of exercises, are furnished by the Scriptures. In the case of men, let some strip and engage in wrestling; let some play at the small ball, especially the game they call Pheninda, [10] in the sun. To others who walk into the country, or go down into the town, the walk is sufficient exercise. And were they to handle the hoe, this stroke of economy in agricultural labour would not be ungentleman like.

I had almost forgot to say that the well-known Pittacus, king of Miletus, practised the laborious exercise of turning the mill. [11] It is respectable for a man to draw water for himself, and to cut billets of wood which he is to use himself. Jacob fed the sheep of Laban that were left in

1 ἀνθρωπογναφεῖα.
2 Matt. xxiii. 27.
3 Matt. xxiii. 25, 26.
4 Isa. iv. 4.
5 [That is, water applied by cloths or sponges. Clement does not oppose bathing, except in excess, and with the processes used in heathen baths. St. John was fond of the bath; and see the story of his encounter with Cerinthus, in Eusebius, book iv. cap. xiv.]

6 Prov. xxxi. 19, 20, Septuagint.
7 Gen. xviii. 6.
8 Gen. xxix. 9.
9 Ibid.
10 φενίνδα or φεννίς.
11 The text has ἦλθεν. The true reading, doubtless, is ἤλαθεν. That Pittacus exercised himself thus, is stated by Isidore of Pelusium, Diogenes, Laertius, Plutarch.

his charge, having as a royal badge "a rod of storax,"[1] which aimed by its wood to change and improve nature. And reading aloud is often an exercise to many. But let not such athletic contests, as we have allowed, be undertaken for the sake of vainglory, but for the exuding of manly sweat. Nor are we to struggle with cunning and showiness, but in a stand-up wrestling bout, by disentangling of neck, hands, and sides. For such a struggle with graceful strength is more becoming and manly, being undertaken for the sake of serviceable and profitable health. But let those others, who profess the practice of illiberal postures in gymnastics, be dismissed. We must always aim at moderation. For as it is best that labour should precede food, so to labour above measure is both very bad, very exhausting, and apt to make us ill. Neither, then, should we be idle altogether, nor completely fatigued. For similarly to what we have laid down with respect to food, are we to do everywhere and with everything. Our mode of life is not to accustom us to voluptuousness and licentiousness, nor to the opposite extreme, but to the medium between these, that which is harmonious and temperate, and free of either evil, luxury and parsimony. And now, as we have also previously remarked, attending to one's own wants is an exercise free of pride, — as, for example, putting on one's own shoes, washing one's own feet, and also rubbing one's self when anointed with oil. To render one who has rubbed you the same service in return, is an exercise of reciprocal justice ; and to sleep beside a sick friend, help the infirm, and supply him who is in want, are proper exercises. "And Abraham," it is said, "served up for three, dinner under a tree, and waited on them as they ate."[2] The same with fishing,[3] as in the case of Peter, if we have leisure from necessary instructions in the Word. But that is the better enjoyment which the Lord assigned to the disciple, when He taught him to "catch men" as fishes in the water.

CHAP. XI. — A COMPENDIOUS VIEW OF THE CHRISTIAN LIFE.

Wherefore the wearing of gold and the use of softer clothing is not to be entirely prohibited. But irrational impulses must be curbed, lest, carrying us away through excessive relaxation, they impel us to voluptuousness. For luxury, that has dashed on to surfeit, is prone to kick up its heels and toss its mane, and shake off the

charioteer, the Instructor ; who, pulling back the reins from far, leads and drives to salvation the human horse — that is, the irrational part of the soul — which is wildly bent on pleasures and vicious appetites, and precious stones, and gold, and variety of dress, and other luxuries.

Above all, we are to keep in mind what was spoken sacredly : "Having your conversation honest among the Gentiles ; that, whereas they speak against you as evil-doers, they may, by the good works which they behold, glorify God."[4]

Clothes.

The Instructor permits us, then, to use simple clothing, and of a white colour, as we said before. So that, accommodating ourselves not to variegated art, but to nature as it is produced, and pushing away whatever is deceptive and belies the truth, we may embrace the uniformity and simplicity of the truth.[5]

Sophocles, reproaching a youth, says : —

"Decked in women's clothes."

For, as in the case of the soldier, the sailor, and the ruler, so also the proper dress of the temperate man is what is plain, becoming, and clean. Whence also in the law, the law enacted by Moses about leprousy rejects what has many colours and spots, like the various scales of the snake. He therefore wishes man, no longer decking himself gaudily in a variety of colours, but white all over from the crown of the head to the sole of the foot, to be clean ; so that, by a transition from the body, we may lay aside the varied and versatile passions of the man, and love the unvaried, and unambiguous, and simple colour of truth. And he who also in this emulates Moses — Plato best of all — approves of that texture on which not more than a chaste woman's work has been employed. And white colours well become gravity. And elsewhere he says, "Nor apply dyes or weaving, except for warlike decorations."[6]

To men of peace and of light, therefore, white is appropriate.[7] As, then, signs, which are very closely allied to causes, by their presence indicate, or rather demonstrate, the existence of the result ; as smoke is the sign of fire, and a good complexion and a regular pulse of health ; so also clothing of this description shows the character of our habits. Temperance is pure and simple ; since purity is a habit which ensures pure conduct unmixed with what is base. Simplicity is a habit which does away with superfluities.

---

[1] Gen. xxx. 37. Not "poplar," as in A. V. [See Abp. Leighton on "Laban's lambs," *Comm. on St. Peter*, part i. p. 360, and questionable note of an admirable editor, same page.]

[2] Gen. xviii. 8.

[3] [The old canons allowed to clergymen the recreation of fishing, but not the chase, or fowling. Of this, the godly Izaak Walton fails not to remind us. *Complete Angler*, p. 38, learned note, and preface by the late Dr. Bethune. New York, 1847.]

[4] 1 Pet. ii. 12.

[5] [Surely the costly and gorgeous ecclesiastical raiment of the Middle Ages is condemned by Clement's primitive maxims.]

[6] Plato's words are : "The web is not to be more than a woman's work for a month. White colour is peculiarly becoming for the gods in other things, but especially in cloth. Dyes are not to be applied except for warlike decorations" — PLATO: *De Legibus*, xii. 992.

[7] [Another law against colours in clerical attire.]

Substantial clothing also, and chiefly what is unfulled, protects the heat which is in the body; not that the clothing has heat in itself, but that it turns back the heat issuing from the body, and refuses it a passage. And whatever heat falls upon it, it absorbs and retains, and being warmed by it, warms in turn the body. And for this reason it is chiefly to be worn in winter.

It also (temperance) is contented. And contentment is a habit which dispenses with superfluities, and, that there may be no failure, is receptive of what suffices for the healthful and blessed life according to the Word.[1]

Let the women wear a plain and becoming dress, but softer than what is suitable for a man, yet not quite immodest or entirely gone in luxury. And let the garments be suited to age, person, figure, nature, pursuits. For the divine apostle most beautifully counsels us "to put on Jesus Christ, and make no provision for the lusts of the flesh."[2]

Ear-rings.

The Word prohibits us from doing violence to nature[3] by boring the lobes of the ears. For why not the nose too? — so that, what was spoken, may be fulfilled: "As an ear-ring in a swine's nose, so is beauty to a woman without discretion."[4] For, in a word, if one thinks himself made beautiful by gold, he is inferior to gold; and he that is inferior to gold is not lord of it. But to confess one's self less ornamental than the Lydian ore, how monstrous! As, then, the gold is polluted by the dirtiness of the sow, which stirs up the mire with her snout, so those women that are luxurious to excess in their wantonness, elated by wealth, dishonour by the stains of amatory indulgences what is the true beauty.

Finger-rings.

The Word, then, permits them a finger-ring of gold.[5] Nor is this for ornament, but for sealing things which are worth keeping safe in the house, in the exercise of their charge of housekeeping.

For if all were well trained, there would be no need of seals, if servants and masters were equally honest. But since want of training produces an inclination to dishonesty, we require seals.

But there are circumstances in which this strictness may relaxed. For allowance must sometimes be made in favour of those women who have not been fortunate[6] in falling in with chaste husbands, and adorn themselves in order to please their husbands. But let desire for the admiration of their husbands alone be proposed as their aim. I would not have them to devote themselves to personal display, but to attract their husbands by chaste love for them — a powerful and legitimate charm. But since they wish their wives to be unhappy in mind, let the latter, if they would be chaste, make it their aim to allay by degrees the irrational impulses and passions of their husbands. And they are to be gently drawn to simplicity, by gradually accustoming them to sobriety. For decency is not produced by the imposition of what is burdensome, but by the abstraction of excess. For women's articles of luxury are to be prohibited, as things of swift wing producing unstable follies and empty delights; by which, elated and furnished with wings, they often fly away from the marriage bonds. Wherefore also women ought to dress neatly, and bind themselves around with the band of chaste modesty, lest through giddiness they slip away from the truth. It is right, then, for men to repose confidence in their wives, and commit the charge of the household to them, as they are given to be their helpers in this.

And if it is necessary for us, while engaged in public business, or discharging other avocations in the country, and often away from our wives, to seal anything for the sake of safety, He (the Word) allows us a signet for this purpose only. Other finger-rings are to be cast off, since, according to the Scripture, "instruction is a golden ornament for a wise man."[7]

But women who wear gold seem to me to be afraid, lest, if one strip them of their jewellery, they should be taken for servants, without their ornaments. But the nobility of truth, discovered in the native beauty which has its seat in the soul, judges the slave not by buying and selling, but by a servile disposition. And it is incumbent on us not to seem, but to be free, trained by God, adopted by God.

Wherefore we must adopt a mode of standing and motion, and a step, and dress, and in a word, a mode of life, in all respects as worthy as possible of freemen. But men are not to wear the ring on the joint; for this is feminine; but to place it on the little finger at its root. For so the hand will be freest for work, in whatever we need it; and the signet will not very easily fall off, being guarded by the large knot of the joint.

And let our seals be either a dove, or a fish, or a ship scudding before the wind, or a musical lyre, which Polycrates used, or a ship's anchor, which Seleucus got engraved as a device; and if there be one fishing, he will remember the

---

1 Κατὰ Λόγον. The reading in the text is κατάλογον.
2 Rom. xiii. 14.
3 [Natural instinct is St. Paul's argument (1 Cor. xi. 14, 15); and that it rules for modesty in man as well as woman, is finely illustrated by an instructive story in Herodotus (book i. 8-12). The wife of Gyges could be guilty of a heathenish revenge, but nature taught her to abhor exposure. "A woman who puts off her raiment, puts off her modesty," said Candaules to her foolish husband.]
4 Prov. xi. 22.
5 [Possibly used thus early as a distinction of matrons.]
6 Εὐτυχούσαις, for which the text has ἐντοχούσαις.
7 Ecclus. xxi. 21.

apostle, and the children drawn out of the water. For we are not to delineate the faces of idols,[1] we who are prohibited to cleave to them; nor a sword, nor a bow, following as we do, peace; nor drinking-cups, being temperate.

Many of the licentious have their lovers[2] engraved,[3] or their mistresses, as if they wished to make it impossible ever to forget their amatory indulgences, by being perpetually put in mind of their licentiousness.

The Hair.

About the hair, the following seems right. Let the head of men be shaven, unless it has curly hair. But let the chin have the hair. But let not twisted locks hang far down from the head, gliding into womanish ringlets. For an ample beard suffices for men. And if one, too, shave a part of his beard, it must not be made entirely bare, for this is a disgraceful sight. The shaving of the chin to the skin is reprehensible, approaching to plucking out the hair and smoothing. For instance, thus the Psalmist, delighted with the hair of the beard, says, "As the ointment that descends on the beard, the beard of Aaron."[4]

Having celebrated the beauty of the beard by a repetition, he made the face to shine with the ointment of the Lord.

Since cropping is to be adopted not for the sake of elegance, but on account of the necessity of the case; the hair of the head, that it may not grow so long as to come down and interfere with the eyes, and that of the moustache similarly, which is dirtied in eating, is to be cut round, not by the razor, for that were not well-bred, but by a pair of cropping scissors. But the hair on the chin is not to be disturbed, as it gives no trouble, and lends to the face dignity and paternal terror.[5]

Moreover, the shape instructs many not to sin, because it renders detection easy. To those who do [not][6] wish to sin openly, a habit that will escape observation and is not conspicuous is most agreeable, which, when assumed, will allow them to transgress without detection; so that, being undistinguishable from others, they may fearlessly go their length in sinning.[7] A cropped head not only shows a man to be grave, but renders the cranium less liable to injury, by accustoming it to the presence of

both cold and heat; and it averts the mischiefs arising from these, which the hair absorbs into itself like a sponge, and so inflicts on the brain constant mischief from the moisture.

It is enough for women to protect[8] their locks, and bind up their hair simply along the neck with a plain hair-pin, nourishing chaste locks with simple care to true beauty. For meretricious plaiting of the hair, and putting it up in tresses, contribute to make them look ugly, cutting the hair and plucking off it those treacherous braidings; on account of which they do not touch their head, being afraid of disordering their hair. Sleep, too, comes on, not without fear lest they pull down without knowing the shape of the braid.

But additions of other people's hair are entirely to be rejected, and it is a most sacrilegious thing for spurious hair to shade the head, covering the skull with dead locks. For on whom does the presbyter lay his hand?[9] Whom does he bless? Not the woman decked out, but another's hair, and through them another head. And if "the man is head of the woman, and God of the man,"[10] how is it not impious that they should fall into double sins? For they deceive the men by the excessive quantity of their hair; and shame the Lord as far as in them lies, by adorning themselves meretriciously, in order to dissemble the truth. And they defame the head, which is truly beautiful.

Consequently neither is the hair to be dyed, nor grey hair to have its colour changed. For neither are we allowed to diversify our dress. And above all, old age, which conciliates trust, is not to be concealed. But God's mark of honour is to be shown in the light of day, to win the reverence of the young. For sometimes, when they have been behaving shamefully, the appearance of hoary hairs, arriving like an instructor, has changed them to sobriety, and paralysed juvenile lust with the splendour of the sight.

Painting the Face.

Nor are the women to smear their faces with the ensnaring devices of wily cunning. But let us show to them the decoration of sobriety. For, in the first place, the best beauty is that which is spiritual, as we have often pointed out. For when the soul is adorned by the Holy Spirit, and inspired with the radiant charms which proceed from Him, — righteousness, wisdom, fortitude, temperance, love of the good, modesty,

---

[1] [How this was followed, is proved by the early Christian devices of the catacombs, contrasted with the engraved gems from Pompeii, in the *Museo Borbonico* at Naples.]

[2] Masculine.

[3] γεγλυμμένους, written on the margin of Codex clxv. for γεγυμνωμένους (naked) of the text. [Royal Library, Naples.]

[4] Ps. cxxxiii. 2.

[5] [Here Clement's rules are arbitrary, and based on their existing ideas of propriety. If it be not improper to shave the head, much less to shave the face, which he allows in part.]

[6] "Not" does not occur in the MSS.

[7] For δεδοικότες, the conjectural emendation δεδυκότες has been adopted.

[8] φυλάσσειν, Sylburg and Bod. Reg., agree better than μαλάσσειν with the context.

[9] [The *chrism* (confirmation) was thus administered then, not with material oil, and was called *anointing*, with reference to 1 John, ii. 27. Consult *Bunsen*, however, who attributes great antiquity to his canons (collected in vol. iii. *Hippolytus*), p. 22, *Church and House Book*.]

[10] 1 Cor. xi. 3. Nov. reads "Christ," as in St. Paul, instead of "God."

than which no more blooming colour was ever seen, — then let coporeal beauty be cultivated too, symmetry of limbs and members, with a fair complexion. The adornment of health is here in place, through which the transition of the artificial image to the truth, in accordance with the form which has been given by God, is effected. But temperance in drinks, and moderation in articles of food, are effectual in producing beauty according to nature ; for not only does the body maintain its health from these, but they also make beauty to appear. For from what is fiery arises a gleam and sparkle ; and from moisture, brightness and grace ; and from dryness, strength and firmness ; and from what is aërial, free-breathing and equipoise ; from which this well-proportioned and beautiful image of the Word is adorned. Beauty is the free flower of health ; for the latter is produced within the body ; while the former, blossoming out from the body, exhibits manifest beauty of complexion. Accordingly, these most decorous and healthful practices, by exercising the body, produce true and lasting beauty, the heat attracting to itself all the moisture and cold spirit. Heat, when agitated by moving causes, is a thing which attracts to itself ; and when it does attract, it gently exhales through the flesh itself, when warmed, the abundance of food, with some moisture, but with excess of heat. Wherefore also the first food is carried off. But when the body is not moved, the food consumed does not adhere, but falls away, as the loaf from a cold oven, either entire, or leaving only the lower part. Accordingly, the *fæces* are in excess in the case of those who do not throw off the excrementitious matters by the rubbings necessitated by exercise. And other superfluous matters abound in their case too, and also perspiration, as the food is not assimilated by the body, but is flowing out to waste. Thence also lusts are excited, the redundance flowing to the *pudenda* by commensurate motions. Wherefore this redundance ought to be liquefied and dispersed for digestion, by which beauty acquires its ruddy hue. But it is monstrous for those who are made in " the image and likeness of God," to dishonour the archetype by assuming a foreign ornament, preferring the mischievous contrivance of man to the divine creation.

The Instructor orders them to go forth " in becoming apparel, and adorn themselves with shamefacedness and sobriety," [1] " subject to their own husbands ; that, if any obey not the word, they may without the word be won by the conversation of the wives ; while they behold," he says, " your chaste conversation. Whose adorning, let it not be that outward adorning of plait-ing the hair, and of wearing of gold, or of putting on of apparel ; but let it be the hidden man of the heart, in that which is not corruptible, even the ornament of a meek and quiet spirit, which is in the sight of God of great price." [2]

For the labour of their own hands, above all, adds genuine beauty to women, exercising their bodies and adorning themselves by their own exertions ; not bringing unornamental ornament wrought by others, which is vulgar and meretricious, but that of every good woman, supplied and woven by her own hands whenever she most requires. For it is never suitable for women whose lives are framed according to God, to appear arrayed in things bought from the market, but in their own home-made work. For a most beautiful thing is à thrifty wife, who clothes both herself and her husband with fair array of her own working ; [3] in which all are glad — the children on account of their mother, the husband on account of his wife, she on their account, and all in God.

In brief, " A store of excellence is a woman of worth, who eateth not the bread of idleness ; and the laws of mercy are on her tongue ; who openeth her mouth wisely and rightly ; whose children rise up and call her blessed," as the sacred Word says by Solomon : " Her husband also, and he praiseth her. For a pious woman is blessed ; and let her praise the fear of the LORD." [4]

And again, " A virtuous woman is a crown to her husband." [5] They must, as far as possible, correct their gestures, looks, steps, and speech. For they must not do as some, who, imitating the acting of comedy, and practising the mincing motions of dancers, conduct themselves in society as if on the stage, with voluptuous movements, and gliding steps, and affected voices, casting languishing glances round, tricked out with the bait of pleasure. " For honey drops from the lips of a woman who is an harlot ; who, speaking to please, lubricates thy throat. But at last thou wilt find it bitterer than bile, and sharper than a two-edged sword. For the feet of folly lead those who practise it to hell after death." [6]

The noble Samson was overcome by the harlot, and by another woman was shorn of his manhood. But Joseph was not thus beguiled by another woman. The Egyptian harlot was conquered. And chastity,[7] assuming to itself bonds, appears superior to dissolute licence. Most excellent is what has been said : —

---

[1] 1 Tim. ii. 9.

[2] 1 Pet. iii. 1–4.
[3] In reference to Prov. xxxi. 22.
[4] Prov. xxxi. 26, 27, 28, 30, quoted from memory, and with variety of reading.
[5] Prov. xii. 4.
[6] Prov. v. 3–5, Septuagint.
[7] We have read from the New College MS. σωφροσύνη for σωφροσύνης.

" In fine, I know not how
  To whisper, nor effeminately,
  To walk about with my neck awry,
  As I see others — lechers there
In numbers in the city, with hair plucked out." [1]

But feminine motions, dissoluteness, and luxury, are to be entirely prohibited. For voluptuousness of motion in walking, " and a mincing gait," as Anacreon says, are altogether meretricious.

"As seems to me," says the comedy, "it is time [2] to abandon meretricious steps and luxury." And the steps of harlotry lean not to the truth ; for they approach not the paths of life. Her tracks are dangerous, and not easily known.[3] The eyes especially are to be sparingly used, since it is better to slip with the feet than with the eyes.[4] Accordingly, the Lord very summarily cures this malady : " If thine eye offend thee, cut it out," [5] He says, dragging lust up from the foundation. But languishing looks, and ogling, which is to wink with the eyes, is nothing else than to commit adultery with the eyes, lust skirmishing through them. For of the whole body, the eyes are first destroyed. "The eye contemplating beautiful objects ($\kappa\alpha\lambda\acute{\alpha}$), gladdens the heart ; " that is, the eye which has learned rightly ($\kappa\alpha\lambda\hat{\omega}s$) to see, gladdens. " Winking with the eye, with guile, heaps woes on men."[6] Such they introduce the effeminate Sardanapalus, king of the Assyrians, sitting on a couch with his legs up, fumbling at his purple robe, and casting up the whites of his eyes. Women that follow such practices, by their looks offer themselves for prostitution. " For the light of the body is the eye," says the Scripture, by which the interior illuminated by the shining light appears. Fornication in a woman is in the raising of the eyes.[7]

" Mortify therefore your members which are upon the earth ; fornication, uncleanness, inordinate affection, and concupiscence, and covetousness, which is idolatry : for which things' sake cometh the wrath of God upon the children of disobedience," [8] cries the apostle.

But we enkindle the passions, and are not ashamed.

Some of these women eating mastich,[9] going about, show their teeth to those that come near. And others, as if they had not fingers, give themselves airs, scratching their heads with pins ; and these made either of tortoise or ivory, or some other dead creature they procure at much pains. And others, as if they had certain efflorescences, in order to appear comely in the eyes of spectators, stain their faces by adorning them with gay-coloured unguents. Such a one is called by Solomon " a foolish and bold woman," who " knows not shame. She sits at the door of her house, conspicuously in a seat, calling to all that pass by the way, who go right on their ways ; " by her style and whole life manifestly saying, " Who among you is very silly ? let him turn to me." And those devoid of wisdom she exhorts, saying, " Touch sweetly secret bread, and sweet stolen water ; " meaning by this, clandestine love (from this point the Bœotian Pindar, coming to our help, says, " The clandestine pursuit of love is something sweet "). But the miserable man " knoweth not that the sons of earth perish beside her, and that she tends to the level of hell." But says the Instructor : " Hie away, and tarry not in the place ; nor fix thine eye on her : for thus shalt thou pass over a strange water, and cross to Acheron." [10] Wherefore thus saith the Lord by Isaiah, " Because the daughters of Sion walk with lofty neck, and with winkings of the eyes, and sweeping their garments as they walk, and playing with their feet ; the Lord shall humble the daughters of Sion, and will uncover their form " [11] — their deformed form. I deem it wrong that servant girls, who follow women of high rank, should either speak or act unbecomingly to them. But I think it right that they should be corrected by their mistresses. With very sharp censure, accordingly, the comic poet Philemon says : " You may follow at the back of a pretty servant girl, seen behind a gentlewoman ; and any one from the Platæicum may follow close, and ogle her." For the wantonness of the servant recoils on the mistress ; allowing those who attempt to take lesser liberties not to be afraid to advance to greater ; since the mistress, by allowing improprieties, shows that she does not disapprove of them. And not to be angry at those who act wantonly, is a clear proof of a disposition inclining to the like. " For like mistress like wench," [12] as they say in the proverb.

Walking.

Also we must abandon a furious mode of walking, and choose a grave and leisurely, but not a lingering step.

Nor is one to swagger in the ways, nor throw back his head to look at those he meets, if they look at him, as if he were strutting on the stage, and pointed at with the finger. Nor, when pushing up hill, are they to be shoved up by

---

[1] From some comic poet.
[2] Some read ὥραν ἀπολείπει. [New College MS.] In the translation the conjecture ὥρα ἀπολείπειν is adopted.
[3] An adaptation of Prov. v. 5, 6.
[4] An imitation of Zeno's saying, " It is better to slip with the feet than the tongue."
[5] Quoting from memory, he has substituted ἔκκοψον for ἔξελε (Matt. v. 29).
[6] Prov. x. 10.
[7] Ecclus. xxvi. 9.
[8] Col. iii. 5, 6.
[9] [A similar practice, very gross and unbecoming, prevails among the lower class of girls brought together in our common schools.]
[10] Prov. ix. 13-18.
[11] τὸ ἄσχημον σχῆμα (Isa. iii. 16, 17), Sept.
[12] ἀ κύων, catella. The literal English rendering is coarser and more opprobrious than the original, which Helen applies to herself (*Iliad*, vi. 344, 356).

their domestics, as we see those that are more luxurious, who appear strong, but are enfeebled by effeminacy of soul.

A true gentleman must have no mark of effeminacy visible on his face, or any other part of his body. Let no blot on his manliness, then, be ever found either in his movements or habits. Nor is a man in health to use his servants as horses to bear him. For as it is enjoined on them, " to be subject to their masters with all fear, not only to the good and gentle, but also to the froward," [1] as Peter says; so fairness, and forbearance, and kindness, are what well becomes the masters. For he says: " Finally, be ye all of one mind, having compassion one of another; love as brethren, be pitiful, be humble," and so forth, " that ye may inherit a blessing," [2] excellent and desirable.

The Model Maiden.

Zeno the Cittiæan thought fit to represent the image of a young maid, and executed the statue thus: " Let her face be clean, her eyebrows not let down, nor her eyelids open nor turned back. Let her neck not be stretched back, nor the members of her body be loose. But let the parts that hang from the body look as if they were well strung; let there be the keenness of a well-regulated mind [3] for discourse, and retention of what has been rightly spoken; and let her attitudes and movements give no ground of hope to the licentious; but let there be the bloom of modesty, and an expression of firmness. But far from her be the wearisome trouble that comes from the shops of perfumers, and goldsmiths, and dealers in wool, and that which comes from the other shops where women, meretriciously dressed, pass whole days as if sitting in the stews."

Amusements and Associates.

And let not men, therefore, spend their time in barbers' shops and taverns, babbling nonsense; and let them give up hunting for the women who sit near, [4] and ceaselessly talking slander against many to raise a laugh.

The game of dice [5] is to be prohibited, and the pursuit of gain, especially by dicing, [6] which many keenly follow. Such things the prodigality of luxury invents for the idle. For the cause is idleness, and a love [7] for frivolities

apart from the truth. For it is not possible otherwise to obtain enjoyment without injury; and each man's preference of a mode of life is a counterpart of his disposition.

But, as appears, only intercourse with good men benefits; on the other hand, the all-wise Instructor, by the mouth of Moses, recognising companionship with bad men as swinish, forbade the ancient people to partake of swine; to point out that those who call on God ought not to mingle with unclean men, who, like swine, delight in corporeal pleasures, in impure food, and in itching with filthy pruriency after the mischievous delights of lewdness.

Further, He says: " Thou art not to eat a kite or swift-winged ravenous bird, or an eagle," [8] meaning: Thou shalt not come near men who gain their living by rapine. And other things also are exhibited figuratively.

With whom, then, are we to associate? With the righteous, He says again, speaking figuratively; for everything " which parts the hoof and chews the cud is clean." For the parting of the hoof indicates the equilibrium of righteousness, and ruminating points to the proper food of righteousness, the word, which enters from without, like food, by instruction, but is recalled from the mind, as from the stomach, to rational recollection. And the spiritual man, having the word in his mouth, ruminates the spiritual food; and righteousness parts the hoof rightly, because it sanctifies us in this life, and sends us on our way to the world to come.

Public Spectacles.

The Instructor will not then bring us to public spectacles; nor inappropriately might one call the racecourse and the theatre " the seat of plagues;" [9] for there is evil counsel as against the Just One, [10] and therefore the assembly against Him is execrated. These assemblies, indeed, are full of confusion [11] and iniquity; and these pretexts for assembling are the cause of disorder — men and women assembling promiscuously for the sight of one another. In this respect the assembly has already shown itself bad: for when the eye is lascivious, [12] the desires grow warm; and the eyes that are accustomed to look impudently at one's neighbours during the leisure granted to them, inflame the amatory desires. Let spectacles, therefore, and plays that are full of scurrility and of abundant gossip, be forbidden. [13] For what base action is it that is

---

1 1 Pet. ii. 18.

2 1 Pet. iii 8. Clement has substituted ταπεινόφρονες for φιλόφρονες (courteous).

3 This passage has been variously amended and translated. The reading of the text has been adhered to, but ὀρθόνου has been coupled with what follows.

4 Sylburg suggests παριούσας (passing by) instead of παριζούσας.

5 κύβος, a die marked on all the six sides. [This prohibition would include cards in modern ethics.]

6 διὰ τῶν ἀστραγάλων. The ἀστράγαλοι were dice marked on four sides only. Clemens seems to use these terms here indifferently.

7 Lowth's conjecture of ἔρως instead of ἐρᾷ has been adopted.

8 Lev. xi. 13, 14; Deut. xiv. 12.

9 Ps. i. 1, Septuagint.

10 Acts iii. 14.

11 ἀναμιξίας adopted instead of the reading ἀμιξίας, which is plainly wrong.

12 λιχνευούσης on the authority of the Pal. ms. Nov. Reg. Bod.

13 [Jeremy Collier's Short View of the Immorality and Profaneness of the English Stage (London, 1698) and the discussions that followed belong to literature, and ought to be republished with historic notes.]

not exhibited in the theatres? And what shameless saying is it that is not brought forward by the buffoons? And those who enjoy the evil that is in them, stamp the clear images of it at home. And, on the other hand, those that are proof against these things, and unimpressible, will never make a stumble in regard to luxurious pleasures.

For if people shall say that they betake themselves to the spectacles as a pastime for recreation, I should say that the cities which make a serious business of pastime are not wise; for cruel contests for glory which have been so fatal are not sport. No more is senseless expenditure of money, nor are the riots that are occasioned by them sport. And ease of mind is not to be purchased by zealous pursuit of frivolities, for no one who has his senses will ever prefer what is pleasant to what is good.

Religion in Ordinary Life.

But it is said we do not all philosophize. Do we not all, then, follow after life? What sayest thou? How hast thou believed? How, pray, dost thou love God and thy neighbour, if thou dost not philosophize? And how dost thou love thyself, if thou dost not love life? It is said, I have not learned letters; but if thou hast not learned to read, thou canst not excuse thyself in the case of hearing, for it is not taught. And faith is the possession not of the wise according to the world, but of those according to God; and it is taught without letters; and its handbook, at once rude and divine, is called love — a spiritual book. It is in your power to listen to divine wisdom, ay, and to frame your life in accordance with it. Nay, you are not prohibited from conducting affairs in the world decorously according to God. Let not him who sells or buys aught name two prices for what he buys or sells; but stating the net price, and studying to speak the truth, if he get not his price, he gets the truth, and is rich in the possession of rectitude. But, above all, let an oath on account of what is sold be far from you; and let swearing, too, on account of other things be banished.

And in this way those who frequent the market-place and the shop philosophize. "For thou shalt not take the name of the LORD thy God in vain: for the LORD will not hold him guiltless that taketh His name in vain."[1]

But those who act contrary to these things — the avaricious, the liars, the hypocrites, those who make merchandise of the truth — the Lord cast out of His Father's court,[2] not willing that the holy house of God should be the house of unrighteous traffic either in words or in material things.

Going to Church.

Woman and man are to go to church[3] decently attired, with natural step, embracing silence, possessing unfeigned love, pure in body, pure in heart, fit to pray to God. Let the woman observe this, further. Let her be entirely covered, unless she happen to be at home. For that style of dress is grave, and protects from being gazed at. And she will never fall, who puts before her eyes modesty, and her shawl; nor will she invite another to fall into sin by uncovering her face. For this is the wish of the Word, since it is becoming for her to pray veiled.[4]

They say that the wife of Æneas, through excess of propriety, did not, even in her terror at the capture of Troy, uncover herself; but, though fleeing from the conflagration, remained veiled.

Out of Church.

Such ought those who are consecrated to Christ appear, and frame themselves in their whole life, as they fashion themselves in the church[5] for the sake of gravity; and to be, not to seem such — so meek, so pious, so loving. But now I know not how people change their fashions and manners with the place. As they say that polypi, assimilated to the rocks to which they adhere, are in colour such as they; so, laying aside the inspiration of the assembly, after their departure from it, they become like others with whom they associate. Nay, in laying aside the artificial mask of solemnity, they are proved to be what they secretly were. After having paid reverence to the discourse about God, they leave within [the church] what they have heard. And outside they foolishly amuse themselves with impious playing, and amatory quavering, occupied with flute-playing, and dancing, and intoxication, and all kinds of trash. They who sing thus, and sing in response, are those who before hymned immortality, — found at last wicked and wickedly singing this most pernicious palinode, "Let us eat and drink, for to-morrow we die." But not to-morrow in truth, but already, are these dead to God; burying their dead,[6] that is, sinking themselves down to death. The apostle very firmly assails them: "Be not deceived; neither adulterers, nor effeminate, nor abusers of themselves with mankind, nor thieves, nor covetous, nor drunkards, nor railers," and whatever else he adds to these, "shall inherit the kingdom of God."[7]

---

[1] Ex. xx. 7.
[2] In allusion to the cleansing of the temple (John ii. 13-17; Matt. xxi. 12, 13; Luke xix. 45, 46).

[3] [This early use of the word "church" for the place or house of worship, is to be noted. See Elucidation ii.]
[4] 1 Cor. xi. 5. [This helps to the due rendering of ἐξουσίαν ἐπὶ τῆς κεφαλῆς in 1 Cor. xi. 10.]
[5] [1 Cor. xi. 22. But I cannot say that the word ἐκκλησία is used for the place of Christian worship, even in this text, where it seems to be in antithesis with the dwelling-house.]
[6] Matt. viii. 22.
[7] 1 Cor. vi. 9, 10.

Love and the Kiss of Charity.

And if we are called to the kingdom of God, let us walk worthy of the kingdom, loving God and our neighbour. But love is not proved by a kiss, but by kindly feeling. But there are those, that do nothing but make the churches resound with a kiss,[1] not having love itself within. For this very thing, the shameless use of a kiss, which ought to be mystic, occasions foul suspicions and evil reports. The apostle calls the kiss holy.[2]

When the kingdom is worthily tested, we dispense the affection of the soul by a chaste and closed mouth, by which chiefly gentle manners are expressed.

But there is another unholy kiss, full of poison, counterfeiting sanctity. Do you not know that spiders, merely by touching the mouth, afflict men with pain? And often kisses inject the poison of licentiousness. It is then very manifest to us, that a kiss is not love. For the love meant is the love of God. "And this is the love of God," says John, "that we keep His commandments;"[3] not that we stroke each other on the mouth. "And His commandments are not grievous." But salutations of beloved ones in the ways, full as they are of foolish boldness, are characteristic of those who wish to be conspicuous to those without, and have not the least particle of grace. For if it is proper mystically "in the closet" to pray to God, it will follow that we are also to greet mystically our neighbour, whom we are commanded to love second similarly to God, within doors, "redeeming the time." "For we are the salt of the earth."[4] "Whosoever shall bless his friend early in the morning with a loud voice, shall be regarded not to differ from cursing."[5]

The Government of the Eyes.

But, above all, it seems right that we turn away from the sight of women. For it is sin not only to touch, but to look; and he who is rightly trained must especially avoid them. "Let thine eyes look straight, and thine eyelids wink right."[6] For while it is possible for one who looks to remain stedfast; yet care must be taken against falling. For it is possible for one who looks to slip; but it is impossible for one, who looks not, to lust. For it is not enough for the chaste to be pure; but they must give all diligence, to be beyond the range of censure, shutting out all ground of suspicion, in order to the consummation of chastity; so that we may not only be faithful, but appear worthy of trust. For this is also consequently to be guarded against, as the apostle says, "that no man should blame us; providing things honourable, not only in the sight of the Lord, but also in the sight of men."[7] "But turn away thine eyes from a graceful woman, and contemplate not another's beauty," says the Scripture.[8] And if you require the reason, it will further tell you, "For by the beauty of woman many have gone astray, and at it affection blazes up like fire;"[9] the affection which arises from the fire which we call love, leading to the fire which will never cease in consequence of sin.

CHAP. XII. — CONTINUATION: WITH TEXTS FROM SCRIPTURE.

I would counsel the married never to kiss their wives in the presence of their domestics. For Aristotle does not allow people to laugh to their slaves. And by no means must a wife be seen saluted in their presence. It is moreover better that, beginning at home with marriage, we should exhibit propriety in it. For it is the greatest bond of chastity, breathing forth pure pleasure. Very admirably the tragedy says: —

"Well! well! ladies, how is it, then, that among men,
Not gold, not empire, or luxury of wealth,
Conferred to such an extent signal delights,
As the right and virtuous disposition
Of a man of worth and a dutiful wife?"

Such injunctions of righteousness uttered by those who are conversant with worldly wisdom are not to be refused. Knowing, then, the duty of each, "pass the time of your sojourning here in fear: forasmuch as ye know that ye were not redeemed with corruptible things, such as silver or gold, from your vain conversation received by tradition from your fathers; but with the precious blood of Christ, as of a lamb without blemish and without spot."[10] "For," says Peter, "the time past of our life may suffice us to have wrought the will of the Gentiles, when we walked in lasciviousness, lusts, excess of wine, revellings, banquetings, and abominable idolatries."[11] We have as a limit the cross of the Lord, by which we are fenced and hedged about from our former sins. Therefore, being regenerated, let us fix ourselves to it in truth, and return to sobriety, and sanctify ourselves; "for the eyes of the LORD are on the righteous, and His ears are open to their prayer; but the face of the LORD is against them that do evil."[12] "And who is he that will harm us, if we

---

1 [The sexes sat apart in the primitive churches, and the kiss of peace was given by women only to women (Bunsen, *Hippol.*, iii. p. 15). Does the author, here, imply that *unholy* kissing had crept in? Among the Germans, even in our days, nothing is more common than to see men, not at all related, salute one another in this way. It was therefore all one with shaking hands, in the apostolic ordinance. For some very fine reflections on the *baiser de paix*, see De Maistre, *Soirées*, ii. p. 199, ed. Paris, 1850.]
2 Rom. xvi. 16.
3 1 John v. 3.
4 Matt. v. 13.
5 Prov. xxvii. 14.
6 Prov. iv. 25.
7 2 Cor. viii. 20, 21.
8 Ecclus. ix. 8.
9 Ecclus. ix. 8.
10 1 Pet. i. 17–19.
11 1 Pet. iv. 3.
12 Ps. xxxiv. 15, 16.

be followers of that which is good?"[1]—"us" for "you." But the best training is good order, which is perfect decorum, and stable and orderly power, which in action maintains consistence in what it does. If these things have been adduced by me with too great asperity, in order to effect the salvation which follows from your correction; they have been spoken also, says the Instructor, by me: "Since he who reproves with boldness is a peacemaker."[2] And if ye hear me, ye shall be saved. And if ye attend not to what is spoken, it is not my concern. And yet it is my concern thus: "For he desires the repentance rather than the death of a sinner."[3] "If ye shall hear me, ye shall eat the good of the land," the Instructor again says, calling by the appellation "the good of the land," beauty, wealth, health, strength, sustenance. For those things which are really good, are what "neither ear hath heard, nor hath ever entered into the heart"[4] respecting Him who is really King, and the realities truly good which await us. For He is the giver and the guard of good things. And with respect to their participation, He applies the same names of things in this world, the Word thus training in God the feebleness of men from sensible things to understanding.

What has to be observed at home, and how our life is to be regulated, the Instructor has abundantly declared. And the things which He is wont to say to children by the way,[5] while He conducts them to the Master, these He suggests, and adduces the Scriptures themselves in a compendious form, setting forth bare injunctions, accommodating them to the period of guidance, and assigning the interpretation of them to the Master.[6] For the intention of His law is to dissipate fear, emancipating free-will in order to faith. "Hear," He says, "O child," who art rightly instructed, the principal points of salvation. For I will disclose my ways, and lay before thee good commandments; by which thou wilt reach salvation. And I lead thee by the way of salvation. Depart from the paths of deceit.

"For the LORD knoweth the way of the righteous, and the way of the ungodly shall perish."[7] "Follow, therefore, O son, the good way which I shall describe, lending to me attentive ears." "And I will give to thee the treasures of darkness, hidden and unseen"[8] by the nations, but seen by us. And the treasures of wisdom are unfailing, in admiration of which the apostle says, "O the depth of the riches and the wisdom!"[9] And by one God are many treasures dispensed; some disclosed by the law, others by the prophets; some to the divine mouth, and others to the heptad of the spirit singing accordant. And the Lord being one, is the same Instructor by all these. Here is then a comprehensive precept, and an exhortation of life, all-embracing: "As ye would that men should do unto you, do ye likewise to them."[10] We may comprehend the commandments in two, as the Lord says, "Thou shalt love the Lord thy God with all thy heart, with all thy soul, and with all thy strength; and thy neighbour as thyself." Then from these He infers, "on this hang the law and the prophets."[11] Further, to him that asked, "What good thing shall I do, that I may inherit eternal life?" He answered, "Thou knowest the commandments?" And on him replying Yea, He said, "This do, and thou shalt be saved." Especially conspicuous is the love of the Instructor set forth in various salutary commandments, in order that the discovery may be readier, from the abundance and arrangement of the Scriptures. We have the Decalogue[12] given by Moses, which, indicating by an elementary principle, simple and of one kind, defines the designation of sins in a way conducive to salvation: "Thou shalt not commit adultery. Thou shalt not worship idols. Thou shalt not corrupt boys. Thou shalt not steal. Thou shalt not bear false witness. Honour thy father and thy mother."[13] And so forth. These things are to be observed, and whatever else is commanded in reading the Bible. And He enjoins on us by Isaiah: "Wash you, and make you clean. Put away iniquities from your souls before mine eyes. Learn to do well. Seek judgment. Deliver the wronged. Judge for the orphan, and justify the widow. And come, and let us reason together, saith the Lord."[14] And we shall find many examples also in other places, — as, for instance, respecting prayer: "Good works are an acceptable prayer to the Lord," says the Scripture.[15] And the manner of prayer is described. "If thou seest," it is said, "the naked, cover him; and thou shalt not overlook those who belong to thy seed. Then shall thy light spring forth early, and thy healing shall spring up quickly; and thy righteousness shall go before thee, and the glory of God shall encompass thee." What, then, is the fruit of such prayer? "Then shalt thou call, and God will hear thee; whilst thou art yet speaking, He will say, I am here."[16]

In regard to fasting it is said, "Wherefore do

1 1 Pet. iii. 13.
2 Prov. x. 10, Sept.
3 Ezek. xviii. 23.
4 1 Cor. ii. 9.
5 [Here the *pædagogue* is the child-guide, leading to the Teacher.]
6 [Important foot-note, Kaye, p. 105.]
7 Ps. i. 6.
8 Isa. xlv. 3.
9 Rom. xi. 33.
10 Luke vi. 31.
11 Matt. xxii. 37, 39, 40.
12 [See Irenæus, vol. i. p. 482, this series. *Stromata*, vi. 360.]
13 Ex. xx.: Deut. v.
14 Isa. i. 16, 17, 18.
15 Where, no one knows.
16 Isa. lviii. 7, 8, 9.

ye fast to me? saith the Lord. Is it such a fast that I have chosen, even a day for a man to humble his soul? Thou shalt not bend thy neck like a circle, and spread sackcloth and ashes under thee. Not thus shall ye call it an acceptable fast."

What means a fast, then? "Lo, this is the fast which I have chosen, saith the Lord. Loose every band of wickedness. Dissolve the knots of oppressive contracts. Let the oppressed go free, and tear every unjust bond. Break thy bread to the hungry; and lead the houseless poor into thy house. If thou see the naked, cover him."[1] About sacrifices too: "To what purpose is the multitude of your sacrifices to me? saith the Lord. I am full of burnt-offerings and of rams; and the fat of lambs, and the blood of bulls and kids I do not wish; nor that ye should come to appear before me. Who hath required this at your hands? You shall no more tread my court. If ye bring fine flour, the vain oblation is an abomination to me. Your new moons and your sabbaths I cannot away with."[2] How, then, shall I sacrifice to the Lord? "The sacrifice of the Lord is," He says, "a broken heart."[3] How, then, shall I crown myself, or anoint with ointment, or offer incense to the Lord? "An odour of a sweet fragrance," it is said,[4] "is the heart that glorifies Him who made it." These are the crowns and sacrifices, aromatic odours, and flowers of God.

Further, in respect to forbearance. "If thy brother," it is said, "sin against thee, rebuke him; and if he repent, forgive him. If he sin against thee seven times in a day, and turn to thee the seventh time, and say, I repent, forgive him."[5] Also to the soldiers, by John, He commands, "to be content with their wages only;" and to the publicans, "to exact no more than is appointed." To the judges He says, "Thou shalt not show partiality in judgment. For gifts blind the eyes of those who see, and corrupt just words. Rescue the wronged."

And to householders: "A possession which is acquired with iniquity becomes less."[6]

Also of "love." "Love," He says, "covers a multitude of sins."[7]

And of civil government: "Render to Cæsar the things which are Cæsar's; and unto God the things which are God's."[8]

Of swearing and the remembrance of injuries: "Did I command your fathers, when they went out of Egypt, to offer burnt-offerings and sacrifices? But I commanded them, Let none of you bear malice in his heart against his neighbour, or love a false oath."[9]

The liars and the proud, too, He threatens; the former thus: "Woe to them that call bitter sweet, and sweet bitter;" and the latter: "Woe unto them that are wise in their own eyes, and prudent in their own sight."[10] "For he that humbleth himself shall be exalted, and he that exalteth himself shall be humbled."[11]

And "the merciful" He blesses, "for they shall obtain mercy."

Wisdom pronounces anger a wretched thing, because "it will destroy the wise."[12] And now He bids us "love our enemies, bless them that curse us, and pray for them that despitefully use us." And He says: "If any one strike thee on the one cheek, turn to him the other also; and if any one take away thy coat, hinder him not from taking thy cloak also."[13]

Of faith He says: "Whatsoever ye shall ask in prayer, believing, ye shall receive."[14] "To the unbelieving nothing is trustworthy," according to Pindar.

Domestics, too, are to be treated like ourselves; for they are human beings, as we are. For God is the same to free and bond, if you consider.

Such of our brethren as transgress, we must not punish, but rebuke. "For he that spareth the rod hateth his son."[15]

Further, He banishes utterly love of glory, saying, "Woe to you, Pharisees! for ye love the chief seat in the synagogues, and greetings in the markets."[16] But He welcomes the repentance of the sinner — loving repentance — which follows sins. For this Word of whom we speak alone is sinless. For to sin is natural and common to all. But to return [to God] after sinning is characteristic not of any man, but only of a man of worth.

Respecting liberality He said: "Come to me, ye blessed, inherit the kingdom prepared for you from the foundation of the world: for I was an hungry, and ye gave Me meat; I was thirsty, and ye gave Me drink; I was a stranger, and ye took Me in; naked, and ye clothed Me; sick, and ye visited Me; in prison, and ye came unto Me." And when have we done any of these things to the Lord?

The Instructor Himself will say again, loving to refer to Himself the kindness of the brethren, "Inasmuch as ye have done it to these least, ye have done it to Me. And these shall go away into everlasting life."[17]

---

[1] Isa. lviii. 6, 7.
[2] Isa. i. 11–14.
[3] Ps. li. 17.
[4] Not in Scripture. [Irenæus, iv. 17, vol. i. 444, this series.]
[5] Luke xvii. 3, 4.
[6] Prov. xiii. 11.
[7] 1 Pet. iv. 8.
[8] Matt. xxii. 21; Mark xii. 17; Luke xx. 25.

[9] In Jer. vii. 22, 23, and Zech. viii. we find the substance of what Clement gives here.
[10] Isa. v. 20, 21.
[11] Luke xiv. 11, xviii. 14.
[12] Prov. xvi. Sept.
[13] Matt. v. 40; Luke vi. 27–29.
[14] Matt. xxi. 22.
[15] Prov. xiii. 24.
[16] Luke xi. 43.
[17] Matt. xxv. 34–36, 40, 46.

Such are the laws of the Word, the consolatory words not on tables of stone which were written by the finger of the Lord, but inscribed on men's hearts, on which alone they can remain imperishable. Wherefore the tablets of those who had hearts of stone are broken, that the faith of the children may be impressed on softened hearts.

However, both the laws served the Word for the instruction of humanity, both that given by Moses and that by the apostles. What, therefore, is the nature of the training by the apostles, appears to me to require to be treated of. Under this head, I, or rather the Instructor by me,[1] will recount; and I shall again set before you the precepts themselves, as it were in the germ.

"Putting away lying, speak every man truth with his neighbour: for we are members one of another. Let not the sun go down upon your wrath; neither give place to the devil. Let him that stole steal no more: but rather let him labour, working with his hands the thing which is good, that he may have to give to him that needeth. Let all bitterness, and wrath, and anger, and clamour, and evil-speaking, be put away from you, with all malice: and be ye kind one to another, tender-hearted, forgiving one another, as God in Christ hath forgiven you. Be therefore wise,[2] followers of God, as dear children; and walk in love, as Christ also hath loved us. Let wives be subject to their own husbands, as to the Lord. And let husbands love their wives, as Christ also hath loved the Church." Let those who are yoked together love one another "as their own bodies." "Children, be obedient to your parents. Parents, provoke not your children to wrath; but bring them up in the nurture and admonition of the Lord. Servants, be obedient to those that are your masters according to the flesh, with fear and trembling, in the singleness of your hearts, as unto Christ; with good-will from the soul doing service. And, ye masters, treat your servants well, forbearing threatening: knowing that both their and your Lord is in heaven; and there is no respect of persons with Him."[3]

"If we live in the Spirit, let us walk in the Spirit. Let us not be desirous of vainglory, provoking one another, envying one another. Bear ye one another's burdens, and so fulfil the law of Christ. Be not deceived; God is not mocked. Let us not be weary in well-doing: for in due time we shall reap, if we faint not."[4]

"Be at peace among yourselves. Now we admonish you, brethren, warn them who are unruly, comfort the feeble-minded, support the weak, be patient toward all men. See that none render evil for evil to any man. Quench not the Spirit. Despise not prophesyings. Prove all things: hold fast that which is good. Abstain from every form of evil."[5]

"Continue in prayer, watching thereunto with thanksgiving. Walk in wisdom towards them that are without, redeeming the time. Let your speech be always with grace, seasoned with salt, that ye may know how ye ought to answer every man."[6]

"Nourish yourselves up in the words of faith. Exercise yourselves unto godliness: for bodily exercise profiteth little; but godliness is profitable for all things, having the promise of the life which now is, and that which is to come."[7]

"Let those who have faithful masters not despise them, because they are brethren; but rather do them service, because they are faithful."[8]

"He that giveth, let him do it with simplicity; he that ruleth, with diligence; he that showeth mercy, with cheerfulness. Let love be without dissimulation. Abhor that which is evil; cleave to that which is good. Be kindly affectioned one to another with brotherly love, in honour preferring one another. Not slothful in business; fervent in spirit, serving the Lord. Rejoicing in hope; patient in tribulation; continuing instant in prayer. Given to hospitality; communicating to the necessities of the saints."[9]

Such are a few injunctions out of many, for the sake of example, which the Instructor, running over the divine Scriptures, sets before His children; by which, so to speak, vice is cut up by the roots, and iniquity is circumscribed.

Innumerable commands such as these are written in the holy Bible appertaining to chosen persons, some to presbyters, some to bishops, some to deacons, others to widows,[10] of whom we shall have another opportunity of speaking. Many things spoken in enigmas, many in parables, may benefit such as fall in with them. But it is not my province, says the Instructor, to teach these any longer. But we need a Teacher of the exposition of those sacred words, to whom we must direct our steps.

'And now, in truth, it is time for me to cease from my instruction, and for you to listen to the Teacher.[11] And He, receiving you who have been trained up in excellent discipline, will teach you the oracles. To noble purpose has

---

[1] δι ἐμαυτοῦ. The reading here adopted is found in Bod. and Reg.
[2] φρόνιμοι, not found in Eph. v. 1.
[3] Eph. iv. 25-29, v. 1, 2, 22, 25, vi. 1, 4-9.
[4] Gal. v. 25, 26, vi. 2, 7, 9.

[5] 1 Thess. v. 13-15, 19-22.
[6] Col. iv. 2, 5, 9.
[7] 1 Tim. iv. 6-8.
[8] 1 Tim. vi. 2.
[9] Rom. xii. 8-13.
[10] [Consult Bunsen's *Handbook*, book iv. pp. 75-82. Thus did primitive Christianity labour to uproot the social estate of heathenism.]
[11] That is, he who undertakes the instruction of those that are full-grown, as Clemens does in the *Stromata*. [Where see his *esoteric* doctrine.]

the Church sung, and the Bridegroom also, the only Teacher, the good Counsel, of the good Father, the true Wisdom, the Sanctuary of knowledge. "And He is the propitiation for our sins," as John says; Jesus, who heals both our body and soul — which are the proper man. "And not for our sins only, but also for the whole world. And by this we know that we know Him, if we keep His commandments. He that saith, I know Him, and keepeth not His commandments, is a liar; and the truth is not in Him. But whoso keepeth His word, in him verily is the love of God perfected. Hereby know we that we are in Him. He that saith he abideth in Him, ought himself to walk even as He also walked." [1] O nurslings of His blessed training! let us complete the fair face of the church; and let us run as children to our good mother. And if we become listeners to the Word, let us glorify the blessed dispensation by which man is trained and sanctified as a child of God, and has his conversation in heaven, being trained from earth, and there receives the Father, whom he learns to know on earth. The Word both does and teaches all things, and trains in all things.

A horse is guided by a bit, and a bull is guided by a yoke, and a wild beast is caught in a noose. But man is transformed by the Word, by whom wild beasts are tamed, and fishes caught, and birds drawn down. He it is, in truth, who fashions the bit for the horse, the yoke for the bull, the noose for the wild beast, the rod for the fish, the snare for the bird. He both manages the state and tills the ground; commands, and helps, and creates the universe.

> "There were figured earth, and sky, and sea,
> The ever-circling sun, and full-orbed moon,
> And all the signs that crown the vault of heaven." [2]

O divine works! O divine commands! "Let this water undulate within itself; let this fire restrain its wrath; let this air wander into ether; and this earth be consolidated, and acquire motion! When I want to form man, I want matter, and have matter in the elements. I dwell with what I have formed. If you know me, the fire will be your slave."

Such is the Word, such is the Instructor, the Creator of the world and of man: and of Himself, now the world's Instructor, by whose command we and the universe subsist, and await judgment. "For it is not he who brings a stealthy vocal word to men," as Bacchylidis says, "who shall be the Word of Wisdom;" but "the blameless, the pure, and faultless sons of God," according to Paul, "in the midst of a crooked and perverse generation, to shine as lights in the world." [3]

All that remains therefore now, in such a celebration of the Word as this, is that we address to the Word our prayer.

PRAYER TO THE PÆDAGOGUS.

Be gracious, O Instructor, to us Thy children, Father, Charioteer of Israel, Son and Father, both in One, O Lord. Grant to us who obey Thy precepts, that we may perfect the likeness of the image, and with all our power know Him who is the good God and not a harsh judge. And do Thou Thyself cause that all of us who have our conversation in Thy peace, who have been translated into Thy commonwealth, having sailed tranquilly over the billows of sin, may be wafted in calm by Thy Holy Spirit, by the ineffable wisdom, by night and day to the perfect day; and giving thanks may praise, and praising thank the Alone Father and Son, Son and Father, the Son, Instructor and Teacher, with the Holy Spirit, all in One, in whom is all, for whom all is One, for whom is eternity, whose members we all are, whose glory the æons [4] are; for the All-good, All-lovely, All-wise, All-just One. To whom be glory both now and for ever. Amen.

And since the Instructor, by translating us into His Church, has united us to Himself, the teaching and all-surveying Word, it were right that, having got to this point, we should offer to the Lord the reward of due thanksgiving — praise suitable to His fair instruction.

A HYMN TO CHRIST THE SAVIOUR.

COMPOSED BY ST. CLEMENT.[5]

I.

Bridle of colts untamed,
    Over our wills presiding;
Wing of unwandering birds,
    Our flight securely guiding.
Rudder of youth unbending,
    Firm against adverse shock;
Shepherd, with wisdom tending
    Lambs of the royal flock:
Thy simple children bring
In one, that they may sing
In solemn lays
Their hymns of praise
With guileless lips to Christ their King.

---

[1] 1 John ii. 2-6.
[2] *Iliad*, xviii. 483-485; spoken of Vulcan making the shield of Achilles.

[3] Phil. ii 15.
[4] Αἰῶνες, "celestial spirits and angels." — GRABE, in a note on Bull's *Defence of the Nicene Creed*. [I wish a more definite reference had been furnished by the learned translator. Even Kaye's reference is not precise. Consulting Grabe's annotations in vain, I was then obliged to go through the foot-notes, where, at last (vol. v. part i. p. 246), I found in comparative obscurity Grabe's language. It may be rendered: "These words I think should be thus construed — *cujus gloria sunt sæcula* — whose glory are the *heavenly spirits* or angels. Concerning which signification of τῶν αἰώνων, note what I have said among divers annotations on Irenæus, p. 32. ed. Benedict."]
[5] [Elucidation III.] The translator has done what he could to render this hymn literally. He has been obliged, however, to add somewhat to it in the way of expansion, for otherwise it would have been impossible to secure anything approaching the flow of English versification. The original is in many parts a mere string of epithets, which no ingenuity could render in rhymed verse without some additions.

II.

King of saints, almighty Word
Of the Father highest Lord;
Wisdom's head and chief;
Assuagement of all grief;
Lord of all time and space,
Jesus, Saviour of our race;
Shepherd, who dost us keep;
    Husbandman, who tillest,
Bit to restrain us, Rudder
    To guide us as Thou willest;
Of the all-holy flock celestial wing;
Fisher of men, whom Thou to life dost bring;
    From evil sea of sin,
      And from the billowy strife,
Gathering pure fishes in,
    Caught with sweet bait of life:
Lead us, Shepherd of the sheep,
    Reason-gifted, holy One;
King of youths, whom Thou dost keep,
    So that they pollution shun:
Steps of Christ, celestial Way;
    Word eternal, Age unending;
Life that never can decay;
    Fount of mercy, virtue-sending;
Life august of those who raise
Unto God their hymn of praise,
              Jesus Christ!

III.

Nourished by the milk of heaven,
To our tender palates given;
Milk of wisdom from the breast
Of that bride of grace exprest;
By a dewy spirit filled
From fair Reason's breast distilled;
Let us sucklings join to raise
With pure lips our hymns of praise
As our grateful offering,
Clean and pure, to Christ our King.
Let us, with hearts undefiled,
Celebrate the mighty Child.
We, Christ-born, the choir of peace;
    We, the people of His love,
Let us sing, nor ever cease,
    To the God of peace above.

We subjoin the following literal translation of the foregoing hymn: —

Bridle of untamed colts, Wing of unwandering birds, sure Helm of babes,[1] Shepherd of royal lambs, assemble Thy simple children to praise holily, to hymn guilelessly with innocent mouths, Christ the guide of children. O King of saints, all-subduing Word of the most high Father, Ruler of wisdom, Support of sorrows, that rejoicest in the ages,[2] Jesus, Saviour of the human race, Shepherd, Husbandman, Helm, Bridle, Heavenly Wing of the all-holy flock, Fisher of men who are saved, catching the chaste fishes with sweet life from the hateful wave of a sea of vices, — Guide [us], Shepherd of rational sheep; guide unharmed children, O holy King,[3] O footsteps of Christ, O heavenly way, perennial Word, immeasurable Age, Eternal Light, Fount of mercy, performer of virtue; noble [is the] life of those who hymn God, O Christ Jesus, heavenly milk of the sweet breasts of the graces of the Bride, pressed out of Thy wisdom. Babes nourished with tender mouths, filled with the dewy spirit of the rational pap, let us sing together simple praises, true hymns to Christ [our] King, holy fee for the teaching of life; let us sing in simplicity the powerful Child. O choir of peace, the Christ-begotten, O chaste people, let us sing together [4] the God of peace.[5]

TO THE PAEDAGOGUS.

Teacher, to Thee a chaplet I present,
Woven of words culled from the spotless mead,
Where Thou dost feed Thy flocks; like to the bee,
That skilful worker, which from many a flower
Gathers its treasures, that she may convey
A luscious offering to the master's hand.
Though but the least, I am Thy servant still,
(Seemly is praise to Thee for Thy behests).
O King, great Giver of good gifts to men,
Lord of the good, Father, of all the Maker,
Who heaven and heaven's adornment, by Thy word
Divine fitly disposed, alone didst make;
Who broughtest forth the sunshine and the day;
Who didst appoint their courses to the stars,
And how the earth and sea their place should keep;
And when the seasons, in their circling course,
Winter and summer, spring and autumn, each [6]
Should come, according to well-ordered plan;
Out of a confused heap who didst create
This ordered sphere, and from the shapeless mass
Of matter didst the universe adorn; —
Grant to me life, and be that life well spent,
Thy grace enjoying; let me act and speak
In all things as Thy Holy Scriptures teach; [7]
Thee and Thy co-eternal Word, All-wise,
From Thee proceeding, ever may I praise;
Give me nor poverty nor wealth, but what is meet,
Father, in life, and then life's happy close.[8]

---

[1] Or, "ships:" νηῶν, instead of νηπίων, has been suggested as better sense and better metre.

[2] Or, "rejoicing in eternity."

[3] By altering the punctuation, we can translate thus: "Guide, O holy King, Thy children safely along the footsteps of Christ."

[4] The word used here is ψάλωμεν, originally signifying, "Let us celebrate on a stringed instrument." Whether it is so used here or not, may be matter of dispute.

[5] [The holy virgin of Nazareth is the author of the first Christian hymn, *The Magnificat*. It is a sequel to the psalms of her father David, and interprets them. To Clement of Alexandria belongs the praise of leading the choir of uninspired Christian poets, whom he thus might seem to invoke to carry on the strain through all time.]

[6] [The hymn suffixed to Thomson's *Seasons* might seem to have been suggested by this ancient example of praise to the Maker. But, to *feel* this hymn, we must reflect upon its superiority, in a moral point of view, to all the Attic Muse had ever produced before.]

[7] [The Scriptures are the rule of faith.]

[8] [Kaye's careful criticism of M. Barbeyrac's captious complaints against Clement, are specially instructive. p. 109.]

ELUCIDATIONS.

I.

(Pædagogue, book ii. cap. 3, p. 247.)

THIS fine paragraph is in many ways interesting. The tourist who has visited the catacombs, is familiar, among tokens of the first rude art of Christians, with relics of various articles, realizing this idea of Clement's, that even our furniture should be distinctively Christian. In Pompeii, one finds lamps and other vessels marked by heathenish devices, some of them gross and revolting. On the contrary, these Christian utensils bear the sacred monograms XP, AΩ, or the figure of the fish, conveying to the user, by the letters of the Greek word for a fish (IXΘΥΣ), the initials of the words "Jesus Christ, Son of God, The Saviour." Often we have the anchor, the palm-branch, or the cross itself. But I never looked at one of those Christian lamps without imagining its owner, singing, as it was lighted, the eventide hymn (of which see Elucidation III.), and reciting probably, therewith, the text, "Let your loins be girded, and your lamps burning," etc. For a valuable elucidation of subjects illustrated by Christian art, see *Testimony of the Catacombs*, by the late Wharton B. Marriott (London, Hatchards, 1870).

II.

(Book iii. Going to Church. p. 290, *supra*.)

Frequent references become necessary, at this point, to the ecclesiastical usages of the early Christians. These have been largely treated of by the great Anglican divines, whose works are recognised as part of the standard literature of Christendom; but the nature of this publication seems to impose on me the duty of choosing from external sources, rather than from authors who have been more or less associated with the controversies of our great "Anglo-Saxon" family. Happily the writings of the late Dr. Bunsen supply us with all that is requisite of this sort. In that very curious and characteristic medley, *Hippolytus and His Age*, he has gathered into a convenient form nearly every point which requires antiquarian elucidation, under the title of *The Church and Home Book of the Ancient Christians*. Its contents he professes to have rescued "from the rubbish in which they were enveloped for centuries, and disencumbered of the fraud and misunderstanding by which they are defaced." Now, while by no means satisfied with this work myself, it affords an interesting specimen of the conclusions to which an earnest and scholarly mind has been brought, in the course of original and industrious research. It is the more interesting, as illustrating a conviction, which he expresses elsewhere, that, in shaping "the Church of the future," all Christians must revert to these records of primitive antiquity, as of practical interest for our own times. The proverbial faults of its author are indeed conspicuous in this work, which, though the product of a mere inquirer, is presented to us with entire self-reliance, as if he were competent to pronounce upon all questions with something like pontifical infallibility. It is also greatly mixed up with his personal theories, which are always interesting, but rarely satisfactory to his readers. In spite of all this, he has brought together, in a condensed form, what is undoubtedly the result of patient investigation. It is the rather useful, because it is the work of a genuine disciple of Niebuhr, who doubts and questions at every step, and who always suspects a fraud. He is committed, by his religious persuasions, to no system whatever, with respect to such matters, and he professes to have produced a manual of Christian antiquity, entirely scientific; that is to say, wholly impartial, indifferent as to consequences, and following only the lead of truth and evidence. In my references to Bunsen, therefore, let it be understood, that, without accepting him as my own master, I yet wish to respect his opinion and to commend his performance to the candid investigation of others.

III.

The one ancient hymn, not strictly liturgical, which probably was not new even to Clement, and to which we have already made reference once or twice, is the following, which we give from Bunsen. He calls it " The Evening Hymn of the Greek Christians," but it was not confined to the Greeks any more than was the Greek of the Gospels and the Creeds. Its proper name is "The Eventide Hymn," or "The Hymn for the Lighting of the Lamps," and was doubtless uttered in the family at " candlelight," as we say a grace before meat. It is thus rendered :—

HYMN.

Serene light of the Holy Glory
Of the Father Everlasting,
Jesus Christ:
Having come to the setting of the sun,
And seeing the evening light,
We praise the Father and the Son,
And the Holy Spirit of God.
It behooveth to praise Thee,
At all times with holy songs,
Son of God, who hast given life;
Therefore the world glorifieth Thee.

The modern Italians, at sunset, recite the *Ave Maria*, which has been imposed upon them by mediæval Rome. Nothing but the coincidence of the hour reminds us of the ancient hymn which it has superseded ; and a healthy mind, one would think, would note the contrast. This pure " hymn to Christ as God," and to the Godhead in unity, gives place to an act of worship addressed to the creature, more than to the Creator. One might indeed call this *Ave Maria* the eventide hymn of modern Italy ; but the scatter-brain processes of Dr. Bunsen come out in the strange reversal of thought, by which he would throw back the utterly incongruous title of its Italian substitute upon a primitive hymn to the Trinity, — " the Ave-Maria hymn, *as we might call it* from the present Italian custom," etc. The strange confusion of ideas which constantly characterizes this author, whenever some association, however remote, strikes his fancy, is well illustrated by this instance. Let it serve as a caution in following his lead. See *Hippolytus* (vol. iii. pp. 68, 138, etc.) and also Routh (*Reliquiæ*, vol. iii. pp. 515–520). Concerning the morning hymn, *Gloria in Excelsis*, which Dr. Bunsen gives from the Alexandrian MS., and to which reference is made in his *Analecta Ante-Nicæna* (iii. 86), see Warren's *Celtic Liturgy* (p. 197, and index references. *Ed.* Oxford, 1881).

THE STROMATA, OR MISCELLANIES

BOOK I

[*Wants the beginning*] . . . . that you may read them under your hand, and may be able to preserve them. Whether written compositions are not to be left behind at all ; or if they are, by whom ? And if the former, what need there is for written compositions ? and if the latter, is the composition of them to be assigned to earnest men, or the opposite ? It were certainly ridiculous for one to disapprove of the writing of earnest men, and approve of those, who are not such, engaging in the work of composition. Theopompus and Timæus, who composed fables and slanders, and Epicurus the leader of atheism, and Hipponax and Archilochus, are to be allowed to write in their own shameful manner. But he who proclaims the truth is to be prevented from leaving behind him what is to benefit posterity. It is a good thing, I reckon, to leave to posterity good children. This is the case with children of our bodies. But words are the progeny of the soul. Hence we call those who have instructed us, fathers. Wisdom is a communicative and philanthropic thing. Accordingly, Solomon says, "My son, if thou receive the saying of my commandment, and hide it with thee, thine ear shall hear wisdom."[2] He points out that the word that is sown is hidden in the soul of the learner, as in the earth, and this is spiritual planting. Wherefore also he adds, "And thou shalt apply thine heart to understanding, and apply it for the admonition of thy son." For soul, methinks, joined with soul, and spirit with spirit, in the sowing of the word, will make that which is sown grow and germinate. And every one who is instructed, is in respect of subjection the son of his instructor. "Son," says he, "forget not my laws."[3]

And if knowledge belong not to all (set an ass to the lyre, as the proverb goes), yet written compositions are for the many. "Swine, for instance, delight in dirt more than in clean water." "Wherefore," says the Lord, "I speak to them in parables : because seeing, they see not ; and hearing, they hear not, and do not understand ; "[4] not as if the Lord caused the ignorance : for it were impious to think so. But He prophetically exposed this ignorance, that existed in them, and intimated that they would not understand the things spoken. And now the Saviour shows Himself, out of His abundance, dispensing goods to His servants according to the ability of the recipient, that they may augment them by exercising activity, and then returning to reckon with them ; when, approving of those that had increased His money, those faithful in little, and commanding them to have the charge over many things, He bade them enter into the joy of the Lord. But to him who had hid the money, entrusted to him to be given out at interest, and had given it back as he had received it, without increase, He said, "Thou wicked and slothful servant, thou oughtest to have given my money to the bankers, and at my coming I should have received mine own." Wherefore the useless servant "shall be cast into outer darkness."[5] "Thou, therefore, be strong," says Paul, "in the grace that is in Christ Jesus. And the things which thou hast heard of me among many witnesses, the same commit thou to faithful men, who shall be able to teach others also."[6] And again : "Study to show thyself approved unto God, a workman that needeth not to be ashamed, rightly dividing the word of truth."

If, then, both proclaim the Word — the one

---

[1] [It is impossible to illustrate the *Stromata* by needed notes, on the plan of this publication. It would double the size of the work, and require time and such scholarship as belongs to experts. Important matters are briefly discussed at the end of each book. Elucidation I.]
[2] Prov. ii. 1, 2.
[3] Prov. iii. 1.
[4] Matt. xiii. 13.
[5] Matt. xviii. 32 ; Luke xix. 22 ; Matt. xxv. 30.
[6] 2 Tim. ii. 1, 2.

by writing, the other by speech — are not both then to be approved, making, as they do, faith active by love? It is by one's own fault that he does not choose what is best; God is free of blame. As to the point in hand, it is the business of some to lay out the word at interest, and of others to test it, and either choose it or not. And the judgment is determined within themselves. But there is that species of knowledge which is characteristic of the herald, and that which is, as it were, characteristic of a messenger, and it is serviceable in whatever way it operates, both by the hand and tongue. "For he that soweth to the Spirit, shall of the Spirit reap life everlasting. And let us not be weary in well-doing."[1] On him who by Divine Providence meets in with it, it confers the very highest advantages, — the beginning of faith, readiness for adopting a right mode of life, the impulse towards the truth, a movement of inquiry, a trace of knowledge; in a word, it gives the means of salvation. And those who have been rightly reared in the words of truth, and received provision for eternal life, wing their way to heaven. Most admirably, therefore, the apostle says, "In everything approving ourselves as the servants of God; as poor, and yet making many rich; as having nothing, yet possessing all things. Our mouth is opened to you."[2] "I charge thee," he says, writing to Timothy, "before God, and Christ Jesus, and the elect angels, that thou observe these things, without preferring one before another, doing nothing by partiality."[3]

Both must therefore test themselves: the one, if he is qualified to speak and leave behind him written records; the other, if he is in a right state to hear and read: as also some in the dispensation of the Eucharist, according to[4] custom, enjoin that each one of the people individually should take his part. One's own conscience is best for choosing accurately or shunning. And its firm foundation is a right life, with suitable instruction. But the imitation of those who have already been proved, and who have led correct lives, is most excellent for the understanding and practice of the commandments. "So that whosoever shall eat the bread and drink the cup of the Lord unworthily, shall be guilty of the body and blood of the Lord. But let a man examine himself, and so let him eat of the bread and drink of the cup."[5] It therefore follows, that every one of those who undertake to promote the good of their neighbours, ought to consider whether he has betaken himself to teaching rashly and out of rivalry to any; if his communication of the word is out of vainglory; if the

only reward he reaps is the salvation of those who hear, and if he speaks not in order to win favour: if so, he who speaks by writings escapes the reproach of mercenary motives. "For neither at any time used we flattering words, as ye know," says the apostle, "nor a cloak of covetousness. God is witness. Nor of men sought we glory, neither of you, nor yet of others, when we might have been burdensome as the apostles of Christ. But we were gentle among you, even as a nurse cherisheth her children."[6]

In the same way, therefore, those who take part in the divine words, ought to guard against betaking themselves to this, as they would to the building of cities, to examine them out of curiosity; that they do not come to the task for the sake of receiving worldly things, having ascertained that they who are consecrated to Christ are given to communicate the necessaries of life. But let such be dismissed as hypocrites. But if any one wishes not to seem, but to be righteous, to him it belongs to know the things which are best. If, then, "the harvest is plenteous, but the labourers few," it is incumbent on us "to pray" that there may be as great abundance of labourers as possible.[7]

But the husbandry is twofold, — the one unwritten, and the other written. And in whatever way the Lord's labourer sow the good wheat, and grow and reap the ears, he shall appear a truly divine husbandman. "Labour," says the Lord, "not for the meat which perisheth, but for that which endureth to everlasting life."[8] And nutriment is received both by bread and by words. And truly "blessed are the peace-makers,"[9] who instructing those who are at war in their life and errors here, lead them back to the peace which is in the Word, and nourish for the life which is according to God, by the distribution of the bread, those "that hunger after righteousness." For each soul has its own proper nutriment; some growing by knowledge and science, and others feeding on the Hellenic philosophy, the whole of which, like nuts, is not eatable. "And he that planteth and he that watereth," "being ministers" of Him "that gives the increase, are one" in the ministry. "But every one shall receive his own reward, according to his own work. For we are God's husbandmen, God's husbandry. Ye are God's building,"[10] according to the apostle. Wherefore the hearers are not permitted to apply the test of comparison. Nor is the word, given for investigation, to be committed to those who have been reared in the arts of all kinds of words, and in the power of inflated attempts at proof; whose

1 Gal. vi. 8, 9.
2 2 Cor. vi. 4, 10, 11.
3 1 Tim. v. 21.
4 [To be noted as apparently allowed, yet exceptionally so.]
5 1 Cor. xi. 27, 28.

6 1 Thess. ii. 5, 6, 7.
7 Matt. ix. 37, 38; Luke x. 2.
8 John vi. 27.
9 Matt. v. 9.
10 1 Cor. iii. 8, 9.

minds are already pre-occupied, and have not been previously emptied. But whoever chooses to banquet on faith, is stedfast for the reception of the divine words, having acquired already faith as a power of judging, according to reason. Hence ensues to him persuasion in abundance. And this was the meaning of that saying of prophecy, "If ye believe not, neither shall ye understand." [1] "As, then, we have opportunity, let us do good to all, especially to the household of faith." [2] And let each of these, according to the blessed David, sing, giving thanks. "Thou shalt sprinkle me with hyssop, and I shall be cleansed. Thou shalt wash me, and I shall be whiter than the snow. Thou shalt make me to hear gladness and joy, and the bones which have been humbled shall rejoice. Turn Thy face from my sins. Blot out mine iniquities. Create in me a clean heart, O God, and renew a right spirit in my inward parts. Cast me not away from Thy face, and take not Thy Holy Spirit from me. Restore to me the joy of Thy salvation, and establish me with Thy princely spirit." [3]

He who addresses those who are present before him, both tests them by time, and judges by his judgment, and from the others distinguishes him who can hear; watching the words, the manners, the habits, the life, the motions, the attitudes, the look, the voice; the road, the rock, the beaten path, the fruitful land, the wooded region, the fertile and fair and cultivated spot, that is able to multiply the seed. But he that speaks through books, consecrates himself before God, crying in writing thus: Not for gain, not for vainglory, not to be vanquished by partiality, nor enslaved by fear nor elated by pleasure; but only to reap the salvation of those who read, which he does, not at present participate in, but awaiting in expectation the recompense which will certainly be rendered by Him, who has promised to bestow on the labourers the reward that is meet. But he who is enrolled in the number of men [4] ought not to desire recompense. For he that vaunts his good services, receives glory as his reward. And he who does any duty for the sake of recompense, is he not held fast in the custom of the world, either as one who has done well, hastening to receive a reward, or as an evil-doer avoiding retribution? We must, as far as we can, imitate the Lord. And he will do so, who complies with the will of God, receiving freely, giving freely, and receiving as a worthy reward the citizenship itself. "The hire of an harlot shall not come into the sanctuary," it is said: accordingly it was forbidden to bring to the altar the price of a dog.

And in whomsoever the eye of the soul has been blinded by ill-nurture and teaching, let him advance to the true light, to the truth, which shows by writing the things that are unwritten. "Ye that thirst, go to the waters," [5] says Esaias. And "drink water from thine own vessels," [6] Solomon exhorts. Accordingly in "The Laws," the philosopher who learned from the Hebrews, Plato, commands husbandmen not to irrigate or take water from others, until they have first dug down in their own ground to what is called the virgin soil, and found it dry. For it is right to supply want, but it is not well to support laziness. For Pythagoras said that, "although it be agreeable to reason to take a share of a burden, it is not a duty to take it away."

Now the Scripture kindles the living spark of the soul, and directs the eye suitably for contemplation; perchance inserting something, as the husbandman when he ingrafts, but, according to the opinion of the divine apostle, exciting what is in the soul. "For there are certainly among us many weak and sickly, and many sleep. But if we judge ourselves, we shall not be judged." [7] Now this work of mine in writing is not artfully constructed for display; but my memoranda are stored up against old age, as a remedy against forgetfulness, truly an image and outline of those vigorous and animated discourses which I was privileged to hear, and of blessed and truly remarkable men.

Of these the one, in Greece, an Ionic; [8] the other in Magna Græcia: the first of these from Cœle-Syria, the second from Egypt, and others in the East. The one was born in the land of Assyria, and the other a Hebrew in Palestine. When I came upon the last [9] (he was the first in power), having tracked him out concealed in Egypt, I found rest. He, the true, the Sicilian bee, gathering the spoil of the flowers of the prophetic and apostolic meadow, engendered in the souls of his hearers a deathless element of knowledge.

Well, they preserving the tradition of the blessed doctrine derived directly from the holy apostles, Peter, James, John, and Paul, the sons receiving it from the father (but few were like the fathers), came by God's will to us also to deposit those ancestral and apostolic seeds. And well I know that they will exult; I do not mean delighted with this tribute, but solely on account of the preservation of the truth, according as they delivered it. For such a sketch as this, will, I think, be agreeable to a soul desirous of preserving from escape the blessed tradition. [10]

---

[1] Isa. vii. 9.
[2] Gal. vi. 10.
[3] Ps. li. 7-12.
[4] i.e., perfect men.

[5] Isa. lv. 1.
[6] Prov. v. 15.
[7] 1 Cor. xi. 31, 32. "You" is the reading of New Testament.
[8] The first probably Tatian, the second Theodotus.
[9] Most likely Pantænus, master of the catechetical school in Alexandria, and the teacher of Clement. [Elucidation II.]
[10] [See Elucidation III., *infra.*]

"In a man who loves wisdom the father will be glad."[1] Wells, when pumped out, yield purer water; and that of which no one partakes, turns to putrefaction. Use keeps steel brighter, but disuse produces rust in it. For, in a word, exercise produces a healthy condition both in souls and bodies. "No one lighteth a candle, and putteth it under a bushel, but upon a candlestick, that it may give light to those who are regarded worthy of the feast."[2] For what is the use of wisdom, if it makes not him who can hear it wise? For still the Saviour saves, "and always works, as He sees the Father."[3] For by teaching, one learns more; and in speaking, one is often a hearer along with his audience. For the teacher of him who speaks and of him who hears is one — who waters both the mind and the word. Thus the Lord did not hinder from doing good while keeping the Sabbath;[4] but allowed us to communicate of those divine mysteries, and of that holy light, to those who are able to receive them. He did not certainly disclose to the many what did not belong to the many; but to the few to whom He knew that they belonged, who were capable of receiving and being moulded according to them. But secret things are entrusted to speech, not to writing, as is the case with God.[5]

And if one say that it is written, "There is nothing secret which shall not be revealed, nor hidden which shall not be disclosed,"[6] let him also hear from us, that to him who hears secretly, even what is secret shall be manifested. This is what was predicted by this oracle. And to him who is able secretly to observe what is delivered to him. that which is veiled shall be disclosed as truth; and what is hidden to the many, shall appear manifest to the few. For why do not all know the truth? why is not righteousness loved, if righteousness belongs to all? But the mysteries are delivered mystically, that what is spoken may be in the mouth of the speaker; rather not in his voice, but in his understanding. "God gave to the Church, some apostles, and some prophets, and some evangelists, and some pastors and teachers, for the perfecting of the saints, for the work of the ministry, for the edifying of the body of Christ."[7]

The writing of these memoranda of mine, I well know, is weak when compared with that spirit, full of grace, which I was privileged to hear.[8] But it will be an image to recall the archetype to him who was struck with the thyr-

sus. For "speak," it is said, "to a wise man, and he will grow wiser; and to him that hath, and there shall be added to him." And we profess not to explain secret things sufficiently — far from it — but only to recall them to memory, whether we have forgot aught, or whether for the purpose of not forgetting. Many things, I well know, have escaped us, through length of time, that have dropped away unwritten. Whence, to aid the weakness of my memory, and provide for myself a salutary help to my recollection in a systematic arrangement of chapters, I necessarily make use of this form. There are then some things of which we have no recollection; for the power that was in the blessed men was great.[8] There are also some things which remained unnoted long, which have now escaped; and others which are effaced, having faded away in the mind itself, since such a task is not easy to those not experienced; these I revive in my commentaries. Some things I purposely omit, in the exercise of a wise selection, afraid to write what I guarded against speaking: not grudging — for that were wrong — but fearing for my readers, lest they should stumble by taking them in a wrong sense; and, as the proverb says, we should be found "reaching a sword to a child." For it is impossible that what has been written should not escape, although remaining unpublished by me. But being always revolved, using the one only voice, that of writing, they answer nothing to him that makes inquiries beyond what is written; for they require of necessity the aid of some one, either of him who wrote, or of some one else who has walked in his footsteps. Some things my treatise will hint; on some it will linger; some it will merely mention. It will try to speak imperceptibly, to exhibit secretly, and to demonstrate silently. The dogmas taught by remarkable sects will be adduced; and to these will be opposed all that ought to be premised in accordance with the profoundest contemplation of the knowledge, which, as we proceed to the renowned and venerable canon of tradition, from the creation of the world,[9] will advance to our view; setting before us what according to natural contemplation necessarily has to be treated of beforehand, and clearing off what stands in the way of this arrangement. So that we may have our ears ready for the reception of the tradition of true knowledge; the soil being previously cleared of the thorns and of every weed by the husbandman, in order to the planting of the vine. For there is a contest, and the prelude to the contest; and there are some mysteries before other mysteries.

Our book will not shrink from making use of what is best in philosophy and other preparatory

---

[1] Prov. xxix. 3.
[2] Matt. v. 15; Mark iv. 21.
[3] John v. 17, 19.
[4] [This reference to the Jewish Sabbath to be noted in connection with what Clement says elsewhere.]
[5] [See Elucidation IV., *infra.*]
[6] Luke viii. 17, xii. 2.
[7] Eph. iv. 11, 12.
[8] [An affectionate reference to Pantænus and his other masters.]
[9] [See Elucidation V., *infra.*]

instruction. "For not only for the Hebrews and those that are under the law," according to the apostle, "is it right to become a Jew, but also a Greek for the sake of the Greeks, that we may gain all."[1] Also in the Epistle to the Colossians he writes, "Admonishing every man, and teaching every man in all wisdom, that we may present every man perfect in Christ."[2] The nicety of speculation, too, suits the sketch presented in my commentaries. In this respect the resources of learning are like a relish mixed with the food of an athlete, who is not indulging in luxury, but entertains a noble desire for distinction.

By music we harmoniously relax the excessive tension of gravity. And as those who wish to address the people, do so often by the herald, that what is said may be better heard; so also in this case. For we have the word, that was spoken to many, before the common tradition. Wherefore we must set forth the opinions and utterances which cried individually to them, by which those who hear shall more readily turn.

And, in truth, to speak briefly: Among many small pearls there is the one; and in a great take of fish there is the beauty-fish; and by time and toil truth will gleam forth, if a good helper is at hand. For most benefits are supplied, from God, through men. All of us who make use of our eyes see what is presented before them. But some look at objects for one reason, others for another. For instance, the cook and the shepherd do not survey the sheep similarly: for the one examines it if it be fat; the other watches to see if it be of good breed. Let a man milk the sheep's milk if he need sustenance: let him shear the wool if he need clothing. And in this way let me produce the fruit of the Greek erudition.[3]

For I do not imagine that any composition can be so fortunate as that no one will speak against it. But that is to be regarded as in accordance with reason, which nobody speaks against, with reason. And that course of action and choice is to be approved, not which is faultless, but which no one rationally finds fault with. For it does not follow, that if a man accomplishes anything not purposely, he does it through force of circumstances. But he will do it, managing it by wisdom divinely given, and in accommodation to circumstances. For it is not he who has virtue that needs the way to virtue, any more than he, that is strong, needs recovery. For, like farmers who irrigate the land beforehand, so we also water with the liquid stream of Greek learning what in it is earthy; so that it

may receive the spiritual seed cast into it, and may be capable of easily nourishing it. The *Stromata* will contain the truth mixed up in the dogmas of philosophy, or rather covered over and hidden, as the edible part of the nut in the shell. For, in my opinion, it is fitting that the seeds of truth be kept for the husbandmen of faith, and no others. I am not oblivious of what is babbled by some, who in their ignorance are frightened at every noise, and say that we ought to occupy ourselves with what is most necessary, and which contains the faith; and that we should pass over what is beyond and superfluous, which wears out and detains us to no purpose, in things which conduce nothing to the great end. Others think that philosophy was introduced into life by an evil influence, for the ruin of men, by an evil inventor. But I shall show, throughout the whole of these *Stromata*, that evil has an evil nature, and can never turn out the producer of aught that is good; indicating that philosophy is in a sense a work of Divine Providence.[3]

CHAP. II. — OBJECTION TO THE NUMBER OF EXTRACTS FROM PHILOSOPHICAL WRITINGS IN THESE BOOKS ANTICIPATED AND ANSWERED.

In reference to these commentaries, which contain as the exigencies of the case demand, the Hellenic opinions, I say thus much to those who are fond of finding fault. First, even if philosophy were useless, if the demonstration of its uselessness does good, it is yet useful. Then those cannot condemn the Greeks, who have only a mere hearsay knowledge of their opinions, and have not entered into a minute investigation in each department, in order to acquaintance with them. For the refutation, which is based on experience, is entirely trustworthy. For the knowledge of what is condemned is found the most complete demonstration. Many things, then, though not contributing to the final result, equip the artist. And otherwise erudition commends him, who sets forth the most essential doctrines so as to produce persuasion in his hearers, engendering admiration in those who are taught, and leads them to the truth. And such persuasion is convincing, by which those that love learning admit the truth; so that philosophy does not ruin life by being the originator of false practices and base deeds, although some have calumniated it, though it be the clear image of truth, a divine gift to the Greeks;[4] nor does it drag us away from the faith, as if we were bewitched by some delusive art, but rather, so to speak, by the use of an ampler circuit, obtains a common exercise demonstrative of the faith. Further, the juxtaposition

---

[1] 1 Cor. ix. 20, 21.
[2] Col. i. 28.
[3] [Every reference of our author to his use of Greek learning and (eclectic) philosophy, is important in questions about his orthodoxy.]

[4] [Noteworthy with his *caveat* about *comparison*. He deals with Greek philosophers as surgeons do with comparative anatomy.]

of doctrines, by comparison, saves the truth, from which follows knowledge.

Philosophy came into existence, not on its own account, but for the advantages reaped by us from knowledge, we receiving a firm persuasion of true perception, through the knowledge of things comprehended by the mind. For I do not mention that the *Stromata*, forming a body of varied erudition, wish artfully to conceal the seeds of knowledge. As, then, he who is fond of hunting captures the game after seeking, tracking, scenting, hunting it down with dogs; so truth, when sought and got with toil, appears a delicious [1] thing. Why, then, you will ask, did you think it fit that such an arrangement should be adopted in your memoranda? Because there is great danger in divulging the secret of the true philosophy to those, whose delight it is unsparingly to speak against everything, not justly; and who shout forth all kinds of names and words indecorously, deceiving themselves and beguiling those who adhere to them. "For the Hebrews seek signs," as the apostle says, "and the Greeks seek after wisdom." [2]

CHAP. III. — AGAINST THE SOPHISTS.

There is a great crowd of this description: some of them, enslaved to pleasures and willing to disbelieve, laugh at the truth which is worthy of all reverence, making sport of its barbarousness. Some others, exalting themselves, endeavour to discover calumnious objections to our words, furnishing captious questions, hunters out of paltry sayings, practisers of miserable artifices, wranglers, dealers in knotty points, as that Abderite says: —

"For mortals' tongues are glib, and on them are many speeches;
And a wide range for words of all sorts in this place and that."

And —

"Of whatever sort the word you have spoken, of the same sort you must hear."

Inflated with this art of theirs, the wretched Sophists, babbling away in their own jargon; toiling their whole life about the division of names and the nature of the composition and conjunction of sentences, show themselves greater chatterers than turtle-doves; scratching and tickling, not in a manly way, in my opinion, the ears of those who wish to be tickled.

"A river of silly words — not a dropping;"

just as in old shoes, when all the rest is worn and is falling to pieces, and the tongue alone remains. The Athenian Solon most excellently enlarges, and writes: —

"Look to the tongue, and to the words of the glozing man,
But you look on no work that has been done;
But each one of you walks in the steps of a fox,
And in all of you is an empty mind."

This, I think, is signified by the utterance of the Saviour, "The foxes have holes, but the Son of man hath not where to lay His head." [3] For on the believer alone, who is separated entirely from the rest, who by the Scripture are called wild beasts, rests the head of the universe, the kind and gentle Word, "who taketh the wise in their own craftiness. For the LORD knoweth the thoughts of the wise, that they are vain;" [4] the Scripture calling those the wise (σοφούς) who are skilled in words and arts, sophists (σοφιστάς). Whence the Greeks also applied the denominative appellation of wise and sophists (σοφοί, σοφισταί) to those who were versed in anything. Cratinus accordingly, having in the *Archilochi* enumerated the poets, said: —

"Such a hive of sophists have ye examined."

And similarly Iophon, the comic poet, in *Flute-playing Satyrs*, says: —

"For there entered
A band of sophists, all equipped."

Of these and the like, who devote their attention to empty words, the divine Scripture most excellently says, "I will destroy the wisdom of the wise, and bring to nothing the understanding of the prudent." [5]

CHAP. IV. — HUMAN ARTS AS WELL AS DIVINE KNOWLEDGE PROCEED FROM GOD.

Homer calls an artificer wise; and of Margites, if that is his work, he thus writes: —

"Him, then, the Gods made neither a delver nor a ploughman,
Nor in any other respect wise; but he missed every art."

Hesiod further said the musician Linus was "skilled in all manner of wisdom;" and does not hesitate to call a mariner wise, seeing he writes: —

"Having no wisdom in navigation."

And Daniel the prophet says, "The mystery which the king asks, it is not in the power of the wise, the Magi, the diviners, the Gazarenes, to tell the king; but it is God in heaven who revealeth it." [6]

Here he terms the Babylonians wise. And that Scripture calls every secular science or art by the one name wisdom (there are other arts and sciences invented over and above by human reason), and that artistic and skilful invention is from God, will be clear if we adduce the follow-

---

[1] Adopting the emendation γλυκύ τι instead of γλυκύτητι.
[2] 1 Cor. i. 22.
[3] Matt. viii. 20; Luke ix. 58.
[4] Job v. 13; 1 Cor. iii. 19, 20; Ps. xciv. 11.
[5] Isa. xxix. 14; 1 Cor. i. 19.
[6] Dan. ii. 27, 28.

ing statement : " And the Lord spake to Moses, See, I have called Bezaleel, the son of Uri, the son of Or, of the tribe of Judah ; and I have filled him with the divine spirit of wisdom, and understanding, and knowledge, to devise and to execute in all manner of work, to work gold, and silver, and brass, and blue, and purple, and scarlet, and in working stone work, and in the art of working wood," and even to "all works." [1] And then He adds the general reason, " And to every understanding heart I have given understanding ; " [2] that is, to every one capable of acquiring it by pains and exercise. And again, it is written expressly in the name of the Lord : " And speak thou to all that are wise in mind, whom I have filled with the spirit of perception." [3]

Those who are wise in mind have a certain attribute of nature peculiar to themselves ; and they who have shown themselves capable, receive from the Supreme Wisdom a spirit of perception in double measure. For those who practise the common arts, are in what pertains to the senses highly gifted : in hearing, he who is commonly called a musician ; in touch, he who moulds clay ; in voice the singer, in smell the perfumer, in sight the engraver of devices on seals. Those also that are occupied in instruction, train the sensibility according to which the poets are susceptible to the influence of measure ; the sophists apprehend expression ; the dialecticians, syllogisms ; and the philosophers are capable of the contemplation of which themselves are the objects. For sensibility finds and invents ; since it persuasively exhorts to application. And practice will increase the application which has knowledge for its end. With reason, therefore, the apostle has called the wisdom of God " manifold," and which has manifested its power " in many departments and in many modes " [4] — by art, by knowledge, by faith, by prophecy — for our benefit. " For all wisdom is from the Lord, and is with Him for ever," as says the wisdom of Jesus. [5]

For if thou call on wisdom and knowledge with a loud voice, and seek it as treasures of silver, and eagerly track it out, thou shalt understand godliness and find divine knowledge." [6] The prophet says this in contradiction to the knowledge according to philosophy, which teaches us to investigate in a magnanimous and noble manner, for our progress in piety. He opposes, therefore, to it the knowledge which is occupied with piety, when referring to knowledge, when he speaks as follows : " For God gives wisdom out of His own mouth, and knowledge along with

understanding, and treasures up help for the righteous." For to those who have been justified [7] by philosophy, the knowledge which leads to piety is laid up as a help.

CHAP. V. — PHILOSOPHY THE HANDMAID OF THEOLOGY.

Accordingly, before the advent of the Lord, philosophy was necessary to the Greeks for righteousness. [8] And now it becomes conducive to piety ; being a kind of preparatory training to those who attain to faith through demonstration. " For thy foot," it is said, " will not stumble, if thou refer what is good, whether belonging to the Greeks or to us, to Providence." [9] For God is the cause of all good things ; but of some primarily, as of the Old and the New Testament ; and of others by consequence, as philosophy. Perchance, too, philosophy was given to the Greeks directly and primarily, till the Lord should call the Greeks. For this was a schoolmaster to bring " the Hellenic mind," as the law, the Hebrews, " to Christ." [10] Philosophy, therefore, was a preparation, paving the way for him who is perfected in Christ. [8]

" Now," says Solomon, " defend wisdom, and it will exalt thee, and it will shield thee with a crown of pleasure." [11] For when thou hast strengthened wisdom with a cope by philosophy, and with right expenditure, thou wilt preserve it unassailable by sophists. The way of truth is therefore one. But into it, as into a perennial river, streams flow from all sides. It has been therefore said by inspiration : " Hear, my son, and receive my words ; that thine may be the many ways of life. For I teach thee the ways of wisdom ; that the fountains fail thee not," [12] which gush forth from the earth itself. Not only did He enumerate several ways of salvation for any one righteous man, but He added many other ways of many righteous, speaking thus : " The paths of the righteous shine like the light." [13] The commandments and the modes of preparatory training are to be regarded as the ways and appliances of life.

" Jerusalem, Jerusalem, how often would I have gathered thy children, as a hen her chickens ! " [14] And Jerusalem is, when interpreted, " a vision of peace." He therefore shows prophetically, that those who peacefully contemplate sacred things are in manifold ways trained to their calling. What then ? He " would," and could not. How often, and where ? Twice ; by

---

[1] Ex xxxi. 2–5.
[2] Ex. xxxi. 6.
[3] Ex. xxviii. 3.
[4] Eph. iii 10; Heb. i. 1.
[5] Ecclus. i. 1.
[6] Prov. ii. 3–5.

[7] [A passage much reflected upon, in questions of Clement's Catholic orthodoxy. See Elucidation VI., *infra*.]
[8] [In connection with note 3, p. 303, *supra*, see Elucidation VII.]
[9] Prov. iii. 23.
[10] Gal. iii. 24 .
[11] Prov. iv. 8, 9.
[12] Prov. iv. 10, 11, 21.
[13] Prov. iv. 18.
[14] Matt. xxiii. 37; Luke xiii. 34.

the prophets, and by the advent. The expression, then, "How often," shows wisdom to be manifold ; and in every mode of quantity and quality, it by all means saves some, both in time and in eternity. "For the Spirit of the Lord fills the earth."[1] And if any should violently say that the reference is to the Hellenic culture, when it is said, "Give not heed to an evil woman ; for honey drops from the lips of a harlot," let him hear what follows : "who lubricates thy throat for the time." But philosophy does not flatter. Who, then, does He allude to as having committed fornication? He adds expressly, "For the feet of folly lead those who use her, after death, to Hades. But her steps are not supported." Therefore remove thy way far from silly pleasure. "Stand not at the doors of her house, that thou yield not thy life to others." And He testifies, "Then shalt thou repent in old age, when the flesh of thy body is consumed." For this is the end of foolish pleasure. Such, indeed, is the case. And when He says, "Be not much with a strange woman,"[2] He admonishes us to use indeed, but not to linger and spend time with, secular culture. For what was bestowed on each generation advantageously, and at seasonable times, is a preliminary training for the word of the Lord. "For already some men, ensnared by the charms of handmaidens, have despised their consort philosophy, and have grown old, some of them in music, some in geometry, others in grammar, the most in rhetoric."[3] "But as the encyclical branches of study contribute to philosophy, which is their mistress ; so also philosophy itself co-operates for the acquisition of wisdom. For philosophy is the study of wisdom, and wisdom is the knowledge of things divine and human ; and their causes." Wisdom is therefore queen of philosophy, as philosophy is of preparatory culture. For if philosophy "professes control of the tongue, and the belly, and the parts below the belly, it is to be chosen on its own account. But it appears more worthy of respect and pre-eminence, if cultivated for the honour and knowledge of God."[4] And Scripture will afford a testimony to what has been said in what follows. Sarah was at one time barren, being Abraham's wife. Sarah having no child, assigned her maid, by name Hagar, the Egyptian, to Abraham, in order to get children. Wisdom, therefore, who dwells with the man of faith (and Abraham was reckoned faithful and righteous), was still barren and without child in that generation, not having

brought forth to Abraham aught allied to virtue. And she, as was proper, thought that he, being now in the time of progress, should have intercourse with secular culture first (by Egyptian the world is designated figuratively) ; and afterwards should approach to her according to divine providence, and beget Isaac."[5]

And Philo interprets Hagar to mean "sojourning."[6] For it is said in connection with this, "Be not much with a strange woman."[7] Sarah he interprets to mean "my princedom." He, then, who has received previous training is at liberty to approach to wisdom, which is supreme, from which grows up the race of Israel. These things show that that wisdom can be acquired through instruction, to which Abraham attained, passing from the contemplation of heavenly things to the faith and righteousness which are according to God. And Isaac is shown to mean "self-taught ; " wherefore also he is discovered to be a type of Christ. He was the husband of one wife Rebecca, which they translate "Patience." And Jacob is said to have consorted with several, his name being interpreted "Exerciser." And exercises are engaged in by means of many and various dogmas. Whence, also, he who is really "endowed with the power of seeing" is called Israel,[8] having much experience, and being fit for exercise.

Something else may also have been shown by the three patriarchs, namely, that the sure seal of knowledge is composed of nature, of education, and exercise.

You may have also another image of what has been said, in Thamar sitting by the way, and presenting the appearance of a harlot, on whom the studious Judas (whose name is interpreted "powerful"), who left nothing unexamined and uninvestigated, looked ; and turned aside to her, preserving his profession towards God. Wherefore also, when Sarah was jealous at Hagar being preferred to her, Abraham, as choosing only what was profitable in secular philosophy, said, "Behold, thy maid is in thine hands : deal with her as it pleases thee ; "[9] manifestly meaning, "I embrace secular culture as youthful, and a handmaid ; but thy knowledge I honour and reverence as true wife." And Sarah afflicted her ; which is equivalent to corrected and admonished her. It has therefore been well said, "My son, despise not thou the correction of God ; nor faint when thou art rebuked of Him. For whom the LORD loveth He chasteneth, and

---

1 [A favourite expression of the Fathers, expressing hope for the heathen. See Elucidation VIII., *infra*.]
2 Prov. v. 2, 3, 5, 8, 9, 11, 20.
3 Philo Judæus, *On seeking Instruction*, 435. See Bohn's translation, ii. 173.
4 Quoted from Philo with some alterations. See Bohn's translation, vol. ii. p. 173.

5 See Philo, *Meeting to seek Instruction*, Bohn's translation, vol. ii. 160.
6 Bohn's trans., vol. ii. 161.
7 Prov. v. 20. Philo, *On meeting to seek Knowledge*, near beginning.
8 Philo, in the book above cited, interprets "Israel," "seeing God." From this book all the instances and etymologies occurring here are taken.
9 Gen. xvi. 6.

courgeth every son whom He receiveth." [1] nd the foresaid Scriptures, when examined in ther places, will be seen to exhibit other mysries. We merely therefore assert here, that hilosophy is characterized by investigation into uth and the nature of things (this is the truth f which the Lord Himself said, "I am the uth" [2]); and that, again, the preparatory aining for rest in Christ exercises the mind, uses the intelligence, and begets an inquiring rewdness, by means of the true philosophy, hich the initiated possess, having found it, or ather received it, from the truth itself.

CHAP. VI. — THE BENEFIT OF CULTURE.

The readiness acquired by previous training onduces much to the perception of such things s are requisite; but those things which can be erceived only by mind are the special exercise r the mind. And their nature is triple according as we consider their quantity, their magniude, and what can be predicated of them. For he discourse which consists of demonstrations, nplants in the spirit of him who follows it, lear faith; so that he cannot conceive of that hich is demonstrated being different; and so does not allow us to succumb to those who ssail us by fraud. In such studies, therefore, he soul is purged from sensible things, and excited, so as to be able to see truth disinctly. For nutriment, and the training which maintained gentle, make noble natures; and oble natures, when they have received such raining, become still better than before both in ther respects, but especially in productiveness, s is the case with the other creatures. Wherere it is said, "Go to the ant, thou sluggard, and ecome wiser than it, which provideth much and aried food in the harvest against the inclemncy of winter." [3] Or go to the bee, and learn ow laborious she is; for she, feeding on the hole meadow, produces one honey-comb. And "thou prayest in the closet," as the Lord aught, "to worship in spirit," [4] thy management will no longer be solely occupied about he house, but also about the soul, what must be estowed on it, and how, and how much; and hat must be laid aside and treasured up in it; nd when it ought to be produced, and to whom. or it is not by nature, but by learning, that eople become noble and good, as people also ecome physicians and pilots. We all in comnon, for example, see the vine and the horse. ut the husbandman will know if the vine be ood or bad at fruit-bearing; and the horseman ill easily distinguish between the spiritless and the swift animal. But that some are naturally predisposed to virtue above others, certain pursuits of those, who are so naturally predisposed above others, show. But that perfection in virtue is not the exclusive property of those, whose natures are better, is proved, since also those who by nature are ill-disposed towards virtue, in obtaining suitable training, for the most part attain to excellence; and, on the other hand, those whose natural dispositions are apt, become evil through neglect.

Again, God has created us naturally social and just; whence justice must not be said to take its rise from implantation alone. But the good imparted by creation is to be conceived of as excited by the commandment; the soul being trained to be willing to select what is noblest.

But as we say that a man can be a believer without learning, [5] so also we assert that it is impossible for a man without learning to comprehend the things which are declared in the faith. But to adopt what is well said, and not to adopt the reverse, is caused not simply by faith, but by faith combined with knowledge. But if ignorance is want of training and of instruction, then teaching produces knowledge of divine and human things. But just as it is possible to live rightly in penury of this world's good things, so also in abundance. And we avow, that at once with more ease and more speed will one attain to virtue through previous training. But it is not such as to be unattainable without it; but it is attainable only when they have learned, and have had their senses exercised. [6] "For hatred," says Solomon, "raises strife, but instruction guardeth the ways of life;" [7] in such a way that we are not deceived nor deluded by those who are practised in base arts for the injury of those who hear. "But instruction wanders reproachless," [8] it is said. We must be conversant with the art of reasoning, for the purpose of confuting the deceitful opinions of the sophists. Well and felicitously, therefore, does Anaxarchus write in his book respecting "kingly rule:" "Erudition benefits greatly and hurts greatly him who possesses it; it helps him who is worthy, and injures him who utters readily every word, and before the whole people. It is necessary to know the measure of time. For this is the end of wisdom. And those who sing at the doors, even if they sing skilfully, are not reckoned wise, but have the reputation of folly." And Hesiod: —

"Of the Muses, who make a man loquacious, divine, vocal."

[1] Prov. iii. 11, 12; Heb. xii. 5, 6.
[2] John xiv. 6.
[3] Prov. vi. 6, 8. [The bee is not instanced in Scripture.]
[4] Matt. vi. 6; John iv. 23.

[5] [Illustrative of the esoteric principle of Clement. See Elucidation IX., *infra*.]
[6] Heb. v. 14.
[7] Prov. x. 12, 17.
[8] Prov. x. 19.

For him who is fluent in words he calls loquacious ; and him who is clever, vocal ; and " divine," him who is skilled, a philosopher, and acquainted with the truth.

CHAP. VII. — THE ECLECTIC PHILOSOPHY PAVES THE WAY FOR DIVINE VIRTUE.

The Greek preparatory culture, therefore, with philosophy itself, is shown to have come down from God to men, not with a definite direction, but in the way in which showers fall down on the good land, and on the dunghill, and on the houses. And similarly both the grass and the wheat sprout ; and the figs and any other reckless trees grow on sepulchres. And things that grow, appear as a type of truths. For they enjoy the same influence of the rain. But they have not the same grace as those which spring up in rich soil, inasmuch as they are withered or plucked up. And here we are aided by the parable of the sower, which the Lord interpreted. For the husbandman of the soil which is among men is one ; He who from the beginning, from the foundation of the world, sowed nutritious seeds ; He who in each age rained down the Lord, the Word. But the times and places which received [such gifts], created the differences which exist. Further, the husbandman sows not only wheat (of which there are many varieties), but also other seeds — barley, and beans, and peas, and vetches, and vegetable and flower seeds. And to the same husbandry belongs both planting and the operations necessary in the nurseries, and gardens, and orchards, and the planting and rearing of all sorts of trees

In like manner, not only the care of sheep, but the care of herds, and breeding of horses, and dogs, and bee-craft, all arts, and to speak comprehensively, the care of flocks and the rearing of animals, differ from each other more or less, but are all useful for life. And philosophy — I do not mean the Stoic, or the Platonic, or the Epicurean, or the Aristotelian, but whatever has been well said by each of those sects, which teach righteousness along with a science pervaded by piety, — this eclectic whole I call philosophy.[1] But such conclusions of human reasonings, as men have cut away and falsified, I would never call divine.

And now we must look also at this, that if ever those who know not how to do well, live well ;[2] for they have lighted on well-doing. Some, too, have aimed well at the word of truth through understanding. "But Abraham was not justified by works, but by faith."[3] It is therefore of no advantage to them after the end of life, even if

they do good works now, if they have not faith. Wherefore also the Scriptures[4] were translated into the language of the Greeks, in order that they might never be able to allege the excuse of ignorance, inasmuch as they are able to hear also what we have in our hands, if they only wish. One speaks in one way of the truth, in another way the truth interprets itself. The guessing at truth is one thing, and truth itself is another. Resemblance is one thing, the thing itself is another. And the one results from learning and practice, the other from power and faith. For the teaching of piety is a gift, but faith is grace. " For by doing the will of God we know the will of God."[5] " Open, then," says the Scripture, " the gates of righteousness ; and I will enter in, and confess to the Lord."[6] But the paths to righteousness (since God saves in many ways, for He is good) are many and various, and lead to the Lord's way and gate. And if you ask the royal and true entrance, you will hear, " This is the gate of the Lord, the righteous shall enter in by it."[7] While there are many gates open, that in righteousness is in Christ, by which all the blessed enter, and direct their step in the sanctity of knowledge. Now Clemens, in his Epistle to the Corinthians, while expounding the differences of those who are approved according to the Church, says expressly, " One may be a believer ; one may be powerful in uttering knowledge ; one may be wise in discriminating between words ; one may be terrible in deeds."

CHAP. VIII. — THE SOPHISTICAL ARTS USELESS.

But the art of sophistry, which the Greeks cultivated, is a fantastic power, which makes false opinions like true by means of words. For it produces rhetoric in order to persuasion, and disputation for wrangling. These arts, therefore, if not conjoined with philosophy, will be injurious to every one. For Plato openly called sophistry " an evil art." And Aristotle, following him, demonstrates it to be a dishonest art which abstracts in a specious manner the whole business of wisdom, and professes a wisdom which it has not studied. To speak briefly, the beginning of rhetoric is the probable, and an attempted proof[9] the process, and the end persuasion, so the beginning of disputation is what is matter of opinion, and the process a contest and the end victory. For in the same manner also, the beginning of sophistry is the apparent and the process twofold ; one of rhetoric, continuous and exhaustive ; and the other of logic and is interrogatory. And its end is admiration

---

[1] [Most important as defining Clement's system, and his use of this word, " philosophy."]
[2] Something seems wanting to complete the sense.
[3] Rom. iv.

[4] [Stillingfleet, *Origines Sacræ*, vol. i. p. 55. Important reference
[5] John vii. 17.
[6] Ps. cxviii. 19.
[7] Ps. cxviii. 20.
[8] [See vol. i. p. 18, First Epistle of Clement, chap. xlviii. S.]
[9] ἐπιχείρημα.

The dialectic in vogue in the schools, on the other hand, is the exercise of a philosopher in matters of opinion, for the sake of the faculty of disputation. But truth is not in these at all. With reason, therefore, the noble apostle, depreciating these superfluous arts occupied about words, says, "If any man do not give heed to wholesome words, but is puffed up by a kind of teaching, knowing nothing, but doting (νοσῶν) about questions and strifes of words, whereof cometh contention, envy, railings, evil surmisings, perverse disputings of men of corrupt minds, destitute of the truth."[1]

You see how he is moved against them, calling their art of logic — on which, those to whom this garrulous mischievous art is dear, whether Greeks or barbarians, plume themselves — a disease (νόσος). Very beautifully, therefore, the tragic poet Euripides says in the *Phœnissæ*, —

"But a wrongful speech
Is diseased in itself, and needs skilful medicines."[2]

For the saving Word[3] is called "wholesome," He being the truth; and what is wholesome (healthful) remains ever deathless. But separation from what is healthful and divine is impiety, and a deadly malady. These are rapacious wolves hid in sheep-skins, men-stealers, and glozing soul-seducers, secretly, but proved to be robbers; striving by fraud and force to catch us who are unsophisticated and have less power of speech.

"Often a man, impeded through want of words, carries
  less weight
In expressing what is right, than the man of eloquence.
But now in fluent mouths the weightiest truths
They disguise, so that they do not seem what they
  ought to seem,"

says the tragedy. Such are these wranglers, whether they follow the sects, or practise miserable dialectic arts. These are they that "stretch the warp and weave nothing," says the Scripture;[4] prosecuting a bootless task, which the apostle has called "cunning craftiness of men, whereby they lie in wait to deceive."[5] "For there are," he says, "many unruly and vain talkers and deceivers."[6] Wherefore it was not said to all, "Ye are the salt of the earth."[7] For there are some even of the hearers of the word who are like the fishes of the sea, which, reared from their birth in brine, yet need salt to dress them for food. Accordingly I wholly approve of the tragedy, when it says: —

"O son, false words can be well spoken,
And truth may be vanquished by beauty of words.

But this is not what is most correct, but nature and
  what is right;
He who practises eloquence is indeed wise,
But I consider deeds always better than words."

We must not, then, aspire to please the multitude. For we do not practise what will please them, but what we know is remote from their disposition. "Let us not be desirous of vainglory," says the apostle, "provoking one another, envying one another."[8]

Thus the truth-loving Plato says, as if divinely inspired, "Since I am such as to obey nothing but the word, which, after reflection, appears to me the best."[9]

Accordingly he charges those who credit opinions without intelligence and knowledge, with abandoning right and sound reason unwarrantably, and believing him who is a partner in falsehood. For to cheat one's self of the truth is bad; but to speak the truth, and to hold as our opinions positive realities, is good.

Men are deprived of what is good unwillingly. Nevertheless they are deprived either by being deceived or beguiled, or by being compelled and not believing. He who believes not, has already made himself a willing captive; and he who changes his persuasion is cozened, while he forgets that time imperceptibly takes away some things, and reason others. And after an opinion has been entertained, pain and anguish, and on the other hand contentiousness and anger, compel. Above all, men are beguiled who are either bewitched by pleasure or terrified by fear. And all these are voluntary changes, but by none of these will knowledge ever be attained.

CHAP. IX. — HUMAN KNOWLEDGE NECESSARY FOR THE UNDERSTANDING OF THE SCRIPTURES.

Some, who think themselves naturally gifted, do not wish to touch either philosophy or logic; nay more, they do not wish to learn natural science. They demand bare faith alone, as if they wished, without bestowing any care on the vine, straightway to gather clusters from the first. Now the Lord is figuratively described as the vine, from which, with pains and the art of husbandry, according to the word, the fruit is to be gathered.

We must lop, dig, bind, and perform the other operations. The pruning-knife, I should think, and the pick-axe, and the other agricultural implements, are necessary for the culture of the vine, so that it may produce eatable fruit. And as in husbandry, so also in medicine: he has learned to purpose, who has practised the various lessons, so as to be able to cultivate and to heal. So also here, I call him truly learned who brings everything to bear on the truth; so that, from

---

[1] 1 Tim. vi. 3–5. [He treats the sophists with Platonic scorn, but adopts St. Paul's enlarged idea of sophistry.]
[2] *Phœnissæ*, 471, 472.
[3] [He has no idea of salvation by any other name, though he regards Gentile illumination as coming through philosophy.]
[4] Where, nobody knows.
[5] Eph. iv. 14.
[6] Tit. i. 10.
[7] Matt. v. 13.

[8] Gal. v. 26.
[9] Plato, *Crito*, vi. p. 46.

geometry, and music, and grammar, and philosophy itself, culling what is useful, he guards the faith against assault. Now, as was said, the athlete is despised who is not furnished for the contest. For instance, too, we praise the experienced helmsman who " has seen the cities of many men," and the physician who has had large experience; thus also some describe the empiric.[1] And he who brings everything to bear on a right life, procuring examples from the Greeks and barbarians, this man is an experienced searcher after truth, and in reality a man of much counsel, like the touch-stone (that is, the Lydian), which is believed to possess the power of distinguishing the spurious from the genuine gold. And our much-knowing gnostic can distinguish sophistry from philosophy, the art of decoration from gymnastics, cookery from physic, and rhetoric from dialectics, and the other sects which are according to the barbarian philosophy, from the truth itself. And how necessary is it for him who desires to be partaker of the power of God, to treat of intellectual subjects by philosophising! And how serviceable is it to distinguish expressions which are ambiguous, and which in the Testaments are used synonymously! For the Lord, at the time of His temptation, skilfully matched the devil by an ambiguous expression. And I do not yet, in this connection, see how in the world the inventor of philosophy and dialectics, as some suppose, is seduced through being deceived by the form of speech which consists in ambiguity. And if the prophets and apostles knew not the arts by which the exercises of philosophy are exhibited, yet the mind of the prophetic and instructive spirit, uttered secretly, because all have not an intelligent ear, demands skilful modes of teaching in order to clear exposition. For the prophets and disciples of the Spirit knew infallibly their mind. For they knew it by faith, in a way which others could not easily, as the Spirit has said. But it is not possible for those who have not learned to receive it thus. "Write," it is said, " the commandments doubly, in counsel and knowledge, that thou mayest answer the words of truth to them who send unto thee."[2] What, then, is the knowledge of answering? or what that of asking? It is dialectics. What then? Is not speaking our business, and does not action proceed from the Word? For if we act not for the Word, we shall act against reason. But a rational work is accomplished through God. "And nothing," it is said, " was made without Him " — the Word of God.[3]

And did not the Lord make all things by the Word? Even the beasts work, driven by compelling fear. And do not those who are called orthodox apply themselves to good works, knowing not what they do?

CHAP. X. — TO ACT WELL OF GREATER CONSEQUENCE THAN TO SPEAK WELL.

Wherefore the Saviour, taking the bread, first spake and blessed. Then breaking the bread,[4] He presented it, that we might eat it, according to reason, and that knowing the Scriptures[5] we might walk obediently. And as those whose speech is evil are no better than those whose practice is evil (for calumny is the servant of the sword, and evil-speaking inflicts pain; and from these proceed disasters in life, such being the effects of evil speech); so also those who are given to good speech are near neighbours to those who accomplish good deeds. Accordingly discourse refreshes the soul and entices it to nobleness; and happy is he who has the use of both his hands. Neither, therefore, is he who can act well to be vilified by him who is able to speak well; nor is he who is able to speak well to be disparaged by him who is capable of acting well. But let each do that for which he is naturally fitted. What the one exhibits as actually done, the other speaks, preparing, as it were, the way for well-doing, and leading the hearers to the practice of good. For there is a saving word, as there is a saving work. Righteousness, accordingly,[6] is not constituted without discourse. And as the receiving of good is abolished if we abolish the doing of good; so obedience and faith are abolished when neither the command, nor one to expound the command, is taken along with us.[7] But now we are benefited mutually and reciprocally by words and deeds; but we must repudiate entirely the art of wrangling and sophistry, since these sentences of the sophists not only bewitch and beguile the many, but sometimes by violence win a Cadmean victory.[8] For true above all is that Psalm, " The just shall live to the end, for he shall not see corruption, when he beholds the wise dying."[9] And whom does he call wise? Hear from the Wisdom of Jesus : " Wisdom is not the knowledge of evil."[10] Such he calls what the arts of speaking and of discussing have invented. "Thou shalt therefore seek wisdom among the wicked, and shalt not find it."[11] And if you inquire again of what sort this is, you are told, " The mouth of the righteous man will distil wisdom."[12] And simi-

---

[1] The empirics were a class of physicians who held practice to be the one thing essential.
[2] Prov. xxii. 2o, 21. The Septuagint and Hebrew both differ from the reading here.
[3] John i. 3.

[4] [" Eat it *according to reason.*" Spiritual food does not stultify reason, nor conflict with the evidence of the senses.]
[5] [This constant appeal to the Scriptures, noteworthy.]
[6] [Matt. xii. 37.]
[7] [Acts viii. 30.]
[8] A victory disastrous to the victor and the vanquished.
[9] Ps. xlviii. 10, 11, Sept.
[10] Ecclus. xix. 22.
[11] Prov. xiv. 6.
[12] Prov. x. 31.

larly with truth, the art of sophistry is called wisdom.

But it is my purpose, as I reckon, and not without reason, to live according to the Word, and to understand what is revealed ;[1] but never affecting eloquence, to be content merely with indicating my meaning. And by what term that which I wish to present is shown, I care not. For I well know that to be saved, and to aid those who desire to be saved, is the best thing, and not to compose paltry sentences like gewgaws. "And if," says the Pythagorean in the *Politicus* of Plato, "you guard against solicitude about terms, you will be richer in wisdom against old age."[2] And in the *Theætetus* you will find again, "And carelessness about names, and expressions, and the want of nice scrutiny, is not vulgar and illiberal for the most part, but rather the reverse of this, and is sometimes necessary."[3] This the Scripture[4] has expressed with the greatest possible brevity, when it said, "Be not occupied much about words." For expression is like the dress on the body. The matter is the flesh and sinews. We must not therefore care more for the dress than the safety of the body. For not only a simple mode of life, but also a style of speech devoid of superfluity and nicety, must be cultivated by him who has adopted the true life, if we are to abandon luxury as treacherous and profligate, as the ancient Lacedæmonians adjured ointment and purple, deeming and calling them rightly treacherous garments and treacherous unguents ; since neither is that mode of preparing food right where there is more of seasoning than of nutriment ; nor is that style of speech elegant which can please rather than benefit the hearers. Pythagoras exhorts us to consider the Muses more pleasant than the Sirens, teaching us to cultivate wisdom apart from pleasure, and exposing the other mode of attracting the soul as deceptive. For sailing past the Sirens one man has sufficient strength, and for answering the Sphinx another one, or, if you please, not even one.[5] We ought never, then, out of desire for vainglory, to make broad the phylacteries. It suffices the gnostic[6] if only one hearer is found for him.[7] You may hear therefore Pindar the Bœotian,[8] who writes, " Divulge not before all the ancient speech. The way of silence is sometimes the surest. And the mighti-

est word is a spur to the fight." Accordingly, the blessed apostle very appropriately and urgently exhorts us "not to strive about words to no profit, but to the subverting of the hearers, but to shun profane and vain babblings, for they increase unto more ungodliness, and their word will eat as doth a canker."[9]

CHAP. XI. — WHAT IS THE PHILOSOPHY WHICH THE APOSTLE BIDS US SHUN?

This, then, "the wisdom of the.world is foolishness with God," and of those who are "the wise the Lord knoweth their thoughts that they are vain."[10] Let no man therefore glory on account of pre-eminence in human thought. For it is written well in Jeremiah, "Let not the wise man glory in his wisdom, and let not the mighty man glory in his might, and let not the rich man glory in his riches : but let him that glorieth glory in this, that he understandeth and knoweth that I am the LORD, that executeth mercy and judgment and righteousness upon the earth : for in these things is my delight, saith the LORD."[11] "That we should trust not in ourselves, but in God who raiseth the dead," says the apostle, "who delivered us from so great a death, that our faith should not stand in the wisdom of men, but in the power of God." "For the spiritual man judgeth all things, but he himself is judged of no man."[12] I hear also those words of his, "And these things I say, lest any man should beguile you with enticing words, or one should enter in to spoil you."[13] And again, "Beware lest any man spoil you through philosophy and vain deceit, after the tradition of men, after the rudiments of the world, and not after Christ ;"[14] branding not all philosophy, but the Epicurean, which Paul mentions in the Acts of the Apostles,[15] which abolishes providence and deifies pleasure, and whatever other philosophy honours the elements, but places not over them the efficient cause, nor apprehends the Creator.[16]

The Stoics also, whom he mentions too, say not well that the Deity, being a body, pervades the vilest matter. He calls the jugglery of logic "the tradition of men." Wherefore also he adds, "Avoid juvenile[17] questions. For such contentions are puerile." "But virtue is no lover of boys," says the philosopher Plato. And our struggle, according to Gorgias Leontinus, requires two virtues — boldness and wisdom, — boldness to undergo danger, and wisdom to understand the enigma. For the Word, like the Olympian

---

[1] [Revelation is complete, and nothing new to be expected. Gal. i. 8, 9.]
[2] Plato's *Politicus*, p. 261 E.
[3] Plato's *Theætetus*, p. 184 C.
[4] [2 Tim. ii. 14.]
[5] The story of Œdipus being a myth.
[6] The possessor of true divine knowledge.
[7] [" Fit audience find though few."
　　　　　　　　　　Paradise Lost, book vii. 31.
Dante has the same thought. Pindar's φωνᾱντα συνετοῑσιν. *Olymp.*, ii. 35.]
[8] [Here I am sorry I cannot supply the proper reference. Clement shows his Attic prejudice in adding the epithet, here and elsewhere (Bœotian), which Pindar felt so keenly, and resents more than once. *Olymp.*, vi. vol. i. p. 75. *Ed.* Heyne, London, 1823.]

[9] 2 Tim. ii. 14, 16, 17.
[10] 1 Cor. iii. 19, 20.
[11] Jer. ix. 23, 24.
[12] 2 Cor. i. 9, 10; 1 Cor. ii. 5, 15.
[13] Col. ii. 4, 8.
[14] Col. ii. 8.
[15] Acts xvii. 18.
[16] [Revived by some " scientists" of our days.]
[17] The apostle says " foolish," 2 Tim. ii. 23.

proclamation, calls him who is willing, and crowns him who is able to continue unmoved as far as the truth is concerned. And, in truth, the Word does not wish him who has believed to be idle. For He says, "Seek, and ye shall find." [1] But seeking ends in finding, driving out the empty trifling, and approving of the contemplation which confirms our faith. "And this I say, lest any man beguile you with enticing words," [2] says the apostle, evidently as having learned to distinguish what· was said by him, and as being taught to meet objections. "As ye have therefore received Christ Jesus the Lord, so walk in Him, rooted and built up in Him, and stablished in the faith." [3] Now persuasion is [the means of] being established in the faith. "Beware lest any man spoil you of faith in Christ by philosophy and vain deceit," which does away with providence, "after the tradition of men;" for the philosophy which is in accordance with divine tradition establishes and confirms providence, which, being done away with, the economy of the Saviour appears a myth, while we are influenced "after the elements of the world, and not after Christ." [4] For the teaching which is agreeable to Christ deifies the Creator, and traces providence in particular events,[5] and knows the nature of the elements to be capable of change and production, and teaches that we ought to aim at rising up to the power which assimilates to God, and to prefer the dispensation [6] as holding the first rank and superior to all training.

The elements are worshipped, — the air by Diogenes, the water by Thales, the fire by Hippasus; and by those who suppose atoms to be the first principles of things, arrogating the name of philosophers, being wretched creatures devoted to pleasure.[7] "Wherefore I pray," says the apostle, "that your love may abound yet more and more, in knowledge and in all judgment, that ye may approve things that are excellent." [8] "Since, when we were children," says the same apostle, "we were kept in bondage under the rudiments of the world. And the child, though heir, differeth nothing from a servant, till the time appointed of the father." [9] Philosophers, then, are children, unless they have been made men by Christ. "For if the son of the bond woman shall not be heir with the son of the free," [10] at least he is the seed of Abraham, though not of promise, receiving what belongs to him by free gift. "But strong meat belongeth to those that are of full age, even

those who by reason of use have their senses exercised to discern both good and evil." [11] "For every one that useth milk is unskilful in the word of righteousness; for he is a babe," [12] and not yet acquainted with the word, according to which he has believed and works, and not able to give a reason in himself. "Prove all things," the apostle says, "and hold fast that which is good," [13] speaking to spiritual men, who judge what is said according to truth, whether it seems or truly holds by the truth. "He who is not corrected by discipline errs, and stripes and reproofs give the discipline of wisdom," the reproofs manifestly that are with love. "For the right heart seeketh knowledge." [14] "For he that seeketh the Lord shall find knowledge with righteousness; and they who have sought it rightly have found peace." [15] "And I will know," it is said, "not the speech of those which are puffed up, but the power." In rebuke of those who are wise in appearance, and think themselves wise, but are not in reality wise, he writes: "For the kingdom of God is not in word." [16] It is not in that which is not true, but which is only probable according to opinion; but he said "in power," for the truth alone is powerful. And again: "If any man thinketh that he knoweth anything, he knoweth nothing yet as he ought to know." For truth is never mere opinion. But the "supposition of knowledge inflates," and fills with pride; "but charity edifieth," which deals not in supposition, but in truth. Whence it is said, "If any man loves, he is known." [17]

CHAP. XII. — THE MYSTERIES OF THE FAITH NOT TO BE DIVULGED TO ALL.

But since this tradition is not published alone for him who perceives the magnificence of the word; it is requisite, therefore, to hide in a mystery the wisdom spoken, which the Son of God taught. Now, therefore, Isaiah the prophet has his tongue purified by fire, so that he may be able to tell the vision. And we must purify not the tongue alone, but also the ears, if we attempt to be partakers of the truth.

Such were the impediments in the way of my writing. And even now I fear, as it is said, "to cast the pearls before swine, lest they tread them under foot, and turn and rend us." [18] For it is difficult to exhibit the really pure and transparent words respecting the true light, to swinish and untrained hearers. For scarcely could anything which they could hear be more ludicrous than these to the multitude; nor any subjects

---

[1] Matt. vii. 7.
[2] Col. ii. 4.
[3] Col. ii. 6, 7.
[4] Col. ii. 8.
[5] [A special Providence notably recognised as Christian truth.]
[6] i.e., of the Gospel.
[7] [The Epicureans whom he censures just before.]
[8] Phil. i. 9, 10.
[9] Gal. iv. 1, 2, 3.
[10] Gen. xxi. 10; Gal. iv. 30.

[11] Heb. v. 14.
[12] Heb. v. 13.
[13] 1 Thess. v. 21.
[14] Prov. xv. 14.
[15] The substance of these remarks is found in Prov. ii.
[16] 1 Cor. iv. 19, 20.
[17] 1 Cor. viii. 1, 2, 3.
[18] Matt. vii. 6.

on the other hand more admirable or more inspiring to those of noble nature. " But the natural man receiveth not the things of the Spirit of God ; for they are foolishness to him." [1] But the wise do not utter with their mouth what they reason in council. " But what ye hear in the ear," says the Lord, " proclaim upon the houses ; " [2] bidding them receive the secret traditions [3] of the true knowledge, and expound them aloft and conspicuously ; and as we have heard in the ear, so to deliver them to whom it is requisite ; but not enjoining us to communicate to all without distinction, what is said to them in parables. But there is only a delineation in the memoranda, which have the truth sowed sparse [4] and broadcast, that it may escape the notice of those who pick up seeds like jackdaws ; but when they find a good husbandman, each one of them will germinate and produce corn.

CHAP. XIII. — ALL SECTS OF PHILOSOPHY CONTAIN A GERM OF TRUTH.

Since, therefore, truth is one (for falsehood has ten thousand by-paths) ; just as the Bacchantes tore asunder the limbs of Pentheus, so the sects both of barbarian and Hellenic philosophy have done with truth, and each vaunts as the whole truth the portion which has fallen to its lot. But all, in my opinion, [5] are illuminated by the dawn of Light. [6] Let all, therefore, both Greeks and barbarians, who have aspired after the truth, — both those who possess not a little, and those who have any portion, — produce whatever they have of the word of truth.

Eternity, for instance, presents in an instant the future and the present, also the past of time. But truth, much more powerful than limitless duration, can collect its proper germs, though they have fallen on foreign soil. For we shall find that very many of the dogmas that are held by such sects as have not become utterly senseless, and are not cut out from the order of nature (by cutting off Christ, as the women of the fable dismembered the man), [7] though appearing unlike one another, correspond in their origin and with the truth as a whole. For they coincide in one, either as a part, or a species, or a genus. For instance, though the highest note is different from the lowest note, yet both compose one harmony. And in numbers an even number differs from an odd number ; but both suit in arithmetic ; as also is the case with figure, the circle, and the

triangle, and the square, and whatever figures differ from one another. Also, in the whole universe, all the parts, though differing one from another, preserve their relation to the whole. So, then, the barbarian and Hellenic philosophy has torn off a fragment of eternal truth not from the mythology of Dionysus, but from the theology of the ever-living Word. And He who brings again together the separate fragments, and makes them one, will without peril, be assured, contemplate the perfect Word, the truth. Therefore it is written in Ecclesiastes : " And I added wisdom above all who were before me in Jerusalem ; and my heart saw many things ; and besides, I knew wisdom and knowledge, parables and understanding. And this also is the choice of the spirit, because in abundance of wisdom is abundance of knowledge." [8] He who is conversant with all kinds of wisdom, will be pre-eminently a gnostic. [9] Now it is written, " Abundance of the knowledge of wisdom will give life to him who is of it." [10] And again, what is said is confirmed more clearly by this saying, " All things are in the sight of those who understand " — all things, both Hellenic and barbarian ; but the one or the other is not all. " They are right to those who wish to receive understanding. Choose instruction, and not silver, and knowledge above tested gold," and prefer also sense to pure gold ; " for wisdom is better than precious stones, and no precious thing is worth it." [11]

CHAP. XIV. — SUCCESSION OF PHILOSOPHERS IN GREECE.

The Greeks say, that after Orpheus and Linus, and the most ancient of the poets that appeared among them, the seven, called wise, were the first that were admired for their wisdom. Of whom four were of Asia — Thales of Miletus, and Bias of Priene, Pittacus of Mitylene, and Cleobulus of Lindos ; and two of Europe, Solon the Athenian, and Chilon the Lacedæmonian ; and the seventh, some say, was Periander of Corinth ; others, Anacharsis the Scythian ; others, Epimenides the Cretan, whom Paul knew as a Greek prophet, whom he mentions in the Epistle to Titus, where he speaks thus : " One of themselves, a prophet of their own, said, *The Cretans are always liars, evil beasts, slow bellies.* And this witness is true." [12] You see how even to the prophets of the Greeks he attributes something of the truth, and is not ashamed, [13] when discours-

---

1 [1] 1 Cor. ii. 14.
2 [2] Matt. x. 27.
3 [3] [See Elucidation X., *infra.*]
4 [4] [A word (sparse) hitherto branded as an " Americanism. "]
5 [5] [Here he expresses merely as an opinion, his " gnostic " ideas as to philosophy, and the salvability of the heathen.]
6 [6] Namely Jesus: John viii. 12.
7 [7] We have adopted the translation of Potter, who supposes a reference to the fate of Pentheus. Perhaps the translation should be : " excluding Christ, as the apartments destined for women exclude the man; " i.e., all males.

8 [8] Eccles. i. 16, 17, 18.
9 [9] [His grudging of the term " gnostic " to unworthy pretenders, illustrates the spirit in which we must refuse to recognise the modern (Trent) theology of the Latins, as in any sense Catholic.]
10 [10] Eccles. vii. 13, according to Sept.
11 [11] Prov. viii. 9, 10, 11.
12 [12] Tit. i. 12, 13.
13 [13] [Though Canon Farrar minimizes the Greek scholarship of St. Paul, as is now the fashion, I think Clement credits him with Greek learning. The apostle's example seems to have inspired the philosophical arguments of Clement, as well as his exuberance of poetical and mythological quotation.]

ing for the edification of some and the shaming of others, to make use of Greek poems. Accordingly to the Corinthians (for this is not the only instance), while discoursing on the resurrection of the dead, he makes use of a tragic Iambic line, when he said, "What advantageth it me if the dead are not raised? Let us eat and drink, for to-morrow we die. Be not deceived; evil communications corrupt good manners."[1] Others have enumerated Acusilaus the Argive among the seven wise men; and others, Pherecydes of Syros. And Plato substitutes Myso the Chenian for Periander, whom he deemed unworthy of wisdom, on account of his having reigned as a tyrant. That the wise men among the Greeks flourished after the age of Moses, will, a little after, be shown. But the style of philosophy among them, as Hebraic and enigmatical, is now to be considered. They adopted brevity, as suited for exhortation, and most useful. Even Plato says, that of old this mode was purposely in vogue among all the Greeks, especially the Lacedæmonians and Cretans, who enjoyed the best laws.

The expression, "Know thyself," some supposed to be Chilon's. But Chamæleon, in his book *About the Gods*, ascribes it to Thales; Aristotle to the Pythian. It may be an injunction to the pursuit of knowledge. For it is not possible to know the parts without the essence of the whole; and one must study the genesis of the universe, that thereby we may be able to learn the nature of man. Again, to Chilon the Lacedæmonian they attribute, "Let nothing be too much."[2] Strato, in his book *Of Inventions*, ascribes the apophthegm to Stratodemus of Tegea. Didymus assigns it to Solon; as also to Cleobulus the saying, "A middle course is best." And the expression, "Come under a pledge, and mischief is at hand," Cleomenes says, in his book *Concerning Hesiod*, was uttered before by Homer in the lines:—

"Wretched pledges, for the wretched, to be pledged."[3]

The Aristotelians judge it to be Chilon's; but Didymus says the advice was that of Thales. Then, next in order, the saying, "All men are bad," or, "The most of men are bad" (for the same apophthegm is expressed in two ways), Sotades the Byzantian says that it was Bias's. And the aphorism, "Practice conquers everything,"[4] they will have it to be Periander's; and likewise the advice, "Know the opportunity," to have been a saying of Pittacus. Solon made laws for the Athenians, Pittacus for the Mitylenians. And at a late date, Pythagoras, the pupil

of Pherecydes, first called himself a philosopher. Accordingly, after the fore-mentioned three men, there were three schools of philosophy, named after the places where they lived: the Italic from Pythagoras, the Ionic from Thales, the Eleatic from Xenophanes. Pythagoras was a Samian, the son of Mnesarchus, as Hippobotus says: according to Aristoxenus, in his life of Pythagoras and Aristarchus and Theopompus, he was a Tuscan; and according to Neanthes, a Syrian or a Tyrian. So that Pythagoras was, according to the most, of barbarian extraction. Thales, too, as Leander and Herodotus relate, was a Phœnician; as some suppose, a Milesian. He alone seems to have met the prophets of the Egyptians. But no one is described as his teacher, nor is any one mentioned as the teacher of Pherecydes of Syros, who had Pythagoras as his pupil. But the Italic philosophy, that of Pythagoras, grew old in Metapontum in Italy. Anaximander of Miletus, the son of Praxiades, succeeded Thales; and was himself succeeded by Anaximenes of Miletus, the son of Eurustratus; after whom came Anaxagoras of Clazomenæ, the son of Hegesibulus.[5] He transferred his school from Ionia to Athens. He was succeeded by Archelaus, whose pupil Socrates was.

"From these turned aside, the stone-mason;
Talker about laws; the enchanter of the Greeks,"

says Timon in his *Satirical Poems*, on account of his quitting physics for ethics. Antisthenes, after being a pupil of Socrates, introduced the Cynic philosophy; and Plato withdrew to the Academy. Aristotle, after studying philosophy under Plato, withdrew to the Lyceum, and founded the Peripatetic sect. He was succeeded by Theophrastus, who was succeeded by Strato, and he by Lycon, then Critolaus, and then Diodorus. Speusippus was the successor of Plato; his successor was Xenocrates; and the successor of the latter, Polemo. And the disciples of Polemo were Crates and Crantor, in whom the old Academy founded by Plato ceased. Arcesilaus was the associate of Crantor; from whom, down to Hegesilaus, the Middle Academy flourished. Then Carneades succeeded Hegesilaus, and others came in succession. The disciple of Crates was Zeno of Citium, the founder of the Stoic sect. He was succeeded by Cleanthes; and the latter by Chrysippus, and others after him. Xenophanes of Colophon was the founder of the Eleatic school, whô, Timæus says, lived in the time of Hiero, lord of Sicily, and Epicharmus the poet; and Apollodorus says that he was born in the fortieth Olympiad, and reached to the times of Darius and Cyrus. Parmenides, accordingly, was the disciple of Xenophanes, and Zeno of him; then came Leu-

---

[1] 1 Cor. xv. 32, 33.
[2] "Nequid nimis." Μηδὲν ἄγαν.
[3] *Odyss.*, viii. 351.
[4] Μελέτη πάντα καθαιρεῖ.

[5] Or Eubulus.

cippus, and then Democritus. Disciples of Democritus were Protagoras of Abdera, and Metrodorus of Chios, whose pupil was Diogenes of Smyrna; and his again Anaxarchus, and his Pyrrho, and his Nausiphanes. Some say that Epicurus was a scholar of his.

Such, in an epitome, is the succession of the philosophers among the Greeks. The periods of the originators of their philosophy are now to be specified successively, in order that, by comparison, we may show that the Hebrew philosophy was older by many generations.[1]

It has been said of Xenophanes that he was the founder of the Eleatic philosophy. And Eudemus, in the *Astrological Histories*, says that Thales foretold the eclipse of the sun, which took place at the time that the Medians and the Lydians fought, in the reign of Cyaxares the father of Astyages over the Medes, and of Alyattus the son of Crœsus over the Lydians. Herodotus in his first book agrees with him. The date is about the fiftieth Olympiad. Pythagoras is ascertained to have lived in the days of Polycrates the tyrant, about the sixty-second Olympiad. Mnesiphilus is described as a follower of Solon, and was a contemporary of Themistocles. Solon therefore flourished about the forty-sixth Olympiad. For Heraclitus, the son of Bauso, persuaded Melancomas the tyrant to abdicate his sovereignty. He despised the invitation of king Darius to visit the Persians.

CHAP. XV. — THE GREEK PHILOSOPHY IN GREAT PART DERIVED FROM THE BARBARIANS.

These are the times of the oldest wise men and philosophers among the Greeks. And that the most of them were barbarians by extraction, and were trained among barbarians, what need is there to say? Pythagoras is shown to have been either a Tuscan or a Tyrian. And Antisthenes was a Phrygian. And Orpheus was an Odrysian or a Thracian. The most, too, show Homer to have been an Egyptian. Thales was a Phœnician by birth, and was said to have consorted with the prophets of the Egyptians; as also Pythagoras did with the same persons, by whom he was circumcised, that he might enter the adytum and learn from the Egyptians the mystic philosophy. He held converse with the chief of the Chaldeans and the Magi; and he gave a hint of the church, now so called, in the common hall[2] which he maintained.

And Plato does not deny that he procured all that is most excellent in philosophy from the barbarians; and he admits that he came into Egypt. Whence, writing in the *Phædo* that the

philosopher can receive aid from all sides, he said: "Great indeed is Greece, O Cebes, in which everywhere there are good men, and many are the races of the barbarians."[3] Thus Plato thinks that some of the barbarians, too, are philosophers. But Epicurus, on the other hand, supposes that only Greeks can philosophise. And in the *Symposium*, Plato, lauding the barbarians as practising philosophy with conspicuous excellence,[4] truly says: "And in many other instances both among Greeks and barbarians, whose temples reared for such sons are already numerous." And it is clear that the barbarians signally honoured their lawgivers and teachers, designating them gods. For, according to Plato, "they think that good souls, on quitting the supercelestial region, submit to come to this Tartarus, and assuming a body, share in all the ills which are involved in birth, from their solicitude for the race of men;" and these make laws and publish philosophy, "than which no greater boon ever came from the gods to the race of men, or will come."[5]

And as appears to me, it was in consequence of perceiving the great benefit which is conferred through wise men, that the men themselves were honoured and philosophy cultivated publicly by all the Brahmins, and the Odrysi, and the Getæ. And such were strictly deified by the race of the Egyptians, by the Chaldeans and the Arabians, called the Happy, and those that inhabited Palestine, by not the least portion of the Persian race, and by innumerable other races besides these. And it is well known that Plato is found perpetually celebrating the barbarians, remembering that both himself and Pythagoras learned the most and the noblest of their dogmas among the barbarians. Wherefore he also called the races of the barbarians, "races of barbarian philosophers," recognising, in the Phædrus, the Egyptian king, and shows him to us wiser than Theut, whom he knew to be Hermes. But in the Charmides, it is manifest that he knew certain Thracians who were said to make the soul immortal. And Pythagoras is reported to have been a disciple of Sonches the Egyptian archprophet; and Plato, of Sechnuphis of Heliopolis; and Eudoxus, of Cnidius of Konuphis, who was also an Egyptian. And in his book, *On the Soul*,[6] Plato again manifestly recognises prophecy, when he introduces a prophet announcing

---

[1] [Clement's Attic scholarship never seduces him from this fidelity to the Scriptures. The argument from superior antiquity was one which the Greeks were sure to feel when demonstrated.]
[2] ὁμακοεῖον.

[3] Greece is ample, O Cebes, in which everywhere there are good men; and many are the races of the barbarians, over all of whom you must search, seeking such a physician, sparing neither money nor pains. — *Phædo*, p. 78 A.
[4] This sense is obtained by the omission of μόνους from the text, which may have crept in in consequence of occurring in the previous text, to make it agree with what Plato says, which is, "And both among Greeks and barbarians, there are many who have shown many and illustrious deeds, generating virtue of every kind, to whom many temples on account of such sons are raised." — *Symp.*, p. 209 E.
[5] Plato, *Timæus*, p. 47 A.
[6] A mistake of Clement for *The Republic*.

the word of Lachesis, uttering predictions to the souls whose destiny is becoming fixed. And in the *Timæus* he introduces Solon, the very wise, learning from the barbarian. The substance of the declaration is to the following effect : " O Solon, Solon, you Greeks are always children. And no Greek is an old man. For you have no learning that is hoary with age." [1]

Democritus appropriated the Babylonian ethic discourses, for he is said to have combined with his own compositions a translation of the column of Acicarus.[2] And you may find the distinction notified by him when he writes, "Thus says Democritus." About himself, too, where, pluming himself on his erudition, he says, " I have roamed over the most ground of any man of my time, investigating the most remote parts. I have seen the most skies and lands, and I have heard of learned men in very great numbers. And in composition no one has surpassed me ; in demonstration, not even those among the Egyptians who are called Arpenodaptæ, with all of whom I lived in exile up to eighty years." For he went to Babylon, and Persis, and Egypt, to learn from the Magi and the priests.

Zoroaster the Magus, Pythagoras showed to be a Persian. Of the secret books of this man, those who follow the heresy of Prodicus boast to be in possession. Alexander, in his book *On the Pythagorean Symbols*, relates that Pythagoras was a pupil of Nazaratus the Assyrian [3] (some think that he is Ezekiel ; but he is not, as will afterwards be shown), and will have it that, in addition to these, Pythagoras was a hearer of the Galatæ and the Brahmins. Clearchus the Peripatetic says that he knew a Jew who associated with Aristotle.[4] Heraclitus says that, not humanly, but rather by God's aid, the Sibyl spoke.[5] They say, accordingly, that at Delphi a stone was shown beside the oracle, on which, it is said, sat the first Sibyl, who came from Helicon, and had been reared by the Muses. But some say that she came from Milea, being the daughter of Lamia of Sidon.[6] And Serapion, in his epic verses, says that the Sibyl, even when dead, ceased not from divination. And he writes that, what proceeded from her into the air after her death, was what gave oracular utterances in voices and omens ; and on her body being changed into earth, and the grass as natural growing out of it, whatever beasts happening to be in that place fed on it exhibited to men an accurate

knowledge of futurity by their entrails. He thinks also, that the face seen in the moon is her soul. So much for the Sibyl.

Numa the king of the Romans was a Pythagorean, and aided by the precepts of Moses, prohibited from making an image of God in human form, and of the shape of a living creature. Accordingly, during the first hundred and seventy years, though building temples, they made no cast or graven image. For Numa secretly showed them that the Best of Beings could not be apprehended except by the mind alone. Thus philosophy, a thing of the highest utility, flourished in antiquity among the barbarians, shedding its light over the nations. And afterwards it came to Greece. First in its ranks were the prophets of the Egyptians ; and the Chaldeans among the Assyrians ; and the Druids among the Gauls ; and the Samanæans among the Bactrians ; and the philosophers of the Celts ; and the Magi of the Persians, who foretold the Saviour's birth, and came into the land of Judæa guided by a star. The Indian gymnosophists are also in the number, and the other barbarian philosophers. And of these there are two classes, some of them called Sarmanæ,[7] and others Brahmins. And those of the Sarmanæ who are called Hylobii [8] neither inhabit cities, nor have roofs over them, but are clothed in the bark of trees, feed on nuts, and drink water in their hands. Like those called Encratites in the present day, they know not marriage nor begetting of children.

Some, too, of the Indians obey the precepts of Buddha ; [9] whom, on account of his extraordinary sanctity, they have raised to divine honours.

Anacharsis was a Scythian, and is recorded to have excelled many philosophers among the Greeks. And the Hyperboreans, Hellanicus relates, dwelt beyond the Riphæan mountains, and inculcated justice, not eating flesh, but using nuts. Those who are sixty years old they take without the gates, and do away with. There are also among the Germans those called sacred women, who, by inspecting the whirlpools of rivers and the eddies, and observing the noises of streams, presage and predict future events.[10] These did not allow the men to fight against Cæsar till the new moon shone.

Of all these, by far the oldest is the Jewish race ; and that their philosophy committed to writing has the precedence of philosophy among the Greeks, the Pythagorean Philo [11] shows at large ; and, besides him, Aristobulus the Peripatetic, and several others, not to waste time, in

---

[1] *Timæus*, p. 22 B.
[2] About which the learned have tortured themselves greatly. The reference is doubtless here to some pillar inscribed with what was deemed a writing of importance. But as to Acicarus nothing is known.
[3] Otherwise Zaratus, or Zabratus, or Zaras, who, Huet says, was Zoroaster.
[4] [Direct testimony, establishing one important fact in the history of philosophy.]
[5] Adopting Lowth's emendation, Σιβύλλην φάναι.
[6] Or, according to the reading in Pausanias, and the statement of Plutarch, " who was the daughter of Poseidon."

[7] Or Samanæi.
[8] Altered for Ἀλλόβιοι in accordance with the note of Montacutius, who cites Strabo as an authority for the existence of a sect of Indian sages called Hylobii, ὑλόβιοι — Silvicolæ.
[9] Βουττα.
[10] Cæsar, *Gallic War*, book i. chap. 50.
[11] Sozomen also calls Philo a Pythagorean.

going over them by name. Very clearly the author Megasthenes, the contemporary of Seleucus Nicanor, writes as follows in the third of his books, *On Indian Affairs:* "All that was said about nature by the ancients is said also by those who philosophise beyond Greece : some things by the Brahmins among the Indians, and others by those called Jews in Syria." Some more fabulously say that certain of those called the Idæan Dactyli were the first wise men ; to whom are attributed the invention of what are called the "Ephesian letters," and of numbers in music. For which reason dactyls in music received their name. And the Idæan Dactyli were Phrygians and barbarians. Herodotus relates that Hercules, having grown a sage and a student of physics, received from the barbarian Atlas, the Phrygian, the columns of the universe ; the fable meaning that he received by instruction the knowledge of the heavenly bodies. And Hermippus of Berytus calls Charon the Centaur wise ; about whom, he that wrote *The Battle of the Titans* says, " that he first led the race of mortals to righteousness, by teaching them the solemnity of the oath, and propitiatory sacrifices and the figures of Olympus." By him Achilles, who fought at Troy, was taught. And Hippo, the daughter of the Centaur, who dwelt with Æolus, taught him her father's science, the knowledge of physics. Euripides also testifies of Hippo as follows : —

> " Who first, by oracles, presaged,
> And by the rising stars, events divine."

By this Æolus, Ulysses was received as a guest after the taking of Troy. Mark the epochs by comparison with the age of Moses, and with the high antiquity of the philosophy promulgated by him.

CHAP. XVI. — THAT THE INVENTORS OF OTHER ARTS WERE MOSTLY BARBARIANS.

And barbarians were inventors not only of philosophy, but almost of every art. The Egyptians were the first to introduce astrology among men. Similarly also the Chaldeans. The Egyptians first showed how to burn lamps, and divided the year into twelve months, prohibited intercourse with women in the temples, and enacted that no one should enter the temples[1] from a woman without bathing. Again, they were the inventors of geometry. There are some who say that the Carians invented prognostication by the stars. The Phrygians were the first who attended to the flight of birds. And the Tuscans, neighbours of Italy, were adepts at the art of the Haruspex. The Isaurians and the Arabians invented augury, as the Telmesians divination by dreams. The Etruscans invented the

trumpet, and the Phrygians the flute. For Olympus and Marsyas were Phrygians. And Cadmus, the inventor of letters among the Greeks, as Euphorus says, was a Phœnician ; whence also Herodotus writes that they were called Phœnician letters. And they say that the Phœnicians and the Syrians first invented letters ; and that Apis, an aboriginal inhabitant of Egypt, invented the healing art before Io came into Egypt. But afterwards they say that Asclepius improved the art. Atlas the Libyan was the first who built a ship and navigated the sea. Kelmis and Damnaneus, Idæan Dactyli, first discovered iron in Cyprus. Another Idæan discovered the tempering of brass ; according to Hesiod, a Scythian. The Thracians first invented what is called a scimitar ($\check{\alpha}\rho\pi\eta$), — it is a curved sword, — and were the first to use shields on horseback. Similarly also the Illyrians invented the shield ($\pi\acute{\epsilon}\lambda\tau\eta$). Besides, they say that the Tuscans invented the art of moulding clay ; and that Itanus (he was a Samnite) first fashioned the oblong shield ($\theta\nu\rho\acute{\epsilon}os$). Cadmus the Phœnician invented stonecutting, and discovered the gold mines on the Pangæan mountain. Further, another nation, the Cappadocians, first invented the instrument called the nabla,[2] and the Assyrians in the same way the dichord. The Carthaginians were the first that constructed a trireme ; and it was built by Bosporus, an aboriginal.[3] Medea, the daughter of Æetas, a Colchian, first invented the dyeing of hair. Besides, the Noropes (they are a Pæonian race, and are now called the Norici) worked copper, and were the first that purified iron. Amycus the king of the Bebryci was the first inventor of boxing-gloves.[4] In music, Olympus the Mysian practised the Lydian harmony ; and the people called Troglodytes invented the sambuca,[5] a musical instrument. It is said that the crooked pipe was invented by Satyrus the Phrygian ; likewise also diatonic harmony by Hyagnis, a Phrygian too ; and notes by Olympus, a Phrygian ; as also the Phrygian harmony, and the half-Phrygian and the half-Lydian, by Marsyas, who belonged to the same region as those mentioned above. And the Doric was invented by Thamyris the Thracian. We have heard that the Persians were the first who fashioned the chariot, and bed, and footstool ; and the Sidonians the first to construct a trireme. The Sicilians, close to Italy, were the first inventors of the phorminx, which is not much inferior to the lyre. And they invented castanets. In the

---

[1] [Elucidation XI. *infra;* also p. 428, *infra.*]

[2] νάβλα and ναυλα, Lat. *nablium*; doubtless the Hebrew נבל (psaltery, A. V.), described by Josephus as a lyre or harp of twelve strings (in Ps. xxxiii. it is said ten), and played with the fingers. Jerome says it was triangular in shape.

[3] αὐτόχθων, Eusebius. The text has αὐτοσχέδιον, off-hand.

[4] Literally, fist-straps, the cæstus of the boxers.

[5] σαμβύκη, a triangular lyre with four strings.

time of Semiramis queen of the Assyrians,[1] they relate that linen garments were invented. And Hellanicus says that Atossa queen of the Persians was the first who composed a letter. These things are reported by Scamo of Mitylene, Theophrastus of Ephesus, Cydippus of Mantinea, also Antiphanes, Aristodemus, and Aristotle ; and besides these, Philostephanus, and also Strato the Peripatetic, in his books *Concerning Inventions*. I have added a few details from them, in order to confirm the inventive and practically useful genius of the barbarians, by whom the Greeks profited in their studies. And if any one objects to the barbarous language, Anacharsis says, " All the Greeks speak Scythian to me." It was he who was held in admiration by the Greeks, who said, " My covering is a cloak ; my supper, milk and cheese." You see that the barbarian philosophy professes deeds, not words. The apostle thus speaks : " So likewise ye, except ye utter by the tongue a word easy to be understood, how shall ye know what is spoken? for ye shall speak into the air. There are, it may be, so many kind of voices in the world, and none of them is without signification. Therefore if I know not the meaning of the voice, I shall be unto him that speaketh a barbarian, and he that speaketh shall be a barbarian unto me." And, " Let him that speaketh in an unknown tongue pray that he may interpret."[2]

Nay more, it was late before the teaching and writing of discourses reached Greece. Alcmæon, the son of Perithus, of Crotona, first composed a treatise on nature. And it is related that Anaxagoras of Clazomenæ, the son of Hegesibulus, first published a book in writing. The first to adapt music to poetical compositions was Terpander of Antissa ; and he set the laws of the Lacedæmonians to music. Lasus of Hermione invented the dithyramb ; Stesichorus of Himera, the hymn ; Alcman the Spartan, the choral song ; Anacreon of Teos, love songs ; Pindar the Theban, the dance accompanied with song. Timotheus of Miletus was the first to execute those musical compositions called νόμοι on the lyre, with dancing. Moreover, the iambus was invented by Archilochus of Paros, and the choliambus by Hipponax of Ephesus. Tragedy owed its origin to Thespis the Athenian, and comedy to Susarion of Icaria. Their dates are handed down by the grammarians. But it were tedious to specify them accurately : presently, however, Dionysus, on whose account the Dionysian spectacles are celebrated, will be shown to be later than Moses. They say that Antiphon of Rhamnusium, the son of Sophilus, first in-

vented scholastic discourses and rhetorical figures, and was the first who pled causes for a fee, and wrote a forensic speech for delivery,[3] as Diodorus says. And Apollodorus of Cuma first assumed the name of critic, and was called a grammarian. Some say it was Eratosthenes of Cyrene who was first so called, since he published two books which he entitled *Grammatica*. The first who was called a grammarian, as we now use the term, was Praxiphanes, the son of Disnysophenes of Mitylene. Zeleucus the Locrian was reported to have been the first to have framed laws (in writing) Others say that it was Menos the son of Zeus, in the time of Lynceus. He comes after Danaus, in the eleventh generation from Inachus and Moses ; as we shall show a little further on. And Lycurgus, who lived many years after the taking of Troy, legislated for the Lacedæmonians a hundred and fifty years before the Olympiads. We have spoken before of the age of Solon. Draco (he was a legislator too) is discovered to have lived about the three hundred and ninth Olympiad. Antilochus, again, who wrote of the learned men from the age of Pythagoras to the death of Epicurus, which took place in the tenth day of the month Gamelion, makes up altogether three hundred and twelve years. Moreover, some say that Phanothea, the wife of Icarius, invented the heroic hexameter ; others Themis, one of the Titanides. Didymus, however, in his* work *On the Pythagorean Philosophy*, relates that Theano of Crotona was the first woman who cultivated philosophy and composed poems The Hellenic philosophy then, according to some, apprehended the truth accidentally, dimly, partially ; as others will have it, was set a-going by the devil. Several suppose that certain powers, descending from heaven, inspired the whole of philosophy. But if the Hellenic philosophy comprehends not the whole extent of the truth, and besides is destitute of strength to perform the commandments of the Lord, yet it prepares the way for the truly royal teaching ; training in some way or other, and moulding the character, and fitting him who believes in Providence for the reception of the truth.[4]

CHAP. XVII. — ON THE SAYING OF THE SAVIOUR, " ALL THAT CAME BEFORE ME WERE THIEVES AND ROBBERS."[5]

But, say they, it is written, " All who were before the Lord's advent are thieves and robbers." All, then, who are in the Word (for it is these that were previous to the incarnation of the Word) are understood generally. But the

---

[1] " King of the Egyptians" in the MSS. of Clement. The correction is made from Eusebius, who extracts the passage.
[2] 1 Cor. xiv. 9, 10, 11, 13.
[3] By one or other of the parties in the case, it being a practice of advocates in ancient times to compose speeches which the litigants delivered.
[4] [Elucidation XII., *infra*.]
[5] John x. 8.

prophets, being sent and inspired by the Lord, were not thieves, but servants. The Scripture accordingly says, "Wisdom sent her servants, inviting with loud proclamation to a goblet of wine." [1]

But philosophy, it is said, was not sent by the Lord, but came stolen, or given by a thief. It was then some power or angel that had learned something of the truth, but abode not in it, that inspired and taught these things, not without the Lord's knowledge, who knew before the constitution of each essence the issues of futurity, but without His prohibition.

For the theft which reached men then, had some advantage; not that he who perpetrated the theft had utility in his eye, but Providence directed the issue of the audacious deed to utility. I know that many are perpetually assailing us with the allegation, that not to prevent a thing happening, is to be the cause of it happening. For they say, that the man who does not take precaution against a theft, or does not prevent it, is the cause of it: as he is the cause of the conflagration who has not quenched it at the beginning; and the master of the vessel who does not reef the sail, is the cause of the shipwreck. Certainly those who are the causes of such events are punished by the law. For to him who had power to prevent, attaches the blame of what happens. We say to them, that causation is seen in doing, working, acting; but the not preventing is in this respect inoperative. Further, causation attaches to activity; as in the case of the shipbuilder in relation to the origin of the vessel, and the builder in relation to the construction of the house. But that which does not prevent is separated from what takes place. Wherefore the effect will be accomplished; because that which could have prevented neither acts nor prevents. For what activity does that which prevents not exert? Now their assertion is reduced to absurdity, if they shall say that the cause of the wound is not the dart, but the shield, which did not prevent the dart from passing through; and if they blame not the thief, but the man who did not prevent the theft. Let them then say, that it was not Hector that burned the ships of the Greeks, but Achilles; because, having the power to prevent Hector, he did not prevent him; but out of anger (and it depended on himself to be angry or not) did not keep back the fire, and was a concurring cause. Now the devil, being possessed of free-will, was able both to repent and to steal; and it was he who was the author of the theft, not the Lord, who did not prevent him. But neither was the gift hurtful, so as to require that prevention should intervene.

But if strict accuracy must be employed in dealing with them, let them know, that that which does not prevent what we assert to have taken place in the theft, is not a cause at all; but that what prevents is involved in the accusation of being a cause. For he that protects with a shield is the cause of him whom he protects not being wounded; preventing him, as he does, from being wounded. For the demon of Socrates was a cause, not by not preventing, but by exhorting, even if (strictly speaking) he did not exhort. And neither praises nor censures, neither rewards nor punishments, are right, when the soul has not the power of inclination and disinclination, but evil is involuntary. Whence he who prevents is a cause; while he who prevents not judges justly the soul's choice. So in no respect is God the author of evil. But since free choice and inclination originate sins, and a mistaken judgment sometimes prevails, from which, since it is ignorance and stupidity, we do not take pains to recede, punishments are rightly inflicted. For to take fever is involuntary; but when one takes fever through his own fault, from excess, we blame him. Inasmuch, then, as evil is involuntary,—for no one prefers evil as evil; but induced by the pleasure that is in it, and imagining it good, considers it desirable;—such being the case, to free ourselves from ignorance, and from evil and voluptuous choice, and above all, to withhold our assent from those delusive phantasies, depends on ourselves. The devil is called "thief and robber;" having mixed false prophets with the prophets, as tares with the wheat. "All, then, that came before the Lord, were thieves and robbers;" not absolutely all men, but all the false prophets, and all who were not properly sent by Him. For the false prophets possessed the prophetic name dishonestly, being prophets, but prophets of the liar. For the Lord says, "Ye are of your father the devil; and the lusts of your father ye will do. He was a murderer from the beginning, and abode not in the truth, because there is no truth in him. When he speaketh a lie, he speaketh of his own; for he is a liar, and the father of it." [2]

But among the lies, the false prophets also told some true things. And in reality they prophesied "in an ecstasy," as [3] the servants of the apostate. And the Shepherd, the angel of repentance, says to Hermas, of the false prophet: "For he speaks some truths. For the devil fills him with his own spirit, if perchance he may be able to cast down any one from what is right." All things, therefore, are dispensed from heaven for good, "that by the Church may be made known the manifold wisdom of God, according

---

[1] Prov. ix. 3.

[2] John viii. 44.
[3] [The devil can quote Scripture. Hermas, p. 27, this volume See, on this important chapter, Elucidation XIII., *infra*.]

to the eternal foreknowledge,[1] which He purposed in Christ."[2] Nothing withstands God: nothing opposes Him: seeing He is Lord and omnipotent. Further, the counsels and activities of those who have rebelled, being partial, proceed from a bad disposition, as bodily diseases from a bad constitution, but are guided by universal Providence to a salutary issue, even though the cause be productive of disease. It is accordingly the greatest achievement of divine Providence, not to allow the evil, which has sprung from voluntary apostasy, to remain useless, and for no good, and not to become in all respects injurious. For it is the work of the divine wisdom, and excellence, and power, not alone to do good (for this is, so to speak, the nature of God, as it is of fire to warm and of light to illumine), but especially to ensure that what happens through the evils hatched by any, may come to a good and useful issue, and to use to advantage those things which appear to be evils, as also the testimony which accrues from temptation.

There is then in philosophy, though stolen as the fire by Prometheus, a slender spark, capable of being fanned into flame, a trace of wisdom and an impulse from God. Well, be it so that "the thieves and robbers" are the philosophers among the Greeks, who from the Hebrew prophets before the coming of the Lord received fragments of the truth, not with full knowledge, and claimed these as their own teachings, disguising some points, treating others sophistically by their ingenuity, and discovering other things, for perchance they had "the spirit of perception."[3] Aristotle, too, assented to Scripture, and declared sophistry to have stolen wisdom, as we intimated before. And the apostle says, "Which things we speak, not in the words which man's wisdom teacheth, but which the Holy Ghost teacheth."[4] For of the prophets it is said, "We have all received of His fulness,"[5] that is, of Christ's. So that the prophets are not thieves. "And my doctrine is not Mine," saith the Lord, "but the Father's which sent me." And of those who steal He says: "But he that speaketh of himself, seeketh his own glory."[6] Such are the Greeks, "lovers of their own selves, and boasters."[7] Scripture, when it speaks of these as wise, does not brand those who are really wise, but those who are wise in appearance.

CHAP. XVIII. — HE ILLUSTRATES THE APOSTLE'S SAYING, "I WILL DESTROY THE WISDOM OF THE WISE."

And of such it is said, "I will destroy the wisdom of the wise: I will bring to nothing the understanding of the prudent." The apostle accordingly adds, "Where is the wise? Where is the scribe? Where is the disputer of this world?" setting in contradistinction to the scribes, the disputers[8] of this world, the philosophers of the Gentiles. "Hath not God made foolish the wisdom of the world?"[9] which is equivalent to, showed it to be foolish, and not true, as they thought. And if you ask the cause of their seeming wisdom, he will say, "because of the blindness of their heart;" since "in the wisdom of God," that is, as proclaimed by the prophets, "the world knew not," in the wisdom "which spake by the prophets," "Him,"[10] that is, God, — "it pleased God by the foolishness of preaching"— what seemed to the Greeks foolishness —"to save them that believe. For the Jews require signs," in order to faith; "and the Greeks seek after wisdom," plainly those reasonings styled "irresistible," and those others, namely, syllogisms. "But we preach Jesus Christ crucified; to the Jews a stumbling-block," because, though knowing prophecy, they did not believe the event: "to the Greeks, foolishness;" for those who in their own estimation are wise, consider it fabulous that the Son of God should speak by man and that God should have a Son, and especially that that Son should have suffered. Whence their preconceived idea inclines them to disbelieve. For the advent of the Saviour did not make people foolish, and hard of heart, and unbelieving, but made them understanding, amenable to persuasion, and believing. But those that would not believe, by separating themselves from the voluntary adherence of those who obeyed, were proved to be without understanding, unbelievers and fools. "But to them who are called, both Jews and Greeks, Christ is the power of God, and the wisdom of God." Should we not understand (as is better) the words rendered, "Hath not God made foolish the wisdom of the world?" negatively: "God hath not made foolish the wisdom of the world?"— so that the cause of their hardness of heart may not appear to have proceeded from God, "making foolish the wisdom of the world." For on all accounts, being wise, they incur greater blame in not believing the proclamation. For the preference and choice of truth is voluntary. But that declaration, "I will destroy the wisdom of the wise," declares Him to have sent forth light, by bringing forth in opposition the despised and contemned barbarian philosophy; as the lamp, when shone upon by the sun, is said to be extinguished, on account of its not then exert-

---

[1] Clement reads πρόγνωσιν for πρόθεσιν.
[2] Eph. iii. 10, 11.
[3] Ex. xxviii. 3.
[4] 1 Cor. ii. 13.
[5] John i. 16.
[6] John vii. 16, 18.
[7] 2 Tim. iii. 2.

[8] Or. "inquirers."
[9] 1 Cor. i. 19, 20.
[10] 1 Cor. i. 21–24; where the reading is Θεόν, not Αὐτόν.

ing the same power. All having been therefore called, those who are willing to obey have been named[1] "called." For there is no unrighteousness with God. Those of either race who have believed, are "a peculiar people."[2] And in the Acts of the Apostles you will find this, word for word, "Those then who received his word were baptized;"[3] but those who would not obey kept themselves aloof. To these prophecy says, "If ye be willing and hear me, ye shall eat the good things of the land;"[4] proving that choice or refusal depends on ourselves. The apostle designates the doctrine which is according to the Lord, "the wisdom of God," in order to show that the true philosophy has been communicated by the Son. Further, he, who has a show of wisdom, has certain exhortations enjoined on him by the apostle: "That ye put on the new man, which after God is renewed in righteousness and true holiness. Wherefore, putting away lying, speak every man truth. Neither give place to the devil. Let him that stole, steal no more; but rather let him labour, working that which is good" (and to work is to labour in seeking the truth; for it is accompanied with rational well-doing), "that ye may have to give to him that has need,"[5] both of worldly wealth and of divine wisdom. For he wishes both that the word be taught, and that the money be put into the bank, accurately tested, to accumulate interest. Whence he adds, "Let no corrupt communication proceed out of your mouth,"—that is "corrupt communication" which proceeds out of conceit,—"but that which is good for the use of edifying, that it may minister grace to the hearers." And the word of the good God must needs be good. And how is it possible that he who saves shall not be good?

CHAP. XIX.—THAT THE PHILOSOPHERS HAVE ATTAINED TO SOME PORTION OF TRUTH.

Since, then, the Greeks are testified to have laid down some true opinions, we may from this point take a glance at the testimonies. Paul, in the Acts of the Apostles, is recorded to have said to the Areopagites, "I perceive that ye are more than ordinarily religious. For as I passed by, and beheld your devotions, I found an altar with the inscription, To The Unknown God. Whom therefore ye ignorantly worship, Him declare I unto you. God, that made the world and all things therein, seeing that He is Lord of heaven and earth, dwelleth not in temples made with hands; neither is worshipped with men's hands, as though He needed anything, seeing He giveth

to all life, and breath, and all things; and hath made of one blood all nations of men to dwell on all the face of the earth, and hath determined the times before appointed, and the bounds of their habitation; that they should seek God, if haply they might feel after Him, and find Him; though He be not far from every one of us: for in Him we live, and move, and have our being; as certain also of your own poets have said, For we also are His offspring."[6] Whence it is evident that the apostle, by availing himself of poetical examples from the *Phenomena* of Aratus, approves of what had been well spoken by the Greeks; and intimates that, by the unknown God, God the Creator was in a roundabout way worshipped by the Greeks; but that it was necessary by positive knowledge to apprehend and learn Him by the Son. "Wherefore, then, I send thee to the Gentiles," it is said, "to open their eyes, and to turn them from darkness to light, and from the power of Satan unto God; that they may receive forgiveness of sins, and inheritance among them that are sanctified by faith which is in Me."[7] Such, then, are the eyes of the blind which are opened. The knowledge of the Father by the Son is the comprehension of the "Greek circumlocution;"[8] and to turn from the power of Satan is to change from sin, through which bondage was produced. We do not, indeed, receive absolutely all philosophy, but that of which Socrates[9] speaks in Plato. "For there are (as they say) in the mysteries many bearers of the thyrsus, but few bacchanals;" meaning, "that many are called, but few chosen." He accordingly plainly adds: "These, in my opinion, are none else than those who have philosophized right; to belong to whose number, I myself have left nothing undone in life, as far as I could, but have endeavoured in every way. Whether we have endeavoured rightly and achieved aught, we shall know when we have gone there, if God will, a little afterwards." Does he not then seem to declare from the Hebrew Scriptures the righteous man's hope, through faith, after death? And in *Demodocus*[10] (if that is really the work of Plato): "And do not imagine that I call it philosophizing to spend life pottering about the arts, or learning many

---

[1] [He thus expounds the *Ecclesia*.]
[2] Tit. ii. 14.
[3] Acts. ii. 41.
[4] Isa. i. 19.
[5] Eph. iv. 24, 25, 27–29.

[6] Acts xvii. 22–28.
[7] Acts xxvi. 17, 18.
[8] Viz., "The Unknown God." [Hereafter to be noted.]
[9] [Not original with Socrates, but a common adage:—

Multi thyrsigeri, pauci Bacchi.

The original Greek hexameter is given by Erasmus, in his *Adagia* (p. 650), with numerous equivalents, among which take this: *Non omnes episcopi qui mitram gerunt bicornem.* He reminds us that Plato borrows it in the *Phædo*, and he quotes the parallel saying of Herodes Atticus, " I see a beard and the cloak, but as yet do not discover the philosopher."]

[10] There is no such utterance in the *Demodocus*. But in the *Amatores*, Basle Edition, p. 237, Plato says: " But it is not so, my friend; nor is it philosophizing to occupy oneself in the arts, nor lead a life of bustling, meddling activity, nor to learn many things: but it is something else. Since I, at least, would reckon this a reproach; and that those who devote themselves to the arts ought to be called mechanics."

things, but something different; since I, at least, would consider this a disgrace." For he knew, I reckon, "that the knowledge of many things does not educate the mind,"[1] according to Heraclitus. And in the fifth book of the *Republic*,[2] he says, "'Shall we then call all these, and the others which study such things, and those who apply themselves to the meaner arts, philosophers?' 'By no means,' I said, 'but like philosophers.' 'And whom,' said he, 'do you call true?' 'Those,' said I, 'who delight in the contemplation of truth. For philosophy is not in geometry, with its postulates and hypotheses; nor in music, which is conjectural; nor in astronomy, crammed full of physical, fluid, and probable causes. But the knowledge of the good and truth itself are requisite, — what is good being one thing, and the ways to the good another.'"[3] So that he does not allow that the curriculum of training suffices for the good, but co-operates in rousing and training the soul to intellectual objects. Whether, then, they say that the Greeks gave forth some utterances of the true philosophy by accident, it is the accident of a divine administration (for no one will, for the sake of the present argument with us, deify chance); or by good fortune, good fortune is not unforeseen. Or were one, on the other hand, to say that the Greeks possessed a natural conception of these things, we know the one Creator of nature; just as we also call righteousness natural; or that they had a common intellect, let us reflect who is its father, and what righteousness is in the mental economy. For were one to name "prediction,"[4] and assign as its cause "combined utterance,"[5] he specifies forms of prophecy. Further, others will have it that some truths were uttered by the philosophers, in appearance.

The divine apostle writes accordingly respecting us: "For now we see as through a glass;"[6] knowing ourselves in it by reflection, and simultaneously contemplating, as we can, the efficient cause, from that, which, in us, is divine. For it is said, "Having seen thy brother, thou hast seen thy God:" methinks that now the Saviour God is declared to us. But after the laying aside of the flesh, "face to face," — then definitely and comprehensively, when the heart becomes pure. And by reflection and direct vision, those among the Greeks who have philosophized accurately, see God. For such, through our weakness, are our true views, as images are seen in the water, and as we see things through pellucid and transparent bodies. Excellently therefore Solomon

says: "He who soweth righteousness, worketh faith."[7] "And there are those who, sewing their own, make increase."[8] And again: "Take care of the verdure on the plain, and thou shalt cut grass and gather ripe hay, that thou mayest have sheep for clothing."[9] You see how care must be taken for external clothing and for keeping. "And thou shalt intelligently know the souls of thy flock."[10] "For when the Gentiles, which have not the law, do by nature the things contained in the law, these, having not the law, are a law unto themselves; uncircumcision observing the precepts of the law,"[11] according to the apostle, both before the law and before the advent. As if making comparison of those addicted to philosophy with those called heretics,[12] the Word most clearly says: "Better is a friend that is near, than a brother that dwelleth afar off."[13] "And he who relies on falsehoods, feeds on the winds, and pursues winged birds."[14] I do not think that philosophy directly declares the Word, although in many instances philosophy attempts and persuasively teaches us probable arguments; but it assails the sects. Accordingly it is added: "For he hath forsaken the ways of his own vineyard, and wandered in the tracks of his own husbandry." Such are the sects which deserted the primitive Church.[12] Now he who has fallen into heresy passes through an arid wilderness, abandoning the only true God, destitute of God, seeking waterless water, reaching an uninhabited and thirsty land, collecting sterility with his hands. And those destitute of prudence, that is, those involved in heresies, "I enjoin," remarks Wisdom, saying, "Touch sweetly stolen bread and the sweet water of theft;"[15] the Scripture manifestly applying the terms bread and water to nothing else but to those heresies, which employ bread and water in the oblation, not according to the canon of the Church. For there are those who celebrate the Eucharist with mere water. "But begone, stay not in her place:" *place* is the synagogue, not the Church. He calls it by the equivocal name, *place*. Then He subjoins: "For so shalt thou pass through the water of another;" reckoning heretical baptism not proper and true water. "And thou shalt pass over another's river," that rushes along and sweeps down to the sea; into which he is cast who, having diverged from the stability which is according to truth, rushes back into the heathenish and tumultous waves of life.

---

[1] According to the emendations of Menagius: "ὡς ἄρα ἡ πολυμάθεια νοῦν οὐχὶ διδάσκει."
[2] [Sect. xix. xx. p. 475.]
[3] Adopting the emendations, δεῖ ἐπιστήμης instead of δι' ἐπιστήμης, and τἀγαθῶν for τἀγαθοῦ, omitting ὥσπερ.
[4] προαναφώνησις.
[5] συνεκφώνησις.
[6] 1 Cor. xiii. 12.

[7] Prov. xi. 21.
[8] Prov. xi. 24.
[9] Prov. xxvii. 25, 26.
[10] Prov. xxvii. 23.
[11] Rom. ii. 14, 15.
[12] [His ideas of the condition of the Gnostics, Montanists, and other heretical sects who divided the primitive unity, is important as illustrating Irenæus. Note his words, *the primitive*, etc.]
[13] Prov. xxvii. 10.
[14] Prov. ix. 12.
[15] Prov. ix. 17.

CHAP. XX. — IN WHAT RESPECT PHILOSOPHY CON-
TRIBUTES TO THE COMPREHENSION OF DIVINE
TRUTH.

As many men drawing down the ship, cannot be called many causes, but one cause consisting of many ; — for each individual by himself is not the cause of the ship being drawn, but along with the rest ; — so also philosophy, being the search for truth, contributes to the comprehension of truth ; not as being the cause of comprehension, but a cause along with other things, and co-operator ; perhaps also a joint cause. And as the several virtues are causes of the happiness of one individual ; and as both the sun, and the fire, and the bath, and clothing are of one getting warm : so while truth is one, many things contribute to its investigation. But its discovery is by the Son. If then we consider, virtue is, in power, one. But it is the case, that when exhibited in some things, it is called prudence, in others temperance, and in others manliness or righteousness. By the same analogy, while truth is one, in geometry there is the truth of geometry ; in music, that of music ; and in the right philosophy, there will be Hellenic truth. But that is the only authentic truth, unassailable, in which we are instructed by the Son of God. In the same way we say, that the drachma being one and the same, when given to the shipmaster, is called the fare ; to the tax-gatherer, tax ; to the landlord, rent ; to the teacher, fees ; to the seller, an earnest. And each, whether it be virtue or truth, called by the same name, is the cause of its own peculiar effect alone ; and from the blending of them arises a happy life. For we are not made happy by names alone, when we say that a good life is happiness, and that the man who is adorned in his soul with virtue is happy. But if philosophy contributes remotely to the discovery of truth, by reaching, by diverse essays, after the knowledge which touches close on the truth, the knowledge possessed by us, it aids him who aims at grasping it, in accordance with the Word, to apprehend knowledge. But the Hellenic truth is distinct from that held by us (although it has got the same name), both in respect of extent of knowledge, certainly of demonstration, divine power, and the like. For we are taught of God, being instructed in the truly " sacred letters " [1] by the Son of God. Whence those, to whom we refer, influence souls not in the way we do, but by different teaching. And if, for the sake of those who are fond of fault-finding, we must draw a distinction, by saying that philosophy is a concurrent and co-operating cause of true apprehension, being the search for truth, then we shall avow it to be a

preparatory training for the enlightened man (τοῦ γνωστικοῦ) ; not assigning as the cause that which is but the joint-cause ; nor as the upholding cause, what is merely co-operative ; nor giving to philosophy the place of a *sine quâ non*. Since almost all of us, without training in arts and sciences, and the Hellenic philosophy, and some even without learning at all, through the influence of a philosophy divine and barbarous, and by power, have through faith received the word concerning God, trained by self-operating wisdom. But that which acts in conjunction with something else, being of itself incapable of operating by itself, we describe as co-operating and concausing, and say that it becomes a cause only in virtue of its being a joint-cause, and receives the name of cause only in respect of its concurring with something else, but that it cannot by itself produce the right effect.

Although at one time philosophy justified the Greeks,[2] not conducting them to that entire righteousness to which it is ascertained to co-operate, as the first and second flight of steps help you in your ascent to the upper room, and the grammarian helps the philosopher. Not as if by its abstraction, the perfect Word would be rendered incomplete, or truth perish ; since also sight, and hearing, and the voice contribute to truth, but it is the mind which is the appropriate faculty for knowing it. But of those things which co-operate, some contribute a greater amount of power ; some, a less. Perspicuity accordingly aids in the communication of truth, and logic in preventing us from falling under the heresies by which we are assailed. But the teaching, which is according to the Saviour, is complete in itself and without defect, being " the power and wisdom of God ; " [3] and the Hellenic philosophy does not, by its approach, make the truth more powerful ; but rendering powerless the assault of sophistry against it, and frustrating the treacherous plots laid against the truth, is said to be the proper " fence and wall of the vineyard." And the truth which is according to faith is as necessary for life as bread ; while the preparatory discipline is like sauce and sweetmeats. " At the end of the dinner, the dessert is pleasant," according to the Theban Pindar. And the Scripture has expressly said, " The innocent will become wiser by understanding, and the wise will receive knowledge." [4] " And he that speaketh of himself," saith the Lord, " seeketh his own glory ; but He that seeketh His glory that sent Him is true, and there is no unrighteousness in Him." [5] On the other hand, therefore, he who appropriates what belongs to the barbarians,

---

1 ἱερὰ γράμματα (2 Tim. iii. 15), translated in A. V. " sacred Scriptures ; " also in contradistinction to the so-called sacred letters of the Egyptians, Chaldeans, etc.

2 [Kaye, p. 426. A most valuable exposition of these passages on justification. See Elucidation XIV., *infra*.]
3 1 Cor. i. 24.
4 Prov. xxi. 11.
5 John vii. 18.

and vaunts it is his own, does wrong, increasing his own glory, and falsifying the truth. It is such an one that is by Scripture called a "thief." It is therefore said, "Son, be not a liar; for falsehood leads to theft." Nevertheless the thief possesses really, what he has possessed himself of dishonestly,[1] whether it be gold, or silver, or speech, or dogma. The ideas, then, which they have stolen, and which are partially true, they know by conjecture and necessary logical deduction: on becoming disciples, therefore, they will know them with intelligent apprehension.

CHAP. XXI.—THE JEWISH INSTITUTIONS AND LAWS OF FAR HIGHER ANTIQUITY THAN THE PHILOSOPHY OF THE GREEKS.

On the plagiarizing of the dogmas of the philosophers from the Hebrews, we shall treat a little afterwards. But first, as due order demands, we must now speak of the epoch of Moses, by which the philosophy of the Hebrews will be demonstrated beyond all contradiction to be the most ancient of all wisdom. This has been discussed with accuracy by Tatian in his book *To the Greeks*, and by Cassian in the first book of his *Exegetics*. Nevertheless our commentary demands that we too should run over what has been said on the point. Apion, then, the grammarian, surnamed Pleistonices, in the fourth book of *The Egyptian Histories*, although of so hostile a disposition towards the Hebrews, being by race an Egyptian, as to compose a work against the Jews, when referring to Amosis king of the Egyptians, and his exploits, adduces, as a witness, Ptolemy of Mendes. And his remarks are to the following effect: Amosis, who lived in the time of the Argive Inachus, overthrew Athyria, as Ptolemy of Mendes relates in his *Chronology*. Now this Ptolemy was a priest; and setting forth the deeds of the Egyptian kings in three entire books, he says, that the exodus of the Jews from Egypt, under the conduct of Moses, took place while Amosis was king of Egypt. Whence it is seen that Moses flourished in the time of Inachus. And of the Hellenic states, the most ancient is the Argolic, I mean that which took its rise from Inachus, as Dionysius of Halicarnassus teaches in his *Times*. And younger by forty generations than it was Attica, founded by Cecrops, who was an aboriginal of double race, as Tatian expressly says; and Arcadia, founded by Pelasgus, younger too by nine generations; and he, too, is said to have been an aboriginal. And more recent than this last by fifty-two generations, was Pthiotis, founded by Deucalion. And from the time of Inachus

to the Trojan war twenty generations or more are reckoned; let us say, four hundred years and more. And if Ctesias says that the Assyrian power is many years older than the Greek, the exodus of Moses from Egypt will appear to have taken place in the forty-second year of the Assyrian empire,[2] in the thirty-second year of the reign of Belochus, in the time of Amosis the Egyptian, and of Inachus the Argive. And in Greece, in the time of Phoroneus, who succeeded Inachus, the flood of Ogyges occurred; and monarchy subsisted in Sicyon first in the person of Ægialeus, then of Europs, then of Telches; in Crete, in the person of Cres. For Acusilaus says that Phoroneus was the first man. Whence, too, the author of *Phoronis* said that he was "the father of mortal men." Thence Plato in the *Timæus*, following Acusilaus, writes: "And wishing to draw them out into a discussion respecting antiquities, he[3] said that he ventured to speak of the most remote antiquities of this city[4] respecting Phoroneus, called the first man, and Niobe, and what happened after the deluge." And in the time of Phorbus lived Actæus, from whom is derived Actaia, Attica; and in the time of Triopas lived Prometheus, and Atlas, and Epimetheus, and Cecrops of double race, and Ino. And in the time of Crotopus occurred the burning of Phaethon, and the deluge[5] of Deucalion; and in the time of Sthenelus, the reign of Amphictyon, and the arrival of Danaus in the Peloponnesus; and under Dardanus happened the building of Dardania, whom, says Homer,

"First cloud-compelling Zeus begat,"—

and the transmigration from Crete into Phœnicia. And in the time of Lynceus took place the abduction of Proserpine, and the dedication of the sacred enclosure in Eleusis, and the husbandry of Triptolemus, and the arrival of Cadmus in Thebes, and the reign of Minos. And in the time of Prœtus the war of Eumolpus with the Athenians took place; and in the time of Acrisius, the removal of Pelops from Phrygia, the arrival of Ion at Athens; and the second Cecrops appeared, and the exploits of Perseus and Dionysus took place, and Orpheus and Musæus lived. And in the eighteenth year of the reign of Agamemnon, Troy was taken, in the first year of the reign of Demophon the son of Theseus at Athens, on the twelfth day of the month Thargelion, as Dionysius the Argive says; but Ægias and Dercylus, in the third book, say that it was on the eighth day of the last division of the month Panemus; Hellanicus says that it was on the twelfth

---

[1] [This ingenious statement explains the author's constant assertion that truth, and to some extent saving truth, was to be found in Greek philosophy.]

[2] The deficiencies of the text in this place have been supplied from Eusebius's *Chronicles*.
[3] i.e., Solon, in his conversation with the Egyptian priests.
[4] πόλει, "city," is not in Plato.
[5] ἐπομβρία.

of the month Thargelion ; and some of the authors of the *Attica* say that it was on the eighth of the last division of the month in the last year of Menestheus, at full moon.

"It was midnight,"

says the author of the *Little Iliad*,

"And the moon shone clear."

Others say, it took place on the same day of Scirophorion. But Theseus, the rival of Hercules, is older by a generation than the Trojan war. Accordingly Tlepolemus, a son of Hercules, is mentioned by Homer, as having served at Troy.

Moses, then, is shown to have preceded the deification of Dionysus six hundred and four years, if he was deified in the thirty-second year of the reign of Perseus, as Apollodorus says in his *Chronology*. From Bacchus to Hercules and the chiefs that sailed with Jason in the ship Argo, are comprised sixty-three years. Æsculapius and the Dioscuri sailed with them, as Apollonius Rhodius testifies in his *Argonautics*. And from the reign of Hercules, in Argos, to the deification of Hercules and of Æsculapius, are comprised thirty-eight years, according to Apollodorus the chronologist ; from this to the deification of Castor and Pollux, fifty-three years. And at this time Troy was taken. And if we may believe the poet Hesiod, let us hear him : —

"Then to Jove, Maia, Atlas' daughter, bore renowned Hermes,
　Herald of the immortals, having ascended the sacred couch.
And Semele, the daughter of Cadmus, too, bore an illustrious son,
Dionysus, the joy-inspiring, when she mingled with him in love." [1]

Cadmus, the father of Semele, came to Thebes in the time of Lynceus, and was the inventor of the Greek letters. Triopas was a contemporary of Isis, in the seventh generation from Inachus. And Isis, who is the same as Io, is so called, it is said, from her going (*ἰέναι*) roaming over the whole earth. Her, Istrus, in his work on the migration of the Egyptians, calls the daughter of Prometheus. Prometheus lived in the time of Triopas, in the seventh generation after Moses. So that Moses appears to have flourished even before the birth of men, according to the chronology of the Greeks. Leon, who treated of the Egyptian divinities, says that Isis by the Greeks was called Ceres, who lived in the time of Lynceus, in the eleventh generation after Moses. And Apis the king of Argos built Memphis, as Aristippus says in the first book of the *Arcadica*. And Aristeas the Argive says that he was named Serapis, and that it is he that the Egyptians

worship. And Nymphodorus of Amphipolis, in the third book of the *Institutions of Asia*, says that the bull Apis, dead and laid in a coffin (*σορός*), was deposited in the temple of the god (*δαίμονος*) there worshipped, and thence was called Soroapis, and afterwards Serapis by the custom of the natives. And Apis is third after Inachus. Further, Latona lived in the time of Tityus. "For he dragged Latona, the radiant consort of Zeus." Now Tityus was contemporary with Tantalus. Rightly, therefore, the Bœotian Pindar writes, "And in time was Apollo born ; " and no wonder when he is found along with Hercules, serving Admetus "for a long year." Zethus and Amphion, the inventors of music, lived about the age of Cadmus. And should one assert that Phemonoe was the first who sang oracles in verse to Acrisius, let him know that twenty-seven years after Phemonoe, lived Orpheus, and Musæus, and Linus the teacher of Hercules. And Homer and Hesiod are much more recent than the Trojan war ; and after them the legislators among the Greeks are far more recent, Lycurgus and Solon, and the seven wise men, and Pherecydes of Syros, and Pythagoras the great, who lived later, about the Olympiads, as we have shown. We have also demonstrated Moses to be more ancient, not only than those called poets and wise men among the Greeks, but than the most of their deities. Nor he alone, but the Sibyl also is more ancient than Orpheus. For it is said, that respecting her appellation and her oracular utterances there are several accounts ; that being a Phrygian, she was called Artemis ; and that on her arrival at Delphi, she sang —

"O Delphians, ministers of far-darting Apollo,
　I come to declare the mind of Ægis-bearing Zeus,
　Enraged as I am at my own brother Apollo."

There is another also, an Erythræan, called Herophile. These are mentioned by Heraclides of Pontus in his work *On Oracles*. I pass over the Egyptian Sibyl, and the Italian, who inhabited the Carmentale in Rome, whose son was Evander, who built the temple of Pan in Rome, called the Lupercal.

It is worth our while, having reached this point, to examine the dates of the other prophets among the Hebrews who succeeded Moses. After the close of Moses's life, Joshua succeeded to the leadership of the people, and he, after warring for sixty-five years, rested in the good land other five-and-twenty. As the book of Joshua relates, the above mentioned man was the successor of Moses twenty-seven years. Then the Hebrews having sinned, were delivered to Chusachar [2] king of Mesopotamia for eight years, as the book of Judges mentions. But

---

[1] [*Theog.*, 938.]

[2] Chushan-rishathaim; Judg. iii. 8.

having afterwards besought the Lord, they receive for leader Gothoniel,[1] the younger brother of Caleb, of the tribe of Judah, who, having slain the king of Mesopotamia, ruled over the people forty years in succession. And having again sinned, they were delivered into the hands of Æglom[2] king of the Moabites for eighteen years. But on their repentance, Aod,[3] a man who had equal use of both hands, of the tribe of Ephraim, was their leader for eighty years. It was he that despatched Æglom. On the death of Aod, and on their sinning again, they were delivered into the hand of Jabim[4] king of Canaan twenty years. After him Deborah the wife of Lapidoth, of the tribe of Ephraim, prophesied; and Ozias the son of Rhiesu was high priest. At her instance Barak the son of Bener,[5] of the tribe of Naphtali, commanding the army, having joined battle with Sisera, Jabim's commander-in-chief, conquered him. And after that Deborah ruled, judging the people forty years. On her death, the people having again sinned, were delivered into the hands of the Midianites seven years. After these events, Gideon, of the tribe of Manasseh, the son of Joas, having fought with his three hundred men, and killed a hundred and twenty thousand, ruled forty years; after whom the son of Ahimelech, three years. He was succeeded by Boleas, the son of Bedan, the son of Charran,[6] of the tribe of Ephraim, who ruled twenty-three years. After whom, the people having sinned again, were delivered to the Ammonites eighteen years; and on their repentance were commanded by Jephtha the Gileadite, of the tribe of Manasseh; and he ruled six years. After whom, Abatthan[7] of Bethlehem, of the tribe of Juda, ruled seven years. Then Ebron[8] the Zebulonite, eight years. Then Eglom of Ephraim, eight years. Some add to the seven years of Abatthan the eight of Ebrom.[9] And after him, the people having again transgressed, came under the power of the foreigners, the Philistines, for forty years. But on their returning [to God], they were led by Samson, of the tribe of Dan, who conquered the foreigners in battle. He ruled twenty years. And after him, there being no governor, Eli the priest judged the people for forty years. He was succeeded by Samuel the prophet; contemporaneously with whom Saul reigned, who held sway for twenty-seven years. He anointed David. Samuel died two years before Saul, while Abimelech was high priest. He anointed Saul as king,

who was the first that bore regal sway over Israel after the judges; the whole duration of whom, down to Saul, was four hundred and sixty-three years and seven months.

Then in the first book of Kings there are twenty years of Saul, during which he reigned after he was renovated. And after the death of Saul, David the son of Jesse, of the tribe of Judah, reigned next in Hebron, forty years, as is contained in the second book of Kings. And Abiathar the son of Abimelech, of the kindred of Eli, was high priest. In his time Gad and Nathan prophesied. From Joshua the son of Nun, then, till David received the kingdom, there intervene, according to some, four hundred and fifty years. But, as the chronology set forth shows, five hundred and twenty-three years and seven months are comprehended till the death of David.

And after this Solomon the son of David reigned forty years. Under him Nathan continued to prophesy, who also exhorted him respecting the building of the temple. Achias of Shilo also prophesied. And both the kings, David and Solomon, were prophets. And Sadoc the high priest was the first who ministered in the temple which Solomon built, being the eighth from Aaron, the first high priest. From Moses, then, to the age of Solomon, as some say, are five hundred and ninety-five years, and as others, five hundred and seventy-six.

And if you count, along with the four hundred and fifty years from Joshua to David, the forty years of the rule of Moses, and the other eighty years of Moses's life previous to the exodus of the Hebrews from Egypt, you will make up the sum in all of six hundred and ten years. But our chronology will run more correctly, if to the five hundred and twenty-three years and seven months till the death of David, you add the hundred and twenty years of Moses and the forty years of Solomon. For you will make up in all, down to the death of Solomon, six hundred and eighty-three years and seven months.

Hiram gave his daughter to Solomon about the time of the arrival of Menelaus in Phœnicia, after the capture of Troy, as is said by Menander of Pergamus, and Lætus in *The Phœnicia*. And after Solomon, Roboam his son reigned for seventeen years; and Abimelech the son of Sadoc was high priest. In his reign, the kingdom being divided, Jeroboam, of the tribe of Ephraim, the servant of Solomon, reigned in Samaria; and Achias the Shilonite continued to prophesy; also Samæas the son of Amame, and he who came from Judah to Jeroboam,[10] and prophesied against the altar. After him his son

---

[1] Othniel.
[2] Eglon.
[3] Ehud.
[4] Jabin.
[5] Abinoam; Judg. iv. 6.
[6] *Sic.* Θωλεᾶς may be the right reading instead of Βωλεᾶς. But Judg. x 1, says Tola, the son of Puah, the son of Dodo.
[7] Ibzan, A. V., Judg. xii. 8; Ἀβαισσάν, *Septuagint.* According to Judg. xii. 11, Elon the Zebulonite succeeded Ibzan.
[8] Not mentioned in Scripture.
[9] *Sic.*

[10] See 1 Kings xiii. 1, 2. The text has ἐπὶ Ῥοβοάμ, which, if retained, must be translated, "in the reign of Roboam." But Jeroboam was probably the original reading.

Abijam, twenty-three years; and likewise his son Asaman.[1] The last, in his old age, was diseased in his feet; and in his reign prophesied Jehu the son of Ananias.

After him Jehosaphat his son reigned twenty-five years.[2] In his reign prophesied Elias the Thesbite, and Michæas the son of Jebla, and Abdias the son of Ananias. And in the time of Michæas there was also the false prophet Zedekias, the son of Chonaan. These were followed by the reign of Joram the son of Jehosaphat, for eight years; during whose time prophesied Elias; and after Elias, Elisæus the son of Saphat. In his reign the people in Samaria ate doves' dung and their own children. The period of Jehosaphat extends from the close of the third book of Kings to the fourth. And in the reign of Joram, Elias was translated, and Elisæus the son of Saphat commenced prophesying, and prophesied for six years, being forty years old.

Then Ochozias reigned a year. In his time Elisæus continued to prophesy, and along with him Adadonæus.[3] After him the mother of Ozias,[4] Gotholia,[5] reigned eight[6] years, having slain the children of her brother.[7] For she was of the family of Ahab. But the sister of Ozias, Josabæa, stole Joas the son of Ozias, and invested him afterwards with the kingdom. And in the time of this Gotholia, Elisæus was still prophesying. And after her reigned, as I said before, Joash, rescued by Josabæa the wife of Jodæ the high priest, and lived in all forty years.

There are comprised, then, from Solomon to the death of Elisæus the prophet, as some say, one hundred and five years : according to others, one hundred and two; and, as the chronology before us shows, from the reign of Solomon an hundred and eighty-one.

Now from the Trojan war to the birth of Homer, according to Philochorus, a hundred and eighty years elapsed; and he was posterior to the Ionic migration. But Aristarchus, in the Archilochian Memoirs, says that he lived during the Ionic migration, which took place a hundred and twenty years after the siege of Troy. But Apollodorus alleges it was an hundred and twenty years after the Ionic migration, while Agesilaus son of Doryssæus was king of the Lacedæmonians : so that he brings Lycurgus the legislator, while still a young man, near him. Euthymenes, in the Chronicles, says that he flourished contemporaneously with Hesiod, in the time of Acastus, and was born in Chios, about the four hundredth year after the capture of Troy. And Archimachus, in the third book of his Eubœan History, is of this opinion. So that both he and Hesiod were later than Elisæus, the prophet. And if you choose to follow the grammarian Crates, and say that Homer was born about the time of the expedition of the Heraclidæ, eighty years after the taking of Troy, he will be found to be later again than Solomon, in whose days occurred the arrival of Menelaus in Phenicia, as was said above. Eratosthenes says that Homer's age was two hundred years after the capture of Troy. Further, Theopompus, in the forty-third book of the Philippics, relates that Homer was born five hundred years after the war at Troy. And Euphorion, in his book about the Aleuades, maintains that he was born in the time of Gyges, who began to reign in the eighteenth Olympiad, who, also he says, was the first that was called tyrant (τύραννος). Sosibius Lacon, again, in his Record of Dates, brings Homer down to the eighth year of the reign of Charillus the son of Polydectus. Charillus reigned for sixty-four years, after whom the son of Nicander reigned thirty-nine years. In his thirty-fourth year it is said that the first Olympiad was instituted; so that Homer was ninety years before the introduction of the Olympic games.

After Joas, Amasias his son reigned as his successor thirty-nine years. He in like manner was succeeded by his son Ozias, who reigned for fifty-two years, and died a leper. And in his time prophesied Amos, and Isaiah his son,[8] and Hosea the son of Beeri, and Jonas the son of Amathi, who was of Geth-chober, who preached to the Ninevites, and passed through the whale's belly.

Then Jonathan the son of Ozias reigned for sixteen years. In his time Esaias still prophesied, and Hosea, and Michæas the Morasthite, and Joel the son of Bethuel.

Next in succession was his son Ahaz, who reigned for sixteen years. In his time, in the fifteenth year, Israel was carried away to Babylon. And Salmanasar the king of the Assyrians carried away the people of Samaria into the country of the Medes and to Babylon.

Again Ahaz was succeeded by Osee,[9] who reigned for eight years. Then followed Hezekiah, for twenty-nine years. For his sanctity, when he had approached his end, God, by Isaiah, allowed him to live for other fifteen years, giving as a sign the going back of the sun. Up to his times Esaias, Hosea, and Micah continued prophesying.

And these are said to have lived after the age

---

1 Asa.
2 So Lowth corrects the text, which has five.
3 Supposed to be " son of Oded" or " Adad," i.e., Azarias.
4 i.e., of Ochozias.
5 Athalia.
6 She was slain in the seventh year of her reign.
7 Not of her brother, but of her son Ahaziah, all of whom she slew except Joash.

8 Clement is wrong in asserting that Amos the prophet was the father of Isaiah. The names are written differently in Hebrew, though the same in Greek.
9 By a strange mistake Hosea king of Israel is reckoned among the kings of Judah.

of Lycurgus, the legislator of the Lacedæmonians. For Dieuchidas, in the fourth book of the *Megarics*, places the era of Lycurgus about the two hundred and ninetieth year after the capture of Troy.

After Hezekiah, his son Manasses reigned for fifty-five years. Then his son Amos for two years. After him reigned his son Josias, distinguished for his observance of the law, for thirty-one years. He "laid the carcases of men upon the carcases of the idols," as is written in the book of Leviticus.[1] In his reign, in the eighteenth year, the passover was celebrated, not having been kept from the days of Samuel in the intervening period.[2] Then Chelkias the priest, the father of the prophet Jeremiah, having fallen in with the book of the law, that had been laid up in the temple, read it and died.[3] And in his days Olda[4] prohesied, and Sophonias,[5] and Jeremiah. And in the days of Jeremiah was Ananias the son of Azor,[6] the false prophet. He[7] having disobeyed Jeremiah the prophet, was slain by Pharaoh Necho king of Egypt at the river Euphrates, having encountered the latter, who was marching on the Assyrians.

Josiah was succeeded by Jechoniah, called also Joachas,[8] his son, who reigned three months and ten days. Necho king of Egypt bound him and led him to Egypt, after making his brother Joachim king in his stead, who continued his tributary for eleven years. After him his namesake[9] Joakim reigned for three months. Then Zedekiah reigned for eleven years; and up to his time Jeremiah continued to prophesy. Along with him Ezekiel[10] the son of Buzi, and Urias[11] the son of Samæus, and Ambacum[12] prophesied. Here end the Hebrew kings.

There are then from the birth of Moses till this captivity nine hundred and seventy-two years; but according to strict chronological accuracy, one thousand and eighty-five, six months, ten days. From the reign of David to the captivity by the Chaldeans, four hundred and fifty-two years and six months; but as the accuracy we have observed in reference to dates makes out, four hundred and eighty-two and six months ten days.

And in the twelfth year of the reign of Zedekiah, forty years before the supremacy of the Persians, Nebuchodonosor made war against the Phœnicians and the Jews, as Berosus asserts in his *Chaldæan Histories*. And Joabas,[13] writing about the Assyrians, acknowledges that he had received the history from Berosus, and testifies to his accuracy. Nebuchodonosor, therefore, having put out the eyes of Zedekiah, took him away to Babylon, and transported the whole people (the captivity lasted seventy years), with the exception of a few who fled to Egypt.

Jeremiah and Ambacum were still prophesying in the time of Zedekiah. In the fifth year of his reign Ezekiel prophesied at Babylon; after him Nahum, then Daniel. After him, again, Haggai and Zechariah prophesied in the time of Darius the First for two years; and then the angel among the twelve.[14] After Haggai and Zechariah, Nehemiah, the chief cup-bearer of Artaxerxes, the son of Acheli the Israelite, built the city of Jerusalem and restored the temple. During the captivity lived Esther and Mordecai, whose book is still extant, as also that of the Maccabees. During this captivity Mishael, Ananias, and Azarias, refusing to worship the image, and being thrown into a furnace of fire, were saved by the appearance of an angel. At that time, on account of the serpent,[15] Daniel was thrown into the den of lions; but being preserved through the providence of God by Ambacub, he is restored on the seventh day. At this period, too, occurred the sign of Jona; and Tobias, through the assistance of the angel Raphael, married Sarah, the demon having killed her seven first suitors; and after the marriage of Tobias, his father Tobit recovered his sight. At that time Zorobabel, having by his wisdom overcome his opponents, and obtained leave from Darius for the rebuilding of Jerusalem, returned with Esdras to his native land; and by him the redemption of the people and the revisal and restoration of the inspired oracles were effected; and the passover of deliverance celebrated, and marriage with aliens dissolved.

Cyrus had, by proclamation, previously enjoined the restoration of the Hebrews. And his promise being accomplished in the time of Darius, the feast of the dedication was held, as also the feast of tabernacles.

There were in all, taking in the duration of the captivity down to the restoration of the people, from the birth of Moses, one thousand one hundred and fifty-five years, six months, and ten days; and from the reign of David, according to some, four hundred and fifty-two;

---

[1] Lev. xxvi. 30.
[2] 2 Kings xxiii. 22.
[3] 2 Kings xxii. 8.
[4] Huldah.
[5] Zephaniah.
[6] ὁ Ἰωσίου, the reading of the text, is probably corrupt.
[7] Josias.
[8] ὁ καὶ Ἰωάχας, instead of which the text has καὶ Ἰωάχας.
[9] The names, however, were not the same. The name of the latter was Jehoiachin. The former in Hebrew is written יהויקים, the latter יהויכין. By copyists they were often confounded, as here by Clement.
[10] Lowth supplies Ἰεζεκιήλ, which is wanting in the text.
[11] He was a contemporary of Jeremiah, but was killed before the time of Zedekiah by Joachin. Jer. xxvi. 20.
[12] Habakkuk.
[13] Juba.
[14] Malachi, my angel or messenger. [Again, p. 331, *infra*.]
[15] On account of killing the serpent, as is related in the apocryphal book, "Bel and the Dragon, or Serpent."

more correctly, five hundred and seventy-two years, six months, and ten days.

From the captivity at Babylon, which took place in the time of Jeremiah the prophet, was fulfilled what was spoken by Daniel the prophet as follows: "Seventy weeks are determined upon thy people, and upon thy holy city, to finish the transgression, and to seal sins, and to wipe out and make reconciliation for iniquity, and to bring in everlasting righteousness, and to seal the vision and the prophet, and to anoint the Holy of Holies. Know therefore, and understand, that from the going forth of the word commanding an answer to be given, and Jerusalem to be built, to Christ the Prince, are seven weeks and sixty-two weeks; and the street shall be again built, and the wall; and the times shall be expended. And after the sixty-two weeks the anointing shall be overthrown, and judgment shall not be in him; and he shall destroy the city and the sanctuary along with the coming Prince. And they shall be destroyed in a flood, and to the end of the war shall be cut off by desolations. And he shall confirm the covenant with many for one week; and in the middle of the week the sacrifice and oblation shall be taken away; and in the holy place shall be the abomination of desolations, and until the consummation of time shall the consummation be assigned for desolation. And in the midst of the week shall he make the incense of sacrifice cease, and of the wing of destruction, even till the consummation, like the destruction of the oblation."[1] That the temple accordingly was built in seven weeks, is evident; for it is written in Esdras. And thus Christ became King of the Jews, reigning in Jerusalem in the fulfilment of the seven weeks. And in the sixty and two weeks the whole of Judæa was quiet, and without wars. And Christ our Lord, "the Holy of Holies," having come and fulfilled the vision and the prophecy, was anointed in His flesh by the Holy Spirit of His Father. In those "sixty and two weeks," as the prophet said, and "in the one week," was He Lord. The half of the week Nero held sway, and in the holy city Jerusalem placed the abomination; and in the half of the week he was taken away, and Otho, and Galba, and Vitellius. And Vespasian rose to the supreme power, and destroyed Jerusalem, and desolated the holy place. And that such are the facts of the case, is clear to him that is able to understand, as the prophet said.

On the completion, then, of the eleventh year, in the beginning of the following, in the reign of Joachim, occurred the carrying away captive to Babylon by Nabuchodonosor the king, in the seventh year of his reign over the As-

syrians, in the second year of the reign of Vaphres over the Egyptians, in the archonship of Philip at Athens, in the first year of the forty-eighth Olympiad. The captivity lasted for seventy years, and ended in the second year of Darius Hystaspes, who had become king of the Persians, Assyrians, and Egyptians; in whose reign, as I said above, Haggai and Zechariah and the angel of the twelve prophesied. And the high priest was Joshua the son of Josedec. And in the second year of the reign of Darius, who, Herodotus says, destroyed the power of the Magi, Zorobabel the son of Salathiel was despatched to raise and adorn the temple at Jerusalem.

The times of the Persians are accordingly summed up thus: Cyrus reigned thirty years; Cambyses, nineteen; Darius, forty-six; Xerxes, twenty-six; Artaxerxes, forty-one; Darius, eight; Artaxerxes, forty-two; Ochus or Arses, three. The sum total of the years of the Persian monarchy is two hundred and thirty-five years.

Alexander of Macedon, having despatched this Darius, during this period, began to reign. Similarly, therefore, the times of the Macedonian kings are thus computed: Alexander, eighteen years; Ptolemy the son of Lagus, forty years; Ptolemy Philadelphus, twenty-seven years; then Euergetes, five-and-twenty years; then Philopator, seventeen years; then Epiphanes, four-and-twenty years; he was succeeded by Philometer, who reigned five-and-thirty years; after him Physcon, twenty-nine years; then Lathurus, thirty-six years; then he that was surnamed Dionysus, twenty-nine years; and last Cleopatra reigned twenty-two years. And after her was the reign of the Cappadocians for eighteen days.

Accordingly the period embraced by the Macedonian kings is, in all, three hundred and twelve years and eighteen days.

Therefore those who prophesied in the time of Darius Hystaspes, about the second year of his reign, — Haggai, and Zechariah, and the angel of the twelve, who prophesied about the first year of the forty-eighth Olympiad, — are demonstrated to be older than Pythagoras, who is said to have lived in the sixty-second Olympiad, and than Thales, the oldest of the wise men of the Greeks, who lived about the fiftieth Olympiad. Those wise men that are classed with Thales were then contemporaneous, as Andron says in the *Tripos*. For Heraclitus being posterior to Pythagoras, mentions him in his book. Whence indisputably the first Olympiad, which was demonstrated to be four hundred and seven years later than the Trojan war, is found to be prior to the age of the above-mentioned prophets, together with those called the seven wise men. Accordingly it is easy to perceive that Solomon, who lived in the time of Menelaus (who was during the Trojan war), was earlier by

---

[1] Dan. ix. 24–27. [Speaker's Commentary, *Excursus, ad locum.*]

many years than the wise men among the Greeks. And how many years Moses preceded him we showed, in what we said above. And Alexander, surnamed Polyhistor, in his work on the Jews, has transcribed some letters of Solomon to Vaphres king of Egypt, and to the king of the Phœnicians at Tyre, and theirs to Solomon; in which it is shown that Vaphres sent eighty thousand Egyptian men to him for the building of the temple, and the other as many, along with a Tyrian artificer, the son of a Jewish mother, of the tribe of Dan,[1] as is there written, of the name of Hyperon.[2] Further, Onomacritus the Athenian, who is said to have been the author of the poems ascribed to Orpheus, is ascertained to have lived in the reign of the Pisistratidæ, about the fiftieth Olympiad. And Orpheus, who sailed with Hercules, was the pupil of Musæus. Amphion precedes the Trojan war by two generations. And Demodocus and Phemius were posterior to the capture of Troy; for they were famed for playing on the lyre, the former among the Phæacians, and the latter among the suitors. And the *Oracles* ascribed to Musæus are said to be the production of Onomacritus, and the *Crateres* of Orpheus the production of Zopyrus of Heraclea, and *The Descent to Hades* that of Prodicus of Samos. Ion of Chios relates in the *Triagmi*,[3] that Pythagoras ascribed certain works [of his own] to Orpheus. Epigenes, in his book respecting *The Poetry attributed to Orpheus*, says that *The Descent to Hades* and the *Sacred Discourse* were the production of Cecrops the Pythagorean; and the *Peplus* and the *Physics* of Brontinus. Some also make Terpander out ancient. Hellanicus, accordingly, relates that he lived in the time of Midas: but Phanias, who places Lesches the Lesbian before Terpander, makes Terpander younger than Archilochus, and relates that Lesches contended with Arctinus, and gained the victory. Xanthus the Lydian says that he lived about the eighteenth Olympiad; as also Dionysius says that Thasus was built about the fifteenth Olympiad: so that it is clear that Archilochus[5] was already known after the twentieth Olympiad. He accordingly relates the destruction of Magnetes as having recently taken place. Simonides is assigned to the time of Archilochus. Callinus is not much older; for Archilochus refers to Magnetes as destroyed, while the latter refers to it as flourishing. Eumelus of Corinth being older, is said to have met Archias, who founded Syracuse.

We were induced to mention these things, because the poets of the epic cycle are placed amongst those of most remote antiquity. Already, too, among the Greeks, many diviners are said to have made their appearance, as the Bacides, one a Bœotian, the other an Arcadian, who uttered many predictions to many. By the counsel of Amphiletus the Athenian,[5] who showed the time for the onset, Pisistratus, too, strengthened his government. For we may pass over in silence Cometes of Crete, Cinyras of Cyprus, Admetus the Thessalian, Aristæas the Cyrenian, Amphiaráus the Athenian, Timoxeus[6] the Corcyræan, Demænetus the Phocian, Epigenes the Thespian, Nicias the Carystian, Aristo the Thessalian, Dionysius the Carthaginian, Cleophon the Corinthian, Hippo the daughter of Chiro, and Bœo, and Manto, and the host of Sibyls, the Samian, the Colophonian, the Cumæan, the Erythræan, the Pythian,[7] the Taraxandrian, the Macetian, the Thessalian, and the Thesprotian. And Calchas again, and Mopsus, who lived during the Trojan war. Mopsus, however, was older, having sailed along with the Argonauts. And it is said that Battus the Cyrenian composed what is called *the Divination* of Mopsus. Dorotheus in the first *Pandect* relates that Mopsus was the disciple of Alcyon and Corone. And Pythagoras the Great always applied his mind to prognostication, and Abaris the Hyperborean, and Aristæas the Proconnesian, and Epimenides the Cretan, who came to Sparta, and Zoroaster the Mede, and Empedocles of Agrigentum, and Phormion the Lacedæmonian; Polyaratus, too, of Thasus, and Empedotimus of Syracuse; and in addition to these, Socrates the Athenian in particular. "For," he says in the *Theages*, "I am attended by a supernatural intimation, which has been assigned me from a child by divine appointment. This is a voice which, when it comes, prevents what I am about to do, but exhorts never."[8] And Execestus, the tyrant of the Phocians, wore two enchanted rings, and by the sound which they uttered one against the other determined the proper times for actions. But he died, nevertheless, treacherously murdered, although warned beforehand by the sound, as Aristotle says in the *Polity of the Phocians*.

Of those, too, who at one time lived as men among the Egyptians, but were constituted gods by human opinion, were Hermes the Theban, and Asclepius of Memphis; Tireseus and Manto, again, at Thebes, as Euripides says. Helenus, too, and Laocoön, and Œnone, and Crenus in

---

[1] The text has David.
[2] Hiram or Huram was his name (1 Kings vii. 13, 40). Clement seems to have mistaken the words ὑπὲρ ὧν occurring in the epistle referred to for a proper name.
[3] Such, according to Harpocration, was the title of this work. In the text it is called Τριγράμμοι. Suidas calls it Τριασμοί.
[4] The passage seems incomplete. The bearing of the date of the building of Thasos on the determination of the age of Archilochus, may be, that it was built by Telesiclus his son.

[5] Called so because he sojourned at Athens. His birthplace was Acarnania.
[6] Another reading is Τιμόθεος: Sylburgius conjectures Τιμόξενος.
[7] The text has Φυτώ, which Sylburgius conjectures has been changed from Πυθώ.
[8] Plato's *Theages*, xi. p. 128.

Ilium. For Crenus, one of the Heraclidæ, is said to have been a noted prophet. Another was Jamus in Elis, from whom came the Jamidæ; and Polyidus at Argos and Megara, who is mentioned by the tragedy. Why enumerate Telemus, who, being a prophet of the Cyclops, predicted to Polyphemus the events of Ulysses' wandering; or Onomacritus at Athens; or Amphiaraus, who campaigned with the seven at Thebes, and is reported to be a generation older than the capture of Troy; or Theoclymenus in Cephalonia, or Telmisus in Caria, or Galeus in Sicily?

There are others, too, besides these: Idmon, who was with the Argonauts, Phemonoe of Delphi, Mopsus the son of Apollo and Manto in Pamphylia, and Amphilochus the son of Amphiaraus in Cilicia, Alcmæon among the Acarnanians, Anias in Delos, Aristander of Telmessus, who was along with Alexander. Philochorus also relates in the first book of the work, *On Divination*, that Orpheus was a seer. And Theopompus, and Ephorus, and Timæus, write of a seer called Orthagoras; as the Samian Pythocles in the fourth book of *The Italics* writes of Caius Julius Nepos.

But some of these "thieves and robbers," as the Scripture says, predicted for the most part from observation and probabilities, as physicians and soothsayers judge from natural signs; and others were excited by demons, or were disturbed by waters, and fumigations, and air of a peculiar kind. But among the Hebrews the prophets were moved by the power and inspiration of God. Before the law, Adam spoke prophetically in respect to the woman, and the naming of the creatures; Noah preached repentance;[1] Abraham, Isaac, and Jacob gave many clear utterances respecting future and present things. Contemporaneous with the law, Moses and Aaron; and after these prophesied Jesus the son of Nave, Samuel, Gad, Nathan, Achias, Samæas, Jehu, Elias, Michæas, Abdiu, Elisæus, Abbadonai, Amos, Esaias, Osee, Jonas, Joel, Jeremias, Sophonias the son of Buzi, Ezekiel, Urias, Ambacum, Naum, Daniel, Misael, who wrote the syllogisms, Aggai, Zacharias, and the angel among the twelve. These are, in all, five-and-thirty prophets. And of women (for these too prophesied), Sara, and Rebecca, and Mariam, and Debbora, and Olda, i.e., Huldah.

Then within the same period John prophesied till the baptism of salvation;[2] and after the birth of Christ, Anna and Simeon.[3] For Zacaharias, John's father, is said in the Gospels to have prophesied before his son. Let us then draw up the chronology of the Greeks from Moses.

From the birth of Moses to the exodus of the Jews from Egypt, eighty years; and the period down to his death, other forty years. The exodus took place in the time of Inachus, before the wandering of Sothis,[4] Moses having gone forth from Egypt three hundred and forty-five years before. From the rule of Moses, and from Inachus to the flood of Deucalion, I mean the second inundation, and to the conflagration of Phaethon, which events happened in the time of Crotopus, forty generations are enumerated (three generations being reckoned for a century). From the flood to the conflagration of Ida, and the discovery of iron, and the Idæan Dactyls, are seventy-three years, according to Thrasyllus; and from the conflagration of Ida to the rape of Ganymede, sixty-five years. From this to the expedition of Perseus, when Glaucus established the Isthmian games in honour of Melicerta, fifteen years; and from the expedition of Perseus to the building of Troy, thirty-four years. From this to the voyage of the Argo, sixty-four years. From this to Theseus and the Minotaur, thirty-two years; then to the seven at Thebes, ten years. And to the Olympic contest, which Hercules instituted in honour of Pelops, three years; and to the expedition of the Amazons against Athens, and the rape of Helen by Theseus, nine years. From this to the deification of Hercules, eleven years; then to the rape of Helen by Alexander, four years. From the taking of Troy to the descent of Æneas and the founding of Lavinium, ten years; and to the government of Ascanius, eight years; and to the descent of the Heraclidæ, sixty-one years; and to the Olympiad of Iphitus, three hundred and thirty-eight years. Eratosthenes thus sets down the dates: "From the capture of Troy to the descent of the Heraclidæ, eighty years. From this to the founding of Ionia, sixty years; and the period following to the protectorate of Lycurgus, a hundred and fifty-nine years; and to the first year of the first Olympiad, a hundred and eight years. From which Olympiad to the invasion of Xerxes, two hundred and ninety-seven years; from which to the beginning of the Peloponnesian war, forty-eight years; and to its close, and the defeat of the Athenians, twenty-seven years; and to the battle at Leuctra, thirty-four years; after which to the death of Philip, thirty-five years. And after this to the decease of Alexander, twelve years."

Again, from the first Olympiad, some say, to the

---

[1] [Not to be lightly passed over. This whole paragraph is of value. Noah is the eighth *preacher* (2 Pet. ii. 5) of righteousness.]

[2] [The baptism of Jesus as distinguished from the baptism of repentance. John is clearly recognised, here, as of the old dispensation. John iv. 1.]

[3] [It is extraordinary that he fails to mention the blessed virgin and her *Magnificat*, the earliest Christian hymn; i.e., the first after the incarnation.]

[4] i.e., of Io, the daughter of Inachus.

building of Rome, are comprehended twenty-four years; and after this to the expulsion of the kings,[1] when consuls were created, about two hundred and forty-three years. And from the taking of Babylon to the death of Alexander, a hundred and eighty-six years. From this to the victory of Augustus, when Antony killed himself at Alexandria, two hundred and ninety-four years, when Augustus was made consul for the fourth time. And from this time to the games which Domitian instituted at Rome, are a hundred and fourteen years; and from the first games to the death of Commodus, a hundred and eleven years.

There are some that from Cecrops to Alexander of Macedon reckon a thousand eight hundred and twenty-eight years; and from Demophon, a thousand two hundred and fifty; and from the taking of Troy to the expedition of the Heraclidæ, a hundred and twenty or a hundred and eighty years. From this to the archonship of Evænetus at Athens, in whose time Alexander is said to have marched into Asia, according to Phanias, are seven hundred and fifty years; according to Ephorus, seven hundred and thirty-five; according to Timæus and Clitarchus, eight hundred and twenty; according to Eratosthenes, seven hundred and seventy-four. As also Duris, from the taking of Troy to the march of Alexander into Asia, a thousand years; and from that to the archonship of Hegesias, in whose time Alexander died, eleven years. From this date to the reign of Germanicus Claudius Cæsar, three hundred and sixty-five years. From which time the years summed up to the death of Commodus are manifest.

After the Grecian period, and in accordance with the dates, as computed by the barbarians, very large intervals are to be assigned.

From Adam to the deluge are comprised two thousand one hundred and forty-eight years, four days. From Shem to Abraham, a thousand two hundred and fifty years. From Isaac to the division of the land, six hundred and sixteen years. Then from the judges to Samuel, four hundred and sixty-three years, seven months. And after the judges there were five hundred and seventy-two years, six months, ten days of kings.

After which periods, there were two hundred and thirty-five years of the Persian monarchy. Then of the Macedonian, till the death of Antony, three hundred and twelve years and eighteen days. After which time, the empire of the Romans, till the death of Commodus, lasted for two hundred and twenty-two years.

Then, from the seventy years' captivity, and the restoration of the people into their own land to the captivity in the time of Vespasian, are comprised four hundred and ten years. Finally, from Vespasian to the death of Commodus, there are ascertained to be one hundred and twenty-one years, six months, and twenty-four days.

Demetrius, in his book, *On the Kings in Judæa*, says that the tribes of Juda, Benjamin, and Levi were not taken captive by Sennacherim; but that there were from this captivity to the last, which Nabuchodonosor made out of Jerusalem, a hundred and twenty-eight years and six months; and from the time that the ten tribes were carried captive from Samaria till Ptolemy the Fourth, were five hundred and seventy-three years, nine months; and from the time that the captivity from Jerusalem took place, three hundred and thirty-eight years and three months.

Philo himself set down the kings differently from Demetrius.

Besides, Eupolemus, in a similar work, says that all the years from Adam to the fifth year of Ptolemy Demetrius, who reigned twelve years in Egypt, when added, amount to five thousand a hundred and forty-nine; and from the time that Moses brought out the Jews from Egypt to the above-mentioned date, there are, in all, two thousand five hundred and eighty years. And from this time till the consulship in Rome of Caius Domitian and Casian, a hundred and twenty years are computed.

Euphorus and many other historians say that there are seventy-five nations and tongues, in consequence of hearing the statement made by Moses: "All the souls that sprang from Jacob, which went down into Egypt, were seventy-five."[2] According to the true reckoning, there appear to be seventy-two generic dialects, as our Scriptures hand down. The rest of the vulgar tongues are formed by the blending of two, or three, or more dialects. A dialect is a mode of speech which exhibits a character peculiar to a locality, or a mode of speech which exhibits a character peculiar or common to a race. The Greeks say, that among them are five dialects — the Attic, Ionic, Doric, Æolic, and the fifth the Common; and that the languages of the barbarians, which are innumerable, are not called dialects, but tongues.

Plato attributes a dialect also to the gods, forming this conjecture mainly from dreams and oracles, and especially from demoniacs, who do not speak their own language or dialect, but that of the demons who have taken possession of them. He thinks also that the irrational creatures have dialects, which those that belong to

---

[1] For Βαβυλῶνος, βασιλέων has been substituted. In an old chronologist, as quoted by Clement elsewhere, the latter occurs: and the date of the expulsion of the kings harmonizes with the number of years here given, which that of the destruction of Babylon does not.

[2] Gen. xlvi. 27, Sept.

the same genus understand.[1] Accordingly, when an elephant falls into the mud and bellows out, any other one that is at hand, on seeing what has happened, shortly turns, and brings with him a herd of elephants, and saves the one that has fallen in. It is said also in Libya, that a scorpion, if it does not succeed in stinging a man, goes away and returns with several more; and that, hanging on one to the other like a chain, they make in this way the attempt to succeed in their cunning design.

The irrational creatures do not make use of an obscure intimation, or hint their meaning by assuming a particular attitude, but, as I think, by a dialect of their own.[1] And some others say, that if a fish which has been taken escape by breaking the line, no fish of the same kind will be caught in the same place that day. But the first and generic barbarous dialects have terms by nature, since also men confess that prayers uttered in a barbarian tongue are more powerful. And Plato, in the *Cratylus*, when wishing to interpret πῦρ (*fire*), says that it is a barbaric term. He testifies, accordingly, that the Phrygians use this term with a slight deviation.

And nothing, in my opinion, after these details, need stand in the way of stating the periods of the Roman emperors, in order to the demonstration of the Saviour's birth. Augustus, forty-three years; Tiberius, twenty-two years; Caius, four years; Claudius, fourteen years; Nero, fourteen years; Galba, one year; Vespasian, ten years; Titus, three years; Domitian, fifteen years; Nerva, one year; Trajan, nineteen years; Adrian, twenty-one years; Antoninus, twenty-one years; likewise again, Antoninus and Commodus, thirty-two. In all, from Augustus to Commodus, are two hundred and twenty-two years; and from Adam to the death of Commodus, five thousand seven hundred and eighty-four years, two months, twelve days.

Some set down the dates of the Roman emperors thus:—

Caius Julius Cæsar, three years, four months, five days; after him Augustus reigned forty-six years, four months, one day. Then Tiberius, twenty-six years, six months, nineteen days. He was succeeded by Caius Cæsar, who reigned three years, ten months, eight days; and he by Claudius for thirteen years, eight months, twenty-eight days. Nero reigned thirteen years, eight months, twenty-eight days; Galba, seven months and six days; Otho, five months, one day; Vitellius, seven months, one day; Vespasian, eleven years, eleven months, twenty-two days; Titus, two years, two months; Domitian, fifteen years, eight months, five days; Nerva, one year, four months, ten days; Trajan, nineteen years,

seven months, ten days; Adrian, twenty years, ten months, twenty-eight days. Antoninus, twenty-two years, three months, and seven days; Marcus Aurelius Antoninus, nineteen years, eleven days; Commodus, twelve years, nine months, fourteen days.

From Julius Cæsar, therefore, to the death of Commodus, are two hundred and thirty-six years, six months. And the whole from Romulus, who founded Rome, till the death of Commodus, amounts to nine hundred and fifty-three years, six months. And our Lord was born in the twenty-eighth year, when first the census was ordered to be taken in the reign of Augustus. And to prove that this is true, it is written in the Gospel by Luke as follows: "And in the fifteenth year, in the reign of Tiberius Cæsar, the word of the Lord came to John, the son of Zacharias." And again in the same book: "And Jesus was coming to His baptism, being about thirty years old,"[2] and so on. And that it was necessary for Him to preach only a year, this also is written:[3] "He hath sent Me to proclaim the acceptable year of the Lord." This both the prophet spake, and the Gospel. Accordingly, in fifteen years of Tiberius and fifteen years of Augustus; so were completed the thirty years till the time He suffered. And from the time that He suffered till the destruction of Jerusalem are forty-two years and three months; and from the destruction of Jerusalem to the death of Commodus, a hundred and twenty-eight years, ten months, and three days. From the birth of Christ, therefore, to the death of Commodus are, in all, a hundred and ninety-four years, one month, thirteen days. And there are those who have determined not only the year of our Lord's birth, but also the day; and they say that it took place in the twenty-eighth year of Augustus, and in the twenty-fifth day of Pachon. And the followers of Basilides hold the day of his baptism as a festival, spending the night before in readings.

And they say that it was the fifteenth year of Tiberius Cæsar, the fifteenth day of the month Tubi; and some that it was the eleventh of the same month. And treating of His passion, with very great accuracy, some say that it took place in the sixteenth year of Tiberius, on the twenty-fifth of Phamenoth; and others the twenty-fifth of Pharmuthi and others say that on the nineteenth of Pharmuthi the Saviour suffered. Further, others say that He was born on the twenty-fourth or twenty-fifth of Pharmuthi.[4]

We have still to add to our chronology the

---

[1] [This assent to Plato's whim, on the part of our author, is suggestive.]

[2] Luke iii. 1, 2, 23.

[3] [A fair parallel to the amazing traditional statement of Irenæus, and his objection to this very idea, vol. i. p. 391, this series. Is?. lxi. 1, 2.]

[4] [Mosheim, *Christ. of First Three Cent.*, i. 432; and Josephus, *Antiquities*, ii. 14.]

following, — I mean the days which Daniel indicates from the desolation of Jerusalem, the seven years and seven months of the reign of Vespasian. For the two years are added to the seventeen months and eighteen days of Otho, and Galba, and Vitellius; and the result is three years and six months, which is "the half of the week," as Daniel the prophet said. For he said that there were two thousand three hundred days from the time that the abomination of Nero stood in the holy city, till its destruction. For thus the declaration, which is subjoined, shows: "How long shall be the vision, the sacrifice taken away, the abomination of desolation, which is given, and the power and the holy place shall be trodden under foot? And he said to him, Till the evening and morning, two thousand three hundred days, and the holy place shall be taken away."[1]

These two thousand three hundred days, then, make six years four months, during the half of which Nero held sway, and it was half a week; and for a half, Vespasian with Otho, Galba, and Vitellius reigned. And on this account Daniel says, "Blessed is he that cometh to the thousand three hundred and thirty-five days."[2] For up to these days was war, and after them it ceased. And this number is demonstrated from a subsequent chapter, which is as follows: "And from the time of the change of continuation, and of the giving of the abomination of desolation, there shall be a thousand two hundred and ninety days. Blessed is he that waiteth, and cometh to the thousand three hundred and thirty-five days."[3]

Flavius Josephus the Jew, who composed the history of the Jews, computing the periods, says that from Moses to David were five hundred and eighty-five years; from David to the second year of Vespasian, a thousand one hundred and seventy-nine; then from that to the tenth year of Antoninus, seventy-seven. So that from Moses to the tenth year of Antoninus there are, in all, two thousand one hundred and thirty-three years.

Of others, counting from Inachus and Moses to the death of Commodus, some say there were three thousand one hundred and forty-two years; and others, two thousand eight hundred and thirty-one years.

And in the Gospel according to Matthew, the genealogy which begins with Abraham is continued down to Mary the mother of the Lord. "For," it is said,[4] "from Abraham to David are fourteen generations; and from David to the carrying away into Babylon are fourteen genera-

tions; and from the carrying away into Babylon till Christ are likewise other fourteen generations," — three mystic intervals completed in six weeks.[5]

CHAP. XXII. — ON THE GREEK TRANSLATION OF THE OLD TESTAMENT.

So much for the details respecting dates, as stated variously by many, and as set down by us.

It is said that the Scriptures both of the law and of the prophets were translated from the dialect of the Hebrews into the Greek language in the reign of Ptolemy the son of Lagos, or, according to others, of Ptolemy surnamed Philadelphus; Demetrius Phalereus bringing to this task the greatest earnestness, and employing painstaking accuracy on the materials for the translation. For the Macedonians being still in possession of Asia, and the king being ambitious of adorning the library he had at Alexandria with all writings, desired the people of Jerusalem to translate the prophecies they possessed into the Greek dialect. And they being the subjects of the Macedonians, selected from those of highest character among them seventy elders, versed in the Scriptures, and skilled in the Greek dialect, and sent them to him with the divine books. And each having severally translated each prophetic book, and all the translations being compared together, they agreed both in meaning and expression. For it was the counsel of God carried out for the benefit of Grecian ears. It was not alien to the inspiration of God, who gave the prophecy, also to produce the translation, and make it as it were Greek prophecy. Since the Scriptures having perished in the captivity of Nabuchodonosor, Esdras[6] the Levite, the priest, in the time of Artaxerxes king of the Persians, having become inspired in the exercise of prophecy restored again the whole of the ancient Scriptures. And Aristobulus, in his first book addressed to Philometor, writes in these words: "And Plato followed the laws given to us, and had manifestly studied all that is said in them." And before Demetrius there had been translated by another, previous to the dominion of Alexander and of the Persians, the account of the departure of our countrymen the Hebrews from Egypt, and the fame of all that happened to them, and their taking possession of the land, and the account of the whole code of laws; so that it is perfectly clear that the above-mentioned philosopher derived a great deal from this source, for he was very learned, as also Pythagoras, who transferred many things from our books to his own system of doctrines. And Numenius, the Pythagorean philosopher, expressly writes: "For what is Plato, but Moses speak-

---

1 Dan. viii. 13, 14.
2 Dan. xii. 12.
3 Dan. xii. 11, 12.
4 Matt. i. 17.

5 [As to our author's chronology, see Elucidation XV., *infra.*]
6 [The work of Ezra, as Clement testifies concerning it, adds immensely to the common ideas of his place in the history of the canon.]

ng in Attic Greek?" This Moses was a theologian and prophet, and as some say, an interpreter of sacred laws. His family, his deeds, and life, are related by the Scriptures themselves, which are worthy of all credit; but have nevertheless to be stated by us also as well as we can.[1]

CHAP. XXIII. — THE AGE, BIRTH, AND LIFE OF MOSES.

Moses, originally of a Chaldean[2] family, was born in Egypt, his ancestors having migrated from Babylon into Egypt on account of a protracted famine. Born in the seventh generation,[3] and having received a royal education, the following are the circumstances of his history. The Hebrews having increased in Egypt to a great multitude, and the king of the country being afraid of insurrection in consequence of their numbers, he ordered all the female children born to the Hebrews to be reared (woman being unfit for war), but the male to be destroyed, being suspicious of stalwart youth. But the child being goodly, his parents nursed him secretly three months, natural affection being too strong for the monarch's cruelty. But at last, dreading lest they should be destroyed along with the child, they made a basket of the papyrus that grew there, put the child in it, and laid it on the banks of the marshy river. The child's sister stood at a distance, and watched what would happen. In this emergency, the king's daughter, who for a long time had not been pregnant, and who longed for a child, came that day to the river to bathe and wash herself; and hearing the child cry, she ordered it to be brought to her; and touched with pity, sought a nurse. At that moment the child's sister ran up, and said that, if she wished, she could procure for her as nurse one of the Hebrew women who had recently had a child. And on her consenting and desiring her to do so, she brought the child's mother to be nurse for a stipulated fee, as if she had been some other person. Thereupon the queen gave the babe the name of Moses, with etymological propriety, from his being drawn out of "the water,"[4] — for the Egyptians call water "mou," — in which he had been exposed to die. For they call Moses one who "who breathed [on being taken] from the water." It is clear that previously the parents gave a name to the child on his circumcision; and he was called Joachim. And he had a third name in heaven, after his ascension,[5] as the mystics say — Melchi. Hav-

ing reached the proper age, he was taught arithmetic, geometry, poetry, harmony, and besides, medicine and music, by those that excelled in these arts among the Egyptians; and besides, the philosophy which is conveyed by symbols, which they point out in the hieroglyphical inscriptions. The rest of the usual course of instruction, Greeks taught him in Egypt as a royal child, as Philo says in his life of Moses. He learned, besides, the literature of the Egyptians, and the knowledge of the heavenly bodies from the Chaldeans and the Egyptians; whence in the Acts[6] he is said "to have been instructed in all the wisdom of the Egyptians." And Eupolemus, in his book *On the Kings in Judea*, says that "Moses was the first wise man, and the first that imparted grammar to the Jews, that the Phœnicians received it from the Jews, and the Greeks from the Phœnicians." And betaking himself to their philosophy,[7] he increased his wisdom, being ardently attached to the training received from his kindred and ancestors, till he struck and slew the Egyptian who wrongfully attacked the Hebrew. And the mystics say that he slew the Egyptian by a word only; as, certainly, Peter in the Acts is related to have slain by speech those who appropriated part of the price of the field, and lied.[8] And so Artapanus, in his work *On the Jews*, relates "that Moses, being shut up in custody by Chenephres, king of the Egyptians, on account of the people demanding to be let go from Egypt, the prison being opened by night, by the interposition of God, went forth, and reaching the palace, stood before the king as he slept, and aroused him; and that the latter, struck with what had taken place, bade Moses tell him the name of the God who had sent him; and that he, bending forward, told it in his ear; and that the king on hearing it fell speechless, but being supported by Moses, revived again." And respecting the education of Moses, we shall find a harmonious account in Ezekiel,[9] the composer of Jewish tragedies in the drama entitled *The Exodus*. He thus writes in the person of Moses: —

"For, seeing our race abundantly increase,
His treacherous snares King Pharaoh 'gainst us laid,
And cruelly in brick-kilns some of us,
And some, in toilsome works of building, plagued.
And towns and towers by toil of ill-starred men
He raised. Then to the Hebrew race proclaimed,
That each male child should in deep-flowing Nile
Be drowned. My mother bore and hid me then
Three months (so afterwards she told). Then took,
And me adorned with fair array, and placed
On the deep sedgy marsh by Nilus bank,
While Miriam, my sister, watched afar.
Then, with her maids, the daughter of the king,
To bathe her beauty in the cleansing stream,

---

[1] [Concerning the LXX., see cap. vii. p. 308, note 4, *supra*.]
[2] This is the account given by Philo, of whose book on the life of Moses this chapter is an epitome, for the most part in Philo's words.
[3] "He was the seventh in descent from the first, who, being a foreigner, was the founder of the whole Jewish race." — PHILO.
[4] [See Ex. ii. 10.]
[5] [Concerning this, see Deut. xxxiii. 5. And as to "mystics," with caution, may be read advantageously, the article "Mysteries," *Encyclop. Britann.*, vol. xxiii. p. 124.]

[6] Acts vii. 22.
[7] Adopting the reading φιλοσοφίαν ἀΐξας instead of φύσιν ἄξας.
[8] Acts v. 1.
[9] [Eusebius, *Præp Evang.*, ix. 4.]

Came near, straight saw, and took and raised me up;
And knew me for a Hebrew.　Miriam
My sister to the princess ran, and said,
' Is it thy pleasure, that I haste and find
A nurse for thee to rear this child
Among the Hebrew women?'　The princess
Gave assent.　The maiden to her mother sped,
And told, who quick appeared.　My own
Dear mother took me in her arms.　Then said
The daughter of the king: ' Nurse me this child,
And I will give thee wages.'　And my name
Moses she called, because she drew and saved
Me from the waters on the river's bank.
And when the days of childhood had flown by,
My mother brought me to the palace where
The princess dwelt, after disclosing all
About my ancestry, and God's great gifts.
In boyhood's years I royal nurture had,
And in all princely exercise was trained,
As if the princess's very son.　But when
The circling days had run their course,
I left the royal palace."

Then, after relating the combat between the
Hebrew and the Egyptian, and the burying of
the Egyptian in the sand, he says of the other
contest : —

" Why strike one feebler than thyself?
And he rejoined: Who made thee judge o'er us,
Or ruler?　Wilt thou slay me, as thou didst
Him yesterday?　And I in terror said,
How is this known?"

Then he fled from Egypt and fed sheep, being
thus trained beforehand for pastoral rule.　For
the shepherd's life is a preparation for sovereignty
in the case of him who is destined to rule over
the peaceful flock of men, as the chase for those
who are by nature warlike.　Thence God brought
him to lead the Hebrews.　Then the Egyptians,
oft admonished, continued unwise ; and the
Hebrews were spectators of the calamities that
others suffered, learning in safety the power of
God.　And when the Egyptians gave no heed
to the effects of that power, through their foolish
infatuation disbelieving, then, as is said, " the
children knew " what was done ; and the Hebrews afterwards going forth, departed carrying
much spoil from the Egyptians, not for avarice,
as the cavillers say, for God did not persuade
them to covet what belonged to others.　But, in
the first place, they took wages for the services
they had rendered the Egyptians all the time ;
and then in a way recompensed the Egyptians,
by afflicting them in requital as avaricious, by
the abstraction of the booty, as they had done
the Hebrews by enslaving them.　Whether, then,
as may be alleged is done in war, they thought
it proper, in the exercise of the rights of conquerors, to take away the property of their enemies, as those who have gained the day do from
those who are worsted (and there was just cause
of hostilities.　The Hebrews came as suppliants
to the Egyptians on account of famine ; and
they, reducing their guests to slavery, compelled
them to serve them after the manner of captives,

giving them no recompense) ; or as in peace,
took the spoil as wages against the will of those
who for a long period had given them no recompense, but rather had robbed them, [it is all
one.]

CHAP. XXIV. — HOW MOSES DISCHARGED THE PART
OF A MILITARY LEADER.

Our Moses then is a prophet, a legislator,
skilled in military tactics and strategy, a poli-
tician, a philosopher.　And in what sense he
was a prophet, shall be by and by told, when
we come to treat of prophecy.　Tactics belong
to military command, and the ability to command an army is among the attributes of kingly
rule.　Legislation, again, is also one of the
functions of the kingly office, as also judicial
authority.

Of the kingly office one kind is divine, — that
which is according to God and His holy Son, by
whom both the good things which are of the
earth, and external and perfect felicity too, are
supplied.　" For," it is said, " seek what is great,
and the little things shall be added." [1]　And
there is a second kind of royalty, inferior to that
administration which is purely rational and divine, which brings to the task of government
merely the high mettle of the soul ; after which
fashion Hercules ruled the Argives, and Alexander the Macedonians.　The third kind is what
aims after one thing — merely to conquer and
overturn ; but to turn conquest either to a good
or a bad purpose, belongs not to such rule.
Such was the aim of the Persians in their cam-
paign against Greece.　For, on the one hand,
fondness for strife is solely the result of passion,
and acquires power solely for the sake of domi-
nation ; while, on the other, the love of good is
characteristic of a soul which uses its high spirit
for noble ends.　The fourth, the worst of all, is
the sovereignty which acts according to the
promptings of the passions, as that of Sardanapalus, and those who propose to themselves
as their end the gratification of the passions to
the utmost.　But the instrument of regal sway
— the instrument at once of that which over-
comes by virtue, and that which does so by force
— is the power of managing (or tact).　And it
varies according to the nature and the material.
In the case of arms and of fighting animals the
ordering power is the soul and mind, by means
animate and inanimate ; and in the case of the
passions of the soul, which we master by virtue,
reason is the ordering power, by affixing the seal
of continence and self-restraint, along with holiness, and sound knowledge with truth, making
the result of the whole to terminate in piety
towards God.　For it is wisdom which regulates

---

[1] Not in Scripture.　The reference may be to Matt. vi. 33.

in the case of those who so practise virtue ; and divine things are ordered by wisdom, and human affairs by politics — all things by the kingly faculty. He is a king, then, who governs according to the laws, and possesses the skill to sway willing subjects. Such is the Lord, who receives all who believe on Him and by Him. For the Father has delivered and subjected all to Christ our King, " that at the name of Jesus every knee may bow, of things in heaven, and things in earth, and things under the earth, and every tongue confess that Jesus Christ is Lord, to the glory of God the Father." [1]

Now, generalship involves three ideas : caution, enterprise, and the union of the two. And each of these consists of three things, acting as they do either by word, or by deeds, or by both together. And all this can be accomplished either by persuasion, or by compulsion, or by inflicting harm in the way of taking vengeance on those who ought to be punished ; and this either by doing what is right, or by telling what is untrue, or by telling what is true, or by adopting any of these means conjointly at the same time.

Now, the Greeks had the advantage of receiving from Moses all these, and the knowledge of how to make use of each of them. And, for the sake of example, I shall cite one or two instances of leadership. Moses, on leading the people forth, suspecting that the Egyptians would pursue, left the short and direct route, and turned to the desert, and marched mostly by night. For it was another kind of arrangement by which the Hebrews were trained in the great wilderness, and for a protracted time, to belief in the existence of one God alone, being inured by the wise discipline of endurance to which they were subjected. The strategy of Moses, therefore, shows the necessity of discerning what will be of service before the approach of dangers, and so to encounter them. It turned out precisely as he suspected, for the Egyptians pursued with horses and chariots, but were quickly destroyed by the sea breaking on them and overwhelming them with their horses and chariots, so that not a remnant of them was left. Afterwards the pillar of fire, which accompanied them (for it went before them as a guide), conducted the Hebrews by night through an untrodden region, training and bracing them, by toils and hardships, to manliness and endurance, that after their experience of what appeared formidable difficulties, the benefits of the land, to which from the trackless desert he was conducting them, might become apparent. Furthermore, he put to flight and slew the hostile occupants of the land, falling upon them from a desert and rugged

line of march (such was the excellence of his generalship). For the taking of the land of those hostile tribes was a work of skill and strategy.

Perceiving this, Miltiades, the Athenian general, who conquered the Persians in battle at Marathon, imitated it in the following fashion. Marching over a trackless desert, he led on the Athenians by night, and eluded the barbarians that were set to watch him. For Hippias, who had deserted from the Athenians, conducted the barbarians into Attica, and seized and held the points of vantage, in consequence of having a knowledge of the ground. The task was then to elude Hippias. Whence rightly Miltiades, traversing the desert and attacking by night the Persians commanded by Dates, led his soldiers to victory.

But further, when Thrasybulus was bringing back the exiles from Phyla, and wished to elude observation, a pillar became his guide as he marched over a trackless region. To Thrasybulus by night, the sky being moonless and stormy, a fire appeared leading the way, which, having conducted them safely, left them near Munychia, where is now the altar of the light-bringer (Phosphorus).

From such an instance, therefore, let our accounts become credible to the Greeks, namely, that it was possible for the omnipotent God to make the pillar of fire, which was their guide on their march, go before the Hebrews by night. It is said also in a certain oracle, —

" A pillar to the Thebans is joy-inspiring Bacchus,"

from the history of the Hebrews. Also Euripides says, in *Antiope*, —

" In the chambers within, the herdsman,
    With chaplet of ivy, pillar of the Evœan god."

The pillar indicates that God cannot be portrayed. The pillar of light, too, in addition to its pointing out that God cannot be represented, shows also the stability and the permanent duration of the Deity, and His unchangeable and inexpressible light. Before, then, the invention of the forms of images, the ancients erected pillars, and reverenced them as statues of the Deity. Accordingly, he who composed the *Phoronis* writes, —

" Callithoe, key-bearer of the Olympian queen :
    Argive Hera, who first with fillets and with fringes
    The queen's tall column all around adorned."

Further, the author of *Europia* relates that the statue of Apollo at Delphi was a pillar in these words : —

" That to the god first-fruits and tithes we may
    On sacred pillars and on lofty column hang."

Apollo, interpreted mystically by " privation of

---

[1] Phil. ii. 10, 11.

many," [1] means the one God. Well, then, that fire like a pillar, and the fire in the desert, is the symbol of the holy light which passed through from earth and returned again to heaven, by the wood [of the cross], by which also the gift of intellectual vision was bestowed on us.

CHAP. XXV. — PLATO AN IMITATOR OF MOSES IN FRAMING LAWS.

Plato the philosopher, aided in legislation by the books of Moses, censured the polity of Minos, and that of Lycurgus, as having bravery alone as their aim; while he praised as more seemly the polity which expresses some one thing, and directs according to one precept. For he says that it becomes us to philosophize with strength, and dignity, and wisdom, — holding unalterably the same opinions about the same things, with reference to the dignity of heaven. Accordingly, therefore, he interprets what is in the law, enjoining us to look to one God and to do justly. Of politics, he says there are two kinds, — the department of law, and that of politics, strictly so called.

And he refers to the Creator, as the Statesman (ὁ πολιτικός) by way of eminence, in his book of this name (ὁ πολιτικός); and those who lead an active and just life, combined with contemplation, he calls statesmen (πολιτικοί). That department of politics which is called "Law," he divides into administrative magnanimity and private good order, which he calls orderliness, and harmony, and sobriety, which are seen when rulers suit their subjects, and subjects are obedient to their rulers; a result which the system of Moses sedulously aims at effecting. Further, that the department of law is founded on generation, that of politics on friendship and consent, Plato, with the aid he received, affirms; and so, coupled with the laws the philosopher in the *Epinomis*, who knew the course of all generation, which takes place by the instrumentality of the planets; and the other philosopher, *Timæus*, who was an astronomer and student of the motions of the stars, and of their sympathy and association with one another, he consequently joined to the "polity" (or "republic"). Then, in my opinion, the end both of the statesman, and of him who lives according to the law, is contemplation. It is necessary, therefore, that public affairs should be rightly managed. But to philosophize is best. For he who is wise will live concentrating all his energies on knowledge, directing his life by good deeds, despising the opposite, and following the pursuits which contribute to truth. And the law is not what is decided by law (for what is seen is not vision), nor every opinion (not certainly what is evil). But

law is the opinion which is good, and what is good is that which is true, and what is true is that which finds "true being," and attains to it. "He who is," [2] says Moses, "sent me." In accordance with which, namely, good opinion, some have called law, right reason, which enjoins what is to be done and forbids what is not to be done.

CHAP. XXVI. — MOSES RIGHTLY CALLED A DIVINE LEGISLATOR, AND, THOUGH INFERIOR TO CHRIST, FAR SUPERIOR TO THE GREAT LEGISLATORS OF THE GREEKS, MINOS AND LYCURGUS.

Whence the law was rightly said to have been given by Moses, being a rule of right and wrong; and we may call it with accuracy the divine ordinance (θεσμός [3]), inasmuch as it was given by God through Moses. It accordingly conducts to the divine. Paul says: "The law was instituted because of transgressions, till the seed should come, to whom the promise was made." Then, as if in explanation of his meaning, he adds: "But before faith came, we were kept under the law, shut up," manifestly through fear, in consequence of sins, "unto the faith which should afterwards be revealed; so that the law was a schoolmaster to bring us to Christ, that we should be justified by faith." [4] The true legislator is he who assigns to each department of the soul what is suitable to it and to its operations. Now Moses, to speak comprehensively, was a living law, governed by the benign Word. Accordingly, he furnished a good polity, which is the right discipline of men in social life. He also handled the administration of justice, which is that branch of knowledge which deals with the correction of transgressors in the interests of justice. Co-ordinate with it is the faculty of dealing with punishments, which is a knowledge of the due measure to be observed in punishments. And punishment, in virtue of its being so, is the correction of the soul. In a word, the whole system of Moses is suited for the training of such as are capable of becoming good and noble men, and for hunting out men like them; and this is the art of command. And that wisdom, which is capable of treating rightly those who have been caught by the Word, is legislative wisdom. For it is the property of this wisdom, being most kingly, to possess and use. It is the wise man, therefore, alone whom the philosophers proclaim king, legislator, general, just, holy, God-beloved. And if we discover these qualities in Moses, as shown from the Scriptures themselves, we may, with the most assured persuasion, pronounce Moses to be truly wise. As then we say that it belongs to the

---

[1] ά privative, and πολλοί, many.

[2] "I AM," A.V.; Ex. iii. 14.
[3] From the ancient derivation of this word from θεος.
[4] Gal. iii. 19, 23, 24.

epherd's art to care for the sheep; for so the good shepherd giveth his life for the heep;"[1] so also we shall say that legislation, inasmuch as it presides over and cares for the ock of men, establishes the virtue of men, by unning into flame, as far as it can, what good here is in humanity.

And if the flock figuratively spoken of as elonging to the Lord is nothing but a flock of men, then He Himself is the good Shepherd and Lawgiver of the one flock, " of the sheep who hear Him," the one who cares for them, seeking," and finding by the law and the word, that which was lost;" since, in truth, the law is spiritual and leads to felicity. For that which has arisen through the Holy Spirit is spiritual. And he is truly a legislator, who not only announces what is good and noble, but understands :. The law of this man who possesses knowledge is the saving precept; or rather, the law is the precept of knowledge. For the Word is the power and the wisdom of God."[2] Again, the expounder of the laws is the same one by whom the law was given; the first expounder of the divine commands, who unveiled the bosom of the Father, the only-begotten Son.

Then those who obey the law, since they have some knowledge of Him, cannot disbelieve or be ignorant of the truth. But those who disbelieve, and have shown a repugnance to engage in the works of the law, whoever else may, certainly confess their ignorance of the truth.

What, then, is the unbelief of the Greeks? Is it not their unwillingness to believe the truth which declares that the law was divinely given by Moses, whilst they honour Moses in their own writers? They relate that Minos received the laws from Zeus in nine years, by frequenting the cave of Zeus; and Plato, and Aristotle, and Ephorus write that Lycurgus was trained in legislation by going constantly to Apollo at Delphi. Chamæleo of Heraclea, in his book *On Drunkenness,* and Aristotle in *The Polity of Locrians,* mention that Zaleucus the Locrian received the laws from Athene.

But those who exalt the credit of Greek legislation as far as in them lies, by referring it to a divine source, after the model of Mosaic prophecy, are senseless in not owning the truth, and the archetype of what is related among them.

CHAP. XXVII. — THE LAW, EVEN IN CORRECTING AND PUNISHING, AIMS AT THE GOOD OF MEN.

Let no one, then, run down law, as if, on account of the penalty, it were not beautiful and good. For shall he who drives away bodily disease appear a benefactor; and shall not he who attempts to deliver the soul from iniquity, as much more appear a friend, as the soul is a more precious thing than the body? Besides, for the sake of bodily health we submit to incisions, and cauterizations, and medicinal draughts; and he who administers them is called saviour and healer,[3] even though amputating parts, not from grudge or ill-will towards the patient, but as the principles of the art prescribe, so that the sound parts may not perish along with them, and no one accuses the physician's art of wickedness; and shall we not similarly submit, for the soul's sake, to either banishment, or punishment, or bonds, provided only from unrighteousness we shall attain to righteousness?

For the law, in its solicitude for those who obey, trains up to piety, and prescribes what is to be done, and restrains each one from sins, imposing penalties even on lesser sins.

But when it sees any one in such a condition as to appear incurable, posting to the last stage of wickedness, then in its solicitude for the rest, that they may not be destroyed by it (just as if amputating a part from the whole body), it condemns such an one to death, as the course most conducive to health. " Being judged by the Lord," says the apostle, " we are chastened, that we may not be condemned with the world."[4] For the prophet had said before, " Chastening, the LORD hath chastised me, but hath not given me over unto death."[5] " For in order to teach thee His righteousness," it is said, " He chastised thee and tried thee, and made thee to hunger and thirst in the desert land; that all His statutes and His judgments may be known in thy heart, as I command thee this day; and that thou mayest know in thine heart, that just as if a man were chastising his son, so the LORD our God shall chastise thee."[6]

And to prove that example corrects, he says directly to the purpose: " A clever man, when he seeth the wicked punished, will himself be severely chastised, for the fear of the Lord is the source of wisdom."[7]

But it is the highest and most perfect good, when one is able to lead back any one from the practice of evil to virtue and well-doing, which is the very function of the law. So that, when one falls into any incurable evil,— when taken possession of, for example, by wrong or covetousness, — it will be for his good if he is put to death. For the law is beneficent, being able to make some righteous from unrighteous, if they will only give ear to it, and by releasing others from present evils; for those who have chosen

---

[1] John x. 11.
[2] 1 Cor. i. 24.

[3] [So, the Good Physician. Jer. viii. 22.]
[4] 1 Cor. xi. 32.
[5] Ps. cxviii. 18.
[6] Deut. viii. 2, 3, 5.
[7] Prov. xxii. 3, 4.

to live temperately and justly, it conducts to immortality. To know the law is characteristic of a good disposition. And again : " Wicked men do not understand the law ; but they who seek the LORD shall have understanding in all that is good." [1]

It is essential, certainly, that the providence which manages all, be both supreme and good. For it is the power of both that dispenses salvation — the one correcting by punishment, as supreme, the other showing kindness in the exercise of beneficence, as a benefactor. It is in your power not to be a son of disobedience, but to pass from darkness to life, and lending your ear to wisdom, to be the legal slave of God, in the first instance, and then to become a faithful servant, fearing the Lord God. And if one ascend higher, he is enrolled among the sons.

But when " charity covers the multitude of sins," [2] by the consummation of the blessed hope, then may we welcome him as one who has been enriched in love, and received into the elect adoption, which is called the beloved of God, while he chants the prayer, saying, " Let the Lord be my God."

The beneficent action of the law, the apostle showed in the passage relating to the Jews, writing thus : " Behold, thou art called a Jew and restest in the law, and makest thy boast in God, and knowest the will of God, and approvest the things that are more excellent, being instructed out of the law, and art confident that thou thyself art a guide of the blind, a light of them who are in darkness, an instructor of the foolish, a teacher of babes, who hast the form of knowledge and of truth in the law." [3] For it is admitted that such is the power of the law, although those whose conduct is not according to the law, make a false pretence, as if they lived in the law. " Blessed is the man that hath found wisdom, and the mortal who has seen understanding ; for out of its mouth," manifestly Wisdom's, " proceeds righteousness, and it bears law and mercy on its tongue." [4] For both the law and the Gospel are the energy of one Lord, who is " the power and wisdom of God ; " and the terror which the law begets is merciful and in order to salvation. " Let not alms, and faith, and truth fail thee, but hang them around thy neck." [5] In the same way as Paul, prophecy upbraids the people with not understanding the law. " Destruction and misery are in their ways, and the way of peace have they not known." [6] " There is no fear of God before their eyes." [7] " Pro-

fessing themselves wise, they became fools." [8] " And we know that the law is good, if a man use it lawfully." [9] " Desiring to be teachers of the law, they understand," says the apostle, " neither what they say, nor whereof they affirm." [10] " Now the end of the commandment is charity out of a pure heart, and a good conscience, and faith unfeigned." [11]

CHAP. XXVIII. — THE FOURFOLD DIVISION OF THE MOSAIC LAW.

The Mosaic philosophy is accordingly divided into four parts, — into the historic, and that which is specially called the legislative, which two properly belong to an ethical treatise ; and the third, that which relates to sacrifice, which belongs to physical science ; and the fourth above all, the department of theology, "vision," [12] which Plato predicates of the truly great mysteries. And this species Aristotle calls metaphysics. Dialectics, according to Plato, is, as he says in *The Statesman*, a science devoted to the discovery of the explanation of things. And it is to be acquired by the wise man, not for the sake of saying or doing aught of what we find among men (as the dialecticians, who occupy themselves in sophistry, do), but to be able to say and do, as far as possible, what is pleasing to God. But the true dialectic, being philosophy mixed with truth, by examining things, and testing forces and powers, gradually ascends in relation to the most excellent essence of all, and essays to go beyond to the God of the universe, professing not the knowledge of mortal affairs, but the science of things divine and heavenly ; in accordance with which follows a suitable course of practice with respect to words and deeds, even in human affairs. Rightly, therefore, the Scripture, in its desire to make us such dialecticians, exhorts us : " Be ye skilful money-changers," [13] rejecting some things, but retaining what is good. For this true dialectic is the science which analyses the objects of thought, and shows abstractly and by itself the individual substratum of existences, or the power of dividing things into genera, which descends to their most special properties, and presents each individual object to be contemplated simply such as it is.

Wherefore it alone conducts to the true wisdom, which is the divine power which deals with the knowledge of entities as entities, which grasps what is perfect, and is freed from all passion ; not without the Saviour, who withdraws by the divine word, the gloom of ignorance

---

[1] Prov. xxviii. 5.
[2] 1 Pet. iv. 8.
[3] Rom. ii. 17-20.
[4] Prov. iii. 13, 16.
[5] Prov. iii. 3.
[6] Isa. lix. 7, 8; Rom. iii. 16, 17.
[7] Ps. xxxvi. 1; Rom. iii. 18.

[8] Rom. i. 22.
[9] 1 Tim. i. 8.
[10] 1 Tim. i. 7.
[11] 1 Tim. i. 5.
[12] ἐποπτεία, the third and highest grade of initiation into the mysteries.
[13] A saying not in Scripture; but by several of the ancient Fathers attributed to Christ or an apostle. [Jones, *Canon*, i. 438.]

arising from evil training, which had overspread the eye of the soul, and bestows the best of gifts, —

"That we might well know or God or man."[1]

It is He who truly shows how we are to know ourselves. It is He who reveals the Father of the universe to whom He wills, and as far as human nature can comprehend. "For no man knoweth the Son but the Father, nor the Father but the Son, and he to whom the Son shall reveal Him."[2] Rightly, then, the apostle says that it was by revelation that he knew the mystery: "As I wrote afore in few words, according as ye are able to understand my knowledge in the mystery of Christ."[3] "According as ye are able," he said, since he knew that some had received milk only, and had not yet received meat, nor even milk simply. The sense of the law is to be taken in three ways,[4] — either as exhibiting a symbol, or laying down a precept for right conduct, or as uttering a prophecy. But I well know that it belongs to men [of full age] to distinguish and declare these things. For the whole Scripture is not in its meaning a single Myconos, as the proverbial expression has it; but those who hunt after the connection of the divine teaching, must approach it with the utmost perfection of the logical faculty.

CHAP. XXIX. — THE GREEKS BUT CHILDREN COMPARED WITH THE HEBREWS.

Whence most beautifully the Egyptian priest in Plato said, "O Solon, Solon, you Greeks are always children, not having in your souls a single ancient opinion received through tradition from antiquity. And not one of the Greeks is an old man;"[5] meaning by old, I suppose, those who know what belongs to the more remote antiquity, that is, our literature; and by young, those who treat of what is more recent and made the subject of study by the Greeks, — things of yesterday and of recent date as if they were old and ancient. Wherefore he added, "and no study hoary with time;" for we, in a kind of barbarous way, deal in homely and rugged metaphor. Those, therefore, whose minds are rightly constituted approach the interpretation utterly destitute of artifice. And of the Greeks, he says that their opinions "differ but little from myths." For neither puerile fables nor stories current among children are fit for listening to. And he called the myths themselves "children," as if the progeny of those, wise in their own conceits

among the Greeks, who had but little insight; meaning by the "hoary studies" the truth which was possessed by the barbarians, dating from the highest antiquity. To which expression he opposed the phrase "child fable," censuring the mythical character of the attempts of the moderns, as, like children, having nothing of age in them, and affirming both in common — their fables and their speeches — to be puerile.

Divinely, therefore, the power which spoke to Hermas by revelation said, "The visions and revelations are for those who are of double mind, who doubt in their hearts if these things are or are not."[6]

Similarly, also, demonstrations from the resources of erudition, strengthen, confirm, and establish demonstrative reasonings, in so far as men's minds are in a wavering state like young people's. "The good commandment," then, according to the Scripture, "is a lamp, and the law is a light to the path; for instruction corrects the ways of life."[7] "Law is monarch of all, both of mortals and of immortals," says Pindar. I understand, however, by these words, Him who enacted law. And I regard, as spoken of the God of all, the following utterance of Hesiod, though spoken by the poet at random and not with comprehension: —

"For the Saturnian framed for men this law:
Fishes, and beasts, and winged birds may eat
Each other, since no rule of right is theirs;
But Right (by far the best) to men he gave."

Whether, then, it be the law which is connate and natural, or that given afterwards, which is meant, it is certainly of God; and both the law of nature and that of instruction are one. Thus also Plato, in *The Statesman*, says that the lawgiver is one; and in *The Laws*, that he who shall understand music is one; teaching by these words that the Word is one, and God is one. And Moses manifestly calls the Lord a covenant: "Behold I am my Covenant with thee,"[8] having previously told him not to seek the covenant in writing.[9] For it is a covenant which God, the Author of all, makes. For God is called Θεός, from θέσις (placing), and order or arrangement. And in the *Preaching*[10] of Peter you will find the Lord called Law and Word. But at this point, let our first Miscellany[11] of gnostic notes, according to the true philosophy, come to a close.

---

[1] "That thou may'st well know whether he be a god or a man." — HOMER.

[2] Matt. xi. 27.

[3] Eph. iii. 3, 4.

[4] The text has τετραχῶς, which is either a mistake for τριχῶς, or belongs to a clause which is wanting. The author asserts the triple sense of Scripture, — the mystic, the moral, and the prophetic. [And thus lays the egg which his pupil Origen was to hatch, and to nurse into a brood of mysticism.]

[5] [*Timæus*, p. 22, B. — S.]

[6] [See *Shepherd of Hermas*, i. p. 14, *ante*. S.]

[7] Prov. vi. 23.

[8] Gen. xvii. 4. "As for me, behold, My covenant is with thee." — A.V.

[9] The allusion here is obscure. The suggestion has been made that it is to ver. 2 of the same chapter, which is thus taken to intimate that the covenant was to be verbal, not written.

[10] Referring to an apocryphal book so called. [This book is not cited as Scripture, but (*valeat quantum*) as containing a saying attributed to St. Peter. Clement quotes it not infrequently. A very full and valuable account of it may be found in Lardner, vol. ii. p. 252, *et seqq.* Not less valuable is the account given by Jones, *On the Canon*, vol. i. p. 355. See all Clement's citations, same volume, p. 345, *et seqq.*]

[11] Στρωματεύς.

ELUCIDATIONS.

I.

(Purpose of the *Stromata*.[1])

THE Alexandrian Gnostics were the pestilent outgrowth of *pseudo-Platonism ;* and nobody could comprehend their root-errors, and their branching thorns and thistles, better than Clement. His superiority in philosophy and classical culture was exhibited, therefore, in his writings, as a necessary preliminary.   Like a good nautical combatant, his effort was to "get to windward," and so bear down upon the enemy (to use an anachronism) with heavy-shotted broadsides.   And we must not blame Clement for his plan of "taking the wind out of their sails," by showing that an eclectic philosophy might be made to harmonize with the Gospel.   His plan was that of melting the gold out of divers ores, and throwing the dross away.   Pure gold, he argues, is gold wherever it may be found, and even in the purse of "thieves and robbers."   So, then, he "takes from them the armour in which they trusted, and divides the spoils."   He will not concede to them the name of "Gnostics," but wrests it from them, just as we reclaim the name of "Catholics" from the Tridentine innovators, who have imposed a modern creed (and are constantly adding to it) upon the Latin churches.   Here, then, let me quote the *Account* of Bishop Kaye.   He says, "The object of Clement, in composing the *Stromata*, was to describe the true ' Gnostic,' or perfect Christian, in order to furnish the believer with a model for his imitation, and to prevent him from being led astray by the representations of the Valentinians and other gnostic sects." . . . "Before we proceed to consider his description of the Gnostic, however, it will be necessary briefly to review his opinions respecting the nature and condition of man."

Here follows a luminous analysis (occupying pp. 229–238 of Kaye's work), after which he says, —

"The foregoing brief notice of Clement's opinions respecting man, his soul, and his fallen state, appeared necessary as an introduction to the description of the *true Gnostic*. By γνῶσις, Clement understood the perfect knowledge of all that relates to God, His nature, and dispensations. He speaks of a twofold knowledge, — one, common to all men, and born of sense ; the other, the genuine γνῶσις, bred from the intellect, the mind, and its reason. This latter is not born with men, but must be gained and by practice formed into a habit. The *initiated* find its perfection in a loving mysticism, which this never-failing love makes lasting."

So, further, this learned analyst, not blindly, but always with scientific conscience and judicial impartiality, expounds his author ; and, without some such guide, I despair of securing the real interest of the youthful student.   Butler's *Analogy* and Aristotle's *Ethics* are always analyzed for learners, by editors of their works ; and hence I have ventured to direct attention to this "guide, philosopher, and friend" of my own inquiries.[2]

II.

(Pantænus and His School.[3])

The catechetical school at Alexandria was already ancient ; for Eusebius describes it as ἐξ ἀρχαίου ἔθους, and St. Jerome dates its origin from the first planting of Christianity.   Many things conspired to make this city the very head of Catholic ·Christendom, at this time ; for the whole

---

[1] Book i. cap. i. p. 299, note 1.   [2] *Ed*. Rivingtons, London, 1835.   [3] Book i. cap. i. p. 301, note 9.

East centred here, and the East was Christendom while the West was yet a missionary field almost entirely. Demetrius, then bishop, at the times with which we are now concerned, sent Pantænus to convert the Hindoos, and, whatever his success or failure there, he brought back reports that Christians were there before him, the offspring of St. Bartholomew's preaching; and, in proof thereof, he brought with him a copy of St. Matthew's Gospel in the Hebrew tongue,[1] which became one of the treasures of the church on the Nile.

But it deserves note, that, because of the learning concentrated in this place, the bishops of Alexandria were, from the beginning, the great authorities as to the Easter cycle and the annual computation of Easter, which new created the science of astronomy as one result. The Council of Nice, in settling the laws for the observance of the Feast of the Resurrection, extended the function of the Alexandrian See in this respect; for it was charged with the duty of giving notice of the day when Easter should fall every year, to all the churches. And easily might an ambitious primate of Egypt have imagined himself superior to all other bishops at that time; for, as Bingham observes,[2] he was the greatest in the world, "for the absoluteness of his power, and the extent of his jurisdiction." And this greatness of Alexandria was *ancient*, we must remember, at the Nicene epoch; for their celebrated canon (VI.) reads, " *Let ancient customs prevail;* so that in Egypt, Lybia, and Pentapolis, the Bishop of Alexandria shall have power over all these." Similar powers and privileges, over their own regions, were recognised in Rome and Antioch.

III.

(Tradition.[3])

The apostles distinguish between vain traditions of the Jews, and their own Christian παραδό-σεις, the *tradita apostolica* (2 Tim. i. 13, 14; 2 Tim. ii. 2; 1 Cor. xi. 2; 2 Thess. ii. 15; 2 Thess. iii. 6; 1 Cor. v. 8; 1 Cor. xvi. 2). Among these were (1) the authentication of their own Scriptures; (2) certain "forms of sound words," afterwards digested into liturgies; (3) the rules for celebrating the Lord's Supper, and of administering baptism; (4) the Christian Passover and the weekly Lord's Day; (5) the Jewish Sabbath and ordinances, how far to be respected while the temple yet stood; (6) the kiss of charity, and other observances of public worship; (7) the *agapæ*, the rules about widows, etc.

In some degree these were the secret of the Church, with which "strangers intermeddled not" lawfully. The Lord's Supper was celebrated after the catechumens and mere hearers had withdrawn, and nobody was suffered to be present without receiving the sacrament. But, after the conversion of the empire, the canons and constitutions universally dispersed made public all these *tradita;* and the liturgies also were everywhere made known. It is idle, therefore, to shelter under theories of the *Disciplina Arcani,* those Middle-Age inventions, of which antiquity shows no trace but in many ways contradicts emphatically; e.g., the Eucharist, celebrated after the withdrawal of the non-communicants, and received, in both kinds, by all present, cannot be pleaded as the "secret" which justifies a ceremony in an unknown tongue and otherwise utterly different; in which the priest alone partakes, in which the cup is denied to the laity and which is exhibited with great pomp before all comers with no general participation.

IV.

(Esoteric Doctrine.[4])

Early Christians, according to Clement, taught to all alike, (1) all things necessary to salvation, (2) all the whole Scriptures, and (3) all the apostolic traditions. This is evident from passages

---

[1] See Jones, *On the Canon*, vol. iii. p. 44.   [2] *Antiquities*, vol. i. p. 66, ed. Bohn.   [3] Book i. cap. i. p. 301, note 10.
[4] Book i. cap. i. p. 302, note 5.

noted here and hereafter. But, in the presence of the heathen, they remembered our Lord's words, and were careful not "to cast pearls before swine." Like St. Paul before Felix, they "reasoned of righteousness, temperance, and judgment to come," when dealing with men who knew not God, preaching Christ to them in a practical way. In their instructions to the churches, they were able to say with the same apostle, "I am pure from the blood of all men, for I have not shunned to declare unto you *all the counsel of God.*" Yet, even in the Church, they fed ·babes with milk, and the more intelligent with the meat of God's word. What that meat was, we discover in the *Stromata*, when our author defines the true Gnostic, who follows whithersoever God leads him in *the divinely inspired Scriptures.* He recognises many who merely taste the Scriptures as *believers;* but the true Gnostic is a *gnomon* of truth, an index to others of the whole knowledge of Christ.

What we teach children in the Sunday school, and what we teach young men in the theological seminary, must illustrate the two ideas ; the same truths to babes in element, but to men in all their bearings and relations.

The defenders of the modern creed of Pius the Fourth (A.D. 1564), finding no authority in Holy Scripture for most of its peculiarities, which are all imposed as requisite to salvation as if it were the Apostles' Creed itself, endeavour to support them, by asserting that they belonged to the secret teaching of the early Church, of which they claim Clement as a witness. But the fallacy is obvious. Either they were thus *secreted,* or they were not. If not, as is most evident (because they contradict what was openly professed), then no ground for the pretence. But suppose they were, what follows? Such secrets were no part of the faith, and could not become so at a later period. If they were kept secret by the new theologians, and taught to "Gnostics" only, they would still be without primitive example, but might be less objectionable. But, no ! they are imposed upon all, as if part of the ancient creeds ; imposed, as if articles of the Catholic faith, on the most illiterate peasant, whose mere *doubt* as to any of them excludes him from the Church here, and from salvation hereafter. Such, then, is a fatal departure from Catholic orthodoxy and the traditions of the ancients. The whole system is a novelty, and the product of the most barren and corrupt period of Occidental history.

The Church, as Clement shows, never made any *secret* of any article of the Christian faith ; and, as soon as she was free from persecution, the whole testimony of the Ante-Nicene Fathers was summed up in the Nicæno-Constantinopolitan Confession. This only is the Catholic faith, and the council forbade any additions thereto, in the way of a symbol. See Professor Shedd's *Christian Doctrine,* vol. ii. p. 438. Ed. 1864, New York.

V.

(p. 302, note 9, Elucidation III., continued.)

This is a valuable passage for the illustration of our author's views of the nature of tradition, (κατὰ τὸν σεμνὸν τῆς παραδόσεως κανόνα) as a canon "from the creation of the world ; " a tradition preluding the tradition of true knowledge ; a divine mystery preparing for the knowledge of mysteries,—clearing the ground from thorns and weeds, beforehand, so that the seed of the Word may not be choked. Now, in this tradition, he includes a true idea of Gentilism as well as of the Hebrew Church and its covenant relations ; in short, whatever a Christian scholar is obliged to learn from "Antiquities" and "Introductions" and "Bible Dictionaries," authenticated by universal and orthodox approbation. These are the providential provisions of the Divine Œconomy, for the communication of truth. Dr. Watts has a sermon on the *Inward Witness to Christianity,* which I find quoted by Vicesimus Knox (Works, vol. vii. p. 73, *et seqq.*) in a choice passage that forcibly expands and expounds some of Clement's suggestions, though without referring to our author.

VI.

(Justification, p. 305, note 7.)

Without reference to my own views on this great subject, and desiring merely to illustrate our author, it shall suffice to remark, here, that to suppose that Clement uses the word *technically*, as we now use the language of the schools and of post-Reformation theologians, would hopelessly confuse the argument of our author. It is clear that he has no idea of any justification apart from the merits of Christ : but he uses the term loosely to express his idea, that as the Law led the Hebrews to the great Healer, who rose from the dead for our justification, in that sense, and in no other, *the truth* that was to be found in Greek Philosophy, although a *minimum*, did the same for heathen who loved truth, and followed it so far as they knew. Whether his views even in this were correct, it would not become me, here, to express any opinion. (See below, Elucidation XIV.)

VII.

(Philosophy, p. 305, note 8.)

It is so important to grasp just what our author understands by this "philosophy," that I had designed to introduce, here, a long passage from Bishop Kaye's lucid exposition. Finding, however, that these elucidations are already, perhaps, over multiplied, I content myself with a reference to his *Account,* etc. (pp. 118–121).

VIII.

(Overflow of the Spirit, p. 306, note 1.)

Here, again, I wished to introduce textual citations from several eminent authors : I content myself with a very short one from Kaye, to illustrate the intricacy, not to say the contradictory character, of some of Clement's positions as to the extent of grace bestowed on the heathen. " Clement says that an act, to be right, must be done through the love of God. He says that every action of the heathen is sinful, since it is not sufficient that an action is right : *its object or aim must also be right"* (*Account,* etc., p. 426). For a most interesting, but I venture to think overdrawn, statement of St. Paul's position as to heathen " wisdom," etc., see Farrar's *Life of St. Paul* (p. 20, *et seqq.,* ed. New York). Without relying on this popular author, I cannot but refer the reader to his *Hulsean Lecture* (1870, p. 135, *et seqq.*).

IX.

(Faith without Learning, p. 307, note 5.)

The compassion of Christ for poverty, misery, for childhood, and for ignorance, is everywhere illustrated in Holy Scripture ; and *faith,* even " as a grain of mustard seed," is magnified, accordingly, in the infinite love of his teaching. Again I am willing to refer to Farrar (though I read him always with something between the lines, before I can adopt his sweeping generalizations) for a fine passage, I should quote entire, did space permit (*The Witness of History to Christ,* p. 172, ed. London, 1872). See also the noble sermon of Jeremy Taylor on John vii. 17 (Works, vol. ii. p. 53, ed. Bohn, 1844).

X.

(The Open Secret, p. 313, note 3.)

The esoteric system of Clement is here expounded in few words : there is nothing in it which may not be proclaimed from the house-tops, for all who have ears to hear. It is the mere swine (with seed-pickers and jack-daws, the σπερμολόγοι of the Athenians) who must be denied the pearls of gnostic truth. And this, on the same merciful principle on which the Master was silent before Pilate, and turned away from cities where they were not prepared to receive his message.

XI.

(Bodily Purity, p. 317, note 1.)

From a familiar quotation, I have often argued that the fine instinct of a woman, even among heathen, enforces a true idea : " If from her husband's bed, as soon as she has bathed : if from adulterous commerce, not at all." This is afterwards noted by our author ; [1] but it is extraordinary to find the mind of the great missionary to our Saxon forefathers, troubled about such questions, even in the seventh century. I have less admiration for the elaborate answers of the great Patriarch of Rome (Gregory), to the scrupulous inquiries of Augustine, than for the instinctive and aphoristic wisdom of poor Theano, in all the darkness of her heathenism. (See Ven. Bede, *Eccles. Hist.*, book i. cap. 27, p. 131. Works, ed. London, 1843.)

XII.

(Clement's View of Philosophy, p. 318, note 4.)

I note the concluding words of this chapter (xvi.), as epitomizing the whole of what Clement means to say on this great subject ; and, for more, see the Elucidation *infra*, on Justification.

XIII.

(The Ecstacy of Sibyl, etc., p. 319, note 3.)

No need to quote Virgil's description (*Æneid*, vi. 46, with Heyne's references in Excursus V.) ; but I would compare with his picture of Sibylline inspiration, that of Balaam (Num. xxiv. 3, 4, 15, 16), and leave with the student an inquiry, how far we may credit to a divine motion, the oracles of the heathen, i.e., some of them. I wish to refer the student, also, as to a valuable bit of introductory learning, to the essay of Isaac Casaubon (*Exercitationes ad Baronii Prolegom.*, pp. 65-85, ed. Genevæ, 1663).

XIV.

(Justification, p. 323, note 2.)

Casaubon, in the work just quoted above (*Exercitat.*, i.) examines this passage of our author, and others, comparing them with passages from St. Chrysostom and St. Augustine, and with Justin Martyr (see vol. i. p. 178, this series, cap. 46). Bishop Kaye (p. 428) justly remarks : " The apparent incorrectness of Clement's language arises from not making that clear distinction which the controversies at the time of the Reformation introduced." The word " incorrectness," though for myself I do not object to it, might be said " to beg the question ; " and hence I should prefer to leave it open to the divers views of readers, by speaking, rather, of his lack of *precision* in the use of a term not then defined with theological delicacy of statement.

XV.

(Chronology, p. 334, note 5.)

Here an invaluable work for comparison and reference must be consulted by the student ; viz., the *Chronicon* of Julius Africanus, in Routh's *Reliquiæ* (tom ii. p. 220, *et seqq.*), with learned annotations, in which (e g., p. 491) Clement's work is cited. Africanus took up chronological science in the imperfect state where it was left by Clement, with whom he was partially contemporary ; for he was Bishop of Emmaus in Palestine (called also Nicopolis), and composed his fine books of chronological history, under Marcus Aurelius.[2] On the Alexandrian era consult a paragraph in *Encyc. Britannica* (vol. v. p. 714). It was adopted for Christian computation, after Africanus. See Eusebius (book vi. cap. 31), and compare (this volume, p. 85) what is said of Theophilus of Antioch, by Abp. Usher.[3]

---

[1] p 428, *infra*.   [2] See also *Fragments*, p. 164, vol. ix., this series, Edin. edition.
[3] For matters further pertaining to Clement, consult Routh, i. 140, i. 148, i. 127, i. 169, ii. 59 (Eusebius, vi. 13), ii. 165, 167, 168, 171-172, 179, 307, 416, 491.

THE STROMATA, OR MISCELLANIES.

BOOK II.

CHAP. I. — INTRODUCTORY.[1]

As Scripture has called the Greeks pilferers of the Barbarian[2] philosophy, it will next have to be considered how this may be briefly demonstrated. For we shall not only show that they have imitated and copied the marvels recorded in our books; but we shall prove, besides, that they have plagiarized and falsified (our writings being, as we have shown, older) the chief dogmas they hold, both on faith and knowledge and science, and hope and love, and also on repentance and temperance and the fear of God, — a whole swarm, verily, of the virtues of truth.

Whatever the explication necessary on the point in hand shall demand, shall be embraced, and especially what is occult in the barbarian philosophy, the department of symbol and enigma; which those who have subjected the teaching of the ancients to systematic philosophic study have affected, as being in the highest degree serviceable, nay, absolutely necessary to the knowledge of truth. In addition, it will in my opinion form an appropriate sequel to defend those tenets, on account of which the Greeks assail us, making use of a few Scriptures, if perchance the Jew also may listen[3] and be able quietly to turn from what he has believed to Him on whom he has not believed. The ingenuous among the philosophers will then with propriety be taken up in a friendly exposure both of their life and of the discovery of new dogmas, not in the way of our avenging ourselves on our detractors (for that is far from being the case with those who have learned to bless those who curse, even though they needlessly discharge on us words of blasphemy), but with a view to their conversion; if by any means these adepts in wisdom may feel ashamed, being brought to their senses by barbarian demonstration; so as to be able, although late, to see clearly of what sort are the intellectual acquisitions for which they make pilgrimages over the seas. Those they have stolen are to be pointed out, that we may thereby pull down their conceit; and of those on the discovery of which through investigation they plume themselves, the refutation will be furnished. By consequence, also we must treat of what is called the curriculum of study — how far it is serviceable;[4] and of astrology, and mathematics, and magic, and sorcery. For all the Greeks boast of these as the highest sciences. "He who reproves boldly is a peacemaker."[5] We have often said already that we have neither practised nor do we study the expressing ourselves in pure Greek; for this suits those who seduce the multitude from the truth. But true philosophic demonstration will contribute to the profit not of the listeners' tongues, but of their minds. And, in my opinion, he who is solicitous about truth ought not to frame his language with artfulness and care, but only to try to express his meaning as he best can. For those who are particular about words, and devote their time to them, miss the things.[6] It is a feat fit for the gardener to pluck without injury the rose that is growing among the thorns; and for the craftsman to find out the pearl buried in the oyster's flesh. And they say that fowls have flesh of the most agreeable quality, when, through not being supplied with abundance of food, they pick their sustenance with difficulty, scraping with their feet. If any one, then, speculating on what is

---

[1] [" The Epistles of the New Testament have all a particular reference *to the condition and usages of the Christian world at the time they were written.* Therefore as they cannot be thoroughly understood, unless that condition and those usages are known and attended to, so further, though they be known, yet if they be discontinued or changed . . . references to such circumstances, now ceased or altered, cannot, at this time, be urged in that manner and with that force which they were to the primitive Christians." This quotation from one of Bishop Butler's *Ethical Sermons* has many bearings on the study of our author; but the sermon itself, with its sequel, *On Human Nature,* may well be read in connection with the *Stromata.* See Butler, *Ethical Discourses,* p. 77. Philadelphia, 1855]

[2] Referring in particular to the Jews.

[3] [Col. iv. 6.]

[4] The text reads ἄχρηστος: Sylburg prefers the reading εὔχρηστος.

[5] Prov. x. 10, Septuagint.

[6] [διαδιδράσκει τὰ πράγματα. A truly Platonic thrust at sophistical rhetoricians.]

similar, wants to arrive [1] at the truth [that is] in the numerous Greek plausibilities, like the real face beneath masks, he will hunt it out with much pains. For the power that appeared in the vision to Hermas said, "Whatever may be revealed to you, shall be revealed." [2]

CHAP. II.—THE KNOWLEDGE OF GOD CAN BE ATTAINED ONLY THROUGH FAITH.

"Be not elated on account of thy wisdom," say the Proverbs. "In all thy ways acknowledge her, that she may direct thy ways, and that thy foot may not stumble." By these remarks he means to show that our deeds ought to be conformable to reason, and to manifest further that we ought to select and possess what is useful out of all culture. Now the ways of wisdom are various that lead right to the way of truth. Faith is the way. "Thy foot shall not stumble" is said with reference to some who seem to oppose the one divine administration of Providence. Whence it is added, "Be not wise in thine own eyes," according to the impious ideas which revolt against the administration of God. "But fear God," who alone is powerful. Whence it follows as a consequence that we are not to oppose God. The sequel especially teaches clearly, that "the fear of God is departure from evil;" for it is said, "and depart from all evil." Such is the discipline of wisdom ("for whom the Lord loveth He chastens" [3]), causing pain in order to produce understanding, and restoring to peace and immortality. Accordingly, the Barbarian philosophy, which we follow, is in reality perfect and true. And so it is said in the book of Wisdom : "For He hath given me the unerring knowledge of things that exist, to know the constitution of the word," and so forth, down to "and the virtues of roots." Among all these he comprehends natural science, which treats of all the phenomena in the world of sense. And in continuation, he alludes also to intellectual objects in what he subjoins : "And what is hidden or manifest I know ; for Wisdom, the artificer of all things, taught me." [4] You have, in brief, the professed aim of our philosophy ; and the learning of these branches, when pursued with right course of conduct, leads through Wisdom, the artificer of all things, to the Ruler of all, — a Being difficult to grasp and apprehend, ever receding and withdrawing from him who pursues. But He who is far off has — oh ineffable marvel ! — come very near. "I am a God that draws near," says the Lord. He is in essence remote ; "for how is it that what is begotten can have approached the Unbegotten ?"

But He is very near in virtue of that power which holds all things in its embrace. "Shall one do aught in secret, and I see him not?" [5] For the power of God is always present, in contact with us, in the exercise of inspection, of beneficence, of instruction. Whence Moses, persuaded that God is not to be known by human wisdom, said, "Show me Thy glory;" [6] and into the thick darkness where God's voice was, pressed to enter — that is, into the inaccessible and invisible ideas respecting Existence. For God is not in darkness or in place, but above both space and time, and qualities of objects. Wherefore neither is He at any time in a part, either as containing or as contained, either by limitation or by section. "For what house will ye build to Me?" saith the Lord. [7] Nay, He has not even built one for Himself, since He cannot be contained. And though heaven be called His throne, not even thus is He contained, but He rests delighted in the creation.

It is clear, then, that the truth has been hidden from us ; and if that has been already shown by one example, we shall establish it a little after by several more. How entirely worthy of approbation are they who are both willing to learn, and able, according to Solomon, "to know wisdom and instruction, and to perceive the words of wisdom, to receive knotty words, and to perceive true righteousness," there being another [righteousness as well], not according to the truth, taught by the Greek laws, and by the rest of the philosophers. "And to direct judgments," it is said — not those of the bench, but he means that we must preserve sound and free of error the judicial faculty which is within us — "That I may give subtlety to the simple, to the young man sense and understanding." [8] "For the wise man," who has been persuaded to obey the commandments, "having heard these things, will become wiser" by knowledge ; and "the intelligent man will acquire rule, and will understand a parable and a dark word, the sayings and enigmas of the wise." [9] For it is not spurious words which those inspired by God and those who are gained over by them adduce, nor is it snares in which the most of the sophists entangle the young, spending their time on nought true. But those who possess the Holy Spirit "search the deep things of God," [10] — that is, grasp the secret that is in the prophecies. "To impart of holy things to the dogs" is forbidden, so long as they remain beasts. For never ought those who are envious and perturbed, and still infidel in conduct, shameless in barking at inves-

1 διεληλυθέναι, suggested by Sylb. as more suitable than the διαλεληθέναι of the text.
2 Hermas—close of third vision, [cap. 13. p. 17, supra.]
3 Prov. iii. 5, 6, 7, 12, 23.
4 Wisd. vii. 17, 20, 21, 22.

5 Jer. xxiii. 23, 24.
6 Ex. xxxiii. 18.
7 Isa. lxvi. 1.
8 ἔννοιαν, not εὔνοιαν, as in the text.
9 Prov. i. 2-6.
10 1 Cor. ii. 10.

tigation, to dip in the divine and clear stream of the living water. " Let not the waters of thy fountain overflow, and let thy waters spread over thine own streets." [1] For it is not many who understand such things as they fall in with; or know them even after learning them, though they think they do, according to the worthy Heraclitus. Does not even he seem to thee to censure those who believe not? " Now my just one shall live by faith," [2] the prophet said. And another prophet also says, " Except ye believe, neither shall ye understand." [3] For how ever could the soul admit the transcendental contemplation of such themes, while unbelief respecting what was to be learned struggled within? But faith, which the Greeks disparage, deeming it futile and barbarous, is a voluntary preconception, [4] the assent of piety — " the subject of things hoped for, the evidence of things not seen," according to the divine apostle. " For hereby," pre-eminently, " the elders obtained a good report. But without faith it is impossible to please God." [5] Others have defined faith to be a uniting assent to an unseen object, as certainly the proof of an unknown thing is an evident assent. If then it be choice, being desirous of something, the desire is in this instance intellectual. And since choice is the beginning of action, faith is discovered to be the beginning of action, being the foundation of rational choice in the case of any one who exhibits to himself the previous demonstration through faith. Voluntarily to follow what is useful, is the first principle of understanding. Unswerving choice, then, gives considerable momentum in the direction of knowledge. The exercise of faith directly becomes knowledge, reposing on a sure foundation. Knowledge, accordingly, is defined by the sons of the philosophers as a habit, which cannot be overthrown by reason. Is there any other true condition such as this, except piety, of which alone the Word is teacher? [6] I think not. Theophrastus says that sensation is the root of faith. For from it the rudimentary principles extend to the reason that is in us, and the understanding. He who believeth then the divine Scriptures with sure judgment, receives in the voice of God, who bestowed the Scripture, a demonstration that cannot be impugned. Faith, then, is not established by demonstration. " Blessed therefore those who, not having seen, yet have believed." [7] The Siren's songs, exhibiting a power above human, fascinated those that came near, conciliating them, almost against their will, to the reception of what was said.

CHAP. III. — FAITH NOT A PRODUCT OF NATURE.

Now the followers of Basilides regard faith as natural, as they also refer it to choice, [representing it] as finding ideas by intellectual comprehension without demonstration; while the followers of Valentinus assign faith to us, the simple, but will have it that knowledge springs up in their own selves (who are saved by nature) through the advantage of a germ of superior excellence, saying that it is as far removed from faith as [8] the spiritual is from the animal. Further, the followers of Basilides say that faith as well as choice is proper according to every interval; and that in consequence of the supramundane selection mundane faith accompanies all nature, and that the free gift of faith is comformable to the hope of each. Faith, then, is no longer the direct result of free choice, if it is a natural advantage.

Nor will he who has not believed, not being the author [of his unbelief], meet with a due recompense; and he that has believed is not the cause [of his belief]. And the entire peculiarity and difference of belief and unbelief will not fall under either praise or censure, if we reflect rightly, since there attaches to it the antecedent natural necessity proceeding from the Almighty. And if we are pulled like inanimate things by the puppet-strings of natural powers, willingness [9] and unwillingness, and impulse, which is the antecedent of both, are mere redundancies. And for my part, I am utterly incapable of conceiving such an animal as has its appetencies, which are moved by external causes, under the dominion of necessity. And what place is there any longer for the repentance of him who was once an unbeliever, through which comes forgiveness of sins? So that neither is baptism rational, nor the blessed seal, [10] nor the Son, nor the Father. But God, as I think, turns out to be the distribution to men of natural powers, which has not as the foundation of salvation voluntary faith.

CHAP. IV. — FAITH THE FOUNDATION OF ALL KNOWLEDGE.

But we, who have heard by the Scriptures that self-determining choice and refusal have been given by the Lord to men, rest in the infallible criterion of faith, manifesting a willing spirit, since we have chosen life and believe God through His voice. And he who has believed the Word knows the matter to be true; for the Word is

---

[1] Prov. v. 16.
[2] Hab. ii. 4.
[3] Isa. vii. 9.
[4] Or anticipation, πρόληψις.
[5] Heb. xi. 1, 2, 6.
[6] Adopting Lowth's conjecture of supplying πλήν before θεοσεβείας.
[7] John xx. 29. [Note this definition of true knowledge, followed by an appeal to the Scriptures as infallible teaching. No need to say that no other infallibility is ever hinted, or dreamed of, by Clement.]

[8] The text reads ἤ: but Sylb. suggests ῇ, which we have adopted. The text has ἀκούσιον only, for which Lowth proposes to read ἑκούσιον.
[9] καὶ τὸ ἑκούσιον is supplied as required by the sense. The text has ἀκούσιον only, for which Lowth proposes to read ἑκούσιον.
[10] Either baptism or the imposition of hands after baptism. [For an almost pontifical decision as to this whole matter, with a very just eulogy of the German (Lutheran) confirmation-office, see Bunsen, Hippol., iii. pp. 214, 369.]

truth. But he who has disbelieved Him that speaks, has disbelieved God.

"By faith we understand that the worlds were framed by the word of God, so that what is seen was not made of things which appear," says the apostle. "By faith Abel offered to God a fuller sacrifice than Cain, by which he received testimony that he was righteous, God giving testimony to him respecting his gifts ; and by it he, being dead, yet speaketh," and so forth, down to "than enjoy the pleasures of sin for a season."[1] Faith having, therefore, justified these before the law, made them heirs of the divine promise. Why then should I review and adduce any further testimonies of faith from the history in our hands ? "For the time would fail me were I to tell of Gideon, Barak, Samson, Jephtha, David, and Samuel, and the prophets," and what follows.[2] Now, inasmuch as there are four things in which the truth resides — Sensation, Understanding, Knowledge, Opinion, — intellectual apprehension is first in the order of nature ; but in our case, and in relation to ourselves, Sensation is first, and of Sensation and Understanding the essence of Knowledge is formed ; and evidence is common to Understanding and Sensation. Well, Sensation is the ladder to Knowledge ; while Faith, advancing over the pathway of the objects of sense, leaves Opinion behind, and speeds to things free of deception, and reposes in the truth.

Should one say that Knowledge is founded on demonstration by a process of reasoning, let him hear that first principles are incapable of demonstration ; for they are known neither by art nor sagacity. For the latter is conversant about objects that are susceptible of change, while the former is practical solely, and not theoretical.[3] Hence it is thought that the first cause of the universe can be apprehended by faith alone. For all knowledge is capable of being taught ; and what is capable of being taught is founded on what is known before. But the first cause of the universe was not previously known to the Greeks ; neither, accordingly, to Thales, who came to the conclusion that water was the first cause ; nor to the other natural philosophers who succeeded him, since it was Anaxagoras who was the first who assigned to Mind the supremacy over material things. But not even he preserved the dignity suited to the efficient cause, describing as he did certain silly vortices, together with the inertia and even foolishness of Mind. Wherefore also the Word says, "Call no man master on earth."[4] For knowledge is a state of mind that results from demonstration ; but faith is a

grace which from what is indemonstrable conducts to what is universal and simple, what is neither with matter, nor matter, nor under matter. But those who believe not, as to be expected, drag all down from heaven, and the region of the invisible, to earth, "absolutely grasping with their hands rocks and oaks," according to Plato. For, clinging to all such things, they asseverate that that alone exists which can be touched and handled, defining body and essence to be identical : disputing against themselves, they very piously defend the existence of certain intellectual and bodiless forms descending somewhere from above from the invisible world, vehemently maintaining that there is a true essence. "Lo, I make new things," saith the Word, "which eye hath not seen, nor ear heard, nor hath it entered into the heart of man."[5] With a new eye, a new ear, a new heart, whatever can be seen and heard is to be apprehended, by the faith and understanding of the disciples of the Lord, who speak, hear, and act spiritually. For there is genuine coin, and other that is spurious ; which no less deceives unprofessionals, that it does not the money-changers ; who know through having learned how to separate and distinguish what has a false stamp from what is genuine. So the money-changer only says to the unprofessional man that the coin is counterfeit. But the reason why, only the banker's apprentice, and he that is trained to this department, learns.

Now Aristotle says that the judgment which follows knowledge is in truth faith. Accordingly, faith is something superior to knowledge, and is its criterion. Conjecture, which is only a feeble supposition, counterfeits faith ; as the flatterer counterfeits a friend, and the wolf the dog. And as the workman sees that by learning certain things he becomes an artificer, and the helmsman by being instructed in the art will be able to steer ; he does not regard the mere wishing to become excellent and good enough, but he must learn it by the exercise of obedience. But to obey the Word, whom we call Instructor, is to believe Him, going against Him in nothing. For how can we take up a position of hostility to God ? Knowledge, accordingly, is characterized by faith ; and faith, by a kind of divine mutual and reciprocal correspondence, becomes characterized by knowledge.

Epicurus, too, who very greatly preferred pleasure to truth, supposes faith to be a preconception of the mind ; and defines preconception to be a grasping at something evident, and at the clear understanding of the thing ; and asserts that, without preconception, no one can either inquire, or doubt, or judge, or even argue. How

---

[1] Heb. xi. 3, 4, 25.
[2] Heb. xi. 32.
[3] Instead of μονονουχί, Petavius and Lowth read μόνον, οὐχί, as above.
[4] Matt. xxiii. 9.
[5] Isa. lxiv. 4; 1 Cor. ii. 9.

can one, without a preconceived idea of what he is aiming after, learn about that which is the subject of his investigation? He, again, who has learned has already turned his preconception[1] into comprehension. And if he who learns, learns not without a preconceived idea which takes in what is expressed, that man has ears to hear the truth. And happy is the man that speaks to the ears of those who hear; as happy certainly also is he who is a child of obedience. Now to hear is to understand. If, then, faith is nothing else than a preconception of the mind in regard to what is the subject of discourse, and obedience is so called, and understanding and persuasion; no one shall learn aught without faith, since no one [learns aught] without preconception. Consequently there is a more ample demonstration of the complete truth of what was spoken by the prophet, " Unless ye believe, neither will ye understand." Paraphrasing this oracle, Heraclitus of Ephesus says, " If a man hope not, he will not find that which is not hoped for, seeing it is inscrutable and inaccessible." Plato the philosopher, also, in *The Laws*, says, " that he who would be blessed and happy, must be straight from the beginning a partaker of the truth, so as to live true for as long a period as possible; for he is a man of faith. But the unbeliever is one to whom voluntary falsehood is agreeable; and the man to whom involuntary falsehood is agreeable is senseless;[2] neither of which is desirable. For he who is devoid of friendliness, is faithless and ignorant." And does he not enigmatically say in *Euthydemus*, that this is " the regal wisdom "? In *The Statesman* he says expressly, " So that the knowledge of the true king is kingly; and he who possesses it, whether a prince or private person, shall by all means, in consequence of this act, be rightly styled royal." Now those who have believed in Christ both are and are called *Chrestoi* (good),[3] as those who are cared for by the true king are kingly. For as the wise are wise by their wisdom, and those observant of law are so by the law; so also those who belong to Christ the King are kings, and those that are Christ's Christians. Then, in continuation, he adds clearly, " What is right will turn out to be lawful, law being in its nature right reason, and not found in writings or elsewhere." And the stranger of Elea pronounces the kingly and statesmanlike man " *a living law*." Such is he who fulfils the law, " doing the will of the Father,"[4] inscribed on a lofty pillar, and set as an example of divine virtue to all who possess

the power of seeing. The Greeks are acquainted with the staves of the Ephori at Lacedæmon, inscribed with the law on wood. But my law, as was said above, is both royal and living; and it is right reason. " Law, which is king of all — of mortals and immortals," as the Bœotian Pindar sings. For Speusippus,[5] in the first book against Cleophon, seems to write like Plato on this wise: " For if royalty be a good thing, and the wise man the only king and ruler, the law, which is right reason, is good;"[6] which is the case. The Stoics teach what is in conformity with this, assigning kinghood, priesthood, prophecy, legislation, riches, true beauty, noble birth, freedom, to the wise man alone. But that he is exceedingly difficult to find, is confessed even by them.

CHAP. V. — HE PROVES BY SEVERAL EXAMPLES THAT THE GREEKS DREW FROM THE SACRED WRITERS.

Accordingly all those above-mentioned dogmas appear to have been transmitted from Moses the great to the Greeks. That all things belong to the wise man, is taught in these words: " And because God hath showed me mercy, I have all things."[7] And that he is beloved of God, God intimates when He says, " The God of Abraham, the God of Isaac, the God of Jacob."[8] For the first is found to have been expressly called " friend;"[9] and the second is shown to have received a new name, signifying " he that sees God;"[10] while Isaac, God in a figure selected for Himself as a consecrated sacrifice, to be a type to us of the economy of salvation.

Now among the Greeks, Minos the king of nine years' reign, and familiar friend of Zeus, is celebrated in song; they having heard how once God conversed with Moses, " as one speaking with his friend."[11] Moses, then, was a sage, king, legislator. But our Saviour surpasses all human nature.[12] He is so lovely, as to be alone loved by us, whose hearts are set on the true beauty, for " He was the true light."[13] He is shown to be a King, as such hailed by unsophisticated children and by the unbelieving and ignorant Jews, and heralded by the prophets. So rich is He, that He despised the whole earth, and the gold above and beneath it, with all glory, when given to Him by the adversary. What need is there to say that He is the only High Priest, who alone possesses

---

1 καταληψιν ποιεῖ τὴν πρόληψιν.

2 οὐ ζῶον is here interpolated into the text, not being found in Plato.

3 Χριστός and χρηστός are very frequently compared in the patristic authors.

4 Matt. xxi. 31.

5 Plato's sister's son and successor.

6 σπουδαῖος.

7 The words of Jacob to Esau slightly changed from the Septuagint: " For God hath shown mercy to me, and I have all things " — οτι ἠλέησέ με ὁ Θεὸς καὶ ἔστι μοι πάντα (Gen. xxxiii. 11).

8 Ex. iii. 16.

9 Jas. ii. 23.

10 So the name Israel is explained, *Stromata*, i. p. 334, Potter; [see p. 300, *supra*.]

11 Ex. xxxiii. 11.

12 [This passage, down to the reference to Plato, is unspeakably sublime. One loves Clement for this exclusive loyalty to the Saviour.]

13 John. i. 9.

the knowledge of the worship of God?[1] He is Melchizedek, "King of peace,"[2] the most fit of all to head the race of men. A legislator too, inasmuch as He gave the law by the mouth of the prophets, enjoining and teaching most distinctly what things are to be done, and what not. Who of nobler lineage than He whose only Father is God? Come, then, let us produce Plato assenting to those very dogmas. The wise man he calls rich in the *Phædrus*, when he says, "O dear Pan, and whatever other gods are here, grant me to become fair within; and whatever external things I have, let them be agreeable to what is within. I would reckon the wise man rich."[3] And the Athenian stranger,[4] finding fault with those who think that those who have many possessions are rich, speaks thus : " For the very rich to be also good is impossible — those, I mean, whom the multitude count rich. Those they call rich, who, among a few men, are owners of the possessions worth most money; which any bad man may possess. " " The whole world of wealth belongs to the believer,"[5] Solomon says, "but not a penny to the unbeliever." Much more, then, is the Scripture to be believed which says, "It is easier for a camel to go through the eye of a needle, than for a rich man "[6] to lead a philosophic life. But, on the other hand, it blesses "the poor ; "[7] as Plato understood when he said, " It is not the diminishing of one's resources, but the augmenting of insatiableness, that is to be considered poverty; for it is not slender means that ever constitutes poverty, but insatiableness, from which the good man being free, will also be rich." And in *Alcibiades* he calls vice a servile thing, and virtue the attribute of freemen. "Take away from you the heavy yoke, and take up the easy one,"[8] says the Scripture ; as also the poets call [vice] a slavish yoke. And the expression, " Ye have sold yourselves to your sins," agrees with what is said above : " Every one, then, who committeth sin is a slave ; and the slave abideth not in the house for ever. But if the Son shall make you free, then shall ye be free, and the truth shall make you free."[9]

And again, that the wise man is beautiful, the Athenian stranger asserts, in the same way as if one were to affirm that certain persons were just, even should they happen to be ugly in their persons. And in speaking thus with respect to eminent rectitude of character, no one who should assert them to be on this account beauti-

ful would be thought to speak extravagantly. And " His appearance was inferior to all the sons of men,"[10] prophecy predicted.

Plato, moreover, has called the wise man a king, in *The Statesman*. The remark is quoted above.

These points being demonstrated, let us recur again to our discourse on faith. Well, with the fullest demonstration, Plato proves, that there is need of faith everywhere, celebrating peace at the same time : " For no man will ever be trusty and sound in seditions without entire virtue. There are numbers of mercenaries full of fight, and willing to die in war ; but, with a very few exceptions, the most of them are desperadoes and villains, insolent and senseless." If these observations are right, "every legislator who is even of slight use, will, in making his laws, have an eye to the greatest virtue. Such is fidelity,"[11] which we need at all times, both in peace and in war, and in all the rest of our life, for it appears to embrace the other virtues. " But the best thing is neither war nor sedition, for the necessity of these is to be deprecated. But peace with one another and kindly feeling are what is best." From these remarks the greatest prayer evidently is to have peace, according to Plato. And faith is the greatest mother of the virtues. Accordingly it is rightly said in Solomon, "Wisdom is in the mouth of the faithful."[12] Since also Xenocrates, in his book on "Intelligence," says "that wisdom is the knowledge of first causes and of intellectual essence." He considers intelligence as twofold, practical and theoretical, which latter is human wisdom. Consequently wisdom is intelligence, but all intelligence is not wisdom. And it has been shown, that the knowledge of the first cause of the universe is of faith, but is not demonstration. For it were strange that the followers of the Samian Pythagoras, rejecting demonstrations of subjects of question, should regard the bare *ipse dixit*[13] as ground of belief; and that this expression alone sufficed for the confirmation of what they heard, while those devoted to the contemplation of the truth, presuming to disbelieve the trustworthy Teacher, God the only Saviour, should demand of Him tests of His utterances. But He says, " He that hath ears to hear, let him hear." And who is he? Let Epicharmus say : —

" Mind sees, mind hears; all besides is deaf and blind."[14]

Rating some as unbelievers, Heraclitus says,

[1] The Stoics defined piety as "the knowledge of the worship of God."
[2] Heb. vii. 2.
[3] Socrates in the *Phædrus*, near the end, [p. 279.]
[4] Introduced by Plato in *The Laws*, conversing with Socrates.
[5] Taken likely from some apocryphal writing.
[6] Matt. xix. 24.
[7] Matt. v. 3.
[8] Matt. xi. 28-30.
[9] John viii. 32-36.
[10] Isa. liii. 3. [That is after he became the Man of Sorrows; not originally.]
[11] πιστότης.
[12] Ecclus. xv. 10.
[13] Laertius, in opposition to the general account, ascribes the celebrated αὐτὸς ἐφα to Pythagoras Zacynthus. Suidas, who with the most ascribes it to the Samian Pythagoras, says that it meant " God has said," as he professed to have received his doctrines from God.
[14] This famous line of Epicharmus the comic poet is quoted by Tertullian (*de Anima*), by Plutarch, by Jamblichus, and Porphyry.

"Not knowing how to hear or to speak;" aided doubtless by Solomon, who says, "If thou lovest to hear, thou shalt comprehend; and if thou incline thine ear, thou shalt be wise." [1]

CHAP. VI. — THE EXCELLENCE AND UTILITY OF FAITH.

"Lord, who hath believed our report?" [2] Isaiah says. For "faith cometh by hearing, and hearing by the word of God," saith the apostle. "How then shall they call on Him in whom they have not believed? And how shall they believe on Him whom they have not heard? And how shall they hear without a preacher? And how shall they preach except they be sent? As it is written, How beautiful are the feet of those that publish glad tidings of good things!" [3] You see how he brings faith by hearing, and the preaching of the apostles, up to the word of the Lord, and to the Son of God. We do not yet understand the word of the Lord to be demonstration.

As, then, playing at ball not only depends on one throwing the ball skilfully, but it requires besides one to catch it dexterously, that the game may be gone through according to the rules for ball; so also is it the case that teaching is reliable when faith on the part of those who hear, being, so to speak, a sort of natural art, contributes to the process of learning. So also the earth co-operates, through its productive power, being fit for the sowing of the seed. For there is no good of the very best instruction without the exercise of the receptive faculty on the part of the learner, not even of prophecy, when there is the absence of docility on the part of those who hear. For dry twigs, being ready to receive the power of fire, are kindled with great ease; and the far-famed stone [4] attracts steel through affinity, as the amber teardrop drags to itself twigs, and the lump sets chaff in motion. And the substances attracted obey them, influenced by a subtle spirit, not as a cause, but as a concurring cause.

There being then a twofold species of vice — that characterized by craft and stealth, and that which leads and drives with violence — the divine Word cries, calling all together; knowing perfectly well those that will not obey; notwithstanding then since to obey or not is in our own power, provided we have not the excuse of ignorance to adduce. He makes a just call, and demands of each according to his strength. For some are able as well as willing, having reached this point through practice and being purified; while others, if they are not yet able, already

have the will. Now to will is the act of the soul, but to do is not without the body. Nor are actions estimated by their issue alone; but they are judged also according to the element of free choice in each, — if he chose easily, if he repented of his sins, if he reflected on his failures and repented (μετέγνω), which is (μετὰ ταῦτα ἔγνω) "afterwards knew." For repentance is a tardy knowledge, and primitive innocence is knowledge. Repentance, then, is an effect of faith. For unless a man believe that to which he was addicted to be sin, he will not abandon it; and if he do not believe punishment to be impending over the transgressor, and salvation to be the portion of him who lives according to the commandments, he will not reform.

Hope, too, is based on faith. Accordingly the followers of Basilides define faith to be, the assent of the soul to any of those things, that do not affect the senses through not being present. And hope is the expectation of the possession of good. Necessarily, then, is expectation founded on faith. Now he is faithful who keeps inviolably what is entrusted to him; and we are entrusted with the utterances respecting God and the divine words, the commands along with the execution of the injunctions. This is the faithful servant, who is praised by the Lord. And when it is said, "God is faithful," it is intimated that He is worthy to be believed when declaring aught. Now His Word declares; and "God" Himself is "faithful." [5] How, then, if to believe is to suppose, do the philosophers think that what proceeds from themselves is sure? For the voluntary assent to a preceding demonstration is not supposition, but it is assent to something sure. Who is more powerful than God? Now unbelief is the feeble negative supposition of one opposed to Him; as incredulity is a condition which admits faith with difficulty. Faith is the voluntary supposition and anticipation of pre-comprehension. Expectation is an opinion about the future, and expectation about other things is opinion about uncertainty. Confidence is a strong judgment about a thing. Wherefore we believe Him in whom we have confidence unto divine glory and salvation. And we confide in Him, who is God alone, whom we know, that those things nobly promised to us, and for this end benevolently created and bestowed by Him on us, will not fail.

Benevolence is the wishing of good things to another for his sake. For He needs nothing; and the beneficence and benignity which flow from the Lord terminate in us, being divine benevolence, and benevolence resulting in beneficence. And if to Abraham on his believing it

---

[1] Ecclus. vi. 33.
[2] Isa. liii. 1.
[3] Rom. x. 17, 14, 15.
[4] Loadstone. [Philosophy of the second century. See note in Migne.]

[5] 1 Cor. i. 9, x. 13.

was counted for righteousness; and if we are the seed of Abraham, then we must also believe through hearing. For we are Israelites, who are convinced not by signs, but by hearing. Wherefore it is said, " Rejoice, O barren, that barest not; break forth and cry, thou that didst not travail with child : for more are the children of the desolate than of her who hath an husband." [1] " Thou hast lived for the fence of the people, thy children were blessed in the tents of their fathers." [2] And if the same mansions are promised by prophecy to us and to the patriarchs, the God of both the covenants is shown to be one. Accordingly it is added more clearly, " Thou hast inherited the covenant of Israel," [3] speaking to those called from among the nations, that were once barren, being formerly destitute of this husband, who is the Word, — desolate formerly, — of the bridegroom. " Now the just shall live by faith," [4] which is according to the covenant and the commandments; since these, which are two in name and time, given in accordance with the [divine] economy — being in power one — the old and the new, are dispensed through the Son by one God. As the apostle also says in the Epistle to the Romans, " For therein is the righteousness of God revealed from faith to faith," teaching the one salvation which from prophecy to the Gospel is perfected by one and the same Lord. " This charge," he says, " I commit to thee, son Timothy, according to the prophecies which went before on thee, that thou by them mightest war the good warfare; holding faith, and a good conscience; which some having put away concerning faith have made shipwreck," [5] because they defiled by unbelief the conscience that comes from God. Accordingly, faith may not, any more, with reason, be disparaged in an offhand way, as simple and vulgar, appertaining to anybody. For, if it were a mere human habit, as the Greeks supposed, it would have been extinguished. But if it grow, and there be no place where it is not; then I affirm, that faith, whether founded in love, or in fear, as its disparagers assert, is something divine; which is neither rent asunder by other mundane friendship, nor dissolved by the presence of fear. For love, on account of its friendly alliance with faith, makes men believers; and faith, which is the foundation of love, in its turn introduces the doing of good; since also fear, the pædagogue of the law, is believed to be fear by those, by whom it is believed. For, if its existence is shown in its working, it is yet believed when about to do and threatening, and when not working and present; and

being believed to exist, it does not itself generate faith, but is by faith tested and proved trustworthy. Such a change, then, from unbelief to faith — and to trust in hope and fear, is divine. And, in truth, faith is discovered, by us, to be the first movement towards salvation; after which fear, and hope, and repentance, advancing in company with temperance and patience, lead us to love and knowledge. Rightly, therefore, the Apostle Barnabas says, " From the portion I have received I have done my diligence to send by little and little to you; that along with your faith you may also have perfect knowledge.[6] Fear and patience are then helpers of your faith; and our allies are long-suffering and temperance. These, then," he says, " in what respects the Lord, continuing in purity, there rejoice along with them, wisdom, understanding, intelligence, knowledge." The fore-mentioned virtues being, then, the elements of knowledge; the result is that faith is more elementary, being as necessary to the Gnostic,[7] as respiration to him that lives in this world is to life. And as without the four elements it is not possible to live, so neither can knowledge be attained without faith. It is then the support of truth.

CHAP. VII. — THE UTILITY OF FEAR.   OBJECTIONS ANSWERED.

Those, who denounce fear, assail the law; and if the law, plainly also God, who gave the law. For these three elements are of necessity presented in the subject on hand : the ruler, his administration, and the ruled. If, then, according to hypothesis, they abolish the law; then, by necessary consequence, each one who is led by lust, courting pleasure, must neglect what is right and despise the Deity, and fearlessly indulge in impiety and injustice together, having dashed away from the truth.

Yea, say they, fear is an irrational aberration,[8] and perturbation of mind. What sayest thou? And how can this definition be any longer maintained, seeing the commandment is given me by the Word? But the commandment forbids, hanging fear over the head of those who have incurred [9] admonition for their discipline.

Fear is not then irrational. It is therefore rational. How could it be otherwise, exhorting as it does, *Thou shalt not kill, Thou shalt not commit adultery, Thou shalt not steal, Thou shalt not bear false witness?* But if they will quibble about the names, let the philosophers term the fear of the law, cautious fear, (εὐλάβεια,)

---

[1] Isa. liv. 1.
[2] Not in Script.
[3] Where?
[4] Rom. i. 17, etc.
[5] 1 Tim. i. 18, 19.

[6] [Clement accepts the Epistle of Barnabas as an apostolic writing. For this quotation, see vol. i. p. 137, this series.]
[7] The man of perfect knowledge.
[8] Instead of ἔκκλισις, it has been proposed to read ἔκλυσις, a term applied by the Stoics to fear; but we have ἔκκλισις immediately after.
[9] According to the correction and translation of Lowth, who reads τῶν οὕτως ἐπιδεχομένων instead of τὸν οὕτως, etc., of the text.

which is a shunning (ἔκκλισις) agreeable to reason. Such Critolaus of Phasela not inaptly called fighters about names (ὀνοματομάχοι). The commandment, then, has already appeared fair and lovely even in the highest degree, when conceived under a change of name. Cautious fear (εὐλάβεια) is therefore shown to be reasonable, being the shunning of what hurts; from which arises repentance for previous sins. "For the fear of the LORD is the beginning of wisdom; good understanding is to all that do it."[1] He calls wisdom a doing, which is the fear of the Lord paving the way for wisdom. But if the law produces fear, the knowledge of the law is the beginning of wisdom; and a man is not wise without law. Therefore those who reject the law are unwise; and in consequence they are reckoned godless (ἄθεοι). Now instruction is the beginning of wisdom. "But the ungodly despise wisdom and instruction,"[2] saith the Scripture.

Let us see what terrors the law announces. If it is the things which hold an intermediate place between virtue and vice, such as poverty, disease, obscurity, and humble birth, and the like, these things civil laws hold forth, and are praised for so doing. And those of the Peripatetic school, who introduce three kinds of good things, and think that their opposites are evil, this opinion suits. But the law given to us enjoins us to shun what are in reality bad things — adultery, uncleanness, pæderasty, ignorance, wickedness, soul-disease, death (not that which severs the soul from the body, but that which severs the soul from truth). For these are vices in reality, and the workings that proceed from them are dreadful and terrible. "For not unjustly," say the divine oracles, "are the nets spread for birds; for they who are accomplices in blood treasure up evils to themselves."[3] How, then, is the law still said to be not good by certain heresies that clamorously appeal to the apostle, who says, "For by the law is the knowledge of sin?"[4] To whom we say, The law did not cause, but showed sin. For, enjoining what is to be done, it reprehended what ought not to be done. And it is the part of the good to teach what is salutary, and to point out what is deleterious; and to counsel the practice of the one, and to command to shun the other. Now the apostle, whom they do not comprehend, said that by the law the knowledge of sin was manifested, not that from it it derived its existence. And how can the law be not good, which trains, which is given as the instructor (παιδαγωγός) to Christ,[5] that being corrected by

fear, in the way of discipline, in order to the attainment of the perfection which is by Christ? "I will not," it is said, "the death of the sinner, as his repentance."[6] Now the commandment works repentance; inasmuch as it deters[7] from what ought not to be done, and enjoins good deeds. By ignorance he means, in my opinion, death. "And he that is near the Lord is full of stripes."[8] Plainly, he, that draws near to knowledge, has the benefit of perils, fears, troubles, afflictions, by reason of his desire for the truth. "For the son who is instructed turns out wise, and an intelligent son is saved from burning. And an intelligent son will receive the commandments."[9] And Barnabas the apostle having said, "Woe to those who are wise in their own conceits, clever in their own eyes,"[10] added, "Let us become spiritual, a perfect temple to God; let us, as far as in us lies, practise the fear of God, and strive to keep His commands, that we may rejoice in His judgments."[11] Whence "the fear of God" is divinely said to be the beginning of wisdom.[12]

CHAP. VIII. — THE VAGARIES OF BASILIDES AND VALENTINUS AS TO FEAR BEING THE CAUSE OF THINGS.

Here the followers of Basilides, interpreting this expression, say, "that the Prince,[13] having heard the speech of the Spirit, who was being ministered to, was struck with amazement both with the voice and the vision, having had glad tidings beyond his hopes announced to him; and that his amazement was called fear, which became the origin of wisdom, which distinguishes classes, and discriminates, and perfects, and restores. For not the world alone, but also the election, He that is over all has set apart and sent forth."

And Valentinus appears also in an epistle to have adopted such views. For he writes in these very words: "And as[14] terror fell on the angels at this creature, because he uttered things greater than proceeded from his formation, by reason of the being in him who had invisibly communicated a germ of the supernal essence, and who spoke with free utterance; so also among the tribes of men in the world, the works of men became terrors to those who made them, — as, for example, images and statues. And the hands of all fashion things to bear the name of God:

---

[1] Ps. cxi. 10.
[2] Prov. i. 7.
[3] Prov. i. 17, 18, "Surely in vain the net is spread in the sight of any bird, and they lay wait for their own blood."
[4] Rom. iii. 20.
[5] Gal. iii. 24.

[6] Ezek. xxxiii. 11, xviii. 23, 32.
[7] Adopting the conjecture which, by a change from the accusative to the nominative, refers "deters," and "enjoins," to the commandment instead of to repentance, according to the teaching of the text.
[8] Judith viii. 27.
[9] Prov. x. 4, 5, 8.
[10] Isa. v. 21.
[11] [See vol. i. p. 139. S.]
[12] Prov. i. 7.
[13] Viz., of the angels, who according to them was Jehovah, the God of the Jews.
[14] Instead of ὡς περίφοβος of the text, we read with Grabe ὡσπερεὶ φόβος.

for Adam formed into the name of man inspired the dread attaching to the pre-existent man, as having his being in him ; and they were terror-stricken, and speedily marred the work."

But there being but one First Cause, as will be shown afterwards, these men will be shown to be inventors of chatterings and chirpings. But since God deemed it advantageous, that from the law and the prophets, men should receive a preparatory discipline by the Lord, the fear of the Lord was called the beginning of wisdom, being given by the Lord, through Moses, to the disobedient and hard of heart. For those whom reason convinces not, fear tames ; which also the Instructing Word, foreseeing from the first, and purifying by each of these methods, adapted the instrument suitably for piety. Consternation is, then, fear at a strange apparition, or at an unlooked-for representation — such as, for example, a message ; while fear is an excessive wonderment on account of something which arises or is. They do not then perceive that they represent by means of amazement the God who is highest and is extolled by them, as subject to perturbation and antecedent to amazement as having been in ignorance. If indeed ignorance preceded amazement ; and if this amazement and fear, which is the beginning of wisdom, is the fear of God, then in all likelihood ignorance as cause preceded both the wisdom of God and all creative work, and not only these, but restoration and even election itself. Whether, then, was it ignorance of what was good or what was evil?

Well, if of good, why does it cease through amazement? And minister and preaching and baptism are [in that case] superfluous to them. And if of evil, how can what is bad be the cause of what is best? For had not ignorance preceded, the minister would not have come down, nor would have amazement seized on "the Prince," as they say ; nor would he have attained to a beginning of wisdom from fear, in order to discrimination between the elect and those that are mundane. And if the fear of the pre-existent man made the angels conspire against their own handiwork, under the idea that an invisible germ of the supernal essence was lodged within that creation, or through unfounded suspicion excited envy, which is incredible, the angels became murderers of the creature which had been entrusted to them, as a child might be, they being thus convicted of the grossest ignorance. Or suppose they were influenced by being involved in foreknowledge. But they would not have conspired against what they foreknew in the assault they made ; nor would they have been terror-struck at their own work, in consequence of foreknowledge, on their perceiving the supernal germ. Or, finally, suppose, trusting to their

knowledge, they dared (but this also were impossible for them), on learning the excellence that is in the Pleroma, to conspire against man. Furthermore also they laid hands on that which was according to the image, in which also is the archetype, and which, along with the knowledge that remains, is indestructible.

To these, then, and certain others, especially the Marcionites, the Scripture cries, though they listen not, "He that heareth Me shall rest with confidence in peace, and shall be tranquil, fearless of all evil." [1]

What, then, will they have the law to be? They will not call it evil, but just ; distinguishing what is good from what is just. But the Lord, when He enjoins us to dread evil, does not exchange one evil for another, but abolishes what is opposite by its opposite. Now evil is the opposite of good, as what is just is of what is unjust. If, then, that absence of fear, which the fear of the Lord produces, is called the beginning of what is good,[2] fear is a good thing. And the fear which proceeds from the law is not only just, but good, as it takes away evil. But introducing absence of fear by means of fear, it does not produce apathy by means of mental perturbation, but moderation of feeling by discipline. When, then, we hear, "Honour the Lord, and be strong : but fear not another besides Him,"[3] we understand it to be meant fearing to sin, and following the commandments given by God, which is the honour that cometh from God. For the fear of God is Δέος [in Greek]. But if fear is perturbation of mind, as some will have it that fear is perturbation of mind, yet all fear is not perturbation. Superstition is indeed perturbation of mind ; being the fear of demons, that produce and are subject to the excitement of passion. On the other hand, consequently, the fear of God, who is not subject to perturbation, is free of perturbation. For it is not God, but falling away from God, that the man is terrified for. And he who fears this — that is, falling into evils — fears and dreads those evils. And he who fears a fall, wishes himself to be free of corruption and perturbation. "The wise man, fearing, avoids evil : but the foolish, trusting, mixes himself with it," says the Scripture ; and again it says, "In the fear of the LORD is the hope of strength."[4]

CHAP. IX. — THE CONNECTION OF THE CHRISTIAN VIRTUES.

Such a fear, accordingly, leads to repentance and hope. Now hope is the expectation of good things, or an expectation sanguine of ab-

---

[1] Prov. i. 33.
[2] The text reads κακῶν. Lowth conjectures the change, which we have adopted, καλῶν.
[3] Prov. vii. 2.
[4] Prov. xiv. 16, 26.

sent good ; and favourable circumstances are assumed in order to good hope, which we have learned leads on to love. Now love turns out to be consent in what pertains to reason, life, and manners, or in brief, fellowship in life, or it is the intensity of friendship and of affection, with right reason, in the enjoyment of associates. And an associate (ἑταῖρος) is another self ; [1] just as we call those, brethren, who are regenerated by the same word. And akin to love is hospitality, being a congenial art devoted to the treatment of strangers. And those are strangers, to whom the things of the world are strange. For we regard as worldly those, who hope in the earth and carnal lusts. "Be not conformed," says the apostle, "to this world : but be ye transformed in the renewal of the mind, that ye may prove what is that good, and acceptable, and perfect, will of God." [2]

Hospitality, therefore, is occupied in what is useful for strangers ; and guests (ἐπίξενοι) are strangers (ξένοι) ; and friends are guests ; and brethren are friends. "Dear brother," [3] says Homer.

Philanthropy, in order to which also, is natural affection, being a loving treatment of men, and natural affection, which is a congenial habit exercised in the love of friends or domestics, follow in the train of love. And if the real man within us is the spiritual, philanthropy is brotherly love to those who participate, in the same spirit. Natural affection, on the other hand, is the preservation of good-will, or of affection ; and affection is its perfect demonstration ; [4] and to be beloved is to please in behaviour, by drawing and attracting. And persons are brought to sameness by consent, which is the knowledge of the good things that are enjoyed in common. For community of sentiment (ὁμογνωμοσύνη) is harmony of opinions (συμφωνία γνωμῶν). "Let your love be without dissimulation," it is said ; "and abhorring what is evil, let us become attached to what is good, to brotherly love," and so on, down to "If it be possible, as much as lieth in you, living peaceably with all men." Then "be not overcome of evil," it is said, "but overcome evil with good." [5] And the same apostle owns that he bears witness to the Jews, "that they have a zeal of God, but not according to knowledge. For, being ignorant of God's righteousness, and seeking to establish their own, they have not submitted themselves to the righteousness of God." [6] For they did not know and do the will of the law ; but what they supposed, that they thought the law wished.

And they did not believe the law as prophesying, but the bare word ; and they followed through fear, not through disposition and faith. "For Christ is the end of the law for righteousness," [7] who was prophesied by the law to every one that believeth. Whence it was said to them by Moses, "I will provoke you to jealousy by them that are not a people ; and I will anger you by a foolish nation, that is, by one that has become disposed to obedience." [8] And by Isaiah it is said, "I was found of them that sought Me not ; I was made manifest to them that inquired not after Me," [9] — manifestly previous to the coming of the Lord ; after which to Israel, the things prophesied, are now appropriately spoken : "I have stretched out My hands all the day long to a disobedient and gainsaying people." Do you see the cause of the calling from among the nations, clearly declared, by the prophet, to be the disobedience and gainsaying of the people ? Then the goodness of God is shown also in their case. For the apostle says, "But through their transgression salvation is come to the Gentiles, to provoke them to jealousy," [10] and to willingness to repent. And the Shepherd, speaking plainly of those who had fallen asleep, recognises certain righteous among Gentiles and Jews, not only before the appearance of Christ, but before the law, in virtue of acceptance before God, — as Abel, as Noah, as any other righteous man. He says accordingly, "that the apostles and teachers, who had preached the name of the Son of God, and had fallen asleep, in power and by faith, preached to those that had fallen asleep before." Then he subjoins : "And they gave them the seal of preaching. They descended, therefore, with them into the water, and again ascended. But these descended alive, and again ascended alive. But those, who had fallen asleep before, descended dead, but ascended alive. By these, therefore, they were made alive, and knew the name of the Son of God. Wherefore also they ascended with them, and fitted into the structure of the tower, and unhewn were built up together : they fell asleep in righteousness and in great purity, but wanted only this seal." [11] "For when the Gentiles, which have not the law, do by nature the things of the law, these, having not the law, are a law unto themselves," [12] according to the apostle.

As, then, the virtues follow one another, why need I say what has been demonstrated already, that faith hopes through repentance, and fear through faith ; and patience and practice in these along with learning terminate in love,

1 ἕτερος ἐγώ, alter ego, deriving ἑταῖρος from ἕτερος.
2 Rom. xii. 2.
3 φίλε κασίγνητε, Iliad, v. 359.
4 ἀπόδεξις has been conjectured in place of ἀπόδειξις.
5 Rom. xii. 9, 10, 18, 21.
6 Rom. x. 2, 3.
7 Rom. x. 4.
8 Rom. x. 19; Deut. xxxii. 21.
9 Isa. xlv. 1, 2; Rom. x. 20, 21.
10 Rom. xi. 11.
11 Hermas, [Similitudes, p. 49, supra.]
12 Rom. ii. 14.

which is perfected by knowledge? But that is necessarily to be noticed, that the Divine alone is to be regarded as naturally wise. Therefore also wisdom, which has taught the truth, is the power of God; and in it the perfection of knowledge is embraced. The philosopher loves and likes the truth, being now considered as a friend, on account of his love, from his being a true servant. The beginning of knowledge is wondering at objects, as Plato says is in his *Theætetus;* and Matthew exhorting in the *Traditions*, says, "Wonder at what is before you;" laying this down first as the foundation of further knowledge. So also in the Gospel to the Hebrews it is written, "He that wonders shall reign, and he that has reigned shall rest. It is impossible, therefore, for an ignorant man, while he remains ignorant, to philosophize, not having apprehended the idea of wisdom; since philosophy is an effort to grasp that which truly is, and the studies that conduce thereto. And it is not the rendering of one[1] accomplished in good habits of conduct, but the knowing how we are to use and act and labour, according as one is assimilated to God. I mean God the Saviour, by serving the God of the universe through the High Priest, the Word, by whom what is in truth good and right is beheld. Piety is conduct suitable and corresponding to God.

CHAP. X. — TO WHAT THE PHILOSOPHER APPLIES HIMSELF.

These three things, therefore, our philosopher attaches himself to: first, speculation; second, the performance of the precepts; third, the forming of good men; — which, concurring, form the Gnostic. Whichever of these is wanting, the elements of knowledge limp. Whence the Scripture divinely says, "And the Lord spake to Moses, saying, Speak to the children of Israel, and thou shalt say to them, I am the LORD your God. According to the customs of the land of Egypt, in which ye have dwelt, ye shall not do; and according to the customs of Canaan, into which I bring you, ye shall not do; and in their usages ye shall not walk. Ye shall perform My judgments, and keep My precepts, and walk in them: I am the LORD your God. And ye shall keep all My commandments, and do them. He that doeth them shall live in them. I am the LORD your God."[2] Whether, then, Egypt and the land of Canaan be the symbol of the world and of deceit, or of sufferings and afflictions; the oracle shows us what must be abstained from, and what, being divine and not worldly, must be observed. And when it is said, "The man that doeth them shall live in

them,"[3] it declares both the correction of the Hebrews themselves, and the training and advancement of us who are nigh:[4] it declares at once their life and ours. For "those who were dead in sins are quickened together with Christ,"[5] by our covenant. For Scripture, by the frequent reiteration of the expression, "I am the LORD your God," shames in such a way as most powerfully to dissuade, by teaching us to follow God who gave the commandments, and gently admonishes us to seek God and endeavour to know Him as far as possible; which is the highest speculation, that which scans the greatest mysteries, the real knowledge, that which becomes irrefragable by reason. This alone is the knowledge of wisdom, from which rectitude of conduct is never disjoined.

CHAP. XI. — THE KNOWLEDGE WHICH COMES THROUGH FAITH THE SUREST OF ALL.

But the knowledge of those who think themselves wise, whether the barbarian sects or the philosophers among the Greeks, according to the apostle, "puffeth up."[6] But that knowledge, which is the scientific demonstration of what is delivered according to the true philosophy, is founded on faith. Now, we may say that it is that process of reason which, from what is admitted, procures faith in what is disputed. Now, faith being twofold — the faith of knowledge and that of opinion — nothing prevents us from calling demonstration twofold, the one resting on knowledge, the other on opinion; since also knowledge and foreknowledge are designated as twofold, that which is essentially accurate, that which is defective. And is not the demonstration, which we possess, that alone which is true, as being supplied out of the divine Scriptures, the sacred writings, and out of the "God-taught wisdom," according to the apostle? Learning, then, is also obedience to the commandments, which is faith in God. And faith is a power of God, being the strength of the truth. For example, it is said, "If ye have faith as a grain of mustard, ye shall remove the mountain."[7] And again, "According to thy faith let it be to thee."[8] And one is cured, receiving healing by faith; and the dead is raised up in consequence of the power of one believing that he would be raised. The demonstration, however, which rests on opinion is human, and is the result of rhetorical arguments or dialectic syllogisms. For the highest demonstration, to which we have alluded, produces intelligent faith by the adducing and opening up of the Scrip-

---

[1] This clause is hopelessly corrupt: the text is utterly unintelligible, and the emendation of Sylburgius is adopted in the translation.
[2] Lev. xviii. 1-5.
[3] Gal. iii. 12.
[4] "Them that are far off, and them that are nigh" (Eph. ii. 13).
[5] Eph. ii. 5.
[6] 1 Cor. viii. 1.
[7] Matt. xvii. 20.
[8] Matt. ix. 29.

tures to the souls of those who desire to learn; the result of which is knowledge (*gnosis*). For if what is adduced in order to prove the point at issue is assumed to be true, as being divine and prophetic, manifestly the conclusion arrived at by inference from it will consequently be inferred truly; and the legitimate result of the demonstration will be knowledge. When, then, the memorial of the celestial and divine food was commanded to be consecrated in the golden pot, it was said, "The omer was the tenth of the three measures." [1] For in ourselves, by the three measures are indicated three criteria; sensation of objects of sense, speech, — of spoken names and words, and the mind, — of intellectual objects. The Gnostic, therefore, will abstain from errors in speech, and thought, and sensation, and action, having heard "that he that looks so as to lust hath committed adultery;" [2] and reflecting that "blessed are the pure in heart, for they shall see God;" [3] and knowing this, "that not what enters into the mouth defileth, but that it is what cometh forth by the mouth that defileth the man. For out of the heart proceed thoughts." [4] This, as I think, is the true and just measure according to God, by which things capable of measurement are measured, the decad which is comprehensive of man; which summarily the three above-mentioned measures pointed out. There are body and soul, the five senses, speech, the power of reproduction — the intellectual or the spiritual faculty, or whatever you choose to call it. And we must, in a word, ascending above all the others, stop at the mind; as also certainly in the universe overleaping the nine divisions, the first consisting of the four elements put in one place for equal interchange: and then the seven wandering stars and the one that wanders not, the ninth, to the perfect number, which is above the nine, [5] and the tenth division, we must reach to the knowledge of God, to speak briefly, desiring the Maker after the creation. Wherefore the tithes both of the ephah and of the sacrifices were presented to God; and the paschal feast began with the tenth day, being the transition from all trouble, and from all objects of sense.

The Gnostic is therefore fixed by faith; but the man who thinks himself wise touches not what pertains to the truth, moved as he is by unstable and wavering impulses. It is therefore reasonably written, "Cain went forth from the face of God, and dwelt in the land of Naid, over against Eden." Now Naid is interpreted *com-*

motion, and Eden *delight*; and Faith, and Knowledge, and Peace are delight, from which he that has disobeyed is cast out. But he that is wise in his own eyes will not so much as listen to the beginning of the divine commandments; but, as if his own teacher, throwing off the reins, plunges voluntarily into a billowy commotion, sinking down to mortal and created things from the uncreated knowledge, holding various opinions at various times. "Those who have no guidance fall like leaves." [6]

Reason, the governing principle, remaining unmoved and guiding the soul, is called its pilot. For access to the Immutable is obtained by a truly immutable means. Thus Abraham was stationed before the Lord, and approaching spoke. [7] And to Moses it is said, "But do thou stand there with Me." [8] And the followers of Simon wish to be assimilated in manners to the standing form which they adore. Faith, therefore, and the knowledge of the truth, render the soul, which makes them its choice, always uniform and equable. For congenial to the man of falsehood is shifting, and change, and turning away, as to the Gnostic are calmness, and rest, and peace. As, then, philosophy has been brought into evil repute by pride and self-conceit, so also gnosis by false gnosis called by the same name; of which the apostle writing says, "O Timothy, keep that which is committed to thy trust, avoiding the profane and vain babblings and oppositions of science (gnosis) falsely so called; which some professing, have erred concerning the faith." [9]

Convicted by this utterance, the heretics reject the Epistles to Timothy. [10] Well, then, if the Lord is the truth, and wisdom, and power of God, as in truth He is, it is shown that the real Gnostic is he that knows Him, and His Father by Him. For his sentiments are the same with him who said, "The lips of the righteous know high things." [11]

CHAP. XII. — TWOFOLD FAITH.

Faith as also Time being double, we shall find virtues in pairs both dwelling together. For memory is related to past time, hope to future. We believe that what is past did, and that what is future will take place. And, on the other hand, we love, persuaded by faith that the past was as it was, and by hope expecting the future. For in everything love attends the Gnostic, who knows one God. "And, behold, all things which He created were very good." [12] He both knows and admires. Godliness adds length of

---

[1] Ex. xvi. 36, Septuagint; "the tenth part of an ephah," A.V.
[2] Matt. v. 28.
[3] Matt. xv. 11, 19.
[4] Matt. v. 8.
[5] The text here reads θεῶν, arising in all probability from the transcriber mistaking the numeral θ for the above.

[6] Prov. xi. 14, Septuagint; "Where no counsel is, the people fall," A.V.
[7] Gen. xviii. 22, 23.
[8] Ex. xxxiv. 2.
[9] 1 Tim. vi. 20, 21.
[10] [See Elucidation III. at the end of this second book.]
[11] Prov. x. 21, Septuagint; "feed many," A.V.
[12] Gen. i. 31.

life ; and the fear of the Lord adds days. As, then, the days are a portion of life in its progress, so also fear is the beginning of love, becoming by development faith, then love. But it is not as I fear and hate a wild beast (since fear is twofold) that I fear the father, whom I fear and love at once. Again, fearing lest I be punished, I love myself in assuming fear. He who fears to offend his father, loves himself. Blessed then is he who is found possessed of faith, being, as he is, composed of love and fear. And faith is power in order to salvation, and strength to eternal life. Again, prophecy is foreknowledge ; and knowledge the understanding of prophecy ; being the knowledge of those things known before by the Lord who reveals all things.

The knowledge, then, of those things which have been predicted shows a threefold result, — either one that has happened long ago, or exists now, or about to be. Then the extremes [1] either of what is accomplished or of what is hoped for fall under faith ; and the present action furnishes persuasive arguments of the confirmation of both the extremes. For if, prophecy being one, one part is accomplishing and another is fulfilled ; hence the truth, both what is hoped for and what is passed is confirmed. For it was first present ; then it became past to us ; so that the belief of what is past is the apprehension of a past event, and a hope which is future the apprehension of a future event.

And not only the Platonists, but the Stoics, say that assent is in our own power. All opinion then, and judgment, and supposition, and knowledge, by which we live and have perpetual intercourse with the human race, is an assent ; which is nothing else than faith. And unbelief being defection from faith, shows both assent and faith to be possessed of power ; for non-existence cannot be called privation. And if you consider the truth, you will find man naturally misled so as to give assent to what is false, though possessing the resources necessary for belief in the truth. "The virtue, then, that encloses the Church in its grasp," as the Shepherd says,[2] "is Faith, by which the elect of God are saved ; and that which acts the man is Self-restraint. And these are followed by Simplicity, Knowledge, Innocence, Decorum, Love," and all these are the daughters of Faith. And again, "Faith leads the way, fear upbuilds, and love perfects." Accordingly he [3] says, the Lord is to be feared in order to edification, but not the devil to destruction. And again, the works of the Lord — that is, His commandments — are to be loved and

done ; but the works of the devil are to be dreaded and not done. For the fear of God trains and restores to love ; but the fear of the works of the devil has hatred dwelling along with it. The same also says " that repentance is high intelligence. For he that repents of what he did, no longer does or says as he did. But by torturing himself for his sins, he benefits his soul. Forgiveness of sins is therefore different from repentance ; but both show what is in our power."

CHAP. XIII. — ON FIRST AND SECOND REPENTANCE.

He, then, who has received the forgiveness of sins ought to sin no more. For, in addition to the first and only repentance from sins (this is from the previous sins in the first and heathen life — I mean that in ignorance), there is forthwith proposed to those who have been called, the repentance which cleanses the seat of the soul from transgressions, that faith may be established. And the Lord, knowing the heart, and foreknowing the future, foresaw both the fickleness of man and the craft and subtlety of the devil from the first, from the beginning ; how that, envying man for the forgiveness of sins, he would present to the servants of God certain causes of sins ; skilfully working mischief, that they might fall together with himself. Accordingly, being very merciful, He has vouchsafed, in the case of those who, though in faith, fall into any transgression, a second repentance ; so that should any one be tempted after his calling, overcome by force and fraud, he may receive still a repentance not to be repented of. " For if we sin wilfully after that we have received the knowledge of the truth, there remaineth no more sacrifice for sins, but a certain fearful looking for of judgment and fiery indignation, which shall devour the adversaries." [4] But continual and successive repentings for sins differ nothing from the case of those who have not believed at all, except only in their consciousness that they do sin. And I know not which of the two is worst, whether the case of a man who sins knowingly, or of one who, after having repented of his sins, transgresses again. For in the process of proof sin appears on each side, — the sin which in its commission is condemned by the worker of the iniquity, and that of the man who, foreseeing what is about to be done, yet puts his hand to it as a wickedness. And he who perchance gratifies himself in anger and pleasure, gratifies himself in he knows what ; and he who, repenting of that in which he gratified himself, by rushing again into pleasure, is near neighbour to him who has sinned wilfully at first. For one, who does again that of which he has repented,

---

[1] i.e., Past and Future, between which lies the Present.
[2] *Pastor of Hermas*, book i. vision iii. chap. viii. vol. i. p. 15.
[3] See *Pastor of Hermas*, book ii. commandt. iv. ch. ii. [vol. i. p. 22], for the sense of this passage.

[4] Heb. x. 26, 27.

and condemning what he does, performs it willingly.

He, then, who from among the Gentiles and from that old life has betaken himself to faith, has obtained forgiveness of sins once. But he who has sinned after this, on his repentance, though he obtain pardon, ought to fear, as one no longer washed to the forgiveness of sins. For not only must the idols which he formerly held as gods, but the works also of his former life, be abandoned by him who has been "born again, not of blood, nor of the will of the flesh,"[1] but in the Spirit; which consists in repenting by not giving way to the same fault. For frequent repentance and readiness to change easily from want of training, is the practice of sin again.[2] The frequent asking of forgiveness, then, for those things in which we often transgress, is the semblance of repentance, not repentance itself. "But the righteousness of the blameless cuts straight paths,"[3] says the Scripture. And again, "The righteousness of the innocent will make his way right."[4] Nay, "as a father pitieth his children, so the LORD pitieth them that fear Him."[5] David writes, "They who sow," then, "in tears, shall reap in joy;"[6] those, namely, who confess in penitence. "For blessed are all those that fear the LORD."[7] You see the corresponding blessing in the Gospel. "Fear not," it is said, "when a man is enriched, and when the glory of his house is increased: because when he dieth he shall leave all, and his glory shall not descend after him."[8] "But I in Thy mercy will enter into Thy house. I will worship toward Thy holy temple, in Thy fear: LORD, lead me in Thy righteousness."[9] Appetite is then the movement of the mind to or from something.[10] Passion is an excessive appetite exceeding the measures of reason, or appetite unbridled and disobedient to the word. Passions, then, are a perturbation of the soul contrary to nature, in disobedience to reason. But revolt and distraction and disobedience are in our own power, as obedience is in our power. Wherefore voluntary actions are judged. But should one examine each one of the passions, he will find them irrational impulses.

CHAP. XIV. — HOW A THING MAY BE INVOLUNTARY.

What is involuntary is not matter for judgment. But this is twofold, — what is done in ignorance, and what is done through necessity. For how will you judge concerning those who are said to sin in involuntary modes? For either one knew not himself, as Cleomenes and Athamas, who were mad; or the thing which he does, as Æschylus, who divulged the mysteries on the stage, who, being tried in the Areopagus, was absolved on his showing that he had not been initiated. Or one knows not what is done, as he who has let off his antagonist, and slain his domestic instead of his enemy; or that by which it is done, as he who, in exercising with spears having buttons on them, has killed some one in consequence of the spear throwing off the button; or knows not the manner how, as he who has killed his antagonist in the stadium, for it was not for his death but for victory that he contended; or knows not the reason why it is done, as the physician gave a salutary antidote and killed, for it was not for this purpose that he gave it, but to save. The law at that time punished him who had killed involuntarily, as e.g., him who was subject involuntarily to gonorrhœa, but not equally with him who did so voluntarily. Although he also shall be punished as for a voluntary action, if one transfer the affection to the truth. For, in reality, he that cannot contain the generative word is to be punished; for this is an irrational passion of the soul approaching garrulity. "The faithful man chooses to conceal things in his spirit."[11] Things, then, that depend on choice are subjects for judgment. "For the Lord searcheth the hearts and reins."[12] "And he that looketh so as to lust"[13] is judged. Wherefore it is said, "Thou shalt not lust."[14] And "this people honoureth Me with their lips," it is said, "but their heart is far from Me."[15] For God has respect to the very thought, since Lot's wife, who had merely voluntarily turned towards worldly wickedness, He left a senseless mass, rendering her a pillar of salt, and fixed her so that she advanced no further, not as a stupid and useless image, but to season and salt him who has the power of spiritual perception.

CHAP. XV. — ON THE DIFFERENT KINDS OF VOLUNTARY ACTIONS, AND THE SINS THENCE PROCEEDING.

What is voluntary is either what is by desire, or what is by choice, or what is of intention. Closely allied to each other are these things — sin, mistake, crime. It is sin, for example, to live luxuriously and licentiously; a misfortune, to wound one's friend in ignorance, taking him for an enemy; and crime, to violate graves or

---

[1] John i. 13.
[2] [The penitential system of the early Church was no mere sponge like that of the later Latins, which turns Christ into "the minister of sin."]
[3] Prov. xi. 5.
[4] Prov. xiii. 6.
[5] Ps. ciii. 13.
[6] Ps. cxxvi. 5.
[7] Ps. cxxviii. 1.
[8] Ps. xlix. 16, 17.
[9] Ps. v. 7, 8.
[10] Adopting the emendation, ὁρμὴ μὲν οὖν φορά.

[11] Prov. xi. 13.
[12] Ps. vii. 9.
[13] Matt. v. 28.
[14] Ex. xx. 17.
[15] Isa. xxix. 13; Matt. xv. 8; Mark vii. 6.

commit sacrilege. Sinning arises from being unable to determine what ought to be done, or being unable to do it; as doubtless one falls into a ditch either through not knowing, or through inability to leap across through feebleness of body. But application to the training of ourselves, and subjection to the commandments, is in our own power; with which if we will have nothing to do, by abandoning ourselves wholly to lust, we shall sin, nay rather, wrong our own soul. For the noted Laius says in the tragedy:—

> "None of these things of which you admonish me have
>   escaped me;
> But notwithstanding that I am in my senses, Nature
>   compels me;"

i.e., his abandoning himself to passion. Medea, too, herself cries on the stage:—

> "And I am aware what evils I am to perpetrate,
> But passion is stronger than my resolutions."[1]

Further, not even Ajax is silent; but, when about to kill himself, cries:—

> "No pain gnaws the soul of a free man like dishonour.
> Thus do I suffer; and the deep stain of calamity
> Ever stirs me from the depths, agitated
> By the bitter stings of rage."[2]

Anger made these the subjects of tragedy, and lust made ten thousand others — Phædra, Anthia, Eriphyle,—

> "Who took the precious gold for her dear husband."

For another play represents Thrasonides of the comic drama as saying:—

> "A worthless wench made me her slave."

Mistake is a sin contrary to calculation; and voluntary sin is crime (ἀδικία); and crime is voluntary wickedness. Sin, then, is on my part voluntary. Wherefore says the apostle, "Sin shall not have dominion over you; for ye are not under the law, but under grace."[3] Addressing those who have believed, he says, "For by His stripes we were healed."[4] Mistake is the involuntary action of another towards me, while a crime (ἀδικία) alone is voluntary, whether my act or another's. These differences of sins are alluded to by the Psalmist, when he calls those blessed whose iniquities (ἀνομίας) God hath blotted out, and whose sins (ἁμαρτίας) He hath covered. Others He does not impute, and the rest He forgives. For it is written, "Blessed are they whose iniquities are forgiven, whose sins are covered. Blessed is the man to whom the LORD will not impute sin, and in whose mouth there is no fraud."[5] This blessedness came on

those who had been chosen by God through Jesus Christ our Lord. For "love hides the multitude of sins."[6] And they are blotted out by Him "who desireth the repentance rather than the death of a sinner."[7] And those are not reckoned that are not the effect of choice; "for he who has lusted has already committed adultery,"[8] it is said. And the illuminating Word forgives sins: "And in that time, saith the LORD, they shall seek for the iniquity of Israel, and it shall not exist; and the sins of Judah, and they shall not be found."[9] "For who is like Me? and who shall stand before My face?"[10] You see the one God declared good, rendering according to desert, and forgiving sins. John, too, manifestly teaches the differences of sins, in his larger Epistle, in these words: "If any man see his brother sin a sin that is not unto death, he shall ask, and he shall give him life: for these that sin not unto death," he says. For "there is a sin unto death: I do not say that one is to pray for it. All unrighteousness is sin; and there is a sin not unto death."[11]

David, too, and Moses before David, show the knowledge of the three precepts in the following words: "Blessed is the man who walks not in the counsel of the ungodly;" as the fishes go down to the depths in darkness; for those which have not scales, which Moses prohibits touching, feed at the bottom of the sea. "Nor standeth in the way of sinners," as those who, while appearing to fear the Lord, commit sin, like the sow, for when hungry it cries, and when full knows not its owner. "Nor sitteth in the chair of pestilences," as birds ready for prey. And Moses enjoined not to eat the sow, nor the eagle, nor the hawk, nor the raven, nor any fish without scales. So far Barnabas.[12] And I heard one skilled in such matters say that "the counsel of the ungodly" was the heathen, and "the way of sinners" the Jewish persuasion, and explain "the chair of pestilence" of heresies. And another said, with more propriety, that the first blessing was assigned to those who had not followed wicked sentiments which revolt from God; the second to those who do not remain in the wide and broad road, whether they be those who have been brought up in the law, or Gentiles who have repented. And "the chair of pestilences" will be the theatres and tribunals, or rather the compliance with wicked and deadly powers, and complicity with their deeds. "But his delight is in the law of the LORD."[13] Peter in his *Preach-*

---

[1] Eurip., *Medea*, 1078.
[2] These lines, which are not found in the Ajax of Sophocles, have been amended by various hands. Instead of συμφορουσα, we have ventured to read συμφοράς,—κηλὶς συμφοράς being a Sophoclean phrase, and συμφορούσα being unsuitable.
[3] Rom. iv. 7, 8.
[4] 1 Pet. ii. 24.
[5] Ps. xxxii. 1, 2; Rom. iv. 7, 8.

[6] 1 Pet. iv. 8.
[7] Ezek. xxxiii. 11.
[8] Matt. v. 28.
[9] Jer. i. 20.
[10] Jer. xlix. 19.
[11] 1 John v. 16, 17.
[12] Ps. i. 1 (quoted from Barnabas, with some additions and omissions). [See vol. i. p. 143, this series.]
[13] Ps. i. 2.

ing called the Lord, Law and Logos. The legislator seems to teach differently the interpretation of the three forms of sin — understanding by the mute fishes sins of word, for there are times in which *silence is better than speech, for silence has a safe recompense;* sins of deed, by the rapacious and carnivorous birds. The sow delights in dirt and dung; and we ought not to have "a conscience" that is "defiled." [1]

Justly, therefore, the prophet says, "The ungodly are not so: but as the chaff which the wind driveth away from the face of the earth. Wherefore the ungodly shall not stand in the judgment" [2] (being already condemned, for "he that believeth not is condemned already" [3]), "nor sinners in the counsel of the righteous," inasmuch as they are already condemned, so as not to be united to those that have lived without stumbling. "For the LORD knoweth the way of the righteous; and the way of the ungodly shall perish." [4]

Again, the Lord clearly shows sins and transgressions to be in our own power, by prescribing modes of cure corresponding to the maladies; showing His wish that we should be corrected by the shepherds, in Ezekiel; blaming, I am of opinion, some of them for not keeping the commandments. "That which was enfeebled ye have not strengthened," and so forth, down to, "and there was none to search out or turn away." [5]

For "great is the joy before the Father when one sinner is saved," [6] saith the Lord. So Abraham was much to be praised, because "he walked as the Lord spake to him." Drawing from this instance, one of the wise men among the Greeks uttered the maxim, "Follow God." [7] "The godly," says Esaias, "framed wise counsels." [8] Now counsel is seeking for the right way of acting in present circumstances, and good counsel is wisdom in our counsels. And what? Does not God, after the pardon bestowed on Cain, suitably not long after introduce Enoch, who had repented? [9] showing that it is the nature of repentance to produce pardon; but pardon does not consist in remission, but in remedy. An instance of the same is the making of the calf by the people before Aaron. Thence one of the wise men among the Greeks uttered the maxim, "Pardon is better than punishment;" as also, "Become surety, and mischief is at hand," is derived from the utterance of Solomon which

says, "My son, if thou become surety for thy friend, thou wilt give thine hand to thy enemy; for a man's own lips are a strong snare to him, and he is taken in the words of his own mouth." [10] And the saying, "Know thyself," has been taken rather more mystically from this, "Thou hast seen thy brother, thou hast seen thy God." [11] Thus also, "Thou shalt love the LORD thy God with all thy heart, and thy neighbour as thyself;" for it is said, "On these commandments the law and the prophets hang and are suspended." [12] With these also agree the following: "These things have I spoken to you, that My joy might be fulfilled: and this is My commandment, That ye love one another, as I have loved you." [13] "For the LORD is merciful and pitiful; and gracious [14] is the LORD to all." [15] "Know thyself" is more clearly and often expressed by Moses, when he enjoins, "Take heed to thyself." [16] "By alms then, and acts of faith, sins are purged." [17] "And by the fear of the LORD each one departs from evil." [18] "And the fear of the Lord is instruction and wisdom." [19]

CHAP. XVI. — HOW WE ARE TO EXPLAIN THE PASSAGES OF SCRIPTURE WHICH ASCRIBE TO GOD HUMAN AFFECTIONS.

Here again arise the cavillers, who say that joy and pain are passions of the soul: for they define joy as a rational elevation and exultation, as rejoicing on account of what is good; and pity as pain for one who suffers undeservedly; and that such affections are moods and passions of the soul. But we, as would appear, do not cease in such matters to understand the Scriptures carnally; and starting from our own affections, interpret the will of the impassible Deity similarly to our perturbations; and as we are capable of hearing; so, supposing the same to be the case with the Omnipotent, err impiously. For the Divine Being cannot be declared as it exists: but as we who are fettered in the flesh were able to listen, so the prophets spake to us; the Lord savingly accommodating Himself to the weakness of men. [20] Since, then, it is the will of God that he, who is obedient to the commands and repents of his sins should be saved, and we rejoice on account of our salvation, the Lord, speaking by the prophets, appropriated our joy to Himself;

---

[1] 1 Cor. viii. 7.
[2] Ps. i. 4, 5.
[3] John iii. 18.
[4] Ps. i. 5, 6.
[5] Ezek. xxxiv. 4–6.
[6] These words are not in Scripture, but the substance of them is contained in Luke xv. 7, 10.
[7] One of the precepts of the seven wise men.
[8] Isa. xxxii. 8, Sept.
[9] Philo explains Enoch's translation allegorically, as denoting reformation or repentance.

[10] Prov. vi. 1, 2.
[11] Quoted as if in Scripture, but not found there. The allusion may be, as is conjectured, to what God said to Moses respecting him and Aaron, to whom he was to be as God; or to Jacob saying to Esau, "I have seen thy face as it were the face of God."
[12] Luke x. 27, etc.
[13] John xv. 11, 12.
[14] χρηστός instead of χριστός which is in the text.
[15] Ps. ciii. 8, cxi. 4.
[16] Ex. x. 28, xxxiv. 12; Deut. iv. 9.
[17] Prob. Ecclus. iii. 29.
[18] Prov. iii. 7.
[19] Ecclus. i. 27.
[20] [This *anthropopathy* is a figure by which God is interpreted to us after the intelligible forms of humanity. Language framed by human usage makes this figure necessary to revelation.]

as speaking lovingly in the Gospel He says, " I was hungry, and ye gave Me to eat : I was thirsty, and ye gave Me to drink. For inasmuch as ye did it to one of the least of these, ye did it to Me." [1] As, then, He is nourished, though not personally, by the nourishing of one whom He wishes nourished ; so He rejoices, without suffering change, by reason of him who has repented being in joy, as He wished. And since God pities richly, being good, and giving commands by the law and the prophets, and more nearly still by the appearance of his Son, saving and pitying, as was said, those who have found mercy ; and properly the greater pities the less ; and a man cannot be greater than man, being by nature man ; but God in everything is greater than man ; if, then, the greater pities the less, it is God alone that will pity us. For a man is made to communicate by righteousness, and bestows what he received from God, in consequence of his natural benevolence and relation, and the commands which he obeys. But God has no natural relation to us, as the authors of the heresies will have it ; neither on the supposition of His having made us of nothing, nor on that of having formed us from matter ; since the former did not exist at all, and the latter is totally distinct from God, unless we shall dare to say that we are a part of Him, and of the same essence as God. And I know not how one, who knows God, can bear to hear this when he looks to our life, and sees in what evils we are involved. For thus it would turn out, which it were impiety to utter, that God sinned in [certain] portions, if the portions are parts of the whole and complementary of the whole ; and if not complementary, neither can they be parts. But God being by nature rich in pity, in consequence of His own goodness, cares for us, though neither portions of Himself, nor by nature His children. And this is the greatest proof of the goodness of God : that such being our relation to Him, and being by nature wholly estranged, He nevertheless cares for us. For the affection in animals to their progeny is natural, and the friendship of kindred minds is the result of intimacy. But the mercy of God is rich toward us, who are in no respect related to Him ; I say either in our essence or nature, or in the peculiar energy of our essence, but only in our being the work of His will. And him who willingly, with discipline and teaching, accepts the knowledge of the truth, He calls to adoption, which is the greatest advancement of all. " Transgressions catch a man ; and in the cords of his own sins each one is bound." [2] And God is without blame. And in reality, " blessed is the man who feareth alway through piety." [3]

CHAP. XVII. — ON THE VARIOUS KINDS OF KNOWLEDGE.

As, then, Knowledge (ἐπιστήμη) is an intellectual state, from which results the act of knowing, and becomes apprehension irrefragable by reason ; so also ignorance is a receding impression, which can be dislodged by reason. And that which is overthrown as well as that which is elaborated by reason, is in our power. Akin to Knowledge is *experience*, cognition (εἴδησις), Comprehension (σύνεσις), perception, and Science. Cognition (εἴδησις) is the knowledge of universals by species ; and Experience is comprehensive knowledge, which investigates the nature of each thing. Perception (νόησις) is the knowledge of intellectual objects ; and Comprehension (σύνεσις) is the knowledge of what is compared, or a comparison that cannot be annulled, or the faculty of comparing the objects with which Judgment and Knowledge are occupied, both of one and each and all that goes to make up one reason. And Science (γνῶσις) is the knowledge of the thing in itself, or the knowledge which harmonizes with what takes place. Truth is the knowledge of the true ; and the mental habit of truth is the knowledge of the things which are true. Now knowledge is constituted by the reason, and cannot be overthrown by another reason.[4] What we do not, we do not either from not being able, or not being willing — or both. Accordingly we don't fly, since we neither can nor wish ; we do not swim at present, for example, since we can indeed, but do not choose ; and we are not as the Lord, since we wish, but cannot be : " for no disciple is above his master, and it is sufficient if we be as the master :" [5] not in essence (for it is impossible for that, which is by adoption, to be equal in substance to that, which is by nature) ; but [we are as Him] only in our [6] having been made immortal, and our being conversant with the contemplation of realities, and beholding the Father through what belongs to Him.

Therefore volition takes the precedence of all ; for the intellectual powers are ministers of the Will. " Will," it is said, " and thou shalt be able." [7] And in the Gnostic, Will, Judgment, and Exertion are identical. For if the determinations are the same, the opinions and judgments will be the same too ; so that both his words, and life, and conduct, are conformable to rule. " And a right heart seeketh knowl-

---

[1] Matt. xxv. 35, 40.
[2] Prov. v. 22.
[3] Prov. xxviii. 14.

[4] ἐνταῦθα τὴν γνῶσιν πολυπραγμονεῖ appears in the text, which, with great probability, is supposed to be a marginal note which got into the text, the indicative being substituted for the imperative.
[5] Matt. x. 24, 25; Luke vi. 40.
[6] Adopting Sylburgius' conjecture of τῷ δέ for τὸ δέ.
[7] Perhaps in allusion to the leper's words to Christ, "If Thou wilt, Thou canst make me clean" (Mark i. 40).

edge, and heareth it." "God taught me wisdom, and I knew the knowledge of the holy." [1]

CHAP. XVIII. — THE MOSAIC LAW THE FOUNTAIN OF ALL ETHICS, AND THE SOURCE FROM WHICH THE GREEKS DREW THEIRS.[2]

It is then clear also that all the other virtues, delineated in Moses, supplied the Greeks with the rudiments of the whole department of morals. I mean valour, and temperance, and wisdom, and justice, and endurance, and patience, and decorum, and self-restraint; and in addition to these, piety.

But it is clear to every one that piety, which teaches to worship and honour, is the highest and oldest cause; and the law itself exhibits justice, and teaches wisdom, by abstinence from sensible images, and by inviting to the Maker and Father of the universe. And from this sentiment, as from a fountain, all intelligence increases. "For the sacrifices of the wicked are abomination to the LORD; but the prayers of the upright are acceptable before Him," [3] since "righteousness is more acceptable before God than sacrifice." Such also as the following we find in Isaiah : "To what purpose to me is the multitude of your sacrifices? saith the LORD;" and the whole section.[4] "Break every bond of wickedness; for this is the sacrifice that is acceptable to the Lord, a contrite heart that seeks its Maker." [5] "Deceitful balances are abomination before God ; but a just balance is acceptable to Him." [6] Thence Pythagoras exhorts "not to step over the balance;" and the profession of heresies is called deceitful righteousness; and "the tongue of the unjust shall be destroyed, but the mouth of the righteous droppeth wisdom." [7] "For they call the wise and prudent worthless." [8] But it were tedious to adduce testimonies respecting these virtues, since the whole Scripture celebrates them. Since, then, they define manliness to be knowledge [9] of things formidable, and not formidable, and what is intermediate; and temperance to be a state of mind which by choosing and avoiding preserves the judgments of wisdom; and conjoined with manliness is patience, which is called endurance, the knowledge of what is bearable and what is unbearable; and magnanimity is the knowledge which rises superior to circumstances. With temperance also is conjoined caution, which is avoidance in accordance with reason. And observance of the commandments, which is the innoxious keeping of them, is the attainment of a secure life. And there is no endurance without manliness, nor the exercise of self-restraint without temperance. And these virtues follow one another; and with whom are the sequences of the virtues, with him is also salvation, which is the keeping of the state of well-being. Rightly, therefore, in treating of these virtues, we shall inquire into them all; for he that has one virtue gnostically, by reason of their accompanying each other, has them all. Self-restraint is that quality which does not overstep what appears in accordance with right reason. He exercises self-restraint, who curbs the impulses that are contrary to right reason, or curbs himself so as not to indulge in desires contrary to right reason. Temperance, too, is not without manliness; since from the commandments spring both wisdom, which follows God who enjoins, and that which imitates the divine character, namely righteousness; in virtue of which, in the exercise of self-restraint, we address ourselves in purity to piety and the course of conduct thence resulting, in conformity with God; being assimilated to the Lord as far as is possible for us beings mortal in nature. And this is being just and holy with wisdom; for the Divinity needs nothing and suffers nothing; whence it is not, strictly speaking, capable of self-restraint, for it is never subjected to perturbation, over which to exercise control; while our nature, being capable of perturbation, needs self-constraint, by which disciplining itself to the need of little, it endeavours to approximate in character to the divine nature. For the good man, standing as the boundary between an immortal and a mortal nature, has few needs; having wants in consequence of his body, and his birth itself, but taught by rational self-control to want few things.

What reason is there in the law's prohibiting a man from "wearing woman's clothing"? [10] Is it not that it would have us to be manly, and not to be effeminate neither in person and actions, nor in thought and word? For it would have the man, that devotes himself to the truth, to be masculine both in acts of endurance and patience, in life, conduct, word, and discipline by night and by day; even if the necessity were to occur, of witnessing by the shedding of his blood. Again, it is said, "If any one who has newly built a house, and has not previously inhabited it; or cultivated a newly-planted vine, and not yet partaken of the fruit; or betrothed a virgin, and not yet married her;" [11] — such the humane law orders to be relieved from military service : from military reasons in the first place, lest, bent on

---

[1] Prov. xxx. 3.
[2] [See p. 192, *supra*, and the note.]
[3] Prov. xv. 8.
[4] Isa. i. 11, etc.
[5] Isa. lviii. 6.
[6] Prov. xi. 1.
[7] Prov. x. 31.
[8] Prov. xvi. 21, misquoted, or the text is corrupt; " The wise in heart shall be called prudent," A.V.
[9] For the use of knowledge in this connection, Philo, Sextus Empiricus, and Zeno are quoted.

[10] Deut. xxii. 5.
[11] " These words are more like Philo Judæus, i. 740, than those of Moses, Deut. xx. 5-7." — POTTER.

their desires, they turn out sluggish in war; for it is those who are untrammelled by passion that boldly encounter perils; and from motives of humanity, since, in view of the uncertainties of war, the law reckoned it not right that one should not enjoy his own labours, and another should, without bestowing pains, receive what belonged to those who had laboured. The law seems also to point out manliness of soul, by enacting that he who had planted should reap the fruit, and he that built should inhabit, and he that had betrothed should marry: for it is not vain hopes which it provides for those who labour; according to the gnostic word: "For the hope of a good man dead or living does not perish,"[1] says Wisdom; "I love them that love me; and they who seek me shall find peace,"[2] and so forth. What then? Did not the women of the Midianites, by their beauty, seduce from wisdom into impiety, through licentiousness, the Hebrews when making war against them? For, having seduced them from a grave mode of life, and by their beauty ensnared them in wanton delights, they made them insane upon idol sacrifices and strange women; and overcome by women and by pleasure at once, they revolted from God, and revolted from the law. And the whole people was within a little of falling under the power of the enemy through female stratagem, until, when they were in peril, fear by its admonitions pulled them back. Then the survivors, valiantly undertaking the struggle for piety, got the upper hand of their foes. "The beginning, then, of wisdom is piety, and the knowledge of holy things is understanding; and to know the law is the characteristic of a good understanding."[3] Those, then, who suppose the law to be productive of agitating fear, are neither good at understanding the law, nor have they in reality comprehended it; for "the fear of the LORD causes life, but he who errs shall be afflicted with pangs which knowledge views not."[4] Accordingly, Barnabas says mystically, "May God who rules the universe vouchsafe also to you wisdom, and understanding, and science, and knowledge of His statutes, and patience. Be therefore God-taught, seeking what the Lord seeks from you, that He may find you in the day of judgment lying in wait for these things." "Children of love and peace," he called them gnostically.[5]

Respecting imparting and communicating, though much might be said, let it suffice to remark that the law prohibits a brother from taking usury: designating as a brother not only him who is born of the same parents, but also one of the same race and sentiments, and a participator

in the same word; deeming it right not to take usury for money, but with open hands and heart to bestow on those who need. For God, the author and the dispenser of such grace, takes as suitable usury the most precious things to be found among men — mildness, gentleness, magnanimity, reputation, renown. Do you not regard this command as marked by philanthropy? As also the following, "To pay the wages of the poor daily," teaches to discharge without delay the wages due for service; for, as I think, the alacrity of the poor with reference to the future is paralyzed when he has suffered want. Further, it is said, "Let not the creditor enter the debtor's house to take the pledge with violence." But let the former ask it to be brought out, and let not the latter, if he have it, hesitate.[6] And in the harvest the owners are prohibited from appropriating what falls from the handfuls; as also in reaping [the law] enjoins a part to be left unreaped; signally thereby training those who possess to sharing and to large-heartedness, by foregoing of their own to those who are in want, and thus providing means of subsistence for the poor.[7] You see how the law proclaims at once the righteousness and goodness of God, who dispenses food to all ungrudgingly. And in the vintage it prohibited the grape-gatherers from going back again on what had been left, and from gathering the fallen grapes; and the same injunctions are given to the olive-gatherers.[8] Besides, the tithes of the fruits and of the flocks taught both piety towards the Deity, and not covetously to grasp everything, but to communicate gifts of kindness to one's neighbours. For it was from these, I reckon, and from the firstfruits that the priests were maintained. We now therefore understand that we are instructed in piety, and in liberality, and in justice, and in humanity by the law. For does it not command the land to be left fallow in the seventh year, and bids the poor fearlessly use the fruits that grow by divine agency, nature cultivating the ground for behoof of all and sundry?[9] How, then, can it be maintained that the law is not humane, and the teacher of righteousness? Again, in the fiftieth year, it ordered the same things to be performed as in the seventh; besides restoring to each one his own land, if from any circumstance he had parted with it in the meantime; setting bounds to the desires of those who covet possession, by measuring the period of enjoyment, and choosing that those who have paid the penalty of protracted penury should not suffer a life-long punishment. "But alms and acts of faith are royal guards, and blessing is on

1 Prov. x 7, xi. 7.
2 Prov. viii. 17.
3 Prov. ix. 10.
4 Prov. xix. 23.
5 [See *Epistle of Barnabas*, vol. p. i. 149, S.]

6 Deut. xxiv. 10, 11.
7 Lev. xix. 9, xxiii. 22; Deut. xxiv. 19.
8 Lev. xix. 10; Deut. xxiv. 20, 21.
9 Ex. xxiii. 10, 11; Lev. xxv. 2-7.

the head of him who bestows; and he who pities the poor shall be blessed." [1] For he shows love to one like himself, because of his love to the Creator of the human race. The above-mentioned particulars have other explanations more natural, both respecting rest and the recovery of the inheritance; but they are not discussed at present.

Now love is conceived in many ways, in the form of meekness, of mildness, of patience, of liberality, of freedom from envy, of absence of hatred, of forgetfulness of injuries. In all it is incapable of being divided or distinguished: its nature is to communicate. Again, it is said, "If you see the beast of your relatives, or friends, or, in general, of anybody you know, wandering in the wilderness, take it back and restore it; [2] and if the owner be far away, keep it among your own till he return, and restore it." It teaches a natural communication, that what is found is to be regarded as a deposit, and that we are not to bear malice to an enemy. "The command of the Lord being a fountain of life" truly, "causeth to turn away from the snare of death." [3] And what? Does it not command us "to love strangers not only as friends and relatives, but as ourselves, both in body and soul?" [4] Nay more, it honoured the nations, and bears no grudge [5] against those who have done ill. Accordingly it is expressly said, "Thou shalt not abhor an Egyptian, for thou wast a sojourner in Egypt;" [6] designating by the term Egyptian either one of that race, or any one in the world. And enemies, although drawn up before the walls attempting to take the city, are not to be regarded as enemies till they are by the voice of the herald summoned to peace. [7]

Further, it forbids intercourse with a female captive so as to dishonour her. "But allow her," it says, "thirty days to mourn according to her wish, and changing her clothes, associate with her as your lawful wife." [8] For it regards it not right that this should take place either in wantonness or for hire like harlots, but only for the birth of children. Do you see humanity combined with continence? The master who has fallen in love with his captive maid it does not allow to gratify his pleasure, but puts a check on his lust by specifying an interval of time; and further, it cuts off the captive's hair, in order to shame disgraceful love: for if it is reason that induces him to marry, he will cleave to her

even after she has become disfigured. Then if one, after his lust, does not care to consort any longer with the captive, it ordains that it shall not be lawful to sell her, or to have her any longer as a servant, but desires her to be freed and released from service, lest on the introduction of another wife she bear any of the intolerable miseries caused through jealousy.

What more? The Lord enjoins to ease and raise up the beasts of enemies when labouring beneath their burdens; remotely teaching us not to indulge in joy at our neighbour's ills, or exult over our enemies; in order to teach those who are trained in these things to pray for their enemies. For He does not allow us either to grieve at our neighbour's good, or to reap joy at our neighbour's ill. And if you find any enemy's beast straying, you are to pass over the incentives of difference, and take it back and restore it. For oblivion of injuries is followed by goodness, and the latter by dissolution of enmity. From this we are fitted for agreement, and this conducts to felicity. And should you suppose one habitually hostile, and discover him to be unreasonably mistaken either through lust or anger, turn him to goodness. Does the law then which conducts to Christ appear humane and mild? And does not the same God, good, while characterized by righteousness from the beginning to the end, employ each kind suitably in order to salvation? "Be merciful," says the Lord, "that you may receive mercy; forgive, that you may be forgiven. As ye do, so shall it be done to you; as ye give, so shall it be given to you; as ye judge, so shall ye be judged; as ye show kindness, so shall kindness be shown to you: with what measure ye mete, it shall be measured to you again." [9] Furthermore, [the law] prohibits those, who are in servitude for their subsistence, to be branded with disgrace; and to those, who have been reduced to slavery through money borrowed, it gives a complete release in the seventh year. Further, it prohibits suppliants from being given up to punishment. True above all, then, is that oracle. "As gold and silver are tried in the furnace, so the Lord chooseth men's hearts. The merciful man is long-suffering; and in every one who shows solicitude there is wisdom. For on a wise man solicitude will fall; and exercising thought, he will seek life; and he who seeketh God shall find knowledge with righteousness. And they who have sought Him rightly have found peace." [10] And Pythagoras seems to me, to have derived his mildness towards irrational creatures from the law. For instance, he interdicted the immediate use of the young in the flocks of sheep, and goats, and herds of cattle, on the instant of their

---

[1] Prov. xx. 28, xi. 26, xiv. 21.
[2] Quoted from Philo, with slight alterations, giving the sense of Ex. xxiii. 4, Deut. xxii. 12, 3.
[3] Prov. xiv. 27.
[4] Lev. xix. 33, 34; Deut. x. 19, xxiii. 7.
[5] μνησιπονηρεῖ (equivalent to μνησικακεῖ in the passage of Philo from which Clement is quoting) has been substituted by Sylb for μισοπονηρεῖ.
[6] Deut. xxiii. 7.
[7] Deut. xx. 10.
[8] Deut. xxi. 10-13.

[9] Matt. v. vi. vii.; Luke vi.
[10] Prov. xix. 11, xiv. 23, xvii. 12.

birth; not even on the pretext of sacrifice allowing it, both on account of the young ones and of the mothers; training man to gentleness by what is beneath him, by means of the irrational creatures. "Resign accordingly," he says, "the young one to its dam for even the first seven days." For if nothing takes place without a cause, and milk comes in a shower to animals in parturition for the sustenance of the progeny, he that tears that, which has been brought forth, away from the supply of the milk, dishonours nature. Let the Greeks, then, feel ashamed, and whoever else inveighs against the law; since it shows mildness in the case of the irrational creatures, while they expose the offspring of men; though long ago and prophetically, the law, in the above-mentioned commandment, threw a check in the way of their cruelty. For if it prohibits the progeny of the irrational creatures to be separated from the dam before sucking, much more in the case of men does it provide beforehand a cure for cruelty and savageness of disposition; so that even if they despise nature, they may not despise teaching. For they are permitted to satiate themselves with kids and lambs, and perhaps there might be some excuse for separating the progeny from its dam. But what cause is there for the exposure of a child? For the man who did not desire to beget children had no right to marry at first; certainly not to have become, through licentious indulgence, the murderer of his children. Again, the humane law forbids slaying the offspring and the dam together on the same day. Thence also the Romans, in the case of a pregnant woman being condemned to death, do not allow her to undergo punishment till she is delivered. The law, too, expressly prohibits the slaying of such animals as are pregnant till they have brought forth, remotely restraining the proneness of man to do wrong to man. Thus also it has extended its clemency to the irrational creatures; that from the exercise of humanity in the case of creatures of different species, we might practise among those of the same species a large abundance of it. Those, too, that kick the bellies of certain animals before parturition, in order to feast on flesh mixed with milk, make the womb created for the birth of the fœtus its grave, though the law expressly commands, "But neither shalt thou seethe a lamb in its mother's milk."[1] For the nourishment of the living animal, it is meant, may not become sauce for that which has been deprived of life; and that, which is the cause of life, may not co-operate in the consumption of the body. And the same law commands "not to muzzle the ox which treadeth out the corn: for the labourer must be reckoned worthy of his food."[2]

And it prohibits an ox and ass to be yoked in the plough together;[3] pointing perhaps to the want of agreement in the case of the animals; and at the same time teaching not to wrong any one belonging to another race, and bring him under the yoke, when there is no other cause to allege than difference of race, which is no cause at all, being neither wickedness nor the effect of wickedness. To me the allegory also seems to signify that the husbandry of the Word is not to be assigned equally to the clean and the unclean, the believer and the unbeliever; for the ox is clean, but the ass has been reckoned among the unclean animals. But the benignant Word, abounding in humanity, teaches that neither is it right to cut down cultivated trees, or to cut down the grain before the harvest, for mischief's sake; nor that cultivated fruit is to be destroyed at all — either the fruit of the soil or that of the soul: for it does not permit the enemy's country to be laid waste.

Further, husbandmen derived advantage from the law in such things. For it orders newly planted trees to be nourished three years in succession, and the superfluous growths to be cut off, to prevent them being loaded and pressed down; and to prevent their strength being exhausted from want, by the nutriment being frittered away, enjoins tilling and digging round them, so that [the tree] may not, by sending out suckers, hinder its growth. And it does not allow imperfect fruit to be plucked from immature trees, but after three years, in the fourth year; dedicating the first-fruits to God after the tree has attained maturity.

This type of husbandry may serve as a mode of instruction, teaching that we must cut the growths of sins, and the useless weeds of the mind that spring up round the vital fruit, till the shoot of faith is perfected and becomes strong.[4] For in the fourth year, since there is need of time to him that is being solidly catechized, the four virtues are consecrated to God, the third alone being already joined to the fourth,[5] the person of the Lord. And a sacrifice of praise is above holocausts: "for He," it is said, "giveth strength to get power."[6] And if your affairs are in the sunshine of prosperity, get and keep strength, and acquire power in knowledge. For by these instances it is shown that both good things and gifts are supplied by God; and that we, becoming ministers of the divine grace, ought to sow the benefits of God, and make those who approach us noble and

---

[1] Deut. xiv. 21.
[2] Deut. xxv. 4; 1 Tim. v. 18.

[3] Deut. xxii. 10.
[4] [See Hermas, *Visions*, note 2, p. 15, this volume.]
[5] So Clement seems to designate the human nature of Christ, — as being a *quartum quid* in addition to the three persons of the Godhead. [A strange note; borrowed from ed. Migne. The incarnation of the second person is a *quartum quid*, of course; but not, in our author's view, "an addition to the three persons of the Godhead."]
[6] Deut. viii. 18.

good; so that, as far as possible, the temperate man may make others continent, he that is manly may make them noble, he that is wise may make them intelligent, and the just may make them just.

CHAP. XIX. — THE TRUE GNOSTIC IS AN IMITATOR OF GOD, ESPECIALLY IN BENEFICENCE.

He is the Gnostic, who is after the image and likeness of God, who imitates God as far as possible, deficient in none of the things which contribute to the likeness as far as compatible, practising self-restraint and endurance, living righteously, reigning over the passions, bestowing of what he has as far as possible, and doing good both by word and deed. "He is the greatest," it is said, "in the kingdom who shall do and teach;"[1] imitating God in conferring like benefits. For God's gifts are for the common good. "Whoever shall attempt to do aught with presumption, provokes God,"[2] it is said. For haughtiness is a vice of the soul, of which, as of other sins, He commands us to repent; by adjusting our lives from their state of derangement to the change for the better in these three things — mouth, heart, hands. These are signs — the hands of action, the heart of volition, the mouth of speech. Beautifully, therefore, has this oracle been spoken with respect to penitents: "Thou hast chosen God this day to be thy God; and God hath chosen thee this day to be His people."[3] For him who hastes to serve the self-existent One, being a suppliant,[4] God adopts to Himself; and though he be only one in number, he is honoured equally with the people. For being a part of the people, he becomes complementary of it, being restored from what he was; and the whole is named from a part.

But nobility is itself exhibited in choosing and practising what is best. For what benefit to Adam was such a nobility as he had? No mortal was his father; for he himself was father of men that are born. What is base he readily chose, following his wife, and neglected what is true and good; on which account he exchanged his immortal life for a mortal life, but not for ever. And Noah, whose origin was not the same as Adam's, was saved by divine care. For he took and consecrated himself to God. And Abraham, who had children by three wives, not for the indulgence of pleasure, but in the hope, as I think, of multiplying the race at the first, was succeeded by one alone, who was heir of his father's blessings, while the rest were separated from the family; and of the twins who sprang

from him, the younger having won his father's favour and received his prayers, became heir, and the elder served him. For it is the greatest boon to a bad man not to be master of himself.[5]

And this arrangement was prophetical and typical. And that all things belong to the wise, Scripture clearly indicates when it is said, "Because God hath had mercy on me, I have all things."[6] For it teaches that we are to desire one thing, by which are all things, and what is promised is assigned to the worthy. Accordingly, the good man who has become heir of the kingdom, it registers also as fellow-citizen, through divine wisdom, with the righteous of the olden time, who under the law and before the law lived according to law, whose deeds have become laws to us; and again, teaching that the wise man is king, introduces people of a different race, saying to him, "Thou art a king before God among us;"[7] those who were governed obeying the good man of their own accord, from admiration of his virtue.

Now Plato the philosopher, defining the end of happiness, says that it is likeness to God as far as possible; whether concurring with the precept of the law (for great natures that are free of passions somehow hit the mark respecting the truth, as the Pythagorean Philo says in relating the history of Moses), or whether instructed by certain oracles of the time, thirsting as he always was for instruction. For the law says, "Walk after the Lord your God, and keep my commandments."[8] For the law calls assimilation following; and such a following to the utmost of its power assimilates. "Be," says the Lord, "merciful and pitiful, as your heavenly Father is pitiful."[9] Thence also the Stoics have laid down the doctrine, that living agreeably to nature is the end, fitly altering the name of God into nature; since also nature extends to plants, to seeds, to trees, and to stones. It is therefore plainly said, "Bad men do not understand the law; but they who love the law fortify themselves with a wall."[10] "For the wisdom of the clever knows its ways; but the folly of the foolish is in error."[11] "For on whom will I look, but on him who is mild and gentle, and trembleth at my words?" says the prophecy.

We are taught that there are three kinds of friendship: and that of these the first and the best is that which results from virtue, for the love that is founded on reason is firm; that the second and intermediate is by way of recompense, and is social, liberal, and useful for life; for the friendship which is the result of favour is mutual.

---

[1] Matt. v. 19.
[2] Num. xv. 30.
[3] Deut. xxvi. 17, 18.
[4] ἱκέτην has been adopted from Philo, instead of οἰκέτην of the text.

[5] [A noteworthy aphorism.]
[6] Gen. xxxiii. 11.
[7] Gen. xxiii. 6.
[8] Deut. xiii. 4.
[9] Luke vi. 36.
[10] Prov. xxviii. 4, 5.
[11] Prov. xiv. 8.

And the third and last *we* assert to be that which is founded on intimacy; others, again, that it is that variable and changeable form which rests on pleasure. And Hippodamus the Pythagorean seems to me to describe friendships most admirably: "That founded on knowledge of the gods, that founded on the gifts of men, and that on the pleasures of animals." There is the friendship of a philosopher, — that of a man and that of an animal. For the image of God is really the man who does good, in which also he gets good : as the pilot at once saves, and is saved. Wherefore, when one obtains his request, he does not say to the giver, Thou hast given well, but, Thou hast received well. So he receives who gives, and he gives who receives. "But the righteous pity and show mercy." [1] "But the mild shall be inhabitants of the earth, and the innocent shall be left in it. But the transgressors shall be extirpated from it." [2] And Homer seems to me to have said prophetically of the faithful, "Give to thy friend." And an enemy must be aided, that he may not continue an enemy. For by help good feeling is compacted, and enmity dissolved. "But if there be present readiness of mind, according to what a man hath it is acceptable, and not according to what he hath not : for it is not that there be ease to others, but tribulation to you, but of equality at the present time," and so forth.[3] "He hath dispersed, he hath given to the poor; his righteousness endureth for ever," the Scripture says.[4] For conformity with the image and likeness is not meant of the body (for it were wrong for what is mortal to be made like what is immortal), but in mind and reason, on which fitly the Lord impresses the seal of likeness, both in respect of doing good and of exercising rule. For governments are directed not by corporeal qualities, but by judgments of the mind. For by the counsels of holy men states are managed well, and the household also.

CHAP. XX. — THE TRUE GNOSTIC EXERCISES PATIENCE AND SELF-RESTRAINT.

Endurance also itself forces its way to the divine likeness, reaping as its fruit impassibility through patience, if what is related of Ananias be kept in mind; who belonged to a number, of whom Daniel the prophet, filled with divine faith, was one. Daniel dwelt at Babylon, as Lot at Sodom, and Abraham, who a little after became the friend of God, in the land of Chaldea. The king of the Babylonians let Daniel down into a pit full of wild beasts; the King of all, the faithful Lord, took him up unharmed. Such patience

will the Gnostic, as a Gnostic, possess. He will bless when under trial, like the noble Job; like Jonas, when swallowed up by the whale, he will pray, and faith will restore him to prophesy to the Ninevites; and though shut up with lions, he will tame the wild beasts; though cast into the fire, he will be besprinkled with dew, but not consumed. He will give his testimony by night; he will testify by day; by word, by life, by conduct, he will testify. Dwelling with the Lord,[5] he will continue his familiar friend, sharing the same hearth according to the Spirit; pure in the flesh, pure in heart, sanctified in word. "The world," it is said, "is crucified to him, and he to the world." [6] He, bearing about the cross of the Saviour, will follow the Lord's footsteps, as God, having become holy of holies.

The divine law, then, while keeping in mind all virtue, trains man especially to self-restraint, laying this as the foundation of the virtues; and disciplines us beforehand to the attainment of self-restraint by forbidding us to partake of such things as are by nature fat, as the breed of swine, which is full-fleshed. For such a use is assigned to epicures. It is accordingly said that one of the philosophers, giving the etymology of $\hat{v}_{\text{S}}$ (sow), said that it was θύς, as being fit only for slaughter (θύσιν) and killing; for life was given to this animal for no other purpose than that it might swell in flesh. Similarly, repressing our desires, it forbade partaking of fishes which have neither fins nor scales; for these surpass other fishes in fleshiness and fatness. From this it was, in my opinion, that the mysteries not only prohibited touching certain animals, but also withdrew certain parts of those slain in sacrifice, for reasons which are known to the initiated. If, then, we are to exercise control over the belly, and what is below the belly, it is clear that we have of old heard from the Lord that we are to check lust by the law.

And this will be completely effected, if we unfeignedly condemn what is the fuel of lust : I mean pleasure. Now they say that the idea of it is a gentle and bland excitement, accompanied with some sensation. Enthralled by this, Menelaus, they say, after the capture of Troy, having rushed to put Helen to death, as having been the cause of such calamities, was nevertheless not able to effect it, being subdued by her beauty, which made him think of pleasure. Whence the tragedians, jeering, exclaimed insultingly against him : —

"But thou, when on her breast thou lookedst, thy sword
Didst cast away, and with a kiss the traitress,
Ever-beauteous wretch,[7] thou didst embrace."

1 Prov. xxi. 26.
2 Prov. ii. 21, 22.
3 2 Cor. viii. 12, 13, 14.
4 Ps. cxii. 9.

5 Substituting ὤν for ἐν τῷ Κυρίῳ after σύνοικος.
6 [Gal vi. 14. S.]
7 κύνα, Eurip., *Andromache*, 629.

And again : —

"Was the sword then by beauty blunted?"

And I agree with Antisthenes when he says, 'Could I catch Aphrodite, I would shoot her; for she has destroyed many of our beautiful and good women." And he says that "Love[1] is a vice of nature, and the wretches who fall under its power call the disease a deity." For in these words it is shown that stupid people are overcome from ignorance of pleasure, to which we ought to give no admittance, even though it be called a god, that is, though it be given by God for the necessity of procreation. And Xenophon, expressly calling pleasure a vice, says: "Wretch, what good dost thou know, or what honourable aim hast thou? which does not even wait for the appetite for sweet things, eating before being hungry, drinking before being thirsty; and that thou mayest eat pleasantly, seeking out fine cooks; and that thou mayest drink pleasantly, procuring costly wines; and in summer runnest about seeking snow; and that thou mayest sleep pleasantly, not only providest soft beds, but also supports[2] to the couches." Whence, as Aristo said, "against the whole tetrachord of pleasure, pain, fear, and lust, there is need of much exercise and struggle."

"For it is these, it is these that go through our bowels,
And throw into disorder men's hearts."

"For the minds of those even who are deemed grave, pleasure makes waxen," according to Plato; since "each pleasure and pain nails to the body the soul" of the man, that does not sever and crucify himself from the passions. "He that loses his life," says the Lord, "shall save it;" either giving it up by exposing it to danger for the Lord's sake, as He did for us, or loosing it from fellowship with its habitual life. For if you would loose, and withdraw, and separate (for this is what the cross means) your soul from the delight and pleasure that is in this life, you will possess it, found and resting in the looked-for hope. And this would be the exercise of death, if we would be content with those desires which are measured according to nature alone, which do not pass the limit of those which are in accordance with nature — by going to excess, or going against nature — in which the possibility of sinning arises. "We must therefore put on the panoply of God, that we may be able to stand against the wiles of the devil; since the weapons of our warfare are not carnal, but mighty through God to the pulling down of strongholds, casting down reasonings, and every lofty thing which exalteth itself against the knowledge of God, and bringing every

thought into captivity unto the obedience of Christ,"[3] says the divine apostle. There is need of a man who shall use in a praiseworthy and discriminating manner the things from which passions take their rise, as riches and poverty, honour and dishonour, health and sickness, life and death, toil and pleasure. For, in order that we may treat things, that are different, indifferently, there is need of a great difference in us, as having been previously afflicted with much feebleness, and in the distortion of a bad training and nurture ignorantly indulged ourselves. The simple word, then, of our philosophy declares the passions to be impressions on the soul that is soft and yielding, and, as it were, the signatures of the spiritual powers with whom we have to struggle. For it is the business, in my opinion, of the malificent powers to endeavour to produce somewhat of their own constitution in everything, so as to overcome and make their own those who have renounced them. And it follows, as might be expected, that some are worsted; but in the case of those who engage in the contest with more athletic energy, the powers mentioned above, after carrying on the conflict in all forms, and advancing even as far as the crown wading in gore, decline the battle, and admire the victors.

For of objects that are moved, some are moved by impulse and appearance, as animals; and some by transposition, as inanimate objects. And of things without life, plants, they say, are moved by transposition in order to growth, if we will concede to them that plants are without life. To stones, then, belongs a permanent state. Plants have a nature; and the irrational animals possess impulse and perception, and likewise the two characteristics already specified.[4] But the reasoning faculty, being peculiar to the human soul, ought not to be impelled similarly with the irrational animals, but ought to discriminate appearances, and not to be carried away by them. The powers, then, of which we have spoken hold out beautiful sights, and honours, and adulteries, and pleasures, and such like alluring phantasies before facile spirits; as those who drive away cattle hold out branches to them. Then, having beguiled those incapable of distinguishing the true from the false pleasure, and the fading and meretricious from the holy beauty, they lead them into slavery. And each deceit, by pressing constantly on the spirit, impresses its image on it; and the soul unwittingly carries about the image of the passion, which takes its rise from the bait and our consent.

The adherents of Basilides are in the habit of

---

[1] Ἔρως, Cupid.
[2] Or, "carpets." Xenoph., *Memorabilia*, II. i. 30; The Words of Virtue to Vice.
[3] Eph. vi. 11.
[4] i.e., Permanent state and nature.
[5] [See Epiphan., *Opp.*, ii. 391, ed. Oehler.]

calling the passions appendages : saying that these are in essence certain spirits attached to the rational soul, through some original perturbation and confusion ; and that, again, other bastard and heterogeneous natures of spirits grow on to them, like that of the wolf, the ape, the lion, the goat, whose properties showing themselves around the soul, they say, assimilate the lusts of the soul to the likeness of the animals. For they imitate the actions of those whose properties they bear. And not only are they associated with the impulses and perceptions of the irrational animals, but they affect [1] the motions and the beauties of plants, on account of their bearing also the properties of plants attached to them. They have also the properties of a particular state, as the hardness of steel. But against this dogma we shall argue subsequently, when we treat of the soul. At present this only needs to be pointed out, that man, according to Basilides, preserves the appearance of a wooden horse, according to the poetic myth, embracing as he does in one body a host of such different spirits. Accordingly, Basilides' son himself, Isidorus, in his book, *About the Soul attached to us*, while agreeing in the dogma, as if condemning himself, writes in these words : "For if I persuade any one that the soul is undivided, and that the passions of the wicked are occasioned by the violence of the appendages, the worthless among men will have no slight pretence for saying, ' I was compelled, I was carried away, I did it against my will, I acted unwillingly ;' though he himself led the desire of evil things, and did not fight against the assaults of the appendages. But we must, by acquiring superiority in the rational part, show ourselves masters of the inferior creation in us." For he too lays down the hypothesis of two souls in us, like the Pythagoreans, at whom we shall glance afterwards.

Valentinus too, in a letter to certain people, writes in these very words respecting the appendages : "There is one good, by whose presence [2] is the manifestation, which is by the Son, and by Him alone can the heart become pure, by the expulsion of every evil spirit from the heart : for the multitude of spirits dwelling in it do not suffer it to be pure ; but each of them performs his own deeds, insulting it oft with unseemly lusts. And the heart seems to be treated somewhat like a caravanserai. For the latter has holes and ruts made in it, and is often filled with dung ; men living filthily in it, and taking no care for the place as belonging to others. So fares it with the heart as long as there is no thought taken for it, being unclean, and the abode of many demons. But when the only good Father visits it, it is

sanctified, and gleams with light. And he who possesses such a heart is so blessed, that "he shall see God." [3]

What, then, let them tell us, is the cause of such a soul not being cared for from the beginning? Either that it is not worthy (and somehow a care for it comes to it as from repentance), or it is a saved nature, as he would have it ; and this, of necessity, from the beginning, being cared for by reason of its affinity, afforded no entrance to the impure spirits, unless by being forced and found feeble. For were he to grant that on repentance it preferred what was better, he will say this unwillingly, being what the truth we hold teaches ; namely, that salvation is from a change due to obedience, but not from nature. For as the exhalations which arise from the earth, and from marshes, gather into mists and cloudy masses ; so the vapours of fleshly lusts bring on the soul an evil condition, scattering about the idols of pleasure before the soul. Accordingly they spread darkness over the light of intelligence, the spirit attracting the exhalations that arise from lust, and thickening the masses of the passions by persistency in pleasures. Gold is not taken from the earth in the lump, but is purified by smelting ; then, when made pure, it is called gold, the earth being purified. For "Ask, and it shall be given you," [4] it is said to those who are able of themselves to choose what is best. And how we say that the powers of the devil, and the unclean spirits, sow into the sinner's soul, requires no more words from me, on adducing as a witness the apostolic Barnabas (and he was one of the seventy, [5] and a fellow-worker of Paul), who speaks in these words : "Before we believed in God, the dwelling-place of our heart was unstable, truly a temple built with hands. For it was full of idolatry, and was a house of demons, through doing what was opposed to God." [6]

He says, then, that sinners exercise activities appropriate to demons ; but he does not say that the spirits themselves dwell in the soul of the unbeliever. Wherefore he also adds, "See that the temple of the Lord be gloriously built. Learn, having received remission of sins ; and having set our hope on the Name, let us become new, created again from the beginning." For what he says is not that demons are driven out of us, but that the sins which like them we commit before believing are remitted. Rightly thus he puts in opposition what follows : "Wherefore God truly dwells in our home. He dwells in us. How? The word of His faith, the calling of His promise, the wisdom of His statutes, the

---

[1] Or, vie with.
[2] παρουσιᾳ substituted by Grabe for παῤῥησιᾳ.

[3] Matt. v. 8. [On the Beatitudes, see book iv. cap. 6, *infra*.]
[4] Matt. vii. 7.
[5] [See note, book ii. cap. 7, p. 352, *supra*.]
[6] Barnabas, *Epist.*, cap. xvi. vol. i. p. 147.

commandments of His communication, [dwell in us]."

"I know that I have come upon a heresy; and its chief was wont to say that he fought with pleasure by pleasure, this worthy Gnostic advancing on pleasure in feigned combat, for he said he was a Gnostic; since he said it was no great thing for a man that had not tried pleasure to abstain from it, but for one who had mixed in it not to be overcome [was something]; and that therefore by means of it he trained himself in it. The wretched man knew not that he was deceiving himself by the artfulness of voluptuousness. To this opinion, then, manifestly Aristippus the Cyrenian adhered — that of the sophist who boasted of the truth. Accordingly, when reproached for continually cohabiting with the Corinthian courtezan, he said, "I possess Lais, and am not possessed by her."

Such also are those who say that they follow Nicolaus, quoting an adage of the man, which they pervert,[1] "that the flesh must be abused." But the worthy man showed that it was necessary to check pleasures and lusts, and by such training to waste away the impulses and propensities of the flesh. But they, abandoning themselves to pleasure like goats, as if insulting the body, lead a life of self-indulgence; not knowing that the body is wasted, being by nature subject to dissolution; while their soul is buried in the mire of vice; following as they do the teaching of pleasure itself, not of the apostolic man. For in what do they differ from Sardanapalus, whose life is shown in the epigram : —

> "I have what I ate — what I enjoyed wantonly;
> And the pleasures I felt in love. But those
> Many objects of happiness are left,
> For I too am dust, who ruled great Ninus."

For the feeling of pleasure is not at all a necessity, but the accompaniment of certain natural needs — hunger, thirst, cold, marriage. If, then, it were possible to drink without it, or take food, or beget children, no other need of it could be shown. For pleasure is neither a function, nor a state, nor any part of us; but has been introduced into life as an auxiliary, as they say salt was to season food. But when it casts off restraint and rules the house, it generates first concupiscence, which is an irrational propension and impulse towards that which gratifies it; and it induced Epicurus to lay down pleasure as the aim of the philosopher. Accordingly he deifies a sound condition of body, and the certain hope respecting it. For what else is luxury than the voluptuous gluttony and the superfluous abundance of those who are abandoned to self-indulgence? Diogenes writes significantly in a tragedy : —

> "Who to the pleasures of effeminate
> And filthy luxury attached in heart,
> Wish not to undergo the slightest toil."

And what follows, expressed indeed in **foul** language, but in a manner worthy of the voluptuaries.

Wherefore the divine law appears to me necessarily to menace with fear, that, by caution and attention, the philosopher may acquire and retain absence of anxiety, continuing without fall and without sin in all things. For peace and freedom are not otherwise won, than by ceaseless and unyielding struggles with our lusts. For these stout and Olympic antagonists are keener than wasps, so to speak; and Pleasure especially, not by day only, but by night, is in dreams with witchcraft ensnaringly plotting and biting. How, then, can the Greeks any more be right in running down the law, when they themselves teach that Pleasure is the slave of fear? Socrates accordingly bids "people guard against enticements to eat when they are not hungry, and to drink when not thirsty, and the glances and kisses of the fair, as fitted to inject a deadlier poison than that of scorpions and spiders." And Antisthenes chose rather "*to be demented than delighted.*" And the Theban Crates says : —

> "Master these, exulting in the disposition of the soul,
> Vanquished neither by gold nor by languishing love,
> Nor are they any longer attendants to the wanton."

And at length infers : —

> "Those, unenslaved and unbended by servile Pleasure,
> Love the immortal kingdom and freedom."

He writes expressly, in other words, "that the stop[2] to the unbridled propensity to amorousness is hunger or a halter."

And the comic poets attest, while they depreciate the teaching of Zeno the Stoic, to be to the following effect : —

> "For he philosophizes a vain philosophy :
> He teaches to want food, and gets pupils
> One loaf, and for seasoning a dry fig, and to **drink** water."

All these, then, are not ashamed clearly to confess the advantage which accrues from caution. And the wisdom which is true and not contrary to reason, trusting not in mere words and oracular utterances, but in invulnerable armour of defence and energetic mysteries, and devoting itself to divine commands, and exercise, and practice, receives a divine power according to its inspiration from the Word.

---

[1] [Clement does not credit the apostasy of the deacon Nicolas (Acts vi. 5), though others of the Fathers surrender him to the Nicolaitans. See book iii. cap. iv. *infra*.]

[2] κατάπαυσμα (in Theodoret), for which the text reads κατάπλασμα.

Already, then, the ægis of the poetic Jove is described as

"Dreadful, crowned all around by Terror,
    And on it Strife and Prowess, and chilling Rout;
    On it, too, the Gorgon's head, dread monster,
    Terrible, dire, the sign of Ægis-bearing Jove." [1]

But to those, who are able rightly to understand salvation, I know not what will appear dearer than the gravity of the Law, and Reverence, which is its daughter. For when one is said to pitch too high, as also the Lord says, with reference to certain ; so that some of those whose desires are towards Him may not sing out of pitch and tune, I do not understand it as pitching too high in reality, but only as spoken with reference to such as will not take up the divine yoke. For to those, who are unstrung and feeble, what is medium seems too high ; and to those, who are unrighteous, what befalls them seems severe justice. For those, who, on account of the favour they entertain for sins, are prone to pardon, suppose truth to be harshness, and severity to be savageness, and him who does not sin with them, and is not dragged with them, to be pitiless. Tragedy writes therefore well of Pluto : —

"And to what sort of a deity wilt thou come, [2] dost thou ask,
    Who knows neither clemency nor favour,
    But loves bare justice alone."

For although you are not yet able to do the things enjoined by the Law, yet, considering that the noblest examples are set before us in it, we are able to nourish and increase the love of liberty ; and so we shall profit more eagerly as far as we can, inviting some things, imitating some things, and fearing others. For thus the righteous of the olden time, who lived according to the law, "were not from a storied oak, or from a rock ; " because they wish to philosophize truly, took and devoted themselves entirely to God, and were classified under faith. Zeno said well of the Indians, that he would rather have seen one Indian roasted, than have learned the whole of the arguments about bearing pain. But we have exhibited before our eyes every day abundant sources of martyrs that are burnt, impaled, beheaded. All these the fear inspired by the law, — leading as a pædagogue to Christ, trained so as to manifest their piety by their blood. "God stood in the congregation of the gods ; He judgeth in the midst of the gods." [3] Who are they ? Those that are superior to Pleasure, who rise above the passions, who know what they do — the Gnostics, who are greater than the world.

"I said, Ye are Gods ; and all sons of the Highest." To whom speaks the Lord ? To those who reject as far as possible all that is of man. And the apostle says, "For ye are not any longer in the flesh, but in the Spirit." [5] And again he says, "Though in the flesh, we do not war after the flesh." [6] "For flesh and blood cannot inherit the kingdom of God, neither doth corruption inherit incorruption." [7] "Lo, ye shall die like men," the Spirit has said, confuting us.

We must then exercise ourselves in taking care about those things which fall under the power of the passions, fleeing like those who are truly philosophers such articles of food as excite lust, and dissolute licentiousness in chambering and luxury ; and the sensations that tend to luxury, which are a solid reward to others, must no longer be so to us. For God's greatest gift is self-restraint. For He Himself has said, "I will never leave thee, nor forsake thee," [8] as having judged thee worthy according to the true election. Thus, then, while we attempt piously to advance, we shall have put on us the mild yoke of the Lord from faith to faith, one charioteer driving each of us onward to salvation, that the meet fruit of beatitude may be won. "*Exercise is*" according to Hippocrates of Cos, "*not only the health of the body, but of the soul — fearlessness of labours — a ravenous appetite for food.*"

CHAP. XXI. — OPINIONS OF VARIOUS PHILOSOPHERS ON THE CHIEF GOOD.

Epicurus, in placing happiness in not being hungry, or thirsty, or cold, uttered that godlike word, saying impiously that he would fight in these points even with Father Jove ; teaching, as if it were the case of pigs that live in filth and not that of rational philosophers, that happiness was victory. For of those that are ruled by pleasure are the Cyrenaics and Epicurus ; for these expressly said that to live pleasantly was the chief end, and that pleasure was the only perfect good. Epicurus also says that the removal of pain is pleasure ; and says that that is to be preferred, which first attracts from itself to itself, being, that is, wholly in motion. Dinomachus and Callipho said that the chief end was for one to do what he could for the attainment and enjoyment of pleasure ; and Hieronymus the Peripatetic said the great end was to live unmolested, and that the only final good was happiness ; and Diodorus likewise, who belonged to the same sect, pronounces the end to be to live undisturbed and well. Epicurus indeed, and the Cyrenaics, say that pleasure is the first duty ; for it is for the sake of pleasure, they say,

---

[1] *Iliad*, v. 739.
[2] After this comes ὡς ἔρωτα, which yields no meaning, and has been variously amended, but not satisfactorily. Most likely some words have dropped out of the text. [The note in ed. Migne, nevertheless, is worth consultation.]
[3] Ps. lxxxii. 1.

[4] Ps. lxxxii. 6.
[5] Rom. viii. 9.
[6] 2 Cor. x. 3.
[7] 1 Cor. xv. 50.
[8] Heb. xiii. 5.

that virtue was introduced, and produced pleasure. According to the followers of Calliphon, virtue was introduced for the sake of pleasure, but that subsequently, on seeing its own beauty, it made itself equally prized with the first principle, that is, pleasure.

But the Aristotelians lay it down, that to live in accordance with virtue is the end, but that neither happiness nor the end is reached by every one who has virtue. For the wise man, vexed and involved in involuntary mischances, and wishing gladly on these accounts to flee from life, is neither fortunate nor happy. For virtue needs time; for that is not acquired in one day which exists [only] in the perfect man; since, as they say, a child is never happy. But human life is a perfect time, and therefore happiness is completed by the three kinds of good things. Neither, then, the poor, nor the mean, nor even the diseased, nor the slave, can be one of them.

Again, on the other hand, Zeno the Stoic thinks the end to be living according to virtue; and, Cleanthes, living agreeably to nature in the right exercise of reason, which he held to consist of the selection of things according to nature. And Antipatrus, his friend, supposes the end to consist in choosing continually and unswervingly the things which are according to nature, and rejecting those contrary to nature. Archedamus, on the other hand, explained the end to be such, that in selecting the greatest and chief things according to nature, it was impossible to overstep it. In addition to these, Panæcius pronounced the end to be, to live according to the means given to us by nature. And finally, Posidonius said that it was to live engaged in contemplating the truth and order of the universe, and forming himself as he best can, nothing influenced by the irrational part of his soul. And some of the later Stoics defined the great end to consist in living agreeably to the constitution of man. Why should I mention Aristo? He said that the end was indifference; but what is indifferent simply abandons the indifferent. Shall I bring forward the opinions of Herillus? Herillus states the end to be to live according to science. For some think that the more recent disciples of the Academy define the end to be, the steady abstraction of the mind to its own impressions. Further, Lycus the Peripatetic used to say that the final end was the true joy of the soul; as Leucimus, that it was the joy it had in what was good. Critolaus, also a Peripatetic, said that it was the perfection of a life flowing rightly according to nature, referring to the perfection accomplished by the three kinds according to tradition.

We must, however, not rest satisfied with these, but endeavour as we best can to adduce the doctrines laid down on the point by the naturalist; for they say that Anaxagoras of Clazomenæ affirmed contemplation and the freedom flowing from it to be the end of life; Heraclitus the Ephesian, complacency. The Pontic Heraclides relates, that Pythagoras taught that the knowledge of the perfection of the numbers [1] was happiness of the soul. The Abderites also teach the existence of an end. Democritus, in his work *On the Chief End*, said it was cheerfulness, which he also called well-being, and often exclaims, "For delight and its absence are the boundary of those who have reached full age;" Hecatæus, that it was sufficiency to one's self; Apollodotus of Cyzicum, that it was delectation; as Nausiphanes, that it was undauntedness,[2] for he said that it was this that was called by Democritus imperturbability. In addition to these still, Diotimus declared the end to be perfection of what is good, which he said was termed well-being. Again, Antisthenes, that it was humility. And those called Annicereans, of the Cyrenaic succession, laid down no definite end for the whole of life; but said that to each action belonged, as its proper end, the pleasure accruing from the action. These Cyrenaics reject Epicurus' definition of pleasure, that is the removal of pain, calling that the condition of a dead man; because we rejoice not only on account of pleasures, but companionships and distinctions; while Epicurus thinks that all joy of the soul arises from previous sensations of the flesh. Metrodorus, in his book *On the Source of Happiness in Ourselves being greater than that which arises from Objects*, says: What else is the good of the soul but the sound state of the flesh, and the sure hope of its continuance?

CHAP. XXII. — PLATO'S OPINION, THAT THE CHIEF GOOD CONSISTS IN ASSIMILATION TO GOD, AND ITS AGREEMENT WITH SCRIPTURE.

Further, Plato the philosopher says that the end is twofold: that which is communicable, and exists first in the ideal forms themselves, which he also calls "the good;" and that which partakes of it, and receives its likeness from it, as is the case in the men who appropriate virtue and true philosophy. Wherefore also Cleanthes, in the second book, *On Pleasure*, says that Socrates everywhere teaches that the just man and the happy are one and the same, and execrated the first man who separated the just from the useful, as having done an impious thing. For those are in truth impious who separate the useful from that which is right according to the law. Plato himself says that happiness (εὐδαι-

---

[1] The text has ἀρετῶν, virtues, for which, in accordance with Pythagoras' well-known opinion, ἀριθμῶν has been substituted from Theodoret.

[2] For καταπληξιν of the text, Heinsius reads ἀκαταπληξιν, which corresponds to the other term ascribed to Democritus — ἀθαμβίην.

μονία) is to possess rightly the dæmon, and that the ruling faculty of the soul is called the dæmon ; and he terms happiness (εὐδαιμονία) the most perfect and complete good. Sometimes he calls it a consistent and harmonious life, sometimes the highest perfection in accordance with virtue ; and this he places in the knowledge of the Good, and in likeness to God, demonstrating likeness to be justice and holiness with wisdom. For is it not thus that some of our writers have understood that man straightway on his creation received what is "according to the image," but that what is according "to the likeness" he will receive afterwards on his perfection ? Now Plato, teaching that the virtuous man shall have this likeness accompanied with humility, explains the following : "He that humbleth himself shall be exalted." [1] He says, accordingly, in *The Laws :* "God indeed, as the ancient saying has it, occupying the beginning, the middle, and the end of all things, goes straight through while He goes round the circumference. And He is always attended by Justice, the avenger of those who revolt from the divine law." You see how he connects fear with the divine law. He adds, therefore : "To which he, who would be happy, cleaving, will follow lowly and beautified." Then, connecting what follows these words, and admonishing by fear, he adds : "What conduct, then, is dear and conformable to God? That which is characterized by one word of old date : *Like will be dear to like*, as to what is in proportion ; but things out of proportion are neither dear to one another, nor to those which are in proportion. And that therefore he that would be dear to God, must, to the best of his power, become such as He is. And in virtue of the same reason, our self-controlling man is dear to God. But he that has no self-control is unlike and diverse." In saying that it was an ancient dogma, he indicates the teaching which had come to him from the law. And having in the *Theatætus* admitted that evils make the circuit of mortal nature and of this spot, he adds : "Wherefore we must try to flee hence as soon as possible. For flight is likeness to God as far as possible. And likeness is to become holy and just with wisdom." Speusippus, the nephew of Plato, says that happiness is a perfect state in those who conduct themselves in accordance with nature, or the state of the good : for which condition all men have a desire, but the good only attained to quietude ; consequently the virtues are the authors of happiness. And Xenocrates the Chalcedonian defines happiness to be the possession of virtue, strictly so called, and of the power subservient to it. Then he clearly says, that the seat in which it resides is the soul ; that by which it is effected, the vir-

tues ; and that of these as parts are formed praiseworthy actions, good habits and dispositions, and motions, and relations ; and that corporeal and external objects are not without these. For Polemo, the disciple of Xenocrates, seems of the opinion that happiness is sufficiency of all good things, or of the most and greatest. He lays down the doctrine, then, that happiness never exists without virtue ; and that virtue, apart from corporeal and external objects, is sufficient for happiness. Let these things be so. The contradictions to the opinions specified shall be adduced in due time. But on us it is incumbent to reach the unaccomplished end, obeying the commands — that is, God — and living according to them, irreproachably and intelligently, through knowledge of the divine will ; and assimilation as far as possible in accordance with right reason is the end, and restoration to perfect adoption by the Son, which ever glorifies the Father by the great High Priest who has deigned to call us brethren and fellow-heirs. And the apostle, succinctly describing the end, writes in the Epistle to the Romans : "But now, being made free from sin, and become servants to God, ye have your fruit unto holiness, and the end everlasting life." [2] And viewing the hope as twofold — that which is expected, and that which has been received — he now teaches the end to be the restitution of the hope. "For patience," he says, "worketh experience, and experience hope : and hope maketh not ashamed ; because the love of God is shed abroad in our hearts by the Holy Spirit that is given to us." [3] On account of which love and the restoration to hope, he says, in another place, "*which rest* is laid up for us." [4] You will find in Ezekiel the like, as follows : "The soul that sinneth, it shall die. And the man who shall be righteous, and shall do judgment and justice, who has not eaten on the mountains, nor lifted his eyes to the idols of the house of Israel, and hath not defiled his neighbour's wife, and hath not approached to a woman in the time of her uncleanness (for he does not wish the seed of man to be dishonoured), and will not injure a man ; will restore the debtor's pledge, and will not take usury ; will turn away his hand from wrong ; will do true judgment between a man and his neighbour ; will walk in my ordinances, and keep my commandments, so as to do the truth ; he is righteous, he shall surely live, saith Adonai the Lord." [5] Isaiah too, in exhorting him that hath not believed to gravity of life, and the Gnostic to attention, proving that man's virtue and God's are not the same, speaks thus : "Seek the Lord, and on finding Him call on Him. And when

---

[1] Luke xiv. 11.

[2] Rom. vi 22.
[3] Rom. v. 4, 5.
[4] Probably Heb. iv. 8, 9.
[5] Ezek. xviii. 4–9.

He shall draw near to you, let the wicked forsake his ways, and the unrighteous man his ways; and let him return to the Lord, and he shall obtain mercy," down to "and your thoughts from my thoughts."[1] "We," then, according to the noble apostle, "wait for the hope of righteousness by faith. For in Christ neither circumcision availeth anything, nor uncircumcision, but faith which worketh by love."[2] And we desire that every one of you show the same diligence to the full assurance of hope," down to "made an high priest for ever, after the order of Melchizedek."[3] Similarly with Paul "the All-virtuous Wisdom" says, "He that heareth me shall dwell trusting in hope."[4] For the restoration of hope is called by the same term "hope." To the expression "will dwell" it has most beautifully added "trusting," showing that such an one has obtained rest, having received the hope for which he hoped. Wherefore also it is added, "and shall be quiet, without fear of any evil." And openly and expressly the apostle, in the first Epistle to the Corinthians, says, "Be ye followers of me, as also I am of Christ,"[5] in order that that may take place. If ye are of me, and I am of Christ, then ye are imitators of Christ, and Christ of God. *Assimilation to God, then, so that as far as possible a man becomes righteous and holy with wisdom,* he lays down as the aim of faith, and the end to be that restitution of the promise which is effected by faith. From these doctrines gush the fountains, which we specified above, of those who have dogmatized about "the end." But of these enough.

CHAP. XXIII. — ON MARRIAGE.

Since pleasure and lust seem to fall under marriage, it must also be treated of. Marriage is the first conjunction of man and woman for the procreation of legitimate children.[6] Accordingly Menander the comic poet says: —

"For the begetting of legitimate children,
　I give thee my daughter."

We ask if we ought to marry; which is one of the points, which are said to be relative. For some must marry, and a man must be in some condition, and he must marry some one in some condition. For every one is not to marry, nor always. But there is a time in which it is suitable, and a person for whom it is suitable, and an age up to which it is suitable. Neither ought every one to take a wife, nor is it every woman one is to take, nor always, nor in every

way, nor inconsiderately. But only he who is in certain circumstances, and such an one and at such time as is requisite, and for the sake of children, and one who is in every respect similar, and who does not by force or compulsion love the husband who loves her. Hence Abraham, regarding his wife as a sister, says, "She is my sister by my father, but not by my mother; and she became my wife,"[7] teaching us that children of the same mothers ought not to enter into matrimony. Let us briefly follow the history. Plato ranks marriage among outward good things, providing for the perpetuity of our race, and handing down as a torch a certain perpetuity to children's children. Democritus repudiates marriage and the procreation of children, on account of the many annoyances thence arising, and abstractions from more necessary things. Epicurus agrees, and those who place good in pleasure, and in the absence of trouble and pain. According to the opinion of the Stoics, marriage and the rearing of children are a thing indifferent; and according to the Peripatetics, a good. In a word, these, following out their dogmas in words, became enslaved to pleasures; some using concubines, some mistresses, and the most youths. And that wise quaternion in the garden with a mistress, honoured pleasure by their acts. Those, then, will not escape the curse of yoking an ass with an ox, who, judging certain things not to suit them, command others to do them, or the reverse. This Scripture has briefly showed, when it says, "What thou hatest, thou shalt not do to another."[8]

But they who approve of marriage say, Nature has adapted us for marriage, as is evident from the structure of our bodies, which are male and female. And they constantly proclaim that command, "Increase and replenish."[9] And though this is the case, yet it seems to them shameful that man, created by God, should be more licentious than the irrational creatures, which do not mix with many licentiously, but with one of the same species, such as pigeons and ringdoves,[10] and creatures like them. Furthermore, they say, "The childless man fails in the perfection which is according to nature, not having substituted his proper successor in his place. For he is perfect that has produced from himself his like, or rather, when he sees that he has produced the same; that is, when that which is begotten attains to the same nature with him who begat." Therefore we must by all means marry, both for our country's sake,

---

[1] Isa. lv. 6, 7, 9.
[2] Gal. v. 5, 6.
[3] Heb. vi. 11-20.
[4] Prov. i. 33.
[5] 1 Cor. xi. 1.
[6] [He places the essence of marriage in the chaste consummation itself, the first after lawful nuptials. Such is the force of this definition, which the note in ed. Migne misrepresents, as if it were a denial that *second* nuptials are marriage.]

[7] Gen. xx. 12.
[8] Tob. iv. 15.
[9] Gen. i. 28.
[10] [The offering of the purification has a beautiful regard to the example of the turtle-dove; and the marriage-ring may have been suggested by the ringdove, a symbol of constancy in nature.]

for the succession of children, and as far as we are concerned, the perfection of the world; since the poets also pity a marriage half-perfect and childless, but pronounce the fruitful one happy. But it is the diseases of the body that principally show marriage to be necessary. For a wife's care and the assiduity of her constancy appear to exceed the endurance of all other relations and friends, as much as to excel them in sympathy; and most of all, she takes kindly to patient watching. And in truth, according to Scripture, she is a needful help.[1] The comic poet then, Menander, while running down marriage, and yet alleging on the other side its advantages, replies to one who had said:—

"I am averse to the thing,
   For you take it awkwardly."

Then he adds:—

"You see the hardships and the things which annoy you
       in it.
   But you do not look on the advantages."

And so forth.

Now marriage is a help in the case of those advanced in years, by furnishing a spouse to take care of one, and by rearing children of her to nourish one's old age.

"For to a man after death his children bring renown,
   Just as corks bear the net,
   Saving the fishing-line from the deep."[2]

according to the tragic poet Sophocles.

Legislators, moreover, do not allow those who are unmarried to discharge the highest magisterial offices. For instance, the legislator of the Spartans imposed a fine not on bachelorhood only, but on monogamy,[3] and late marriage, and single life. And the renowned Plato orders the man who has not married to pay a wife's maintenance into the public treasury, and to give to the magistrates a suitable sum of money as expenses. For if they shall not beget children, not having married, they produce, as far as in them lies, a scarcity of men, and dissolve states and the world that is composed of them, impiously doing away with divine generation. It is also unmanly and weak to shun living with a wife and children. For of that of which the loss is an evil, the possession is by all means a good; and this is the case with the rest of things. But the loss of children is, they say, among the chiefest evils: the possession of children is consequently a good thing; and if it be so, so also is marriage. It is said:—

"Without a father there never could be a child,
   And without a mother conception of a child could not
      be.
   Marriage makes a father, as a husband a mother."[4]

Accordingly Homer makes a thing to be earnestly prayed for:—

"A husband and a house;"

yet not simply, but along with good agreement. For the marriage of other people is an agreement for indulgence; but that of philosophers leads to that agreement which is in accordance with reason, bidding wives adorn themselves not in outward appearance, but in character; and enjoining husbands not to treat their wedded wives as mistresses, making corporeal wantonness their aim; but to take advantage of marriage for help in the whole of life, and for the best self-restraint.

Far more excellent, in my opinion, than the seeds of wheat and barley that are sown at appropriate seasons, is man that is sown, for whom all things grow; and those seeds temperate husbandmen ever sow. Every foul and polluting practice must therefore be purged away from marriage; that the intercourse of the irrational animals may not be cast in our teeth, as more accordant with nature than human conjunction in procreation. Some of these, it must be granted, desist at the time in which they are directed, leaving creation to the working of Providence.

By the tragedians, Polyxena, though being murdered, is described nevertheless as having, when dying, taken great care to fall decently,—

"Concealing what ought to be hid from the eyes of
       men."

Marriage to her was a calamity. To be subjected, then, to the passions, and to yield to them, is the extremest slavery; as to keep them in subjection is the only liberty. The divine Scripture accordingly says, that those who have transgressed the commandments are sold to strangers, that is, to sins alien to nature, till they return and repent. Marriage, then, as a sacred image, must be kept pure from those things which defile it.[5] We are to rise from our slumbers with the Lord, and retire to sleep with thanksgiving and prayer,—

"Both when you sleep, and when the holy light comes,"

confessing the Lord in our whole life; possessing piety in the soul, and extending self-control to the body. For it is pleasing to God to lead decorum from the tongue to our actions. Filthy speech is the way to effrontery; and the end of both is filthy conduct.

---

[1] Gen. ii. 18. [A beautiful tribute to the true wife.]
[2] The corrections of Stanley on these lines have been adopted. They occur in the *Choephoræ* of Æschylus, 503, but may have been found in Sophocles, as the tragic poets borrowed from one another.
[3] i.e., not entering into a second marriage after a wife's death. But instead of μονογαμίου some read κακογαμίου — bad marriage.

[4] [To be a *mother*, indeed, one must be first a *wife*: the woman who has a child out of wedlock is not entitled to this holy name.]
[5] [A holy marriage, as here so beautifully defined, was something wholly unknown to Roman and Greek civilization. Here we find the Christian family established.]

Now that the Scripture counsels marriage, and allows no release from the union, is expressly contained in the law, "Thou shalt not put away thy wife, except for the cause of fornication;" and it regards as fornication, the marriage of those separated while the other is alive. Not to deck and adorn herself beyond what is becoming, renders a wife free of calumnious suspicion, while she devotes herself assiduously to prayers and supplications; avoiding frequent departures from the house, and shutting herself up as far as possible from the view of all not related to her, and deeming housekeeping of more consequence than impertinent trifling. "He that taketh a woman that has been put away," it is said, "committeth adultery; and if one puts away his wife, he makes her an adulteress,"[1] that is, compels her to commit adultery. And not only is he who puts her away guilty of this, but he who takes her, by giving to the woman the opportunity of sinning; for did he not take her, she would return to her husband. What, then, is the law?[2] In order to check the impetuosity of the passions, it commands the adulteress to be put to death, on being convicted of this; and if of priestly family, to be committed to the flames.[3] And the adulterer also is stoned to death, but not in the same place, that not even their death may be in common. And the law is not at variance with the Gospel, but agrees with it. How should it be otherwise, one Lord being the author of both? She who has committed fornication liveth in sin, and is dead to the commandments; but she who has repented, being as it were born again by the change in her life, has a regeneration of life; the old harlot being dead, and she who has been regenerated by repentance having come back again to life. The Spirit testifies to what has been said by Ezekiel, declaring, "I desire not the death of the sinner, but that he should turn."[4] Now they are stoned to death; as through hardness of heart dead to the law which they believed not. But in the case of a priestess the punishment is increased, because "to whom much is given, from him shall more be required."[5]

Let us conclude this second book of the *Stromata* at this point, on account of the length and number of the chapters.

---

[1] Matt. v. 32, xix. 9.
[2] Lev. xx. 10; Deut. xxii. 22.
[3] Lev. xxi. 9.
[4] Ezek. xxxiii. 11.
[5] Luke xii. 48.

ELUCIDATIONS.

I.

(On the Greeks, cap. i. note 3, p. 347.)

THE admirable comments of Stier on the Greeks, who said to Philip, "*We would see Jesus*,"[6] seem to me vindicated by the history of the Gospel, and by the part which the Greeks were called to take in its propagation. Clement seems to me the man of Providence, who gives rich significance to "the corn of wheat," and its multiplication in Gentile discipleship. And in this I am a convert to Stier's view, against my preconceptions. That the Greeks who were at Jerusalem at the Passover were other than Hellenistic Jews, or Greek proselytes, always seemed to me improbable; but, more and more, I discover a design in this narrative, which seems to me thoroughly sustained by the history of the Gentile churches, which were Greek everywhere originally, and for the use of which the Septuagint had been prepared in the providence of God. To say nothing of the New-Testament Scriptures, the whole symbolic and liturgic system of the early Christians and all the Catholic councils which were Greek in their topography, language, and legislation, confirm the sublime thought which Stier has elucidated. "The Pharisees said, *The world is gone after him;* and there were certain Greeks," etc. So the story is introduced. Jesus is told of their desire to see him; and he answers, "The hour is come that the Son of man should be glorified;" and he goes on to speak of his death as giving life to the world. I feel grateful to Stier for his bold originality in

---

[6] Reden Jesu. St. John xii. 23–26.

treating the subject ; and I trust others will find that it invests the study of the ante-Nicene Fathers with a fresh interest, and throws back from their writings a peculiar reflex light on the New-Testament Scriptures themselves.

II.

(See p. 352, note 9.)

Μόνος ὁ σοφὸς ἐλεύθερος. Stier, in his comments [1] on St. John (viii. 32–36), may well be compared with this chapter of Clement's. The eighteenth chapter of this book must also be kept in view if we would do full justice to the true position of Clement, who recognises nothing in heathen philosophy as true wisdom, save as it flows from God, in Moses, and through the Hebrew Church. That Greek philosophy, so viewed, did lead to Christ, and that this great principle is recognised in the apostolic teachings, seems to me indisputable. This illustrates what has been noted above in Elucidation I.

III.

(See p. 359.)

Clement notes that the false Gnostics rejected the Epistles to Timothy,[2] chiefly because of I Tim. vi. 20. Beausobre (*Histoire du Manichéisme*, tom. ii. p. v.) doubts as to Basilides, whether he is open to this charge ; but Jerome accuses him expressly of rejecting the pastoral epistles, and that to the Hebrews. For this, and Neander's qualifying comment, see Kaye, p. 263. Clement is far from charging Basilides, personally, with an immoral life, or from lending his sanction to impurity ; but a study of the Gnostic sects, with whom our Alexandrian doctor was forced to contend, will show that they were introducing, under the pretence of Christianity, such abominations as made their defeat and absolute overthrow a matter of life and death for the Church. To let *such teachers* be confounded with Christians, was to neutralize the very purpose for which the Church existed. Now, it was in the deadly grapple with such loathsome errorists, that the idea of " Catholic orthodoxy " became so precious to the primitive faithful. They were forced to make even the heathen comprehend the existence of that world-wide confederation of churches already explained,[3] and to exhibit their Scriptural creed and purity of discipline, in the strongest contrast with these pestilent " armies of the aliens," who were neither Gnostics nor Christians indeed, much less Catholic or Orthodox teachers and believers.

Now, if in dealing with counterfeits Clement was obliged to meet them on their own grounds, and defeat them on a plan, at once intelligible to the heathen, and enabling all believers to " fight the good fight of faith" successfully, we must concede that he knew better than we can, what was suited to the Alexandrian schools, their intellect, and their false mysticism. His works were a great safeguard to those who came after him ; though they led to the false system of exposition by which Origen so greatly impaired his services to the Church, and perhaps to other evils, which, in the issue, shook the great patriarchate of Alexandria to its foundations. It is curious to trace the influence of Clement, through Tertullian and St. Augustine, upon the systems of the schoolmen, and again, through them, on the Teutonic reformers. The mysticism of Fénelon as well, may be traced, more than is generally credited, to the old Alexandrian school, which was itself the product of some of the most subtle elements of our nature, sanctified, but not wholly controlled, by the wisdom that is from above. Compare the interminable controversies of the period, in the writings of Fénelon and Bossuet ; and, for a succinct history, see *L'Histoire de l'église de France*, par l'Abbé Guettée, tom. xi. p. 156 *et seqq.*

---

[1] "Words of Jesus." Translation (vol. v. p. 354, ed. Edinburgh, 1856).   [2] *Stromata*, Book ii. cap. xi. p. 358, *supra*.
[3] Quotation from Milman, p. 166, this volume.

THE STROMATA, OR MISCELLANIES.

BOOK III.[1]

CAPUT I.—BASILIDIS SENTENTIAM DE CONTINENTIA ET NUPTIIS REFUTAT.

Ac Valentiniani quidem, qui desuper ex divinis emissionibus deduxere conjugationes, acceptum habent matrimonium : Basilidis autem sectatores, "Cum interrogassent, inquiunt, apostoli, nun sit melius uxorem non ducere, dicunt respondisse Dominum : 'Non omnes capiunt verbum hoc. Sunt enim eunuchi alii a nativitate, alii vero a necessitate.'"[2] Hoc dictum autem sic interpretantur : "Quidam ex quo nati sunt, naturaliter feminam aversantur, qui quidem hoc naturali utentes temperamento, recte faciunt, si uxorem non ducant. Hi, inquiunt, eunuchi sunt ex nativitate. Qui autem sunt a necessitate, ii sunt theatrici exercitatores, qui, gloriæ studio retracti, se continent. Quinetiam qui casu aliquo excisi sunt, eunuchi facti sunt per necessitatem. Qui itaque eunuchi fiunt per necessitatem, non fiunt eunuchi secundum logon, seu rationem. Qui autem regni sempiterni gratia seipsos castrarunt, id ad declinandas, inquiunt, conjugii molestias fecerunt, quod procurandæ rei familiaris onus ac sollicitudinem timerent. Et illud : 'Melius est nubere quam uri,'[3] dicentem Apostolum aiunt velle : Ne animam tuam in ignem injicias, noctu et interdiu resistens, et timens ne a continentia excidas. Nam cum in resistendo occupata fuerit anima, a spe est divisa"—Patienter igitur sustine," inquit his verbis Isidorus in *Moralibus*, "contentiosam mulierem, ne a Dei gratia avellaris ; et cum ignem in semine excreveris, cum

bona ores conscientia. Quando autem, inquit, tua gratiarum actio delapsa fuerit in petitionem, et deinceps steteris, ut tamen labi ac titubare non desinas, duc uxorem. Sin est aliquis juvenis, vel pauper, vel infirmus, et non ei libet logo, seu rationi, convenienter uxorem ducere, is a fratre ne discedat ; dicat : Ingressus sum in sancta, nihil possum pati. Quod si eum suspicio aliqua subeat, dicat : Frater, impone mihi manum, ne peccem ; et confestim tum in mente, tum in corpore opem experietur. Velit modo quod bonum est perficere, et assequetur. Nonnunquam autem ore tenus dicimus : Nolumus peccare ; animus autem noster propendet in pectatum. Qui est ejusmodi, propter metum, quod vult, non facit, ne ei constituatur supplicium. At hominum generi quædam necessaria sunt ac naturalia duntaxat. Quod indumentis egeat, necessarium simul est et naturale : est autem venerea voluptas naturalis, sed non necessaria." Has voces adduxi ad reprehendendos Basilidianos, qui non recte vivunt, ut qui vel peccandi potestatem habeant propter perfectionem, vel omnino quidem natura salvi futuri sint, etsi nunc peccent, quod naturæ dignitate sunt electi. Neque vero primi dogmatum architecti eorumdem perpetrandorum potestatem illis faciunt. Ne ergo Christi nomen suspicientes, et iis, qui sunt in gentibus intemperantissimi, incontinentius viventes, nomini maledictum inurant. "Qui enim sunt ejusmodi, pseudapostoli, operarii dolosi," usque ad illud : "Quorum finis erit secundum opera eorum."[4] Est ergo continentia, corporis despicientia secundum confessionem in Deum ; non solum enim in rebus venereis, sed etiam in aliis, quæ anima perperam concupiscit, non contenta necessariis, versatur continentia. Est autem et in lingua, et in acquirendo, et in utendo, et in concupiscendo continentia. Non docet autem ea solummodo esse temperantes, siquidem præbet nobis temperantiam, ut quæ sit divina potestas et gratia. Dicendum est ergo, quidnam nostris videatur de

---

[1] After much consideration, the Editors have deemed it best to give the whole of this Book in Latin. [In the former Book, Clement has shown, not without a decided leaning to chaste celibacy, that marriage is a holy estate, and consistent with the perfect man in Christ. He now enters upon the refutation of the false-Gnostics and their licentious tenets. Professing a stricter rule to begin with, and despising the ordinances of the Creator, their result was the grossest immorality in practice. The melancholy consequences of an enforced celibacy are, here, all foreseen and foreshown; and this Book, though necessarily offensive to our Christian tastes, is most useful as a commentary upon the history of monasticism, and the celibacy of priests, in the Western churches. The resolution of the Edinburgh editors to give this Book to scholars *only*, in the Latin, is probably wise. I subjoin a succint analysis, in the elucidations.]

[2] Matt. xix. 11. 12.

[3] 1 Cor. vii. 9.

[4] 2 Cor. ix. 13, 15.

eo, quod est propositum. Nos quidem castitatem, et eos, quibus hoc a Deo datum est, beatos decimus : monogamiam autem, et quæ consistit in uno solum matrimonio, honestatem admiramur ; dicentes tamen oportere aliorum misereri, et " alterum alterius onera portare," [1] ne " quis, cum " recte " stare videatur," [2] ipse quoque " cadat." De secundis autem nuptiis : " Si uraris," inquit Apostolus, " jungere matrimonio." [3]

CAPUT II. — CARPOCRATIS ET EPIPHANIS SENTENTIAM DE FEMINARUM COMMUNITATE REFUTAT.

Qui autem a Carpocrate descendunt et Epiphane, censent oportere uxores esse communes ; a quibus contra nomen Christi maximum emanavit probrum. Hic autem Epiphanes, cujus etiam scripta feruntur, filius erat Carpocratis, et matris Alexandriæ nomine, ex patre quidem Alexandrinus, ex matre vero Cephalleneus. Vixit autem solum septemdecim annos, et Samæ, quæ est urbs Cephalleniæ, ut deus est honore affectus. Quo in loco templum ex ingentibus lapidibus, altaria, delubra, museum, ædificatum est et consecratum ; et cum est nova luna, convenientes Cephallenei, diem natalem, quo in deos relatus est Epiphanes, sacrificant, libantque, et convivantur, et hymnos canunt. A patre autem didicit et orbem disciplinarum et Platonis philosophiam. Fuit autem princeps monadicæ [4] cognitionis. A quo etiam profluxit hæresis eorum, qui nunc sunt, Carpocratianorum. Is ergo dicit in libro *De justitia*, " Justitiam Dei esse quamdam cum æqualitate communionem. Æquale quidem certe cœlum undequaque extensum totam terram cingit. Et nox ex æquo stellas omnes ostendit ; et diei auctorem et lucis patrem, solem, Deus ex alto æqualem effudit omnibus, qui possunt videre (illi autem omnes communiter respiciunt), quoniam non discernit divitem vel pauperem vel populi principem, insipientes et sapientes, feminas et masculos, liberos, servos. Sed neque secus facit in brutis. Cum autem omnibus animantibus æque ipsum communem effuderit, bonis et malis justitiam suam confirmat, cum nemo possit plus habere, neque auferre a proximo, ut ipse illius lucem habeat duplicatam. Sol facit omnibus animantibus communia exoriri nutrimenta, communi justitia ex æquo data omnibus : et ad ea, quæ sunt hujusmodi, similiter se habet genus boum, ut boves ; et suum, ut sues, et ovium, ut oves ; et reliqua omnia. Justitia enim in iis apparet esse communitas. Deinde per communitatem omnia similiter secundum sua genera seminantur, et commune nutrimentum editur humi pascentibus jumentis omnibus, et omnibus ex æquo ; ut quod nulla

lege circumscriptum sit, sed ejus, qui donat, jubentis suppeditatione, convenienter justeque adsit omnibus. Sed neque generationi posita est lex, esset enim jamdiu abolita : ex æquo autem seminant et generant, habentia innatam a justitia communionem : ex æquo communiter omnibus oculum ad videndum, creator et pater omnium, sua justitia legem ferens, præbuit, non discernens feminam a masculo, non id quod est rationis particeps, ab experte rationis, et, ut semel dicam, nullum a nullo ; sed æqualitate et communitate visum similiter dividens, uno jussu omnibus est largitus. Leges autem, inquit, hominum, cum ignorationem castigare non possent, contra leges facere docuerunt : legum enim proprietas dissecuit divinæ legis communionem et arrodit ; non intelligens dictum Apostoli dicentis : ' Per legem peccatum cognovi.' Et meum et tuum dicit subiisse per leges, ut quæ non amplius communiter fruantur (sunt enim communia), neque terra, neque possessionibus, sed neque matrimonio. Fecit enim vites communiter omnibus, quæ neque passerem, neque furem abnegant ; et frumentum similiter, et alios fructus. Violata autem communio et æqualitas, genuit furem pecorum et fructuum. Cum ergo Deus communiter omnia fecisset homini, et feminam cum masculo communiter conjunxisset, et omnia similiter animantia conglutinasset, pronuntiavit justitiam, communionem cum æqualitate. Qui autem sic nati sunt, communionem, quæ eorum conciliat generationem, abnegaverunt. Et dicit, si unam ducens habeat, cum omnium possint esse participes, sicut reliqua fecit animantia." Hæc cum his verbis dixisset, subjungit rursus his verbis : " Intensam enim et vehementiorem ingeneravit masculis cupiditatem ad generum perpetuitatem, quam nec lex, nec mos, nec aliquid aliud potest abolere : est enim Dei decretum." Et quomodo amplius hic in nostra examinetur oratione, cum legem et Evangelium per hæc aperte destruat ? Illa enim dicit : " Non mœchaberis." [5] Hoc autem dicit : " Quicunque respicit ad concupiscentiam, jam mœchatus est." [6] Illud enim : " Non concupisces," [7] quod a lege dicitur, ostendit unum esse Deum, qui prædicatur per legem et prophetas et Evangelium. Dicit enim : " Non concupisces uxorem proximi tui." Proximus autem non est Judæus Judæo : frater enim est et eumdem habet Spiritum ; restat ergo, ut propinquum dicat eum qui est alterius gentis. Quomodo autem non propinquus, qui aptus est esse Spiritus particeps ? Non solum enim Hebræorum, sed etiam gentium pater est Abraham. Si autem quæ est adulterata, et qui in eam fornicatus est, capite punitur : [8]

---

1 Gal. vi. 2.
2 1 Cor. x. 12.
3 1 Cor. vii. 9.
4 *Vid.* Irenæum, lib. i. c. 2, p. 51.

5 Ex. xx. 13.
6 Matt. v. 28.
7 Ex. xx. 17.
8 Deut. xxii. 22.

clarum est utique præceptum, quod dicit : " Non concupisces uxorem propinqui tui," loqui de gentibus : ut cum quis secundum legem et ab uxore proximi et a sorore abstinuerit, aperte audiat a Domino : " Ego autem dico, non concupisces." Additio autem hujus particulæ, " ego," majorem præcepti vim ostendit. Quod autem cum Deo bellum gerat Carpocrates, et Epiphanes etiam in eo, qui vulgo jactatur, libro *De justitia*, patet ex eo quod subjungit his verbis : " Hinc ut qui ridiculum dixerit, legislatoris hoc verbum audiendum est : 'Non concupisces :' usque ad id, quod magis ridicule dicit : 'Res proximi tui.' Ipse enim, qui dedit cupiditatem, ut quæ contineret generationem, jubet eam auferre, cum a nullo eam auferat animali. Illud autem : ' Uxorem proximi tui,' quo communionem cogit ad proprietatem, dixit adhuc magis ridicule." Et hæc quidem dogmata constituunt egregii Carpocratiani. Hos dicunt et aliquos alios similium malorum æmulatores, ad cœnas convenientes (neque enim dixerim " agapen" eorum congressionem) [1] viros simul et mulieres, postquam cibis venerem excitantibus se expleverint, lumine amoto, quod eorum fornicatoriam hanc justitiam pudore afficiebat, aversa lucerna, coire quomodo velint, et cum quibus velint : meditatus autem in ejusmodi " agape " communionem, interdiu jam, a quibus velint mulieribus exigere Carpocrateæ (divinæ enim nefas est discere) legis obedientiam. Has leges, ut sentio, ferre opportuit Carpocratem canum et suum et hircorum libidinibus. Mihi autem videtur, Platonem quoque male intellexisse, in *Republica* dicentem, oportere esse communes omnium uxores : ut qui diceret eas quidem, quæ nondum nupserant, esse communes eorum, qui essent petituri, quemadmodum theatrum quoque est commune spectatorum ; esse autem unamquamque uniuscujusque qui præoccupasset, et non amplius communem esse eam quæ nupsisset. Xanthus autem in iis, quæ scribuntur *Magica :* " Coeunt autem," inquit, " magi cum matribus et filiabus : et fas esse aiunt coire cum sororibus, et communes esse uxores, non vi et clam, sed utrisque consentientibus, cum velit alter ducere uxorem alterius." De his et similibus hæresibus existimo Judam prophetice dixisse in epistola : " Similiter quidem hi quoque somniantes " (non enim vigilantes ad veritatem se applicant), usque ad illud : " Et os eorum loquitur superba." [2]

CAPUT III. — QUATENUS PLATO ALIIQUE E VETERIBUS PRÆIVERINT MARCIONITIS ALIISQUE HÆRETICIS, QUI A NUPTIIS IDEO ABSTINENT QUIA CREATURAM MALAM EXISTIMANT ET NASCI HOMINES IN PŒNAM OPINANTUR.

Jam vero si et ipse Plato et Pythagorei, sicut etiam postea Marcionitæ, malam existimarunt esse generationem, longe abfuit, ut communes ipse poneret uxores. Sed Marcionitæ [3] quidem dicunt malam esse naturam, ex mala materia, et a justo factam opifice ac Creatore. Qua quidem ratione nolentes implere mundum, qui factus est a Creatore, volunt abstinere a nuptiis, resistentes suo Creatori, et contendentes ad bonum, qui vocavit : sed non ad eum, qui, ut dicunt, Deus est diversis moribus præditus. Unde cum nihil hic velint relinquere proprium, non sunt ex destinato animi proposito continentes, sed propter odium conceptum adversum eum, qui creavit, nolentes iis uti, quæ ab ipso sunt creata. Sed hi quidem, qui propter impium, quod cum Deo gerunt, bellum, emoti sunt ab iis cogitationibus, quæ sunt secundum naturam, Dei longanimitatem contemnentes et benignitatem, etsi nolunt uxorem ducere, cibis tamen utuntur creatis, et aerem respirant Creatoris, ut qui et ejus sint opera, et in iis, quæ sunt ejus, permaneant, et inauditam ac novam quamdam, ut aiunt, annuntiatam audiunt cognitionem, etiamsi hoc quoque nomine mundi Domino deberent agere gratias, quod hic acceperint Evangelium. Sed adversus eos quidem, cum de principiis tractabimus, accuratissime disseremus. Philosophi autem, quorum mentionem fecimus, a quibus cum malam esse generationem impie didicissent Marcionitæ, tanquam suo dogmate gloriantur, non eam volunt esse natura malam, sed anima, quæ veritatem divulgavit. Animam enim, quam esse divinam fatentur, in hunc mundum deducunt, tanquam in locum supplicii. Oportet autem animas in corpus immissas expiari ex eorum sententia. Non convenit autem amplius hoc dogma Marcionistis, sed iis, qui censent in corpora intrudi, et iis alligari, et quasi ex vase in vas aliud transfundi animas. Adversus quos fuerit aliud dicendi tempus, quando de anima tractabimus. Videtur itaque Heraclitus maledictis insequi generationem : " Quoniam autem," inquit, " nati volunt vivere, et mortes habere, vel potius quiescere ; filios quoque relinquunt, ut mortes fiant." Clarum est autem cum eo convenire Empedoclem quoque dicentem : —

> Deflevi et luxi, insolitum cernens miser orbem.

Et amplius : —

> Mortua nam ex vivis fecit, species commutans.

Et rursus : —

> Hei mihi! quam infelix hominum genus atque misellum
> Litibus ex quantis prognati et planctibus estis ?

Dicit autem Sibylla quoque : —

> Mortales homines, caro qui tantum, et nihil estis ;

Similiter atque poeta, qui scribit : —

> Haud homine infelix tellus mage quidquam alit alma.

---

[1] [Elucidation II.]
[2] Jude 8–17.

Quin etiam Theognis malam ostendit esse generationem, dicens hoc modo : —

> Optima non nasci res est mortalibus ægris,
>
> Nec nitidi solis luce micante frui,
> Extemplo aut natum portas invadere Ditis.

His autem consequentia scribit quoque Euripides, poeta tragicus : —

> Nam nos decebat convenire publice, et
> Deflere natum, quod tot ingreditur mala :
> Ast mortuum, cuique jam quies data est,
> Efferre lætis gratulationibus.

Et rursus similia sic dicit : —

> Quis novit, an vivere quidem siet mori,
> Siet mori autem vivere?

Idem quod hi, videtur Herodotus quoque inducere dicentem Solonem : "O Crœse, quivis homo nihil est aliud quam calamitas." Jam vero ejus de Cleobide et Bitone fabula plane nihil aliud vult, quam vituperare generationem, laudare autem mortem.

Et qualis folii, est hominum generatio talis, ait Homerus. Plato autem in *Cratylo*, Orpheo tribuit eum sermonem, quo anima puniri in corpore dicitur : "Nempe corpus hoc animæ σῆμα," *monumentum*, "quidam esse tradunt : quasi ipsa præsenti in tempore sit sepulta ; atque etiam quia anima per corpus σημαίνει," *significat*, "quæcunque significare potest : iedo σῆμα jure vocari. Videatur mihi præterea Orpheus nomen hoc ob id potissimum imposuisse, quod anima in corpore hoc delictorum luat pœnas." Operæ pretium est autem meminisse etiam eorum, quæ dicit Philolaus. Sic enim dicit hic Pythagoreus : "Testantur autem veteres quoque theologi et vates, ad luenda supplicia animam conjunctam esse corpori, et in eo tanquam in *monumento* esse sepultam." Quin etiam Pindarus de iis, quæ sunt in Eleusine, mysteriis loquens, infert : "Beatus, qui cum illa sub terra viderit communia, novit quidem vitæ finem, novit autem datum Jovis imperium." Et Plato similiter in *Phædone* non veretur hoc modo scribere : "Porro autem hi, qui nobis hæc constituerunt mysteria, non aliquid aliud," usque ad : "Et cum diis habitatione." Quid vero, cum dicit : "Quandiu corpus habuerimus, et anima nostra cum ejusmodi malo admista fuerit, illud, quod desideramus, nunquam satis assequemur?" annon significat generationem esse causam maximorum malorum? Jam vero in *Phædone* quoque testatur : "Evenit enim, ut qui recte philosophantur, non animadvertantur ab aliis in nullam rem aliam suum studium conferre, quam ut emoriantur, et sint mortui." Et rursus : "Ergo hic quoque philosophi anima corpus maxime vilipendit, et ab eo fugit, ipsa autem secum seorsim esse quærit." Nunquid autem consentit cum divino Apostolo, qui dicit : "Infelix ego homo, quis me liberabit a corpore mortis hujus?"[1] nisi forte eorum consensionem, qui trahuntur in vitium, "corpus mortis" dicit tropice. Atque coitum quoque, qui est principium generationis, vel ante Marcionem videtur Plato aversari in primo *De republica :* ubi cum laudasset senectutem, subjungit : "Velim scias, quod quo magis me deficiunt aliæ," nempe corporis, "voluptates, eo magis confabulandi cupiditas, et voluptas, quam ex ea re capio, augetur." Et cum rei venereæ injecta esset mentio : "Bona verba quæso," inquit : "ego vero lubenter isthinc, tanquam ad insano aliquo et agresti domino, effugi." Rursus in *Phædone*, vituperans generationem, dicit : "Quæ ergo de his in arcanis dicitur, hæc est oratio, quod nos homines sumus in custodia aliqua." Et rursus : "Qui autem pie præ cæteris vixisse inveniuntur, hi sunt, qui ex his terrenis locis, tanquam e carcere, soluti atque liberati, ad puram in altioribus locis habitationem transcendunt." Sed tamen quamvis ita se habeat, recte a Deo mundum administrari existimat ; unde dicit : "Non oportet autem seipsum solvere, nec effugere." Et ut paucis dicam, non dedit Marcioni occasionem, ut malam existimaret materiam, cum ipse pie de mundo hæc dixerit : "Ab eo enim, qui ipsum construxit, habet omnia bona : a priori autem deformitate incommoda et injusta omnia, quæ intra cœlum nascuntur, mundus ipse sustinet, et animantibus inserit." Adhuc autem subjungit manifestius : "Cujus quidem defectus est coporea temperatura, priscæ naturæ comes ; nam quiddam valde deforme erat, et ordinis expers, priusquam præsenti ornatu decoraretur." Nihilominus autem in *Legibus* quoque deflet humanum genus, sic dicens : "Dii autem hominum genus laboribus naturæ pressum miserati, remissiones ipsis statuerunt laborum, solemnium videlicet festorum vicissitudines." Et in *Epinomide* persequitur etiam causas, cur sint hominum miserti, et sic dicit : "Ab initio ipsum esse genitum, est grave cuilibet animanti : primum quidem, quod eorum constitutionis sint participes, quæ in utero gestantur ; deinde ipsum nasci, et præterea nutriri et erudiri, per innumerabiles labores universa fiunt, ut omnes dicimus." Quid vero? annon Heraclitus generationem quoque dicit esse mortem? Pythagoras autem similiter atque Socrates in *Gorgia*, cum dicit : "Mors est, quæcunque experrecti videmus : quæcunque autem dormientes, somnus." Sed de his quidem satis. Quando autem tractabimus de principiis, tunc et has repugnantias, quas et innuunt philosophi, et suis dogmatibus decernunt Marcionistæ, considerabimus. Cæterum satis dilucide ostensas esse existimo, externorum alienorumque dogmatum occasiones Marcionem ingrate et indocte accepisse a Platone. Nobis autem procedat sermo de continentia. Dicebamus autem

---

[1] Rom. vii. 24.

Græcos adversus liberorum generationem multa dixisse, incommoda, quæ comitari eam solent, respicientes : quæ cum impie excepissent Marcionitæ, impie fuisse ingratos in Creatorem. Dicit enim tragœdia : —

> Non nascier præstat homines, quam nascier.
> Dein filios acerbis cum coloribus
> Enitor, ast enixa, si stolidi scient,
> Afflictor, intuendo quod servo malos,
> Bonosque perdo. Si bonos servo, tamen

> Mihi miscellum cor timore liquitur.
> Quid hic boni ergo est ? unicam annon sufficit
> Effundere animam, nisi crucieris amplius ?

Et adhuc similiter : —

> Vetus stat mihi persuasio,
> Plantare filios nunquam hominem oportuit,
> Dum cernit ad quot gignimus natos mala.

In his autem, quæ deinceps sequuntur, malorum quoque causam evidenter reducit ad principia, sic dicens : —

> O ! miser natus, malisque obnoxius
> Editus, homo, es, vitæ tuæque miseriam
> Hinc inchoasti : cœpit æther omnibus
> Spiramen unde alens tradere mortalibus ;
> Mortalis ægre ne feras mortalia.

Rursus autem his similia tradit : —

> Mortalium omnium beatus non fuit
> Quisquam, molestia et nemo carens fuit.

Et deinde rursus : —

> Heu ! quanta, quotque hominibus eveniunt mala,
> Quam varia, quorum terminus nullus datur.

Et adhuc similiter : —

> Nemo beatus semper est mortalium.

Hac itaque ratione dicunt etiam Pythagoreos abstinere a rebus venereis. Mihi autem contra videntur uxores quidem ducere, ut liberos suscipiant, velle autem a venerea voluptate se continere post susceptos liberos. Proinde mystice uti fabis prohibent, non quod sit legumen flatum excitans, et concoctu difficile, et somnia efficiat turbulenta ; neque quod hominis capiti sit similis, ut vult ille versiculus : —

Idem est namque fabam atque caput corrodere patris ;

sed potius quod fabæ, si comedantur, steriles efficiant mulieres. Theophrastus quidem certe in quinto libro *De causis plantarum*, fabarum siliquas, si ponantur ad radices arborum quæ nuper sunt plantatæ, refert plantas exsiccare. Quinetiam gallinæ domesticæ, quæ eas assidue comedunt, efficiuntur steriles.

CAPUT IV. — QUIBUS PRÆTEXTIBUS UTANTUR HÆRETICI AD OMNIS GENERIS LICENTIAM ET LIBIDINEM EXERCENDAM.

Ex iis autem, qui ab hæresi ducuntur, Marcionis quidem Pontici fecimus mentionem, qui propter certamen, quod adversus Creatorem suscepit, mundanarum rerum usum recusat.

Ei autem continentiæ causa est, si modo est ea dicenda continentia, ipse Creator, cui se adversari existimans gigas iste cum Deo pugnans, est invitus continens, dum in creationem et Dei opus invehitur. Quod si usurpent vocem Domini, qui dicit Philippo : " Sine mortuos sepelire mortuos suos, tu autem sequere me : " [1] at illud considerent, quod similem carnis formationem fert quoque Philippus, non habens cadaver pollutum. Quomodo ergo cum carnem haberet, non habuit cadaver ? Quoniam surrexit ex monumento, Domino ejus vitia morte afficiente, vixit autem Christo. Meminimus autem nefariæ quoque ex Carpocratis sententia mulierum communionis. Cum autem de dicto Nicolai loqueremur, illud prætermisimus : Cum formosam, aiunt, haberet uxorem, et post Servatoris assumptionem ei fuisset ab apostolis exprobrata zelotypia, in medium adducta muliere, permisit cui vellet eam nubere. Aiunt enim hanc actionem illi voci consentaneam, quæ dicit, quod " carne abuti oporteat." Proinde ejus factum et dictum absolute et inconsiderate sequentes, qui ejus hæresim persequuntur, impudenter effuseque fornicantur. Ego autem audio Nicolaum quidem nulla unquam alia, quam ea, quæ ei nupserat, uxore usum esse ; et ex illius liberis, filias quidem consenuisse virgines, filium autem permansisse incorruptum. Quæ cum ita se habeant, vitii erat depulsio atque expurgatio, in medium apostolorum circumactio uxoris, cujus dicebatur laborare zelotypia : et continentia a voluptatibus, quæ magno studio parari solent, docebat illud, " abuti carne," hoc est, exercere carnem. Neque enim, ut existimo, volebant, convenienter Domini præcepto, " duobus dominis servire," [2] voluptati et Deo. Dicunt itaque Matthiam [3] quoque sic docuisse : " Cum carne quidem pugnare, et ea uti, nihil ei impudicum largiendo ad voluptatem ; augere autem animam per fidem et cognitionem." Sunt autem, qui etiam publicam venerem pronuntiant mysticam communionem ; et sic ipsum nomen contumelia afficiunt. Sicut enim operari eum dicimus, tum qui malum aliquod facit, tum etiam qui bonum, idem nomen utrique tribuentes ; haud aliter " communio " usurpari solet ; nam bona quidem est in communicatione tum pecuniæ, tum nutrimenti et vestitus : illi autem quamlibet veneream conjunctionem impie vocaverunt " communionem." Dicunt itaque ex iis quemdam, cum ad nostram virginem vultu formosam accessisset, dixisse : Scriptum est : " Da omni te petenti : " [4] illam autem honeste admodum respondisse, ut quæ non intelligeret hominis petulantiam : At tu matrem conveni de matrimonio. O impietatem ! etiam voces Domini

---

[1] Matt. viii. 22 ; Luke ix. 60.
[2] Matt. vi. 24 ; Luke xvi. 13.
[3] [Elucidation IV.]
[4] Matt. v. 24 ; Luke vi. 30.

ementiuntur isti intemperantiæ communicatores, fratresque libidinis, non solum probrum philosophiæ, sed etiam totius vitæ; qui veritatem, quantum in eis situm est, adulterant ac corrumpunt, vel potius defodiunt; homines infelicissimi carnalem concubitus communionem consecrant, et hanc ipsos putant ad regnum Dei perducere. Ad lupanaria ergo deducit hæc communio, et cum eis communicaverint sues et hirci, maximaque apud illos in spe fuerint meretrices, quæ in prostibulis præsto sunt, et volentes omnes admittunt. "Vos autem non sic Christum didicistis, siquidem ipsum audiistis, et in eo docti estis, quemadmodum est veritas in Christo Jesu, ut deponatis quæ sunt secundum veterem conversationem, veterem hominem, qui corrumpitur secundum desideria deceptionis. Renovamini autem spiritu mentis vestræ, et induatis novum hominem, qui creatus est secundum Deum in justitia et sanctitate veritatis,"[1] ad Dei similitudinem. "Efficimini ergo Dei imitatores, ut filii dilecti, et ambulate in dilectione, sicut Christus quoque dilexit nos, et tradidit seipsum pro nobis oblationem et hostiam Deo in odorem suavitatis. Fornicatio autem, et omnis immunditia, vel avaritia, ne nominetur quidem in vobis, sicut decet sanctos, et turpitudo, et stultiloquium."[2] Etenim docens Apostolus meditari vel ipsa voce esse castos, scribit: "Hoc enim scitote, quod omnis fornicator," et cætera, usque ad illud: "Magis autem arguite."[3] Effluxit autem eis dogma ex quodam apocrypho libro. Atque adeo afferam dictionem, quæ mater eorum intemperantiæ et origo est: et sive ipsi hujus libri scriptores se fateantur, en eorum vecordiam, licet Deo eum falso ascribant libidinis intemperantia ducti: sive ab aliis, eos perverse audientes, hoc præclarum dogma acceperint, sic porro se habent ejus verba: "Unum erant omnia: postquam autem ejus unitati visum est non esse solam, exiit ab eo inspiratio, et cum ea iniit communionem, et fecit dilectum. Exhinc autem egressa est ab ipso inspiratio, cum qua cum communionem iniisset, fecit potestates, quæ nec possunt videri nec audiri," usque ad illud, "unamquamque in nomine proprio." Si enim hi quoque, sicut Valentiniani, spiritales posuissent communiones, suscepisset forte aliquis eorum opinionem: carnalis autem libidinis communionem ad sanctam inducere prophetiam, est ejus qui desperat salutem. Talia etiam statuunt Prodici quoque asseclæ, qui seipsos falso nomine vocant Gnosticos: seipsos quidem dicentes esse natura filios primi Dei; ea vero nobilitate et libertate abutentes, vivunt ut volunt; volunt autem libidinose; se nulla re teneri arbitrati, ut "domini sabbati," et qui sint quovis genere superiores, filii regales. Regi autem, inquiunt, lex scripta

non est. Primum quidem, quod non faciant omnia quæ volunt: multa enim eos prohibebunt, etsi cupiant et conentur. Quinetiam quæ faciunt, non faciunt ut reges, sed ut mastigiæ: clanculum enim committunt adulteria, timentes ne deprehendantur, et vitantes ne condemnntur, et metuentes ne supplicio afficiantur. Quomodo etiam res est libera, intemperantia et turpis sermo? "Omnis enim, qui peccat, est servus," inquit Apostolus.[4] Sed quomodo vitiam ex Deo instituit, qui seipsum præbuit dedititium cuivis concupiscentiæ? cum dixerit Dominus: "Ego autem dico: Ne concupiscas." Vultne autem aliquis sua sponte peccare, et decernere adulteria esse committenda, voluptatibusque et deliciis se explendum, et aliorum violanda matrimonia, cum aliorum etiam, qui inviti peccant, misereamur? Quod si in externum mundum venerint, qui in alieno non fuerint fideles, verum non habebunt. Afficit autem hospes aliquis cives contumelia, et eis injuriam facit; et non potius ut peregrinus, utens necessariis, vivit, cives non offendens? Quomodo autem, cum eadem faciant, ac ii, quos gentes odio habent, quod legibus obtemperare nolint, nempe iniqui, et incontinentes, et avari, et adulteri, dicunt se solos Deum nosse? Oporteret enim eos, cum in alienis adsunt, recte vivere, ut revera regiam indolem ostenderent. Jam vero' et humanos legislatores, et divinam legem habent sibi infensam, cum inique et præter leges vivere instituerint. Is certe, qui scortatorem "confodit," a Deo pius esse ostenditur in Numeris. "Et si dixerimus," inquit Joannes in epistola, "quod societatem habemus cum eo," nempe Deo, "et in tenebris ambulamus, mentimur, et veritatem non facimus. Si autem in luce ambulamus, sicut et ipse est in luce, societatem habemus cum ipso, et sanguis Jesu filii ejus emundat nos a peccato."[5] Quomodo ergo sunt hi hujus mundi hominibus meliores, qui hæc faciunt, et vel pessimis hujus mundi sunt similes? sunt enim, ut arbitror, similes natura, qui sunt factis similes. Quibus autem se esse censent nobilitate superiores, eos debent etiam superare moribus, ut vitent ne includantur in carcere. Revera enim, ut dixit Dominus: "Nisi abundaverit justitia vestra plus quam scribarum et Pharisæorum, non intrabitis in regnum Dei."[6] De abstinentia autem a cibis ostenditur a Daniele.[7] Ut semel autem dicam, de obedientia dicit psallens David: "In quo diriget junior viam suam?"[8] Et statim audit: "In custodiendo sermones tuos in toto corde." Et dicit Jeremias: "Hæc autem dicit Dominus: Per vias gentium ne ambulaveritis."[9] Hinc moti

---

1 Eph. iv. 20-24.
2 Eph. v. 1-4.
3 Eph. v. 5-11.

4 Rom. vi. 16.
5 Num. xxv. 8; 1 John i. 6, 7.
6 Matt. v. 20.
7 Dan. i. 1.
8 Ps. cxviii. 9.
9 Jer. x. 2.

aliqui alii, pusilli et nullius pretii, dicunt forma-
tum fuisse hominem a diversis potestatibus : et
quæ sunt quidem usque ad umbilicum esse artis
divinioris ; quæ autem subter, minoris ; qua de
causa coitum quoque appetere.   Non animad-
vertunt autem, quod superiores quoque partes
nutrimentum appetunt, et quibusdam libidinan-
tur.   Adversantur autem Christo quoque, qui
dixit Pharisæis, eundem Deum et "internum"
nostrum et " externum " fecisse hominem.[1]
Quinetiam appetitio non est corporis, etsi fiat
per corpus.   Quidam alii, quos etiam vocamus
Antitactas, hoc est "adversarios" et repugnantes, dicunt quod Deus quidem universorum noster est natura pater, et omnia quæcunque fecit,
bona sunt ; unus autem quispiam ex iis, qui ab
ipso facti sunt, seminatis zizaniis, malorum naturam generavit : quibus etiam nos omnes impli-
cavit, ut nos efficeret Patri adversarios.   Quare
nos etiam ipsi huic adversamur ad Patrem ulcis-
cendum, contra secundi voluntatem facientes.
Quoniam ergo hic dixit : " Non mœchaberis : "
nos, inquiunt, mœchamur, ut ejus mandatum dis-
solvamus.   Quibus responderimus quoque, quod
pseudoprophetas, et eos qui veritatem simulant,
ex operibus cognosci accepimus : si male audiunt autem vestra opera, quomodo adhuc dicetis
vos veritatem tenere?   Aut enim nullum est
malum, et non est utique dignus reprehensione
is, quem vos insimulatis, ut qui Deo sit adversa-
tus, neque fuit alicujus mali effector ; una enim
cum malo arbor quoque interimitur : aut si est
malum ac consistit, dicant nobis, quid dicunt
esse ea, quæ data sunt, præcepta, de justitia, de
continentia, de toleratia, de patientia, et iis,
quæ sunt hujusmodi, bona an mala? et si fuerit
quidem malum præceptum, quod plurima prohibet facere turpia, adversus seipsum legem feret
vitium, ut seipsum dissolvat, quod quidem non
potest fieri ; sin autem bonum, cum bonis adver-
sentur præceptis, se bono adversari, et mala
facere confitentur.   Jam vero ipse quoque Servator, cui soli censent esse parendum, odio habere, et maledictis insequi prohibuit · et, " Cum
adversario," inquit, "vadens, ejus amicus conare
discedere."[2]   Aut ergo Christi quoque negabunt
suasionem, adversantes adversario : aut, si sint
amici, contra eum certamen suscipere nolunt.
Quid vero? an nescitis, viri egregii (loquor enim
tanquam præsentibus), quod cum præceptis,
quæ se recte habent, pugnantes, propriæ saluti
resistis?   Non enim ea, quæ sunt utiliter edicta,
sed vos ipsos evertitis.   Et Dominus : " Luce-
ant " quidem, inquit, "bona vestra opera : "[3]
vos autem libidines et intemperantias vestras
manifestas redditis.   Et alioqui si vultis legislatoris præcepta dissolvere, quanam de causa, illud

quidem : " Non mœchaberis ; " et hoc : "Stuprum puero non inferes," et quæcunque ad continentiam conferunt, dissolvere conamini, propter
vestram intemperantiam   non dissolvitis autem,
quæ ab ipso fit, hiemem, ut media adhuc hieme
æstatem faciatis : neque terram navigabilem,
mare autem pedibus pervium, facitis, ut qui
historias composuerunt, barbarum Xerxem dicunt voluisse facere?   Cur vero non omnibus
præceptis repugnatis?   Nam cum ille dicat ;
"Crescite et multiplicamini,"[4] oporteret vos, qui
adversamini, nullo modo uti coitu.   Et cum
dixit : " Dedi vobis omnia ad vescendum "[5] et
fruendum, vos nullo frui oportuit.   Quinetiam
eo dicente : "Oculum pro oculo,"[6] oportuit vos
decertationem contraria non rependere decerta-
tione.   Et cum furem jusserit reddere "quadru-
plum,"[7] oportuit vos furi aliquid etiam adhere.
Rursus vero similiter, cum præcepto : "Diliges
Deum tuum ex toto corde tuo,"[8] repugnetis,
oportuit nec universorum quidem Deum diligere.
Et rursus, cum dixerit : "Non facies sculptile
neque fusile,"[9] consequens erat ut etiam sculp-
tilia adoraretis.   Quomodo ergo non impie facitis, qui Creatori quidem, ut dicitis, resistitis ;
quæ sunt autem meretricibus et adulteris similia,
sectamini?   Quomodo autem non sentitis vos
eum majorem facere, quem pro imbecillo habe-
tis ; si quidem id fit, quod hic vult ; non autem
illud, quod voluit bonus? contra enim ostenditur
quodam modo a vobis ipsis, imbecillum esse,
quem vestrum patrem dicitis.   Recensent etiam
ex quibusdam locis propheticis decerptas dictio-
nes, et male consarcinatas, quæ allegorice dicta
sunt tanquam recto ductu et citra figuram dicta
sumentes.   Dicunt enim scriptum esse : " Deo
restiterunt, et salvi facti sunt : "[10] illi autem "Deo
impudenti " addunt ; et hoc eloquium tanquam
consilium præceptum accipiunt : et hoc ad salutem conferre existimant, quod Creatori resis-
tant.   At "impudenti" quidem "Deo," non est
scriptum.   Si autem sic quoque habeat, eum,
qui vocatus est diabolus, inteligite impudentem :
vel quod hominem calumniis impetat, vel quod
accuset peccatores, vel quod sit apostata.   Populus ergo, de quo hoc dictum est, cum castigaretur
propter sua peccata, ægre ferentes et gementes,
his verbis, quæ dicta sunt, murmurabant, quod
aliæ quidem gentes cum inique se gerant non
puniantur, ipsi autem in singulis vexentur ; adeo
ut Jeremias quoque dixerit : " Cur via impiorum
prosperatur?"[11] quod simile est ie, quod prius
allatum est ex Malachia : "Deo restiterunt, et
salvi facti sunt."   Nam prophetæ divinitus in-

---

[1] Luke xi. 40.
[2] Matt. v. 25; Luke xii. 58.
[3] Matt. v. 16.

[4] Gen. i. 28, ix. 1.
[5] Gen. i. 29, ix. 2, 3.
[6] Ex. xxi. 24.
[7] Ex. xxii 1.
[8] Deut. vi 5.
[9] Deut. xxvii. 15.
[10] Mal. iii. 15
[11] Jer. xii. 1.

spirati, non solum quæ a Deo audierint, se loqui profitentur; sed et ipsi etiam solent ea, quæ vulgo jactantur a populo, exceptionis modo, edicere, et tanquam quæstiones ab hominibus motas referre: cujusmodi est illud dictum, cujus mentio jam facta est. Nunquid autem ad hos verba sua dirigens, scribit Apostolus in Epistola ad Romanos: " Et non sicut blasphemamur, et sicut dicunt aliqui nos dicere: Faciamus mala, ut eveniant bona, quorum justa est damnatio?" [1] Ii sunt, qui inter legendum tono vocis pervertunt Scripturas ad proprias voluptates, et quorumdam accentuum et punctorum transpositione, quæ prudenter et utiliter præcepta sunt, as suas trahunt delicias. "Qui irritatis Deum sermonibus vestris," inquit Malachias, "et dicitis, in quonam eum irritavimus; Dum vos dicitis: Quicunque facit malum, bonus est coram Domino, et ipse in eis complacuit; et ubi est Deus justitiæ?" [2]

CAPUT V. — DUO GENERA HÆRETICORUM NOTAT: PRIUS ILLORUM QUI OMNIA OMNIBUS LICERE PRONUNTIANT, QUOS REFUTAT.

Ne ergo hunc locum ungue amplius fodicantes, plurium absurdarum hæresium meminerimus; nec rursus dum in singulis adversus unamquamque dicere necesse habemus, propterea pudore afficiamur, et nimis prolixos hos faciamus commentarios, age in duo dividentes omnes hæreses, eis respondeamus.[3] Aut enim docent indiscrete vivere: aut modum excedentes, per inpietatem et odium profitentur continentiam. Prius autem tractandum est de prima parte. Quod si quodlibet vitæ genus licet eligere, tum eam scilicet etiam licet, quæ est continens: et si electus tute poterit quodlibet vitæ genus sectari, manifestum est eam, quæ temperanter et secundum virtutem agitur, longe tutissimam esse. Nam cum "domino sabbati," etiamsi intemperanter vivat, nulla ratio reddenda sit, multo magis qui vitam moderate et temperate instituit, nulli erit rationi reddendæ obnoxius. "Omnia enim licent, sed non omnia expediunt," [4] ait Apostolus. Quod si omnia licent, videlicet moderatum quoque esse et temperantem. Quemadmodum ergo is est laudandus, qui libertate sua usus est ad vivendum ex virtute: ita multo magis qui dedit nobis liberam nostri potestatem, et concessit vivere ut vellemus, est venerandus et adorandus, quod non permiserit, ut nostra electio et vitatio cuiquam necessario serviret. Si est autem uterque æque securus, et qui incontinentiam, et qui continentiam elegerit, non est tamen ex æquo honestum et decorum. Qui enim impegit in voluptates, gratificatur corpori: temperans autem animam corporis dominam liberat a perturba-

tionibus. Et si dicant nos "vocatos fuisse in libertatem, solummodo ne præbeamus libertatem, in occasionem carni," [5] ex sententia Apostoli. Si autem cupiditati est obsequendum, et quæ probrosa est et turpis vita tanquam indifferens est eligenda, ut ipsi dicunt; aut cupiditatibus est omnino parendum, et si hoc ita est, facienda sunt quævis impudicissima et maxime nefaria, eos sequendo, qui nobis persuadent: aut sunt aliquæ declinandæ cupiditates, et non est amplius vivendum indifferenter, neque est impudenter serviendum vilissimis et abjectissimis nostris partibus, ventri et pudendis, dum cupidate ducti nostro blandimur cadaveri. Nutritur enim et vivificatur cupiditas, dum ei voluptates ministrantur: quemadmodum rursus si impediatur et interturbetur, flaccescit. Quomodo autem fieri potest, ut qui victus est a voluptatibus corporis, Domino assimiletur, aut Dei habeat cognitionem? Omnis enim voluptatis principium est cupiditas: cupiditas autem est molestia et sollicitudo, quæ propter egestatem aliquid appetit. Quare nihil aliud mihi videntur, qui hanc vitæ rationem suscipiunt, quam quod dicitur,

Ultra ignominiam sentire dolores;

ut qui malum a se accersitum, nunc et in posterum eligant. Si ergo "omnia licerent," nec timendum esset ne a spe excideremus propter malas actiones, esset fortasse eis aliquis prætextus, cur male viverent et miserabiliter. Quoniam autem vita beata nobis ostensa est per præcepta, quam oportet omnes sequentes, nec aliquid eorum, quæ dicta sunt, perperam intelligentes, nec eorum, quæ convenit, aliquid, etsi sit vel minimum, contemnentes, sequi quo logos ducit; quia, si ab eo aberraverimus, in malum immortale incidamus necesse est; si divinam autem Scripturam secuti fuerimus, per quam ingrediuntur, qui crediderunt, ut Domino, quoad fieri potest, assimilentur, non est vivendum indifferenter, sed pro viribus mundos esse oportet a voluptatibus et cupiditatibus, curaque est gerenda animæ, qua apud solum Deum perseverandum est. Mens enim, quæ est munda et ab omni vitio libera, est quodammodo apta ad potestatem Dei suscipiendam, cum divina in ea assurgat imago: "Et quicunque habet hanc spem in Domino, seipsum," inquit, "mundum castumque facit, quatenus ille est castus." [6] Ut ii autem accipiant Dei cognitionem, qui adhuc ducuntur ab affectibus, minime potest fieri: ergo nec ut finem assequantur, cum nullam habeant Dei cognitionem. Et eum quidem, qui hunc finem non assequitur, accusare videtur Dei ignoratio; ut Deus autem ignoretur, efficit vitæ institutio. Omnino enim fieri non potest, ut

1 Rom. iii. 8.
2 Mal. ii. 17.
3 [Elucidation V.]
4 1 Cor. vi. 13, x. 23.
5 Gal. v. 13.
6 John iii. 3.

quis simul sit et scientia præditus, et blandiri corpori non erubescat. Neque enim potest unquam convenire, quod voluptas sit bonum, cum eo, quod bonum sit solum pulchrum et honestum : vel etiam cum eo, quod solus sit pulcher Dominus, et solus bonus Deus, et solus amabilis. "In Christo autem circumcisi estis, circumcisione non manu facta, in exspoliatione corporis carnis, in circumcisione Christi.[1] Si ergo cum Christo consurrexistis, quæ sursum sunt quærite, quæ sursum sunt sapite, non quæ sunt super terram. Mortui enim estis, et vita vestra absconsa est cum Christo in Deo ; " non autem ea, quam exercent, fornicatio. "Mortificate ergo membra, quæ sunt super terram, fornicationem, immunditiam, passionem, desiderium, propter quæ venit ira Dei. Deponant ergo ipsi quoque iram, indignationem, vitium, maledictum, turpem sermonem ex ore suo, exuentes veterem hominem cum concupiscentiis, et induentes novum, qui renovatur in agnitionem, ad imaginem ejus, qui creavit ipsum."[2] Vitæ enim institutio aperte eos arguit, qui mandata novere : qualis enim sermo, talis est vita. Arbor autem cognoscitur ex fructibus, non ex floribus et foliis ac ramis. Cognitio ergo est ex fructu et vitæ institutione, non ex sermone et flore. Non enim nudum sermonem dicimus esse cognitionem, sed quamdam divinam scientiam, et lucem illam, quæ innata animæ ex præceptorum obedientia, omnia, quæ per generationem oriuntur, manifesta facit, et hominem instruit, ut seipsum cognoscat, et qua ratione compos fieri possit, edocet. Quod enim oculus est in corpore, hoc est in mente cognitio. Neque dicant libertatem, qua quis voluptati servit, sicut ii, qui bilem dicunt dulcem. Nos enim didicimus libertatem, qua Dominus noster nos liberat a voluptatibus, et a cupiditatibus, et aliis perturbationibus solvens. "Qui dicit : Novi Dominum, et mandata ejus non servat, mendax est, et in eo veritas non est,"[3] ait Joannes.

CAPUT VI. — SECUNDUM GENUS HÆRETICORUM AGGREDITUR, ILLORUM SCILICET QUI EX IMPIA DE DEO OMNIUM CONDITORE SENTENTIA, CONTINENTIAM EXERCENT.

Adversus autem alterum genus hæreticorum,[4] qui speciose per continentiam impie se gerunt, tum in creaturam, tum in sanctum Opificem, qui est solus Deus omnipotens ; et dicunt non esse admittendum matrimonium et liberorum procreationem, nec in mundum esse inducendos alios infelices futuros, nec suppeditandum morti nutrimentum, hæc sunt opponenda : primum quidem illud Joannis : "Et nunc antichristi multi

facti sunt, unde scimus quod novissima hora est. Ex nobis exierunt, sed non erant ex nobis. Nam si fuissent ex nobis, permansissent utique nobiscum."[5]   Deinde sunt etiam evertendi, et dissolvenda, quæ ab eis afferuntur, hoc modo : "Salomæ interroganti, quousque vigebit mors," non quasi vita esset mala, et mala creatura, "Dominus, Quoadusque, inquit, vos mulieres paritis," sed quasi naturalem docens consequentiam : ortum enim omnino sequitur interitus. Vult ergo lex quidem nos a deliciis omnique probro et dedecore educere. Et hic est ejus finis, ut nos ab injustitia ad justitiam deducamur, honesta eligendo matrimonia, et liberorum procreationem, bonamque vitæ institutionem. Dominus autem "Non venit ad solvendam legem, sed ad implendam : "[6] ad implendam autem, non ut cui aliquid deesset, sed quod legis prophetiæ per ejus adventum completæ fuerint. Nam recta vitæ institutio, iis etiam, qui juste vixerunt ante legem, per Logon prædicabatur. Vulgus ergo hominum, quod non novit continentiam, corpore vitam degit, sed non spiritu : sine spiritu autem corpus nihil aliud est quam terra et cinis. Jam adulterium judicat Dominus ex cogitatione. Quid enim? annon licet etiam continenter uti matrimonio, et non conari dissolvere, quod "conjunxit Deus?"[7]   Talia enim docent conjugii divisores, propter quod nomen probris ac maledictis appetitur inter gentes. Sceleratum autem dicentes isti esse coitum, qui ipsi quoque suam essentiam ex coitu accepere, quomodo non fuerint scelerati? Eorum autem, qui sunt sanctificati, sanctum quoque, ut puto, semen est. Ac nobis quidem debet esse sanctificatus, non solum spiritus, sed et mores, et vita, et corpus. Nam quanam ratione dicit Paulus apostolus esse "sanctificatam mulierem a viro," aut "virum a muliere?"[8]   Quid est autem, quod Dominus quoque dixit iis, qui interrogabant de divortio: "An liceat uxorem dimittere, cum Moyses id permiserit?"   "Ad duritiam cordis vestri, inquit, Moyses hæc scripsit. Vos autem non legistis, quod protoplasto Deus dixit : 'Eritis duo in carne una? Quare qui dimittit uxorem, præterquam fornicationis causa, facit eam mœchari.[9] Sed post resurrectionem, inquit, nec uxorem ducunt, nec nubunt.' "[10]   Etenim de ventre et cibis dictum est : "Escæ ventri, et venter escis ; Deus autem et illum et has destruet ; "[11] hos impetens, qui instar caprorum et hircorum sibi vivendum esse censent, ne secure ac sine terrore comessent et coirent. Si resurrectionem itaque receperint, ut ipsi dicunt, et ideo matrimonium infirmant et abrogant ; nec comedant, nec bibant : "destrui"

---

[1] Col. ii. 11.
[2] Col. iii. 4, 10.
[3] 1 John ii 4.
[4] [Elucidation VI.]

[5] 1 John ii. 18, 19.
[6] Matt. v. 17.
[7] Matt. xix. 6; Mark x. 9.
[8] 1 Cor. vii 14.
[9] Matt. xix. 3; Mark x. 2.
[10] Matt. xxii. 30; Mark xii. 23; Luke xx. 35.
[11] 1 Cor. vi. 13.

enim "ventrem et cibos," dicit Apostolus in resurrectione. Quomodo ergo esuriunt, et sitiunt, et carnis patiuntur affectiones, et alia, quæ non patietur, qui per Christum accepit perfectam, quæ speratur, resurrectionem? Quin etiam ii, qui colunt idola, a cibis et venere abstinent. "Non est" autem, inquit, "regnum Dei cibus est potus." [1] Certe magis quoque curæ est, qui angelos colunt et dæmones, simul a vino et animatis et rebus abstinere venereis. Quemadmodum autem humilitas est mansuetudo, non autem afflictio corporis : ita etiam continentia est animæ virtus, quæ non est in manifesto, sed in occulto. Sunt autem etiam, qui matrimonium aperte dicunt fornicationem, et decernunt id traditum esse a diabolo. Dicunt autem gloriosi isti jactatores se imitari Dominum, qui neque uxorem duxit, neque in mundo aliquid possedit ; se magis quam alii Evangelium intellexisse gloriantes. Eis autem dicit Scriptura : "Deus superbis resistit, humilibus autem dat gratiam." [2] Deinde nesciunt causam cur Dominas uxorem non duxerit. Primum quidem, propriam sponsam habuit Ecclesiam : deinde vero, nec homo erat communis, ut opus haberet etiam adjutore aliquo secundum carnem ; neque erat ei necesse procreare filios, qui manet in æternum, et natus est solus Dei Filius. Hic ipse autem Dominus dicit : "Quod Deus conjunxit, homo ne separet." [3] Et rursus : "Sicut autem erat in diebus Noe, erant nubentes, et nuptui dantes, ædificantes, et plantantes ; et sicut erat in diebus Lot, ita erit adventus Filii hominis." [4] Et quod hoc non dicit ad gentes, ostendit, cum subjungit : "Num cum venerit Filius hominis, inveniet fidem in terra?" [5] Et rursus : "Væ prægnantibus et lactantibus in illis diebus." [6] Quanquam hæc quoque dicuntur allegorice. Propterea nec "tempora" præfiniit, "quæ Pater posuit in sua potestate," [7] ut permaneret mundus per generationes. Illud autem : "Non omnes capiunt verbum hoc : sunt enim eunuchi, qui sic nati sunt ; et sunt eunuchi, qui castrati sunt ab hominibus ; et sunt eunuchi, qui seipsos castrarunt propter regnum cœlorum. Qui potest capere, capiat ; " [8] nesciunt quod, postquam de divortio esset locutus, cum quidam rogassent : "Si sic sit causa uxoris, non expedit homini uxorem ducere ; " tunc dixit Dominus : "Non omnes capiunt verbum hoc, sed quibus datum est." [9] Hoc enim qui rogabant, volebant ex eo scire, an uxore damnata et ejecta propter fornicationem, concedat aliam ducere. Aiunt autem athletas quoque

non paucos abstinere a venere, propter exercitationem corporis continentes : quemadmodum Crotoniatem Astylum, et Crisonem Himeræum. Quinetiam Amœbeus citharœdus, cum recenter matrimonio junctus esset, a sponsa abstinuit : et Cyrenæus Aristoteles amantem Laidem solus despexit. Cum meretrici itaque jurasset, se eam esse in patriam abducturum, si sibi adversus decertantes advesarios in aliquibus opem tulisset, postquam id perfecisset, lepide a se dictum jusjurandum exsequens, cum curasset imaginem ejus quam simillimam depingi, eam Cyrenæ statuit, ut scribit Ister in libro *De proprietate certaminum*. Quare nec castitas est bonum, nisi fiat propter delectionem Dei. Jam de iis, qui matrimonium abhorrent, dicit beatus Paulus : "In novissimis diebus deficient quidam a fide, attendentes spiritibus erroris, et doctrinis dæmoniorum, prohibentium nubere, abstinere a cibis." [10] Et rursus dicit : "Nemo vos seducat in voluntaria humilitatis religione, et parcimonia corporis." [11] Idem autem illa quoque scribit : "Alligatus es uxori? ne quæras solutionem. Solutus es ab uxore? ne quæras uxorem." [12] Et rursus : "Unusquisque autem suam uxorem habeat, ne tentet vos Satanas." [13] Quid vero? non etiam justi veteres creaturam cum gratiarum actione participabant? Aliqui autem etiam liberos susceperunt, continenter versati in matrimonio. Et Eliæ quidem corvi alimentum afferebant, panes et carnes. Quinetiam Samuel propheta armum, quem ex iis, quæ comedisset, reliquerat, allatum, dedit edendum Sauli. Hi autem, qui se eos dicunt vitæ institutis excellere, cum illorum actionibus ne poterunt quidem conferri. "Qui" itaque "non comedit, comedentem ne spernat. Qui autem comedit, eum qui non comedit non judicet : Deus enim ipsum accepit." [14] Quin etiam Dominus de seipso dicens : "Venit," inquit, "Joannes, nec comedens, nec bibens, et dicunt : dæmonium habet ; venit Filius hominis comedans et bibens, et dicunt : Ecce homo vorax et vini potor, amicus publicanorum, et peccator." [15] An etiam reprobant apostolos? Petrus enim et Philippus [16] filios procrearunt : Philippus autem filias quoque suas viris locavit. Et Paulus quidem certe non veretur in quadam epistola suam appellare "conjugem," quam non circumferebat, quod non magno ei esset opus ministerio. Dicit itaque in quadam epistola : "Non habemus potestatem sororem uxorem circumducendi, sicut et reliqui apostoli?" [17] Sed hi quidem, ut erat consentaneum, ministerio, quod divelli non poterat, prædicationi scilicet, attendentes, non ut ux-

---

[1] Rom. xiv. 17.
[2] Jas. iv. 6; 1 Pet. v. 5.
[3] Matt. xix. 6; Mark x. 9.
[4] Matt. xxiv. 37; Luke xvii. 28.
[5] Luke xviii. 8.
[6] Matt. xxiv. 19; Mark xiii. 17; Luke xxi. 23.
[7] Acts i. 7.
[8] Matt. xix. 11, 12.
[9] Matt. xix. 10, 11.

[10] 1 Tim. iv. 1, 3.
[11] Col. ii. 18, 23.
[12] 1 Cor. vii. 27.
[13] 1 Cor. vii. 2, 5.
[14] Rom. xiv. 3.
[15] Matt. xi. 18, 19.
[16] [Elucidation VII.]
[17] 1 Cor. ix. 5.

ores, sed ut sorores circumducebant mulieres, quæ una ministraturæ essent apud mulieres quæ domos custodiebant : per quas etiam in gynæceum, absque ulla reprehensione malave suspicione, ingredi posset doctrina Domini. Scimus enim quæcunque de feminis diaconis in altera ad Timotheum præstantissimus [1] docet Paulus. Atqui hic ipse exclamavit : "Non est regnum Dei esca et potus : " neque vero abstinentia a vino et carnibus ; "sed justitia, et pax, et gaudium in Spiritu sancto." [2] Quis eorum, ovilla pelle indutus, zona pellicea accinctus, circuit ut Elias? Quis cilicium induit, cætera nudus, et discalceatus, ut Isaias? vel subligaculum tantum habet lineum, ut Jeremias? Joannis autem vitæ institutum gnosticum quis imitabitur? Sed sic quoque viventes, gratias Creatori agebant beati prophetæ. Carpocratis autem justitia, et eorum, qui æque atque ipse impudicam prosequuntur communionem, hoc modo dissolvitur ; simul enim ac dixerit : "Te petenti des ; " subjungit : "Et eum, qui velit mutuo accipere, ne averseris ; " [3] hanc docens communionem, non autem illam incestam et impudicam. Quomodo autem fuerit is qui petit et accipit, et is qui mutuatur, si nullus sit qui habeat et det mutuo? Quid vero? quando dicit Dominus : "Esurivi, et me pavistis ; sitii, et potum mihi dedistis ; hospes eram, et me collegistis ; nudus, et me vestiistis ; " [4] deinde subjungit : "Quatenus fecistis uni horum minimorum, mihi fecistis." [5] Nunquid easdem quoque tulit leges in Veteri Testamento? "Qui dat mendico, fœneratur Deo." [6] Et : "Ne abstinueris a benefaciendo egeno," [7] inquit. Et rursus : "Eleemosynæ et fides ne te deficiant," [8] inquit. "Paupertas" autem "virum humiliat, ditant autem manus virorum." [9] Subjungit autem : "Qui pecuniam suam non dedit ad usuram, fit acceptus." Et : "Pretium redemptionis anima, propriæ judicantur divitiæ." [10] Annon aperte indicat, quod sicut mundus componitur ex contrariis, nempe ex calido et frigido, humido et sicco, ita etiam ex iis qui dant, et ex iis qui accipiunt? Et rursus cum dixit : "Si vis perfectus esse, vende quæ habes, et da pauperibus," refellit eum qui gloriabatur quod "omnia a juventute præcepta servaverat ; " non enim impleverat illud : "Diliges proximum tuum sicut teipsum : " [11] tunc autem cum a Domino perficeretur, docebatur communicare et impertiri per charitatem. Honeste ergo non prohibuit esse divitem, sed esse divitem injuste et inexplebiliter.

"Possessio (enim,) quæ cum iniquitate acceleratur, minor redditur." [12] "Sunt (enim,) qui seminantes multiplicant, et qui colligentes minus habent." [13] De quibus scriptum est : "Dispersit, dedit pauperibus, justitia ejus manet in sæculum sæculi." [14] Qui enim "seminat et plura colligit," is est, qui per terrenam et temporalem communicationem ac distributionem, cœlestia acquirit et æterna. Est autem alius, qui nemini impertit, et incassum "thesauros in terra colligit, ubi ærugo et tinea destruunt." [15] De quo scriptum est : "Qui colligit mercedes, colligit in saccum perforatum." [16] Hujus "agrum" Dominus in Evangelio dicit "fuisse fertilem : " [17] deinde cum vellet fructus reponere, et esset "majora horrea ædificaturus," sibi dixisse per prosopopœiam : "Habes bona multa reposita tibi in multos annos, ede, bibe, lætare : " "Stulte ergo, inquit, hac nocte animam tuam a te repetunt ; quæ ergo parasti, cujus erunt?"

CAPUT VII. — QUA IN RE CHRISTIANORUM CONTINENTIA EAM QUAM SIBI VINDICANT PHILOSOPHI ANTECELLAT.

Humana ergo continentia,[18] ea, inquam, quæ est ex sententia philosophorum Græcorum, profitetur pugnare cum cupiditate, et in factis ei non inservire ; quæ est autem ex nostra sententia continentia, non concupiscere ; non ut quis concupiscens se fortiter gerat, sed ut etiam a concupiscendo se contineat. Non potest autem ea aliter comparari continentia, nisi gratia Dei. Et ideo dixit : "Petite, et dabitur vobis." [19] Hanc gratiam Moyses quoque accepit, qui indigo corpore erat indutus, ut quadraginta diebus neque esuriret, neque sitiret. Quemadmodum autem melius est sanum esse, quam ægrotantem disserere de sanitate : ita lucem esse, quam loqui de luce ; et quæ est ex veritate continentia, ea quæ docetur a philosophis. Non enim ubi est lux, illic tenebræ : ubi autem sola insidet cupiditas, etiamsi quiescat a corporea operatione, at memoria cum eo, quod non est præsens, congreditur. Generatim autem nobis procedat oratio de matrimonio, nutrimento, et aliis, ut nihil faciamus ex cupiditate, velimus autem ea sola, quæ sunt necessaria. Non sumus enim filii cupiditatis, sed voluntatis ; et eum, qui uxorem duxit propter liberorum procreationem, exercere oportet continentiam, ut ne suam quidem concupiscat uxorem, quam debet diligere, honesta et moderata voluntate operam dans liberis. Non enim "carnis curam gerere ad concupiscentias" didicimus ; "honeste autem tanquam in die,"

---

[1] [De diaconissa primitiva, confer *Bunsenium*, apud *Hippol.*, vol. iii. p. 41.]
[2] Rom. xiv. 17.
[3] Matt. v. 42.
[4] Matt. xxv. 35, 36.
[5] Matt. xxv. 40.
[6] Prov. xix. 17.
[7] Prov. iii. 27.
[8] Prov. iii. 3.
[9] Prov. x. 4.
[10] Prov. xiii. 8.
[11] Matt. xix. 16; Mark x. 17; Luke xviii. 18.

[12] Prov. xiii. 11.
[13] Prov. xi 23.
[14] Ps. cxi. 9.
[15] Matt. vi. 19.
[16] Hagg. i. 6.
[17] Luke xii. 16-20.
[18] [Elucidation VIII.]
[19] Matt. vii. 7.

Christo, et Dominica lucida vitæ institutione, "ambulantes, non in comessationibus et ebrietatibus, non in cubilibus et impudicitiis, non in litibus et contentionibus."[1]   Verumenimvero non oportet considerare continentiam in uno solum genere, nempe in rebus venereis, sed etiam in quibuscunque aliis, quæ luxuriosa concupiscit anima, non contenta necessariis, sed sollicita de deliciis.   Continentia est pecuniam despicere ; voluptatem, possessionem, spectaculum magno et excelso animo contemnere ; os continere, ratione quæ sunt mala vincere.   Jam vero angeli quoque quidam, cum fuissent incontinentes, victi cupiditate, huc e cœlo deciderunt. Valentinus autem in Epistola ad Agathopodem : "Cum omnia, inquit, sustinuisset, erat continens, divinitatem sibi comparavit Jesus ; edebat et bibebat peculiari modo, non reddens cibos ; tanta ei inerat vis continentiæ, ut etiam nutrimentum in eo non interierit, quoniam ipse non habuit interitum."   Nos ergo propter dilectionem in Dominum, et propter ipsum honestum, amplectimur continentiam, templum Spiritus sanctificantes.   Honestum enim est, "propter regnum cœlorum seipsum castrare "[2] ab omni cupiditate, et "emundare conscientiam a mortuis operibus, ad serviendum Deo viventi."[3] Qui autem propter odium adversus carnem susceptum a conjugali conjunctione, et eorum qui conveniunt ciborum participatione, liberari desiderant, indocti sunt et impii, et absque ratione continentes, sicut aliæ gentes plurimæ.   Brachmanes quidem certe neque animatum comedunt, neque vinum bibunt ; sed aliqui quidem ex iis quotidie sicut nos cibum capiunt ; nonnulli autem ex iis tertio quoque die, ut ait Alexander Polyhistor in *Indicis ;* mortem autem contemnunt, et vivere nihili faciunt ; credunt enim esse regenerationem : aliqui autem colunt Herculem et Pana.   Qui autem ex Indis vocantur Σεμνοί, hoc est, *venerandi,* nudi totam vitam transigunt : ii veritatis exercent, et futura prædicunt, et colunt quamdam pyramidem, sub qua existimant alicujus dei ossa reposita.   Neque vero Gymnosophistæ, nec qui dicuntur Σεμνοί, utuntur mulieribus, hoc enim præter naturam et iniquum esse existimant ; qua de causa seipsos castos conservant.   Virgines autem sunt etiam mulieres, quæ dicuntur Σεμναί, hoc est, *venerandæ.* Videntur autem observare cœlestia, et per eorum significationem quædam futura prædicere.

CAPUT VIII. — LOCA S. SCRIPTURÆ AB HÆRETICIS IN VITUPERIUM MATRIMONII ADDUCTA EXPLICAT ; ET PRIMO VERBA APOSTOLI ROM. VI. 14, AB HÆRETICORUM PERVERSA INTERPRETATIONE VINDICAT.[4]

Quoniam autem qui introducunt indifferentiam, paucas quasdam Scripturas detorquentes, titillanti suæ voluptati eas suffragari existimant ; tum præcipue illam quoque : " Peccatum enim vestri non dominabitur ; non estis enim sub lege, sed sub gratia ; "[5] et aliquas alias hujusmodi, quarum post hæc non est rationi consentaneum ut faciam mentionem (non enim navem instruo piraticam), age paucis eorum argumentum perfringamus.   Ipse enim egregius Apostolus in verbis, quæ prædictæ dictioni subjungit, intentati criminis afferet solutionem : " Quid ergo ? peccabimus, quia non sumus sub lege, sed sub gratia ? Absit."[6]   Adeo divine et prophetice e vestigio dissolvit artem voluptatis sophisticam. Non intelligunt ergo, ut videtur, quod " omnes nos oportet manifestari ante tribunal Christi, ut referat unusquisque per corpus ea quæ fecit, sive bonum, sive malum : "[7] ut quæ per corpus fecit aliquis, recipiat.   " Quare si quis est in Christo, nova creatura est," nec amplius peccatis dedita : " Vetera præterierunt," vitam antiquam exuimus : " Ecce enim nova facta sunt,"[8] castitas ex fornicatione, et continentia ex incontinentia, justitia ex injustitia.   " Quæ est enim participatio justitiæ et injustitiæ ? aut quæ luci cum tenebris societas ? quæ est autem conventio Christo cum Belial ? quæ pars est fideli cum infideli ? quæ est autem consensio templo Dei cum idolis ?[9]   Has ergo habentes promissiones, mundemus nos ipsos ab omni inquinamento carnis et spiritus, perficientes sanctitatem in timore Dei."[10]

CAPUT IX. — DICTUM CHRISTI AD SALOMEN EXPONIT, QUOD TANQUAM IN VITUPERIUM NUPTIARUM PROLATUM HÆRETICI ALLEGABANT.

Qui autem Dei creaturæ resistunt per speciosam illam continentiam, illa quoque dicunt, quæ ad Salomen dicta sunt, quorum prius de minimus : habentur autem, ut existimo, in Evangelio secundum Ægyptios.[11]   Aiunt enim ipsum dixisse Servatorem : " Veni ad dissolvendum opera feminæ ; " feminæ quidem, cupiditatis ; opera autem generationem et interitum.   Quid ergo dixerint ? Desiit hæc administratio ? Non dixerint : manet enim mundus in eadem œconomia.   Sed non falsum dixit Dominus ; revera enim opera dissolvit cupiditatis, avaritiam, contentionem, gloriæ cupiditatem, mulierum insanum amorem, pædicatum, ingluviem, luxum et profusionem, et quæ sunt his similia.   Horum autem ortus, est animæ interitus : siquidem " delictis mortui " efficimur.[12]   Ea vero femina est intemperantia.   Ortum autem et interitum

---

[1] Rom. xiii. 12, 13, 14.
[2] Matt. xix. 12.
[3] Heb. ix. 14.
[4] [Elucidation IX.]

[5] Rom. vi 14.
[6] Rom. vi. 15.
[7] 2 Cor. v. 10.
[8] 2 Cor. v. 16, 17.
[9] 2 Cor. vi. 14, 15, 16.
[10] 2 Cor. vii. 1.
[11] [Elucidation X.]
[12] Eph. ii. 5.

creaturarum propter ipsorum naturas fieri necesse est, usque ad perfectam distinctionem et restitutionem electionis, per quam, quæ etiam sunt mundo permistæ et confusæ substantiæ, proprietati suæ restituuntur. Unde merito cum de consummatione Logos locutus fuerat, ait Salome : "Quousque morientur homines?" Hominem autem vocat Scriptura dupliciter : et eum, qui apparet, et animam ; et eum rursus, qui servatur, et eum qui non. Mors autem animæ dicitur peccatum. Quare caute et considerate respondet Dominus : "Quoadusque pepererint mulieres," hoc est quandiu operabuntur cupiditates. "Et ideo quemadmodum per unum hominem peccatum ingressum est in mundum, per peccatum quoque mors ad omnes homines pervasit, quatenus omnes peccaverunt; et regnavit mors ab Adam usque ad Moysen,"[1] inquit Apostolus : naturali autem divinæ œconomiæ necessitate mors sequitur generationem : et corporis et animæ conjunctionem consequitur eorum dissolutio. Si est autem propter doctrinam et agnitionem generatio, restitutionis causa erit dissolutio. Quomodo autem existimatur mulier causa mortis, propterea quod pariat : ita etiam dicetur dux vitæ propter eamdem causam. Proinde quæ prior inchoavit transgressionem, *Vita* est appellata,[2] propter causam successionis : et eorum, qui generantur, et qui peccant, tam justorum quam injustorum, mater est, unoquoque nostrum seipsum justificante, vel contra inobedientem constituente. Unde non ego quidem arbitror Apostolum abhorrere vitam, quæ est in carne, cum dicit : "Sed in omni fiducia, ut semper, nunc quoque Christus magnificabitur in corpore meo, sive per vitam, sive per mortem. Mihi enim vivere Christus et mori lucrum. Si autem vivere in carne, et hoc quoque mihi fructus operis, quid eligam nescio, et coarctor ex duobus, cupiens resolvi, et esse cum Christo : multo enim melius : manere autem in carne, est magis necessarium propter vos."[3] Per hæc enim, ut puto, aperte ostendit, exitus quidem e corpore perfectionem, esse in Dei dilectionem : ejus autem præsentiæ in carne, ex grato animo profectam tolerantiam, propter eos, qui salute indigent. Quid vero? non etiam ea, quæ deinceps sequuntur, ex iis, quæ dicta sunt ad Salomen, subjungunt ii, qui quidvis potius quam quæ est ex veritate, evangelicam regulam sunt secuti? Cum ea enim dixisset : "Recte ergo feci, quæ non peperi :" scilicet, quod generatio non esset ut oportet assumpta ; excipit Dominus, dicens : "Omni herba vescere, ea autem, quæ habet amaritudinem, ne vescaris." Per hæc enim significat, esse in nostra potestate, et non esse necessarium ex prohibitione præcepti, vel con-

tinentiam, vel etiam matrimonium ; et quod matrimonium creationi aliquid affert auxilii, præterea explicans. Ne quis ergo eum deliquisse existimet, qui secundum Logon matrimonium inierit, nisi existimet amaram esse filiorum educationem : contra tamen, permultis videtur esse molestissimum liberis carere. Neque amara cuiquam videatur liberorum procreatio, eo quod negotiis implicatos a divinis abstrahat. Est enim, qui vitam solitariam facile ferre non valens, expetit matrimonium : quandoquidem res grata, qua quis temperanter fruitur, et innoxia : et unusquisque nostrum eatenus sui dominus est, ut eligat, an velit liberos procreare. Intelligo autem, quod aliqui quidem, qui prætextu matrimonii difficultatum ab eo abstinuerunt, non convenienter sanctæ cognitioni ad inhumanitatem et odium hominum defluxerunt, et perit apud ipsos charitas ; alii autem matrimonio ligati, et luxui ac voluptatibus dediti, lege quodammodo eos comitante, fuerunt, ut ait Propheta, "assimilati jumentis."[4]

CAPUT X. — VERBA CHRISTI MATT. XVIII. 20, MYSTICE EXPONIT.[5]

Quinam sunt autem illi "duo et tres, qui congregantur in nomine Domini, in" quorum "medio" est Dominus?[6] annon virum et mulierem et filium tres dicit, quoniam mulier cum viro per Deum conjungitur? Quod si accinctus quis esse velit et expeditus, non volens procreare liberos, propter eam, quæ est in procreandis liberis, molestiam et occupationem, "maneat," inquit Apostolus, absque uxore "ut ego."[7] Quidam vero effatum Domini exponunt, ac si dixisset, cum pluribus quidem esse Creatorem ac præsidem generationis Deum ; cum uno autem, nempe electo, Servatorem, qui alterius, boni scilicet, Dei Filius sit. Hoc autem non ita habet : sed est quidem etiam cum iis, qui honeste ac moderate in matrimonio versati sunt, et liberos susceperunt, Deus per Filium : est autem etiam cum eo, qui secundum Logon, seu rationem, fuit continens, idem Deus. Fuerint autem aliter quoque tres quidem, ira, cupiditas, et ratio : caro autem at anima et spiritus, alia ratione. Forte autem et vocationem et electionem secundam, et tertium genus, quod in primo honore collocatur, innuit trias prius dicta : cum quibus est, quæ omnia considerat, Dei potestas, absque divisione cadens in divisionem. Qui ergo animæ naturalibus, ita ut oportet, utitur operationibus, desiderat quidem ea, quæ sunt convenientia, odio autem habet ea, quæ lædunt, sicut jubent mandata : "Benedices" enim, inquit, "benedicenti, et maledices male-

[1] Rom. v. 12–14.
[2] Gen. iii. 20.
[3] Phil. i. 20–24.

[4] Ps. xlviii. 21.
[5] [Elucidation XI.]
[6] Matt. xviii. 20.
[7] 1 Cor. vii. 7.

dicenti." Quando autem his, ira scilicet et cupiditate, superior factus, et creaturæ amore vere affectus propter eum, qui est Deus et effector omnium, gnostice vitam instituerit, et Salvatori similis evadens, facilem temperantiæ habitum acquisiverit, et cognitionem, fidem, ac dilectionem conjunxerit, simplici hac in parte judicio utens, et vere spiritalis factus, nec earum, quæ ex ira et cupiditate procedunt, cogitationum omnino capax, ad Domini imaginem ab ipso artifice efficitur homo perfectus, is sane dignus jam est, qui frater a Domino nominetur, is simul est amicus et filius. Sic ergo "duo et tres" in eodem "congregantur," nempe in homine gnostico. Poterit etiam multorum quoque concordia ex tribus æstimata, cum quibus est Dominus, significare unam Ecclesiam, unum hominem, genus unum. Annon cum uno quidem Judæo erat Dominus, cum legem tulit : at prophetans, et Jeremiam mittens Babylonem, quinetiam eos qui erant ex gentibus vocans per prophetiam, congregavit duos populos : tertius autem est unus, qui ex duobus "creatur in novum hominem, quo inambulat et inhabitat" in ipsa Ecclesia? Et lex simul et prophetæ, una cum Evangelio, in nomine Christi congregantur in unam cognitionem. Qui ergo propter odium uxorem non ducunt, vel propter concupiscentiam carne indifferenter abutuntur, non sunt in numero illorum qui servantur, cum quibus est Dominus.

CAPUT XI. — LEGIS ET CHRISTI MANDATUM DE NON CONCUPISCENDO EXPONIT.[1]

His sic ostensis, age Scripturas, quæ adversantur sophistis hæreticis, jam adducamus, et regulam continentiæ secundum logon seu rationem observandam declaremus. Qui vero intelligit, quæ Scriptura cuique hæresi contraria sit, eam tempestive adhibendo refutabit eos, qui dogmata mandatis contraria fingunt. Atque ut ab alto rem repetamus, lex quidem, sicut prius diximus, illud, "Non concupisces uxorem proximi tui,"[2] prius exclamavit ante conjunctam Domini in Novo Testamento vocem, quæ dicit ex sua ipsius persona : "Audivistis legem præcipientem : Non mœchaberis. Ego autem dico : Non concupisces."[3] Quod enim vellet lex viros uti moderate uxoribus, et propter solam liberorum susceptionem, ex eo clarum est, quod prohibet quidem eum, qui non habet uxorem, statim cum "captiva" habere consuetudinem.[4] Quod si semel desideraverit, ei, cum tonsa fuerit capillos, permittere ut lugeat triginta diebus. Si autem ne sic quidem emarcescat cupiditas, tunc liberis operam dare, cum quæ dominatur impulsio, probata sit præfinito tempore consentanea rationi

appetitio. Unde nullum ex veteribus ex Scriptura ostenderis, qui cum prægnante rem habuerit : sed postquam gestavit uterum, et postquam editum fetum a lacte depulit, rursus a viris cognitas fuisse uxores. Jam hunc scopum et institutum invenies servantem Moysis patrem, cum triennium post Aaronem editum intermisisset, genuisse Moysem. Et rursus Levitica tribus, servans hanc naturæ legem a Deo traditam, aliis numero minor ingressa est in terram promissam. Non enim facile multiplicatur genus, cum viri quidem seminant, legitimo juncti matrimonio ; exspectant autem non solum uteri gestationem, sed etiam a lacte depulsionem. Unde merito Moyses, quoque Judæos paulatim provehens ad continentiam, cum "tribus diebus"[5] deinceps consequentibus a venerea voluptate abstinuissent, jussit audire verba Dei. "Nos ergo Dei templa sumus, sicut dixit propheta : Inhabitabo in eis, et inambulabo, et ero eorum Deus, et ipsi erunt meus populus," si ex præceptis vitam instituamus, sive singuli nostrum, sive tota simul Ecclesia. "Quare egredimini e medio ipsorum, et separamini, dicit Dominus, et immundum ne tangatis ; et ego vos suscipiam, et ero vobis in patrem, et vos eritis mihi in filios et filias, dicit Dominus omnipotens."[6] Non ab iis, qui uxores duxerunt, ut aiunt, sed a gentibus, quæ adhuc vivebant in fornicatione, præterea autem a prius quoque dictis hæresibus, ut immundis et impiis, prophetice nos jubet separari. Unde etiam Paulus quoque verba dirigens ad eos, qu ierant iis, qui dicti sunt, similes : "Has ergo promissiones habete, inquit, dilecti : mundemus corda nostra ab omni inquinamento carnis et spiritus, perficientes sanctitatem in timore Dei.[7] Zelo enim vos zelo Dei ; despondi enim vos uni viro, virginem castam exhibere Christo."[8] Et Ecclesia quidem alii non jungitur matrimonio, cum sponsum habeat : sed unusquisque nostrum habet potestatem ducendi, quamcunque velit, legitimam uxorem, in primis, inquam, nuptiis. "Vereor autem, ne sicut serpens seduxit Evam in astutia, corrumpantur sensus vestri a simplicitate, quæ in Christo est,"[9] pie admodum et doctoris instar dixit Apostolus. Quocirca admirabilis quoque Petrus : "Charissimi, inquit, obsecro vos tanquam advenas et peregrinos, abstinete vos a carnalibus desideriis, quæ militant adversus animam, conversationem vestram inter gentes habentes bonam : quoniam sic est voluntas Dei, ut bene facientes obmutescere faciatis imprudentium hominum ignorantiam ; quasi liberi, et non quasi velamen habentes malitiæ libertatem, sed ut servi Dei."[10] Similiter etiam scribit Paulus in

---

1 [Elucidation XII.]
2 Ex. xx. 17.
3 Matt. v. 27, 28.
4 Deut. xxi. 11, 12, 13.

5 Ex. xix. 20.
6 2 Cor. vi. 16, 17, 18.
7 2 Cor. vii. 1.
8 2 Cor. xi. 2.
9 2 Cor. xi. 3.
10 1 Pet. ii. 11, 12, 15, 16.

Epistola ad Romanos : " Qui mortui sumus peccato, quomodo adhuc vivemus in ipso ? Quoniam vetus homo noster simul est crucifixus, ut destruatur corpus peccati," [1] usque ad illud : " Neque exhibete membra vestra, arma injustitiæ peccato." [2] Atque adeo cum in hunc locum devenerim, videor mihi non esse prætermissurus, quin notem, quod eumdem Deum per legem et prophetas et Evangelium prædicet Apostolus. Illud enim : " Non concupisces," quod scriptum est in Evangelio, legi attribuit in Epistola ad Romanos, sciens esse unum eum, qui prædicavit per legem et prophetas, Patrem, et qui per ipsum est annuntiatus. Dicit enim : " Quid dicemus ? Lex estne peccatum ? Absit. Sed peccatum non cognovi, nisi per legem. Concupiscentiam enim non cognovissem, nisi lex diceret : Non concupisces." [3] Quod si ii, qui sunt diversæ sententiæ, repugnantes, existiment Paulum verba sua dirigentem adversus Creatorem, dixisse ea, quæ deinceps sequuntur : " Novi enim, quod non habitat in me, hoc est, in carne mea, bonum ; " [4] legant ea, quæ prius dicta sunt ; et ea, quæ consequuntur. Prius enim dixit : " Sed inhabitans in me peccatum ; " propter quod consentaneum erat dicere illud : " Non habitat in carne mea bonum." [5] Consequenter subjunxit : " Si autem quod nolo, hoc ego facio, non utique ego id operor, sed quod inhabitat in me peccatum : " quod " repugnans," inquit, " legi " Dei et " mentis meæ, captivat me in lege peccati, quæ est in membris meis. Miser ego homo, quis me liberabit de corpore mortis hujus ? " [6] Et rursus (nunquam enim quovis modo juvando defatigatur) non veretur veluti concludere : " Lex enim spiritus liberavit me a lege peccati et mortis : " quoniam " per Filium Deus condemnavit peccatum in carne, ut justificatio legis impleatur in nobis, qui non secundum carnem ambulamus, sed secundum spiritum." [7] Præter hæc adhuc declarans ea, quæ prius dicta sunt, exclamat : " Corpus quidem mortuum propter peccatum : " significans id non esse templum, sed sepulcrum animæ. Quando enim sanctificatum fuerit Deo, " Spiritus ejus," infert, " qui suscitavit Jesum a mortuis, habitat in vobis : qui vivificabit etiam mortalia vestra corpora, per ejus Spiritum, qui habitat in vobis." [8] Rursus itaque voluptarios increpans, illa adjicit : " Prudentia enim carnis, mors ; quoniam qui ex carne vivunt, ea, quæ sunt carnis, cogitant ; et prudentia carnis est cum Deo gerere inimicitias ; legi enim Dei non subjicitur. Qui autem sunt in carne," non ut quidam decernunt, " Deo placere non possunt,"

sed ut prius diximus. Deinde ut eos distinguat, dicit Ecclesiæ : " Vos autem non estis in carne, sed in spiritu, si quidem spiritus Dei habitat in vobis. Si quis autem spiritum Christi non habet, is non est ejus. Si autem Christus in vobis, corpus quidem est mortuum per peccatum, spiritus autem vivus per justitiam. Debitores itaque sumus, fratres, non carni, ut secundum carnem vivamus. Si enim secundum carnem vivitis, estis morituri : si vero spiritu facta carnis mortificaveritis, vivetis. Quicunque enim spiritu Dei aguntur, ii sunt filii Dei." Et adversus nobilitatem et adversus libertatem, quæ exsecrabiliter ab iis, qui sunt diversæ sententiæ, introducitur, qui de libidine gloriantur, subjungit dicens : " Non enim accepistis spiritum servitutis rursus in timorem, sed accepistis spiritum adoptionis filiorum, in quo clamamus, Abba Pater ; " [9] hoc est, ad hoc accepimus, ut cognoscamus eum, quem oramus, qui est vere Pater, qui rerum omnium solus est Pater, qui ad salutem erudit et castigat ut pater, et timorem minatur.

CAPUT XII. — VERBA APOSTOLI 1 COR. VII. 5, 39, 40, ALIAQUE S. SCRIPTURÆ LOCA EODEM SPECTANTIA EXPLICAT.

Quod autem " ex consensu ad tempus orationi vacat " conjugium, doctrina est continentiæ. Adjecit enim illud quidem, " ex consensu," ne quis dissolveret matrimonium ; " ad tempus autem," [10] ne, dum ex necessitate exercet continentiam is, qui uxorem duxerit, labatur in peccatum, et dum suo conjugio parcit, alienum concupiscat. Qua ratione eum, qui se indecore gerere existimat, quod virginem alat, recte eam dicit esse nuptum daturum. Verum unusquisque, tam is qui castitatem, delegit, quam is qui propter liberorum procreationem seipsum conjunxit matrimonio, in suo proposito firmiter debet perseverare, nec in deterius deflectere. Si enim vitæ suæ institutum augere ac intendere poterit, majorem sibi apud Deum acquirit dignitatem, propter puram et ex ratione profectam continentiam. Si autem eam, quam elegit, regulam superaverit, in majorem deinde ad spem gloriam recidet. Habet enim sicut castitas, ita etiam matrimonium propria munera et ministeria, quæ ad Dominum pertinent, filiorum, inquam, curam gerere et uxoris. Quod enim honeste causatur is, qui est in matrimonio perfectus, est conjugii necessitudo, ut qui omnium curam ac providentiam in domo communi ostenderit. Ac proinde " episcopos," inquit, oportet constitui, qui ex domo propria toti quoque Ecclesiæ præesse sint meditati. " Unusquisque " ergo, " in quo vocatus est " [11] opere ministerium peragat, ut liber in Christo fiat, et debitam ministerio suo mercedem

---

[1] Rom. vi. 2, 6.
[2] Rom. vi. 13.
[3] Rom. vii. 7.
[4] Rom. vii. 18.
[5] Rom. vii. 17.
[6] Rom. vii. 20, 23, 24
[7] Rom. viii. 2, 3, 4.
[8] Rom. viii. 10, 11.

[9] Rom. viii. 5, 6, 7, 8, 9, 10, 12, 13, 14, 15.
[10] 1 Cor. vii. 5.
[11] 1 Cor. vii. 24.

accipiat. Et rursus de lege disserens, utens allegoria : " Nam quæ sub viro est mulier," inquit, " viventi viro alligata est lege," [1] et quæ sequuntur. Et rursus : " Mulier est alligata, quandiu vivit vir ejus ; sin autem mortuus fuerit, libera est ut nubat, modo in Domino. Beata est autem si sic permanserit, mea quidem sententia." [2] Sed in priore quidem particula, " mortificati estis," inquit, " legi," non matrimonio, " ut efficiamini vos alteri, qui excitatus est ex mortuis," [3] sponsa et Ecclesia ; quam castam esse oportet, et ab iis quæ sunt intus, cogitationibus, quæ sunt contrariæ veritati ; et ab iis, qui tentant extrinsecus, hoc est ab iis, qui sectantur hæreses, et persuadent vobis fornicari ab uno viro, nempe omnipotenti Deo : " Ne sicut serpens decepit Evam," [4] quæ " vita " dicitur, nos quoque inducti callidis hæresium illecebris, transgrediamur mandata. Secunda autem particula statuit monogamiam : non enim, ut quidam existimarunt, mulieris cum viro alligationem, carnis cum corruptelâ connexionem, significari putandum est ; impiorum enim hominum, qui matrimonii inventionem diabolo aperte tribuunt, opinionem reprehendit, unde in periculum venit legislator ne incessatur maledictis. Tatianum arbitror Syrum talia audere dogmata tradere.[5] His verbis quidem certe scribit in libro *De perfectione secundum Servatorem :* Consensum quidem conjungit orationi : communio autem corruptelæ, interitus solvit interpellationem. Admodum certe circumspecte arcet per concessionem. Nam cum rursus permisit " simul convenire propter Satanam et intemperantiam," [6] pronuntiavit eum, qui est obtemperaturus, " serviturum duobus dominis :" [7] per consensum quidem, Deo ; per dissensionem autem, intemperantiæ et fornicationi et diabolo. Hæc autem dicit, Apostolum exponens. Sophistice autem eludit veritatem, per verum, falsum confirmans : intemperantiam enim et fornicationem, diabolica vitia et affectiones nos quoque confitemur ; intercedit autem moderati matrimonii consensio, quæ tum ad precationem continenter deducit, tum ad procreandos liberos cum honestate conciliat. " Cognitio " quidem certe a Scriptura dictum est tempus liberorum procreationis, cum dixit : " Cognovit autem Adam Evam uxorem suam ; et concepit, et peperit filium, et nominavit nomen ejus Seth : Suscitavit enim mihi Deus aliud semen pro Abel." [8] Vides, quemnam maledictis incessant, qui honestam ac moderatam incessunt seminationem, et diabolo attribuunt generationem. Non enim simpliciter Deum dixit,

qui articuli præmissione, nempe ὁ Θεός dicens, significavit eum, qui est omnipotens. Quod ab Apostolo autem subjungitur : " Et rursus simul convenite propter Satanam," [9] in eum finem dicitur, ut occasionem tollat ad alias declinandi cupiditates. Non enim penitus repellit naturæ appetitiones, qui fit ad tempus, consensus : per quem rursus inducit Apostolus conjugationem matrimonii, non ad intemperantiam et fornicationem et opus diaboli, sed ne subjugetur intemperantiæ, fornicationi, et diabolo. Distinguit autem veterem quoque hominem et novum Tatianus, sed non ut dicimus, " Veterem " quidem " virum," legem ; " novum " autem, Evangelium. Assentimur ei nos quoque, sed non eo modo, quo vult ille, dissolvens legem ut alterius Dei : sed idem vir et Dominus, dum vetera renovat, non amplius concedit polygamiam (nam hanc quidem expetebat Deus, quando oportebat homines augeri et multiplicari), sed monogamiam introducit propter liberorum procreationem et domus curam, ad quam data est mulier adjutrix : et si cui Apostolus propter intemperantiam et ustionem, veniam secundi concedit matrimonii ; nam hic quoque non peccat quidem ex Testamento (non est enim a lege prohibitus), non implet autem summam illam vitæ perfectionem, quæ agitur ex Evangelio. Gloriam autem sibi acquirit cœlestem, qui apud se manserit, eam, quæ est morte dissoluta, impollutam servans conjunctionem, et grato ac lubente animo paret œconomiæ, per quam effectum est, ut divelli non possit a Domini ministerio. Sed nec eum, qui ex conjugali surgit cubili, similiter ut olim, tingi nunc quoque jubet divina per Dominum providentia : non enim necessario a liberorum abducit procreatione, qui credentes per unum baptismum ad consuetudinem omni ex parte perfectam abluit, Dominus, qui etiam multa Moysis baptismata per unum comprehendit baptismum. Proinde lex, ut per carnalem generationem nostram prædiceret regenerationem, genitali seminis facultati baptismum olim adhibuit, non vero quod ab hominis generatione abhorreret. Quod enim apparet homo generatus, hoc valet seminis dejectio. Non sunt ergo multi coitus genitales, sed matricis susceptio fatetur generationem, cum in naturæ officina semen formatur in fetum. Quomodo autem vetus quidem est solum matrimonium et legis inventum, alienum autem est, quod est ex Domino, matrimonium, cum idem Deus servetur a nobis ? " Non " enim " quod Deus conjunxit, homo " jure " dissolverit ; " [10] multo autem magis quæ jussit Pater, servabit quoque Filius. Si autem idem simul est et legislator et evangelista, nunquam ipse secum pugnat. Vivit enim lex, cum sit spiritalis, et gnostice intelligatur : nos autem

---

[1] Rom. vii. 2.
[2] 1 Cor. vii. 39, 40.
[3] Rom. vii. 4.
[4] 2 Cor. xi. 3.
[5] [Elucidation XIII.]
[6] 1 Cor. vii. 5.
[7] Matt. vi. 24.
[8] Gen. iv. 25.

[9] 1 Cor. vii. 5.
[10] Matt. xix. 6.

"mortui" sumus "legi per corpus Christi, ut gigneremur alteri, qui resurrrexit ex mortuis," qui prædictus fuit a lege, "ut Deo fructificaremus." [1] Quare "lex quidem est sancta, et mandatum sanctum, et justum, et bonum." [2] Mortui ergo sumus legi, hoc est, peccato, quod a lege significatur, quod ostendit, non autem generat lex, per jussionem eorum quæ sunt facienda, et prohibitionem eorum quæ non facienda; reprehendens subjectum peccatum, "ut appareat peccatum." Si autem peccatum est matrimonium, quod secundum legem initur, nescio quomodo quis dicet se Deum nosse, dicens Dei jussum esse peccatum. Quod si "lex sancta" est, sanctum est matrimonium. Mysterium ergo hoc ad Christum et Ecclesiam ducit Apostolus: quemadmodum "quod ex carne generatur, caro est; ita quod ex spiritu, spiritus," [3] non solum in pariendo, sed etiam in discendo. Jam "sancti sunt filii," [4] Deo gratæ oblectationes verborum Dominicorum, quæ desponderunt animam. Sunt ergo separata fornicatio et matrimonium, quoniam a Deo longe abest diabolus. "Et vos ergo mortui estis legi per corpus Christi, ut vos gigneremini alteri, qui surrexit a mortuis." [5] Simul autem proxime exauditur, si fueritis obedientes: quamdoquidem etiam ex veritate legis eidem Domino obedimus, qui præcipit eminus. Nunquid autem de ejusmodi hominibus merito aperte "dicit Spiritus, quod in posterioribus temporibus deficient quidam a fide, attendentes spiritibus erroris, et doctrinis dæmoniorum, in hypocrisi falsiloquorum, cauteriatam habentium conscientiam, et prohibentium nubere, abstinere a cibis, quos Deus creavit ad participationem cum gratiarum actione fidelibus, et qui agnoverunt veritatem, quod omnis creatura Dei bona est, et nihil est rejiciendum quod sumitur cum gratiarum actione. Sanctificatur enim per verbum Dei et orationem?" [6] Omnino igitur non est prohibendum jungi matrimonio, neque carnibus vesci, aut vinum bibere. Scriptum est enim: "Bonum est carnem non comedere, nec vinum bibere, si quis comedat per offendiculum." [7] Et: "Bonum est manere sicut ego." [8] Sed et qui utitur, "cum gratiarum actione," [9] et qui rursus non utitur, ipse quoque "cum gratiarum actione," et cum moderata ac temperanti vivat perceptione, logo seu rationi convenienter. Et, ut in summa dicam, omnes Apostoli epistolæ, quæ moderationem docent et continentiam, cum et de matrimonio, et de liberorum procreatione, et de domus administratione innumerabilia præcepta con-

tineant, nusquam honestum moderatumque matrimonium prohibuerunt aut abrogarunt: sed legis cum Evangelio servantes convenientiam, utrumque admittunt: et eum, qui deo agendo gratias, moderate utitur matrimonio; et eum, qui, ut vult Dominus, vivit in castitate, quemadmodum "vocatus est unusquisque" inoffense et perfecte eligens. "Et erat terra Jacob laudata supra omnem terram," [10] inquit propheta, ipse vas spiritus gloria afficiens. Insectatur autem aliquis generationem, in eam dicens interitum cadere, eamque perire: et detorquet aliquis ad filiorum procreationem illud dictum Servatoris: "Non oportere in terra thesauros recondere, ubi tinea et ærugo demolitur;" [11] nec erubescit his addere ea, quæ dicit propheta: "Omnes vos sicut vestimentum veterascetis, et tinea vos exedet." [12] Sed neque nos contradicimus Scripturæ, neque in nostra corpora cadere interitum, eaque esse fluxa, negamus. Fortasse autem iis, quos ibi alloquitur propheta, ut peccatoribus, prædicit interitum. Servator autem de liberorum procreatione nil dixit, sed ad impertiendum ac communicandum eos hortatur, qui solum opibus abundare, egentibus autem nolebant opem ferre. Quamobrem dicit: "Operamini non cibum, qui perit; sed eum, qui manet in vitam æternam." [13] Similiter autem afferunt etiam illud dictum de resurrectione mortuorum: "Filii illius sæculi nec nubunt, nec nubuntur." [14] Sed hanc interrogationem et eos qui interrogant, si quis consideraverit, inveniet Dominum non reprobare matrimonium, sed remedium afferre exspectationi carnalis cupiditatis in resurrectione. Illud autem, "filiis hujus sæculi," [15] non dixit ad distinctionem alicujus alius sæculi, sed perinde ac si diceret: Qui in hoc nati sunt sæculo, cum per generationem sint filii, et gignunt et gignuntur; quoniam non absque generatione hanc quis vitam prætergreditur: sed hæc generatio, quæ similem suscipit interitum, non amplius competit ei qui ab hac vita est separatus. "Unus est ergo Pater noster, qui est in cœlis:" [16] sed is ipse quoque Pater est omnium per creationem. "Ne vocaveritis ergo, inquit, vobis patrem super terram." [17] Quasi diceret: Ne existimetis eum, qui carnali vos sevit satu, auctorem et causam vestræ essentiæ, sed adjuvantem causam generationis, vel ministrum potius. Sic ergo nos rursus conversos vult effici ut pueros, eum, qui vere Pater est, agnoscentes, regeneratos per aquam, cum hæc sit alia satio in creatione. At, inquit, "Qui est cælebs, curat quæ sunt Domini; qui autem duxit uxorem, quomodo placebit uxori." Quid vero?

1 Rom. vii. 4.
2 Rom. vii. 12.
3 John iii. 6.
4 1 Cor. vii. 14.
5 Rom. vii. 4.
6 1 Tim. iv. 1, 2, 3, 4, 5.
7 Rom. xiv. 21.
8 1 Cor. vii. 8.
9 Rom. xiv. 19.

10 Sophon. iii. 19.
11 Matt. vi. 19.
12 Isa. l. 9.
13 John vi. 27.
14 Luke xx. 35.
15 Luke xx. 34.
16 Matt. xxiii. 9.
17 Matt. xxiii. 9.

annon licet etiam eis, qui secundum Deum placent uxori, Deo gratias agere? Annon permittitur etiam ei, qui uxorem duxit, una cum conjugio etiam esse sollicitum de iis quæ sunt Domini? Sed quemadmodum "quæ non nupsit, sollicita est de iis, quæ sunt Domini, ut sit sancta corpore et spiritu:"[1] ita etiam quæ nupsit, et de iis, quæ sunt mariti, et de iis, quæ sunt Domini, est in Domino sollicita, ut sit sancta et corpore et spiritu. Ambæ enim sunt sanctæ in Domino: hæc quidem ut uxor, illa vero ut virgo. Ad eos autem pudore afficiendos et reprimendos, qui sunt proclives ad secundas nuptias, apte Apostolus alto quodam tono eloquitur; inquit enim: "Ecce, omne peccatum est extra corpus; qui autem fornicatur, in proprium corpus peccat."[2] Si quis autem matrimonium audet dicere fornicationem, rursus, legem et Dominum insectans, maledictis impetit. Quemadmodum enim avaritia et plura habendi cupiditas dicitur fornicatio, ut quæ adversetur sufficientiæ: et ut idololatria est ab uno in multos Dei distributio, ita fornicatio est ab uno matrimonio ad plura prolapsio. Tribus enim modis, ut diximus, fornicatio et adulterium sumitur apud Apostolum. De his dicit propheta: "Peccatis vestris venundati estis." Et rursus: "Pollutus es in terra aliena:"[3] conjunctionem sceleratam existimans, quæ cum alieno corpore facta est, et non cum eo, quod datur in conjugio, ad liberorum procreationem. Unde etiam Apostolus: "Volo, inquit, juniores nubere, filios procreare, domui præesse, nullam dare occasionem adversario maledicti gratia. Jam enim quædam diverterunt post Satanam."[4] Quin et unius quoque uxoris virum utique admittit; seu sit presbyter, seu diaconus, seu laicus, utens matrimonio citra reprehensionem: "Servabitur autem per filiorum procreationem."[5] Et rursus Servator dicens Judæos "generationem pravam et adulteram," docet eos legem non cognovisse, ut lex vult: "sed seniorum traditionem, et hominum præcepta sequentes," adulterare legem, perinde ac si non esset data vir et dominus eorum virginitatis. Fortasse autem eos quoque innuit esse alienis mancipatos cupiditatibus, propter quas assidue quoque servientes peccatis, vendebantur alienigenis. Nam apud Judæos non erant admissæ communes mulieres: verum prohibitum erat adulterium. Qui autem dicit: "Uxorem duxi, non possum venire,"[6] ad divinam cœnam, est quidem exemplum ab eos arguendos, qui propter voluptates abscedunt a divino mandato: alioquin nec qui justi fuere ante adventum, nec qui post adventum uxores duxerunt,

servabuntur, etiamsi sint apostoli. Quod si illud attulerint, quod propheta quoque dicit: "Inveteravi inter omnes inimicos meos,"[7] per inimicos peccata intelligant. Unum quoddam autem est peccatum, non matrimonium, sed fornicatio: alioqui generationem quoque dicunt peccatum, et creatorem generationis.

CAPUT XIII. — JULII CASSIANI HÆRETICI VERBIS RESPONDET; ITEM LOCO QUEM EX EVANGELIO APOCRYPHO IDEM ADDUXERAT.

Talibus argumentis utitur quoque Julius Cassianus,[8] qui fuit princeps sectæ Docetarum. In opere certe De continentia, vel De castitate, his verbis dicit: "Nec dicat aliquis, quod quoniam talia habemus membra, ut aliter figurata sit femina, aliter vero masculus: illa quidem ad suscipiendum, hic vero ad seminandum, concessam esse a Deo consuetudinem. Si enim a Deo, ad quem tendimus, esset hæc constitutio, non beatos dixisset esse eunuchos; neque propheta dixisset, eos 'non esse arborem infrugiferam;[9] transferens ab arbore ad hominem, qui sua sponte et ex instituto se castrat tali cogitatione." Et pro impia opinione adhuc decertans, subjungit: "Quomodo autem non jure quis reprehenderit Servatorem, si nos transformavit, et ab errore liberavit, et a conjunctione membrorum, et additamentorum, et pudendorum?" in hoc eadem decernens cum Tatiano: hic autem prodiit ex schola Valentini. Propterea dicit Cassianus: "Cum interrogaret Salome, quando cognoscentur, ea, de quibus interrogabat, ait Dominus: Quando pudoris indumentum conculcaveritis, et quando duo facta fuerint unum, et masculum cum femina, nec masculum nec femineum." Primum quidem, in nobis traditis quatuor Evangeliis non habemus hoc dictum, sed in eo, quod est secundum Ægyptios. Deinde mihi videtur ignorare, iram quidem, masculam appetitionem; feminam vero, significare cupiditatem: quorum operationem pœnitentia et pudor consequuntur. Cum quis ergo neque iræ neque cupiditati obsequens, quæ quidem et consuetudine et mala educatione auctæ, obumbrant et contegunt rationem, sed quæ ex iis proficiscitur exuens caliginem, et pudore affectus ex pœnitentia, spiritum et animam unierit in obedientia Logi seu rationis; tunc, ut ait Paulus, "non inest in nobis nec masculus, nec femina." Recedens enim anima ab ea figura, qua discernitur masculus et femina, traducitur ad unionem, cum ea nutrum sit. Existimat autem hic vir præclarus plus, quam par sit, Platonice, animam, cum sit ab initio divina, cupiditate effeminatam, huc venire ad generationem et interitum.

---

[1] 1 Cor. vii. 32, 33, 34.
[2] 1 Cor. vi. 18.
[3] Isa. l. 1.
[4] 1 Tim. v. 14, 15.
[5] 1 Tim. ii. 15.
[6] Luke xiv. 20.

[7] Ps. vi. 8.
[8] [Elucidation XIV.]
[9] Isa. lvi. 3.

CAPUT XIV. — 2 COR. XI. 3, ET EPH. IV. 24,
EXPONIT.

Jam vero vel invitum cogit Paulum genera-tionem ex deceptione deducere, cum dicit: "Vereor autem, ne sicut serpens Evam decepit, corrupti sint sensus vestri a simplicitate, quæ est in Christo." [1] Sed certum est, Dominum quoque "venisse" ad ea, "quæ aberraverant." [2] Aber-raverunt autem, non ab alto repetita origine in eam, quæ hic est, generationem (est enim ge-neratio creatura Omnipotentis, qui nunquam ex melioribus ad deteriora deduxerit animam); sed ad eos, qui sensibus seu cogitationibus aberra-verant, ad nos, inquam, venit Servator : qui quidem ex nostra in præceptis inobedientia corrupti sunt, dum nimis avide voluptatem persequeremur ; cum utique protoplastus noster tempus præve-nisset, et ante debitum tempus matrimonii gratiam appetiisset et aberrasset : quoniam "quicunque aspicit mulierem ad concupiscendum eam, jam mœchatus est eam," [3] ut qui voluntatis tempus non exspectaverit. Is ipse ergo erat Dominus, qui tunc quoque damnabat cupiditatem, quæ prævenit matrimonium. Cum ergo dicit Aposto-lus : "Induite novum hominem, qui secundum Deum creatur," [4] nobis dicit, qui ab Omnipo-tentis voluntate efficti sumus, sicut sumus efficti. "Veterem" autem dixit, non recipiens ad ge-nerationem et regenerationem, sed ad vitam ino-bedientiæ et obedientiæ. "Pelliceas" autem "tunicas" [5] existimat Cassianus esse corpora : in quo postea et eum, et qui idem cum eo sentiunt, aberrasse ostendemus, cum de ortu hominis, iis consequenter, quæ prius dicenda sunt, aggredie-mur expositionem. "Quoniam, inquit, qui a terrenis reguntur, et generant, et generantur : *Nostra autem conversatio est in cœlo, ex quo etiam Salvatorem exspectamus.*" [6] Recte ergo nos hæc quoque dicta esse scimus, quoniam ut hospites et advenæ peregrinantes debemus vitam instituere ; qui uxorem habent, ut non habentes ; qui possident, ut non possidentes ; qui liberos procreant, ut mortales gignentes, ut relicturi pos-sessiones, ut etiam sine uxore victuri, si opus sit ; non cum immodico actione, et animo excelso.

CAPUT XV. — I COR. VII. 1 ; LUC. XIV. 26 ; ISA.
LVI. 2, 3, EXPLICAT.

Et rursus cum dicit : "Bonum est homini uxorem non tangere, sed propter fornicationes unusquisque suam uxorem habeat ; " [7] id ve-luti exponens, rursus dicit : "Ne vos tentet Sa-tanas." [8] Non enim iis, qui continenter utuntur matrimonio propter solam liberorum procrea-tionem, dicit, "propter intemperantiam ; " sed iis, qui finem liberorum procreationis cupiunt transilire : ne, cum nimium annuerit noster adver-sarius, excitet appetitionem ad alienas voluptates. Fortasse autem quoniam iis, qui juste vivunt, resistit propter æmulationem, et adversus eos contendit, volens eos ad suos ordines traducere, per laboriosam continentiam eis vult præbere occasionem. Merito ergo dicit : "Melius est matrimonio jungi quam uri," [9] ut "vir reddat debitum uxori, et uxor viro, et ne frustrentur invicem " [10] hoc divino ad generationem dato auxilio. "Qui autem, inquiunt, non oderit pa-trem, vel matrem, vel uxorem, vel filios, non potest meus esse discipulus." [11] Non jubet odisse proprium genus : "Honora " enim, inquit, "pa-trem et matrem, ut tibi bene sit : " [12] sed ne abdu-caris, inquit, per appetitiones a ratione alienas, sed neque civilibus moribus conformis fias. Do-mus enim constat ex genere, civitates autem ex domibus ; quemadmodum Paulus quoque eos, qui occupantur in matrimonio, "mundo dixit placere." [13] Rursus dicit Dominus : "Qui uxorem duxit, ne expellat ; et qui non duxit, ne ducat ; " [14] qui ex proposito castitatis professus est uxorem non ducere maneat cælebs. Utrisque ergo idem Dominus per prophetam Isaiam convenientes dat promissiones sic dicens : "Ne dicat eunuchus : Sum lignum aridum ; " hæc enim dicit Dominus eunuchis : "Si custodieritis sabbata mea, et fe-ceritis quæcunque præcipio, dabo vobis locum meliorem filiis et filiabus." [15] Non sola enim justificat castitas, sed nec sabbatum eunuchi, nisi fecerit mandata. Infert autem iis, qui uxorem duxerunt, et dicit : "Electi mei non laborabunt in vanum, neque procreabunt filios in exsecra-tionem, quia semen est benedictum a Domino." [16] Ei enim, qui secundum Logon filios procreavit et educavit, et erudivit in Domino, sicut etiam ei, qui genuit per veram catechesim et institu-tionem, merces quædam est proposita, sicut etiam electo semini. Alii autem "exsecrationem " ac-cipiunt esse ipsam liberorum procreationem, et non intelligunt adversus illos ipsos ea dicere Scripturam. Qui enim sunt revera electi Domini, non dogmata decernunt, nec filios progignunt, qui sunt ad exsecrationem, et hæreses. Eunu-chus ergo, non qui per vim excisas habet partes, sed nec qui cælebs est, dictus est, sed qui non gignit veritatem. Lignum hic prius erat aridum ; si autem Logo obedierit, et sabbata custodieri, per abstinentiam a peccatis, et fecerit mandata erit honorabilior iis, qui absque recta vitæ insti-tutione solo sermone erudiuntur. "Filioli, modi-

---

[1] 2 Cor. xi. 3.
[2] Matt. xviii. 11, 12.
[3] Matt. v. 28.
[4] Eph. iv 24.
[5] Gen. iii. 21.
[6] Phil. iii. 20.
[7] 1 Cor. vii. 1, 2.
[8] 1 Cor. vii. 5.

[9] 1 Cor. vii. 9.
[10] 1 Cor. vii. 3, 5.
[11] Luke xiv. 26.
[12] Ex. xx. 12.
[13] 1 Cor. vii. 33.
[14] 1 Cor. vii. 10, 11.
[15] Isa. lvi. 3, 4, 5.
[16] Isa. lxv. 23.

cum adhuc sum vobiscum," [1] inquit Magister. Quare Paulus quoque scribens ad Galatas, dicit : " Filioli mei, quos iterum parturio, donec formetur in vobis Christus." [2] Rursus ad Corinthios scribens : " Si enim decies mille pædagogos," inquit, " habeatis in Christo, sed non multos patres. In Christo enim per Evangelium ego vos genui." [3] Propterea "non ingrediatur eunuchus in Ecclesiam Dei," [4] qui est sterilis, et non fert fructum, nec vitæ institutione, nec sermone. Sed " qui se " quidem " castrarunt " ab omni peccato " propter regnum cœlorum," [5] ii sunt beati, qui a mundo jejunant.

CAPUT XVI. — JER. XX. 14 ; JOB XIV. 3 ; PS. L. 5 ; I COR. IX. 27, EXPONIT.

" Exsecranda " autem " dies in qua natus sum, et ut non sit optanda," [6] inquit Jeremias : non absolute exsecrandam dicens generationem, sed populi peccata ægre ferens et inobedientiam. Subjungit itaque : " Cur enim natus sum ut viderem labores et dolores, et in perpetuo probro fuerunt dies mei ? " [7] Quin etiam omnes, qui prædicabant veritatem, propter eorum, qui audiebant, inobedientiam, quærebantur ad pœnam, et veniebant in periculum. " Cur enim non fuit uterus matris meæ sepulcrum, ne viderem afflictionem Jacob et laborem generis Israel ? " [8] ait Esdras propheta. " Nullus est a sorde mundus," ait Job, " nec si sit quidem una dies vita ejus." [9] Dicant ergo nobis, ubi fornicatus est infans natus ? vel quomodo sub Adæ cecidit exsecrationem, qui nihil est operatus ? Restat ergo eis, ut videtur, consequenter, ut dicant malam esse generationem, non solum corporis, sed etiam animæ, per quam exsistit corpus. Et quando dixit David : " In peccatis conceptus sum, et in iniquitatibus concepit me mater mea : " [10] dicit prophetice quidem matrem Evam ; sed Eva quidem fuit " mater viventium ; " et si is " in peccatis fuit conceptus," at non ipse in peccato, neque vero ipse peccatum. Utrum vero quicunque etiam a peccato ad fidem convertitur, a peccandi consuetudine tanquam a "matre" converti dicatur ad "vitam," feret mihi testimonium unus ex duodecim prophetis, qui dixit : " Si dedero primogenita pro impietate fructum ventris mei, pro peccatis animæ meæ." [11] Non accusat eum, qui dixit : " Crescite et multiplicamini : " [12] sed primos post generationem motus, quorum tem-

pore Deum non cognoscimus, dicit "impietates." Si quis autem ea ratione dicit malam generationem, idem eam dicat bonam, quatenus in ipso veritatem cognoscimus. "Abluamini juste, et ne peccetis. Ignorationem enim Dei quidam habent," [13] videlicet qui peccant. "Quoniam nobis est colluctatio non adversus carnem et sanguinem, sed adversus spiritalia." [14] Potentes autem sunt· ad tentandum "principes tenebrarum hujus mundi," et ideo datur venia. Et ideo Paulus quoque : "Corpus meum," inquit, "castigo, et in servitutem redigo ; quoniam qui certat, omnia continet," hoc est, in omnibus continet, non ab omnibus abstinens, sed continenter utens iis, quæ utenda judicavit, "illi quidem ut corruptibilem coronam accipiant ; nos autem ut incorruptibilem," [15] in lucta vincentes, non autem sine pulvere coronam accipientes. Jam nonnulli quoque præferunt viduam virgini, ut quæ, quam experta est, voluptatem magno animo contempserit.

CAPUT XVII. — QUI NUPTIAS ET GENERATIONEM MALAS ASSERUNT, II ET DEI CREATIONEM ET IPSAM EVANGELII DISPENSATIONEM VITUPERANT.

Sin autem malum est generatio, in malo blasphemi dicant fuisse Dominum qui fuit particeps generationis, in malo Virginem quæ genuit. Hei mihi ! quot et quanta mala ! Dei voluntatem maledictis incessunt, et mysterium creationis, dum invehuntur in generationem. Et hinc "Docesin" fingit Cassianus ; hinc etiam Marcioni, et Valentino quoque est corpus animale ; quoniam homo, inquiunt, operam dans veneri, "assimilatus est jumentis." [16] Atqui profecto, cum libidine vere insaniens, aliena inire voluerit, tunc revera, qui talis est, efferatur : "Equi in feminas furentes facti sunt, unusquisque hinniebat ad uxorem proximi sui." [17] Quod si dicat serpentem, a brutis animantibus accepta consilii sui ratione, Adamo persuasisse ut cum Eva coire consentiret, tanquam alioqui, ut quidam existimant, protoplasti hac natura usuri non fuissent : rursus vituperatur creatio, ut quæ rationis expertium animantium natura homines fecerit imbecilliores, quorum exempla consecuti sunt, qui a Deo primi formati fuere. Sin autem natura quidem eos sicut bruta deduxit ad filiorum procreationem ; moti autem sunt citius quam oportuit, fraude inducti, cum adhuc essent juvenes ; justum quidem est Dei judicium in eos qui non exspectarunt ejus voluntatem : sancta est autem generatio, per quam mundus consistit, per quam essentiæ, per quam naturæ, per quam angeli, per quam potestates, per quam

---

[1] John xiii. 33.
[2] Gal. iv. 19.
[3] 1 Cor iv. 15.
[4] Deut. xxiii. 1.
[5] Matt. xix. 12.
[6] Jer. xx. 14.
[7] Jer. xx. 18.
[8] 4 Esdr. v. 35.
[9] Job xiv. 4, 5.
[10] Ps. l. 7.
[11] Mic. vi. 7.
[12] Gen. i. 28.

[13] 1 Cor. xv. 34. Clement reads here ἐκνίψατε, " wash," instead of ἐκνήψατε, " awake."
[14] Eph. vi. 12.
[15] 1 Cor. ix. 27, 25.
[16] Ps. xlviii. 13, 21.
[17] Jer. v. 8.

animæ, per quam præcepta, per quam lex, per quam Evangelium, per quam Dei cognitio. "Et omnis caro fenum, et omnis gloria ejus quasi flos feni; et fenum quidem exsiccatur, flos autem decidit, sed verbum Domini manet,"[1] quod unxit animam et uniit spiritui. Quomodo autem, quæ est in Ecclesia nostra,[2] œconomia ad finem perduci potuisset absque corpore, cum etiam ipse, qui est caput Ecclesiæ, in carne quidem informis et specie carens vitam transiit, ut doceret nos respicere ad naturam divinæ causæ informem et incorpoream? "Arbor enim vitæ," inquit propheta, "est in bono desiderio,"[3] docens bona et munda desideria, quæ sunt in Domino vivente. Jam vero volunt viri cum uxore in matrimonio consuetudinem, quæ dicta est "cognitio," esse peccatum: eam quippe indicari ex esu "ligni boni et mali,"[4] per significationem hujus vocabuli "cognovit,"[5] quæ mandati transgressionem notat. Si autem hoc ita est, veritatis quoque cognitio, est esus ligni vitæ. Potest ergo honestum ac moderatum matrimonium illius quoque ligni esse particeps. Nobis autem prius dictum est, quod licet bene et male uti matrimonio; et hoc est lignum "cognitionis," si non transgrediamur leges matrimonii. Quid vero? annon Servator noster, sicut animam, ita etiam corpus curavit ab affectionibus? Neque vero si esset caro inimica animæ, inimicam per sanitatis restitutionem adversus ipsam muniisset. "Hoc autem dico, fratres, quod caro et sanguis regnum Dei non possunt possidere, neque corruptio possidet incorruptionem."[6] Peccatun enim, cum sit "corruptio," non potest habere societatem cum incorruptione," quæ est justitia. "Adeo stulti," inquit, "estis? cum spiritu cœperitis, nunc carne consummamini."[7]

CAPUT XVIII. — DUÀS EXTREMAS OPINIONES ESSE VITANDAS: PRIMAM ILLORUM QUI CREATORIS ODIO A NUPTIIS ABSTINENT; ALTERAM ILLORUM QUI HINC OCCASIONEM ARRIPIUNT NEFARIIS LIBIDINIBUS INDULGENDI.

Justitiam ergo et salutis harmoniam, quæ est veneranda firmaque, alii quidem, ut ostendimus, nimium intenderunt, blaspheme ac maledice cum quavis impietate suscipientes continentiam; cum pie liceret castitatem, quæ secundum sanam regulam instituitur, eligere; gratias quidem agendo propter datam ipsis gratiam, non habendo autem odio creaturam, neque eos aspernando, qui juncti sunt matrimonio; est enim creatus mundus, creata est etiam castitas; ambo autem agant

gratias in iis, in quibus sunt collocati, si modo ea quoque norunt, in quibus sunt collocati. Alii autem effrenati se petulanter et insolenter gesserunt, revera "effecti equi in feminas insanientes, et ad proximorum suorum uxores hinnientes;"[8] ut qui et ipsi contineri non possint, et proximis suis persuadeant ut dent operam voluptati; infeliciter illas audientes Scripturas: "Quæ tibi obtigit, partem pone nobiscum, crumenam autem unam possideamus communem, et unum fiat nobis marsupium."[9] Propter eos idem propheta dicit, nobis consulens: "Ne ambulaveris in via cum ipsis, declina pedem tuum a semitis eorum. Non enim injuste tenduntur retia pennatis. Ipsi enim, cum sint sanguinum participes, thesauros malorum sibi recondunt;"[10] hoc est, sibi affectantes immunditiam, et proximos similia docentes, bellatores, percussores caudis suis,[11] ait propheta, quas quidem Græci κέρκους appellant. Fuerint autem ii, quos significat prophetia, libidinosi intemperantes, qui sunt caudis suis pugnaces, tenebrarum "iræque filii,"[12] cæde polluti, manus sibi afferentes, et homicidæ propinquorum. "Expurgate ergo vetus fermentum, ut sitis novo conspersio,"[13] nobis exclamat Apostolus. Et rursus, propter quosdam ejusmodi homines indignans, præcipit, "Ne conversari quidem, si quis frater nominetur vel fornicator, vel avarus, vel idololatra, vel maledicus, vel ebriosus, vel raptor; cum eo, qui est talis, ne una quidem comedere. Ego enim per legem legi mortuus sum," inquit; "ut Deo vivam, cum Christo sum crucifixus; vivo autem non amplius ego," ut vivebam per cupiditates; "vivit autem in me Christus," caste et beate per obedientiam præceptorum. Quare tunc quidem in carne vivebam carnaliter: "quod autem nunc vivo in carne, in fide vivo Filii Dei."[14] — "In viam gentium ne abieritis, et ne ingrediamini in urbem Samaritanorum,"[15] a contraria vitæ institutione nos dehortans dicit Dominus; quoniam "Iniquorum virorum mala est conversatio; et hæ sunt viæ omnium, qui ea, quæ sunt iniqua, efficiunt."[16] — "Væ homini illi," inquit Dominus; "bonum esset ei, si non natus esset, quam ut unum ex electis meis scandalizaret.[17] Melius esset, ut ei mola circumponeretur, et in mari demergeretur, quam ut unum ex meis perverteret.[18] Nomen enim Dei blasphematur propter ipsos."[19] Unde præclare Apostolus: "Scripsi," inquit, "vobis in epistola, non conversari cum fornicatoribus,"[20]

1 Isa. xl. 6, 7, 8.
2 [Elucidation XV.]
3 Prov. xiii. 12.
4 Gen. iii. 5.
5 Gen. iv. 1.
6 1 Cor. xv. 50.
7 Gal. iii. 3.

8 Jer. v. 8.
9 Prov. i. 14.
10 Prov. i. 15, 16, 17.
11 Apoc. ix. 10.
12 Eph. ii. 3.
13 1 Cor. v. 7.
14 Gal. ii. 19, 20.
15 Matt. x. 5.
16 Prov. i. 18, 19.
17 Matt. xxvi. 24.
18 Matt. xviii. 6 seqq.
19 Rom. ii. 24.
20 1 Cor. v. 11.

usque ad illud : " Corpus autem non fornicationi, sed Domino, et Dominus corpori." [1]. Et quod matrimonium non dicat fornicationem, ostendit eo, quod subjungit : " An nescitis, quod qui adhæret meretrici, unum est corpus ? " [2] An meretricem quis dicet virginem, priusquam nubat ? " Et ne fraudetis," inquit, " vos invicem, nisi ex consensu ad tempus : " [3] per dictionem, " fraudetis," ostendens matrimonii debitum esse liberorum procreationem : quod quidem in iis, quæ præcedunt, ostendit, dicens : " Mulieri vir debitum reddat ; similiter autem mulier quoque viro ; " [4] post quam exsolutionem, in domo custodienda, et in ea quæ est in Christo fide, adjutrix est. Et adhuc apertius, dicens : " Iis, qui sunt juncti matrimonio, præcipio, inquit, non ego, sed Dominus, uxorem a viro non separari ; sin autem separata fuerit, maneat innupta, vel viro reconcilietur ; et virum uxorem non dimittere. Reliquis autem dico ego, non Dominus : Si quis frater," [5] usque ad illud : " Nunc autem sancta est." [6] Quid autem ad hæc dicunt, qui in legem invehuntur, et in matrimonium, quasi sit solum a lege concessum, non autem etiam in Novo Testamento ? Quid ad has leges latas possunt dicere, qui sationem abhorrent et generationem ? cum " episcopum " quoque, " qui domui recte præsit," [7] Ecclesiæ ducem constituat ; domum autem Dominicam " unius mulieris " constituat conjugium. [8] " Omnia " ergo dicit esse " munda mundis ; pollutis autem et infidelibus nihil est mundum, sed polluta est eorum et mens, et conscientia." [9] De ea autem voluptate, quæ est

præter regulam : " Ne erretis," inquit ; " nec fornicatores, nec idololatræ, nec adulteri, nec molles, nec masculorum concubitores, neque avari, neque fures, neque ebriosi, neque maledici, nec raptores, regnum Dei possidebunt ; et nos quidem abluti sumus," [10] qui in his eramus ; qui autem in hanc tingunt intemperantiam, ex temperantia in fornicationem baptizant, voluptatibus et affectibus esse indulgendum decernentes, incontinentes ex moderatis fieri docentes, et in spe sua membrorum suorum impudentiæ affixi ; ut a regno Dei abdicentur, non autem ut inscribantur, qui ad eos ventitant, efficientes ; sub falso nominatæ cognitionis titulo, eam, quæ ad exteriores ducit tenebras, viam ingredientes. " Quod reliquum est, fratres, quæcunque vera, quæcunque honesta, quæcunque justa, quæcunque casta, quæcunque amabilia, quæcunque bonæ famæ ; si qua virtus, et si qua laus, ea considerate ; quæ et didicistis ; quæ etiam accepistis et audiistis et vidistis in me, ea facite ; et Deus pacis erit vobiscum." [11] Et Petrus similia dicit in Epistola : " Ut fides vestra et spes sit in Deum, cum animas vestras castas effeceritis in obedientia veritatis ; " [12] quasi filii obedientiæ, non configurati prioribus desideriis, quæ fuerunt in ignorantia ; sed secundum eum, qui vocavit vos, sanctum, et ipsi sancti sitis in omni conversatione. Quoniam scriptum est : " Sancti eritis, quoniam ego sanctus sum." [13] Verumtamen quæ adversus eos, qui cognitionem falso nomine simulant, necessario suscepta est a nobis disputatio, nos longius, quam par sit, abduxit, et orationem effecit prolixiorem. Unde tertius quoque liber Stromateus eorum, quæ sunt de vera philosophia, commentariorum, hunc finem habeat.

---

[1] 1 Cor. vi. 13.
[2] 1 Cor. vi. 16.
[3] 1 Cor. vii. 5.
[4] 1 Cor. vii. 3.
[5] 1 Cor. vii. 10, 11, 12.
[6] 1 Cor. vii. 14.
[7] 1 Tim. iii. 2, 4; Tit. i. 6.
[8] [Elucidation XVI.]
[9] Tit. i. 15.

[10] 1 Cor. vi. 9, 10, 11.
[11] Phil. iv. 8, 9.
[12] 1 Pet. i. 21, 22.
[13] 1 Pet. i. 14, 15, 16.

ELUCIDATIONS.

I.

(See p. 381, cap. i.)

IN his third book, Clement exposes the Basilidians and others who perverted the rule of our Lord, which permissively, but not as of obligation, called some to the self-regimen of a single life, on condition of their possessing the singular gift requisite to the same. True continence, he argues, implies the command of the tongue, and all manner of concupiscence, such as greed of wealth, or luxury in using it. If, by a divine faculty and gift of grace, it enables us to practise temperance, very well ; but more is necessary. As to marriage, he states what seems to him to be the truth. We honour celibate chastity, and esteem them blest to whom this is God's gift. We also admire a single marriage, and the dignity which pertains to one marriage only; admitting, nevertheless, that we ought to compassionate others, and to bear one another's burdens, lest any one, when he thinks he stands, should himself also fall. The apostle enjoins, with respect to a second marriage, "If thou art tempted by concupiscence, resort to a lawful wedlock."

Our author then proceeds to a castigation of Carpocrates, and his son Epiphanes, an Alexandrian on his father's side, who, though he lived but seventeen years, his mother being a Cephallenian, received divine honours at Sama, where a magnificent temple, with altars and shrines, was erected to him; the Cephallenians celebrating his apotheosis, by a new-moon festival, with sacrifices, libations and hymns, and convivialities. This youth acquired, from his father, a knowledge of Plato's philosophy and of the circle of the sciences. He was the author of the jargon about monads,[1] of which see Irenæus; and from him comes the heresy of those subsequently known as Carpocratians. He left a book, *De Justitia*, in which he contends for what he represents as Plato's idea of a community of women in sexual relations. Justly does our author reckon him a destroyer alike of law and Gospel, unworthy even of being classed with decent heretics; and he attributes to his followers all those abominations which had been charged upon the Christians. This illustrates the terrible necessity, which then existed, of drawing a flaming line of demarcation between the Church, and the wolves in sheeps' clothing, who thus dishonoured the name of Christ, by associating such works of the devil with the adoption of a nominal discipleship. It should be mentioned that Mosheim questions the story of Epiphanes. (See his *Hist. of the First Three Centuries*, vol. i. p. 448.)

II.

(See p. 383, cap. ii. note 1.)

The early disappèarance of the Christian *agapæ* may probably be attributed to the terrible abuse of the word here referred to, by the licentious Carpocratians. The genuine *agapæ* were of apostolic origin (2 Pet. ii. 13; Jude 12), but were often abused by hypocrites, even under the apostolic eye (1 Cor. xi. 21). In the Gallican Church, a survival or relic of these feasts of charity is seen in the *pain béni;* and, in the Greek churches. in the ἀντίδωρον, or *eulogiæ* distributed to non-communicants at the close of the Eucharist, from the loaf out of which the bread of oblation is supposed to have been cut.

III.

(See p. 383, note 3.)

Next, he treats of the Marcionites, who rejected marriage on the ground that the material creation is in itself evil. Promising elsewhere to deal with this general false principle, he refutes Marcion, and with him the Greeks who have condemned the generative law of nature, specifying Heraclitus, Empedocles, the Sibyl, Homer, and others; but he defends Plato against Marcion, who represents him as teaching the depravity of matter. He proceeds to what the dramatists have exhibited of human misery. He shows the error of those who represent the Pythagoreans as on that account denying themselves the intimacies of conjugal society; for he says they practised this restraint, only after having given themselves a family. He explains the prohibition of the bean, by Pythagoras, on the very ground, that it occasioned sterility in women according to Theophrastus. Clement expounds the true meaning of Christ's words, perverted by those who abstained from marriage not in honour of encraty, but as an insane impeachment of the divine wisdom in the material creation.

---

[1] See vol. i. p. 332, note 4, this series.

IV.

(See p. 385, note 3.)

He refutes the Carpocratians, also, in their slanders against the deacon Nicolas, showing that the Nicolaitans had abused his name and words. Likewise, concerning Matthias, he exposes a similar abuse. He castigates one who seduced a maiden into impurity by an absurd perversion of Scripture, and thoroughly exposes this blasphemous abuse of the apostolic text. He subjoins another refutation of one of those heretics, and allows that some might adopt the opinion of his dupes, if, as the Valentinians would profess, only spiritual communion were concerned.

Seeing, however, that these heretics, and the followers of Prodicus, who wrongfully call themselves *gnostics*, claimed a practical indulgence in all manner of disgusting profligacies, he convicts them by arguments derived from right reason and from the Scriptures, and by human laws as well. Further, he exposes the folly of those who pretended that the less honourable parts of man are not the work of the Creator, and overwhelms their presumption by abundant argument, exploding, at the same time, their corruptions of the sacred text of the Scriptures.

V.

(See p. 388, note 3.)

To relieve himself of a more particular struggle with each individual heresy, he proceeds to reduce them under two heads : (1) Those who teach a reckless mode of life (ἀδιαφόρως ζῆν), and (2) those who impiously affect continence. To the first, he opposes the plain propriety and duty of a decorous way of living continently ; showing, that as it cannot be denied that there are certain abominable and filthy lusts, which, as such, must be shunned, therefore there is no such thing as living " indifferently " with respect to them. He who lives to the flesh, moreover, is condemned ; nor can the likeness and image of God be regained, or eternal life be ensured, save by a strict observance of divine precepts. Further, our author shows that true Christian liberty consists, not, as they vociferate, in self-indulgence, but, on the contrary, is founded in an entire freedom from perturbations of mind and passion, and from all filthy lusts.

VI.

(See p. 389, note 4.)

As to the second class of heretics, he reproves the contemners of God's ordinance, who boast of a false continence, and scorn holy matrimony and the creation of a family. He contends with them by the authority of St. John, and first answers objections of theirs, based on certain apocryphal sayings of Christ to Salome ; next, somewhat obscurely, he answers their notions of laws about marriage imposed in the Old Law, and, as they pretend, abrogated in the New; thirdly, he rebukes their perpetual clatter about the uncleanness of conjugal relations ; and, fourth, he pulverizes their arguments derived from the fact, that the children of the resurrection " neither marry, nor are given in marriage."

Then he gives his attention to another class of heretics boasting that they followed the example of Christ, and presuming to teach that marriage is of the devil. He expounds the exceptional celibacy of the Messiah, by the two natures of the Godman, which need nothing but a reverent statement to expose the fallacy of arguing from His example in this particular, seeing He, alone, of all the sons of men, is thus supreme over all considerations of human nature, pure and simple, as it exists in the sons of Adam. Moreover, He espoused the Church, which is His wife. Clement expounds very wisely those sayings of our Lord which put honour upon voluntary celibacy, where the gift has been imparted, for His better service.

And here let it be noted, how continually the heresies of these times seem to turn on this matter of the sexes. It is impossible to cleanse a dirty house, without raising a dust and a bad smell; and heathenism, which had made lust into a religion, and the worship of its gods a school of gross vice, penetrating all classes of society, could not be exorcised, and give place to faith, hope and charity, without this process of conflict, in which Clement distinguishes himself. At the same time, the wisdom of our Lord's precepts and counsels are manifest, in this history. Alike He taught the sanctity and blessedness of marriage and maternity, and the exceptional blessedness of the celibate when received as a gift of God, for a peculiar ministry. Thus heathen morals were rebuked and castigated, womanhood was lifted to a sphere of unwonted honour, and the home was created and sanctified in the purity and chastity of the Christian wife; while yet a celibate chastity was recognised as having a high place in the Christian system. The Lord prescribes to all, whether married or unmarried, a law of discipline and evangelical encraty. The Christian homes of England and America may be pointed out, thank God, as illustrating the divine wisdom; while the degraded monasteries of Italy and Spain and South America, with the horrible history of enforced celibacy in the Latin priesthood, are proofs of the unwisdom of those who imported into the Western churches the very heresies and abortive argumentations which Clement disdains, while he pulverizes them and blows them away, thoroughly purging his floor, and burning up this chaff.

VII.

(See p. 390, note 16.)

Here it is specially important to observe what Clement demonstrates, not only from the teachings of the apostles, of Elijah and Samuel and the Master Himself, but, finally and irrefragably, from the apostolic example. He names St. Peter here as elsewhere, and notes his memorable history as a married man.[1] He supposes St. Paul himself to have been married; and he instances St. Philip the deacon, and his married daughters, besides giving the right exposition of a passage which Carpocrates had shamefully distorted from its plain significance.

VIII.

(See p. 391, note 18.)

He passes to a demonstration of the superiority of Christian continence over the sort of self-constraint lauded by Stoics and other philosophers. God only can enable man to practise a genuine continence, not merely contending with depraved lusts, but eradicating them. Here follow some interesting examples drawn from the brahmins and fakirs of India; interesting tokens, by the way, of the assaults the Gospel had already made upon their strongholds about the Ganges.

IX.

(See p. 392, note 4.)

Briefly he explains another text, "Sin shall not have dominion over you," which the heretics wrested from the purpose and intent of St. Paul. He also returns to a passage from the apocryphal Gospel of the Hebrews, and to the pretended conversation of Christ with Salome, treating it, perhaps, with more consideration than it merits.

---

[1] See the touching story of St. Peter's words to his wife as she was led to martyrdom (*Stromata*, book vii. p. 451, Edinburgh Edition).

X.

(See p. 392, note 11.)

But this Gospel of the Hebrews, and another apocryphal Gospel, that of the Egyptians, may be worthy of a few words just here. Jones (*On the Canon*, vol. i. p. 206) very learnedly maintains that Clement "never saw it," nor used it for any quotation of his own. And, as for a Gospel written in the Hebrew tongue, Clement could not read Hebrew; the single citation he makes out of it, being, probably, at second hand. Greatly to the point is the argument of Lardner,[1] therefore, who says, as settling the question of the value of these books, "If Clement, who lived at Alexandria, and was so well acquainted with almost all sorts of books, had (but a slight, or) no knowledge at all of them, how obscure must they have been; how little regarded by Catholic Christians."

XI.

(See p. 393, note 5; also Elucidation xvii. p. 408, *infra*.)

Ingenious is Clement's exposition of that saying of our Lord, "Where two or three are met together in my name," etc. He explodes a monstrous exposition of the text, and ingeniously applies it to the Christian family. The husband and the wife living in chaste matrimony, and the child which God bestows, are three in sweet society, who may claim and enjoy the promise. This reflects great light upon the Christian home, as it rose, like a flower, out of the "Church in the house." Family prayers, the graces before and after meat, the hymn "On lighting the lamps at eventide," and the *complines*, or prayers at bedtime, are all the products of the divine contract to be with the "two or three" who are met in His name to claim that inconceivably precious promise. Other texts from St. Matthew are explained, in their Catholic verity, by our venerable author.

XII.

(See p. 394, note 1.)

He further expounds the Catholic idea of marriage, and rescues, from heretical adulteration, the precept of Moses (Ex. xix. 15); introducing a lucid parallel, with the Apostolic command,[2] "Come out from among them, and be separate," etc. He turns the tables on his foul antagonists; showing them that this very law obliges the Catholic Christian to separate himself alike from the abominations of the heathen, and from the depraved heretics who abuse the word of God, and "wrest the Scriptures to their own destruction." This eleventh chapter of the third book abounds in Scriptural citations and expositions, and is to be specially praised for asserting the purity of married life, in connection with the inspired law concerning fasting and abstinence (1 Cor. vii. 3–5), laid down by the reasonably ascetic St. Paul.

XIII.

(See p. 396, note 5.)

The melancholy example of Tatian is next instanced, in his departures from orthodox encraty. Against poor Tatian's garrulity, he proves the sanctity of marriage, alike in the New and the Old Testaments. A curious argument he adduces against the *ceremonial* washing prescribed by the

---

[1] Works, ii. 252. See, also, the apocryphal collection in this series, hereafter.
[2] 2 Cor. vi. 17. Compare Ex. xxix. 45, and Lev. xxvi. 12.

aw (Lev. xv. 18), but not against the same as a dictate of natural instinct. He considers that particular ceremonial law a protest against the polygamy which God tolerated, but never authorized, under Moses ; and its abrogation (i.e., by the Synod of Jerusalem), is a testimony that there is no uncleanness, whatever, in the chaste society of the married pair, in Christ. He rescues other texts from the profane uses of the heretics, proving that our duty to abstain from laying up treasures here, merely favours the care of the poor and needy ; and that the saying, that " the children of the kingdom neither marry nor are given in marriage," respects only their estate after the resurrection. So the command about " caring for the things of God," is harmonized with 'married life. But our author dwells on the apostle's emphatic counsels against second marriages. It is noteworthy how deeply Clement's orthodoxy has rooted itself in the Greek churches, where the clergy must be once married, but are not permitted to marry a second time.

A curious objection is met and dismissed. The man who excused himself " because he had married a wife," was a great card for heretical manipulations ; but no need of saying that Clement knows how to turn this, also, upon their own hands.

XIV.

(See p. 398, note 8.)

Julius Cassianus (assigned by Lardner to A.D. 190) was an Alexandrian Encratite, of whom, whatever his faults, Clement speaks not without respect. He is quoted with credit in the *Stromata* (book i. cap. xxi. p. 324), but comes into notice here, as having led off the school of Docetism. But Clement does not treat him as he does the vulgar and licentious errorist. He reproves him for his use of the Gospel according to the Egyptians, incidentally testifying to the Catholic recognition of only four Gospels. He refutes a Platonic idea of Cassian, as to the pre-existence of the soul. Also, he promises a full explanation, elsewhere, of " the coats of skins " (which Cassian seems to have thought the flesh itself), wherewith Adam and Eve were clothed. Lardner refers us to Beausobre for a curious discussion of this matter. Clement refutes a false argument from Christ's hyperbole of hatred to wife and children and family ties, and also gives lucid explanations of passages from Isaiah, Jeremiah, and Ezra, which had been wrested to heretical abuse. In a similar manner, he overthrows what errorists had built upon Job's saying, " who can bring a clean thing out of the unclean ; " as also their false teachings on the texts, " In sin hath my mother conceived me," " the fruit of my body for the sin of my soul," and the apostolic instance of the athlete who is " temperate in all things."

XV.

(See p. 400, cap. xvii. and 401, note 2.)

He proclaims the purity of physical generation, because of the parturition of the Blessed Virgin ; castigating the docetism of Cassian, who had presumed to speak of the body of Jesus as a phantasm, and the grosser blasphemies of Marcion and Valentinus, equally destructive to the Christ of the Gospel.[1] He overturns the whims of these latter deceivers, about Adam's society with his wife, and concludes that our Lord's assumption of the flesh of His mother, was a sufficient corroboration of that divine law by which the generations of mankind are continued.

XVI.

(See p. 402, note 8.)

From all which Clement concludes that his two classes of heretics are alike wanderers from Catholic orthodoxy ; whether, on the one hand, under divers pretexts glorifying an unreal continence

---

[1] In using the phrase *ecclesia nostra* (ἡ κατὰ τὴν Ἐκκλησίαν καθ' ἡμας), which I take to refer to the Church Militant, we encounter a formula which we use differently in our day.

against honourable marriage, or, on the other, persuading themselves as speciously to an unlimited indulgence of their sinful lusts and passions. Once more he quotes the Old Testament and the New, which denounce uncleanness, but not the conjugal relations. He argues with indignation upon those who degrade the estate to which a bishop is called as " the husband of one wife, ruling his own house and children well." Then he reverts to his idea of " the two or three," maintaining that a holy marriage makes the bishop's home " a house of the Lord " (see note 75, p. 1211, *ed.* Migne). And he concludes the book by repeating his remonstrance against the claim of these heretics to be veritable *Gnostics*, — a name he will by no means surrender to the enemies of truth.

XVII.

(On Matt. xviii. 20, p. 393; and, see *Supra*, Elucidation XI.)

To the interpretation I have thought preferable, and which I ventured to enlarge, it should be added that our author subjoins others, founded on flesh, soul, and spirit ; on vocation, election, and the Gnostic accepting both ; and on the Jew and the Gentile, and the Church gathered from each race.

Over and over again Clement asserts that a life of chaste wedlock is not to be accounted imperfect.

On the celibate in practice, see *Le Célibat des Prêtres*, par l'abbé Chavard, Genève, 1874.

XVIII.

The *Commentaria* of Le Nourry have been my guide to the brief analysis of these Elucidations, though I have not always allowed the learned Benedictine to dictate an opinion, or to control my sense of our author's argument.

THE STROMATA, OR MISCELLANIES.

BOOK IV.

CHAP. I. — ORDER OF CONTENTS.

IT will follow, I think, that I should treat of martyrdom, and of who the perfect man is. With these points shall be included what follows in accordance with the demands of the points to be spoken about, and how both bond and free must equally philosophize, whether male or female in sex. And in the sequel, after finishing what is to be said on faith and inquiry, we shall set forth the department of symbols; so that, on cursorily concluding the discourse on ethics, we shall exhibit the advantage which has accrued to the Greeks from the barbarian philosophy. After which sketch, the brief explanation of the Scriptures both against the Greeks and against the Jews will be presented, and whatever points we were unable to embrace in the previous *Miscellanies* (through having respect necessarily to the multitude of matters), in accordance with the commencement of the proem, purposing to finish them in one commentary. In addition to these points, afterwards on completing the sketch, as far as we can in accordance with what we propose, we must give an account of the physical doctrines of the Greeks and of the barbarians, respecting elementary principles, as far as their opinions have reached us, and argue against the principal views excogitated by the philosophers.

It will naturally fall after these, after a cursory view of theology, to discuss the opinions handed down respecting prophecy; so that, having demonstrated that the Scriptures which we believe are valid from their omnipotent authority, we shall be able to go over them consecutively, and to show thence to all the heresies one God and Omnipotent Lord to be truly preached by the law and the prophets, and besides by the blessed Gospel. Many contradictions against the heterodox await us while we attempt, in writing, to do away with the force of the allegations made by them, and to persuade them against their will, proving by the Scriptures themselves.

On completing, then, the whole of what we propose in the commentaries, on which, if the Spirit will, we ministering to the urgent need, (for it is exceedingly necessary, before coming to the truth, to embrace what ought to be said by way of preface), shall address ourselves to the true gnostic science of nature, receiving initiation into the minor mysteries before the greater; so that nothing may be in the way of the truly divine declaration of sacred things, the subjects requiring preliminary detail and statement being cleared away, and sketched beforehand. The science of nature, then, or rather observation, as contained in the gnostic tradition according to the rule of the truth, depends on the discussion concerning cosmogony, ascending thence to the department of theology. Whence, then, we shall begin our account of what is handed down, with the creation as related by the prophets, introducing also the tenets of the heterodox, and endeavouring as far as we can to confute them. But it shall be written if God will, and as He inspires; and now we must proceed to what we proposed, and complete the discourse on ethics.

CHAP. II. — THE MEANING OF THE NAME STROMATA OR MISCELLANIES.

Let these notes of ours, as we have often said for the sake of those that consult them carelessly and unskilfully, be of varied character — and as the name itself indicates, patched together — passing constantly from one thing to another, and in the series of discussions hinting at one thing and demonstrating another. "For those who seek for gold," says Heraclitus, "dig much earth and find little gold." But those who are of the truly golden race, in mining for what is allied to them, will find the much in little. For the word will find one to understand it. The Miscellanies of notes contribute, then, to the recollection and expression of truth in the case of him who is able to investigate with reason.

And you must prosecute, in addition to these, other labours and researches; since, in the case of people who are setting out on a road with which they are unacquainted, it is sufficient merely to point out the direction. After this they must walk and find out the rest for themselves. As, they say, when a certain slave once asked at the oracle what he should do to please his master, the Pythian priestess replied, "You will find if you seek." It is truly a difficult matter, then, as turns out, to find out latent good; since

> "Before virtue is placed exertion,
> And long and steep is the way to it,
> And rough at first; but when the summit is reached,
> Then is it easy, though difficult [before]."

"For narrow," in truth, "and strait is the way" of the Lord. And it is to the "violent that the kingdom of God belongs." [1]

Whence, "Seek, and ye shall find," holding on by the truly royal road, and not deviating. As we might expect, then, the generative power of the seeds of the doctrines comprehended in this treatise is great in small space, as the "universal herbage of the field," [2] as Scripture saith. Thus the Miscellanies of notes have their proper title, wonderfully like that ancient oblation culled from all sorts of things of which Sophocles writes : —

> "For there was a sheep's fleece, and there was a vine,
> And a libation, and grapes well stored;
> And there was mixed with it fruit of all kinds,
> And the fat of the olive, and the most curious
> Wax-formed work of the yellow bee."

Just so our *Stromata*, according to the husbandman of the comic poet Timocles, produce "figs, olives, dried figs, honey, as from an all-fruitful field;" on account of which exuberance he adds : —

> "Thou speakest of a harvest-wreath not of husbandry."

For the Athenians were wont to cry : —

> "The harvest-wreath bears figs and fat loaves,
> And honey in a cup, and olive oil to anoint you."

We must then often, as in winnowing sieves, shake and toss up this the great mixture of seeds, in order to separate the wheat.

CHAP. III. — THE TRUE EXCELLENCE OF MAN.

The most of men have a disposition unstable and heedless, like the nature of storms. "Want of faith has done many good things, and faith evil things." And Epicharmus says, "Don't forget to exercise incredulity; for it is the sinews of the soul." Now, to disbelieve truth brings death, as to believe, life; and again, to believe the lie and to disbelieve the truth hurries to destruction. The same is the case with self-restraint and licentiousness. To restrain one's self from doing good is the work of vice; but to keep from wrong is the beginning of salvation. So the Sabbath, by abstinence from evils, seems to indicate self-restraint. And what, I ask, is it in which man differs from beasts, and the angels of God, on the other hand, are wiser than he? "Thou madest him a little lower than the angels." [3] For some do not interpret this Scripture of the Lord, although He also bore flesh, but of the perfect man and the gnostic, inferior in comparison with the angels in time, and by reason of the vesture [of the body]. I call then wisdom nothing but science, since life differs not from life. For to live is common to the mortal nature, that is to man, with that to which has been vouchsafed immortality; as also the faculty of contemplation and of self-restraint, one of the two being more excellent. On this ground Pythagoras seems to me to have said that God alone is wise, since also the apostle writes in the Epistle to the Romans, "For the obedience of the faith among all nations, being made known to the only wise God through Jesus Christ;" [4] and that he himself was a philosopher, on account of his friendship with God. Accordingly it is said, "God talked with Moses as a friend with a friend." [5] That, then, which is true being clear to God, forthwith generates truth. And the gnostic loves the truth. "Go," it is said, "to the ant, thou sluggard, and be the disciple of the bee;" thus speaks Solomon. [6] For if there is one function belonging to the peculiar nature of each creature, alike of the ox, and horse, and dog, what shall we say is the peculiar function of man? He is like, it appears to me, the Centaur, a Thessalian figment, compounded of a rational and irrational part, of soul and body. Well, the body tills the ground, and hastes to it; but the soul is raised to God: trained in the true philosophy, it speeds to its kindred above, turning away from the lusts of the body, and besides these, from toil and fear, although we have shown that patience and fear belong to the good man. For if "by the law is the knowledge of sin," [7] as those allege who disparage the law, and "till the law sin was in the world;" [8] yet "without the law sin was dead," [9] we oppose them. For when you take away the cause of fear, sin, you have taken away fear; and much more, punishment, when you have taken away that which gives rise to lust. "For the law is not made for the just

---

[1] Matt. vii. 14, xi. 12, vii. 7.
[2] Job v. 25.

[3] Ps. viii. 5.
[4] Rom. xvi. 26, 27.
[5] Ex. xxxiii. 11.
[6] Prov. vi. 6, 8.
[7] Rom. iii. 20.
[8] Rom. v. 13.
[9] Rom. vii. 6.

man," [1] says the Scripture. Well, then, says Heraclitus, "They would not have known the name of Justice if these things had not been." And Socrates says, "that the law was not made for the sake of the good." But the cavillers did not know even this, as the apostle says, "that he who loveth his brother worketh not evil;" for this, "Thou shalt not kill, thou shalt not commit adultery, thou shalt not steal; and if there be any other commandment, it is comprehended in the word, Thou shalt love thy neighbour as thyself." [2] So also is it said, "Thou shalt love the Lord thy God with all thy heart, and thou shalt love thy neighbour as thyself." [3] And "if he that loveth his neighbour worketh no evil," and if "every commandment is comprehended in this, the loving our neighbour," the commandments, by menacing with fear, work love, not hatred. Wherefore the law is productive of the emotion of fear. "So that the law is holy," and in truth "spiritual," [4] according to the apostle. We must, then, as is fit, in investigating the nature of the body and the essence of the soul, apprehend the end of each, and not regard death as an evil. "For when ye were the servants of sin," says the apostle, "ye were free from righteousness. What fruit had ye then in those things in which ye are now ashamed? For the end of those things is death. But now, being made free from sin, and become servants to God, ye have your fruit unto holiness, and the end everlasting life. For the wages of sin is death: but the gift of God is eternal life, through Jesus Christ our Lord." [5] The assertion, then, may be hazarded, that it has been shown that death is the fellowship of the soul in a state of sin with the body; and life the separation from sin. And many are the stakes and ditches of lust which impede us, and the pits of wrath and anger which must be overleaped, and all the machinations we must avoid of those who plot against us, — who would no longer see the knowledge of God "through a glass."

"The half of virtue the far-seeing Zeus takes
From man, when he reduces him to a state of slavery."

As slaves the Scripture views those "under sin" and "sold to sin," the lovers of pleasure and of the body; and beasts rather than men, "those who have become like to cattle, horses, neighing after their neighbours' wives." [6] The licentious is "the lustful ass," the covetous is the "savage wolf," and the deceiver is "a serpent." The severance, therefore, of the soul from the body, made a life-long study, produces in the phi-

losopher gnostic alacrity, so that he is easily able to bear natural death, which is the dissolution of the chains which bind the soul to the body. "For the world is crucified to me, and I to the world," the [apostle] says; "and now I live, though in the flesh, as having my conversation in heaven." [7]

CHAP. IV. — THE PRAISES OF MARTYRDOM.

Whence, as is reasonable, the gnostic, when called, obeys easily, and gives up his body to him who asks; and, previously divesting himself of the affections of this carcase, not insulting the tempter, but rather, in my opinion, training him and convincing him, —

"From what honour and what extent of wealth fallen,"

as says Empedocles, here for the future he walks with mortals. He, in truth, bears witness to himself that he is faithful and loyal towards God; and to the tempter, that he in vain envied him who is faithful through love; and to the Lord, of the inspired persuasion in reference to His doctrine, from which he will not depart through fear of death; further, he confirms also the truth of preaching by his deed, showing that God to whom he hastes is powerful. You will wonder at his love, which he conspicuously shows with thankfulness, in being united to what is allied to him, and besides by his precious blood, shaming the unbelievers. He then avoids denying Christ through fear by reason of the command; nor does he sell his faith in the hope of the gifts prepared, but in love to the Lord he will most gladly depart from this life; perhaps giving thanks both to him who afforded the cause of his departure hence, and to him who laid the plot against him, for receiving an honourable reason which he himself furnished not, for showing what he is, to him by his patience, and to the Lord in love, by which even before his birth he was manifested to the Lord, who knew the martyr's choice. With good courage, then, he goes to the Lord, his friend, for whom he voluntarily gave his body, and, as his judges hoped, his soul, hearing from our Saviour the words of poetry, "Dear brother," by reason of the similarity of his life. We call martyrdom perfection, not because the man comes to the end of his life as others, but because he has exhibited the perfect work of love. And the ancients laud the death of those among the Greeks who died in war, not that they advised people to die a violent death, but because he who ends his life in war is released without the dread of dying, severed from the body without experiencing previous suffering or being enfeebled in his soul, as the people that suffer in diseases. For they de-

---

[1] 1 Tim. i. 9.
[2] Rom. xiii. 8–10.
[3] Luke x. 27.
[4] Rom. vii. 12, 14.
[5] Rom. vi. 20–23.
[6] Jer. v. 8, etc.

[7] Gal. vi. 14; Phil. iii. 20.

part in a state of effeminacy and desiring to live; and therefore they do not yield up the soul pure, but bearing with it their lusts like weights of lead; all but those who have been conspicuous in virtue. Some die in battle with their lusts, these being in no respect different from what they would have been if they had wasted away by disease.

If the confession to God is martyrdom, each soul which has lived purely in the knowledge of God, which has obeyed the commandments, is a witness both by life and word, in whatever way it may be released from the body, — shedding faith as blood along its whole life till its departure. For instance, the Lord says in the Gospel, "Whosoever shall leave father, or mother, or brethren," and so forth, "for the sake of the Gospel and my name,"[1] he is blessed; not indicating simple martyrdom, but the gnostic martyrdom, as of the man who has conducted himself according to the rule of the Gospel, in love to the Lord (for the knowledge of the Name and the understanding of the Gospel point out the gnosis, but not the bare appellation), so as to leave his worldly kindred, and wealth, and every possession, in order to lead a life free from passion. "Mother" figuratively means country and sustenance; "fathers" are the laws of civil polity: which must be contemned thankfully by the high-souled just man; for the sake of being the friend of God, and of obtaining the right hand in the holy place, as the Apostles have done.

Then Heraclitus says, "Gods and men honour those slain in battle;" and Plato in the fifth book of the *Republic* writes, "Of those who die in military service, whoever dies after winning renown, shall we not say that he is chief of the golden race? Most assuredly." But the golden race is with the gods, who are in heaven, in the fixed sphere, who chiefly hold command in the providence exercised towards men. Now some of the heretics who have misunderstood the Lord, have at once an impious and cowardly love of life; saying that the true martyrdom is the knowledge of the only true God (which we also admit), and that the man is a self-murderer and a suicide who makes confession by death; and adducing other similar sophisms of cowardice. To these we shall reply at the proper time; for they differ with us in regard to first principles. Now we, too, say that those who have rushed on death (for there are some, not belonging to us, but sharing the name merely, who are in haste to give themselves up, the poor wretches dying through hatred to the Creator[2]) — these, we say, banish themselves without being martyrs, even though they are punished publicly. For

they do not preserve the characteristic mark of believing martyrdom, inasmuch as they have not known the only true God, but give themselves up to a vain death, as the Gymnosophists of the Indians to useless fire.

But since these falsely named[3] calumniate the body, let them learn that the harmonious mechanism of the body contributes to the understanding which leads to goodness of nature. Wherefore in the third book of the *Republic*, Plato, whom they appeal to loudly as an authority that disparages generation, says, "that for the sake of harmony of soul, care must be taken for the body," by which, he who announces the proclamation of the truth, finds it possible to live, and to live well. For it is by the path of life and health that we learn gnosis. But is he who cannot advance to the height without being occupied with necessary things, and through them doing what tends to knowledge, not to choose to live well? In living, then, living well is secured. And he who in the body has devoted himself to a good life, is being sent on to the state of immortality.

CHAP. V. — ON CONTEMPT FOR PAIN, POVERTY, AND OTHER EXTERNAL THINGS.

Fit objects for admiration are the Stoics, who say that the soul is not affected by the body, either to vice by disease, or to virtue by health; but both these things, they say, are indifferent. And indeed Job, through exceeding continence, and excellence of faith, when from rich he became poor, from being held in honour dishonoured, from being comely unsightly, and sick from being healthy, is depicted as a good example, putting the Tempter to shame, blessing his Creator; bearing what came second, as the first, and most clearly teaching that it is possible for the gnostic to make an excellent use of all circumstances. And that ancient achievements are proposed as images for our correction, the apostle shows, when he says, "So that my bonds in Christ are become manifest in all the palace, and to all the rest; and several of the brethren in the Lord, waxing confident by my bonds, are much more bold to speak the word of God without fear,"[4] — since martyrs' testimonies are examples of conversion gloriously sanctified. "For what things the Scripture speaks were written for our instruction, that we, through patience and the consolation of the Scriptures, might have the hope of consolation."[5] When pain is present, the soul appears to decline from it, and to deem release from present pain a precious thing. At that moment it slackens from studies, when the other virtues also are

---

[1] Matt. xix. 29.
[2] Demiurgus.

[3] [οἱ ψευδώνυμοι, i.e., the gnostic heretics. Clement does not approve of the surrender of a good name to false pretenders.]
[4] Phil. i. 13, 14.
[5] Rom. xv. 4.

neglected. And yet we do not say that it' is virtue itself which suffers, for virtue is not affected by disease. But he who is partaker of both, of virtue and the disease, is afflicted by the pressure of the latter; and if he who has not yet attained the habit of self-command be not a high-souled man, he is distraught; and the inability to endure it is found equivalent to fleeing from it.

The same holds good also in the case of poverty. For it compels the soul to desist from necessary things, I mean contemplation and from pure sinlessness, forcing him, who has not wholly dedicated himself to God in love, to occupy himself about provisions; as, again, health and abundance of necessaries keep the soul free and unimpeded, and capable of making a good use of what is at hand. "For," says the apostle, "such shall have trouble in the flesh. But I spare you. For I would have you without anxiety, in order to decorum and assiduity for the Lord, without distraction." [1]

These things, then, are to be abstained from, not for their own sakes, but for the sake of the body; and care for the body is exercised for the sake of the soul, to which it has reference. For on this account it is necessary for the man who lives as a gnostic to know what is suitable. Since the fact that pleasure is not a good thing is admitted from the fact that certain pleasures are evil, by this reason good appears evil, and evil good. And then, if we choose some pleasures and shun others, it is not every pleasure that is a good thing.

Similarly, also, the same rule holds with pains, some of which we endure, and others we shun. But choice and avoidance are exercised according to knowledge; so that it is not pleasure that is the good thing, but knowledge by which we shall choose a pleasure at a certain time, and of a certain kind. Now the martyr chooses the pleasure that exists in prospect through the present pain. If pain is conceived as existing in thirst, and pleasure in drinking, the pain that has preceded becomes the efficient cause of pleasure. But evil cannot be the efficient cause of good. Neither, then, is the one thing nor the other evil. Simonides accordingly (as also Aristotle) writes, "that to be in good health is the best thing, and the second best thing is to be handsome, and the third best thing is to be rich without cheating."

And Theognis of Megara says:—

> "You must, to escape poverty, throw
> Yourself, O Cyrnus, down from
> The steep rocks into the deep sea."

On the other hand, Antiphanes, the comic poet, says, " Plutus (Wealth), when it has taken hold

of those who see better than others, makes them blind." Now by the poets he is proclaimed as blind from his birth:—

> "And brought him forth blind who saw not the sun."

Says the Chalcidian Euphorion:—

> "Riches, then, and extravagant luxuries,
> Were for men the worst training for manliness."

Wrote Euripides in *Alexander*:—

> "And it is said,
> Penury has attained wisdom through misfortune;
> But much wealth will capture not
> Sparta alone, but every city."

"It is not then the only coin that mortals have, that which is white silver or golden, but virtue too," as Sophocles says.

CHAP. VI. — SOME POINTS IN THE BEATITUDES.

Our holy Saviour applied poverty and riches, and the like, both to spiritual things and objects of sense. For when He said, "Blessed are they that are persecuted for righteousness' sake," [2] He clearly taught us in every circumstance to seek for the martyr who, if poor for righteousness' sake, witnesses that the righteousness which he loves is a good thing; and if he "hunger and thirst for righteousness' sake," testifies that righteousness is the best thing. Likewise he, that weeps and mourns for righteousness' sake, testifies to the best law that it is beautiful. As, then, "those that are persecuted," so also "those that hunger and thirst" for righteousness' sake, are called "blessed" by Him who approves of the true desire, which not even famine can put a stop to. And if "they hunger after righteousness itself," they are blessed. "And blessed are the poor," whether "in spirit" or in circumstances — that is, if for righteousness' sake. It is not the poor simply, but those that have wished to become poor for righteousness' sake, that He pronounces blessed — those who have despised the honours of this world in order to attain "the good;" likewise also those who, through chastity, have become comely in person and character, and those who are of noble birth, and honourable, having through righteousness attained to adoption, and therefore "have received power to become the sons of God," [3] and "to tread on serpents and scorpions," and to rule over demons and "the host of the adversary." [4] And, in fine, the Lord's discipline [5] draws the soul away gladly from the body, even if it wrench itself away in its removal. "For he that loveth his life shall lose it, and he that loseth his life shall find it," [6] if we only join that which is mortal of us with

[1] 1 Cor. vii. 28, 32, 35.

[2] Matt. v. 10.
[3] John i. 12.
[4] Luke x. 19.
[5] [Canons Apostolical (so called), li. liii. But see Elucidation I.]
[6] [Matt. x. 39; John xii. 25. S.]

the immortality of God. It is the will of God [that we should attain] the knowledge of God, which is the communication of immortality. He therefore, who, in accordance with the word of repentance, knows his life to be sinful will lose it — losing it from sin, from which it is wrenched; but losing it, will find it, according to the obedience which lives again to faith, but dies to sin. This, then, is what it is "to find one's life," "to know one's self."

The conversion, however, which leads to divine things, the Stoics say, is affected by a change, the soul being changed to wisdom. And Plato: "On the soul taking a turn to what is better, and a change from a kind of nocturnal day." Now the philosophers also allow the good man an exit from life in accordance with reason, in the case of one depriving him of active exertion, so that the hope of action is no longer left him. And the judge who compels us to deny Him whom we love, I regard as showing who is and who is not the friend of God. In that case there is not left ground for even examining what one prefers — the menaces of man or the love of God. And abstinence from vicious acts is found, somehow, [to result in] the diminution and extinction of vicious propensities, their energy being destroyed by inaction. And this is the import of "Sell what thou hast, and give to the poor, and come, follow Me"[1] — that is, follow what is said by the Lord. Some say that by what "thou hast" He designated the things in the soul, of a nature not akin to it, though how these are bestowed on the poor they are not able to say. For God dispenses to all according to desert, His distribution being righteous. Despising, therefore, the possessions which God apportions to thee in thy magnificence, comply with what is spoken by me; haste to the ascent of the Spirit, being not only justified by abstinence from what is evil, but in addition also perfected, by Christlike beneficence.[2] In this instance He convicted the man, who boasted that he had fulfilled the injunctions of the law, of not loving his neighbour; and it is by beneficence that the love which, according to the gnostic ascending scale, is Lord of the Sabbath, proclaims itself.[3] We must then, according to my view, have recourse to the word of salvation neither from fear of punishment nor promise of a gift, but on account of the good itself. Such, as do so, stand on the right hand of the sanctuary; but those who think that by the gift of what is perishable they shall receive in exchange what belongs to immortality are in the parable of the two brothers called "hire-

lings." And is there not some light thrown here on the expression "in the likeness and image," in the fact that some live according to the likeness of Christ, while those who stand on the left hand live according to their image? There are then two things proceeding from the truth, one root lying beneath both, — the choice being, however, not equal, or rather the difference that is in the choice not being equal. To choose by way of imitation differs, as appears to me, from the choice of him who chooses according to knowledge, as that which is set on fire differs from that which is illuminated. Israel, then, is the light of the likeness which is according to the Scripture. But the image is another thing. What means the parable of Lazarus, by showing the image of the rich and poor? And what the saying, "No man can serve two masters, God and Mammon?" — the Lord so terming the love of money. For instance, the covetous, who were invited, responded not to the invitation to the supper, not because of their possessing property, but of their inordinate affection to what they possessed. "The foxes," then, have holes. He called those evil and earthly men who are occupied about the wealth which is mined and dug from the ground, foxes. Thus also, in reference to Herod: "Go, tell that fox, Behold, I cast out devils, and perform cures to-day and to-morrow, and the third day I shall be perfected."[4] For He applied the name "fowls of the air" to those who were distinct from the other birds — those really pure, those that have the power of flying to the knowledge of the heavenly Word. For not riches only, but also honour, and marriage, and poverty, have ten thousand cares for him who is unfit for them.[5] And those cares He indicated in the parable of the fourfold seed, when He said that "the seed of the word which fell unto the thorns" and hedges was choked by them, and could not bring forth fruit. It is therefore necessary to learn how to make use of every occurrence, so as by a good life, according to knowledge, to be trained for the state of eternal life. For it said, "I saw the wicked exalted and towering as the cedars of Lebanon; and I passed," says the Scripture, "and, lo, he was not; and I sought him, and his place was not found. Keep innocence, and look on uprightness: for there is a remnant to the man of peace."[6] Such will he be who believes unfeignedly with his whole heart, and is tranquil in his whole soul. "For the different people honour me with their lips, but their heart is far from the Lord."[7] "They bless

---

[1] Matt. xix. 21.
[2] κυριακῇ εὐποιΐα.
[3] [If love, exerting itself in doing good, overruled the letter of the Sabbatic law, rise to this supremacy of love, which is, of itself, "the fulfilling of the law."]

[4] Luke xiii. 32.
[5] [He regards the estate of marriage and the estate of poverty, as gifts redounding to the benefit of those who accept them as such, and adapt themselves to the same, as stewards.]
[6] Ps. xxxvii 35–37.
[7] Isa. xxix 13 (ὁ ἑτερος inserted).

with their mouth, but they curse in their heart." [1] "They loved Him with their mouth, and lied to Him with their tongue ; but their heart was not right with Him, and they were not faithful to His covenant." Wherefore "let the false lips become speechless, and let the LORD destroy the boastful tongue : those who say, We shall magnify our tongue, and our lips are our own ; who is Lord over us ? For the affliction of the poor and the groaning of the needy now will I arise, saith the LORD ; I will set him in safety ; I will speak out in his case." [2] For it is to the humble that Christ belongs, who do not exalt themselves against His flock. "Lay not up for yourselves, therefore, treasures on the earth, where moth and rust destroy, and thieves break through and steal," [3] says the Lord, in reproach perchance of the covetous, and perchance also of those who are simply anxious and full of cares, and those too who indulge their bodies. For amours, and diseases, and evil thoughts "break through" the mind and the whole man. But our true "treasure" is where what is allied to our mind is, since it bestows the communicative power of righteousness, showing that we must assign to the habit of our old conversation what we have acquired by it, and have recourse to God, beseeching mercy. He is, in truth, "the bag that waxeth not old," the provisions of eternal life, "the treasure that faileth not in heaven." [4] "For I will have mercy on whom I will have mercy ," [5] saith the Lord. And they say those things to those who wish to be poor for righteousness' sake. For they have heard in the commandment that "the broad and wide way leadeth to destruction, and many there are who go in by it." [6] It is not of anything else that the assertion is made, but of profligacy, and love of women, and love of glory, and ambition, and similar passions. For so He says, "Fool, this night shall thy soul be required of thee ; and whose shall those things be which thou hast prepared ? " [7] And the commandment is expressed in these very words, "Take heed, therefore, of covetousness. For a man's life does not consist in the abundance of those things which he possesses. For what shall it profit a man, if he shall gain the whole world, and lose his own soul ? or what shall a man give in exchange for his soul ? " [8] "Wherefore I say, Take no thought for your life, what ye shall eat ; neither for your body, what ye shall put on. For your life is more than meat, and your body than raiment." [9]

And again, "For your Father knoweth that ye have need of all these things." "But seek first the kingdom of heaven, and its righteousness," for these are the great things, and the things which are small and appertain to this life "shall be added to you." [10] Does He not plainly then exhort us to follow the gnostic life, and enjoin us to seek the truth in word and deed ? Therefore Christ, who trains the soul, reckons one rich, not by his gifts, but by his choice. It is said, therefore, that Zaccheus, or, according to some, Matthew, the chief of the publicans, on hearing that the Lord had deigned to come to him, said, "Lord, and if I have taken anything by false accusation, I restore him fourfold ; " on which the Saviour said, "The Son of man, on coming to-day, has found that which was lost." [11] Again, on seeing the rich cast into the treasury according to their wealth, and the widow two mites, He said "that the widow had cast in more than they all," for "they had contributed of their abundance, but she of her destitution." And because He brought all things to bear on the discipline of the soul, He said, "Blessed are the meek : for they shall inherit the earth." [12] And the meek are those who have quelled the battle of unbelief in the soul, the battle of wrath, and lust, and the other forms that are subject to them. And He praises those meek by choice, not by necessity. For there are with the Lord both rewards and "many mansions," corresponding to men's lives. "Whosoever shall receive," says He, "a prophet in the name of a prophet, shall receive a prophet's reward ; and whosoever shall receive a righteous man in the name of a righteous man, shall receive a righteous man's reward ; and whoso shall receive one of the least of these my disciples, shall not lose his reward." [13] And again, the differences of virtue according to merit, and the noble rewards, He indicated by the hours unequal in number ; and in addition, by the equal reward given to each of the labourers — that is, salvation, which is meant by the penny — He indicated the equality of justice ; and the difference of those called He intimated, by those who worked for unequal portions of time. They shall work, therefore, in accordance with the appropriate mansions of which they have been deemed worthy as rewards, being fellow-workers in the ineffable administration and service. [14] "Those, then," says Plato, "who seem called to a holy life, are those who, freed and released from those earthly localities as from prisons, have reached the pure dwelling-place on high." In clearer terms again he

1 Ps. lxii. 4.
2 Ps. xii. 3-5.
3 Matt. vi. 19.
4 Luke xii. 33.
5 Rom. ix. 15.
6 Matt. vii 13.
7 Luke xii. 20.
8 Matt. xvi. 26.
9 Matt. vi. 31 ; Luke xii. 22, 23.

10 Matt. vi. 32, 33 ; Luke xii. 30, 31.
11 Luke xix. 8, 9, 10.
12 Matt. v. 5.
13 Matt. x. 41, 42.
14 Translated as completed, and amended by Heinsius. In the text it is plainly mutilated and corrupt.

expresses the same thing : "Those who by philosophy have been sufficiently purged from those things, live without bodies entirely for all time. Although they are enveloped in certain shapes ; in the case of some, of air, and others, of fire." He adds further : "And they reach abodes fairer than those, which it is not easy, nor is there sufficient time now to describe." Whence with reason, "blessed are they that mourn : for they shall be comforted ; " [1] for they who have repented of their former evil life shall attain to "the calling" ($\kappa\lambda\hat{\eta}\sigma\iota\nu$), for this is the meaning of being comforted ($\pi\alpha\rho\alpha\kappa\lambda\eta\theta\hat{\eta}\nu\alpha\iota$). And there are two styles of penitents.[2] That which is more common is fear on account of what is done ; but the other which is more special, the shame which the spirit feels in itself arising from conscience. Whether then, here or elsewhere (for no place is devoid of the beneficence of God), He again says, "Blessed are the merciful : for they shall obtain mercy." And mercy is not, as some of the philosophers have imagined, pain on account of others' calamities, but rather something good, as the prophets say. For it is said, "I will have mercy, and not sacrifice." [3] And He [4] means by the merciful, not only those who do acts of mercy, but those who wish to do them, though they be not able ; who do as far as purpose is concerned. For sometimes we wish by the gift of money or by personal effort to do mercy, as to assist one in want, or help one who is sick, or stand by one who is in any emergency ; and are not able either from poverty, or disease, or old age (for this also is natural disease), to carry out our purpose, in reference to the things to which we are impelled, being unable to conduct them to the end we wished. Those, who have entertained the wish whose purpose is equal, share in the same honour with those who have the ability, although others have the advantage in point of resources.[5] And since there are two paths of reaching the perfection of salvation, works and knowledge, He called the "pure in heart blessed, for they shall see God." [6] And if we really look to the truth of the matter, knowledge is the purification of the leading faculty of the soul, and is a good activity. Some things accordingly are good in themselves, and others by participation in what is good, as we say good actions are good. But without things intermediate which hold the place of material, neither good nor bad actions are constituted, such I mean as life, and health, and other necessary

things or circumstantials. Pure then as respects corporeal lusts, and pure in respect of holy thoughts, he means those are, who attain to the knowledge of God, when the chief faculty of the soul has nothing spurious to stand in the way of its power. When, therefore, he who partakes gnostically of this holy quality devotes himself to contemplation, communing in purity with the divine, he enters more nearly into the state of impassible identity, so as no longer to have science and possess knowledge, but to be science and knowledge.

"Blessed, then, are the peacemakers," [7] who have subdued and tamed the law which wars against the disposition of the mind, the menaces of anger, and the baits of lust, and the other passions which war against the reason ; who, having lived in the knowledge both of good works and true reason, shall be reinstated in adoption, which is dearer. It follows that the perfect peacemaking is that which keeps unchanged in all circumstances what is peaceful ; calls Providence holy and good ; and has its being in the knowledge of divine and human affairs, by which it deems the opposites that are in the world to be the fairest harmony of creation. They also are peacemakers, who teach those who war against the stratagems of sin to have recourse to faith and peace. And it is the sum of all virtue, in my opinion, when the Lord teaches us that for love to God we must gnostically despise death. "Blessed are they," says He, "who are persecuted for righteousness' sake, for they shall be called the sons of God ; " [8] or, as some of those who transpose the Gospels [9] say, "Blessed are they who are persecuted by righteousness, for they shall be perfect." And, "Blessed are they who are persecuted for my sake ; for they shall have a place where they shall not be persecuted." And, "Blessed are ye when men shall hate you, when they shall separate you, when they shall cast out your name as evil, for the Son of man's sake ; " [10] if we do not detest our persecutors, and undergo punishments at their hands, not hating them under the idea that we have been put to trial more tardily than we looked for ; but knowing this also, that every instance of trial is an occasion for testifying.

CHAP. VII. — THE BLESSEDNESS OF THE MARTYR.

Then he who has lied and shown himself unfaithful, and revolted to the devil's army, in what evil do we think him to be? He belies, therefore, the Lord, or rather he is cheated of his own hope who believes not God ; and he believes not who does not what He has commanded.

---

[1] Matt. v. 4.
[2] [Clement describes the *attrition* of the schoolmen (which they say suffices) with the *contrition* exacted by the Gospel. He knows nothing but the latter, as having promise of the Comforter.]
[3] Hos. vi. 6; Matt. ix. 13, xii. 7.
[4] [Matt. v. 7. S.]
[5] [A cheering comment on the widow's mites, and the apostolic principle of 2 Cor. viii. 12.]
[6] [Matt. v. 8. S.]

[7] [Matt. v. 9. S].
[8] Matt. v. 10.
[9] [Note that thus in the second century there were those (scholiasts) who interlined and transposed the Gospels, in MSS.]
[10] Luke vi. 22.

And what? Does not he, who denies the Lord, deny himself? For does he not rob his Master of His authority, who deprives himself of his relation to Him? He, then, who denies the Saviour, denies life; for "the light was life."[1] He does not term those men of little faith, but faithless and hypocrites,[2] who have the name inscribed on them, but deny that they are really believers. But the faithful is called both servant and friend. So that if one loves himself, he loves the Lord, and confesses to salvation that he may save his soul. Though you die for your neighbour out of love, and regard the Saviour as our neighbour (for God who saves is said to be nigh in respect to what is saved); you do so, choosing death on account of life, and suffering for your own sake rather than his. And is it not for this that he is called brother? he who, suffering out of love to God, suffered for his own salvation; while he, on the other hand, who dies for his own salvation, endures for love to the Lord. For he being life, in what he suffered, wished to suffer that we might live by his suffering.

"Why call ye me Lord, Lord," He says, "and do not the things which I say?"[3] For "the people that loveth with their lips, but have their heart far away from the Lord,"[4] is another people, and trust in another, and have willingly sold themselves to another; but those who perform the commandments of the Lord, in every action "testify," by doing what He wishes, and consistently naming the Lord's name; and "testifying" by deed to Him in whom they trust, that they are those "who have crucified the flesh, with the affections and lusts." "If we live in the Spirit, let us also walk in the Spirit."[5] "He that soweth to his flesh, shall of the flesh reap corruption; but he that soweth to the Spirit, shall of the Spirit reap life everlasting."[6]

But to those miserable men, witness to the Lord by blood seems a most violent death, not knowing that such a gate of death is the beginning of the true life; and they will understand neither the honours after death, which belong to those who have lived holily, nor the punishments of those who have lived unrighteously and impurely.[7] I do not say only from our Scriptures (for almost all the commandments indicate them); but they will not even hear their own discourses. For the Pythagorean Theano writes, "Life were indeed a feast to the wicked, who, having done evil, then die; were not the soul immortal, death would be a godsend." And

Plato in the *Phædo*, "For if death were release from everything," and so forth. We are not then to think according to the *Telephus* of Æschylus, "that a single path leads to Hades." The ways are many, and the sins that lead thither. Such deeply erring ones as the unfaithful are, Aristophanes properly makes the subjects of comedy. "Come," he says, "ye men of obscure life, ye that are like the race of leaves, feeble, wax figures, shadowy tribes, evanescent, fleeting, ephemeral." And Epicharmus, "This nature of men is inflated skins." And the Saviour has said to us, "The spirit is willing, but the flesh is weak."[8] "Because the carnal mind is enmity against God," explains the apostle: "for it is not subject to the law of God, neither indeed can be. And they that are in the flesh cannot please God." And in further explanation continues, that no one may, like Marcion,[9] regard the creature as evil. "But if Christ be in you, the body is dead because of sin; but the Spirit is life because of righteousness." And again: "For if ye live after the flesh, ye shall die. For I reckon that the sufferings of this present time are not worthy to be compared to the glory which shall be revealed in us. If we suffer with Him, that we also may be glorified together as joint-heirs of Christ. And we know that all things work together for good to them that love God, to them that are called according to the purpose. For whom He did foreknow, He also did predestinate to be conformed to the image of His Son, that He might be the first-born among many brethren. And whom He did predestinate, them He also called; and whom He called, them He also justified; and whom He justified, them He also glorified."[10]

You see that martyrdom for love's sake is taught. And should you wish to be a martyr for the recompense of advantages, you shall hear again. "For we are saved by hope: but hope that is seen is not hope: for what a man seeth, why doth he yet hope for? But if we hope for that we see not, then do we with patience wait for it."[11] "But if we also suffer for righteousness' sake," says Peter, "blessed are we. Be not afraid of their fear, neither be troubled. But sanctify the Lord God in your hearts: and be ready always to give an answer to him that asks a reason of the hope that is in you, but with meekness and fear, having a good conscience; so that in reference to that for which you are spoken against, they may be ashamed who calumniate your good conversation in Christ. For it is better to suffer for well-doing, if the will of God, than for evil-doing." But if one should cap-

---

[1] John i. 4.
[2] Matt. vi 30.
[3] Luke vi. 46.
[4] Isa. xxix. 15.
[5] Gal. v, 24, 25.
[6] Gal. vi. 8.
[7] [This is important testimony as to the primitive understanding of the awards of a future life.]

[8] Matt. xxvi. 41.
[9] [See book iii., cap. iii., *supra*.]
[10] Rom. viii. 7, 8, 10, 13, 17, 18, 28, 29, 30.
[11] Rom. viii. 24, 25.

tiously say, And how is it possible for feeble flesh to resist the energies and spirits of the Powers?[1] well, let him know this, that, confiding in the Almighty and the Lord, we war against the principalities of darkness, and against death. "Whilst thou art yet speaking," He says, "Lo, here am I." See the invincible Helper who shields us. "Think it not strange, therefore, concerning the burning sent for your trial, as though some strange thing happened to you; But, as you are partakers in the sufferings of Christ, rejoice; that at the revelation of His glory ye may rejoice exultant. If ye be reproached in the name of Christ, happy are ye; for the Spirit of glory and of God resteth on you."[2] As it is written, "Because for Thy sake we are killed all the day long; we are accounted as sheep for the slaughter. Nay, in all these things we are more than conquerors, through Him that loved us."[3]

"What you wish to ascertain from my mind,
　You shall not ascertain, not were you to apply
Horrid saws from the crown of my head to the soles of
　my feet,
Not were you to load me with chains,"

says a woman acting manfully in the tragedy. And Antigone, contemning the proclamation of Creon, says boldly:—

"It was not Zeus who uttered this proclamation."

But it is God that makes proclamation to us, and He must be believed. "For with the heart man believeth unto righteousness; and with the mouth confession is made unto salvation. Wherefore the Scripture saith, "Whosoever believeth on Him shall not be put to shame."[4] Accordingly Simonides justly writes, "It is said that virtue dwells among all but inaccessible rocks, but that she speedily traverses a pure place. Nor is she visible to the eyes of all mortals. He who is not penetrated by heart-vexing sweat will not scale the summit of manliness." And Pindar says:—

"But the anxious thoughts of youths, revolving with
　toils,
Will find glory: and in time their deeds
Will in resplendent ether splendid shine."

Æschylus, too, having grasped this thought, says:—
　　　"To him who toils is due,

As product of his toil, glory from the gods."

"For great Fates attain great destinies," according to Heraclitus:—

"And what slave is there, who is careless of death?"

"For God hath not given us the spirit of bondage again to fear; but of power, and love, and of a sound mind. Be not therefore ashamed of the testimony of our Lord, or of me his pris-

oner," he writes to Timothy.[5] Such shall he be "who cleaves to that which is good," according to the apostle,[6] "who hates evil, having love unfeigned; for he that loveth another fulfilleth the law."[7] If, then, this God, to whom we bear witness, be as He is, the God of hope, we acknowledge our hope, speeding on to hope, "saturated with goodness, filled with all knowledge."[8]

The Indian sages say to Alexander of Macedon: "You transport men's bodies from place to place. But you shall not force our souls to do what we do not wish. Fire is to men the greatest torture, this we despise." Hence Heraclitus preferred one thing, glory, to all else; and professes "that he allows the crowd to stuff themselves to satiety like cattle."

"For on account of the body are many toils,
　For it we have invented a roofed house,
And discovered how to dig up silver, and sow the land,
　And all the rest which we know by names."

To the multitude, then, this vain labour is desirable. But to us the apostle says, "Now we know this, that our old man is crucified with Him, that the body of sin might be destroyed, that henceforth we should not serve sin."[9] Does not the apostle then plainly add the following, to show the contempt for faith in the case of the multitude? "For I think that God hath set forth us the apostles last, as appointed to death: we are made a spectacle to the world, and to angels, and to men. Up to this present hour we both hunger, and thirst, and are naked, and are beaten, and are feeble, and labour, working with our hands. Being reviled, we bless; being persecuted, we endure; being defamed, we entreat; we are become as it were the offscourings of the world."[10] Such also are the words of Plato in the *Republic*:[11] "The just man, though stretched on the rack, though his eyes are dug out, will be happy." The Gnostic will never then have the chief end placed in life, but in being always happy and blessed, and a kingly friend of God. Although visited with ignominy and exile, and confiscation, and above all, death, he will never be wrenched from his freedom, and signal love to God. "The charity which bears all things, endures all things,"[12] is assured that Divine Providence orders all things well. "I exhort you," therefore it is said, "Be followers of me." The first step to salvation[13] is the instruction accompanied with fear, in consequence of which we abstain from what is wrong; and the second is

---

1　In allusion to Eph. vi. 12.
2　1 Pet. iv. 12, 13, 14.
3　Rom. viii. 36, 37.
4　Rom. x. 10, 11.

5　2 Tim. i. 7, 8; Rom. viii. 15.
6　Rom. xii. 9.
7　Rom. xiii. 8.
8　Instead of μέγιστοι, read from Rom. xv. 13, 14, μεστοί.
9　Rom. vi. 6.
10　1 Cor. iv. 9, 11, 12, 13.
11　[ii. 5. Compare Cicero's *Rep.*, iii. 17.]
12　1 Cor. xiii. 7.
13　For σώματος　ωτηρίας.

hope, by reason of which we desire the best things; but love, as is fitting, perfects, by training now according to knowledge. For the Greeks, I know not how, attributing events to unreasoning necessity, own that they yield to them unwillingly. Accordingly Euripides says :—

"What I declare, receive from me, madam:
No mortal exists who has not toil;
He buries children, and begets others,
And he himself dies. And thus mortals are afflicted."

Then he adds : —

"We must bear those things which are inevitable according to nature, and go through them:
Not one of the things which are necessary is formidable for mortals."

And for those who are aiming at perfection there is proposed the rational gnosis, the foundation of which is "the sacred Triad." "Faith, hope, love; but the greatest of these is love." [1] Truly, "all things are lawful, but all things are not expedient," says the apostle : "all things are lawful for me, but all things edify not." [2] And, "Let no one seek his own advantage, but also that of his neighbour," [3] so as to be able at once to do and to teach, building and building up. For that "the earth is the Lord's, and the fulness thereof," is admitted; but the conscience of the weak is supported. "Conscience, I say, not his own, but that of the other; for why is my liberty judged of by another conscience? For if I by grace am partaker, why am I evil spoken of for that for which I give thanks? Whether therefore ye eat, or drink, or whatsoever ye do, do all to the glory of God." [4] "For though we walk in the flesh, we do not war after the flesh; for the weapons of our warfare are not carnal, but mighty through God to the demolition of fortifications, demolishing thoughts, and every high thing which exalteth itself against the knowledge of Christ." [5] Equipped with these weapons, the Gnostic says: O Lord, give opportunity, and receive demonstration; let this dread event pass; I contemn dangers for the love I bear to Thee.

"Because alone of human things
Virtue receives not a recompense from without,
But has itself as the reward of its toils."

"Put on therefore, as the elect of God, holy and beloved, bowels of mercies, kindness, humbleness, meekness, long-suffering. And above all these, love, which is the bond of perfection. And let the peace of God reign in your hearts, to which also ye are called in one body; and be thankful," [6] ye who, while still in the body, like the just men of old, enjoy impassibility and tranquillity of soul.

CHAP. VIII. — WOMEN AS WELL AS MEN, SLAVES AS WELL AS FREEMEN, CANDIDATES FOR THE MARTYR'S CROWN.

Since, then, not only the Æsopians, and Macedonians, and the Lacedæmonians endured when subjected to torture, as Eratosthenes says in his work, *On Things Good and Evil;* but also Zeno of Elea, when subjected to compulsion to divulge a secret, held out against the tortures, and confessed nothing; who, when expiring, bit out his tongue and spat it at the tyrant, whom some term Nearchus, and some Demulus. Theodotus the Pythagorean acted also similarly, and Paulus the friend of Lacydes, as Timotheus of Pergamus says in his work on *The Fortitude of Philosophers,* and Achaicus in *The Ethics.* Posthumus also, the Roman, when captured by Peucetion, did not divulge a single secret; but putting his hand on the fire, held it to it as if to a piece of brass, without moving a muscle of his face. I omit the case of Anaxarchus, who exclaimed, "Pound away at the sack which holds Anaxarchus, for it is not Anaxarchus you are pounding," when by the tyrant's orders he was being pounded with iron pestles. Neither, then, the hope of happiness nor the love of God takes what befalls ill, but remains free, although thrown among the wildest beasts or into the all-devouring fire; though racked with a tyrant's tortures. Depending as it does on the divine favour, it ascends aloft unenslaved, surrendering the body to those who can touch it alone. A barbarous nation, not cumbered with philosophy, select, it is said, annually an ambassador to the hero Zamolxis. Zamolxis was one of the disciples of Pythagoras. The one, then, who is judged of the most sterling worth is put to death, to the distress of those who have practised philosophy, but have not been selected, at being reckoned unworthy of a happy service.

So the Church is full of those, as well chaste women as men, who all their life have contemplated the death which rouses up to Christ. [7] For the individual whose life is framed as ours is, may philosophize without Learning, whether barbarian, whether Greek, whether slave — whether an old man, or a boy, or a woman. [8] For self-control is common to all human beings who have made choice of it. And we admit that the same nature exists in every race, and the same virtue. As far as respects human nature, the woman does not possess one nature, and the man exhibit another, but the same : so also with virtue. If, consequently, a self-restraint and righteousness, and whatever qualities are regarded as

---

[1] 1 Cor. xiii. 13. [Not without allusion to the grand Triad, however. p. 101, this volume.]
[2] 1 Cor. x. 23.
[3] 1 Cor. x. 24.
[4] 1 Cor. x. 26, 28, 29, 30, 31.
[5] 2 Cor. x. 3, 4, 5.
[6] Col. iii. 12, 14, 15.

[7] [The Edin. translator says "*courted* the death;" but surely (μελετησάντων) the original merely states the condition of Christians in the second century, "dying daily," and accepting in daily contemplation the very probable death " by which they should glorify God."]
[8] [Note the Catholic democracy of Christianity, which levels up and not downward.]

following them, is the virtue of the male, it belongs to the male alone to be virtuous, and to the woman to be licentious and unjust. But it is offensive even to say this. Accordingly woman is to practise self-restraint and righteousness, and every other virtue, as well as man, both bond and free; since it is a fit consequence that the same nature possesses one and the same virtue.[1] We do not say that woman's nature is the ·same as man's, as she is woman. For undoubtedly it stands to reason that some difference should exist between each of them, in virtue of which one is male and the other female. Pregnancy and parturition, accordingly, we say belong to woman, as she is woman, and not as she is a human being. But if there were no difference between man and woman, both would do and suffer the same things. As then there is sameness, as far as respects the soul, she will attain to the same virtue; but as there is difference as respects the peculiar construction of the body, she is destined for child-bearing and housekeeping. "For I would have you know," says the apostle, "that the head of every man is Christ; and the head of the woman is the man: for the man is not of the woman, but the woman of the man. For neither is the man without the woman, nor the man without the woman, in the Lord."[2] For as we say that the man ought to be continent, and superior to pleasures; so also we reckon that the woman should be continent and practised in fighting against pleasures. "But I say, Walk in the Spirit, and ye shall not fulfil the lusts of the flesh," counsels the apostolic command; "for the flesh lusteth against the spirit, and the spirit against the flesh. These, then, are contrary" (not as good to evil, but as fighting advantageously), he adds therefore, "so that ye cannot do the things that ye would. Now the works of the flesh are manifest, which are, fornication, uncleanness, profligacy, idolatry, witchcrafts, enmities, strifes, jealousies, wrath, contentions, dissensions, heresies, envyings, drunkenness, revellings, and such like; of which I tell you before, as I have also said before, that they which do such things shall not inherit the kingdom of God. But the fruit of the Spirit is love, joy, peace, long-suffering, gentleness, temperance, goodness, faith, meekness."[3] He calls sinners, as I think, "flesh," and the righteous "spirit." Further, manliness is to be assumed in order to produce confidence and forbearance, so as "to him that strikes on the one cheek, to give to him the other; and to him that takes away the cloak, to yield to him the coat also," strongly restraining anger. For we do not train our women like Amazons to manliness in war; since we wish the men even to be peaceable. I hear that the Sarmatian women practise war no less than the men; and the women of the Sacæ besides, who shoot backwards, feigning flight as well as the men. I am aware, too, that the women near Iberia practise manly work and toil, not refraining from their tasks even though near their delivery; but even in the very struggle of her pains, the woman, on being delivered, taking up the infant, carries it home. Further, the females no less than the males manage the house, and hunt, and keep the flocks:—

"Cressa the hound ran keenly in the stag's track."

Women are therefore to philosophize equally with men, though the males are preferable at everything, unless they have become effeminate.[4] To the whole human race, then, discipline and virtue are a necessity, if they would pursue after happiness. And how recklessly Euripides writes sometimes this and sometimes that! On one occasion, "For every wife is inferior to her husband, though the most excellent one marry her that is of fair fame." And on another:—

"For the chaste is her husband's slave,
    While she that is unchaste in her folly despises her
        consort.
. . . . For nothing is better and more excellent,
    Than when as husband and wife ye keep house,
    Harmonious in your sentiments."

The ruling power is therefore the head. And if "the Lord is head of the man, and the man is head of the woman," the man, "being the image and glory of God, is lord of the woman."[5] Wherefore also in the Epistle to the Ephesians it is written, "Subjecting yourselves one to another in the fear of God. Wives, submit yourselves to your own husbands, as to the Lord. For the husband is head of the wife, as also Christ is the head of the Church; and He is the Saviour of the body. Husbands, love your wives, as also Christ loved the Church. So also ought men to love their wives as their own bodies: he that loveth his wife loveth himself. For no man ever yet hated his own flesh."[6] And in that to the Colossians it is said, "Wives, submit yourselves to your own husbands, as is fit in the Lord.[7] Husbands, love your wives, and be not bitter against them. Children, obey your parents in all things; for this is well pleasing to the Lord. Fathers, provoke not your children to anger, lest they be discouraged. Servants, be obedient in all things to those who

---

[1] [This vindication of the equality of the sexes is a comment on what the Gospel found woman's estate, and on what it created for her among Christians.]

[2] 1 Cor. xi. 3, 8, 11.

[3] [Gal. v. 16, 17, 19-23. S.]

[4] [The Edin. trans. has "best at everything," but I have corrected it in closer accord with the comparative degree in the Greek.]

[5] 1 Cor. xi. 3, 7.

[6] Eph. v. 21-29.

[7] [It is a sad token of our times that some women resent this law of the Christian family. In every society there must be presidency even among equals; and even Christ, though "equal to the Father," in the Catholic theology, is yet subordinate. See Bull, *Defens. Fid., Nicæn. Works*, vol. v. p. 685.]

are your masters according to the flesh; not with eye-service, as men-pleasers; but with singleness of heart, fearing the Lord. And whatsoever ye do, do it heartily, as serving the Lord and not men; knowing that of the Lord ye shall receive the reward of the inheritance: for ye serve the Lord Christ. For the wrong-doer shall receive the wrong, which he hath done; and there is no respect of persons. Masters, render to your servants justice and equity; knowing that ye also have a Master in heaven, where there is neither Greek nor Jew, circumcision and uncircumcision, barbarian, Scythian, bond, free: but Christ is all, and in all." [1] And the earthly Church is the image of the heavenly, as we pray also "that the will of God may be done upon the earth as in heaven." [2] "Putting on, therefore, bowels of mercy, gentleness, humbleness, meekness, long-suffering; forbearing one another, and forgiving one another, if one have a quarrel against any man; as also Christ hath forgiven us, so also let us. And above all these things put on charity, which is the bond of perfectness. And let the peace of God rule in your hearts, to which ye are called in one body; and be thankful." [3] For there is no obstacle to adducing frequently the same Scripture in order to put Marcion [4] to the blush, if perchance he be persuaded and converted; by learning that the faithful ought to be grateful to God the Creator, who hath called us, and who preached the Gospel in the body. From these considerations the unity of the faith is clear, and it is shown who is the perfect man; so that though some are reluctant, and offer as much resistance as they can, though menaced with punishments at the hand of husband or master, both the domestic and the wife will philosophize. Moreover, the free, though threatened with death at a tyrant's hands, and brought before the tribunals, and all his substances imperilled, will by no means abandon piety; nor will the wife who dwells with a wicked husband, or the son if he has a bad father, or the domestic if he has a bad master, ever fail in holding nobly to virtue. But as it is noble for a man to die for virtue, and for liberty, and for himself, so also is it for a woman. For this is not peculiar to the nature of males, but to the nature of the good. Accordingly, both the old man, the young, and the servant will live faithfully, and if need be die; which will be to be made alive by death. So we know that both children, and women, and servants have often, against their fathers', and masters', and hus-

bands' will, reached the highest degree of excellence. Wherefore those who are determined to live piously ought none the less to exhibit alacrity, when some seem to exercise compulsion on them; but much more, I think, does it become them to show eagerness, and to strive with uncommon vigour, lest, being overcome, they abandon the best and most indispensable counsels. For it does not, I think, admit of comparison, whether it be better to be a follower of the Almighty than to choose the darkness of demons. For the things which are done by us on account of others we are to do always, endeavouring to have respect to those for whose sake 'it is proper that they be done, regarding the gratification rendered in their case, as what is to be our rule; but the things which are done for our own sake rather than that of others, are to be done with equal earnestness, whether they are like to please certain people or not. If some indifferent things have obtained such honour as to appear worthy of adoption, though against the will of some; much more is virtue to be regarded by us as worth contending for, looking the while to nothing but what can be rightly done, whether it seem good to others or not. Well then, Epicurus, writing to Menoeceus, says, "Let not him who is young delay philosophizing, and let not the old man grow weary of philosophizing; for no one is either not of age or past age for attending to the health of his soul. And he who says that the time for philosophizing is not come or is past, is like the man who says that the time for happiness is not come or has gone. So that young [5] as well as old ought to philosophize: the one, in order that, while growing old, he may grow young in good things out of favour accruing from what is past; and the other, that he may be at once young and old, from want of fear for the future."

CHAP. IX. — CHRIST'S SAYINGS RESPECTING MARTYRDOM.

On martyrdom the Lord hath spoken explicitly, and what is written in different places we bring together. "But I say unto you, Whosoever shall confess in Me before men, the Son of man also shall confess before the angels of God; but whosoever shall deny Me before men, him will I deny before the angels." [6] "Whosoever shall be ashamed of Me or of My words in this adulterous and sinful generation, of him shall the Son of man also be ashamed when He cometh in the glory of His Father with His angels.

---

[1] Col. iii. 18-25, iv. 1, iii. 11.
[2] Matt. vi. 10.
[3] Col. iii. 12-15. [Again let us note this Catholic democracy of the Christian brotherhood (see p. 416, *supra*), for which indeed we should be thankful as Christ's freemen.]
[4] [Book iii. cap. iii., *supra*.]

[5] [He who studies the Sapiential books of the Bible and Apocrypha and the Sermon on the Mount, is a philosopher of the sort here commended.]
[6] Luke xii. 8.

Whosoever therefore shall confess in Me before men, him will I also confess before my Father in heaven." [1] "And when they bring you before synagogues, and rulers, and powers, think not beforehand how ye shall make your defence, or what ye shall say. For the Holy Spirit shall teach you in the same hour what ye must say." [2] In explanation of this passage, Heracleon, the most distinguished of the school of Valentinians, says expressly, "that there is a confession by faith and conduct, and one with the voice. The confession that is made with the voice, and before the authorities, is what the most reckon the only confession. Not soundly: and hypocrites also can confess with this confession. But neither will this utterance be found to be spoken universally; for all the saved have confessed with the confession made by the voice, and departed. [3] Of whom are Matthew, Philip, Thomas, Levi, and many others. And confession by the lip is not universal, but partial. But that which He specifies now is universal, that which is by deeds and actions corresponding to faith in Him. This confession is followed by that which is partial, that before the authorities, if necessary, and reason dictate. For he will confess rightly with his voice who has first confessed by his disposition. [3] And he has well used, with regard to those who confess, the expression 'in Me,' and applied to those who deny the expression 'Me.' For those, though they confess Him with the voice, yet deny Him, not confessing Him in their conduct. But those alone confess 'in Him,' who live in the confession and conduct according to Him, in which He also confesses, who is contained in them and held by them. Wherefore 'He never can deny Himself.' And those deny Him who are not in Him. For He said not, 'Whosoever shall deny' in Me, but 'Me.' For no one who is in Him will ever deny Him. And the expression 'before men' applies both to the saved and the heathen similarly by conduct before the one, and by voice before the other. Wherefore they never can deny Him. But those deny Him who are not in Him." So far Heracleon. And in other things he seems to be of the same sentiments with us in this section; but he has not adverted to this, that if some have not by conduct and in their life "confessed Christ before men," they are manifested to have believed with the heart; by confessing Him with the mouth at the tribunals, and not denying Him when tortured to the death. And the disposition being confessed, and especially not being changed by death at any time, cuts away all passions which were engendered by corporeal desire. For there is, so to speak, at the close of life a sudden repentance in action, and a true confession toward Christ, in the testimony of the voice. But if the Spirit of the Father testifies in us, how can we be any more hypocrites, who are said to bear testimony with the voice alone? But it will be given to some, if expedient, to make a defence, that by their witness and confession all may be benefited — those in the Church being confirmed, and those of the heathen who have devoted themselves to the search after salvation wondering and being led to the faith; and the rest seized with amazement. So that confession is by all means necessary. [4] For it is in our power. But to make a defence for our faith is not universally necessary. For that does not depend on us. "But he that endureth to the end shall be saved." For who of those who are wise would not choose to reign in God, and even to serve? So some "confess that they know God," according to the apostle; "but in works they deny Him, being abominable and disobedient, and to every good work reprobate." [5] And these, though they confess nothing but this, will have done at the end one good work. Their witness, then, appears to be the cleansing away of sins with glory. For instance, the Shepherd [6] says: "You will escape the energy of the wild beast, if your heart become pure and blameless." Also the Lord Himself says: "Satan hath desired to sift you; but I have prayed." [7] Alone, therefore, the Lord, for the purification of the men who plotted against Him and disbelieved Him, "drank the cup;" in imitation of whom the apostles, that they might be in reality Gnostics, and perfect, suffered for the Churches which they founded. So, then, also the Gnostics who tread in the footsteps of the apostles ought to be sinless, and, out of love to the Lord, to love also their brother; so that, if occasion call, enduring without stumbling, afflictions for the Church, "they may drink the cup." Those who witness in their life by deed, and at the tribunal by word, whether entertaining hope or surmising fear, are better than those who confess salvation by their mouth alone. But if one ascend also to love, he is a really blessed and true martyr, having confessed perfectly both to the commandments and to God, by the Lord; whom having loved, he acknowledged a brother, giving himself up wholly for God, resigning pleasantly and lovingly the man when asked, like a deposit. [8]

---

[1] Matt. x. 32.
[2] Luke xii. 11, 12.
[3] [Rom. x. 10. The indifference of our times is based on an abuse of the principle that God sees *the heart*, and needs no public (sacramental) profession of faith. Had this been Christ's teaching, there would have been no martyrs and no visible Church to hand down the faith.]

[4] [Absolutely necessary (i.e., open profession of Christ) to the conversion of others, and the perpetuation of the Christian Church.]
[5] Tit. i. 16.
[6] [See p. 18, this volume.]
[7] Luke xxii. 31, 32.
[8] [As a reflection of the condition and fidelity of Christians, still "sheep for the slaughter." At such a period the tone and argument of this touching chapter are suggestive.]

CHAP. X. — THOSE WHO OFFERED THEMSELVES FOR MARTYRDOM REPROVED.

When, again, He says, "When they persecute you in this city, flee ye to the other,"[1] He does not advise flight, as if persecution were an evil thing; nor does He enjoin them by flight to avoid death, as if in dread of it, but wishes us neither to be the authors nor abettors of any evil to any one, either to ourselves or the persecutor and murderer. For He, in a way, bids us take care of ourselves. But he who disobeys is rash and foolhardy. If he who kills a man of God sins against God, he also who presents himself before the judgment-seat becomes guilty of his death. And such is also the case with him who does not avoid persecution, but out of daring presents himself for capture. Such a one, as far as in him lies, becomes an accomplice in the crime of the persecutor. And if he also uses provocation, he is wholly guilty, challenging the wild beast. And similarly, if he afford any cause for conflict or punishment, or retribution or enmity, he gives occasion for persecution. Wherefore, then, we are enjoined not to cling to anything that belongs to this life; but "to him that takes our cloak to give our coat," not only that we may continue destitute of inordinate affection, but that we may not by retaliating make our persecutors savage against ourselves, and stir them up to blaspheme the name.[2]

CHAP. XI. — THE OBJECTION, WHY DO YOU SUFFER IF GOD CARES FOR YOU, ANSWERED.

But, say they, if God cares for you, why are you persecuted and put to death? Has He delivered you to this? No, we do not suppose that the Lord wishes us to be involved in calamities, but that He foretold prophetically what would happen — that we should be persecuted for His name's sake, slaughtered, and impaled. So that it was not that He wished us to be persecuted, but He intimated beforehand what we shall suffer by the prediction of what would take place, training us to endurance, to which He promised the inheritance, although we are punished not alone, but along with many. But those, it is said, being malefactors, are righteously punished. Accordingly, they unwillingly bear testimony to our righteousness, we being unjustly punished for righteousness' sake. But the injustice of the judge does not affect the providence of God. For the judge must be master of his own opinion — not pulled by strings, like inanimate machines, set in motion only by external causes. Accordingly he is judged in respect to his judgment, as we also, in accordance with our choice of things desirable, and our endurance.

Although we do not wrong, yet the judge looks on us as doing wrong, for he neither knows nor wishes to know about us, but is influenced by unwarranted prejudice; wherefore also he is judged.[3] Accordingly they persecute us, not from the supposition that we are wrong-doers, but imagining that by the very fact of our being Christians we sin against life in so conducting ourselves, and exhorting others to adopt the like life.

But why are you not helped when persecuted? say they. What wrong is done us, as far as we are concerned, in being released by death to go to the Lord, and so undergoing a change of life, as if a change from one time of life to another? Did we think rightly, we should feel obliged to those who have afforded the means for speedy departure, if it is for love that we bear witness; and if not, we should appear to the multitude to be base men. Had they also known the truth, all would have bounded on to the way, and there would have been no choice. But our faith, being the light of the world, reproves unbelief. "Should Anytus and Melitus kill me, they will not hurt me in the least; for I do not think it right for the better to be hurt by the worse," [says Socrates]. So that each one of us may with confidence say, "The Lord is my helper; I will not fear: what shall man do to me?"[4] "For the souls of the righteous are in the hand of the Lord, and no plague shall touch them."[5]

CHAP. XII. — BASILIDES' IDEA OF MARTYRDOM REFUTED.

Basilides, in the twenty-third book of the *Exegetics*, respecting those that are punished by martyrdom, expresses himself in the following language: "For I say this, Whosoever fall under the afflictions mentioned, in consequence of unconsciously transgressing in other matters, are brought to this good end by the kindness of Him who brings them, but accused on other grounds; so that they may not suffer as condemned for what are owned to be iniquities, nor reproached as the adulterer or the murderer, but because they are Christians; which will console them, so that they do not appear to suffer. And if one who has not sinned at all incur suffering — a rare case — yet even he will not suffer aught through the machinations of power, but will suffer as the child which seems not to have sinned would suffer." Then further on he adds: "As, then, the child which has not sinned before, or committed actual sin in itself, but has that which committed sin, when subjected to

---

[1] Matt. x. 23.
[2] [An excellent rendering, which the Latin translator misses (see ed. Migne, *ad loc.*), the reference being to Jas. ii. 7.]

[3] [Self-condemned. A pathetic description of the indifference of the Roman law to the rights of the people. Pilates all were these judges of Christ's followers or Gallios at best.]
[4] Ps. cxviii. 6.
[5] Wisd. iii. 1. [This is pronounced canonical Scripture by the Trent theology, and yet the same theology asserts a purgatory to which none but the faithful are committed.]

suffering, gets good, reaping the advantage of many difficulties; so also, although a perfect man may not have sinned in act, while he endures afflictions, he suffers similarly with the child. Having within him the sinful principle, but not embracing the opportunity of committing sin, he does not sin; so that he is not to be reckoned as not having sinned. For as he who wishes to commit adultery is an adulterer, although he does not succeed in committing adultery; and he that wishes to commit murder is a murderer, although he is unable to kill; so also, if I see the man without sin, whom I specify, suffering, though he have done nothing bad, I should call him bad, on account of his wishing to sin. For I will affirm anything rather than call Providence evil." Then, in continuation, he says expressly concerning the Lord, as concerning man: "If then, passing from all these observations, you were to proceed to put me to shame by saying, perchance impersonating certain parties, This man has then sinned; for this man has suffered; — if you permit, I will say, He has not sinned; but was like a child suffering. If you were to insist more urgently, I would say, That the man you name is man, but that God is righteous: 'For no one is pure,' as one said, 'from pollution.'"[1] But the hypothesis of Basilides[2] says that the soul, having sinned before in another life, endures punishment in this — the elect soul with honour by martyrdom, the other purged by appropriate punishment. How can this be true, when the confessing and suffering punishment or not depends on ourselves? For in the case of the man who shall deny, Providence, as held by Basilides, is done away with. I will ask him, then, in the case of a confessor who has been arrested, whether he will confess and be punished in virtue of Providence or not? For in the case of denying he will not be punished. But if, for the sake of escaping and evading the necessity of punishing such an one, he shall say that the destruction of those who shall deny is of Providence, he will be a martyr against his will. And how any more is it the case, that there is laid up in heaven the very glorious recompense to him who has witnessed, for his witnessing? If Providence did not permit the sinner to get the length of sinning, it is unjust in both cases; both in not rescuing the man who is dragged to punishment for righteousness' sake, and in having rescued him who wished to do wrong, he having done it as far as volition was concerned, but [Providence] having prevented the deed, and unjustly favoured the sin-

ner. And how impious, in deifying the devil, and in daring to call the Lord a sinful man! For the devil tempting us, knowing what we are, but not knowing if we will hold out, but wishing to dislodge us from the faith, attempts also to bring us into subjection to himself. Which is all that is allowed to him, partly from the necessity of saving us, who have taken occasion from the commandment, from ourselves; partly for the confusion of him who has tempted and failed; for the confirmation of the members of the Church, and the conscience of those who admire the constancy [displayed]. But if martyrdom be retribution by way of punishment, then also faith and doctrine, on account of which martyrdom comes, are co-operators in punishment — than which, what other absurdity could be greater? But with reference to these dogmas, whether the soul is changed to another body, also of the devil, at the proper time mention will be made. But at present, to what has been already said, let us add the following: Where any more is faith in the retribution of sins committed before martyrdom takes place? And where is love to God, which is persecuted and endures for the truth? And where is the praise of him who has confessed, or the censure of him who has denied? And for what use is right conduct, the mortification of the lusts, and the hating of no creature? But if, as Basilides himself says, we suppose one part of the declared will of God to be the loving of all things because all things bear a relation to the Whole, and another "not to lust after anything," and a third "not to hate anything," by the will of God these also will be punishments, which it were impious to think. For neither did the Lord suffer by the will of the Father, nor are those who are persecuted persecuted by the will of God; since either of two things is the case: either persecution in consequence of the will of God is a good thing, or those who decree and afflict are guiltless. But nothing is without the will of the Lord of the universe. It remains to say that such things happen without the prevention of God; for this alone saves both the providence and the goodness of God. We must not therefore think that He actively produces afflictions (far be it that we should think this!); but we must be persuaded that He does not prevent those that cause them, but overrules for good the crimes of His enemies: "I will therefore," He says, "destroy the wall, and it shall be for treading under foot."[3] Providence being a disciplinary art;[4] in the case of others for each individual's sins, and in the case of the Lord and His apostles for ours. To this

---

1 Job xiv. 4.
2 [This exposition of Basilides is noteworthy. It is very doubtful, whether, even in poetry, the Platonic idea of pre-existence should be encouraged by Christians, as, e.g., in that sublimest of modern lyrics, Wordsworth's ode on *Immortality and Childhood*.]

3 Isa. v. 5.
4 The text has παιδευτικῆς τέχνης τῆς τοιάδε, for which Sylburgius suggests τοιᾶσδε, as translated above.

point says the divine apostle : " For this is the will of God, even your sanctification, that ye abstain from fornication : that each one of you should know how to possess his vessel in sanctification and honour ; not in the lust of concupiscence, as the Gentiles who know not the Lord : that none of you should overreach or take advantage of his brother in any matter ; because the Lord is the avenger in respect of all such, as we also told you before, and testified. For God hath not called us unto uncleanness, but to holiness. Wherefore he that despiseth, despiseth not man, but God, who hath also given His Holy Spirit to you." [1] Wherefore the Lord was not prohibited from this sanctification of ours. If, then, one of them were to say, in reply, that the martyr is punished for sins committed before this embodying, and that he will again reap the fruit of his conduct in this life, for that such are the arrangements of the [divine administration], we shall ask him if the retribution takes place by Providence. For if it be not of the divine administration, the economy of expiations is gone, and their hypothesis falls to the ground ; but if expiations are by Providence, punishments are by Providence too. But Providence, although it begins, so to speak, to move with the Ruler, yet is implanted in substances along with their origin by the God of the universe. Such being the case, they must confess either that punishment is not just, and those who condemn and persecute the martyrs do right, or that persecutions even are wrought by the will of God. Labour and fear are not, then, as they say, incident to affairs as rust to iron, but come upon the soul through its own will. And on these points there is much to say, which will be reserved for future consideration, taking them up in due course.

CHAP. XIII. — VALENTINIAN'S VAGARIES ABOUT THE ABOLITION OF DEATH REFUTED.

Valentinian, in a homily, writes in these words : " Ye are originally immortal, and children of eternal life, and ye would have death distributed to you, that ye may spend and lavish it, and that death may die in you and by you ; for when we dissolve the world, and are not yourselves dissolved, ye have dominion over creation and all corruption." For he also, similarly with Basilides, supposes a class saved by nature, and that this different race has come hither to us from above for the abolition of death, and that the origin of death is the work of the Creator of the world. Wherefore also he so expounds that Scripture, " No man shall see the face of God, and live," as if He were the cause

of death. Respecting this God, he makes those allusions when writing in these expressions : " As much as the image is inferior to the living face, so much is the world inferior to the living Æon. What is, then, the cause of the image ? The majesty of the face, which exhibits the figure to the painter, to be honoured by his name ; for the form is not found exactly to the life, but the name supplies what is wanting in the effigy. The invisibility of God co-operates also in order to the faith of that which has been fashioned." For the Creator, called God and Father, he designated as " Painter," and " Wisdom," whose image that which is formed is, to the glory of the invisible One ; since the things which proceed from a pair are complements, and those which proceed from one are images. But since what is seen is no part of Him, the soul comes from what is intermediate, which is different ; and this is the inspiration of the different spirit, and generally what is breathed into the soul, which is the image of the spirit. And in general, what is said of the Creator, who was made according to the image, they say was foretold by a sensible image in the book of Genesis respecting the origin of man ; and the likeness they transfer to themselves, teaching that the addition of the different spirit was made; unknown to the Creator. When, then, we treat of the unity of the God who is proclaimed in the law, the prophets, and the Gospel, we shall also discuss this ; for the topic is supreme.[2] But we must advance to that which is urgent. If for the purpose of doing away with death the peculiar race has come, it is not Christ who has abolished death, unless He also is said to be of the same essence with them. And if He abolished it to this end, that it might not touch the peculiar race, it is not these, the rivals of the Creator, who breathe into the image of their intermediate spirit the life from above — in accordance with the principle of their dogma — that abolish death. But should they say that this takes place by His mother,[3] or should they say that they, along with Christ, war against death, let them own their secret dogma that they have the hardihood to assail the divine power of the Creator, by setting to rights His creation, as if they were superior, endeavouring to save the vital image which He was not able to rescue from corruption. Then the Lord would be superior to God the Creator ; for the son would never contend with the father, especially among the gods. But the point that the Creator of all things, the omnipotent Lord, is the Father of the Son, we have deferred till the discussion of these points, in which we have under-

---

[1] 1 Thess. iv. 3–8.

[2] [Kaye, p. 322.]
[3] [See the Valentinian jargon about the Demiurge (rival of the true Creator), in Irenæus, vol. i. p. 322, this series.]

taken to dispute against the heresies, showing that He alone is the God proclaimed by Him.

But the apostle, writing to us with reference to the endurance of afflictions, says, " And this is of God, that it is given to you on behalf of Christ, not only to believe on Him, but also to suffer for His sake ; having the same conflict which ye saw in me, and now hear to be in me. If there is therefore any consolation in Christ, if any comfort of love, if any communion of spirit, if any bowels and mercies, fulfil ye my joy, that ye may be of the same mind, having the same love, unanimous, thinking one thing. And if he is offered on the sacrifice and service of faith, joying and rejoicing "[1] with the Philippians, to whom the apostle speaks, calling them " fellow-partakers of joy,"[2] how does he say that they are of one soul, and having a soul? Likewise, also, writing respecting Timothy and himself, he says, " For I have no one like-souled, who will nobly care for your state. For all seek their own, not the things which are Jesus Christ's."[3]

Let not the above-mentioned people, then, call us, by way of reproach, " natural men " (ψυχικοί), nor the Phrygians[4] either ; for these now call those who do not apply themselves to the new prophecy " natural men " (ψυχικοί), with whom we shall discuss in our remarks on " Prophecy."[5] The perfect man ought therefore to practise love, and thence to haste to the divine friendship, fulfilling the commandments from love. And loving one's enemies does not mean loving wickedness, or impiety, or adultery, or theft ; but the thief, the impious, the adulterer, not as far as he sins, and in respect of the actions by which he stains the name of man, but as he is a man, and the work of God. Assuredly sin is an activity, not an existence : and therefore it is not a work of God. Now sinners are called enemies of God — enemies, that is, of the commands which they do not obey, as those who obey become friends, the one named so from their fellowship, the others from their estrangement, which is the result of free choice ; for there is neither enmity nor sin without the enemy and the sinner. And the command " to covet nothing," not as if the things to be desired did not belong to us, does not teach us not to entertain desire, as those suppose who teach that the Creator is different from the first God, not as if creation was loathsome and bad (for such opinions are impious). But we say that the things of the world are *not our own*, not as if they were monstrous, not as if they did not belong to God, the Lord of the universe, but because we do not

continue among them for ever ; being, in respect of possession, not ours, and passing from one to another in succession ; but belonging to us, for whom they were made in respect of use, so long as it is necessary to continue with them. In accordance, therefore, with natural appetite, things disallowed are to be used rightly, avoiding all excess and inordinate affection.

CHAP. XIV. — THE LOVE OF ALL, EVEN OF OUR ENEMIES.

How great also is benignity ! " Love your enemies," it is said, " bless them who curse you, and pray for them who despitefully use you,"[6] and the like ; to which it is added, " that ye may be the children of your Father who is in heaven," in allusion to resemblance to God. Again, it is said, " Agree with thine adversary quickly, whilst thou art in the way with him."[7] The adversary is not the body, as some would have it, but the devil, and those assimilated to him, who walks along with us in the person of men, who emulate his deeds in this earthly life. It is inevitable, then, that those who confess themselves to belong to Christ, but find themselves in the midst of the devil's works, suffer the most hostile treatment. For it is written, " Lest he deliver thee to the judge, and the judge deliver thee to the officers of Satan's kingdom." " For I am persuaded that neither death," through the assault of persecutors, " nor life " in this world, " nor angels," the apostate ones, " nor powers " (and Satan's power is the life which he chose, for such are the powers and principalities of darkness belonging to him), " nor things present," amid which we exist during the time of life, as the hope entertained by the soldier, and the merchant's gain, " nor height, nor depth, nor any other creature," in consequence of the energy proper to a man, — opposes the faith of him who acts according to free choice. " Creature " is synonymous with activity, being our work, and such activity " shall not be able to separate us from the love of God, which is in Christ Jesus our Lord."[8] You have got a compendious account of the gnostic martyr.

CHAP. XV. — ON AVOIDING OFFENCE.

" We know that we all have knowledge " — common knowledge in common things, and the knowledge that there is one God. For he was writing to believers ; whence he adds, " But knowledge (*gnosis*) is not in all," being communicated to few. And there are those who say that the knowledge about things sacrificed to idols is not promulgated among all, " lest our liberty prove a stumbling-block to the weak. For by

---

1 Phil. i. 29, 30, ii. 1, 2, 17.
2 Phil. i. 7.
3 Phil. ii. 20, 21.
4 [Kaye, p. 405.]
5 [The valuable note of Routh, on a fragment of Melito, should be consulted. *Reliquiæ*, vol. i. p. 140.]

6 Matt. v. 44, 45.
7 Matt. v. 25.
8 Rom. viii. 38, 39.

thy knowledge he that is weak is destroyed." [1] Should they say, "Whatsoever is sold in the shambles, ought that to be bought?" adding, by way of interrogation, "asking no questions," [2] as if equivalent to "asking questions," they give a ridiculous interpretation. For the apostle says, "All other things buy out of the shambles, asking no questions," with the exception of the things mentioned in the Catholic epistle of all the apostles, [3] "with the consent of the Holy Ghost," which is written in the Acts of the Apostles, and conveyed to the faithful by the hands of Paul himself. For they intimated "that they must of necessity abstain from things offered to idols, and from blood, and from things strangled, and from fornication, from which keeping themselves, they should do well." It is a different matter, then, which is expressed by the apostle: "Have we not power to eat and to drink? Have we not power to lead about a sister, a wife, as the rest of the apostles, as the brethren of the Lord and Cephas? But we have not used this power," he says, "but bear all things, lest we should occasion hindrance to the Gospel of Christ;" namely, by bearing about burdens, when it was necessary to be untrammelled for all things; or to become an example to those who wish to exercise temperance, not encouraging each other to eat greedily of what is set before us, and not to consort inconsiderately with woman. And especially is it incumbent on those entrusted with such a dispensation to exhibit to disciples a pure example. "For though I be free from all men, I have made myself servant to all," it is said, "that I might gain all. And every one that striveth for mastery is temperate in all things." [4] "But the earth is the Lord's, and the fulness thereof." [5] For conscience' sake, then, we are to abstain from what we ought to abstain. "Conscience, I say, not his own," for it is endued with knowledge, "but that of the other," lest he be trained badly, and by imitating in ignorance what he knows not, he become a despiser instead of a strong-minded man. "For why is my liberty judged of by another conscience? For if I by grace am a partaker, why am I evil spoken of for that for which I give thanks? Whatever ye do, do all to the glory of God" [6] — what you are commanded to do by the rule of faith.

CHAP. XVI. — PASSAGES OF SCRIPTURE RESPECTING THE CONSTANCY, PATIENCE, AND LOVE OF THE MARTYRS.

"With the heart man believeth unto righteousness, and with the mouth confession is made unto salvation. Wherefore the Scripture saith, Whosoever believeth on Him shall not be ashamed; that is, the word of faith which we preach: for if thou confess the word with thy mouth that Jesus is Lord, and believe in thy heart that God hath raised Him from the dead, thou shalt be saved." [7] There is clearly described the perfect righteousness, fulfilled both in practice and contemplation. Wherefore we are "to bless those who persecute us. Bless, and curse not." [8] "For our rejoicing is this, the testimony of a good conscience, that in holiness and sincerity we know God" by this inconsiderable instance exhibiting the work of love, that "not in fleshly wisdom, but by the grace of God, we have had our conversation in the world." [9] So far the apostle respecting knowledge; and in the second Epistle to the Corinthians he calls the common "teaching of faith" the savour of knowledge. "For unto this day the same veil remains on many in the reading of the Old Testament," [10] not being uncovered by turning to the Lord. Wherefore also to those capable of perceiving he showed resurrection, that of the life still in the flesh, creeping on its belly. Whence also he applied the name "brood of vipers" to the voluptuous, who serve the belly and the pudenda, and cut off one another's heads for the sake of worldly pleasures. "Little children, let us not love in word, or in tongue," says John, teaching them to be perfect, "but in deed and in truth; hereby shall we know that we are of the truth." [11] And if "God be love," piety also is love: "there is no fear in love; but perfect love casteth out fear." [12] "This is the love of God, that we keep His commandments." [13] And again, to him who desires to become a Gnostic, it is written, "But be thou an example of the believers, in word, in conversation, in love, in faith, in purity." [14] For perfection in faith differs, I think, from ordinary faith. And the divine apostle furnishes the rule for the Gnostic in these words, writing as follows: "For I have learned, in whatsoever state I am, to be content. I know both how to be abased, and I know how to abound. Everywhere and in all things I am instructed both to be full and to be hungry, both to abound and to lack. I can do all things through Him who strengtheneth me." [15] And also when discussing with others in order to put them, to shame, he does not shrink from saying, "But call to mind the former days, in which, after ye were illuminated, ye endured a great fight of

---

[1] 1 Cor. viii. 1, 7, 9, 11.
[2] 1 Cor. x. 25.
[3] Acts xv. 24, etc.
[4] 1 Cor. ix. 19-25.
[5] 1 Cor. x. 26.
[6] 1 Cor. x. 28-31.

[7] Rom. x 10, 11, 8, 9.
[8] Rom. xii. 14.
[9] 2 Cor. i. 12.
[10] 2 Cor. iii. 14.
[11] 1 John iii. 18, 19.
[12] 1 John iv. 16, 18.
[13] 1 John v. 3.
[14] 1 Tim. iv. 12.
[15] Phil. iv. 11-13.

afflictions; partly, whilst ye were made a gazing-stock, both by reproaches and afflictions; and partly, whilst ye became companions of them that were so used. For ye had compassion of me in my bonds, and took with joy the spoiling of your goods, knowing that you have a better and enduring substance. Cast not away therefore your confidence, which hath great recompense of reward. For ye have need of patience, that, after doing the will of God, ye may obtain the promise. For yet a little while, and He that cometh will come, and will not tarry. Now the just shall live by faith: and if any man draw back, my soul shall have no pleasure in him. But we are not of them that draw back unto perdition, but of them that believe to the saving of the soul."[1] He then brings forward a swarm of divine examples. For was it not "by faith," he says, this endurance, that they acted nobly who "had trial of mockeries and scourgings, and, moreover, of bonds and imprisonments? They were stoned, they were tempted, were slain with the sword. They wandered about in sheep-skins and goat-skins, being destitute, afflicted, tormented, of whom the world was not worthy. They wandered in deserts, in mountains, in dens, and caves of the earth. And all having received a good report, through faith, received not the promise of God" (what is expressed by a parasiopesis is left to be understood, viz., "alone"). He adds accordingly, "God having provided some better thing for us (for He was good), that they should not without us be made perfect. Wherefore also, having encompassing us such a cloud," holy and transparent, "of witnesses, laying aside every weight, and the sin which doth so easily beset us, let us run with patience the race set before us, looking unto Jesus, the author and finisher of our faith."[2] Since, then, he specifies one salvation in Christ of the righteous,[3] and of us he has expressed the former unambiguously, and saying nothing less respecting Moses, adds, "Esteeming the reproach of Christ greater riches than the treasures of Egypt: for he had respect to the recompense of the reward. By faith he forsook Egypt, not fearing the wrath of the king: for he endured as seeing Him who is invisible."[4] The divine Wisdom says of the martyrs, "They seemed in the eyes of the foolish to die, and their departure was reckoned a calamity, and their migration from us an affliction. But they are in peace. For though in the sight of men they were punished, their hope was full of immortality."[5] He then adds, teaching martyrdom to be a glorious purification, "And being chastened a little, they shall be benefited much; because God proved

them," that is, suffered them to be tried, to put them to the proof, and to put to shame the author of their trial, "and found them worthy of Himself," plainly to be called sons. "As gold in the furnace He proved them, and as a whole burned-offering of sacrifice He accepted them. And in the time of their visitation they will shine forth, even as sparks run along the stubble. They shall judge the nations, and rule over the peoples, and the Lord shall reign over them forever."[6]

CHAP. XVII. — PASSAGES FROM CLEMENT'S EPISTLE TO THE CORINTHIANS ON MARTYRDOM.

Moreover, in the Epistle to the Corinthians, the Apostle[7] Clement also, drawing a picture of the Gnostic, says:[8] "For who that has sojourned among you has not proved your perfect and firm faith? and has not admired your sound and gentle piety? and has not celebrated the munificent style of your hospitality? and has not felicitated your complete and sure knowledge? For ye did all things impartially, and walked in the ordinances of God;" and so forth.

Then more clearly: "Let us fix our eyes on those who have yielded perfect service to His magnificent glory. Let us take Enoch, who, being by his obedience found righteous, was translated; and Noah, who, having believed, was saved; and Abraham, who for his faith and hospitality was called the friend of God, and was the father of Isaac." "For hospitality and piety, Lot was saved from Sodom." "For faith and hospitality, Rahab the harlot was saved." "From patience and faith they walked about in goat-skins, and sheep-skins, and folds of camels' hair, proclaiming the kingdom of Christ. We name His prophets Elias, and Eliseus, and Ezekiel, and John."

"For Abraham, who for his free faith was called 'the friend of God,' was not elated by glory, but modestly said, 'I am dust and ashes.'[9] And of Job it is thus written: 'Job was just and blameless, true and pious, abstaining from all evil.'"[10] He it was who overcame the tempter by patience, and at once testified and was testified to by God; who keeps hold of humility, and says, "No one is pure from defilement, not even if his life were but for one day."[11] "Moses, 'the servant who was faithful in all his house,' said to Him who uttered the oracles from the bush, 'Who am I, that Thou sendest me? I am slow of speech, and of a stammering tongue,' to minister the voice of God in human speech. And again: 'I am smoke from a pot.'" "For

---

[1] Heb. x. 32–39.
[2] Heb. xi. 36–40, xii. 1, 2.
[3] Who lived before Christ. [Moses was a Christian.]
[4] Heb. xi. 26, 27. [Moses suffered "the reproach of Christ."]
[5] Wisd. iii. 2, 3, 4.
[6] Wisd. iii. 5, 6, 7, 8.
[7] [The use of this title is noticeable here, on many accounts, as historic.]
[8] [See vol. i. p. 5-11, et seqq. S.]
[9] Gen. xviii. 27.
[10] Job i. 1.
[11] Job xiv. 4, 5, Sept.

God resisteth the proud, but giveth grace to the humble." [1]

"David too, of whom the Lord, testifying, says, 'I found a man after my own heart, David the son of Jesse. With my holy oil I anointed him.' [2] But he also says to God, 'Pity me, O God, according to Thy mercy; and according to the multitude of Thy tender mercies, blot out my transgression. Wash me thoroughly from mine iniquity, and cleanse me from my sin. For I know my transgression, and my sin is ever before me.'" [3] Then, alluding to sin which is not subject to the law, in the exercise of the moderation of true knowledge, he adds, "Against Thee only have I sinned, and done evil in Thy sight." [4] For the Scripture somewhere says, "The Spirit of the Lord is a lamp, searching the recesses of the belly." [5] And the more of a Gnostic a man becomes by doing right, the nearer is the illuminating Spirit to him. "Thus the Lord draws near to the righteous, and none of the thoughts and reasonings of which we are the authors escape Him — I mean the Lord Jesus," the scrutinizer by His omnipotent will of our heart, "whose blood was consecrated [6] for us. Let us therefore respect those who are over us, and reverence the elders; let us honour the young, and let us teach the discipline of God." For blessed is he who shall do and teach the Lord's commands worthily; and he is of a magnanimous mind, and of a mind contemplative of truth. "Let us direct our wives to what is good; let them exhibit," says he, "the lovable disposition of chastity; let them show the guileless will of their meekness; let them manifest the gentleness of their tongue by silence; let them give their love not according to their inclinations, but equal love in sanctity to all that fear God. Let our children share in the discipline that is in Christ; let them learn what humility avails before God; what is the power of holy love before God, how lovely and great is the fear of the Lord, saving all that walk in it holily, with a pure heart: for He is the Searcher of the thoughts and sentiments, whose breath is in us, and when He wills He will take it away."

"Now all those things are confirmed by the faith that is in Christ. 'Come, ye children,' says the Lord, 'hearken to me, and I will teach you the fear of the Lord. Who is the man that desireth life, that loveth to see good days?' [7] Then He subjoins the gnostic mystery of the numbers seven and eight. 'Stop thy tongue from evil, and thy lips from speaking guile. Depart from evil, and do good. Seek peace,

and pursue it.' [8] For in these words He alludes to knowledge (*gnosis*), with abstinence from evil and the doing of what is good, teaching that it is to be perfected by word and deed. 'The eyes of the Lord are on the righteous, and His ears are to their prayer. But the face of God is against those that do evil, to root out their memory from the earth. The righteous cried, and the Lord heard, and delivered him out of all his distresses.' [9] 'Many are the stripes of sinners; but those who hope in the Lord, mercy shall compass about.'" [10] "A multitude of mercy," he nobly says, "surrounds him that trusts in the Lord."

For it is written in the Epistle to the Corinthians, "Through Jesus Christ our foolish and darkened mind springs up to the light. By Him the Sovereign Lord wished us to taste the knowledge that is immortal." And, showing more expressly the peculiar nature of knowledge, he added: "These things, then, being clear to us, looking into the depths of divine knowledge, we ought to do all things in order which the Sovereign Lord commanded us to perform at the appointed seasons. Let the wise man, then, show his wisdom not in words only, but in good deeds. Let the humble not testify to himself, but allow testimony to be borne to him by another. Let not him who is pure in the flesh boast, knowing that it is another who furnishes him with continence. Ye see, brethren, that the more we are subjected to peril, the more knowledge are we counted worthy of."

CHAP. XVIII. — ON LOVE, AND THE REPRESSING OF OUR DESIRES.

"The decorous tendency of our philanthropy, therefore," according to Clement, "seeks the common good;" whether by suffering martyrdom, or by teaching by deed and word, — the latter being twofold, unwritten and written. This is love, to love God and our neighbour. "This conducts to the height which is unutterable. [11] 'Love covers a multitude of sins. [12] Love beareth all things, suffereth all things.' [13] Love joins us to God, does all things in concord. In love, all the chosen of God were perfected. Apart from love, nothing is well pleasing to God." "Of its perfection there is no unfolding," it is said. "Who is fit to be found in it, except those whom God counts worthy?" To the point the Apostle Paul speaks, "If I give my body, and have not love, I am sounding brass, and a tinkling cymbal." [14] If it is not from a disposition determined by gnostic love that I shall testify, he means;

---

[1] Jas. iv. 6; 1 Pet. v. 5.
[2] Ps. lxxxix. 21.
[3] Ps. li. 1-4.
[4] Ps. li. 6.
[5] Prov. xx. 27.
[6] ἡγιάσθη. Clemens Romanus has ἐδόθη. [Vol. i. p. 11, this series.]
[7] Ps. xxxiv. 12.
[8] Ps. xxxiv. 13, 14.
[9] Ps. xxxiv. 15-17.
[10] Ps. xxxii. 10.
[11] [See vol. i. p. 18. S.]
[12] Jas. v. 20; 1 Pet. iv. 8.
[13] 1 Cor. xiii. 7.
[14] 1 Cor. xiii. 1, 3.

but if through fear and expected reward, moving my lips in order to testify to the Lord that I shall confess the Lord, I am a common man, sounding the Lord's name, not knowing Him. "For there is the people that loveth with the lips; and there is another which gives the body to be burned." "And if I give all my goods in alms," he says, not according to the principle of loving communication, but on account of recompense, either from him who has received the benefit, or the Lord who has promised; "and if I have all faith so as to remove mountains," and cast away obscuring passions, and be not faithful to the Lord from love, "I am nothing," as in comparison of him who testifies as a Gnostic, and the crowd, and being reckoned nothing better.

"Now all the generations from Adam to this day are gone. But they who have been perfected in love, through the grace of God, hold the place of the godly, who shall be manifested at the visitation of the kingdom of Christ." Love permits not to sin; but if it fall into any such case, by reason of the interference of the adversary, in imitation of David, it will sing: "I will confess unto the Lord, and it will please Him above a young bullock that has horns and hoofs. Let the poor see it, and be glad." For he says, "Sacrifice to God a sacrifice of praise, and pay to the Lord thy vows; and call upon me in the day of trouble, and I will deliver thee, and thou shalt glorify me."[1] "For the sacrifice of God is a broken spirit."[2]

"God," then, being good, "is love," it is said.[3] Whose "love worketh no ill to his neighbour,"[4] neither injuring nor revenging ever, but, in a word, doing good to all according to the image of God. "Love is," then, "the fulfilling of the law;"[4] like as Christ, that is the presence of the Lord who loves us; and our loving teaching of, and discipline according to Christ. By love, then, the commands not to commit adultery, and not to covet one's neighbour's wife, are fulfilled, [these sins being] formerly prohibited by fear.

The same work, then, presents a difference, according as it is done by fear, or accomplished by love, and is wrought by faith or by knowledge. Rightly, therefore, their rewards are different. To the Gnostic "are prepared what eye hath not seen, nor ear heard, nor hath entered into the heart of man;" but to him who has exercised simple faith He testifies a hundredfold in return for what he has left, — a promise which has turned out to fall within human comprehension.

Come to this point, I recollect one who called himself a Gnostic. For, expounding the words, "But I say unto you, he that looketh on a woman to lust after, hath committed adultery,"[5] he thought that it was not bare desire that was condemned; but if through the desire the act that results from it proceeding beyond the desire is accomplished in it. For dream employs phantasy and the body. Accordingly, the historians relate the following decision of Bocchoris the just.[6] A youth, falling in love with a courtezan, persuades the girl, for a stipulated reward, to come to him next day. But his desire being unexpectedly satiated, by laying hold of the girl in a dream, by anticipation, when the object of his love came according to stipulation, he prohibited her from coming in. But she, on learning what had taken place, demanded the reward, saying that in this way she had sated the lover's desire. They came accordingly to the judge. He, ordering the youth to hold out the purse containing the reward in the sun, bade the courtezan take hold of the shadow; facetiously bidding him pay the image of a reward for the image of an embrace.

Accordingly one dreams, the soul assenting to the vision. But he dreams waking, who looks so as to lust; not only, as that Gnostic said, if along with the sight of the woman he imagine in his mind intercourse, for this is already the act of lust, as lust; but if one looks on beauty of person (the Word says), and the flesh seem to him in the way of lust to be fair, looking on carnally and sinfully, he is judged because he admired. For, on the other hand, he who in chaste love looks on beauty, thinks not that the flesh is beautiful, but the spirit, admiring, as I judge, the body as an image, by whose beauty he transports himself to the Artist, and to the true beauty; exhibiting the sacred symbol, the bright impress of righteousness to the angels that wait on the ascension;[7] I mean the unction of acceptance, the quality of disposition which resides in the soul that is gladdened by the communication of the Holy Spirit. This glory, which shone forth on the face of Moses, the people could not look on. Wherefore he took a veil for the glory, to those who looked carnally. For those, who demand toll, detain those who bring in any worldly things, who are burdened with their own passions. But him that is free of all things which are subject to duty, and is full of knowledge, and of the righteousness of works, they pass on with their good wishes, blessing the man with his work. "And his life shall not fall away" — the leaf of the living tree that is nourished "by the water-courses."[8] Now

---

[1] Ps. l. 14, 15.
[2] Ps. li. 17.
[3] 1 John iv 8, 16.
[4] Rom. xiii. 10.

[5] Matt. v. 28.
[6] [Or, "the Wise." See Rawlinson, *Herodotus*, ii. p. 317.]
[7] i.e., of blessed souls.
[8] Ps. i. 3.

the righteous is likened to fruit-bearing trees, and not only to such as are of the nature [1] of tall-growing ones. And in the sacrificial oblations, according to the law, there were those who looked for blemishes in the sacrifices. They who are skilled in such matters distinguish propension [2] (ὄρεξις) from lust (ἐπιθυμία) ; and assign the latter, as being irrational, to pleasures and licentiousness ; and propension, as being a rational movement, they assign to the necessities of nature.

CHAP. XIX. — WOMEN AS WELL AS MEN CAPABLE OF PERFECTION.

In this perfection it is possible for man and woman equally to share. It is not only Moses, then, that heard from God, "I have spoken to thee once, and twice, saying, I have seen this people, and lo, it is stiff-necked. Suffer me to exterminate them, and blot out their name from under heaven ; and I will make thee into a great and wonderful nation much greater than this ; " who answers not regarding himself, but the common salvation : "By no means, O Lord ; forgive this people their sin, or blot me out of the book of the living." [3] How great was his perfection, in wishing to die together with the people, rather than be saved alone !

But Judith too, who became perfect among women, in the siege of the city, at the entreaty of the elders went forth into the strangers' camp, despising all danger for her country's sake, giving herself into the enemy's hand in faith in God ; and straightway she obtained the reward of her faith, — though a woman, prevailing over the enemy of her faith, and gaining possession of the head of Holofernes. And again, Esther perfect by faith, who rescued Israel from the power of the king and the satrap's cruelty : a woman alone, afflicted with fastings,[4] held back ten thousand armed [5] hands, annulling by her faith the tyrant's decree ; him indeed she appeased, Haman she restrained, and Israel she preserved scathless by her perfect prayer to God. I pass over in silence Susanna and the sister of Moses, since the latter was the prophet's associate in commanding the host, being superior to all the women among the Hebrews who were in repute for their wisdom ; and the former in her surpassing modesty, going even to death condemned by licentious admirers, remained the unwavering martyr of chastity.

Dion, too, the philosopher, tells that a certain woman Lysidica, through excess of modesty,

bathed in her clothes ; and that Philotera, when she was to enter the bath, gradually drew back her tunic as the water covered the naked parts ; and then rising by degrees, put it on. And did not Leæna of Attica manfully bear the torture? She being privy to the conspiracy of Harmodius and Aristogeiton against Hipparchus, uttered not a word, though severely tortured. And they say that the Argolic women, under the guidance of Telesilla the poetess, turned to flight the doughty Spartans by merely showing themselves ; and that she produced in them fearlessness of death. Similarly speaks he who composed the Danais respecting the daughters of Danaus : —

"And then the daughters of Danaus swiftly armed themselves,
Before the fair-flowing river, majestic Nile[4] "

and so forth.

And the rest of the poets sing of Atalanta's swiftness in the chase, of Anticlea's love for children, of Alcestis's love for her husband, of the courage of Makæria and of the Hyacinthides. What shall I say? Did not Theano the Pythagorean make such progress in philosophy, that to him who looked intently at her, and said, "Your arm is beautiful," she answered "Yes, but it is not public." Characterized by the same propriety, there is also reported the following reply.[6] When asked when a woman after being with her husband attends the Thesmophoria, said, "From her own husband at once, from a stranger never." Themisto too, of Lampsacus, the daughter of Zoilus, the wife of Leontes of Lampsacus, studied the Epicurean philosophy, as Myia the daughter of Theano the Pythagorean, and Arignote, who wrote the history of Dionysius.

And the daughters of Diodorus, who was called Kronus, all became dialecticians, as Philo the dialectician says in the Menexenus, whose names are mentioned as follows — Menexene, Argia, Theognis, Artemesia, Pantaclea. I also recollect a female Cynic, — she was called Hipparchia, a Maronite, the wife of Crates, — in whose case the so-called dog-wedding was celebrated in the Pœcile. Arete of Cyrene, too, the daughter of Aristippus, educated her son Aristippus, who was surnamed Mother-taught. Lastheneia of Arcis, and Axiothea of Phlius, studied philosophy with Plato. Besides, Aspasia of Miletus, of whom the writers of comedy write much, was trained by Socrates in philosophy, by Pericles in rhetoric. I omit, on account of the length of the discourse, the rest ; enumerating neither the poetesses Corinna, Telesilla, Myia, and Sappho ; nor the painters, as Irene the daughter of Cratinus, and Anaxandra the daughter of Nealces, according to the account of-

[1] The text has θυσίαν, for which φύσιν has been suggested as probably the true reading.
[2] ὄρεξις the Stoics define to be a desire agreeable to reason ; ἐπιθυμία, a desire contrary to reason.
[3] Ex. xxxii. 9, 10, 32.
[4] So rendered by the Latin translator, as if the reading were τεθ-λιμμένη.
[5] Sylburguis' conjecture of ὡπλισμένας instead of ὁπλισαμένας is here adopted.

[6] [Theano. See, also, p. 417. Elucidation II.]

Didymus in the Symposiaci. The daughter of Cleobulus, the sage and monarch of the Lindii, was not ashamed to wash the feet of her father's guests. Also the wife of Abraham, the blessed Sarah, in her own person prepared the cakes baked in the ashes for the angels ; and princely maidens among the Hebrews fed sheep. Whence also the Nausicaä of Homer went to the washing-tubs.

The wise woman, then, will first choose to persuade her husband to be her associate in what is conducive to happiness. And should that be found impracticable, let her by herself earnestly aim at virtue, gaining her husband's consent in everything, so as never to do anything against his will, with exception of what is reckoned as contributing to virtue and salvation. But if one keeps from such a mode of life either wife or maid-servant, whose heart is set on it ; what such a person in that case plainly does is nothing else than determine to drive her away from righteousness and sobriety, and to choose to make his own house wicked and licentious.

It is not then possible that man or woman can be conversant with anything whatever, without the advantage of education, and application, and training ; and virtue, we have said, depends not on others, but on ourselves above all. Other things one can repress, by waging war against them ; but with what depends on one's self, this is entirely out of the question, even with the most strenuous persistence. For the gift is one conferred by God, and not in the power of any other. Whence licentiousness should be regarded as the evil of no other one than of him who is guilty of licentiousness ; and temperance, on the other hand, as the good of him who is able to practise it.

CHAP. XX. — A GOOD WIFE.

The woman who, with propriety, loves her husband, Euripides describes, while admonishing, —

"That when her husband says aught,
　She ought to regard him as speaking well if she say nothing ;
　And if she will say anything, to do her endeavour to gratify her husband."

And again he subjoins the like : —

"And that the wife should sweetly look sad with her husband,
　Should aught evil befall him,
　And have in common a share of sorrow and joy."

Then, describing her as gentle and kind even in misfortunes, he adds : —

"And I, when you are ill, will, sharing your sickness bear it ;
　And I will bear my share in your misfortunes."

And : —

"Nothing is bitter to me,
For with friends one ought to be happy,
For what else is friendship but this ? "

The marriage, then, that is consummated according to the word, is sanctified, if the union be under subjection to God, and be conducted "with a true heart, in full assurance of faith, having hearts sprinkled from an evil conscience, and the body washed with pure water, and holding the confession of hope ; for He is faithful that promised." And the happiness of marriage ought never to be estimated either by wealth or beauty, but by virtue.

"Beauty," says the tragedy, —

"Helps no wife with her husband ;
　But virtue has helped many ; for every good wife
　Who is attached to her husband knows how to practise sobriety."

Then, as giving admonitions, he says : —

"First, then, this is incumbent on her who is endowed with mind,
　That even if her husband be ugly, he must appear good-looking ;
　For it is for the mind, not the eye, to judge."

And so forth.

For with perfect propriety Scripture has said that woman is given by God as "an help" to man. It is evident, then, in my opinion, that she will charge herself with remedying, by good sense and persuasion, each of the annoyances that originate with her husband in domestic economy. And if he do not yield, then she will endeavour, as far as possible for human nature, to lead a sinless life ; whether it be necessary to die, in accordance with reason, or to live ; considering that God is her helper and associate in such a course of conduct, her true defender and Saviour both for the present and for the future ; making Him the leader and guide of all her actions, reckoning sobriety and righteousness her work, and making the favour of God her end. Gracefully, therefore, the apostle says in the Epistle to Titus, "that the elder women should be of godly behaviour, should not be slanderers, not enslaved to much wine ; that they should counsel the young women to be lovers of their husbands, lovers of their children, discreet, chaste, housekeepers, good, subject to their own husbands ; that the word of God be not blasphemed." [1] But rather, he says, " Follow peace with all men, and holiness, without which no man shall see the Lord : looking diligently, lest there be any fornicator or profane person, as Esau, who for one morsel surrendered his birthright ; and lest any root of bitterness springing up trouble you, and thereby many be defiled." [2] And then, as putting the finishing stroke to the question about marriage, he adds : " Marriage is honourable in all, and the bed undefiled : but whoremongers and adulterers God will judge." [3]

---

[1] Tit. ii. 3-5.
[2] Heb. xiii. 14-16.
[3] Heb. xiii. 4.

And one aim and one end, as far as regards perfection, being demonstrated to belong to the man and the woman, Peter in his Epistle says, "Though now for a season, if need be, ye are in heaviness through manifold temptations; that the trial of your faith, being much more precious than that of gold which perisheth, though it be tried with fire, might be found unto praise, and honour, and glory at the revelation of Jesus Christ; whom, having not seen, ye love; in whom, though now ye see Him not, yet believing, ye rejoice with joy unspeakable, and full of glory, receiving the end of your faith, the salvation of your souls." [1] Wherefore also Paul rejoices for Christ's sake that he was "in labours. more abundantly, in stripes above measure, in deaths oft." [2]

CHAP. XXI. — DESCRIPTION OF THE PERFECT MAN, OR GNOSTIC.

Here I find perfection apprehended variously in relation to Him who excels in every virtue. Accordingly one is perfected as pious, and as patient, and as continent, and as a worker, and as a martyr, and as a Gnostic. But I know no one of men perfect in all things at once, while still human, though according to the mere letter of the law, except Him alone who for us clothed Himself with humanity. Who then is perfect? He who professes abstinence from what is bad. Well, this is the way to the Gospel and to well-doing. But gnostic perfection in the case of the legal man is the acceptance of the Gospel, that he that is after the law may be perfect. For so he, who was after the law, Moses, foretold that it was necessary to hear in order that we might, according to the apostle, receive Christ, the fulness of the law.[3] But now in the Gospel the Gnostic attains proficiency not only by making use of the law as a step, but by understanding and comprehending it, as the Lord who gave the Covenants delivered it to the apostles. And if he conduct himself rightly (as assuredly it is impossible to attain knowledge (*gnosis*) by bad conduct); and if, further, having made an eminently right confession, he become a martyr out of love, obtaining considerable renown as among men; not even thus will he be called perfect in the flesh beforehand; since it is the close of life which claims this appellation, when the gnostic martyr has first shown the perfect work, and rightly exhibited it, and having thankfully shed his blood, has yielded up the ghost: blessed then will he be, and truly proclaimed perfect, "that the excellency of the power may be of God, and not of us," as the apostle says. Only let us preserve free-will and love: "troubled on

every side, yet not distressed; perplexed, but not in despair; persecuted, but not forsaken; cast down, but not destroyed." [4] For those who strive after perfection, according to the same apostle, must "give no offence in anything, but in everything approve themselves not to men, but to God." And, as a consequence, also they ought to yield to men; for it is reasonable, on account of abusive calumnies. Here is the specification: "in much patience, in afflictions, in necessities, in distresses, in stripes, in imprisonments, in tumults, in labours, in watchings, in fastings, in pureness, in knowledge, in long-suffering, in kindness, in the Holy Ghost, in love unfeigned, in the word of truth, in the power of God," [5] that we may be the temples of God, purified "from all filthiness of the flesh and of the spirit." "And I," He says, "will receive you; and I will be to you for a Father, and ye shall be to Me for sons and daughters, saith the Lord Almighty." [6] "Let us then," he says, "perfect holiness in the fear of God." For though fear beget pain, "I rejoice," he says, "not that ye were made sorry, but that ye showed susceptibility to repentance. For ye sorrowed after a godly sort, that ye might receive damage by us in nothing. For godly sorrow worketh repentance unto salvation not to be regretted; but the sorrow of the world worketh death. For this same thing that ye sorrowed after a godly sort, what earnestness it wrought in you; yea, what clearing of yourselves; yea, what compunction; yea, what fear; yea, what desire; yea, what zeal; yea, revenge! In all things ye have showed yourselves clear in the matter." [7] Such are the preparatory exercises of gnostic discipline. And since the omnipotent God Himself "gave some apostles, and some prophets, and some evangelists, and some pastors and teachers, for the perfecting of the saints, for the work of the ministry, for the edifying of the body of Christ, till we all attain to the unity of the faith, and of the knowledge of the Son of God, to a perfect man, to the measure of the stature of the fulness of Christ;" [8] we are then to strive to reach manhood as befits the Gnostic, and to be as perfect as we can while still abiding in the flesh, making it our study with perfect concord here to concur with the will of God, to the restoration of what is the truly perfect nobleness and relationship, to the fulness of Christ, that which perfectly depends on our perfection.

And now we perceive where, and how, and when the divine apostle mentions the perfect man, and how he shows the differences of the perfect. And again, on the other hand: "The

---

[1] 1 Pet. i. 6–9.
[2] 2 Cor. xi. 23.
[3] Deut. xviii. 15; Rom. x. 4.

[4] 2 Cor. iv. 8, 9.
[5] 2 Cor. vi. 3–7.
[6] 2 Cor. vii. 1, vi. 16, 17, 18.
[7] 2 Cor. vii. 1–11.
[8] Eph. iv. 11, 12, 13.

manifestation of the Spirit is given for our profit. For to one is given the word of wisdom by the Spirit ; to another the word of knowledge according to the same Spirit ; to another faith through the same Spirit ; to another the gifts of healing through the same Spirit ; to another the working of miracles ; to another prophecy ; to another discernment of spirits ; to another diversities of tongues ; to another the interpretation of tongues : and all these worketh the one and the same Spirit, distributing to each one according as He wills." [1] Such being the case, the prophets are perfect in prophecy, the righteous in righteousness, and the martyrs in confession, and others in preaching, not that they are not sharers in the common virtues, but are proficient in those to which they are appointed. For what man in his senses would say that a prophet was not righteous ? For what ? did not righteous men like Abraham prophesy ?

" For to one God has given warlike deeds,
To another the accomplishment of the dance,
To another the lyre and song," [2]

says Homer. "But each has his own proper gift of God," [3] — one in one way, another in another. But the apostles were perfected in all. You will find, then, if you choose, in their acts and writings, knowledge, life, preaching, righteousness, purity, prophecy. We must know, then, that if Paul is young in respect to time [4] — having flourished immediately after the Lord's ascension — yet his writings depend on the Old Testament, breathing and speaking of them. For faith in Christ and the knowledge of the Gospel are the explanation and fulfilment of the law ; and therefore it was said to the Hebrews, "If ye believe not, neither shall you understand ; " [5] that is, unless you believe what is prophesied in the law, and oracularly delivered by the law, you will not understand the Old Testament, which He by His coming expounded.

CHAP. XXII. — THE TRUE GNOSTIC DOES GOOD, NOT FROM FEAR OF PUNISHMENT OR HOPE OF REWARD, BUT ONLY FOR THE SAKE OF GOOD ITSELF.

The man of understanding and perspicacity is, then, a Gnostic. And his business is not abstinence from what is evil (for this is a step to the highest perfection), or the doing of good out of fear. For it is written, " Whither shall I flee, and where shall I hide myself from Thy presence? If I ascend into heaven, Thou art there ; if I go away to the uttermost parts of the sea, there is Thy right hand ; if I go down into the depths, there is Thy Spirit." [6] Nor any more is

he to do so from hope of promised recompense. For it is said, " Behold the Lord, and His reward is before His face, to give to every one according to his works ; what eye hath not seen, and ear hath not heard, and hath not entered into the heart of man what God hath prepared for them that love Him." [7] But only the doing of good out of love, and for the sake of its own excellence, is to be the Gnostic's choice. Now, in the person of God it is said to the Lord, " Ask of Me, and I will give the heathen for Thine inheritance ; " [8] teaching Him to ask a truly regal request — that is, the salvation of men without price, that we may inherit and possess the Lord. For, on the contrary, to desire knowledge about God for any practical purpose, that this may be done, or that may not be done, is not proper to the Gnostic ; but the knowledge itself suffices as the reason for contemplation. For I will dare aver that it is not because he wishes to be saved that he, who devotes himself to knowledge for the sake of the divine science itself, chooses knowledge. For the exertion of the intellect by exercise is prolonged to a perpetual exertion. And the perpetual exertion of the intellect is the essence of an intelligent being, which results from an uninterrupted process of admixture, and remains eternal contemplation, a living substance. Could we, then, suppose any one proposing to the Gnostic whether he would choose the knowledge of God or everlasting salvation ; and if these, which are entirely identical, were separable, he would without the least hesitation choose the knowledge of God, deeming that property of faith, which from love ascends to knowledge, desirable, for its own sake. This, then, is the perfect man's first form of doing good, when it is done not for any advantage in what pertains to him, but because he judges it right to do good ; and the energy being vigorously exerted in all things, in the very act becomes good ; not, good in some things, and not good in others ; but consisting in the habit of doing good, neither for glory, nor, as the philosophers say, for reputation, nor from reward either from men or God ; but so as to pass life after the image and likeness of the Lord.

And if, in doing good, he be met with anything adverse, he will let the recompense pass without resentment as if it were good, he being just and good " to the just and the unjust." To such the Lord says, " Be ye, as your Father is perfect."

To him the flesh is dead ; but he himself lives alone, having consecrated the sepulchre into a holy temple to the Lord, having turned towards God the old sinful soul.

Such an one is no longer continent, but has

1 1 Cor. xii. 7-11.
2 *Iliad*, xiii. 730.
3 1 Cor. vii. 7.
4 [Elucidation III.]
5 Isa. vii. 9
6 Ps. cxxxix. 7-10.

7 Isa. xl. 10, lxii. 11; Ps. lxii. 12; Rev. xxii. 12; Rom. ii. 6.
8 Ps. ii. 8.

reached a state of passionlessness, waiting to put on the divine image. " If thou doest alms," it is said, " let no one know it ; and if thou fastest, anoint thyself, that God alone may know,"[1] and not a single human being. Not even he himself who shows mercy ought to know that he does show mercy ; for in this way he will be sometimes merciful, sometimes not. And when he shall do good by habit, he will imitate the nature of good, and his disposition will be his nature and his practice. There is no necessity for removing those who are raised on high, but there is necessity for those who are walking to reach the requisite goal, by passing over the whole of the narrow way. For this is to be drawn by the Father, to become worthy to receive the power of grace from God, so as to run without hindrance. And if some hate the elect, such an one knows their ignorance, and pities their minds for its folly.

As is right, then, knowledge itself loves and teaches the ignorant, and instructs the whole creation to honour God Almighty. And if such an one teaches to love God, he will not hold virtue as a thing to be lost in any case, either awake or in a dream, or in any vision ; since the habit never goes out of itself by falling from being a habit. Whether, then, knowledge be said to be habit or disposition ; on account of diverse sentiments never obtaining access, the guiding faculty, remaining unaltered, admits no alteration of appearances by framing in dreams visionary conceptions out of its movements by day. Wherefore also the Lord enjoins " to watch," so that our soul may never be perturbed with passion, even in dreams ; but also to keep the life of the night pure and stainless, as if spent in the day. For assimilation to God, as far as we can, is preserving the mind in its relation to the same things. And this is the relation of mind as mind.

But the variety of disposition arises from inordinate affection to material things. And for this reason, as they appear to me, to have called night Euphrone ; since then the soul, released from the perceptions of sense, turns in on itself, and has a truer hold of intelligence ($\phi\rho\acute{o}\nu\eta\sigma\iota\varsigma$).[2] Wherefore the mysteries are for the most part celebrated by night, indicating the withdrawal of the soul from the body, which takes place by night. " Let us not then sleep, as do others ; but let us watch and be sober. For they that sleep, sleep in the night ; and they that are drunken, are drunken in the night. But let us who are of the day be sober, putting on the breastplate of faith and love, and as an helmet the hope of salvation."[3] And as to what, again,

they say of sleep, the very same things are to be understood of death. For each exhibits the departure of the soul, the one more, the other less ; as we may also get this in Heraclitus : " Man touches night in himself, when dead and his light quenched ; and alive, when he sleeps he touches the dead ; and awake, when he shuts his eyes, he touches the sleeper."[4] " For blessed are those that have seen the Lord,"[5] according to the apostle ; " for it is high time to awake out of sleep. For now is our salvation nearer than when we believed. The night is far spent, the day is at hand. Let us therefore cast off the works of darkness, and put on the armour of light."[6] By day and light he designates figuratively the Son, and by the armour of light metaphorically the promises.

So it is said that we ought to go washed to sacrifices and prayers, clean and bright ; and that this external adornment and purification are practised for a sign. Now purity is to think holy thoughts. Further, there is the image of baptism, which also was handed down to the poets from Moses as follows : —

" And she having drawn water, and wearing on her body clean clothes."[7]

It is Penelope that is going to prayer : —

" And Telemachus,
Having washed his hands in the hoary sea, prayed to Athene."[8]

It was a custom of the Jews to wash frequently after being in bed. It was then well said, —

" Be pure, not by washing of water, but in the mind."

For sanctity, as I conceive it, is perfect pureness of mind, and deeds, and thoughts, and words too, and in its last degree sinlessness in dreams.

And sufficient purification to a man, I reckon, is thorough and sure repentance. If, condemning ourselves for our former actions, we go forward, after these things taking thought,[9] and divesting our mind both of the things which please us through the senses, and of our former transgressions.

If, then, we are to give the etymology of $\epsilon\pi\iota\sigma\tau\acute{\eta}\mu\eta$, knowledge, its signification is to be derived from $\sigma\tau\acute{a}\sigma\iota\varsigma$, placing ; for our soul, which was formerly borne, now in one way, now in another, it settles in objects. Similarly faith is to be explained etymologically, as the settling ($\sigma\tau\acute{a}\sigma\iota\varsigma$) of our soul respecting that which is.

But we desire to learn about the man who is always and in all things righteous ; who, neither dreading the penalty proceeding from the law,

---

[1] Matt. vi. 2, etc.
[2] Euphrone is plainly " kindly, cheerful."
[3] 1 Thess. v. 6-8.

[4] As it stands in the text the passage is unintelligible, and has been variously amended successfully.
[5] Clement seems to have read Κύριον for καιρόν in Rom. xiii. 11.
[6] Rom. xiii. 11, 12.
[7] Homer, Odyss., iv. 750, 760; xvii. 48, 58.
[8] Odyss., ii. 261.
[9] Explaining μετανοέω etymologically.

nor fearing to entertain hatred of evil in the case of those who live with him and who prosecute the injured, nor dreading danger at the hands of those who do wrong, remains righteous. For he who, on account of these considerations, abstains from anything wrong, is not voluntarily kind, but is good from fear. Even Epicurus says, that the man who in his estimation was wise, " would not do wrong to any one for the sake of gain; for he could not persuade himself that he would escape detection." So that, if he knew he would not be detected, he would, according to him, do evil. And such are the doctrines of darkness. If, too, one shall abstain from doing wrong from hope of the recompense given by God on account of righteous deeds, he is not on this supposition spontaneously good. For as fear makes that man just, so reward makes this one; or rather, makes him appear to be just. But with the hope after death — a good hope to the good, to the bad the reverse — not only they who follow after Barbarian wisdom, but also the Pythagoreans, are acquainted. For the latter also proposed hope as an end to those who philosophize. Whereas Socrates[1] also, in the *Phædo*, says " that good souls depart hence with a good hope;" and again, denouncing the wicked, he sets against this the assertion, " For they live with an evil hope." With him Heraclitus manifestly agrees in his dissertations concerning men: "There awaits man after death what they neither hope nor think." Divinely, therefore, Paul writes expressly, "Tribulation worketh patience, and patience experience, and experience hope; and hope maketh not ashamed."[2] For the patience is on account of the hope in the future. Now hope is synonymous with the recompense and restitution of hope; which maketh not ashamed, not being any more vilified.

But he who obeys the mere call, as he is called, neither for fear, nor for enjoyments, is on his way to knowledge (γνῶσις). For he does not consider whether any extrinsic lucrative gain or enjoyment follows to him; but drawn by the love of Him who is the true object of love, and led to what is requisite, practises piety. So that not even were we to suppose him to receive from God leave to do things forbidden with impunity; not even if he were to get the promise that he would receive as a reward the good things of the blessed; but besides, not even if he could persuade himself that God would be hoodwinked with reference to what he does (which is impossible), would he ever wish to do aught contrary to right reason, having once made choice of what is truly good and worthy of choice on its own account, and therefore to be loved. For it is not in the food of the belly, that we have heard good to be situated. But he has heard that " meat will not commend us,"[3] nor marriage, nor abstinence from marriage in ignorance; but virtuous gnostic conduct. For the dog, which is an irrational animal, may be said to be continent, dreading as it does the uplifted stick, and therefore keeping away from the meat. But let the predicted promise be taken away, and the threatened dread cancelled, and the impending danger removed, and the disposition of such people will be revealed.

CHAP. XXIII. — THE SAME SUBJECT CONTINUED.

For it is not suitable to the nature of the thing itself, that they should apprehend in the truly gnostic manner the truth, that all things which were created for our use are good; as, for example, marriage and procreation, when used in moderation; and that it is better than good to become free of passion, and virtuous by assimilation to the divine. But in the case of external things, agreeable or disagreeable, from some they abstain, from others not. But in those things from which they abstain from disgust, they plainly find fault with the creature and the Creator; and though in appearance they walk faithfully, the opinion they maintain is impious. That command, " Thou shalt not lust," needs neither the necessity arising from fear, which compels to keep from things that are pleasant; nor the reward, which by promise persuades to restrain the impulses of passion.

And those who obey God through the promise, caught by the bait of pleasure, choose obedience not for the sake of the commandment, but for the sake of the promise. Nor will turning away from objects of sense, as a matter of necessary consequence, produce attachment to intellectual objects. On the contrary, the attachment to intellectual objects naturally becomes to the Gnostic an influence which draws away from the objects of sense; inasmuch as he, in virtue of the selection of what is good, has chosen what is good according to knowledge (γνωστικῶς), admiring generation, and by sanctifying the Creator sanctifying assimilation to the divine. But I shall free myself from lust, let him say, O Lord, for the sake of alliance with Thee. For the economy of creation is good, and all things are well administered: nothing happens without a cause. I must be in what is Thine, O Omnipotent One. And if I am there, I am near Thee. And I would be free of fear that I may be able to draw near to Thee, and to be satisfied with little, practising Thy just choice between things good and things like.

Right mystically and sacredly the apostle, teaching us the choice which is truly gracious,

---

[1] [Elucidation IV.]
[2] Rom. v. 3-5.

[3] 1 Cor. viii. 8.

not in the way of rejection of other things as bad, but so as to do things better than what is good, has spoken, saying, "So he that giveth his virgin in marriage doeth well; and he that giveth her not doeth better; as far as respects seemliness and undistracted attendance on the Lord." [1]

Now we know that things which are difficult are not essential; but that things which are essential have been graciously made easy of attainment by God. Wherefore Democritus well says, that "nature and instruction" are like each other. And we have briefly assigned the cause. For instruction harmonizes man, and by harmonizing makes him natural; and it is no matter whether one was made such as he is by nature, or transformed by time and education. The Lord has furnished both; that which is by creation, and that which is by creating again and renewal through the covenant. And that is preferable which is advantageous to what is superior; but what is superior to everything is mind. So, then, what is really good is seen to be most pleasant, and of itself produces the fruit which is desired — tranquillity of soul. "And he who hears Me," it is said, "shall rest in peace, confident, and shall be calm without fear of any evil." [2] "Rely with all thy heart and thy mind on God." [3]

On this wise it is possible for the Gnostic already to have become God. "I said, Ye are gods, and [4] sons of the highest." And Empedocles says that the souls of the wise become gods, writing as follows: —

"At last prophets, minstrels, and physicians,
And the foremost among mortal men, approach;
Whence spring gods supreme in honours."

Man, then, generically considered, is formed in accordance with the idea of the connate spirit. For he is not created formless and shapeless in the workshop of nature, where mystically the production of man is accomplished, both art and essence being common. But the individual man is stamped according to the impression produced in the soul by the objects of his choice. Thus we say that Adam was perfect, as far as respects his formation; for none of the distinctive characteristics of the idea and form of man were wanting to him; but in the act of coming into being he received perfection. And he was justified by obedience; this was reaching manhood, as far as depended on him. And the cause lay in his choosing, and especially in his choosing what was forbidden. God was not the cause.

For production is twofold — of things procreated, and of things that grow. And manliness in man, who is subject to perturbation, as they say, makes him who partakes of it essentially fearless and invincible; and anger is the mind's satellite in patience, and endurance, and the like; and self-constraint and salutary sense are set over desire. But God is impassible, free of anger, destitute of desire. And He is not free of fear, in the sense of avoiding what is terrible; or temperate, in the sense of having command of desires. For neither can the nature of God fall in with anything terrible, nor does God flee fear; just as He will not feel desire, so as to rule over desires. Accordingly that Pythagorean saying was mystically uttered respecting us, "that man ought to become one;" for the high priest himself is one, God being one in the immutable state of the perpetual flow [5] of good things. Now the Saviour has taken away wrath in and with lust, wrath being lust of vengeance. For universally liability to feeling belongs to every kind of desire; and man, when deified purely into a passionless state, becomes a unit. As, then, those, who at sea are held by an anchor, pull at the anchor, but do not drag it to them, but drag themselves to the anchor; so those who, according to the gnostic life, draw God towards them, imperceptibly bring themselves to God: for he who reverences God, reverences himself. In the contemplative life, then, one in worshipping God attends to himself, and through his own spotless purification beholds the holy God holily; for self-control, being present, surveying and contemplating itself uninterruptedly, is as far as possible assimilated to God.

CHAP. XXIV. — THE REASON AND END OF DIVINE PUNISHMENTS.

Now that is in our power, of which equally with its opposite we are masters, — as, say, to philosophize or not, to believe or disbelieve. In consequence, then, of our being equally masters of each of the opposites, what depends on us is found possible. Now the commandments may be done or not done by us, who, as is reasonable, are liable to praise and blame. And those, again, who are punished on account of sins committed by them, are punished for them alone; for what is done is past, and what is done can never be undone. The sins committed before faith are accordingly forgiven by the Lord, not that they may be undone, but as if they had not been done. "But not all," says Basilides, [6] "but only sins involuntary and in ignorance, are forgiven;" as would be the case were it a man, and not God, that conferred such a boon. To such an one Scripture says, "Thou thoughtest that I would be like thee." [7] But if we are punished

---

[1] 1 Cor. vii. 38, 35.
[2] Prov. i. 33.
[3] Prov. iii. 5.
[4] Ps. lxxxii. 6.

[5] θεῖν . . . θεός.
[6] [Elucidation V.]
[7] Ps. l. 21.

for voluntary sins, we are punished not that the sins which are done may be undone, but because they were done. But punishment does not avail to him who has sinned, to undo his sin, but that he may sin no more, and that no one else fall into the like. Therefore the good God corrects for these three causes: First, that he who is corrected may become better than his former self; then that those who are capable of being saved by examples may be driven back, being admonished; and thirdly, that he who is injured may not be readily despised, and be apt to receive injury. And there are two methods of correction — the instructive and the punitive, which we have called the disciplinary. It ought to be known, then, that those who fall into sin after baptism [1] are those who are subjected to discipline; for the deeds done before are remitted, and those done after are purged. It is in reference to the unbelieving that it is said, "that they are reckoned as the chaff which the wind drives from the face of the earth, and the drop which falls from a vessel." [2]

CHAP. XXV. — TRUE PERFECTION CONSISTS IN THE KNOWLEDGE AND LOVE OF GOD.

"Happy he who possesses the culture of knowledge, and is not moved to the injury of the citizens or to wrong actions, but contemplates the undecaying order of immortal nature, how and in what way and manner it subsists. To such the practice of base deeds attaches not." Rightly, then, Plato says, "that the man who devotes himself to the contemplation of ideas will live as a god among men; now the mind is the place of ideas, and God is mind." He says that he who contemplates the unseen God lives as a god among men. And in the *Sophist*, Socrates calls the stranger of Elea, who was a dialectician, "god:" "Such are the gods who, like stranger guests, frequent cities. For when the soul, rising above the sphere of generation, is by itself apart, and dwells amidst ideas," like the Coryphæus in Theætetus, now become as an angel, it will be with Christ, being rapt in contemplation, ever keeping in view the will of God; in reality

"Alone wise, while these flit like shadows." [3]

"For the dead bury their dead." Whence Jeremiah says: "I will fill it with the earth-born dead whom mine anger has smitten." [4]

God, then, being not a subject for demonstration, cannot be the object of science. But the Son is wisdom, and knowledge, and truth, and all else that has affinity thereto. He is also susceptible of demonstration and of description. And all the powers of the Spirit, becoming collectively one thing, terminate in the same point — that is, in the Son. But He is incapable of being declared, in respect of the idea of each one of His powers. And the Son is neither simply one thing as one thing, nor many things as parts, but one thing as all things; whence also He is all things. For He is the circle of all powers rolled and united into one unity. Wherefore the Word is called the Alpha and the Omega, of whom alone the end becomes beginning, and ends again at the original beginning without any break. Wherefore also to believe in Him, and by Him, is to become a unit, being indissolubly united in Him; and to disbelieve is to be separated, disjoined, divided.

"Wherefore thus saith the Lord, Every alien son is uncircumcised in heart, and uncircumcised in flesh" (that is, unclean in body and soul): "there shall not enter one of the strangers into the midst of the house of Israel, but the Levites." [5] He calls those that would not believe, but would disbelieve, strangers. Only those who live purely being true priests of God. Wherefore, of all the circumcised tribes, those anointed to be high priests, and kings, and prophets, were reckoned more holy. Whence He commands them not to touch dead bodies, or approach the dead; not that the body was polluted, but that sin and disobedience were incarnate, and embodied, and dead, and therefore abominable. It was only, then, when a father and mother, a son and daughter died, that the priest was allowed to enter, because these were related only by flesh and seed, to whom the priest was indebted for the immediate cause of his entrance into life. And they purify themselves seven days, the period in which Creation was consummated. For on the seventh day the rest is celebrated; and on the eighth he brings a propitiation, as is written in Ezekiel, according to which propitiation the promise is to be received. [6] And the perfect propitiation, I take it, is that propitious faith in the Gospel which is by the law and the prophets, and the purity which shows itself in universal obedience, with the abandonment of the things of the world; in order to that grateful surrender of the tabernacle, which results from the enjoyment of the soul. Whether, then, the time be that which through the seven periods enumerated returns to the chiefest rest, [7] or the seven heavens, which some reckon one above the other; or whether also the fixed sphere which borders on the intellectual world be called the eighth, the expression denotes that the Gnostic ought to rise out of the sphere of creation and of sin. After these seven days, sacrifices are offered for sins. For there is still fear of

---

[1] λουτρόν. [See Elucidation VI.]
[2] Ps. i. 4; Isa. xl. 15.
[3] Hom., *Odyss.*, x. 495.
[4] Jer. xxxiii. 5.

[5] Ezek. xliv. 9, 10.
[6] Ezek. xliv. 27.
[7] The jubilee. [Elucidation VII.]

change, and it touches the seventh circle. The righteous Job says: "Naked came I out of my mother's womb, and naked shall I return there;"[1] not naked of possessions, for that were a trivial and common thing; but, as a just man, he departs naked of evil and sin, and of the unsightly shape which follows those who have led bad lives. For this was what was said, "Unless ye be converted, and become as children,"[2] pure in flesh, holy in soul by abstinence from evil deeds; showing that He would have us to be such as also He generated us from our mother—the water.[3] For the intent of one generation succeeding another is to immortalize by progress. "But the lamp of the wicked shall be put out."[4] That purity in body and soul which the Gnostic partakes of, the all-wise Moses indicated, by employing repetition in describing the incorruptibility of body and of soul in the person of Rebecca, thus: "Now the virgin was fair, and man had not known her."[5] And Rebecca, interpreted, means "glory of God;" and the glory of God is immortality.[6] This is in reality righteousness, not to desire other things, but to be entirely the consecrated temple of the Lord. Righteousness is peace of life and a well-conditioned state, to which the Lord dismissed her when He said, "Depart into peace."[7] For Salem is, by interpretation, peace; of which our Saviour is enrolled King, as Moses says, Melchizedek king of Salem, priest of the most high God, who gave bread and wine, furnishing consecrated food for a type of the Eucharist. And Melchizedek is interpreted "righteous king;" and the name is a synonym for righteousness and peace. Basilides, however, supposes that Righteousness and her daughter Peace dwell stationed in the eighth sphere.

But we must pass from physics to ethics, which are clearer; for the discourse concerning these will follow after the treatise in hand. The Saviour Himself, then, plainly initiates us into the mysteries, according to the words of the tragedy:[8]—

"Seeing those who see, he also gives the orgies."

And if you ask,

"These orgies, what is their nature?"

You will hear again:—

"It is forbidden to mortals uninitiated in the Bacchic rites to know."

And if any one will inquire curiously what they are, let him hear:—

"It is not lawful for thee to hear, but they are worth knowing;
The rites of the God detest him who practises impiety."

Now God, who is without beginning, is the perfect beginning of the universe, and the producer of the beginning. As, then, He is being, He is the first principle of the department of action, as He is good, of morals; as He is mind, on the other hand, He is the first principle of reasoning and of judgment. Whence also He alone is Teacher, who is the only Son of the Most High Father, the Instructor of men.

CHAP. XXVI. — HOW THE PERFECT MAN TREATS THE BODY AND THE THINGS OF THE WORLD.

Those, then, who run down created existence and vilify the body are wrong; not considering that the frame of man was formed erect for the contemplation of heaven, and that the organization of the senses tends to knowledge; and that the members and parts are arranged for good, not for pleasure. Whence this abode becomes receptive of the soul which is most precious to God; and is dignified with the Holy Spirit through the sanctification of soul and body, perfected with the perfection of the Saviour. And the succession of the three virtues is found in the Gnostic, who morally, physically, and logically occupies himself with God. For wisdom is the knowledge of things divine and human; and righteousness is the concord of the parts of the soul; and holiness is the service of God. But if one were to say that he disparaged the flesh, and generation on account of it, by quoting Isaiah, who says, "All flesh is grass, and all the glory of man as the flower of grass: the grass is withered, and the flower has fallen; but the word of the LORD endureth for ever;"[9] let him hear the Spirit interpreting the matter in question by Jeremiah, "And I scattered them like dry sticks, that are made to fly by the wind into the desert. This is the lot and portion of your disobedience, saith the LORD. As thou hast forgotten Me, and hast trusted in lies, so will I discover thy hinder parts to thy face; and thy disgrace shall be seen, thy adultery, and thy neighing," and so on.[10] For "the flower of grass," and "walking after the flesh," and "being carnal," according to the apostle, are those who are in their sins. The soul of man is confessedly the better part of man, and the body the inferior. But neither is the soul good by nature, nor, on the other hand, is the body bad by nature. Nor is that which is not good straightway bad. For there are things which occupy a middle place, and among them are things to be preferred, and things to be re-

---

1 Job i. 21.
2 Matt. xviii. 3.
3 i. e., Baptism.
4 Job [xviii. 5; Prov. xiii. 9.]
5 Gen. xxiv. 16.
6 [On Clement's Hebrew, see Elucidation VIII.]
7 Mark v. 34.
8 Eurip., *Bacchæ*, 465, etc.

9 Isa. xl. 6–8.
10 Jer. xiii. 24–27.

jected. The constitution of man, then, which has its place among things of sense, was necessarily composed of things diverse, but not opposite — body and soul.

Always therefore the good actions, as better, attach to the better and ruling spirit ; and voluptuous and sinful actions are attributed to the worse, the sinful one.

Now the soul of the wise man and Gnostic, as sojourning in the body, conducts itself towards it gravely and respectfully, not with inordinate affections, as about to leave the tabernacle if the time of departure summon. " I am a stranger in the earth, and a sojourner with you," it is said.[1] And hence Basilides says, that he apprehends that the election are strangers to the world, being supramundane by nature. But this is not the case. For all things are of one God. And no one is a stranger to the world by nature, their essence being one, and God one. But the elect man dwells as a sojourner, knowing all things to be possessed and disposed of ; and he makes use of the things which the Pythagoreans make out to be the threefold good things. The body, too, as one sent on a distant pilgrimage, uses inns and dwellings by the way, having care of the things of the world, of the places where he halts ; but leaving his dwelling-place and property without excessive emotion ; readily following him that leads him away from life ; by no means and on no occasion turning back ; giving thanks for his sojourn, and blessing [God] for his departure, embracing the mansion that is in heaven. " For we know, that, if the earthly house of our tabernacle be dissolved, we have a building of God, an house not made with hands, eternal in the heavens. For we that are in this tabernacle do groan, desiring to be clothed upon with our house which is from heaven : if so be that being clothed we shall not be found naked. For we walk by faith, not by sight,"[2] as the apostle says ; " and we are willing rather to be absent from the body, and present with God." The rather is in comparison. And comparison obtains in the case of things that fall under resemblance ; as the more valiant man is more valiant among the valiant, and most valiant among cowards. Whence he adds, " Wherefore we strive, whether present or absent, to be accepted with Him,"[3] that is, God, whose work and creation are all things, both the world and things supramundane. I admire Epicharmus, who clearly says : —

" Endowed with pious mind, you will not, in dying, Suffer aught evil. The spirit will dwell in heaven above ; "

and the minstrel[4] who sings : —

" The souls of the wicked flit about below the skies on earth,
In murderous pains beneath inevitable yokes of evils ;
But those of the pious dwell in the heavens,
Hymning in songs the Great, the Blessed One."

The soul is not then sent down from heaven to what is worse. For God works all things up to what is better. But the soul which has chosen the best life — the life that is from God and righteousness — exchanges earth for heaven. With reason therefore, Job, who had attained to knowledge, said, " Now I know that thou canst do all things ; and nothing is impossible to Thee. For who tells me of what I know not, great and wonderful things with which I was unacquainted ? And I felt myself vile, considering myself to be earth and ashes."[5] For he who, being in a state of ignorance, is sinful, "is earth and ashes ;" while he who is in a state of knowledge, being assimilated as far as possible to God, is already spiritual, and so elect. And that Scripture calls the senseless and disobedient " earth," will be made clear by Jeremiah the prophet, saying, in reference to Joachim and his brethren " Earth, earth, hear the word of the Lord ; Write this man, as man excommunicated."[6] And another prophet says again, " Hear, O heaven ; and give ear, O earth,"[7] calling understanding " ear," and the soul of the Gnostic, that of the man who has applied himself to the contemplation of heaven and divine things, and in this way has become an Israelite, "heaven." For again he calls him who has made ignorance and hardness of heart his choice, " earth." And the expression " give ear " .he derives from the "organs of hearing," " the ears," attributing carnal things to those who cleave to the things of sense. Such are they of whom Micah the prophet says, " Hear the word of the Lord, ye peoples who dwell with pangs."[8] And Abraham said, " By no means. The Lord is He who judgeth the earth ; "[9] " since he that believeth not, is," according to the utterance of the Saviour, " condemned already."[10] And there is written in the Kings[11] the judgment and sentence of the Lord, which stands thus : " The Lord hears the righteous, but the wicked He saveth not, because they do not desire to know God." For the Almighty will not accomplish what is absurd. What do the heresies say to this utterance, seeing Scripture proclaims the Almighty God to be good, and not the author of evil and wrong, if indeed ignorance arises from one not knowing ? But God does nothing absurd. " For this God," it is said, " is our God, and there is none to save besides Him."[12] " For there is no unrighteous-

---

[1] Gen. xxiii. 4 ; Ps. xxxix. 12.
[2] 2 Cor. v. 1, 2, 3, 7.
[3] 2 Cor. v. 9.
[4] Pindar, according to Theodoret.

[5] Job xlii. 2, 3, 6.
[6] Jer. xxii. 29, 30.
[7] Isa. i. 2.
[8] Mic. i. 2, where, however, the concluding words are not found.
[9] Gen. xviii. 25.
[10] John iii. 18.
[11] Where ?
[12] Isa. xlv. 21.

ness with God," [1] according to the apostle. And clearly yet the prophet teaches the will of God, and the gnostic proficiency, in these words: "And now, Israel, what doth the LORD God require of thee, but to fear the LORD thy God, and walk in all His ways, and love Him, and serve Him alone?" [2] He asks of thee, who hast the power of choosing salvation. What is it, then, that the Pythagoreans mean when they bid us "pray with the voice"? As seems to me, not that they thought the Divinity could not hear those who speak silently, but because they wished prayers to be right, which no one would be ashamed to make in the knowledge of many. We shall, however, treat of prayer in due course by and by. But we ought to have works that cry aloud, as becoming "those who walk in the day." [3] "Let thy works shine," [4] and behold a man and his works before his face. "For behold God and His works." [5] For the gnostic must, as far as is possible, imitate God. And the poets call the elect in their pages godlike and gods, and equal to the gods, and equal in sagacity to Zeus, and having counsels like the gods, and resembling the gods, — nibbling, as seems to me, at the expression, "in the image and likeness." [6]

Euripides accordingly says, "Golden wings are round my back, and I am shod with the winged sandals of the Sirens; and I shall go aloft into the wide ether, to hold converse with Zeus."

But I shall pray the Spirit of Christ to wing me to my Jerusalem. For the Stoics say that heaven is properly a city, but places here on earth are not cities; for they are called so, but are not. For a city is an important thing, and the people a decorous body, and a multitude of men regulated by law as the church by the word — a city on earth impregnable — free from tyranny; a product of the divine will on earth as in heaven. Images of this city the poets create with their pen. For the Hyperboreans, and the Arimaspian cities, and the Elysian plains, are commonwealths of just men. And we know Plato's city placed as a pattern in heaven.[7]

---

[1] Rom. ix. 14.
[2] Deut. x. 12.
[3] Rom. xiii. 13.
[4] Matt. v. 16.
[5] Isa. lxii. 11.

[6] Gen. i. 26.
[7] [Elucidation IX.]

ELUCIDATIONS.

I.

(The Lord's Discipline, book iv. cap. vi. p. 413.)

ἡ κυριακὴ ἄσκησις. Casaubon explains this as *Dominica exercitatio* (the *religion* which the Lord taught), and quotes the apostolic canons (li. and lii.), which, using this word (ἄσκησις), ordain certain fasts *on account of pious exercise*. Baronius, *more suo*, grasps at this word ἄσκησις, as a peg to hang the system of monkery upon. Casaubon answers: "If so, then all the early Christians were monks and nuns; as this word is always used by the Fathers for the Christian discipline, or Christianity itself." Such are the original *ascetics*, nothing more. The Christian Fathers transferred the word from heathen use to that of the Church, to signify the training to which *all the faithful* should subject themselves, in obedience to St. Paul (1 Cor. ix. 24-27). See Isaaci Casauboni, *De Annalibus Baronianis Exercitationes*, p. 171.

II.

(Theano, cap. xix. p. 431.)

The translator has not been happy in this rendering, but I retain it as in the Edinburgh Edition, which leaves one in doubt whether this second saying was Theano's; for, possibly, the translator meant to leave it so. But the Migne note is very good: "Jamblichus mentions two Theanos, one the wife of Brontinus, or Brotinus, and the other of Pythagoras. Both alike were devoted to the Pythagorean philosophy; and it is not certain, therefore, to which of them these *dicta* belong."

Theodoret quotes both, but decides not this doubt. Hoffman says, "There were many of the name;" and he mentions five different ones. Suidas makes mention of Theano of Crotona as the wife of Pythagoras, "the first woman who philosophized and wrote poetry;" and Hoffman doubts not this lady is the one quoted by Clement. She seems to have presided over the school of her husband after his death. Of the beauty and morality of the second *dictum*, I have spoken already (p. 348, Elucidation XI.); and I think it worth whole volumes of casuistry on a subject which (naturâ duce, sub lege Logi) the Gospel modestly leaves to natural decency and enlightened conscience. (See Clement's fine remarks, on p. 435.)

III.

(St. Paul, note 4, p. 434.)

Better rendered, " Paul is more recent (or later) in respect of time." This seems a strangely apologetic way to speak of this glorious apostle; though the reference may be to his own words (1 Cor. xv. 8), "as of one born out of due time." And it suggests to me, that, among the Alexandrian Christians, there were many Jewish converts who said, "I am of Apollos," and with whom the name of the great apostle of the Gentiles was still unsavoury. This goes to confirm the Pauline origin of the Epistle to the Hebrews, so far as it accounts for (what is testified by Eusebius, vi. 14) his omission of his own name from his treatise, lest it should prejudice his argument with his Hebrew kinsmen. Apollos may have sent it to Alexandria.

IV.

(Socrates, cap. xxii. p. 436.)

Who can read the *Phædo*, and think of Plato and Socrates, without hope that the mystery of redemption applies to them in some effectual way, under St. Paul's maxims (Rom. ii. 26, 27)? It would torture me in reading such sayings as are quoted here, were I not able reverently to indulge such hope, and then *to desist from speculation*. Cannot we be silent where Scripture is silent, and leave all to Him who loved the Gentiles, and died for them on the cross? I suspect the itch of our times, on this and like subjects, to be presumption (2 Cor. x. 5) "against the obedience of Christ." As if our own concern for the heathen were greater than His who died for the unjust, praying for His murderers! Why not leave the ransomed world to the world's Redeemer? The cross bore the inscription in Greek, and Latin also; for the Jews scorned it in Hebrew: and who can doubt that those outstretched arms embraced all mankind?

V.

(Basilides answered, cap. xxiv. p. 437.)

Note the pith and point of this chapter, and the beauty of Clement's *dictum*, "So it would be, were it a man and not God that justifies! As it is written, Thou thoughtest that I was altogether such an one as thyself." (Compare Matt. xx. 14.) But let us not overlook his exposition of the ends and purposes of chastisement. The great principle which he lays down destroys the whole Trent theology about penance, and annihilates the logical base of its figment about "Purgatory." "Punishment does not avail to him who has sinned, to undo his sin." The precious blood of Christ "speaketh better things."

VI.

(Sin after Baptism, cap. xxiv. p. 438.)

Not to broach any opinion of my own, it is enough to remark, that this reference to primitive discipline shows that a defined penitential system in the early Church was aimed at by the Montanists, and inspired their deadly animosity, not merely as a theory, but as a system.   Although differing on many points with Dr. Bunsen (he is both Baron and Doctor, and I give him the more honourable title of the two), I feel it due to my contract with the reader of this series to refer him to what he says of the baptismal vow, etc. (*Hippol.*, iii. p. 187), as furnishing a valuable commentary on the text, and on the whole plan of Alexandrian teaching and discipline.

VII.

(Jubilee, cap. xxv. p. 438.)

Here the reader may feel that an Elucidation is requisite to any intelligent idea of what Clement means to say.   " We wish he would explain his explanation " of Ezekiel.   Let me give a brief rendering of the annotations in Migne, as all that can here be furnished.   (1) The *tabernacle* is the body, as St. Paul uses the word (2 Cor. v. 1–4), and St. Peter (2 Ep. i. 13, 14).   (2) The *seven periods* are the Sabbatical weeks of years leading up to the year of Jubilee.   (3) The ἀπλανὴς χώρα refers to the old system of astronomy, and its division of the heavens into an octave of *spheres*, of which the seven inner spheres are those of the seven planets ; the fixt stars being in the eighth, which "borders on the intellectual world," — the abode of spirits, according to Clement.   The Miltonic student will recall the perplexity with which, perhaps, in early years, he first read : —

> " They pass the planets seven, and pass the fixt,
> And that crystalline sphere whose balance weighs
> The trepidation talked, and that first moved.
>
> *Paradise Lost*, book iii. 481.

The Copernican system was, even in Milton's time, not generally accepted ; but, for one who had personally conversed with Galileo, this seems incorrigibly bad.   The true system would have given greater dignity, and in fact a better topography, to his great poem.

VIII.

(Rebecca, p. 439.)

Le Nourry, as well as Barbeyrac (see Kaye, pp. 109 and 473), regards Clement as ignorant of the Hebrew language.   Kaye, though he shows that some of the attempts to demonstrate this are fanciful, inclines to the same opinion ; remarking that he borrows his interpretations from Philo. On the passage here under consideration, he observes, that, " having said repeatedly [1] that Rebekah in Hebrew is equivalent to ὑπομονή in Greek, he now makes it equivalent to Θεοῦ δόξα. He elsewhere refers our Saviour's exclamation, Eli, Eli, etc., to the Greek word ἥλιος, and the name Jesus to ἰᾶσθαι."

IX.

(Plato's City, cap. xxvi. p. 441.)

This is worth quoting from the *Republic* (book ix. p. 423, Jowett) : " In heaven there is laid up a pattern of such a city ; and he who desires may behold this, and, beholding, govern himself accordingly.   He will act according to the laws of that city, and of no other."   Sublime old Gentile !   Did not the apostle of the Gentiles think of Socrates, when he wrote Heb. xii. 28, and xiii. 14 ? On this noble passage, of which Clement has evidently thought very seriously, Schleiermacher's remarks seem to me cold and unsatisfactory.   (See his *Introductions*, translated by Dobson ; ed. Cambridge, 1836.)

---

[1] e.g., this vol., p. 309.

THE STROMATA, OR MISCELLANIES

BOOK V.

CHAP. I. — ON FAITH.

OF the Gnostic so much has been cursorily, as it were, written. We proceed now to the sequel, and must again contemplate faith; for there are some that draw the distinction, that faith has reference to the Son, and knowledge to the Spirit. But it has escaped their notice that, in order to believe truly in the Son, we must believe that He is the Son, and that He came, and how, and for what, and respecting His passion; and we must know who is the Son of God. Now neither is knowledge without faith, nor faith without knowledge. Nor is the Father without the Son; for the Son is with the Father. And the Son is the true teacher respecting the Father; and that we may believe in the Son, we must know the Father, with whom also is the Son. Again, in order that we may know the Father, we must believe in the Son, that it is the Son of God who teaches; for from faith to knowledge by the Son is the Father. And the knowledge of the Son and Father, which is according to the gnostic rule — that which in reality is gnostic — is the attainment and comprehension of the truth by the truth.

We, then, are those who are believers in what is not believed, and who are Gnostics as to what is unknown; that is, Gnostics as to what is unknown and disbelieved by all, but believed and known by a few; and Gnostics, not describing actions by speech, but Gnostics in the exercise of contemplation. Happy is he who speaks in the ears of the hearing. Now faith is the ear of the soul. And such the Lord intimates faith to be, when He says, "He that hath ears to hear, let him hear;"[1] so that by believing he may comprehend what He says, as He says it. Homer, too, the oldest of the poets, using the word "hear" instead of "perceive" — the specific for the generic term — writes: —

"Him most they heard."[2]

For, in fine, the agreement and harmony of the faith of both[3] contribute to one end — salvation. We have in the apostle an unerring witness: "For I desire to see you, that I may impart unto you some spiritual gift, in order that ye may be strengthened; that is, that I may be comforted in you, by the mutual faith of you and me."[4] And further on again he adds, "The righteousness of God is revealed from faith to faith."[5] The apostle, then, manifestly announces a twofold faith, or rather one which admits of growth and perfection; for the common faith lies beneath as a foundation.[6] To those, therefore, who desire to be healed, and are moved by faith, He added, "Thy faith hath saved thee."[7] But that which is excellently built upon is consummated in the believer, and is again perfected by the faith which results from instruction and the word, in order to the performance of the commandments. Such were the apostles, in whose case it is said that "faith removed mountains and transplanted trees."[8] Whence, perceiving the greatness of its power, they asked "that faith might be added to them;"[9] a faith which salutarily bites the soil "like a grain of mustard," and grows magnificently in it, to such a degree that the reasons of things sublime rest on it. For if one by nature knows God, as Basilides thinks, who calls intelligence of a superior order at once faith and kingship, and a creation worthy of the essence of the Creator; and explains that near Him exists not power, but essence and nature and substance; and says that faith is not the rational assent of the soul exercising free-will, but an undefined beauty, belonging immediately to the creature; — the precepts both of the Old and of the New Testament are, then, superfluous, if one is saved by

---

[1] Matt. xi. 15.
[2] *Odyss.*, vi. 185.

[3] Teacher and scholar.
[4] Rom. i. 11, 12.
[5] Rom. i. 17.
[6] ["The common faith" (ἡ κοινὴ πίστις) is no "secret," then, and cannot be in its nature.]
[7] Matt. ix. 22.
[8] Matt. xvii. 20; Luke xvii. 6; 1 Cor. xiii. 2.
[9] Luke xvii. 5.

nature, as Valentinus would have it, and is a believer and an elect man by nature, as Basilides thinks; and nature would have been able, one time or other, to have shone forth, apart from the Saviour's appearance. But were they to say that the visit of the Saviour was necessary, then the properties of nature are gone from them, the elect being saved by instruction, and purification, and the doing of good works. Abraham, accordingly, who through hearing believed the voice, which promised under the oak in Mamre, "I will give this land to thee, and to thy seed," was either elect or not. But if he was not, how did he straightway believe, as it were naturally? And if he was elect, their hypothesis is done away with, inasmuch as even previous to the coming of the Lord an election was found, and that saved: "For it was reckoned to him for righteousness."[1] For if any one, following Marcion, should dare to say that the Creator (Δημιουργόν) saved the man that believed on him, even before the advent of the Lord, (the election being saved with their own proper salvation); the power of the good Being will be eclipsed; inasmuch as late only, and subsequent to the Creator spoken of by them in words of good omen, it made the attempt to save, and by his instruction, and in imitation of him. But if, being such, the good Being save, according to them; neither is it his own that he saves, nor is it with the consent of him who formed the creation that he essays salvation, but by force or fraud. And how can he any more be good, acting thus, and being posterior? But if the locality is different, and the dwelling-place of the Omnipotent is remote from the dwelling-place of the good God; yet the will of him who saves, having been the first to begin, is not inferior to that of the good God. From what has been previously proved, those who believe not are proved senseless: "For their paths are perverted, and they know not peace," saith the prophet.[2] "But foolish and unlearned questions" the divine Paul exhorted to "avoid, because they gender strifes."[3] And Æschylus exclaims:—

"In what profits not, labour not in vain."

For that investigation, which accords with faith, which builds, on the foundation of faith,[4] the august knowledge of the truth, we know to be the best. Now we know that neither things which are clear are made subjects of investigation, such as if it is day, while it is day; nor things unknown, and never destined to become clear, as whether the stars are even or odd in number;

nor things convertible; and those are so which can be said equally by those who take the opposite side, as if what is in the womb is a living creature or not. A fourth mode is, when, from either side of those, there is advanced an unanswerable and irrefragable argument. If, then, the ground of inquiry, according to all of these modes, is removed, faith is established. For we advance to them the unanswerable consideration, that it is God who speaks and comes to our help in writing, respecting each one of the points regarding which I investigate. Who, then, is so impious as to disbelieve God, and to demand proofs from God as from men? Again, some questions demand the evidence of the senses,[5] as if one were to ask whether the fire be warm, or the snow white; and some admonition and rebuke, as the question if you ought to honour your parents. And there are those that deserve punishment, as to ask proofs of the existence of Providence. There being then a Providence, it were impious to think that the whole of prophecy and the economy in reference to a Saviour did not take place in accordance with Providence. And perchance one should not even attempt to demonstrate such points, the divine Providence being evident from the sight of all its skilful and wise works which are seen, some of which take place in order, and some appear in order. And He who communicated to us being and life, has communicated to us also reason, wishing us to live rationally and rightly. For the Word of the Father of the universe is not the uttered word (λόγος προφορικός), but the wisdom and most manifest kindness of God, and His power too, which is almighty and truly divine, and not incapable of being conceived by those who do not confess—the all-potent will. But since some are unbelieving, and some are disputatious, all do not attain to the perfection of the good. For neither is it possible to attain it without the exercise of free choice; nor does the whole depend on our own purpose; as, for example, what is destined to happen. "For by grace we are saved:" not, indeed, without good works; but we must, by being formed for what is good, acquire an inclination for it. And we must possess the healthy mind which is fixed on the pursuit of the good; in order to which we have the greatest need of divine grace, and of right teaching, and of holy susceptibility, and of the drawing of the Father to Him. For, bound in this earthly body, we apprehend the objects of sense by means of the body; but we grasp intellectual objects by means of the logical faculty itself. But if one expect to apprehend all things by the senses, he has fallen far from the truth. Spiritually, therefore, the apostle writes respecting the knowledge of God,

---

[1] Gen. xv. 6; Rom. iv. 3.
[2] Isa. lix. 8.
[3] 2 Tim. ii. 23.
[4] [All such expressions noteworthy for manifold uses among divines.]
[5] [Fatal to not a little of the scholastic theology, and the Trent dogmas.]

" For now we see as through a glass, but then face to face." [1] For the vision of the truth is given but to few. Accordingly, Plato says in the *Epinomis*, " I do not say that it is possible for all to be blessed and happy ; only a few. Whilst we live, I pronounce this to be the case. But there is a good hope that after death I shall attain all." To the same effect is what we find in Moses : " No man shall see My face, and live." [2] For it is evident that no one during the period of life has been able to apprehend God clearly. But " the pure in heart shall see God," [3] when they arrive at the final perfection. For since the soul became too enfeebled for the apprehension of realities, we needed a divine teacher. The Saviour is sent down — a teacher and leader in the acquisition of the good — the secret and sacred token of the great Providence. " Where, then, is the scribe ? where is the searcher of this world ? Hath not God made foolish the wisdom of this world ? " [4] it is said. And again, " I will destroy the wisdom of the wise, and bring to nothing the understanding of the prudent," [5] plainly of those wise in their own eyes, and disputatious. Excellently therefore Jeremiah says, " Thus saith the LORD, Stand in the ways, and ask for the eternal paths, what is the good way, and walk in it, and ye shall find expiation for your souls." [6] Ask, he says, and inquire of those who know, without contention and dispute. And on learning the way of truth, let us walk on the right way, without turning till we attain to what we desire. It was therefore with reason that the king of the Romans (his name was Numa), being a Pythagorean, first of all men, erected a temple to Faith and Peace. " And to Abraham, on believing, righteousness was reckoned." [7] He, prosecuting the lofty philosophy of aerial phenomena, and the sublime philosophy of the movements in the heavens, was called Abram, which is interpreted " sublime father." [8] But afterwards, on looking up to heaven, whether it was that he saw the Son in the spirit, as some explain, or a glorious angel, or in any other way recognised God to be superior to the creation, and all the order in it, he receives in addition the Alpha, the knowledge of the one and only God, and is called Abraam, having, instead of a natural philosopher, become wise, and a lover of God. For it is interpreted, " elect father of sound." For by sound is the uttered word : the mind is its father ; and the mind of the good man is elect. I cannot forbear praising exceedingly the poet

of Agrigentum, who celebrates faith as follows : —

" Friends, I know, then, that there is truth in the myths
Which I will relate. But very difficult to men,
And irksome to the mind, is the attempt of faith." [9]

Wherefore also the apostle exhorts, " that your faith should not be in the wisdom of men," who profess to persuade, " but in the power of God," [10] which alone without proofs, by mere faith, is able to save. " For the most approved of those that are reputable knows how to keep watch. And justice will apprehend the forgers and witnesses of lies," says the Ephesian. [11] For he, having derived his knowledge from the barbarian philosophy, is acquainted with the purification by fire of those who have led bad lives, which the Stoics afterwards called the Conflagration (ἐκπύρωσις), in which also they teach that each will arise exactly as he was, so treating of the resurrection ; while Plato says as follows, that the earth at certain periods is purified by fire and water : " There have been many destructions of men in many ways ; and there shall be very great ones by fire and water ; and others briefer by innumerable causes." And after a little he adds : " And, in truth, there is a change of the objects which revolve about earth and heaven ; and in the course of long periods there is the destruction of the objects on earth by a great conflagration." Then he subjoins respecting the deluge : " But when, again, the gods deluge the earth to purify it with water, those on the mountains, herdsmen and shepherds, are saved ; those in your cities are carried down by the rivers into the sea." And we showed in the first Miscellany [12] that the philosophers of the Greeks are called thieves, inasmuch as they have taken without acknowledgment their principal dogmas from Moses and the prophets. To which also we shall add, that the angels who had obtained the superior rank, having sunk into pleasures, told to the women [13] the secrets which had come to their knowledge ; while the rest of the angels concealed them, or rather, kept them against the coming of the Lord. Thence emanated the doctrine of providence, and the revelation of high things ; and prophecy having already been imparted to the philosophers of the Greeks, the treatment of dogma arose among the philosophers, sometimes true when they hit the mark, and sometimes erroneous, when they comprehended not the secret of the prophetic allegory. And this it is proposed briefly to indicate in running over the points requiring mention. Faith, then, we say, we are to show must not be

---

[1] 1 Cor. xiii. 12.
[2] Ex. xxxiii. 20.
[3] Matt. v. 8.
[4] 1 Cor. i. 20.
[5] 1 Cor. i. 19.
[6] Jer. vi. 16.
[7] Rom. iv. 3, 5, 9, 22.
[8] Philo Judæus, *De Abrahame,* p. 413, vol. ii. Bohn. [But see Elucidation I.]

[9] Empedocles.
[10] 1 Cor. ii. 5.
[11] Heraclitus.
[12] [See p. 318, *supra.*]
[13] [See vol. i. p. 190, this series.]

inert and alone, but accompanied with investigation. For I do not say that we are not to inquire at all. For " Search, and thou shalt find," [1] it is said.

> " What is sought may be captured,
> But what is neglected escapes,"

according to Sophocles.

The like also says Menander the comic poet : —

> " All things sought,
> The wisest say, need anxious thought."

But we ought to direct the visual faculty of the soul aright to discovery, and to clear away obstacles ; and to cast clean away contention, and envy, and strife, destined to perish miserably from among men.

For very beautifully does Timon of Phlius write : —

> " And Strife, the Plague of Mortals, stalks vainly shrieking,
> The sister of Murderous Quarrel and Discord,
> Which rolls blindly over all things. But then
> It sets its head towards men, and casts them on hope."

Then a little below he adds : —

> " For who hath set these to fight in deadly strife ?
> A rabble keeping pace with Echo; for, enraged at those silent,
> It raised an evil disease against men, and many perished ; "

of the speech which denies what is false, and of the dilemma, of that which is concealed, of the Sorites, and of the Crocodilean, of that which is open, and of ambiguities and sophisms. To inquire, then, respecting God, if it tend not to strife, but to discovery, is salutary. For it is written in David, " The poor eat, and shall be filled ; and they shall praise the LORD that seek Him. Your heart shall live for ever." [2] For they who seek Him after the true search, praising the Lord, shall be filled with the gift that comes from God, that is, knowledge. And their soul shall live ; for the soul is figuratively termed the heart, which ministers life : for by the Son is the Father known.

We ought not to surrender our ears to all who speak and write rashly. For cups also, which are taken hold of by many by the ears, are dirtied, and lose the ears ; and besides, when they fall they are broken. In the same way also, those, who have polluted the pure hearing of faith by many trifles, at last becoming deaf to the truth, become useless and fall to the earth. It is not, then, without reason that we commanded boys to kiss their relations, holding them by the ears ; indicating this, that the feeling of love is engendered by hearing. And " God," who is known to those who love, " is love," [3] as " God,"

who by instruction is communicated to the faithful, " is faithful ; " [4] and we must be allied to Him by divine love : so that by like we may see like, hearing the word of truth guilelessly and purely, as children who obey us. And this was what he, whoever he was, indicated who wrote on the entrance to the temple at Epidaurus the inscription : —

> " Pure he must be who goes within
> The incense-perfumed fane."

And purity is " to think holy thoughts." " Except ye become as these little children, ye shall not enter," it is said, " into the kingdom of heaven." [5] For there the temple of God is seen established on three foundations — faith, hope, and love.

CHAP. II. — ON HOPE.

Respecting faith we have adduced sufficient testimonies of writings among the Greeks. But in order not to exceed bounds, through eagerness to collect a very great many also respecting hope and love, suffice it merely to say that in the *Crito* Socrates, who prefers a good life and death to life itself, thinks that we have hope of another life after death.

Also in the *Phædrus* he says, " That only when in a separate state can the soul become partaker of the wisdom which is true, and surpasses human power ; and when, having reached the end of hope by philosophic love, desire shall waft it to heaven, then," says he, " does it receive the commencement of another, an immortal life." And in the *Symposium* he says, " That there is instilled into all the natural love of generating what is like, and in men of generating men alone, and in the good man of the generation of the counterpart of himself. But it is impossible for the good man to do this without possessing the perfect virtues, in which he will train the youth who have recourse to him." And as he says in the *Theætetus,* " He will beget and finish men. For some procreate by the body, others by the soul ; " since also with the barbarian philosophers to teach and enlighten is called to regenerate ; and " I have begotten you in Jesus Christ," [6] says the good apostle somewhere.

Empedocles, too, enumerates friendship among the elements, conceiving it as a combining love : —

> " Which do you look at with your mind; and don't sit gaping with your eyes."

Parmenides, too, in his poem, alluding to hope, speaks thus : —

[1] Matt. vii. 7.
[2] Ps. xxii. 26.
[3] 1 John iv. 16.
[4] 1 Cor. i. 9, x. 13.
[5] Matt. xviii. 3. [Again this tender love of children.]
[6] 1 Cor. iv. 15.

"Yet look with the mind certainly on what is absent as
    present,
For it will not sever that which is from the grasp it
    has of that which is
Not, even if scattered in every direction over the
    world or combined."

CHAP. III. — THE OBJECTS OF FAITH AND HOPE PERCEIVED BY THE MIND ALONE.

For he who hopes, as he who believes, sees
intellectual objects and future things with the
mind. If, then, we affirm that aught is just,
and affirm it to be good, and we also say that
truth is something, yet we have never seen any
of such objects with our eyes, but with our mind
alone. Now the Word of God says, "I am the
truth." [1] The Word is then to be contemplated
by the mind. "Do you aver," it was said, [2] "that
there are any true philosophers?" "Yes," said
I, "those who love to contemplate the truth."
In the *Phædrus* also, Plato, speaking of the
truth, shows it as an idea. Now an idea is a
conception of God; and this the barbarians have
termed the Word of God. The words are as
follow: "For one must then dare to speak the
truth, especially in speaking of the truth. For
the essence of the soul, being colourless, formless, and intangible, is visible only to God, [3] its
guide." Now the Word issuing forth was the
cause of creation; then also he generated himself, "when the Word had become flesh," [4] that
He might be seen. The righteous man will
seek the discovery that flows from love, to which
if he hastes he prospers. For it is said, "To him
that knocketh, it shall be opened: ask, and it
shall be given to you." [5] "For the violent that
storm the kingdom" [6] are not so in disputatious
speeches; but by continuance in a right life and
unceasing prayers, are said "to take it by force,"
wiping away the blots left by their previous sins.

"You may obtain wickedness, even in great abundance. [7]
And him who toils God helps;
For the gifts of the Muses, hard to win,
Lie not before you, for any one to bear away."

The knowledge of ignorance is, then, the first
lesson in walking according to the Word. An
ignorant man has sought, and having sought, he
finds the teacher; and finding has believed, and
believing has hoped; and henceforward having
loved, is assimilated to what was loved — endeavouring to be what he first loved. Such is
the method Socrates shows Alcibiades, who thus
questions: "Do you not think that I shall know
about what is right otherwise?" "Yes, if you
have found out." "But you don't think I have

found out?" "Certainly, if you have sought."
"Then you don't think that I have sought?"
"Yes, if you think you do not know." [8] So
with the lamps of the wise virgins, lighted at
night in the great darkness of ignorance, which
the Scripture signified by "night." Wise souls,
pure as virgins, understanding themselves to be
situated amidst the ignorance of the world, kindle the light, and rouse the mind, and illumine
the darkness, and dispel ignorance, and seek
truth, and await the appearance of the Teacher.
"The mob, then," said I, "cannot become a philoso-
    pher." [9]

"Many rod-bearers there are, but few Bacchi,"
according to Plato. "For many are called, but
few chosen." [10] "Knowledge is not in all," [11] says
the apostle. "And pray that we may be delivered from unreasonable and wicked men: for
all men have not faith." [12] And the *Poetics* of
Cleanthes, the Stoic, writes to the following
effect: —

"Look not to glory, wishing to be suddenly wise,
And fear not the undiscerning and rash opinon of the
    many;
For the multitude has not an intelligent, or wise, or
    right judgment,
And it is in few men that you will find this." [13]

And more sententiously the comic poet briefly
says: —

"It is a shame to judge of what is right by much noise."

For they heard, I think, that excellent wisdom,
which says to us, "Watch your opportunity in
the midst of the foolish, and in the midst of the
intelligent continue." [14] And again, "The wise
will conceal sense." [15] For the many demand
demonstration as a pledge of truth, not satisfied
with the bare salvation by faith.

"But it is strongly incumbent to disbelieve the dominant
    wicked,
And as is enjoined by the assurance of our muse,
Know by dissecting the utterance within your breast."

"For this is habitual to the wicked," says Empedocles, "to wish to overbear what is true by
disbelieving it." And that our tenets are probable and worthy of belief, the Greeks shall know,
the point being more thoroughly investigated in
what follows. For we are taught what is like by
what is like. For says Solomon, "Answer a fool
according to his folly." [15] Wherefore also, to
those that ask the wisdom that is with us, we are
to hold out things suitable, that with the greatest
possible ease they may, through their own ideas,
be likely to arrive at faith in the truth. For "I

---

1 John xiv. 6.
2 By Plato.
3 In Plato we have νῷ instead of Θεῷ.
4 John i. 14.
5 Matt. vii. 7.
6 Matt. xi. 12.
7 Hesiod, first line, *Works and Days*, 285. The other three are
variously ascribed to different authors.

8 Plato, *Alcibiades*, book i.
9 Plato, *Republic*, vi. p. 678.
10 Matt. xx. 16.
11 1 Cor. viii. 7.
12 2 Thess. iii. 1, 2.
13 Quoted by Socrates in the *Phædo*, p. 52.
14 Ecclus. xxvii. 12.
15 Prov. x. 14.
16 Prov. xxvi. 5.

became all things to all men, that I might gain all men." [1] Since also "the rain" of the divine grace is sent down "on the just and the unjust." [2] "Is He the God of the Jews only, and not also of the Gentiles? Yes, also of the Gentiles: if indeed He is one God," [3] exclaims the noble apostle.

CHAP. IV. — DIVINE THINGS WRAPPED UP IN FIG-
URES BOTH IN THE SACRED AND IN HEATHEN
WRITERS.

But since they will believe neither in what is good justly nor in knowledge unto salvation, we ourselves reckoning what they claim as belonging to us, because all things are God's; and especially since what is good proceeded from us to the Greeks, let us handle those things as they are capable of hearing. For intelligence or rectitude this great crowd estimates not by truth, but by what they are delighted with. And they will be pleased not more with other things than with what is like themselves. For he who is still blind and dumb, not having understanding, or the undazzled and keen vision of the contemplative soul, which the Saviour confers, like the uninitiated at the mysteries, or the unmusical at dances, not being yet pure and worthy of the pure truth, but still discordant and disordered and material, must stand outside of the divine choir. · "For we compare spiritual things with spiritual." [4] Wherefore, in accordance with the method of concealment, the truly sacred Word, truly divine and most necessary for us, deposited in the shrine of truth, was by the Egyptians indicated by what were called among them *adyta*, and by the Hebrews by the veil. Only the consecrated — that is, those devoted to God, circumcised in the desire of the passions for the sake of love to that which is alone divine — were allowed access to them. For Plato also thought it not lawful for "the impure to touch the pure."

Thence the prophecies and oracles are spoken in enigmas, and the mysteries are not exhibited incontinently to all and sundry, but only after certain purifications and previous instructions.

"For the Muse was not then
    Greedy of gain or mercenary;
    Nor were Terpsichore's sweet,
    Honey-toned, silvery soft-voiced
    Strains made merchandise of."

Now those instructed among the Egyptians learned first of all that style of the Egyptian letters which is called Epistolographic; and second, the Hieratic, which the sacred scribes practise; and finally, and last of all, the Hieroglyphic, of which one kind which is by the first

elements is literal (Kyriologic), and the other Symbolic. Of the Symbolic, one kind speaks literally by imitation, and another writes as it were figuratively; and another is quite allegorical, using certain enigmas.

Wishing to express Sun in writing, they make a circle; and Moon, a figure like the Moon, like its proper shape. But in using the figurative style, by transposing and transferring, by changing and by transforming in many ways as suits them, they draw characters. In relating the praises of the kings in theological myths, they write in anaglyphs. [5] Let the following stand as a specimen of the third species — the Enigmatic. For the rest of the stars, on account of their oblique course, they have figured like the bodies of serpents; but the sun, like that of a beetle, because it makes a round figure of ox-dung, [6] and rolls it before its face. And they say that this creature lives six months under ground, and the other division of the year above ground, and emits its seed into the ball, and brings forth; and that there is not a female beetle. All then, in a word, who have spoken of divine things, both Barbarians and Greeks, have veiled the first principles of things, and delivered the truth in enigmas, and symbols, and allegories, and metaphors, and such like tropes. [7] Such also are the oracles among the Greeks. And the Pythian Apollo is called Loxias. Also the maxims of those among the Greeks called wise men, in a few sayings indicate the unfolding of matter of considerable importance. Such certainly is that maxim, "Spare Time:" either because life is short, and we ought not to expend this time in vain; or, on the other hand, it bids you spare your personal expenses; so that, though you live many years, necessaries may not fail you. Similarly also the maxim "*Know thyself*" shows many things; both that thou art mortal, and that thou wast born a human being; and also that, in comparison with the other excellences of life, thou art of no account, because thou sayest that thou art rich or renowned; or, on the other hand, that, being rich or renowned, you are not honoured on account of your advantages alone. And it says, Know for what thou wert born, and whose image thou art; and what is thy essence, and what thy creation, and what thy relation to God, and the like. And the Spirit says by Isaiah the prophet, "I will give thee treasures, hidden, dark." [8] Now wisdom, hard to hunt, is the treasures of God and unfailing riches. But those, taught in theology by those prophets, the poets, philosophize much by way of a hidden sense. I mean Orpheus, Linus, Musæus, Homer, and

---

[1] 1 Cor. ix. 22.
[2] Matt. v. 45.
[3] Rom. iii. 29, 30.
[4] 1 Cor. ii. 13.

[5] Bas relief.
[6] [Elucidation II.]
[7] [Prov. i. 6.]
[8] Isa. xlv. 3.

Hesiod, and those in this fashion wise. The persuasive style of poetry is for them a veil for the many. Dreams and signs are all more or less obscure to men, not from jealousy (for it were wrong to conceive of God as subject to passions), but in order that research, introducing to the understanding of enigmas, may haste to the discovery of truth. Thus Sophocles the tragic poet somewhere says : —

"And God I know to be such an one,
Ever the revealer of enigmas to the wise,
But to the perverse bad, although a teacher in few words," —

putting bad instead of simple. Expressly then respecting all our Scripture, as if spoken in a parable, it is written in the Psalms, "Hear, O My people, My law : incline your ear to the words of My mouth. I will open My mouth in parables, I will utter My problems from the beginning." [1] Similarly speaks the noble apostle to the following effect : "Howbeit we speak wisdom among those that are perfect ; yet not the wisdom of this world, nor of the princes of this world, that come to nought. But we speak the wisdom of God hidden in a mystery ; which none of the princes of this world knew. For had they known it, they would not have crucified the Lord of glory." [2]

The philosophers did not exert themselves in contemning the appearance of the Lord. It therefore follows that it is the opinion of the wise among the Jews which the apostle inveighs against it. Wherefore he adds, " But we preach, as it is written, what eye hath not seen, and ear hath not heard, and hath not entered into the heart of man, what God hath prepared for them that love Him. For God hath revealed it to us by the Spirit. For the Spirit searcheth all things, even the deep things of God." [3] For he recognises the spiritual man and the Gnostic as the disciple of the Holy Spirit dispensed by God, which is the mind of Christ. " But the natural man receiveth not the things of the Spirit, for they are foolishness to him." [4] Now the apostle, in contradistinction to gnostic perfection, calls the common faith [5] *the foundation*, and sometimes *milk*, writing on this wise : " Brethren, I could not speak to you as to spiritual, but as to carnal, to babes in Christ. I have fed you with milk, not with meat : for ye were not able. Neither yet are ye now able. For ye are yet carnal : for whereas there is among you envy and strife, are ye not carnal, and walk as men ?" [6] Which things are the choice of those men who are sinners. But those who abstain from these things give

their thoughts to divine things, and partake of gnostic food. " According to the grace," it is said, " given to me as a wise master builder, I have laid the foundation. And another buildeth on it gold and silver, precious stones." [7] Such is the gnostic superstructure on the foundation of faith in Christ Jesus. But " the stubble, and the wood, and the hay," are the additions of heresies. " But the fire shall try every man's work, of what sort it is." In allusion to the gnostic edifice also in the Epistle to the Romans, he says, " For I desire to see you, that I may impart unto you a spiritual gift, that ye may be established." [8] It was impossible that gifts of this sort could be written without disguise.

CHAP. V. — ON THE SYMBOLS OF PYTHAGORAS.

Now the Pythagorean symbols were connected with the Barbarian philosophy in the most recondite way. For instance, the Samian counsels "not to have a swallow in the house ;" that is, not to receive a loquacious, whispering, garrulous man, who cannot contain what has been communicated to him. " For the swallow, and the turtle, and the sparrows of the field, know the times of their entrance," [9] says the Scripture ; and one ought never to dwell with trifles. And the turtle-dove murmuring shows the thankless slander of fault-finding, and is rightly expelled the house.

"Don't mutter against me, sitting by one in one place, another in another." [10]

The swallow too, which suggests the fable of Pandion, seeing it is right to detest the incidents reported of it, some of which we hear Tereus suffered, and some of which he inflicted. It pursues also the musical grasshoppers, whence he who is a persecutor of the word ought to be driven away.

" By sceptre-bearing Here, whose eye surveys Olympus,
I have a rusty closet for tongues, "

says Poetry. Æschylus also says : —

" But, I, too, have a key as a guard on my tongue."

Again Pythagoras commanded, "When the pot is lifted off the fire, not to leave its mark in the ashes, but to scatter them ;" and " people on getting up from bed, to shake the bed-clothes." For he intimated that it was necessary not only to efface the mark, but not to leave even a trace of anger ; and that on its ceasing to boil, it was to be composed, and all memory of injury to be wiped out. " And let not the sun," says the Scripture, " go down upon your wrath." [11] And he that said, " Thou shalt not desire," [12] took away all memory of wrong ; for wrath is found

---

1 Ps. lxxviii. 1, 2.
2 1 Cor. ii. 6-8.
3 1 Cor. ii. 9, 10.
4 1 Cor. ii. 14.
5 [See cap. i. p. 444, note 6, *supra*.]
6 1 Cor. iii. 1-3.

7 1 Cor. iii. 10-13.
8 Rom. i. 11.
9 Jer. viii. 6.
10 *Iliad*, IX. 311.
11 Eph. iv. 26.
12 Ex. xx. 17.

to be the impulse of concupiscence in a mild soul, especially seeking irrational revenge. In the same way "the bed is ordered to be shaken up," so that there may be no recollection of effusion in sleep,[1] or sleep in the day-time; nor, besides, of pleasure during the night. And he intimated that the vision of the dark ought to be dissipated speedily by the light of truth. "Be angry, and sin not," says David, teaching us that we ought not to assent to the impression, and not to follow it up by action, and so confirm wrath.

Again, "Don't sail on land" is a Pythagorean saw, and shows that taxes and similar contracts, being troublesome and fluctuating, ought to be declined. Wherefore also the Word says that the tax-gatherers shall be saved with difficulty.[2]

And again, "Don't wear a ring, nor engrave on it the images of the gods," enjoins Pythagoras; as Moses ages before enacted expressly, that neither a graven, nor molten, nor moulded, nor painted likeness should be made; so that we may not cleave to things of sense, but pass to intellectual objects: for familiarity with the sight disparages the reverence of what is divine; and to worship that which is immaterial by matter, is to dishonour it by sense.[3] Wherefore the wisest of the Egyptian priests decided that the temple of Athene should be hypæthral, just as the Hebrews constructed the temple without an image. And some, in worshipping God, make a representation of heaven containing the stars; and so worship, although Scripture says, "Let Us make man in Our image and likeness."[4] I think it worth while also to adduce the utterance of Eurysus the Pythagorean, which is as follows, who in his book *On Fortune*, having said that the "Creator, on making man, took Himself as an exemplar," added, "And the body is like the other things, as being made of the same material, and fashioned by the best workman, who wrought it, taking Himself as the archetype." And, in fine, Pythagoras and his followers, with Plato also, and most of the other philosophers, were best acquainted with the Lawgiver, as may be concluded from their doctrine. And by a happy utterance of divination, not without divine help, concurring in certain prophetic declarations, and seizing the truth in portions and aspects, in terms not obscure, and not going beyond the explanation of the things, they honoured it on as certaining the appearance of relation with the truth. Whence the Hellenic philosophy is like the torch of wick which men kindle, artificially stealing the light from the sun. But on the

proclamation of the Word all that holy light shone forth. Then in houses by night the stolen light is useful; but by day the fire blazes, and all the night is illuminated by such a sun of intellectual light.

Now Pythagoras made an epitome of the statements on righteousness in Moses, when he said, "Do not step over the balance;" that is, do not transgress equality in distribution, honouring justice so.

"Which friends to friends for ever, binds,
To cities, cities — to allies, allies,
For equality is what is right for men;
But less to greater ever hostile grows,
And days of hate begin,"

as is said with poetic grace.

Wherefore the Lord says, "Take My yoke, for it is gentle and light."[5] And on the disciples, striving for the pre-eminence, He enjoins equality with simplicity, saying "that they must become as little children."[6] Likewise also the apostle writes, that "no one in Christ is bond or free, or Greek or Jew. For the creation in Christ Jesus is new, is equality, free of strife — not grasping — just." For envy, and jealousy, and bitterness, stand without the divine choir.

Thus also those skilled in the mysteries forbid "to eat the heart;" teaching that we ought not to gnaw and consume the soul by idleness and by vexation, on account of things which happen against one's wishes. Wretched, accordingly, was the man whom Homer also says, wandering alone, "ate his own heart." But again, seeing the Gospel supposes two ways — the apostles, too, similarly with all the prophets — and seeing they call that one "narrow and confined" which is circumscribed according to the commandments and prohibitions, and the opposite one, which leads to perdition, "broad and roomy," open to pleasures and wrath, and say, "Blessed is the man who walketh not in the counsel of the ungodly, and standeth not in the way of sinners."[7] Hence also comes the fable of Prodicus of Ceus about Virtue and Vice.[8] And Pythagoras shrinks not from prohibiting to walk on the public thoroughfares, enjoining the necessity of not following the sentiments of the many, which are crude and inconsistent. And Aristocritus, in the first book of his *Positions against Heracliodorus*, mentions a letter to this effect: "Atœeas king of the Scythians to the people of Byzantium: Do not impair my revenues in case my mares drink your water;" for the Barbarian indicated symbolically that he would make war on them. Likewise also the poet Euphorion introduces Nestor saying, —

"We have not yet wet the Achæan steeds in Simois."

---

[1] [Jude 23.]
[2] It is so said of the rich: Matt. xix. 23; Mark x. 23; Luke xviii. 24.
[3] [Against images. But see *Catechism of the Council of Trent*, part iii. cap. 2, quæst. xxiv.]
[4] Gen. i. 26.

[5] Matt. xi. 29, 30.
[6] Matt. xviii. 3.
[7] Ps. i. 1.
[8] [See *Pædagogue*, ii. 11, p. 265, *supra*.]

Therefore also the Egyptians place Sphinxes [1] before their temples, to signify that the doctrine respecting God is enigmatical and obscure; perhaps also that we ought both to love and fear the Divine Being: to love Him as gentle and benign to the pious; to fear Him as inexorably just to the impious; for the sphinx shows the image of a wild beast and of a man together.

CHAP. VI. — THE MYSTIC MEANING OF THE TABERNACLE AND ITS FURNITURE.

It were tedious to go over all the Prophets and the Law, specifying what is spoken in enigmas; for almost the whole Scripture gives its utterances in this way. It may suffice, I think, for any one possessed of intelligence, for the proof of the point in hand, to select a few examples.

Now concealment is evinced in the reference of the seven circuits around the temple, which are made mention of among the Hebrews; and the equipment on the robe, indicating by the various symbols, which had reference to visible objects, the agreement which from heaven reaches down to earth. And the covering and the veil were variegated with blue, and purple, and scarlet, and linen. And so it was suggested that the nature of the elements contained the revelation of God. For purple is from water, linen from the earth; blue, being dark, is like the air, as scarlet is like fire.

In the midst of the covering and veil, where the priests were allowed to enter, was situated the altar of incense, the symbol of the earth placed in the middle of this universe; and from it came the fumes of incense. And that place intermediate between the inner veil, where the high priest alone, on prescribed days, was permitted to enter, and the external court which surrounded it — free to all the Hebrews — was, they say, the middlemost point of heaven and earth. But others say it was the symbol of the intellectual world, and that of sense. The covering, then, the barrier of popular unbelief, was stretched in front of the five pillars, keeping back those in the surrounding space.

So very mystically the five loaves are broken by the Saviour, and fill the crowd of the listeners. For great is the crowd that keep to the things of sense, as if they were the only things in existence. "Cast your eyes round, and see," says Plato, "that none of the uninitiated listen." Such are they who think that nothing else exists, but what they can hold tight with their hands; but do not admit as in the department of existence, actions and processes of generation, and the whole of the unseen. For such are those who keep by the five senses. But the knowledge

of God is a thing inaccessible to the ears and like organs of this kind of people. Hence the Son is said to be the Father's face, being the revealer of the Father's character to the five senses by clothing Himself with flesh. "But if we live in the Spirit, let us also walk in the Spirit." [2] "For we walk by faith, not by sight," [3] the noble apostle says. Within the veil, then, is concealed the sacerdotal service; and it keeps those engaged in it far from those without.

Again, there is the veil of the entrance into the holy of holies. Four pillars there are, the sign of the sacred tetrad of the ancient covenants.[4] Further, the mystic name of four letters which was affixed to those alone to whom the adytum was accessible, is called Jave, which is interpreted, "Who is and shall be." The name of God, too, among the Greeks contains four letters.

Now the Lord, having come alone into the intellectual world, enters by His sufferings, introduced into the knowledge of the Ineffable, ascending above every name which is known by sound. The lamp, too, was placed to the south of the altar of incense; and by it were shown the motions of the seven planets, that perform their revolutions towards the south. For three branches rose on either side of the lamp, and lights on them; since also the sun, like the lamp, set in the midst of all the planets, dispenses with a kind of divine music the light to those above and to those below.

The golden lamp conveys another enigma as a symbol of Christ, not in respect of form alone, but in his casting light, "at sundry times and divers manners," [5] on those who believe on Him and hope, and who see by means of the ministry of the First-born. And they say that the seven eyes of the Lord "are the seven spirits resting on the rod that springs from the root of Jesse." [6]

North of the altar of incense was placed a table, on which there was "the exhibition of the loaves;" for the most nourishing of the winds are those of the north. And thus are signified certain seats of churches conspiring so as to form one body and one assemblage.[7]

And the things recorded of the sacred ark signify the properties of the world of thought, which is hidden and closed to the many.

And those golden figures, each of them with six wings, signify either the two bears, as some will have it, or rather the two hemispheres. And the name cherubim meant "much knowledge." But both together have twelve wings, and by the zodiac and time, which moves on it, point out

---

[1] [Rawlinson, *Herod.*, ii. 223.]

[2] Gal. v. 25.
[3] 2 Cor. v. 7.
[4] [Elucidation III.]
[5] Heb. i. 1.
[6] Rev. v. 6: Isa. xi. 10. [Elucidation IV.]
[7] ["The communion of saints."]

the world of sense. It is of them, I think, that Tragedy, discoursing of Nature, says : —

> " Unwearied Time circles full in perennial flow,
>   Producing itself. And the twin-bears
> On the swift wandering motions of their wings,
>   Keep the Atlantean pole."

And Atlas,[1] the unsuffering pole, may mean the fixed sphere, or better perhaps, motionless eternity. But I think it better to regard the ark, so called from the Hebrew word Thebotha,[2] as signifying something else. It is interpreted, *one instead of one in all places*. Whether, then, it is the eighth region and the world of thought, or God, all-embracing, and without shape, and invisible, that is indicated, we may for the present defer saying. But it signifies the repose which dwells with the adoring spirits, which are meant by the cherubim.

For He who prohibited the making of a graven image, would never Himself have made an image in the likeness of holy things.[3] Nor is there at all any composite thing, and creature endowed with sensation, of the sort in heaven. But the face is a symbol of the rational soul, and the wings are the lofty ministers and energies of powers right and left ; and the voice is delightsome glory in ceaseless contemplation. Let it suffice that the mystic interpretation has advanced so far.

Now the high priest's robe is the symbol of the world of sense. The seven planets are represented by the five stones and the two carbuncles, for Saturn and the Moon. The former is southern, and moist, and earthy, and heavy ; the latter aerial, whence she is called by some Artemis, as if Aerotomos (cutting the air) ; and the air is cloudy. And co-operating as they did in the production of things here below, those that by Divine Providence are set over the planets are rightly represented as placed on the breast and shoulders ; and by them was the work of creation, the first week. And the breast is the seat of the heart and soul.

Differently, the stones might be the various phases of salvation ; some occupying the upper, some the lower parts of the entire body saved. The three hundred and sixty bells, suspended from the robe, is the space of a year, " the acceptable year of the Lord," proclaiming and resounding the stupendous manifestation of the Saviour. Further, the broad gold mitre indicates the regal power of the Lord, " since the Head of the Church " is the Saviour.[4] The mitre that is on it [i.e., the head] is, then, a sign of most princely rule ; and otherwise we have heard it

said, " The Head of Christ is the God and Father of our Lord Jesus Christ."[5] Moreover, there was the breastplate, comprising the ephod, which is the symbol of work, and the oracle (λογίον) ; and this indicated the Word (λόγος) by which it was framed, and is the symbol of heaven, made by the Word,[6] and subjected to Christ, the Head of all things, inasmuch as it moves in the same way, and in a like manner. The luminous emerald stones, therefore, in the ephod, signify the sun and moon, the helpers of nature. The shoulder, I take it, is the commencement of the hand.

The twelve stones, set in four rows on the breast, describe for us the circle of the zodiac, in the four changes of the year. It was otherwise requisite that the law and the prophets should be placed beneath the Lord's head, because in both Testaments mention is made of the righteous. For were we to say that the apostles were at once prophets and righteous, we should say well, " since one and the self-same Holy Spirit works in all."[7] And as the Lord is above the whole world, yea, above the world of thought, so the name engraven on the plate has been regarded to signify, above all rule and authority ; and it was inscribed with reference both to the written commandments and the manifestation to sense. And it is the name of God that is expressed ; since, as the Son sees the goodness of the Father, God the Saviour works, being called the first principle of all things, which was imaged forth from the invisible God first, and before the ages, and which fashioned all things which came into being after itself. Nay more, the oracle[8] exhibits the prophecy which by the Word cries and preaches, and the judgment that is to come ; since it is the same Word which prophesies, and judges, and discriminates all things.

And they say that the robe prophesied the ministry in the flesh, by which He was seen in closer relation to the world. So the high priest, putting off his consecrated robe (the universe, and the creation in the universe, were consecrated by Him assenting that, what was made, was good), washes himself, and puts on the other tunic — a holy-of holies one, so to speak — which is to accompany him into the adytum ; exhibiting, as seems to me, the Levite and Gnostic, as the chief of other priests (those bathed in water, and clothed in faith alone, and expecting their own individual abode), himself distinguishing the objects of the intellect from the things of sense, rising above other priests,

---

[1] 'Α — τλας, unsuffering.
[2] The Chaldaic אָרְבוֹתָא. The Hebrew is תֵּבָה, Sept. κιβωτός, Vulg. *arca*.
[3] [Elucidation V.]
[4] Eph. v. 23.

[5] 1 Cor. xi. 3; 2 Cor. xi. 31.
[6] And the whole place is very correctly called the Logeum (λογεῖον), since everything in heaven has been created and arranged in accordance with right reason (λόγοις) and proportion (Philo, vol. iii. p. 195, Bohn's translation).
[7] 1 Cor. xii. 11.
[8] i.e., the oracular breastplate.

hasting to the entrance to the world of ideas, to wash himself from the things here below, not in water, as formerly one was cleansed on being enrolled in the tribe of Levi. But purified already by the gnostic Word in his whole heart, and thoroughly regulated, and having improved that mode of life received from the priest to the highest pitch, being quite sanctified both in word and life, and having put on the bright array of glory, and received the ineffable inheritance of that spiritual and perfect man, "which eye hath not seen and ear hath not heard, and it hath not entered into the heart of man ; " and having become son and friend, he is now replenished with insatiable contemplation face to face. For there is nothing like hearing the Word Himself, who by means of the Scripture inspires fuller intelligence. For so it is said, " And he shall put off the linen robe, which he had put on when he entered into the holy place ; and shall lay it aside there, and wash his body in water in the holy place, and put on his robe." [1] But in one way, as I think, the Lord puts off and puts on by descending into the region of sense ; and in another, he who through Him has believed puts off and puts on, as the apostle intimated, the consecrated stole. Thence, after the image of the Lord, the worthiest were chosen from the sacred tribes to be high priests, and those elected to the kingly office and to prophecy were anointed.

CHAP. VII. — THE EGYPTIAN SYMBOLS AND ENIGMAS OF SACRED THINGS.

Whence also the Egyptians did not entrust the mysteries they possessed to all and sundry, and did not divulge the knowledge of divine things to the profane ; but only to those destined to ascend the throne, and those of the priests that were judged the worthiest, from their nurture, culture, and birth. Similar, then, to the Hebrew enigmas in respect to concealment, are those of the Egyptians also. Of the Egyptians, some show the sun on a ship, others on a crocodile. And they signify hereby, that the sun, making a passage through the delicious and moist air, generates time ; which is symbolized by the crocodile in some other sacerdotal account. Further, at Diospolis in Egypt, on the temple called Pylon, there was figured a boy as the symbol of production, and an old man as that of decay. A hawk, on the other hand, was the symbol of God, as a fish of hate ; and, according to a different symbolism, the crocodile of impudence. The whole symbol, then, when put together, appears to teach this : "Oh ye who are born and die, God hates impudence."

And there are those who fashion ears and eyes of costly material, and consecrate them, dedicating them in the temples to the gods — by this plainly indicating that God sees and hears all things. Besides, the lion is with them the symbol of strength and prowess, as the ox clearly is of the earth itself, and husbandry and food, and the horse of fortitude and confidence ; while, on the other hand, the sphinx, of strength combined with intelligence — as it had a body entirely that of a lion, and the face of a man. Similarly to these, to indicate intelligence, and memory, and power, and art, a man is sculptured in the temples. And in what is called among them the Komasiæ of the gods, they carry about golden images — two dogs, one hawk, and one ibis ; and the four figures of the images they call four letters. For the dogs are symbols of the two hemispheres, which, as it were, go round and keep watch ; the hawk, of the sun, for it is fiery and destructive (so they attribute pestilential diseases to the sun) ; the ibis, of the moon, likening the shady parts to that which is dark in plumage, and the luminous to the light. And some will have it that by the dogs are meant the tropics, which guard and watch the sun's passage to the south and north. The hawk signifies the equinoctial line, which is high and parched with heat, as the ibis the ecliptic. For the ibis seems, above other animals, to have furnished to the Egyptians the first rudiments of the invention of number and measure, as the oblique line did of circles.

CHAP. VIII. — THE USE OF THE SYMBOLIC STYLE BY POETS AND PHILOSOPHERS.

But it was not only the most highly intellectual of the Egyptians, but also such of other barbarians as prosecuted philosophy, that affected the symbolical style. They say, then, that Idanthuris king of the Scythians, as Pherecydes of Syros relates, sent to Darius, on his passing the Ister in threat of war, a symbol, instead of a letter, consisting of a mouse, a frog, a bird, a javelin, a plough. And there being a doubt in reference to them, as was to be expected, Orontopagas the Chiliarch said that they were to resign the kingdom ; taking dwellings to be meant by the mouse, waters by the frog, air by the bird, land by the plough, arms by the javelin. But Xiphodres interpreted the contrary ; for he said, " If we do not take our flight like birds, or like mice get below the earth, or like frogs beneath the water, we shall not escape their arrows ; for we are not lords of the territory."

It is said that Anacharsis the Scythian, while asleep, covered the pudenda with his left hand, and his mouth with his right, to intimate that both ought to be mastered, but that it was a greater thing to master the tongue than voluptuousness.

---

[1] Lev. xvi. 23, 24.

And why should I linger over the barbarians, when I can adduce the Greeks as exceedingly addicted to the use of the method of concealment? Androcydes the Pythagorean says the far-famed so-called Ephesian letters were of the class of symbols. For he said that ἄσκιον (shadowless) meant darkness, for it has no shadow; and κατάσκιον (shadowy) light, since it casts with its rays the shadow; and λίξ is the earth, according to an ancient appellation; and τετράς is the year, in reference to the seasons; and δαμναμενεύς is the sun, which overpowers (δαμά-ζων); and τὰ αἴσια is the true voice. And then the symbol intimates that divine things have been arranged in harmonious order — darkness to light, the sun to the year, and the earth to nature's processes of production of every sort. Also Dionysius Thrax, the grammarian, in his book, *Respecting the Exposition of the Symbolical Signification in Circles*, says expressly, "Some signified actions not by words only, but also by symbols: by words, as is the case of what are called the Delphic maxims, 'Nothing in excess,' 'Know thyself,' and the like; and by symbols, as the wheel that is turned in the temples of the gods, derived from the Egyptians, and the branches that are given to the worshippers. For the Thracian Orpheus says: —

"Whatever works of branches are a care to men on
     earth,
 Not one has one fate in the mind, but all things
 Revolve around; and it is not lawful to stand at one
     point,
 But each one keeps an equal part of the race as they
     began."

The branches either stand as the symbol of the first food, or they are that the multitude may know that fruits spring and grow universally, remaining a very long time; but that the duration of life allotted to themselves is brief. And it is on this account that they will have it that the branches are given; and perhaps also that they may know, that as these, on the other hand, are burned, so also they themselves speedily leave this life, and will become fuel for fire.

Very useful, then, is the mode of symbolic interpretation for many purposes; and it is helpful to the right theology, and to piety, and to the display of intelligence, and the practice of brevity, and the exhibition of wisdom. "For the use of symbolical speech is characteristic of the wise man," appositely remarks the grammarian Didymus, "and the explanation of what is signified by it." And indeed the most elementary instruction of children embraces the interpretation of the four elements; for it is said that the Phrygians call water Bedu, as also Orpheus says: [1] —

"And bright water is poured down, the Bedu of the
     nymphs."

Dion Thytes also seems to write similarly: —

"And taking Bedu, pour it on your hands, and turn to
     divination."

On the other hand, the comic poet, Philydeus, understands by Bedu the air, as being (Biodoros) life-giver, in the following lines: —

"I pray that I may inhale the salutary Bedu,
 Which is the most essential part of health;
 Inhale the pure, the unsullied air."

In the same opinion also concurs Neanthes of Cyzicum, who writes that the Macedonian priests invoke Bedu, which they interpret to mean *the air*, to be propitious to them and to their children. And Zaps some have ignorantly taken for fire (from ζέσιν, *boiling*); for so the sea is called, as Euphorion, in his reply to Theoridas: —

"And Zaps, destroyer of ships, wrecked it on the rocks."

And Dionysius Iambus similarly: —

"Briny Zaps moans about the maddened deep."

Similarly Cratinus the younger, the comic poet: —

"Zaps casts forth shrimps and little fishes."

And Simmias of Rhodes: —

"Parent of the Ignetes and the Telchines briny Zaps
     was born." [2]

And χθών is the earth (κεχυμένη), spread forth to bigness. And Plectron, according to some, is the sky (πόλος), according to others, it is the air, which strikes (πλήσσοντα) and moves to nature and increase, and which fills all things. But these have not read Cleanthes the philosopher, who expressly calls Plectron the sun; for darting his beams in the east, as if striking the world, he leads the light to its harmonious course. And from the sun it signifies also the rest of the stars.

And the Sphinx is not the comprehension [3] of the universe, and the revolution of the world, according to the poet Aratus; but perhaps it is the spiritual tone which pervades and holds together the universe. But it is better to regard it as the ether, which holds together and presses all things; as also Empedocles says: —

"But come now, first will I speak of the Sun, the first
     principle of all things,
 From which all, that we look upon, has sprung,
 Both earth, and billowy deep, and humid air;
 Titan and Ether too, which binds all things around."

And Apollodorus of Corcyra says that these lines were recited by Branchus the seer, when purifying the Milesians from plague; for he, sprinkling

---

2 This line has given commentators considerable trouble. Diodorus says that the Telchines — fabled sons of Ocean — were the first inhabitants of Rhodes.
3 σύνεσις. Sylburgius, with much probability, conjectures σύνδεσις, binding together.

the multitude with branches of laurel, led off the hymn somehow as follows : —

"Sing Boys Hecaergus and Hecaerga."

And the people accompanied him, saying, " Bedu,[1] Zaps, Chthon, Plectron, Sphinx, Cnaxzbi, Chthyptes, Phlegmos, Drops." Callimachus relates the story in iambics. Cnaxzbi is, by derivation, the plague, from its gnawing ($\kappa\nu\alpha\acute{\iota}\epsilon\iota\nu$) and destroying ($\delta\iota\alpha\phi\theta\epsilon\acute{\iota}\rho\epsilon\iota\nu$), and $\theta\bar{\upsilon}\psi\alpha\iota$ is to consume with a thunderbolt. Thespis the tragic poet says that something else was signified by these, writing thus : " Lo, I offer to thee a libation of white Cnaxzbi, having pressed it from the yellow nurses. Lo, to thee, O two-horned Pan, mixing Chthyptes cheese with red honey, I place it on thy sacred altars. Lo, to thee I pour as a libation the sparkling gleam of Bromius." He signifies, as I think, the soul's first milk-like nutriment of the four-and-twenty elements, after which solidified milk comes as food. And last, he teaches of the blood of the vine of the Word, the sparkling wine, the perfecting gladness of instruction. And Drops is the operating Word, which, beginning with elementary training, and advancing to the growth of the man, inflames and illumines man up to the measure of maturity.

The third is said to be a writing copy for children — $\mu\acute{\alpha}\rho\pi\tau\epsilon\varsigma$, $\sigma\phi\acute{\iota}\gamma\xi$, $\kappa\lambda\acute{\omega}\psi$, $\zeta\upsilon\nu\chi\theta\eta\delta\acute{o}\nu$. And it signifies, in my opinion, that by the arrangement of the elements and of the world, we must advance to the knowledge of what is more perfect, since eternal salvation is attained by force and toil ; for $\mu\acute{\alpha}\rho\psi\alpha\iota$ is to grasp. And the harmony of the world is meant by the Sphinx ; and $\zeta\upsilon\nu$-$\chi\theta\eta\delta\acute{o}\nu$ means difficulty ; and $\kappa\lambda\acute{\omega}\psi$ means at once the secret knowledge of the Lord and day. Well ! does not Epigenes, in his book on the Poetry of Orpheus, in exhibiting the peculiarities found in Orpheus,[2] say that by " the curved rods " ($\kappa\epsilon\rho\alpha\acute{\iota}\sigma\iota$) is meant "ploughs ; " and by the warp ($\sigma\tau\acute{\eta}\mu\omicron\sigma\iota$), the furrows ; and the woof ($\mu\acute{\iota}\tau\omicron\varsigma$) is a figurative expression for the seed ; and that the tears of Zeus signify a shower ; and that the "parts" ($\mu\omicron\hat{\iota}\rho\alpha\iota$) are, again, the phases of the moon, the thirtieth day, and the fifteenth, and the new moon, and that Orpheus accordingly calls them " white-robed," as being parts of the light? Again, that the Spring is called "flowery," from its nature ; and Night " still," on account of rest ; and the Moon " Gorgonian," on account of the face in it ; and that the time in which it is necessary to sow is called Aphrodite by the " Theologian."[3] In the same way, too, the Pythagoreans figuratively called the planets the " dogs of Persephone ; " and to the sea they applied the metaphorical appellation of " the tears of Kronus." Myriads on myriads of enigmatical utterances by both poets and philosophers are to be found ; and there are also whole books which present the mind of the writer veiled, as that of Heraclitus On Nature, who on this very account is called "Obscure." Similar to this book is the Theology of Pherecydes of Syrus ; for Euphorion the poet, and the Causes of Callimachus, and the Alexandra of Lycophron, and the like, are proposed as an exercise in exposition to all the grammarians.

It is, then, proper that the Barbarian philosophy, on which it is our business to speak, should prophecy also obscurely and by symbols, as was evinced. Such are the injunctions of Moses : " These common things, the sow, the hawk, the eagle, and the raven, are not to be eaten."[4] For the sow is the emblem of voluptuous and unclean lust of food, and lecherous and filthy licentiousness in venery, always prurient, and material, and lying in the mire, and fattening for slaughter and destruction.

Again, he commands to eat that which parts the hoof and ruminates ; "intimating," says Barnabas, "that we ought to cleave to those who fear the Lord, and meditate in their heart on that portion of the word which they have received, to those who speak and keep the Lord's statutes, to those to whom meditation is a work of gladness, and who ruminate on the word of the Lord. And what is the parted hoof? That the righteous walks in this world, and expects the holy eternity to come." Then he adds, "See how well Moses enacted. But whence could they understand or comprehend these things? We who have rightly understood speak the commandments as the Lord wished ; wherefore He circumcised our ears and hearts, that we may comprehend these things. And when he says, 'Thou shalt not eat the eagle, the hawk, the kite, and the crow ; ' he says, 'Thou shalt not adhere to or become like those men who know not how to procure for themselves subsistence by toil and sweat, but live by plunder, and lawlessly.' For the eagle indicates robbery, the hawk injustice, and the raven greed. It is also written, 'With the innocent man thou wilt be innocent, and with the chosen choice, and with the perverse thou shalt pervert.'[5] It is incumbent on us to cleave to the saints, because they that cleave to them shall be sanctified."[6]

Thence Theognis writes : —

"For from the good you will learn good things ;
  But if you mix with the bad, you will destroy any mind
  you may have."

---

[1] Βέδυ, Ζάψ, Χθών, Πλῆκτρον, Σφίγξ, Κναξζβί, Χθύπτης, Φλεγμός, Δρώψ. On the interpretation of which, much learning and ingenuity have been expended.
[2] [See valuable references and note on the Sibylline and Orphic sayings. Leighton, Works, vol. vi. pp. 131, 178.]
[3] Orpheus.

[4] Lev. xi. ; Deut. xiv.
[5] Ps. xviii. 25, 26.
[6] [Epistle of Barnabas, vol. i, p. 143, 144. S.]

And when, again, it is said in the ode, " For He hath triumphed gloriously : the horse and his rider hath He cast into the sea ; " [1] the many-limbed and brutal affection, lust, with the rider mounted, who gives the reins to pleasures, " He has cast into the sea," throwing them away into the disorders of the world. Thus also Plato, in his book *On the Soul*, says that the charioteer and the horse that ran off — the irrational part, which is divided in two, into anger and concupiscence — fall down ; and so the myth intimates that it was through the licentiousness of the steeds that Phaëthon was thrown out. Also in the case of Joseph : the brothers having envied this young man, who by his knowledge was possessed of uncommon foresight, stripped off the coat of many colours, and took and threw him into a pit (the pit was empty, it had no water), rejecting the good man's varied knowledge, springing from his love of instruction ; or, in the exercise of the bare faith, which is according to the law, they threw him into the pit empty of water, selling him into Egypt, which was destitute of the divine word. And the pit was destitute of knowledge ; into which being thrown and stript of his knowledge, he that had become unconsciously wise, stript of knowledge, seemed like his brethren. Otherwise interpreted, the coat of many colours is lust, which takes its way into a yawning pit. " And if one open up or hew out a pit," it is said, " and do not cover it, and there fall in there a calf or ass, the owner of the pit shall pay the price in money, and give it to his neighbour ; and the dead body shall be his." [2] Here add that prophecy : " The ox knoweth his owner, and the ass his master's crib : but Israel hath not understood Me." [3] In order, then, that none of those, who have fallen in with the knowledge taught by thee, may become incapable of holding the truth, and disobey and fall away, it is said, Be thou sure in the treatment of the word, and shut up the living spring in the depth from those who approach irrationally, but reach drink to those that thirst for truth. Conceal it, then, from those who are unfit to receive the depth of knowledge, and so cover the pit. The owner of the pit, then, the Gnostic, shall himself be punished, incurring the blame of the others stumbling, and of being overwhelmed by the greatness of the word, he himself being of small capacity ; or transferring the worker into the region of speculation, and on that account dislodging him from off-hand faith. " And will pay money," rendering a reckoning, and submitting his accounts to the " omnipotent Will."

This, then, is the type of " the law and the prophets which were until John ; " [4] while he, though speaking more perspicuously as no longer prophesying, but pointing out as now present, Him, who was proclaimed symbolically from the beginning, nevertheless said, " I am not worthy to loose the latchet of the Lord's shoe." [5] For he confesses that he is not worthy to baptize so great a Power ; for it behooves those, who purify others, to free the soul from the body and its sins, as the foot from the thong. Perhaps also this signified the final exertion of the Saviour's power toward us — the immediate, I mean — that by His presence, concealed in the enigma of prophecy, inasmuch as he, by pointing out to sight Him that had been prophesied of, and indicating the Presence which had come, walking forth into the light, loosed the latchet of the oracles of the [old] economy, by unveiling the meaning of the symbols.

And the observances practised by the Romans in the case of wills have a place here ; those balances and small coins to denote justice, and freeing of slaves, and rubbing of the ears. For these observances are, that things may be transacted with justice ; and those for the dispensing of honour ; and the last, that he who happens to be near, as if a burden were imposed on him, should stand and hear and take the post of mediator.

CHAP. IX. — REASONS FOR VEILING THE TRUTH IN SYMBOLS.

But, as appears, I have, in my eagerness to establish my point, insensibly gone beyond what is requisite. For life would fail me to adduce the multitude of those who philosophize in a symbolical manner. For the sake, then, of memory and brevity, and of attracting to the truth, such are the Scriptures of the Barbarian philosophy.

For only to those who often approach them, and have given them a trial by faith and in their whole life, will they supply the real philosophy and the true theology. They also wish us to require an interpreter and guide. For so they considered, that, receiving truth at the hands of those who knew it well, we would be more earnest and less liable to deception, and those worthy of them would profit. Besides, all things that shine through a veil show the truth grander and more imposing ; as fruits shining through water, and figures through veils, which give added reflections to them. For, in addition to the fact that things unconcealed are perceived in one way, the rays of light shining round reveal defects. Since, then, we may draw several meanings, as we do from what is expressed in

---

[1] Ex. xv. 1.
[2] Ex. xxi. 33, 36.
[3] Isa. i. 3.

[4] Matt. xi. 13; Luke xvi. 16.
[5] Mark i. 7; Luke iii. 16; John i. 27.

veiled form, such being the case, the ignorant and unlearned man fails. But the Gnostior apprehends. Now, then, it is not wished that all things should be exposed indiscriminately to all and sundry, or the benefits of wisdom communicated to those who have not even in a dream been purified in soul, (for it is not allowed to hand to every chance comer what has been procured with such laborious efforts) ; nor are the mysteries of the word to be expounded to the profane.

They say, then, that Hipparchus the Pythagorean, being guilty of writing the tenets of Pythagoras in plain language, was expelled from the school, and a pillar raised for him as if he had been dead. Wherefore also in the Barbarian philosophy they call those dead who have fallen away from the dogmas, and have placed the mind in subjection to carnal passions. " For what fellowship hath righteousness and iniquity?" according to the divine apostle. " Or what communion hath light with darkness? or what concord hath Christ with Belial? or what portion hath the believer with the unbeliever?"[1] For the honours of the Olympians and of mortals lie apart. "Wherefore also go forth from the midst of them, and be separated, saith the Lord, and touch not the unclean thing ; and I will receive you, and will be to you for a Father, and ye shall be my sons and daughters."[2]

It was not only the Pythagoreans and Plato, then, that concealed many things ; but the Epicureans too say that they have things that may not be uttered, and do not allow all to peruse those writings. The Stoics also say that by the first Zeno things were written which they do not readily allow disciples to read, without their first giving proof whether or not they are genuine philosophers. And the disciples of Aristotle say that some of their treatises are esoteric, and others common and exoteric. Further, those who instituted the mysteries, being philosophers, buried their doctrines in myths, so as not to be obvious to all. Did they then, by veiling human opinions, prevent the ignorant from handling them ; and was it not more beneficial for the holy and blessed contemplation of realities to be concealed? But it was not only the tenets of the Barbarian philosophy, or the Pythagorean myths. But even those myths in Plato (in the *Republic*, that of Hero the Armenian ; and in the *Gorgias*, that of Æacus and Rhadamanthus ; and in the *Phædo*, that of Tartarus ; and in the *Protagoras*, that of Prometheus and Epimetheus ; and besides these, that of the war between the Atlantini and the Athenians in the Atlanticum) are to be expounded allegorically, not absolutely in all their expressions, but in those which ex-

press the general sense. And these we shall find indicated by symbols under the veil of allegory. Also the association of Pythagoras, and the twofold intercourse with the associates which designates the majority, hearers (ἀκουσματικοί), and the others that have a genuine attachment to philosophy, disciples (μαθηματικοί), yet signified that something was spoken to the multitude, and something concealed from them. Perchance, too, the twofold species of the Peripatetic teaching — that called probable, and that called knowable — came very near the distinction between opinion on the one hand, and glory and truth on the other.

" To win the flowers of fair renown from men,
    Be not induced to speak aught more than right."

The Ionic muses accordingly expressly say, "That the majority of people, wise in their own estimation, follow minstrels and make use of laws, knowing that many are bad, few good ; but that the best pursue glory : for the best make choice of the everlasting glory of men above all. But the multitude cram themselves like brutes, measuring happiness by the belly and the pudenda, and the basest things in us." And the great Parmenides of Elea is introduced describing thus the teaching of the two ways : —

" The one is the dauntless heart of convincing truth ;
    The other is in the opinions of men, in whom is no
    true faith."

CHAP. X. — THE OPINION OF THE APOSTLES ON VEILING THE MYSTERIES OF THE FAITH.

Rightly, therefore, the divine apostle says, " By revelation the mystery was made known to me (as I wrote before in brief, in accordance with which, when ye read, ye may understand my knowledge in the mystery of Christ), which in other ages was not made known to the sons of men, as it is now revealed to His holy apostles and prophets."[3] For there is an instruction of the perfect, of which, writing to the Colossians, he says, " We cease not to pray for you, and beseech that ye may be filled with the knowledge of His will in all wisdom and spiritual understanding ; that ye may walk worthy of the Lord to all pleasing ; being fruitful in every good work, and increasing in the knowledge of God ; strengthened with all might according to the glory of His power."[4] And again he says, "According to the disposition of the grace of God which is given me, that ye may fulfil the word of God ; the mystery which has been hid from ages and generations, which now is manifested to His saints : to whom God wished to make known what is the riches of the glory of this mystery among the nations."[5] So that, on the one hand, then, are

---

[1] 2 Cor. vi. 14, 15.
[2] 2 Cor. vi. 17, 18.

[3] Eph. iii. 3-5.
[4] Col. i. 9-11.
[5] Col. i. 25-27.

the mysteries which were hid till the time of the apostles, and were delivered by them as they received from the Lord, and, concealed in the Old Testament, were manifested to the saints. And, on the other hand, there is "the riches of the glory of the mystery in the Gentiles," which is faith and hope in Christ; which in another place he has called the "foundation."[1] And again, as if in eagerness to divulge this knowledge, he thus writes: "Warning every man in all wisdom, that we may present every man (the whole man) perfect in Christ;" not every man simply, since no one would be unbelieving. Nor does he call every man who believes in Christ perfect; but he[2] says all the man, as if he said the whole man, as if purified in body and soul. For that the knowledge does not appertain to all, he expressly adds: "Being knit together in love, and unto all the riches of the full assurance of knowledge, to the acknowledgment of the mystery of God in Christ, in whom are hid all the treasures of wisdom and of knowledge."[3] "Continue in prayer, watching therein with thanksgiving."[4] And thanksgiving has place not for the soul and spiritual blessings alone, but also for the body, and for the good things of the body. And he still more clearly reveals that knowledge belongs not to all, by adding: "Praying at the same time for you, that God would open to us a door to speak the mystery of Christ, for which I am bound; that I may make it known as I ought to speak."[5] For there were certainly, among the Hebrews, some things delivered unwritten. "For when ye ought to be teachers for the time," it is said, as if they had grown old in the Old Testament, "ye have again need that one teach you which be the first principles of the oracles of God; and are become such as have need of milk, and not of solid food. For every one that partaketh of milk is unskilful in the word of righteousness; for he is a babe, being instructed with the first lessons. But solid food belongs to those who are of full age, who by reason of use have their senses exercised so as to distinguish between good and evil. Wherefore, leaving the first principles of the doctrine of Christ, let us go on to perfection."[6]

Barnabas, too, who in person preached the word along with the apostle in the ministry of the Gentiles, says, "I write to you most simply, that ye may understand." Then below, exhibiting already a clearer trace of gnostic tradition, he says, "What says the other prophet Moses to them? Lo, thus saith the Lord God, Enter ye into the good land which the Lord God sware,

the God of Abraham, and Isaac, and Jacob; and ye received for an inheritance that land, flowing with milk and honey.[7] What says knowledge? Learn, hope, it says, in Jesus, who is to be manifested to you in the flesh. For man is the suffering land; for from the face of the ground was the formation of Adam. What, then, does it say in reference to the good land, flowing with milk and honey? Blessed be our Lord, brethren, who has put into our hearts wisdom, and the understanding of His secrets. For the prophet says, "Who shall understand the Lord's parable but the wise and understanding, and he that loves his Lord?" It is but for few to comprehend these things. For it is not in the way of envy that the Lord announced in a Gospel, "My mystery is to me, and to the sons of my house;" placing the election in safety, and beyond anxiety; so that the things pertaining to what it has chosen and taken may be above the reach of envy. For he who has not the knowledge of good is wicked: for there is one good, the Father; and to be ignorant of the Father is death, as to know Him is eternal life, through participation in the power of the incorrupt One. And to be incorruptible is to participate in divinity; but revolt from the knowledge of God brings corruption. Again the prophet says: "And I will give thee treasures, concealed, dark, unseen; that they may know that I am the LORD."[8] Similarly David sings: "For, lo, Thou hast loved truth; the obscure and hidden things of wisdom hast Thou showed me."[9] "Day utters speech to day"[10] (what is clearly written), "and night to night proclaims knowledge" (which is hidden in a mystic veil); "and there are no words or utterances whose voices shall not be heard" by God, who said, "Shall one do what is secret, and I shall not see him?"

Wherefore instruction, which reveals hidden things, is called illumination, as it is the teacher only who uncovers the lid of the ark, contrary to what the poets say, that "Zeus stops up the jar of good things, but opens that of evil." "For I know," says the apostle, "that when I come to you, I shall come in the fulness of the blessing of Christ;"[11] designating the spiritual gift, and the gnostic communication, which being present he desires to impart to them present as "the fulness of Christ, according to the revelation of the mystery sealed in the ages of eternity, but now manifested by the prophetic Scriptures, according to the command of the eternal God, made known to all the nations, in order to the obedience of faith," that is, those

---

1 Col. i. 27.
2 [Elucidation VI.]
3 Col. ii. 2, 3.
4 Col. iv. 2.
5 Col. iv. 3, 4.
6 Heb. v. 12, 13, 14, vi. 1.

7 [Ex. xxxiii. 1; Lev. xx. 24. S.]
8 Isa. xlv. 3.
9 Ps. li. 6, Sept.
10 Ps. xix. 2, 3.
11 Rom. xv. 29.

of the nations who believe that it is. But only to a few of them is shown what those things are which are contained in the mystery.

Rightly then, Plato, in the Epistles, treating of God, says: "We must speak in enigmas; that should the tablet come by any mischance on its leaves either by sea or land, he who reads may remain ignorant." For the God of the universe, who is above all speech, all conception, all thought, can never be committed to writing, being inexpressible even by His own power. And this too Plato showed, by saying: "Considering, then, these things, take care lest some time or other you repent on account of the present things, departing in a manner unworthy. The greatest safeguard is not to write, but learn; for it is utterly impossible that what is written will not vanish."

Akin to this is what the holy Apostle Paul says, preserving the prophetic and truly ancient secret from which the teachings that were good were derived by the Greeks: "Howbeit we speak wisdom among them who are perfect; but not the wisdom of this world, or of the princes of this world, that come to nought; but we speak the wisdom of God hidden in a mystery." [1] Then proceeding, he thus inculcates the caution against the divulging of his words to the multitude in the following terms: "And I, brethren, could not speak to you as to spiritual, but as to carnal, even to babes in Christ. I have fed you with milk, not with meat: for ye were not yet able; neither are ye now able. For ye are yet carnal." [2]

If, then, "the milk" is said by the apostle to belong to the babes, and "meat" to be the food of the full-grown, milk will be understood to be catechetical instruction — the first food, as it were, of the soul. And meat is the mystic contemplation; for this is the flesh and the blood of the Word, that is, the comprehension of the divine power and essence. "Taste and see that the Lord is Christ," [3] it is said. For so He imparts of Himself to those who partake of such food in a more spiritual manner; when now the soul nourishes itself, according to the truth-loving Plato. For the knowledge of the divine essence is the meat and drink of the divine Word. Wherefore also Plato says, in the second book of the *Republic*, "It is those that sacrifice not a sow, but some great and difficult sacrifice," who ought to inquire respecting God. And the apostle writes, "Christ our passover was sacrificed for us;" [4] — a sacrifice hard to procure, in truth, the Son of God consecrated for us.

CHAP. XI. — ABSTRACTION FROM MATERIAL THINGS NECESSARY IN ORDER TO ATTAIN TO THE TRUE KNOWLEDGE OF GOD.

Now the sacrifice which is acceptable to God is unswerving abstraction from the body and its passions. This is the really true piety. And is not, on this account, philosophy rightly called by Socrates the practice of Death? For he who neither employs his eyes in the exercise of thought, nor draws aught from his other senses, but with pure mind itself applies to objects, practises the true philosophy. This is, then, the import of the silence of five years prescribed by Pythagoras, which he enjoined on his disciples; that, abstracting themselves from the objects of sense, they might with the mind alone contemplate the Deity. It was from Moses that the chief of the Greeks drew these philosophical tenets.[5] For he commands holocausts to be skinned and divided into parts. For the gnostic soul must be consecrated to the light, stript of the integuments of matter, devoid of the frivolousness of the body and of all the passions, which are acquired through vain and lying opinions, and divested of the lusts of the flesh. But the most of men, clothed with what is perishable, like cockles, and rolled all round in a ball in their excesses, like hedgehogs, entertain the same ideas of the blessed and incorruptible God as of themselves. But it has escaped their notice, though they be near us, that God has bestowed on us ten thousand things in which He does not share: birth, being Himself unborn; food, He wanting nothing; and growth, He being always equal; and long life and immortality, He being immortal and incapable of growing old. Wherefore let no one imagine that hands, and feet, and mouth, and eyes, and going in and coming out, and resentments and threats, are said by the Hebrews to be attributes of God. By no means; but that certain of these appellations are used more sacredly in an allegorical sense, which, as the discourse proceeds, we shall explain at the proper time.

"Wisdom of all medicines is the Panacea," writes Callimachus in the *Epigrams*. "And one becomes wise from another, both in past times and at present," says Bacchylides in the *Pæans;* "for it is not very easy to find the portals of unutterable words." Beautifully, therefore, Isocrates writes in the *Panathenaic*, having put the question, "Who, then, are well trained?" adds, "First, those who manage well the things which occur each day, whose opinion jumps with opportunity, and is able for the most part to hit on what is beneficial; then those who behave becomingly and rightly to those who approach them, who take lightly and easily annoy-

---

[1] 1 Cor. ii. 6, 7.
[2] 1 Cor. iii. 1–3.
[3] Ps. xxxiv. 8; according to the reading Χριστός for χρηστός.
[4] 1 Cor. v. 7.

[5] [See p. 316, note 4, *supra.*]

ances and molestations offered by others, but conduct themselves as far as possible, to those with whom they have intercourse, with consummate care and moderation ; further, those who have the command of their pleasures, and are not too much overcome by misfortunes, but conduct themselves in the midst of them with manliness, and in a way worthy of the nature which we share ; fourth — and this is the greatest — those who are not corrupted by prosperity, and are not put beside themselves, or made haughty, but continue in the class of sensible people." Then he puts on the top-stone of the discourse : "Those who have the disposition of their soul well suited not to one only of these things, but to them all — those I assert to be wise and perfect men, and to possess all the virtues."

Do you see how the Greeks deify the gnostic life (though not knowing how to become acquainted with it)? And what knowledge it is, they know not even in a dream. If, then, it is agreed among us that knowledge is the food of reason, "blessed truly are they," according to the Scripture, "who hunger and thirst after truth : for they shall be filled" with everlasting food. In the most wonderful harmony with these words, Euripides, the philosopher of the drama, is found in the following words, — making allusion, I know not how, at once to the Father and the Son : —

"To thee, the Lord of all, I bring
    Cakes and libations too, O Zeus,
    Or Hades would'st thou choose be called ;
    Do thou accept my offering of all fruits,
    Rare, full, poured forth."

For a whole burnt-offering and rare sacrifice for us is Christ. And that unwittingly he mentions the Saviour, he will make plain, as he adds : —

"For thou who, 'midst the heavenly gods,
    Jove's sceptre sway'st, dost also share
    The rule of those on earth."

Then he says expressly : —

"Send light to human souls that fain would know
    Whence conflicts spring, and what the root of ills,
    And of the blessed gods to whom due rites
    Of sacrifice we needs must pay, that so
    We may from troubles find repose."

It is not then without reason that in the mysteries that obtain among the Greeks, lustrations hold the first place ; as also the laver among the Barbarians. After these are the minor[1] mysteries, which have some foundation of instruction and of preliminary preparation for what is to come after ; and the great mysteries, in which nothing remains to be learned of the universe, but only to contemplate and comprehend nature and things.

We shall understand the mode of purification by confession, and that of contemplation by analysis, advancing by analysis to the first notion, beginning with the properties underlying it ; abstracting from the body its physical properties, taking away the dimension of depth, then that of breadth, and then that of length. For the point which remains is a unit, so to speak, having position ; from which if we abstract position, there is the conception of unity.

If, then, abstracting all that belongs to bodies and things called incorporeal, we cast ourselves into the greatness of Christ, and thence advance into immensity by holiness, we may reach somehow to the conception of the Almighty, knowing not what He is, but what He is not. And form and motion, or standing, or a throne, or place, or right hand or left, are not at all to be conceived as belonging to the Father of the universe, although it is so written. But what each of these means will be shown in its proper place. The First Cause is not then in space, but above both space, and time, and name, and conception.

Wherefore also Moses says, "Show Thyself to me,"[2] — intimating most clearly that God is not capable of being taught by man, or expressed in speech, but to be known only by His own power. For inquiry was obscure and dim ; but the grace of knowledge is from Him by the Son. Most clearly Solomon shall testify to us, speaking thus : "The prudence of man is not in me : but God giveth me wisdom, and I know holy things."[3] Now Moses, describing allegorically the divine prudence, called it the tree of life planted in Paradise ; which Paradise may be the world in which all things proceeding from creation grow. In it also the Word blossomed and bore fruit, being "made flesh," and gave life to those "who had tasted of His graciousness ;" since it was not without the wood of the tree that He came to our knowledge. For our life was hung on it, in order that we might believe. And Solomon again says : "She is a tree of immortality to those who take hold of her."[4] "Behold, I set before thy face life and death, to love the LORD thy God, and to walk in His ways, and hear His voice, and trust in life. But if ye transgress the statutes and the judgments which I have given you, ye shall be destroyed with destruction. For this is life, and the length of thy days, to love the LORD thy God."[5] Again : "Abraham, when he came to the place which God told him of on the third day, looking up, saw the place afar off."[6] For the

---

1 [Analogies in Bunsen, *Hippol.*, iii. 75, and notes, p. 123.]

2 Ex. xxxiii. 18.
3 Prov. xxx. 2.
4 Prov. iii. 18.
5 Deut. xxx. 15, 16, etc.
6 Gen. xxii. 3, 4.

first day is that which is constituted by the sight of good things; and the second is the soul's[1] best desire; on the third, the mind perceives spiritual things, the eyes of the understanding being opened by the Teacher who rose on the third day. The three days may be the mystery of the seal,[2] in which God is really believed. It is consequently afar off that he sees the place. For the region of God is hard to attain; which Plato called the region of ideas, having learned from Moses that it was a place which contained all things universally. But it is seen by Abraham afar off, rightly, because of his being in the realms of generation, and he is forthwith initiated by the angel. Thence says the apostle: "Now we see as through a glass, but then face to face," by those sole pure and incorporeal applications of the intellect. In reasoning, it is possible to divine respecting God, if one attempt without any of the senses, by reason, to reach what is individual; and do not quit the sphere of existences, till, rising up to the things which transcend it, he apprehends by the intellect itself that which is good, moving in the very confines of the world of thought, according to Plato.

Again, Moses, not allowing altars and temples to be constructed in many places, but raising one temple of God, announced that the world was only-begotten, as Basilides says, and that God is one, as does not as yet appear to Basilides. And since the gnostic Moses does not circumscribe within space Him that cannot be circumscribed, he set up no image in the temple to be worshipped; showing that God was invisible, and incapable of being circumscribed; and somehow leading the Hebrews to the conception of God by the honour for His name in the temple. Further, the Word, prohibiting the constructing of temples and all sacrifices, intimates that the Almighty is not contained in anything, by what He says: "What house will ye build to Me? saith the Lord. Heaven is my throne,"[3] and so on. Similarly respecting sacrifices: "I do not desire the blood of bulls and the fat of lambs,"[4] and what the Holy Spirit by the prophet in the sequel forbids.

Most excellently, therefore, Euripides accords with these, when he writes:—

"What house constructed by the workmen's hands,
With folds of walls, can clothe the shape divine?"

And of sacrifices he thus speaks:—

"For God needs nought, if He is truly God.
These of the minstrels are the wretched myths."

"For it was not from need that God made the world; that He might reap honours from men and the other gods and demons, winning a kind of revenue from creation, and from us, fumes, and from the gods and demons, their proper ministries," says Plato. Most instructively, therefore, says Paul in the Acts of the Apostles: "The God that made the world, and all things in it, being the Lord of heaven and earth, dwelleth not in temples made with hands; neither is worshipped by men's hands, as if He needed anything; seeing that it is He Himself that giveth to all breath, and life, and all things."[5] And Zeno, the founder of the Stoic sect, says in this book of the *Republic*, "that we ought to make neither temples nor images; for that no work is worthy of the gods." And he was not afraid to write in these very words: "There will be no need to build temples. For a temple is not worth much, and ought not to be regarded as holy. For nothing is worth much, and holy, which is the work of builders and mechanics." Rightly, therefore, Plato too, recognising the world as God's temple, pointed out to the citizens a spot in the city where their idols were to be laid up. "Let not, then, any one again," he says, "consecrate temples to the gods. For gold and silver in other states, in the case of private individuals and in the temples, is an invidious possession; and ivory, a body which has abandoned the life, is not a sacred votive offering; and steel and brass are the instruments of wars; but whatever one wishes to dedicate, let it be wood of one tree, as also stone for common temples." Rightly, then, in the great Epistle he says: "For it is not capable of expression, like other branches of study. But as the result of great intimacy with this subject, and living with it, a sudden light, like that kindled by a coruscating fire, arising in the soul, feeds itself." Are not these statements like those of Zephaniah the prophet? "And the Spirit of the Lord took me, and brought me up to the fifth heaven, and I beheld angels called Lords; and their diadem was set on in the Holy Spirit; and each of them had a throne sevenfold brighter than the light of the rising sun; and they dwelt in temples of salvation, and hymned the ineffable, Most High God."[6]

CHAP. XII.— GOD CANNOT BE EMBRACED IN WORDS OR BY THE MIND.

"For both is it a difficult task to discover the Father and Maker of this universe; and having found Him, it is impossible to declare Him to all. For this is by no means capable of expression, like the other subjects of instruction," says the truth-loving Plato. For he that had heard right well that the all-wise Moses, ascending the mount for holy contemplation, to the summit of

---

[1] Or, "the desire of a very good soul," according to the text which reads Ἡ ψυχῆς ἀρίστης. The other reading is ἀρίστη.
[2] Baptism. [Into the Triad.]
[3] Isa. lxvi. 1.
[4] Ps. l. 13.

[5] Acts xvii. 24, 25.
[6] From some apocryphal writing.

intellectual objects, necessarily commands that the whole people do not accompany him. And when the Scripture says, "Moses entered into the thick darkness where God was," this shows to those capable of understanding, that God is invisible and beyond expression by words. And "the darkness"—which is, in truth, the unbelief and ignorance of the multitude—obstructs the gleam of truth. And again Orpheus, the theologian, aided from this quarter, says:—

"One is perfect in himself, and all things are made the progeny of one,"

or, "are born;" for so also is it written. He adds:—

"Him
No one of mortals has seen, but He sees all."

And he adds more clearly:—

"Him see I not, for round about, a cloud
Has settled; for in mortal eyes are small,
And mortal pupils—only flesh and bones grow there."

To these statements the apostle will testify: "I know a man in Christ, caught up into the third heaven, and thence into Paradise, who heard unutterable words which it is not lawful for a man to speak,"—intimating thus the impossibility of expressing God, and indicating that what is divine is unutterable by human [1] power; if, indeed, he begins to speak above the third heaven, as it is lawful to initiate the elect souls in the mysteries there. For I know what is in Plato (for the examples from the barbarian philosophy, which are many, are suggested now by the composition which, in accordance with promises previously given, waits the suitable time). For doubting, in *Timæus*, whether we ought to regard several worlds as to be understood by many heavens, or this one, he makes no distinction in the names, calling the world and heaven by the same name. But the words of the statement are as follows: "Whether, then, have we rightly spoken of one heaven, or of many and infinite? It were more correct to say one, if indeed it was created according to the model." Further, in the Epistle of the Romans to the Corinthians [2] it is written, "An ocean illimitable by men and the worlds after it." Consequently, therefore, the noble apostle exclaims, "Oh the depth of the riches both of the wisdom and the knowledge of God!" [3]

And was it not this which the prophet meant, when he ordered unleavened cakes [4] to be made, intimating that the truly sacred mystic word, respecting the unbegotten and His powers, ought to be concealed? In confirmation of these things, in the Epistle to the Corinthians the apostle plainly says: "Howbeit we speak wisdom among those who are perfect, but not the wisdom of this world, or of the princes of this world, that come to nought. But we speak the wisdom of God hidden in a mystery." [5] And again in another place he says: "To the acknowledgment of the mystery of God in Christ, in whom are hid all the treasures of wisdom and knowledge." [6] These things the Saviour Himself seals when He says: "To you it is given to know the mysteries of the kingdom of heaven." [7] And again the Gospel says that the Saviour spake to the apostles the word in a mystery. For prophecy says of Him: "He will open His mouth in parables, and will utter things kept secret from the foundation of the world." [8] And now, by the parable of the leaven, the Lord shows concealment; for He says, "The kingdom of heaven is like leaven, which a woman took and hid in three measures of meal, till the whole was leavened." [9] For the tripartite soul is saved by obedience, through the spiritual power hidden in it by faith; or because the power of the word which is given to us, being strong [10] and powerful, draws to itself secretly and invisibly every one who receives it, and keeps it within himself, and brings his whole system into unity.

Accordingly Solon has written most wisely respecting God thus:—

"It is most difficult to apprehend the mind's invisible measure
Which alone holds the boundaries of all things."

For "the divine," says the poet of Agrigentum, [11]—

"Is not capable of being approached with our eyes,
Or grasped with our hands; but the highway
Of persuasion, highest of all, leads to men's minds."

And John the apostle says: "No man hath seen God at any time. The only-begotten God, who is in the bosom of the Father, He hath declared Him," [12]—calling invisibility and ineffableness the bosom of God. Hence some have called it the Depth, as containing and embosoming all things, inaccessible and boundless.

This discourse respecting God is most difficult to handle. For since the first principle of everything is difficult to find out, the absolutely first and oldest principle, which is the cause of all other things being and having been, is difficult to exhibit. For how can that be expressed which is neither genus, nor difference, nor species, nor individual, nor number; nay more, is

---

[1] ἀγία is the reading of the text. This is with great probability supposed to be changed from ἀνη, a usual contraction for ἀνθρωπινη.
[2] [i.e., as written by St. Clement of Rome. See vol. 1, p. 10. S.]
[3] Rom. xi. 33.
[4] Alluding to Gen. xviii. 6; the word used is ἐγκρυφίαι, which Clement, following Philo, from its derivation, takes to signify occult mysteries.

[5] 1 Cor. ii. 6, 7.
[6] Col. ii. 2, 3.
[7] Matt. xiii. 11; Mark iv. 11; Luke viii. 10.
[8] Ps. lxxviii. 2.
[9] Matt. xiii. 33.
[10] According to the conjecture of Sylburgius, σύντονος is adopted for σύντομος.
[11] Empedocles.
[12] John i. 18.

neither an event, nor that to which an event happens? No one can rightly express Him wholly. For on account of His greatness He is ranked as the All, and is the Father of the universe. Nor are any parts to be predicated of Him. For the One is indivisible; wherefore also it is infinite, not considered with reference to inscrutability, but with reference to its being without dimensions, and not having a limit. And therefore it is without form and name. And if we name it, we do not do so properly, terming it either the One, or the Good, or Mind, or Absolute Being, or Father, or God, or Creator, or Lord. We speak not as supplying His name; but for want, we use good names, in order that the mind may have these as points of support, so as not to err in other respects. For each one by itself does not express God; but all together are indicative of the power of the Omnipotent. For predicates are expressed either from what belongs to things themselves, or from their mutual relation. But none of these are admissible in reference to God. Nor any more is He apprehended by the science of demonstration. For it depends on primary and better known principles. But there is nothing antecedent to the Unbegotten.

It remains that we understand, then, the Unknown, by divine grace, and by the word alone that proceeds from Him; as Luke in the Acts of the Apostles relates that Paul said, "Men of Athens, I perceive that in all things ye are too superstitious.[1] For in walking about, and beholding the objects of your worship, I found an altar on which was inscribed, To the Unknown God. Whom therefore ye ignorantly worship, Him declare I unto you."[2]

CHAP. XIII. — THE KNOWLEDGE OF GOD A DIVINE GIFT, ACCORDING TO THE PHILOSOPHERS.

Everything, then, which falls under a name, is originated, whether they will or not. Whether, then, the Father Himself draws to Himself every one who has led a pure life, and has reached the conception of the blessed and incorruptible nature; or whether the free-will which is in us, by reaching the knowledge of the good, leaps and bounds over the barriers, as the gymnasts say; yet it is not without eminent grace that the soul is winged, and soars, and is raised above the higher spheres, laying aside all that is heavy, and surrendering itself to its kindred element.

Plato, too, in Meno, says that virtue is God-given, as the following expressions show: "From this argument then, O Meno, virtue is shown to come to those, in whom it is found, by divine providence." Does it not then appear that "the gnostic disposition" which has come to all is

enigmatically called "divine providence?" And he adds more explicitly: "If, then, in this whole treatise we have investigated well, it results that virtue is neither by nature, nor is it taught, but is produced by divine providence, not without intelligence, in those in whom it is found." Wisdom which is God-given, as being the power of the Father, rouses indeed our free-will, and admits faith, and repays the application of the elect with its crowning fellowship.

And now I will adduce Plato himself, who clearly deems it fit to believe the children of God. For, discoursing on gods that are visible and born, in Timæus, he says: "But to speak of the other demons, and to know their birth, is too much for us. But we must credit those who have formerly spoken, they being the offspring of the gods, as they said, and knowing well their progenitors, although they speak without probable and necessary proofs." I do not think it possible that clearer testimony could be borne by the Greeks, that our Saviour, and those anointed to prophesy (the latter being called the sons of God, and the Lord being His own Son), are the true witnesses respecting divine things. Wherefore also they ought to be believed, being inspired, he added. And were one to say in a more tragic vein, that we ought not to believe,

"For it was not Zeus that told me these things,"

yet let him know that it was God Himself that promulgated the Scriptures by His Son. And he, who announces what is his own, is to be believed. "No one," says the Lord, "hath known the Father but the Son, and he to whom the Son shall reveal Him."[3] This, then, is to be believed, according to Plato, though it is announced and spoken "without probable and necessary proofs," but in the Old and New Testament. "For except ye believe," says the Lord, "ye shall die in your sins."[4] And again: "He that believeth hath everlasting life."[5] "Blessed are all they that put their trust in Him."[6] For trusting is more than faith. For when one has believed[7] that the Son of God is our teacher, he trusts[8] that his teaching is true. And as "instruction," according to Empedocles, "makes the mind grow," so trust in the Lord makes faith grow.

We say, then, that it is characteristic of the same persons to vilify philosophy, and run down faith, and to praise iniquity and felicitate a libidinous life. But now faith, if it is the voluntary assent of the soul, is still the doer of good things, the foundation of right conduct; and if Aristotle defines strictly when he teaches that ποιεῖν is applied to the irrational creatures and to inanimate

---

[1] [Elucidation VII.]
[2] Acts xvii. 22, 23.

[3] Matt. xi. 27; Luke x. 22.
[4] John viii. 24.
[5] John iii. 15, 16, 36, v. 24.
[6] Ps. ii. 12.
[7] The text ἐπίστηται, but the sense seems to require ἐπίστευσε.
[8] πέποιθεν has confidence.

things, while πράττειν is applicable to men only, let him correct those who say that God is the maker (ποιητής) of the universe. And what is done (πρακτόν), he says, is as good or as necessary. To do wrong, then, is not good, for no one does wrong except for some other thing; and nothing that is necessary is voluntary. To do wrong, then, is voluntary, so that it is not necessary. But the good differ especially from the bad in inclinations and good desires. For all depravity of soul is accompanied with want of restraint; and he who acts from passion, acts from want of restraint and from depravity.

I cannot help admiring in every particular that divine utterance: "Verily, verily, I say unto you, He that entereth not in by the door into the sheepfold, but climbeth up some other way, the same is a thief and a robber. But he that entereth in by the door is the shepherd of the sheep. To him the porter openeth." Then the Lord says in explanation, "I am the door of the sheep."[1] Men must then be saved by learning the truth through Christ, even if they attain philosophy. For now that is clearly shown "which was not made known to other ages, which is now revealed to the sons of men."[2] For there was always a natural manifestation of the one Almighty God, among all right-thinking men; and the most, who had not quite divested themselves of shame with respect to the truth, apprehended the eternal beneficence in divine providence. In fine, then, Xenocrates the Chalcedonian was not quite without hope that the notion of the Divinity existed even in the irrational creatures. And Democritus, though against his will, will make this avowal by the consequences of his dogmas; for he represents the same images as issuing, from the divine essence, on men and on the irrational animals.[3] Far from destitute of a divine idea is man, who, it is written in Genesis, partook of inspiration, being endowed with a purer essence than the other animate creatures. Hence the Pythagoreans say that mind comes to man by divine providence, as Plato and Aristotle avow; but we assert that the Holy Spirit inspires him who has believed. The Platonists hold that mind is an effluence of divine dispensation in the soul, and they place the soul in the body. For it is expressly said by Joel, one of the twelve prophets, "And it shall come to pass after these things, I will pour out of My Spirit on all flesh, and your sons and your daughters shall prophesy."[4] But it is not as a portion of God that the Spirit is in each of us. But how this dispensation takes place, and what the Holy Spirit is, shall be shown by us in the books on prophecy, and in those on the soul. But "incredulity is good at concealing the depths of knowledge," according to Heraclitus; "for incredulity escapes from ignorance."

CHAP. XIV. — GREEK PLAGIARISM FROM THE HEBREWS.

Let us add in completion what follows, and exhibit now with greater clearness the plagiarism of the Greeks from the Barbarian philosophy.

Now the Stoics say that God, like the soul, is essentially body and spirit. You will find all this explicitly in their writings. Do not consider at present their allegories as the gnostic truth presents them; whether they show one thing and mean another, like the dexterous athletes. Well, they say that God pervades all being; while we call Him solely Maker, and Maker by the Word. They were misled by what was said in the book of Wisdom: "He pervades and passes through all by reason of His purity;"[5] since they did not understand that this was said of Wisdom, which was the first of the creation of God.

So be it, they say. But the philosophers, the Stoics, and Plato, and Pythagoras, nay more, Aristotle the Peripatetic, suppose the existence of matter among the first principles; and not one first principle. Let them then know that what is called matter by them, is said by them to be without quality, and without form, and more daringly said by Plato to be non-existence. And does he not say very mystically, knowing that the true and real first cause is one, in these very words: "Now, then, let our opinion be so. As to the first principle or principles of the universe, or what opinion we ought to entertain about all these points, we are not now to speak, for no other cause than on account of its being difficult to explain our sentiments in accordance with the present form of discourse." But undoubtedly that prophetic expression, "Now the earth was invisible and formless," supplied them with the ground of material essence.

And the introduction of "chance" was hence suggested to Epicurus, who misapprehended the statement, "Vanity of vanities, and all is vanity." And it occurred to Aristotle to extend Providence as far as the moon from this psalm: "Lord, Thy mercy is in the heavens; and Thy truth reacheth to the clouds."[6] For the explanation of the prophetic mysteries had not yet been revealed previous to the advent of the Lord.

Punishments after death, on the other hand, and penal retribution by fire, were pilfered from the Barbarian philosophy both by all the poetic Muses and by the Hellenic philosophy. Plato,

[1] John x. 1–3. 7.
[2] Eph. iii. 5.
[3] [Elucidation VIII.]
[4] Joel ii. 28.
[5] Wisd. vii. 24.
[6] Ps. xxxvi. 5.

accordingly, in the last book of the *Republic*, says in these express terms : " Then these men fierce and fiery to look on, standing by, and hearing the sound, seized and took some aside ; and binding Aridæus and the rest hand, foot, and head, and throwing them down, and flaying them, dragged them along the way, tearing their flesh with thorns." For the fiery men are meant to signify the angels, who seize and punish the wicked. " Who maketh," it is said, " His angels spirits ; His ministers flaming fire." [1] It follows from this that the soul is immortal. For what is tortured or corrected being in a state of sensation lives, though said to suffer. Well ! Did not Plato know of the rivers of fire and the depth of the earth, and Tartarus, called by the Barbarians Gehenna, naming, as he does prophetically, [2] Cocytus, and Acheron, and Pyriphlegethon, and introducing such corrective tortures for discipline ?

But indicating " the angels," as the Scripture says, " of the little ones, and of the least, which see God," and also the oversight reaching to us exercised by the tutelary angels, [3] he shrinks not from writing, " That when all the souls have selected their several lives, according as it has fallen to their lot, they advance in order to Lachesis ; and she sends along with each one, as his guide in life, and the joint accomplisher of his purposes, the demon which he has chosen." Perhaps also the demon of Socrates suggested to him something similar.

Nay, the philosophers, having so heard from Moses, taught that the world was created. [4] And so Plato expressly said, " Whether was it that the world had no beginning of its existence, or derived its beginning from some beginning? For being visible, it is tangible ; and being tangible, it has a body." Again, when he says, " It is a difficult task to find the Maker and Father of this universe," he not only showed that the universe was created, but points out that it was generated by him as a son, and that he is called its father, as deriving its being from him alone, and springing from non-existence. The Stoics, too, hold the tenet that the world was created.

And that the devil so spoken of by the Barbarian philosophy, the prince of the demons, is a wicked spirit, Plato asserts in the tenth book of the *Laws*, in these words : " Must we not say that spirit which pervades the things that are moved on all sides, pervades also heaven ? Well, what? One or more? Several, say I, in reply for you. Let us not suppose fewer than two — that which is beneficent, and that which is able to accomplish the opposite." Similarly in the *Phædrus* he writes as follows : " Now there are other evils. But

some demon has mingled pleasure with the most things at present." Further, in the tenth book of the *Laws*, he expressly emits that apostolic sentiment, [5] " Our contest is not with flesh and blood, but principalities, with powers, with the spiritual things of those which are in heaven ; " writing thus : " For since we are agreed that heaven is full of many good beings ; but it is also full of the opposite of these, and more of these ; and as we assert such a contest is deathless, and requiring marvellous watchfulness."

Again the Barbarian philosophy knows the world of thought and the world of sense — the former archetypal, and the latter the image of that which is called the model ; and assigns the former to the Monad, as being perceived by the mind, and the world of sense to the number six. For six is called by the Pythagoreans marriage, as being the genital number ; and he places in the Monad the invisible heaven and the holy earth, and intellectual light. For " in the beginning," it is said, " God made the heaven and the earth ; and the earth was invisible." And it is added, " And God said, Let there be light ; and there was light." [6] And in the material cosmogony He creates a solid heaven (and what is solid is capable of being perceived by sense), and a visible earth, and a light that is seen. Does not Plato hence appear to have left the ideas of living creatures in the intellectual world, and to make intellectual objects into sensible species according to their genera? Rightly then Moses says, that the body which Plato calls " the earthly tabernacle " was formed of the ground, but that the rational soul was breathed by God into man's face. For there, they say, the ruling faculty is situated ; interpreting the access by the senses into the first man as the addition of the soul.

Wherefore also man is said " to have been made in [God's] image and likeness." For the image of God is the divine and royal Word, the impassible man ; and the image of the image is the human mind. And if you wish to apprehend the likeness by another name, you will find it named in Moses, a divine correspondence. For he says, " Walk after the Lord your God, and keep His commandments." [7] And I reckon all the virtuous, servants and followers of God. Hence the Stoics say that the end of philosophy is to live agreeable to nature ; and Plato, likeness to God, as we have shown in the second Miscellany. And Zeno the Stoic, borrowing from Plato, and he from the Barbarian philosophy, says that all the good are friends of one another. For Socrates says in the *Phædrus*, " that it has not been ordained that the bad should be a friend

---

1 Ps. civ. 4.
2 Eusebius reads ποιητικῶς.
3 [Guardian angels. Matt. xviii. 10.]
4 γενητόν.

5 [Compare Tayler Lewis, *Plato against the Atheists*, p. 342.]
6 Gen. i. 1-3.
7 Deut. xiii. 4.

to the bad, nor the good be not a friend to the good ; " as also he showed sufficiently in the *Lysis*, that friendship is never preserved in wickedness and vice. And the Athenian stranger similarly says, " that there is conduct pleasing and conformable to God, based on one ancient ground-principle, That like loves like, provided it be within measure. But things beyond measure are congenial neither to what is within nor what is beyond measure. Now it is the case that God is the measure to us of all things." Then proceeding, Plato[1] adds : " For every good man is like every other good man ; and so being like to God, he is liked by every good man and by God." At this point I have just recollected the following. In the end of the *Timæus* he says : " You must necessarily assimilate that which perceives to that which is perceived, according to its original nature ; and it is by so assimilating it that you attain to the end of the highest life proposed by the gods to men,[2] for the present or the future time." For those have equal power with these. He, who seeks, will not stop till he find ; and having found, he will wonder ; and wondering, he will reign ; and reigning, he will rest. And what? Were not also those expressions of Thales derived from these ? The fact that God is glorified for ever, and that He is expressly called by us the Searcher of hearts, he interprets. For Thales being asked, What is the divinity? said, What has neither beginning nor end. And on another asking, " If a man could elude the knowledge of the Divine Being while doing aught? " said, " How could he who cannot do so while thinking? "

Further, the Barbarian philosophy recognises good as alone excellent, and virtue as sufficient for happiness, when it says, " Behold, I have set before your eyes good and evil, life and death, that ye may choose life."[3] For it calls good, " life," and the choice of it excellent, and the choice of the opposite " evil." And the end of good and of life is to become a lover of God : " For this is thy life and length of days," to love that which tends to the truth. And these points are yet clearer. For the Saviour, in enjoining to love God and our neighbour, says, " that on these two commandments hang the whole law and the prophets." Such are the tenets promulgated by the Stoics ; and before these, by Socrates, in the *Phædrus*, who prays, " O Pan, and ye other gods, give me to be beautiful within." And in the *Theætetus* he says expressly, " For he that speaks well (καλῶς) is both beautiful and good." And in the *Protagoras* he avers to the companions of Protagoras that he has met with one more beautiful than Alcibiades, if indeed that which is wisest is most beautiful. For he said that virtue was the soul's beauty, and, on the contrary, that vice was the soul's deformity. Accordingly, Antipatrus the Stoic, who composed three books on the point, " That, according to Plato, only the beautiful is good," shows that, according to him, virtue is sufficient for happiness ; and adduces several other dogmas agreeing with the Stoics. And by Aristobulus, who lived in the time of Ptolemy Philadelphus, who is mentioned by the composer of the epitome of the books of the Maccabees, there were abundant books to show that the Peripatetic philosophy was derived from the law of Moses and from the other prophets. Let such be the case.

Plato plainly calls us brethren, as being of one God and one teacher, in the following words : " For ye who are in the state are entirely brethren (as we shall say to them, continuing our story). But the God who formed you, mixed gold in the composition of those of you who are fit to rule, at your birth, wherefore you are most highly honoured ; and silver in the case of those who are helpers ; and steel and brass in the case of farmers and other workers." Whence, of necessity, some embrace and love those things to which knowledge pertains ; and others matters of opinion. Perchance he prophesies of that elect nature which is bent on knowledge ; if by the supposition he makes of three natures he does not describe three polities, as some supposed : that of the Jews, the silver ; that of the Greeks, the third ; and that of the Christians, with whom has been mingled the regal gold, the Holy Spirit, the golden.[4]

And exhibiting the Christian life, he writes in the *Theætetus* in these words : " Let us now speak of the highest principles. For why should we speak of those who make an abuse of philosophy? These know neither the way to the forum, nor knew they the court or the senate-house, or any other public assembly of the state. As for laws and decrees spoken or[5] written, they neither see nor hear them. But party feelings of political associations and public meetings, and revels with musicians [occupy them] ; but they never even dream of taking part in affairs. Has any one conducted himself either well or ill in the state, or has aught evil descended to a man from his forefathers? — it escapes their attention as much as do the sands of the sea. And the man does not even know that he does not know all these things ; but in reality his body alone is situated and dwells in the state,[6] while the man himself flies, according to Pindar, beneath the earth and above the sky, astronomizing, and exploring all nature on all sides.

---

[1] The text has πάλιν: Eusebius reads Πλάτων.
[2] The text has ἀνθρώπῳ: Plato and Eusebius, ἀνθρώποις.
[3] Deut. xxx. 15, 19, 20.

[4] τὴν χρυσῆν is supplied, according to a very probable conjecture.
[5] " Spoken or " supplied from Plato and Eusebius.
[6] μόνον ἐν τῇ πόλει is here supplied from Plato. [Note in Migne.]

Again, with the Lord's saying, "Let your yea be yea, and your nay nay," may be compared the following: "But to admit a falsehood, and destroy a truth, is in nowise lawful." With the prohibition, also, against swearing agrees the saying in the tenth book of the *Laws*: "Let praise and an oath in everything be absent."

And in general, Pythagoras, and Socrates, and Plato say that they hear God's voice while closely contemplating the fabric of the universe, made and preserved unceasingly by God. For they heard Moses say, "He said, and it was done," describing the word of God as an act.

And founding on the formation of man from the dust, the philosophers constantly term the body earthy. Homer, too, does not hesitate to put the following as an imprecation: —

"But may you all become earth and water."

As Esaias says, "And trample them down as clay." And Callimachus clearly writes: —

"That was the year in which
Birds, fishes, quadrupeds,
Spoke like Prometheus' clay."

And the same again: —

"If thee Prometheus formed,
And thou art not of other clay."

Hesiod says of Pandora: —

"And bade Hephæstus, famed, with all his speed,
Knead earth with water, and man's voice and mind
Infuse."

The Stoics, accordingly, define nature to be artificial fire, advancing systematically to generation. And God and His Word are by Scripture figuratively termed fire and light. But how? Does not Homer himself, is not Homer himself, paraphrasing the retreat of the water from the land, and the clear uncovering of the dry land, when he says of Tethys and Oceanus: —

"For now for a long time they abstain from
Each other's bed and love?"[1]

Again, power in all things is by the most intellectual among the Greeks ascribed to God; Epicharmus — he was a Pythagorean — saying: —

"Nothing escapes the divine. This it behoves thee to know.
He is our observer. To God nought is impossible."

And the lyric poet: —

"And God from gloomy night
Can raise unstained light,
And can in darksome gloom obscure
The day's refulgence pure."

He alone who is able to make night during the period of day is God.

In the *Phænomena* Aratus writes thus: —

"With Zeus let us begin; whom let us ne'er,
Being men, leave unexpressed. All full of Zeus,
The streets, and throngs of men, and full the sea,
And shores, and everywhere we Zeus enjoy."

He adds: —

"For we also are
His offspring; . . . ."

that is, by creation.

"Who, bland to men,
Propitious signs displays, and to their tasks
Arouses. For these signs in heaven He fixed,
The constellations spread, and crowned the year
With stars; to show to men the seasons' tasks,
That all things may proceed in order sure.
Him ever first, Him last too, they adore:
Hail Father, marvel great — great boon to men."

And before him, Homer, framing the world in accordance with Moses on the Vulcan-wrought shield, says: —

"On it he fashioned earth, and sky, and sea,
And all the signs with which the heaven is crowned."[2]

For the Zeus celebrated in poems and prose compositions leads the mind up to God. And already, so to speak, Democritus writes, "that a few men are in the light, who stretch out their hands to that place which we Greeks now call the air. Zeus speaks all, and he hears all, and distributes and takes away, and he is king of all." And more mystically the Bœotian Pindar, being a Pythagorean, says: —

"One is the race of gods and men,
And of one mother both have breath;"

that is, of matter: and names the one creator of these things, whom he calls Father, chief artificer, who furnishes the means of advancement on to divinity, according to merit.

For I pass over Plato; he plainly, in the Epistle to Erastus and Coriscus, is seen to exhibit the Father and Son somehow or other from the Hebrew Scriptures, exhorting in these words: "In invoking by oath, with not illiterate gravity, and with culture, the sister of gravity, God the author of all, and invoking Him by oath as the Lord, the Father of the Leader, and author; whom if ye study with a truly philosophical spirit, ye shall know." And the address in the *Timæus* calls the creator, Father, speaking thus: "Ye gods of gods, of whom I am Father; and the Creator of your works." So that when he says, "Around the king of all, all things are, and because of Him are all things; and he [or that] is the cause of all good things; and around the second are the things second in order; and around the third, the third," I understand nothing else than the Holy Trinity to be meant; for the third is the Holy Spirit, and the Son is the second, by whom all things were made according to the will of the Father.[3]

---

[1] *Iliad*, xiv. 206.

[2] *Iliad*, xviii. 483.
[3] [On the Faith, see p. 444, note 6, *supra*.]

And the same, in the tenth book of the *Republic*, mentions Eros the son of Armenius, who is Zoroaster. Zoroaster, then, writes: "These were composed by Zoroaster, the son of Armenius, a Pamphylian by birth: having died in battle, and been in Hades, I learned them of the gods." This Zoroaster, Plato says, having been placed on the funeral pyre, rose again to life in twelve days. He alludes perchance to the resurrection, or perchance to the fact that the path for souls to ascension lies through the twelve signs of the zodiac; and he himself says, that the descending pathway to birth is the same. In the same way we are to understand the twelve labours of Hercules, after which the soul obtains release from this entire world.

I do not pass over Empedocles, who speaks thus physically of the renewal of all things, as consisting in a transmutation into the essence of fire, which is to take place. And most plainly of the same opinion is Heraclitus of Ephesus, who considered that there was a world everlasting, and recognised one perishable — that is, in its arrangement, not being different from the former, viewed in a certain aspect. But that he knew the imperishable world which consists of the universal essence to be everlastingly of a certain nature, he makes clear by speaking thus: "The same world of all things, neither any of the gods, nor any one of men, made. But there was, and is, and will be ever-living fire, kindled according to measure,[1] and quenched according to measure." And that he taught it to be generated and perishable, is shown by what follows: "There are transmutations of fire, — first, the sea; and of the sea the half is land, the half fiery vapour." For he says that these are the effects of power. For fire is by the Word of God, which governs all things, changed by the air into moisture, which is, as it were, the germ of cosmical change; and this he calls sea. And out of it again is produced earth, and sky, and all that they contain. How, again, they are restored and ignited, he shows clearly in these words: "The sea is diffused and measured according to the same rule which subsisted before it became earth." Similarly also respecting the other elements, the same is to be understood. The most renowned of the Stoics teach similar doctrines with him, in treating of the conflagration and the government of the world, and both the world and man properly so called, and of the continuance of our souls.

Plato, again, in the seventh book of the *Republic*, has called "the day here nocturnal," as I suppose, on account of "the world-rulers of this darkness;"[2] and the descent of the soul into the body, sleep and death, similarly with Heraclitus. And was not this announced, oracularly, of the Saviour, by the Spirit, saying by David, "I slept, and slumbered; I awoke: for the LORD will sustain me?"[3] For He not only figuratively calls the resurrection of Christ rising from sleep; but to the descent of the Lord into the flesh he also applies the figurative term sleep. The Saviour Himself enjoins, "Watch;"[4] as much as to say, "Study how to live, and endeavour to separate the soul from the body."

And the Lord's day Plato prophetically speaks of in the tenth book of the *Republic*, in these words: "And when seven days have passed to each of them in the meadow, on the eighth they are to set out and arrive in four days."[5] By the meadow is to be understood the fixed sphere, as being a mild and genial spot, and the locality of the pious; and by the seven days each motion of the seven planets, and the whole practical art which speeds to the end of rest. But after the wandering orbs the journey leads to heaven, that is, to the eighth motion and day. And he says that souls are gone on the fourth day, pointng out the passage through the four elements. But the seventh day is recognised as sacred, not by the Hebrews only, but also by the Greeks; according to which the whole world of all animals and plants revolve. Hesiod says of it: —

"The first, and fourth, and seventh day were held sacred."

And again: —

"And on the seventh the sun's resplendent orb."

And Homer: —

"And on the seventh then came the sacred day."

And: —

"The seventh was sacred."

And again: —

"It was the seventh day, and all things were accomplished."

And again: —

"And on the seventh morn we leave the stream of Acheron."

Callimachus the poet also writes: —

"It was the seventh morn, and they had all things done."

And again: —

"Among good days is the seventh day, and the seventh race."

And: —

"The seventh is among the prime, and the seventh is perfect."

[1] Μέτρα is the reading of the text, but is plainly an error for μέτρῳ, which is the reading of Eusebius.
[2] Eph. vi. 12.
[3] Ps. iii. 5.
[4] Matt. xxiv. 42, etc.
[5] [The bearing of this passage on questions of Sabbatical and Dominical observances, needs only to be indicated.]

And : —

"Now all the seven were made in starry heaven,
    In circles shining as the years appear."

The Elegies of Solon, too, intensely deify the seventh day.

And how? Is it not similar to Scripture when it says, "Let us remove the righteous man from us, because he is troublesome to us?"[1] when Plato, all but predicting the economy of salvation, says in the second book of the *Republic* as follows: "Thus he who is constituted just shall be scourged, shall be stretched on the rack, shall be bound, have his eyes put out; and at last, having suffered all evils, shall be crucified."[2]

And the Socratic Antisthenes, paraphrasing that prophetic utterance, "To whom have ye likened me? saith the Lord,"[3] says that "God is like no one; wherefore no one can come to the knowledge of Him from an image."

Xenophon too, the Athenian, utters these similar sentiments in the following words: "He who shakes all things, and is Himself immoveable, is manifestly one great and powerful. But what He is in form, appears not. No more does the sun, who wishes to shine in all directions, deem it right to permit any one to look on himself. But if one gaze on him audaciously, he loses his eyesight."

"What flesh can see with eyes the Heavenly, True,
    Immortal God, whose dwelling is the poles?
    Not even before the bright beams of the sun
    Are men, as being mortal, fit to stand,"—

the Sibyl had said before. Rightly, then, Xenophanes of Colophon, teaching that God is one and incorporeal, adds: —

"One God there is 'midst gods and men supreme;
    In form, in mind, unlike to mortal men."

And again: —

"But men have the idea that gods are born,
    And wear their clothes, and have both voice and
        shape."

And again: —

"But had the oxen or the lions hands,
    Or could with hands depict a work like men,
    Were beasts to draw the semblance of the gods,
    The horses would them like to horses sketch,
    To oxen, oxen, and their bodies make
    Of such a shape as to themselves belongs."

Let us hear, then, the lyric poet Bacchylides speaking of the divine: —

"Who to diseases dire[4] never succumb,
    And blameless are; in nought resembling men."

And also Cleanthes, the Stoic, who writes thus in a poem on the Deity:[5] —

"If you ask what is the nature of the good, listen —
    That which is regular, just, holy, pious,
    Self-governing, useful, fair, fitting,
    Grave, independent, always beneficial,
    That feels no fear or grief, profitable, painless,
    Helpful, pleasant, safe, friendly,
    Held in esteem, agreeing with itself: honourable,
    Humble, careful, meek, zealous,
    Perennial, blameless, ever-during."

And the same, tacitly vilifying the idolatry of the multitude, adds: —

"Base is every one who looks to opinion,
    With the view of deriving any good from it."

We are not, then, to think of God according to the opinion of the multitude.

"For I do not think that secretly,
    Imitating the guise of a scoundrel,
    He would go to thy bed as a man,"

says Amphion to Antiope. And Sophocles plainly writes: —

"His mother Zeus espoused,
    Not in the likeness of gold, nor covered
    With swan's plumage, as the Pleuronian girl
    He impregnated; but an out and out man."

He further proceeds, and adds: —

"And quick the adulterer stood on the bridal steps."

Then he details still more plainly the licentiousness of the fabled Zeus: —

"But he nor food nor cleansing water touched,
    But heart-stung went to bed, and that whole night
    Wantoned."

But let these be resigned to the follies of the theatre.

Heraclitus plainly says: "But of the word which is eternal men are not able to understand, both before they have heard it, and on first hearing it." And the lyrist Melanippides says in song: —

"Hear me, O Father, Wonder of men,
    Ruler of the ever-living soul."

And Parmenides the great, as Plato says in the *Sophist*, writes of God thus: —

"Very much, since unborn and indestructible He is,
    Whole, only-begotten, and immoveable, and unorigi-
        nated."

Hesiod also says: —

"For He of the immortals all is King and Lord.
    With God[6] none else in might may strive."

Nay more, Tragedy, drawing away from idols, teaches to look up to heaven. Sophocles, as Hecatæus, who composed the histories in the work about Abraham and the Egyptians, says, exclaims plainly on the stage: —

"One in very truth, God is One,
    Who made the heaven and the far-stretching earth,

---

[1] Wisd. ii. 12.
[2] [See Leighton, *Works*, vol. v. p. 62, the very rich and copious note of the editor, William West, of Nairn, Scotland. Elucidation IX.]
[3] Isa. xl. 18, 25.
[4] H. Stephanus, in his *Fragments* of Bacchylides, reads αἰκελείων (foul) instead of ἀεὶ καὶ λίαν of the text.
[5] Quoted in *Exhortation to the Heathen*, p. 192, *ante*, and is here corrected from the text there.

[6] This is quoted in *Exhortation to the Heathen*, p. 192, ch. vii. The reading varies, and it has been variously amended. Θεῷ is substituted above for σέο. Perhaps the simplest of the emendations proposed on this passage is the change of σέο into σοί, *with Thee*.

The Deep's blue billow, and the might of winds.
But of us mortals, many erring far
In heart, as solace for our woes, have raised
Images of gods — of stone, or else of brass,
Or figures wrought of gold or ivory;
And sacrifices and vain festivals
To these appointing, deem ourselves devout."

And Euripides on the stage, in tragedy, says : —

"Dost thou this lofty, boundless Ether see,
Which holds the earth around in the embrace
Of humid arms? This reckon Zeus,
And this regard as God."

And in the drama of Pirithous, the same writes those lines in tragic vein : —

"Thee, self-sprung, who on Ether's wheel
Hast universal nature spun,
Around whom Light and dusky spangled Night,
The countless host of stars, too, ceaseless dance."

For there he says that the creative mind is self-sprung. What follows applies to the universe, in which are the opposites of light and darkness. Æschylus also, the son of Euphorion, says with very great solemnity of God : —

"Ether is Zeus, Zeus earth, and Zeus the heaven;
The universe is Zeus, and all above."

I am aware that Plato assents to Heraclitus, who writes : "The one thing that is wise alone will not be expressed, and means the name of Zeus." And again, "Law is to obey the will of one." And if you wish to adduce that saying, "He that hath ears to hear, let him hear," you will find it expressed by the Ephesian [1] to the following effect : "Those that hear without understanding are like the deaf. The proverb witnesses against them, that when present they are absent."

But do you want to hear from the Greeks expressly of one first principle? Timæus the Locrian, in the work on Nature, shall testify in the following words : "There is one first principle of all things unoriginated. For were it originated, it would be no longer the first principle ; but the first principle would be that from which it originated." For this true opinion was derived from what follows : "Hear," it is said, "O Israel ; the LORD thy God is one, and Him only shalt thou serve." [2]

"Lo [3] He all sure and all unerring is,"

says the Sibyl.

Homer also manifestly mentions the Father and the Son by a happy hit of divination in the following words : —

"If Outis,[4] alone as thou art, offers thee violence,
And there is no escaping disease sent by Zeus, —
For the Cyclopes heed not Ægis-bearing Zeus." [5]

And before him Orpheus said, speaking of the point in hand : —

"Son of great Zeus, Father of Ægis-bearing Zeus."

And Xenocratês the Chalcedonian, who mentions the supreme Zeus and the inferior Zeus, leaves an indication of the Father and the Son. Homer, while representing the gods as subject to human passions, appears to know the Divine Being, whom Epicurus does not so revere. He says accordingly : —

"Why, son of Peleus, mortal as thou art,
With swift feet me pursuest, a god
Immortal? Hast thou not yet known
That I am a god?" [6]

For he shows that the Divinity cannot be captured by a mortal, or apprehended either with feet, or hands, or eyes, or by the body at all. "To whom have ye likened the Lord? or to what likeness have ye likened Him?" says the Scripture.[7] Has not the artificer made the image? or the goldsmith, melting the gold, has gilded it, and what follows.

The comic poet Epicharmus speaks in the *Republic* clearly of the Word in the following terms : —

"The life of men needs calculation and number alone,
And we live by number and calculation, for these save mortals." [8]

He then adds expressly : —

"Reason governs mortals, and alone preserves manners."

Then : —

"There is in man reasoning; and there is a divine Reason.[9]
Reason is implanted in man to provide for life and sustenance,
But divine Reason attends the arts in the case of all,
Teaching them always what it is advantageous to do.
For it was not man that discovered art, but God brought it;
And the Reason of man derives its origin from the divine Reason."

The Spirit also cries by Isaiah : "Wherefore the multitude of sacrifices? saith the LORD. I am full of holocausts of rams, and the fat of lambs and the blood of bulls I wish not ;" and a little after adds : "Wash you, and be clean. Put away wickedness from your souls," [10] and so forth.

Menander, the comic poet, writes in these very words : —

"If one by offering sacrifice, a crowd
Of bulls or kids, O Pamphilus, by Zeus.
Or such like things; by making works of art,
Garments of gold or purple, images

---

1 Heraclitus.
2 Deut. vi 4.
3 See *Exhortation*, p. 194, where for "So" read "Lo."
4 "Οὖτις, Noman, Nobody; a fallacious name assumed by Ulysses (with a primary allusion to μῆτις, μῆτις, *Odyss.*, xx. 20), to deceive Polyphemus." — LIDDELL and SCOTT. The third line is 274 of same book.
5 *Odyss.*, ix. 410.

6 *Iliad*, xxii. 8.
7 Isa. xl. 18, 25.
8 All these lines from Epicharmus : they have been rendered as amended by Grotius.
9 λόγος [or Word].
10 Isa. i 11, 16.

Of ivory or emerald, deems by these
God can be made propitious, he does err,
And has an empty mind.   For the man must prove
A man of worth, who neither maids deflowers,
Nor an adulterer is, nor steals, nor kills
For love of worldly wealth, O Pamphilus.
Nay, covet not a needle's thread.   For God
Thee sees, being near beside thee." . . . [1]

" I am a God at hand," it is said by Jeremiah,[2] " and not a God afar off.   Shall a man do aught in secret places, and I shall not see him ? "

And again Menander, paraphrasing that Scripture, " Sacrifice a sacrifice of righteousness, and trust in the Lord," [3] thus writes : —

" And not a needle even that is
Another's ever covet, dearest friend ;
For God in righteous works delights, and so
Permits him to increase his worldly wealth,
Who toils, and ploughs the land both night and day.
But sacrifice to God, and righteous be,
Shining not in bright robes, but in thy heart ;
And when thou hear'st the thunder, do not flee,
Being conscious to thyself of nought amiss,
Good sir, for thee God ever present sees." [4]

" Whilst thou art yet speaking," says the Scripture, " I will say, Lo, here I am." [5]

Again Diphilus, the comic poet, discourses as follows on the judgment : —

" Think'st thou, O Niceratus, that the dead,
Who in all kinds of luxury in life have shared,
Escape the Deity, as if forgot ?
There is an eye of justice, which sees all.
For two ways, as we deem, to Hades lead —
One for the good, the other for the bad.
But if the earth hides both for ever, then
Go plunder, steal, rob, and be turbulent.
But err not.   For in Hades judgment is,
Which God the Lord of all will execute,
Whose name too dreadful is for me to name,
Who gives to sinners length of earthly life.
If any mortal thinks, that day by day,
While doing ill, he eludes the gods' keen sight,
His thoughts are evil ; and when justice has
The leisure, he shall then detected be
So thinking.   Look, whoe'er you be that say
That there is not a God.   There is, there is.
If one, by nature evil, evil does,
Let him redeem the time ; for such as he
Shall by and by due punishment receive." [6]

And with this agrees the tragedy [7] in the following lines : —

" For there shall come, shall come [8] that point of time,
When Ether, golden-eyed, shall ope its store
Of treasured fire ; and the devouring flame,
Raging, shall burn all things on earth below,
And all above." . . .

And after a little he adds : —

" And when the whole world fades,
And vanished all the abyss of ocean's waves,
And earth of trees is bare ; and wrapt in flames,
The air no more begets the winged tribes,
Then He who all destroyed, shall all restore."

We shall find expressions similar to these also in the Orphic hymns, written as follows : —

" For having hidden all, brought them again
To gladsome light, forth from his sacred heart,
Solicitous."

And if we live throughout holily and righteously, we are happy here, and shall be happier after our departure hence ; not possessing happiness for a time, but enabled to rest in eternity.

" At the same hearth and table as the rest
Of the immortal gods, we sit all free
Of human ills, unharmed,"

says the philosophic poetry of Empedocles. And so, according to the Greeks, none is so great as to be above judgment, none so insignificant as to escape its notice.

And the same Orpheus speaks thus : —

" But to the word divine, looking, attend,
Keeping aright the heart's receptacle
Of intellect, and tread the straight path well,
And only to the world's immortal King
Direct thy gaze." [9]

And again, respecting God, saying that He was invisible, and that He was known to but one, a Chaldean by race — meaning either by this Abraham or his son — he speaks as follows : —

" But one a scion of Chaldean race ;
For he the sun's path knew right well,
And how the motion of the sphere about
The earth proceeds, in circle moving
Equally around its axis, how the winds
Their chariot guide o'er air and sea."

Then, as if paraphrasing the expression, " Heaven is my throne, and earth is my footstool," [10] he adds : —

" But in great heaven, He is seated firm
Upon a throne of gold, and 'neath His feet
The earth.   His right hand round the ocean's bound
He stretches ; and the hills' foundations shake
To the centre at His wrath, nor can endure
His mighty strength.   He all celestial is,
And all things finishes upon the earth.
He the Beginning, Middle is, and End.
But Thee I dare not speak.   In limbs
And mind I tremble.   He rules from on high."

And so forth.   For in these he indicates these prophetic utterances : " If Thou openest the heaven, trembling shall seize the mountains from Thy presence ; and they shall melt, as wax melteth before the fire ; " [11] and in Isaiah, " Who hath measured the heaven with a span, and the whole earth with His fist ? " [12]   Again, when it is said : —

---

[1] This passage, with four more lines, is quoted by Justin Martyr [De Monarchia, vol. i. p. 291, this series], and ascribed by him to Philemon.
[2] Jer. xxiii. 23, 24.
[3] Ps. iv. 5.
[4] In Justin Martyr, in the place above quoted, these lines are joined to the preceding.   They are also quoted by Eusebius, but differently arranged.   The translation adopts the arrangement of Grotius.
[5] Isa. lxv. 24.
[6] These lines are quoted by Justin (De Monarchia [vol. i. p. 291, this series]), but ascribed by him part to Philemon, part to Euripides.
[7] Ascribed by Justin to Sophocles.
[8] Adopting the reading κεῖνος instead of καινός in the text.

[9] Quoted in Exhortation, p. 193.
[10] Isa lxvi. 1.
[11] Isa. lxiv. 1, 2, xl. 12.
[12] [On the Orphica, see Lewis' Plato cont. Ath., p. 99.]

Ruler of Ether, Hades, Sea, and Land,
Who with Thy bolts Olympus' strong-built home
Dost shake. Whom demons dread, and whom the
    throng
Of gods do fear. Whom, too, the Fates obey,
Relentless though they be. O deathless One,
Our mother's Sire! whose wrath makes all things reel;
Who mov'st the winds, and shroud'st in clouds the
    world,
Broad Ether cleaving with Thy lightning gleams, —
Thine is the order 'mongst the stars, which run
As Thine unchangeable behests direct.
Before Thy burning throne the angels wait,
Much-working, charged to do all things for men.
Thy young Spring shines, all prank'd with purple
    flowers;
Thy Winter with its chilling clouds assails;
Thine Autumn noisy Bacchus distributes."

Then he adds, naming expressly the Almighty
God : —

"Deathless Immortal, capable of being
To the immortals only uttered! Come,
Greatest of gods, with strong Necessity.
Dread, invincible, great, deathless One,
Whom Ether crowns." . . .

By the expression "Sire of our Mother" (μητρο-
πάτωρ) he not only intimates creation out of
nothing, but gives occasion to those who introduce emissions of imagining a consort of the
Deity.   And he paraphrases those prophetic
Scriptures — that in Isaiah, "I am He that fixes
the thunder, and creates the wind ; whose hands
have founded the host of heaven;"[1] and that
in Moses, "Behold, behold that I am He, and
there is no god beside me : I will kill, and I will
make to live ; I will smite, and I will heal : and
there is none that shall deliver out of my hands."[2]

"And He, from good, to mortals planteth ill,
And cruel war, and tearful woes,"

according to Orpheus.
    Such also are the words of the Parian Archil-
ochus.

"O Zeus, thine is the power of heaven, and thou
Inflict'st on men things violent and wrong."[3]

Again let the Thracian Orpheus sing to us : —

"His right hand all around to ocean's bound
He stretches; and beneath His feet is earth."

These are plainly derived from the following :
"The Lord will save the inhabited cities, and
grasp the whole land in His hand like a nest;"[4]
"It is the Lord that made the earth by His
power," as saith Jeremiah, "and set up the earth
by His wisdom."[5]   Further, in addition to these,
Phocylides, who calls the angels demons, explains in the following words that some of them
are good, and others bad (for we also have
learned that some are apostate) : —

"Demons there are — some here, some there — set over
    men;
Some, on man's entrance [into life], to ward off ill."

Rightly, then, also Philemon, the comic poet
demolishes idolatry in these words : —

"Fortune is no divinity to us :
There's no such god.   But what befalls by chance
And of itself to each, is Fortune called."

And Sophocles the tragedian says : —

"Not even the gods have all things as they choose,
Excepting Zeus; for he beginning is and end."

And Orpheus : —

"One Might, the great, the flaming heaven, was
One Deity.   All things one Being were; in whom
All these revolve fire, water, and the earth."

And so forth.
    Pindar, the lyric poet, as if in Bacchic frenzy,
plainly says : —

"What is God?   The All."

And again : —

"God, who makes all mortals."

And when he says, —

"How little, being a man, dost thou expect
Wisdom for man?   'Tis hard for mortal mind
The counsels of the gods to scan; and thou
Wast of a mortal mother born,"

he drew the thought from the following : "Who
hath known the mind of the LORD, or who was
His counsellor?"[6]   Hesiod, too, agrees with
what is said above, in what he writes : —

"No prophet, sprung of men that dwell on earth,
Can know the mind of Ægis-bearing Zeus."

Similarly, then, Solon the Athenian, in the *Elegies*,
following Hesiod, writes : —

"The immortal's mind to men is quite unknown."

Again Moses, having prophesied that the woman
would bring forth in trouble and pain, on account of transgression, a poet not undistinguished
writes : —

                    "Never by day
From toil and woe shall they have rest, nor yet
By night from groans.   Sad cares the gods to men
Shall give."

Further, when Homer says, —

"The Sire himself the golden balance held,"[7]

he intimates that God is just.
    And Menander, the comic poet, in exhibiting
God, says : —

"To each man, on his birth, there is assigned
A tutelary Demon, as his life's good guide.
For that the Demon evil is, and harms
A good life, is not to be thought."

Then he adds : —

"Ἅπαντα δ' ἀγαθὸν εἶναι τὸν Θεόν,"

[1] Amos iv. 13.
[2] Deut. xxxii. 39.
[3] For οὐρανοὺς ὁρᾷς we read ἀνθρώπους (which is the reading of
Eusebius); and ὁρῆς (Sylburgius's conjecture), also from Eusebius,
instead of ἃ θέμις ἀθέμιστα.
[4] Isa. x. 14.
[5] Jer. x. 12.
[6] Isa. xl. 13.
[7] *Iliad*, viii. 69.

meaning either "that every one good is God," or, what is preferable, " that God in all things is good."

Again, Æschylus the tragedian, setting forth the power of God, does not shrink from calling Him the Highest, in these words : —

> "Place God apart from mortals; and think not
> That He is, like thyself, corporeal.
> Thou know'st Him not. Now He appears as fire,
> Dread force; as water now; and now as gloom;
> And in the beasts is dimly shadowed forth,
> In wind, and cloud, in lightning, thunder, rain ;
> And minister to Him the seas and rocks,
> Each fountain and the water's floods and streams.
> The mountains tremble, and the earth, the vast
> Abyss of sea, and towering height of hills,
> When on them looks the Sovereign's awful eye:
> Almighty is the glory of the Most High God."[1]

Does he not seem to you to paraphrase that text, "At the presence of the Lord the earth trembles?"[2] In addition to these, the most prophetic Apollo is compelled — thus testifying to the glory of God — to say of Athene, when the Medes made war against Greece, that she besought and supplicated Zeus for Attica. The oracle is as follows : —

> "Pallas cannot Olympian Zeus propitiate,
> Although with many words and sage advice she prays;
> But he will give to the devouring fire many temples of the immortals,
> Who now stand shaking with terror, and bathed in sweat;"[3]

and so forth.

Thearidas, in his book *On Nature*, writes : "There was then one really true beginning [first principle] of all that exists — one. For that Being in the beginning is one and alone."

> "Nor is there any other except the Great King,"

says Orpheus. In accordance with whom, the comic poet Diphilus says very sententiously,[4] the

> "Father of all,
> To Him alone incessant reverence pay,
> The inventor and the author of such blessings."

Rightly therefore Plato "accustoms the best natures to attain to that study which formerly we said was the highest, both to see the good and to accomplish that ascent. And this, as appears, is not the throwing of the potsherds ;[5] but the turning round of the soul from a nocturnal day to that which is a true return to that which really is, which we shall assert to be the true philosophy." Such as are partakers of this he judges[6] to belong to the golden race, when he says : "Ye are all brethren ; and those who are of the golden race are most capable of judging most accurately in every respect."[7]

The Father, then, and Maker of all things is apprehended by all things, agreeably to all, by innate power and without teaching, — things inanimate, sympathizing with the animate creation ; and of living beings some are already immortal, working in the light of day. But of those that are still mortal, some are in fear, and carried still in their mother's womb ; and others regulate themselves by their own independent reason. And of men all are Greeks and Barbarians. But no race anywhere of tillers of the soil, or nomads, and not even of dwellers in cities, can live, without being imbued with the faith of a superior being.[8] Wherefore every eastern nation, and every nation touching the western shore ; or the north, and each one towards the south,[9] — all have one and the same preconception respecting Him who hath appointed government ; since the most universal of His operations equally pervade all. Much more did the philosophers among the Greeks, devoted to investigation, starting from the Barbarian philosophy, attribute providence[10] to the "Invisible, and sole, and most powerful, and most skilful and supreme cause of all things most beautiful ;" — not knowing the inferences from these truths, unless instructed by us, and not even how God is to be known naturally ; but only, as we have already often said, by a true periphrasis.[11] Rightly therefore the apostle says, "Is He the God of the Jews only, and not also of the Greeks ?" — not only saying prophetically that of the Greeks believing Greeks would know God ;[12] but also intimating that in power the Lord is the God of all, and truly Universal King. For they know neither what He is, nor how He is Lord, and Father, and Maker, nor the rest of the system of the truth, without being taught by it. Thus also the prophetic utterances have the same force as the apostolic word. For Isaiah says, "If ye say, We trust in the LORD our God : now make an alliance with my Lord the king of the Assyrians." And he adds : "And now, was it without the LORD that we came up to this land to make war against it?"[13] And Jonah, himself a prophet, intimates the same thing in what he says : "And the shipmaster came to him, and

---

[1] These lines of Æschylus are also quoted by Justyn Martyr (*De Monarchia*, vol. i. p. 290). Dread force, ἄπλατος ὁρμή: Eusebius reads ὁρμῇ, dative. J. Langus has suggested (ἄπλαστος) uncreated; ἄπληστος (insatiate) has also been suggested.) The epithet of the text, which means primarily unapproachable, then dread or terrible, is applied by Pindar to fire.
[2] Ps. lxviii. 8. [Comp. Coleridge's *Hymn in Chamounix*.]
[3] This Pythian oracle is given by Herodotus, and is quoted also by Eusebius and Theodoret.
[4] γνωμικώτατα. Eusebius reads γενικώτατον, agreeing with πατέρα.
[5] A game in which a potsherd with a black and white side was cast on a line; and as the black or white turned up, one of the players fled and the other pursued.

[6] Eusebius has κρίνει, which we have adopted, for κρίνειν of the text.
[7] Plato, *Rep.*, book vii.
[8] [Pearson, *On the Creed*, p 47.]
[9] According to the reading in Eusebius, πᾶν ἔθνος ἐῷον πᾶν δὲ ἑσπερίων ἠόνων, βόρειόν τε καὶ τό, κ.τ.λ.
[10] Instead of πρόνοιαν, Eusebius has προνομίαν (privilege).
[11] Clement seems to mean that they knew God only in a roundabout and inaccurate way. The text has περίφασιν: but περίφρασιν, which is in Eusebius, is preferable.
[12] [See p. 379, Elucidation I., *supra*.]
[13] Isa xxxvi 7, 8, 10.

said to him, Why dost thou snore? Rise, call on thy God, that He may save us, and that we may not perish."[1] For the expression "thy God" he makes as if to one who knew Him by way of knowledge; and the expression, "that God may save us," revealed the consciousness in the minds of heathens who had applied their mind to the Ruler of all, but had not yet believed. And again the same: "And he said to them, I am the servant of the LORD; and I fear the LORD, the God of heaven." And again the same: "And he said, Let us by no means perish for the life of this man." And Malachi the prophet plainly exhibits God saying, "I will not accept sacrifice at your hands. For from the rising of the sun to its going down, My name is glorified among the Gentiles; and in every place sacrifice is offered to Me."[2] And again: "Because I am a great King, saith the LORD omnipotent; and My name is manifest among the nations." What name? The Son declaring the Father among the Greeks who have believed.

Plato in what follows gives an exhibition of free-will: "Virtue owns not a master; and in proportion as each one honours or dishonours it, in that proportion he will be a partaker of it. The blame lies in the exercise of free choice." But God is blameless. For He is never the author of evil.

"O warlike Trojans," says the lyric poet,[3] —

"High ruling Zeus, who beholds all things,
Is not the cause of great woes to mortals;
But it is in the power of all men to find
Justice, holy, pure,
Companion of order,
And of wise Themis
The sons of the blessed are ye
In finding her as your associate."

And Pindar expressly introduces also Zeus Soter, the consort of Themis, proclaiming him King, Saviour, Just, in the following lines: —

"First, prudent Themis, of celestial birth,
On golden steeds, by Ocean's rock,
The Fates brought to the stair sublime,
The shining entrance of Olympus,
Of Saviour Zeus for aye[4] to be the spouse,
And she, the Hours, gold-diademed, fair-fruited, good,
　　brought forth."[5]

He, then, who is not obedient to the truth, and is puffed up with human teaching, is wretched and miserable, according to Euripides: —

"Who these things seeing, yet apprehends not God,
But mouthing lofty themes, casts far
Perverse deceits; stubborn in which, the tongue
Its shafts discharges, about things unseen,
Devoid of sense."

Let him who wishes, then, approaching to the true instruction, learn from Parmenides the Eleatic, who promises: —

"Ethereal nature, then, and all the signs
In Ether thou shalt know, and the effects,
All viewless, of the sacred Sun's clear torch
And whence produced. The round-eyed Moon's
Revolving influences and nature thou
Shalt learn; and the ensphering heaven shalt know;
Whence sprung; and how Necessity took it
And chained so as to keep the starry bounds."

And Metrodorus, though an Epicurean, spoke thus, divinely inspired: "Remember, O Menestratus, that, being a mortal endowed with a circumscribed life, thou hast in thy soul ascended, till thou hast seen endless time, and the infinity of things; and what is to be, and what has been;" when with the blessed choir, according to Plato, we shall gaze on the blessed sight and vision; we following with Zeus, and others with other deities, if we may be permitted so to say, to receive initiation into the most blessed mystery: which we shall celebrate, ourselves being perfect and untroubled by the ills which awaited us at the end of our time; and introduced to the knowledge of perfect and tranquil visions, and contemplating them in pure sunlight; we ourselves pure, and now no longer distinguished by that, which, when carrying it about, we call the body, being bound to it like an oyster to its shell.

The Pythagoreans call heaven the Antichthon [the opposite Earth]. And in this land, it is said by Jeremiah, "I will place thee among the children, and give thee the chosen land as inheritance of God Omnipotent;"[6] and they who inherit it shall reign over the earth. Myriads on myriads of examples[7] rush on my mind which I might adduce. But for the sake of symmetry the discourse must now stop, in order that we may not exemplify the saying of Agatho the tragedian: —

"Treating our by-work as work,
And doing our work as by-work."

It having been, then, as I think, clearly shown in what way it is to be understood that the Greeks were called thieves by the Lord, I willingly leave the dogmas of the philosophers. For were we to go over their sayings, we should gather together directly such a quantity of notes, in showing that the whole of the Hellenic wisdom was derived from the Barbarian philosophy. But this speculation, we shall, nevertheless, again touch on, as necessity requires, when we collect the opinions current among the Greeks respecting first principles.

But from what has been said, it tacitly devolves on us to consider in what way the Hellenic books

---

[1] Jonah i. 6, 9, 14.
[2] Mal. i. 10, 11, 14. [The prophetic present-future.]
[3] Perhaps Bacchylides.
[4] ἀρχαίαν.
[5] The reading of H. Stephanus, ἀγαθὰς Ὧρας, is adopted in the translation. The text has ἀγαθὰ σωτῆρας. Some supply Ὧρας, and at the same time retain σωτῆρας.

[6] Jer iii. 19.
[7] [This strong testimony of Clement is worthy of special note.]

are to be perused by the man who is able to pass through the billows in them. Therefore

"Happy is he who possesses the wealth of the divine mind,"

as appears according to Empedocles,

"But wretched he, who cares for dark opinion about the Gods."

He divinely showed knowledge and ignorance to be the boundaries of happiness and misery. "For it behoves philosophers to be acquainted with very many things," according to Heraclitus; and truly must

"He, who seeks to be good, err in many things."

It is then now clear to us, from what has been said, that the beneficence of God is eternal, and that, from an unbeginning principle, equal natural righteousness reached all, according to the worth of each several race, — never having had a beginning. For God did not make a beginning of being Lord and Good, being always what He is. Nor will He ever cease to do good, although He bring all things to an end. And each one of us is a partaker of His beneficence, as far as He wills. For the difference of the elect is made by the intervention of a choice worthy of the soul, and by exercise.

Thus, then, let our fifth Miscellany of gnostic notes in accordance with the true philosophy be brought to a close.

ELUCIDATIONS.

I.

(Clement's Hebrew, p. 446, note 8.)

On this matter having spoken in a former Elucidation (see Elucidation VIII. p. 443), I must here translate a few words from Philo Judæus. He says, "Before Abram was called, such was his name; but afterward he was named *Abraam,* by the simple duplication of one letter, which nevertheless enfolds a great significance. For *Abram* is expounded to mean *sublime father,* but *Abraam* means *elect father of sound.*" Philo goes on to give his personal fancies in explication of this whim. But, with Clement, Philo was an *expert,* to whom all knowledge was to be credited in his specialty. This passage, however, confirms the opinion of those who pronounce Clement destitute of Hebrew, even in its elements. No need to say that *Abram* means something like what Philo gives us, but *Abraham* is expounded in the Bible itself (Gen. xvii. 3, 4, 5). The text of the LXX. seems to have been dubious to our author's mind, and hence he falls back on Philo. But this of itself appears decisive as to Clement's Hebrew scholarship.

II.

(The Beetle, cap. iv. p. 449, note 6.)

Cicero notes the *scarabæus* on the tongue, as identifying Apis,[1] the calf-god of the Egyptians. Now, this passage of our author seems to me to clear up the Scriptural word *gillulim* in Deut. xxix. 17, where the English margin reads, literally enough, *dungy-gods.* The word means, *things rolled about* (Lev. xxvi. 30; Hab. ii. 18, 19; 1 Kings xv. 12); on which compare Leighton (*St. Peter,* pp. 239, 746, and note). Scripture seems to prove that this story of Clement's about the beetle of the Egyptians, was known to the ancient Hebrews, and was the point in their references to the *gillulim* (see *Herod.,* book iii. cap. 28., or Rawlinson's *Trans.,* vol. ii. 353). The note in Migne *ad loc.* is also well-worthy to be consulted.

III.

(The Tetrad, cap. vi. p. 452, note 4.)

It is important to observe that "the patriarchal dispensation," as we too carelessly speak, is pluralized by Clement. He clearly distinguishes the *three* patriarchal dispensations, as given in Adam, Noah, and Abraham; and then comes the Mosaic. The editor begs to be pardoned for refer-

---

[1] *De Nat. Deor.,* ed. Delphin., vol. xiv. p. 852.

ring to his venerated and gifted father's division (sustained by Clement's authority), which he used to insist should be further enlarged so as to subdivide the first and the last, making *seven* complete, and thus honouring the system of sevens which runs through all Scripture. Thus *Adam* embraces *Paradise*, and the *first covenant* after the fall; and the *Christian covenant* embraces *a millenial period*. So that we have (1) *Paradise*, (2) Adam, (3) Noah, (4) Abraham, (5) Moses, (6) CHRIST, (7) a *millenial period*, preluding the Judgment and the Everlasting Kingdom. My venerated and most erudite instructor in theology, the late Dr. Jarvis, in his *Church of the Redeemed*, expounds a dispensation as identified by (1) a covenant, original or renewed, (2) a sign or sacrament, and (3) a closing judgment. (See pp. 4, 5, and elsewhere in the great work I have named.) Thus (1) the Tree of Life, (2) the institution of sacrifice, (3) the rainbow, (4) circumcision, (5) the ark, (6) the baptismal and eucharistic sacraments, and (7) the same renewed and glorified by the conversion of nations are the symbols. The covenants and the judgments are easily identified, ending with the universal Judgment.

Dr. Jarvis died, leaving his work unfinished; but the *Church of the Redeemed* is a book complete in itself, embodying the results of a vast erudition, and of a devout familiarity with Scripture. It begins with Adam, and ends with the downfall of Jerusalem (the typical judgment), which closed the Mosaic dispensation. It is written in a pellucid style, and with a fastidious use of the English language; and it is the noblest introduction to the understanding of the New Testament, with which I am acquainted. That such a work should be almost unknown in American literature, of which it should be a conspicuous ornament, is a sad commentary upon the taste of the period when it was given to the public.[1]

IV.

(The Golden Candlestick, cap. vi. p. 452, note 6.)

The seven gifts of the Spirit seem to be prefigured in this symbol, corresponding to the seven (spirits) lamps before the throne in the vision of St. John (see Rev. i. 4, iii. 1, iv. 5, and v. 6; also Isa. xi. 1, 2, and Zech. iii. 9, and iv. 10). The prediction of Isaiah intimates the anointing of Jesus at his baptism, and the outpouring of these gifts upon the Christian Church.

V.

(Symbols, cap. vi. p. 453, note 3.)

Clement regards the symbols of the divine law as *symbols* merely, and not *images* in the sense of the Decalogue. Whatever we may think of this distinction, his argument destroys the fallacy of the *Trent Catechism*, which pleads the Levitical symbols in favour of *images* in "the likeness of holy things," and which virtually abrogates the second commandment. Images of God the Father (crowned with the Papal tiara) are everywhere to be seen in the Latin churches, and countless images of all heavenly things are everywhere *worshipped* under the fallacy which Clement rejects. Pascal exposes the distinctions without a difference, by which God's laws are evacuated of all force in Jesuit theology; but the hair-splitting distinctions, about "bowing down to images and *worshipping* them," which infect the Trent theology, are equal to the worst of Pascal's instances.[2] It is with profound regret that I insert this testimony; but it seems necessary, because garblings of patristic authorities, which begin to appear in America, make an accurate and intelligent study of the *Ante-Nicene Fathers* a necessity for the American theologian.

---

[1] Boston, 1850. [2] In the *Provincial Letters, passim*.

VI.

(Perfection, cap. x. p. 459, note 2.)

The τέλειοι of the ancient canons were rather the *complete* than the *perfect*, as understood by the ancients. Clement's *Gnostic* is "complete," and goes on to moral perfection. Now, does not St. Paul make a similar distinction between babes in Christ, and those "*complete* in Him"? (Col. ii. 10.) The πεπληρωμένοι of this passage, referring to the "thoroughly furnished" Christian (fully equipped for his work and warfare), has thrown light on many passages of the Fathers and of the old canons, in my experience ; and I merely make the suggestion for what it may be worth. See Bunsen's *Church and Home Book* (*Hippol.*, iii. 82, 83, *et seqq.*) for the rules (1) governing all Christians, and (2) those called "the faithful," by way of eminence. So, in our days, not all *believers* are *communicants*.

VII.

(The Unknown God, cap. xii. p. 464, note 1.)

Must we retain "too superstitious," even in the Revised Version? (Which see *ad loc.*) Bunsen's rendering of δεισιδαιμονία, by *demon-fear*,[1] is not English ; but it suggests the common view of scholars, upon the passage, and leads me to suppose that the learned and venerable company of revisers could not agree on any English that would answer. That St. Paul paid the Athenians a compliment, as *devout in their way*, i.e., God-fearing towards their divinities, will not be denied. Clement seems to have so understood it, and hence his constant effort to show that we must recognise, in dealing with Gentiles, whatever of elementary good God has permitted to exist among them. May we not admit this principle, at least so far as to believe that Divine Providence led the Athenians to set up the very inscription which was to prompt Christ's apostle to an ingenious interpretation, and to an equally ingenious use of it, so avoiding a direct conflict with their laws? This they had charged on him (Acts xvii. 18), as before on Socrates.

VIII.

(Xenocrates and Democritus, cap. xiii. p. 465, note 3.)

My grave and studious reader will forgive me, here, for a reference to *Stromata* of a widely different sort. *Dulce est desipere*, etc. One sometimes finds instruction and relief amid the intense nonsense of "agnostic" and other "philosophies" of our days, in turning to a healthful intellect which "answers fools according to their folly." I confess myself an occasional reader of the vastly entertaining and suggestive *Noctes* of Christopher North, which may be excused by the famous example of a Father of the Church, who delighted in Aristophanes.[2] To illustrate this passage of Clement, then, let me refer to Professor Wilson's intense sympathy with animals. See the real eloquence of his reference to the dogs of Homer and of Sir Walter Scott.[3] "The Ettrick Shepherd" somewhere wondered, whether some dogs are not gifted with souls ; and, in the passage referred to, it is asked, whether the dog of Ulysses could have been destitute of an immortal spirit. On another occasion, Christopher breaks out with something like this : "Let me prefer the man who thinks so, to the miserable atheist whose creed is dust." He looks upon his dog "Fro," and continues (while the noble animal seems listening), "Yes, better a thousand times, O Fro, to believe that 'my faithful dog shall bear me company,' than that the soul of a Newton perishes at death," etc. How often have I regaled myself with the wholesome tonic of such dog-loving sport, after turning with disgust from some God-hating and man-destroying argument of "modern science," falsely so called.

---

[1] *Hippol.*, vol. iii. p 200. [2] Chrysostom. [3] Vol iv. pp. 104–107. American ed., 1854, Redfield, New York.

IX.

(Plato's Prophecy, cap. xiv. p. 470, note 2.)

My references at this point are worthy of being enlarged upon. I subjoin the following as additional. On this sublime passage, Jones of Nayland remarks,[1] "The greatest moral philosopher of the Greeks declared, with a kind of prescience, that, if a man *perfectly just* were to come upon earth, he would be impoverished and scourged, and bound as a criminal ; and, when he had suffered all manner of indignities, would be put to the shameful death of (suspension or) crucifixion." "Several of the Fathers," he adds, "have taken notice of this extraordinary passage in Plato, looking upon it as a prediction of the sufferings of the JUST ONE, Jesus Christ." He refers us to Grotius (*De Veritate*, iv. sec. 12) and to Meric Casaubon (*On Credulity*, p. 135). The passage from Plato (*Rep.*, ii. 5) impressed the mind of Cicero. (See his *Rep.*, iii. 17.)

---

[1] Works, vol. iv. p. 205.

THE STROMATA, OR MISCELLANIES.

BOOK VI.

CHAP. I. — PLAN.[1]

THE sixth and also the seventh Miscellany of gnostic notes, in accordance with the true philosophy, having delineated as well as possible the ethical argument conveyed in them, and having exhibited what the Gnostic is in his life, proceed to show the philosophers that he is by no means impious, as they suppose, but that he alone is truly pious, by a compendious exhibition of the Gnostic's form of religion, as far as it is possible, without danger, to commit it to writing in a book of reference. For the Lord enjoined " to labour for the meat which endureth to eternity."[2] And the prophet says, " Blessed is he that soweth into all waters, whose ox and ass tread,"[3] [that is,] the people, from the Law and from the Gentiles, gathered into one faith.

" Now the weak eateth herbs," according to the noble apostle.[4] *The Instructor*, divided by us into three books, has already exhibited the training and nurture up from the state of childhood, that is, the course of life which from elementary instruction grows by faith; and in the case of those enrolled in the number of men, prepares beforehand the soul, endued with virtue, for the reception of gnostic knowledge. The Greeks, then, clearly learning, from what shall be said by us in these pages, that in profanely persecuting the God-loving man, they themselves act impiously; then, as the notes advance, in accordance with the style of the *Miscellanies*, we must solve the difficulties raised both by Greeks and Barbarians with respect to the coming of the Lord.

In a meadow the flowers blooming variously, and in a park the plantations of fruit-trees, are not separated according to their species from those of other kinds. If some, culling varieties, have composed learned collections, Meadows, and Helicons, and Honeycombs, and Robes; then, with the things which come to recollection by haphazard, and are expurgated neither in order nor expression, but purposely scattered, the form of the *Miscellanies* is promiscuously variegated like a meadow. And such being the case, my notes shall serve as kindling sparks; and in the case of him, who is fit for knowledge, if he chance to fall in with them, research made with exertion will turn out to his benefit and advantage. For it is right that labour should precede not only food but also, much more knowledge, in the case of those that are advancing to the eternal and blessed salvation by the "strait and narrow way," which is truly the Lord's.

Our knowledge, and our spiritual garden, is the Saviour Himself; into whom we are planted, being transferred and transplanted, from our old life, into the good land. And transplanting contributes to fruitfulness. The Lord, then, into whom we have been transplanted, is the Light and the true Knowledge.

Now knowledge is otherwise spoken of in a twofold sense: that, commonly so called, which appears in all men (similarly also comprehension and apprehension), universally, in the knowledge of individual objects; in which not only the rational powers, but equally the irrational, share, which I would never term knowledge, inasmuch as the apprehension of things through the senses comes naturally. But that which *par excellence* is termed knowledge, bears the impress of judgment and reason, in the exercise of which there will be rational cognitions alone, applying purely to objects of thought, and resulting from the bare energy of the soul. " He is a good man," says David,[5] " who pities " (those ruined through error), " and lends " (from the communication of the word of truth) not at haphazard, for " he will dispense his words in judgment: " with profound calculation, " he hath dispersed, he hath given to the poor."

---

[1] [On Clement's *plan*, see Elucidation I. p. 342, *supra*.]
[2] John vi. 27.
[3] Isa. xxxii. 20.
[4] Rom. xiv. 2.
[5] Ps. cxii. 5, 9.

CHAP. II. — THE SUBJECT OF PLAGIARISMS RESUMED. THE GREEKS PLAGIARIZED FROM ONE ANOTHER.

Before handling the point proposed, we must, by way of preface, add to the close of the fifth book what is wanting. For since we have shown that the symbolical style was ancient, and was employed not only by our prophets, but also by the majority of the ancient Greeks, and by not a few of the rest of the Gentile Barbarians, it was requisite to proceed to the mysteries of the initiated. I postpone the elucidation of these till we advance to the confutation of what is said by the Greeks on first principles; for we shall show that the mysteries belong to the same branch of speculation. And having proved that the declaration of Hellenic thought is illuminated all round by the truth, bestowed on us in the Scriptures, taking it according to the sense, we have proved, not to say what is invidious, that the theft of the truth passed to them.

Come, and let us adduce the Greeks as witnesses against themselves to the theft. For, inasmuch as they pilfer from one another, they establish the fact that they are thieves; and although against their will, they are detected, clandestinely appropriating to those of their own race the truth which belongs to us. For if they do not keep their hands from each other, they will hardly do it from our authors. I shall say nothing of philosophic dogmas, since the very persons who are the authors of the divisions into sects, confess in writing, so as not to be convicted of ingratitude, that they have received from Socrates the most important of their dogmas. But after availing myself of a few testimonies of men most talked of, and of repute among the Greeks, and exposing their plagiarizing style, and selecting them from various periods, I shall turn to what follows.

Orpheus, then, having composed the line : —

"Since nothing else is more shameless and wretched
    than woman," —

Homer plainly says : —

"Since nothing else is more dreadful and shameless
    than a woman." [1]

And Musæus having written : —

"Since art is greatly superior to strength," —

Homer says : —

"By art rather than strength is the woodcutter greatly
    superior." [2]

Again, Musæus having composed the lines : —

"And as the fruitful field produceth leaves,
    And on the ash trees some fade, others grow,
    So whirls the race of man its leaf," [3] —

Homer transcribes : —

"Some of the leaves the wind strews on the ground.
    The budding wood bears some; in time of spring,
    They come. So springs one race of men, and one
        departs." [4]

Again, Homer having said : —

"It is unholy to exult over dead men," [5] —

Archilochus and Cratinus write, the former : —

"It is not noble at dead men to sneer ;"

and Cratinus in the *Lacones :* —

"For men 'tis dreadful to exult
    Much o'er the stalwart dead."

Again, Archilochus, transferring that Homeric line : —

"I erred, nor say I nay : instead of many" [6] —

writes thus : —

"I erred, and this mischief hath somehow seized
    another."

As certainly also that line : —

"Even-handed [7] war the slayer slays." [8]

He also, altering, has given forth thus : —

"I will do it.
    For Mars to men in truth is even-handed." [7]

Also, translating the following : —

"The issues of victory among men depend on the
    gods," [9]

he openly encourages youth, in the following iambic : —

"Victory's issues on the gods depend."

Again, Homer having said : —

"With feet unwashed sleeping on the ground," [10]

Euripides writes in *Erechtheus:* —

"Upon the plain spread with no couch they sleep,
    Nor in the streams of water lave their feet."

Archilochus having likewise said : —

"But one with this and one with that
    His heart delights," —

in correspondence with the Homeric line : —

"For one in these deeds, one in those delights," [11] —

Euripides says in *Œneus:* —

---

[1] *Odyss.*, xi. 427.
[2] Homer, *Iliad*, xxiii. 315: μέγ' ἀμείνων is found in the *Iliad* as in Musæus. In the text occurs instead περιγίνεται, which is taken from line 318.
    "By art rather than strength is the woodcutter greatly superior;
    By art the helmsman on the dark sea
    Guides the swift ship when driven by winds;
    By art one charioteer excels (περιγίνεται) another.
                                      Iliad, xxiii. 315-318.

[3] φύλλον, for which Sylburg suggests φῦλον.
[4] *Iliad*, vi. 147-149.
[5] *Odyss.*, xxii. 412.
[6] *Iliad*, ix 116.
[7] Ξυνός. So Livy, "communis Mars;" and Cicero, "cum omnis belli Mars communis."
[8] *Iliad*, xviii. 309.
[9] The text has: Νίκης ἀνθρώποισι θεῶν ἐκ πείρατα κεῖται. In *Iliad*, vii. 101, 102, we read: —
                            αὐτὰρ ὕπερθεν
            Νίκης πείρατ' ἔχονται ἐν ἀθανάτοισι θεοῖσιν.
[10] *Iliad*, xvi. 235.
[11] *Odyss.*, xiv. 228.

"But one in these ways, one in those, has more delight."

And I have heard Æschylus saying : —

"He who is happy ought to stay at home ;
There should he also stay, who speeds not well."

And Euripides, too, shouting the like on the stage : —

"Happy the man who, prosperous, stays at home."

Menander, too, on comedy, saying : —

"He ought at home to stay, and free remain,
Or be no longer rightly happy."

Again, Theognis having said : —

"The exile has no comrade dear and true," —

Euripides has written : —

"Far from the poor flies every friend."

And Epicharmus, saying : —

"Daughter, woe worth the day!
Thee who art old I marry to a youth ; "[1]

and adding : —

"For the young husband takes some other girl,
And for another husband longs the wife," —

Euripides[2] writes : —

"'Tis bad to yoke an old wife to a youth ;
For he desires to share another's bed,
And she, by him deserted, mischief plots."

Euripides having, besides, said in the *Medea :* —

"For no good do a bad man's gifts," —

Sophocles in *Ajax Flagellifer* utters this iambic : —

"For foes' gifts are no gifts, nor any boon."[3]

Solon having written : —

"For surfeit insolence begets,
When store of wealth attends."

Theognis writes in the same way : —

"For surfeit insolence begets,
When store of wealth attends the bad."

Whence also Thucydides, in the *Histories,* says : "Many men, to whom in a great degree, and in a short time, unlooked-for prosperity comes, are wont to turn to insolence." And Philistus[4] likewise imitates the same sentiment, expressing himself thus : "And the many things which turn out prosperously to men, in accordance with reason, have an incredibly dangerous[5] tendency to misfortune. For those who meet with unlooked success beyond their expectations, are for the most part wont to turn to insolence."
Again, Euripides having written : —

"For children sprung of parents who have led
A hard and toilsome life, superior are ; "

Critias writes : "For I begin with a man's origin : how far the best and strongest in body will he be, if his father exercises himself, and eats in a hardy way, and subjects his body to toilsome labour ; and if the mother of the future child be strong in body, and give herself exercise."
Again, Homer having said of the Hephæstus-made shield : —

"Upon it earth and heaven and sea he made,
And Ocean's rivers' mighty strength portrayed," —

Pherecydes of Syros says : "Zas makes a cloak large and beautiful, and works on it earth and Ogenus, and the palace of Ogenus."
And Homer having said : —

"Shame, which greatly hurts a man or helps,"[6] —

Euripides writes in *Erechtheus :* —

"Of shame I find it hard to judge ;
'Tis needed. 'Tis at times a great mischief."

Take, by way of parallel, such plagiarisms as the following, from those who flourished together, and were rivals of each other. From the *Orestes* of Euripides : —

"Dear charm of sleep, aid in disease."

From the *Eriphyle* of Sophocles : —

"Hie thee to sleep, healer of that disease."

And from the *Antigone* of Sophocles : —

"Bastardy is opprobrious in name ; but the nature is equal ; "[7]

And from the *Aleuades* of Sophocles : —

"Each good thing has its nature equal."

Again, in the *Ctimenus*[8] of Euripides : —

"For him who toils, God helps ; "

And in the *Minos* of Sophocles : —

"To those who act not, fortune is no ally ; "

And from the *Alexander* of Euripides : —

"But time will show ; and learning, by that test,
I shall know whether thou art good or bad ; "

And from the *Hipponos* of Sophocles : —

"Besides, conceal thou nought ; since Time,
That sees all, hears all, all things will unfold."

But let us similarly run over the following ; for Eumelus having composed the line,

"Of Memory and Olympian Zeus the daughters nine,"

Solon thus begins the elegy : —

"Of Memory and Olympian Zeus the children bright."

---

[1] The text is corrupt and unintelligible. It has been restored as above.
[2] In some lost tragedy.
[3] Said by Ajax of the sword received from Hector, with which he killed himself.
[4] The imitator of Thucydides, said to be weaker but clearer than his model. He is not specially clear here.
[5] The text has, ἀσφαλέστερα παρὰ δόξαν καὶ κακοπραγίαν: for which Lowth reads, ἐπισφαλέστερα πρὸς κακοπραγίαν, as translated above.

[6] *Iliad*, xxiv. 44, 45. Clement's quotation differs somewhat from the passage as it stands in Homer.
[7] The text has δοίη, which Stobæus has changed into δ' ἴση, as above. Stobæus gives this quotation as follows : —

"The bastard has equal strength with the legitimate ;
Each good thing has its nature legitimate."

[8] As no play bearing this name is mentioned by any one else, various conjectures have been made as to the true reading ; among which are Clymene Temenos or Temenides.

Again, Euripides, paraphrasing the Homeric line : —

"What, whence art thou? Thy city and thy parents, where?"[1]

employs the following iambics in *Ægeus :* —

"What country shall we say that thou hast left
To roam in exile, what thy land — the bound
Of thine own native soil? Who thee begat?
And of what father dost thou call thyself the son?"

And what? Theognis[2] having said : —

"Wine largely drunk is bad; but if one use
It with discretion, 'tis not bad, but good,"—

does not Panyasis write?

"Above the gods' best gift to men ranks wine,
In measure drunk; but in excess the worst."

Hesiod, too, saying : —

"But for the fire to thee I'll give a plague,[3]
For all men to delight themselves withal,"—

Euripides writes : —

"And for the fire
Another fire greater and unconquerable,
Sprung up in the shape of women."[4]

And in addition, Homer, saying : —

"There is no satiating the greedy paunch,
Baneful, which many plagues has caused to men."[5]

Euripides says : —

"Dire need and baneful paunch me overcome;
From which all evils come."

Besides, Callias the comic poet having written : —

"With madmen, all men must be mad, they say,"—

Menander, in the *Poloumenoi*, expresses himself similarly, saying : —

"The presence of wisdom is not always suitable:
One sometimes must with others play[6] the fool."

And Antimachus of Teos having said : —

"From gifts, to mortals many ills arise,"—

Augias composed the line : —

"For gifts men's mind and acts deceive."

And Hesiod having said : —

"Than a good wife, no man a better thing
Ere gained; than a bad wife, a worse,"—

Simonides said : —

"A better prize than a good wife no man
Ere gained, than a bad one nought worse."

Again, Epicharmas having said : —

"As destined long to live, and yet not long,
Think of thyself,"—

Euripides writes : —

"Why? seeing the wealth we have uncertain is,
Why don't we live as free from care, as pleasant
As we may?"

Similarly also, the comic poet Diphilus having said : —

"The life of men is prone to change,"—

Posidippus says : —

"No man of mortal mould his life has passed
From suffering free. Nor to the end again
Has continued prosperous."

Similarly[7] speaks to thee Plato, writing of man as a creature subject to change.

Again, Euripides having said : —

"Oh life to mortal men of trouble full,
How slippery in everything art thou!
Now grow'st thou, and thou now decay'st away.
And there is set no limit, no, not one,
For mortals of their course to make an end,
Except when Death's remorseless final end
Comes, sent from Zeus,"—

Diphilus writes : —

"There is no life which has not its own ills,
Pains, cares, thefts, and anxieties, disease;
And Death, as a physician, coming, gives
Rest to their victims in his quiet sleep."[8]

Furthermore, Euripides having said : —

"Many are fortune's shapes,
And many things contrary to expectation the gods perform,"—

The tragic poet Theodectes similarly writes : —

"The instability of mortals' fates."

And Bacchylides having said : —

"To few[9] alone of mortals is it given
To reach hoary age, being prosperous all the while,
And not meet with calamities,"—

Moschion, the comic poet, writes : —

"But he of all men is most blest,
Who leads throughout an equal life."

And you will find that, Theognis having said : —

"For no advantage to a man grown old
A young wife is, who will not, as a ship
The helm, obey,"—

Aristophanes, the comic poet, writes : —

"An old man to a young wife suits but ill."

For Anacreon, having written : —

---

[1] *Odyss.*, xiv. 187.
[2] [See, *supra*, book ii. cap. ii. p. 242.] In Theognis the quotation stands thus : —

Οἶνον τοι πίνειν πουλὸν κακόν, ἢν δέ τις αὐτὸν
Πίνῃ ἐπισταμένως, οὐ κακὸς ἀλλ᾽ ἀγαθός.

"To drink much wine is bad; but if one drink
It with discretion, 'tis not bad, but good."

[3] From Jupiter's address (referring to Pandora) to Prometheus, after stealing fire from heaven. The passage in Hesiod runs thus : —

"You rejoice at stealing fire and outwitting my mind;
But I will give you, and to future men, a great plague.
And for the fire will give to them a bane in which
All will delight their heart, embracing their own bane.'

[4] Translated as arranged by Grotius.
[5] *Odyss.*, xvii. 286.
[6] συμμανῆναι is doubtless here the true reading, for which the text has συμβῆναι.

[7] The text has κατ᾽ ἄλλα. And although Sylburgius very properly remarks, that the conjecture κατάλληλα instead is uncertain, it is so suitable to the sense here, that we have no hesitation in adopting it.
[8] The above is translated as amended by Grotius.
[9] παύροισι, "few," instead of παρ᾽οἷσι, and πράσσοντας instead of πράσσοντα, and δύαις, "calamities," instead of δύᾳ, are adopted from *Lyric Fragments*.

"Luxurious love I sing,
　With flowery garlands graced,
　He is of gods the king,
　He mortal men subdues,"—

Euripides writes : —

"For love not only men attacks,
　And women; but disturbs
　The souls of gods above, and to the sea
　Descends."

But not to protract the discourse further, in our anxiety to show the propensity of the Greeks to plagiarism in expressions and dogmas, allow us to adduce the express testimony of Hippias, the sophist of Elea, who discourses on the point in hand, and speaks thus : " Of these things some perchance are said by Orpheus, some briefly by Musæus; some in one place, others in other places ; some by Hesiod, some by Homer, some by the rest of the poets; and some in prose compositions, some by Greeks, some by Barbarians. And I from all these, placing together the things of most importance and of kindred character, will make the present discourse new and varied."

And in order that we may see that philosophy and history, and even rhetoric, are not free of a like reproach, it is right to adduce a few instances from them. For Alcmæon of Crotona having said, " It is easier to guard against a man who is an enemy than a friend," Sophocles wrote in the *Antigone* : —

"For what sore more grievous than a bad friend ? "

And Xenophon said : " No man can injure enemies in any way other than by appearing to be a friend."

And Euripides having said in *Telephus:* —

"Shall we Greeks be slaves to Barbarians ? "—

Thrasymachus, in the oration for the Larissæans, says : " Shall we be slaves to Archelaus — Greeks to a Barbarian ? "

And Orpheus having said : —

"Water is the change for soul, and death for water ;
　From water is earth, and what comes from earth is
　　again water,
　And from that, soul, which changes the whole
　　ether ; "

and Heraclitus, putting together the expressions from these lines, writes thus : —

"It is death for souls to become water, and death for water to become earth; and from earth comes water, and from water soul."

And Athamas the Pythagorean having said, " Thus was produced the beginning of the universe ; and there are four roots — fire, water, air, earth : for from these is the origination of what is produced," — Empedocles of Agrigentum wrote : —

"The four roots of all things first do thou hear —
　Fire, water, earth, and ether's boundless height :
　For of these all that was, is, shall be, comes."

And Plato having said, " Wherefore also the gods, knowing men, release sooner from life those they value most," Menander wrote : —

"Whom the gods love, dies young."

And Euripides having written in the *Œnomaus :* —

"We judge of things obscure from what we see ; "

and in the *Phœnix :* —

"By signs the obscure is fairly grasped,"—

Hyperides says, " But we must investigate things unseen by learning from signs and probabilities." And Isocrates having said, " We must conjecture the future by the past," Andocides does not shrink from saying, " For we must make use of what has happened previously as signs in reference to what is to be." Besides, Theognis having said : —

"The evil of counterfeit silver and gold is not intolerable,
　O Cyrnus, and to a wise man is not difficult of detection ;
　But if the mind of a friend is hidden in his breast,
　If he is false,[1] and has a treacherous heart within,
　This is the basest thing for mortals, caused by God,
　And of all things the hardest to detect,"—

Euripides writes : —

"Oh Zeus, why hast thou given to men clear tests
　Of spurious gold, while on the body grows
　No mark sufficing to discover clear
　The wicked man ? "

Hyperides himself also says, " There is no feature of the mind impressed on the countenance of men."

Again, Stasinus having composed the line : —

"Fool, who, having slain the father, leaves the children,"—

Xenophon[2] says, " For I seem to myself to have acted in like manner, as if one who killed the father should spare his children." And Sophocles having written in the *Antigone:* —

"Mother and father being in Hades now,
　No brother ever can to me spring forth,"—

Herodotus says, " Mother and father being no more, I shall not have another brother." In addition to these, Theopompus having written : —

"Twice children are old men in very truth ; "

And before him Sophocles in *Peleus:* —

"Peleus, the son of Æacus, I, sole housekeeper,
　Guide, old as he is now, and train again,
　For the aged man is once again a child,"—

Antipho the orator says, " For the nursing of the old is like the nursing of children." Also the

---

[1] ψυδνός = ψυδρός — which, however, occurs nowhere but here — is adopted as preferable to ψεδνός (bald), which yields no sense, or ψυχρός. Sylburgius MS. Paris; Ruhnk reads ψυδρός.
[2] A mistake for Herodotus.

philosopher Plato says, "The old man then, as seems, will be twice a child." Further, Thucydides having said, "We alone bore the brunt at Marathon," [1] — Demosthenes said, "By those who bore the brunt at Marathon." Nor will I omit the following. Cratinus having said in the *Pytine* : [2] —

"The preparation perchance you know,"

Andocides the orator says, "The preparation, gentlemen of the jury, and the eagerness of our enemies, almost all of you know." Similarly also Nicias, in the speech on the deposit, against Lysias, says, "The preparation and the eagerness of the adversaries, ye see, O gentlemen of the jury." After him Æschines says, "You see the preparation, O men of Athens, and the line of battle." Again, Demosthenes having said, "What zeal and what canvassing, O men of Athens, have been employed in this contest, I think almost all of you are aware ; " and Philinus similarly, "What zeal, what forming of the line of battle, gentlemen of the jury, have taken place in this contest, I think not one of you is ignorant." Isocrates, again, having said, "As if she were related to his wealth, not him," Lysias says in the *Orphics*, "And he was plainly related not to the persons, but to the money." Since Homer also having written : —

"O friend, if in this war, by taking flight,
We should from age and death exemption win,
I would not fight among the first myself,
Nor would I send thee to the glorious fray ;
But now — for myriad fates of death attend
In any case, which man may not escape
Or shun — come on. To some one we shall bring
Renown, or some one shall to us," [3] —

Theopompus writes, "For if, by avoiding the present danger, we were to pass the rest of our time in security, to show love of life would not be wonderful. But now, so many fatalities are incident to life, that death in battle seems preferable." And what? Chilo the sophist having uttered the apophthegm, "Become surety, and mischief is at hand," did not Epicharmus utter the same sentiment in other terms, when he said, "Suretyship is the daughter of mischief, and loss that of suretyship ? " [4] Further, Hippocrates the physician having written, "You must look to time, and locality, and age, and disease," Euripides says in *Hexameters* : [5] —

"Those who the healing art would practise well,
Must study people's modes of life, and note
The soil, and the diseases so consider."

Homer again, having written : —

"I say no mortal man can doom escape," —

Archinus says, "All men are bound to die either sooner or later ; " and Demosthenes, "To all men death is the end of life, though one should keep himself shut up in a coop."

And Herodotus, again, having said, in his discourse about Glaucus the Spartan, that the Pythian said, "In the case of the Deity, to say and to do are equivalent," Aristophanes said : —

"For to think and to do are equivalent."

And before him, Parmenides of Elea said : —

"For thinking and being are the same."

And Plato having said, "And we shall show, not absurdly perhaps, that the beginning of love is sight ; and hope diminishes the passion, memory nourishes it, and intercourse preserves it ; " does not Philemon the comic poet write : —

"First all see, then admire ;
Then gaze, then come to hope ;
And thus arises love ? "

Further, Demosthenes having said, "For to all of us death is a debt," and so forth, Phanocles writes in *Loves*, or *The Beautiful* : —

"But from the Fates' unbroken thread escape
Is none for those that feed on earth."

You will also find that Plato having said, "For the first sprout of each plant, having got a fair start, according to the virtue of its own nature, is most powerful in inducing the appropriate end ; " the historian writes, "Further, it is not natural for one of the wild plants to become cultivated, after they have passed the earlier period of growth ; " and the following of Empedocles : —

"For I already have been boy and girl,
And bush, and bird, and mute fish in the sea," —

Euripides transcribes in *Chrysippus* : —

"But nothing dies
Of things that are ; but being dissolved,
One from the other,
Shows another form."

And Plato having said, in the *Republic*, that women were common, Euripides writes in the *Protesilaus* : —

"For common, then, is woman's bed."

Further, Euripides having written : —

"For to the temperate enough sufficient is," —

Epicurus expressly says, "Sufficiency is the greatest riches of all."

Again, Aristophanes having written : —

"Life thou securely shalt enjoy, being just
And free from turmoil, and from fear live well," —

Epicurus says, "The greatest fruit of righteousness is tranquillity."

---

[1] Instead of Μαραθωνίται, as in the text, we read from Thucydides Μαραθῶνί τε.
[2] Πυτίνη (not, as in the text, Ποιτίνη), a flask covered with plaited osiers. The name of a comedy by Cratinus (Liddell and Scott's *Lexicon*). [Elucidation I.]
[3] *Iliad*, xii. 322, Sarpedon to Glaucus.
[4] Grotius's correction has been adopted, ἐγγύας δὲ ζαμία, instead of ἐγγύα δὲ ζαμίας.
[5] In the text before *In Hexameters* we have τηρήσει, which has occasioned much trouble to the critics. Although not entirely satisfactory, yet the most probable is the correction θέλουσι as above.

Let these species, then, of Greek plagiarism of sentiments, being such, stand as sufficient for a clear specimen to him who is capable of perceiving.

And not only have they been detected pirating and paraphrasing thoughts and expressions, as will be shown; but they will also be convicted of the possession of what is entirely stolen. For stealing entirely what is the production of others, they have published it as their own; as Eugamon of Cyrene did the entire book on the Thesprotians from Musæus, and Pisander of Camirus the Heraclea of Pisinus of Lindus, and Panyasis of Halicarnassus, the capture of Œchalia from Cleophilus of Samos.

You will also find that Homer, the great poet, took from Orpheus, from the *Disappearance* of Dionysus, those words and what follows verbatim: —

"As a man trains a luxuriant shoot of olive."[1]

And in the *Theogony*, it is said by Orpheus of Kronos: —

"He lay, his thick neck bent aside; and him
All-conquering Sleep had seized."

These Homer transferrred to the Cyclops.[2] And Hesiod writes of Melampous: —

"Gladly to hear, what the immortals have assigned
To men, the brave from cowards clearly marks;"

and so forth, taking it word for word from the poet Musæus.

And Aristophanes the comic poet has, in the first of the *Thesmophoriazusæ*, transferred the words from the *Empiprameni* of Cratinus. And Plato the comic poet, and Aristophanes in *Dædalus*, steal from one another. *Cocalus*, composed by Araros,[3] the son of Aristophanes, was by the comic poet Philemon altered, and made into the comedy called *Hypobolimæns*.

Eumelus and Acusilaus the historiographers changed the contents of Hesiod into prose, and published them as their own. Gorgias of Leontium and Eudemus of Naxus, the historians, stole from Melesagoras. And, besides, there is Bion of Proconnesus, who epitomized and transcribed the writings of the ancient Cadmus, and Archilochus, and Aristotle, and Leandrus, and Hellanicus, and Hecatæus, and Androtion, and Philochorus. Dieuchidas of Megara transferred the beginning of his treatise from the *Deucalion* of Hellanicus. I pass over in silence Heraclitus of Ephesus, who took a very great deal from Orpheus.

From Pythagoras Plato derived the immortality of the soul; and he from the Egyptians. And many of the Platonists composed books, in which they show that the Stoics, as we said in the beginning, and Aristotle, took the most and principal of their dogmas from Plato. Epicurus also pilfered his leading dogmas from Democritus. Let these things then be so. For life would fail me, were I to undertake to go over the subject in detail, to expose the selfish plagiarism of the Greeks, and how they claim the discovery of the best of their doctrines, which they have received from us.

CHAP. III. — PLAGIARISM BY THE GREEKS OF THE MIRACLES RELATED IN THE SACRED BOOKS OF THE HEBREWS.

And now they are convicted not only of borrowing doctrines from the Barbarians, but also of relating as prodigies of Hellenic mythology the marvels found in our records, wrought through divine power from above, by those who led holy lives, while devoting attention to us. And we shall ask at them whether those things which they relate are true or false. But they will not say that they are false; for they will not with their will condemn themselves of the very great silliness of composing falsehoods, but of necessity admit them to be true. And how will the prodigies enacted by Moses and the other prophets any longer appear to them incredible? For the Almighty God, in His care for all men, turns some to salvation by commands, some by threats, some by miraculous signs, some by gentle promises.

Well, the Greeks, when once a drought had wasted Greece for a protracted period, and a dearth of the fruits of the earth ensued, it is said, those that survived of them, having, because of the famine, come as suppliants to Delphi, asked the Pythian priestess how they should be released from the calamity. She announced that the only help in their distress was, that they should avail themselves of the prayers of Æacus. Prevailed on by them, Æacus, ascending the Hellenic hill, and stretching out pure[4] hands to heaven, and invoking the common[5] God, besought him to pity wasted Greece. And as he prayed, thunder sounded, out of the usual course of things, and the whole surrounding atmosphere was covered with clouds. And impetuous and continued rains, bursting down, filled the whole region. The result was a copious and rich fertility wrought by the husbandry of the prayers of Æacus.

"And Samuel called on the LORD," it is said, "and the LORD gave forth His voice, and rain in the day of harvest."[6] Do you see that "He who sendeth His rain on the just and on the

---

[1] *Iliad*, xvii. 53.
[2] i.e., Polyphemus, *Odyss*., ix. 372.
[3] According to the correction of Casaubon, who, instead of ἀραρότως of the text, reads 'Αραρώς. Others ascribed the comedy to Aristophanes himself.

[4] i.e., washed.
[5] Eusebius reads, "invoking the common Father, God," viz., Πανελλήνιος Ζεύς, as Pausanias relates.
[6] 1 Sam. xi. 18.

unjust "[1] by the subject powers is the one God? And the whole of our Scripture is full of instances of God, in reference to the prayers of the just, hearing and performing each one of their petitions.

Again, the Greeks relate, that in the case of a failure once of the Etesian winds, Aristæus once sacrificed in Ceus to Isthmian Zeus. For there was great devastation, everything being burnt up with the heat in consequence of the winds, which had been wont to refresh the productions of the earth, not blowing, and he easily called them back.

And at Delphi, on the expedition of Xerxes against Greece, the Pythian priestess having made answer : —

" O Delphians, pray the winds, and it will be better," —

they having erected an altar and performed sacrifice to the winds, had them as their helpers. For, blowing violently around Cape Sepias, they shivered the whole preparations of the Persian expedition. Empedocles of Agrigentum was called " Checker of Winds." Accordingly it is said, that when, on a time, a wind blew from the mountain of Agrigentum, heavy and pestiferous for the inhabitants, and the cause also of barrenness to their wives, he made the wind to cease. Wherefore he himself writes in the lines : —

" Thou shalt the might of the unwearied winds make still,
    Which rushing to the earth spoil mortals' crops,
    And at thy will bring back the avenging blasts."

And they say that he was followed by some that used divinations, and some that had been long vexed by sore diseases.[2] They plainly, then, believed in the performance of cures, and signs and wonders, from our Scriptures. For if certain powers move the winds and dispense showers, let them hear the psalmist : " How amiable are thy tabernacles, O LORD of hosts ! "[3] This is the Lord of powers, and principalities, and authorities, of whom Moses speaks ; so that we may be with Him. " And ye shall circumcise your hard heart, and shall not harden your neck any more. For He is Lord of lords and God of gods, the great God and strong,"[4] and so forth. And Isaiah says, " Lift your eyes to the height, and see who hath produced all these things."[5]

And some say that plagues, and hail-storms, and tempests, and the like, are wont to take place, not alone in consequence of material disturbance, but also through anger of demons and bad angels. For instance, they say that the Magi at Cleone, watching the phenomena of the skies, when the clouds are about to discharge hail, avert the threatening of wrath by incantations and sacrifices. And if at any time there is the want of an animal, they are satisfied with bleeding their own finger for a sacrifice. The prophetess Diotima, by the Athenians offering sacrifice previous to the pestilence, effected a delay of the plague for ten years. The sacrifices, too, of Epimenides of Crete, put off the Persian war for an equal period. And it is considered to be all the same whether we call these spirits gods or angels. And those skilled in the matter of consecrating statues, in many of the temples have erected tombs of the dead, calling the souls of these Dæmons, and teaching them to be worshipped by men ; as having, in consequence of the purity of their life, by the divine foreknowledge, received the power of wandering about the space around the earth in order to minister to men. For they knew that some souls were by nature kept in the body. But of these, as the work proceeds, in the treatise on the angels, we shall discourse.

Democritus, who predicted many things from observation of celestial phenomena, was called " Wisdom " (Σοφία). On his meeting a cordial reception from his brother Damasus, he predicted that there would be much rain, judging from certain stars. Some, accordingly, convinced by him, gathered their crops ; for being in summer-time, they were still on the threshing-floor. But others lost all, unexpected and heavy showers having burst down.

How then shall the Greeks any longer disbelieve the divine appearance on Mount Sinai, when the fire burned, consuming none of the things that grew on the mount ; and the sound of trumpets issued forth, breathed without instruments? For that which is called the descent on the mount of God is the advent of divine power, pervading the whole world, and proclaiming " the light that is inaccessible."[6]

For such is the allegory, according to the Scripture. But the fire was seen, as Aristobulus[7] says, while the whole multitude, amounting to not less than a million, besides those under age, were congregated around the mountain, the circuit of the mount not being less than five days' journey. Over the whole place of the vision the burning fire was seen by them all encamped as it were around ; so that the descent was not local. For God is everywhere.

Now the compilers of narratives say that in the island of Britain[8] there is a cave situated under a mountain, and a chasm on its summit ;

---

[1] Matt. v. 45.
[2] Instead of νοῦσον σιδηρόν, the sense requires that we should, with Sylburgius, read νούσοισι δηρόν.
[3] Ps. lxxxiv. 1.
[4] Deut. x. 16, 17.
[5] Isa. xl. 26.

[6] 1 Tim. vi. 16.
[7] [Of this Aristobulus, see 2 Maccab. i. 10, and Euseb., *Hist.*, book vii. cap. 32.   Elucidation II.]
[8] [See the unsatisfactory note in ed. Migne, *ad locum.*]

and that, accordingly, when the wind falls into the cave, and rushes into the bosom of the cleft, a sound is heard like cymbals clashing musically. And often in the woods, when the leaves are moved by a sudden gust of wind, a sound is emitted like the song of birds.

Those also who composed the *Persics* relate that in the uplands, in the country of the Magi, three mountains are situated on an extended plain, and that those who travel through the locality, on coming to the first mountain, hear a confused sound as of several myriads shouting, as if in battle array; and on reaching the middle one, they hear a clamour louder and more distinct; and at the end hear people singing a pæan, as if victorious. And the cause, in my opinion, of the whole sound, is the smoothness and cavernous character of the localities; and the air, entering in, being sent back and going to the same point, sounds with considerable force. Let these things be so. But it is possible for God Almighty,[1] even without a medium, to produce a voice and vision through the ear, showing that His greatness has a natural order beyond what is customary, in order to the conversion of the hitherto unbelieving soul, and the reception of the commandment given. But there being a cloud and a lofty mountain, how is it not possible to hear a different sound, the wind moving by the active cause? Wherefore also the prophet says, " Ye heard the voice of words, and saw no similitude." [2] You see how the Lord's voice, the Word, without shape, the power of the Word, the luminous word of the Lord, the truth from heaven, from above, coming to the assembly of the Church, wrought by the luminous immediate ministry.

CHAP. IV. — THE GREEKS DREW MANY OF THEIR PHILOSOPHICAL TENETS FROM THE EGYPTIAN AND INDIAN GYMNOSOPHISTS.

We shall find another testimony in confirmation, in the fact that the best of the philosophers, having appropriated their most excellent dogmas from us, boast, as it were, of certain of the tenets which pertain to each sect being culled from other Barbarians, chiefly from the Egyptians — both other tenets, and that especially of the transmigration of the soul. For the Egyptians pursue a philosophy of their own. This is principally shown by their sacred ceremonial. For first advances the Singer, bearing some one of the symbols of music. For they say that he must learn two of the books of Hermes, the one of which contains the hymns of the gods, the second the regulations for the king's life. And

after the Singer advances the Astrologer,[3] with a horologe in his hand, and a palm, the symbols of astrology. He must have the astrological books of Hermes, which are four in number, always in his mouth. Of these, one is about the order of the fixed stars that are visible, and another about the conjunctions and luminous appearances of the sun and moon; and the rest respecting their risings. Next in order advances the sacred Scribe, with wings on his head, and in his hand a book and rule, in which were writing ink and the reed, with which they write. And he must be acquainted with what are called hieroglyphics, and know about cosmography and geography, the position of the sun and moon, and about the five planets; also the description of Egypt, and the chart of the Nile; and the description of the equipment of the priests and of the places consecrated to them, and about the measures and the things in use in the sacred rites. Then the Stole-keeper follows those previously mentioned, with the cubit of justice and the cup for libations. He is acquainted with all points called Pædeutic (relating to training) and Moschophatic (sacrificial). There are also ten books which relate to the honour paid by them to their gods, and containing the Egyptian worship; as that relating to sacrifices, first-fruits, hymns, prayers, processions, festivals, and the like. And behind all walks the Prophet, with the water-vase carried openly in his arms; who is followed by those who carry the issue of loaves. He, as being the governor of the temple, learns the ten books called " Hieratic;" and they contain all about the laws, and the gods, and the whole of the training of the priests. For the Prophet is, among the Egyptians, also over the distribution of the revenues. There are then forty-two books of Hermes indispensably necessary; of which the six-and-thirty containing the whole philosophy of the Egyptians are learned by the forementioned personages; and the other six, which are medical, by the Pastophoroi (image-bearers), — treating of the structure of the body, and of diseases, and instruments, and medicines, and about the eyes, and the last about women.[4] Such are the customs of the Egyptians, to speak briefly.

The philosophy of the Indians, too, has been celebrated. Alexander of Macedon, having taken ten of the Indian Gymnosophists, that seemed the best and most sententious, proposed to them problems, threatening to put to death him that did not answer to the purpose; ordering one, who was the eldest of them, to decide.

The first, then, being asked whether he thought that the living were more in number than the dead, said, The living; for that the

---

[1] [See interesting remarks of Professor Cook, *Religion and Chemistry* (first edition), p. 44. This whole passage of our author, on the *sounds* of Sinai and the angelic trumpets, touches a curious matter, which must be referred, as here, to the unlimited power of God.]

[2] Deut. iv. 12.

[3] Ὡροσκόπος. [Elucidation III.]

[4] [Elucidation IV.]

dead were not. The second, on being asked whether the sea or the land maintained larger beasts, said, The land; for the sea was part of it. And the third being asked which was the most cunning of animals? The one, which has not hitherto been known, man. And the fourth being interrogated, For what reason they had made Sabba, who was their prince, revolt, answered, Because they wished him to live well rather than die ill. And the fifth being asked, Whether he thought that day or night was first, said, One day. For puzzling questions must have puzzling answers. And the sixth being posed with the query, How shall one be loved most? By being most powerful; in order that he may not be timid. And the seventh being asked, How any one of men could become God? said, If he do what it is impossible for man to do. And the eighth being asked, Which is the stronger, life or death? said, Life, which bears such ills. And the ninth being interrogated, Up to what point it is good for a man to live? said, Till he does not think that to die is better than to live. And on Alexander ordering the tenth to say something, for he was judge, he said, "One spake worse than another." And on Alexander saying, Shall you not, then, die first, having given such a judgment? he said, And how, O king, wilt thou prove true, after saying that thou wouldest kill first the first man that answered very badly?

And that the Greeks are called pilferers of all manner of writing, is, as I think, sufficiently demonstrated by abundant proofs.[1]

CHAP. V. — THE GREEKS HAD SOME KNOWLEDGE OF THE TRUE GOD.

And that the men of highest repute among the Greeks knew God, not by positive knowledge, but by indirect expression,[2] Peter says in the *Preaching:* "Know then that there is one God, who made the beginning of all things, and holds the power of the end; and is the Invisible, who sees all things; incapable of being contained, who contains all things; needing nothing, whom all things need, and by whom they are; incomprehensible, everlasting, unmade, who made all things by the 'Word of His power,' that is, according to the gnostic scripture, His Son."[3]

Then he adds: "Worship this God not as the Greeks," — signifying plainly, that the excellent among the Greeks worshipped the same God as we, but that they had not learned by perfect knowledge that which was delivered by the Son. "Do not then worship," he did not say, the God whom the Greeks worship, but "as the Greeks," — changing the manner of the worship of God, not announcing another God. What, then, the expression "not as the Greeks" means, Peter himself shall explain, as he adds: "Since they are carried away by ignorance, and know not God" (as we do, according to the perfect knowledge); "but giving shape to the things[4] of which He gave them the power for use — stocks and stones, brass and iron, gold and silver — matter; — and setting up the things which are slaves for use and possession, worship them.[5] And what God hath given to them for food — the fowls of the air, and the fish of the sea, and the creeping things of the earth, and the wild beasts with the four-footed cattle of the field, weasels and mice, cats and dogs and apes, and their own proper food — they sacrifice as sacrifices to mortals; and offering dead things to the dead, as to gods, are unthankful to God, denying His existence by these things." And that it is said, that we and the Greeks know the same God, though not in the same way, he will infer thus: "Neither worship as the Jews; for they, thinking that they only know God, do not know Him, adoring as they do angels and archangels, the month and the moon. And if the moon be not visible, they do not hold the Sabbath, which is called the first;[6] nor do they hold the new moon, nor the feast of unleavened bread, nor the feast, nor the great day."[7] Then he gives the finishing stroke to the question: "So that do ye also, learning holily and righteously what we deliver to you; keep them, worshipping God in a new way, by Christ." For we find in the Scriptures, as the Lord says: "Behold, I make with you a new covenant, not as I made with your fathers in Mount Horeb."[8] He made a new covenant with us; for what belonged to the Greeks and Jews is old. But we, who worship Him in a new way, in the third form, are Christians. For clearly, as I think, he showed that the one and only God was known by the Greeks in a Gentile way, by the Jews Judaically, and in a new and spiritual way by us.

And further, that the same God that furnished both the Covenants was the giver of Greek philosophy to the Greeks, by which the Almighty is glorified among the Greeks, he shows. And it is clear from this. Accordingly, then, from the

---

[1] [Instructive remarks on the confusions, etc., in Greek authors, may be seen in Schliemann, *Mycenæ*, p. 36, ed. New York, 1878.]

[2] We have the same statement made, *Stromata*, i. 19, p. 322, *ante*, Potter p. 372; also v. 14, p. 465, *ante*, Potter p. 730, — in all of which Lowth adopts περιφρασιν as the true reading, instead of περιφασιν. In the first of these passages Clement instances as one of the circumlocutions or roundabout expressions by which God was known to the Greek poets and philosophers, "*The Unknown God.*" Joannes Clericus proposes to read παράφασιν (*palpitatio*), touching, feeling after. [See *Strom.*, p. 321, and p. 464, note 1.]

[3] i.e., "The Word of God's power is His Son."

[4] Instead of ἦν . . . ἐξουσίας, as in the text, we read ὧν ἐξουσίαν.

[5] None of the attempts to amend this passage are entirely successful. The translation adopts the best suggestions made.

[6] [A strange passage; but its "darkness visible" seems to lend some help to the understanding of the puzzle about the *second-first* Sabbath of Luke vi. 1.]

[7] i.e., of atonement.

[8] Jer. xxxi. 31, 32; Heb. viii. 8-10.

Hellenic training, and also from that of the law, are gathered into the one race of the saved people those who accept faith : not that the three peoples are separated by time, so that one might suppose three natures, but trained in different Covenants of the one Lord, by the word of the one Lord. For that, as God wished to save the Jews by giving to them prophets, so also by raising up prophets of their own in their own tongue, as they were able to receive God's beneficence, He distinguished the most excellent of the Greeks from the common herd, in addition to " *Peter's Preaching*," the Apostle Paul will show, saying : "Take also the Hellenic books, read the Sibyl, how it is shown that God is one, and how the future is indicated. And taking Hystaspes, read, and you will find much more luminously and distinctly the Son of God described, and how many kings shall draw up their forces against Christ, hating Him and those that bear His name, and His faithful ones, and His patience, and His coming." Then in one word he asks us, "Whose is the world, and all that is in the world? Are they not God's?"[1] Wherefore Peter says, that the Lord said to the apostles : "If any one of Israel, then, wishes to repent, and by my name to believe in God, his sins shall be forgiven him, after twelve years. Go forth into the world, that no one may say, We have not heard."

CHAP. VI. — THE GOSPEL WAS PREACHED TO JEWS AND GENTILES IN HADES.[2]

But as the proclamation [of the Gospel] has come now at the fit time, so also at the fit time were the Law and the Prophets given to the Barbarians, and Philosophy to the Greeks, to fit their ears for the Gospel. "Therefore," says the Lord who delivered Israel, " in an acceptable time have I heard thee, and in a day of salvation have I helped thee. And I have given thee for a Covenant to the nations ; that thou mightest inhabit the earth, and receive the inheritance of the wilderness ; saying to those that are in bonds, Come forth ; and to those that are in darkness, Show yourselves." For if the "prisoners" are the Jews, of whom the Lord said, "Come forth, ye that will, from your bonds," — meaning the voluntary bound, and who have taken on them " *the burdens grievous to be borne*"[3] by human injunction — it is plain that "those in darkness" are they who have the ruling faculty of the soul buried in idolatry.

For to those who were righteous according to the law, faith was wanting. Wherefore also the Lord, in healing them, said, "Thy faith hath saved thee."[4] But to those that were righteous according to philosophy, not only faith in the Lord, but also the abandonment of idolatry, were necessary. Straightway, on the revelation of the truth, they also repented of their previous conduct.

Wherefore the Lord preached the Gospel to those in Hades. Accordingly the Scripture says, "Hades says to Destruction, We have not seen His form, but we have heard His voice."[5] It is not plainly the place, which, the words above say, heard the voice, but those who have been put in Hades, and have abandoned themselves to destruction, as persons who have thrown themselves voluntarily from a ship into the sea. They, then, are those that hear the divine power and voice. For who in his senses can suppose the souls of the righteous and those of sinners in the same condemnation, charging Providence with injustice ?

But how? Do not [the Scriptures] show that the Lord preached[6] the Gospel to those that perished in the flood, or rather had been chained, and to those kept " in ward and guard "?[7] And it has been shown also,[8] in the second book of the *Stromata*, that the apostles, following the Lord, preached the Gospel to those in Hades. For it was requisite, in my opinion, that as here, so also there, the best of the disciples should be imitators of the Master ; so that He should bring to repentance those belonging to the Hebrews, and they the Gentiles ; that is, those who had lived in righteousness according to the Law and Philosophy, who had ended life not perfectly, but sinfully. For it was suitable to the divine administration, that those possessed of greater worth in righteousness, and whose life had been pre-eminent, on repenting of their transgressions, though found in another place, yet being confessedly of the number of the people of God Almighty, should be saved, each one according to his individual knowledge.

And, as I think, the Saviour also exerts His might because it is His work to save ; which accordingly He also did by drawing to salvation those who became willing, by the preaching [of the Gospel], to believe on Him, wherever they were. If, then, the Lord descended to Hades for no other end but to preach the Gospel, as He did descend ; it was either to preach the Gospel to all or to the Hebrews only. If, accordingly, to all, then all who believe shall be saved, although they may be of the Gentiles, on making their profession there ; since God's pun-

---

[1] Most likely taken from some apocryphal book bearing the name of Paul.
[2] [The ideas on which our author bases his views of Christ's descent into the invisible world, are well expounded by Kaye, p. 189.]
[3] Matt. xxiii. 4; Luke xi. 46.

[4] Matt. ix. 22, etc.
[5] The passage which seems to be alluded to here is Job xxviii. 22, " Destruction and Death say, We have heard the fame thereof with our ears."
[6] εὐηγγελίσθαι used actively for εὐαγγελίσαι, as also immediately after εὐηγγελισμένοι for εὐαγγελισάμενοι.
[7] 1 Pet. iii. 19, 20.
[8] Potter, p. 452. [See ii. p. 357, *supra*.]

ishments are saving and disciplinary, leading to conversion, and choosing rather the repentance than the death of a sinner;[1] and especially since souls, although darkened by passions, when released from their bodies, are able to perceive more clearly, because of their being no longer obstructed by the paltry flesh.

If, then, He preached only to the Jews, who wanted the knowledge and faith of the Saviour, it is plain that, since God is no respecter of persons, the apostles also, as here, so there, preached the Gospel to those of the heathen who were ready for conversion. And it is well said by the Shepherd, "They went down with them therefore into the water, and again ascended. But these descended alive, and again ascended alive. But those who had fallen asleep, descended dead, but ascended alive."[2] Further, the Gospel[3] says, "that many bodies of those that slept arose," — plainly as having been translated to a better state.[4] There took place, then, a universal movement and translation through the economy of the Saviour.[5]

One righteous man, then, differs not, as righteous, from another righteous man, whether he be of the Law or a Greek. For God is not only Lord of the Jews, but of all men, and more nearly the Father of those who know Him. For if to live well and according to the law is to live, also to live rationally according to the law is to live; and those who lived rightly before the Law were classed under faith,[6] and judged to be righteous, — it is evident that those, too, who were outside of the Law, having lived rightly, in consequence of the peculiar nature of the voice,[7] though they are in Hades and in ward,[8] on hearing the voice of the Lord, whether that of His own person or that acting through His apostles, with all speed turned and believed. For we remember that the Lord is "the power of God,"[9] and power can never be weak.

So I think it is demonstrated that the God being good, and the Lord powerful, they save with a righteousness and equality which extend to all that turn to Him, whether here or elsewhere. For it is not here alone that the active power of God is beforehand, but it is everywhere and is always at work. Accordingly, in the *Preaching of Peter*, the Lord says to the disciples after the resurrection, "I have chosen you twelve disciples, judging you worthy of me," whom the Lord wished to be apostles, having judged them faithful, sending them into the world to the men on the earth, that they may know that there is one God, showing clearly what would take place by the faith of Christ; that they who heard and believed should be saved; and that those who believed not, after having heard, should bear witness, not having the excuse to allege, We have not heard.

What then? Did not the same dispensation obtain in Hades, so that even there, all the souls, on hearing the proclamation, might either exhibit repentance, or confess that their punishment was just, because they believed not? And it were the exercise of no ordinary arbitrariness, for those who had departed before the advent of the Lord (not having the Gospel preached to them, and having afforded no ground from themselves, in consequence of believing or not) to obtain either salvation or punishment. For it is not right that these should be condemned without trial, and that those alone who lived after the advent should have the advantage of the divine righteousness. But to all rational souls it was said from above, "Whatever one of you has done in ignorance, without clearly knowing God, if, on becoming conscious, he repent, all his sins will be forgiven him."[10] "For, behold," it is said, "I have set before your face death and life, that ye may choose life."[11] God says that He set, not that He made both, in order to the comparison of choice. And in another Scripture He says, "If ye hear Me, and be willing, ye shall eat the good of the land. But if ye hear Me not, and are not willing, the sword shall devour you: for the mouth of the LORD hath spoken these things."[12]

Again, David expressly (or rather the Lord in the person of the saint, and the same from the foundation of the world is each one who at different periods is saved, and shall be saved by faith) says, "My heart was glad, and my tongue rejoiced, and my flesh shall still rest in hope. For Thou shalt not leave my soul in hell, nor wilt Thou give Thine holy one to see corruption. Thou hast made known to me the paths of life, Thou wilt make me full of joy in Thy presence."[13] As, then, the people was precious to the Lord, so also is the entire holy people; he also who is converted from the Gentiles, who was prophesied under the name of proselyte, along with the Jew. For rightly the Scripture says, that "the ox and the bear shall come together."[14] For the Jew is designated by the ox, from the animal under the yoke being reckoned clean, according

---

[1] Ezek. xviii. 23, 32, xxxiii. 11, etc.
[2] *Hermas*, book iii. chap. xvi. p. 49. Quoted also in *Stromata*, ii. p. 357, *ante*, from which the text here is corrected; Potter, 452.
[3] Matt. xxvii. 52.
[4] τάξιν.
[5] [In connection with John v. 25, we may suppose that the opening of the graves, at the passion and resurrection, is an intimation of some sublime mystery, perhaps such as here intimated.]
[6] Rom. iii. 29, x. 12, etc.
[7] Apparently God's voice to them. Sylburgius proposes to read φύσεως instead of φωνῆς here.
[8] 1 Pet. iii. 19.
[9] 1 Cor. i. 24.

[10] Alluding apparently to such passages as Acts iii. 17, 19, and xvii. 30.
[11] Deut. xxx. 15, 19.
[12] Isa. i. 19, 20.
[13] Ps. xvi. 9-11; Acts ii. 26-28.
[14] Isa. xi. 7.

to the law; for the ox both parts the hoof and chews the cud. And the Gentile is designated by the bear, which is an unclean and wild beast. And this animal brings forth a shapeless lump of flesh, which it shapes into the likeness of a beast solely by its tongue. For he who is converted from among the Gentiles is formed from a beastlike life to gentleness by the word; and, when once tamed, is made clean, just as the ox. For example, the prophet says, "The sirens, and the daughters of the sparrows, and all the beasts of the field, shall bless me." [1] Of the number of unclean animals, the wild beasts of the field are known to be, that is, of the world; since those who are wild in respect of faith, and polluted in life, and not purified by the righteousness which is according to the law, are called wild beasts. But changed from wild beasts by the faith of the Lord, they become men of God, advancing from the wish to change to the fact. For some the Lord exhorts, and to those who have already made the attempt he stretches forth His hand, and draws them up. "For the Lord dreads not the face of any one, nor will He regard greatness; for He hath made small and great, and cares alike for all." [2] And David says, "For the heathen are fixed in the destruction they have caused; their foot is taken in the snare which they hid." [3] "But the LORD was a refuge to the poor, a help in season also in affliction." [4] Those, then, that were in affliction had the Gospel seasonably proclaimed. And therefore it said, "Declare among the heathen his pursuits," [5] that they may not be judged unjustly.

If, then, He preached the Gospel to those in the flesh that they might not be condemned unjustly, how is it conceivable that He did not for the same cause preach the Gospel to those who had departed this life before His advent? "For the righteous LORD loveth righteousness: His countenance beholdeth uprightness." [6] "But he that loveth wickedness hateth his own soul." [7]

If, then, in the deluge all sinful flesh perished, punishment having been inflicted on them for correction, we must first believe that the will of God, which is disciplinary and beneficent, [8] saves those who turn to Him. Then, too, the more subtle substance, the soul, could never receive any injury from the grosser element of water, its subtle and simple nature rendering it impalpable, called as it is incorporeal. But whatever is gross, made so in consequence of sin, this is cast away

along with the carnal spirit which lusts against the soul. [9]

Now also Valentinus, the Coryphæus of those who herald community, in his book on *The Intercourse of Friends*, writes in these words: "Many of the things that are written, though in common books, are found written in the church of God. For those sayings which proceed from the heart are vain. For the law written in the heart is the People [10] of the Beloved — loved and loving Him." For whether it be the Jewish writings or those of the philosophers that he calls "the Common Books," he makes the truth common. And Isidore, [11] at once son and disciple to Basilides, in the first book of the *Expositions of the Prophet Parchor*, writes also in these words: "The Attics say that certain things were intimated to Socrates, in consequence of a dæmon attending on him. And Aristotle says that all men are provided with dæmons, that attend on them during the time they are in the body, — having taken this piece of prophetic instruction and transferred it to his own books, without acknowledging whence he had abstracted this statement." And again, in the second book of his work, he thus writes: "And let no one think that what we say is peculiar to the elect, was said before by any philosophers. For it is not a discovery of theirs. For having appropriated it from our prophets, they attributed it to him who is wise according to them." Again, in the same: "For to me it appears that those who profess to philosophize, do so that they may learn what is the winged oak, [12] and the variegated robe on it, all of which Pherecydes has employed as theological allegories, having taken them from the prophecy of Cham."

CHAP. VII. — WHAT TRUE PHILOSOPHY IS, AND WHENCE SO CALLED.

As we have long ago pointed out, what we propose as our subject is not the discipline which obtains in each sect, but that which is really philosophy, strictly systematic Wisdom, which furnishes acquaintance with the things which pertain to life. And we define Wisdom to be certain knowledge, being a sure and irrefragable apprehension of things divine and human, comprehending the present, past, and future, which the Lord hath taught us, both by His advent and by the prophets. And it is irrefragable by reason, inasmuch as it has been communicated. And so it is wholly true according to [God's] intention, as being known through means of the Son. And in one aspect

---

1 Isa. xliii. 20.
2 Wisd. vi. 7.
3 Ps. ix. 15.
4 Ps. ix. 9.
5 Ps. ix. 11.
6 Ps. xi. 7.
7 Ps. xi. 6, Septuagint version.
8 Sylburgius' conjecture, εὐεργετικόν, seems greatly preferable to the reading of the text, ἐνεργητικόν.

9 [Kaye, p. 189.]
10 Grabe reads λόγος for λαός, "Word of the Beloved," etc.
11 [See Epiphan, *Opp.*, ii. 391, ed. Oehler, Berlin, 1859; also Mosheim, *First Three Centuries*, vol. i. p. 434.]
12 Grabe suggests, instead of ὄρυς here, ὄρυοψ, a kind of woodpecker, mentioned by Aristophanes.

it is eternal, and in another it becomes useful in time. Partly it is one and the same, partly many and indifferent — partly without any movement of passion, partly with passionate desire — partly perfect, partly incomplete.

This wisdom, then — rectitude of soul and of reason, and purity of life — is the object of the desire of philosophy, which is kindly and lovingly disposed towards wisdom, and does everything to attain it.

Now those are called philosophers, among us, who love Wisdom, the Creator and Teacher of all things, that is, the knowledge of the Son of God; and among the Greeks, those who undertake arguments on virtue. Philosophy, then, consists of such dogmas found in each sect (I mean those of philosophy) as cannot be impugned, with a corresponding life, collected into one selection; and these, stolen from the Barbarian God-given grace, have been adorned by Greek speech. For some they have borrowed, and others they have misunderstood. And in the case of others, what they have spoken, in consequence of being moved, they have not yet perfectly worked out; and others by human conjecture and reasoning, in which also they stumble. And they think that they have hit the truth perfectly; but as we understand them, only partially. They know, then, nothing more than this world. And it is just like geometry, which treats of measures and magnitudes and forms, by delineation on plane-surfaces; and just as painting appears to take in the whole field of view in the scenes represented. But it gives a false description of the view, according to the rules of the art, employing the signs that result from the incidents of the lines of vision. By this means, the higher and lower points in the view, and those between, are preserved; and some objects seem to appear in the foreground, and others in the background, and others to appear in some other way, on the smooth and level surface. So also the philosophers copy the truth, after the manner of painting. And always in the case of each one of them, their self-love is the cause of all their mistakes. Wherefore one ought not, in the desire for the glory that terminates in men, to be animated by self-love; but loving God, to become really holy with wisdom. If, then, one treats what is particular as universal, and regards that, which serves, as the Lord, he misses the truth, not understanding what was spoken by David by way of confession: "I have eaten earth [ashes] like bread." [1] Now, self-love and self-conceit are, in his view, earth and error. But if so, science and knowledge are derived from instruction. And if there

is instruction, you must seek for the master. Cleanthes claims Zeno, and Metrodorus Epicurus, and Theophrastus Aristotle, and Plato Socrates. But if I come to Pythagoras, and Pherecydes, and Thales, and the first wise men, I come to a stand in my search for their teacher. Should you say the Egyptians, the Indians, the Babylonians, and the Magi themselves, I will not stop from asking their teacher. And I lead you up to the first generation of men; and from that point I begin to investigate Who is their teacher. No one of men; for they had not yet learned. Nor yet any of the angels: for in the way that angels, in virtue of being angels, speak, men do not hear; nor, as we have ears, have they a tongue to correspond; nor would any one attribute to the angels organs of speech, lips I mean, and the parts contiguous, throat, and windpipe, and chest, breath and air to vibrate. And God is far from calling aloud in the unapproachable sanctity, separated as He is from even the archangels.

And we also have already heard that angels learned the truth, and their rulers over them; [2] for they had a beginning. It remains, then, for us, ascending to seek their teacher. And since the unoriginated Being is one, the Omnipotent God; one, too, is the First-begotten, "by whom all things were made, and without whom not one thing ever was made." [3] "For one, in truth, is God, who formed the beginning of all things;" pointing out "the first-begotten Son," Peter writes, accurately comprehending the statement, "In the beginning God made the heaven and the earth." [4] And He is called Wisdom by all the prophets. This is He who is the Teacher of all created beings, the Fellow-counsellor of God, who foreknew all things; and He from above, from the first foundation of the world, "in many ways and many times," [5] trains and perfects; whence it is rightly said, "Call no man your teacher on earth." [6]

You see whence the true philosophy has its handles; though the Law be the image and shadow of the truth: for the Law is the shadow of the truth. But the self-love of the Greeks proclaims certain men as their teachers. As, then, the whole family runs back to God the Creator; [7] so also all the teaching of good things, which justifies, does to the Lord, and leads and contributes to this.

But if from any creature they received in any way whatever the seeds of the Truth, they did not nourish them; but committing them to a barren and rainless soil, they choked them with

---

[1] Ps. cii. 9. The text reads, γῆν σποδόν. Clement seems to have read in Ps. cii. 9, γῆν and σποδόν. The reading of the Septuagint may have crept into the text from the margin. [Elucidation V.]

[2] [See the interesting passage in Justin Martyr (and note), vol. i. p. 164, this series.]
[3] John i. 3.
[4] Gen. i. 1.
[5] Heb. i. 1.
[6] Matt. xxiii. 8-10.
[7] Eph. iii. 14, 15.

weeds, as the Pharisees revolted from the Law, by introducing human teachings,— the cause of these being not the Teacher, but those who choose to disobey. But those of them who believed the Lord's advent and the plain teaching of the Scriptures, attain to the knowledge of the law; as also those addicted to philosophy, by the teaching of the Lord, are introduced into the knowledge of the true philosophy: " For the oracles of the Lord are pure oracles, melted in the fire, tried in the earth,[1] purified seven times." [2]　Just as silver often purified, so is the just man brought to the test, becoming the Lord's coin and receiving the royal image. Or, since Solomon also calls the " tongue of the righteous man gold that has been subjected to fire," [3] intimating that the doctrine which has been proved, and is wise, is to be praised and received, whenever it is amply tried by the earth: that is, when the gnostic soul is in manifold ways sanctified, through withdrawal from earthy fires.　And the body in which it dwells is purified, being appropriated to the pureness of a holy temple.　But the first purification which takes place in the body, the soul being first, is abstinence from evil things, which some consider perfection, and is, in truth, the perfection of the common believer — Jew and Greek. But in the case of the Gnostic, after that which is reckoned perfection in others, his righteousness advances to activity in well-doing.　And in whomsoever the increased force [4] of righteouness advances to the doing of good, in his case perfection abides in the fixed habit of well-doing after the likeness of God.　For those who are the seed of Abraham, and besides servants of God, are " the called;" and the sons of Jacob are the elect — they who have tripped up the energy of wickedness.

If, then, we assert that Christ Himself is Wisdom, and that it was His working which showed itself in the prophets, by which the gnostic tradition may be learned, as He Himself taught the apostles during His presence; then it follows that the gnosis, which is the knowledge and apprehension of things present, future, and past, which is sure and reliable, as being imparted and revealed by the Son of God, is wisdom.

And if, too, the end of the wise man is contemplation, that of those who are still philosophers aims at it, but never attains it, unless by the process of learning it receives the prophetic utterance which has been made known, by which it grasps both the present, the future, and the past — how they are, were, and shall be.

And the *gnosis* itself is that which has descended by transmission to a few, having been imparted unwritten by the apostles. Hence, then, knowledge or wisdom ought to be exercised up to the eternal and unchangeable habit of contemplation.

CHAP. VIII. — PHILOSOPHY IS KNOWLEDGE GIVEN BY GOD.

For Paul too, in the Epistles, plainly does not disparage philosophy; but deems it unworthy of the man who has attained to the elevation of the Gnostic, any more to go back to the Hellenic " philosophy," figuratively calling it " the rudiments of this world," [5] as being most rudimentary, and a preparatory training for the truth. Wherefore also, writing to the Hebrews, who were declining again from faith to the law, he says, " Have ye not need again of one to teach you which are the first principles of the oracles of God, and are become such as have need of milk, and not of strong meat? " [6] So also to the Colossians, who were Greek converts, " Beware lest any man spoil you by philosophy and vain deceit, after the tradition of men, after the rudiments of this world, and not after Christ," [7] — enticing them again to return to philosophy, the elementary doctrine.

And should one say that it was through human understanding that philosophy was discovered by the Greeks, still I find the Scriptures saying that understanding is sent by God. The psalmist, accordingly, considers understanding as the greatest free gift, and beseeches, saying, " I am Thy servant; give me understanding." [8] And does not David, while asking the abundant experience of knowledge, write, " Teach me gentleness, and discipline, and knowledge: for I have believed in Thy commandments? " [9] He confessed the covenants to be of the highest authority, and that they were given to the more excellent. Accordingly the psalm again says of God, " He hath not done thus to any nation; and He hath not shown His judgments to them." [10] The expression " He hath not done so " shows that *He hath done*, but not " thus." The " thus," then, is put comparatively, with reference to pre-eminence, which obtains in our case. The prophet might have said simply, " He hath not done," without the " thus."

Further, Peter in the Acts says, " Of a truth, I perceive that God is no respecter of persons; but in every nation he that feareth Him, and worketh righteousness, is accepted by Him." [11]

[1] " Tried in a furnace of earth;" Jerome, " tried in the fire, separated from earth."
[2] Ps. xii. 6.
[3] Prov. x. 20.
[4] The Latin translator appears to have read what seems the true reading, ἐπίτασις, and not, as in the text, ἐπίστασις.

[5] Col. ii. 8. [This is an interesting comment on the apostles' system, and very noteworthy.]
[6] Heb. v. 12.
[7] Col. ii. 8.
[8] Ps. cxix. 125.
[9] Ps. cxix. 66.
[10] Ps. cxlvii. 20.
[11] Acts x. 34, 35.

The absence of respect of persons in God is not then in time, but from eternity. Nor had His beneficence a beginning; nor any more is it limited to places or persons. For His beneficence is not confined to parts. "Open ye the gates of righteousness," it is said; "entering into them, I will confess to the LORD. This is the gate of the LORD. The righteous shall enter by it."[1] Explaining the prophet's saying, Barnabas adds, "There being many gates open, that which is in righteousness is the gate which is in Christ, by which all who enter are blessed." Bordering on the same meaning is also the following prophetic utterance: "The LORD is on many waters;"[2] not the different covenants alone, but the modes of teaching, those among the Greek and those among the Barbarians, conducing to righteousness. And already clearly David, bearing testimony to the truth, sings, "Let sinners be turned into Hades, and all the nations that forget God."[3] They forget, plainly, Him whom they formerly remembered, and dismiss Him whom they knew previous to forgetting Him. There was then a dim knowledge of God also among the nations. So much for those points.

Now the Gnostic must be erudite. And since the Greeks say that Protagoras having led the way, the opposing of one argument by another was invented, it is fitting that something be said with reference to arguments of this sort. For Scripture says, "He that says much, shall also hear in his turn."[4] And who shall understand a parable of the Lord, but the wise, the intelligent, and he that loves his Lord? Let such a man be faithful; let him be capable of uttering his knowledge; let him be wise in the discrimination of words; let him be dexterous in action; let him be pure. "The greater he seems to be, the more humble should he be," says Clement in the Epistle to the Corinthians, — "such an one as is capable of complying with the precept, 'And some pluck from the fire, and on others have compassion, making a difference.'"[5]

The pruning-hook is made, certainly, principally for pruning; but with it we separate twigs that have got intertwined, cut the thorns which grow along with the vines, which it is not very easy to reach. And all these things have a reference to pruning. Again, man is made principally for the knowledge of God; but he also measures land, practises agriculture, and philosophizes; of which pursuits, one conduces to life, another to living well, a third to the study of the things which are capable of demonstration. Further, let those who say that philosophy took its rise from the devil know this, that

the Scripture says that "the devil is transformed into an angel of light."[6] When about to do what? Plainly, when about to prophesy. But if he prophesies as an angel of light, he will speak what is true. And if he prophesies what is angelical, and of the light, then he prophesies what is beneficial when he is transformed according to the likeness of the operation, though he be different with respect to the matter of apostasy. For how could he deceive any one, without drawing the lover of knowledge into fellowship, and so drawing him afterwards into falsehood? Especially he will be found to know the truth, if not so as to comprehend it, yet so as not to be unacquainted with it.

Philosophy is not then false, though the thief and the liar speak truth, through a transformation of operation. Nor is sentence of condemnation to be pronounced ignorantly against what is said, on account of him who says it (which also is to be kept in view, in the case of those who are now alleged to prophesy); but what is said must be looked at, to see if it keep by the truth.

And in general terms, we shall not err in alleging that all things necessary and profitable for life came to us from God, and that philosophy more especially was given to the Greeks, as a covenant peculiar to them — being, as it is, a stepping-stone to the philosophy which is according to Christ — although those who applied themselves to the philosophy of the Greeks shut their ears voluntarily to the truth, despising the voice of Barbarians, or also dreading the danger suspended over the believer, by the laws of the state.

And as in the Barbarian philosophy, so also in the Hellenic, "tares were sown" by the proper husbandman of the tares; whence also heresies grew up among us along with the productive wheat; and those who in the Hellenic philosophy preach the impiety and voluptuousness of Epicurus, and whatever other tenets are disseminated contrary to right reason, exist among the Greeks as spurious fruits of the divinely bestowed husbandry. This voluptuous and selfish philosophy the apostle calls "the wisdom of this world;" in consequence of its teaching the things of this world and about it alone, and its consequent subjection, as far as respects ascendancy, to those who rule here. Wherefore also this fragmentary philosophy is very elementary, while truly perfect science deals with intellectual objects, which are beyond the sphere of the world, and with the objects still more spiritual than those which "eye saw not, and ear heard not, nor did it enter into the heart of men," till the Teacher told the account of them to us;

---

1 Ps. cxviii. 19, 20.
2 Ps. xxix. 3.
3 Ps. ix. 17.
4 Job xi. 2.
5 Jude 22, 23.

6 2 Cor. xi. 14.

unveiling the holy of holies; and in ascending order, things still holier than these, to those who are truly and not spuriously heirs of the Lord's adoption. For we now dare aver (for here is the faith that is characterized by knowledge [1]) that such an one knows all things, and comprehends all things in the exercise of sure apprehension, respecting matters difficult for us, and really pertaining to the true gnosis,[2] such as were James, Peter, John, Paul, and the rest of the apostles. For prophecy is full of knowledge (*gnosis*), inasmuch as it was given by the Lord, and again explained by the Lord to the apostles. And is not knowledge (*gnosis*) an attribute of the rational soul, which trains itself for this, that by knowledge it may become entitled to immortality? For both are powers of the soul, both knowledge and impulse. And impulse is found to be a movement after an assent. For he who has an impulse towards an action, first receives the knowledge of the action, and secondly the impulse. Let us further devote our attention to this. For since learning is older than action; (for naturally, he who does what he wishes to do learns it first; and knowledge comes from learning, and impulse follows knowledge; after which comes action;) knowledge turns out the beginning and author of all rational action. So that rightly the peculiar nature of the rational soul is characterized by this alone; for in reality impulse, like knowledge, is excited by existing objects. And knowledge (*gnosis*) is essentially a contemplation of existences on the part of the soul, either of a certain thing or of certain things, and when perfected, of all together. Although some say that the wise man is persuaded that there are some things incomprehensible, in such wise as to have respecting them a kind of comprehension, inasmuch as he comprehends that things incomprehensible are incomprehensible; which is common, and pertains to those who are capable of perceiving little. For such a man affirms that there are some things incomprehensible.

But that Gnostic of whom I speak, himself comprehends what seems to be incomprehensible to others; believing that nothing is incomprehensible to the Son of God, whence nothing incapable of being taught. For He who suffered out of His love for us, would have suppressed no element of knowledge requisite for our instruction. Accordingly this faith becomes sure demonstration; since truth follows what has been delivered by God. But if one desires extensive knowledge, " he knows things ancient, and conjectures things future; he understands knotty sayings, and the solutions of enigmas. The disciple of wisdom foreknows signs and omens, and the issues of seasons and of times." [3]

CHAP. IX. — THE GNOSTIC FREE OF ALL PERTURBATIONS OF THE SOUL.

The Gnostic is such, that he is subject only to the affections that exist for the maintenance of the body, such as hunger, thirst, and the like. But in the case of the Saviour, it were ludicrous [to suppose] that the body, as a body, demanded the necessary aids in order to its duration. For He ate, not for the sake of the body, which was kept together by a holy energy, but in order that it might not enter into the minds of those who were with Him to entertain a different opinion of Him; in like manner as certainly some afterwards supposed that He appeared in a phantasmal shape (δοκήσει). But He was entirely impassible (ἀπαθής); inaccessible to any movement of feeling — either pleasure or pain. While the apostles, having most gnostically mastered, through the Lord's teaching, anger, and fear, and lust, were not liable even to such of the movements of feeling, as seem good, courage, zeal, joy, desire, through a steady condition of mind, not changing a whit; but ever continuing unvarying in a state of training after the resurrection of the Lord.

And should it be granted that the affections specified above, when produced rationally, are good, yet they are nevertheless inadmissible in the case of the perfect man, who is incapable of exercising courage: for neither does he meet what inspires fear, as he regards none of the things that occur in life as to be dreaded; nor can aught dislodge him from this — the love he has towards God. Nor does he need cheerfulness of mind; for he does not fall into pain, being persuaded that all things happen well. Nor is he angry; for there is nothing to move him to anger, seeing he ever loves God, and is entirely turned towards Him alone, and therefore hates none of God's creatures. No more does he envy; for nothing is wanting to him, that is requisite to assimilation, in order that he may be excellent and good. Nor does he consequently love any one with this common affection, but loves the Creator in the creatures. Nor, consequently, does he fall into any desire and eagerness; nor does he want, as far as respects his soul, aught appertaining to others, now that he associates through love with the Beloved One, to whom he is allied by free choice, and by the habit which results from training, approaches closer to Him, and is blessed through the abundance of good things.

So that on these accounts he is compelled to

---

[1] γνωστική.
[2] γνωστικῶν, for which Hervetus, reading γνωστικόν, has translated, " qui vere est cognitione præditus." This is suitable and easier, but doubtful.

[3] Wisd. vii. 17, 18.

become like his Teacher in impassibility. For the Word of God is intellectual, according as the image of mind is seen [1] in man alone. Thus also the good man is godlike in form and semblance as respects his soul. And, on the other hand, God is like man. For the distinctive form of each one is the mind by which we are characterized. Consequently, also, those who sin against man are unholy and impious. For it were ridiculous to say that the gnostic and perfect man must not eradicate anger and courage, inasmuch as without these he will not struggle against circumstances, or abide what is terrible. But if we take from him desire, he will be quite overwhelmed by troubles, and therefore depart from this life very basely. Unless possessed of it, as some suppose, he will not conceive a desire for what is like the excellent and the good. If, then, all alliance with what is good is accompanied with desire, how, it is said, does he remain impassible who desires what is excellent?

But these people know not, as appears, the divinity of love. For love is not desire on the part of him who loves; but is a relation of affection, restoring the Gnostic to the unity of the faith, — independent of time and place. But he who by love is already in the midst of that in which he is destined to be, and has anticipated hope by knowledge, does not desire anything, having, as far as possible, the very thing desired. Accordingly, as to be expected, he continues in the exercise of gnostic love, in the one unvarying state.

Nor will he, therefore, eagerly desire to be assimilated to what is beautiful, possessing, as he does, beauty by love. What more need of courage and of desire to him, who has obtained the affinity to the impassible God which arises from love, and by love has enrolled himself among the friends of God?

We must therefore rescue the gnostic and perfect man from all passion of the soul. For knowledge (*gnosis*) produces practice, and practice habit or disposition; and such a state as this produces impassibility, not moderation of passion. And the complete eradication of desire reaps as its fruit impassibility. But the Gnostic does not share either in those affections that are commonly celebrated as good, that is, the good things of the affections which are allied to the passions: such, I mean, as gladness, which is allied to pleasure; and dejection, for this is conjoined with pain; and caution, for it is subject to fear. Nor yet does he share in high spirit, for it takes its place alongside of wrath; although some say that these are no longer evil, but already good. For it is impossible that he who has been once made perfect by love, and feasts eternally and insatiably on the boundless joy of contemplation,

should delight in small and grovelling things. For what rational cause remains any more to the man who has gained "the light inaccessible," [2] for reverting to the good things of the world? Although not yet true as to time and place, yet by that gnostic love through which the inheritance and perfect restitution follow, the giver of the reward makes good by deeds what the Gnostic, by gnostic choice, had grasped by anticipation through love.

For by going away to the Lord, for the love he bears Him, though his tabernacle be visible on earth, he does not withdraw himself from life. For that is not permitted to him. But he has withdrawn his soul from the passions. For that is granted to him. And on the other hand he lives, having put to death his lusts, and no longer makes use of the body, but allows it the use of necessaries, that he may not give cause for dissolution.

How, then, has he any more need of fortitude, who is not in the midst of dangers, being not present, but already wholly with the object of love? And what necessity for self-restraint to him who has not need of it? For to have such desires, as require self-restraint in order to their control, is characteristic of one who is not yet pure, but subject to passion. Now, fortitude is assumed by reason of fear and cowardice. For it were no longer seemly that the friend of God, whom "God hath fore-ordained before the foundation of the world" [3] to be enrolled in the highest "adoption," should fall into pleasures or fears, and be occupied in the repression of the passions. For I venture to assert, that as he is predestinated through what he shall do, and what he shall obtain, so also has he predestinated himself by reason of what he knew and whom he loved; not having the future indistinct, as the multitude live, conjecturing it, but having grasped by gnostic faith what is hidden from others. And through love, the future is for him already present. For he has believed, through prophecy and the advent, on God who lies not. And what he believes he possesses, and keeps hold of the promise. And He who hath promised is truth. And through the trustworthiness of Him who has promised, he has firmly laid hold of the end of the promise by knowledge. And he, who knows the sure comprehension of the future which there is in the circumstances, in which he is placed, by love goes to meet the future. So he, that is persuaded that he will obtain the things that are really good, will not pray to obtain what is here, but that he may always cling to the faith which hits the mark and succeeds. And besides, he will pray that as many as possible may become like him, to the glory of God,

---

[1] Adopting the various reading καθ᾿ ὅ, and the conjecture ὁρᾶται, instead of καθ᾿ ὅν and ὁράσει in the text, as suggested by Sylburgius.

[2] 1 Tim. vi. 16.
[3] Eph. i. 4, 5.

which is perfected through knowledge. For he who is made like the Saviour is also devoted to saving; performing unerringly the commandments as far as the human nature may admit of the image. And this is to worship God by deeds and knowledge of the true righteousness. The Lord will not wait for the voice of this man in prayer. "Ask," He says, "and I will do it; think, and I will give."[1]

For, in fine, it is impossible that the immutable should assume firmness and consistency in the mutable. But the ruling faculty being in perpetual change, and therefore unstable, the force of habit is not maintained. For how can he who is perpetually changed by external occurrences and accidents, ever possess habit and disposition, and in a word, grasp of scientific knowledge ($\epsilon\pi\iota\sigma\tau\eta\mu\eta$)? Further, also, the philosophers regard the virtues as habits, dispositions, and sciences. And as knowledge (*gnosis*) is not born with men, but is acquired,[2] and the acquiring of it in its elements demands application, and training, and progress; and then from incessant practice it passes into a habit; so, when perfected in the mystic habit, it abides, being infallible through love. For not only has he apprehended the first Cause, and the Cause produced by it, and is sure about them, possessing firmly firm and irrefragable and immoveable reasons; but also respecting what is good and what is evil, and respecting all production, and to speak comprehensively, respecting all about which the Lord has spoken, he has learned, from the truth itself, the most exact truth from the foundation of the world to the end. Not preferring to the truth itself what appears plausible, or, according to Hellenic reasoning, necessary; but what has been spoken by the Lord he accepts as clear and evident, though concealed from others; and he has already received the knowledge of all things. And the oracles we possess give their utterances respecting what exists, as it is; and respecting what is future, as it shall be; and respecting what is past, as it was.

In scientific matters, as being alone possessed of scientific knowledge, he will hold the pre-eminence, and will discourse on the discussion respecting the good, ever intent on intellectual objects, tracing out his procedure in human affairs from the archetypes above; as navigators direct the ship according to the star; prepared to hold himself in readiness for every suitable action; accustomed to despise all difficulties and dangers when it is necessary to undergo them; never doing anything precipitate or incongruous either to himself or the common weal; foreseeing; and inflexible by pleasures both of waking hours and of dreams. For, accustomed to spare living and frugality, he is moderate, active, and grave; requiring few necessaries for life; occupying himself with nothing superfluous. But desiring not even these things as chief, but by reason of fellowship in life, as necessary for his sojourn in life, as far as necessary.

CHAP. X. — THE GNOSTIC AVAILS HIMSELF OF THE HELP OF ALL HUMAN KNOWLEDGE.

For to him knowledge (*gnosis*) is the principal thing. Consequently, therefore, he applies to the subjects that are a training for knowledge, taking from each branch of study its contribution to the truth. Prosecuting, then, the proportion of harmonies in music; and in arithmetic noting the increasing and decreasing of numbers, and their relations to one another, and how the most of things fall under some proportion of numbers; studying geometry, which is abstract essence, he perceives a continuous distance, and an immutable essence which is different from these bodies. And by astronomy, again, raised from the earth in his mind, he is elevated along with heaven, and will revolve with its revolution; studying ever divine things, and their harmony with each other; from which Abraham starting, ascended to the knowledge of Him who created them. Further, the Gnostic will avail himself of dialectics, fixing on the distinction of genera into species, and will master[3] the distinction of existences, till he come to what are primary and simple.

But the multitude are frightened at the Hellenic philosophy, as children are at masks, being afraid lest it lead them astray. But if the faith (for I cannot call it knowledge) which they possess be such as to be dissolved by plausible speech, let it be by all means dissolved,[4] and let them confess that they will not retain the truth. For truth is immoveable; but false opinion dissolves. We choose, for instance, one purple by comparison with another purple. So that, if one confesses that he has not a heart that has been made right, he has not the table of the money-changers or the test of words.[5] And how can he be any longer a money-changer, who is not able to prove and distinguish spurious coin, even offhand?

Now David cried, "The righteous shall not be shaken for ever;"[6] neither, consequently, by deceptive speech nor by erring pleasure.

---

[1] Quoted afterwards, chap. xii., and book vii. chap. ii.
[2] The text has ἐπίμικτος, which on account of its harshness has been rejected by the authorities for ἐπίκτητος.

[3] Our choice lies between the reading of the text, προσίσεται: that of Hervetus, προσοίσεται: the conjecture of Sylburgius, προσείσεται, or προσήσεται, used a little after in the phrase προσήσεται τὴν ἀλήθειαν.
[4] There is some difficulty in the sentence as it stands. Hervetus omits in his translation the words rendered here, "let it be by all means dissolved." We have omitted διὰ τούτους, which follows immediately after, but which is generally retained and translated "by these," i.e., philosophers.
[5] τῶν λόγων, Sylburgius; τὸν λόγον is the reading of the text.
[6] Ps. cxii. 6.

Whence he shall never be shaken from his own heritage. "He shall not be afraid of evil tidings;"[1] consequently neither of unfounded calumny, nor of the false opinion around him. No more will he dread cunning words, who is capable of distinguishing them, or of answering rightly to questions asked. Such a bulwark are dialectics, that truth cannot be trampled under foot by the Sophists. "For it behoves those who praise in the holy name of the Lord," according to the prophet, "to rejoice in heart, seeking the Lord. Seek then Him, and be strong. Seek His face continually in every way."[2] "For, having spoken at sundry times and in divers manners,"[3] it is not in one way only that He is known.

It is, then, not by availing himself of these as virtues that our Gnostic will be deeply learned. But by using them as helps in distinguishing what is common and what is peculiar, he will admit the truth. For the cause of all error and false opinion, is inability to distinguish in what respect things are common, and in what respects they differ. For unless, in things that are distinct, one closely watch speech, he will inadvertently confound what is common and what is peculiar And where this takes place, he must of necessity fall into pathless tracts and error.

The distinction of names and things also in the Scriptures themselves produces great light in men's souls. For it is necessary to understand expressions which signify several things, and several expressions when they signify one thing. The result of which is accurate answering. But it is necessary to avoid the great futility which occupies itself in irrelevant matters; since the Gnostic avails himself of branches of learning as auxiliary preparatory exercises, in order to the accurate communication of the truth, as far as attainable and with as little distraction as possible, and for defence against reasonings that plot for the extinction of the truth. He will not then be deficient in what contributes to proficiency in the curriculum of studies and the Hellenic philosophy; but not principally, but necessarily, secondarily, and on account of circumstances. For what those labouring in heresies use wickedly, the Gnostic will use rightly.

Therefore the truth that appears in the Hellenic philosophy, being partial, the real truth, like the sun glancing on the colours both white and black, shows what like each of them is. So also it exposes all sophistical plausibility. Rightly, then, was it proclaimed also by the Greeks: —

"Truth the queen is the beginning of great virtue."[4]

CHAP. XI. — THE MYSTICAL MEANINGS IN THE PROPORTIONS OF NUMBERS, GEOMETRICAL RATIOS, AND MUSIC.

As then in astronomy we have Abraham as an instance, so also in arithmetic we have the same Abraham. "For, hearing that Lot was taken captive, and having numbered his own servants, born in his house, 318 ($\tau\iota\eta$[5])," he defeats a very great number of the enemy.

They say, then, that the character representing 300 is, as to shape, the type of the Lord's sign,[6] and that the *Iota* and the *Eta* indicate the Saviour's name; that it was indicated, accordingly, that Abraham's domestics were in salvation, who having fled to the Sign and the Name became lords of the captives, and of the very many unbelieving nations that followed them.

Now the number 300 is, 3 by 100. Ten is allowed to be the perfect number. And 8 is the first cube, which is equality in all the dimensions — length, breadth, depth. "The days of men shall be," it is said, "120 ($\rho\kappa'$) years."[7] And the sum is made up of the numbers from 1 to 15 added together.[8] And the moon at 15 days is full.

On another principle, 120 is a triangular[9] number, and consists of the equality[10] of the number 64, [which consists of eight of the odd numbers beginning with unity],[11] the addition of which (1, 3, 5, 7, 9, 11, 13, 15) in succession generate squares;[12] and of the inequality of the number 56, consisting of seven of the even numbers beginning with 2 (2, 4, 6, 8, 10, 12, 14), which produce the numbers that are not squares[13]

Again, according to another way of indicating, the number 120 consists of four numbers — of one triangle, 15; of another, a square, 25; of a third, a pentagon, 35; and of a fourth, a hexagon, 45. The 5 is taken according to the same ratio in each mode. For in triangular numbers, from the unity 5 comes 15; and in squares, 25; and of those in succession, proportionally. Now 25, which is the number 5 from unity, is said to be the symbol of the Levitical tribe. And the

---

[5] Gen. xiv. 14. In Greek numerals.
[6] The Lord's sign is the cross, whose form is represented by T; Iη (the other two letters of τιη, 318) are the first two letters of the name Ἰησοῦς (Jesus).
[7] Gen. vi. 3.
[8] The sum of the numbers from 1 to 15 inclusive is 120.
[9] "Triangular numbers are those which can be disposed in a triangle, as 3 ∴, 6 ∴∴, etc, being represented by the formula $\frac{x^2+x}{2}$" (Liddell and Scott's *Lexicon*). Each side of the triangle of coures contains an equal number of units, the sum of which amounts to the number. [Elucidation VI.]
[10] This number is called equality, because it is composed of eight numbers, an even number; as fifty-six is called inequality, because it is composed of seven numbers, an odd number.
[11] The clause within brackets has been suggested by Hervetus to complete the sense.
[12] That is, 1 + 3 + 5 + 7 + 9 + 11 + 13 + 15 = 120; and 1 + 3 = 4 + 5 = 9 + 7 = 16 + 9 = 25 + 11 = 36 + 13 = 49 + 15 = 64, giving us the numbers 4, 9, 16, 25, 36, 49, 64, the squares of 2, 3, 4, 5, 6, 7, 8.
[13] ἑτερομήκεις, the product of two unequal factors, i.e., 2 + 4 + 6 + 8 + 10 + 12 + 14 = 56; and 2 + 4 = 6 = 3 × 2, 6 + 4 = 10 = 5 × 2, and so on.

---

[1] Ps. cxii. 7.
[2] Ps. cv. 3, 4.
[3] Heb. i. 1.
[4] Pindar.

number 35 depends also on the arithmetic, geometric, and harmonic scale of doubles — 6, 8, 9, 12; the addition of which makes 35. In these days, the Jews say that seven months' children are formed. And the number 45 depends on the scale of triples — 6, 9, 12, 18 — the addition of which makes 45; and similarly, in these days they say that nine months' children are formed.

Such, then, is the style of the example in arithmetic. And let the testimony of geometry be the tabernacle that was constructed, and the ark that was fashioned, — constructed in most regular proportions, and through divine ideas, by the gift of understanding, which leads us from things of sense to intellectual objects, or rather from these to holy things, and to the holy of holies. For the squares of wood indicate that the square form, producing right angles, pervades all, and points out security. And the length of the structure was three hundred cubits, and the breadth fifty, and the height thirty; and above, the ark ends in a cubit, narrowing to a cubit from the broad base like a pyramid, the symbol of those who are purified and tested by fire. And this geometrical proportion has a place, for the transport of those holy abodes, whose differences are indicated by the differences of the numbers set down below.

And the numbers introduced are sixfold, as three hundred is six times fifty; and tenfold, as three hundred is ten times thirty; and containing one and two-thirds (ἐπιδίμοιροι), for fifty is one and two-thirds of thirty.

Now there are some who say that three hundred cubits are the symbol of the Lord's sign;[1] and fifty, of hope and of the remission given at Pentecost; and thirty, or as in some, twelve, they say points out the preaching [of the Gospel]; because the Lord preached in His thirtieth year; and the apostles were twelve. And the structure's terminating in a cubit is the symbol of the advancement of the righteous to oneness and to "the unity of the faith."[2]

And the table which was in the temple was six cubits;[3] and its four feet were about a cubit and a half.

They add, then, the twelve cubits, agreeably to the revolution of the twelve months, in the annual circle, during which the earth produces and matures all things; adapting itself to the four seasons. And the table, in my opinion, exhibits the image of the earth, supported as it is on four feet, summer, autumn, spring, winter, by which the year travels. Wherefore also it is said that the table has "wavy chains;"[4] either

because the universe revolves in the circuits of the times, or perhaps it indicated the earth surrounded with ocean's tide.

Further, as an example of music, let us adduce David, playing at once and prophesying, melodiously praising God. Now the Enarmonic[5] suits best the Dorian harmony, and the Diatonic the Phrygian, as Aristoxenus says. The harmony, therefore, of the Barbarian psaltery, which exhibited gravity of strain, being the most ancient, most certainly became a model for Terpander, for the Dorian harmony, who sings the praise of Zeus thus: —

"O Zeus, of all things the Beginning, Ruler of all;
O Zeus, I send thee this beginning of hymns."

The lyre, according to its primary signification, may by the psalmist be used figuratively for the Lord; according to its secondary, for those who continually strike the chords of their souls under the direction of the Choir-master, the Lord. And if the people saved be called the lyre, it will be understood to be in consequence of their giving glory musically, through the inspiration of the Word and the knowledge of God, being struck by the Word so as to produce faith. You may take music in another way, as the ecclesiastical symphony at once of the law and the prophets, and the apostles along with the Gospel, and the harmony which obtained in each prophet, in the transitions of the persons.

But, as seems, the most of those who are inscribed with the Name,[6] like the companions of Ulysses, handle the word unskilfully, passing by not the Sirens, but the rhythm and the melody, stopping their ears with ignorance; since they know that, after lending their ears to Hellenic studies, they will never subsequently be able to retrace their steps.

But he who culls what is useful for the advantage of the catechumens, and especially when they are Greeks (and the earth is the Lord's, and the fulness thereof[7]), must not abstain from erudition, like irrational animals; but he must collect as many aids as possible for his hearers. But he must by no means linger over these studies, except solely for the advantage accruing from them; so that, on grasping and obtaining this, he may be able to take his departure home to the true philosophy, which is a strong cable for the soul, providing security from everything.

Music is then to be handled for the sake of the embellishment and composure of manners. For instance, at a banquet we pledge each other while the music is playing;[8] soothing by song the eagerness of our desires, and glorifying God

---

[1] The cross.
[2] Eph. iv. 13.
[3] Ex. xxv. 23. The table is said to be two cubits in length, a cubit in breadth, and a cubit and a half in height; therefore it was six cubits round.
[4] Ex. xxv. 24.

[5] The three styles of Greek music were the ἐναρμονικόν, διάτονον, and χρωματικόν.
[6] i.e., of Christ.
[7] 1 Cor. x. 26, etc.
[8] ψάλλοντες is substituted by Lowth for ψάλλειν of the text; ἐν τῷ ψάλλειν has also been proposed.

for the copious gift of human enjoyments, for His perpetual supply of the food necessary for the growth of the body and of the soul. But we must reject superfluous music, which enervates men's souls, and leads to variety, — now mournful, and then licentious and voluptuous, and then frenzied and frantic.

The same holds also of astronomy. For treating of the description of the celestial objects, about the form of the universe, and the revolution of the heavens, and the motion of the stars, leading the soul nearer to the creative power, it teaches to quickness in perceiving the seasons of the year, the changes of the air, and the appearance of the stars; since also navigation and husbandry derive from this much benefit, as architecture and building from geometry. This branch of learning, too, makes the soul in the highest degree observant, capable of perceiving the true and detecting the false, of discovering correspondences and proportions, so as to hunt out for similarity in things dissimilar; and conducts us to the discovery of length without breadth, and superficial extent without thickness, and an indivisible point, and transports to intellectual objects from those of sense.

The studies of philosophy, therefore, and philosophy itself, are aids in treating of the truth. For instance, the cloak was once a fleece; then it was shorn, and became warp and woof; and then it was woven. Accordingly the soul must be prepared and variously exercised, if it would become in the highest degree good. For there is the scientific and the practical element in truth; and the latter flows from the speculative; and there is need of great practice, and exercise, and experience.

But in speculation, one element relates to one's neighbours and another to one's self. Wherefore also training ought to be so moulded as to be adapted to both. He, then, who has acquired a competent acquaintance with the subjects which embrace the principles which conduce to scientific knowledge (*gnosis*), may stop and remain for the future in quiet, directing his actions in conformity with his theory.

But for the benefit of one's neighbours, in the case of those who have proclivities for writing, and those who set themselves to deliver the word, both is other culture beneficial, and the reading of the Scriptures of the Lord is necessary, in order to the demonstration of what is said, and especially if those who hear are accessions from Hellenic culture.

Such David describes the Church: "The queen stood on thy right hand, enveloped in a golden robe, variegated;"[1] and with Hellenic and superabundant accomplishments, "clothed

variegated with gold-fringed garments."[2] And the Truth says by the Lord, "For who had known Thy counsel, hadst Thou not given wisdom, and sent Thy Holy Spirit from the Highest; and so the ways of those on earth were corrected, and men learned Thy decrees, and were saved by wisdom?" For the Gnostic knows things ancient by the Scripture, and conjectures things future: he understands the involutions of words and the solutions of enigmas. He knows beforehand signs and wonders, and the issues of seasons and periods, as we have said already. Seest thou the fountain of instructions that takes its rise from wisdom? But to those who object, What use is there in knowing the causes of the manner of the sun's motion, for example, and the rest of the heavenly bodies, or in having studied the theorems of geometry or logic, and each of the other branches of study?— for these are of no service in the discharge of duties, and the Hellenic philosophy is human wisdom, for it is incapable of teaching[3] the truth — the following remarks are to be made. First, that they stumble in reference to the highest of things — namely, the mind's free choice. "For they," it is said, "who keep holy holy things, shall be made holy; and those who have been taught will find an answer."[4] For the Gnostic alone will do holily, in accordance with reason all that has to be done, as he hath learned through the Lord's teaching, received through men.

Again, on the other hand, we may hear: "For in His hand, that is, in His power and wisdom, are both we and our words, and all wisdom and skill in works; for God loves nothing but the man that dwells with wisdom."[5] And again, they have not read what is said by Solomon; for, treating of the construction of the temple, he says expressly, "And it was Wisdom as artificer that framed it; and Thy providence, O Father, governs throughout."[6] And how irrational, to regard philosophy as inferior to architecture and shipbuilding! And the Lord fed the multitude of those that reclined on the grass opposite to Tiberias with the two fishes and the five barley loaves, indicating the preparatory training of the Greeks and Jews previous to the divine grain, which is the food cultivated by the law. For barley is sooner ripe for the harvest than wheat; and the fishes signified the Hellenic philosophy that was produced and moved in the midst of the Gentile billow, given, as they were, for copious food to those lying on the ground, increasing no more, like the fragments of the

---

[1] Ps. xlv. 9.

[2] Ps. xlv. 14. [Elucidation VII.]
[3] διδακτικήν, proposed by Sylburgius, seems greatly preferable to the reading of the text, διδακτήν, and has been adopted above.
[4] Wisd. vi. 10.
[5] Wisd. vii. 16.
[6] Wisd. xiv. 2, 3.

loaves, but having partaken of the Lord's blessing, and breathed into them the resurrection of Godhead[1] through the power of the Word. But if you are curious, understand one of the fishes to mean the curriculum of study, and the other the philosophy which supervenes. The gatherings[2] point out the word of the Lord.

"And the choir of mute fishes rushed to it,"

says the Tragic Muse somewhere.

"I must decrease," said the prophet John,[3] and the Word of the Lord alone, in which the law terminates, "increase." Understand now for me the mystery of the truth, granting pardon if I shrink from advancing further in the treatment of it, by announcing this alone: "All things were made by Him, and without Him was not even one thing."[4] Certainly He is called "the chief corner stone; in whom the whole building, fitly joined together, groweth into an holy temple of God,"[5] according to the divine apostle.

I pass over in silence at present the parable which says in the Gospel: "The kingdom of heaven is like a man who cast a net into the sea, and out of the multitude of the fishes caught, makes a selection of the better ones."[6]

And now the wisdom which we possess announces the four virtues[7] in such a way as to show that the sources of them were communicated by the Hebrews to the Greeks. This may be learned from the following: "And if one loves justice, its toils are virtues. For temperance and prudence teach justice and fortitude; and than these there is nothing more useful in life to men."

Above all, this ought to be known, that by nature we are adapted for virtue; not so as to be possessed of it from our birth, but so as to be adapted for acquiring it.

CHAP. XII. — HUMAN NATURE POSSESSES AN ADAPTATION FOR PERFECTION; THE GNOSTIC ALONE ATTAINS IT.

By which consideration[8] is solved the question propounded to us by the heretics, Whether Adam was created perfect or imperfect? Well, if imperfect, how could the work of a perfect God — above all, that work being man — be imperfect? And if perfect, how did he transgress the commandments? For they shall hear from

us that he was not perfect in his creation, but adapted to the reception of virtue. For it is of great importance in regard to virtue to be made fit for its attainment. And it is intended that we should be saved by ourselves. This, then, is the nature of the soul, to move of itself. Then, as we are rational, and philosophy being rational, we have some affinity with it. Now an aptitude is a movement towards virtue, not virtue itself. All, then, as I said, are naturally constituted for the acquisition of virtue.

But one man applies less, one more, to learning and training. Wherefore also some have been competent to attain to perfect virtue, and others have attained to a kind of it. And some, on the other hand, through negligence, although in other respects of good dispositions, have turned to the opposite. Now much more is that knowledge which excels all branches of culture in greatness and in truth, most difficult to acquire, and is attained with much toil. "But, as seems, they know not the mysteries of God. For God created man for immortality, and made him an image of His own nature;"[9] according to which nature of Him who knows all, he who is a Gnostic, and righteous, and holy with prudence, hastes to reach the measure of perfect manhood. For not only are actions and thoughts, but words also, pure in the case of the Gnostic: "Thou hast proved mine heart; Thou hast visited me by night," it is said; "Thou hast subjected me to the fire, and unrighteousness was not found in me: so that my mouth shall not speak the works of men."[10]

And why do I say the works of men? He recognises sin itself, which is not brought forward in order to repentance (for this is common to all believers); but what sin is. Nor does he condemn this or that sin, but simply all sin; nor is it what one has done ill that he brings up, but what ought not to be done. Whence also repentance is twofold: that which is common, on account of having transgressed; and that which, from learning the nature of sin, persuades, in the first instance, to keep from sinning, the result of which is not sinning.

Let them not then say, that he who does wrong and sins transgresses through the agency of demons; for then he would be guiltless. But by choosing the same things as demons, by sinning, being unstable, and light, and fickle in his desires, like a demon, he becomes a demoniac man. Now he who is bad, having become, through evil, sinful by nature, becomes depraved, having what he has chosen; and being sinful, sins also in his actions. And again, the good man does right. Wherefore we call not only the virtues, but also right actions, good. And of things that are

---

[1] That is, resurrection effected by divine power
[2] Such seems the only sense possible of this clause, — obtained, however, by substituting for συνάλογοι λογου, κ.τ.λ., σύλλογοι λόγον, κ.τ.λ.
[3] John iii. 30.
[4] John i. 3.
[5] Eph. ii. 20, 21.
[6] Matt. xiii. 47, 48.
[7] Prudence, fortitude, justice, temperance. [Known as the philosophical virtues.]
[8] i.e., that mentioned in the last sentence of chap xi., which would more appropriately be transferred to chap. xii.

[9] Wisd. ii. 22, 25.
[10] Ps. xvii. 3, 4.

good we know that some are desirable for themselves, as knowledge; for we hunt for nothing from it when we have it, but only [seek] that it be with us, and that we be in uninterrupted contemplation, and strive to reach it for its own sake. But other things are desirable for other considerations, such as faith, for escape from punishment, and the advantage arising from reward, which accrue from it. For, in the case of many, fear is the cause of their not sinning; and the promise is the means of pursuing obedience, by which comes salvation. Knowledge, then, desirable as it is for its own sake, is the most perfect good; and consequently the things which follow by means of it are good. And punishment is the cause of correction to him who is punished; and to those who are able to see before them he becomes an example, to prevent them falling into the like.

Let us then receive knowledge, not desiring its results, but embracing itself for the sake of knowing. For the first advantage is the habit of knowledge (γνωστική), which furnishes harmless pleasures and exultation both for the present and the future. And exultation is said to be gladness, being a reflection of the virtue which is according to truth, through a kind of exhilaration and relaxation of soul. And the acts which partake of knowledge are good and fair actions. For abundance in the actions that are according to virtue, is the true riches, and destitution in decorous [1] desires is poverty. For the use and enjoyment of necessaries are not injurious in quality, but in quantity, when in excess. Wherefore the Gnostic circumscribes his desires in reference both to possession and to enjoyment, not exceeding the limit of necessity. Therefore, regarding life in this world as necessary for the increase of science (ἐπιστήμη) and the acquisition of knowledge (γνῶσις), he will value highest, not living, but living well. He will therefore prefer neither children, nor marriage, nor parents, to love for God, and righteousness in life. To such an one, his wife, after conception, is as a sister, and is judged as if of the same father; then only recollecting her husband, when she looks on the children; as being destined to become a sister in reality after putting off the flesh, which separates and limits the knowledge of those who are spiritual by the peculiar characteristics of the sexes. For souls, themselves by themselves, are equal. Souls are neither male nor female, when they no longer marry nor are given in marriage. And is not woman translated into man, when she is become equally unfeminine, and manly, and perfect? Such, then, was the laughter of Sarah [2]

when she received the good news of the birth of a son; not, in my opinion, that she disbelieved the angel, but that she felt ashamed of the intercourse by means of which she was destined to become the mother of a son.

And did not Abraham, when he was in danger on account of Sarah's beauty, with the king of Egypt, properly call her sister, being of the same father, but not of the same mother? [3]

To those, then, who have repented and not firmly believed, God grants their requests through their supplications. But to those who live sinlessly and gnostically, He gives, when they have but merely entertained the thought. For example, to Anna, on her merely conceiving the thought, conception was vouchsafed of the child Samuel. [4] "Ask," says the Scripture, "and I will do. Think, and I will give." For we have heard that God knows the heart, not judging [5] the soul from [external] movement, as we men; nor yet from the event. For it is ridiculous to think so. Nor was it as the architect praises the work when accomplished that God, on making the light and then seeing it, called it good. But He, knowing before He made it what it would be, praised that which was made, He having potentially made good, from the first by His purpose that had no beginning, what was destined to be good actually. Now that which has future He already said beforehand was good, the phrase concealing the truth by hyperbaton. Therefore the Gnostic prays in thought during every hour, being by love allied to God. And first he will ask forgiveness of sins; and after, that he may sin no more; and further, the power of well-doing and of comprehending the whole creation and administration by the Lord, that, becoming pure in heart through the knowledge, which is by the Son of God, he may be initiated into the beatific vision face to face, having heard the Scripture which says, "Fasting with prayer is a good thing." [6]

Now fastings signify abstinence from all evils whatsoever, both in action and in word, and in thought itself. As appears, then, righteousness is quadrangular; [7] on all sides equal and like in word, in deed, in abstinence from evils, in beneficence, in gnostic perfection; nowhere, and in no respect halting, so that he does not appear unjust and unequal. As one, then, is righteous, so certainly is he a believer. But as he is a believer, he is not yet also righteous — I mean ac-

---

[1] Sylburgius proposes κοσμικάς, worldly, instead of κοσμίας, decorous; in which case the sentence would read: "and [true] poverty, destitution in worldly desires."
[2] Gen. xviii. 12.

[3] The reading of the text has, "not of the same mother, much less of the same father," which contradicts Gen. xx. 12, and has been therefore amended as above.
[4] 1 Sam. 1. 13.
[5] Or, "judging from the motion of the soul;" the text reading here οὐ κινήματος ψυχῆς, for which, as above, is proposed, οὐκ ἐκ κινήματος ψυχῆν.
[6] Tob. xii. 8.
[7] Metaphorical expression for perfect. The phrase "a quadrangular man" is found in Plato and Aristotle. [The proverbial τετράγωνος ἄνευ ψόγου, of the Nicomach. Ethics, i. 10, and of Plato in the Protagoras, p 154. Ed. Bipont, 1782.]

cording to the righteousness of progress and perfection, according to which the Gnostic is called righteous.

For instance, on Abraham becoming a believer, it was reckoned to him for righteousness, he having advanced to the greater and more perfect degree of faith. For he who merely abstains from evil conduct is not just, unless he also attain besides beneficence and knowledge; and for this reason some things are to be abstained from, others are to be done. "By the armour of righteousness on the right hand and on the left," [1] the apostle says, the righteous man is sent on to the inheritance above,—by some [arms] defended, by others putting forth his might. For the defence of his panoply alone, and abstinence from sins, are not sufficient for perfection, unless he assume in addition the work of righteousness—activity in doing good.

Then our dexterous man and Gnostic is revealed in righteousness already even here, as Moses, glorified in the face of the soul,[2] as we have formerly said, the body bears the stamp of the righteous soul. For as the mordant of the dyeing process, remaining in the wool, produces in it a certain quality and diversity from other wool; so also in the soul the pain is gone, but the good remains; and the sweet is left, but the base is wiped away. For these are two qualities characteristic of each soul, by which is known that which is glorified, and that which is condemned.

And as in the case of Moses, from his righteous conduct, and from his uninterrupted intercourse with God, who spoke to him, a kind of glorified hue settled on his face; so also a divine power of goodness clinging to the righteous soul in contemplation and in prophecy, and in the exercise of the function of governing, impresses on it something, as it were, of intellectual radiance, like the solar ray, as a visible sign of righteousness, uniting the soul with light, through unbroken love, which is God-bearing and God-borne. Thence assimilation to God the Saviour arises to the Gnostic, as far as permitted to human nature, he being made perfect "as the Father who is in heaven." [3]

It is He Himself who says, "Little children, a little while I am still with you." [4] Since also God Himself remains blessed and immortal, neither molested nor molesting another; [5] not in consequence of being by nature good, but in consequence of doing good in a manner peculiar to Himself. God being essentially, and

proving Himself actually, both Father and good, continues immutably in the self-same goodness. For what is the use of good that does not act and do good?

CHAP. XIII. — DEGREES OF GLORY IN HEAVEN CORRESPONDING WITH THE DIGNITIES OF THE CHURCH BELOW.

He, then, who has first moderated his passions and trained himself for impassibility, and developed to the beneficence of gnostic perfection, is here equal to the angels. Luminous already, and like the sun shining in the exercise of beneficence, he speeds by righteous knowledge through the love of God to the sacred abode, like as the apostles. Not that they became apostles through being chosen for some distinguished peculiarity [6] of nature, since also Judas was chosen along with them. But they were capable of becoming apostles on being chosen by Him who foresees even ultimate issues. Matthias, accordingly, who was not chosen along with them, on showing himself worthy of becoming an apostle, is substituted for Judas.

Those, then, also now, who have exercised themselves in the Lord's commandments, and lived perfectly and gnostically according to the Gospel, may be enrolled in the chosen body of the apostles. Such an one is in reality a presbyter of the Church, and a true minister (deacon) of the will of God, if he do and teach what is the Lord's; not as being ordained [7] by men, nor regarded righteous because a presbyter, but enrolled in the presbyterate [8] because righteous. And although here upon earth he be not honoured with the chief seat,[9] he will sit down on the four-and-twenty thrones,[10] judging the people, as John says in the Apocalypse.

For, in truth, the covenant of salvation, reaching down to us from the foundation of the world, through different generations and times, is one, though conceived as different in respect of gift. For it follows that there is one unchangeable gift of salvation given by one God, through one Lord, benefiting in many ways. For which cause the middle wall [11] which separated the Greek from the Jew is taken away, in order that there might be a peculiar people. And so both meet in the one unity of faith; and the selection out of both is one. And the chosen of the chosen are those who by reason of perfect knowledge are called [as the best] from the

---

[1] 2 Cor. vi. 7.
[2] Ex. xxxiv. 29.
[3] Matt. v. 48.
[4] John xiii. 33.
[5] This is cited by Diogenes Laertius as the first dictum of Epicurus. It is also referred to as such by Cicero, *De Natura Deorum*, and by others.

[6] In opposition to the heretical opinion, that those who are saved have an innate original excellence, on account of which they are saved. [Elucidation VIII.]
[7] Or, "elected"—χειροτονούμενος. Acts xiv. 23, "And when they had ordained (χειροτονήσαντες) them elders in every church." A different verb (καθίστημι) is used in Tit. i. 5.
[8] Presbytery or eldership.
[9] πρωτοκαθεδρία, Mark xii. 39, Luke xx. 46.
[10] Rev. iv. 4, xi. 16.
[11] Eph ii. 14, 15, 16, iv. 13.

Church itself, and honoured with the most august glory — the judges and rulers — four-and-twenty (the grace being doubled) equally from Jews and Greeks. Since, according to my opinion, the grades [1] here in the Church, of bishops, presbyters, deacons, are imitations of the angelic glory, and of that economy which, the Scriptures say, awaits those who, following the footsteps of the apostles, have lived in perfection of righteousness according to the Gospel. For these taken up in the clouds, the apostle [2] writes, will first minister [as deacons], then be classed in the presbyterate, by promotion in glory (for glory differs [3] from glory) till they grow into " a perfect man." [4]

CHAP. XIV. — DEGREES OF GLORY IN HEAVEN.

Such, according to David, " rest in the holy hill of God," [5] in the Church far on high, in which are gathered the philosophers of God, " who are Israelites indeed, who are pure in heart, in whom there is no guile ; " [6] who do not remain in the seventh seat, the place of rest, but are promoted, through the active beneficence of the divine likeness, to the heritage of beneficence which is the eighth grade ; devoting themselves to the pure vision [7] of insatiable contemplation.

" And other sheep there are also," saith the Lord, " which are not of this fold " [8] — deemed worthy of another fold and mansion, in proportion to their faith. " But My sheep hear My voice," [9] understanding gnostically the commandments. And this is to be taken in a magnanimous and worthy acceptation, along with also the recompense and accompaniment of works. So that when we hear, " Thy faith hath saved thee," [10] we do not understand Him to say absolutely that those who have believed in any way whatever shall be saved, unless also works follow. But it was to the Jews alone that He spoke this utterance, who kept the law and lived blamelessly, who wanted only faith in the Lord. No one, then, can be a believer and at the same time be licentious ; but though he quit the flesh, he must put off the passions, so as to be capable of reaching his own mansion.

Now to know is more than to believe, as to be dignified with the highest honour after being saved is a greater thing than being saved. Accordingly the believer, through great discipline, divesting himself of the passions, passes to the mansion which is better than the former one,

viz., to the greatest torment, taking with him the characteristic of repentance from the sins he has committed after baptism. He is tortured then still more — not yet or not quite attaining what he sees others to have acquired. Besides, he is also ashamed of his transgressions. The greatest torments, indeed, are assigned to the believer. For God's righteousness is good, and His goodness is righteous. And though the punishments cease in the course of the completion of the expiation and purification of each one, yet those have very great and permanent grief who [11] are found worthy of the other fold, on account of not being along with those that have been glorified through righteousness.

For instance, Solomon, calling the Gnostic, wise, speaks thus of those who admire the dignity of his mansion : " For they shall see the end of the wise, and to what a degree the Lord has established him." [12] And of his glory they will say, " This was he whom we once held up to derision, and made a byword of reproach ; fools that we were ! We thought his life madness, and his end dishonourable. How is he reckoned among the sons of God, and his inheritance among the saints ? " [13]

Not only then the believer, but even the heathen, is judged most righteously. For since God knew in virtue of His prescience that he would not believe, He nevertheless, in order that he might receive his own perfection gave him philosophy, but gave it him previous to faith. And He gave the sun, and the moon, and the stars to be worshipped ; " which God," the Law says, [14] made for the nations, that they might not become altogether atheistical, and so utterly perish. But they, also in the instance of this commandment, having become devoid of sense, and addicting themselves to graven images, are judged unless they repent ; some of them because, though able, they would not believe God ; and others because, though willing, they did not take the necessary pains to become believers. There were also, however, those who, from the worship of the heavenly bodies, did not return to the Maker of them. For this was the way given to the nations to rise up to God, by means of the worship of the heavenly bodies. But those who would not abide by those heavenly bodies assigned to them, but fell away from them to stocks and stones, " were counted," it is said, " as chaff-dust and as a drop from a jar," [15] beyond salvation, cast away from the body.

As, then, to be simply saved is the result of

---

1 προκοπαί. [Book vii. cap. 1, *infra*.]
2 1 Thess. iv. 17.
3 1 Cor. xv. 41.
4 Eph. iv. 13.
5 Ps. xv 1.
6 John i 47: Matt v. 8.
7 ἐποπτεία, the third and highest grade of initiation of the Eleusinian mysteries (Liddell and Scott's *Lexicon*).
8 John x. 16.
9 John x. 27.
10 Mark v. 34, etc.

11 The text here has ὅτι, for which has been substituted (Potter and Sylb.) οἱ, as above ; τήν after αὐλῆς (fold) requires to be omitted also in rendering the sentence as we have done.
12 Wisd. iv. 17.
13 Wisd. v. 3-5.
14 Deut. iv. 19.
15 Isa. xl. 15.

medium [1] actions, but to be saved rightly and becomingly [2] is right action, so also all action of the Gnostic may be called right action; that of the simple believer, intermediate action, not yet perfected according to reason, not yet made right according to knowledge; but that of every heathen again is sinful. For it is not simply doing well, but doing actions with a certain aim, and acting according to reason, that the Scriptures exhibit as requisite. [3]

As, then, lyres ought not to be touched by those who are destitute of skill in playing the lyre, nor flutes by those who are unskilled in fluteplaying, neither are those to put their hand to affairs who have not knowledge, and know not how to use them in the whole [4] of life.

The struggle for freedom, then, is waged not alone by the athletes of battles in wars, but also in banquets, and in bed, and in the tribunals, by those who are anointed by the word, who are ashamed to become the captives of pleasures.

"I would never part with virtue for unrighteous gain." But plainly, unrighteous gain is pleasure and pain, toil and fear; and, to speak comprehensively, the passions of the soul, the present of which is delightful, the future vexatious. "For what is the profit," it is said, "if you gain the world and lose the soul?" [5] It is clear, then, that those who do not perform good actions, do not know what is for their own advantage. And if so, neither are they capable of praying aright, so as to receive from God good things; nor, should they receive them, will they be sensible of the boon; nor, should they enjoy them, will they enjoy worthily what they know not; both from their want of knowledge how to use the good things given them, and from their excessive stupidity, being ignorant of the way to avail themselves of the divine gifts.

Now stupidity is the cause of ignorance. And it appears to me that it is the vaunt of a boastful soul, though of one with a good conscience, to exclaim against what happens through circumstances: —

"Therefore let them do what they may; [6]
For it shall be well with me; and Right
Shall be my ally, and I shall not be caught doing evil."

But such a good conscience preserves sanctity towards God and justice towards men; keeping

the soul pure with grave thoughts, and pure words, and just deeds. By thus receiving the Lord's power, the soul studies to be God; regarding nothing bad but ignorance, and action contrary to right reason. And giving thanks always for all things to God, by righteous hearing and divine reading, by true investigation, by holy oblation, by blessed prayer; lauding, hymning, blessing, praising, such a soul is never at any time separated from God. [7] Rightly then is it said, "And they who trust in Him shall understand the truth, and those faithful in love shall abide by Him." [8] You see what statements Wisdom makes about the Gnostics.

Conformably, therefore, there are various abodes, according to the worth of those who have believed. [9] To the point Solomon says, "For there shall be given to him the choice grace of faith, and a more pleasant lot in the temple of the Lord." [10] For the comparative shows that there are lower parts in the temple of God, which is the whole Church. And the superlative remains to be conceived, where the Lord is. These chosen abodes, which are three, are indicated by the numbers in the Gospel — the thirty, the sixty, the hundred. [11] And the perfect inheritance belongs to those who attain to "a perfect man," according to the image of the Lord. And the likeness is not, as some imagine, that of the human form; for this consideration is impious. Nor is the likeness to the first cause that which consists in virtue. For this utterance is also impious, being that of those who have imagined that virtue in man and in the sovereign God is the same. "Thou hast supposed iniquity," He says, "[in imagining] that I will be like to thee." [12] But "it is enough for the disciple to become as the Master," [13] saith the Master. To the likeness of God, then, he that is introduced into adoption and the friendship of God, to the just inheritance of the lords and gods is brought; if he be perfected, according to the Gospel, as the Lord Himself taught.

CHAP. XV. — DIFFERENT DEGREES OF KNOWLEDGE.

The Gnostic, then, is impressed with the closest likeness, that is, with the mind of the Master; which He being possessed of, commanded and recommended to His disciples and to the prudent. Comprehending this, as He who taught wished, and receiving it in its grand sense, he teaches worthily "on the housetops" [14] those capable of being built to a lofty height; and begins the doing of what is spoken, in accordance

---

[1] The author reckons three kinds of actions, the first of which is κατόρθωμα, right or perfect action, which is characteristic of the perfect man and Gnostic alone, and raises him (εἰς τὴν ἀνωτάτω δόξαν) to the height of glory. The second is the class of τῶν μέσων, medium, or intermediate actions, which are done by less perfect believers, and procure a lower grade of glory. In the third place he reckons sinful actions (ἁμαρτητικάς), which are done by those who fall away from salvation (Potter).

[2] [2 Pet. i. 11.]

[3] To produce this sense, καθῆκεν of the text is by Potter changed into καθήκειν.

[4] On the authority of one of the MS., Sylburgius reads ὅλον instead of λόγον in the text.

[5] Matt. viii. 26; Mark viii. 36; Luke ix. 25.

[6] From the Acharneis of Aristophanes, quoted also by Cicero; with various readings in each. Heinsius substitutes παλαμάσθων for παλαμᾶσθαι of the text.

[7] [Bunsen, Hippol., iii. p. 141.]

[8] Wisd. iii. 9.

[9] [1 Cor. xv. 41.]

[10] Wisd. iii. 14.

[11] Matt. xiii. 8.

[12] Ps. l. 21.

[13] Matt. xxv. 10.

[14] Matt. x. 27; Luke xii. 3.

with the example of life. For He enjoined what is possible. And, in truth, the kingly man and Christian ought to be ruler and leader. For we are commanded to be lords over not only the wild beasts without us, but also over the wild passions within ourselves.

Through the knowledge, then, as appears, of a bad and good life is the Gnostic saved, understanding and executing "more than the scribes and Pharisees."[1] "Exert thyself, and prosper, and reign," writes David, "because of truth, and meekness, and righteousness; and thy right hand shall guide thee marvellously,"[2] that is, the Lord. "Who then is the wise? and he shall understand these things. Prudent? and he shall know them. For the ways of the LORD are right,"[3] says the prophet, showing that the Gnostic alone is able to understand and explain the things spoken by the Spirit obscurely. "And he who understands in that time shall hold his peace,"[4] says the Scripture, plainly in the way of declaring them to the unworthy. For the Lord says, "He that hath ears to hear, let him hear,"[5] declaring that hearing and understanding belong not to all. To the point David writes: "Dark water is in the clouds of the skies. At the gleam before Him the clouds passed, hail and coals of fire;"[6] showing that the holy words are hidden. He intimates that transparent and resplendent to the Gnostics, like the innocuous hail, they are sent down from God; but that they are dark to the multitude, like extinguished coals out of the fire, which, unless kindled and set on fire, will not give forth fire or light. "The Lord, therefore," it is said, "gives me the tongue of instruction, so as to know in season when it is requisite to speak a word;"[7] not in the way of testimony alone, but also in the way of question and answer. "And the instruction of the Lord opens my mouth."[8] It is the prerogative of the Gnostic, then, to know how to make use of speech, and when, and how, and to whom. And already the apostle, by saying, "After the rudiments of the world, and not after Christ,"[9] makes the asseveration that the Hellenic teaching is elementary, and that of Christ perfect, as we have already intimated before.

"Now the wild olive is inserted into the fatness of the olive,"[10] and is indeed of the same species as the cultivated olives. For the graft uses as soil the tree in which it is engrafted. Now all the plants sprouted forth simultaneously in consequence of the divine order. Wherefore also, though the wild olive be wild, it crowns the Olympic victors. And the elm teaches the vine to be fruitful, by leading it up to a height. Now we see that wild trees attract more nutriment, because they cannot ripen. The wild trees, therefore, have less power of secretion than those that are cultivated. And the cause of their wildness is the want of the power of secretion. The engrafted olive accordingly receives more nutriment from its growing in the wild one; and it gets accustomed, as it were, to secrete the nutriment, becoming thus assimilated[11] to the fatness of the cultivated tree.

So also the philosopher, resembling the wild olive, in having much that is undigested, on account of his devotion to the search, his propensity to follow, and his eagerness to seize the fatness of the truth; if he get besides the divine power, through faith, by being transplanted into the good and mild knowledge, like the wild olive, engrafted in the truly fair and merciful Word, he both assimilates the nutriment that is supplied, and becomes a fair and good olive tree. For engrafting makes worthless shoots noble, and compels the barren to be fruitful by the art of culture and by gnostic skill.

Different modes of engrafting illustrative of different kinds of conversion.

They say that engrafting is effected in four modes: one, that in which the graft must be fitted in between the wood and the bark; resembling the way in which we instruct plain people belonging to the Gentiles, who receive the word superficially. Another is, when the wood is cleft, and there is inserted in it the cultivated branch. And this applies to the case of those who have studied philosophy; for on cutting through their dogmas, the acknowledgment of the truth is produced in them. So also in the case of the Jews, by opening up the Old Testament, the new and noble plant of the olive is inserted. The third mode of engrafting applies to rustics and heretics, who are brought by force to the truth. For after smoothing off both suckers with a sharp pruning-hook, till the pith is laid bare, but not wounded, they are bound together. And the fourth is that form of engrafting called budding. For a bud (eye) is cut out of a trunk of a good sort, a circle being drawn round in the bark along with it, of the size of the palm. Then the trunk is stripped, to suit the eye, over an equal circumference. And so the graft is inserted, tied round, and daubed with clay, the bud being kept uninjured and unstained. This is the style of gnostic teaching, which is capable of looking into things themselves. This mode is, in truth, of most

---

[1] Matt. v. 20.
[2] Ps. xlv. 4.
[3] Hos. xiv. 9.
[4] Amos v. 13.
[5] Matt. xi. 15.
[6] Ps. xviii. 11, 12.
[7] Isa. l. 4.
[8] Isa. l. 5.
[9] Col. ii. 8.
[10] Rom. xi. 17.

[11] i.e., the graft is assimilated; so the Latin translator. But in the text we have συνεξομοιουμένη, dative, agreeing with fatness, which seems to be a mistake.

service in the case of cultivated trees. And " the engrafting into the good olive " mentioned by the apostle, may be [engrafting into] Christ Himself; the uncultivated and unbelieving nature being transplanted into Christ — that is, in the case of those who believe in Christ. But it is better [to understand it] of the engrafting [1] of each one's faith in the soul itself. For also the Holy Spirit is thus somehow transplanted by distribution, according to the circumscribed capacity of each one, but without being circumscribed.

Knowledge and love.

Now, discoursing on knowledge, Solomon speaks thus : " For wisdom is resplendent and fadeless, and is easily beheld by those who love her. She is beforehand in making herself known to those who desire her. He that rises early for her shall not toil wearily. For to think about her is the perfection of good sense. And he that keeps vigils for her shall quickly be relieved of anxiety. For she goes about, herself seeking those worthy of her (for knowledge belongs not to all) ; and in all ways she benignly shows herself to them." [2] Now the paths are the conduct of life, and the variety that exists in the covenants. Presently he adds : " And in every thought she meets them," [3] being variously contemplated, that is, by all discipline. Then he subjoins, adducing love, which perfects by syllogistic reasoning and true propositions, drawing thus a most convincing and true inference, " For the beginning of her is the truest desire of instruction," that is, of knowledge ; " prudence is the love of instruction, and love is the keeping of its laws ; and attention to its laws is the confirmation of immortality ; and immortality causes nearness to God. The desire of wisdom leads, then, to the kingdom." [4]

For he teaches, as I think, that true instruction is desire for knowledge ; and the practical exercise of instruction produces love of knowledge. And love is the keeping of the commandments which lead to knowledge. And the keeping of them is the establishment of the commandments, from which immortality results. " And immortality brings us near to God."

True knowledge found in the teaching of Christ alone.

If, then, the love of knowledge produces immortality, and leads the kingly man near to God the King, knowledge ought to be sought till it is found. Now seeking is an effort at grasping, and finds the subject by means of certain signs. And discovery is the end and cessation of inquiry, which has now its object in its grasp. And this is knowledge. And this discovery, properly so called, is knowledge, which is the apprehension of the object of search. And they say that a proof is either the antecedent, or the coincident, or the consequent. The discovery, then, of what is sought respecting God, is the teaching through the Son ; and the proof of our Saviour being the very Son of God is the prophecies which preceded His coming, announcing Him ; and the testimonies regarding Him which attended His birth in the world ; in addition, His powers proclaimed and openly shown after His ascension.

The proof of the truth being with us, is the fact of the Son of God Himself having taught us. For if in every inquiry these universals are found, a person and a subject, that which is truly the truth is shown to be in our hands alone. For the Son of God is the person of the truth which is exhibited ; and the subject is the power of faith, which prevails over the opposition of every one whatever, and the assault of the whole world.

But since this is confessedly established by eternal facts and reasons, and each one who thinks that there is no Providence has already been seen to deserve punishment and not contradiction, and is truly an atheist, it is our aim to discover what doing, and in what manner living, we shall reach the knowledge of the sovereign God, and how, honouring the Divinity, we may become authors of our own salvation. Knowing and learning, not from the Sophists, but from God Himself, what is well-pleasing to Him, we endeavour to do what is just and holy. Now it is well-pleasing to Him that we should be saved ; and salvation is effected through both well-doing and knowledge, of both of which the Lord is the teacher.

If, then, according to Plato, it is only possible to learn the truth either from God or from the progeny of God, with reason we, selecting testimonies from the divine oracles, boast of learning the truth by the Son of God, prophesied at first, and then explained.

Philosophy and heresies, aids in discovering the truth.

But the things which co-operate in the discovery of truth are not to be rejected. Philosophy, accordingly, which proclaims a Providence, and the recompense of a life of felicity, and the punishment, on the other hand, of a life of misery, teaches theology comprehensively ; but it does not preserve accuracy and particular points ; for neither respecting the Son of God, nor respecting the economy of Providence, does it treat similarly with us ; for it did not know the worship of God.

---

1 Or inoculation (ἐνοφθαλμισμός).
2 Wisd. vi. 12-15.
3 Wisd. ii. 16.
4 Wisd. vi. 17-20

Wherefore also the heresies of the Barbarian philosophy, although they speak of one God, though they sing the praises of Christ, speak without accuracy, not in accordance with truth; for they discover another God, and receive Christ not as the prophecies deliver. But their false dogmas, while they oppose the conduct that is according to the truth, are against us. For instance, Paul circumcised Timothy because of the Jews who believed, in order that those who had received their training from the law might not revolt from the faith through his breaking such points of the law as were understood more carnally, knowing right well that circumcision does not justify; for he professed that "all things were for all" by conformity, preserving those of the dogmas that were essential, "that he might gain all."[1] And Daniel, under the king of the Persians, wore "the chain,"[2] though he despised not the afflictions of the people.

The liars, then, in reality are not those who for the sake of the scheme of salvation conform, nor those who err in minute points, but those who are wrong in essentials, and reject the Lord, and as far as in them lies deprive the Lord of the true teaching; who do not quote or deliver the Scriptures in a manner worthy of God and of the Lord;[3] for the deposit rendered to God, according to the teaching of the Lord by His apostles, is the understanding and the practice of the godly tradition. "And what ye hear in the ear"—that is, in a hidden manner, and in a mystery (for such things are figuratively said to be spoken in the ear)—"proclaim," He says, "on the housetops," understanding them sublimely, and delivering them in a lofty strain, and according to the canon of the truth explaining the Scriptures; for neither prophecy nor the Saviour Himself announced the divine mysteries simply so as to be easily apprehended by all and sundry, but express them in parables. The apostles accordingly say of the Lord, that "He spake all things in parables, and without a parable spake He nothing unto them;"[4] and if "all things were made by Him, and without Him was not anything made that was made,"[5] consequently also prophecy and the law were by Him, and were spoken by Him in parables. "But all things are right," says the Scripture,[6] "before those who understand," that is, those who receive and observe, according to the ecclesiastical rule, the exposition of the Scriptures explained by Him; and the ecclesiastical rule is the concord and harmony of the law and the

prophets in the covenant delivered at the coming of the Lord. Knowledge is then followed by practical wisdom, and practical wisdom by self-control: for it may be said that practical wisdom is divine knowledge, and exists in those who are deified; but that self-control is mortal, and subsists in those who philosophize, and are not yet wise. But if virtue is divine, so is also the knowledge of it; while self-control is a sort of imperfect wisdom which aspires after wisdom, and exerts itself laboriously, and is not contemplative. As certainly righteousness, being human, is, as being a common thing, subordinate to holiness, which subsists through the divine righteousness;[7] for the righteousness of the perfect man does not rest on civil contracts, or on the prohibition of law, but flows from his own spontaneous action and his love to God.

Reasons for the meaning of Scripture being veiled.

For many reasons, then, the Scriptures hide the sense. First, that we may become inquisitive, and be ever on the watch for the discovery of the words of salvation. Then it was not suitable for all to understand, so that they might not receive harm in consequence of taking in another sense the things declared for salvation by the Holy Spirit. Wherefore the holy mysteries of the prophecies are veiled in the parables—preserved for chosen men, selected to knowledge in consequence of their faith; for the style of the Scriptures is parabolic. Wherefore also the Lord, who was not of the world, came as one who was of the world to men. For He was clothed with all virtue; and it was His aim to lead man, the foster-child of the world, up to the objects of intellect, and to the most essential truths by knowledge, from one world to another.

Wherefore also He employed metaphorical description; for such is the parable,—a narration based on some subject which is not the principal subject, but similar to the principal subject, and leading him who understands to what is the true and principal thing; or, as some say, a mode of speech presenting with vigour, by means of other circumstances, what is the principal subject.

And now also the whole economy which prophesied of the Lord appears indeed a parable to those who know not the truth, when one speaks and the rest hear that the Son of God—of Him who made the universe—assumed flesh, and was conceived in the virgin's womb (as His material body was produced), and subsequently,

---

[1] 1 Cor. ix. 19. [Note τὰ κύρια τῶν δογμάτων.]
[2] Dan. v. 7, 29.
[3] [The Scriptures the authority; the canon of interpretation is the harmony of law and Gospel as first opened by Christ Himself in the walk to Emmaus. Luke xxiv. 13.]
[4] Matt. xiii. 34.
[5] John i. 3.
[6] Prov. viii. 9.

[7] Heinsius, in a note, remarks that Plato regarded ὁσιότης and δικαιοσύνη as identical, while others ascribe the former to the immortals (as also θέμις); ὁσιότης, as the greater, comprehends δικαιοσύνη. He also amends the text. Instead of κοινόν he reads ὡς κοινόν τι, supplies κατά before θείαν δικαιοσύνην, and changes ὑπάρχουσαν into ὑπαρχούσῃ.

as was the case, suffered and rose again, being "to the Jews a stumbling-block, and to the Greeks foolishness," as the apostle says.

But on the Scriptures being opened up, and declaring the truth to those who have ears, they proclaim the very suffering endured by the flesh, which the Lord assumed, to be "the power and wisdom of God." And finally, the parabolic style of Scripture being of the greatest antiquity, as we have shown, abounded most, as was to be expected, in the prophets, in order that the Holy Spirit might show that the philosophers among the Greeks, and the wise men among the Barbarians besides, were ignorant of the future coming of the Lord, and of the mystic teaching that was to be delivered by Him. Rightly then, prophecy, in proclaiming the Lord, in order not to seem to some to blaspheme while speaking what was beyond the ideas of the multitude, embodied its declarations in expressions capable of leading to other conceptions. Now all the prophets who foretold the Lord's coming, and the holy mysteries accompanying it, were persecuted and killed. As also the Lord Himself, in explaining the Scriptures to them, and His disciples who preached the word like Him, and subsequently to His life, used parables.[1] Whence also Peter, in his *Preaching*, speaking of the apostles, says: "But we, unrolling the books of the prophets which we possess, who name Jesus Christ, partly in parables, partly in enigmas, partly expressly and in so many words, find His coming and death, and cross, and all the rest of the tortures which the Jews inflicted on Him, and His resurrection and assumption to heaven previous to the capture[2] of Jerusalem. As it is written, *These things are all that He behoves to suffer, and what should be after Him.* Recognising them, therefore, we have believed in God in consequence of what is written respecting Him."

And after a little again he draws the inference that the Scriptures owed their origin to the divine providence, asserting as follows: "For we know that God enjoined these things, and we say nothing apart from the Scriptures."

Now the Hebrew dialect, like all the rest, has certain properties, consisting in a mode of speech which exhibits the national character. Dialect is accordingly defined as a style of speech produced by the national character. But prophecy is not marked by those dialects. For in the Hellenic writings, what are called changes of figures purposely produce obscurations, deduced after the style of our prophecies. But this is effected through the voluntary departure from

direct speech which takes place in metrical or offhand diction. A figure, then, is a form of speech transferred from what is literal to what is not literal, for the sake of the composition, and on account of a diction useful in speech.

But prophecy does not employ figurative forms in the expressions for the sake of beauty of diction. But from the fact that truth appertains not to all, it is veiled in manifold ways, causing the light to arise only on those who are initiated into knowledge, who seek the truth through love. The proverb, according to the Barbarian philosophy, is called a mode of prophecy, and the parable is so called, and the enigma in addition. Further also, they are called "wisdom;" and again, as something different from it, "instruction and words of prudence," and "turnings of words," and "true righteousness;" and again, "teaching to direct judgment," and "subtlety to the simple," which is the result of training, "and perception and thought," with which the young catechumen is imbued.[3] "He who hears these prophets, being wise, will be wiser. And the intelligent man will acquire rule, and will understand a parable and a dark saying, the words and enigmas of the wise."[4]

And if it was the case that the Hellenic dialects received their appellation from Hellen, the son of Zeus, surnamed Deucalion, from the chronology which we have already exhibited, it is comparatively easy to perceive by how many generations the dialects that obtained among the Greeks are posterior to the language of the Hebrews.

But as the work advances, we shall in each section, noting the figures of speech mentioned above by the prophet,[5] exhibit the gnostic mode of life, showing it systematically according to the rule of the truth.

Did not the Power also, that appeared to Hermas in the Vision, in the form of the Church, give for transcription the book which she wished to be made known to the elect? And this, he says, he transcribed to the letter, without finding how to complete the syllables.[6] And this signified that the Scripture is clear to all, when taken according to the bare reading; and that this is the faith which occupies the place of the rudiments. Wherefore also the figurative expression is employed, "reading according to the letter;" while we understand that the gnostic unfolding of the Scriptures, when faith has already reached an advanced state, is likened to reading according to the syllables.

Further, Esaias the prophet is ordered to take "a new book, and write in it"[7] certain things:

---

1 μετ' αὐτὸν τὸ ζῆν παρεβάλοντο. The translation of Hervetus, which we have followed, supposes the reading αὐτοῦ instead of αὐτόν. Others, retaining the latter, translated τὸ ζῆν παρεβάλοντο (sacrificed life). But the former is most to the author's purpose.
2 If we retain the reading of the text, we must translate "founding," and understand the reference to be to the descent of the new Jerusalem. But it seems better to change the reading as above.

3 Prov. i. 1–4.
4 Prov. i. 5, 6. [Elucidation IX.]
5 i.e., Solomon.
6 [This volume, p. 11, *supra*.]
7 Isa. viii. 1.

the Spirit prophesying that through the exposition of the Scriptures there would come afterwards the sacred knowledge, which at that period was still unwritten, because not yet known. For it was spoken from the beginning to those only who understand. Now that the Saviour has taught the apostles, the unwritten rendering[1] of the written [Scripture] has been handed down also to us, inscribed by the power of God on hearts new, according to the renovation of the book. Thus those of highest repute among the Greeks, dedicate the fruit of the pomegranate to Hermes, who they say is speech, on account of its interpretation. For speech conceals much. Rightly, therefore, Jesus the son of Nave saw Moses, when taken up [to heaven], double,— one Moses with the angels, and one on the mountains, honoured with burial in their ravines. And Jesus saw this spectacle below, being elevated by the Spirit, along also with Caleb. But both do not see similarly But the one descended with greater speed, as if the weight he carried was great; while the other, on descending after him, subsequently related the glory which he beheld, being able to perceive more than the other, as having grown purer; the narrative, in my opinion, showing that knowledge is not the privilege of all. Since some look at the body of the Scriptures, the expressions and the names as to the body of Moses; while others see through to the thoughts and what is signified by the names, seeking the Moses that is with the angels.

Many also of those who called to the Lord said, "Son of David, have mercy on me."[2] A few, too, knew Him as the Son of God; as Peter, whom also He pronounced blessed, "for flesh and blood revealed not the truth to him, but His Father in heaven,"[3] — showing that the Gnostic recognises the Son of the Omnipotent, not by His flesh conceived in the womb, but by the Father's own power. That it is therefore not only to those who read simply that the acquisition of the truth is so difficult, but that not even to those whose prerogative the knowledge of the truth is, is the contemplation of it vouchsafed all at once, the history of Moses teaches, until, accustomed to gaze, as the Hebrews on the glory of Moses, and the prophets of Israel on the visions of angels, so we also become able to look the splendours of truth in the face.

CHAP. XVI. — GNOSTIC EXPOSITION OF THE DECA-
LOGUE.

Let the Decalogue be set forth cursorily by us as a specimen for gnostic exposition.

The number " Ten."

That ten is a sacred number, it is superfluous to say now. And if the tables that were written were the work of God, they will be found to exhibit physical creation. For by the " finger of God " is understood the power of God, by which the creation of heaven and earth is accomplished; of both of which the tables will be understood to be symbols. For the writing and handiwork of God put on the table is the creation of the world.

And the Decalogue, viewed as an image of heaven, embraces sun and moon, stars, clouds, light, wind, water, air, darkness, fire. This is the physical Decalogue of the heaven.

And the representation of the earth contains men, cattle, reptiles, wild beasts; and of the inhabitants of the water, fishes and whales; and again, of the winged tribes, those that are carnivorous, and those that use mild food; and of plants likewise, both fruit-bearing and barren. This is the physical Decalogue of the earth.

And the ark which held them[4] will then be the knowledge of divine and human things and wisdom.[5]

And perhaps the two tables themselves may be the prophecy of the two covenants. They were accordingly mystically renewed, as ignorance along with sin abounded. The commandments are written, then, doubly, as appears, for twofold spirits, the ruling and the subject. "For the flesh lusteth against the Spirit, and the Spirit against the flesh."[6]

And there is a ten in man himself: the five senses, and the power of speech, and that of reproduction; and the eighth is the spiritual principle communicated at his creation; and the ninth the ruling faculty of the soul; and tenth, there is the distinctive characteristic of the Holy Spirit, which comes to him through faith.

Besides, in addition to these ten human parts, the law appears to give its injunctions[7] to sight, and hearing, and smell, and touch, and taste, and to the organs subservient to these, which are double — the hands and the feet. For such is the formation of man. And the soul is introduced, and previous to it the ruling faculty, by which we reason, not produced in procreation; so that without it there is made up the number ten, of the faculties by which all the activity of man is carried out. For in order, straightway on man's entering existence, his life begins with sensations. We accordingly assert that rational and ruling power is the cause of the constitution

---

[1] [In the walk to Emmaus, and by the Spirit bringing all things to remembrance. John xiv. 26.]
[2] Mark x. 48, etc.
[3] Matt. xvi. 17.

[4] i.e., the Commandments.
[5] For perfect wisdom, which is knowledge of things divine and human, which comprehends all that relates to the oversight of the flock of men, becomes, in reference to life, art (*Instructor*, book ii. chap. ii. p. 244, *supra*).
[6] Gal. v. 17.
[7] The text reads ἐντολαῖς, which, however, Hervetus, Heinsius, and Sylburgius, all concur in changing to the accusative, as above.

of the living creature; also that this, the irrational part, is animated, and is a part of it. Now the vital force, in which is comprehended the power of nutrition and growth, and generally of motion, is assigned to the carnal spirit, which has great susceptibility of motion, and passes in all directions through the senses and the rest of the body, and through the body is the primary subject of sensations. But the power of choice, in which investigation, and study, and knowledge, reside, belongs to the ruling faculty. But all the faculties are placed in relation to one — the ruling faculty: it is through that man lives, and lives in a certain way.

Through the corporeal spirit, then, man perceives, desires, rejoices, is angry, is nourished, grows. It is by it, too, that thoughts and conceptions advance to actions. And when it masters the desires, the ruling faculty reigns.

The commandment, then, "Thou shalt not lust," says, thou shalt not serve the carnal spirit, but shall rule over it; "For the flesh lusteth against the Spirit,"[1] and excites to disorderly conduct against nature; "and the Spirit against the flesh" exercises sway, in order that the conduct of the man may be according to nature.

Is not man, then, rightly said "to have been made in the image of God?" — not in the form of his [corporeal] structure; but inasmuch as God creates all things by the Word (λόγῳ), and the man who has become a Gnostic performs good actions by the faculty of reason (τῷ λογικῷ), properly therefore the two tables are also said to mean the commandments that were given to the twofold spirits, — those communicated before the law to that which was created, and to the ruling faculty; and the movements of the senses are both copied in the mind, and manifested in the activity which proceeds from the body. For apprehension results from both combined. Again, as sensation is related to the world of sense, so is thought to that of intellect. And actions are twofold — those of thought, those of act.

The First Commandment.

The first commandment of the Decalogue shows that there is one only Sovereign God;[2] who led the people from the land of Egypt through the desert to their fatherland; that they might apprehend His power, as they were able, by means of the divine works, and withdraw from the idolatry of created things, putting all their hope in the true God.

The Second Commandment.

The second word[3] intimated that men ought not to take and confer the august power of God (which is the name, for this alone were many even yet capable of learning), and transfer His title to things created and vain, which human artificers have made, among which "He that is" is not ranked. For in His uncreated identity, "He that is" is absolutely alone.

The Fourth Commandment.

And the fourth[4] word is that which intimates that the world was created by God, and that He gave us the seventh day as a rest, on account of the trouble that there is in life. For God is incapable of weariness, and suffering, and want. But we who bear flesh need rest. The seventh day, therefore, is proclaimed a rest — abstraction from ills — preparing for the Primal Day,[5] our true rest; which, in truth, is the first creation of light, in which all things are viewed and possessed. From this day the first wisdom and knowledge illuminate us. For the light of truth — a light true, casting no shadow, is the Spirit of God indivisibly divided to all, who are sanctified by faith, holding the place of a luminary, in order to the knowledge of real existences. By following Him, therefore, through our whole life, we become impassible; and this is to rest.[6]

Wherefore Solomon also says, that before heaven, and earth, and all existences, Wisdom had arisen in the Almighty; the participation of which — that which is by power, I mean, not that by essence — teaches a man to know by apprehension things divine and human. Having reached this point, we must mention things by the way; since the discourse has turned on the seventh and the eighth. For the eighth may possibly turn out to be properly the seventh, and the seventh manifestly the sixth, and the latter properly the Sabbath, and the seventh a day of work. For the creation of the world was concluded in six days. For the motion of the sun from solstice to solstice is completed in six months — in the course of which, at one time the leaves fall, and at another plants bud and seeds come to maturity. And they say that the embryo is perfected exactly in the sixth month, that is, in one hundred and eighty days in addition to the two and a half, as Polybus the physician relates in his book On the Eighth Month, and Aristotle the philosopher in his book On Nature. Hence the Pythagoreans, as I think, reckon six the perfect number, from the creation of the world, according to the prophet, and call it Me-

---

[1] Gal. v. 17.
[2] Ex. xx. 2, 3.
[3] i. e., commandment. The Decalogue is in Hebrew called "the ten words."

[4] The text has τρίτος, but Sylburgius reads τέταρτος, the third being either omitted, or embraced in what is said of the second. The next mentioned is the fifth.
[5] i.e., Christ. [And the first day, or the Christian Sabbath.]
[6] [Barnabas, vol. i. chap. xv. p. 146, this series.]

seuthys [1] and Marriage, from its being the middle of the even numbers, that is, of ten and two. For it is manifestly at an equal distance from both.

And as marriage generates from male and female, so six is generated from the odd number three, which is called the masculine number, and the even number two, which is considered the feminine. For twice three are six.

Such, again, is the number of the most general motions, according to which all origination takes place — up, down, to the right, to the left, forward, backward. Rightly, then, they reckon the number seven motherless and childless, interpreting the Sabbath, and figuratively expressing the nature of the rest, in which " they neither marry nor are given in marriage any more." [2] For neither by taking from one number and adding to another of those within ten is seven produced ; nor when added to any number within the ten does it make up any of them.

And they called eight a cube, counting the fixed sphere along with the seven revolving ones, by which is produced " the great year," as a kind of period of recompense of what has been promised.

Thus the Lord, who ascended the mountain, the fourth,[3] becomes the sixth, and is illuminated all round with spiritual light, by laying bare the power proceeding from Him, as far as those selected to see were able to behold it, by the Seventh, the Voice, proclaimed to be the Son of God ; in order that they, persuaded respecting Him, might have rest ; while He by His birth, which was indicated by the sixth conspicuously marked, becoming the eighth, might appear to be God in a body of flesh, by displaying His power, being numbered indeed as a man, but being concealed as to who He was. For six is reckoned in the order of numbers, but the succession of the letters acknowledges the character which is not written. In this case, in the numbers themselves, each unit is preserved in its order up to seven and eight. But in the number of the characters, *Zeta* becomes six and *Eta* seven.

And the character [4] having somehow slipped into writing, should we follow it out thus, the seven became six, and the eight seven.

Wherefore also man is said to have been made on the sixth day, who became faithful to Him who is the sign (τῷ ἐπισήμῳ [5]), so as straightway to receive the rest of the Lord's inheritance. Some such thing also is indicated by the sixth

hour in the scheme of salvation, in which man was perfected. Further, of the eight, the intermediates are seven ; and of the seven, the intervals are shown to be six. For that is another ground, in which seven glorifies eight, and " the heavens declare to the heavens the glory of God." [6]

The sensible types of these, then, are the sounds we pronounce. Thus the Lord Himself is called " Alpha and Omega, the beginning and the end," [7] " by whom all things were made, and without whom not even one thing was made." [8] God's resting is not, then, as some conceive, that God ceased from doing. For, being good, if He should ever cease from doing good, then would He cease from being God, which it is sacrilege even to say. The resting is, therefore, the ordering that the order of created things should be preserved inviolate, and that each of the creatures should cease from the ancient disorder. For the creations on the different days followed in a most important succession ; so that all things brought into existence might have honour from priority, created together in thought, but not being of equal worth. Nor was the creation of each signified by the voice, inasmuch as the creative work is said to have made them at once. For something must needs have been named first. Wherefore those things were announced first, from which came those that were second, all things being originated together from one essence by one power. For the will of God was one, in one identity. And how could creation take place in time, seeing time was born along with things which exist.

And now the whole world of creatures born alive, and things that grow, revolves in sevens. The first-born princes of the angels, who have the greatest power, are seven.[9] The mathematicians also say that the planets, which perform their course around the earth, are seven ; by which the Chaldeans think that all which concerns mortal life is effected through sympathy, in consequence of which they also undertake to tell things respecting the future.

And of the fixed stars, the Pleiades are seven. And the Bears, by the help of which agriculture and navigation are carried through, consist of seven stars. And in periods of seven days the moon undergoes its changes. In the first week she becomes half moon ; in the second, full moon ; and in the third, in her wane, again half moon ; and in the fourth she disappears. Further, as Seleucus the mathematician lays down, she has seven phases. First, from being invisible she becomes crescent-shaped, then half

---

[1] μεσευθύς, μέσος and εὐθύς, between the even ones, applied by the Pythagoreans to 6, a half-way between 2 and 10, the first and the last even numbers of the dinary scale.
[2] Luke xx. 35.
[3] i.e., with the three disciples.
[4] The numeral ϛ΄ = 6. This is said to be the *Digamma* in its original place in the alphabet, and afterwards used in its MSS. and old editions as a short form of στ (Liddell and Scott's *Lexicon*).
[5] That is, Christ, who answers to the numerai six.

[6] Ps. xix. 1.
[7] Rev. xxi. 6.
[8] John i. 3.
[9] [By Rabbinical tradition. But see Calmet, *Dict. Bib.*, p. 78.]

moon, then gibbous and full; and in her wane again gibbous, and in like manner half moon and crescent-shaped.

"On a seven-stringed lyre we shall sing new hymns,"

writes a poet of note, teaching us that the ancient lyre was seven-toned. The organs of the senses situated on our face are also seven — two eyes, two passages of hearing, two nostrils, and the seventh the mouth.

And that the changes in the periods of life take place by sevens, the *Elegies of Solon* teach thus : —

"The child, while still an infant, in seven years,
Produces and puts forth its fence of teeth;
And when God seven years more completes,
He shows of puberty's approach the signs;
And in the third, the beard on growing cheek
With down o'erspreads the bloom of changing skin;
And in the fourth septenniad, at his best
In strength, of manliness he shows the signs;
And in the fifth, of marriage, now mature,
And of posterity, the man bethinks;
Nor does he yet desire vain works to see.
The seventh and eighth septenniads see him now
In mind and speech mature, till fifty years;
And in the ninth he still has vigour left,
But strength and body are for virtue great
Less than of yore; when, seven years more, God brings
To end, then not too soon may he submit to die."

Again, in diseases the seventh day is that of the crisis; and the fourteenth, in which nature struggles against the causes of the diseases. And a myriad such instances are adduced by Hermippus of Berytus, in his book *On the Number Seven*, regarding it as holy.[1] And the blessed David delivers clearly to those who know the mystic account of seven and eight, praising thus : "Our years were exercised like a spider. The days of our years in them are seventy years; but if in strength, eighty years. And that will be to reign." [2] That, then, we may be taught that the world was originated, and not suppose that God made it in time, prophecy adds : "This is the book of the generation : also of the things in them, when they were created in the day that God made heaven and earth." [3] For the expression "when they were created" intimates an indefinite and dateless production. But the expression "in the day that God made," that is, in and by which God made "all things," and "without which not even one thing was made," points out the activity exerted by the Son. As David says, "This is the day which the LORD hath made ; let us be glad and rejoice in it ; " [4] that is, in consequence of the knowledge [5] imparted by Him, let us celebrate the divine festi-

val; for the Word that throws light on things hidden, and by whom each created thing came into life and being, is called day.

And, in fine, the Decalogue, by the letter *Iota*,[6] signifies the blessed name, presenting Jesus, who is the Word.

The Fifth Commandment.

Now the fifth in order is the command on the honour of father and mother. And it clearly announces God as Father and Lord. Wherefore also it calls those who know Him sons and gods. The Creator of the universe is their Lord and Father ; and the mother is not, as some say, the essence from which we sprang, nor, as others teach, the Church, but the divine knowledge and wisdom, as Solomon says, when he terms wisdom " the mother of the just," and says that it is desirable for its own sake. And the knowledge of all, again, that is lovely and venerable, proceeds from God through the Son.

The Seventh Commandment.

This is followed by the command respecting adultery. Now it is adultery, if one, abandoning the ecclesiastical and true knowledge, and the persuasion respecting God, accedes to false and incongruous opinion, either by deifying any created object, or by making an idol of anything that exists not, so as to overstep, or rather step from, knowledge. And to the Gnostic false opinion is foreign, as the true belongs to him, and is allied with him. Wherefore the noble apostle calls one of the kinds of fornication, idolatry,[7] in following the prophet, who says : " [My people] hath committed fornication with stock and stone. They have said to the stock, Thou art my father ; and to the stone, Thou hast begotten me." [8]

The Sixth Commandment.

Then follows the command about murder. Now murder is a sure destruction. He, then, that wishes to extirpate the true doctrine of God and of immortality, in order to introduce falsehood, alleging either that the universe is not under Providence, or that the world is uncreated, or affirming anything against true doctrine, is most pernicious.

The Eighth Commandment.

And after this is the command respecting theft. As, then, he that steals what is another's, doing great wrong, rightly incurs ills suitable to

---

[1] [The honour put upon this number in the Holy Scriptures is obvious to all, and it seems to be wrought into nature by the author of Scripture. But see Dan. viii. 13, the original, and (*Palmoni*) Eng. margin.]
[2] Ps. xc. 9, 10.
[3] Gen. ii. 4.
[4] Ps. cxviii. 24.
[5] [1 Cor. v. 7.]

[6] The first letter of the name of Jesus, and used as the sign of ten.
[7] In close conjunction with idolatry, fornication is mentioned, Col. iii. 5, Gal. v. 20, 1 Pet. iv. 3.
[8] Jer. ii. 27, iii. 9.

his deserts; so also does he, who arrogates to himself divine works by the art of the statuary or the painter, and pronounces himself to be the maker of animals and plants. Likewise those, too, who mimic the true philosophy are thieves. Whether one be a husbandman or the father of a child, he is an agent in depositing seeds. But it is God who, ministering the growth and perfection of all things, brings the things produced to what is in accordance with their nature. But the most, in common also with the philosophers, attribute growth and changes to the stars as the primary cause, robbing the Father of the universe, as far as in them lies, of His tireless might.

The elements, however, and the stars — that is, the administrative powers — are ordained for the accomplishment of what is essential to the administration, and are influenced and moved by what is commanded to them, in the way in which the Word of the Lord leads, since it is the nature of the divine power to work all things secretly. He, accordingly, who alleges that he has conceived or made anything which pertains to creation, will suffer the punishment of his impious audacity.

The Tenth Commandment.[1]

And the tenth is the command respecting all lusts. As, then, he who entertains unbecoming desires is called to account; in the same way he is not allowed to desire things false, or to suppose that, of created objects, those that are animate have power of themselves, and that inanimate things can at all save or hurt. And should one say that an antidote cannot heal or hemlock kill, he is unwittingly deceived. For none of these operates except one makes use of the plant and the drug; just as the axe does not without one to cut with it, or a saw without one sawing with it. And as they do not work by themselves, but have certain physical qualities which accomplish their proper work by the exertion of the artisan; so also, by the universal providence of God, through the medium of secondary causes, the operative power is propagated in succession to individual objects.

CHAP. XVII. — PHILOSOPHY CONVEYS ONLY AN IMPERFECT KNOWLEDGE OF GOD.

But, as appears, the philosophers of the Greeks, while naming God, do not know Him. But their philosophical speculations, according to Empedocles, "as passing over the tongue of the multitude, are poured out of mouths that know little of the whole." For as art changes the light of the sun into fire by passing it through

a glass vessel full of water, so also philosophy, catching a spark from the divine Scripture, is visible in a few. Also, as all animals breathe the same air, some in one way, others in another, and to a different purpose; so also a considerable number of people occupy themselves with the truth, or rather with discourse concerning the truth. For they do not say aught respecting God, but expound Him by attributing their own affections to God. For they spend life in seeking the probable, not the true. But truth is not taught by imitation, but by instruction. For it is not that we may seem good[2] that we believe in Christ, as it is not alone for the purpose of being seen, while in the sun, that we pass into the sun. But in the one case for the purpose of being warmed; and in the other, we are compelled to be Christians in order to be excellent and good. For the kingdom belongs pre-eminently to the violent,[3] who, from investigation, and study, and discipline, reap this fruit, that they become kings.

He, then, who imitates opinion shows also preconception. When then one, having got an inkling of the subject, kindles it within in his soul by desire and study, he sets everything in motion afterwards in order to know it. For that which one does not apprehend, neither does he desire it, nor does he embrace the advantage flowing from it. Subsequently, therefore, the Gnostic at last imitates the Lord, as far as allowed to men, having received a sort of quality akin to the Lord Himself, in order to assimilation to God. But those who are not proficient in knowledge cannot judge the truth by rule. It is not therefore possible to share in the gnostic contemplations, unless we empty ourselves of our previous notions. For the truth in regard to every object of intellect and of sense is thus simply universally declared. For instance, we may distinguish the truth of painting from that which is vulgar, and decorous music from licentious. There is, then, also a truth of philosophy as distinct from the other philosophies, and a true beauty as distinct from the spurious. It is not then the partial truths, of which truth is predicated, but the truth itself, that we are to investigate, not seeking to learn names. For what is to be investigated respecting God is not one thing, but ten thousand. There is a difference between declaring God, and declaring things about God. And to speak generally, in everything the accidents are to be distinguished from the essence.

Suffice it for me to say, that the Lord of all is God; and I say the Lord of all absolutely, nothing being left by way of exception.

Since, then, the forms of truth are two —

---

[1] [The ninth is not altogether omitted, but is supposed to be included in the eighth. False testimony is theft of another's credit, or of another's truth. Migne, *Strom.*, vi. 361. Elucidation X.]

[2] ἀγαθοὶ εἶς are supplied here to complete.
[3] [Matt. xi. 4.]

the names and the things — some discourse of names, occupying themselves with the beauties of words : such are the philosophers among the Greeks. But we who are Barbarians have the things. Now it was not in vain that the Lord chose to make use of a mean form of body ; so that no one praising the grace and admiring the beauty might turn his back on what was said, and attending to what ought to be abandoned, might be cut off from what is intellectual. We must therefore occupy ourselves not with the expression, but the meaning.

To those, then, who are not gifted[1] with the power of apprehension, and are not inclined to knowledge, the word is not entrusted ; since also the ravens imitate human voices, having no understanding of the thing which they say. And intellectual apprehension depends on faith. Thus also Homer said : —

"Father of men and gods,"[2] —

knowing not who the Father is, or how He is Father.

And as to him who has hands it is natural to grasp, and to him who has sound eyes to see the light ; so it is the natural prerogative of him who has received faith to apprehend knowledge, if he desires, on "the foundation" laid, to work, and build up "gold, silver, precious stones."[3]

Accordingly he does not profess to wish to participate, but begins to do so. Nor does it belong to him to *intend*, but to *be* regal, and illuminated, and gnostic. Nor does it appertain to him to wish to grasp things in name, but in fact.

For God, being good, on account of the principal part of the whole creation, seeing He wishes to save it, was induced to make the rest also ; conferring on them at the beginning this first boon, that of existence. For that to be is far better than not to be, will be admitted by every one. Then, according to the capabilities of their nature, each one was and is made, advancing to that which is better.

So there is no absurdity in philosophy having been given by Divine Providence as a preparatory discipline for the perfection which is by Christ ; unless philosophy is ashamed at learning from Barbarian knowledge how to advance to truth.[4] But if "the very hairs are numbered, and the most insignificant motions," how shall not philosophy be taken into account? For to Samson power was given in his hair, in order that he might perceive that the worthless arts that refer to the things in this life, which lie and remain on the ground after the departure of the soul, were not given without divine power.

But it is said Providence, from above, from

what is of prime importance, as from the head, reaches to all, "as the ointment," it is said, "which descends to Aaron's beard, and to the skirt of his garment"[5] (that is, of the great High Priest, "by whom all things were made, and without whom not even one thing was made"[6]) ; not to the ornament of the body ; for Philosophy is outside of the People, like raiment.[7] The philosophers, therefore, who, trained to their own peculiar power of perception by the spirit of perception, when they investigate, not a part of philosophy, but philosophy absolutely, testify to the truth in a truth-loving and humble spirit ; if in the case of good things said by those even who are of different sentiments they advance to understanding, through the divine administration, and the ineffable Goodness, which always, as far as possible, leads the nature of existences to that which is better. Then, by cultivating the acquaintance not of Greeks alone, but also of Barbarians, from the exercise common to their proper intelligence, they are conducted to Faith. And when they have embraced the foundation of truth, they receive in addition the power of advancing further to investigation. And thence they love to be learners, and aspiring after knowledge, haste to salvation.

Thus Scripture says, that "the spirit of perception" was given to the artificers from God.[8] And this is nothing else than Understanding, a faculty of the soul, capable of studying existences, — of distinguishing and comparing what succeeds as like and unlike, — of enjoining and forbidding, and of conjecturing the future. And it extends not to the arts alone, but even to philosophy itself.

Why, then, is the serpent called wise? Because even in its wiles there may be found a connection, and distinction, and combination, and conjecturing of the future. And so very many crimes are concealed ; because the wicked arrange for themselves so as by all means to escape punishment.

And Wisdom being manifold, pervading the whole world, and all human affairs, varies its appellation in each case. When it applies itself to first causes, it is called Understanding ($\nu\acute{o}\eta\sigma\iota\varsigma$). When, however, it confirms this by demonstrative reasoning, it is termed Knowledge, and Wisdom, and Science. When it is occupied in what pertains to piety, and receives without speculation the primal Word[9] in consequence of the maintenance of the operation in it, it is called Faith. In the sphere of things of sense, establishing that which appears as being truest, it is

---

[1] οὐκ ἀντιληπτικοῖς is substituted here for οὖν ἀντιληπτοῖς of the text.
[2] *Iliad*, i. 544.
[3] 1 Cor. iii. 12.
[4] [See p. 303, *supra*, this volume.]
[5] Ps. cxxxiii. 2.
[6] John i. 3.
[7] i.e., the body is the Jewish people, and philosophy is something external to it, like the garment.
[8] Ex. xxviii. 3.
[9] Christ.

Right Opinion. In operations, again, performed by skill of hand, it is Art But when, on the other hand, without the study of primary causes, by the observation of similarities, and by transposition, it makes any attempt or combination, it is called Experiment. But belonging to it, and supreme and essential, is the Holy Spirit, which above all he who, in consequence of [divine] guidance, has believed, receives after strong faith. Philosophy, then, partaking of a more exquisite perception, as has been shown from the above statements, participates in Wisdom.

Logical discussion, then, of intellectual subjects, with selection and assent, is called Dialectics ; which establishes, by demonstration, allegations respecting truth, and demolishes the doubts brought forward.

Those, then, who assert that philosophy did not come hither from God, all but say that God does not know each particular thing, and that He is not the cause of all good things ; if, indeed, each of these belongs to the class of individual things. But nothing that exists could have subsisted at all, had God not willed. And if He willed, then philosophy is from God, He having willed it to be such as it is, for the sake of those who not otherwise than by its means would abstain from what is evil. For God knows all things — not those only which exist, but those also which shall be — and how each thing shall be. And foreseeing the particular movements, " He surveys all things, and hears all things," seeing the soul naked within ; and possesses from eternity the idea of each thing individually. And what applies to theatres, and to the parts of each object, in looking at, looking round, and taking in the whole in one view, applies also to God. For in one glance He views all things together, and each thing by itself ; but not all things, by way of primary intent.

Now, then, many things in life take their rise in some exercise of human reason, having received the kindling spark from God. For instance, health by medicine, and soundness of body through gymnastics, and wealth by trade, have their origin and existence in consequence of Divine Providence indeed, but in consequence, too, of human co-operation. Understanding also is from God.

But God's will is especially obeyed by the free-will of good men. Since many advantages are common to good and bad men : yet they are nevertheless advantageous only to men of goodness and probity, for whose sake God created them. For it was for the use of good men that the influence which is in God's gifts was originated. Besides, the thoughts of virtuous men are produced through the inspiration [1] of God ; the soul being disposed in the way it is, and the divine will being conveyed to human souls, particular divine ministers contributing to such services. For regiments of angels are distributed over the nations and cities.[2] And, perchance, some are assigned to individuals.[3]

The Shepherd, then, cares for each of his sheep ; and his closest inspection is given to those who are excellent in their natures, and are capable of being most useful. Such are those fit to lead and teach, in whom the action of Providence is conspicuously seen ; whenever either by instruction, or government, or administration, God wishes to benefit. But He wishes at all times. Wherefore He moves those who are adapted to useful exertion in the things which pertain to virtue, and peace, and beneficence. But all that is characterized by virtue proceeds from virtue, and leads back to virtue. And it is given either in order that men may become good, or that those who are so may make use of their natural advantages. For it co-operates both in what is general and what is particular. How absurd, then, is it, to those who attribute disorder and wickedness to the devil, to make him the bestower of philosophy, a virtuous thing ! For he is thus all but made more benignant to the Greeks, in respect of making men good, than the divine providence and mind.

Again, I reckon it is the part of law and of right reason to assign to each one what is appropriate to him, and belongs to him, and falls to him. For as the lyre is only for the harper, and the flute for the flute-player ; so good things are the possessions of good men. As the nature of the beneficent is to do good, as it is of the fire to warm, and the light to give light, and a good man will not do evil, or light produce darkness, or fire cold ; so, again, vice cannot do aught virtuous. For its activity is to do evil, as that of darkness to dim the eyes.

Philosophy is not, then, the product of vice, since it makes men virtuous ; it follows, then, that it is the work of God, whose work it is solely to do good. And all things given by God are given and received well.

Further, if the practice of philosophy does not belong to the wicked, but was accorded to the best of the Greeks, it is clear also from what source it was bestowed — manifestly from Providence, which assigns to each what is befitting in accordance with his deserts." [4]

Rightly, then, to the Jews belonged the Law,

---

[1] ἐπίπνοιαν, preferred by Sylburgius and the Latin translator to the reading ἐπίνοιαν.

[2] " When the Most High divided the nations, as He separated the sons of Adam, He set the bounds of the nations according to the angels of God" (Deut. xxxii. 8, Sept.). The Hebrew and the Latin and A. V. have, " according to the number of the children of Israel." [See this chapter, further, infra.]

[3] Lowth proposes to read κατὰ τοὺς ἐπὶ μέρους instead of καὶ τῶν, etc.; and Montfaucon, instead of ἐνίοις ἁγίοις for ἀνθρώποις. But the sense is, in any case, as given above.

[4] [Here I venture to commend, as worthy of note, the speculations of Edward King, on Matt. xxv. 32. Morsels of Criticism, vol. i. p. 333. Ed. London, 1788.]

and to the Greeks Philosophy, until the Advent; and after that came the universal calling to be a peculiar people of righteousness, through the teaching which flows from faith, brought together by one Lord, the only God of both Greeks and Barbarians, or rather of the whole race of men. We have often called by the name philosophy that portion of truth attained through philosophy, although but partial.[1]

Now, too what is good in the arts as arts,[2] have their beginning from God. For as the doing of anything artistically is embraced in the rules of art, so also acting sagaciously is classed under the head of sagacity ($\phi\rho\acute{o}\nu\eta\sigma\iota\varsigma$). Now sagacity is virtue, and it is its function to know other things, but much more especially what belongs to itself. And Wisdom ($\Sigma o\phi\acute{\iota}a$) being power, is nothing but the knowledge of good things, divine and human.

But "the earth is God's, and the fulness thereof,"[3] says the Scripture, teaching that good things come from God to men; it being through divine power and might that the distribution of them comes to the help of man.

Now the modes of all help and communication from one to another are three. One is, by attending to another, as the master of gymnastics, in training the boy. The second is, by assimilation, as in the case of one who exhorts another to benevolence by practising it before. The one co-operates with the learner, and the other benefits him who receives. The third mode is that by command, when the gymnastic master, no longer training the learner, nor showing in his own person the exercise for the boy to imitate, prescribes the exercise by name to him, as already proficient in it.

The Gnostic, accordingly, having received from God the power to be of service, benefits some by disciplining them, by bestowing attention on them; others, by exhorting them, by assimilation; and others, by training and teaching them, by command. And certainly he himself is equally benefited by the Lord. Thus, then, the benefit that comes from God to men becomes known — angels at the same time lending encouragement.[4] For by angels, whether seen or not, the divine power bestows good things. Such was the mode adopted in the advent of the Lord. And sometimes also the power "breathes" in men's thoughts and reasonings, and "puts in" their hearts "strength" and a keener perception, and furnishes "prowess" and "boldness of alacrity"[5] both for researches and deeds.

But exposed for imitation and assimilation are truly admirable and holy examples of virtue in the actions put on record. Further, the department of action is most conspicuous both in the testaments of the Lord, and in the laws in force among the Greeks, and also in the precepts of philosophy.

And to speak comprehensively, all benefit appertaining to life, in its highest reason, proceeding from the Sovereign God, the Father who is over all, is consummated by the Son, who also on this account "is the Saviour of all men," says the apostle, "but especially of those who believe."[6] But in respect of its immediate reason, it is from those next to each, in accordance with the command and injunction of Him who is nearest the First Cause, that is, the Lord.

CHAP. XVIII. — THE USE OF PHILOSOPHY TO THE GNOSTIC.

Greek philosophy the recreation of the Gnostic.

Now our Gnostic always occupies himself with the things of highest importance. But if at any time he has leisure and time for relaxation from what is of prime consequence, he applies himself to Hellenic philosophy in preference to other recreation, feasting on it as a kind of dessert at supper.[7] Not that he neglects what is superior; but that he takes this in addition, as long as proper, for the reasons I mentioned above. But those who give their mind to the unnecessary and superfluous points of philosophy, and addict themselves to wrangling sophisms alone, abandon what is necessary and most essential, pursuing plainly the shadows of words.

It is well indeed to know all. But the man whose soul is destitute of the ability to reach to acquaintance with many subjects of study, will select the principal and better subjects alone. For real science ($\epsilon\pi\iota\sigma\tau\acute{\eta}\mu\eta$, which we affirm the Gnostic alone possesses) is a sure comprehension ($\kappa\alpha\tau\acute{a}\lambda\eta\psi\iota\varsigma$), leading up through true and sure reasons to the knowledge ($\gamma\nu\hat{\omega}\sigma\iota\varsigma$) of the cause. And he, who is acquainted with what is true respecting any one subject, becomes of course acquainted with what is false respecting it.

Philosophy necessary.

For truly it appears to me to be a proper point for discussion, Whether we ought to philosophize: for its terms are consistent.

But if we are not to philosophize, what then? (For no one can condemn a thing without first knowing it): the consequence, even in that case, is that we must philosophize.[8]

---

[1] [Cap. xviii., *infra*.]
[2] For ὡς ἐν τέχναις it is proposed to read ὡς ἂν αἱ τέχναι.
[3] Ps. xxiv. 1; 1 Cor. x. 26.
[4] [See *supra*, this chapter; and, *infra*, book vii. cap. i.]
[5] "Blue-eyed Athene inspired him with prowess." — *Iliad*, x. 482.
"And put excessive boldness in his breast." — *Iliad*, xvii. 570.
"To Diomede son of Tydeus Pallas Athene gave strength and boldness." — *Iliad*, v. 1, 2.

[6] 1 Tim. iv. 10.
[7] [The proportion to be observed between the study of what is secular and that of the Scriptures, according to Clement.]
[8] The author's meaning is, that it is only by a process of philosophical reasoning that you can decide whether philosophy is possible, valid, or useful. You must philosophize in order to decide whether you ought or ought not to philosophize.

First of all, idols are to be rejected.

Such, then, being the case, the Greeks ought by the Law and the Prophets to learn to worship one God only, the only Sovereign ; then to be taught by the apostle, " but to us an idol is nothing in the world," [1] since nothing among created things can be a likeness of God ; and further, to be taught that none of those images which they worship can be similitudes : for the race of souls is not in form such as the Greeks fashion their idols. For souls are invisible ; not only those that are rational, but those also of the other animals. And their bodies never become parts of the souls themselves, but organs — partly as seats, partly as vehicles — and in other cases possessions in various ways. But it is not possible to copy accurately even the likenesses of the organs ; since, were it so, one might model the sun, as it is seen, and take the likeness of the rainbow in colours.

After abandoning idols, then, they will hear the Scripture, " Unless your righteousness exceed the righteousness of the scribes and Pharisees " [2] (who justified themselves in the way of abstinence from what was evil), — so as, along with such perfection as they evinced, and " the loving of your neighbour," to be able also to do good, — you shall not " be kingly." [3]

For intensification of the righteousness which is according to the law shows the Gnostic. So one who is placed in the head, which is that which rules its own body — and who advances to the summit of faith, which is the knowledge (*gnosis*) itself, for which all the organs of perception exist — will likewise obtain the highest inheritance.

The primacy of knowledge the apostle shows to those capable of reflection, in writing to those Greeks of Corinth, in the following terms : " But having hope, when your faith is increased, that we shall be magnified in you according to our rule abundantly, to preach the Gospel beyond you." [4] He does not mean the extension of his preaching locally : for he says also that in Achaia faith abounded ; and it is related also in the Acts of the Apostles that he preached the word in Athens.[5] But he teaches that knowledge (*gnosis*), which is the perfection of faith, goes beyond catechetical instruction, in accordance with the magnitude of the Lord's teaching and the rule of the Church.[6] Wherefore also he proceeds to add, " And if I am rude in speech, yet I am not in knowledge." [7]

Whence is the knowledge of truth ?

But let those who vaunt on account of having apprehended the truth tell us from whom they boast of having heard it. They will not say from God, but will admit that it was from men. And if so, it is either from themselves that they have learned it lately, as some of them arrogantly boast, or from others like them. But human teachers, speaking of God, are not reliable, as men. For he that is man cannot speak worthily the truth concerning God : the feeble and mortal [cannot speak worthily] of the Unoriginated and Incorruptible — the work, of the Workman. Then he who is incapable of speaking what is true respecting himself, is he not much less reliable in what concerns God ? For just as far as man is inferior to God in power, so much feebler is man's speech than Him ; although he do not declare God, but only speak about God and the divine word. For human speech is by nature feeble, and incapable of uttering God. I do not say His name. For to name it is common, not to philosophers only, but also to poets. Nor [do I say] His essence ; for this is impossible, but the power and the works of God.

Those even who claim God as their teacher, with difficulty attain to a conception of God, grace aiding them to the attainment of their modicum of knowledge ; accustomed as they are to contemplate the will [of God] by the will, and the Holy Spirit by the Holy Spirit. " For the Spirit searches the deep things of God. But the natural man receiveth not the things of the Spirit." [8]

The only wisdom, therefore, is the God-taught wisdom we possess ; on which depend all the sources of wisdom, which make conjectures at the truth.

Intimations of the Teacher's advent.

Assuredly of the coming of the Lord, who has taught us, to men, there were a myriad indicators, heralds, preparers, precursors, from the beginning, from the foundation of the world, intimating beforehand by deeds and words, prophesying that He would come, and where, and how, what should be the signs. From afar certainly Law and Prophecy kept Him in view beforehand. And then the precursor pointed Him out as present. After whom the heralds point out by their teaching the virtue of His manifestation.

Universal diffusion of the Gospel a contrast to philosophy.

The philosophers, however, chose to [teach philosophy] to the Greeks alone,[9] and not even to all of them ; but Socrates to Plato, and Plato

---

[1] I Cor. viii. 4.
[2] Matt. v. 20 ; Jas. ii. 8
[3] βασιλικοί, Jas. ii. 8 (royal law).
[4] 2 Cor. x. 15, 16.
[5] Acts xvii.
[6] [Canon-law referred to as already recognised. And see 2 Cor. x. 13–15 (Greek), as to a certain ecclesiastical rule or canon observed by the apostles. It may refer, primarily, to (Gal. ii. 9) limitations of apostolic work and jurisdiction. See Bunsen, iii. 217.]
[7] 2 Cor xi. 6.

[8] I Cor. ii. 10, 14.
[9] Following Hervetus, the Latin translator, who interpolates into the text here, as seems necessary, οἱ φιλόσοφοι τοῖς Ἕλλησι.

to Xenocrates, Aristotle to Theophrastus, and Zeno to Cleanthes, who persuaded their own followers alone.

But the word of our Teacher remained not in Judea alone, as philosophy did in Greece; but was diffused over the whole world, over every nation, and village, and town, bringing already over to the truth whole houses, and each individual of those who heard it by him himself, and not a few of the philosophers themselves.

And if any one ruler whatever prohibit the Greek philosophy, it vanishes forthwith.[1] But our doctrine on its very first proclamation was prohibited by kings and tyrants together, as well as particular rulers and governors, with all their mercenaries, and in addition by innumerable men, warring against us, and endeavouring as far as they could to exterminate it. But it flourishes the more. For it dies not, as human doctrine dies, nor fades as a fragile gift. For no gift of God is fragile. But it remains unchecked, though prophesied as destined to be persecuted to the end. Thus Plato writes of poetry: "A poet is a light and a sacred thing, and cannot write poetry till he be inspired and lose his senses." And Democritus similarly: "Whatever things a poet writes with divine afflatus, and with a sacred spirit, are very beautiful." And we know what sort of things poets say. And shall no one be amazed at the prophets of God Almighty becoming the organs of the divine voice?

Having then moulded, as it were, a statue of the Gnostic, we have now shown who he is; indicating in outline, as it were, both the greatness and beauty of his character. What he is as to the study of physical phenomena shall be shown afterwards, when we begin to treat of the creation of the world.

---

[1] [The imperishable nature of the Gospel, forcibly contrasted with the evanescence of philosophy.]

ELUCIDATIONS.

I.

(Gentlemen of the Jury, cap. ii. p. 485.)

THIS strange rendering of ὦ ἄνδρες δικασταὶ (which we were taught to translate *O judices*, in our school-days) occurs three times on this page, and I felt bound to retain it. But why import such an anachronism into the author's work, and the forensic eloquence of the Athenians? Better do violence to idiom, like our English Bible ("men and brethren"), and say, *O men and judges.* Why not *judges?* See Sharon Turner (*Anglo-Saxons*, i. p. 476) and Freeman (*Norman Conquest*, v. p. 451).

II.

(Aristobulus, cap. iii. p. 487, note 7.)

In addition to the note *in loc.*, it may be well to mention the *Stromata* (book i. cap. xv. p. 316), as another place where this name occurs. The learned Calmet (Works, tom. ix. p. 121), in his *Dict. Critic.*, has a valuable statement as to the difficulties connected with this name and the probability that there were two so called, who have been confused in the citations and references of authors.

III.

(Egyptians, cap. iv. p. 488.)

The paradoxical genius of Warburton ought not to dissuade us from enjoying the amusement and instruction to be found in his *Divine Legation*. In many respects he reminds me of this great Alexandrian Father, and they are worthy of being studied together. Let me instance, in connection with this subject, the second book, e.g. p. 151, on *Metempsychosis* (Hurd's Edition, vol. ii. 1811).

IV.

(Egyptian Women, book vi. cap. iv. p. 488.)

" *Last*, about women," says our author ; and one would infer *least*. But Rawlinson (*Herod.*, vol. ii. p. 47, ed. New York) has a long and learned note on this subject. " Queens made offerings with the kings, and the monuments show that an order of women were employed in the service of the gods." . . . Then he says, " A sort of monastic institution seems to have originated in Egypt at an early time, and to have been imitated afterwards, when *the real conventual system* was set on foot by the Christians, in the same country." This may be worthy of being borne in mind, when we come to the cœnobitic life of the Thebaid, which lies, indeed, beyond the limits of our ante-Nicene researches. But persecution had already driven Christians to the desert ; and the ascetic type of piety, with which the age and its necessities imprinted the souls of many devout women, may have led them at a very early period to the " imitation " of which Rawlinson speaks. The " widows " recognised by the ante-Nicene canons, would naturally become the founders of " widows' houses," such as are to be seen among the pious Moravians in our times. (See Bunsen, *Hippol.*, iii. p. 81.)

V.

(Philosophy, cap. vii. p. 493.)

In justice to Clement's eulogies of philosophy, we must constantly bear in mind his reiterated definitions. We have here a very important outline of his *Christian Eclecticism*, which, so far from clashing with St. Paul's scornful references to Gentile wisdom, seems to me in absolute correspondence with his reference to "science *falsely so called*" (1 Tim. vi. 20). So, when the apostle identifies philosophy with " the rudiments of the world," he adds, " and not after Christ." Now, Clement's eclectic system yokes all true philosophy to the chariot-wheels of the Messiah, as in this instance ; making all true science hinge upon " the knowledge of the Son of God." How these chapters shine in contrast even with Plato.

VI.

(Numbers, cap. xi. p. 499.)

The marvellous system of numbers which runs through all revelation, and which gives us the name *Palmoni* (English margin) in a remarkable passage of Daniel (viii. 13), has lately excited fresh interest among the learned in England and America. Doubtless the language of St. John (Rev. xiii. 18), " Here is wisdom," etc., influenced the early Church in what seems to us purely fanciful conjectures and combinations like these. Two unpretending little books have lately struck me as quite in the spirit of the ante-Nicene Fathers : *The Number Counted*, and the *Name Counted*, by J. A. Upjohn (Appleton, Wis., 1883).

VII.

(The Gnostic, cap. xi. p. 501.)

The Gnostic " conjectures things future," i.e., by the Scriptures. " He shall show you things to come," said the Divine Master, speaking of the Blessed Comforter. To what extent did these ancients, in their esoteric conjectures, anticipate the conversion of the empire, and the evils that were to follow? This they could not publish ; but the inquiry deserves thought, and there are clues for inquirers.

VIII.

(Ultimate Issues, cap. xiii. p. 504.)

With reference to the choice of Judas to be an apostle, and like mysteries, this seems to me a bit of calm philosophy, worthy of the childlike faith of the early Christians. I confess great obligations to a neglected American author, with reference to such discussions (see Bledsoe, *Theodicy*, New York, 1854).

IX.

(Enigmas, cap. xv. p. 510.)

We are often troubled by this Oriental tendency to teach by myths and mysteries; but the text here quoted from the Proverbs, goes far to show that it is rooted in human nature, and that God himself has condescended to adopt it. Like every gift of God, it is subject to almost inevitable corruption and abuse.

X.

(Omissions, cap. xvi. p. 515.)

The omissions in Clement's Decalogue are worthy of remark, and I can only account for them by supposing a defective text. Kaye might have said more on the subject; but he suggests this as the solution of the difficulty, when he says (p. 201), "*As the text now stands*, Clement interprets only eight out of the ten."

P.S.—I have foreborne to say anything on "the descent into hell," in my annotations (on cap. vi.), for obvious reasons of propriety; but, for an entire system of references to the whole subject, I name Ezra Abbot's *Catalogue*, appended to Alger's *History*, etc. (Philadelphia, 1864.)

THE STROMATA, OR MISCELLANIES.

BOOK VII.

It is now time to show the Greeks that the
Gnostic alone is truly pious; so that the philosophers, learning of what description the true
Christian is, may condemn their own stupidity
in rashly and inconsiderately persecuting the
[Christian] name, and without reason calling
those impious who know the true God. And
clearer arguments must be employed, I reckon,
with the philosophers, so that they may be able,
from the exercise they have already had through
their own training, to understand, although they
have not yet shown themselves worthy to partake of the power of believing.

The prophetic sayings we shall not at present
advert to, as we are to avail ourselves of the
Scriptures subsequently at the proper places.
But we shall point out summarily the points
indicated by them, in our delineation of Christianity, so that by taking the Scriptures at once
(especially as they do not yet comprehend their
utterances), we may not interrupt the continuity
of the discourse. But after pointing out the
things indicated, proofs shall be shown in abundance to those who have believed.

But if the assertions made by us appear to
certain of the multitude to be different from the
Scriptures of the Lord, let it be known that it is
from that source that they have breath and life;
and taking their rise from them, they profess to
adduce the sense only, not the words. For further treatment, not being seasonable, will rightly
appear superfluous. Thus, not to look at what
is urgent would be excessively indolent and
defective; and " blessed, in truth, are they
who, investigating the testimonies of the LORD,
shall seek Him with their whole heart." [1] And
the law and the prophets witness of the Lord.

It is, then, our purpose to prove that the
Gnostic alone is holy and pious, and worships the
true God in a manner worthy of Him; and that
worship meet for God is followed by loving and
being loved by God. He accordingly judges all
excellence to be honourable according to its
worth; and judges that among the objects perceived by our senses, we are to esteem rulers,
and parents, and every one advanced in years;
and among subjects of instruction, the most
ancient philosophy and primeval prophecy; and
among intellectual ideas, what is oldest in origin,
the timeless and unoriginated First Principle,
and Beginning of existences — the Son — from
whom we are to learn the remoter Cause, the
Father, of the universe, the most ancient and
the most beneficent of all; not capable of expression by the voice, but to be reverenced with
reverence, and silence, and holy wonder, and
supremely venerated; declared by the Lord, as
far as those who learned were capable of comprehending, and understood by those chosen by
the Lord to acknowledge; " whose senses," says
the apostle, " were exercised." [2]

The service of God, then, in the case of the
Gnostic, is his soul's continual study [3] and occupation, bestowed on the Deity in ceaseless love.
For of the service bestowed on men, one kind
is that whose aim is improvement, the other
ministerial. The improvement of the body is
the object of the medical art, of the soul of
philosophy. Ministerial service is rendered to
parents by children, to rulers by subjects.

Similarly, also, in the Church, the elders
attend to the department which has improvement for its object; and the deacons to the
ministerial. In both these ministries the angels [4]
serve God, in the management of earthly affairs;
and the Gnostic himself ministers to God, and

---

[1] Ps. cxix. 2.

[2] Heb. v. 14.
[3] Or, as rendered by the Latin translator, " continual care for his
soul and occupation, bestowed on the Deity," etc.
[4] [Book vi. cap. 13, *supra*.]

exhibits to men the scheme of improvement, in the way in which he has been appointed to discipline men for their amendment. For he is alone pious that serves God rightly and unblameably in human affairs. For as that treatment of plants is best through which their fruits are produced and gathered in, through knowledge and skill in husbandry, affording men the benefit accruing from them; so the piety of the Gnostic, taking to itself the fruits of the men who by his means have believed, when not a few attain to knowledge and are saved by it, achieves by his skill the best harvest. And as Godliness (θεοπρέπεια) is the habit which preserves what is becoming to God, the godly man is the only lover of God, and such will he be who knows what is becoming, both in respect of knowledge and of the life which must be lived by him, who is destined to be divine (θεῷ), and is already being assimilated to God. So then he is in the first place a lover of God. For as he who honours his father is a lover of his father, so he who honours God is a lover of God.

Thus also it appears to me that there are three effects of gnostic power: the knowledge of things; second, the performance of whatever the Word suggests; and the third, the capability of delivering, in a way suitable to God, the secrets veiled in the truth.

He, then, who is persuaded that God is omnipotent, and has learned the divine mysteries from His only-begotten Son, how can he be an atheist (ἄθεος)? For he is an atheist who thinks that God does not exist. And he is superstitious who dreads the demons; who deifies all things, both wood and stone; and reduces to bondage spirit, and man who possesses the life of reason.[1]

CHAP. II.—THE SON THE RULER AND SAVIOUR OF ALL.

To know[2] God is, then, the first step of faith; then, through confidence in the teaching of the Saviour, to consider the doing of wrong in any way as not suitable to the knowledge of God.

So the best thing on earth is the most pious man; and the best thing in heaven, the nearer in place and purer, is an angel, the partaker of the eternal and blessed life. But the nature of the Son, which is nearest to Him who is alone the Almighty One, is the most perfect, and most holy, and most potent, and most princely, and most kingly, and most beneficent. This is the highest excellence, which orders all things in accordance with the Father's will, and holds the helm of the universe in the best way, with unwearied and tireless power, working all things in which it operates, keeping in view its hidden designs. For from His own point of view the Son of God is never displaced; not being divided, not severed, not passing from place to place; being always everywhere, and being contained nowhere; complete mind, the complete paternal light; all eyes, seeing all things, hearing all things, knowing all things, by His power scrutinizing the powers. To Him is placed in subjection all the host of angels and gods; He, the paternal Word, exhibiting[3] the holy administration for Him who put [all] in subjection to Him.

Wherefore also all men are His; some through knowledge, and others not yet so; and some as friends, some as faithful servants, some as servants merely. This is the Teacher, who trains the Gnostic by mysteries, and the believer by good hopes, and the hard of heart by corrective discipline through sensible operation. Thence His providence is in private, in public, and everywhere.

And that He whom we call Saviour and Lord is the Son of God, the prophetic Scriptures explicitly prove. So the Lord of all, of Greeks and of Barbarians, persuades those who are willing. For He does not compel him[4] who (through choosing and fulfilling, from Him, what pertains to laying hold of it the hope) is able to receive salvation from Him.

It is He who also gave philosophy to the Greeks by means of the inferior angels. For by an ancient and divine order the angels are distributed among the nations.[5] But the glory of those who believe is "the Lord's portion." For either the Lord does not care for all men; and this is the case either because He is unable (which is not to be thought, for it would be a proof of weakness), or because He is unwilling, which is not the attribute of a good being. And He who for our sakes assumed flesh capable of suffering, is far from being luxuriously indolent. Or He does care for all, which is befitting for Him who has become Lord of all. For He is Saviour; not [the Saviour] of some, and of others not. But in proportion to the adaptation possessed by each, He has dispensed His beneficence both to Greeks and Barbarians, even to those of them that were predestinated, and in due time called, the faithful and elect. Nor can He who called all equally, and assigned special honours to those who have believed in a specially excellent way, ever envy any. Nor can He who is the Lord of all, and serves above all the will of the good and almighty Father, ever be hindered

---

[1] Potter's text has καταδεδουλωμένον — which Lowth changes into καταδεδουλωμένος, nominative; and this has been adopted in the translation. The thought is the same as in *Exhortation to the Heathen* [cap. ii. p. 177, *supra*.]

[2] This sentence has been thus rendered by Sylburgius and by Bp. Kaye. Lowth, however, suggests the supplying of ἐνεργεῖ, or something similar, to govern πεποίθησιν, confidence.

[3] Ἀναδεδειγμένῳ. Instead of this, ἀναδεδεγμένῳ, "having received," has been suggested by Sylburgius.

[4] By omitting "him" (τόν), as Sylburgius does, the translation would run thus: "For He compels no one to receive salvation from Him, because he is able to choose and fulfil from himself what pertains to the laying hold of the hope."

[5] Deut. xxxii. 8, 9, Septuagint, quoted already more than once.

by another. But neither does envy touch the Lord, who without beginning was impassible ; nor are the things of men such as to be envied by the Lord. But it is another, he whom passion hath touched, who envies. And it cannot be said that it is from ignorance that the Lord is not willing to save humanity, because He knows not how each one is to be cared for. For ignorance applies not to the God who, before the foundation of the world, was the counsellor of the Father. For He was the Wisdom " in which " the Sovereign God " delighted." [1] For the Son is the power of God, as being the Father's most ancient Word before the production of all things, and His Wisdom. He is then properly called the Teacher of the beings formed by Him. Nor does He ever abandon care for men, by being drawn aside from pleasure, who, having assumed flesh, which by nature is susceptible of suffering, trained it to the condition of impassibility.

And how is He Saviour and Lord, if not the Saviour and Lord of all? But He is the Saviour of those who have believed, because of their wishing to know ; and the Lord of those who have not believed, till, being enabled to confess him, they obtain the peculiar and appropriate boon which comes by Him.

Now the energy of the Lord has a reference to the Almighty ; and the Son is, so to speak, an energy of the Father. Therefore, a hater of man, the Saviour can never be ; who, for His exceeding love to human flesh, despising not its susceptibility to suffering, but investing Himself with it, came for the common salvation of men ; for the faith of those who have chosen it, is common. Nay more, He will never neglect His own work, because man alone of all the other living creatures was in his creation endowed with a conception of God. Nor can there be any other better and more suitable government for men than that which is appointed by God.

It is then always proper for the one who is superior by nature to be over the inferior, and for him who is capable of managing aught well to have the management of it assigned to him. Now that which truly rules and presides is the Divine Word and His providence, which inspects all things, and despises the care of nothing belonging to it.

Those, then, who choose to belong to Him, are those who are perfected through faith. He, the Son, is, by the will of the Almighty Father, the cause of all good things, being the first efficient cause of motion — a power incapable of being apprehended by sensation. For what He was, was not seen by those who, through the weakness of the flesh, were incapable of taking in [the reality]. But, having assumed sensitive

flesh, He came to show man what was possible through obedience to the commandments. Being, then, the Father's power, He easily prevails in what He wishes, leaving not even the minutest point of His administration unattended to. For otherwise the whole would not have been well executed by Him.

But, as I think, characteristic of the highest power is the accurate scrutiny of all the parts, reaching even to the minutest, terminating in the first Administrator of the universe, who by the will of the Father directs the salvation of all ; some overlooking, who are set under others, who are set over them, till you come to the great High Priest. For on one original first Principle, which acts according to the [Father's] will, the first and the second and the third depend. Then at the highest extremity of the visible world is the blessed band of angels ; [2] and down to ourselves there are ranged, some under others, those who, from One and by One, both are saved and save.

As, then, the minutest particle of steel is moved by the spirit of the Heraclean stone, [3] when diffused [4] over many steel rings ; so also, attracted by the Holy Spirit, the virtuous are added by affinity to the first abode, and the others in succession down to the last. But those who are bad from infirmity, having fallen from vicious insatiableness into a depraved state, neither controlling nor controlled, rush round and round, whirled about by the passions, and fall down to the ground.

For this was the law from the first, that virtue should be the object of voluntary choice. Wherefore also the commandments, according to the Law, and before the Law, not given to the upright (for the law is not appointed for a righteous man [5]), ordained that he should receive eternal life and the blessed prize, who chose them.

But, on the other hand, they allowed him who had been delighted with vice to consort with the objects of his choice ; and, on the other hand, that the soul, which is ever improving in the acquisition [6] of virtue and the increase of righteousness, should obtain a better place in the universe, as tending in each step of advancement towards the habit of impassibility, till " it come to a perfect man," [7] to the excellence at once of knowledge and of inheritance.

These salutary revolutions, in accordance with the order of change, are distinguished both by times, and places, and honours, and cognitions, and heritages, and ministries, according to the

2 [So called from *Heraclea* in Lydia.]
3 The magnet. [So called from the Lydian Magnesia.]
4 Lowth here reads ἐκτεινομένῳ, agreeing with πνεύματι, instead of ἐκτεινομένη, as in the Oxford text.
5 1 Tim. i. 9.
6 Instead of ἐπίγνωσιν, the corrupt reading of the text, ἐπίκτησιν (as above), ἐπίδοσιν, and ἐπ' ἐξήγησιν have been proposed.
7 Eph. iv. 13.

particular order of each change, up to the transcendent and continual contemplation of the Lord in eternity.

Now that which is lovable leads, to the contemplation of itself, each one who, from love of knowledge, applies himself entirely to contemplation. Wherefore also the Lord, drawing the commandments, both the first which He gave, and the second, from one fountain, neither allowed those who were before the law to be without law, nor permitted those who were unacquainted with the principles of the Barbarian philosophy to be without restraint. For, having furnished the one with the commandments, and the other with philosophy, He shut up unbelief to the Advent. Whence[1] every one who believes not is without excuse. For by a different process of advancement, both Greek and Barbarian, He leads to the perfection which is by faith.[2]

And if any one of the Greeks, passing over the preliminary training of the Hellenic philosophy, proceeds directly to the true teaching, he distances others, though an unlettered man, by choosing[3] the compendious process of salvation by faith to perfection.

Everything, then, which did not hinder a man's choice from being free, He made and rendered auxiliary to virtue, in order that there might be revealed somehow or other, even to those capable of seeing but dimly, the one only almighty, good God — from eternity to eternity saving by His Son.

And, on the other hand, He is in no respect whatever the cause of evil. For all things are arranged with a view to the salvation of the universe by the Lord of the universe, both generally and particularly. It is then the function of the righteousness of salvation to improve everything as far as practicable. For even minor matters are arranged with a view to the salvation of that which is better, and for an abode suitable for people's character. Now everything that is virtuous changes for the better; having as the proper[4] cause of change the free choice of knowledge, which the soul has in its own power. But necessary corrections, through the goodness of the great overseeing Judge, both by the attendant angels, and by various acts of anticipative judgment, and by the perfect judgment, compel egregious sinners to repent.

---

[1] The text has ὅτε but the sense seems to require, as Sylburgius suggests, ὅθεν or ὥστε.
[2] [The salvability of the heathen through Christ, is everywhere conspicuous in our author's system; but there is a solemn dignity in the concluding paragraphs of this chapter, which deserves reflection. It would not be becoming for me to express my own views upon the subject here, but it is one assuming fresh importance in our day].
[3] Instead of ἐλόμενος, Sylburgius proposes ἀλάμενος, making a leap by faith to perfection.
[4] The reading varies here. For οἰκήσεις of the text, Heinsius and the Latin translator adopt οἰκείαν, which, on the whole, seems preferable to οἴκησιν or ἠκούσης.

CHAP. III. — THE GNOSTIC AIMS AT THE NEAREST LIKENESS POSSIBLE TO GOD AND HIS SON.

Now I pass over other things in silence, glorifying the Lord. But I affirm that gnostic souls, that surpass in the grandeur of contemplation the mode of life of each of the holy ranks, among whom the blessed abodes of the gods are allotted by distribution, reckoned holy among the holy, transferred entire from among the entire, reaching places better than the better places, embracing the divine vision not in mirrors or by means of mirrors, but in the transcendently clear and absolutely pure insatiable vision which is the privilege of intensely loving souls, holding festival through endless ages, remain honoured with the indentity of all excellence. Such is the vision attainable by "the pure in heart."[5] This is the function of the Gnostic, who has been perfected, to have converse with God through the great High Priest, being made like the Lord, up to the measure of his capacity, in the whole service of God, which tends to the salvation of men, through care of the beneficence which has us for its object; and on the other side through worship, through teaching and through beneficence in deeds. The Gnostic even forms and creates himself; and besides also, he, like to God, adorns those who hear him; assimilating as far as possible the moderation which, arising from practice, tends to impassibility, to Him who by nature possesses impassibility; and especially having uninterrupted converse and fellowship with the Lord. Mildness, I think, and philanthropy, and eminent piety, are the rules of gnostic assimilation. I affirm that these virtues "are a sacrifice acceptable in the sight of God;"[6] Scripture alleging that "the humble heart with right knowledge is the holocaust of God;"[7] each man who is admitted to holiness being illuminated in order to indissoluble union.

For "to bring themselves into captivity," and to slay themselves, putting to death "the old man, who is through lusts corrupt," and raising the new man from death, "from the old conversation," by abandoning the passions, and becoming free of sin, both the Gospel and the apostle enjoin.[8]

It was this, consequently, which the Law intimated, by ordering the sinner to be cut off, and translated from death to life, to the impassibility that is the result of faith; which the teachers of the Law, not comprehending, inasmuch as they regarded the law as contentious, they have given a handle to those who attempt idly to calumniate the Law. And for this reason we rightly do not sacrifice to God, who, needing

---

[5] Matt. v. 8.
[6] Phil. iv. 18.
[7] Ps. li. 17, 19.
[8] Rom. vi. 6, 7; 2 Cor. x 5; Eph. iv. 22-24; Col. iii. 8, 9, etc.

nothing, supplies all men with all things; but we glorify Him who gave Himself in sacrifice for us, we also sacrificing ourselves; from that which needs nothing to that which needs nothing, and to that which is impassible from that which is impassible. For in our salvation alone God delights. We do not therefore, and with reason too, offer sacrifice to Him who is not overcome by pleasures, inasmuch as the fumes of the smoke stop far beneath, and do not even reach the thickest clouds; but those they reach are far from them. The Deity neither is, then, in want of aught, nor loves pleasure, or gain, or money, being full, and supplying all things to everything that has received being and has wants. And neither by sacrifices nor offerings, nor on the other hand by glory and honour, is the Deity won over; nor is He influenced by any such things; but He appears only to excellent and good men, who will never betray justice for threatened fear, nor by the promise of considerable gifts.

But those who have not seen the self-determination of the human soul, and its incapability of being treated as a slave in what respects the choice of life, being disgusted at what is done through rude injustice, do not think that there is a God. On a par with these in opinion, are they who, falling into licentiousness in pleasures, and grievous pains, and unlooked-for accidents, and bidding defiance to events, say that there is no God, or that, though existing, He does not oversee all things. And others there are, who are persuaded that those they reckon gods are capable of being prevailed upon by sacrifices and gifts, favouring, so to speak, their profligacies; and will not believe that He is the only true God, who exists in the invariableness of righteous goodness.

The Gnostic, then, is pious, who cares first for himself, then for his neighbours, that they may become very good. For the son gratifies a good father, by showing himself good and like his father; and in like manner the subject, the governor. For believing and obeying are in our own power.

But should any one suppose the cause of evils to be the weakness of matter, and the involuntary impulses of ignorance, and (in his stupidity) irrational necessities; he who has become a Gnostic has through instruction superiority over these, as if they were wild beasts; and in imitation of the divine plan, he does good to such as are willing, as far as he can. And if ever placed in authority, like Moses, he will rule for the salvation of the governed; and will tame wildness and faithlessness, by recording honour for the most excellent, and punishment for the wicked, in accordance with reason for the sake of discipline.

For pre-eminently a divine image, resembling God, is the soul of a righteous man; in which, through obedience to the commands, as in a consecrated spot, is enclosed and enshrined the Leader of mortals and of immortals, King and Parent of what is good, who is truly law, and right, and eternal Word, being the one Saviour individually to each, and in common to all.

He is the true Only-begotten, the express image of the glory of the universal King and Almighty Father, who impresses on the Gnostic the seal of the perfect contemplation, according to His own image; so that there is now a third divine image, made as far as possible like the Second Cause, the Essential Life, through which we live the true life; the Gnostic, as we regard him, being described as moving amid things sure and wholly immutable.

Ruling, then, over himself and what belongs to him, and possessing a sure grasp, of divine science, he makes a genuine approach to the truth. For the knowledge and apprehension of intellectual objects must necessarily be called certain scientific knowledge, whose function in reference to divine things is to consider what is the First Cause, and what that "by whom all things were made, and without whom nothing was made;"[1] and what things, on the other hand, are as pervasive, and what is comprehensive; what conjoined, what disjoined; and what is the position which each one of them holds, and what power and what service each contributes. And again, among human things, what man himself is, and what he has naturally or preternaturally; and how, again, it becomes him to do or to suffer; and what are his virtues and what his vices; and about things good, bad, and indifferent; also about fortitude, and prudence, and self-restraint, and the virtue which is in all respects complete, namely, righteousness.

Further, he employs prudence and righteousness in the acquisition of wisdom, and fortitude, not only in the endurance of circumstances, but also in restraining[2] pleasure and desire, grief and anger; and, in general, to withstand[3] everything which either by any force or fraud entices us. For it is not necessary to endure vices and virtues, but it is to be persuaded to bear things that inspire fear.

Accordingly, pain is found beneficial in the healing art, and in discipline, and in punishment; and by it men's manners are corrected to their advantage. Forms of fortitude are endurance, magnanimity, high spirit, liberality, and grandeur. And for this reason he neither meets with the blame or the bad opinion of the multitude; nor is he subjected to opinions or flatteries. But in

---

[1] John i. 3.
[2] κρατεῖν is hear supplied to complete the sense.
[3] ἀντιτάσσεσθαι is suggested instead of ἀντιτάσσεται of the text.

the indurance of toils and at the same time [1] in the discharge of any duty, and in his manly superiority to all circumstances, he appears truly a man (ἀνήρ) among the rest of human beings. And, on the other hand, maintaining prudence, he exercises moderation in the calmness of his soul; receptive of what is commanded, as of what belongs to him, entertaining aversion to what is base, as alien to him; become decorous and supramundane,[2] he does everything with decorum and in order, and transgresses in no respect, and in nothing. Rich he is in the highest degree in desiring nothing, as having few wants; and being in the midst of abundance of all good through the knowledge of the good. For it is the first effect of his righteousness, to love to spend his time and associate with those of his own race both in earth and heaven. So also he is liberal of what he possesses. And being a lover of men, he is a hater of the wicked, entertaining a perfect aversion to all villany. He must consequently learn to be faithful both to himself and his neighbours, and obedient to the commandments. For he is the true servant of God who spontaneously subjects himself to His commands. And he who already, not through the commandments, but through knowledge itself, is pure in heart, is the friend of God. For neither are we born by nature possessing virtue, nor after we are born does it grow naturally, as certain parts of the body; since then it would neither be voluntary nor praiseworthy. Nor is virtue, like speech, perfected by the practice that results from everyday occurrences (for this is very much the way in which vice originates). For it is not by any art, either those of acquisition, or those which relate to the care of the body, that knowledge is attained. No more is it from the curriculum of instruction. For that is satisfied if it can only prepare and sharpen the soul. For the laws of the state are perchance able to restrain bad actions; but persuasive words, which but touch the surface, cannot produce a scientific permanence of the truth.

Now the Greek philosophy, as it were, purges the soul, and prepares it beforehand for the reception of faith, on which the Truth builds up the edifice of knowledge.

This is the true athlete—he who in the great stadium, the fair world, is crowned for the true victory over all the passions. For He who prescribes the contest is the Almighty God, and He who awards the prize is the only-begotten Son of God. Angels and gods are spectators; and the contest, embracing all the varied exercises, is "not against flesh and blood,"[3] but against the spiritual powers of inordinate passions that work through the flesh. He who obtains the mastery in these struggles, and overthrows the tempter, menacing, as it were, with certain contests, wins immortality. For the sentence of God in most righteous judgment is infallible. The spectators[4] are summoned to the contest, and the athletes contend in the stadium; the one, who has obeyed the directions of the trainer, wins the day. For to all, all rewards proposed by God are equal; and He Himself is unimpeachable. And he who has power receives mercy, and he that has exercised will is mighty.

So also we have received mind, that we may know what we do. And the maxim "Know thyself" means here to know for what we are born. And we are born to obey the commandments, if we choose to be willing to be saved. Such is the Nemesis,[5] through which there is no escaping from God. Man's duty, then, is obedience to God, who has proclaimed salvation manifold by the commandments. And confession is thanksgiving. For the beneficent first begins to do good. And he who on fitting considerations readily receives and keeps the commandments, is faithful (πιστός); and he who by love requites benefits as far as he is able, is already a friend. One recompense on the part of men is of paramount importance — the doing of what is pleasing to God. As being His own production, and a result akin to Himself, the Teacher and Saviour receives acts of assistance and of improvement on the part of men as a personal favour and honour; as also He regards the injuries inflicted on those who believe on Him as ingratitude and dishonour to Himself. For what other dishonour can touch God? Wherefore it is impossible to render a recompense at all equivalent to the boon received from the Lord.

And as those who maltreat property insult the owners, and those who maltreat soldiers insult the commander, so also the ill-usage of His consecrated ones is contempt for the Lord.

For, just as the sun not only illumines heaven and the whole world, shining over land and sea, but also through windows and small chinks sends his beams into the innermost recesses of houses, so the Word diffused everywhere casts His eyeglance on the minutest circumstances of the actions of life.

CHAP. IV. — THE HEATHENS MADE GODS LIKE THEMSELVES, WHENCE SPRINGS ALL SUPERSTITION.

Now, as the Greeks represent the gods as possessing human forms, so also do they as possessing human passions. And as each of them

---

[1] ἅμα is here, on the authority of a MS., and with the approval of Sylburguis, to be substituted for ἄλμα.
[2] κόσμιος καὶ ὑπερκόσμιος. The author plays on the double meaning of κόσμος, world or order.
[3] Eph. vi. 12.

[4] τὸ θέατρον used for the place, the spectacle, and the spectators.
[5] Ἀδράστεια, a name given to Nemesis, said to be from an altar erected to her by Adrastus; but as used here, and when employed as an adjective qualifying Nemesis, it has reference to διδράσκω.

depict their forms similar to themselves, as Xenophanes says, " Ethiopians as black and apes, the Thracians ruddy and tawny ; " so also they assimilate their souls to those who form them : the Barbarians, for instance, who make them savage and wild ; and the Greeks, who make them more civilized, yet subject to passion.

Wherefore it stands to reason, that the ideas entertained of God by wicked men must be bad, and those by good men most excellent. And therefore he who is in soul truly kingly and gnostic, being likewise pious and free from superstition, is persuaded that He who alone is God is honourable, venerable, august, beneficent, the doer of good, the author of all good things, but not the cause of evil. And respecting the Hellenic superstition we have, as I think, shown enough in the book entitled by us *The Exhortation*, availing ourselves abundantly of the history bearing on the point. There is no need, then, again to make a long story of what has already been clearly stated. But in as far as necessity requires to be pointed out on coming to the topic, suffice it to adduce a few out of many considerations in proof of the impiety of those who make the Divinity resemble the worst men. For either those Gods of theirs are injured by men, and are shown to be inferior to men on being injured by us ; or, if not so, how is it that they are incensed at those by whom they are not injured, like a testy old wife roused to wrath ?

As they say that Artemis was enraged at the Ætolians on account of Œneus.[1] For how, being a goddess, did she not consider that he had neglected to sacrifice, not through contempt, but out of inadvertence, or under the idea that he had sacrificed ?

And Latona,[2] arguing her case with Athene, on account of the latter being incensed at her for having brought forth in the temple, says : —

> " Man-slaying spoils
> Torn from the dead you love to see. And these
> To you are not unclean. But you regard
> My parturition here a horrid thing,
> Though other creatures in the temple do
> No harm by bringing forth their young."

It is natural, then, that having a superstitious dread of those irascible [gods], they imagine that all events are signs and causes of evils. If a mouse bore through an altar built of clay, and for want of something else gnaw through an oil flask ; if a cock that is being fattened crow in the evening, they determine this to be a sign of something.

Of such a one Menander gives a comic description in *The Superstitious Man* : —

> " *A.* Good luck be mine, ye honoured gods !
> Tying my right shoe's string,
> I broke it."
> " *B.* Most likely, silly fool,
> For it was rotten, and you, niggard, you
> Would not buy new ones."[3]

It was a clever remark of Antiphon, who (when one regarded it as an ill omen that the sow had eaten her pigs), on seeing her emaciated through the niggardliness of the person that kept her, said, Congratulate yourself on the omen that, being so hungry, she did not eat your own children.

"And what wonder is it," says Bion, "if the mouse, finding nothing to eat, gnaws the bag?" For it were wonderful if (as Arcesilaus argued in fun) "the bag had eaten the mouse."

Diogenes accordingly remarked well to one who wondered at finding a serpent coiled round a pestle : "Don't wonder ; for it would have been more surprising if you had seen the pestle coiled round the serpent, and the serpent straight."

For the irrational creatures must run, and scamper, and fight, and breed, and die ; and these things being natural to them, can never be unnatural to us.

" And many birds beneath the sunbeams walk."

And the comic poet Philemon treats such points in comedy : —

> " When I see one who watches who has sneezed,
> Or who has spoke ; or looking, who goes on,
> I straightway in the market sell him off.
> Each one of us walks, talks, and sneezes too,
> For his own self, not for the citizens :
> According to their nature things turn out."

Then by the practice of temperance men seek health : and by cramming themselves, and wallowing in potations at feasts, they attract diseases.

There are many, too, that dread inscriptions set up. Very cleverly Diogenes, on finding in the house of a bad man the inscription, "Hercules, for victory famed, dwells here ; let nothing bad enter," remarked, "And how shall the master of the house go in?"

The same people, who worship every stick and greasy stone, as the saying is, dreads tufts of tawny wool, and lumps of salt, and torches, and squills, and sulphur, bewitched by sorcerers, in certain impure rites of expiation. But God, the true God, recognises as holy only the character of the righteous man, — as unholy, wrong and wickedness.

You may see the eggs,[4] taken from those who have been purified, hatched if subjected to the necessary warmth. But this could not take

---

[1] *Iliad*, ix. 533, etc.
[2] The text has Ἡ αὐτή, which is plainly unsuitable ; hence the suggestion ἡ Λητώ.

[3] These lines are quoted by Theodoret, and have been amended and arranged by Sylburgius and Grotius. The text has Ἀγαθόν τι; Theodoret and Grotius omit τί as above.
[4] Which were used in lustrations, ᾠά. The text has ὦτα.

place if they had had transferred to them the sins of the man that had undergone purification. Accordingly the comic poet Diphilus facetiously writes, in comedy, of sorcerers, in the following words : —

" Purifying Prœtus' daughters, and their father
Prœtus Abantades, and fifth, an old wife to boot,
So many people's persons with one torch, one squill,
With sulphur and asphalt of the loud-sounding sea,
From the placid-flowing, deep-flowing ocean.
But blest air through the clouds send Anticyra
That I may make this bug into a drone."

For well Menander remarks : [1] —

" Had you, O Phidias, any real ill,
You needs must seek for it a real cure ;
Now 'tis not so. And for the unreal ill
I've found an unreal cure   Believe that it
Will do thee good. Let women in a ring
Wipe thee, and from three fountains water bring.
Add salt and lentils ; sprinkle then thyself.
Each one is pure, who's conscious of no sin."

For instance, the tragedy says : —

Menelaus. " What disease, Orestes, is destroying thee ? "
Orestes. "Conscience. For horrid deeds I know I've done." [2]

For in reality there is no other purity but abstinence from sins. Excellently then Epicharmus says : —

" If a pure mind thou hast,
In thy whole body thou art pure."

Now also we say that it is requisite to purify the soul from corrupt and bad doctrines by right reason ; and so thereafter to the recollection of the principal heads of doctrine. Since also before the communication of the mysteries they think it right to apply certain purifications to those who are to be initiated ; so it is requisite for men to abandon impious opinion, and thus turn to the true tradition.

CHAP. V. — THE HOLY SOUL A MORE EXCELLENT TEMPLE THAN ANY EDIFICE BUILT BY MAN.

For is it not the case that rightly and truly we do not circumscribe in any place that which cannot be circumscribed ; nor do we shut up in temples made with hands that which contains all things ? What work of builders, and stone-cutters, and mechanical art can be holy ? Superior to these are not they who think that the air, and the enclosing space, or rather the whole world and the universe, are meet for the excellency of God ?

It were indeed ridiculous, as the philosophers themselves say, for man, the plaything [3] of God, to make God, and for God to be the plaything [4] of art ; since what is made is similar and the same to that of which it is made, as that which

is made of ivory is ivory, and that which is made of gold golden. Now the images and temples constructed by mechanics are made of inert matter ; so that they too are inert, and material, and profane ; and if you perfect the art, they partake of mechanical coarseness. Works of art cannot then be sacred and divine.

And what can be localized, there being nothing that is not localized ? Since all things are in a place. And that which is localized having been formerly not localized, is localized by something. If, then, God is localized by men, He was once not localized, and did not exist at all. For the non-existent is what is not localized ; since whatever does not exist is not localized. And what exists cannot be localized by what does not exist ; nor by another entity. For it is also an entity. It follows that it must be by itself. And how shall anything generate itself ? Or how shall that which exists place itself as to being ? Whether, being formerly not localized, has it localized itself ? But it was not in existence ; since what exists not is not localized. And its localization being supposed, how can it afterwards make itself what it previously was ?

But how can He, to whom the things that are belong, need anything ? But were God possessed of a human form, He would need, equally with man, food, and shelter, and house, and the attendant incidents. Those who are like in form and affections will require similar sustenance. And if sacred (τὸ ἱερόν) has a twofold application, designating both God Himself and the structure raised to His honour,[5] how shall we not with propriety call the Church holy, through knowledge, made for the honour of God, sacred (ἱερόν) to God, of great value, and not constructed by mechanical art, nor embellished by the hand of an impostor, but by the will of God fashioned into a temple ? For it is not now the place, but the assemblage of the elect,[6] that I call the Church. This temple is better for the reception of the greatness of the dignity of God. For the living creature which is of high value, is made sacred by that which is worth all, or rather which has no equivalent, in virtue of the exceeding sanctity of the latter. Now this is the Gnostic, who is of great value, who is honoured by God, in whom God is enshrined, that is, the knowledge respecting God is consecrated. Here, too, we shall find the divine likeness and the holy image in the righteous soul, when it is blessed in being purified and performing blessed deeds. Here also we shall find that which is localized, and that which is being localized, — the former in the case of those who are already Gnostics, and the latter in the case of those

---

[1] Translated as arranged and amended by Grotius.
[2] Euripides, *Orestes*, 395, 396
[3] A Platonic phrase: παιγνιον Θεοῦ.
[4] So Sylburgius, who, instead of παιδιᾶς τέχνης of the text, reads παιδιὰν τέχνης.

[5] God Himself is ἱερός, and everything dedicated to Him.
[6] Montacutius suggests ἐκκλήτων, from its connection with Ἐκκλησία, instead of ἐκλεκτῶν. [Notes 3 and 5, p. 290, *supra.*]

capable of becoming so, although not yet worthy of receiving the knowledge of God. For every being destined to believe is already faithful in the sight of God, and set up for His honour, an image, endowed with virtue, dedicated to God.

CHAP. VI. — PRAYERS AND PRAISE FROM A PURE MIND, CEASELESSLY OFFERED, FAR BETTER THAN SACRIFICES.

As, then, God is not circumscribed by place, neither is ever represented by the form of a living creature ; so neither has He similar passions, nor has He wants like the creatures, so as to desire sacrifice, from hunger, by way of food. Those creatures which are affected by passion are all mortal. And it is useless to bring food to one who is not nourished.

And that comic poet Pherecrates, in *The Fugitives*, facetiously represents the gods themselves as finding fault with men on the score of their sacred rites : —

> " When to the gods you sacrifice,
> Selecting what our portion is,
> 'Tis shame to tell, do ye not take,
> And both the thighs, clean to the groins,
> The loins quite bare, the backbone, too,
> Clean scrape as with a file,
> Them swallow, and the remnant give
> To us as if to dogs? And then,
> As if of one another 'shamed,
> With heaps of salted barley hide." [1]

And Eubulus, also a comic poet, thus writes respecting sacrifices : —

> " But to the gods the tail alone
> And thigh, as if to pæderasts you sacrifice."

And introducing Dionysus in Semele, he represents him disputing : —

> " First if they offer aught to me, there are
> Who offer blood, the bladder, not the heart
> Or caul. For I no flesh do ever eat
> That's sweeter than the thigh." [2]

And Menander writes : —

> " The end of the loin,
> The bile, the bones uneatable, they set
> Before the gods ; the rest themselves consume."

For is not the savour of the holocausts avoided by the beasts? And if in reality the savour is the guerdon of the gods of the Greeks, should they not first deify the cooks, who are dignified with equal happiness, and worship the chimney itself, which is closer still to the much-prized savour?

And Hesiod says that Zeus, cheated in a division of flesh by Prometheus, received the white bones of an ox, concealed with cunning art, in shining fat : —

> " Whence to the immortal gods the tribes of men
> The victim's white bones on the altars burn."

But they will by no means say that the Deity, enfeebled through the desire that springs from want, is nourished. Accordingly, they will represent Him as nourished without desire like a plant, and like beasts that burrow. They say that these grow innoxiously, nourished either by the density in the air, or from the exhalations proceeding from their own body. Though if the Deity, though needing nothing, is according to them nourished, what necessity has He for food, wanting nothing? But if, by nature needing nothing, He delights to be honoured, it is not without reason that we honour God in prayer ; and thus the best and holiest sacrifice with righteousness we bring, presenting it as an offering to the most righteous Word, by whom we receive knowledge, giving glory by Him for what[3] we have learned.

The altar, then, that is with us here, the terrestrial one, is the congregation of those who devote themselves to prayers, having as it were one common voice and one mind.

Now, if nourishing substances taken in by the nostrils are diviner than those taken in by the mouth, yet they infer respiration. What, then, do they say of God? Whether does He exhale like the tribe of oaks?[4] Or does He only inhale, like the aquatic animals, by the dilatation of their gills? Or does He breathe all round, like the insects, by the compression of the section by means of their wings? But no one, if he is in his senses, will liken God to any of these.

And the creatures that breathe by the expansion of the lung towards the thorax draw in the air. Then if they assign to God viscera, and arteries, and veins, and nerves, and parts, they will make Him in nothing different from man.

Now breathing together ($\sigma\acute{v}\mu\pi\nu o\iota a$) is properly said of the Church. For the sacrifice of the Church is the word breathing as incense[6] from holy souls, the sacrifice and the whole mind being at the same time unveiled to God. Now the very ancient altar in Delos they celebrated as holy ; which alone, being undefiled by slaughter and death, they say Pythagoras approached. And will they not believe us when we say that the righteous soul is the truly sacred altar, and that incense arising from it is holy prayer? But I believe sacrifices were invented by men to be a pretext for eating flesh.[7] But without such idolatry he who wished might have partaken of flesh.

For the sacrifices of the Law express figura-

---

[1] Translated as arranged by Grotius.
[2] These lines are translated as arranged by Grotius, who differs in some parts from the text.

[3] $\acute{\epsilon}\phi'$ o$\acute{\iota}$ς, substituted by Lowth for $\ddot{a}$ in the text.
[4] $\delta\rho\upsilon\tilde{\omega}\nu$, a probable conjecture of Gataker for the reading of the text, $\delta a\iota\mu\acute{o}\nu\omega\nu$.
[5] $\acute{a}\nu\theta\rho\acute{\omega}\pi o\upsilon$ supplied by Lowth.
[6] [Again the spiritualizing of incense.]
[7] [This is extraordinary language in Clement, whose views of Gentilism are so charitable. Possibly it is mere pleasantry, though he speaks of idolatry only. He recognises the divine institution of sacrifice, elsewhere.]

tively the piety which we practise, as the turtle-dove and the pigeon offered for sins point out that the cleansing of the irrational part of the soul is acceptable to God.   But if any one of the righteous does not burden his soul by the eating of flesh, he has the advantage of a rational reason, not as Pythagoras and his followers dream of the transmigration of the soul.

Now Xenocrates, treating by himself of "the food derived from animals," and Polemon in his work *On Life according to Nature*, seem clearly to say that animal food is unwholesome, inasmuch as it has already been elaborated and assimilated to the souls of the irrational creatures.

So also, in particular, the Jews abstain from swine's flesh on the ground of this animal being unclean ; since more than the other animals it roots up, and destroys the productions of the ground.   But if they say that the animals were assigned to men — and we agree with them — yet it was not entirely for food.   Nor was it all animals, but such as do not work.   Wherefore the comic poet Plato says not badly in the drama of *The Feasts* : —

> " For of the quadrupeds we should not slay
> In future aught but swine.   For these have flesh
> Most toothsome ; and about the pig is nought
> For us, excepting bristles, mud, and noise."

Whence Æsop said not badly, that "swine squeaked out very loudly, because, when they were dragged, they knew that they were good for nothing but for sacrifice."

Wherefore also Cleanthes says, "that they have soul[1] instead of salt," that their flesh may not putrefy.   Some, then, eat them as useless, others as destructive of fruits.   And others do not eat them, because the animal has a strong sensual propensity.

So, then, the law sacrifices not the goat, except in the sole case of the banishment of sins ;[2] since pleasure is the metropolis of vice.   It is to the point also that it is said that the eating of goat's flesh contributes to epilepsy.   And they say that the greatest increase is produced by swine's flesh.   Wherefore it is beneficial to those who exercise the body ; but to those who devote themselves to the development of the soul it is not so, on account of the hebetude that results from the eating of flesh.   Perchance also some Gnostic will abstain from the eating of flesh for the sake of training, and in order that the flesh may not grow wanton in amorousness.   " For wine," says Androcydes, " and gluttonous feeds of flesh make the body strong, but the soul more sluggish."   Accordingly such food, in order to clear understanding, is to be rejected.

Wherefore also the Egyptians, in the purifications practised among them, do not allow the priests to feed on flesh ; but they use chickens, as lightest ; and they do not touch fish, on account of certain fables, but especially on account of such food making the flesh flabby.   But now terrestrial animals and birds breathe the same air as our vital spirits, being possessed of a vital principle cognate with the air.   But it is said that fishes do not breathe this air, but that which was mixed with the water at the instant of its first creation, as well as with the rest of the elements, which is also a sign of the permanence of matter.[3]

Wherefore we ought to offer to God sacrifices not costly, but such as He loves.   And that compounded incense which is mentioned in the Law, is that which consists of many tongues and voices in prayer,[4] or rather of different nations and natures, prepared by the gift vouchsafed in the dispensation for " the unity of the faith," and brought together in praises, with a pure mind, and just and right conduct, from holy works and righteous prayer.   For in the elegant language of poetry, —

> " Who is so great a fool, and among men
> So very easy of belief, as thinks
> The gods, with fraud of fleshless bones and bile
> All burnt, not fit for hungry dogs to eat,
> Delighted are, and take this as their prize,
> And favour show to those who treat them thus,"

though they happen to be tyrants and robbers?

But we say that the fire sanctifies[5] not flesh, but sinful souls ; meaning not the all-devouring vulgar fire,[6] but that of wisdom, which pervades the soul passing through the fire.

CHAP. VII. — WHAT SORT OF PRAYER THE GNOSTIC EMPLOYS, AND HOW IT IS HEARD BY GOD.

Now we are commanded to reverence and to honour the same one, being persuaded that He is Word, Saviour, and Leader, and by Him, the Father, not on special days, as some others, but doing this continually in our whole life, and in every way.   Certainly the elect race justified by the precept says, " Seven times a day have I praised Thee."[7]   Whence not in a specified place,[8] or selected temple, or at certain festivals and on appointed days, but during his whole life, the Gnostic in every place, even if he be alone by himself, and wherever he has any of those who have exercised the like faith, honours God,

---

[1] ψυχή, animal life.
[2] i.e., in the institution of the scape-goat.

[3] Or, of water.   For instead of ὑλικῆς in the text, it is proposed to read ὑδατικῆς.
[4] [Again, for the Gospel-day, he *spiritualizes* the incense of the Law.]
[5] Consult Matt. iii. 11; Luke iii. 16; Heb. iv. 12.   [See what is said of the philosophic ἐκπύρωσις (book v. cap. i. p. 446, *supra*, this volume) by our author.   These passages bear on another theological matter, of which see Kaye, p. 466.]
[6] [See useful note of Kaye, p. 309.]
[7] Ps. cxix. 164.
[8] [It is hardly needful to say that our author means " *not merely* in a specified place," etc.   See p. 290, *supra*, as to time and place.]

that is, acknowledges his gratitude for the knowledge of the way to live.

And if the presence of a good man, through the respect and reverence which he inspires, always improves him with whom he associates, with much more reason does not he who always holds uninterrupted converse with God by knowledge, life, and thanksgiving, grow at every step superior to himself in all respects — in conduct, in words, in disposition? Such an one is persuaded that God is ever beside him, and does not suppose that He is confined in certain limited places; so that under the idea that at times he is without Him, he may indulge in excesses night and day.

Holding festival, then, in our whole life, persuaded that God is altogether on every side present, we cultivate our fields, praising; we sail the sea, hymning; in all the rest of our conversation we conduct ourselves according to rule.[1] The Gnostic, then, is very closely allied to God, being at once grave and cheerful in all things, — grave on account of the bent of his soul towards the Divinity, and cheerful on account of his consideration of the blessings of humanity which God hath given us.

Now the excellence of knowledge is evidently presented by the prophet when he says, "Benignity, and instruction, and knowledge teach me,"[2] magnifying the supremacy of perfection by a climax.

He is, then, the truly kingly man; he is the sacred high priest of God. And this is even now observed among the most sagacious of the Barbarians, in advancing the sacerdotal caste to the royal power. He, therefore, never surrenders himself to the rabble that rules supreme over the theatres, and gives no admittance even in a dream to the things which are spoken, done, and seen for the sake of alluring pleasures; neither, therefore, to the pleasures of sight, nor the various pleasures which are found in other enjoyments, as costly incense and odours, which bewitch the nostrils, or preparations of meats, and indulgences in different wines, which ensnare the palate, or fragrant bouquets of many flowers, which through the senses effeminate the soul. But always tracing up to God the grave enjoyment of all things, he offers the first-fruits of food, and drink, and unguents to the Giver of all, acknowledging his thanks in the gift and in the use of them by the Word given to him. He rarely goes to convivial banquets of all and sundry, unless the announcement to him of the friendly and harmonious character of the entertainment induce him to go. For he is convinced that God knows and perceives all things — not the words only, but also the thought; since even

our sense of hearing, which acts through the passages of the body, has the apprehension [belonging to it] not through corporeal power, but through a psychical perception, and the intelligence which distinguishes significant sounds. God is not, then, possessed of human form, so as to hear; nor needs He senses, as the Stoics have decided, "especially hearing and sight; for He could never otherwise apprehend." But the susceptibility of the air, and the intensely keen perception of the angels,[3] and the power which reaches the soul's consciousness, by ineffable power and without sensible hearing, know all things at the moment of thought. And should any one say that the voice does not reach God, but is rolled downwards in the air, yet the thoughts of the saints cleave not the air only, but the whole world. And the divine power, with the speed of light, sees through the whole soul. Well! Do not also volitions speak to God, uttering their voice? And are they not conveyed by conscience? And what voice shall He wait for, who, according to His purpose, knows the elect already, even before his birth, knows what is to be as already existent? Does not the light of power shine down to the very bottom of the whole soul; "the lamp of knowledge," as Scripture says, searching "the recesses"? God is all ear and all eye, if we may be permitted to use these expressions.

In general, then, an unworthy opinion of God preserves no piety, either in hymns, or discourses, or writings, or dogmas, but diverts to grovelling and unseemly ideas and notions. Whence the commendation of the multitude differs nothing from censure, in consequence of their ignorance of the truth. The objects, then, of desires and aspirations, and, in a word, of the mind's impulses, are the subjects of prayers. Wherefore, no man desires a draught, but to drink what is drinkable; and no man desires an inheritance, but to inherit. And in like manner no man desires knowledge, but to know; or a right government, but to take part in the government. The subjects of our prayers, then, are the subjects of our requests, and the subjects of requests are the objects of desires. Prayer, then, and desire, follow in order, with the view of possessing the blessings and advantages offered.

The Gnostic, then, who is such by possession, makes his prayer and request for the truly good things which appertain to the soul, and prays, he himself also contributing his efforts to attain to the habit of goodness, so as no longer to have the things that are good as certain lessons belonging to him, but to be good.

Wherefore also it is most incumbent on such

---

[1] [See p. 200, this volume; also, *infra*, this chapter, p. 537.]
[2] Ps. cxix. 66.

[3] [Pious men have been strict in their conduct when quite alone, from a devout conviction of the presence of angelic guardians.]

to pray, knowing as they do the Divinity rightly, and having the moral excellence suitable to him; who know what things are really good, and what are to be asked, and when and how in each individual case. It is the extremest stupidity to ask of them who are no gods, as if they were gods; or to ask those things which are not beneficial, begging evils for themselves under the appearance of good things.

Whence, as is right, there being only one good God, that some good things be given from Him alone, and that some remain, we and the angels pray. But not similarly. For it is not the same thing to pray that the gift remain, and to endeavour to obtain it for the first time.

The averting of evils is a species of prayer; but such prayer is never to be used for the injury of men, except that the Gnostic, in devoting attention to righteousness, may make use of this petition in the case of those who are past feeling.

Prayer is, then, to speak more boldly, converse with God. Though whispering, consequently, and not opening the lips, we speak in silence, yet we cry inwardly.[1] For God hears continually all the inward converse. So also we raise the head and lift the hands to heaven, and set the feet in motion[2] at the closing utterance of the prayer, following the eagerness of the spirit directed towards the intellectual essence; and endeavouring to abstract the body from the earth, along with the discourse, raising the soul aloft, winged with longing for better things, we compel it to advance to the region of holiness, magnanimously despising the chain of the flesh. For we know right well, that the Gnostic willingly passes over the whole world, as the Jews certainly did over Egypt, showing clearly, above all, that he will be as near as possible to God.

Now, if some assign definite hours for prayer —as, for example, the third, and sixth, and ninth—yet the Gnostic prays throughout his whole life, endeavouring by prayer to have fellowship with God.[3] And, briefly, having reached to this, he leaves behind him all that is of no service, as having now received the perfection of the man that acts by love. But the distribution of the hours into a threefold division, honoured with as many prayers, those are acquainted with, who know the blessed triad of the holy abodes.[4]

Having got to this point, I recollect the doctrines about there being no necessity to pray,

introduced by certain of the heterodox, that is, the followers of the heresy of Prodicus. That they may not then be inflated with conceit about this godless wisdom of theirs, as if it were strange, let them learn that it was embraced before by the philosophers called Cyrenaics.[5] Nevertheless, the unholy knowledge (*gnosis*) of those falsely called [Gnostics] shall meet with confutation at a fitting time; so that the assault on them, by no means brief, may not, by being introduced into the commentary, break the discourse in hand, in which we are showing that the only really holy and pious man is he who is truly a Gnostic according to the rule of the Church, to whom alone the petition made in accordance with the will of God is granted,[6] on asking and on thinking. For as God can do all that He wishes, so the Gnostic receives all that he asks. For, universally, God knows those who are and those who are not worthy of good things; whence He gives to each what is suitable. Wherefore to those that are unworthy, though they ask often, He will not give; but He will give to those who are worthy.

Nor is petition superfluous, though good things are given without claim.

Now thanksgiving and request for the conversion of our neighbours is the function of the Gnostic; as also the Lord prayed, giving thanks for the accomplishment of His ministry, praying that as many as possible might attain to knowledge; that in the saved, by salvation, through knowledge, God might be glorified, and He who is alone good and alone Saviour might be acknowledged through the Son from age to age. But also faith, that one will receive, is a species of prayer gnostically laid up in store.

But if any occasion of converse with God becomes prayer, no opportunity of access to God ought to be omitted. Without doubt, the holiness of the Gnostic, in union with [God's] blessed Providence, exhibits in voluntary confession the perfect beneficence of God. For the holiness of the Gnostic, and the reciprocal benevolence of the friend of God, are a kind of corresponding movement of providence. For neither is God involuntarily good, as the fire is warming; but in Him the imparting of good things is voluntary, even if He receive the request previously. Nor shall he who is saved be saved against his will, for he is not inanimate; but he will above all voluntarily and of free choice speed to salvation. Wherefore also man received the commandments in order that he might be self-impelled, to whatever he wished of things to be chosen and to be avoided. Wherefore God does not do good by necessity, but from His free choice benefits those

1 [I Sam. i. 13. See this same chapter, *infra*, p. 535.]
2 [This is variously explained. It seems to refer to some change of position in Christian assemblies, at the close of worship or in ascriptions of praise.]
3 [See, *supra*, cap. vii. note 8, p. 532.]
4 [The *third, sixth,* and *ninth* hours were deemed sacred to the three persons of the Trinity, respectively. Also they were honoured as the hours of the beginning, middle, and close of our Lord's passion.]

5 [Of these, see ed. Migne, *ad locum.*]
6 According to Heinsius' reading, who substitutes ἀπονενεμημένη for ἀπονενεμημένῳ.

who spontaneously turn. For the Providence which extends to us from God is not ministerial, as that service which proceeds from inferiors to superiors. But in pity for our weakness, the continual dispensations of Providence work, as the care of shepherds towards the sheep, and of a king towards his subjects ; we ourselves also conducting ourselves obediently towards our superiors, who take the management of us, as appointed, in accordance with the commission from God with which they are invested.

Consequently those who render the most free and kingly service, which is the result of a pious mind and of knowledge, are servants and attendants of the Divinity. Each place, then, and time, in which we entertain the idea of God, is in reality sacred.

When, then, the man who chooses what is right, and is at the same time of thankful heart, makes his request in prayer, he contributes to the obtaining of it, gladly taking hold in prayer of the thing desired. For when the Giver of good things perceives the susceptibility on our part, all good things follow at once the conception of them. Certainly in prayer the character is sifted, how it stands with respect to duty.

But if voice and expression are given us, for the sake of understanding, how can God not hear the soul itself, and the mind, since assuredly soul hears soul, and mind, mind ? Whence God does not wait for loquacious tongues, as interpreters among men, but knows absolutely the thoughts of all ; and what the voice intimates to us, that our thought, which even before the creation He knew would come into our mind, speaks to God. Prayer, then, may be uttered without the voice, by concentrating the whole spiritual nature within on expression by the mind, in undistracted turning towards God.

And since the dawn is an image of the day of birth, and from that point the light which has shone forth at first from the darkness increases, there has also dawned on those involved in darkness a day of the knowledge of truth. In correspondence with the manner of the sun's rising, prayers are made looking towards the sunrise in the east. Whence also the most ancient temples looked towards the west, that people might be taught to turn to the east when facing the images.[1] " Let my prayer be directed before Thee as incense, the uplifting of my hands as the evening sacrifice,"[2] say the Psalms.

In the case of wicked men, therefore, prayer is most injurious, not to others alone, but to themselves also. If, then, they should ask and receive what they call pieces of good fortune, these injure them after they receive them, being

ignorant how to use them. For they pray to possess what they have not, and they ask things which seem, but are not, good things.[3] But the Gnostic will ask the permanence of the things he possesses, adaptation for what is to take place, and the eternity of those things which he shall receive. And the things which are really good, the things which concern the soul, he prays that they may belong to him, and remain with him. And so he desires not anything that is absent, being content with what is present. For he is not deficient in the good things which are proper to him ; being already sufficient for himself, through divine grace and knowledge. But having become sufficient in himself, he stands in no want of other things. But knowing the sovereign will, and possessing as soon as he prays, being brought into close contact with the almighty power, and earnestly desiring to be spiritual, through boundless love, he is united to the Spirit.

Thus he, being magnanimous, possessing, through knowledge, what is the most precious of all, the best of all, being quick in applying himself to contemplation, retains in his soul the permanent energy of the objects of his contemplation, that is the perspicacious keenness of knowledge. And this power he strives to his utmost to acquire, by obtaining command of all the influences which war against the mind ; and by applying himself without intermission to speculation, by exercising himself in the training of abstinence from pleasures, and of right conduct in what he does ; and besides, furnished with great experience both in study and in life, he has freedom of speech, not the power of a babbling tongue, but a power which employs plain language, and which neither for favour nor fear conceals aught of the things which may be worthily said at the fitting time, in which it is highly necessary to say them. He, then, having received the things respecting God from the mystic choir of the truth itself, employs language which urges the magnitude of virtue in accordance with its worth ; and shows its results with an inspired elevation of prayer, being associated gnostically, as far as possible, with intellectual and spiritual objects.

Whence he is always mild and meek, accessible, affable, long-suffering, grateful, endued with a good conscience. Such a man is rigid, not alone so as not to be corrupted, but so as not to be tempted. For he never exposes his soul to submission, or capture at the hands of Pleasure and Pain. If the Word, who is Judge, call ; he, having grown inflexible, and not indulging a whit the passions, walks unswervingly where justice advises him to go ; being very well persuaded that all things are managed consummately well,

---

[1] [Christians adopted this habit at an early period, on various grounds, as will hereafter appear in this series.]
[2] Ps. cxli. 2.

[3] [Jas. iv. 3.]

and that progress to what is better goes on in the case of souls that have chosen virtue, till they come to the Good itself, to the Father's vestibule, so to speak, close to the great High Priest. Such is our Gnostic, faithful, persuaded that the affairs of the universe are managed in the best way. Particularly, he is well pleased with all that happens. In accordance with reason, then, he asks for none of those things in life required for necessary use; being persuaded that God, who knows all things, supplies the good with whatever is for their benefit, even though they do not ask.

For my view is, that as all things are supplied to the man of art according to the rules of art, and to the Gentile in a Gentile way, so also to the Gnostic all things are supplied gnostically. And the man who turns from among the Gentiles will ask for faith, while he that ascends to knowledge will ask for the perfection of love. And the Gnostic, who has reached the summit, will pray that contemplation may grow and abide, as the common man will for continual good health.

Nay, he will pray that he may never fall from virtue; giving his most strenuous co-operation in order that he may become infallible. For he knows that some of the angels, through carelessness, were hurled to the earth, not having yet quite reached that state of oneness, by extricating themselves from the propensity to that of duality.

But him, who from this has trained himself to the summit of knowledge and the elevated height of the perfect man, all things relating to time and place help on, now that he has made it his choice to live infallibly, and subjects himself to training in order to the attainment of the stability of knowledge on each side. But in the case of those in whom there is still a heavy corner, leaning downwards, even that part which has been elevated by faith is dragged down. In him, then, who by gnostic training has acquired virtue which cannot be lost, habit becomes nature. And just as weight in a stone, so the knowledge of such an one is incapable of being lost. Not without, but through the exercise of will, and by the force of reason, and knowledge, and Providence, is it brought to become incapable of being lost. Through care it becomes incapable of being lost. He will employ caution so as to avoid sinning, and consideration to prevent the loss of virtue.

Now knowledge appears to produce consideration, by teaching to perceive the things that are capable of contributing to the permanence of virtue. The highest thing is, then, the knowledge of God; wherefore also by it virtue is so preserved as to be incapable of being lost. And he who knows God is holy and pious. The Gnostic has consequently been demonstrated by us to be the only pious man.

He rejoices in good things present, and is glad on account of those promised, as if they were already present. For they do not elude his notice, as if they were still absent, because he knows by anticipation what sort they are. Being then persuaded by knowledge how each future thing shall be, he possesses it. For want and defect are measured with reference to what appertains to one. If, then, he possesses wisdom, and wisdom is a divine thing, he who partakes of what has no want will himself have no want. For the imparting of wisdom does not take place by activity and receptivity moving and stopping each other, or by aught being abstracted or becoming defective. Activity is therefore shown to be undiminished in the act of communication. So, then, our Gnostic possesses all good things, as far as possible; but not likewise in number; since otherwise he would be incapable of changing his place through the due inspired stages of advancement and acts of administration.

Him God helps, by honouring him with closer oversight. For were not all things made for the sake of good men, for their possession and advantage, or rather salvation? He will not then deprive, of the things which exist for the sake of virtue, those for whose sake they were created. For, evidently in honour of their excellent nature and their holy choice, he inspires those who have made choice of a good life with strength for the rest of their salvation; exhorting some, and helping others, who of themselves have become worthy. For all good is capable of being produced in the Gnostic; if indeed it is his aim to know and do everything intelligently. And as the physician ministers health to those who co-operate with him in order to health, so also God ministers eternal salvation to those who co-operate for the attainment of knowledge and good conduct; and since what the commandments enjoin are in our own power, along with the performance of them, the promise is accomplished.

And what follows seems to me to be excellently said by the Greeks. An athlete of no mean reputation among those of old, having for a long time subjected his body to thorough training in order to the attainment of manly strength, on going up to the Olympic games, cast his eye on the statue of the Pisæan Zeus, and said: " O Zeus, if all the requisite preparations for the contest have been made by me, come, give me the victory, as is right." For so, in the case of the Gnostic, who has unblameably and with a good conscience fulfilled all that depends on him, in the direction of learning, and training, and well-doing, and pleasing God, the whole contributes to carry salvation on to perfection. From us, then, are demanded the things which are in our own power, and of the things which pertain to us, both present and absent, the choice, and desire, and possession, and use, and permanence.

Wherefore also he who holds converse with God must have his soul immaculate and stainlessly pure, it being essential to have made himself perfectly good.

But also it becomes him to make all his prayers gently with the good. For it is a dangerous thing to take part in others' sins. Accordingly the Gnostic will pray along with those who have more recently believed, for those things in respect of which it is their duty to act together. And his whole life is a holy festival.[1] His sacrifices are prayers, and praises, and readings in the Scriptures before meals, and psalms and hymns during meals and before bed, and prayers also again during night. By these he unites himself to the divine choir, from continual recollection, engaged in contemplation which has everlasting remembrance.

And what? Does he not also know the other kind of sacrifice, which consists in the giving both of doctrines and of money to those who need? Assuredly. But he does not use wordy prayer by his mouth; having learned to ask of the Lord what is requisite. In every place, therefore, but not ostensibly and visibly to the multitude, he will pray. But while engaged in walking, in conversation, while in silence, while engaged in reading and in works according to reason, he in every mood prays.[2] If he but form the thought in the secret chamber of his soul, and call on the Father "with unspoken groanings,"[3] He is near, and is at his side, while yet speaking. Inasmuch as there are but three ends of all action, he does everything for its excellence and utility; but doing aught for the sake of pleasure,[4] he leaves to those who pursue the common life.

CHAP. VIII. — THE GNOSTIC SO ADDICTED TO TRUTH AS NOT TO NEED TO USE AN OATH.

The man of proved character in such piety is far from being apt to lie and to swear. For an oath is a decisive affirmation, with the taking of the divine name. For how can he, that is once faithful, show himself unfaithful, so as to require an oath; and so that his life may not be a sure and decisive oath? He lives, and walks, and shows the trustworthiness of his affirmation in an unwavering and sure life and speech. And if the wrong lies in the judgment of one who does and says [something], and not in the suffering of one who has been wronged,[5] he will neither lie nor commit perjury so as to wrong the Deity, knowing that it by nature is incapable of being harmed. Nor yet will he lie or commit any transgression, for the sake of the neighbour whom he has learned to love, though he be not on terms of intimacy. Much more, consequently, will he not lie or perjure himself on his own account, since he never with his will can be found doing wrong to himself.

But he does not even swear, preferring to make averment, in affirmation by "yea," and in denial by "nay." For it is an oath to swear, or to produce[6] anything from the mind in the way of confirmation in the shape of an oath. It suffices, then, with him, to add to an affirmation or denial the expression "I say truly," for confirmation to those who do not perceive the certainty of his answer. For he ought, I think, to maintain a life calculated to inspire confidence towards those without, so that an oath may not even be asked; and towards himself and those with whom he associates,[7] good feeling, which is voluntary righteousness.

The Gnostic swears truly, but is not apt to swear, having rarely recourse to an oath, just as we have said. And his speaking truth on oath arises from his accord with the truth. This speaking truth on oath, then, is found to be the result of correctness in duties. Where, then, is the necessity for an oath to him who lives in accordance with the extreme of truth?[8] He, then, that does not even swear will be far from perjuring himself. And he who does not transgress in what is ratified by compacts, will never swear; since the ratification of the violation and of the fulfilment is by actions; as certainly lying and perjury in affirming and swearing are contrary to duty. But he who lives justly, transgressing in none of his duties, when the judgment of truth is scrutinized, swears truth by his acts. Accordingly, testimony by the tongue is in his case superfluous.

Therefore, persuaded always that God is everywhere, and fearing not to speak the truth, and knowing that it is unworthy of him to lie, he is satisfied with the divine consciousness and his own alone.[9] And so he lies not, nor does aught contrary to his compacts. And so he swears not even when asked for his oath; nor does he

---

[1] [See, supra, this chapter, p. 533, note 1.]
[2] [Supra, p. 535, also note 1, 534.]
[3] Rom. viii. 26.
[4] τὸ δὲ ἐπιτελεῖν διὰ τὸν δύσοιστον κοινὸν βίον is the reading of the text: which Potter amends, so as to bring out what is plainly the idea of the author, the reference to pleasure as the third end of actions, and the end pursued by ordinary men, by changing διά into ἡδέα, which is simple, and leaves δύσοιστον (intolerable) to stand. Sylburgius notes that the Latin translator renders as if he read διὰ τὴν ἡδονήν, which is adopted above.

[5] Or, "persecuted;" for ἀδικουμένου (Lowth) and διωκομένου (Potter and Latin translator) have been both suggested instead of the reading of the text, διακονουμένου.
[6] προσφέρεσθαι and προφέρεσθαι are both found here.
[7] συνιέντας, and (Sylburgius) συνιόντας.
[8] [Our Lord answered when adjured by the magistrate; but Christians objected to all extra-judicial oaths, their whole life being sworn to truth.]
[9] [This must be noted, because our author seems to tolerate a departure from strict truth in the next chapter.]

ever deny, so as to speak falsehood, though he should die by tortures.

CHAP. IX. — THOSE WHO TEACH OTHERS, OUGHT TO EXCEL IN VIRTUES.

The gnostic dignity is augmented and increased by him who has undertaken the first place in the teaching of others, and received the dispensation by word and deed of the greatest good on earth, by which he mediates contact and fellowship with the Divinity. And as those who worship terrestrial things pray to them as if they heard, confirming compacts before them; so, in men who are living images, the true majesty of the Word is received by the trustworthy teacher; and the beneficence exerted towards them is carried up to the Lord, after whose image he who is a true man by instruction creates and harmonizes, renewing to salvation the man who receives instruction. For as the Greeks called steel *Ares*, and wine *Dionysus*, on account of a certain relation; so the Gnostic, considering the benefit of his neighbours as his own salvation, may be called a living image of the Lord, not as respects the peculiarity of form, but the symbol of power and similarity of preaching.

Whatever, therefore, he has in his mind, he bears on his tongue, to those who are worthy to hear, speaking as well as living from assent and inclination. For he both thinks and speaks the truth; unless at any time, medicinally, as a physician for the safety of the sick, he may deceive or tell an untruth, according to the Sophists.[1]

To illustrate: the noble apostle circumcised Timothy, though loudly declaring and writing that circumcision made with hands profits nothing.[2] But that he might not, by dragging all at once away from the law to the circumcision of the heart through faith those of the Hebrews who were reluctant listeners, compel them to break away from the synagogue, he, "accommodating himself to the Jews, became a Jew that he might gain all."[3] He, then, who submits to accommodate himself merely for the benefit of his neighbours, for the salvation of those for whose sake he accommodates himself, not partaking in any dissimulation through the peril impending over the just from those who envy them, such an one by no means acts with compulsion.[4] But for the benefit of his neighbours alone, he will do things which would not have

been done by him primarily, if he did not do them on their account. Such an one gives himself for the Church, for the disciples whom he has begotten in faith; for an example to those who are capable of receiving the supreme economy of the philanthropic and God-loving Instructor, for confirmation of the truth of his words, for the exercise of love to the Lord. Such an one is unenslaved by fear, true in word, enduring in labour, never willing to lie by uttered word, and in it always securing sinlessness; since falsehood, being spoken with a certain deceit, is not an inert word, but operates to mischief.

On every hand, then, the Gnostic alone testifies to the truth in deed and word. For he always does rightly in all things, both in word and action, and in thought itself.

Such, then, to speak cursorily, is the piety of the Christian. If, then, he does these things according to duty and right reason, he does them piously and justly. And if such be the case, the Gnostic alone is really both pious, and just, and God-fearing.

The Christian is not impious. For this was the point incumbent on us to demonstrate to the philosophers; so that he will never in any way do aught bad or base (which is unjust). Consequently, therefore, he is not impious; but he alone fears God, holily and dutifully worshipping the true God, the universal Ruler, and King, and Sovereign, with the true piety.

CHAP. X. — STEPS TO PERFECTION.

For knowledge (*gnosis*), to speak generally, a perfecting of man as man, is consummated by acquaintance with divine things, in character, life, and word, accordant and conformable to itself and to the divine Word. For by it faith is perfected, inasmuch as it is solely by it that the believer becomes perfect. Faith is an internal good, and without searching for God, confesses His existence, and glorifies Him as existent. Whence by starting from this faith, and being developed by it, through the grace of God, the knowledge respecting Him is to be acquired as far as possible.

Now we assert that knowledge (*gnosis*) differs from the wisdom (σοφία), which is the result of teaching. For as far as anything is knowledge, so far is it certainly wisdom; but in as far as aught is wisdom, it is not certainly knowledge. For the term wisdom appears only in the knowledge of the uttered word.

But it is not doubting in reference to God, but believing, that is the foundation of knowledge. But Christ is both the foundation and the superstructure, by whom are both the beginning and the ends. And the extreme points, the beginning and the end—I mean faith and love—are not taught. But knowledge, conveyed from

---

[1] [Philo is here quoted by editors, and a passage from Plato. "Sophists," indeed! With insane persons, and in like cases, looser moralists have argued thus, but Clement justly credits it to *Sophistry*. Elucidation I.]

[2] Rom. ii. 25; Eph. ii. 11. [Plainly, he introduces this example of an *apparent* inconsistency, because only so far he supposes the Gnostic may allow himself, without playing false, to temporize.]

[3] 1 Cor. ix. 19, etc.

[4] This sentence is obscure, and has been construed and amended variously.

communication through the grace of God as a deposit, is entrusted to those who show themselves worthy of it; and from it the worth of love beams forth from light to light. For it is said, "To him that hath shall be given:"[1] to faith, knowledge; and to knowledge, love; and to love, the inheritance.

And this takes place, whenever one hangs on the Lord by faith, by knowledge, by love, and ascends along with Him to where the God and guard of our faith and love is. Whence at last (on account of the necessity for very great preparation and previous training in order both to hear what is said, and for the composure of life, and for advancing intelligently to a point beyond the righteousness of the law) it is that knowledge is committed to those fit and selected for it. It leads us to the endless and perfect end, teaching us beforehand the future life that we shall lead, according to God, and with gods; after we are freed from all punishment and penalty which we undergo, in consequence of our sins, for salutary discipline. After which redemption the reward and the honours are assigned to those who have become perfect; when they have got done with purification, and ceased from all service, though it be holy service, and among saints. Then become pure in heart, and near to the Lord, there awaits them restoration to everlasting contemplation; and they are called by the appellation of gods, being destined to sit on thrones with the other gods that have been first put in their places by the Saviour.

Knowledge is therefore quick in purifying, and fit for that acceptable transformation to the better. Whence also with ease it removes [the soul] to what is akin to the soul, divine and holy, and by its own light conveys man through the mystic stages of advancement; till it restores the pure in heart to the crowning place of rest; teaching to gaze on God, face to face, with knowledge and comprehension. For in this consists the perfection of the gnostic soul, in its being with the Lord, where it is in immediate subjection to Him, after rising above all purification and service.

Faith is then, so to speak, a comprehensive knowledge of the essentials;[2] and knowledge is the strong and sure demonstration of what is received by faith, built upon faith by the Lord's teaching, conveying [the soul] on to infallibility, science, and comprehension. And, in my view, the first saving change is that from heathenism to faith, as I said before; and the second, that from faith to knowledge. And the latter terminating in love, thereafter gives the loving to the loved, that which knows to that which is known. And, perchance, such an one has already attained the condition of "being equal to the angels."[3] Accordingly, after the highest excellence in the flesh, changing always duly to the better, he urges his flight to the ancestral hall, through the holy septenniad [of heavenly abodes] to the Lord's own mansion; to be a light, steady, and continuing eternally, entirely and in every part immutable.

The first mode of the Lord's operation mentioned by us is an exhibition of the recompense resulting from piety. Of the very great number of testimonies that there are, I shall adduce one, thus summarily expressed by the prophet David: "Who shall ascend to the hill of the LORD, or who shall stand in His holy place? He who is guiltless in his hands, and pure in his heart; who hath not lifted up his soul to vanity, or sworn deceitfully to his neighbour. He shall receive blessing from the LORD, and mercy from God his Saviour. This is the generation of them that seek the Lord, that seek the face of the God of Jacob."[4] The prophet has, in my opinion, concisely indicated the Gnostic. David, as appears, has cursorily demonstrated the Saviour to be God, by calling Him "the face of the God of Jacob," who preached and taught concerning the Spirit. Wherefore also the apostle designates as "the express image ($\chi\alpha\rho\alpha\kappa\tau\hat{\eta}\rho\alpha$) of the glory of the Father"[5] the Son, who taught the truth respecting God, and expressed the fact that the Almighty is the one and only God and Father, "whom no man knoweth but the Son, and he to whom the Son shall reveal Him."[6] That God is one is intimated by those "who seek the face of the God of Jacob;" whom being the only God, our Saviour and God characterizes as the Good Father. And "the generation of those that seek Him" is the elect race, devoted to inquiry after knowledge. Wherefore also the apostle says, "I shall profit you nothing, unless I speak to you, either by revelation, or by knowledge, or by prophecy, or by doctrine."[7]

Although even by those who are not Gnostics some things are done rightly, yet not according to reason; as in the case of fortitude. For some who are naturally high-spirited, and have afterwards without reason fostered this disposition, rush to many things, and act like brave men, so as sometimes to succeed in achieving the same things; just as endurance is easy for mechanics. But it is not from the same cause, or with the same object; not were they to give their whole body. "For they have not love," according to the apostle.[8]

---

[1] Luke xix. 26.
[2] [Τῶν κατεπειγόντων γνῶσις. This definition must be borne in mind. It destroys all pretences that anything belonging to the faith, i.e., dogma, might belong to an esoteric system.]
[3] Luke xx. 36.
[4] Ps. xxiv. 3–6.
[5] Heb. i. 3.
[6] Matt. xi. 27.
[7] 1 Cor. xiv. 6.
[8] 1 Cor. xiii. 3.

All the action, then, of a man possessed of knowledge is right action; and that done by a man not possessed of knowledge is wrong action, though he observe a plan; since it is not from reflection that he acts bravely, nor does he direct his action in those things which proceed from virtue to virtue, to any useful purpose.

The same holds also with the other virtues. So too the analogy is preserved in religion. Our Gnostic, then, not only is such in reference to holiness; but corresponding to the piety of knowledge are the commands respecting the rest of the conduct of life. For it is our purpose at present to describe the life of the Gnostic,[1] not to present the system of dogmas, which we shall afterwards explain at the fitting time, preserving the order of topics.

CHAP. XI. — DESCRIPTION OF THE GNOSTIC'S LIFE.

Respecting the universe, he conceives truly and grandly in virtue of his reception of divine teaching. Beginning, then, with admiration of the Creation, and affording of himself a proof of his capability for receiving knowledge, he becomes a ready pupil of the Lord. Directly on hearing of God and Providence, he believed in consequence of ethe admiration he entertained. Through the power of impulse thence derived he devotes his energies in every way to learning, doing all those things by means of which he shall be able to acquire the knowledge of what he desires. And desire blended with inquiry arises as faith advances. And this is to become worthy of speculation, of such a character, and such importance. So shall the Gnostic taste of the will of God. For it is not his ears, but his soul, that he yields up to the things signified by what is spoken. Accordingly, apprehending essences and things through the words, he brings his soul, as is fit, to what is essential; apprehending (e.g.) in the peculiar way in which they are spoken to the Gnostic, the commands, "Do not commit adultery," "Do not kill;" and not as they are understood by other people.[2] Training himself, then, in scientific speculation, he proceeds to exercise himself in larger generalizations and grander propositions; knowing right well that "He that teacheth man knowledge," according to the prophet, is the Lord, the Lord acting by man's mouth. So also He assumed flesh.

As is right, then, he never prefers the pleasant to the useful; not even if a beautiful woman were to entice him, when overtaken by circumstances, by wantonly urging him: since Joseph's master's wife was not able to seduce him from his stedfastness; but as she violently held his coat, divested himself of it, — becoming bare of sin, but clothed with seemliness of character. For if the eyes of the master — the Egyptian, I mean — saw not Joseph, yet those of the Almighty looked on. For we hear the voice, and see the bodily forms; but God scrutinizes the thing itself, from which the speaking and the looking proceed.

Consequently, therefore, though disease, and accident, and what is most terrible of all, death, come upon the Gnostic, he remains inflexible in soul, — knowing that all such things are a necessity of creation, and that, also by the power of God, they become the medicine of salvation, benefiting by discipline those who are difficult to reform; allotted according to desert, by Providence, which is truly good.

Using the creatures, then, when the Word prescribes, and to the extent it prescribes, in the exercise of thankfulness to the Creator, he becomes master of the enjoyment of them.

He never cherishes resentment or harbours a grudge against any one, though deserving of hatred for his conduct. For he worships the Maker, and loves him, who shares life, pitying and praying for him on account of his ignorance. He indeed partakes of the affections of the body, to which, susceptible as it is of suffering by nature, he is bound. But in sensation he is not the primary subject of it.

Accordingly, then, in involuntary circumstances, by withdrawing himself from troubles to the things which really belong to him, he is not carried away with what is foreign to him. And it is only to things that are necessary for him that he accommodates himself, in so far as the soul is preserved unharmed. For it is not in supposition or seeming that he wishes to be faithful; but in knowledge and truth, that is, in sure deed and effectual word.[3] Wherefore he not only praises what is noble, but endeavours himself to be noble; changing by love from a good and faithful servant into a friend, through the perfection of habit, which he has acquired in purity from true instruction and great discipline.

Striving, then, to attain to the summit of knowledge (gnosis); decorous in character; composed in mien; possessing all those advantages which belong to the true Gnostic; fixing his eye on fair models, on the many patriarchs who have lived rightly, and on very many prophets and angels reckoned without number, and above all, on the Lord, who taught and showed it to be possible for him to attain that highest life of all, — he therefore loves not all the good things of the world, which are within

---

[1] [Here, also, the morality of the true Gnostic is distinguished from the system of dogmas, την των δογματων θεωρίαν. Elucidation II.]

[2] [Others see the letter only, but the true Gnostic penetrates to the spirit, of the law.]

[3] [Here is no toleration of untruth. See p. 538, supra.]

his grasp, that he may not remain on the ground, but the things hoped for, or rather already known, being hoped for so as to be apprehended.

So then he undergoes toils, and trials, and afflictions, not as those among the philosophers who are endowed with manliness, in the hope of present troubles ceasing, and of sharing again in what is pleasant; but knowledge has inspired him with the firmest persuasion of receiving the hopes of the future. Wherefore he contemns not alone the pains of this world, but all its pleasures.

They say, accordingly, that the blessed Peter, on seeing his wife led to death, rejoiced on account of her call and conveyance home, and called very encouragingly and comfortingly, addressing her by name, "Remember thou the Lord." Such was the marriage of the blessed, and their perfect disposition towards those dearest to them.[1]

Thus also the apostle says, "that he who marries should be as though he married not,"[2] and deem his marriage free of inordinate affection, and inseparable from love to the Lord; to which the true husband exhorted his wife to cling on her departure out of this life to the Lord.

Was not then faith in the hope after death conspicuous in the case of those who gave thanks to God even in the very extremities of their punishments? For firm, in my opinion, was the faith they possessed, which was followed by works of faith.

In all circumstances, then, is the soul of the Gnostic strong, in a condition of extreme health and strength, like the body of an athlete.

For he is prudent in human affairs, in judging what ought to be done by the just man; having obtained the principles from God from above, and having acquired, in order to the divine resemblance, moderation in bodily pains and pleasures. And he struggles against fears boldly, trusting in God. Certainly, then, the gnostic soul, adorned with perfect virtue, is the earthly image of the divine power; its development being the joint result of nature, of training, of reason, all together. This beauty of the soul becomes a temple of the Holy Spirit, when it acquires a disposition in the whole of life corresponding to the Gospel. Such an one consequently withstands all fear of everything terrible, not only of death, but also poverty and disease, and ignominy, and things akin to these; being unconquered by pleasure, and lord over irrational desires. For he well knows what is and what is not to be done; being perfectly aware what things are really to be dreaded, and what not.

Whence he bears intelligently what the Word intimates to him to be requisite and necessary; intelligently discriminating what is really safe (that is, good), from what appears so; and things to be dreaded from what seems so, such as death, disease, and poverty; which are rather so in opinion than in truth.

This is the really good man, who is without passions; having, through the habit or disposition of the soul endued with virtue, transcended the whole life of passion. He has everything dependent on himself for the attainment of the end. For those accidents which are called terrible are not formidable to the good man, because they are not evil. And those which are really to be dreaded are foreign to the gnostic Christian, being diametrically opposed to what is good, because evil; and it is impossible for contraries to meet in the same person at the same time. He, then, who faultlessly acts the drama of life which God has given him to play, knows both what is to be done and what is to be endured.

Is it not then from ignorance of what is and what is not to be dreaded that cowardice arises? Consequently the only man of courage is the Gnostic, who knows both present and future good things; along with these, knowing, as I have said, also the things which are in reality not to be dreaded. Because, knowing vice alone to be hateful, and destructive of what contributes to knowledge, protected by the armour of the Lord, he makes war against it.

For if anything is caused through folly, and the operation or rather co-operation of the devil, this thing is not straightway the devil or folly. For no action is wisdom. For wisdom is a habit. And no action is a habit. The action, then, that arises from ignorance, is not already an evil through ignorance, but not ignorance. For neither perturbations of mind nor sins are vices, though proceeding from vice.

No one, then, who is irrationally brave is a Gnostic;[3] since one might call children brave, who, through ignorance of what is to be dreaded, undergo things that are frightful. So they touch fire even. And the wild beasts that rush close on the points of spears, having a brute courage, might be called valiant. And such people might perhaps call jugglers valiant, who tumble on swords with a certain dexterity, practising a mischievous art for sorry gain. But he who is truly brave, with the peril arising from the bad feeling of the multitude before his eyes, courageously awaits whatever comes. In this way he is distin-

---

[1] [The bearing of this beautiful anecdote upon clerical wedlock and the sanctity of the married life must be obvious.]

[2] [1 Cor. vii. 29. S.]

[3] [Brute bravery is here finely contrasted with real courage: a distinction rarely recognised by the multitude. Thus the man who trembles, yet goes into peril in view of duty, is the real hero. Yet the insensible brute, who does not appreciate the danger, often passes for his superior, with the majority of men.]

guished from others that are called martyrs, inasmuch as some furnish occasions for themselves, and rush into the heart of dangers, I know not how (for it is right to use mild language) ; while they, in accordance with right reason, protect themselves ; then, on God really calling them, promptly surrender themselves, and confirm the call, from being conscious of no precipitancy, and present the man to be proved in the exercise of true rational fortitude.   Neither, then, enduring lesser dangers from fear of greater, like other people, nor dreading censure at the hands of their equals, and those of like sentiments, do they continue in the confession of their calling ; but from love to God they willingly obey the call, with no other aim in view than pleasing God, and not for the sake of the reward of their toils.

For some suffer from love of glory, and others from fear of some other sharper punishment, and others for the sake of pleasures and delights after death, being children in faith ; blessed indeed, but not yet become men in love to God, as the Gnostic is.   For there are, as in the gymnastic contests, so also in the Church, crowns for men and for children.   But love is to be chosen for itself, and for nothing else.   Therefore in the Gnostic, along with knowledge, the perfection of fortitude is developed from the discipline of life, he having always studied to acquire mastery over the passions.

Accordingly, love makes its own athlete fearless and dauntless, and confident in the Lord, anointing and training him ; as righteousness secures for him truthfulness in his whole life.[1] For it was a compendium of righteousness to say, " Let your yea be yea ; and your nay, nay." [2]

And the same holds with self-control.   For it is neither for love of honour, as the athletes for the sake of crowns and fame ; nor on the other hand, for love of money, as some pretend to exercise self-control, pursuing what is good with terrible suffering.   Nor is it from love of the body for the sake of health.   Nor any more is any man who is temperate from rusticity, who has not tasted pleasures, truly a man of self-control.   Certainly those who have led a laborious life, on tasting pleasures, forthwith break down the inflexibility of temperance into pleasures. Such are they who are restrained by law and fear.   For on finding a favourable opportunity they defraud the law, by giving what is good the slip.   But self-control, desirable for its own sake, perfected through knowledge, abiding ever, makes the man lord and master of himself ; so that the Gnostic is temperate and passionless, incapable of being dissolved by pleasures and pains, as they say adamant is by fire.

The cause of these, then, is love, of all science the most sacred and most sovereign.

For by the service of what is best and most exalted, which is characterized by unity, it renders the Gnostic at once friend and son, having in truth grown " a perfect man, up to the measure of full stature." [3]

Further, agreement in the same thing is consent.   But what is the same is one.   And friendship is consummated in likeness ; the community lying in oneness.   The Gnostic, consequently, in virtue of being a lover of the one true God, is the really perfect man and friend of God, and is placed in the rank of son.   For these are names of nobility and knowledge, and perfection in the contemplation of God ; which crowning step of advancement the gnostic soul receives, when it has become quite pure, reckoned worthy to behold everlastingly God Almighty, " face," it is said, " to face."   For having become wholly spiritual, and having in the spiritual Church gone to what is of kindred nature, it abides in the rest of God.

CHAP. XII. — THE TRUE GNOSTIC IS BENEFICENT, CONTINENT, AND DESPISES WORLDLY THINGS.

Let these things, then, be so.   And such being the attitude of the Gnostic towards the body and the soul — towards his neighbours, whether it be a domestic, or a lawful enemy, or whosoever — he is found equal and like.   For he does not " despise his brother," who, according to the divine law, is of the same father and mother.   Certainly he relieves the afflicted, helping him with consolations, encouragements, and the necessaries of life ; giving to all that need, though not similarly, but justly, according to desert ; furthermore, to him who persecutes and hates, even if he need it ; caring little for those who say to him that he has given out of fear, if it is not out of fear that he does so, but to give help.   For how much more are those, who towards their enemies are devoid of love of money, and are haters of evil, animated with love to those who belong to them?

Such an one from this proceeds to the accurate knowledge of whom he ought chiefly to give to, and how much, and when, and how.

And who could with any reason become the enemy of a man who gives no cause for enmity in any way?   And is it not just as in the case of God?   We say that God is the adversary of no one, and the enemy of no one (for He is the Creator of all, and nothing that exists is what He wills it not to be ; but we assert that the disobedient, and those who walk not according to His commandments, are enemies to Him, as being those who are hostile to His covenant).

---

[1] [Again note our author's fidelity to the law of intrepid truthfulness, and compare pp. 538, 540.]
[2] [Jas. v. 12. S.]

[3] Eph. iv. 13.

We shall find the very same to be the case with the Gnostic, for he can never in any way become an enemy to any one ; but those may be regarded enemies to him who turn to the contrary path.

In particular, the habit of liberality[1] which prevails among us is called "righteousness;" but the power of discriminating according to desert, as to greater and less, with reference to those who are proper subjects of it, is a form of the very highest righteousness.

There are things practised in a vulgar style by some people, such as control over pleasures. For as, among the heathen, there are those who, from the impossibility of obtaining what one sees,[2] and from fear of men, and also for the sake of greater pleasures, abstain from the delights that are before them ; so also, in the case of faith, some practise self-restraint, either out of regard to the promise or from fear of God. Well, such self-restraint is the basis of knowledge, and an approach to something better, and an effort after perfection. For "the fear of the LORD," it is said, "is the beginning of wisdom."[3] But the perfect man, out of love, "beareth all things, endureth all things,"[4] "as not pleasing man, but God."[5] Although praise follows him as a consequence, it is not for his own advantage, but for the imitation and benefit of those who praise him.

According to another view, it is not he who merely controls his passions that is called a continent man, but he who has also achieved the mastery over good things, and has acquired surely the great accomplishments of science, from which he produces as fruits the activities of virtue. Thus the Gnostic is never, on the occurrence of an emergency, dislodged from the habit peculiar to him. For the scientific possession of what is good is firm and unchangeable, being the knowledge of things divine and human. Knowledge, then, never becomes ignorance ; nor does good change into evil. Wherefore also he eats, and drinks, and marries, not as principal ends of existence, but as necessary. I name marriage even, if the Word prescribe, and as is suitable. For having become perfect, he[6] has the apostles for examples ; and one is not really shown to be a man in the choice of single life ; but he surpasses men, who, disciplined by marriage, procreation of children, and care for the house, without pleasure or pain, in his solicitude for the house has been inseparable from God's love, and with-

stood all temptation arising through children, and wife, and domestics, and possessions. But he that has no family is in a great degree free of temptation. Caring, then, for himself alone, he is surpassed by him who is inferior, as far as his own personal salvation is concerned, but who is superior in the conduct of life, preserving certainly, in his care for the truth, a minute image.

But we must as much as possible subject the soul to varied preparatory exercise, that it may become susceptible to the reception of knowledge. Do you not see how wax is softened and copper purified, in order to receive the stamp applied to it? Just as death is the separation of the soul from the body, so is knowledge as it were the rational death urging the spirit away, and separating it from the passions, and leading it on to the life of well-doing, that it may then say with confidence to God, "I live as Thou wishest." For he who makes it his purpose to please men cannot please God, since the multitude choose not what is profitable, but what is pleasant. But in pleasing God, one as a consequence gets the favour of the good among men. How, then, can what relates to meat, and drink, and amorous pleasure, be agreeable to such an one? since he views with suspicion even a word that produces pleasure, and a pleasant movement and act of the mind. "For no one can serve two masters, God and Mammon,"[7] it is said ; meaning not simply money, but the resources arising from money bestowed on various pleasures. In reality, it is not possible for him who magnanimously and truly knows God, to serve antagonistic pleasures.

There is one alone, then, who from the beginning was free of concupiscence — the philanthropic Lord, who for us became man. And whosoever endeavour to be assimilated to the impress given by Him, strive, from exercise, to become free of concupiscence. For he who has exercised concupiscence and then restrained himself, is like a widow who becomes again a virgin by continence. Such is the reward of knowledge, rendered to the Saviour and Teacher, which He Himself asked for, — abstinence from what is evil, activity in doing good, by which salvation is acquired.

As, then, those who have learned the arts procure their living by what they have been taught, so also is the Gnostic saved, procuring life by what he knows. For he who has not formed the wish to extirpate the passion of the soul, kills himself. But, as seems, ignorance is the starvation of the soul, and knowledge its sustenance.

Such are the gnostic souls, which the Gospel

---

[1] [The habit of beneficence is a form of virtue, which the Gospel alone has bred among mankind.]
[2] ὁρᾷ; or, desires, ἐρᾷ, as Sylburgius suggests.
[3] Prov. i. 7.
[4] 1 Cor. xiii. 7.
[5] 1 Thess. ii. 4.
[6] [This striking tribute to chaste marriage as consistent with Christian perfection exemplified by apostles, and in many things superior to the selfishness of celibacy, is of the highest importance in the support of a true Catholicity, against the false. p. 541, note 1.]

[7] Matt. vi. 24; Luke xvi. 13.

likened to the consecrated virgins who wait for the Lord. For they are virgins, in respect of their abstaining from what is evil. And in respect of their waiting out of love for the Lord, and kindling their light for the contemplation of things, they are wise souls, saying, " Lord, for long we have desired to receive Thee ; we have lived according to what Thou hast enjoined, transgressing none of Thy commandments. Wherefore also we claim the promises. And we pray for what is beneficial, since it is not requisite to ask of Thee what is most excellent. And we shall take everything for good ; even though the exercises that meet us, which Thine arrangement brings to us for the discipline of our stedfastness, appear to be evil."

The Gnostic, then, from his exceeding holiness, is better prepared to fail when he asks, than to get when he does not ask.

His whole life is prayer and converse with God.[1] And if he be pure from sins, he will by all means obtain what he wishes. For God says to the righteous man, "Ask, and I will give thee ; think, and I will do." If beneficial, he will receive it at once ; and if injurious, he will never ask it, and therefore he will not receive it. So it shall be as he wishes.

But if one say to us, that some sinners even obtain according to their requests, [we should say] that this rarely takes place, by reason of the righteous goodness of God. And it is granted to those who are capable of doing others good. Whence the gift is not made for the sake of him that asked it ; but the divine dispensation, foreseeing that one would be saved by his means, renders the boon again righteous. And to those who are worthy, things which are really good are given, even without their asking.

Whenever, then, one is righteous, not from necessity or out of fear or hope, but from free choice, this is called the royal road, which the royal race travel. But the byways are slippery and precipitous. If, then, one take away fear and honour, I do not know if the illustrious among the philosophers, who use such freedom of speech, will any longer endure afflictions.

Now lusts and other sins are called " briars and thorns." Accordingly the Gnostic labours in the Lord's vineyard, planting, pruning, watering ; being the divine husbandman of what is planted in faith. Those, then, who have not done evil, think it right to receive the wages of ease. But he who has done good out of free choice, demands the recompense as a good workman. He certainly shall receive double wages — both for what he has not done, and for what good he has done.

Such a Gnostic is tempted by no one except with God's permission, and that for the benefit of those who are with him ; and he strengthens them for faith, encouraging them by manly endurance. And assuredly it was for this end, for the establishment and confirmation of the Churches, that the blessed apostles were brought into trial and to martyrdom.

The Gnostic, then, hearing a voice ringing in his ear, which says, "Whom I shall strike, do thou pity," beseeches that those who hate him may repent. For the punishment of malefactors, to be consummated in the highways, is for children to behold ;[2] for there is no possibility of the Gnostic, who has from choice trained himself to be excellent and good, ever being instructed or delighted with such spectacles.[3] And so, having become incapable of being softened by pleasures, and never falling into sins, he is not corrected by the examples of other men's sufferings. And far from being pleased with earthly pleasures and spectacles is he who has shown a noble contempt for the prospects held out in this world, although they are divine.

" Not every one," therefore, " that says Lord, Lord, shall enter into the kingdom of God ; but he that doeth the will of God."[4] Such is the gnostic labourer, who has the mastery of worldly desires even while still in the flesh ; and who, in regard to things future and still invisible, which he knows, has a sure persuasion, so that he regards them as more present than the things within reach. This able workman rejoices in what he knows, but is cramped on account of his being involved in the necessities of life ; not yet deemed worthy of the active participation in what he knows. So he uses this life as if it belonged to another, — so far, that is, as is necessary.

He knows also the enigmas of the fasting of those days[5] — I mean the Fourth and the Preparation. For the one has its name from Hermes, and the other from Aphrodite. He fasts in his life, in respect of covetousness and voluptuousness, from which all the vices grow. For we have already often above shown the three varieties of fornication, according to the apostle — love of pleasure, love of money, idolatry. He fasts, then, according to the Law, abstaining from bad deeds, and, according to the perfection of the Gospel, from evil thoughts. Temptations are applied to him, not for his purification, but, as we have said, for the good of his neighbours,

---

[1] [" Rapt into still communion that transcends
      The imperfect offices of prayer and praise."
                WORDSWORTH: *Excursion*, book i. 208.]

[2] According to the text, instead of " to behold," as above, it would be " not to behold." Lowth suggests the omission of " not," (μὴ). Retaining it, and translating " is not even for children to behold," the clause yields a suitable sense.
[3] ὑπὸ τοιούτων is here substituted by Heinsius for ὑπὸ τῶν αὐτῶν.
[4] Matt. vii. 21.
[5] [The stationary days, Wednesday and Friday. See constitutions *called* Apostolical, v. 19, and vii. 24; also Hermas, *Shepherd*, p. 33, this volume, and my note.]

if, making trial of toils and pains, he has despised and passed them by.

The same holds of pleasure. For it is the highest achievement for one who has had trial of it, afterwards to abstain. For what great thing is it, if a man restrains himself in what he knows not? He, in fulfilment of the precept, according to the Gospel, keeps the Lord's day,[1] when he abandons an evil disposition, and assumes that of the Gnostic, glorifying the Lord's resurrection in himself. Further, also, when he has received the comprehension of scientific speculation, he deems that he sees the Lord, directing his eyes towards things invisible, although he seems to look on what he does not wish to look on; chastising the faculty of vision, when he perceives himself pleasurably affected by the application of his eyes; since he wishes to see and hear that alone which concerns him.

In the act of contemplating the souls of the brethren, he beholds the beauty of the flesh also, with the soul itself, which has become habituated to look solely upon that which is good, without carnal pleasure. And they are really brethren; inasmuch as, by reason of their elect creation, and their oneness of character, and the nature of their deeds, they do, and think, and speak the same holy and good works, in accordance with the sentiments with which the Lord wished them as elect to be inspired.

For faith shows itself in their making choice of the same things; and knowledge, in learning and thinking the same things; and hope, in desiring[2] the same things.

And if, through the necessity of life, he spend a small portion of time about his sustenance, he thinks himself defrauded, being diverted by business.[3] Thus not even in dreams does he look on aught that is unsuitable to an elect man. For thoroughly[4] a stranger and sojourner in the whole of life is every such one, who, inhabiting the city, despises the things in the city which are admired by others, and lives in the city as in a desert, so that the place may not compel him, but his mode of life show him to be just.

This Gnostic, to speak compendiously, makes up for the absence of the apostles, by the rectitude of his life, the accuracy of his knowledge, by benefiting his relations, by "removing the mountains" of his neighbours, and putting away

the irregularities of their soul. Although each of us is his[5] own vineyard and labourer.

He, too, while doing the most excellent things, wishes to elude the notice of men, persuading the Lord along with himself that he is living in accordance with the[6] commandments, preferring these things from believing them to exist. "For where any one's mind is, there also is his treasure."[7]

He impoverishes himself, in order that he may never overlook a brother who has been brought into affliction, through the perfection that is in love, especially if he know that he will bear want himself easier than his brother. He considers, accordingly, the other's pain his own grief; and if, by contributing from his own indigence in order to do good, he suffer any hardship, he does not fret at this, but augments his beneficence still more. For he possesses in its sincerity the faith which is exercised in reference to the affairs of life, and praises the Gospel in practice and contemplation. And, in truth, he wins his praise "not from men, but from God,"[8] by the performance of what the Lord has taught.

He, attracted by his own hope, tastes not the good things that are in the world, entertaining a noble contempt for all things here; pitying those that are chastised after death, who through punishment unwillingly make confession; having a clear conscience with reference to his departure, and being always ready, as "a stranger and pilgrim," with regard to the inheritances here; mindful only of those that are his own, and regarding all things here as not his own; not only admiring the Lord's commandments, but, so to speak, being by knowledge itself partaker of the divine will; a truly chosen intimate of the Lord and His commands in virtue of being righteous; and princely and kingly as being a Gnostic; despising all the gold on earth and under the earth, and dominion from shore to shore of ocean, so that he may cling to the sole service of the Lord. Wherefore also, in eating, and drinking, and marrying (if the Word enjoin), and even in seeing dreams,[9] he does and thinks what is holy.

So is he always pure for prayer. He also prays in the society of angels, as being already of angelic rank, and he is never out of their holy keeping; and though he pray alone, he has the choir of the saints[10] standing with him.

He recognises a twofold [element in faith], both the activity of him who believes, and the

---

[1] [Rom. vi. 5. The original of Clement's argument seems to me to imply that he is here speaking of the Paschal festival, and the true keeping of it by a moral resurrection (1 Cor. v. 7, 8). But the weekly Lord's day enforces the same principle as the great dominical anniversary.]

[2] ποθεῖν suggested by Lowth instead of ποιεῖν.

[3] [The peril of wealth and "business," thus enforced in the martyr-age, is too little insisted upon in our day; if, indeed, it is not wholly overlooked.]

[4] ἀτεχνῶς adopted instead of ἀτέχνως of the text, and transferred to the beginning of this sentence from the close of the preceding, where it appears in the text.

[5] See Matt. xx. 21. Mark xi. 23; 1 Cor. xiii. 2, etc.

[6] Or His, i.e., the Lord's.

[7] Referring to Matt. vi. 21.

[8] Rom. ii. 29.

[9] [Again, the sanctity of chaste marriage. The Fathers attach responsibility to the conscience for impure dreams. See supra, this page.]

[10] ἁγίων, as in the best authorities; or ἀγγέλων, as in recent editions. ["Where two or three are gathered," etc. This principle is insisted upon by the Fathers, as the great idea of public worship. And see the Trisgion, Bunsen's Hippolytus, vol. iii. p. 63.]

excellence of that which is believed according to its worth; since also righteousness is twofold, that which is out of love, and that from fear. Accordingly it is said, "The fear of the LORD is pure, remaining for ever and ever."[1] For those that from fear turn to faith and righteousness, remain for ever. Now fear works abstinence from what is evil; but love exhorts to the doing of good, by building up to the point of spontaneousness; that one may hear from the Lord, "I call you no longer servants, but friends," and may now with confidence apply himself to prayer.

And the form of his prayer is thanksgiving for the past, for the present, and for the future as already through faith present. This is preceded by the reception of knowledge. And he asks to live the allotted life in the flesh as a Gnostic, as free from the flesh, and to attain to the best things, and flee from the worse. He asks, too, relief in those things in which we have sinned, and conversion to the acknowledgment of them.[2]

He follows, on his departure, Him who calls, as quickly, so to speak, as He who goes before calls, hasting by reason of a good conscience to give thanks; and having got there with Christ, shows himself worthy, through his purity, to possess, by a process of blending, the power of God communicated by Christ. For he does not wish to be warm by participation in heat, or luminous by participation in flame, but to be wholly light.

He knows accurately the declaration, "Unless ye hate father and mother, and besides your own life, and unless ye bear the sign [of the cross]."[3] For he hates the inordinate affections of the flesh, which possess the powerful spell of pleasure; and entertains a noble contempt for all that belongs to the creation and nutriment of the flesh. He also withstands the corporeal[4] soul, putting a bridle-bit on the restive irrational spirit: "For the flesh lusteth against the Spirit,"[5] And "to bear the sign of [the cross]" is to bear about death, by taking farewell of all things while still alive; since there is not equal love in "having sown the flesh,"[6] and in having formed the soul for knowledge.

He having acquired the habit of doing good, exercises beneficence well, quicker than speaking; praying that he may get a share in the sins of his brethren, in order to confession and conversion on the part of his kindred; and eager to give a share to those dearest to him of his own good things. And so these are to him, friends. Promoting, then, the growth of the seeds deposited in him, according to the husbandry enjoined by the Lord, he continues free of sin, and becomes continent, and lives in spirit with those who are like him, among the choirs of the saints, though still detained on earth.

He, all day and night, speaking and doing the Lord's commands, rejoices exceedingly, not only on rising in the morning and at noon, but also when walking about, when asleep, when dressing and undressing;[7] and he teaches his son, if he has a son. He is inseparable from the commandment and from hope, and is ever giving thanks to God, like the living creatures figuratively spoken of by Esaias, and submissive in every trial, he says, "The LORD gave, and the LORD hath taken away."[8] For such also was Job; who after the spoiling of his effects, along with the health of his body, resigned all through love to the Lord. For "he was," it is said, "just, holy, and kept apart from all wickedness."[9] Now the word "holy" points out all duties toward God, and the entire course of life. Knowing which, he was a Gnostic. For we must neither cling too much to such things, even if they are good, seeing they are human, nor on the other hand detest them, if they are bad; but we must be above both [good and bad], trampling the latter under foot, and passing on the former to those who need them. But the Gnostic is cautious in accommodation, lest he be not perceived, or lest the accommodation become disposition.

CHAP. XIII. — DESCRIPTION OF THE GNOSTIC CONTINUED.

He never remembers those who have sinned against him, but forgives them. Wherefore also he righteously prays, saying, "Forgive us; for we also forgive."[10] For this also is one of the things which God wishes, to covet nothing, to hate no one. For all men are the work of one will. And is it not the Saviour, who wishes the Gnostic to be perfect as "the heavenly Father,"[11] that is, Himself, who says, "Come, ye children, hear from me the fear of the LORD?"[12] He wishes him no longer to stand in need of help by angels, but to receive it from Himself, having become worthy, and to have protection from Himself by obedience.

Such an one demands from the Lord, and does not merely ask. And in the case of his brethren in want, the Gnostic will not ask himself for abundance of wealth to bestow, but will pray that the supply of what they need may be furnished to them. For so the Gnostic gives his prayer to those who are in need, and by his

---

1 Ps. xix. 9.
2 Luke xviii. 18.
3 Luke xiv. 26, 27.
4 i.e., The sentient soul, which he calls the irrational spirit, in contrast with the rational soul.
5 Gal. v. 17.
6 In allusion to Gal. vi. 8, where, however, the apostle speaks of sowing to the flesh.

7 [See, *supra*, cap. vii. p. 533.]
8 Job i. 21.
9 Job i. 1.
10 Matt. vi. 12; Luke xi. 4.
11 Matt. v. 48.
12 Ps. xxxiv. 11.

prayer they are supplied, without his knowledge, and without vanity.

Penury and disease, and such trials, are often sent for admonition, for the correction of the past, and for care for the future. Such an one prays for relief from them, in virtue of possessing the prerogative of knowledge, not out of vainglory; but from the very fact of his being a Gnostic, he works. beneficence, having become the instrument of the goodness of God.

They say in the traditions [1] that Matthew the apostle constantly said, that "if the neighbour of an elect man sin, the elect man has sinned. For had he conducted himself as the Word prescribes, his neighbour also would have been filled with such reverence for the life he led as not to sin."

What, then, shall we say of the Gnostic himself? "Know ye not," says the apostle, "that ye are the temple of God?" [2] The Gnostic is consequently divine, and already holy, God-bearing, and God-borne. Now the Scripture, showing that sinning is foreign to him, sells those who have fallen away to strangers, saying, "Look not on a strange woman, to lust," [3] plainly pronounces sin foreign and contrary to the nature of the temple of God. Now the temple is great, as the Church, and it is small, as the man who preserves the seed of Abraham. He, therefore, who has God resting in him will not desire aught else. At once leaving all hindrances, and despising all matter which distracts him, he cleaves the heaven by knowledge. And passing through the spiritual Essences, and all rule and authority, he touches the highest thrones, hasting to that alone for the sake of which alone he knew.

Mixing, then, "the serpent with the dove," [4] he lives at once perfectly and with a good conscience, mingling faith with hope, in order to the expectation of the future. For he is conscious of the boon he has received, having become worthy of obtaining it; and is translated from slavery to adoption, as the consequence of knowledge; knowing God, or rather known of Him, for the end, he puts forth energies corresponding to the worth of grace. For works follow knowledge, as the shadow the body.

Rightly, then, he is not disturbed by anything which happens; nor does he suspect those things, which, through divine arrangement, take place for good. Nor is he ashamed to die, having a good conscience, and being fit to be seen by the Powers. Cleansed, so to speak, from all the stains of the soul, he knows right well that it will be better with him after his departure.

Whence he never prefers pleasure and profit to the divine arrangement, since he trains himself by the commands, that in all things he may be well pleasing to the Lord, and praiseworthy in the sight of the world, since all things depend on the one Sovereign God. The Son of God, it is said, came to His own, and His own received Him not. Wherefore also in the use of the things of the world he not only gives thanks and praises the creation, but also, while using them as is right, is praised; since the end he has in view terminates in contemplation by gnostic activity in accordance with the commandments.

Thence now, by knowledge collecting materials to be the food of contemplation, having embraced nobly the magnitude of knowledge, he advances to the holy recompense of translation hence. For he has heard the Psalm which says : "Encircle Zion, and encompass it, tell upon its towers." [5] For it intimates, I think, those who have sublimely embraced the Word, so as to become lofty towers, and to stand firmly in faith and knowledge.

Let these statements concerning the Gnostic, containing the germs of the matter in as brief terms as possible, be made to the Greeks. But let it be known that if the [mere] believer do rightly one or a second of these things, yet he will not do so in all nor with the highest knowledge, like the Gnostic.

CHAP. XIV. — DESCRIPTION OF THE GNOSTIC FURNISHED BY AN EXPOSITION OF 1 COR. VI. 1, ETC.

Now, of what I may call the passionlessness which we attribute to the Gnostic (in which the perfection of the believer, "advancing by love, comes to a perfect man, to the measure of full stature," [6] by being assimilated to God, and by becoming truly angelic), many other testimonies from the Scripture, occur to me to adduce. But I think it better, on account of the length of the discourse, that such an honour should be devolved on those who wish to take pains, and leave it to them to elaborate the dogmas by the selection of Scriptures.

One passage, accordingly, I shall in the briefest terms advert to, so as not to leave the topic unexplained.

For in the first Epistle to the Corinthians the divine apostle says : " Dare any of you, having a matter against the other, go to law before the unrighteous, and not before the saints? Know ye not that the saints shall judge the world?" [7] and so on.

The section being very long, we shall exhibit the meaning of the apostle's utterance by em-

---

[1] [See book ii. p. 358, also book vii. cap. 17, *infra*.]
[2] 1 Cor. iii. 16.
[3] These words are not found in Scripture. Solomon often warns against strange women, and there are our Lord's words in Matt. v. 28.
[4] Matt. x. 16.

[5] Ps. xlviii. 12.
[6] Eph. iv. 13.
[7] 1 Cor. vi. 1, 2.

ploying such of the apostolic expressions as are most pertinent, and in the briefest language, and in a sort of cursory way, interpreting the discourse in which he describes the perfection of the Gnostic. For he does not merely instance the Gnostic as characterized by suffering wrong rather than do wrong; but he teaches that he is not mindful of injuries, and does not allow him even to pray against the man who has done him wrong. For he knows that the Lord expressly enjoined "to pray for enemies." [1]

To say, then, that the man who has been injured goes to law before the unrighteous, is nothing else than to say that he shows a wish to retaliate, and a desire to injure the second in return, which is also to do wrong likewise himself.

And his saying, that he wishes "some to go to law before the saints," points out those who ask by prayer that those who have done wrong should suffer retaliation for their injustice, and intimates that the second are better than the former; but they are not yet obedient,[2] if they do not, having become entirely free of resentment, pray even for their enemies.

It is well, then, for them to receive right dispositions from repentance, which results in faith. For if the truth seems to get enemies who entertain bad feeling, yet it is not hostile to any one. "For God makes His sun to shine on the just and on the unjust,"[3] and sent the Lord Himself to the just and the unjust. And he that earnestly strives to be assimilated to God, in the exercise of great absence of resentment, forgives seventy times seven times, as it were all his life through, and in all his course in this world (that being indicated by the enumeration of sevens) shows clemency to each and any one; if any during the whole time of his life in the flesh do the Gnostic wrong. For he not only deems it right that the good man should resign his property alone to others, being of the number of those who have done him wrong; but also wishes that the righteous man should ask of those judges forgiveness for the offences of those who have done him wrong. And with reason, if indeed it is only in that which is external and concerns the body, though it go to the extent of death even, that those who attempt to wrong him take advantage of him; none of which truly belong to the Gnostic.

And how shall one "judge" the apostate "angels," who has become himself an apostate from that forgetfulness of injuries, which is according to the Gospel? "Why do ye not rather suffer wrong?" he says; "why are ye not rather defrauded? Yea, ye do wrong and defraud,"[4]

manifestly by praying against those who transgress in ignorance, and deprive of the philanthropy and goodness of God, as far as in you lies, those against whom you pray, "and these your brethren," — not meaning those in the faith only, but also the proselytes. For whether he who now is hostile shall afterwards believe, we know not as yet. From which the conclusion follows clearly, if all are not yet brethren to us, they ought to be regarded in that light. And now it is only the man of knowledge who recognises all men to be the work of one God, and invested with one image in one nature, although some may be more turbid than others; and in the creatures he recognises the operation, by which again he adores the will of God.

"Know ye not that the unrighteous shall not inherit the kingdom of God?"[5] He acts unrighteously who retaliates, whether by deed or word, or by the conception of a wish, which, after the training of the Law, the Gospel rejects.

"And such were some of you" — such manifestly as those still are whom you do not forgive; "but ye are washed,"[6] not simply as the rest, but with knowledge; ye have cast off the passions of the soul, in order to become assimilated, as far as possible, to the goodness of God's providence by long-suffering, and by forgiveness "towards the just and the unjust," casting on them the gleam of benignity in word and deeds, as the sun.

The Gnostic will achieve this either by greatness of mind, or by imitation of what is better. And that is a third cause. "Forgive, and it shall be forgiven you;" the commandment, as it were, compelling to salvation through superabundance of goodness.

"But ye are sanctified." For he who has come to this state is in a condition to be holy, falling into none of the passions in any way, but as it were already disembodied and already grown holy without[7] this earth.

"Wherefore," he says, "ye are justified in the name of the Lord." Ye are made, so to speak, by Him to be righteous as He is, and are blended as far as possible with the Holy Spirit. For "are not all things lawful to me? yet I will not be brought under the power of any,"[8] so as to do, or think, or speak aught contrary to the Gospel. "Meats for the belly, and the belly for meats, which God shall destroy,"[9] — that is, such as think and live as if they were made for eating, and do not eat that they may live as a consequence, and apply to knowledge as the primary end. And does he not say that these are, as it were, the fleshy parts of the holy body? As a

---

1 Matt. v. 44.
2 εὐπειθείς here substituted by Sylburgius for ἀπειθείς. May not the true reading be ἀπαθείς, as the topic is ἀπάθεια?
3 Matt. v. 45.
4 1 Cor. vi. 7, 8.

5 1 Cor. vi. 9.
6 1 Cor. vi. 11.
7 ἄνευ: or above, ἄνω.
8 1 Cor. vi. 12.
9 1 Cor. vi. 13.

body, the Church of the Lord, the spiritual and holy choir, is symbolized.[1] Whence those, who are merely called, but do not live in accordance with the word, are the fleshy parts. "Now" this spiritual "body," the holy Church, "is not for fornication." Nor are those things which belong to heathen life to be adopted by apostasy from the Gospel. For he who conducts himself heathenishly in the Church, whether in deed, or word, or even in thought, commits fornication with reference to the Church and his own body. He who in this way "is joined to the harlot," that is, to conduct contrary to the Covenant, becomes another "body," not holy, "and one flesh," and has a heathenish life and another hope. "But he that is joined to the Lord in spirit" becomes a spiritual body by a different kind of conjunction.

Such an one is wholly a son, an holy man, passionless, gnostic, perfect, formed by the teaching of the Lord; in order that in deed, in word, and in spirit itself, being brought close to the Lord, he may receive the mansion that is due to him who has reached manhood thus.

Let the specimen suffice to those who have ears. For it is not required to unfold the mystery, but only to indicate what is sufficient for those who are partakers in knowledge to bring it to mind; who also will comprehend how it was said by the Lord, "Be ye perfect as your father, perfectly,"[2] by forgiving sins, and forgetting injuries, and living in the habit of passionlessness. For as we call a physician perfect, and a philosopher perfect, so also, in my view, do we call a Gnostic perfect. But not one of those points, although of the greatest importance, is assumed in order to the likeness of God. For we do not say, as the Stoics do most impiously, that virtue in man and God is the same. Ought we not then to be perfect, as the Father wills? For it is utterly impossible for any one to become perfect as God is. Now the Father wishes us to be perfect by living blamelessly, according to the obedience of the Gospel.

If, then, the statement being elliptical, we understand what is wanting, in order to complete the section for those who are incapable of understanding what is left out, we shall both know the will of God, and shall walk at once piously and magnanimously, as befits the dignity of the commandment.

CHAP. XV. — THE OBJECTION TO JOIN THE CHURCH ON ACCOUNT OF THE DIVERSITY OF HERESIES ANSWERED.

Since it comes next to reply to the objections alleged against us by Greeks and Jews; and since, in some of the questions previously discussed, the sects also who adhere to other teaching give their help, it will be well first to clear away the obstacles before us, and then, prepared thus for the solution of the difficulties, to advance to the succeeding Miscellany.

First, then, they make this objection to us, saying, that they ought not to believe on account of the discord of the sects. For the truth is warped when some teach one set of dogmas, others another.

To whom we say, that among you who are Jews, and among the most famous of the philosophers among the Greeks, very many sects have sprung up. And yet you do not say that one ought to hesitate to philosophize or Judaize, because of the want of agreement of the sects among you between themselves. And then, that heresies should be sown among the truth, as "tares among the wheat," was foretold by the Lord; and what was predicted to take place could not but happen.[3] And the cause of this is, that everything that is fair is followed by a foul blot. If one, then, violate his engagements, and go aside from the confession which he makes before us, are we not to stick to the truth because he has belied his profession? But as the good man must not prove false or fail to ratify what he has promised, although others violate their engagements; so also are we bound in no way to transgress the canon of the Church.[4] And especially do we keep our profession in the most important points, while they traverse it.

Those, then, are to be believed, who hold firmly to the truth. And we may broadly make use of this reply, and say to them, that physicians holding opposite opinions according to their own schools, yet equally in point of fact treat patients. Does one, then, who is ill in body and needing treatment, not have recourse to a physician, on account of the different schools in medicine? No more, then, may he who in soul is sick and full of idols, make a pretext of the heresies, in reference to the recovery of health and conversion to God.

Further, it is said that it is on account of "those that are approved that heresies exist."[5] [The apostle] calls "approved," either those who in reaching faith apply to the teaching of the Lord with some discrimination (as those are called skilful[6] money-changers, who distinguish the spurious coin from the genuine by the false

---

[1] [Ps. lxxiii. 1. The "Israelite indeed" is thus recognised as the wheat, although tares grow with it in the Militant Church. See cap. xv., *infra*.]

[2] Matt. v.; *sic.* τέλειοι, τελείως.

[3] [Matt. xiii 28. But for our Lord's foreshowing, the existence of so much evil in the Church would be the greatest stumbling-block of the faithful.]

[4] [The "eccleisastical canon" here recognised, marks the existence, at this period, of canon-law. See Bunsen, *Hippol.*, book iii. p. 105.]

[5] 1 Cor. xi. 19.

[6] δοκίμους, same word as above translated "approved."

stamp), or those who have already become approved both in life and knowledge.

For this reason, then, we require greater attention and consideration in order to investigate how precisely we ought to live, and what is the true piety. For it is plain that, from the very reason that truth is difficult and arduous of attainment, questions arise from which spring the heresies, savouring of self-love and vanity, of those who have not learned or apprehended truly, but only caught up a mere conceit of knowledge. With the greater care, therefore, are we to examine the real truth, which alone has for its object the true God. And the toil is followed by sweet discovery and reminiscence.

On account of the heresies, therefore, the toil of discovery must be undertaken; but we must not at all abandon [the truth]. For, on fruit being set before us, some real and ripe, and some made of wax, as like the real as possible, we are not to abstain from both on account of the resemblance. But by the exercise of the apprehension of contemplation, and by reasoning of the most decisive character, we must distinguish the true from the seeming.

And as, while there is one royal highway, there are many others, some leading to a precipice, some to a rushing river or to a deep sea, no one will shrink from travelling by reason of the diversity, but will make use of the safe, and royal, and frequented way; so, though some say this, some that, concerning the truth, we must not abandon it; but must seek out the most accurate knowledge respecting it. Since also among garden-grown vegetables weeds also spring up, are the husbandmen, then, to desist from gardening?

Having then from nature abundant means for examining the statements made, we ought to discover the sequence of the truth. Wherefore also we are rightly condemned, if we do not assent to what we ought to obey, and do not distinguish what is hostile, and unseemly, and unnatural, and false, from what is true, consistent, and seemly, and according to nature. And these means must be employed in order to attain to the knowledge of the real truth.

This pretext is then, in the case of the Greeks, futile; for those who are willing may find the truth. But in the case of those who adduce unreasonable excuses, their condemnation is unanswerable. For whether do they deny or admit that there is such a thing as demonstration? I am of opinion that all will make the admission, except those who take away the senses. There being demonstration, then, it is necessary to condescend to questions, and to ascertain by way of demonstration by the Scriptures themselves how the heresies failed, and how in the truth alone and in the ancient Church is both

the exactest knowledge, and the truly best set of principles (αἵρεσις).[1]

Now, of those who diverge from the truth, some attempt to deceive themselves alone, and some also their neighbours. Those, then, who are called (δοξόσοφοι) wise in their own opinions, who think that they have found the truth, but have no true demonstration, deceive themselves in thinking that they have reached a resting-place. And of whom there is no inconsiderable multitude, who avoid investigations for fear of refutations, and shun instructions for fear of condemnation. But those who deceive those who seek access to them are very astute; who, aware that they know nothing, yet darken the truth with plausible arguments.

But, in my opinion, the nature of plausible arguments is of one character, and that of true arguments of another. And we know that it is necessary that the appellation of the heresies should be expressed in contradistinction to the truth; from which the Sophists, drawing certain things for the destruction of men, and burying them in human arts invented by themselves, glory rather in being at the head of a School than presiding over the Church.[2]

CHAP. XVI. — SCRIPTURE THE CRITERION BY WHICH TRUTH AND HERESY ARE DISTINGUISHED.[3]

But those who are ready to toil in the most excellent pursuits, will not desist from the search after truth, till they get the demonstration from the Scriptures themselves.

There are certain criteria common to men, as the senses; and others that belong to those who have employed their wills and energies in what is true, — the methods which are pursued by the mind and reason, to distinguish between true and false propositions.

Now, it is a very great thing to abandon opinion, by taking one's stand between accurate knowledge and the rash wisdom of opinion, and to know that he who hopes for everlasting rest knows also that the entrance to it is toilsome "and strait." And let him who has once received the Gospel, even in the very hour in which he has come to the knowledge of salvation, "not turn back, like Lot's wife," as is said; and let him not go back either to his former life, which adheres to the things of sense, or to heresies. For they form the character, not knowing the true God. "For he that loveth father or mother more than Me," the Father and Teacher of the truth, who regenerates and creates anew, and

---

[1] [A most important testimony to the primitive rule of faith. Negatively it demonstrates the impossibility of any primitive conception of the modern Trent doctrine, that the holder of a particular see is the arbiter of truth and the end of controversy.]

[2] [A just comment on the late Vatican Council, and its shipwreck of the faith. See Janus, *Pope and Council*, p. 182.]

[3] [One of the most important testimonies of primitive antiquity. Elucidation III.]

nourishes the elect soul, "is not worthy of Me"
— He means, to be a son of God and a disciple
of God, and at the same time also to be a friend,
and of kindred nature. "For no man who looks
back, and puts his hand to the plough, is fit for
the kingdom of God."[1]

But, as appears, many even down to our own
time regard Mary, on account of the birth of
her child, as having been in the puerperal state,
although she was not. For some say that, after
she brought forth, she was found, when examined, to be a virgin.[2]

Now such to us are the Scriptures of the Lord,
which gave birth to the truth and continue virgin,
in the concealment of the mysteries of the truth.
"And she brought forth, and yet brought not
forth,"[3] says the Scripture; as having conceived
of herself, and not from conjunction. Wherefore
the Scriptures have conceived to Gnostics; but
the heresies, not having learned them, dismissed
them as not having conceived.

Now all men, having the same judgment,
some, following the Word speaking, frame for
themselves proofs; while others, giving themselves up to pleasures, wrest Scripture, in accordance with their lusts.[4] And the lover of
truth, as I think, needs force of soul. For those
who make the greatest attempts must fail in
things of the highest importance; unless, receiving from the truth itself the rule of the truth,
they cleave to the truth. But such people, in
consequence of falling away from the right path,
err in most individual points; as you might
expect from not having the faculty for judging of
what is true and false, strictly trained to select
what is essential. For if they had, they would
have obeyed the Scriptures.[5]

As, then, if a man should, similarly to those
drugged by Circe, become a beast; so he, who
has spurned the ecclesiastical tradition, and
darted off to the opinions of heretical men, has
ceased to be a man of God and to remain faithful to the Lord. But he who has returned from
this deception, on hearing the Scriptures, and
turned his life to the truth, is, as it were, from
being a man made a god.

For we have, as the source of teaching, the
Lord, both by the prophets, the Gospel, and the
blessed apostles, "in divers manners and at
sundry times,"[6] leading from the beginning of
knowledge to the end. But if one should suppose that another origin[7] was required, then no
longer truly could an origin be preserved.

He, then, who of himself believes the Scripture and voice of the Lord, which by the Lord
acts to the benefiting of men, is rightly [regarded] faithful. Certainly we use it as a
criterion in the discovery of things.[8] What is
subjected to criticism is not believed till it is so
subjected; so that what needs criticism cannot
be a first principle. Therefore, as is reasonable,
grasping by faith the indemonstrable first principle, and receiving in abundance, from the first
principle itself, demonstrations in reference to
the first principle, we are by the voice of the
Lord trained up to the knowledge of the truth.

For we may not give our adhesion to men on
a bare statement by them, who might equally
state the opposite. But if it is not enough
merely to state the opinion, but if what is stated
must be confirmed, we do not wait for the testimony of men, but we establish the matter that is
in question by the voice of the Lord, which is the
surest of all demonstrations, or rather is the only
demonstration; in which knowledge those who
have merely tasted the Scriptures are believers;
while those who, having advanced further, and
become correct expounders of the truth, are
Gnostics. Since also, in what pertains to life,
craftsmen are superior to ordinary people, and
model what is beyond common notions; so,
consequently, we also, giving a complete exhibition of the Scriptures from the Scriptures
themselves, from faith persuade by demonstration.[9]

And if those also who follow heresies venture
to avail themselves of the prophetic Scriptures;
in the first place they will not make use of all
the Scriptures, and then they will not quote them
entire, nor as the body and texture of prophecy
prescribe. But, selecting ambiguous expressions,
they wrest them to their own opinions, gathering
a few expressions here and there; not looking
to the sense, but making use of the mere words.
For in almost all the quotations they make, you
will find that they attend to the names alone,
while they alter the meanings; neither knowing,
as they affirm, nor using the quotations they
adduce, according to their true nature.

But the truth is not found by changing the
meanings (for so people subvert all true teaching), but in the consideration of what perfectly
belongs to and becomes the Sovereign God, and
in establishing each one of the points demonstrated in the Scriptures again from similar Scriptures. Neither, then, do they want to turn to the

---

[1] Luke ix. 62.
[2] [A reference to the sickening and profane history of an apocryphal book, hereafter to be noted. But this language is most noteworthy as an absolute refutation of modern Mariolatry.]
[3] Tertullian, who treats of the above-mentioned topic, attributes these words to Ezekiel; but they are sought for in vain in Ezekiel, or in any other part of Scripture. [The *words* are not found in Ezekiel, but such was his understanding of Ezek. xliv. 2.]
[4] [2 Pet. iii. 16.]
[5] [Nothing is Catholic dogma, according to our author, that is not proved by the Scriptures.]
[6] Heb. i. 1.

[7] [Absolutely exclusive of any other source of dogma, than "the faith once delivered to the saints." Jude 3; Gal. i. 6–9.]
[8] [τῇ κυριακῇ γραφῇ . . . αὐτῇ χρώμεθα κριτηρίῳ. Can anything be more decisive, save what follows?]
[9] [An absolute demonstration of the rule of Catholic faith against the Trent dogmas.]

truth, being ashamed to abandon the claims of self-love ; nor are they able to manage their opinions, by doing violence to the Scriptures. But having first promulgated false dogmas to men ; plainly fighting against almost the whole Scriptures, and constantly confuted by us who contradict them ; for the rest, even now partly they hold out against admitting the prophetic Scriptures, and partly disparage us as of a different nature, and incapable of understanding what is peculiar to them. And sometimes even they deny their own dogmas, when these are confuted, being ashamed openly to own what in private they glory in teaching. For this may be seen in all the heresies, when you examine the iniquities of their dogmas. For when they are overturned by our clearly showing that they are opposed to the Scriptures,[1] one of two things may be seen to have been done by those who defend the dogma. For they either despise the consistency of their own dogmas, or despise the prophecy itself, or rather their own hope. And they invariably prefer what seems to them to be more evident to what has been spoken by the Lord through the prophets and by the Gospel, and, besides, attested and confirmed by the apostles.

Seeing, therefore, the danger that they are in (not in respect of one dogma, but in reference to the maintenance of the heresies) of not discovering the truth ; for while reading the books we have ready at hand, they despise them as useless, but in their eagerness to surpass common faith, they have diverged from the truth. For, in consequence of not learning the mysteries of ecclesiastical knowledge, and not having capacity for the grandeur of the truth, too indolent to descend to the bottom of things, reading superficially, they have dismissed the Scriptures.[2] Elated, then, by vain opinion, they are incessantly wrangling, and plainly care more to *seem* than to *be* philosophers. Not laying as foundations the necessary first principles of things ; and influenced by human opinions, then making the end to suit them, by compulsion ; on account of being confuted, they spar with those who are engaged in the prosecution of the true philosophy, and undergo everything, and, as they say, ply every oar, even going the length of impiety, by disbelieving the Scriptures,[2] rather than be removed from the honours of the heresy and the boasted first seat in their churches ; on account of which also they eagerly embrace that convivial couch of honour in the Agape, falsely so called.

The knowledge of the truth among us from what is already believed, produces faith in what is not yet believed ; which [faith] is, so to speak, the essence of demonstration. But, as appears, no heresy has at all ears to hear what is useful, but opened only to what leads to pleasure. Since also, if one of them would only obey the truth, he would be healed.

Now the cure of self-conceit (as of every ailment) is threefold : the ascertaining of the cause, and the mode of its removal ; and thirdly, the training of the soul, and the accustoming it to assume a right attitude to the judgments come to. For, just like a disordered eye, so also the soul that has been darkened by unnatural dogmas cannot perceive distinctly the light of truth, but even overlooks what is before it.

They say, then, that in muddy water eels are caught by being blinded. And just as knavish boys bar out the teacher, so do these shut out the prophecies from their Church, regarding them with suspicion by reason of rebuke and admonition. In fact, they stitch together a multitude of lies and figments, that they may appear acting in accordance with reason in not admitting the Scriptures. So, then, they are not pious, inasmuch as they are not pleased with the divine commands, that is, with the Holy Spirit. And as those almonds are called empty in which the contents are worthless, not those in which there is nothing ; so also we call those heretics empty, who are destitute of the counsels of God and the traditions of Christ ; bitter, in truth, like the wild almond, their dogmas originating with themselves, with the exception of such truths as they could not, by reason of their evidence, discard and conceal.

As, then, in war the soldier must not leave the post which the commander has assigned him, so neither must we desert the post assigned by the Word, whom we have received as the guide of knowledge and of life. But the most have not even inquired, if there is one that we ought to follow, and who this is, and how he is to be followed. For as is the Word, such also must the believer's life be, so as to be able to follow God, who brings all things to end from the beginning by the right course.

But when one has transgressed against the Word, and thereby against God ; if it is through becoming powerless in consequence of some impression being suddenly made, he ought to see to have the impressions of reasons at hand. And if it is that he has become " common," as the Scripture[3] says, in consequence of being overcome by the habits which formerly had sway over him, the habits must be entirely put a stop to, and the soul trained to oppose them. And if it appears that conflicting dogmas draw some away, these must be taken out of the way,

---

[1] [Opposition to the Scriptures is the self-refutation of false dogma.]
[2] [See, e.g., *Epochs of the Papacy*, p. 469. New York, 1883.]

[3] An apocryphal Scripture probably.

and recourse is to be had to those who reconcile dogmas, and subdue by the charm of the Scriptures such of the untutored as are timid, by explaining the truth by the connection of the Testaments.[1]

But, as appears, we incline to ideas founded on opinion, though they be contrary, rather than to the truth. For it is austere and grave. Now, since there are three states of the soul — ignorance, opinion, knowledge — those who are in ignorance are the Gentiles, those in knowledge, the true Church, and those in opinion, the Heretics. Nothing, then, can be more clearly seen than those, who know, making affirmations about what they know, and the others respecting what they hold on the strength of opinion, as far as respects affirmation without proof.

They accordingly despise and laugh at one another. And it happens that the same thought is held in the highest estimation by some, and by others condemned for insanity. And, indeed, we have learned that voluptuousness, which is to be attributed to the Gentiles, is one thing; and wrangling, which is preferred among the heretical sects, is another; and joy, which is to be appropriated to the Church, another; and delight, which is to be assigned to the true Gnostic, another. And as, if one devote himself to Ischomachus, he will make him a farmer; and to Lampis, a mariner; and to Charidemus, a military commander; and to Simon, an equestrian; and to Perdices, a trader; and to Crobylus, a cook; and to Archelaus, a dancer; and to Homer, a poet; and to Pyrrho, a wrangler; and to Demosthenes, an orator; and to Chrysippus, a dialectician; and to Aristotle, a naturalist; and to Plato, a philosopher: so he who listens to the Lord, and follows the prophecy given by Him, will be formed perfectly in the likeness of the teacher — made a god going about in flesh.[2]

Accordingly, those fall from this eminence who follow not God whither He leads. And He leads us in the inspired Scriptures.

Though men's actions are ten thousand in number, the sources of all sin are but two, ignorance and inability. And both depend on ourselves; inasmuch as we will not learn, nor, on the other hand, restrain lust. And of these, the one is that, in consequence of which people do not judge well, and the other that, in consequence of which they cannot comply with right judgments. For neither will one who is deluded in his mind be able to act rightly, though perfectly able to do what he knows; nor, though capable of judging what is requisite, will he keep himself free of blame, if destitute of power in action. Consequently, then, there are assigned two kinds

of correction applicable to both kinds of sin: for the one, knowledge and clear demonstration from the testimony of the Scriptures; and for the other, the training according to the Word, which is regulated by the discipline of faith and fear. And both develop into perfect love. For the end of the Gnostic here is, in my judgment, twofold, — partly scientific contemplation, partly action.

Would, then, that these heretics would learn and be set right by these notes, and turn to the sovereign God! But if, like the deaf serpents, they listen not to the song called new, though very old, may they be chastised by God, and undergo paternal admonitions previous to the Judgment, till they become ashamed and repent, but not rush through headlong unbelief, and precipitate themselves into judgment.

For there are partial corrections, which are called chastisements, which many of us who have been in transgression incur, by falling away from the Lord's people. But as children are chastised by their teacher, or their father, so are we by Providence. But God does not punish, for punishment is retaliation for evil. He chastises, however, for good to those who are chastised, collectively and individually.

I have adduced these things from a wish to avert those, who are eager to learn, from the liability to fall into heresies, and out of a desire to stop them from superficial ignorance, or stupidity, or bad disposition, or whatever it should be called. And in the attempt to persuade and lead to the truth those who are not entirely incurable, I have made use of these words. For there are some who cannot bear at all to listen to those who exhort them to turn to the truth; and they attempt to trifle, pouring out blasphemies against the truth, claiming for themselves the knowledge of the greatest things in the universe, without having learned, or inquired, or laboured, or discovered the consecutive train of ideas, — whom one should pity rather than hate for such perversity.

But if one is curable, able to bear (like fire or steel) the outspokenness of the truth, which cuts away and burns their false opinions, let him lend the ears of the soul. And this will be the case, unless, through the propensity to sloth, they push truth away, or through the desire of fame, endeavour to invent novelties. For those are slothful who, having it in their power to provide themselves with proper proofs for the divine Scriptures from the Scriptures themselves, select only what contributes to their own pleasures. And those have a craving for glory who voluntarily evade, by arguments of a diverse sort, the things delivered by the blessed apostles and teachers, which are wedded to inspired words; opposing the divine tradition by human teach-

---

[1] [At every point in this chapter, the student may recognise the primitive rule of faith clearly established.]

[2] [Strong as this language is, it is based on 2 Pet. i. 4.]

ings, in order to establish the heresy.[1] For, in truth, what remained to be said—in ecclesiastical knowledge I mean—by such men, Marcion, for example, or Prodicus, and such like, who did not walk in the right way? For they could not have surpassed their predecessors in wisdom, so as to discover anything in addition to what had been uttered by them; for they would have been satisfied had they been able to learn the things laid down before.

Our Gnostic then alone, having grown old in the Scriptures, and maintaining apostolic and ecclesiastic orthodoxy in doctrines, lives most correctly in accordance with the Gospel, and discovers the proofs, for which he may have made search (sent forth as he is by the Lord), from the law and the prophets. For the life of the Gnostic, in my view, is nothing but deeds and words corresponding to the tradition of the Lord. But " all have not knowledge. For I would not have you to be ignorant, brethren," says the apostle, " that all were under the cloud, and partook of spiritual meat and drink ; "[2] clearly affirming that all who heard the word did not take in the magnitude of knowledge in deed and word. Wherefore also he added : " But with all of them He was not well pleased." Who is this? He who said, " Why do you call Me Lord, and do not the will of My Father ? "[3] That is the Saviour's teaching, which to us is spiritual food, and drink that knows no thirst, the water of gnostic life. Further it is said, knowledge is said " to puff up." To whom we say : Perchance seeming knowledge is said to puff up, if one[4] suppose the expression means " to be swollen up." But if, as is rather the case, the expression of the apostle means, " to entertain great and true sentiments," the difficulty is solved. Following, then, the Scriptures, let us establish what has been said : "Wisdom," says Solomon, " has inflated her children." For the Lord did not work conceit by the particulars of His teaching ; but He produces trust in the truth and expansion of mind, in the knowledge that is communicated by the Scriptures, and contempt for the things which drag into sin, which is the meaning of the expression " inflated." It teaches the magnificence of the wisdom implanted in her children by instruction. Now the apostle says, " I will know not the speech of those that are puffed up, but the power ; "[5] if ye understand the Scriptures magnanimously (which means truly ; for nothing is greater than truth). For in that lies the power of the children of wisdom who are puffed up. He says, as it were,

I shall know if ye rightly entertain great thoughts respecting knowledge. " For God," according to David, " is known in Judea," that is, those that are Israelites according to knowledge. For Judea is interpreted "Confession." It is, then, rightly said by the apostle, " This *Thou, shalt not commit adultery, Thou shalt not steal, Thou shalt not covet;* and if there be any other commandment, it is comprehended in this word, *Thou shalt love thy neighbour as thyself.*"[6]

For we must never, as do those who follow the heresies, adulterate the truth, or steal the canon of the Church, by gratifying our own lusts and vanity, by defrauding our neighbours ; whom above all it is our duty, in the exercise of love to them, to teach to adhere to the truth. It is accordingly expressly said, " Declare among the heathen His statutes," that they may not be judged, but that those who have previously given ear may be converted. But those who speak treacherously with their tongues have the penalties that are on record.[7]

CHAP. XVII. — THE TRADITION OF THE CHURCH PRIOR TO THAT OF THE HERESIES.

Those, then, that adhere to impious words, and dictate them to others, inasmuch as they do not make a right but a perverse use of the divine words, neither themselves enter into the kingdom of heaven, nor permit those whom they have deluded to attain the truth. But not having the key of entrance, but a false (and as the common phrase expresses it), a counterfeit key (ἀντικλεῖς), by which they do not enter in as we enter in, through the tradition of the Lord, by drawing aside the curtain ; but bursting through the side-door, and digging clandestinely through the wall of the Church, and stepping over the truth, they constitute themselves the Mystagogues[8] of the soul of the impious.

For that the human assemblies which they held were posterior to the Catholic Church,[9] requires not many words to show.

For the teaching of our Lord at His advent, beginning with Augustus and Tiberius, was completed in the middle of the times of Tiberius.[10]

---

[1] [The divine tradition is here identified with " things delivered by the blessed apostles."]

[2] 1 Cor. x. 1, 3, 4.

[3] Luke vi. 46, combined with Matt. vii. 21.

[4] εἰ τις instead of ἥτις.

[5] 1 Cor. iv. 19.

[6] Rom. xiii. 9.

[7] [When we reach *The Commonitory* of Vincent of Lerins (A.D. 450), we shall find a strict adherence to what is taught by Clement.]

[8] Those who initiate into the mysteries.

[9] [See the quotation from Milman, p. 166, *supra*.]

[10] Ἡ μὲν γὰρ τοῦ Κυρίου κατὰ τὴν παρουσίαν διδασκαλία, ἀπὸ Αὐγούστου καὶ Τιβερίου Καίσαρος ἀρξαμένη, μεσούντων τῶν Αὐγούστου χρόνων τελειοῦται. In the translation, the change recommended, on high authority, of Αὐγούστου into Τιβερίου in the last clause, is adopted, as on the whole the best way of solving the unquestionable difficulty here. If we retain Αὐγούστου, the clause must then be made parenthetical, and the sense would be: " For the teaching of the Lord on His advent, beginning with Augustus and Tiberius (in the middle of the times of Augustus), was completed." The objection to this (not by any means conclusive) is, that it does not specify the end of the period.

The first 15 years of the life of our Lord were the last 15 of the reign of Augustus; and in the 15th year of the reign of his successor Tiberius our Lord was baptized. Clement elsewhere broaches the singular opinion, that our Lord's ministry lasted only a year, and, consequently that He died in the year in which He was baptized. As

And that of the apostles, embracing the ministry of Paul, ends with Nero. It was later, in the times of Adrian the king, that those who invented the heresies arose ; and they extended to the age of Antoninus the elder, as, for instance, Basilides, though he claims (as they boast) for his master, Glaucias, the interpreter of Peter.

Likewise they allege that Valentinus was a hearer of Theudas.[1] And he was the pupil of Paul. For Marcion, who arose in the same age with them, lived as an old man with the younger[2] [heretics]. And after him Simon heard for a little the preaching of Peter.

Such being the case, it is evident, from the high antiquity and perfect truth of the Church, that these later heresies, and those yet subsequent to them in time, were new inventions falsified [from the truth].

From what has been said, then, it is my opinion that the true Church, that which is really ancient, is one, and that in it those who according to God's purpose are just, are enrolled.[3] For from the very reason that God is one, and the Lord one, that which is in the highest degree honourable is lauded in consequence of its singleness, being an imitation of the one first principle. In the nature of the One, then, is associated in a joint heritage the one Church, which they strive to cut asunder into many sects.

Therefore in substance and idea, in origin, in pre-eminence, we say that the ancient and Catholic[4] Church is alone, collecting as it does into the unity of the one faith — which results from the peculiar Testaments, or rather the one Testament in different times by the will of the one God, through one Lord — those already ordained, whom God predestinated, knowing before the foundation of the world that they would be righteous.

But the pre-eminence of the Church, as the principle of union, is, in its oneness, in this surpassing all things else, and having nothing like or equal to itself. But of this afterwards.

Augustus reigned, according to one of the chronologies of Clement, 43, and according to the other 46 years 4 months 1 day, and Tiberius 22 or 26 years 6 months 19 days, the period of the teaching of the Gospel specified above began during the reign of Augustus, and ended during the reign of Tiberius.

[1] Θεοδάδι ἀκηκοέναι is the reading, which eminent authorities (Bentley, Grabe, etc.) have changed into Θεοδᾶ (or Θευδᾶ) διακηκοέναι.

[2] Much learning and ingenuity have been expended on this sentence, which, read as it stands in the text, appears to state that Marcion was an old man while Basilides and Valentinus were young men; and that Simon (Magus) was posterior to them in time. Marcion was certainly not an old man when Valentinus and Basilides were young men, as they flourished in the first half of the second century, and he was born about the beginning of it. The difficulty in regard to Simon is really best got over by supposing that Clement, speaking of these heresiarchs in ascending order, describes Marcion as further back in time; which sense μεθ' ὃν of course will bear, although it does seem somewhat harsh, as "after" thus means "before."

[3] [This chapter illustrates what the Nicene Fathers understood by their language about the "One Holy Catholic and Apostolic Church."]

[4] [I restore this important word of the Greek text, enfeebled by the translator, who renders it by the word "universal", which, though not wrong, disguises the force of the argument.]

Of the heresies, some receive their appellation from a [person's] name, as that which is called after Valentinus, and that after Marcion, and that after Basilides, although they boast of adducing the opinion of Matthew [without truth] ; for as the teaching, so also the tradition of the apostles was one. Some take their designation from a place, as the Peratici ; some from a nation, as the [heresy] of the Phrygians ; some from an action, as that of the Encratites ; and some from peculiar dogmas, as that of the Docetæ, and that of the Hæmatites ; and some from suppositions, and from individuals they have honoured, as those called Cainists, and the Ophians ; and some from nefarious practices and enormities, as those of the Simonians called Entychites.

CHAP. XVIII. — THE DISTINCTION BETWEEN CLEAN AND UNCLEAN ANIMALS IN THE LAW SYMBOLICAL OF THE DISTINCTION BETWEEN THE CHURCH, AND JEWS, AND HERETICS.

After showing a little peep-hole to those who love to contemplate the Church from the law of sacrifices respecting clean and unclean animals (inasmuch as thus the common Jews and the heretics are distinguished mystically from the divine Church), let us bring the discourse to a close.

For such of the sacrifices as part the hoof, and ruminate, the Scripture represents as clean and acceptable to God ; since the just obtain access to the Father and to the Son by faith. For this is the stability of those who part the hoof, those who study the oracles of God night and day, and ruminate them in the soul's receptacle for instructions ; which gnostic exercise the Law expresses under the figure of the rumination of the clean animal. But such as have neither the one nor the other of those qualities it separates as unclean.

Now those that ruminate, but do not part the hoof, indicate the majority of the Jews, who have indeed the oracles of God, but have not faith, and the step which, resting on the truth, conveys to the Father by the Son. Whence also this kind of cattle are apt to slip, not having a division in the foot, and not resting on the twofold support of faith. For "no man," it is said, "knoweth the Father, but he to whom the Son shall reveal Him."[5]

And again, those also are likewise unclean that part the hoof, but do not ruminate.[6] For these point out the heretics, who indeed go upon the name of the Father and the Son, but are in-

---

[5] Luke x. 22.

[6] [The swine, e.g., has the parted hoof, but does not ruminate; hence he is the hypocrite, — an outward sign with no inward quality to correspond, the foulest of the unclean.]

capable of triturating and grinding down the clear declaration of the oracles, and who, besides, perform the works of righteousness coarsely and not with precision, if they perform them at all. To such the Lord says, "Why will ye call me Lord, Lord, and do not the things which I say?"[1]

And those that neither part the hoof nor chew the cud are entirely unclean.

"But ye Megareans," says Theognis, "are neither third, nor fourth,
Nor twelfth, neither in reckoning nor in number,"

"but as chaff which the wind drives away from the face of the earth,"[2] "and as a drop from a vessel."[3]

These points, then, having been formerly thoroughly treated, and the department of ethics having been sketched summarily in a fragmentary way, as we promised; and having here and there interspersed the dogmas which are the germs[4] of true knowledge, so that the discovery of the sacred traditions may not be easy to any one of the uninitiated, let us proceed to what we promised.

Now the Miscellanies are not like parts laid out, planted in regular order for the delight of the eye, but rather like an umbrageous and shaggy hill, planted with laurel, and ivy, and apples, and olives, and figs; the planting being purposely a mixture of fruit-bearing and fruitless trees, since the composition aims at concealment, on account of those that have the daring to pilfer and steal the ripe fruits; from which, however, the husbandmen, transplanting shoots and plants, will adorn a beautiful park and a delightful grove.

The Miscellanies, then, study neither arrangement nor diction; since there are even cases in which the Greeks on purpose wish that ornate diction should be absent, and imperceptibly cast in the seed of dogmas, not according to the truth, rendering such as may read laborious and quick at discovery. For many and various are the baits for the various kinds of fishes.

And now, after this seventh Miscellany of ours, we shall give the account of what follows in order from another commencement.[5]

[1] Luke vi. 46.
[2] Ps. i. 4.
[3] Isa. xl. 15.
[4] [Clement regards dogma as framing practical morals. The comment is found in the history of nations, nominally Christian.]

[5] [The residue is lost, for the eighth book has little connection with the Gnostic as hitherto developed.]

ELUCIDATIONS

I.

(Deception, cap. ix. p. 538.)

More and more, the casuistry exposed by Pascal in the *Provincial Letters*[1] becomes an important subject for the investigation of Americans. Nobody who has any pretensions to scholarship can afford to be ignorant of these letters; for they belong to literature, and not merely to theology. But they belong in a sense to the past; not that "the Society of Jesus" has ceased to maintain all that Pascal has exposed, and to practise even worse, but that the Latin churches have, since the days of Pascal, been formally subjected to a system of casuistry, in some respects superficially reformed, but in all other respects radically bad, and corrosive to society. In Pascal's day this casuistry could only be charged upon individuals, and upon societies and communities: the Roman Church everywhere adopted it, but was not formally committed to it. But in the system of Liguori this corrupt morality has been made authoritative and *dogmatic;* so that in all the Latin churches it becomes the base of the confessional. For moral purposes, it is the Bible of the millions who resort to their confessors and "directors." These remarks, however, are here introduced merely with reference to the morals of Clement with regard to truth.[2]

I have briefly indicated, in the footnotes, the points which are to be noted in forming an opinion of our author's conceptions of this vital principle. They seem to me conformed to the Gospel; to the teachings of Him who allows no hair-splittings, but says, "Let your yea be yea,

[1] A good translation of the letters was published in New York, in 1864, by Hurd & Houghton.
[2] For a good article on St. Alphonsus de'Liguori, see the *Encyc. Britannica.*

and your nay, nay." But, as the text stood in the Edinburgh translation, it did injustice to Clement in one passage, which I have modified. It reads, " He (the Gnostic) both thinks and speaks the truth, unless, at any time, medicinally, as a physician for the safety of the sick, he may *lie*, or tell an untruth." To this, Clement adds significantly, "according to the Sophists." That is to say, our author tolerates the Christian who has not got beyond the *Sophists* with respect to benevolent deceptions. As *killing* is not always *murder*, so some, even among stern moralists, have maintained that *deception* by word of mouth is not always *lying*. This is the extent to which Clement tolerates sophistry, and he goes on to demand the practice of *truth* in Gospel terms. Now, thank God, the English word " lie " is always infamous ; and there is nothing like it, in this respect, in other languages. The Sophists themselves did not so understand the Greek word (ψεῦδος), when they apply it to the benevolent deception of a physician, or to the untruths used benevolently with the insane. Nothing infamous attaches to the French word *mensonge* when used for what are deemed "innocent deceptions." With this whole system of sophistry I have no patience at all ; but, in justice to the Sophists, let us not make them worse than they were. They did not understand that such deceptions were *lies*. Hence, for " lie," I have used the word *deceive*, correcting a needless rendering of the text, and one to which Clement should not be made to extend even a contemptuous toleration.

In this respect, the holy Jeremy Taylor and Dr. Johnson go further than Clement, and seem to allow that benevolent deceptions may be innocent. Sanderson sustains a sterner morality, and is more generally accepted. Liguori's system is *verbally* as strong as the Gospel itself : lying is a mortal sin, and never justifiable. But, when he comes to the definition of a lie, it is made so feeble, that the worst liar that ever lived need never resort to it. He may practise all manner of subterfuge, and even perjury, without telling a lie. As, e.g., if he points up his sleeve, while he swears that he did not see the criminal *there*, he tells no lie : it is the business of the judge and jury to watch his fingers, etc.

II.

(True Gnostic, cap. x. p. 540, note 1.)

This unfortunate word *Gnostic* hides the force of Clement's teaching, throughout this work. Here he virtually expounds it, and we see that it refers even more to the heart than to the head. It carries with it *the conduct of life* by knowledge ; i.e., by " the true Light which lighteneth every man that cometh into the world." (See p. 607, footnote.)

III.

(The Scriptures, cap. xvi. p. 550, note 3.)

The Primitive Fathers never dream of anything as *dogma* which cannot be proved by the Scriptures, save only that the apostolic traditions, *clearly proved to be such*, must be referred to in proving what is Holy Scripture. It is not possible to graft on this principle the slightest argument for any tradition not indisputably apostolic, so far as the *de fide* is concerned. *Quod semper* is the touchstone, in their conceptions, of all orthodoxy. No matter who may teach this or that, *now* or in any post-apostolic age, their test is Holy Scripture, and the inquiry, Was it *always* so taught and understood?

THE STROMATA, OR MISCELLANIES.

BOOK VIII.

CHAP. I. — THE OBJECT OF PHILOSOPHICAL AND THEOLOGICAL INQUIRY — THE DISCOVERY OF TRUTH.[1]

BUT the most ancient of the philosophers were not carried away to disputing and doubting, much less are we, who are attached to the really true philosophy, on whom the Scripture enjoins examination and investigation. For it is the more recent of the Hellenic philosophers who, by empty and futile love of fame, are led into useless babbling in refuting and wrangling. But, on the contrary, the Barbarian philosophy, expelling all contention, said, "Seek, and ye shall find; knock, and it shall be opened unto you; ask, and it shall be given you."[2]

Accordingly, by investigation, the point proposed for inquiry and answer knocks at the door of truth, according to what appears. And on an opening being made through the obstacle in the process of investigation, there results scientific contemplation. To those who thus knock, according to my view, the subject under investigation is opened.

And to those who thus ask questions, in the Scriptures, there is given from God (that at which they aim) the gift of the God-given knowledge, by way of comprehension, through the true illumination of logical investigation. For it is impossible to find, without having sought; or to have sought, without having examined; or to have examined, without having unfolded and opened up the question by interrogation, to produce distinctness; or again, to have gone through the whole investigation, without thereafter receiving as the prize the knowledge of the point in question.

But it belongs to him who has sought, to find; and to him to seek, who thinks previously that he does not know. Hence drawn by desire to the discovery of what is good, he seeks thought-fully, without love of strife or glory, asking, answering, and besides considering the statements made. For it is incumbent, in applying ourselves not only to the divine Scriptures, but also to common notions, to institute investigations, the discovery ceasing at some useful end.

For another place and crowd await turbulent people, and forensic sophistries. But it is suitable for him, who is at once a lover and disciple of the truth, to be pacific even in investigations, advancing by scientific demonstration, without love of self, but with love of truth, to comprehensive knowledge.

CHAP. II. — THE NECESSITY OF PERSPICUOUS DEFINITION.

What better or clearer method, for the commencement of instruction of this nature, can there be than discussion of the term advanced, so distinctly, that all who use the same language may follow it? Is the term for demonstration of such a kind as the word *Blityri*, which is a mere sound, signifying nothing? But how is it that neither does the philosopher, nor the orator, — no more does the judge, — adduce demonstration as a term that means nothing; nor is any of the contending parties ignorant of the fact, that the meaning does not exist?

Philosophers, in fact, present demonstration as having a substantial existence, one in one way, another in another. Therefore, if one would treat aright of each question, he cannot carry back the discourse to another more generally admitted fundamental principle than what is admitted to be signified by the term by all of the same nation and language.

Then, starting from this point, it is necessary to inquire if the proposition has this signification or not. And next, if it is demonstrated to have, it is necessary to investigate its nature accurately, of what kind it is, and whether it ever passes over the class assigned. And if it suffices not to say, absolutely, only that which one thinks (for

---

[1] [This book is a mere fragment, an imperfect exposition of logic, and not properly part of the *Stromata*. Kaye, 221.]
[2] Matt. vii. 7.; Luke xi. 9. [Elucidation I.]

one's opponent may equally allege, on the other side, what he likes) ; then what is stated must be confirmed. If the decision of it be carried back to what is likewise matter of dispute, and the decision of that likewise to another disputed point, it will go on *ad infinitum,* and will be incapable of demonstration. But if the belief of a point that is not admitted be carried back to one admitted by all, that is to be made the commencement of instruction. Every term, therefore, advanced for discussion is to be converted into an expression that is admitted by those that are parties in the discussion, to form the starting point for instruction, to lead the way to the discovery of the points under investigation. For example, let it be the term "sun" that is in question. Now the Stoics say that it is "an intellectual fire kindled from the waters of the sea." Is not the definition, consequently, obscurer than the term, requiring another demonstration to prove if it be true? It is therefore better to say, in the common and distinct form of speech, "that the brightest of the heavenly bodies is named the sun." For this expression is more credible and clearer, and is likewise admitted by all.

CHAP. III. — DEMONSTRATION DEFINED.

Similarly, also, all men will admit that demonstration is discourse,[1] agreeable to reason, producing belief in points disputed, from points admitted.

Now, not only demonstration and belief and knowledge, but foreknowledge also, are used in a twofold manner. There is that which is scientific and certain, and that which is merely based on hope.

In strict propriety, then, that is called demonstration which produces in the souls of learners scientific belief. The other kind is that which merely leads to opinion. As also, both he that is really a man, possessing common judgment, and he that is savage and brutal, — each is a man. Thus also the Comic poet said that "man is graceful, so long as he is man." The same holds with ox, horse, and dog, according to the goodness or badness of the animal. For by looking to the perfection of the genus, we come to those meanings that are strictly proper. For instance, we conceive of a physician who is deficient in no element of the power of healing, and a Gnostic who is defective in no element of scientific knowledge.

Now demonstration differs from syllogism ; inasmuch as the point demonstrated is indicative of one thing, being one and identical ; as we say that to be with child is the proof of being no longer a virgin. But what is apprehended by syllogism, though one thing, follows from several ; as, for example, not one but several proofs are adduced of Pytho having betrayed the Byzantines, if such was the fact. And to draw a conclusion from what is admitted is to *syllogize* ; while to draw a conclusion from what is true is to *demonstrate.*

So that there is a compound advantage of demonstration : from its assuming, for the proof of points in question, true premisses, and from its drawing the conclusion that follows from them. If the first have no existence, but the second follow from the first, one has not demonstrated, but syllogized. For, to draw the proper conclusion from the premisses, is merely to syllogize. But to have also each of the premisses true, is not merely to have syllogized, but also to have demonstrated.

And to conclude, as is evident from the word, is to bring to the conclusion. And in every train of reasoning, the point sought to be determined is the end, which is also called the conclusion. But no simple and primary statement is termed a syllogism, although true ; but it is compounded of three such, at the least, — of two as premisses, and one as conclusion.

Now, either all things require demonstration, or some of them are self-evident. But if the first, by demanding the demonstration of each demonstration we shall go on *ad infinitum ;* and so demonstration is subverted. But if the second, those things which are self-evident will become the starting points [and fundamental grounds] of demonstration.

In point of fact, the philosophers admit that the first principles of all things are indemonstrable. So that if there is demonstration at all, there is an absolute necessity that there be something that is self-evident, which is called primary and indemonstrable.

Consequently all demonstration is traced up to indemonstrable faith.[2]

It will also turn out that there are other starting points for demonstrations, after the source which takes its rise in faith, — the things which appear clearly to sensation and understanding. For the phenomena of sensation are simple, and incapable of being decompounded ; but those of understanding are simple, rational, and primary. But those produced from them are compound, but no less clear and reliable, and having more to do with the reasoning faculty than the first. For therefore the peculiar native power of reason, which we all have by nature, deals with agreement and disagreement. If, then, any argument be found to be of such a kind, as from points already believed to be capable of producing

---

[1] It is necessary to read λόγον here, though not in the text, on account of ἐκπορίζοντα which follows; and as εὐλογον εἶναι λόγον occurs afterwards, it seems better to retain εὐλογον than to substitute λόγον for it.

[2] [We begin, that is, with axioms: and he ingeniously identifies faith with axiomatic truth. Hence the faith not esoteric.]

belief in what is not yet believed, we shall aver that this is the very essence of demonstration.

Now it is affirmed that the nature of demonstration, as that of belief, is twofold : that which produces in the souls of the hearers persuasion merely, and that which produces knowledge.

If, then, one begins with the things which are evident to sensation and understanding, and then draw the proper conclusion, he truly demonstrates. But if [he begin] with things which are only probable and not primary, that is evident neither to sense nor understanding, and if he draw the right conclusion, he will syllogize indeed, but not produce a scientific demonstration ; but if [he draw] not the right conclusion, he will not syllogize at all.

Now demonstration differs from analysis. For each one of the points demonstrated, is demonstrated by means of points that are demonstrated ; those having been previously demonstrated by others ; till we get back to those which are self-evident, or to those evident to sense and to understanding ; which is called Analysis. But demonstration is, when the point in question reaches us through all the intermediate steps. The man, then, who practises demonstration, ought to give great attention to the truth, while he disregards the terms of the premises, whether you call them axioms, or premises, or assumptions. Similarly, also, special attention must be paid to what suppositions a conclusion is based on ; while he may be quite careless as to whether one choose to term it a conclusive or syllogistic proposition.

For I assert that these two things must be attended to by the man who would demonstrate — to assume true premises, and to draw from them the legitimate conclusion, which some also call "the inference," as being what is inferred from the premises.

Now in each proposition respecting a question, there must be different premises, related, however, to the proposition laid down ; and what is advanced must be reduced to definition. And this definition must be admitted by all. But when premises irrelevant to the proposition to be established are assumed, it is impossible to arrive at any right result ; the entire proposition — which is also called the question of its nature — being ignored.

In all questions, then, there is something which is previously known, — that which being self-evident is believed without demonstration ; which must be made the starting point in their investigation, and the criterion of apparent results.

CHAP. IV. — TO PREVENT AMBIGUITY, WE MUST BEGIN WITH CLEAR DEFINITION.

For every question is solved from pre-existing knowledge. And the knowledge pre-existing of

each object of investigation is sometimes merely of the essence, while its functions are unknown (as of stones, and plants, and animals, of whose operations we are ignorant), or [the knowledge] of the properties, or powers, or (so to speak) of the qualities inherent in the objects. And sometimes we may know some one or more of those powers or properties, — as, for example, the desires and affections of the soul, — and be ignorant of the essence, and make it the object of investigation. But in many instances, our understanding having assumed all these, the question is, in which of the essences do they thus inhere ; for it is after forming conceptions of both — that is, both of essence and operation — in our mind, that we proceed to the question. And there are also some objects, whose operations, along with their essences, we know, but are ignorant of their modifications.

Such, then, is the method of the discovery [of truth]. For we must begin with the knowledge of the questions to be discussed. For often the form of the expression deceives and confuses and disturbs the mind, so that it is not easy to discover to what class the thing is to be referred ; as, for example, whether the fœtus be an animal. For, having a conception of an animal and a fœtus, we inquire if it be the case that the fœtus is an animal ; that is, if the substance which is in the fœtal state possesses the power of motion, and of sensation besides. So that the inquiry is regarding functions and sensations in a substance previously known. Consequently the man who proposes the question is to be first asked, what he calls an animal. Especially is this to be done whenever we find the same term applied to various purposes ; and we must examine whether what is signified by the term is disputed, or admitted by all. For were one to say that he calls whatever grows and is fed an animal, we shall have again to ask further, whether he considered plants to be animals ; and then, after declaring himself to this effect, he must show what it is which is in the fœtal state, and is nourished.

For Plato calls plants animals, as partaking of the third species of life alone, that of appetency.[1] But Aristotle, while he thinks that plants are possessed of a life of vegetation and nutrition, does not consider it proper to call them animals ; for that alone, which possesses the other life — that of sensation — he considers warrantable to be called an animal. The Stoics do not call the power of vegetation, life.

Now, on the man who proposes the question denying that plants are animals, we shall show that he affirms what contradicts himself. For, having defined the animal by the fact of its

---

[1] Ἐπιθυμητικοῦ, which accords with what Plato says in the *Timæus*, p. 1078. Lowth, however, reads φυτικοῦ.

nourishment and growth, but having asserted that a plant is not an animal, it appears that he says nothing else than that what is nourished and grows is both an animal and not an animal.

Let him, then, say what he wants to learn. Is it whether what is in the womb grows and is nourished, or is it whether it possesses any sensation or movement by impulse? For, according to Plato, the plant is animate, and an animal; but, according to Aristotle, not an animal, for it wants sensation, but is animate. Therefore, according to him, an animal is an animate sentient being. But according to the Stoics, a plant is neither animate nor an animal; for an animal is an animate being. If, then, an animal is animate, and life is sentient nature, it is plain that what is animate is sentient. If, then, he who has put the question, being again interrogated if he still calls the animal in the fœtal state an animal on account of its being nourished and growing, he has got his answer.

But were he to say that the question he asks is, whether the fœtus is already sentient, or is capable of moving itself in consequence of any impulse, the investigation of the matter becomes clear, the fallacy in the name no longer remaining. But if he do not reply to the interrogation, and will not say what he means, or in respect of what consideration it is that he applies the term " animal " in propounding the question, but bids us define it ourselves, let him be noted as disputatious.

But as there are two methods, one by question and answer, and the other the method of exposition, if he decline the former, let him listen to us, while we expound all that bears on the problem. Then when we have done, he may treat of each point in turn. But if he attempt to interrupt the investigation by putting questions, he plainly does not want to hear.

But if he choose to reply, let him first be asked, To what thing he applies the name, animal. And when he has answered this, let him be again asked, what, in his view, the fœtus means, whether that which is in the womb, or things already formed and living; and again, if the fœtus means the seed deposited, or if it is only when members and a shape are formed that the name of embryos is to be applied. And on his replying to this, it is proper that the point in hand be reasoned out to a conclusion, in due order, and taught.

But if he wishes us to speak without him answering, let him hear. Since you will not say in what sense you allege what you have propounded (for I would not have thus engaged in a discussion about meanings, but I would now have looked at the things themselves), know that you have done just as if you had propounded the question, Whether a dog were an animal?

For I might have rightly said, Of what dog do you speak? For I shall speak of the land dog and the sea dog, and the constellation in heaven, and of Diogenes too, and all the other dogs in order. For I could not divine whether you inquire about all or about some one. What you shall do subsequently is to learn now, and say distinctly what it is that your question is about. Now if you are shuffling about names, it is plain to everybody that the name *fœtus* is neither an animal nor a plant, but a name, and a sound, and a body, and a being, and anything and everything rather than an animal. And if it is this that you have propounded, you are answered.

But neither is that which is denoted by the name *fœtus* an animal. But that is incorporeal, and may be called a thing and a notion, and everything rather than an animal. The nature of an animal is different. For it was clearly shown respecting the very point in question, I mean the nature of the embryo, of what sort it is. The question respecting the meanings expressed by the name animal is different.

I say, then, if you affirm that an animal is what has the power of sensation and of moving itself from appetency, that an animal is not simply what moves through appetency and is possessed of sensation. For it is also capable of sleeping, or, when the objects of sensation are not present, of not exercising the power of sensation. But the natural power of appetency or of sensation is the mark of an animal. For something of this nature is indicated by these things. First, if the fœtus is not capable of sensation or motion from appetency; which is the point proposed for consideration. Another point is; if the fœtus is capable of ever exercising the power of sensation or moving through appetency. In which sense no one makes it a question, since it is evident.

But the question was, whether the embryo is already an animal, or still a plant. And then the name animal was reduced to definition, for the sake of perspicuity. But having discovered that it is distinguished from what is not an animal by sensation and motion from appetency; we again separated this from its adjuncts; asserting that it was one thing for that to be such *potentially*, which is not yet possessed of the power of sensation and motion, but will some time be so, and another thing to be already so *actually;* and in the case of such, it is one thing to exert its powers, another to be able to exert them, but to be at rest or asleep. And this is the question.

For the embryo is not to be called an animal from the fact that it is nourished; which is the allegation of those who turn aside from the essence of the question, and apply their minds to what happens otherwise. But in the case of all conclusions alleged to be found out, demonstration is applied in common, which is discourse (λόγος), establishing one thing from others. But the grounds from which the point in question is to be established, must be admitted and known by the learner. And the foundation of all these is what is evident to sense and to intellect.

Accordingly the primary demonstration is composed of all these. But the demonstration which, from points already demonstrated thereby, concludes some other point, is no less reliable than the former. It cannot be termed primary, because the conclusion is not drawn from primary principles as premises.

The first species, then, of the different kinds of questions, which are three, has been exhibited, — I mean that, in which the essence being known, some one of its powers or properties is unknown. The second variety of propositions was that in which we all know the powers and properties, but do not know the essence ; as, for example, in what part of the body is the principal faculty of the soul.

CHAP. V. — APPLICATION OF DEMONSTRATION TO SCEPTICAL SUSPENSE OF JUDGMENT.

Now the same treatment which applies to demonstration applies also to the following question.

Some, for instance, say that there cannot be several originating causes for one animal. It is impossible that there can be several homogeneous originating causes of an animal ; but that there should be several heterogeneous, is not absurd.

Suppose the Pyrrhonian suspense of judgment, as they say, [the idea] that nothing is certain : it is plain that, beginning with itself, it first invalidates itself. It either grants that something is true, that you are not to suspend your judgment on all things ; or it persists in saying that there is nothing true. And it is evident, that first it will not be true. For it either affirms what is true or it does not affirm what is true. But if it affirms what is true, it concedes, though unwillingly, that something is true. And if it does not affirm what is true, it leaves true what it wished to do away with. For, in so far as the scepticism which demolishes is proved false, in so far the positions which are being demolished are proved true ; like the dream which says that all dreams are false. For in confuting itself, it is confirmatory of the others.

And, in fine, if it is true, it will make a beginning with itself, and not be scepticism of anything else but of itself first. Then if [such a man] apprehends that he is a man, or that he is sceptical, it is evident that he is not sceptical.[1]

---

[1] [The young student must be on his guard as to the philosophical *scepticism* here treated, which is not the habit of *unbelief* commonly so called.]

And how shall he reply to the interrogation? For he is evidently no sceptic in respect to this. Nay, he affirms even that he does doubt.

And if we must be persuaded to suspend our judgment in regard to everything, we shall first suspend our judgment in regard to our suspense of judgment itself, whether we are to credit it or not.

And if this position is true, that we do not know what is true, then absolutely nothing is allowed to be true by it. But if he will say that even this is questionable, whether we know what is true ; by this very statement he grants that truth is knowable, in the very act of appearing to establish the doubt respecting it.

But if a philosophical sect is a leaning toward dogmas, or, according to some, a leaning to a number of dogmas which have consistency with one another and with phenomena, tending to a right life ; and dogma is a logical conception, and conception is a state and assent of the mind : not merely sceptics, but every one who dogmatizes is accustomed in certain things to suspend his judgment, either through want of strength of mind, or want of clearness in the things, or equal force in the reasons.

CHAP. VI. — DEFINITIONS, GENERA, AND SPECIES.

The introductions and sources of questions are about these points and in them.

But before definitions, and demonstrations, and divisions, it must be propounded in what ways the question is stated ; and equivocal terms are to be treated ; and synonyms stated accurately according to their significations.

Then it is to be inquired whether the proposition belongs to those points, which are considered in relation to others, or is taken by itself. Further, If it is, what it is, what happens to it ; or thus, also, if it is, what it is, why it is. And to the consideration of these points, the knowledge of Particulars and Universals, and the Antecedents and the Differences, and their divisions, contribute.

Now, Induction aims at generalization and definition ; and the divisions are the species, and what a thing is, and the individual. The contemplation of the How adduces the assumption of what is peculiar ; and doubts bring the particular differences and the demonstrations, and otherwise augment the speculation and its consequences ; and the result of the whole is scientific knowledge and truth.

Again, the summation resulting from Division becomes Definition. For Definition is adopted before division and after : before, when it is admitted or stated ; after, when it is demonstrated. And by Sensation the Universal is summed up from the Particular. For the starting point of Induction is Sensation ; and the end is the Universal.

Induction, accordingly, shows not *what* a thing is, but *that* it is, or is not. Division shows what it is; and Definition similarly with Division teaches the essence and what a thing is, but not if it is; while Demonstration explains the three points, *if* it is, *what* it is, and *why* it is.

There are also Definitions which contain the Cause. And since it may be known when we see, when we see the Cause; and Causes are four — the matter, the moving power, the species, the end; Definition will be fourfold.

Accordingly we must first take the genus, in which are the points that are nearest those above; and after this the next difference. And the succession of differences, when cut and divided, completes the " What it is." There is no necessity for expressing all the differences of each thing, but those which form the species.

Geometrical analysis and synthesis are similar to logical division and definition; and by division we get back to what is simple and more elementary. We divide, therefore, the genus of what is proposed for consideration into the species contained in it; as, in the case of man, we divide animal, which is the genus, into the species that appear in it, the mortal, and the immortal. And thus, by continually dividing those genera that seem to be compound into the simpler species, we arrive at the point which is the subject of investigation, and which is incapable of further division.

For, after dividing " the animal " into mortal and immortal, then into terrestrial and aquatic; and the terrestrial again into those who fly and those who walk; and so dividing the species which is nearest to what is sought, which also contains what is sought, we arrive by division at the simplest species, which contains nothing else, but what is sought alone.

For again we divide that which walks into rational and irrational; and then selecting from the species, apprehended by division, those next to man, and combining them into one formula, we state the definition of a man, who is an animal, mortal, terrestrial, walking, rational.

Whence Division furnishes the class of matter, seeking for the definition the simplicity of the name; and the definition of the artisan and maker, by composition and construction, presents the knowledge of the thing as it is; not of those things of which we have general notions. To these notions we say that explanatory expressions belong. For to these notions, also, divisions are applicable.

Now one Division divides that which is divided into species, as a genus; and another into parts, as a whole; and another into accidents.

The division, then, of a whole into the parts, is, for the most part, conceived with reference to magnitude; that into the accidents can never be entirely explicated, if, necessarily, essence is inherent in each of the existences.

Whence both these divisions are to be rejected, and only the division of the genus into species is approved, by which both the identity that is in the genus is characterized, and the diversity which subsists in the specific differences.

The species is always contemplated in a part. On the other hand, however, if a thing is part of another, it will not be also a species. For the hand is a part of a man, but it is not a species. And the genus exists in the species. For [the genus] is both in man and the ox. But the whole is not in the parts. For the man is not in his feet. Wherefore also the species is more important than the part; and whatever things are predicated of the genus will be all predicated of the species.

It is best, then, to divide the genus into two, if not into three species. The species then being divided more generically, are characterized by sameness and difference. And then being divided, they are chacterized by the points generically indicated.

For each of the species is either an essence; as when we say, Some substances are corporeal and some incorporeal; or how much, or what relation, or where, or when, or doing, or suffering.

One, therefore, will give the definition of whatever he possesses the knowledge of; as one can by no means be acquainted with that which he cannot embrace and define in speech. And in consequence of ignorance of the definition, the result is, that many disputes and deceptions arise. For if he that knows the thing has the knowledge of it in his mind, and can explain by words what he conceives; and if the explanation of the thought is definition; then he that knows the thing must of necessity be able also to give the definition.

Now in definitions, difference is assumed, which, in the definition, occupies the place of sign. The faculty of laughing, accordingly, being added to the definition of man, makes the whole — a rational, mortal, terrestrial, walking, laughing animal. For the things added by way of difference to the definition are the signs of the properties of things; but do not show the nature of the things themselves. Now they say that the difference is the assigning of what is peculiar; and as that which has the difference differs from all the rest, that which belongs to it alone, and is predicated conversely of the thing, must in definitions be assumed by the first genus as principal and fundamental.

Accordingly, in the larger definitions the number of the species that are discovered are in the ten Categories; and in the least, the principal points of the nearest species being taken, mark the essence and nature of the thing. But the least consists of three, the genus and two essentially necessary species. And this is done for the sake of brevity.

We say, then, Man is the laughing animal. And we must assume that which pre-eminently happens to what is defined, or its peculiar virtue, or its peculiar function, and the like.

Accordingly, while the definition is explanatory of the essence of the thing, it is incapable of accurately comprehending its nature. By means of the principal species, the definition makes an exposition of the essence, and almost has the essence in the quality.

CHAP. VII. — ON THE CAUSES OF DOUBT OR ASSENT.

The causes productive of scepticism are two things principally. One is the changefulness and instability of the human mind, whose nature it is to generate dissent, either that of one with another, or that of people with themselves. And the second is the discrepancy which is in things; which, as to be expected, is calculated to be productive of scepticism.

For, being unable either to believe in all views, on account of their conflicting nature; or to disbelieve all, because that which says that all are untrustworthy is included in the number of those that are so; or to believe some and disbelieve others on account of the equipoise, we are led to scepticism.

But among the principal causes of scepticism is the instability of the mind, which is productive of dissent. And dissent is the proximate cause of doubt. Whence life is full of tribunals and councils; and, in fine, of selection in what is said to be good and bad; which are the signs of a mind in doubt, and halting through feebleness, on account of conflicting matters. And there are libraries full of books,[1] and compilations and treatises of those who differ in dogmas, and are confident that they themselves know the truth that there is in things.

CHAP. VIII. — THE METHOD OF CLASSIFYING THINGS AND NAMES.

In language there are three things: — Names, which are primarily the symbols of conceptions, and by consequence also of subjects. Second, there are Conceptions, which are the likenesses and impressions of the subjects. Whence in all, the conceptions are the same; in consequence of the same impression being produced by the subjects in all. But the names are not so, on account of the difference of languages. And thirdly, the Subject-matters by which the Conceptions are impressed in us.

The names are reduced by grammar into the twenty-four general elements; for the elements must be determined. For of Particulars there

is no scientific knowledge, seeing they are infinite. But it is the property of science to rest on general and defined principles. Whence also Particulars are resolved into Universals. And philosophic research is occupied with Conceptions and Real subjects. But since of these the Particulars are infinite, some elements have been found, under which every subject of investigation is brought; and if it be shown to enter into any one or more of the elements, we prove it to exist; but if it escape them all, that it does not exist.

Of things stated, some are stated without connection; as, for example, "man" and "runs," and whatever does not complete a sentence, which is either true or false. And of things stated in connection, some point out "essence," some "quality," some "quantity," some "relation," some "where," some "when," some "position," some "possession," some "action," some "suffering," which we call the elements of material things after the first principles. For these are capable of being contemplated by reason.

But immaterial things are capable of being apprehended by the mind alone, by primary application.

And of those things that are classed under the ten Categories, some are predicated by themselves (as the nine Categories), and others in relation to something.

And, again, of the things contained under these ten Categories, some are *Univocal*, as ox and man, as far as each is an animal. For those are Univocal terms, to both of which belongs the common name, animal; and the same principle, that is definition, that is animate essence. And Heteronyms are those which relate to the same subject under different names, as ascent or descent; for the way is the same whether upwards or downwards. And the other species of Heteronyms, as horse and black, are those which have a different name and definition from each other, and do not possess the same subject. But they are to be called different, not Heteronyms. And Polyonyms are those which have the same definition, but a different name, as, hanger, sword, scimitar. And Paronyms are those which are named from something different, as "manly" from "manliness."

Equivocal terms have the same name, but not the same definition, as man—both the animal and the picture. Of Equivocal terms, some receive their Equivocal name fortuitously, as Ajax, the Locrian, and the Salaminian; and some from intention; and of these, some from resemblance, as man both the living and the painted; and some from analogy, as the foot of Mount Ida, and our foot, because they are beneath; some from action, as the foot of a vessel, by which the vessel

---

[1] [The Alexandrians must have recognised this as an *ad hominem* remark. But see Eccles. xii. 12.]

sails, and our foot, by which we move. Equivocal terms are designated from the same and to the same ; as the book and scalpel are called surgical, both from the surgeon who uses them, and with reference to the surgical matter itself.

CHAP. IX. — ON THE DIFFERENT KINDS OF CAUSES.

Of Causes, some are Procatarctic and some Synectic, some Co-operating, some Causes *sine quâ non.*

Those that afford the occasion of the origin of anything first, are Procatarctic ; as beauty is the cause of love to the licentious ; for when seen by them, it alone produces the amorous inclination, but not necessarily.

Causes are Synectic (which are also univocally perfect of themselves) whenever a cause is capable of producing the effect of itself, independently.

Now all the causes may be shown in order in the case of the learner. The father is the Procatarctic cause of learning, the teacher the Synectic, and the nature of the learner the co-operating cause, and time holds the relation of the Cause *sine quâ non.*

Now that is properly called a cause which is capable of effecting anything actively ; since we say that steel is capable of cutting, not merely while cutting, but also while not cutting. Thus, then, the capability of causing (τὸ παρεκτικόν) signifies both ; both that which is now acting, and that which is not yet acting, but which possesses the power of acting.

Some, then, say that causes are properties of bodies ; and others of incorporeal substances ; others say that the body is properly speaking cause, and that what is incorporeal is so only catachrestically, and a quasi-cause. Others, again, reverse matters, saying that corporeal substances are properly causes, and bodies are so improperly ; as, for example, that cutting, which is an action, is incorporeal, and is the cause of cutting which is an action and incorporeal, and, in the case of bodies, of being cut, — as in the case of the sword and what is cut [by it].

The cause of things is predicated in a threefold manner. One, What the cause is, as the statuary ; a second, Of what it is the cause of becoming, a statue ; and a third, To what it is the cause, as, for example, the material : for he is the cause to the brass of becoming a statue. The being produced, and the being cut, which are causes to what they belong, being actions, are incorporeal.

According to which principle, causes belong to the class of predicates (κατηγορημάτων), or, as others say, of *dicta* (λεκτῶν) (for Cleanthes and Archedemus call predicates *dicta*) ; or rather, some causes will be assigned to the class of predicates, as that which is cut, whose case is to be cut ; and some to that of axioms, — as, for example, that of a ship being made, whose case again is, that a ship is constructing. Now Aristotle denominates the name of such things as a house, a ship, burning, cutting, an appellative. But the case is allowed to be incorporeal. Therefore that sophism is solved thus : What you say passes through your mouth. Which is true. You name a house. Therefore a house passes through your mouth. Which is false. For we do not speak the house, which is a body, but the case, in which the house is, which is incorporeal.

And we say that the house-builder builds the house, in reference to that which is to be produced. So we say that the cloak is woven ; for that which makes is the indication of the operation. That which makes is not the attribute of one, and the cause that of another, but of the same, both in the case of the cloak and of the house. For, in as far as one is the cause of anything being produced, in so far is he also the maker of it. Consequently, the cause, and that which makes, and that through which (δι' ὅ), are the same. Now, if anything is "a cause" and "that which effects," it is certainly also "that through which." But if a thing is "that through which," it does not by any means follow that it is also "the cause." Many things, for instance, concur in one result, through which the end is reached ; but all are not causes. For Medea would not have killed her children, had she not been enraged. Nor would she have been enraged, had she not been jealous. Nor would she have been this, if she had not loved. Nor would she have loved, had not Jason sailed to Colchi. Nor would this have taken place, had the Argo not been built. Nor would this have taken place, had not the timbers been cut from Pelion. For though in all these things there is the case of "that through which," they are not all "causes" of the murder of the children, but only Medea was the cause. Wherefore, that which does not hinder does not act. Wherefore, that which does not hinder is not a cause, but that which hinders is. For it is in acting and doing something that the cause is conceived.

Besides, what does not hinder is separated from what takes place ; but the cause is related to the event. That, therefore, which does not hinder cannot be a cause. Wherefore, then, it is accomplished, because that which can hinder is not present. Causation is then predicated in four ways : The efficient cause, as the statuary ; and the material, as the brass ; and the form, as the character ; and the end, as the honour of the Gymnasiarch.

The relation of the cause *sine quâ non* is held by the brass in reference to the production of the statue ; and likewise it is a [true] cause. For everything without which the effect is incapable of being produced, is of necessity a cause; but a cause not absolutely. For the cause *sine quâ non* is not Synectic, but Co-operative. And everything that acts produces the effect, in conjunction with the aptitude of that which is acted on. For the cause disposes. But each thing is affected according to its natural constitution; the aptitude being causative, and occupying the place of causes *sine quâ non*. Accordingly, the cause is inefficacious without the aptitude; and is not a cause, but a co-efficient. For all causation is conceived in action. Now the earth could not make itself, so that it could not be the cause of itself. And it were ridiculous to say that the fire was not the cause of the burning, but the logs, — or the sword of the cutting, but the flesh, — or the strength of the antagonist the cause of the athlete being vanquished, but his own weakness.

The Synectic cause does not require time. For the cautery produces pain at the instant of its application to the flesh. Of Procatarctic causes, some require time till the effect be produced, and others do not require it, as the case of fracture.

Are not these called independent of time, not by way of privation, but of diminution, as that which is sudden, not that which has taken place without time?

Every cause, apprehended by the mind as a cause, is occupied with something, and is conceived in relation to something; that is, some effect, as the sword for cutting; and to some object, as possessing an aptitude, as the fire to the wood. For it will not burn steel. The cause belongs to the things which have relation to something. For it is conceived in its relation to another thing. So that we apply our minds to the two, that we may conceive the cause as a cause.

The same relation holds with the creator, and maker, and father. A thing is not the cause of itself. Nor is one his own father. For so the first would become the second. Now the cause acts and affects. That which is produced by the cause is acted on and is affected. But the same thing taken by itself cannot both act and be affected, nor can one be son and father. And otherwise the cause precedes in being what is done by it, as the sword, the cutting. And the same thing cannot precede at the same instant as to matter, as it is a cause, and at the same time, also, be after and posterior as the effect of a cause.

Now *being* differs from *becoming*, as the cause from the effect, the father from the son. For the same thing cannot both *be* and *become* at the same instant; and consequently it is not the cause of itself. Things are not causes of one another, but causes to each other. For the splenetic affection preceding is not the cause of fever, but of the occurrence of fever; and the fever which precedes is not the cause of spleen, but of the affection increasing.

Thus also the virtues are causes to each other, because on account of their mutual correspondence they cannot be separated. And the stones in the arch are causes of its continuing in this category, but are not the causes of one another. And the teacher and the learner are to one another causes of progressing as respects the predicate.

And mutual and reciprocal causes are predicated, some of the same things, as the merchant and the retailer are causes of gain; and sometimes one of one thing and others of another, as the sword and the flesh; for the one is the cause to the flesh of being cut, and the flesh to the sword of cutting. [It is well said,] "An eye for an eye, life for life." For he who has wounded another mortally, is the cause to him of death, or of the occurrence of death. But on being mortally wounded by him in turn, he has had him as a cause in turn, not in respect of being a cause to him, but in another respect. For he becomes the cause of death to him, not that it was death returned the mortal stroke, but the wounded man himself. So that he was the cause of one thing, and had another cause. And he who has done wrong becomes the cause to another, to him who has been wronged. But the law which enjoins punishment to be inflicted is the cause not of injury, but to the one of retribution, to the other of discipline. So that the things which are causes, are not causes to each other as causes.

It is still asked, if many things in conjunction become many causes of one thing. For the men who pull together are the causes of the ship being drawn down; but along with others, unless what is a joint cause be a cause.

Others say, if there are many causes, each by itself becomes the cause of one thing. For instance, the virtues, which are many, are causes of happiness, which is one; and of warmth and pain, similarly, the causes are many. Are not, then, the many virtues one in power, and the sources of warmth and of pain so, also? and does not the multitude of the virtues, being one in kind, become the cause of the one result, happiness?

But, in truth, Procatarctic causes are more than one both generically and specifically; as, for example, cold, weakness, fatigue, dyspepsia, drunkenness, generically, of any disease; and specifically, of fever. But Synectic causes are so, generically alone, and not also specifically.

For of pleasant odour, which is one thing generically, there are many specific causes, as frankincense, rose, crocus, styrax, myrrh, ointment. For the rose has not the same kind of sweet fragrance as myrrh.

And the same thing becomes the cause of contrary effects; sometimes through the magnitude of the cause and its power, and sometimes in consequence of the susceptibility of that on which it acts. According to the nature of the force, the same string, according to its tension or relaxation, gives a shrill or deep sound. And honey is sweet to those who are well, and bitter to those who are in fever, according to the state of susceptibility of those who are affected. And one and the same wine inclines some to rage, and others to merriment. And the same sun melts wax and hardens clay.

Further, of causes, some are apparent; others are grasped by a process of reasoning; others are occult; others are inferred analogically.

And of causes that are occult, some are occult temporarily, being hidden at one time, and at another again seen clearly; and some are occult by nature, and capable of becoming at no time visible. And of those who are so by nature, some are capable of being apprehended; and these some would not call occult, being apprehended by analogy, through the medium of signs, as, for example, the symmetry of the passages of the senses, which are contemplated by reason. And some are not capable of being apprehended; which cannot in any mode fall under apprehension; which are by their very definition occult.

Now some are Procatarctic, some Synectic, some Joint-causes, some Co-operating causes. And there are some according to nature, some beyond nature. And there are some of disease and by accident, some of sensations, some of the greatness of these, some of times and of seasons.

Procatarctic causes being removed, the effect remains. But a Synectic cause is that, which being present, the effect remains, and being removed, the effect is removed.

The Synectic is also called by the synonymous expression "perfect in itself." Since it is of itself sufficient to produce the effect.

And if the cause manifests an operation sufficient in itself, the co-operating cause indicates assistance and service along with the other. If, accordingly, it effects nothing, it will not be called even a co-operating cause; and if it does effect something, it is wholly the cause of this, that is, of what is produced by it. That is, then, a co-operating cause, which being present, the effect was produced — the visible visibly, and the occult invisibly.

The Joint-cause belongs also to the genus of causes, as a fellow-soldier is a soldier, and as a fellow-youth is a youth.

The Co-operating cause further aids the Synectic, in the way of intensifying what is produced by it. But the Joint-cause does not fall under the same notion. For a thing may be a Joint-cause, though it be not a Synectic cause. For the Joint-cause is conceived in conjunction with another, which is not capable of producing the effect by itself, being a cause along with a cause. And the Co-operating cause differs from the Joint-cause in this particular, that the Joint-cause produces the effect in that which by itself does not act. But the Co-operating cause, while effecting nothing by itself, yet by its accession to that which acts by itself, co-operates with it, in order to the production of the effect in the intensest degree. But especially is that which becomes co-operating from being Procatarctic, effective in intensifying the force of the cause.[1]

---

[1] [The book reaches no conclusion, and is evidently a fragment, merely. See Elucidation II.; also Kaye, p. 224.]

ELUCIDATIONS.

I.

(Scripture, cap. i. p. 558.)

ON the 18th of July, 1870, Pius the Ninth, by the bull *Pastor Æternus* proclaiming himself *infallible*, and defining that every Roman bishop from the times of the apostles were equally so, placed himself in conflict, not merely with Holy Scripture (which repeatedly proves the fallibility of St. Peter himself, when speaking apart from his fellow-apostles), but with the torrent of all antiquity. Yes, and with the great divines of his own communion, such as Bossuet; including divers pontiffs, and the Gallicans generally. But note, here, what St. Clement says of the Holy Scripture, and of the search after truth. Is it conceivable, that he knew of any living infallible oracle, when he wrote this book, never once hinting the existence of any such source of absolute gnostic perfection? A like ignorance of such an oracle characterizes Vincent of Lerins, the great expounder of the rule of faith as understood by the four great councils of antiquity.

Clearly, Clement had never seen in Irenæus the meaning read into his words by the modern flatterers of the Roman See.[1] The discovery of 1870 comes just eighteen centuries too late for practical purposes.

II.

(Of Book the Eighth, note 1, p. 567.)

In the place of this book, according to some MSS., Photius found the tract τίς ὁ σωζόμενος πλούσιος; in other MSS., a book beginning as this does. He accused the *Stromata* of unsound opinions; but, this censure not being supported by anything we possess, some imagine that the eighth book is lost, and that it is no great loss after all. A rash judgment as to its value; but possibly this, which is *called* the eighth book, is from the lost *Hypotyposes*. Kaye's suggestion is, that, as the seventh book closed with a promise of something quite fresh, we may discover it in this contribution towards forming his Gnostic, to further knowledge.

It should be regarded as of great importance, that Christianity appears as the friend of all knowledge, and of human culture, from the very start. To our author's versatile genius, much credit is due for the elements out of which Christian universities took their rise.

---

[1] Vol. i. p. 415, and Elucidation I. p. 460, this series.

FRAGMENTS OF CLEMENS ALEXANDRINUS.

[TRANSLATED BY REV. WILLIAM WILSON, M.A.]

FRAGMENTS.

I.—FROM THE LATIN TRANSLATION OF CASSIODORUS.[1]

I. — COMMENTS [2] ON THE FIRST EPISTLE OF PETER.

CHAP. i. 3. "Blessed be the God and Father of our Lord Jesus Christ, who by His great mercy hath regenerated us." For if God generated us of matter, He afterwards, by progress in life, regenerated us.

"The Father of our Lord, by the resurrection of Jesus Christ:" who, according to your faith, rises again in us; as, on the other hand, He dies in us, through the operation of our unbelief. For He said again, that the soul never returns a second time to the body in this life; and that which has become angelic does not become unrighteous or evil, so as not to have the opportunity of again sinning by the assumption of flesh; but that in the resurrection the soul [3] returns to the body, and both are joined to one another according to their peculiar nature, adapting themselves, through the composition of each, by a kind of congruity like [4] a building of stones.

Besides, Peter says,[5] "Ye also, as living stones, are built up a spiritual house;" meaning the place of the angelic abode, guarded in heaven [6]. "For you," he says, "who are kept by the power of God, by faith and contemplation, to receive the end of your faith, the salvation of your souls."

Hence it appears that the soul is not naturally immortal; but is made immortal by the grace of God, through faith and righteousness, and by knowledge. "Of which salvation," he says,[7] "the prophets have inquired and searched diligently," and what follows. It is declared by this that the prophets spake with wisdom, and that the Spirit of Christ was in them, according to the possession of Christ, and in subjection to Christ. For God works through archangels and kindred angels, who are called spirits of Christ.

"Which are now," he says,[8] "reported unto you by them that have preached the Gospel unto you." The old things which were done by the prophets and escape the observation of most, are now revealed to you by the evangelists. "For to you," he says,[9] "they are manifested by the Holy Ghost, who was sent;" that is the Paraclete, of whom the Lord said, "If I go not away, He will not come." [10] "Unto whom," [11] it is said, "the angels desire to look;" not the apostate angels, as most suspect, but, what is a divine truth, angels who desire to obtain the advantage of that perfection.

"By precious blood," he says,[12] "as of a lamb without blemish and without spot." Here he touches on the ancient Levitical and sacerdotal celebrations; but means a soul pure through righteousness which is offered to God.

"Verily foreknown before the foundation of the world." [13] Inasmuch as He was foreknown before every creature, because He was Christ.

---

[1] [M. Aurelius Cassiodorus (whose name is also Senator) was an author and public man of the sixth century, and a very voluminous writer. He would shine with a greater lustre were he not so nearly lost in the brighter light of Boëthius, his illustrious contemporary. After the death of his patron, Theodoric, he continued for a time in the public service, and in high positions, but, at seventy years of age, began another career, and for twenty years devoted himself to letters and the practice of piety in a monastery which he established in the Neapolitan kingdom, near his native Squillace. Died about A. D. 560.]

[2] Comments, ie., *Adumbrationes.* Cassiodorus says that he had in his translation corrected what he considered erroneous in the original. So Fell states; and he is also inclined to believe that these fragments are from Clement's lost work, the ʽΥποτυπώσεις, of which he believes *The Adumbrationes* of Cassiodorus to be a translation.

[3] "Utramque" is the reading, which is plainly corrupt. We have conjectured "animam." The rest of the sentence is so ungrammatical and impracticable as it stands, that it is only by taking considerable liberties with it that it is translateable at all.

[4] The text here has *like a drag-net or (sicut sagena vel),* which we have omitted, being utterly incapable of divining any conceivable resemblance or analogy which a drag-net can afford for the re-union of the soul and body. "Sagena" is either a blunder for something else which we cannot conjecture, or the sentence is here, as elsewhere, mutilated. But it is possible that it may have been the union of the blessed to each other, and their conjunction with one another according to their affinities, which was the point handled in the original sentences, of which we have only these obscure and confusing remains. [A very good conjecture, on the strength of which the text might have been left as it stood.]

[5] Chap. ii. 5.

[6] "Cœli," plainly a mistake for "cœlo" or "cœlis." There is apparently a *hiatus* here. "The angelic abode, guarded in heaven," most probably is the explanation of "an inheritance incorruptible and undefiled, reserved in heaven."

[7] Ver. 10.

[8] Ver. 12.

[9] *Ibid.*

[10] John xvi. 7.

[11] *Ibid.*

[12] Ver. 19.

[13] Ver. 20.

"But manifested in the last times" by the generation of a body.

"Being born again, not of corruptible seed." [1] The soul, then, which is produced along with the body is corruptible, as some think.

"But the word of the Lord," he says,[2] "endureth for ever:" as well prophecy as divine doctrine.

"But ye are a chosen generation, a royal priesthood." [3] That we are a chosen race by the election of God is abundantly clear. He says royal, because we are called to sovereignty and belong to Christ; and priesthood on account of the oblation which is made by prayers and instructions, by which are gained the souls which are offered to God.

"Who, when He was reviled," he says,[4] "reviled not; when He suffered, threatened not." The Lord acted so in His goodness and patience. "But committed Himself to him that judged Him unrighteously:" [5] whether Himself, so that, regarding Himself in this way, there is a transposition.[6] He indeed gave Himself up to those who judged according to an unjust law; because He was unserviceable to them, inasmuch as He was righteous: or, He committed to God those who judged unrighteously, and without cause insisted on His death, so that they might be instructed by suffering punishment.

"For he that will love life, and see good days;" [7] that is, who wishes to become eternal and immortal. And He calls the Lord life, and the days good, that is holy.

"For the eyes of the Lord," he says, "are upon the righteous, and His ears on their prayers:" he means the manifold inspection of the Holy Spirit. "The face of the Lord is on them that do evil;" [8] that is, whether judgment, or vengeance, or manifestation.

"But sanctify the Lord Christ," he says, "in your hearts." [9] For so you have in the Lord's prayer, "Hallowed be Thy name." [10]

"For Christ," he says,[11] "hath once suffered for our sins, the just for the unjust, that he might present [12] us to God; being put to death in the flesh, but quickened in the spirit." He says these things, reducing them to their faith. That is, He became alive in our spirits.

"Coming," he says,[13] "He preached to those who were once unbelieving." They saw not His form, but they heard His voice.

"When the long-suffering of God" [14] holds out. God is so good, as to work the result by the teaching of salvation.

"By the resurrection," it is said,[15] "of Jesus Christ:" that, namely, which is effected in us by faith.

"Angels being subjected to Him," [16] which are the first order; and "principalities" being subject, who are of the second order; and "powers" being also subject, which are said to belong to the third order.

"Who shall give account," he says,[17] "to Him who is ready to judge the quick and the dead."

These are trained through previous judgments.[18] Therefore he adds, "For this cause was the Gospel preached also to the dead" — to us, namely, who were at one time unbelievers. "That they might be judged according to men," he says,[19] "in the flesh, but live according to God in the spirit." Because, that is, they have fallen away from faith; whilst they are still in the flesh they are judged according to preceding judgments, that they might repent. Accordingly, he also adds, saying, "That they might live according to God in the spirit." So Paul also; for he, too, states something of this nature when he says, "Whom I have delivered to Satan, that he might live in the spirit;" [20] that is, "as good stewards of the manifold grace of God." Similarly also Paul says, "Variously, and in many ways, God of old spake to our fathers." [21]

"Rejoice," it is said, [22] "that ye are partakers in the sufferings of Christ:" that is, if ye are righteous, ye suffer for righteousness' sake, as Christ suffered for righteousness. "Happy are ye, for the Spirit of God, who is the Spirit of His glory and virtue, resteth on you." This possessive "His" signifies also an angelic spirit: inasmuch as the glory of God those are, through whom, according to faith and righteousness, He is glorified, to honourable glory, according to the advancement of the saints who are brought in. "The Spirit of God on us," may be thus understood; that is, who through faith comes on the soul, like a gracefulness of mind and beauty of soul.

"Since," it is said,[23] "it is time for judgment beginning at the house of God." For judgment will overtake these in the appointed persecutions.

"But the God of all grace," he says.[24] "Of all grace," he says, because He is good, and the giver of all good things.

---

[1] Ver. 23.
[2] Ver. 25.
[3] Chap. ii. 9.
[4] Ver. 23.
[5] Sic.
[6] Hyperbaton.
[7] Chap. iii. 10.
[8] Ver. 12.
[9] Ver. 15.
[10] Matt. vi. 9.
[11] Ver. 18.
[12] Offerret.
[13] Ver. 20.

[14] Ibid.
[15] Ver. 21.
[16] Ver. 22.
[17] Chap. iv. 5.
[18] Ver. 6.
[19] Ibid
[20] 1 Cor. v. 5.
[21] Heb. i. 1.
[22] Ver. 13.
[23] Ver. 17.
[24] Chap. v. 10.

"Marcus, my son, saluteth you."[1] Mark, the follower of Peter, while Peter publicly preached the Gospel at Rome before some of Cæsar's equites, and adduced many testimonies to Christ, in order that thereby they might be able to commit to memory what was spoken, of what was spoken by Peter, wrote entirely what is called the Gospel according to Mark. As Luke also may be recognised[2] by the style, both to have composed the Acts of the Apostles, and to have translated Paul's Epistle to the Hebrews.

II. — COMMENTS ON THE EPISTLE OF JUDE.

Jude, who wrote the Catholic Epistle, the brother of the sons of Joseph, and very religious, whilst knowing the near relationship of the Lord, yet did not say that he himself was His brother. But what said he?[3] "Jude, a servant of Jesus Christ," — of Him as Lord; but "the brother of James." For this is true; he was His brother, (the son)[4] of Joseph. "For[5] certain men have entered unawares, ungodly men, who had been of old ordained and predestined to the judgment of our God;" not that they might become impious, but that, being now impious, they were ordained to judgment. "For the Lord God," he says,[6] "who once delivered a people out of Egypt, afterward destroyed them that believed not;" that is, that He might train them through punishment. For they were indeed punished, and they perished on account of those that are saved, until they turn to the Lord. "But the angels," he says,[7] "that kept not their own pre-eminence," that, namely, which they received through advancement, "but left their own habitation," meaning, that is, the heaven and the stars, became, and are called apostates. "He hath reserved these to the judgment of the great day, in chains, under darkness." He means the place near the earth,[8] that is, the dark air. Now he called "chains" the loss of the honour in which they had stood, and the lust of feeble things; since, bound by their own lust, they cannot be converted. "As Sodom and Gomorrha," he says.[9] . . . By which the Lord signifies that pardon had been granted;[10] and that on being disciplined they had repented. "Similarly[11] to the same," he says,[12] "also those dreamers," — that is, who dream in their imagi-

nation lusts and wicked desires, regarding as good not that which is truly good, and superior to all good, — "defile the flesh, despise dominion, and speak evil of majesty," that is, the only Lord,[13] who is truly our Lord, Jesus Christ, and alone worthy of praise. They "speak evil of majesty," that is, of the angels.

"When Michael, the archangel,[14] disputing with the devil, debated about the body of Moses." Here he confirms the assumption of Moses. He is here called Michael, who through an angel near to us debated with the devil.

"But these," he says,[15] "speak evil of those things which they know not; but what they know naturally, as brute beasts, in these things they corrupt themselves." He means that they eat, and drink, and indulge in uncleanness, and says that they do other things that are common to them with animals, devoid of reason.

"Woe unto them!" he says,[16] "for they have gone in the way of Cain." For so also we lie under Adam's sin through similarity of sin. "Clouds," he says,[17] "without water; who do not possess in themselves the divine and fruitful word." Wherefore, he says, "men of this kind are carried about both by winds and violent blasts."[18] "Trees," he says, "of autumn, without fruit," — unbelievers, that is, who bear no fruit of fidelity. "Twice dead," he says: once, namely, when they sinned by transgressing, and a second time when delivered up to punishment, according to the predestined judgments of God; inasmuch as it is to be reckoned death, even when each one does not forthwith deserve the inheritance. "Waves," he says,[19] "of a raging sea." By these words he signifies the life of the Gentiles, whose end is abominable ambition.[20] "Wandering stars," — that is, he means those who err and are apostates are of that kind of stars which fell from the seats of the angels, — "to whom," for their apostasy, "the blackness of darkness is reserved for ever. Enoch also, the seventh from Adam," he says,[21] "prophesied of these." In these words he verifies the prophecy. "Those," he says,[22] "separating" the faithful from the unfaithful, be convicted according to their own unbelief. And again those separating from the flesh.[23] He says, "Animal[24] not having

---

1 Ver. 13.
2 The reading is "agnosceret." To yield any sense it must have been "agnoscatur" or "agnosceretur."
3 Ver. 1.
4 "Son" supplied.
5 Ver. 4.
6 Ver. 5.
7 Ver. 6.
8 Terris.
9 Ver. 7.
10 "Quibus significat Dominus remissius esse," the reading here, defies translation and emendation. We suppose a hiatus here, and change "remissius" into "remissum" to get the above sense. The statement cannot apply to Sodom and Gomorrha.
11 Similiter iisdem.
12 Ver. 8.

13 Dominus — Dominium, referring to the clause "despise dominion." [Jude 8.]
14 Ver. 9.
15 Ver. 10.
16 Ver. 11.
17 Ver. 12.
18 Spiritibus.
19 Ver. 13.
20 The reading "vitam Gentilem significat quorum ambitionis abominabilis est finis," is manifestly corrupt. "The end of whose ambition is abominable" would be obtained by a slighter change than what is given above.
21 Ver. 14.
22 Ver. 19.
23 "Discernentes a carnibus," — a sentence which has got either displaced or corrupted, or both.
24 Animales.

the spirit;" that is, the spirit which is by faith, which supervenes through the practice of right-eousness.

"But ye, beloved," he says,[1] "building up yourselves on your most holy faith, in the Holy Spirit." "But some," he says,[2] "save, pluck-ing them from the fire;"[3] "but of some have compassion in fear," that is, teach those who fall into the fire to free themselves. "Hating," he says,[4] "that spotted garment, which is carnal:" that of the soul, namely; the spotted garment is a spirit polluted by carnal lusts.[5]

"Now to Him," he says,[6] "who is able to keep you without stumbling, and present you faultless before the presence of His glory in joy." In the presence of His glory: he means in the presence of the angels, to be presented faultless, having become angels.[7] When Daniel speaks of the people and comes into the presence of the Lord, he does not say this, because he saw God: for it is impossible that any one whose heart is not pure should see God; but he says this, that everything that the people did was in the sight of God, and was manifest to Him; that is, that nothing is hid from the Lord.

Now, in the Gospel according to Mark, the Lord being interrogated by the chief of the priests if He was the Christ, the Son of the blessed God, answering, said, "I am;[8] and ye shall see the Son of man sitting at the right hand of power."[9] But powers[10] mean the holy angels. Further, when He says "at the right hand of God," He means the self-same [beings], by reason of the equality and likeness of the angelic and holy powers, which are called by the name of God. He says, therefore, that He sits at the right hand; that is, that He rests in pre-eminent honour. In the other Gospels, however, He is said not to have replied to the high priest, on his asking if He was the Son of God. But what said He? "You say."[11] Answering suffi-ciently well. For had He said, It is as you understand, he would have said what was not true, not confessing Himself to be the Son of God; [for] they did not entertain this opinion of Him; but by saying "You say,"[12] He spake truly. For what they had no knowledge of, but expressed in words, that he confessed to be true.

[1] Ver. 20.
[2] Ver. 22.
[3] Ver. 23.
[4] Ver. 23.
[5] By a slight change of punctuation, and by substituting "macu-lata" for "macula," we get the sense as above. Animæ videlicet tunica macula est" is the reading of the text.
[6] Ver. 24.
[7] We have here with some hesitation altered the punctuation. In the text, "To be presented" begins a new sentence.
[8] Mark xiv. 62. There is blundering here as to the differences between the evangelists' accounts, as a comparison of them shows.
[9] Virtutis.
[10] Virtutes.
[11] Matt. xxvi. 64: "Thou hast said: nevertheless, I say unto you, Hereafter ye shall see the Son of man sitting on the right hand of power, and coming in the clouds of heaven."
[12] i.e., It is as you say.

III. — COMMENTS ON THE FIRST EPISTLE OF JOHN.

Chap. i. 1. "That which was from the begin-ning; which we have seen with our eyes; which we have heard."

Following the Gospel according to John, and in accordance with it, this Epistle also contains the spiritual principle.

What therefore he says, "from the begin-ning," the Presbyter explained to this effect, that the beginning of generation is not sepa-rated from the beginning of the Creator. For when he says, "That which was from the begin-ning," he touches upon the generation without beginning of the Son, who is co-existent with the Father. There was, then, a Word import-ing an unbeginning eternity; as also the Word itself, that is, the Son of God, who being, by equality of substance, one with the Father, is eternal and uncreate. That He was always the Word, is signified by saying, "In the beginning was the Word." But by the expression, "we have seen with our eyes," he signifies the Lord's presence in the flesh, "and our hands have handled," he says, "of the Word of life." He means not only His flesh, but the virtues of the Son, like the sunbeam which penetrates to the lowest places, — this sunbeam coming in the flesh became palpable to the disciples. It is ac-cordingly related in traditions, that John, touch-ing the outward body itself, sent his hand deep down into it, and that the solidity of the flesh offered no obstacle, but gave way to the hand of the disciple.

"And our hands have handled of the Word of life;" that is, He who came in the flesh became capable of being touched. As also,

Ver. 2. "The life was manifested." For in the Gospel he thus speaks: "And what was made, in Him was life, and the life was the light of men."[13]

"And we show unto you that eternal life, which was with the Father, and was manifested unto you."

He signifies by the appellation of Father, that the Son also existed always, without beginning.

Ver. 5. "For God," he says, "is light."

He does not express the divine essence, but wishing to declare the majesty of God, he has applied to the Divinity what is best and most excellent in the view of men. Thus also Paul, when he speaks of "light inaccessible."[14] But John himself also in this same Epistle says, "God is love:"[15] pointing out the excellences of God, that He is kind and merciful; and because He is light, makes men righteous, according to the advancement of the soul,

[13] John i. 3, 4.
[14] 1 Tim. vi. 16.
[15] 1 John iv. 16.

through charity. God, then, who is ineffable in respect of His substance, is light.

"And in Him is no darkness at all," — that is, no passion, no keeping up of evil respecting any one, [He] destroys no one, but gives salvation to all. Light moreover signifies, either the precepts of the Law, or faith, or doctrine. Darkness is the opposite of these things. Not as if there were another way; since there is only one way according to the divine precepts. For the work of God is unity. Duality and all else that exists, except unity, arises from perversity of life.

Ver. 7. "And the blood of Jesus Christ His Son," he says, "cleanses us." For the doctrine of the Lord, which is very powerful, is called His blood.

Ver. 10. "If we say that we have not sinned, we make Him a liar, and His word is not in us." His doctrine, that is, or word is truth.

Chap. ii. 1. "And if any man sin," he says, "we have an advocate [1] with the Father, Jesus Christ." For so the Lord is an advocate with the Father for us. So also is there, an advocate, whom, after His assumption, He vouchsafed to send. For these primitive and first-created virtues are unchangeable as to substance, and along with subordinate angels and archangels, whose names they share, effect divine operations. Thus also Moses names the virtue of the angel Michael, by an angel near to himself and of lowest grade. The like also we find in the holy prophets; but to Moses an angel appeared near and at hand. Moses heard him and spoke to him, manifestly, face to face. On the other prophets, through the agency of angels, an impression was made, as of beings hearing and seeing.

On this account also, they alone heard, and they alone saw; as also is seen in the case of Samuel.[2] Elisæus also alone heard the voice by which he was called.[3] If the voice had been open and common, it would have been heard by all. In this instance it was heard by him alone, in whom the impression made by the angel worked.

Ver. 2. "And not only for our sins," — that is, for those of the faithful, — is the Lord the propitiator, does he say, "but also for the whole world." He, indeed, saves all; but some [He saves], converting them by punishments; others, however, who follow voluntarily [He saves] with dignity of honour; so "that every knee should bow to Him, of things in heaven, and things on earth, and things under the earth;"[4] that is, angels, men, and souls that before His advent have departed from this temporal life.

Ver. 3. "And by this we know that we know Him, if we keep His commandments." For the Gnostic [5] [he who knows] also does the works which pertain to the province of virtue. But he who performs the works is not necessarily also a Gnostic. For a man may be a doer of right works, and yet not a knower of the mysteries of science. Finally, knowing that some works are performed from fear of punishment, and some on account of the promise of reward, he shows the perfection of the man gifted with knowledge, who fulfils his works by love. Further, he adds, and says : —

Ver. 5. "But whoso keepeth His word, in him verily is the love of God perfected: hereby know we that we are in Him," — by faith and love.

Ver. 7. "I write no new commandment unto you, but an old commandment, which ye had from the beginning," — through the Law, that is, and the prophets; where it is said, God is one. Accordingly, also, he infers, "For the old commandment is the word which ye have heard." Again, however, he says : —

Ver. 8. "This is the commandment; for the darkness" of perversion, that is, "has passed away, and, lo, the true light hath already shone," — that is, through faith, through knowledge, through the Covenant working in men, through prepared judgments.

Ver. 9. "He that saith he is in the light," — in the light, he means in the truth, — "and hateth," he says, "his brother." By his brother, he means not only his neighbour, but also the Lord. For unbelievers hate Him and do not keep His commandments. Therefore also he infers : —

Ver. 10. "He that loveth his brother abideth in the light; and there is none occasion of stumbling in him."

Vers. 12–14. He then indicates the stages of advancement and progress of souls that are still located in the flesh; and calls those whose sins have been forgiven, for the Lord's name's sake, "little children," for many believe on account of the name only. He styles "fathers" the perfect, "who have known what was from the beginning," and received with understanding, — the Son, that is, of whom he said above, "that which was from the beginning."

"I write," says he, "to you, young men, because ye have overcome the wicked one." Young man strong in despising pleasures. "The wicked one" points out the eminence of the devil. "The children," moreover, know the Father; having fled from idols and gathered together to the one God.

Ver. 15. "For the world," he says, "is in the

---

[1] Consolatorem.
[2] 1 Sam. iii. 3, 4.
[3] 1 Kings xix.
[4] Phil. ii. 10.

[5] "Intellector" in Latin translation. [See p. 607, footnote.]

wicked one." Is not the world, and all that is in the world, called God's creation and very good? Yes. But,

Ver. 16. "The lust of the flesh, the lust of the eyes, and the ambition of the world," which arise from the perversion of life, "are not of the Father, but of the world," and of you.

Ver. 17. "Therefore also the world shall pass away, and the lust thereof; but he that doeth the will of God" and His commandments "abideth for ever."

Ver. 19. "They went out from us; but they were not of us"—neither the apostate angels, nor men falling away;—"but that they may be manifested that they are not of us." With sufficient clearness he distinguishes the class of the elect and that of the lost, and that which remaining in faith "has an unction from the Holy One," which comes through faith. He that abideth not in faith.

Ver. 22. "A liar" and "an antichrist, who denieth that Jesus is the Christ." For Jesus, Saviour and Redeemer, is also Christ the King.

Ver. 23. "He who denies the Son," by ignoring Him, "has not the Father, nor does he know Him." But he who knoweth the Son and the Father, knows according to knowledge, and when the Lord shall be manifested at His second advent, shall have confidence and not be confounded. Which confusion is heavy punishment.

Ver. 29. "Every one," he says, "who doeth righteousness is born of God;" being regenerated, that is, according to faith.

Chap. iii. 1. "For the world knoweth us not, as it knew Him not." He means by the world those who live a worldly life in pleasures.

Ver. 2. "Beloved," says he, "now are we the sons of God," not by natural affection, but because we have God as our Father. For it is the greater love that, seeing we have no relationship to God, He nevertheless loves us and calls us His sons. "And it hath not yet appeared what we shall be;" that is, to what kind of glory we shall attain. "For if He shall be manifested,"—that is, if we are made perfect,—"we shall be like Him," as reposing and justified, pure in virtue, "so that we may see Him" (His countenance) "as He is," by comprehension.

Ver. 8. "He that doeth unrighteousness is of the devil," that is, of the devil as his father, following and choosing the same things. "The devil sinneth from the beginning," he says. From the beginning from which he began to sin, incorrigibly persevering in sinning.

Ver. 9. He says, "Whosoever is born of God does not commit sin, for His seed remaineth in him;" that is, His word in him who is born again through faith.

Ver. 10. "Thus we know the children of God,

as likewise the children of the devil," who choose things like the devil; for so also they are said to be of the wicked one.

Ver. 15. "Every one who hateth his brother is a murderer." For in him through unbelief Christ dies. Rightly, therefore, he continues, "And ye know that no murderer and unbeliever hath eternal life abiding in him." For the living Christ[1] abides in the believing soul.

Ver. 16. "For He Himself laid down His life for us;" that is, for those who believe; that is, for the apostles. If then He laid down His life for the apostles, he means His apostles themselves: as if he said, We, I say, the apostles, for whom He laid down His life, "ought to lay down our lives for the brethren;" for the salvation of their neighbours was the glory of the apostles.

Ver. 20. He says, "For God is greater than our heart;" that is, the virtue of God [is greater] than conscience, which will follow the soul. Wherefore he continues, and says, "and knoweth all things."

Ver. 21. "Beloved, if our heart condemn us not, it will have confidence before God."

Ver. 24. "And hereby we know that He dwelleth in us by His Spirit, which He hath given us;" that is, by superintendence and foresight of future events.

Chap. iv. 18. He says, "Perfect love casteth out fear." For the perfection of a believing man is love.

Chap. v. 6. He says, "This is He who came by water and blood;" and again,—

Ver. 8. "For there are three that bear witness, the spirit," which is life, "and the water," which is regeneration and faith, "and the blood," which is knowledge; "and these three are one." For in the Saviour are those saving virtues, and life itself exists in His own Son.

Ver. 14. "And this is the confidence which we have towards Him, that if we ask anything according to His will, He will hear us." He does not say absolutely what we shall ask, but what we ought to ask.

Ver. 19. "And the whole word lieth in the wicked one;" not the creation, but worldly men, and those who live according to their lusts.

Ver. 20. "And the Son of God hath come and given us understanding," which comes to us, that is, by faith, and is also called the Holy Spirit.

IV. — COMMENTS ON THE SECOND EPISTLE OF JOHN.

The second Epistle of John, which is written to Virgins, is very simple. It was written to a Babylonian lady, by name Electa, and indicates

---

[1] The text reads "Christi," which yields no suitable sense, and or which we have substituted "Christus."

the election of the holy Church. He establishes in this Epistle that the following out of the faith is not without charity, and so that no one divide Jesus Christ; but only to believe that Jesus Christ has come in the flesh. For he who has the Son by apprehension in his intellect knows also the Father, and grasps with his mind intelligibly the greatness of His power working without beginning of time.

Ver. 10. He says, "If any come unto you and bring not this doctrine, receive him not into your house, neither bid him God speed; for he that biddeth him God speed is partaker of his evil deeds." He forbids us to salute such, and to receive them to our hospitality. For this is not harsh in the case of a man of this sort. But he admonishes them neither to confer nor dispute with such as are not able to handle divine things with intelligence, lest through them they be seduced from the doctrine of truth, influenced by plausible reasons. Now, I think that we are not even to pray with such, because in the prayer which is made at home, after rising from prayer, the salutation of joy is also the token of peace.

II.—NICETAS[1] BISHOP OF HERACLEA. FROM HIS CATENA.

I.—JOB I. 21.

But Job's words may be more elegantly understood thus: "Naked" of evil and sin was I formed from the earth at the beginning, as if from a "mother's womb: naked to the earth shall I also depart;" naked,[2] not of possessions, for that were a trivial and common thing, but of evil and sin, and of the unsightly shape which follows those who have led bad lives. Obviously, all of us human beings are born naked, and again are buried naked, swathed only in graveclothes. For God hath provided for us another life, and made the present life the way for the course which leads to it; appointing the supplies derived from what we possess merely as provisions for the way; and on our quitting this way, the wealth, consisting of the things which we possessed, journeys no farther with us. For not a single thing that we possess is properly our own: of one possession alone, that is godliness, are we properly owners. Of this, death, when it overtakes us, will not rob us; but from all else it will eject us, though against our will. For it is for the support of life that we all have received what we possess; and after enjoying merely the use of it, each one departs, obtaining from life a brief remembrance. For this is the end of all prosperity; this is the conclusion of the good

things of this life. Well, then, does the infant, on opening its eyes, after issuing from the womb, immediately begin with crying, not with laughter. For it weeps, as if bewailing life, at whose hands from the outset it tastes of deadly gifts. For immediately on being born its hands and feet are swaddled; and swathed in bonds it takes the breast. O introduction to life, precursor of death! The child has but just entered on life, and straightway there is put upon it the raiment of the dead: for nature reminds those that are born of their end. Wherefore also the child, on being born, wails, as if crying plaintively to its mother. Why, O mother, didst thou bring me forth to this life, in which prolongation of life is progress to death? Why hast thou brought me into this troubled world, in which, on being born, swaddling bands are my first experience? Why hast thou delivered me to such a life as this, in which both a pitiable youth wastes away before old age, and old age is shunned as under the doom of death? Dreadful, O mother, is the course of life, which has death as the goal of the runner. Bitter is the road of life we travel, with the grave as the wayfarer's inn. Perilous the sea of life we sail; for it has Hades as a pirate to attack us. Man alone is born in all respects naked, without a weapon or clothing born with him; not as being inferior to the other animals, but that nakedness and your bringing nothing with you may produce thought; and that thought may bring out dexterity, expel sloth, introduce the arts for the supply of our needs, and beget variety of contrivances. For, naked, man is full of contrivances, being pricked on by his necessity, as by a goad, how to escape rains, how to elude cold, how to fence off blows, how to till the earth, how to terrify wild beasts, how to subdue the more powerful of them. Wetted with rain, he contrived a roof; having suffered from cold, he invented clothing; being struck, he constructed a breastplate; bleeding his hands with the thorns in tilling the ground, he availed himself of the help of tools; in his naked state liable to become a prey to wild beasts, he discovered from his fear an art which frightened what frightened him. Nakedness begat one accomplishment after another; so that even his nakedness was a gift and a master-favour. Accordingly, Job also being made naked of wealth, possessions, of the blessing of children, of a numerous offspring, and having lost everything in a short time, uttered this grateful exclamation: "Naked came I out of the womb, naked also shall I depart thither;" — to God, that is, and to that blessed lot and rest.

II. — FROM THE SAME.

Job xxxiv. 7. Calmness is a thing which, of all other things, is most to be prized. As an exam-

---

[1] [His *Catena* on Job was edited by Patrick Young, London, 1637.]
[2] This down to "lives" is quoted in *Strom.*, book iv. ch. xxv. p. 439, *supra*.

ple of this, the word proposes to us the blessed Job. For it is said of him, "What man is like Job, who drinketh up scorning like water?" For truly enviable, and, in my judgment, worthy of all admiration, a man is, if he has attained to such a degree of long-suffering as to be able with ease to grapple with the pain, truly keen, and not easily conquered by everybody, which arises from being wronged.

III. — FROM NICETAS' CATENA ON MATTHEW.

Matt. v. 42. Alms are to be given, but with judgment, and to the deserving, that we may obtain a recompense from the Most High. But woe to those who have and who take under false pretences, or who are able to help themselves and want to take from others. For he who has, and, to carry out false pretences or out of laziness, takes, shall be condemned.

IV. — FROM THE SAME.

Matt. xiii. 31, 32. The word which proclaims the kingdom of heaven is sharp and pungent as mustard, and represses bile, that is, anger, and checks inflammation, that is, pride ; and from this word the soul's true health and eternal soundness[1] flow. To such increased size did the growth of the word come, that the tree which sprang from it (that is the Church of Christ established over the whole earth) filled the world, so that the fowls of the air — that is, divine angels and lofty souls — dwelt in its branches.

V. — FROM THE SAME.

Matt. xiii. 46. A pearl, and that pellucid and of purest ray, is Jesus, whom of the lightning flash of Divinity the Virgin bore. For as the pearl, produced in flesh and the oyster-shell and moisture, appears to be a body moist and transparent, full of light and spirit ; so also God the Word, incarnate, is intellectual light,[2] sending His rays, through a body luminous and moist.

III. — FROM THE CATENA ON LUKE, EDITED BY CORDERIUS.

Luke iii. 22. God here assumed the "likeness" not of a man, but "of a dove," because He wished, by a new apparition of the Spirit in the likeness of a dove, to declare His simplicity and majesty.

Luke xvi. 17. Perhaps by the iota and tittle His righteousness cries, "If ye come right unto Me, I will also come right to you ; but if crooked, I also will come crooked, saith the Lord of hosts ; " intimating that the ways of sinners are intricate and crooked. For the way right and agreeable to nature which is intimated by the iota of Jesus, is His goodness, which constantly directs those who believe from hearing. "There shall not, therefore, pass from the law one iota or one tittle," neither from the right and good the mutual promises, nor from the crooked and unjust the punishment assigned to them. "For the Lord doeth good to the good, but those who turn aside into crooked ways God will lead with the workers of iniquity."[3]

IV. — FROM THE BOOKS OF THE HYPOTYPOSES.

ŒCUMENIUS FROM BOOK III. ON I COR. XI. 10.

"Because of the angels." By the angels he means righteous and virtuous men. Let her be veiled then, that she may not lead them to stumble into fornication. For the real angels in heaven see her though veiled.

THE SAME, BOOK IV. ON 2 COR. V. 16.

"And if we have known Christ after the flesh." As "after the flesh" in our case is being in the midst of sins, and being out of them is "not after the flesh ; " so also "after the flesh" in the case of Christ was His subjection to natural affections, and His not being subject to them is to be "not after the flesh." But, he says, as He was released, so also are we.

THE SAME, BOOK IV. ON 2 COR. VI. 11.

"Our heart is enlarged," to teach you all things. But ye are straitened in your own bowels, that is, in love to God, in which ye ought to love me.

THE SAME, BOOK V. ON GAL. V. 24.

"And they that are Christ's [have crucified] the flesh." And why mention one aspect of virtue after another? For there are some who have crucified themselves as far as the passions are concerned, and the passions as far as respects themselves. According to this interpretation the "and" is not superfluous. "And they that are Christ's" — that is, striving after Him — "have crucified their own flesh."

MOSCHUS : SPIRITUAL MEADOW, BOOK V. CHAP. 176.

Yes, truly, the apostles were baptised, as Clement the Stromatist relates in the fifth book of the Hypotyposes. For, in explaining the apostolic statement, "I thank God that I baptised none of you," he says, Christ is said to have baptised Peter alone, and Peter Andrew, and Andrew John, and they James and the rest.[4]

---

[1] εὐκρασία.
[2] φωτός here has probably taken the place of φωτεινοῦ. [This passage is in the *Stromata;* and also a similar figure, p. 347, this series.]

[3] Ps. cxxv. 4, 5.
[4] [See Kaye, p. 442, and the eleventh chapter entire.]

EUSEBIUS : ECCLESIASTICAL HISTORY, BOOK VI. ii. 1.

Now Clement, writing in the sixth book of the Hypotyposes, makes this statement. For he says that Peter and James and John, after the Saviour's ascension, though pre-eminently honoured by the Lord, did not contend for glory, but made James the Just, bishop of Jerusalem.

EUSEBIUS : ECCLESIASTICAL HISTORY, II. 15.

So, then, through the visit of the divine word to them, the power of Simon was extinguished, and immediately was destroyed along with the man himself. And such a ray of godliness shone forth on the minds of Peter's hearers, that they were not satisfied with the once hearing or with the unwritten teaching of the divine proclamation, but with all manner of entreaties importuned Mark, to whom the Gospel is ascribed, he being the companion of Peter, that he would leave in writing a record of the teaching which had been delivered to them verbally ; and did not let the man alone till they prevailed upon him ; and so to them we owe the Scripture called the " Gospel by Mark." On learning what had been done, through the revelation of the Spirit, it is said that the apostle was delighted with the enthusiasm of the men, and sanctioned the composition for reading in the Churches. Clemens gives the narrative in the sixth book of the Hypotyposes.

EUSEBIUS : IBID.

Then, also, as the divine Scripture says, Herod, on the execution of James, seeing that what was done pleased the Jews, laid hands also on Peter ; and having put him in chains, would have presently put him to death, had not an angel in a divine vision appeared to him by night, and wondrously releasing him from his bonds, sent him away to the ministry of preaching.

EUSEBIUS : ECCLESIASTICAL HISTORY, VI. 14.

And in the Hypotyposes, in a word, he has made abbreviated narratives of the whole testamentary Scripture ; and has not passed over the disputed books, — I mean Jude and the rest of the Catholic Epistles and Barnabas, and what is called the Revelation of Peter. And he says that the Epistle to the Hebrews is Paul's, and was written to the Hebrews in the Hebrew language ; but that Luke, having carefully translated it, gave it to the Greeks, and hence the same colouring in the expression is discoverable in this Epistle and the Acts ; and that the name " Paul an Apostle " was very properly not prefixed, for, he says, that writing to the Hebrews, who were prejudiced against him and suspected, he with great wisdom did not repel them in the beginning by putting down his name.

EUSEBIUS : BOOK VII.

1 Tim. ii. 6. " In his times ; " that is, when men were in a condition of fitness for faith.

1 Tim. iii. 16. " Was seen of angels." O mystery ! The angels saw Christ while He was with us, not having seen Him before. Not as by men.

1 Tim. v. 8. " And especially those of his own house." He provides for his own and those of his own house, who not only provides for his relatives, but also for himself, by extirpating the passions.

1 Tim. v. 10. " If she have washed the feet of saints ; " that is, if she has performed without shame the meanest offices for the saints.

1 Tim. v. 21. " Without prejudice ; " [1] that is, without falling under the doom and punishment of disobedience through making any false step.

1 Tim. vi. 13. " Who witnessed before Pontius Pilate." For He testified by what he did that He was Christ the Son of God.

2 Tim. ii. 2. " By many witnesses ; " [2] that is, the law and the prophets. For these the apostle made witnesses of his own preaching.

EUSEBIUS : ECCLESIASTCAL HISTORY, BOOK. VII. ii. 1.

To James the Just, and John and Peter, the Lord after His resurrection imparted knowledge (τὴν γνῶσιν.) These imparted it to the rest of the apostles, and the rest of the apostles to the Seventy, of whom Barnabas was one.

EUSEBIUS : THE SAME, II. 2.

And of this James, Clement also relates an anecdote worthy of remembrance in the seventh book of the Hypotyposes, from a tradition of his predecessors. He says that the man who brought him to trial, on seeing him bear his testimony, was moved, and confessed that he was a Christian himself. Accordingly, he says, they were both led away together, and on the way the other asked James to forgive him. And he, considering a little, said, " Peace be to thee," and kissed him. And so both were beheaded together.

EUSEBIUS : THE SAME, VI. 14.

And now, as the blessed Presbyter used to say, since the Lord, as the Apostle of the Almighty, was sent to the Hebrews, Paul, as having been sent to the Gentiles, did not subscribe himself apostle of the Hebrews, out of modesty and reverence for the Lord, and because, being the herald and apostle of the Gentiles, his writing to the Hebrews was something over and above [his assigned function.]

---

1 προκρίματος, " without preferring one before another." — A. V.
2 διά. A. V. " before."

EUSEBIUS : THE SAME.

Again, in the same books Clement has set down a tradition which he had received from the elders before him, in regard to the order of the Gospels, to the following effect. He says that the Gospels containing the genealogies were written first, and that the Gospel according to Mark was composed in the following circumstances : —

Peter having preached the word publicly at Rome, and by the Spirit proclaimed the Gospel, those who were present, who were numerous, entreated Mark, inasmuch as he had attended him from an early period, and remembered what had been said, to write down what had been spoken. On his composing the Gospel, he handed it to those who had made the request to him ; which coming to Peter's knowledge, he neither hindered nor encouraged. But John, the last of all, seeing that what was corporeal was set forth in the Gospels, on the entreaty of his intimate friends, and inspired by the Spirit, composed a spiritual Gospel.

V. — FROM THE BOOK ON PROVIDENCE.

S. MAXIMUS, VOL. II. 114.

Being is in God. God is divine being, eternal and without beginning, incorporeal and illimitable, and the cause of what exists. Being is that which wholly subsists. Nature is the truth of things, or the inner reality of them. According to others, it is the production of what has come to existence ; and according to others, again, it is the providence of God, causing the being, and the manner of being, in the things which are produced.

S. MAXIMUS : IN THE SAME, P. 152.

Willing is a natural power, which desires what is in accordance with nature. Willing is a natural appetency, corresponding with the nature of the rational creature. Willing is a natural spontaneous movement of the self-determining mind, or the mind voluntarily moved about anything. Spontaneity is the mind moved naturally, or an intellectual self-determining movement of the soul.

VI. — FROM THE BOOK ON THE SOUL.

MAXIMUS AND ANTONIUS MELISSA.[1]

Souls that breathe free of all things, possess life, and though separated from the body, and found possessed of a longing for it, are borne immortal to the bosom of God : as in the winter season the vapours of the earth attracted by the sun's rays rise to him.

THE BAROCC. MS.[2]

All souls are immortal, even those of the wicked, for whom it were better that they were not deathless. For, punished with the endless vengeance of quenchless fire, and not dying, it is impossible for them to have a period put to their misery.

VII. — FRAGMENT FROM THE BOOK ON SLANDER.

ANTONIUS MELISSA, BOOK. II. SERMON 69.[3]

Never be afraid of the slanderer who addresses you. But rather say, Stop, brother ; I daily commit more grievous errors, and how can I judge him ? For you will gain two things, healing with one plaster both yourself and your neighbour. He shows what is really evil. Whence, by these arguments, God has contrived to make each one's disposition manifest.

ANTONIUS MELISSA, BOOK I. SERMON 64, AND BOOK II. SERMON 87. ALSO MAXIMUS, SERMON 59, P. 669 ; JOHN OF DAMASCUS, BOOK II.

It is not abstaining from deeds that justifies the believer, but purity and sincerity of thoughts.

VIII.—OTHER FRAGMENTS FROM ANTONIUS MELISSA.

I. — BOOK I. SERMON 17, ON CONFESSION.

Repentance then becomes capable of wiping out every sin, when on the occurrence of the soul's fault it admits no delay, and does not let the impulse pass on to a long space of time. For it is in this way that evil will be unable to leave a trace in us, being plucked away at the moment of its assault like a newly planted plant.

As the creatures called crabs are easy to catch, from their going sometimes forward and sometimes backward ; so also the soul, which at one time is laughing, at another weeping, and at another giving way to luxury, can do no good.

He who is sometimes grieving, and is sometimes enjoying himself and laughing, is like a man pelting the dog of voluptuousness with bread, who chases it in appearance, but in fact invites it to remain near him.

2. BOOK I. SERMON 51, ON PRAISE.

Some flatterers were congratulating a wise man. He said to them, If you stop praising me, I think myself something great after your departure ; but if you do not stop praising me, I guess my own impurity.

Feigned praise is worth less than true censure.

---

[1] Sermon 53, *On The Soul*, p. 156. [Anton. Melissa, a Greek monk of the twelfth century, has left works not infrequently referred to by modern authors. Flourished A. D. 1140.]

[2] 143, fol. 181, p. 1, chapter *On Care For The Soul*.
[3] On *Slanderers and Insult*. The evidence on which this is ascribed to Clement is very slender.

3. BOOK II. SERMON 46, ON THE LAZY AND INDO-
LENT.

To the weak and infirm, what is moderate
appears excessive.

4. BOOK II. SERMON 55, ON YOUR NEIGHBOUR —
THAT YOU ARE TO BEAR HIS BURDENS, ETC.

The reproof that is given with knowledge is
very faithful. Sometimes also the knowledge of
those who are condemned is found to be the
most perfect demonstration.

5. BOOK II. SERMON 74, ON THE PROUD, AND THOSE
DESIROUS OF VAINGLORY.

To the man who exalts and magnifies himself is attached the quick transition and the fall
to low estate, as the divine word teaches.

6. BOOK II. SERMON 87.

Pure speech and a spotless life are the throne
and true temple of God.

IX. — FRAGMENT OF THE TREATISE ON
MARRIAGE.

MAXIMUS, SERMON III. P. 538, ON MODESTY AND
CHASTITY. ALSO, JOHN OF DAMASCUS, BOOK III.
— PARALLEL CHAP. 27.

It is not only fornication, but also the giving
in marriage prematurely, that is called fornication ; when, so to speak, one not of ripe age is
given to a husband, either of her own accord or
by her parents.

X. — FRAGMENTS OF OTHER LOST BOOKS.

MAXIMUS, SERMON 2. — JOHN OF DAMASCUS, II.
CHAP. 70. — ANTONIUS MELISSA, BOOK I. SER-
MON 52.

Flattery is the bane of friendship. Most
men are accustomed to pay court to the good
fortune of princes, rather than to the princes
themselves.

MAXIMUS, SERMON 13, P. 574. — ANTONIUS ME-
LISSA, SERMON 32, P. 45, AND SERMON 33, P. 57.

The lovers of frugality shun luxury as the
bane of soul and body. The possession and
use of necessaries has nothing injurious in
quality, but it has in quantity above measure.
Scarcity of food is a necessary benefit.

MAXIMUS, SERMON 52, P. 654. — ANTONIUS ME-
LISSA, BOOK I. SERMON 54.

The vivid remembrance of death is a check
upon diet ; and when the diet is lessened, the
passions are diminished along with it.

MAXIMUS, SERMON 55, P. 661.

Above all, Christians are not allowed to correct with violence the delinquencies of sins.
For it is not those that abstain from wickedness
from compulsion, but those that abstain from
choice, that God crowns. It is impossible for
a man to be steadily good except by his own
choice. For he that is made good by compulsion of another is not good ; for he is not what
he is by his own choice. For it is the freedom
of each one that makes true goodness and
reveals real wickedness. Whence through these
dispositions God contrived to make His own disposition manifest.

XI. — FRAGMENTS FOUND IN GREEK ONLY
IN THE OXFORD EDITION.

FROM THE LAST WORK ON THE PASSOVER.

Quoted in the Paschal Chronicle.

Accordingly, in the years gone by, Jesus went
to eat the passover sacrificed by the Jews, keeping the feast. But when he had preached He
who was the Passover, the Lamb of God, led as
a sheep to the slaughter, presently taught His
disciples the mystery of the type on the thirteenth
day, on which also they inquired, "Where wilt
Thou that we prepare for Thee to eat the passover?"[1] It was on this day, then, that both
the consecration of the unleavened bread and
the preparation for the feast took place. Whence
John naturally describes the disciples as already
previously prepared to have their feet washed
by the Lord. And on the following day our
Saviour suffered, He who was the Passover, pro-
pitiously sacrificed by the Jews.

THE SAME.

Suitably, therefore, to the fourteenth day, on
which He also suffered, in the morning, the
chief priests and the scribes, who brought Him
to Pilate, did not enter the Prætorium, that they
might not be defiled, but might freely eat the
passover in the evening. With this precise determination of the days both the whole Scriptures agree, and the Gospels harmonize. The
resurrection also attests it. He certainly rose
on the third day, which fell on the first day of
the weeks of harvest, on which the law prescribed
that the priest should offer up the sheaf.

MACARIUS CHRYSOCEPHALUS : PARABLE OF THE
PRODIGAL SON, LUKE XV. ORATION ON LUKE
XV., TOWARDS THE CLOSE.

1. What choral dance and high festival is held
in heaven, if there is one that has become an
exile and a fugitive from the life led under the
Father, knowing not that those who put them-

[1] Matt. xxvi. 17.

selves far from Him shall perish; if he has squandered the gift, and substance, and inheritance of the Father; if there is one whose faith has failed, and whose hope is spent, by rushing along with the Gentiles into the same profligacy of debauchery; and then, famished and destitute, and not even filled with what the swine eat, has arisen and come to his Father!

But the kind Father waits not till the son comes to Him. For perchance he would never be able or venture to approach, did he not find Him gracious. Wherefore, when he merely wishing, when he straightway made a beginning, when he took the first step, while he was yet a great way off, He [the Father] was moved with compassion, and ran, and fell upon his neck and kissed him. And then the son, taking courage, confessed what he had done.

Wherefore the Father bestows on him the glory and honour that was due and meet, putting on him the best robe, the robe of immortality; and a ring, a royal signet and divine seal, — impress of consecration, signature of glory, pledge of testimony (for it is said, "He hath set to his seal that God is true,")[1] and shoes, not those perishable ones which he hath set his foot on holy ground is bidden take off, nor such as he who is sent to preach the kingdom of heaven is forbidden to put on, but such as wear not, and are suited for the journey to heaven, becoming and adorning the heavenly path, such as unwashed feet never put on, but those which are washed by our Teacher and Lord.

Many, truly, are the shoes of the sinful soul, by which it is bound and cramped. For each man is cramped by the cords of his own sins. Accordingly, Abraham swears to the king of Sodom, "I will not take of all that is thine, from a thread to a shoe-latchet."[2] On account of these being defiled and polluted on the earth, every kind of wrong and selfishness engrosses life. As the Lord reproves Israel by Amos, saying, "For three iniquities of Israel, yea, for four, I will not turn him back; because they have given away the righteous for silver, and the needy for a pair of shoes, which tread upon the dust of the ground."[3]

2. Now the shoes which the Father bids the servant give to the repentant son who has betaken himself to Him, do not impede or drag to the earth (for the earthly tabernacle weighs down the anxious mind); but they are buoyant, and ascending, and waft to heaven, and serve as such a ladder and chariot as he requires who has turned his mind towards the Father. For, beautiful after being first beautifully adorned with all these things without, he enters into the gladness within. For "Bring out" was said by Him who had first said, "While he was yet a great way off, he ran and fell upon his neck." For it is here[4] that all the preparation for entrance to the marriage to which we are invited must be accomplished. He, then, who has been made ready to enter will say, "This my joy is fulfilled."[5] But the unlovely and unsightly man will hear, "Friend, how camest thou in here, without having a wedding garment?"[6] And the fat and unctuous food, — the delicacies abundant and sufficing of the blessed, — the fatted calf is killed; which is also again spoken of as a lamb (not literally); that no one may suppose it small; but it is the great and greatest. For not small is "the Lamb of God who taketh away the sin of the world,"[7] who "was led as a sheep to the slaughter," the sacrifice full of marrow, all whose fat, according to the sacred law, was the Lord's. For He was wholly devoted and consecrated to the Lord; so well grown, and to such excessive size, as to reach and extend over all, and to fill those who eat Him and feed upon Him. For He is both flesh and bread, and has given Himself as both to us to be eaten.

To the sons, then, who come to Him, the Father gives the calf, and it is slain and eaten. But those who do not come to Him He pursues and disinherits, and is found to be a most powerful bull. Here, by reason of His size and prowess, it is said of Him, "His glory is as that of an unicorn."[8] And the prophet Habakkuk sees Him bearing horns, and celebrates His defensive attitude — "horns in His hands."[9] Wherefore the sign shows His power and authority, — horns that pierce on both sides, or rather, on all sides, and through everything. And those who eat are so strengthened, and retain such strength from the life-giving food in them, that they themselves are stronger than their enemies, and are all but armed with the horns of a bull; as it is said, "In thee shall we butt our enemies."[10]

3. Gladness there is, and music, and dances; although the elder son, who had ever been with and ever obedient to the Father, takes it ill, when he who never had himself been dissipated or profligate sees the guilty one made happy.

Accordingly the Father calls him, saying, "Son, thou art ever with me." And what greater joy and feast and festivity can be than being continually with God, standing by His side and serving Him? "And all that is mine is thine." And blessed is the heir of God, for whom the

---

[4] We have ventured to substitute ἐνταῦθα instead of ἐντεῦθεν. He is showing that the preparation must be made before we go in.
[5] John iii. 29.
[6] Matt. xxii. 12.
[7] John i. 29.
[8] Numb. xxiii. 22.
[9] Hab. iii. 4.
[10] Ps. xliv. 5.

---

[1] John iii. 33.
[2] Gen. xiv. 23.
[3] Amos ii. 6.

Father holds possession, — the faithful, to whom the whole world of possessions belongs.

"It was meet that we should be glad, and rejoice ; for thy brother was dead, and is alive again." Kind Father, who givest all things life, and raisest the dead. "And was lost, and is found." And "blessed is the man whom Thou hast chosen and accepted,"[1] and whom having sought, Thou dost find. "Blessed are those whose iniquities are forgiven, whose sins are covered."[2] It is for man to repent of sins ; but let this be accompanied with a change that will not be checked. For he who does not act so shall be put to shame, because he has acted not with his whole heart, but in haste.

And it is ours to flee to God. And let us endeavour after this ceaselessly and energetically. For He says, "Come unto Me, all ye that labour and are heavy laden, and I will give you rest."[3] And prayer and confession with humility are voluntary acts. Wherefore it is enjoined, "First tell thy sins, that thou mayest be justified."[4] What afterwards we shall obtain, and what we shall be, it is not for us to judge.

4. Such is the strict meaning of the parable.[5] The repentant son came to the pitying Father, never hoping for these things, — the best robe, and the ring, and the shoes, — or to taste the fatted calf, or to share in gladness, or enjoy music and dances ; but he would have been contented with obtaining what in his own estimation he deemed himself worth. "Make me," he had made up his mind to say, "as one of thy hired servants." But when he saw the Father's welcome meeting him, he did not say this, but said what he had in his mind to say first, "Father, I have sinned against Heaven, and before thee." And so both his humility and his accusation became the cause of justification and glory. For the righteous man condemns himself in his first words. So also the publican departed justified rather than the Pharisee. The son, then, knew not either what he was to obtain, or how to take or use or put on himself the things given him ; since he did not take the robe himself, and put it on. But it is said, "Put it on him." He did not himself put the ring on his finger, but those who were bidden "Put a ring on his hand." Nor did he put the shoes on himself, but it was they who heard, "and shoes on his feet."

And these things were perhaps incredible to him and to others, and unexpected before they took place ; but gladly received and praised were the gifts with which he was presented.

5. The parable exhibits this thought, that the exercise of the faculty of reason has been accorded to each man. Wherefore the prodigal is introduced, demanding from his father his portion, that is, of the state of mind, endowed by reason. For the possession of reason is granted to all, in order to the pursuit of what is good, and the avoidance of what is bad. But many who are furnished by God with this make a bad use of the knowledge that has been given them, and land in the profligacy of evil practices, and wickedly waste the substance of reason, — the eye on disgraceful sights, the tongue on blasphemous words, the smell on fœtid licentious excesses of pleasures, the mouth on swinish gluttony, the hands on thefts, the feet on running into plots, the thoughts on impious counsels, the inclinations on indulgence on the love of ease, the mind on brutish pastime. They preserve nothing of the substance of reason unsquandered. Such an one, therefore, Christ represents in the parable, — as a rational creature, with his reason darkened, and asking from the Divine Being what is suitable to reason ; then as obtaining from God, and making a wicked use of what had been given, and especially of the benefits of baptism, which had been vouchsafed to him ; whence also He calls him a prodigal ; and then, after the dissipation of what had been given him, and again his restoration by repentance, [He represents] the love of God shown to him.

6. For He says, "Bring hither the fatted calf, kill it, and let us eat and be merry ; for this my son" — a name of nearest relationship, and significative of what is given to the faithful — "was dead and lost," — an expression of extremest alienation ; for what is more alien to the living than the lost and dead? For neither can be possessed any more. But having from the nearest relationship fallen to extremest alienation, again by repentance he returned to near relationship. For it is said, "Put on him the best robe," which was his the moment he obtained baptism. I mean the glory of baptism, the remission of sins, and the communication of the other blessings, which he obtained immediately he had touched the font.

"And put a ring on his hand." Here is the mystery of the Trinity ; which is the seal impressed on those who believe.

"And put shoes on his feet," for "the preparation of the Gospel of peace,"[6] and the whole course that leads to good actions.

7. But whom Christ finds lost, after sin committed since baptism, those Novatus, enemy of God, resigns to destruction. Do not let us then reckon any fault if we repent ; guarding against falling, let us, if we have fallen, retrace our steps. And while dreading to offend, let us, after offend-

---

1 Ps. lxv. 4.
2 Ps. xxxii. 1.
3 Matt. xi. 28.
4 Isa. xliii. 26.
5 Here Grabe notes that what follows is a new exposition of the parable, and is by another and a later hand, as is shown by the refutation of Novatus towards the end.

6 Eph. vi. 15.

ing, avoid despair, and be eager to be confirmed; and on sinking, let us haste to rise up again. Let us obey the Lord, who calls to us, "Come unto Me, all ye that labour, and I will give you rest." [1] Let us employ the gift of reason for actions of prudence. Let us learn now abstinence from what is wicked, that we may not be forced to learn in the future. Let us employ life as a training school for what is good; and let us be roused to the hatred of sin. Let us bear about a deep love for the Creator; let us cleave to Him with our whole heart; let us not wickedly waste the substance of reason, like the prodigal. Let us obtain the joy laid up, in which Paul exulting, exclaimed, "Who shall separate us from the love of Christ?" [2] To Him belongs glory and honour, with the Father and the Holy Spirit, world without end. Amen.

MACARIUS CHRYSOCEPHALUS: ORATION VIII. ON MATT. VIII., AND BOOK VII. ON LUKE XIII.

Therefore God does not here take the semblance of man, but of a dove, because He wished to show the simplicity and gentleness of the new manifestation of the Spirit by the likeness of the dove. For the law was stern, and punished with the sword; but grace is joyous, and trains by the word of meekness. Hence the Lord also says to the apostles, who said that He should punish with fire those who would not receive Him, after the manner of Elias: "Ye know not what manner of spirit ye are of." [3]

FROM THE SAME. — BOOK XIII. CHAP. IX.

Possibly by the "iota and the tittle" His righteousness exclaims, "If ye come right to me, I also will come right to you; if ye walk crooked, I also will walk crooked, saith the Lord of hosts," [4] alluding to the offences of sinners under the name of crooked ways. For the straight way, and that according to nature, which is pointed out by the iota of Jesus, is His goodness, which is immoveable towards those who have obediently believed. There shall not then pass away from the law neither the iota nor the tittle; that is, neither the promise that applies to the straight in the way, nor the punishment threatened against those that diverge. For the Lord is good to the straight in the way; but "those that turn aside after their crooked ways He shall lead forth with those that work iniquity." [5] "And with the innocent He is innocent, and with the froward He is froward;" [6] and to the crooked He sends crooked ways.

His own luminous image God impressed as with a seal, even the greatest, — on man made in His likeness, that he might be ruler and lord over all things, and that all things might serve him. Wherefore God judges man to be wholly His, and His own image. He is invisible; but His image, man, is visible. Whatever one, then, does to man, whether good or bad, is referred to Himself. Wherefore from Him judgment shall proceed, appointing to all according to desert; for He will avenge His own image.

XII.—FRAGMENTS NOT GIVEN IN THE OXFORD EDITION.

1. IN ANASTASIUS SINAITA, QUEST. 96.

As it is possible even now for man to form men, according to the original formation of Adam, He no longer now creates, on account of His having granted once for all to man the power of generating men, saying to our nature, "Increase, and multiply, and replenish the earth." [7] So also, by His omnipotent and omniscient power, He arranged that the dissolution and death of our bodies should be effected by a natural sequence and order, through the change of their elements, in accordance with His divine knowledge and comprehension.

2. JOANNES VECCUS, PATRIARCH OF CONSTANTINOPLE, ON THE PROCESSION OF THE SPIRIT. IN LEO ALLATIUS, VOL. I. P. 248.

Further, Clement the Stromatist, in the various definitions which he framed, that they might guide the man desirous of studying theology in every dogma of religion, defining what spirit is, and how it is called spirit, says: "Spirit is a substance, subtle, immaterial, and which issues forth without form."

3. FROM THE UNPUBLISHED DISPUTATION AGAINST ICONOCLASTS, OF NICEPHORUS OF CONSTANTINOPLE; EDITED IN GREEK AND LATIN BY LE NOURRY IN HIS APPARATUS TO THE LIBRARY OF THE FATHERS, VOL. I. P. 1334 A.B. FROM CLEMENT THE PRESBYTER OF ALEXANDRIA'S BOOK AGAINST JUDAIZERS.

Solomon the son of David, in the books styled "The Reigns of the Kings," comprehending not only that the structure of the true temple was celestial and spiritual, but had also a reference to the flesh, which He who was both the son and Lord of David was to build up, both for His own presence, where, as a living image, He resolved to make His shrine, and for the church that was to rise up through the union of faith, says expressly, "Will God in very deed dwell with men on the earth?" [8]

---

[1] Matt. xi. 28.
[2] Rom. viii. 35.
[3] Luke ix. 55.
[4] Lev. xxvi. 24.
[5] Ps. cxxv. 5.
[6] Ps. xviii. 26.

[7] Gen. i. 28.
[8] 1 Kings viii. 27.

He dwells on the earth clothed in flesh, and His abode with men is effected by the conjunction and harmony which obtains among the righteous, and which build and rear a new temple. For the righteous are the earth, being still encompassed with the earth; and earth, too, in comparison with the greatness of the Lord. Thus also the blessed Peter hesitates not to say, "Ye also, as living stones, are built up, a spiritual house, a holy temple, to offer up spiritual sacrifices, acceptable to God by Jesus Christ." [1]

And with reference to the body, which by circumscription He consecrated as a hallowed place for Himself upon earth, He said, "Destroy this temple, and in three days I will raise it up again. The Jews therefore said, In forty-six years was this temple built, and wilt thou raise it up in three days? But He spake of the temple of His body." [2]

4. FROM MS. MARKED 2431 IN THE LIBRARY OF THE MOST CHRISTIAN KING. — IBID. P. 1336 A. FROM THE VERY HOLY AND BLESSED CLEMENT, PRESBYTER OF ALEXANDRIA, THE STROMATIST'S BOOK ON PROVIDENCE.

What is God? "God," as the Lord saith, "is a Spirit." Now spirit is properly substance, incorporeal, and uncircumscribed. And that is incorporeal which does not consist of a body, or whose existence is not according to breadth, length, and depth. And that is uncircumscribed [3] which has no place, which is wholly in all, and in each entire, and the same in itself.

5. FROM THE SAME MS. — IBID. 1335 D.

Φύσις (nature) is so called from τὸ πεφυκέναι (to be born). The first substance is everything which subsists by itself, as a stone is called a substance. The second is a substance capable of increase, as a plant grows and decays. The third is animated and sentient substance, as animal, horse. The fourth is animate, sentient, rational substance, as man. Wherefore each one of us is made as consisting of all, having an immaterial soul and a mind, which is the image of God.

6. IN JOHN OF DAMASCUS — PARALLEL. — VOL. II. P. 307.

The fear of God, who is impassible, is free of perturbation. For it is not God that one dreads, but the falling away from God. He who dreads this, dreads falling into what is evil, and dreads

what is evil. And he that fears a fall wishes himself to be immortal and passionless.

7. THE SAME, P. 341.

Let there be a law against those who dare to look at things sacred and divine irreverently, and in a way unworthy of God, to inflict on them the punishment of blindness.

8. THE SAME, P. 657.

Universally, the Christian is friendly to solitude, and quiet, and tranquillity, and peace.

9. FROM THE CATENA ON THE PENTATEUCH, PUBLISHED IN LATIN BY FRANCIS ZEPHYRUS, P. 146.

That mystic name which is called the Tetragrammaton, by which alone they who had access to the Holy of Holies were protected, is pronounced Jehovah, which means, "Who is, and who shall be." The candlestick which stood at the south of the altar signified the seven planets, which seem to us to revolve around the meridian,[4] on either side of which rise three branches; since the sun also, like the lamp, balanced in the midst of the planets by divine wisdom, illumines by its light those above and below. On the other side of the altar was situated the table on which the loaves were displayed, because from that quarter of the heaven vital and nourishing breezes blow.

10. FROM J. A. CRAMER'S CATENÆ GRÆCORUM PATRUM IN NOV. TEST. OXFORD 1840, VOL. III.

On Acts vii. 24, 25. The mystics say that it was by his word alone that Moses slew the Egyptian; as certainly afterwards it is related in the Acts that [Peter] slew with his word those who kept back part of the price of the land, and lied.

11. THE SAME, VOL. IV. P. 291.

On Rom. viii. 38. "Or life, that of our present existence," and "death," — that caused by the assault of persecutors, and "angels, and principalities, and powers," apostate spirits.

12. P. 369, CHAP. X. 3.

And having neither known nor done the requirement of the law, what they conceived, that they also thought that the law required. And they did not believe the law, as prophesying, but the bare word; and followed it from fear, but not with their disposition and in faith.

13. VOL. VI. P. 385.

On 2 Cor. v. 16. "And if we have known Christ after the flesh."

---

[1] 1 Pet. ii. 5.
[2] John ii. 19-21.
[3] With an exclamation of surprise at the Latin translator giving a translation which is utterly unintelligible, Capperonn amends the text, substituting οὐ τόπος οὐδεὶς τῷ, etc., for οὐ τόπος οὐδεὶς τόπος τὸ, etc., and translates accordingly. The emendation is adopted, with the exception of the τῷ, instead of which τό is retained.

[4] See Stromata, book v. chap. vi. p. 452, which is plainly the source from which this extract is taken.

And so far, he says, no one any longer lives after the flesh. For that is not life, but death. For Christ also, that He might show this,[1] ceased to live after the flesh. How? Not by putting off the body! Far be it! For with it as His own He shall come, the Judge of all. But by divesting Himself of physical affections, such as hunger, and thirst, and sleep, and weariness. For now He has a body incapable of suffering and of injury.

As "after the flesh" in our case is being in the midst of sins, and being out of them is to be "not after the flesh;" so also after the flesh, in the case of Christ, was His subjection to natural affections, and not to be subject to them was not to be "after the flesh." "But," he says, "as He was released, so also are we." Let there be no longer, he says, subjection to the influences of the flesh. Thus Clement, the fourth book of the *Hypotyposes*.

14. FROM THE SAME, P. 391.

On 2 Cor. vi. 11. "Our heart is enlarged."

For as heat is wont to expand, so also love. For love is a thing of warmth. As if he would say, I love you not only with mouth, but with heart, and have you all within. Wherefore he says: "ye are not straitened in us, since desire itself expands the soul." "Our heart is enlarged" to teach you all things; "but ye are straitened in your own bowels," that is, in love to God, in which you ought to love me.

Thus Clement, in the fourth book of the *Hypotyposes*.

15. FROM VOL. VII. P. 286.

Heb. i. 1. "At sundry times and divers manners."

Since the Lord, being the Apostle of the Almighty, was sent to the Hebrews, it was out of modesty that Paul did not subscribe himself apostle of the Hebrews, from reverence for the Lord, and because he was the herald and apostle of the Gentiles, and wrote the Epistle to the Hebrews in addition [to his proper work].[3]

16. FROM THE SAME.

The same work contains a passage from *The Instructor*, book i. chap. vi.[4] The passage is

that beginning, "For the blood is found to be," down to "potent charms of affection."

Portions, however, are omitted. There are a good many various readings; but although the passage in question, as found in Cramer's work, is printed in full in Migne's edition, on the alleged ground of the considerable variation from the text of Clement, the variation is not such as to make a translation of the passage as found in Cramer of any special interest or value.

We have noted the following readings:—

γίνεται, where, the verb being omitted, we have inserted *is:* There is an obstruction, etc.

σύριγγας, tubes, instead of σήραγγας (hollows), hollows of the breasts.

γειτνιαζουσῶν, for γειτνιουσῶν, neighbouring (arteries).

ἐπιλήψει, for ἐμπεριλήψει, interruption (such as this).

ἀποκλήρωσις occurs as in the text, for which the emendation ἀπολήρησις, as specified in the note, has been adopted.

ἥτις ἐστί, omitted here, which is "sweet through grace," is supplied.

P. 142.

γάλα, milk, instead of μάννα, manna, (that food) manna.

P. 149.

χρὴ δὲ κατανοῆσαι τὴν φύσιν (but it is necessary to consider nature), for οὐ κατανενοηκότες, τ. φ., through want of consideration of nature.

κατακλειομένη, agreeing with food, for κατακλειομένῳ, agreeing with heat (enclosed within).

γίνεται for γὰρ (which is untranslated), (the blood) is (a preparation) for milk.

P. 144.

τοίνυν τὸν λόγον is supplied, and εἰκότως omitted in the clause, Paul using appropriate figurative language.

P. 145.

πλὴν is supplied before ἀλλὰ τὸ ἐν αὐτῇ, and the blood in it, etc., is omitted.

P. 146.

"For Diogenes Apolloniates will have it" is omitted.

πάντῃ, rendered "in all respects," is connected with the preceding sentence.

P. 147.

ὅτι τοίνυν, for Ὡς δ'. And that (milk is produced).

τηνικαῦτα for τηνικάδε in the clause, "and the

---

[1] We omit ὅτι, which the text has after δείξῃ, which seems to indicate the omission of a clause, but as it stands is superfluous. The Latin translator retains it; and according to his rendering, the translation would be, "showed that He ceased."

[2] This extract, down to "are we," has already been given among the extracts from the *Hypotyposes*, p. 578.

[3] This extract, almost verbatim, has been already given from Eusebius, among the extracts from the *Hypotyposes*, p. 579.

[4] See p. 219, and the argument following, *supra*.

grass and meadows are juicy and moist," not translated.

προειρημένῳ, above mentioned (milk), omitted.

τρυφῆς for τροφῆς, (sweet) nutriment.

τῷ omitted before γλυκεῖ, sweet (wine), and καθάπερ, "as, when suffering."

τὸ λιπαρόν for τῷ λιπαρῷ, and ἀριδήλως for ἀριδήλου, in the sentence: "Further, many use the fat of milk, called butter, for the lamp, plainly," etc.

N. B.

[Le Nourry decides that the *Adumbrations* were not translated from the *Hypotyposes*, but Kaye (p. 473) thinks on insufficient grounds. See, also (p. 5), Kaye's learned note.]

CLEMENS ALEXANDRINUS

ON THE

SALVATION OF THE RICH MAN.

[TRANSLATED BY REV. WILLIAM WILSON, M.A.]

WHO IS THE RICH MAN THAT SHALL BE SAVED?

I. THOSE who bestow laudatory addresses on the rich [1] appear to me to be rightly judged not only flatterers and base, in vehemently pretending that things which are disagreeable give them pleasure, but also godless and treacherous; godless, because neglecting to praise and glorify God, who is alone perfect and good, "of whom are all things, and by whom are all things, and for whom are all things," [2] they invest [3] with divine honours men wallowing in an execrable and abominable life, and, what is the principal thing, liable on this account to the judgment of God; and treacherous, because, although wealth is of itself sufficient to puff up and corrupt the souls of its possessors, and to turn them from the path by which salvation is to be attained, they stupefy them still more, by inflating the minds of the rich with the pleasures of extravagant praises, and by making them utterly despise all things except wealth, on account of which they are admired; bringing, as the saying is, fire to fire, pouring pride on pride, and adding conceit to wealth, a heavier burden to that which by nature is a weight, from which somewhat ought rather to be removed and taken away as being a dangerous and deadly disease. For to him who exalts and magnifies himself, the change and downfall to a low condition succeeds in turn, as the divine word teaches. For it appears to me to be far kinder, than basely to flatter the rich and praise them for what is bad, to aid them in working out their salvation in every possible way; asking this of God, who surely and sweetly bestows such things on His own children; and thus by the grace of the Saviour healing their souls, enlightening them and leading them to the attainment of the truth; and whosoever obtains this and distinguishes himself in good works shall gain the prize of everlasting life. Now prayer that runs its course till the last day of life needs a strong and tranquil soul; and the conduct of life needs a good and righteous disposition, reaching out towards all the commandments of the Saviour.

II. Perhaps the reason of salvation appearing more difficult to the rich than to poor men, is not single but manifold. For some, merely hearing, and that in an off-hand way, the utterance of the Saviour, "that it is easier for a camel to go through the eye of a needle than for a rich man to enter into the kingdom of heaven," [4] despair of themselves as not destined to live, surrender all to the world, cling to the present life as if it alone was left to them, and so diverge more from the way to the life to come, no longer inquiring either whom the Lord and Master calls rich, or how that which is impossible to man becomes possible to God. But others rightly and adequately comprehend this, but attaching slight importance to the works which tend to salvation, do not make the requisite preparation for attaining to the objects of their hope. And I affirm both of these things of the rich who have learned both the Saviour's power and His glorious salvation. With those who are ignorant of the truth I have little concern.

III. Those then who are actuated by a love of the truth and love of their brethren, and neither are rudely insolent towards such rich as are called, nor, on the other hand, cringe to them for their own avaricious ends, must first by the word relieve them of their groundless despair, and show with the requisite explanation of the oracles of the Lord that the inheritance of the kingdom of heaven is not quite cut off from them if they obey the commandments; then admonish them that they entertain a causeless fear, and that the Lord gladly receives them, provided they are willing; and then, in addition, exhibit and teach how and by what deeds and disposi-

---

[1] [The solemn words of our Lord about the perils of wealth and "the deceitfulness of riches" are much insisted on by Hermas, especially in the beautiful opening of the *Similitudes* (book iii.); and it seems remarkable, that, even in the age of martyrs and confessors, such warnings should have seemed needful. Clement is deeply impressed with the duty of enforcing such doctrine; and perhaps the germ of this very interesting essay is to be found in that eloquent passage in his *Stromata* (book ii. cap. 5, pp. 351, 352), to which the reader may do well to recur, using it as a preface to the following pages. Elucidation I.]

[2] Rom. xi. 36.

[3] This clause is defective in the MS., and is translated as supplemented by Fell from conjecture.

[4] Matt. xix. 24.

tions they shall win the objects of hope, inasmuch as it is neither out of their reach, nor, on the other hand, attained without effort; but, as is the case with athletes — to compare things small and perishing with things great and immortal — let the man who is endowed with worldly wealth reckon that this depends on himself. For among those, one man, because he despaired of being able to conquer and gain crowns, did not give in his name for the contest; while another, whose mind was inspired with this hope, and yet did not submit to the appropriate labours, and diet, and exercises, remained uncrowned, and was balked in his expectations. So also let not the man that has been invested with worldly wealth proclaim himself excluded at the outset from the Saviour's lists, provided he is a believer and one who contemplates the greatness of God's philanthropy; nor let him, on the other hand, expect to grasp the crowns of immortality without struggle and effort, continuing untrained, and without contest. But let him go and put himself under the Word as his trainer, and Christ the President of the contest; and for his prescribed food and drink let him have the New Testament of the Lord; and for exercises, the command-ments; and for elegance and ornament, the fair dispositions, love, faith, hope, knowledge of the truth, gentleness, meekness, pity, gravity: so that, when by the last trumpet the signal shall be given for the race and departure hence, as from the stadium of life, he may with a good conscience present himself victorious before the Judge who confers the rewards, confessedly worthy of the Fatherland on high, to which he returns with crowns and the acclamations of angels.

IV. May the Saviour then grant to us that, having begun the subject from this point, we may contribute to the brethren what is true, and suitable, and saving, first touching the hope itself, and, second, touching the access to the hope. He indeed grants to those who beg, and teaches those who ask, and dissipate signorance and dis-pels despair, by introducing again the same words about the rich, which become their own inter-preters and infallible expounders. For there is nothing like listening again to the very same statements, which till now in the Gospels were distressing you, hearing them as you did without examination, and erroneously through puerility: "And going forth into the way, one approached and kneeled, saying, Good Master, what good thing shall I do that I may inherit everlasting life? And Jesus saith, Why callest thou Me good? There is none good but one, *that is,* God. Thou knowest the commandments. Do not commit adultery, Do not kill, Do not steal, Do not bear false witness, Defraud not, Honour thy father and thy mother. And he answering

saith to Him, All these have I observed. And Jesus, looking upon him, loved him, and said, One thing thou lackest. If thou wouldest be perfect, sell what thou hast and give to the poor, and thou shalt have treasure in heaven: and come, follow Me. And he was sad at that say-ing, and went away grieved: for he was rich, having great possessions. And Jesus looked round about, and saith to His disciples, How hardly shall they that have riches enter into the kingdom of God! And the disciples were as-tonished at His words. But Jesus answereth again, and saith unto them, Children, how hard is it for them that trust in riches to enter into the kingdom of God! More easily shall a camel enter through the eye of a needle than a rich man into the kingdom of God. And they were astonished out of measure, and said, Who then can be saved? And He, looking upon them, said, What is impossible with men is possible with God. For with God all things are possible. Peter began to say to Him, Lo, we have left all and followed Thee. And Jesus answered and said, Verily I say unto you, Whosoever shall leave what is his own, parents, and brethren, and possessions, for My sake and the Gospel's, shall receive an hundred-fold now in this world, lands, and possessions, and house, and brethren, with persecutions; and in the world to come is life everlasting. But many that are first shall be last, and the last first."[1]

V. These things are written in the Gospel ac-cording to Mark; and in all the rest correspond-ingly; although perchance the expressions vary slightly in each, yet all show identical agreement in meaning.

But well knowing that the Saviour teaches nothing in a merely human way, but teaches all things to His own with divine and mystic wis-dom, we must not listen to His utterances carnally; but with due investigation and intelli-gence must search out and learn the meaning hidden in them. For even those things which seem to have been simplified to the disciples by the Lord Himself are found to require not less, even more, attention than what is expressed enigmatically, from the surpassing superabun-dance of wisdom in them. And whereas the things which are thought to have been explained by Him to those within — those called by Him the children of the kingdom — require still more consideration than the things which seemed to have been expressed simply, and respecting which therefore no questions were asked by those who heard them, but which, pertaining to the entire design of salvation, and to be contem-plated with admirable and supercelestial depth of mind, we must not receive superficially with

---

[1] Mark x. 17-31. Clement does not give always Mark's *ipsissi-ma verba.*

our ears, but with application of the mind to the very spirit of the Saviour, and the unuttered meaning of the declaration.

VI. For our Lord and Saviour was asked pleasantly a question most appropriate for Him, — the Life respecting life, the Saviour respecting salvation, the Teacher respecting the chief doctrines taught, the Truth respecting the true immortality, the Word respecting the word of the Father, the Perfect respecting the perfect rest, the Immortal respecting the sure immortality. He was asked respecting those things on account of which He descended, which He inculcates, which He teaches, which He offers, in order to show the essence of the Gospel, that it is the gift of eternal life. For He foresaw as God, both what He would be asked, and what each one would answer Him. For who should do this more than the Prophet of prophets, and the Lord of every prophetic spirit? And having been called "good," and taking the starting note from this first expression, He commences His teaching with this, turning the pupil to God, the good, and first and only dispenser of eternal life, which the Son, who received it of Him, gives to us.

VII. Wherefore the greatest and chiefest point of the instructions which relate to life must be implanted in the soul from the beginning, — to know the eternal God, the giver of what is eternal, and by knowledge and comprehension to possess God, who is first, and highest, and one, and good. For this is the immutable and immoveable source and support of life, the knowledge of God, who really is, and who bestows the things which really are, that is, those which are eternal, from whom both being and the continuance [1] of it are derived to other beings. For ignorance of Him is death ; but the knowledge and appropriation of Him, and love and likeness to Him, are the only life.

VIII. He then who would live the true life is enjoined first to know Him "whom no one knows, except the Son reveal (Him)." [2] Next is to be learned the greatness of the Saviour after Him, and the newness of grace ; for, according to the apostle, "the law was given by Moses, grace and truth came by Jesus Christ ; " [3] and the gifts granted through a faithful servant are not equal to those bestowed by the true Son. If then the law of Moses had been sufficient to confer eternal life, it were to no purpose for the Saviour Himself to come and suffer for us, accomplishing the course of human life from His birth to His cross ; and to no purpose for him who had done all the commandments of the law from his youth to fall on his knees and beg from

another immortality. For he had not only fulfilled the law, but had begun to do so from his very earliest youth. For what is there great or pre-eminently illustrious in an old age which is unproductive of faults? But if one in juvenile frolicsomeness and the fire of youth shows a mature judgment older than his years, this is a champion admirable and distinguished, and hoary pre-eminently in mind.

But, nevertheless, this man being such, is perfectly persuaded that nothing is wanting to him as far as respects righteousness, but that he is entirely destitute of life. Wherefore he asks it from Him who alone is able to give it. And with reference to the law, he carries confidence ; but the Son of God he addresses in supplication. He is transferred from faith to faith. As perilously tossing and occupying a dangerous anchorage in the law, he makes for the Saviour to find a haven.

IX. Jesus, accordingly, does not charge him with not having fulfilled all things out of the law, but loves him, and fondly welcomes his obedience in what he had learned ; but says that he is not perfect as respects eternal life, inasmuch as he had not fulfilled what is perfect, and that he is a doer indeed of the law, but idle at the true life. Those things, indeed, are good. Who denies it? For "the commandment is holy," [4] as far as a sort of training with fear and preparatory discipline goes, leading as it did to the culmination of legislation and to grace. [5] But Christ is the fulfilment "of the law for righteousness to every one that believeth ; " and not as a slave making slaves, but sons, and brethren, and fellow-heirs, who perform the Father's will.

X. "If thou wilt be perfect." [6] Consequently he was not yet perfect. For nothing is more perfect than what is pefect. And divinely the expression " if thou wilt " showed the self-determination of the soul holding converse with Him. For choice depended on the man as being free ; but the gift on God as the Lord. And He gives to those who are willing and are exceedingly earnest, and ask, that so their salvation may become their own. For God compels not (for compulsion is repugnant to God), but supplies to those who seek, and bestows on those who ask, and opens to those who knock. If thou wilt, then, if thou really willest, and art not deceiving thyself, acquire what thou lackest. One thing is lacking thee, — the one thing which abides, the good, that which is now above the law, which the law gives not, which the law contains not, which is the prerogative of those who live. He forsooth who had fulfilled all the demands of the

---

[1] Instead of μείναι Fell here suggests μὴ εἶναι, non-being.
[2] Matt. xi. 27.
[3] John i. 17.

[4] Rom. vii. 12.
[5] Gal. iii. 24.
[6] Matt. xix. 21.

law from his youth, and had gloried in what was magnificent, was not able to complete the whole [1] with this one thing which was specially required by the Saviour, so as to receive the eternal life which he desired. But he departed displeased, vexed at the commandment of the life, on account of which he supplicated. For he did not truly wish life, as he averred, but aimed at the mere reputation of the good choice. And he was capable of busying himself about many things; but the one thing, the work of life, he was powerless, and disinclined, and unable to accomplish. Such also was what the Lord said to Martha, who was occupied with many things, and distracted and troubled with serving; while she blamed her sister, because, leaving serving, she set herself at His feet, devoting her time to learning: "Thou art troubled about many things, but Mary hath chosen the good part, which shall not be taken away from her." [2] So also He bade him leave his busy life, and cleave to One and adhere to the grace of Him who offered everlasting life.

XI. What then was it which persuaded him to flight, and made him depart from the Master, from the entreaty, the hope, the life, previously pursued with ardour? — "Sell thy possessions." And what is this? He does not, as some conceive off-hand, bid him throw away the substance he possessed, and abandon his property; but bids him banish from his soul his notions about wealth, his excitement and morbid feeling about it, the anxieties, which are the thorns of existence, which choke the seed of life. For it is no great thing or desirable to be destitute of wealth, if without a special object, — not except on account of life. For thus those who have nothing at all, but are destitute, and beggars for their daily bread, the poor dispersed on the streets, who know not God and God's righteousness, simply on account of their extreme want and destitution of subsistence, and lack even of the smallest things, were most blessed and most dear to God, and sole possessors of everlasting life.

Nor was the renunciation of wealth and the bestowment of it on the poor or needy a new thing; for many did so before the Saviour's advent, — some because of the leisure (thereby obtained) for learning, and on account of a dead wisdom; and others for empty fame and vainglory, as the Anaxagorases, the Democriti, and the Crateses.

XII. Why then command as new, as divine, as alone life-giving, what did not save those of former days? And what peculiar thing is it

that the new creature [3] the Son of God intimates and teaches? It is not the outward act which others have done, but something else indicated by it, greater, more godlike, more perfect, the stripping off of the passions from the soul itself and from the disposition, and the cutting up by the roots and casting out of what is alien to the mind. For this is the lesson peculiar to the believer, and the instruction worthy of the Saviour. For those who formerly despised external things relinquished and squandered their property, but the passions of the soul, I believe, they intensified. For they indulged in arrogance, pretension, and vainglory, and in contempt of the rest of mankind, as if they had done something superhuman. How then would the Saviour have enjoined on those destined to live for ever what was injurious and hurtful with reference to the life which He promised? For although such is the case, one, after ridding himself of the burden of wealth, may none the less have still the lust and desire for money innate and living; and may have abandoned the use of it, but being at once destitute of and desiring what he spent, may doubly grieve both on account of the absence of attendance, and the presence of regret. For it is impossible and inconceivable that those in want of the necessaries of life should not be harassed in mind, and hindered from better things in the endeavour to provide them somehow, and from some source.

XIII. And how much more beneficial the opposite case, for a man, through possessing a competency, both not himself to be in straits about money, and also to give assistance to those to whom it is requisite so to do! For if no one had anything, what room would be left among men for giving? And how can this dogma fail to be found plainly opposed to and conflicting with many other excellent teachings of the Lord? "Make to yourselves friends of the mammon of unrighteousness, that when ye fail, they may receive you into the everlasting habitations." [4] "Acquire treasures in heaven, where neither moth nor rust destroys, nor thieves break through." [5] How could one give food to the hungry, and drink to the thirsty, clothe the naked, and shelter the houseless, for not doing which He threatens with fire and the outer darkness, if each man first divested himself of all these things? Nay, He bids Zaccheus and Matthew, the rich tax-gathers, entertain Him hospitably. And He does not bid them part

---

[1] The reading of the MS. is πραθῆναι, which is corrupt. We have changed it into περιθεῖναι. Various other emendations have been proposed. Perhaps it should be προσθεῖναι, "to add."
[2] Luke x. 41, 42.

[3] The application of the words ἡ καινὴ κτίσις to Christ has been much discussed. Segaar has a long note on it, the purport of which he thus sums up: ἡ καινὴ κτίσις is a creature to whom nothing has ever existed on earth equal or like. man but also God, through whom is true light and everlasting life. [The translator has largely availed himself of the valuable edition and notes of Charles Segaar (ed. Utrecht, 1816), concerning whom see Elucidation II.]
[4] Luke xvi. 9.
[5] Matt. vi. 19.

with their property, but, applying the just and removing the unjust judgment, He subjoins, "To-day salvation has come to this house, forasmuch as he also is a son of Abraham."[1] He so praises the use of property as to enjoin, along with this addition, the giving a share of it, to give drink to the thirsty, bread to the hungry, to take the houseless in, and clothe the naked. But if it is not possible to supply those needs without substance, and He bids people abandon their substance, what else would the Lord be doing than exhorting to give and not to give the same things, to feed and not to feed, to take in and to shut out, to share and not to share? which were the most irrational of all things.

XIV. Riches, then, which benefit also our neighbours, are not to be thrown away. For they are possessions, inasmuch as they are possessed, and goods, inasmuch as they are useful and provided by God for the use of men; and they lie to our hand, and are put under our power, as material and instruments which are for good use to those who know the instrument. If you use it skilfully, it is skilful; if you are deficient in skill, it is affected by your want of skill, being itself destitute of blame. Such an instrument is wealth. Are you able to make a right use of it? It is subservient to righteousness. Does one make a wrong use of it? It is, on the other hand, a minister of wrong. For its nature is to be subservient, not to rule. That then which of itself has neither good nor evil, being blameless, ought not to be blamed; but that which has the power of using it well and ill, by reason of its possessing voluntary choice. And this is the mind and judgment of man, which has freedom in itself and self-determination in the treatment of what is assigned to it. So let no man destroy wealth, rather than the passions of the soul, which are incompatible with the better use of wealth. So that, becoming virtuous and good, he may be able to make a good use of these riches. The renunciation, then, and selling of all possessions, is to be understood as spoken of the passions of the soul.

XV. I would then say this. Since some things are within and some without the soul, and if the soul make a good use of them, they also are reputed good, but if a bad, bad;— whether does He who commands us to alienate our possessions repudiate those things, after the removal of which the passions still remain, or those rather, on the removal of which wealth even becomes beneficial? If therefore he who casts away worldly wealth can still be rich in the passions, even though the material [for their gratification] is absent,— for the disposition produces its own effects, and strangles the reason, and presses it down and inflames it with its inbred lusts,— it is then of no advantage to him to be poor in purse while he is rich in passions. For it is not what ought to be cast away that he has cast away, but what is indifferent; and he has deprived himself of what is serviceable, but set on fire the innate fuel of evil through want of the external means [of gratification]. We must therefore renounce those possessions that are injurious, not those that are capable of being serviceable, if one knows the right use of them. And what is managed with wisdom, and sobriety, and piety, is profitable; and what is hurtful must be cast away. But things external hurt not. So then the Lord introduces the use of external things, bidding us put away not the means of subsistence, but what uses them badly. And these are the infirmities and passions of the soul.

XVI. The presence of wealth in these is deadly to all, the loss of it salutary. Of which, making the soul pure,— that is, poor and bare,— we must hear the Saviour speaking thus, "Come, follow Me." For to the pure in heart He now becomes the way. But into the impure soul the grace of God finds no entrance. And that (soul) is unclean which is rich in lusts, and is in the throes of many worldly affections. For he who holds possessions, and gold, and silver, and houses, as the gifts of God; and ministers from them to the God who gives them for the salvation of men; and knows that he possesses them more for the sake of the brethren than his own; and is superior to the possession of them, not the slave of the things he possesses; and does not carry them about in his soul, nor bind and circumscribe his life within them, but is ever labouring at some good and divine work, even should he be necessarily some time or other deprived of them, is able with cheerful mind to bear their removal equally with their abundance. This is he who is blessed by the Lord, and called poor in spirit, a meet heir of the kingdom of heaven, not one who could not live rich.

XVII. But he who carries his riches in his soul, and instead of God's Spirit bears in his heart gold or land, and is always acquiring possessions without end, and is perpetually on the outlook for more, bending downwards and fettered in the toils of the world, being earth and destined to depart to earth,— whence can he be able to desire and to mind the kingdom of heaven,— a man who carries not a heart, but land or metal, who must perforce be found in the midst of the objects he has chosen? For where the mind of man is, there is also his treasure. The Lord acknowledges a twofold treasure, — the good: "For the good man, out of the good treasure of his heart, bringeth forth good;"

[1] Luke v. 29; xix. 9.

and the evil : for "the evil man, out of the evil treasure, bringeth forth evil : for out of the abundance of the heart the mouth speaketh." [1]   As then treasure is not one with Him, as also it is with us, that which gives the unexpected great gain in the finding, but also a second, which is profitless and undesirable, an evil acquisition, hurtful ; so also there is a richness in good things, and a richness in bad things, since we know that riches and treasure are not by nature separated from each other.   And the one sort of riches is to be possessed and acquired, and the other not to be possessed, but to be cast away.

In the same way spiritual poverty is blessed. Wherefore also Matthew added, " Blessed are the poor." [2]   How?   " In spirit."   And again, " Blessed are they that hunger and thirst after the righteousness of God." [3]   Wherefore wretched are the contrary kind of poor, who have no part in God, and still less in human property, and have not tasted of the righteousness of God.

XVIII. So that (the expression) rich men that shall with difficulty enter into the kingdom, is to be apprehended in a scholarly [4] way, not awkwardly, or rustically, or carnally.   For if the expression is used thus, salvation does not depend on external things, whether they be many or few, small or great, or illustrious or obscure, or esteemed or disesteemed ; but on the virtue of the soul, on faith, and hope, and love, and brotherliness, and knowledge, and meekness, and humility, and truth, the reward of which is salvation.   For it is not on account of comeliness of body that any one shall live, or, on the other hand, perish.   But he who uses the body given to him chastely and according to God, shall live ; and he that destroys the temple of God shall be destroyed.   An ugly man can be profligate, and a good-looking man temperate.   Neither strength and great size of body makes alive, nor does any of the members destroy.   But the soul which uses them provides the cause for each. Bear then, it is said, when struck on the face ; [5] which a man strong and in good health can obey. And again, a man who is feeble may transgress from refractoriness of temper.   So also a poor and destitute man may be found intoxicated with lusts ; and a man rich in worldly goods temperate, poor in indulgences, trustworthy, intelligent, pure, chastened.

If then it is the soul which, first and especially, is that which is to live, and if virtue springing up around it saves, and vice kills ; then it is clearly manifest that by being poor in those things, by riches of which one destroys it, it is

saved, and by being rich in those things, riches of which ruin it, it is killed.   And let us no longer seek the cause of the issue elsewhere than in the state and disposition of the soul in respect of obedience to God and purity, and in respect of transgression of the commandments and accumulation of wickedness.

XIX. He then is truly and rightly rich who is rich in virtue, and is capable of making a holy and faithful use of any fortune ; while he is spuriously rich who is rich, according to the flesh, and turns life into outward possession, which is transitory and perishing, and now belongs to one, now to another, and in the end to nobody at all.   Again, in the same way there is a genuine poor man, and another counterfeit and falsely so called. He that is poor in spirit, and that is the right thing, and he that is poor in a worldly sense, which is a different thing.   To him who is poor in worldly goods, but rich in vices, who is not poor in spirit [6] and rich toward God, it is said, Abandon the alien possessions that are in thy soul, that, becoming pure in heart, thou mayest see God ; which is another way of saying, Enter into the kingdom of heaven.   And how may you abandon them?   By selling them.   What then? Are you to take money for effects, by effecting an exchange of riches, by turning your visible substance into money?   Not at all.   But by introducing, instead of what was formerly inherent in your soul, which you desire to save, other riches which deify and which minister everlasting life, dispositions in accordance with the command of God ; for which there shall accrue to you endless reward and honour, and salvation, and everlasting immortality.   It is thus that thou dost rightly sell the possessions, many are superfluous, which shut the heavens against thee by exchanging them for those which are able to save.   Let the former be possessed by the carnal poor, who are destitute of the latter.   But thou, by receiving instead spiritual wealth, shalt have now treasure in the heavens.

XX. The wealthy and legally correct man, not understanding these things figuratively, nor how the same man can be both poor and rich, and have wealth and not have it, and use the world and not use it, went away sad and downcast, leaving the state of life, which he was able merely to desire but not to attain, making for himself the difficult impossible.   For it was difficult for the soul not to be seduced and ruined by the luxuries and flowery enchantments that beset remarkable wealth ; but it was not impossible, even surrounded with it, for one to lay hold of salvation, provided he withdrew himself from material wealth,

---

[1] Matt. xii. 34, 35.
[2] Matt. v. 3.
[3] Matt. v. 6.
[4] μαθηματικῶς.   Fell suggests instead of this reading of the text, πνευματικῶς or μεμελημένως.
[5] Matt. v. 39.

[6] ὁ κατὰ πνεῦμα οὐ πτωχὸς . . . φησί. Segaar omits οὐ, and so makes ὁ κατὰ πνεῦμα, κ.τ.λ. the nominative to φησί.   It seems better, with the Latin translator, to render as above, which supposes the change of ὁ into ὅς.

— to that which is grasped by the mind and taught by God, and learned to use things indifferent rightly and properly, and so as to strive after eternal life. And the disciples even themselves were at first alarmed and amazed. Why were they so on hearing this? Was it that they themselves possessed much wealth? Nay, they had long ago left their very nets, and hooks, and rowing boats, which were their sole possessions. Why then do they say in consternation, "Who can be saved?" They had heard well and like disciples what was spoken in parable and obscurely by the Lord, and perceived the depth of the words. For they were sanguine of salvation on the ground of their want of wealth. But when they became conscious of not having yet wholly renounced the passions (for they were neophytes and recently selected by the Saviour), they were excessively astonished, and despaired of themselves no less than that rich man who clung so terribly to the wealth which he preferred to eternal life. It was therefore a fit subject for all fear on the disciples' part; if both he that possesses wealth and he that is teeming with passions were the rich, and these alike shall be expelled from the heavens. For salvation is the privilege of pure and passionless souls.

XXI. But the Lord replies, "Because what is impossible with men is possible with God." This again is full of great wisdom. For a man by himself working and toiling at freedom from passion achieves nothing. But if he plainly shows himself very desirous and earnest about this, he attains it by the addition of the power of God. For God conspires with willing souls. But if they abandon their eagerness, the spirit which is bestowed by God is also restrained. For to save the unwilling is the part of one exercising compulsion; but to save the willing, that of one showing grace. Nor does the kingdom of heaven belong to sleepers and sluggards, "but the violent take it by force."[1] For this alone is commendable violence, to force God, and take life from God by force. And He, knowing those who persevere firmly, or rather violently, yields and grants. For God delights in being vanquished in such things.

Therefore on hearing those words, the blessed Peter, the chosen, the pre-eminent, the first of the disciples, for whom alone and Himself the Saviour paid tribute,[2] quickly seized and comprehended the saying. And what does he say? "Lo, we have left all and followed Thee." Now if by all he means his own property, he boasts of leaving four oboli perhaps in all,[3] and forgets to show the kingdom of heaven to be their recompense. But if, casting away what we were now

speaking of, the old mental possessions and soul diseases, they follow in the Master's footsteps, this now joins them to those who are to be enrolled in the heavens. For it is thus that one truly follows the Saviour, by aiming at sinlessness and at His perfection, and adorning and composing the soul before it as a mirror, and arranging everything in all respects similarly.

XXII. "And Jesus answering said, Verily I say unto you, Whosoever shall leave what is his own, parents, and children, and wealth, for My sake and the Gospel's, shall receive an hundredfold."[4] But let neither this trouble you, nor the still harder saying delivered in another place in the words, "Whoso hateth not father, and mother, and children, and his own life besides, cannot be My disciple."[5] For the God of peace, who also exhorts to love enemies, does not introduce hatred and dissolution from those that are dearest. But if we are to love our enemies, it is in accordance with right reason that, ascending from them, we should love also those nearest in kindred. Or if we are to hate our blood-relations, deduction teaches us that much more are we to spurn from us our enemies. So that the reasonings would be shown to destroy one another. But they do not destroy each other, nor are they near doing so. For from the same feeling and disposition, and on the ground of the same rule, one loving his enemy may hate his father, inasmuch as he neither takes vengeance on an enemy, nor reverences a father more than Christ. For by the one word he extirpates hatred and injury, and by the other shamefacedness towards one's relations, if it is detrimental to salvation. If then one's father, or son, or brother, be godless, and become a hindrance to faith and an impediment to the higher life, let him not be friends or agree with him, but on account of the spiritual enmity, let him dissolve the fleshly relationship.

XXIII. Suppose the matter to be a law-suit. Let your father be imagined to present himself to you and say, "I begot and reared thee. Follow me, and join with me in wickedness, and obey not the law of Christ;" and whatever a man who is a blasphemer and dead by nature would say.

But on the other side hear the Saviour: "I regenerated thee, who wert ill born by the world to death. I emancipated, healed, ransomed thee. I will show thee the face of the good Father God. Call no man thy father on earth. Let the dead bury the dead; but follow thou Me. For I will bring thee to a rest[6] of ineffable and unutterable blessings, which eye hath not seen, nor ear heard, nor have entered into the

---

[1] Matt. xi. 12. [Elucidation III.]
[2] Matt. xvii. 27.
[3] The text is the reading on the margin of the first edition. The reading of the MS., τοῦ λόγου, is amended by Segaar into τὸ τοῦ λόγου, "as the saying is."

[4] Mark x. 29, 30, [quoted inexactly. S.]
[5] Luke xiv. 26.
[6] Segaar amends ἀνάπαυσιν to ἀπόλαυσιν "enjoyment."

heart of men; into which angels desire to look, and see what good things God hath prepared for the saints and the children who love Him." [1] I am He who feeds thee, giving Myself as bread, of which he who has tasted experiences death no more, and supplying day by day the drink of immortality. I am teacher of supercelestial lessons. For thee I contended with Death, and paid thy death, which thou owedst for thy former sins and thy unbelief towards God."

Having heard these considerations on both sides, decide for thyself and give thy vote for thine own salvation. Should a brother say the like, should a child, should a wife, should any one whosoever, in preference to all let Christ in thee be conqueror. For He contends in thy behalf.

XXIV. You may even go against wealth. Say, "Certainly Christ does not debar me from property. The Lord does not envy." But do you see yourself overcome and overthrown by it? Leave it, throw it away, hate, renounce, flee. "Even if thy right eye offend thee," quickly "cut it out." [2] Better is the kingdom of God to a man with one eye, than the fire to one who is unmutilated. Whether hand, or foot, or soul, hate it. For if it is destroyed here for Christ's sake, it will be restored to life yonder.

XXV. And to this effect similarly is what follows. "Now at this present time not to have lands, and money, and houses, and brethren, with persecutions." For it is neither penniless, nor homeless, nor brotherless people that the Lord calls to life, since He has also called rich people; but, as we have said above, also brothers, as Peter with Andrew, and James with John the sons of Zebedee, but of one mind with each other and Christ. And the expression "with persecutions" rejects the possessing of each of those things. There is a persecution which arises from without, from men assailing the faithful, either out of hatred, or envy, or avarice, or through diabolic agency. But the most painful is internal persecution, which proceeds from each man's own soul being vexed by impious lusts, and diverse pleasures, and base hopes, and destructive dreams; when, always grasping at more, and maddened by brutish loves, and inflamed by the passions which beset it like goads and stings, it is covered with blood, (to drive it on) to insane pursuits, and to despair of life, and to contempt of God.

More grievous and painful is this persecution, which arises from within, which is ever with a man, and which the persecuted cannot escape; for he carries the enemy about everywhere in himself. Thus also burning which attacks from without works trial, but that from within produces death. War also made on one is easily put an end to, but that which is in the soul continues till death.

With such persecution, if you have worldly wealth, if you have brothers allied by blood and other pledges, abandon the whole wealth of these which leads to evil; procure peace for yourself, free yourself from protracted persecutions; turn from them to the Gospel; choose before all the Saviour and Advocate and Paraclete of your soul, the Prince of life. "For the things which are seen are temporary; but the things which are not seen are eternal." [3] And in the present time are things evanescent and insecure, but in that to come is eternal life.

XXVI. "The first shall be last, and the last first." [4] This is fruitful in meaning and exposition, [5] but does not demand investigation at present; for it refers not only to the wealthy alone, but plainly to all men, who have once surrendered themselves to faith. So let this stand aside for the present. But I think that our proposition has been demonstrated in no way inferior to what we promised, that the Saviour by no means has excluded the rich on account of wealth itself, and the possession of property, nor fenced off salvation against them; if they are able and willing to submit their life to God's commandments, and prefer them to transitory objects, and if they would look to the Lord with steady eye, as those who look for the nod of a good helmsman, what he wishes, what he orders, what he indicates, what signal he gives his mariners, where and whence he directs the ship's course. For what harm does one do, who, previous to faith, by applying his mind and by saving has collected a competency? Or what is much less reprehensible than this, if at once by God, who gave him his life, he has had his home given him in the house of such men, among wealthy people, powerful in substance, and pre-eminent in opulence? For if, in consequence of his involuntary birth in wealth, a man is banished from life, rather is he wronged by God, who created him, in having vouchsafed to him temporary enjoyment, and in being deprived of eternal life. And why should wealth have ever sprung from the earth at all, if it is the author and patron of death?

But if one is able in the midst of wealth to turn from its power, and to entertain moderate sentiments, and to exercise self-command, and to seek God alone, and to breathe God and walk with God, such a poor man submits to the commandments, being free, unsubdued, free of disease, unwounded by wealth. But if not, "sooner

---

[1] 1 Cor. ii. 9; 1 Pet. i. 12.
[2] Matt. v. 9.

[3] 2 Cor. iv. 18.
[4] Mark x. 31.
[5] σαφηνισμόν, here adopted instead of the reading σοφισμόν, which yields no suitable sense.

shall a camel enter through a needle's eye, than such a rich man reach the kingdom of God." [1]

Let then the camel, going through a narrow and strait way before the rich man, signify something loftier; which mystery of the Saviour is to be learned in the "Exposition of first Principles and of Theology." [2]

XXVII. Well, first let the point of the parable, which is evident, and the reason why it is spoken, be presented. Let it teach the prosperous that they are not to neglect their own salvation, as if they had been already fore-doomed, nor, on the other hand, to cast wealth into the sea, or condemn it as a traitor and an enemy to life, but learn in what way and how to use wealth and obtain life. For since neither does one perish by any means by fearing because he is rich, nor is by any means saved by trusting and believing that he shall be saved, come let them look what hope the Saviour assigns them, and how what is unexpected may become ratified, and what is hoped for may come into possession.

The Master accordingly, when asked, "Which is the greatest of the commandments?" says, "Thou shalt love the Lord thy God with all thy soul, and with all thy strength;" [3] that no commandment is greater than this (He says), and with exceeding good reason; for it gives command respecting the First and the Greatest, God Himself, our Father, by whom all things were brought into being, and exist, and to whom what is saved returns again. By Him, then, being loved beforehand, and having received existence, it is impious for us to regard ought else older or more excellent; rendering only this small tribute of gratitude for the greatest benefits; and being unable to imagine anything else whatever by way of recompense to God, who needs nothing and is perfect; and gaining immortality by the very exercise of loving the Father to the extent of one's might and power. For the more one loves God, the more he enters within God.

XXVIII. The second in order, and not any less than this, He says, is, "Thou shalt love thy neighbour as thyself," [4] consequently God above thyself. And on His interlocutor inquiring, "Who is my neighbour?" [5] He did not, in the same way with the Jews, specify the blood-relation, or the fellow-citizen, or the proselyte, or him that had been similarly circumcised, or the man who uses one and the same law. But He introduces one on his way down from the upland region from Jerusalem to Jericho, and represents him stabbed by robbers, cast half-dead on the way, passed by by the priest, looked sideways at by the Levite, but pitied by the vilified and excommunicated Samaritan; who did not, like those, pass casually, but came provided with such things as the man in danger required, such as oil, bandages, a beast of burden, money for the inn-keeper, part given now, and part promised. "Which," said He, "of them was neighbour to him that suffered these things?" and on his answering, "He that showed mercy to him," (replied), [6] Go thou also, therefore, and do likewise, since love buds into well-doing.

XXIX. In both the commandments, then, He introduces love; but in order distinguishes it. And in the one He assigns to God the first part of love, and allots the second to our neighbour. Who else can it be but the Saviour Himself? or who more than He has pitied us, who by the rulers of darkness were all but put to death with many wounds, fears, lusts, passions, pains, deceits, pleasures? Of these wounds the only physician is Jesus, who cuts out the passions thoroughly by the root, — not as the law does the bare effects, the fruits of evil plants, but applies His axe to the roots of wickedness. He it is that poured wine on our wounded souls (the blood of David's vine), that brought the oil which flows from the compassions of the Father,[7] and bestowed it copiously. He it is that produced the ligatures of health and of salvation that cannot be undone, — Love, Faith, Hope. He it is that subjected angels, and principalities, and powers, for a great reward to serve us. For they also shall be delivered from the vanity of the world through the revelation of the glory of the sons of God. We are therefore to love Him equally with God. And he loves Christ Jesus who does His will and keeps His commandments. "For not every one that saith unto Me, Lord, Lord, shall enter into the kingdom of heaven; but he that doeth the will of My Father." [8] And "Why call ye Me Lord, Lord, and do not the things which I say?" [9] "And blessed are ye who see and hear what neither righteous men nor prophets" (have seen or heard), [10] if ye do what I say.

XXX. He then is first who loves Christ; and second, he who loves and cares for those who have believed on Him. For whatever is done to a disciple, the Lord accepts as done to Himself, and reckons the whole as His. "Come, ye blessed of My Father, inherit the kingdom prepared for you from the foundation of the world. For I was an hungered, and ye gave Me to eat: I was thirsty, and ye gave Me to drink: and I was a stranger, and ye took Me in: I was naked and ye clothed Me: I was sick, and

[1] Mark x. 25.
[2] A work mentioned elsewhere.
[3] Matt. xxii. 36–38.
[4] Matt. xxii. 39.
[5] Luke x. 29.
[6] Luke x. 36, 37.
[7] Combefisius reads "Spirit."
[8] Matt. vii. 21.
[9] Luke vi. 46.
[10] Matt. xiii. 16, 17.

ye visited Me : I was in prison, and ye came to Me. Then shall the righteous answer, saying, Lord, when saw we Thee hungry, and fed Thee? or thirsty, and gave Thee drink? And when saw we Thee a stranger, and took Thee in? or naked, and clothed Thee? Or when saw we Thee sick, and visited Thee? or in prison, and came to Thee? And the King answering, shall say to them, Verily I say unto you, inasmuch as ye have done it unto one of the least of these My brethren, ye have done it unto Me."

Again, on the opposite side, to those who have not performed these things, " Verily I say unto you, inasmuch as ye have not done it unto one of the least of these, ye have not done it to Me." [1] And in another place, " He that receiveth you, receiveth Me ; and he that receiveth not you, rejecteth Me." [2]

XXXI. Such He names children, and sons, and little children, and friends, and little ones here, in reference to their future greatness above. " Despise not," He says, " one of these little ones ; for their angels always behold the face of My Father in heaven." [3] And in another place, " Fear not, little flock, for it is your Father's good pleasure to give you the kingdom of heaven." [4] Similarly also He says that " the least in the kingdom of heaven " that is His own disciple " is greater than John, the greatest among those born of women." [5] And again, " He that receiveth a righteous man or a prophet in the name of a righteous man or a prophet, shall receive their reward ; and he that giveth to a disciple in the name of a disciple a cup of cold water to drink, shall not lose his reward." [6] Wherefore this is the only reward that is not lost. And again, " Make to you friends of the mammon of unrighteousness, that, when ye fail, they may receive you into everlasting habitations ; " [7] showing that by nature all property which a man possesses in his own power is not his own. And from this unrighteousness it is permitted to work a righteous and saving thing, to refresh some one of those who have an everlasting habitation with the Father.

See then, first, that He has not commanded you to be solicited or to wait to be importuned, but yourself to seek those who are to be benefited and are worthy disciples of the Saviour. Excellent, accordingly, also is the apostle's saying, " For the Lord loveth a cheerful giver ; " [8] who delights in giving, and spares not, sowing so that he may also thus reap, without murmuring, and disputing, and regret, and communicat-

ing, which is pure [9] beneficence. But better than this is the saying spoken by the Lord in another place, " Give to every one that asketh thee." [10] For truly such is God's delight in giving. And this saying is above all divinity, [11] — not to wait to be asked, but to inquire oneself who deserves to receive kindness.

XXXII. Then to appoint such a reward for liberality, — an everlasting habitation ! O excellent trading ! O divine merchandise ! One purchases immortality for money ; and, by giving the perishing things of the world, receives in exchange for these an eternal mansion in the heavens ! Sail to this mart, if you are wise, O rich man ! If need be, sail round the whole world. [12] Spare not perils and toils, that you may purchase here the heavenly kingdom. Why do transparent stones and emeralds delight thee so much, and a house that is fuel for fire, or a plaything of time, or the sport of the earthquake, or an occasion for a tyrant's outrage ? Aspire to dwell in the heavens, and to reign with God. This kingdom a man imitating God will give thee. By receiving a little here, there through all ages He will make thee a dweller with Him. Ask that you may receive ; haste ; strive ; fear lest He disgrace thee. For He is not commanded to receive, but thou to give. The Lord did not say, Give, or bring, or do good, or help, but make a friend. But a friend proves himself such not by one gift, but by long intimacy. For it is neither the faith, nor the love, nor the hope, nor the endurance of one day, but " he that endureth to the end shall be saved." [13]

XXXIII. How then does man give these things ? For I will give not only to friends, but to the friends of friends. And who is it that is the friend of God ? Do not you judge who is worthy or who is unworthy. For it is possible you may be mistaken in your opinion. As in the uncertainty of ignorance it is better to do good to the undeserving for the sake of the deserving, than by guarding against those that are less good to fail to meet in with the good. For though sparing, and aiming at testing, who will receive meritoriously or not, it is possible for you to neglect some [14] that are loved by God ; the penalty for which is the punishment of eternal fire. But by offering to all in turn that need, you must of necessity by all means find some one of those who have power with God to save. " Judge not, then, that ye be not judged. With what measure ye mete, it shall be measured to you again ; [15] good measure, pressed and shaken,

---

[1] Matt. xxv. 34, etc.
[2] Matt. x. 40; Luke x. 16.
[3] Matt. xviii. 10.
[4] Luke xii. 32.
[5] Matt. xi. 11.
[6] Matt. x. 41.
[7] Luke xvi. 9.
[8] 2 Cor. ix. 7.

[9] καθαρά, Segaar, for καθά of the MS.
[10] Luke vi. 30.
[11] This, the reading of the MS., has been altered by several editors, but is justly defended by Segaar.
[12] γῆν ὅλην, for which Fell reads τὴν ὅλην.
[13] Matt. x. 22.
[14] τινῶν, for which the text has τιμῶν.
[15] Matt. vii. 1, 2; Luke vi. 37, 38.

and running over, shall be given to you." Open thy compassion to all who are enrolled the disciples of God ; not looking contemptuously to personal appearance, nor carelessly disposed to any period of life.   Nor if one appears penniless, or ragged, or ugly, or feeble, do thou fret in soul at this and turn away.   This form is cast around us from without, the occasion of our entrance into this world, that we may be able to enter into this common school.   But within dwells the hidden Father, and His Son,[1] who died for us and rose with us.

XXXIV. This visible appearance cheats death and the devil ; for the wealth within, the beauty, is unseen by them.   And they rave about the carcase, which they despise as weak, being blind to the wealth within ; knowing not what a " treasure in an earthen vessel "[2] we bear, protected as it is by the power of God the Father, and the blood of God the Son,[3] and the dew of the Holy Spirit.   But be not deceived, thou who hast tasted of the truth, and been reckoned worthy of the great redemption.   But contrary to what is the case with the rest of men, collect for thyself an unarmed, an unwarlike, a bloodless, a passionless, a stainless host, pious old men, orphans dear to God, widows armed with meekness, men adorned with love.   Obtain with thy money such guards, for body and for soul, for whose sake a sinking ship is made buoyant, when steered by the prayers of the saints alone ; and disease at its height is subdued, put to flight by the laying on of hands ; and the attack of robbers is disarmed, spoiled by pious prayers ; and the might of demons is crushed, put to shame in its operations by strenuous commands.

XXXV. All these warriors and guards are trusty.   No one is idle, no one is useless.   One can obtain your pardon from God, another comfort you when sick, another weep and groan in sympathy for you to the Lord of all, another teach some of the things useful for salvation, another admonish with confidence, another counsel with kindness.   And all can love truly, without guile, without fear, without hypocrisy, without flattery, without pretence.   O sweet service of loving [souls] !   O blessed thoughts of confident [hearts] !   O sincere faith of those who fear God alone !   O truth of words with those who cannot lie !   O beauty of deeds with those who have been commissioned to serve God, to persuade God, to please God, not to touch thy flesh ! to speak, but[4] to the King of eternity dwelling in thee.

XXXVI. All the faithful, then, are good and godlike, and worthy of the name by which they are encircled as with a diadem.   There are, besides, some, the elect of the elect, and so much more or less distinguished by drawing themselves, like ships to the strand, out of the surge of the world and bringing themselves to safety ; not wishing to seem holy, and ashamed if one call them so ; hiding in the depth of their mind the ineffable mysteries, and disdaining to let their nobleness be seen in the world ; whom the Word calls " the light of the world, and the salt of the earth."[5]   This is the seed, the image and likeness of God, and His true son and heir, sent here as it were on a sojourn, by the high administration and suitable arrangement of the Father, by whom the visible and invisible things of the world were created ; some for their service, some for their discipline, some for their instruction ; and all things are held together so long as the seed remains here ; and when it is gathered, these things shall be very quickly dissolved.

XXXVII. For what further need has God of the mysteries of love ?[6]   And then thou shalt look into the bosom of the Father, whom God the only-begotten Son alone hath declared. And God Himself is love ; and out of love to us became feminine.[7]   In His ineffable essence He is Father ; in His compassion to us He became Mother.   The Father by loving became feminine : and the great proof of this is He whom He begot of Himself ; and the fruit brought forth by love is love.

For this also He came down.   For this He clothed Himself with man.   For this He voluntarily subjected Himself to the experiences of men, that by bringing Himself to the measure of our weakness whom He loved, He might correspondingly bring us to the measure of His own strength.   And about to be offered up and giving Himself a ransom, He left for us a new Covenant-testament : My love I give unto you. And what and how great is it?   For each of us He gave His life, — the equivalent for all.   This He demands from us in return for one another. And if we owe our lives to the brethren, and have made such a mutual compact with the Saviour, why should we any more hoard and shut up worldly goods, which are beggarly, foreign to us and transitory?   Shall we shut up from each other what after a little shall be the property of the fire?   Divinely and weightily John says, " He that loveth not his brother is a murderer,"[8] the seed of Cain, a nursling of the devil.   He has not God's compassion.   He has no hope of better things.   He is sterile ; he is barren ; he is not

---

[1] παῖς.
[2] 2 Cor. iv. 7.
[3] παιδός.
[4] Perhaps ἀλλά has got transposed, and we should read, "but to speak to the king," etc.

[5] Matt. v. 13, 14.
[6] Segaar reads : For what more should I say ?   Behold the mysteries of love.
[7] Ἐθηλύνθη, which occurs immediately after this, has been suggested as the right reading here.   The text has ἐθηράθη.
[8] 1 John iii. 14, 15.

a branch of the ever-living supercelestial vine. He is cut off; he waits the perpetual fire.

XXXVIII. But learn thou the more excellent way, which Paul shows for salvation. "Love seeketh not her own,"[1] but is diffused on the brother. About him she is fluttered, about him she is soberly insane. "Love covers a multitude of sins."[2] "Perfect love casteth out fear."[3] "Vaunteth not itself, is not puffed up; rejoiceth not in iniquity, but rejoiceth in the truth; beareth all things, believeth all things, hopeth all things, endureth all things. Love never faileth. Prophecies are done away, tongues cease, gifts of healing fail on the earth. But these three abide, Faith, Hope, Love. But the greatest of these is Love."[4] And rightly. For Faith departs when we are convinced by vision, by seeing God. And Hope vanishes when the things hoped for come. But Love comes to completion, and grows more when that which is perfect has been bestowed. If one introduces it into his soul, although he be born in sins, and has done many forbidden things, he is able, by increasing love, and adopting a pure repentance, to retrieve his mistakes. For let not this be left to despondency and despair by you, if you learn who the rich man is that has not a place in heaven, and what way he uses his property.

XXXIX. If one should escape the superfluity of riches, and the difficulty they interpose in the way of life, and be able to enjoy the eternal good things; but should happen, either from ignorance or involuntary circumstances, after the seal[5] and redemption, to fall into sins or transgressions so as to be quite carried away; such a man is entirely rejected by God. For to every one who has turned to God in truth, and with his whole heart, the doors are open, and the thrice-glad Father receives His truly repentant son. And true repentance is to be no longer bound in the same sins for which He denounced death against Himself, but to eradicate them completely from the soul. For on their extirpation God takes up His abode again in thee. For it is said there is great and exceeding joy and festival in the heavens with the Father and the angels when one sinner turns and repents.[6] Wherefore also He cries, "I will have mercy, and not sacrifice."[7] "I desire not the death, but the repentance of the sinner."[8] "Though your sins be as scarlet wool, I will make them white as snow; though they be blacker than darkness, I will wash and make them like white wool."[9] For it is in the power of God alone to grant the forgiveness of sins, and not to impute transgressions; since also the Lord commands us each day to forgive the repenting brethren.[10] "And if we, being evil, know to give good gifts,"[11] much more is it the nature of the Father of mercies, the good Father of all consolation, much pitying, very merciful, to be long-suffering, to wait for those who have turned. And to turn is really to cease from our sins, and to look no longer behind.

XL. Forgiveness of past sins, then, God gives; but of future, each one gives to himself. And this is to repent, to condemn the past deeds, and beg oblivion of them from the Father, who only of all is able to undo what is done, by mercy proceeding from Him, and to blot out former sins by the dew of the Spirit. "For by the state in which I find you will I judge,"[12] also, is what in each case the end of all cries aloud. So that even in the case of one who has done the greatest good deeds in his life, but at the end has run headlong into wickedness, all his former pains are profitless[13] to him, since at the catastrophe of the drama he has given up his part; while it is possible for the man who formerly led a bad and dissolute life, on afterwards repenting, to overcome in the time after repentance the evil conduct of a long time. But it needs great carefulness, just as bodies that have suffered by protracted disease need regimen and special attention. Thief, dost thou wish to get forgiveness? steal no more. Adulterer, burn no more. Fornicator, live for the future chastely. Thou who hast robbed, give back, and give back more than [thou tookest]. False witness, practise truth. Perjurer, swear no more, and extirpate the rest of the passions, wrath, lust, grief, fear; that thou mayest be found at the end to have previously in this world been reconciled to the adversary. It is then probably impossible all at once to eradicate inbred passions; but by God's power and human intercession, and the help of brethren, and sincere repentance, and constant care, they are corrected.

XLI. Wherefore it is by all means necessary for thee, who art pompous, and powerful, and rich, to set over thyself some man of God as a trainer and governor. Reverence, though it be but one man; fear, though it be but one man. Give yourself to hearing, though it be but one speaking freely, using harshness, and at the same time healing. For it is good for the eyes not to continue always wanton, but to weep and smart sometimes, for greater health. So also nothing is more pernicious to the soul than

---

[1] 1 Cor. xiii. 5.
[2] 1 Pet. iv. 8.
[3] 1 John iv. 18.
[4] 1 Cor. xiii. 4-8, 13.
[5] i.e., of baptism.
[6] Luke xv. 10.
[7] Hos. vi. 6; Matt. ix 13.
[8] Ezek. xviii. 23.
[9] Isa. i. 18.

[10] Matt. vi. 14.
[11] Luke xi. 13.
[12] Quoted with a slight variation by Justin Martyr, *Dialogue with Trypho*, ch. xlvii., vol 1. p. 219, and supposed by Grabe to be a quotation from the Apocryphal Gospel to the Hebrews.
[13] Ἀνόνητοι, for which the text has ἀνόητοι.

uninterrupted pleasure. For it is blinded by melting away, if it remain unmoved by bold speech. Fear this man when angry ; be pained at his groaning ; and reverence him when making his anger to cease ; and anticipate him when he is deprecating punishment. Let him pass many sleepless nights for thee, interceding for thee with God, influencing the Father with the magic of familiar litanies. For He does not hold out against His children when they beg His pity. And for you he will pray purely, held in high honour as an angel of God, and grieved not by you, but for you. This is sincere repentance. "God is not mocked," [1] nor does He give heed to vain words. For He alone searches the marrow and reins of the heart, and hears those that are in the fire, and listens to those who supplicate in the whale's belly ; and is near to all who believe, and far from the ungodly if they repent not.

XLII. And that you may be still more confident, that repenting thus truly there remains for you a sure hope of salvation, listen to a tale,[2] which is not a tale but a narrative,[3] handed down and committed to the custody of memory, about the Apostle John. For when, on the tyrant's death, he returned to Ephesus from the isle of Patmos, he went away, being invited, to the contiguous territories of the nations, here to appoint bishops, there to set in order whole Churches, there to ordain such as were marked out by the Spirit.

Having come to one of the cities not far off (the name of which some give[4]), and having put the brethren to rest in other matters, at last, looking to the bishop appointed, and seeing a youth, powerful in body, comely in appearance, and ardent, said, "This (youth) I commit to you in all earnestness, in the presence of the Church, and with Christ as witness." And on his accepting and promising all, he gave the same injunction and testimony. And he set out for Ephesus. And the presbyter taking home the youth committed to him, reared, kept, cherished, and finally baptized him. After this he relaxed his stricter care and guardianship, under the idea that the seal of the Lord he had set on him was a complete protection to him. But on his obtaining premature freedom, some youths of his age, idle, dissolute, and adepts in evil courses, corrupt him. First they entice him by many costly entertainments ; then afterwards by night issuing forth for highway robbery, they take him along with them. Then they dared to execute together something greater. And he by degrees got accustomed ; and from greatness of nature, when he had gone aside from the right path, and

like a hard-mouthed and powerful horse, had taken the bit between his teeth, rushed with all the more force down into the depths. And having entirely despaired of salvation in God, he no longer meditated what was insignificant, but having perpetrated some great exploit, now that he was once lost, he made up his mind to a like fate with the rest. Taking them and forming a band of robbers, he was the prompt captain of the bandits, the fiercest, the bloodiest, the cruelest.

Time passed, and some necessity having emerged, they send again for John. He, when he had settled the other matters on account of which he came, said, "Come now, O bishop, restore to us the deposit which I and the Saviour committed to thee in the face of the Church over which you preside, as witness." The other was at first confounded, thinking that it was a false charge about money which he did not get ; and he could neither believe the allegation regarding what he had not, nor disbelieve John. But when he said " I demand the young man, and the soul of the brother," the old man, groaning deeply, and bursting into tears, said, " He is dead." "How and what kind of death?" " He is dead," he said, " to God. For he turned wicked and abandoned, and at last a robber ; and now he has taken possession of the mountain in front of the church, along with a band like him." Rending, therefore, his clothes, and striking his head with great lamentation, the apostle said, " It was a fine guard of a brother's soul I left ! But let a horse be brought me, and let some one be my guide on the way." He rode away, just as he was, straight from the church. On coming to the place, he is arrested by the robbers' outpost ; neither fleeing nor entreating, but crying, " It was for this I came. Lead me to your captain ; " who meanwhile was waiting, all armed as he was. But when he recognised John as he advanced, he turned, ashamed, to flight. The other followed with all his might, forgetting his age, crying, " Why, my son, dost thou flee from me, thy father, unarmed, old? Son, pity me. Fear not ; thou hast still hope of life. I will give account to Christ for thee. If need be, I will willingly endure thy death, as the Lord did death for us. For thee I will surrender my life. Stand, believe ; Christ hath sent me."

And he, when he heard, first stood, looking down ; then threw down his arms, then trembled and wept bitterly. And on the old man approaching, he embraced him, speaking for himself with lamentations as he could, and baptized a second time with tears, concealing only his right hand. The other pledging, and assuring him on oath that he would find forgiveness for himself from the Saviour, beseeching and falling on his knees, and kissing his right hand itself, as now

---

[1] Gal. vi. 7.
[2] μῦθος.
[3] λόγος.
[4] Said to be Smyrna.

purified by repentance, led him back to the church. Then by supplicating with copious prayers, and striving along with him in continual fastings, and subduing his mind by various utterances [1] of words, did not depart, as they say, till he restored him to the Church, presenting in him a great example of true repentance and a great token of regeneration, a trophy of the resurrection for which we hope ; when at the end of the world, the angels, radiant with joy, hymning and opening the heavens, shall receive into the celestial abodes those who truly repent ; and before all, the Saviour Himself goes to meet them, welcoming them ; holding forth the shadowless, ceaseless light ; conducting them·to the Father's bosom, to eternal life, to the kingdom of heaven.

Let one believe these things, and the disciples of God, and God, who is surety, the Prophecies, the Gospels, the Apostolic words ; living in accordance with them, and lending his ears, and

practising the deeds, he shall at his decease see the end and demonstration of the truths taught. For he who in this world welcomes the angel of penitence will not repent at the time that he leaves the body, nor be ashamed when he sees the Saviour approaching in His glory and with His army. He fears not the fire.

But if one chooses to continue and to sin perpetually in pleasures, and values indulgence here above eternal life, and turns away from the Saviour, who gives forgiveness ; let him no more blame either God, or riches, or his having fallen, but his own soul, which voluntarily perishes. But to him who directs his eye to salvation and desires it, and asks with boldness and vehemence for its bestowal, the good Father who is in heaven will give the true purification and the changeless life. To whom, by His Son Jesus Christ, the Lord of the living and dead, and by the Holy Spirit, be glory, honour, power, eternal majesty, both now and ever, from generation to generation, and from eternity to eternity. Amen.

---

[1] ῥήσεσι λόγων, for which Cod. Reg. Gall. reads σειρῆσι λόγων.

ELUCIDATIONS

I.

(Note 1, p. 591.)

THE kingdom of Christ was set up in great weakness, that nothing might be wanting to the glory of His working by the Spirit, in its triumph over the darkness of the world. " Not many wise men after the flesh, not many mighty, not many noble," were called.[1] And so it continued for a long time. Under Commodus, however (A.D. 180–192), a temporary respite was conceded ; partly because his favourite Marcia took their part for some reason, and partly because his cruelty gratified itself in another direction. " Our circumstances," says Eusebius, " were changed to a milder aspect ; as there was peace prevailing, by the grace of God, throughout the world in the churches. Then, also, the saving-doctrine brought the minds of men to a devout veneration of the Supreme God, from every race on earth, so that, now, many of those *eminent at Rome for their wealth and kindred, with their whole house and family,* yielded themselves to salvation." What happened near the court of a fickle tyrant was far more likely to be common in Antioch and Alexandria. Men's consciences had no doubt been with the Christians, as Pilate's was with their Master ; and now, when it became less perilous, they began to laugh at idols, and even to enroll themselves with Christians. Some, no doubt, like Joseph and Nicodemus, gave themselves to the Lord ; but others, " with a form of godliness, denied the power thereof." Clement detected the great evil that began to threaten, and this beautiful tract is the product of his watchful observation. For he was gifted, also, with that great characteristic of noble mind, a faculty of foreseeing "whereunto such things must grow." His love and solicitude for the Church, lest its simplicity should pass away with its poverty, dictated this solemn and most timely warning.

And it is worthy of grateful remark, how admirably sustained was this primitive spirit among all the early witnesses for truth. They were not of this world, and they dreaded its influence. How richly the Word dwelt in them, is manifest from their amazing familiarity with the Scriptures.

---

[1] 1 Cor. i. 26, 27.

That they sometimes misquote or confuse quotations, or mix a Scriptural saying with some current proverb or an apocryphal gloss, is surely not surprising, when copies of the Scriptures were few and costly, when no concordances and books of reference were at hand, and when their whole apparatus for Biblical study was so extremely incomplete.

To the genius of this great Alexandrian Father, we are all debtors to this day. Had he not, unfortunately, allied much of his wisdom with the hateful name of the *Gnostic*,[1] which he failed to wrest from the pseudo-Gnostics, with whom it is irrevocably associated, we may be sure his expositions of Christian philosophy would be more useful in our times.

II.

(Segaar, note 3, p. 594.)

Charles Segaar, S.T.D., born in 1724, was Greek professor at Utrecht, from 1766 to 1803, after filling several important and laborious positions as a pastor and preacher. He died Dec. 22, 1803. He has left a great reputation as "the most theological of philologists, and the most philological of theologians." Had he gone over the entire text of Clement, and edited all his works, with the care and ability displayed in his critical edition of the Τίς ὁ σωζόμενος πλούσιος, the world would have been greatly enriched by his influence on the cultivation of patristic literature. In his eloquent preface to this tract, he bewails the neglect into which that fundamental department of Christian learning had fallen; praising the labours of Anglican scholars, who, in the former century, had devoted themselves to the production of valuable editions of the Fathers. He speaks of himself as from early years inflamed with a singular love of such studies and especially of the Greek Fathers, and adds an expression of the extreme gratification with which he had read and pondered the *Quis dives Salvandus*, among the admirable works of Clement of Alexandria. He corrects Ghisler's error in crediting it to Origen (edition of 1623), and reminds us that there is but a single MS. from which it is derived, viz., that of the Vatican.

Apart from the value of Segaar's annotations, his work is very useful to Greek scholars, for its varied erudition, much wealth of his learning being expended upon single words and their idiomatic uses. The sort of work devoted to this tract is precisely what I covet for my countrymen; and I look forward with hope to the day as not remote, when from regions now unnamed, in this vast domain of our republican America, critical editions of all of the *Ante-Nicene Fathers* shall be given to the republic of letters, with a beauty of typography hitherto unknown. The valuable *Patrologia* of Migne might well be made the base of a Phœnix-like edition of the same series. It was only fit for such a base; for its print and paper are disgraceful, and the inaccuracy and carelessness of its references and editorial work are only pardonable when one reflects on the small cost at which it was afforded. The plates have perished in flames; but the restoration of the whole work is worthy of the ambition of American scholars, and of the patronage of wealth now sordid but capable of being ennobled by being made useful to mankind.

III.

(Willing Souls, cap. xxi. p. 597.)

On the subject of free-will, so profusely illustrated by Clement, I have foreborne to add any comments. But Segaar's *Excursus* (iv. p. 410) is worthy of being consulted. On Clement's ideas of *Hades* and the *intermediate state*, I have made no comment; but Segaar's endeavour to state judicially the view of our author (*Excursus*, x. p. 421), though in some particulars it seems to me unsatisfactory, is also worthy of examination.

If a number of other important points have been apparently overlooked in my Elucidations, it is because I fear I have already gone beyond the conditions and limitations of my work.

---

[1] For Gnostic, *Intellector* is used, p. 577 Why not use the Latin word *perfector?* The idea is not simply *perfectus*: Clement's *Gnostic* is a *gnomon*, actively indexing the mind of Christ.

INDEXES.

HERMAS

INDEX OF SUBJECTS

609

HERMAS.

INDEX OF TEXTS.

TATIAN

INDEX OF SUBJECTS

Albigenses, 62.
Alexander, flattered by his preceptor, Aristotle, 65.
Alphabet, 65.
Anitus and Miletus, 66.
Anaxagoras, 73.
Apion, the grammarian, 80.
Apollo and Daphne, 73.
Argives, their kings, 80.
Aristippus, 65.
Aristotle, 65.
Astronomy, 65, 68.

Baptism, the renunciation of, 73.
Beausobre, 72.
Berosus, 80.
Busiris, 66.

Catholics, early, 62.
Chaldeans, 80; witness to Moses, 80.
Christianity, Western, effect of Montanism on, 62.
Christians, two classes of, 62; worship God only, 66; their doctrine of Creation, 67; belief in the resurrection, 67; unjustly hated, 76; philosophy of, 77; older than that of Greece, 77; doctrines of, 78; opposed to dissensions, 78; fitted for all men, 78; free schools of, 78; hymns of, 79.
Chronology, 78, 81.
Chrysostom, 69, 79.
Coliseum, 75.
Constellations, origin of, 69.
Corates, 66.
Creation, 67.
Crescens, loathsome character of, 73; persecutes Justin, 73.
Cretans, always liars, 76.
Cross, mystery of, 71.

Democritus, 72.
Demons, 68; turned into gods, 68; teach the doctrine of fate, 68; economize astronomy, 68; to be punished, 78; vain display of, 72; false promises of, 72; deceptions of, 73.
Demon worship, depravity of, 73.
Diogenes, 65.
Doctrines of the Greeks and Christians compared, 74.

Egyptians, 80.
Elijah, 62.
Empedocles, 66.
Encratites, the, 63.
Euripides, 66.
Eusebius, reference to, 61, 62.
Eventide, hymn of, 79.

Free-will, 69.

Geometry, 65.
Gladiators, 75.
God only to be feared, 66; a spirit, 66; Greek notions of, 74; compared with Christian ideas, 74.
Gods of the heathen, 68; absurdities concerning, 69.
Gospels, the four, testimony of the *Diatessaron* to, 61.
Greeks, not the inventors of the arts, 65; foolish solemnities of, 74; their play-actors, 75; other amusements, 75; idols of, 76; studies of, 76; legislation, 77.
Greek studies, ridiculed, 76.

Hellebore, 72.
Hercules, 66, 69.
Heraclitus, 66.
Herodotus, 79.
Holy Ghost, 62.
Homer, 77; his period, 78.
Hus, reference to, 62.

Idioms, communication of, 71.
Irenæus, reference to Tatian, 61.

John the Baptist, 62.
Judaism, 61
Justin Martyr, Tatian's relation to, 61.

Kaye, Bishop, reference to, 70.

Latin Church, sophistries of, 62.
Life, human shortening of, 71.
Logos, 67, 68.

Magic, 65.
Man, fall of, 67.
Marriage, 62.
Marsyas, 65.
Matter, not eternal, 67.

Mill, reference to, 61.
Modern science anticipated, 67.
Montanism, 62.
Moses, his antiquity, 80; his time, 80; compared with heathen heroes, 81; superior antiquity of, 81.
Mythology, 68.

Orpheus, 65.

Paganism, 61.
Pherecydes, 66.
Philosophers, their vices, 65; and absurdities, 66; ridicule of, 66; boastings and quarrels, 75.
Philosophy, Grecian and Christian, compared, 77.
Phœnicians, 80.
Phrygians, reference to, 62.
Pindar, quoted, 74.
Plato, 65, 66.
Psychic natures, 71.
Pugilists, 75.
Pythagoras, 66.

Resurrection, 67.
Rousseau quoted, 82.

Socrates, 66.
Solon, 80.
Soul, immortal, 70.
Southey, Robert, his remarks concerning John Wesley, 62.
Spirit, the Holy, 71.
Spirits, two kinds, 70.
St. Jerome, 61, 62.
St. Paul, 62.

Tatian, Introductory Note, 61; equivocal position of, 61; influenced by Justin, 61; his falling away, 61; possible mental decline, 61; Tatian an Assyrian, 61, 62; some of his works very valuable, 61; some have perished, 61; his *Diatessaron*, 61; his *encraty*, 62; his Address to the Greeks, sole surviving work, 62; Epiphanius describes him as from Mesopotamia, 62; embraced Christianity at Rome, 63; Address to the Greeks, 65; his conversion, 77; visit to Rome, 79; disgusted with

TATIAN.

INDEX OF TEXTS.

THEOPHILUS.

INDEX OF SUBJECTS.

THEOPHILUS

INDEX OF TEXTS

ATHENAGORAS

INDEX OF SUBJECTS

Angels, 141; the fallen, 142.

Atheists, Christians not such, 130; charge retorted on heathen, 131; absurdity of this charge, 134.

Athenagoras, his place among primitive apologists, 125; a trophy of St. Paul's preaching, 125; Paris edition of, 126; his writings harmonized with Justin Martyr and others, by Bishop Kaye, 126; notes of Gesner and Stephans, 126; no historical information concerning him, 127; rare mention of his name in history, 127; beauty and merit of his writings, 127; Introductory Notes, 125-127; Plea for the Christians, 129; On the Resurrection, 149.

Body, functions of, 152; the resurrection of, 152; differs from the mortal, 152.

Calvin, quoted, 157.

Christian morality, 146.

Christianity, at the period of Athenagoras, 125; its shackles falling; 125; bolder tone of, 125; its conflict with heresies, 125; Sibylline predictions of, 125, 132; entreats a fair hearing, 148; his treatise of the resurrection, 149.

Christians, plea in their behalf addressed to Marcus Aurelius and Commodus, 129; injustice towards, 129; claim to legal protection, 130; false charges against, 130; superiority of their theology, 132; worship the Trinity, 133; their moral teaching, 134; why they do not offer sacrifices, 134; inconsistency of their accusers, 135; distinguish God from matter, 135; do not worship the universe, 136; calumnies against, confuted, 145; elevated morality of, 146; their conjugal chastity, 146; contrasted with their accusers, 147; condemn cruelty, 147; abolish gladiatorial shows, 147; abhor fœticide, 147; refuse worship to the emperors, 148.

Creator, 150; who makes, can restore, 150.

Death, 157; and sleep, 157; analogy of, 157.

De Maistre, cited, 131.

Demons, 143; tempt to idolatry, 143; artifices of, 143.

Digestion and nutrition consistent with resurrection, 151.

Divine Providence denied by the poets and philosophers, 142.

Doctrine, Christian, 132.

Germans, 126; their criticisms, 126; valuable editorial labours, 125; lack of sympathy with the primitive writers, 126; and of devout exegesis, 126.

Giants, their progeny, 142.

God, testimony of the poets to unity, 131; opinions of philosophers concerning, 131; distinguished from matter, 135.

Heathen, their gods, 136; and idols, 136; recent invention of, 136; a poetic fiction, 137; absurd representations of gods, 138; impure ideas concerning the gods, 138; their shameful poetry, 139; pretended explanations of mythology, 140; their gods but men, 143.

Human flesh, not the proper food of man, 153.

Judgment, 156; necessary to soul and body, 158.

Logos, 133, 146.

Man, argument from his nature, 156; and from changes in his life, 158; and from his liability to judgment, 160; from his actions, 160; and from such good and evil, 161; and from laws of his nature, 161; and from the objects of his existence, 162.

Marriage, chastity of Christians with respect to, 146.

Philosophers, opinions of, 131; respecting the gods, 137; Thales and Plato, 140; deny a Providence, 142; Aristotle, 142; Plato and Pythagoras sustain the possibility of resurrection, 148.

Plato, opinion of, 140.

Poets, testimony of, 131; describe the gods as originally men, 144; reasons for this, 145.

Polytheism, absurdities of, 132.

Prophets, testimony of, 133.

Pusey, quoted, 157.

Resurrection, 149; not impossible 150; objections to, 151; canibalism no impediment, 153; nor man's impotency, 153; will of the Creator concerning, 154; argument continued, 155; not merely for judgment, 156; children to rise again, 156; argument from man's nature, 156; probability of, 158; from changes in man's life, 158; if none, man less favoured than brutes, 159; concluding argument, 162; its beauty and force, 162.

Rewards and punishments, 158.

St. Paul, his preaching on Mars Hill, 125; its apparent sterility, 125; Athenagoras its trophy, 125.

Sibyl, prediction of Christianity, 125, 132; quotation from, 145.

Sleep, 157.

Soul and body, judgment of, 158.

Telemachus, heroic history of, 147.

Thales, opinion of, 140.

Universe, not worshipped by Christians, 136; the Ptolemaic system of, 136.

ATHENAGORAS.

INDEX OF TEXTS.

CLEMENT OF ALEXANDRIA.

INDEX OF SUBJECTS.

[INCLUDING THE INTRODUCTIONS AND NOTES.]

CLEMENT OF ALEXANDRIA.

INDEX OF TEXTS.